CIVIL ENGINEERING
ESTIMATING, COSTING AND VALUATION

(*Including Quantity Surveying, Contracting and Accounts*)

Prof. V.N. VAZIRANI
M.Sc. (Structures)
Formerly, Delhi College of Engineering, Delhi.

S.P. CHANDOLA
C.E., M.Sc. (Structures) ; M.I. Struct. E (London);
F.I.E. (India)
Formerly, Prof. Delhi College of Engineering, Delhi
Ex. Chief Engineer and Managing Director,
Farrods (E.A.) Ltd.

Revised by :
S.V. DEODHAR
Dean and Professor SVITS, Indore
Formerly, Director S.S.V.P. Sansthan BSD College of Engg.,
Dhule, (M.S.)

KHANNA PUBLISHERS
Operational Office
B-35/9, G.T. Karnal Road Industrial Area,
(Near Telephone Exchange), Delhi-110033
Phones : 011-27224179, 011-45033819 • *Mob.* 09811541460
email : contactus@khannapublishers.in

Published by :

Romesh Chander Khanna & Vineet Khanna
for **KHANNA PUBLISHERS**
2-B, Nath Market, Nai Sarak
Delhi- 110 006 (India)

Website : www.khannapublishers.in

Hologram & Description

To all readers of our books, to prevent yourself from being defrauded by piraters, please make sure that there is an Hologram on the cover of our books with the below specifications. If you find any book without Hologram and Description, please mail us at **contactus@khannapublishers.in**

Thanking you

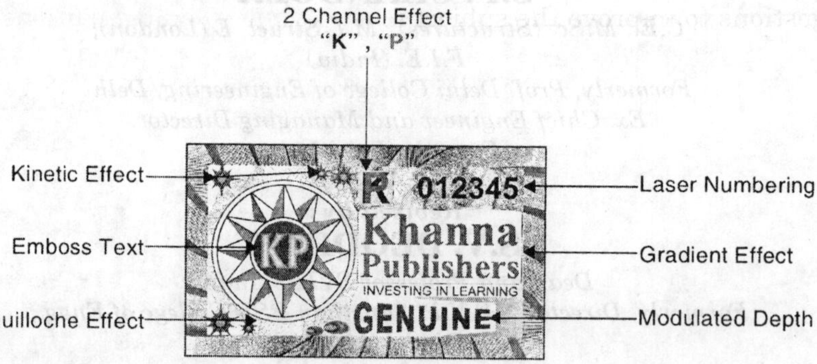

ISBN No. 978-81-7409-127-7

First Edition : 1968
Sixth Edition : 2015
First Reprint : 2021

***Price :* ₹ 549.00**

Preface

The primary purpose of Estimating and Costing is the preparation for submission of a project according to Administrative Approval and Technical Sanction. The various elements of engineering involved in it *viz.* planning, preparing bill of quantities and abstracts of cost, drawing and detailing (specially at the actual construction stage) and organisation of labour and material with a view to provide a durable structure most economically.

Keeping this in mind all topics related to and interelated to any type of project is dealt in detail in this book. While preparing the content matter due consideration is given to the present the subject matter in clear and practical manner as per practice and B.S.I. Specifications.

Latest information and schedule of rates is given throughout the text. The book contains sample examples of different variety along with clear illustrations and tables.

Another feature of the book is new chapters on contract and contracting, valuation and safety in construction and a vast Appendix towards the end wherein, Important tables and Technical data have been given for practical use in field.

The authors hope that this book will serve its purpose for the students of Degree, Diploma, A.M.I.E. and other professional and practising engineers.

Though great care has been taken to avoid any mistakes, authors will be greatful if any mistake is highlighted to them.

We sincerely hope that this book will serve its purpose and we look forward for critical comments, suggestions to improve the subject matter in forthcoming editions.

V. N. VAZIRANI
S. P. CHANDOLA
S.V. DEODHAR

Contents

PART-I. ESTIMATING & COSTING

PART-II. CONTRACTS AND ACCOUNTS

Part—I

ESTIMATING AND COSTING

Part—I

ESTIMATING AND COSTING

1

Procedure of Estimating

1.1. INTRODUCTION

For all Engineering Projects, small or big, heavy construction works or light construction works, it is necessary to know the probable cost, which can only be known by estimating. To keep the estimated cost within the limitations, specifications, designs and drawings are amended accordingly. In estimating, knowledge of mensuration, understanding of drawings and designs, correctness of specifications and schedule of rates are essential. Correct estimate is that, in which, during the actual execution of work, there are (*i*) no deviations in the estimated quantities of different items of work; (*ii*) no extra and additional items; (*iii*) no increase in the cost and (*iv*) no provision of lump-sum items. All this depends upon the knowledge of the estimater.

The calculations of different items of works (*i.e.* quantities) are carried out with the help of the drawings, specifications and designs.

1.2. METHOD OF ESTIMATING

For the preparation of detailed estimate, drawings, designs, specifications and schedule of rates, prevailing in that locality or city are needed. For calculation work, "details of measurement form, abstract of cost form, abstract of quantities form, material statement form and labour statement forms" etc., are needed. These are given below in Tables 1.1 to 1.5. Generally Delhi Schedule of Rates 1997 have been used.

Table 1.1. Details of Measurement Form

S. No.	*Description of Item*	*No.*	*Length (L)*	*Breadth (B)*	*Height or Depth (H)*	*Contents*	*Total*	*Remark*

Table 1.2. Abstract of Cost Form

S. No.	*Detail of Work*	*Quantity*	*Unit*	*Rate.* ₹ *P.*	*Amount* ₹ *P.*	*Remark*

Table 1.3. Abstract of Quantity Form

S. No.	*Detail of Work*	*Quantity*	*Remark*

Table 1.4. Material Statement Form

S. No.	*Particular of Work*	*Cement*	*M.S. Bar*	*Sand*	*Bricks*	*Grit*	*Wood*	*Lime*	*Paint*

Table 1.5. Labour Statement Form

S. No.	*Particular of Work*	*Mistry*	*Mason*	*Carpenter*	*Fitter*	*Black-smith*	*Bhisti*	*Beldar*

The above forms are used for calculating the details for different items of works, cost quantities, material and labour required.

The "abstract of quantity", "material statement" and "labour statement are needed for the planning and execution of work with the help of "network planning and scheduling" (C.P.M. or other methods). Detail about the resources, *i.e.* money, manpower, material and machinery required, are also known.

1.3. REDUCING CALCULATIONS

To save the time and labour, there are certain items, where detail calculations can be avoided with the help of the calculated items. The quantities of such items are reduced in the following ways :

1. Foundation concrete

$$= \frac{\text{Quantity of earthwork in excavation in foundation}}{\text{Depth of excavation}} \times \text{Thickness of concrete.}$$

2. Sand filling under floors

$$= \frac{\text{Quantity of earth filling in plinth}}{\text{Height of earth filling}} \times \text{Height of sand filling.}$$

Similarly the quantity of lime concrete under floors can be calculated.

3. Inside white washing. Quantity is equal to the inside plastering.
4. Outside colour washing. Quantity is equal to the outside plastering or pointing.

1.4. DEDUCTION FOR OPENINGS

Deductions on account of openings are given below.

Deduction for Openings in Masonry

1. *Rectangular openings* doors, window and, ventilators.

Quantities to be deducted $= h$ (m) $\times$ b (m) $\times$ Thickness of the wall (m)
= cum (See Fig. 1.1)

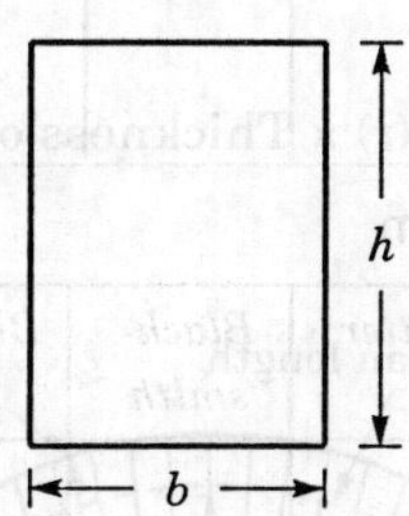

Fig. 1.1

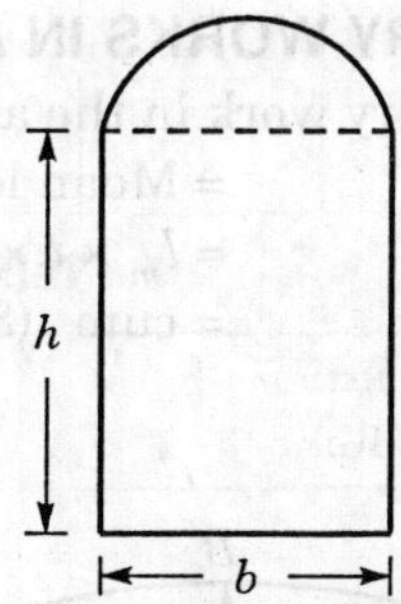

Fig. 1.2

2. *Doors and windows with small segmental arches.*

Quantities to be deducted $= h$ (m) $\times$ b (m) $\times$ Thickness of wall (m)
= cum

Segmental portion is considered as solid to cover the additional expenses in the arch masonry. (See Fig. 1.2)

3. *Segmental arch openings.*

R is the rise.

Area of semi-circular portion = $3/4 \times b \times R$

Quantities to be deducted

$= h \times b \times$ Thickness of the wall + $3/4 \times b \times R \times$ Thickness of wall

$= \{h \times b + (3/4 \times b \times R)\} \times$ Thickness of wall. (See Fig. 1.3)

4. *Semicircular arch openings.*

Quantities to be deducted = {Area of rectangle + Area of semi-circle} × Thickness of wall

$$= \left\{(b \times h) + \pi\left(\frac{b}{2}\right)^2 \times \frac{1}{2}\right\} \times \text{Thickness of wall}$$

$$= \left\{(b \times h) + \pi\left(\frac{b}{2}\right)^2 \times \frac{1}{2}\right\} \times \text{Thickness of wall} \quad \text{(See Fig. 1.4)}$$

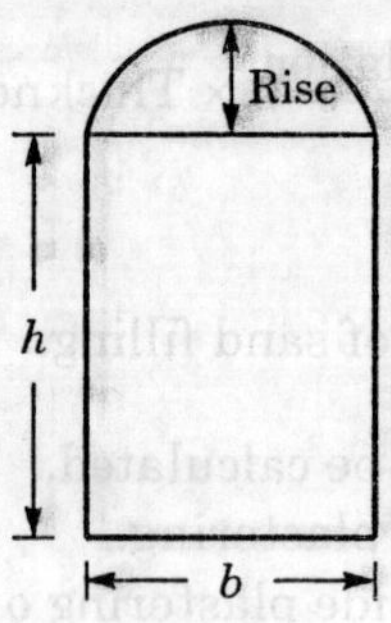

Fig. 1.3

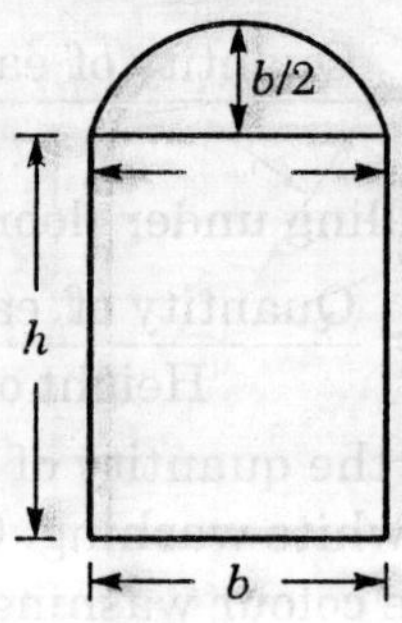

Fig. 1.4

5. *Elliptical openings.*

Major axis $AC = D$

Minor axis $BD = d$; then area $A = 1/4\pi Dd = 0.7854\, Dd$.

Deduction $= \dfrac{AC}{2} \times \dfrac{BD}{2} \times \pi \times$ Thickness of wall = cum (See Fig. 1.5)

1.5. MASONRY WORKS IN ARCHES

(*a*) Masonry work in the arch

= Mean length (l_m) × Thickness of arch (t) × Thickness of the wall

$= l_m \times t \times$ Thickness of the wall

= cum (See Fig. 1.6)

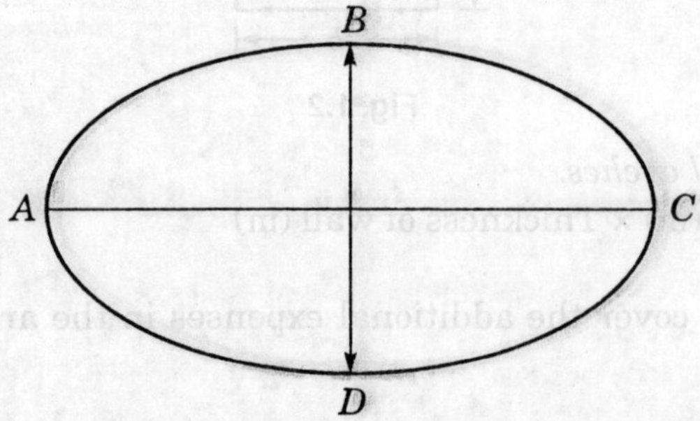

Fig. 1.5

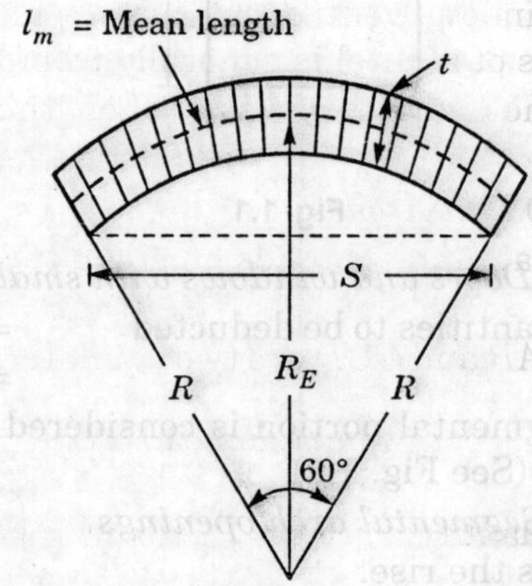

Fig. 1.6

(b) *Arch over doors and windows* is generally segmental with an angle of 60° at the centre. The 60° arch forms an equilateral triangle, with two radii and span as its sides.

l_m = Mean length of the arch
R_m = Mean radius
S = Span
R = Radius
$R = S$

and $$R_M = R + \frac{t}{2}$$

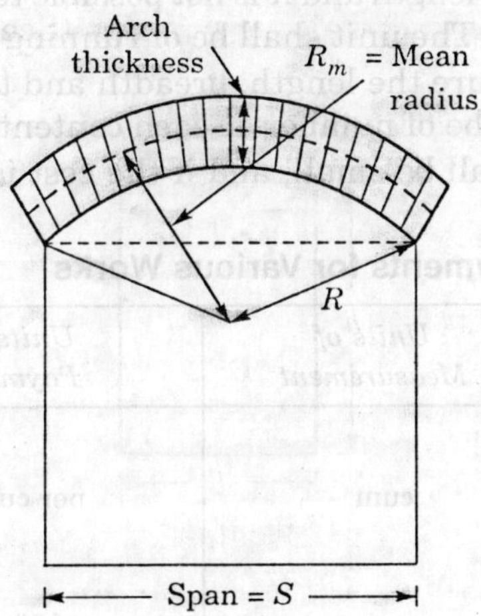

Fig. 1.7

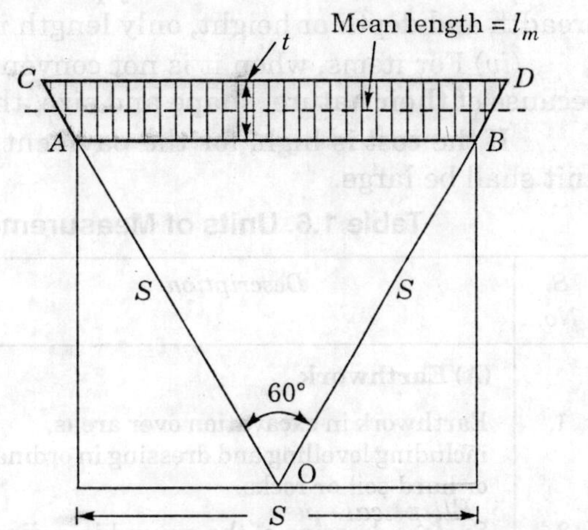

Fig. 1.8

$$\frac{l_m}{\text{Circumference (mean)}} = \frac{60°}{360°} = \frac{1}{6}$$

$$l_m = \frac{1}{6} \times 2\pi R_m = \frac{1}{6} \times \pi \times \text{dia (mean arch)}$$

Quantity of masonry $= l_m \times$ Breadth of wall $\times$ Thickness of arch
$= l_m \times$ Breadth of wall $\times t$.

Doors, windows and ventilators have lintels. The length of the lintel is equal to the span of the window, ventilator or door plus bearing on each end, which is generally 15 cm. The thickness of a lintel is generally from 10 to 15 cm.

The quantity of lintel = Length × Thickness of the lintel × Thickness of the wall
= cum (See Fig. 1.7)

(c) *Flat Arches*

Flat arch subtends an angle of 60° at the centre

$$OA = AB = OB = S$$

OAB and OCD are two equilateral triangles

$$l_m \text{ (mean length)} = S + \frac{t}{2}$$

Quantity $= l_m \times b \times t = \left(S + \frac{t}{2}\right) \times b \times t.$

1.6. UNIT OF MEASUREMENT AND UNIT OF PAYMENT OF DIFFERENT ITEMS OF WORKS

The units of different items of works depend upon the nomenclature of item; cost of materials used, their nature, size and shape after the completion of item itself. In general the units are based on the following principles :

(i) For items, where it is possible to measure, length, breadth and height or depth, easily, volume is calculated, the unit shall be in cubic contents.

(ii) For items, when it is only possible to measure, length and breadth only, area is calculated, the unit shall be of square contents.

(iii) For items, when it is only possible to measure, length and it is not possible to measure breadth and depth or height, only length is calculated. The unit shall be of running contents.

(iv) For items, when it is not convenient to measure the length, breadth and thickness, because of their nature, shape and size, the unit shall be of number or each contents.

If the cost is high, for the payment, the unit shall be small, and if the cost is low, the unit shall be large.

Table 1.6. Units of Measurements and Payments for Various Works

S. No.	*Description*	*Units of Measurement*	*Units of Payment*
	(A) Earthwork		
1.	Earthwork in excavation over areas, including levelling and dressing in ordinary or hard soil or rocks.	cum	per cum
2.	Surface dressing of the ground in ordinary or hard soil or rocks.	sq m	per 100 sq m
3.	Earthwork in excavation in foundation trenches in ordinary or hard soil or rocks.	cum	per cum
4.	Ploughing the existing ground and watering the same.	sq m	per 100 sq m
5.	Banking excavated earth in layers in ordinary or hard soil.	cum	per cum
6.	Earthwork in filling with available earth in trenches, plinth etc.	cum	per cum
7.	Excavating trenches of required width and depths for pipes etc.	metre	per metre
8.	Pumping out water caused by springs, tidal or river seepage, broken water, mains or drains and the like.	litre	per kilo litre
9.	Timbering in trenches including strutting and shoring complete.	sq m	per sq m
10.	Excavating holes in rocks for blasting.	No.	per No.
11.	Blasting of rock, or quarrying of stones etc.	cum	per cum
12.	Clearing jungle including uprooting of rank vegetation, grass, bushwood and removal of rubbish.	sq m	per 100 sq m

S. No.	Description	Units of Measurement	Units of Payment
13.	Felling trees of girth including cutting of trunks and branches etc. (Girth specified)	No.	per No.
14.	Filling in plinth with stand under floors.	cum	per cum
	(B) Concrete work		
1.	Providing and laying in foundation and plinth lime concrete.	cum	per cum
2.	Providing and laying cement concrete in foundations and plinth, R.C.C. work, etc.	cum	per cum
3.	Centring and shuttering including strutting, propping etc. and removed of form work for R.C.C. work.	sq m	per cum
4.	Precast cement concrete work or R.C.C. work.	cum	per cum
5.	Reinforced cement concrete work in foundations, walls, slabs, etc.	cum	per cum
6.	Laying concrete in or under water and/or liquid mud.	cum/m depth	per m depth
7.	Providing and laying Damp Proof course with cement concrete of specified thickness	sq m	per sq m
8.	Providing and mixing water proofing material in cement concrete work.	kg	per kg
9.	Applying a coat of bitumen on damp proof course.	sq m	per sq m
10.	Providing and laying in foundations mud concrete.	cum	per cum
	(C) Reinforced Cement Concrete		
1.	Reinforced cement concrete work 1 : 2 : 4 mix in foundations, footings, column bases, mass concrete, lintels, beams, slabs, columns, stair-cases, etc.	cum	per cum
2.	Centring and shuttering including shuttering, propping etc. and removal of formwork for all types of R.C.C. work.	sq m	per sq m
3.	Providing and fixing expanded metal mesh of sizes in R.C.C. work.	sq m	per sq m
4.	Mild steel reinforced for R.C.C. work including bending, binding and placing in position.	kg	per kg
5.	Hard drawn steel wire fabric for R.C.C. work.	kg	per kg
6.	Rendering smooth the top of suspended floors of R.C.C. work.	sq m	per sq m
7.	Applying cement slurry on R.C.C. work slabs, etc.	sq m	per sq m

(Contd.)

S. No.	*Description*	*Units of Measurement*	*Units of Payment*
8.	Precast cement concrete jali of specified thickness	sq m	per sq m
9.	Filling in position bitumen mix filler for expansion joints.	metre	per cm depth, per cm width per 100 m
10.	Fixing in position copper plate as per design for expansion joints.	kg	per kg
11.	Fixing 6 mm thick asbestos sheet covering over expansion joints of specified width.	metre	per metre
12.	Extra for laying R.C.C. in or under water.	cum/m depth	per cum per m depth
	(D) Brickwork		
1.	Brickwork in foundations and plinth in lime mortar.	cum	per cum
2.	Brickwork in foundations and plinth in cement mortar.	cum	per cum
3.	Brickwork in foundations and plinth in mud mortar.	cum	per cum
4.	Brickwork in superstructure.	cum	per cum
5.	Brickwork in square, or rectangular pillars, or circular pillars, or curved on plan, or making tapered surface.	cum	per cum
6.	Brickwork in arches in cement mortar.	cum	per cum
7.	Centring for arches.	sq m	per sq m
8.	Half brick masonry work, in cement mortar.	sq m	per sq m
9.	Brick tile masonry work in cement mortar.	cum	per cum
10.	Brick tile masonry work 5 cum thick in cement mortar, in partitions.	sq m	per sq m
11.	Constructing brick masonry chullah with holes, in cement mortar.	No.	per No.
12.	Asbestos cement flue.	metre	per metre
13.	Honeycomb brickwork 10 cm thick, in cement mortar.	sq m	per sq m
14.	Joining old brick with new brickwork.	sq m	per sq m
15.	10 cm thick brick drip course at junctions of roof and wall.	metre	per metre
16.	10 cm thick and 5 cm projected brick string course in cement mortar.	metre	per metre
17.	Moulding and cornices in brickwork with cement plaster.	m per cm girth	per m per cm girth
18.	Foam concrete block partitions 100 mm thick.	sq m	per sq m

S. No.	Description	Units of Measurement	Units of Payment
19.	Forming cavity 5 to 7.5 cm wide in cavity walls.	sq m	per sq m
20.	Brick band 10 cm thick and 5 cm projected from wall face.	metre	per metre
	(E) Stonework		
1.	Random rubble masonry with hard stone in foundations, plinths and superstructure, in lime or cement mortar.	cum	per cum
2.	Stonework in plain Ashlar cyclopean in superstructure.	cu dm	per 100 cu dm
3.	Stonework, plain, in copings, cornices, string courses and plinth courses, etc.	cu dm	per 10 cu dm
4.	40 mm thick stonework for wall lining.	sq m	per sq m
5.	Fixing gun metal cramps or dowels of required shape.	No.	per No.
6.	30 mm thick stone shelves.	sq m	per sq m
	(F) Marble Work		
1.	Marble work in steps, jambs, walls, pillars and other plain works.	cu dm	10 cu dm
2.	Marble work for wall lining.	sq m	per sq m
3.	Fixing metal cramps, dowels and copper pins	No.	per No.
4.	Providing and fixing 40 mm thick marble Jali.	sq m	per sq m
	(G) Woodwork		
1.	Woodwork in frames of doors, windows and other frames.	cu dm	10 cu dm
2.	50 mm thick, doors, windows and other shutters.	sq m	per sq m
3.	Plain jaffri work.	sq m	per sq m
4.	50 × 50 × 50 mm wood plugs.	No.	per No.
5.	40 mm thick lining work.	sq m	per sq m
6.	50 × 20 mm moulded beading.	metre	per metre
7.	15 mm thick and 100 mm wide pelmet.	metre	per metre
8.	Curtain rails.	metre	per metre
9.	40 mm thick wooden partitions.	sq m	per sq m
10.	M.S. grills of required pattern.	kg	per kg
11.	M.S. wire gauge, or steel wire fabric, or expanded metal.	sq m	per sq m
12.	40 cm long, 40 mm × 5 mm flat iron hold fasts.	No.	per No.
13.	Wooden joists.	cu dm	10 cu dm

(Contd.)

S. No.	Description	Units of Measurement	Units of Payment
14.	Sal ballies 100 mm diameter.	metre	per metre
15.	All types of fittings—brass or iron.	No.	per No.
	(H) Steel work		
1.	Steel work in single sections such as joists, tee, angles, flat and channels etc.	kg	per quintal
2.	Steel work in built-up sections, trusses and framed work.	kg	per quintal
3.	Collapsible steel shutters, sliding shutters, M.S. sheet garage shutters, of specified sizes.	sq m	per sq m
4.	Wire springs, bearings etc.	No.	per No.
5.	Steel or aluminium doors, windows and ventilators etc.	sq m	per sq m
6.	Clamps rings, and fan clamps.	No.	per No.
7.	M.S. round holding down bolts, and M.S. rivets etc.	kg	per quintal
8.	Welding by gas or electric plant.	cm	per cm length
	(I) Flooring		
1.	Brick flooring in cement mortar or dry brick flooring.	sq m	per sq m
2.	40 mm thick cement concrete flooring.	sq m	per sq m
3.	Cement concrete pavement.	cum	per cum
4.	30 cm high cement plaster skirting.	sq m	per sq m
5.	40 mm thick marble chips flooring.	sq m	per sq m
6.	30 cm high marble chips skirting.	sq m	per sq m
7.	Glass, aluminium or copper strips of specified sizes.	metre	per metre
8.	Special surface finishings.	sq m	per sq m
9.	20 mm thick precast tiles	sq m	per sq m
10.	Marble stone flooring 20 mm thick.	sq m	per sq m
11.	15 mm thick skirting, dado, walls, and other finishings.	sq m	per sq m
12.	40 mm thick Kota stone flooring, or sand stone flooring.	sq m	per sq m
13.	40 mm thick wooden flooring.	sq m	per sq m
14.	40 mm wide aluminium strip.	metre	per metre
	(J) Roofing		
1.	G.I. sheet roofing.	sq m	per sq m
2.	G.I. ridges, and hips, etc.	metre	per metre

S. No.	Description	Units of Measurement	Units of Payment
3.	Wind ties of 40 × 6 mm flat iron section.	metre	per metre
4.	A.C. sheet roofing.	sq m	per sq m
5.	A.C. ridges, hips etc.	metre	per metre
6.	Gutters, nozzles, J-hooks etc.	No.	per No.
7.	40 mm thick stone slab roofing.	sq m	per sq m
8.	10 cm thick mud phuska.	sq m	per sq m
9.	Filling cinder.	cum	per cum
10.	100 mm thick lime concrete terracing.	sq m	per sq m
11.	Gola in lime concrete.	metre	per metre
12.	Water purnalas.	metre	per metre
13.	Painting top of roof with bitumen.	sq m	per sq m
14.	Khurras 45 × 45 cm and 5 cm thick.	No.	per No.
15.	20 mm thick ceiling.	sq m	per sq m
16.	C.I. rain water pipe 100 mm diameter.	metre	per metre
17.	M.S. holder bat clamps.	No.	per No.
18.	C.I. bend, shoes, branches, offset etc.	No.	per No.
	(K) Finishing		
1.	12 mm thick lime plaster, or cement plaster.	sq m	per sq m
2.	Flushbands or moulded bands, 12 mm thick.	cm/m	per cm per m
3.	Pointing on brickwork.	sq m	per sq m
4.	White washing or colour washing or distempering or painting or varnishing or polishing etc.	sq m	per sq m
5.	Painting or rain water pipes etc.	metre	per metre
6.	Lettering.	letters/cm	per letter/cm
	(L) Repair to building		
1.	Repair to plaster in patches.	sq m	per sq m
2.	Fixing doors, windows, or any other frames in openings.	No.	per No.
3.	Providing and fixing glass panes.	sq m	per sq m
4.	Regarding mud phuska.	sq m	per sq m
5.	Replacing sand stone slabs.	sq m	per sq m
	(M) Dismantling and Demolishing		
1.	Demolishing lime concrete or cement concrete.	cum	per cum
2.	Demolishing brickwork.	cum	per cum
3.	Demolishing stone masonry work.	cum	per cum

(Contd.)

S. No.	Description	Units of Measurement	Units of Payment
4.	Cutting reinforcement bars in R.C.C. or R.B. work.	kg	per quintal
5.	Dismantling wood work.	cum	per cum
6.	Dismantling steel work.	kg	per quintal
7.	Dismantling flooring.	sq m	per sq m
8.	Demolishing mud phuska.	cum	per cum
9.	Dismantling A.C. sheet or G.I. sheet roofing.	sq m	per sq m
10.	Dismantling arch roofing.	sq m	per sq m
11.	Dismantling tiled roofing.	sq m	per sq m
12.	Dismantling rain water pipes.	metre	per metre
	(N) Miscellaneous Works		
1.	Constructing wooden cupboards of specified wood as per drawings.	No.	per No.
2.	Rough cast plaster 12 mm thick.	sq m	per sq m
3.	Pebble dash plaster.	sq m	per sq m
4.	Making plinth protection 50 mm thick	sq m	per sq m
5.	Brick edging 10 cm wide 10 cm deep.	metre	per metre
6.	Finishing edges of floors.	metre	per metre
7.	Upholstering soda chains.	No.	per No.
	Road Work		
	Road		
1.	Preparation of subgrade.	sq m	per 100 sq m
2.	Consolidation of subgrade.	sq m	per 100 sq m
3.	Supplying stone for soling.	cum	per cum
4.	Supplying of bricks.	No.	per 100 No.
5.	Laying stone soling.	cum	per cum
6.	Supplying moorum or aggregate or bajri etc.	cum	per cum
7.	Laying wearing course including consolidation.	cum	per cum
8.	Supplying and laying kerb stone.	metre	per metre
9.	Brick edging.	metre	per metre
10.	Scarifying metalled road surface.	sq m	per 100 sq m
	Fencing		
1.	R.C.C. Standard Post.	No.	per No.
2.	1.2 m high fencing as per design with G.I. barbed wire.	metre	per metre

S. No.	Description	Units of Measurement	Units of Payment
	Road Signs and Stones		
1.	R.C.C. standard sign boards as per design	No.	per No.
	Surfacing		
1.	Painting with paving bitumen of road surfaces.	sq m	per sq m
2.	Premix carpet surfacing.	sq m	per sq m
3.	Seal coat.	sq m	per sq m
4.	Joint fitler in expansion joints.	metre	per cm depth per cm width per metre
	Horticultural Work		
1.	Trenching in soil.	cum	per cum
2.	Supplying of good earth.	cum	per cum
3.	Supplying of sludge.	cum	per cum
4.	Rough dressing of ground.	sq m	per 100 sq m
5.	Grassing with "Doob" grass in lawns.	sq m	per 100 sq m
6.	Digging holes in soil 1.2 m dia and 1.2 m deep.	No.	per No.
7.	Tree guards as per drawing and design.	No.	per No.
	Sanitary Installations, Water Supply and Drainage		
	(A) Sanitary Installations		
1.	Providing and fixing Indian type W.C. pan with trap and flushing cistern etc. complete.	No.	per No.
2.	Providing and fixing white flat back or wall-corner type lipped front urinal basin with flushing cistern etc. complete.	No.	per No.
3.	Providing, and fixing white wash basin complete.	No.	per No.
4.	Providing and fixing kitchen sink.	No.	per No.
5.	Providing and fixing draining boards.	No.	per No.
6.	Providing and fixing bath tubs.	No.	per No.
7.	Providing and fixing bevelled edge mirror of superior glass.	No.	per No.
8.	Glass shelf, or towel rails, or toilet paper holder, or liquid soap container, or soap dish etc.	No.	per No.
9.	Providing and fixing C.I. soil, waste and vent pipe 100 mm dia.	metre	per metre
10.	Providing and fixing M.S. holder bat clamp; C.I. bend or heel rest bend, or junctions, or branch, or door piece or terminal guard, or collor, or passover pipe, or lead caulked joints, or trapes etc.	No.	per No.
11.	Painting C.I. cistern.	No.	per No.

(Contd.)

S. No.	Description	Units of Measurement	Units of Payment
12.	Painting C.I. soil waste, vent pipe and fittings.	metre	per metre
13.	Providing and fixing G.I. pipes complete with G.I. fittings.	metre	per metre
14.	Making connection of G.I. distribution branch with G.I. main.	No.	per No.
15.	Providing and fixing brass bib cock, or stop cock, or valves; or mouth cover; or unions, or shower rose etc.	No.	per No.
16.	M.S. sheet or R.C.C. storage tank.	No.	per No.
17.	C.I. pipes and specials for water supply.	kg	per quintal
18.	C.I. pipes of specified dia.	metre	per metre
19.	C.I. standard types of fittings.	No.	per No.
20.	C.I. sluice valves and hydrants.	No.	per No.
21.	R.C.C. pipes of specified dia.	metre	per metre
22.	R.C.C. fittings standard types.	No.	per No.
23.	Stoneware pipes of specified dia.	metre	per metre
24.	S.W. gully trap etc.	No.	per No.
25.	Manhole, or M.S. foot rests, or C.I. cover, or vent shafts etc.	No.	per No.
26.	Boring with 100 mm dia for tube well	metre	per metre
27.	Disinfecting C.I. water mains.	metre	per metre
28.	Cutting C.I. pipe with steel saw.	No.	per each cut

Table 1.7. Approximate Breakup of Construction Cost–Stage Wise Percentage to Total Cost

S. No.	Stage	Load bearing structure %	Framed structure G + 1 structure %	Framed structure G + 1 structure %
1.	Excavation and foundation up to plinth level	15	15	12.5
2.	Super structure up to roof level	23	7.5	7
3.	R.C. roof slab i/c form work i/c beam, column in framed structure	15	35	36
4.	Roof finishes	4.5	4	3.5
5.	Doors, windows, steel grills, ventilators and similar openings	12	9	8.5
6.	Plastering and pointing	6.0	6.0	6.5
7.	Colouring and painting	2.5	2	2.5
8.	Flooring	5.0	5.5	4.0
9.	Water supply and sanitary electrical etc.	15	14	15
10.	Miscellaneous	2.0	2.0	2.0
	Total	100	100	100

2

Types of Estimate

2.1. INTRODUCTION

The term estimate is used to express the probable cost of carrying out any project. It is necessary to know the expenditure of any project before it is started.

For the preparation of estimate the knowledge of drawing, designs, specifications, conditions of contract, location of project, material rates, labour rates, and other information in connection of project are essential.

2.2. VARIOUS SYSTEMS FOR PREPARATION OF ESTIMATE

1. Approximate estimation / Preliminary estimate method

(*a*) Plinth area method (*b*) Cubic content method

(*c*) Bay method (*d*) Approximate quantities method

(*e*) Number of unit estimate

2. Detailed estimation method

(*a*) Long wall-short wall method also called as individual wall method or wall to wall method or in to in and out to out method

(*b*) Center line method (*c*) Crossing method

All these methods have been dealt in details later on. However crossing method is not that common.

3. Other types of estimates

(*a*) Revised estimate (*b*) Supplementary estimate

(*c*) Supplementary and revised estimate

(*d*) Annual repair and maintenance estimate

(*e*) Special repair estimate (*f*) Addition and alteration estimate.

1. **Preliminary Estimate.** The object of this type of estimate is only to know the approximate amount of expenditure which is needed to obtain administrative approval by the competent authority. Detail drawings etc. are not required and it is prepared on the basis of plinth area, cubical contents and number of units, etc.

(*i*) **Plinth Area Estimate.** This estimate is prepared on the basis of plinth area of the building multiplied by the plinth area rate.

(*a*) **Plinth Area Method.** This is the most common method used to find the approximate cost of any building either to be constructed or existing one. In this method plinth area of building under consideration is calculated from drawings and multiplied by plinth area rate of similar building already constructed in recent past, having more or less similar specifications. The plinth area rate is calculated by actual cost of construction divided by plinth area of that building. As on today the plinth area rate of a building having a height of 3.5 M is approximately ₹ 5000 to 8000 per square meter depending on specifications. It means if a house having an plinth area of 110 square meter is to be constructed and if market plinth area rate of construction for similar house with more or less same specifications is ₹ 6500/- per square meter, then construction cost of this house will be approximately 100 × 6500 = 650000/- *i.e.* ₹ 6.5 Lacks. This method is very simple and can be used by a common man also. Each and every person constructing his/her house wants to know the approximate amount likely to be required in construction to make budget prevision. This method helps in it. many a time labour. contract rate of is also finalized by per square meter of construction. For example present rate of labour contract per square meter varies from ₹ 1200 to ₹ 2000 per square meter.

(*ii*) **Cubic Rate Estimate.** This estimate is prepared on the basis of cubical contents of the public halls, or cinema halls ; or library buildings etc. multiplied by the cube rate. For such types of buildings this estimate is more accurate.

(*b*) **Cubic Content Method.** In case of plinth area rate, height is not taken into consideration, while in cubic content method, height plays an important role. In this method instead of plinth area, cubic content rate is calculated and cubic content of building under consideration is multiplied by cubic content rate to arrive at approximate building cost. Cubic content rate is always less than that of plinth area rate. In above case a building having 100 square meter of floor area and a height of 3.5M has a cubic contnet of 3.5*100 = 350 cubic meter. If plinth area rate is ₹ 6500/- per square meter than its cubic content rate will be 6500/ 3.50 = ₹ 1857 per cubic meter. This method is more accurate method but however in general is used for buildings other than residential.

(*c*) **Bay Method.** This method is more accurate but can be used for buildings having identical bay type of construction. In this method detailed estimate of one bay is made and than this cost arrived of one bay is multiplied by number of bays to find total cost of building. This method is very useful for industrial sheds having identical bays.

(*d*) **Approximate quantity method estimate.** This type of estimate is prepared to know the approximate quantity of different types of work in the building. Generally this method is adopted. This will give only the idea of approximate cost of the building. Such type of estimate may be needed for applying for loans or to work out the valuation of the property. Only drawing is enough for this type of estimate.

(*e*) **Number of unit estimate.** This estimate is prepared on the unit basis, for the plan purposes, such as school, colleges, polytechnics, hospitals etc. The expenditure is calculated by the multiplication of rate with unit.

2. **Detailed estimate.** This is an accurate estimate, in which the correct quantities of various type of items of work are calculated with the help of detailed drawings, specifications and designs. The abstract of cost is also prepared. This is required for obtaining the technical sanction, calling of tenders, calculating the quantities of different types of materials and the labour needed. Various methods of detailed estimate are

(*a*) Long wall-short wall method also called as individual wall method or wall to wall method or in to in and out to out method

(*b*) Center line method (*c*) Crossing method

All these methods have been dealt in details later on. However crossing method is not that common.

3. Other Type of Estimate

(*a*) **Revised estimate.** This type of estimate is prepared whenever there is increase in the sanctioned amount of expenditure by more than 5 per cent and for which revised administrative sanction is required, due to some changes in the original proposal. All items of works are again calculated in details; and abstract of cost is prepared. Item-wise, comparative statement is prepared and the difference in the amount is added algebraically and the total amount is thus computed, for which revised sanction is obtained for the completion of project, by giving reasons for such sanction.

(*b*) **Supplementary estimate.** Supplementary estimate is prepared, whenever, during the progress of the project, any change is ordered in the original proposal, for the betterment and development of the project. For such changes, an estimate for the additional items of work is prepared and amount is worked out, for which the sanction is obtained, or required.

(*c*) **Supplementary and revised estimate.** Supplementary estimate is required to be revised as for prevaling clause. This estimate is called as supplementary and revised estimate.

(*d*) **Annual repair and maintenance of estimate (A.R. & M.O. estimate).** All the buildings, roads and other assets are maintained in proper condition for the users. Annual repair work, such as white-washing, colour-washing, painting, etc., and daily repairs of building for sanitory, water supply and other building works, are carried out, for which the estimates are prepared, according to the authorised expenditure on such building on yearly basis. The total expenditure is divided into generally three types *i.e.* (*a*) Estimate for such items of works, which are to be done by contract, (*b*) Estimate of material, which will be obtained through suppliers, and (*c*) The estimate of labour, (*i.e.* work charged staff) which will be required for day to day maintenance work. For preparing this estimate "Property Register" is maintained in the Engineering Department in which name of building, cost of the building, the year of completion and type of construction is given. With the help of this, the total amount of expenditure which can be incurred is calculated and the different estimates are prepared accordingly.

(*e*) **Special repair estimate.** In all the buildings the useful lie of woodwork, flooring and plastering etc. is not as much as of the other works, therefore, special repair is carried out to maintain such items of work in proper condition, for which special repair estimate is prepared.

(*f*) **Addition and alteration estimate.** This is the type of estimate, which is prepared for making certain addition or alteration in the building, by making partitions or creating some more doors, windows etc. in the walls. This is prepared as detailed estimate for any new work.

3

Standard Specification for Building Work

Introduction. Specification embrace endless details, ranging over a scope which cannot possibly be converted in any text book. Certain fundamental ideas have been dealt herewith in brief.

Legally the specifications form an integral part of the construction contract. It describes the work and materials to be used in construction in details. It indicates the nature, character and the form of the finished work and prescribe the special characteristics of the materials which can to be used therein, more particularly about the data not shown on drawings.

A combination of drawings and specifications gives the contractor the complete idea about the work he has to perform and materials he has to use in the construction.

Specifications in general should be definite and explicit. These should be lucidly written in the simplest possible language with clauses in a logical order. The description should be exact and complete. A common fault in specifications is indefiniteness of description, arising because of not having actual idea of work and materials or due to obscurity in the language used. Words like "Proper" or "Insufficient" which do not give or "As far as possible" clear idea should be written by an experienced engineer who has complete ideas of construction further they should be concise as far as possible, because fewer words will involve less risk of legal difficulties as this being an legal document.

Specifications are generally of two types :

(*i*) General or brief specifications or (*ii*) Detailed specifications.

General specifications states the clauses of work to be employed in various parts of the building or other work. These specifications only serve as the guideline to the person preparing estimate or designing the work. Hence though they are attached to the contract document but do not form the part of the contract document to be challenged in law.

Detailed specifications law down the rules with regard the quality of material and workmanship. These form a part of the contract document. Being beyond scope of this book.

3.1. BRICK WORK

3.1.1. Classification

Classification of bricks is based on its compressive strength in accordance to IS : 3495-1966. For example, sub-class B has a crushing strength of 200 kg/cm^2. Water absorption varies from 10 to 20% after 24 hours immersion in water. A class designation varies from 450 to 500.

Each brick is further sub-divided into A and B based on shape and tolerances.

3.1.2. Size of Bricks

Nominal size of Modular brick is 20 cm × 10 cm × 10 cm corresponding to actual size 19 cm × 9 cm × 9 cm. Size of conventional FPS brick is 9‴ × 4½″ × 3‴ corresponding to the actual size 9‴ × $4\frac{3}{8}$″ × $2\frac{3}{4}$‴.

3.1.3 Brickwork General

Bricks shall be thoroughly soaked in water for at least one hour before use. (The absence of bubbling when soaked brick is immersed in water is the test for thorough soaking).

Bricks shall be laid in English bond unless otherwise specified. All vertical joints shall be completely filled with mortar without any void in brickwork.

In case of one brick thick or half brick thick wall at least one face shall be kept smooth and plane even if the other side is slightly rough.

All fixtures, pipes, outlets of water etc. shall be embedded in cement mortar. The flue of chimney shall be done with mud gobar mortar (3 mud : 1 gobar).

3.1.4. Joints

The face joints shall be raked to a minimum depth of 15 mm. Where plaster or pointing is not to be done, the joints shall be struck flush.

The face of brickwork shall be cleared on the same day it is laid and all mortar droppings removed.

3.1.5. Protection and Curing

Green work shall be protected from rain by suitable covering. Masonry in cement or composite mortar shall be kept constantly moist on all the faces for a minimum period of seven days.

3.1.6. Brickwork in Arches

Masonry in archwork may be gauged or 'plain'. Cut or specially moulded bricks shall be used in gauged archwork and ordinary bricks shall be used in plain archwork.

Circular plain arches shall be built in half brick concentric rings taking care to break joints transversely. Thickness of joints shall be between 5 and 15 mm. As soon as the arch is completed, the haunch shall be loaded by filling up the spandrels upto the crown level of the arch.

Flat arches shall be gauged arches using cut or moulded bricks. The extrados shall be kept horizontal while the intrados shall be given slight camber (1/100 of span). The bricks shall be laid with radial through joints to the full depth of the arch. Voussiors shall break joints with each other.

In the case of skew back arches bricks forming skew back shall be dressed or cut so as to give true radial bearing as the end voussiors.

The bricks of the spandrel wall at their junctions with the extrados of arch shall be cut to fit in the curvature of the arch.

The centring and shuttering for the arch shall be strong enough to bear the loads that are likely to come upon it during construction without any settlement or deformation. Dead load consists of the load of the arch with the haunch fillings while the live load consists of the load from workmen during the construction. The shuttering shall be tightened with wedges for easy easement.

3.1.7. Half Brickwork (Plain or Reinforced)

Half brickwork is built by laying bricks in stretcher courses. This type of work may be an independent wall or may form leaf/leaves of a cavity wall.

In case of reinforced half brick wall 25 mm × 1.6 mm hoop iron is embedded in the mortar in every third course. Alternately two 6 mm bars may be embedded in every fourth course.

3.1.8. Honeycomb Brickwork

All joints of honeycomb brickwork shall be struck flush to give a uniform surface. The thickness of this work shall be half brick unless otherwise specified. The opening shall be so provided as to give 2 cm bearing on either side.

3.1.9. Mouldings and Cornices

The bricks used for mouldings shall be either purpose moulded cut to required shape. Normally cornices shall not project by more than 20 cm. Each layer of brick shall not project more than one fourth its length. In case projection exceeding 20 cm is required special arrangement such as provision of metal cramps shall be made.

Corbelling shall be roughly brought to required shape by plastering and finished shape shall be given using metal or wooden templates while mortar is green. Curing shall be done for seven days.

3.1.10. Brick Drip Course

Brick drip course is provided above the junction of the roof with the parapet wall. Specially moulded bricks are used for this purpose. Fig. 3.1 shows details of providing the drip course.

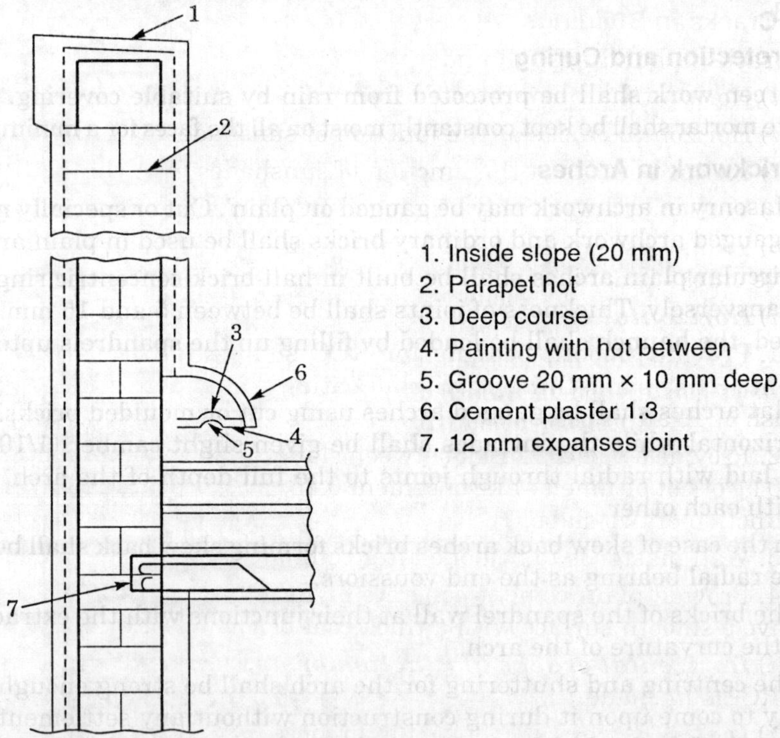

Fig. 3.1. Brick drip course.

3.1.11. Joining Old Brick with New Brickwork

When old brickwork is required to be joined with new work, the old brickwork shall be toothed to the full width of the new wall and depth of quantum of brick in alternate courses. The new brick shall be inserted into the toothing and the layers of new brickwork shall be made to match to those of old work after adjusting thickness of mortar joints. In case the old brickwork consists of FPS bricks, three layers of new brickwork shall be made equal to four layers of old brickwork.

3.1.12. Cavity Walls

The cavity wall may consist of one or both leaves of brick or one of brick and the other of concrete or other material. These leaves are tied by means of specially made wall ties. These ties are spread not more than four brick length apart horizontally and not more than five brick courses staggered vertically. These ties are sloped away from the inner leaf of the cavity wall. At least five ties per square metre of the surface area are provided.

These ties are of mild steel, flat iron suitably twisted to prevent water flowing along it or they may be of round bars bent to oval shape and twisted in the middle. Before inserting into position these ties are given bitumen coating as anti corrosive treatment.

3.1.13. Mortar Droppings

During construction of cavity walls mortar droppings have to be taken care of in particular. This is prevented by providing wooden battens over ties during the construction.

3.1.14. Brickwork with Tile Bricks

The work shall be carried out in the same manner as for common bricks except that brick tiles shall be used instead of conventional bricks.

3.1.15. Cracks in Buildings

Cracks in buildings fall under the following categories :

(*i*) Horizontal at floor or roof level.

(*ii*) Horizontal cracks at the junction of sunshades with the wall.

(*iii*) Inclined cracks at the junction of sunshades with the wall.

(*iv*) Vertical cracks at the junction of RCC beams or pillars.

(*v*) Transverse cracks in RCC slabs in sunshades, verandah and room. Minimisation of the above cracks is done as below :

(*i*) ***Horizontal cracks***

1. Provide smooth bearing for RCC slabs and beams with 6 mm cement mortar (1 cement : 3 fine sand) finished with a floating coat of neat cement over which a thick coat of lime wash or Kraft paper.

2. Provide a gap of 12 mm between slab and masonry and fill this gap with bituminous filler (80 kg of hot bitumen : 1 kg of cement 0.25 cum of coarse sand). Provide similar treatment at the junction of two slabs.

3. Wall plaster is to be done after ceiling plaster has been done.

4. Provide plain cement concrete or RCC bed plate under the beams. The bed plate shall have a smooth surface with a thick coat of lime wash or Kraft paper.

(*ii*) ***Horizontal cracks at junction of sun shades.*** Keep wall plaster separated from that of RCC sun shade.

(*iii*) ***Inclined cracks.*** Provide flat arches for openings upto 1.2 metres. Also RCC lintels to dry as much as possible before plastering the wall.

(*iv*) ***Vertical cracks.*** These cracks are caused due to expansion of RCC beam. These cracks can be avoided by providing continuous beam over the pillar.

(*v*) ***Transverse cracks in the slab in sunshades etc.*** These cracks are avoided by providing expansion joints at every 5 metres in sunshades and 12 metres in continuous slabs.

3.2. STONE MASONRY AND PRECAST CONCRETE BLOCK WORK

3.2.1. Uncoursed Rubble Masonry Random Rubble Polygonal Faced Masonry

As far as possible the following stones shall be used for this masonry.

Granite, trapstone, sand stone and quartzite. The percentage of water absorption shall be below 5.

Cement, lime, pozzolana or combination thereof shall be used as mortar.

Hammer dressing on sides and bed shall be done. The face stone shall be dressed in such a manner as to close up with the adjoining stone in the masonry. The face stones shall be so dresses that no projection exceeds 40 mm from the general wall surface and there is no depression from this surface exceeding 10 mm.

All connected walls in a structure shall be raised regularly and uniformly.

Stones shall be laid in an uncoursed manner to produce polygonal or other specified facing. If part of the masonry is left behind, the wall shall be raked back at an angle not exceeding 45°. Toother joints in masonry shall not be permitted.

Masonry work shall be raised regularly and uniformly and the height done in any one day shall not exceed 1 metre.

Proper bonding shall be achieved by closely filling in adjacent stones as well as by using bond stones as described below. Bond stones or through stones running right across the thickness of the wall shall be provided in walls upto 60 cm thick. In thicker walls two stones shall be provided across the thickness of the wall in such a way that an overlaped 15 cm is provided. At least one bond stone shall be provided for every 0.5 sq metre of wall surface. During construction and for subsequent verification, the bond stone shall be marked.

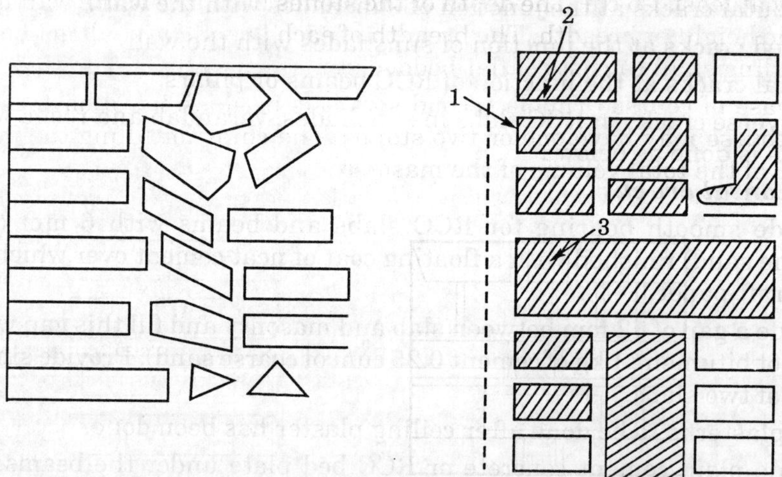

1. Exposed face project
2. 25 mm thick
3. Bonding of brick
4. Plam slai at aler 10 cu mlaol

Fig. 3.2. Uncoursed Rubble/Random Rubble/Polygonal rubble masonry.

The quoins or corner stones shall be properly selected and neatly hammer dressed to form the required corner angle. It shall be laid header and stretcher alternatively. No quoin stone shall be smaller than 0.025 cum.

Jambs shall be made with stones specified for quoins. However, these stones shall have their length equal to the thickness of the wall upto 60 cm, and a line of headers shall be provided for walls thicker than 60 cm.

All joints shall be completely filled with mortar and their thickness shall not exceed 25 mm. Where plastering or pointing is not to be done the joint shall be finished flush simultaneously during the progress of laying while the mortar has not set.

This type of masonry is shown in Fig. 3.2.

Scaffolding shall be strong and sound. Holes left in the masonry after removal of scaffolding shall be made good before plastering.

Where cement or composite mortar is used the surface shall be kept moist for a period of seven days. Green work shall be protected from rain by suitable covering.

3.2.2. Coursed Rubble Masonry

Material for coursed rubble masonry is the same as for uncoursed one. For the first sort course, rubble masonry face stones are hammer dressed so as to give rectangular blocks. The bed joints are chisel dressed for a depth of 5 cm back from the face while the side joints are dressed for a depth of 4 cm back from the face. The bushing on the face shall not project more than 4 cm on an exposed face and not more than 1 cm on the face to be plastered.

For second sort coursed rubble masonry dressing of the stones shall be as for uncoursed masonry. However, no portion of the dressed surface shall show a depression of more than 1 cm against 0.6 cm for the first sort.

For coursed rubble masonry (First sort), the height of each course shall be between 15 cm and 30 cm. Face stones shall be laid in alternate header and stretcher fashion. They shall break joints by at least 7.5 cm. The depth of the stones from face of the wall inwards shall not be less than the height or breadth. The breadth of each face stone shall not be less than 15 cm. The interior filling shall consists of flat bedded stones carefully laid on their proper beds.

In the case of coursed rubble second sort it is permissible to have courses of varying height and a course may have one or two stones. The chips for filling the interstics shall be limited to 15% of the total volume of the masonry.

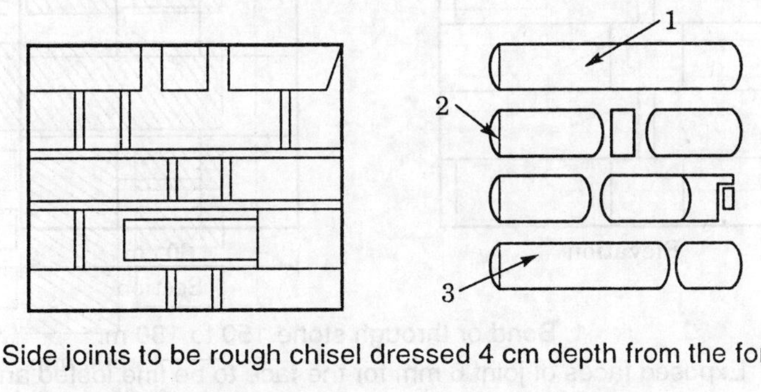

Side joints to be rough chisel dressed 4 cm depth from the for

1. Bond or through stone
2. Exposed face bushing to be not more than 4 cm.
3. Quoin stone 4 cm long (nutrim)

Fig. 3.3. Coursed rubble masonry.

Bond stones shall be provided as for uncoursed masonry but there shall be one bond stone for every 1 metre length of every course.

Quoins shall not be smaller than 0.025 cum in volume and shall not be less than 30 cm in length and 25% of these stones shall not be less than 50 cm in length. Quoins shall be of the same height as the course to which it belongs and shall be at least 40 cm in length.

All joints shall be completely and properly filled with mortar and shall not be more than 10 mm thick. On faces where no plastering is to be done joints shall be struck flush and finished simultaneously while laying the stones. When plastering or pointing is to be provided joints shall be raked to minimum depth of 2 cm.

This type of masonry is illustrated in Fig. 3.3.

3.2.3. Stone Work in Plain Ashlar Masonry

Stones for ashlar masonry shall be hard, sound, durable, and tough. They shall be free from decay, weathering and undesirable particles. Water absorption shall not exceed 5%.

All faces shall be so cut and dressed with chisel so as to give true horizontal and vertical joints. In a 60 cm long edge variation shall not exceed 1 mm.

Stones shall be wetted before laying. They shall be floated with mortar and properly bedded with wooded mallet.

Stones shall be laid in header-stretcher or any other. They shall break joints for at least half the height of the course. The height of the course shall be uniform and not less than 15 cm. Ashlar masonry work may be a composite one as well with ashlar stone facing and brick-work or coursed/uncoursed rubble backing. Bond stones shall be provided at the rate of not less than one per 1.8 m length in each course. They shall be through stones running across the wall upto 60 cm thickness.

The thickness of the joints shall not exceed 5 mm. A uniform recess of 15 mm depth shall be made with the help of steel plate to receive pointing to be done later.

Curing and protection shall be as for coursed stone masonry. Single, scoffolding shall not be permitted.

Fig. 3.4 illustrates this type of masonry.

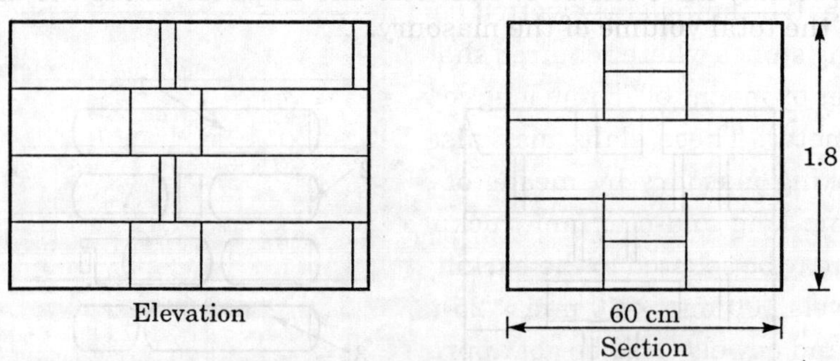

1. Bond or through stone 150 to 180 m.
Exposed faces of joint 6 mm for the face to be fine losted and the remaining faces and beds to be chisel dressed.

Fig. 3.4. Ashlar masonry.

3.2.4. Stone Work Sunk or Moulded, Ashlar Moulded and Carved Columns

Stone used for this purpose shall be hard, durable and tough. It shall be free from cracks and weathering.

Every stone shall be cut to the required size and shape and chisel dressed on all beds and joints. The face shall be brought to the required shape. The vertical surface shall not show a variation of more than 3 mm when a straight edge is placed against the surface. The surface and the moulding obtained shall be the finest possible by means of chiselling.

3.2.5. Stone Work in Arches and Domes

Stone for the work shall be hard, durable and sound. It shall be free from cracks and weathering effect.

Every stone shall be cut to the required wedge shape and size and chisel dressed on all beds and joints. No point on the dressed surface shall have a deviation of more than 3 mm from a 60 cm long straight edge. A full size layout of each unit shall be prepared to facilitate cutting of the stones to required size and shape. Centring and shuttering and false work required for the arch or dome shall be unyielding. Fig. 3.5 illustrates stone work in arches.

3.2.6. Stone Work in Wall Lining

Stone shall be of special variety such as red/ white sand stone, trap stone etc.

The face of the stone slabs shall be chiselled in such a way that a smooth surface free from waviness is obtained. The deviation from straight over a straight length of 60 cm shall not exceed 1 mm. Finished thickness of the slab shall be within + 2 mm. To prevent absorption of water from the mortar, the stone shall be sufficiently wetted before laying. The adjoining stones where required shall be secured to each other by means of 75 mm long copper pins of 6 mm diameter. These slabs may also be secured to the backing masonry by means of gun metal cramps 25 mm long and of 6 mm thickness. Alternately stones may be secured to the backing by means of stone dowels 100 mm × 50 mm × 25 mm. Such pins, cramps and dowels shall be got approved before incorporation in the work. 1 : 2 (Cement : Coarse sand) mortar shall be used for fixing them. See Fig. 3.7, 3.8.

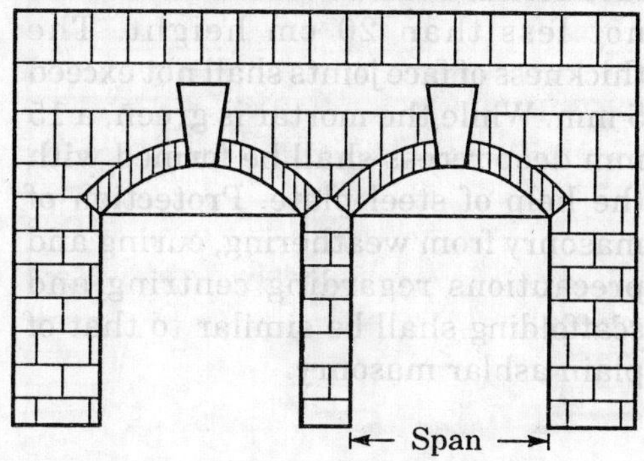

All exposed faces and all joints 6 mm from face shall be fine looted

Face joint to do not more than 5 mm thick.

Fig. 3.5. Semi Circular Arch.

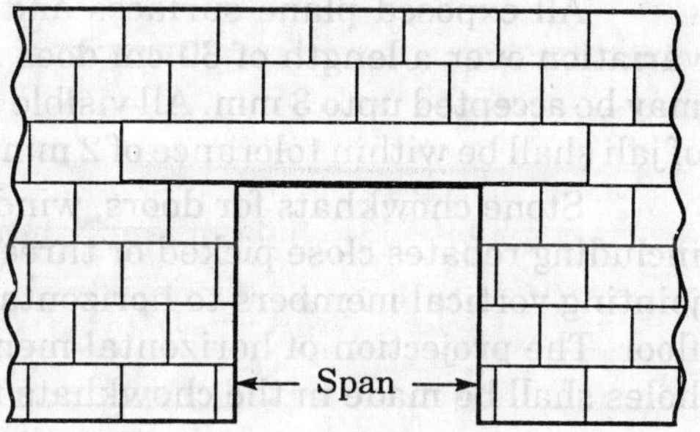

All exposed faces and all joints 6 mm from the face shall to fine looted.

Fig. 3.6. Flat Arch.

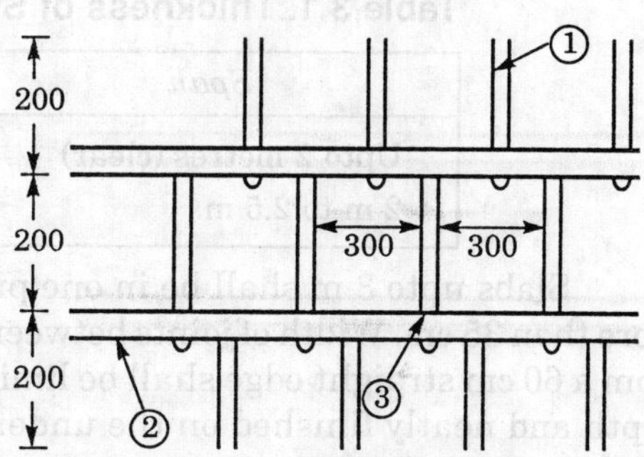

1. Exposed faces and side joints from the face to be fine beder
2. Face joint to be not more than 5 mm thick.
3. Gun metal cramp 4 m + 6 mm × 300 m.

Fig. 3.7. Details of fixing stone Veneer work. (All dimensions in mm)

The face work and backing masonry shall be built together. The face stones shall be laid in courses of not less than 20 cm height. The thickness of face joints shall not exceed 5 mm. While the mortar is green, a 15 mm deep recess shall be formed with the help of steel plate. Protection of masonry from weathering, curing and precautions regarding centring and scaffolding shall be similar to that of plain ashlar masonry.

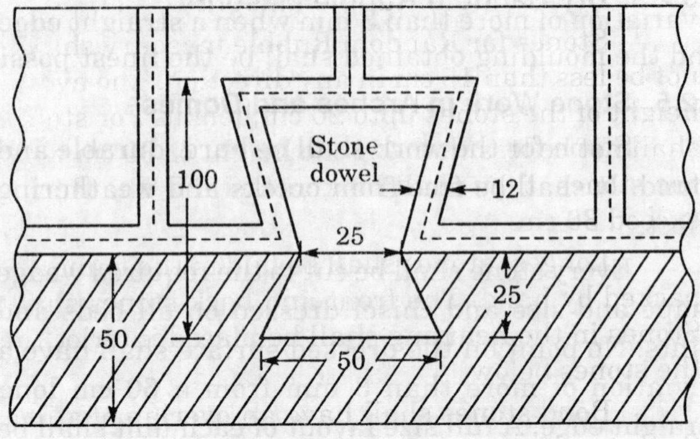

Fig. 3.8. Stone Dowel.
(All dimensions in mm)

3.2.7. Stone Shelves, Coping, Cornices etc.

Stones used for shelves, copings, cornices, string courses, and jail work shall be hard, sound and durable.

All exposed plane surfaces and sides shall be chisel dressed in such a way that the variation over a length of 60 cm does not exceed 1 mm. In the case of shelves this variation may be accepted upto 3 mm. All visible angles and edges shall be free from chipping. Thickness of jali shall be within tolerance of 2 mm. Fixing shall be done in specified cement : sand mortar.

Stone chowkhats for doors, windows and clerestorey windows shall have exposed faces including rebates close picked or three line dressed. Mortice and tenon joint shall be used for jointing vertical members to horizontal members and shall be embedded 15 cm deep into the floor. The projection of horizontal members shall not be less than 15 cm wide. Recesses and holes shall be made in the chowkhats for fixing hinges and bolt staple.

Stone slabs for lintels sills and roofing shall be sawn or split in a plane parallel to the natural bed of the stone obtained from approved quarry. Thickness of stone slabs are given in table 3.1.

Table 3.1. Thickness of Stone Slabs for Lintels, Sills and Roofing

Span	*Thickness (cm)*
Upto 2 metres (clear)	7.5 to 10
2 m to 2.5 m	10 to 12.5

Slabs upto 3 m shall be in one piece. Width of the slab shall not be less than 25 cm nor more than 35 cm. Width of joints between the adjoining slabs shall not exceed 25 mm. Depression from a 60 cm straight edge shall be limited to 2 cm. Joints shall be filled with mortar to the full depth and neatly finished on the underside.

3.2.8. Stone Chajjas

Stones for chajjas shall be hard, sound and durable. The finished thickness shall be as specified with a tolerance of 2 mm. The chajja shall have a bearing of 20 cm on the wall measured horizontally. 45 cm long and 12 mm dia bars shall be used for anchoring each slab. The lower end of such bar shall be bent for fixing into the masonry joint.

Specifications for curing, protection, scaffolding etc. shall be as for plain ashlar masonry work.

3.2.9. Dry Random Rubble Masonry

Stones for Random Rubble masonry shall be as for coursed rubble masonry. They shall not be less than 15 cm in any direction. The average length shall not be less than 1½ times the height of the stones upto 20 cm height. For stones exceeding 20 cm height the average length shall not be less than 1½ the height or 30 cm whichever is more. To obtain largest bedding for the stones, they shall be knocked off. The thickness of joint in front and rear face shall not exceed 30 cm.

Longest stones shall be laid in the foundation. They shall be laid close to each other and packed by hand. The front and back stones shall be laid alternately headers and stretchers. Stones in the hearting shall be placed interlocking each other. Stones shall break joints with the stones below.

Bond stones shall have an overlap of at least 20 cm. These stones shall be provided at the rate of 2 per square metre of the front face area. These stones shall not be less than 300 sq cm at any section.

3.2.10. Laterite Stone Masonry Work

The stone shall be compact in texture, sound, durable and shall be obtained from an approved quarry. Absorption shall not be more than 20% after 24 hours immersion. The stone shall be dressed into regular rectangular blocks and shall not be less than 15 cm in width and height. Breadth shall not be less than height. The length shall generally be twice the breadth plus one mortar joint. The stones shall be laid in alternate courses of headers and stretchers. All connected masonry shall be raised uniformly.

Quoins may be provided where specified, otherwise they may be dispensed with. The quantity of approved quality of mortar required for the work is 0.18 cum to 0.20 cum.

On faces where no plastering or pointing is to be done the joint shall be struck flush and finished simultaneously while the mortar is green. Precautions for protection against weathering, curing, scaffolding etc. shall be as for uncoursed rubble or random rubble masonry.

3.2.11. Precast Concrete Block Masonry

The solid material in the blocks shall be between 50% and 75% of the volume of blocks calculated from overall dimensions. The blocks shall be free from cracks, broken edges and honey combing. The block shall be considered as solid if the solid material in the block is not less than 75% of the total volume of the block calculated from the overall dimensions of the block.

The concrete mix used for making the blocks shall not be richer than one part by volume of cement to 6 parts by volume of combined aggregate. Standard size of the blocks shall be as given in table 3.2.

Table 3.2. Standard Size of Concrete Precast Block

Size Designation	*Nominal size (cm)*			*Actual size (cm)*		
	L	*B*	*H*	*L*	*B*	*H*
A	40	30	20	39	30	19
B	40	20	20	39	20	19
C	40	10	20	39	10	19

Precast blocks may be machine made or hand made. Faces of blocks shall be flat and rectangular. They shall be rendered smooth or plastered using 1 : 3 mortar (Cement 1 : Coarse sand 3). Average compressive strength of the blocks shall not be less than 50 kg/cm^2 of the gross area. These blocks shall be stacked and stored such that they are not in contact with moisture at site.

Lime cement cinder blocks shall conform to IS : 3115-1965 while lime cement cinder hollow blocks shall conform to IS : 5498-1969.

Load bearing light weight concrete blocks (solid or hollow) shall conform to IS : 3590-1966.

Autoclave cellular concrete blocks shall conform to IS : 5482-1969. Non load bearing Gypsum partition blocks (Solid and hollow type) shall conform to IS : 2849-1964. Solid cement blocks shall conform to IS : 1725-1960.

Any standard mortar specified (cement lime sand, cement sand, lime pozzolana sand etc.) may be used for block masonry work. For most of the work, the joints shall be 10 mm thick. Before or during the laying operation the blocks need not be wetted. In hot weather, the blocks may be only slightly moistened to prevent absorption of water by the masonry. For all building, slabs and blocks for external work, special quoin blocks shall be cast. The return face of these blocks shall be equal to half the normal face. Proper half length closer shall be cast and not cut from the normal blocks. Return ends of blocks for door and window reveals and quoins shall be finished with a fair-face finished face in the mould. Only double scaffolding shall be used.

The blocks shall be suitably finished or pointed as specified.

3.2.12. Stone Block Masonry

The minimum quantity of stone pieces to be used in a block shall be 35% of the volume of the block. The size of the stones used shall be between 5 to 15 cm.

The size of the blocks shall be as given in table 3.3.

Table 3.3. Size of Stone Blocks for Masonry

Size Designation	*Nominal size (cm)*			*Actual size (cm)*		
	L	*B*	*H*	*L*	*B*	*H*
Load bearing	30	20	15	29	19	14
Partition	30	10	10	29	10	10

For bond purposes blocks of 1/3 and 2/3 of the size given above shall be used.

Minimum compressive strength of these blocks shall be 50 kg/cm^2. The various steps involved in the preparation of the blocks are as given below :

1. Place the moulds in a row. For easy removal of the blocks from the mould apply grease and kerosene oil in the ratio of 1 : 4.

2. Lay 2 or 3 large size stones (12 cm say).

3. Fill the gap between the stone pieces in the lower side of the mould upto about 5 cm height with cement concrete 1 : 5 : 8 (cement : fine aggregate : 20 mm gauge stones)/cement concrete 1 : 4 : 8 with stones of 20 mm nominal gauge/cement concrete 1 : 5 : 10 and compact with trowel.

4. Fill up the remaining portion by means of 60 to 75 mm pieces of stones in the gap and pour the same cement concrete mix upto the top. Compact by rodding/tamping.

5. Put a wooden piece on top of the block cast and pull the mould up after 3 or 4 minutes.

6. After 24 hours turn the blocks upside down and keep the stone texture exposed. Cure the block in water for seven days and air dry them for 21 days before use.

Mortar as specified may be used.

Before laying, the blocks are slightly wetted, 1/3 and 2/3 size stones shall be used for bonding. The thickness of joints shall not exceed 1 cm.

3.3. MARBLE WORK

IS : 1130-1969 shall be followed for marble work.

The following varieties of marble shall be used :

(*i*) *White variety*. Makrana first/second quality, Abu white, Abu panthar, White veined.

(*ii*) *Black variety*. Black Bainslana, Black Zebra from Kissangarh, Abu and Narnaul. Makrana Zebra Marble from Dhobi Doongri.

(*iii*) Green variety from Baroda, Abu, Falma and Bundi.

(*iv*) Plain pink from Makrana and Bar, Pink Adanga from Makrana and Bar and Bundi, Grey from Makrana and Bundi.

(*v*) *Brown variety*. From Bar and Narnaul.

The stone shall be hard, dense and homogeneous with crystalline and coarse grains and shall be free from stains, cracks, decay and weathering.

Every stone shall be cut to the required size and shape and chisel dressed on all beds and joints. The exposed faces and joint 12 mm from the face shall be fine tooled such that straight edge in contact with the face shall be in contact all along. Beyond the depth of 12 mm from the face the joints shall be dressed with a slight splay so that the thickness of the joint increases in an inverted 'V' shape.

A sample of the dressed and rubbed stone shall be prepared for approval and the approved sample shall be exhibited on for future reference and comparison.

Only specified mortar shall be used.

Stones shall be laid as in plain ashlar masonry work. The thickness of joints shall not be more than 1.5 mm on the exposed face. Beyond the depth of 12 mm from the face, the thickness of joint shall increase in an inverted 'V' shape so as to give a good mortar bond between two stones. The inverted 'V' shaped portion of the joint shall be filled with the bedding mortar and the face 12 mm portion with pointing mortar.

The work shall be kept constantly moist for a period of seven days.

After marble work is cured, it shall be rubbed with carbo-randum stone of different grades Nos. 60, 80 and 120 in succession so as to give a plain and smooth surface.

Scaffolding and protection shall be as for plain ashlar masonry. In case of marble work in wall lining etc. (Veneer work) marble shall be cut into slabs of required thickness. In order to ensure good binding with the hearting or backing the back shall not be dressed but kept rough. The dressed and rubbed slabs shall be of the specified thickness with a tolerance of 2 mm. Stonework for wall lining shall be taken to match the grains of veneer work. Thickness of face joints shall be uniform straight and as fine as possible but the thickness of joints shall not exceed 1.5 mm. The face joint upto 12 mm depth shall be filled with specified mortar for pointing.

Curing, finishing protection and scaffolding shall be the same as for marble work.

Marble jali work shall be carried out in the same way as wall lining. Fixing shall be done with the adjoining grooves, rebates etc.

Thickness of marble jali shall be as indicated in the drawing. All exposed faces shall be fine tooled to a uniform and smooth finish.

3.4. FORM WORK

3.4.1. Indian Standards to be Followed

IS : 303-1960. Specifications for Plywood for general purposes.

IS : 1658-1966. Fibre hard boards.

IS : 1730-1961. Steel plates.

IS : 808-1957. Steel angles.

IS : 723-1961. Mild steel wire nails.

3.4.2. Materials

Timber for formwork shall be free from shakes, loose knots, wormholes or other defects. The strength of planks, scantlings, and battens shall be strong enough to take up the design load. Plywood used for lining shall comply with IS : 303-1960.

Hard board shall conform IS : 1658-1966.

Ballies used for formwork shall be of salt. It shall be of the variety known as 'gollas' following tolerances are permitted. (See Table 3.4).

Table 3.4. Tolerances for Sal Ballies Diameters

S. No.	*Length*	*Mean diameter or diameter at centre*	*Tolerances in diameter at the thinner end*
1.	Ballies below 3 m length	Not less than specified diameter.	The diameter at the thinner end shall not be less than specified diameter by more than 10 mm.
2.	Ballies exceeding 3 m length	Not less than specified diameter.	The diameter at the near end shall not be less than specified diameter by more than 20 mm.

Ballies to be used as props shall not be less than 10 mm minimum measured at mid length and 80 mm at the end. Bamboos shall be of mature growth free splits, rot, borer holes and other defects.

Bricks used in formwork shall conform to the relevant specifications.

Steel plates shall conform to IS : 1730-1961.

Steel angles shall conform to IS : 808-1957.

For steel forms refined mineral oil shall be used while for wooden forms refined paraffin mineral oil shall be used. Surface treatment for formwork shall be prepared by dissolving yellow soap in water.

Mild steel nails shall be bright finished and of adequate strength.

They shall conform to IS : 723-1961.

Ropes for use in formwork shall be from good quality munj ban or from other approved quality.

3.4.3. Workmanship

Depending upon the quality of work formwork is classified as :

(*i*) Rough finish (*ii*) Fair finish

(*iii*) Decorative fine finish (*iv*) Medium smooth finish

Formwork shall be rigid and strong enough to take up the load without undergoing change in shape and dimensions. It should be possible to remove all the side pieces without removing the bottom members.

In case during concreting or after concreting but before removal of the formwork, there is buldging or sagging of the formwork, all the concrete shall be removed and the work redone after strengthening the formwork.

The props shall consist of ballies or brick masonry pillars. In case shuttering has to support two or more floors, the centring and shuttering shall be capable of supporting load of at least two floors below it. The props of the upper floor must rest on the props of lower floor. The surface of plank coming in contact with concrete shall be accurately sawn and planed on the sides. All angles of the formwork shall be sharp and well defined. Form lining shall be such as will not discolour the concrete.

Forms shall be cleaned of all wood shavings dirt and other matter. Oil shall be applied in such a way as to cover the entire surface.

Shuttering for beams and slabs shall have a camber of 4 mm per metre (1 in 250).

Formwork shall not be struck unless concrete has developed twice the stress to which it may be subjected to after removal of the forms.

Table 3.5 gives the period after which formwork may be removed.

Table 3.5. Period Specified for Removal of Formwork

S. No.	*Part of Structure*	*Period in Days*
1.	Sides of foundations, columns etc.	2 days
2.	Underside of slabs	7 to 21 days for spans of upto 4.5, 6, and over 6 metres
3.	Dams, Shells, Vaults, folded plates etc.	As per instruction of Engineer-in-charge

3.5. WOOD WORK AND JOINERY

3.5.1. Indian Standards to be Followed

IS : 286–1973. Moisture content for timbers.

IS : 1761–1960. Transparent glass sheets for glazing.

IS : 419–1967. Putty for use on window frames.

IS : 2202 (Part I)–1973. Wooden flush door shutters. Ply wood face panels.

IS : 2202 (Part II)–1966. Wooden flush door shutters (partial board face panels).

IS : 2191–(Part I)–1973. Wooden (Cellular and hollow core type) plywood face panels.

IS : 2191–(Part II)–1966. Wooden flush door shutters (Cellular particle board face panel).

IS : 1341–1962. Steel butt hinges.

IS : 205–1966. Non ferrous metal butt hinges.

IS : 362–1962. Parliament hinges.

IS : 1003 (Part I) 1966. Timber panelled glazed shutters, Doors.

IS : 1003 (Part II) 1966. Timber panelled glazed shutters. Window and ventilator shutter.

IS : 6198–1971. Ledged braced and battened door shutters.

IS : 303–1975. Plywood for general purposes.

IS : 3087–1965. Wood particle boards.

IS : 1658–1966. Fibre hard boards.

IS : 2098–1964. Asbestos sheet building boards.

IA : 1328–1970. Veneered decorative plywood.

3.5.2. Materials

3.5.2.1. Sawn timber. The various sawn timbers are used.

(*i*) **First class Indian teak wood.** The timber shall be of high quality and well seasoned and free from dead knots and cracks. No individual hard knot shall be more than 6 sq cm and aggregate area of such knots shall not exceed 1% of the area of the piece.

(*ii*) **Second class teak wood.** Second class teak wood shall be similar to first class except that no individual knot shall be more than 15 sq cm. and total area of such knots in any single piece shall not be more than 2% of the area of the piece.

(*iii*) **First class deodar wood.** Timber shall be of very good quality free from cracks, dead knots and cracks. It shall be properly seasoned. No individual hard and sound knot shall be more than 6 sq cm and total area of such knots shall not exceed 1% of the area of the piece. There shall be at least four annual rings per cm width of the cross-section.

(*iv*) **Second class deodar wood.** Same as for first class deodar except that there shall be at least 3 growth rings instead of four and any single knot shall not be more than 15 sq cm in area and total area of knots in any one piece shall not be more than 2% of the area of the piece.

(*v*) **First class kail wood.** The timber shall be of good quality free from dead knots, cracks and sap wood. It shall be well seasoned. Individual sound knot shall not be more than 6 sq cm in area and total area of knots in any one piece shall not exceed 1% of the area of the piece. Number of growth rings per cm width of the cross-section shall not be less than 5.

(*vi*) **Kail wood second class.** Same as for kail wood first class except that the size of individual sound knot shall not be more than 15 sq cm and total area of sound knots in any piece shall not be greater than 2% of the area of the piece. Number of growth rings per cm width of the section shall not be less than 2.

(*vii*) **Other varieties of timber.** Timber used as first class shall be free from knots cracks and sap wood. It shall be well seasoned. First class variety shall have sound knots such that they do not occupy an area exceeding 1% of the piece while second class variety may have such knots upto 2% of the area of the piece.

(*viii*) **Maximum permissible moisture content.** For purpose of permissible moisture India has been divided into four zones. Moisture content permissible for these zones is given in Table 3.6.

Table 3.6. Permissible Moisture Content (Maximum %)

Thickness Zone I AARH of timber 30-40%		*Zone II AARH 40-50%*	*Zone III AARH 50-57%*	*Zone IV AARH above 67%*
Greater than 50 mm	10	12	14	16
Less than 50 mm	8	10	12	14

Note. AARH-Average annual relative humidity percentage moisture content

$$= \frac{W_1 - W_2}{W_1} \times 100.$$

where W_1 = Initial weight of test section, W_2 = Oven dry weight of test section.

(*ix*) **Glazing material.** Glass panes for glazing work in doors and windows shall not be thinner than 2 mm for panes upto 0.1 sq m and not less than 3 mm for glass panes larger than 0.1 sq m.

(*x*) **Putty for glazing in wooden frames of doors and windows.** Putty shall be prepared by mixing one part of white lead with three parts of finely powdered chalk and then making a homogeneous stiff paste in boiled linseed oil.

(*xi*) **Ready made shutters.** Ready made shutters shall conform to IS specifications.

3.5.3. Workmanship

Work shall be carried out as per drawings and specifications. The various items of workmanship are :

3.5.3.1. Jointings. The jointing of timber frames shall be done by pinning with hard wood or bamboo pins of 10 to 15 mm dia.

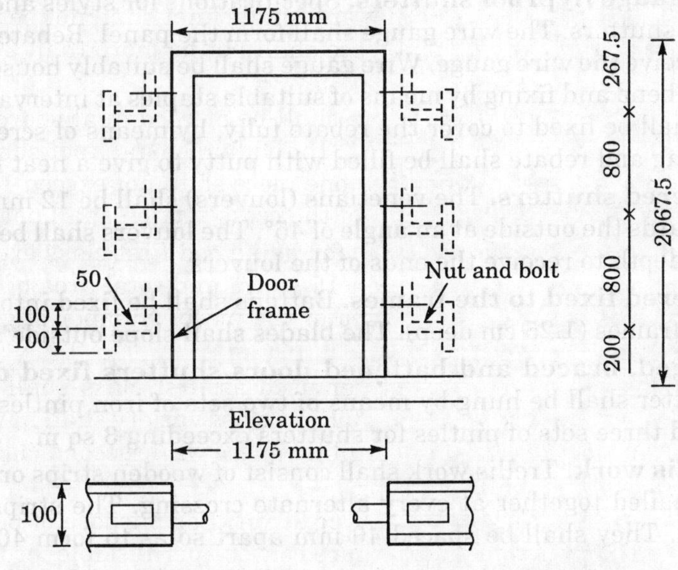

Fig. 3.9. Fixing hold fasts to door frames.

The door and window frames shall have rebates to house the shutter, the depth of such rebates shall be 1.25 cm.

3.5.3.2. Surface treatment. Woodwork shall be oiled, painted or polished as specified.

3.5.3.3. Fixing in position. Frames shall be fixed as per Fig. 3.9.

Where doors have not been provided with sills the frame shall be temporarily braced at the sill level.

For roof trusses a full sized truss diagram shall be laid on a level platform. From this diagram, templates for joints shall be made. Trusses shall be hoisted and placed in position and secured to the walls by means of holding-down bolts.

3.5.3.4. Panelled, glazed or panelled add glazed shutters for doors, windows and clerestorey window. The wooden members shall be planed, smooth and accurate. They shall be cut to exact shape and size without patching or plugging of any kind.

The thickness of styles and rails shall normally be as specified. The minimum thickness of panels where width of panels is not more than 30 cm shall be 15 mm. Where the width of panel is more than 30 cm or more thickness of panels may be 20 mm.

Styles and rails shall be properly and accurately mortised and tenoned. They shall be made of single piece. The tenons shall pass clear through styles. The styles and rails shall have 12 mm groove to receive the panel.

Ready made shutters shall be of correct size. Adding of battens to make up the size shall not be permitted.

3.5.3.5. Battened and framed door shutters. The battens shall be 20 mm thick and 75 to 100 mm wide. They shall be planed smooth. They shall be rebate jointed and glued together. The battens shall be framed into styles and rails by means of feather joints and fixed into 12 mm grooves made in the styles and rails.

3.5.3.6. Lodged and battened or ledged and battened door and window shutters. The battens shall be 20 mm thick and 75 to 100 mm wide. They shall be fixed together by 25 mm thick horizontal ledges and inclined braces. The ledges shall be 175 mm wide and braces 125 mm wide. Tee type hinges shall be provided in ledges only.

3.5.3.7. Wire gauge flyproof shutters. Specifications for styles and rails shall be the same as for panelled shutters. The wire gauge shall form the panel. Rebates shall be made in styles and rails to receive the wire gauge. Wire gauge shall be suitably housed in the rebate by giving a right angled bend and fixing by means of suitable staples at intervals of about 75 mm. A wooden beading shall be fixed to cover the rebate fully, by means of screws and nails. The space between beading and rebate shall be filled with putty to give a neat finish.

3.5.3.8. Louvered shutters. The venetians (louvers) shall be 12 mm thick. The blade shall slope down towards the outside at an angle of 45°. The louvers shall be fixed in the styles by making 1.25 mm depth to receive the ends of the louvers.

3.5.3.9. Louvered fixed to the frames. Battens shall be fixed into the frames in the grooves made in the frames (1.25 cm deep). The blades shall slope outside at an angle of 45°.

3.5.3.10. Ledged, braced and battened doors shutters fixed directly into the wall. Each door shutter shall be hung by means of two sets of iron pintles for shutters upto the size of 3 sq m and three sets of pintles for shutters exceeding 3 sq m.

3.5.3.11. Trellis work. Trellis work shall consist of wooden strips or laths 40 × 12 mm section planed and nailed together at every alternate crossing. The strips shall cross each other at right angles. They shall be spaced 40 mm apart so as to form 40 × 40 mm square opening.

3.5.3.12. Trellis door and window shutters. Shutter frame shall consist of two style rail bottom rail each of section 75 mm × 4 mm. To this frame of styles and rails shall be fixed the trellis work,

3.5.3.13. Trellis work using half round bamboos. The width of the split bamboos shall be 35 mm to 40 mm. They shall be fixed to wooden frames so as to form square openings of 40 × 40 mm. The strips shall be nailed to the frame at alternate crossings. The work shall be finished by 40 mm wide beading of bamboo strip round the edges of the work.

3.5.3.14. Compound gates. Standard gate is shown in Fig. 3.10. It shall be fixed to the masonry pillars of the compound wall with four sets of pintles. These pintles shall be fixed in concrete blocks.

3.5.3.15. Plain teak wood panelling high skirting over walls. The thickness of panel shall be 15 mm upto width of 40 mm and 30 mm for greater width. The chair rail, the vertical member between panels (styles), the top rail shall be 75 mm × 50 mm size. The panels shall be fixed into grooves made in the chair, rails, styles and top rail.

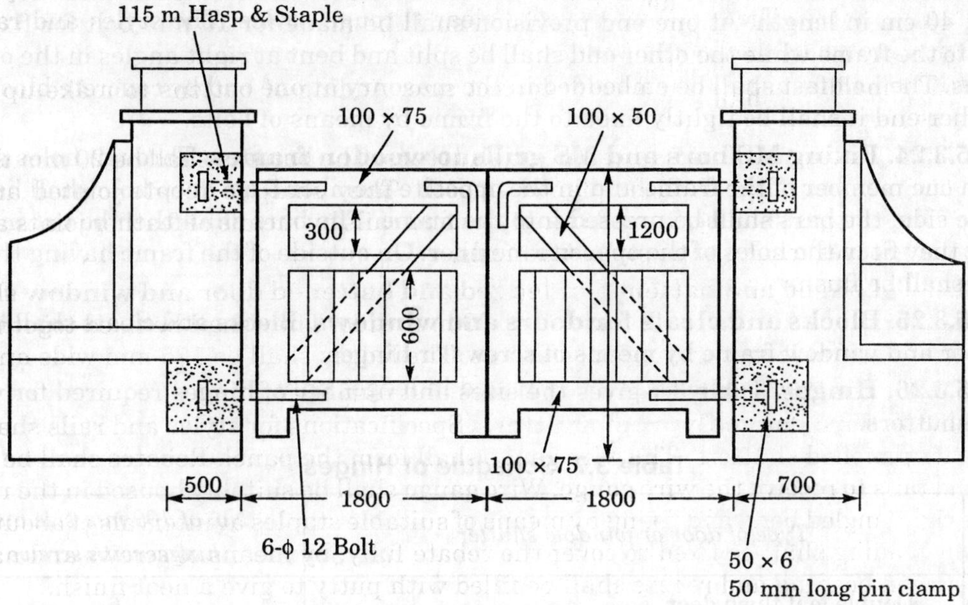

Fig. 3.10. Compound Gate.

The panelling shall be fixed into the walls with the help of wooden plugs fixed into the walls.

Suitable approved wood preservative shall be applied on the back side of the panelling work.

3.5.3.16. Providing wooden plugs in the walls. Plugs shall be made of second class teak or other hard wood. They shall be trapezoidal having cross-section of 50 × 50 mm at the base and 40 × 40 mm at the top and a depth of 40 mm. They shall be embedded into the wall in 1 : 3 mortar.

3.5.3.17. Plain frame panelling for wall lining or partition. The styles shall be 75 × 40 mm. For width of panels upto 40 cm the thickness shall be 15 mm and for greater width its thickness shall be 20 mm. When made of more than one piece they shall be joined together by tongued and grooved joint. They shall be made of one piece of not more than 20 cm width and not less than 12.5 cm width.

The exposed side of the panel shall be planed smooth and even.

3.5.3.18. Teak wood moulding and architraves. The finished work shall give a neat and presentable appearance.

3.5.3.19. Pelmets. Wooden planks for pelmets shall be planed smooth. They shall be fixed to the wall by means of 25 × 3 mm MS brackets 10 cm in length. They shall be bent in the form of angle and wooden plugs fixed in the walls using wood screws, two such brackets shall be used for pelmets upto 1.5 metres in length. For longer pelmets additional brackets shall be provided at the rate of one per additional one metre length.

3.5.3.20. Curtain rods. Curtain rods shall be fixed to the pelmets at the end.

3.5.3.21. Panelled or glazed partition walls. Panels may be of solid planks, asbestos, plywood glass, or any other specified material. They shall be planed smooth and even. When glass is used as panels, putty shall be used in addition to beading.

3.5.3.22. Wooden shelves. They shall be planed smooth and fixed over the iron brackets.

3.5.3.23. Holdfasts. For doors and windows holdfasts shall be made from 40 × 3 mm flat iron, 40 cm in length. At one end provision shall be made for 10 mm bolt for fixing the holdfast to the frame while the other end shall be split and bent at right angles in the opposite directions. The holdfast shall be embedded in the masonry at one end by concrete block while at the other end it shall be tightly fixed to the frame by means of bolts.

3.5.3.24. Fixing MS bars and MS grills to wooden frames. Through holes shall be drilled in one member of the frame and in the opposite member 5 cm deep hole shall be made. From one side, the bars shall be pressed into the frame. The bars shall then be cut in such a way that they fit in the holes of the opposite member. On outside of the frame having the holes the bars shall be flush.

3.5.3.25. Blocks and cleats for doors and windows. Blocks and cleats shall be fixed to the door and window frame by means of screws or hinges.

3.5.3.26. Hinges. Table 3.7 gives the sizes and number of hinges required for various types of shutters.

Table 3.7. Schedule of Hinges

S. No.	*Type of door or window shutter*	*No. of 100 mm size butt hinges with screws*
1.	Double leaf flush door	6
2.	Double-leaf panelled, glazed, panelled and glazed, battened and framed, trellis wire gauges etc.	6
3.	Single leaf flush-shutter exceeding 80 cm in width	4
4.	Single leaf flush shutter less than 80 cm in width	3
5.	As per serial 2 but single leaf shutter exceeding 80 cm in width	4
6.	As per serial 5 but shutter less than 80 cm in width	3
7.	As per serial 2 but window shutter	4
8.	As per serial 7 but single leaf	2
9.	Clerestorey window shutter, bottom hung	2

3.6. STEEL, ALUMINIUM AND IRON WORK

3.6.1. Indian Standards to be Followed

IS : 1956–1962. Glossary of terms relating to iron and steel.

IS : 814–(Part II)–1974. Specifications for covered electrodes, for welding sheets.

IS : (Part I)–1974. Specifications for covered electrodes, for other than welding sheets.

IS : 815-1974. Specifications and costing of covered electrodes.

IS : 818–1968. Code of practice for safety and health requirements in electric and gas welding.

IS : 1182–1967. Recommended practice for Radiographic examination of fusion welded butt joints.

IS : 1182–1973. Specifications for rolling and cutting tolerances for rolled steel products.

IS : 1148–1964. Specifications for rivet bars for structural purposes.

IS : 806–1968. Specifications for steel tubes in building construction.

IS : 1161–1968. Specifications for structural purposes.

IS : 816–1969. Code of practice for use of metal arc weld.

IS : 3600–(Part I)–1973. Method of testing fusion welded joints.

IS : 6227–1971. Use of metal arc welding in tubular structure.

IS : 6248–1971. Rolling shutters and rolling grills.

IS : 733–1967. Wrought Aluminium and Aluminium alloys.

IS : 1081–1960. Fixing and glazing of metal.

IS : 4351–1967. Specifications for steel door frames.

IS : 1948–1961. Specifications for aluminium Doors, and Windows.

IS : 1949–1961. Aluminium Windows for Industrial Buildings.

IS : 1361–1959. Steel Windows for Industrial buildings.

IS : 239 (Part I)–1973. MS Tubes

IS : 1239 (Part II)–1969. MS Tubular pipe fittings.

IS : 1200 (Part III)–1974. Steel Work and Iron Work.

IS : 1038–1969. Steel doors, windows and ventilators.

IS : 1200 (Part XIV)–1970. Method of measurement–Glazing.

IS : 2062–1969. Structural Steel (Fusion welding quality).

IS : 1977–1969. Structural Steel (ordinary quality).

IS : 226–1975. Structural Steel (Standard quality).

IS : 823–1964. Manual steel arc welding.

IS : 102–1962. Ready mixed paints.

IS : 1363–1967. Hexagonal bolts, nuts etc.

IS : 813–1961–Symbols for welding.

IS : 817–1966. Training and testing metal arc welders.

IS : 800–1962. Use of Structural Steel in building construction.

IS : 737–1965. Wrought Aluminium and Aluminium Sheets.

IS : 617–1969. Aluminium alloy ignots.

3.6.2. Materials

The various materials used in Iron Steel and Aluminium are as below :

3.6.2.1. Structural steel. The various qualities of mild steel for structural works are :

(*i*) St 42–S. Shall conform to IS : 226–1975. Used for riveted steel work, bolted work, steel work involving welding.

(*ii*) St 42–W. Shall conform to IS : 2062–1969. Used for welded steel work.

(*iii*) St 32–0. Shall conform to IS : 1977–1969. Used for general purposes such as door and window frames.

(*iv*) St 42–0-Shall conform to IS : 1977–1969. Shall be used for structures not subjected to dynamic loading.

3.6.2.2. Steel Tubes for Structural Purposes. Shall conform to IS : 1161–1968.

All finished steel shall be neatly rolled to dimensions, sections and weights. Steel sections and tubes shall be well protected against rubbing.

Rivets shall be manufactured from mild steel bars conforming to IS : 1184–1973.

Black bolts shall be made from rods.

Turned and fitted bolts shall be made in an automatic lathe machine.

Components of collapsible steel shutters shall be of mild steel.

MS steel sliding shutters shall be fabricated of mild steel components.

MS sheet Garage doors shall be fabricated of mild steel shutters. Rolling shutters shall conform to IS : 6248–1971. The shutters shall be complete with accessories. Self coiling type shutters shall be used upto a maximum of 8 m^2 clear area. Gear operated type shutter shall be used for a maximum of 25 m^2 clear area. Shutters shall be constructed with interlocking lath sections. The guide channels shall be of mild steel deep sections.

3.6.2.3. Steel Doors, Windows and Ventilators. Steel doors, windows and ventilators, shall be manufactured from fusion welding quality steel. In case of composite units different units shall be coupled by using coupling section.

3.6.2.4. MS Clamps and Rings for Chicks. MS clamps shall be fabricated from MS flat iron 20 mm × 6 mm while rings shall be made of 6 mm diameter bars.

3.6.2.5. Fan Clamps. These shall be made from 16 mm M.S. bars.

3.6.2.6. Aluminium Doors, Windows and Ventilators. Aluminium alloys used in the manufacture of extruded window sections shall conform to IS : 733–1967. Coupling sections shall also conform to these specifications.

3.6.3. Workmanship

Workmanship in steel works may be classified into the following categories :

3.6.3.1. Structural Steel Work. Structural steel work may further be divided into the following categories :

(*i*) *Steel work in single section of RS Joists, Channels etc.* All straightening and shaping to form shall be done by applying pressure and not by hammering. All operations shall be done in cold state unless otherwise specified.

(*ii*) *Steel work in riveted, bolted or welded sections.* To ensure maximum efficiency and accuracy, steel tape shall be used for measurements.

Templates shall be laid on the steel members and holes for riveting and bolting marked therein.

(*iii*) *Fabrication. Stiffeners shall be formed by pressure.* Metal shall not be cut and welded in marking these.

Bars shall be thickened at the ends so as to provide for the screwed threads.

All stiffeners shall bear tightly both at the top and bottom without being drawn or caulked.

Web splice plates and fillers under stiffeners shall be cut to fit within 3 mm of flange angles.

The erection clearance for cleated ends of members shall be limited to 15 mm. At the ends of beams with web cleats erection clearance shall be limited to 3 mm.

Connecting angles and channels shall be fabricated and placed in position with perfect accuracy.

Holes for rivets and black bolts shall be larger by 0.4 to 0.6 mm. Holes shall have their axis perpendicular to the surface bored through.

As far as possible, work of fabrication shall be completed in the workshop.

In case of welding, holes shall be made for bolts for temporary fastening only.

(*iv*) *Riveting.* Shanks for rivets shall project beyond the plate surface sufficiently so as to fill the hole thoroughly.

Far testing rivets a hammer weighing about 0.25 kg shall be used.

(*v*) *Bolting*. All bolt heads and nuts shall be hexagonal and of equal size. The screwed heads shall conform to IS : 1363–1960.

Where turned and fitted bolts are required to be used in place of rivets, these shall be provided with washers not less than 6 mm thick.

The faces of bolt heads and nuts abutting against steel members shall be machine finished.

Bolts, nuts and washers shall be thoroughly cleaned and dipped in double boiled linseed oil before use.

(*vi*) *Welding*. Welding shall generally be done by electric process. Gas welding shall not be permitted for structural steel work.

After the erection of the member, use of welding should be very restricted.

Various types of welding are :

1. *Fillet weld*. Used more frequently in structural connections.

2. *Butt weld*. The metal piece shall be filled or chiselled to the required shape for butt welding at throat. Butt Welding shall conform to IS : 816–1969. (See Fig. 3.11).

In welded structures, holes are necessary for service bolts. Surfaces which are to be welded together shall be free from loose mill scale, rust, paint or grease.

Before welding is started the plates shall be brought together and firmly clamped at specified distances. During the operation of welding the following points shall be taken into consideration.

1. Welds shall be made in flat position
2. Filler metal does not overflow
3. The base metal is not undercut
4. The floating metal floats the slag and the gas bubbles to the surface behind the advancing pool.
5. The surface shall be free from defects such as porosity, cavities etc. Intermittent occurrences of lack of penetration bead may be disregarded.
6. Fusion shall be complete over the whole area.
7. Gas cavities and Flux Entrapment.

In case of fusion or non-fusion welding of cast iron isolated blow holes in weld metal shall result in rejection.

8. **Bend testing.** For stress relieved welds. (For ductility) elongation shall not be less than 30%. For not stress relieved welds it shall be not less than 25%.

9. **Steel tube structure.** While assembling, the components shall be assembled in such a way that they are not twisted or damaged in any other way.

The threaded portion of the bolt shall not be within the thickness of the parts bolted together. To allow the nuts to be completely tightened washers of appropriate thickness shall be provided.

The cap or base plate shall be true and square to the axis of the column.

The end of the member shall be completely sealed when it is not completely sealed by virtue of welding connection. To provide for welded, riveted or bolted connections the ends of the tubes may be suitably flattened.

Tubes shall be protected before exposure to the weather. If they are not galvanised they shall be painted or oiled.

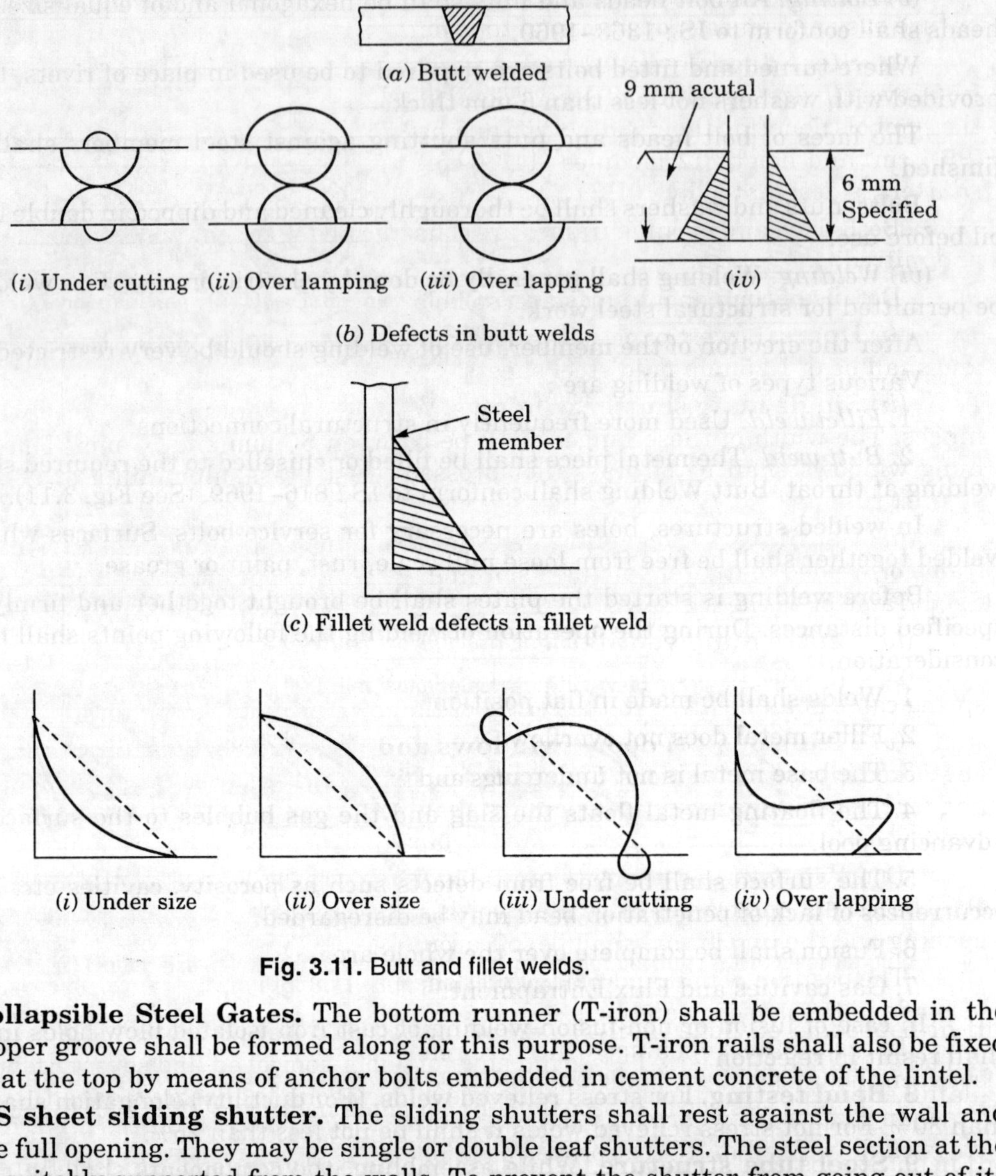

Fig. 3.11. Butt and fillet welds.

10. Collapsible Steel Gates. The bottom runner (T-iron) shall be embedded in the floor and proper groove shall be formed along for this purpose. T-iron rails shall also be fixed to the lintel at the top by means of anchor bolts embedded in cement concrete of the lintel.

11. MS sheet sliding shutter. The sliding shutters shall rest against the wall and shall provide full opening. They may be single or double leaf shutters. The steel section at the top shall be suitably supported from the walls. To prevent the shutter from going out of its support, two channel sections shall be fixed vertically below the extreme clamps in the wall and the floor.

12. MS Sheet Gauge Doors. These shall normally be provided as double leaf shutters. They shall be fixed to the wall masonry with four pin clamps. The pin clamp shall consist of 50 × 6 mm flat iron 45 cm long. It shall be bent and forked at one end and shall be provided with 20 mm diameter pin at the other end. The pin shall be firmly riveted or welded to the pin clamp. The other end shall be embedded in masonry by means of cement concrete block.

13. Rolling shutters. The lath curtain (shutter) shall be laid on the ground and the side guide channels shall be bound with it, with ropes etc. The shutter shall then be placed in position and top fixed with suspension shaft with bolts and nuts. The side guide channels and the cover frame shall then be fixed to the wall through the plate welded to the guides. To ensure easy and smooth operation of the shutter fixing shall be done accurately.

14. **Steel doors, windows and ventilators.** IS : 1038–1968 gives details regarding type, overall sizes, position of steel doors, windows and ventilators. They are designated by the symbols denoting their width, type and height. For example, a window of width 10 modules (99.4 cm) and height 12 modules (119.4 cm) having horizontal glazing bars and wide hung shutters is designated by 10HS12.

Both fixed and opening frames are constructed of sections which have been cut to length and mitred.

Details of component parts are, so below :

(*i*) **Doors.** Lowest panel of the door called as kick panel shall be double tray construction and shall be of 1.25 mm mild steel sheets.

(*ii*) **Single hung shutter windows.** Window shutters shall be hung on projecting type hinges. The width of these hinges shall be between 65 mm and 75 mm. The handle of side hung windows shall be of brass (hot pressed), cast brass, aluminium or of steel protected against rusting.

(*iii*) **Ventilators.** Steel butt hinges for top hung ventilators shall be riveted to the fixed frame or welded to it after cutting a slot in it. The locking bracket shall either be fitted to the fixed frame or to the window.

(*iv*) **Centre hung ventilator.** These shall be hung on two pairs of brass or aluminium cup pivots riveted to the inner or and outer frames of the ventilator. A brass or aluminium spring catch shall be fitted in the centre of the top bar of the ventilator.

(*v*) **Fixing of steel doors, windows and ventilators.** Steel doors and windows shall be stocked in upright positions. Fixing lugs and fixing screws are to be provided for the quantities and for the positions required. Openings shall be so designed that the outer flange of the door, window or ventilator from the section overlaps the steel section by 10 mm.

Door, windows and ventilator units shall not be 'built-in' as the work proceeds but opening shall be left out and frames fitted afterwards so that the minimum specified clearance between opening and the unit frame shall be left around.

The position of unit and fixing holes shall be marked on the jamb. Necessary holes shall be made in the masonry and lugs screws etc. fixed in cement concrete blocks.

In case of flush openings which are rendered smooth, wedges shall be removed and gap between the unit and the jamb shall be filled with cement mortar.

In RCC work where lugs cannot be embedded due to reinforcement bars etc. wooden plugs shall be fixed in RCC at proper positions while laying concrete.

Wooden openings are normally rebated and mastic shall be applied to jambs, sill and channel before fixing in position.

In case of openings in steel work, mastic shall be applied to the steel frame and a mild steel or hard wood fillet shall be provided round the frame to close the gap between opening and the frame.

Screws and lugs shall be provided as shown in Table 3.8.

Table 3.8. Provision of Screws and Lugs in Doors, Windows and Ventilators

S. No.	*Place of fixing*	*Size of Screw or lug*
1.	Wooden frame rebated from the outside.	38 mm No. 10 galvanised wood screws.
2.	Plugs in concrete work or brick work rebated from outside.	38 mm No. 10 galvanised wood screws.
3.	Plugs in concrete work or brick work rebated from outside (plain or square jambs).	65 mm No. 10 galvanised wood screws.
4.	Direct to brick work or masonry.	Slotted and steel adjustable lugs.
5.	To steel work.	Fixing clips and 8 mm galvanised bolts and hexagonal nuts.

15. **MS Clamps and Rings for chicks.**

(*i*) *MS Clamps*. One of the flats shall be bent of right angles for 2.5 cm length and the other shall be tapered to a point. The length of the clamp shall not be less than 15 cm.

(*ii*) *MS Rings*. The internal diameter of the rings shall be 40 mm.

16. **Fan Clamps.** Fan clamps shall be fixed during the laying of the RCC slab. (See. 3.12)

17. **Aluminium doors, windows and ventilators.** IS : 1948–1961 covers specifications for Aluminium doors, windows and ventilators.

Fabrication is similar to corresponding steel members, however, brazing for corner joints may also be done.

(*i*) *Doors*. Same as for steel doors except that the kick panel shall be 1.25 mm Aluminium alloy sheet. The hinges shall normally be of 50 mm projecting type. A suitable lock for the openable from inside as well as from outside shall be provided.

Single and double shutters shall be provided with a Three-way bolting device.

(*ii*) *Side hung shutter windows*. For fixing Aluminium alloy hinges, slots shall be cut in the fixed frame and the hinges inserted inside and may be riveted to the frame. Friction hinges may be provided for side hung shutter windows.

Handle for side hung shutters shall be of cast Aluminium conforming to IS Designation A-5-M of IS : 617–1959 and mounted on a handle plate.

(*iii*) *Ventilator*

(*a*) **Top-hung ventilator.** The Aluminium hinges or top hung ventilators shall be either cast or fabricated out of extruded sections and shall be riveted to the fixed rails.

(*b*) **Centre-hung ventilator.** This shall be hung on two pairs of cup pivots. The opening portion of the ventilator shall be so balanced that it remains open at any desired angle under normal weather conditions.

Outer frames shall be provided with fixing holes centrally in the web of the section.

Aluminium doors, windows and ventilators may be supplied in either matt scratch-brush or polished finish. They may additionally be anodised.

A thick layer of clear transparent lacquer based or methacrylate or cellulose butyrate shall be applied on Aluminium doors, windows and ventilators to protect the surface from wet cement during installation. This lacquer shall be removed after completion of the installation.

(*c*) **Dimensions for holes for metric bolts.** (See Table 3.9).

Table 3.9. Dimensions for Holes for Metric Bolts

Roll thread Diameter *d*	*Clearance (medium)* *(All dimensions in millimetre)*	*Holes Diameter D* *(coarse)*
1.6	1.8	2
2	2.4	2.6
2.5	2.9	3.1
3	3.4	3.6
4	4.5	4.8
5	5.5	5.8
6	6.6	7
7	7.6	8
8	9	. 10
10	11	12
12	14	15
14	16	17
16	18	19
18	20	21
20	22	24
22	24	26
24	26	28
27	30	32
30	33	35
33	36	38
36	39	42
39	42	45

3.7. BUILDER'S HARDWARE

3.7.1. Materials

Relevant Indian Standards shall apply.

3.7.2. Workmanship

Fittings shall be fixed truely vertical or horizontal as the case may be.

Screws shall be driven home with screw driver. These shall in no case be hammered in.

Where required all recesses and seats shall be cut to the exact size.

No gap shall be left between the fittings and the surface which receives these fittings.

Fittings shall be properly cleaned and left in the original finish condition.

3.8. GLAZING

3.8.1. IS Codes to be followed

IS : 1761–1960. Transparent sheet glass for glazing

IS : 2835–1975. Transparent sheet glass.

IS : 5427–1969. Wired and figured glass

IS : 419–1967. Putty for use on window frames

IS : 3548–1966. Glazing in buildings

IS : 1200–1970. (Part IV) Method of measurement of Buildings and Civil Engineering Works-Glazing.

3.8.2. Material

Various materials used for Glazing are :

3.8.2.1. Sheet Glass ordinary quality. Sheet glass shall conform to IS : 1761–1960.

Blisters exceeding 4 mm shall not be permitted. Such blisters shall not be more than 30 per square metre. They shall be uniformly distributed.

Standard thicknesses are : (mm)

2, 2.5, 3, 4, 5, 5.5, 6.5.

3.8.2.2. Sheet glass selected quality. This variety of glass is meant for use in the manufacture of laminated safety glass.

Standard thicknesses of selected quality sheet glass are : 5 mm, 6 mm.

3.8.2.3. Plate glass, Ordinary Glazing Quality. This type of glass is the superior transparent quality having practically no defects.

3.8.2.4. Wired glass and wired figured glass. This type of glass is used for glazing partition walls, doors and windows of buildings and for industrial establishments. Wired glass and wired figured glass shall conform to the tests specified in IS : 5437–1969.

3.8.2.5. Putty. The material shall be homogeneous paste. It shall be free from dust, grit and other visible impurities.

3.8.3. Workmanship

1. **Glazing**. Size of glass for glazing shall allow a clearance of 2.5 mm between the edge of the glass and the wood or the metal surrounding.

2. **Wooden Beading.** For glass panes not exceeding 0.5 sq m in area and having thickness of upto 4 mm, the size of beading shall be 1 cm × 2 cm.

For glass size of more than 4 mm thickness the size of beading shall be 1.5 cm × 3 cm.

3. **Putty.** Sufficient compound shall be applied to the rebate so that when glass has been pressed into the rebate, at least 1.5 mm thick compound remains.

No voids shall be left between the glass and the bead.

4. **Glazing of metal doors, windows and ventilators.** Glazing shall normally be done with glazing putty outside. Quantity of putty shall not be less than 185 gms/metre of glass perimeter.

A thin layer of putty shall be applied between glass panes and sash bars as well as between glass panes and beading.

5. **Frosting and obscuring.** Frosting shall be done thoroughly, uniformly and evenly so as to avoid any patchy look.

6. **Grinding, polishing and rounding of edges.** The edges of glass or glazing sheet shall render a uniform look throughout the length and shall present a neat appearance.

3.9. PAVING AND FLOOR FINISHES

3.9.1. Indian Standards to be followed :

IS : 455–1967. Portland Blast Furnace slag Cement.

IS : 269–1967. Rapid hardening, Ordinary, and Low Heat portland cement.

IS : 2114–1962. Laying in situ terrazzo floor finish.

IS : 1237–1959. Cement Concrete Flooring Tiles.
IS : 777–1970. Glazed Earthenware Tiles.
IS : 2541–1974. Use of Lime Concrete in Buildings.
IS : 2571–1970. Laying in Situ Cement Concrete Flooring.
IS : 451–1961. Wood screws.
IS : 5389–1969. Hardwood parquet and wood Block Floors.
IS : 653–1962. Sheet Linoleum.
IS : 1198–1959. Laying and maintenance of Linoleum Floors.
IS : 4631–1968. Laying of Epoxy Resin Floor topping.
IS : 3962–1966. Flexible PVC Flooring.
IS ; 5318–1969. Laying PVC sheet and Tile flooring.
IS : 809–1970. Rubber Flooring.
IS : 382–1970. Coarse and Fine Aggregates.
IS: 1443–1972. Cement Concrete Flooring Tiles.
IS : 5766–1970. Laying Burnt clay brick flooring.
IS : 5491–1969. Laying in situ granolithic concrete floor topping.
IS : 4971–1968. Laying of Industrial floor finishes.

3.9.2. Terrazzo Flooring

Salient features of Terrazzo flooring are :

3.9.2.1. The minimum thickness of top layer for various sizes of chips are given in Table 3.10.

Table 3.10. Sizes of Chips

Grade No.	*Size of Chips mm*	*Thickness of Top Layer mm*
00	1–2	5
0	2–4	5
1	4–7	5
2	7–10	8
3	10–15	8
4	15–20	10
5	20–25	10

3.9.2.2. Cement used for the floor finish work shall be ordinary Portland Cement/white cement/coloured cement.

Pigments used shall conform to IS : 2114–1962.

3.9.2.3. Dividing strips. The material for dividing strips shall be such that it has similar resistance to wear as the flooring. Copper, brass, aluminium or plastic may be used for this purpose. The thickness of the strip shall not be less than 1.5 mm and width not less than 25 mm. Spacing of such cut portions shall not be closer than 30 cm.

3.9.2.4. Workmanship. Terrazzo finish shall be laid over a layer of base concrete. When terrazzo floor is to be laid over RCC slab a cushioning layer of 75 mm thick lime concrete shall be provided.

Terrazzo flooring shall consist of an under layer of cement concrete and topping layer of terrazzo which shall be laid monolithically.

The under layer shall be of 1 : 2 : 4 cement concrete. The maximum size of aggregate shall be 10 mm.

Topping shall have a mix of cement, marble powder, marble aggregate and water. Cement and marble powder shall be mixed in the ratio of 3 : 1 by weight. Table 3.11 gives the ratio of marble aggregates to be mixed with cement marble powder.

Table 3.11. Proportion of Aggregates to Marble Mix

Size of Aggregate	*Ratio of Aggregate to Binder Mix*
Grade 00, 0 and 1	1–3/4 parts
Grade 00, 2 and 3	1–1/2 parts
Grade 00, 4 and 5	1–1/4 parts

The thickness of base concrete and cushioning layer shall not be less than 10 cm and 7.5 cm respectively. Minimum thickness of under layer and topping shall not be less than 40 mm. While laying the under layer and the topping area shall be divided into panels of not more than 2 sq m with the longer dimension being not longer than 2 m.

To obtain various shades of the binder reference shall be made to IS : 2114–1962. For this purpose pigments are mixed with ordinary cement or white cement.

Mixing shall be done in a trough or tub and complete quantities of cement and pigment required for one unit shall be mixed at the beginning of the work. Coloured cement/cement and pigment mixed shall be dry mixed with marble powder. Aggregates shall be mixed to the dry mix prepared as above. Water shall be added in small quantities to the mix thus obtained. The mix shall be plastic but not so wet as may cause its flow.

3.9.2.5. Laying

(*i*) *Laying of underlayer*. The base shall be divided into panels with the help of dividing strips. It shall be wetted with water. After cleaning it shall be smeared with cement slurry using 2.75 kg/sq m. The top surface shall be kept rough to provide a good bond with the terrazzo.

(*ii*) *Terrazzo topping*. The topping shall be laid while the underlayer is still plastic. This is achieved between 18–24 hours after laying. The terrazzo mix shall be laid to a uniform thickness. The terrazzo surface shall be tamped and trowelled to be brought to required level with the help of straight edge. The maximum amount of marble chips should come up to the surface and no part of the surface shall be left without the chips.

The surface shall be left dry for 18–24 hours. Thereafter it shall be kept under a pool of water for a minimum period of four days.

Grinding and finishing shall be done either by hand or by machine. First grinding shall be done with carborundum stone of 60 grid size. It shall be allowed to dry for 24 hours and cured for 4 days.

The second grinding shall be done with carborundum stone of 80 grit size. The surface shall be prepared as for first grinding. The third grinding shall be done with carborundum stone of 120–150 grit size. The surface shall then be washed again and allowed to dry for 12 hours followed by wet curing for 4 days. The fourth grinding shall be done with carborundum stone of 320–400 grit size. The surface shall then be cleaned and rubbed hard with felt and slightly moistened with oxalic acid powder at 5 gms per sq m of the surface. Floor polishing machine fitted with belt or hessian bobs shall then be run over it until the floor shines.

3.9.3. Boulders and Decorative Designs

Boulders and decorative designs shall be laid before the main flooring.

3.9.4. Terrazzo Skirting and Dados

The under layer for terrazzo on vertical surface shall be of stiff cement mortar 1 : 3 (Cement : coarse sand). Combined thickness of under layer and topping shall not be less than 20 mm with a minimum of 6 mm topping layer.

3.9.5. Terrazzo Tile Flooring

Terrazzo tile flooring shall conform to IS : 1237–1959. Metric sizes of tiles are as given in Table 3.12.

Table 3.12. Metric Sizes of Tiles (cm)

Length (cm)		*Breadth (cm)*		*Thickness (cm)*
Nominal	*Actual*	*Nominal*	*Actual*	*Not less than*
20	19.85	20	19.85	2.0
30	29.85	30	29.85	2.5
25	24.85	25	24.85	2.2

Tiles shall be laid on a subgrade of concrete of RCC slab. Over subgrade concrete or RCC slab, a layer of average thickness of 25 mm of lime mortar 1 : 1 : 2 (lime putty : Surkhi : Coarse sand) or 1 : 2 (lime putty : coarse sand) shall be provided as bedding for the tiles.

The subgrade concrete or RCC slab shall be cleaned, wetted and mopped. Lime mortar shall then be spread evenly and smoothly tamped and levelled with screed battens. The surface shall be left rough to provide a good bond to the tiles.

The bedding shall be allowed to harden for a day before laying the tiles. Over the bedding a neat cement slurry at the rate of 3.4 kg per sq m of the surface shall be spread over the bedding to cover an area of 20 tiles. The joints shall be as thin as possible but in no case more than 1.5 mm in width.

Tiles which are fixed in the walls shall go under about 10 mm of plaster skirting or dado. In case full tiles cannot be used tiles shall be cut to size and smoothened at the edges.

After the tiles have been laid the surplus cement slurry and the joints shall be cleaned with a wire brush to a depth of about 5 mm and then grouted with grey or white cement.

The floor shall be kept wet for a minimum period of 7 days.

The first grinding shall be done with carborundum stone of 48 to 60 grade grit size. Water shall be properly used during grinding. It shall then be covered with a thin coat of grey or white cement with or without pigment to match the colour of the tile. This grout shall be kept moist for a week.

The second grinding shall be done with carborundum of 120 grit size. This shall be followed by grouting and curing.

The final grinding shall be done with carborundum of 220 to 350 grit size using plenty of water.

Oxalic acid powder shall then be dusted at 33 gms sq m of surface rubbed with pads of woollen rags.

Polishing shall be done in the same way as for terrazzo finish.

3.9.6. Terrazzo Tiles in Risers of Steps, Skirting and Dado

The minimum thickness of finished tiles shall be 12 mm.

The finished thickness of upper layer shall not be less than 5 mm.

Brick walls shall be raked to depth of 15 mm. The concrete surface shall be roughened with steel wire brushes.

The wall surface shall be uniformly covered with a backing of 10 mm thick backing of cement mortar 1 : 3 (Cement : Coarse sand) Before hardening of the cushioning layer takes place, each tile shall be covered with a thin layer of grey cement paste.

Top of skirting or dado shall be truely horizontal. Whenever required tiles will be cut/ sawn and thin edges smoothened before use.

Curing, grinding and polishing shall be as for terrazzo tile flooring but it shall be done manually only after 14 days of laying.

3.9.7. Chequered Tile Flooring

The tiles shall be of nominal sizes such as 20 cm × 20 cm, 25 cm × 25 cm and 30 cm × 30 cm. The centre to centre distance of chequers shall not be less than 2.5 cm nor more than 5 cm. The thickness of the tiles shall not be less than 22 mm. The depth of the grooves shall not be less than 3 mm. The thickness of the upper layer shall not be less than 6 mm. Before delivery at site the tiles shall be given first grinding.

Laying of tiles shall be the same as for flooring tiles except that polishing of tiles and the chequered grooves shall be done manually.

3.9.8. Chequered Tiles in Stair Treads

The main features are :

3.9.8.1. Materials. Same as far chequered tiles for flooring except the following :

1. The length of the tiles shall be 33 cm. This includes nosing.
2. The nosing edge shall be rounded.
3. The minimum thickness of the tile shall be 28 mm.
4. In the front portion of the tile for a minimum length of 75 mm from and including the nosing shall have grooves running parallel to the nosing and at centres not exceeding 25 mm.

Beyond that the tiles shall have the normal chequered pattern.

5. The nosing shall have the same wearing layer as the top.

3.9.8.2. Workmanship. RCC or brick treads shall be cleaned, wetted and mopped before laying bedding. A minimum of 12 mm thick bedding of lime mortar (1 : 1 : 1) lime putty, surkhi, course sand or 1 : 2 (Lime putty : Course sand) shall be spread uniformly and tamped shall be laid and allowed to harden for a day. Before laying the tiles cement slurry shall be applied over the surface of the treads at the rate of 3.4 kg per sq m of the surface of treads.

The joints shall be as thin as possible.

Where required full tiles shall be cut or sawn to the required size.

Curing grinding and polishing shall be similar to terrazzo tile flooring. The grinding, however, shall be done manually.

3.9.9. White Glazed Tiled Work

The various stages of the work are :

3.9.9.1 Materials. White glazed tiles shall conform to IS : 777–1970. They shall be free from cracks, crazing spots, chipped edges and corners. Nominal sizes of the tiles are 15 × 15 cm and 10 × 10 cm. The usual thickness of these tiles is 10 mm.

3.9.9.2. Workmanship. The bedding over which tiles are laid shall consist of 12 mm 1 : 3 (Cement : Sand) mortar. Before applying the bedding the subgrade shall be cleaned wetted and mopped. The bedding shall be allowed to harden. Before applying the tiles, they shall be covered with cement slurry of honey like consistency at 3.3 kg per sq m of tile surface.

After laying the tiles the excess cement grout is cleaned.

The joints shall be cleaned of grey cement grout with wire brushes or trowel upto the depth of 5 mm and all dust and loose mortar is removed. White cement shall then be used for flush pointing the joints.

3.9.10. White Glazed Tiles in Risers of Steps, Skirting and Dado

The various stages of work are :

3.9.10.1. Materials. Tiles shall conform to IS : 777–1970.

3.9.10.2. Workmanship. The wall surface shall be covered with 1 : 3 (Cement: Coarse sand) cement sand mortar and allowed to harden. The plaster is roughened with wire brushes or by scratching diagonal lines 1.5 mm deep diagonally 7.5 centres both ways. The back of the tiles shall be buttered with grey cement slurry and edges with white cement slurry. Top of skirting or dado shall be truely horizontal. Risers of steps, skirting or dado shall rest on top of treads or flooring.

The joints shall be cleaned and flush pointed with white cement. The surface shall be kept wet for seven days.

3.9.11. White Glazed Tiles (Specials)

The specials consist of internal and external angles, beads, cornices and corner pieces. They shall have the same thickness as that of the tiles with which they are used.

The surface shall be prepared in the same manner as for terrazzo tiles.

The wall surface shall be covered with 10 mm thick layer of 1 : 3 cement sand mortar. It shall be allowed to harden and with wire brushes or by scratching diagonal lines 1.5 mm deep at 7.5 cm centres both ways.

After curing, the surface shall be washed and cleaned.

3.9.12. Marble Stone Flooring

The slabs shall be from approved quarry. They shall be hand or machine cut.

The sides and top surface shall be machine rubbed or table rubbed with coarse sand before using. Thickness of the slabs shall be 25, 30 or 40 mm.

Base concrete or RCC slab shall serve as sub-base.

Bedding shall be either of lime mortar 1 : 1 : 1 (lime putty : surkhi : coarse sand) of average thickness of 25 mm or cement mortar 1 : 6 (Cement : Coarse sand) of average thickness 20 mm. Minimum thickness at any piece shall not be less than 10 mm.

Sub-grade shall be cleaned, wetted and mopped. Mortar of specified mix is then spread over the area to receive one marble slab. The slab shall then be washed and cleaned. It shall then be pressed over the mortar and brought in with the level of adjoining slab. The slab shall then be lifted and set aside. The mortar is then allowed to harden. Over this surface cement slurry of honey like consistency at the rate of 3.4 kg per sq m of surface is spread. The edges of the slab shall then be buttered with grey or white cement to match the shade of the marble slab.

The floor shall be cured for a minimum period of seven days. Unevenness at the meeting edges of the slabs shall be removed by fine chiselling. Finishing shall be done as for terrazzo flooring except that cement slurry with or without pigment shall not be applied on the surface before each polishing.

3.9.13. Marble Stone in Risers of Steps and Skirting

3.9.13.1. Materials. Same as for marble stone flooring. The thickness of the slab shall, however, be 25 mm.

3.9.13.2. Workmanship. The specifications shall be the same as for terrazzo tile in skirting etc.

The risers of steps and skirting shall be set in grey or white cement.

The gap between the rear of the slab and the wall shall be filled and packed with 1 : 3 cement sand mortar.

Curing, polishing and finishing shall be as for terrazzo tile flooring.

3.9.14. Kota Stone Flooring

3.9.14.1. Materials. The slabs shall be hard, sound, dense and homogeneous. It shall be free from cracks decay and weathering.

3.9.14.2. Workmanship. Each slab shall be cut to the required shape and size.

Thickness of the slab shall be 25, 30 or 49 mm as specified.

Laying

Same as for marble flooring.

Curing, polishing and finishing shall be as for terrazzo tile.

Flooring

Same as terrazzo tile flooring with the following modifications. The first polishing with coarse grained carborundum stone shall not be done.

Cement slurry with or without pigment, shall not be applied to the surface before polishing.

3.9.15. Kota Stone in Risers of Steps, Skirting and Dado

3.9.15.1. Materials. Stone shall be hard, sound and dense and free from cracks and other defects. The thickness of the slab shall be 25 mm or as specified.

3.9.15.2. Workmanship. The surface shall be prepared in the same way as for 'Marble stone in risers of steps and skirting'. The joints of the slab shall be set in grey cement with pigments to match the colour of the slabs.

Curing, Polishing and Finishing

Same as for terrazzo tile flooring except that first polishing with coarse grade carborundum stone shall not be done.

3.9.16. Sand Stone Flooring (Rough Dressed)

3.9.16.1. Material. The slabs shall be red or white as specified. They shall be free from cracks, decay and weathering. They shall also be hard, sound and durable. They shall be hand or machine cut.

3.9.16.2. Workmanship. The subgrade shall be as for marble stone slab flooring. The bedding for the stone slabs shall be 20 mm thick 1 : 5 (Cement : Coarse sand) cement sand mortar or 25 mm thick 1 : 1 : 1 (lime putty : Surkhi : Coarse sand).

Every slab shall be cut to required shape and size. It shall be rough chisel dressed on top in such a way that the dressed surface shall not be more than 6 mm from the straight edge placed on it. The sides shall also be chisel dressed to a minimum depth of 20 mm. Thickness of the slab shall be 20 mm or as specified. For laying the slab, the surface of the subgrade shall be cleaned, wetted and mopped. The bedding of specified mortar shall be spread under each slab. The slab shall be pressed over the bedding and levelled. The thickness of the joint shall not exceed 5 mm. All surplus mortar shall be removed from the surface of the slab. Where pointing of other mix is specified, the mortar from the joints shall be raked to a depth of 12 mm. The pointing shall be cured for a minimum period of seven days.

3.9.17. Sand Stone Flooring (Fine Dressed)

3.9.17.1. Materials. Same as for rough dressed stones.

3.9.17.2. Workmanship. Subgrade bedding shall be the same as for Rough Chiselled sand stone flooring.

Every slab shall be chisel dressed on all sides to a minimum depth of 20 mm.

Thickness of the slab shall be 20 mm or as specified.

Laying shall be as for sand stone flooring (Rough dressed).

Finishing shall be same as for sand stone flooring except that slight unevenness, if any between the edges of the joints shall be removed by chiselling in a slant.

3.9.18. Sand Stone Flooring (Fine dressed and Rubbed)

3.9.18.1. Materials. Same as for rough dressed sand stone slabs.

3.9.18.2. Workmanship. Subgrade and bedding shall be as for Rough dressed sand stone flooring.

Dressing of slabs shall be similar to that of sand stone flooring. The dressed top sides shall, however, be table rubbed with coarse sand.

The slabs shall be laid with 3 or 5 mm thick joints. The sides of the slabs shall be buttered with cement mortar 1 : 2 (cement : Stone dust) admixed with pigment to match the shade of the slab.

Finishing shall be as for Fine dressed Stone Floor unevenness and chisel marks shall be removed by rubbing with coarse grained carborundum.

3.9.19. Cement Concrete Flooring

3.9.19.1. Materials. Materials as specified for Cement Concrete work.

3.9.19.2. Workmanship. Subgrade shall be as for brick flooring.

In case cement concrete flooring is to be laid over RCC slab, the surface of RCC slab shall be roughened while the concrete is still green.

The formwork for structural slab shall be given in the structural concrete itself and any laitance or scum shall be brushed away. Topping shall be laid in position thoroughly compacted after structural concrete has stiffened but is still plastic.

Trowelling of a rich mix of dry cement and fine aggregate on the surface shall not be permitted.

When the finishing is to be laid over a structural slab without a cushioning layer the structural concrete shall be thoroughly brushed after 3 to 4 hours of its laying with coir or steel brush to remove any scum. Panels over the structural steel shall then be formed. Before laying the topping cement slurry shall be brushed into the prepared surface.

When floor finish is laid over cushioning layer of lime concrete the sub-floor shall be thoroughly cleaned by scrubbing with steel wire brushes. In the preparation and laying of concrete IS : 2541–1974 shall be followed.

Panels for concrete floors shall be such that border shall have mitred joints at the corners of the room and intermediate joints shall be in straight line with the panel joints.

Generally no panel of the floor finish shall exceed 4 m in any direction when the floor finish is laid monolithically with the base concrete. When floor finish is laid over hardened concrete no dimension of the panel shall exceed 2 m. Length of the panel shall in no case exceed 1½ times its breadth.

Battens for shuttering shall be fixed in position with their top at proper level providing slope where required.

Use of dry cement or cement and sand mixes sprinkled on the surface to stiffen the concrete or absorb excessive moisture shall not be allowed. While the concrete is still green cement slurry made by mixing 2.2 kg of cement per sq m of surface shall be spread.

Floor finish over ramps, stairs and other similar situations where they are liable to get wet shall be finished in chequered pattern.

Where required the junctions of floors with wall plaster shall be rounded off so as to be at a radius of 25 mm.

Curing of concrete floor shall be as for normal concrete.

In the case of lavatories and bathrooms, flooring shall be laid after fixing sanitary fittings such as water closet squatting pans and floor traps.

3.9.20. Cement Concrete Tile Flooring

3.9.20.1. Materials. Cement concrete tiles shall conform to IS : 1237–1959.

Pigments to be admixed with the mortar shall conform to IS : 2114–1962.

3.9.20.2. Workmanship. Subgrade shall be the same as for Terrazzo tiles.

Bedding shall either be in cement mortar (1 : 6, cement : coarse sand) or lime mortar (1 : 1 : 1, lime putty, surkhi, coarse sand).

Before laying the tiles the base shall be cleaned off all dust, dirt and scum. In case cement mortar is used as bedding, mortar shall be spread evenly over the base for two rows of tiles and three to five metres in length. Thickness of bedding shall not be less than 10 mm at any place. When lime mortar is used for bedding the area over which mortar is spread shall be as much as can be covered with tiles the next day.

In order that the tiles have a rigid surface over which they are laid the actual laying of tiles shall commence the next day. Neat cement slurry of honey like consistency shall be spread over the mortar bedding over an area sufficient to receive 20 tiles. The tiles shall then be fixed over this grout one after the other.

Tiles which are fixed in the floor adjoining the wall shall go atleast 10 mm under the plaster.

Where a full tile cannot be used, it shall be cut to proper size and shape.

The flooring shall be cured for seven days.

Grinding shall commence after 14 days when the tiles and the joints are properly set. As far as possible, machine grinding shall be given preference to manual grinding.

Procedure for grinding and polishing shall be the same as for Terrazzo Tiles.

3.9.21. Chequered or Grooved Tiles

The procedure is the same as for cement concrete tiles.

3.9.22. Cement Concrete Tiles in Skirting, Dado and Stair case Treads

3.9.22.1 Materials. Same as Cement Concrete Tile Flooring.

3.9.22.2. Workmanship. Preparation of the subgrade.

Same as for Terrazzo Tiles.

Laying. Same as for Terrazzo Tiles.

Curring, grinding and polishing. Same as for Terrazzo Tiles.

3.9.23. Brick Flooring

3.9.23.1. Materials. Bricks shall be of specified class and size. The classification of bricks shall be based on IS : 3102–1971.

3.9.23.2. Workmanship. Flooring shall be laid on concrete subgrade where specified as such. Where subgrade is not provided, the earth below shall be properly rammed, consolidated and sloped.

If lime subgrade is specified, the subgrade shall be allowed to set for seven days and floorings shall be laid in the next three days.

Where lean concrete has been specified as subgrade, the flooring shall be commenced within 48 hours of laying of the subgrade, otherwise the surface shall be roughened with steel wire brushes wetted and covered with cement slurry using 2.75 kg of cement per sq m of the surfaces.

The bricks shall be laid in the specified pattern i.e. plain diagonal, herring bond or together.

Bricks shall be laid on 12 mm thick mortar and each brick shall be properly bedded.

Dry brick flooring shall be laid on a bed of 12 mm brick mud mortar. The joints of dry brick flooring shall be as thin as possible but not thicker than 5 mm.

Before laying, the bricks shall be soaked in water. Soaking shall, however, not be done in case of dry brick flooring.

3.9.24. Parquet (Wood Block) Flooring

3.9.24.1. Materials. The size of the blocks shall be 225 × 75 mm or as specified.

The longitudinal edges of the blocks shall be dovetail grooved near the bottom. The thickness of the blocks shall be 38 mm or as specified with a tolerance of 3 mm (plus or minus).

3.9.24.2. Workmanship. Subgrade. As for cement concrete flooring.

Levelling course. The levelling course shall be of cement concrete 1 : 2 : 4 (Cement : Coarse sand : 10 mm nominal size stone aggregate). The cement concrete shall be placed in position and levelled with trowel. The finished level of the concrete shall be lower than the proposed level of the floor by the thickness of the wooden blocks plus 1.5 mm.

Laying. The blocks shall be laid dry in the specified pattern. They shall fit closely and where required the sides and ends shall be corrected by further planing.

A small area thoroughly cleaned of the levelling course, shall be coated with a thin layer of hot bitumen applied at a temperature not less than 180°C at the rate of 2.45 kg per sq m.

The wooden blocks shall then be taken in turn serially and dipped in the same hot bitumen for about half their depth to coat the bottom part and the sides. It shall be quickly set and pressed in place.

When all the blocks have been set in position, the surface shall be cleaned of any bitumen droppings and planed or machine levelled smooth.

The floor shall be finally finished by rubbing with sand paper.

No wood of any kind shall however be placed within 60 cm of any fire place or flame.

The floor shall be waxed or polished with readymade polish.

3.9.25. Linoleum Flooring

3.9.25.1. Materials. Linoleum shall conform to specifications given in IS : 653–1962.

The Engineer-in-Charge shall approve the sample before the start of the work.

Adhesive used for the work shall conform to IS : 1198–1958.

It shall be of heavy consistency with short drying time.

3.9.25.2. Workmanship. Linoleum shall be placed on clean firm and dry base.

The sub floor shall be perfectly level.

If the temperature is below 18°C, linoleum shall not be laid. Linoleum has the special property of shrinking in length and expanding in width after being unrolled. Before being unrolled it should be kept at 20°C temperature for 48 hours and then laid flat for 2 to 3 days before it is cut to size. Linoleum shall be cut to shape and size by a sharp straight edge.

The lengths for borders shall be cut and adjusted followed by panel portions. Initially, the adjacent pieces shall overlap by 12 mm but subsequently with the help of 'Gauge' the overlapping is cut along the line and adjacent sheets butt against each other without any gap or overlap.

When all the pieces have been properly fitted and matched, they shall be removed for application of the adhesive. After application of the approved adhesive, allowing the time specified by the manufacturers of the adhesive to elapse, the sheets shall be rolled with a cast iron 70 kg roller (linoleum roller) working from centre to the walls to ensure that they stick evenly to the base. In case any air pocket is left, the entire operation has to be repeated including brushing more adhesive on the base and rerolling.

Linoleum shall not be used for covers skirting and dado. Recommended thicknesses for linoleum flooring are as given in Table 3.13.

Table 3.13. Recommended Thicknesses of Linoleum for Flooring

S. No.	*Situation*	*Thickness (mm)*
1.	For public buildings, cinemas, restaurants, shops etc.	6 to 6.7
2.	Hotels, ships etc.	3.2 to 4.5
3.	Houses :	3.2
4.	Houses in lightly used areas	less than 3.2

Any adhesive which is likely to contaminate the flooring shall be removed as soon as possible and at any rate within the setting time of the adhesive.

After the flooring has been securely fixed it shall be cleaned with soap and warm water and then waxed.

Care shall be taken not to crease the linoleum sheets.

Excess water is likely to get into the joints. The surface shall not be exposed to sharp edges or points.

3.9.26. PVC Flooring

3.9.26.1. Materials. PVC sheets shall conform to IS : 3462–1966. The flexible type may be packed with hesian or other fabrics.

Adhesive used shall be as prescribed by the manufacturers.

3.9.26.2. Workmanship

General. Same as for linoleum flooring.

Laying. The sheets shall be kept in the area where they are to be fixed for a period of 24 hours. During this period the temperature range shall be between 20°C to 30°C. This temperature shall be maintained during laying and 48 hours thereafter.

Sheets shall initially be laid as a trial to required pattern without using any adhesive. Adhesive shall then be applied using a notched trowel to the sub floor and to the back side of PVC sheet. PVC sheet requires about half an hour for setting. PVC sheeting shall be carefully taken and placed in position from one end onwards slowly so that no air pockets are left between the sheet and the background surface. It shall be rolled with a roller to develop proper contact.

The next shall be laid edge to edge with the sheet already laid.

Tiles shall be laid from centre of the area in the same way as sheets.

Any excess adhesive that comes out during rolling shall be wiped out and removed. In case the adhesive oozing out has become hard, it shall be removed with a solution of one part of Butyle Acetate and three parts of turpentine oil.

PVC sheets shall not be laid under humid conditions.

The surface shall not be used before 24 hours have elapsed after applying the flooring.

It is recommended that PVC flooring shall be laid after other finishes such as plastering, white washing etc. have been completed.

3.9.27. Rubber Flooring

3.9.27.1. Materials. Rubber tiles shall conform to IS : 809–1957.

The standard size of the rubber tiles are :

20 × 20 cm, 30 × 30 cm and 45 × 45 cm.

Where exact number of tiles cannot be fitted, tiles shall be cut to the desired size and shape.

The Engineer-in-charge shall get the sample of the tiles approved before they are used in the work.

The adhesive for the tiles shall be the one recommended by the manufacturers.

3.9.27.2. Workmanship. General. As for Linoleum flooring.

Laying. Rubber flooring shall be laid either in one layer of 6 mm or two layers of 6 mm thick each as specified. They shall be fixed to the floor with a film of smooth but heavy consistency of rubber or resin base.

In case any tendency to curl is noticed the tiles shall be weighed down to firmly press smoothen the tiles flat. Coves of wood or metal may be used to cover or mask the joints between the rubber flooring and the wall facing.

Finishing. Any adhesive sticking on the sides of the tiles shall be removed immediately before it hardens.

After a week of its laying the surface shall be cleaned with mild soap and wet cloth.

Care shall be taken to see that no air pockets are left below the rubber tiles.

In situations, exposed to direct sunlight or rains, rubber flooring shall not be used.

3.9.28. Granolithic Concrete Flooring

3.9.28.1. Materials. Cement concrete under layer.

The mix for under layer shall be 1 : 2 : 4 cement concrete (Cement : Coarse sand : 12.5 mm nominal size stones).

Topping. Topping of specified thickness shall consist of 1 : 1 : 2 cement concrete (Cement : Coarse sand : stone saggregates) Coarse aggregate shall be from granite, Basalt, Trap or Quartzite.

The aggregates shall further conform to IS : 383–1963.

The grading of fine and coarse aggregates shall be as given in Tables 3.14 and 3.15 respectively.

Table 3.14. Grading of Fine Aggregates. The Grading shall be within the Limits of Zone I or Zone II

IS Sieve Designation	*Percentage by Weight Passing IS Sieves*	
	Grading Zone I	*Grading Zone II*
10 mm	100	100
4.75	90–100	90–100
2.36	60–95	75–100
1.18	30–70	55–90
600 micron	15–34	35–54
300 micron	5–26	8–30
150 micron	0–10	0–10

Table 3.15. Grading for Coarse Aggregates

IS Sieve Designation	*Percentage of Weight Passing Sieve*
12.5 mm	90–100
10 mm	40–85
4.75 mm	0–10
2.36 mm	–

Water. Generally potable water is suitable.

3.9.28.2. Workmanship

General. Where flooring is likely to be subjected to heavy loading which are likely to cause large wear and tear of the floor granolithic floor shall be used. Abrasive resistance of the floor is increased by using metallic or non-metallic materials for the topping.

Cement concrete under layer

Granolithic concrete topping shall be laid on cement concrete flooring of specified thickness.

Laying. Floor topping may be laid either monolithically with the base concrete or laid separately on hardened base.

When the topping is laid monolithically with the base concrete the topping shall be laid within two to three hours of laying of the base concrete. Straight edge and spirit level shall be used to ensure proper levelled surface. The surface is rendered even and smoothly finished by floating with wooden floats.

When topping is laid separately over the base concrete, the base is cleaned from dirt or mortar droppings etc. The surface of the underlayer shall be wetted with water for a few hours and surplus water removed. Screed strips shall be fixed in position and neat cement slurry at the rate of 2.75 kg per sq m of surface shall be spread over the under-layer surface.

When floor topping has to be laid monolithically over suspended slab, the topping shall be laid while the suspended slab is still green. The topping is laid over roughened surface to ensure proper bond between the two concretes.

The mix for structural concrete shall be as stiff as possible subject to satisfactory workability.

In case topping on suspended floor has to be provided over hardened suspended floor, a cushioning layer of lime concrete is given over the suspended slab.

Before laying granolithic topping over the lime concrete the surface shall be given a cover of neat cement slurry at the rate 2.75 kg per sq m of the surface.

Curing. As for cement concrete flooring.

3.10. ROOF COVERINGS

3.10.1. IS Codes to be Followed :

IS : 1969–1969. Galvanised Steel Sheets.
IS : 730–1966. Fasteners for corrugated sheet roofing.
IS : 459–1970. Unreinforced corrugated and semi-corrugated AC sheets.
IS : 3007 (Part I) 1964. Laying of AC sheets.
IS : 3007 (Part II)-1965. Laying of AC semi-corrugated sheets.
IS : 654–1962. Clay Roofing Tiles. Mangalore pattern.
IS : 1964–1959. Ridge and ceiling tiles.
IS : 280–1962. Mild steel wire for general use.
IS : 883–1966. Timber in Buildings.
IS : 723–1961. Mild steel wire nails.

3.10.2. Corrugated Sheet Roofing

Normal pitch of trusses shall be one vertical and 2 horizontal. The slope of roof shall however, not be flatter than 1 vertical to 5 horizontal.

Thickness of sheets. As specified.

Ridges and Hips. These shall be 600 mm overall in width. Shall be galvanised class-3.

Valleys and Flashings. Gutters shall be designed to carry the maximum discharge from the roofs.

Wind ties. These shall be of wood or steel of the sizes specified.

3.10.3. Corrugated Asbestos Cement Sheet Roofing

Supporting structure such as rafters, trusses etc. shall be of woodwork or steel work.

3.10.4. Corrugated and Semi-corrugated AC Cement Sheets

All sheets shall conform to IS : 459-1970.

Thickness of sheets shall be as specified.

Ridges and Hips. These shall be of the same thickness as the AC sheets.

Other accessories. These shall be as per recommendations of the manufacturers.

Eaves and Valley gutters. These shall be suitable for the location and size of the concerned item.

3.10.5. Thatch Roofing

Bamboos used for thatching shall be of matured growth and free from all defects such as splits, bonet holes etc.

3.10.6. Stone Roofing

The materials shall conform to corresponding item of 'Stone masonry'.

3.10.7. Tiles

Flat Tiles. Flat Tiles for use with Mangalore tiles shall have one of its dimensions equal to the gauge of Mangalore Tiles.

Pan Tiles. Pan tiles shall be free from cracks flaws etc. They shall have clear sharp edges.

Allahabad Tiles. Sizes of the tiles shall be 300 mm × 375 mm trough shaped flat tiles and 150 mm × 360 mm half round tiles.

3.10.8. Terraced Roof

Materials used for the roofing such as cement, bricks, coarse and fine aggregates etc. shall conform to their respective specifications.

3.10.9. Mud Roofing

Standard size of the tile : 300 × 150 × 30 mm and 300 × 150 × 50 mm.

The work shall generally conform to the respective work under 'Brick work'.

Battens shall be of RCC or timber as specified.

Cement, sand, surkhi etc. shall conform to their respective specifications.

Mud. Soil for mud roofing shall be free from vegetable matter gravel kankar etc. Surki and sarkanda shall be new one of the best quality.

3.10.10. CGI Sheet Roofing

Spacing of purlins. One purlin shall be provided at the ridge and one at the eaves. Spacing of other purlins shall be as given in Table 3.16.

Table 3.16. Spacing of Purlins

Thickness of Sheet (in cm)	*Maximum Spacing (in metres)*
1.25	2.4
1.0	2.0
0.80	1.80
0.63	1.60

Purlins shall coincide with the centre line of end lap. The top surface of the purlins shall be painted before sheets are fixed over them.

Laying of sheets. Sheets shall be laid on the purlins to a true plain with the lines of corrugations parallel or normal to the sides of area covered. The drip course shall cover the junction by at least 750 mm.

Laps. Laps shall be as shown in Table 3.17.

Table 3.17. Laps in CGI Sheet Roofing

Situation	*Lap in mm (Minimum)*
End lap. For slopes 1 vertical to 2 horizontal	150
For flatter slopes	200

Side lap. Two ridges of corrugations on each side.

Cutting of sheets. Sheets shall be cut along the lines of corrugations at hips and valleys.

Fixing of sheets. Sheets shall be fixed to the purlins or other roof members such as hip or valley rafters etc. J or L galvanised hook bolts and galvanised nuts 8 mm diameter with bitumen limpet washers shall be used for this purpose. Length of such bolts shall be on as required basis. A minimum of three bolts shall be fixed at the ends of corrugations in each sheet in every purlin and the spacing shall not exceed 300 mm. Sheets shall be joined together at the side laps by galvanised iron bolts with a bitumen or and GI Limpet washer. Where the overlaps at the sides extend to two corrugations. The spacing of the seam bolts shall not exceed 600 mm along each of the staggered rows.

Holes for all bolts shall be drilled and not punched. Holes in the washers shall be of exact diameter of the hook bolts.

Ridges and Hips. The overlap for ridges and hips on either side over the CGI sheet and legs shall be minimum 225 mm.

Ridges shall be fixed to purlins with 8 mm diameter GI hook bolts and nuts and bitumen and GI limpet washers.

End laps of ridges and hips shall be joined together by galvanised iron seam bolts and GI washers.

Ridges and hips shall fit in squarely on the sheets.

Valleys and fastenings. Whenever the edge of a roof sheeting or valley gutter is turned up against a wall, the edge shall be weather proofed with a flashing. Flashing shall be bent up to shape and fixed.

Valleys shall be bent to shape and shall have end lap and projection on either side under CGS sheet not less than 225 mm.

Gutters. The longitudinal edges shall be turned back to the extent of 12 mm and beaten to form a rounded edge.

Wind Ties. Wind ties shall be of wooden batten 50 mm × 25 mm or 40 mm × 6 mm flat iron section. Fixing shall be done with the same loose bolts which secure the sheets to the purlins.

Slot holes shall be cut in the wind ties to allow for expansion and construction.

Black sheet roofing. When ungalvanised or unpainted sheets are used, and painting is to be done after erection, laps shall be painted before erection.

3.10.11. Nainital Pattern Roof (Plain or corrugated sheets)

The sheets shall be laid over timber boarding with battens at side joints of sheets covered with rolls made from plain sheets. Sheets shall have their edges curved by a bending machine or by hammering with a wooden mallet with a curved head on a wooden platform. The edge is finished off by hammering with the same mallet round a wooden bar of required shape.

Fixing. Sheet prepared as above is fixed to roof boarding at its upper edge by a 25 mm screw placed 40 mm from the upper edge and midway between the battens. The sheet shall have a minimum end lap of 150 mm.

The sheet for rolls shall then be cut to the required size and hammered round a roll of 75 mm in diameter until it gets the required shape. The roll shall then be slid in position and secured to the batten with one 40 mm screw placed at 40 mm from the upper edge of the roll.

The ridge shall be of plain sheets, formed by two wings each 0.6 m wide, with upper edge curved and covered with a separate roll. The ridge wings shall be secured by galvanised iron clips 30 mm × 20 mm × 6 mm fixed with 50 mm screws to each batten at their lower edge.

3.10.12. Asbestos Cement Corrugated Sheets

Spacing of purlins. Maximum spacing of purlins shall be 1.6 m for 7 mm thick sheets and 1.4 m for 6 mm thick sheets.

Ridge purlins shall be fixed at 75 mm to 115 mm from the apex of the roof.

Laying and fixing of sheets. Sheets shall be laid on the purlins and other roof members as per Code of practice.

Overhang. The free overhang of sheets at the eaves shall not exceed 300 mm in case of 6 mm thick sheets and 400 mm in case of 7 mm sheets.

The width of the mitre shall be equal to the width of the side lap.

Lap. End lap shall be 150 mm minimum.

Side lap. The sheets shall be laid with a side lap of a corrugation.

Table 3.18 shows number and length of bolts and number of Bituminous felt and galvanised iron washers.

Table 3.18. Bolts, Nuts and Washers

S. No.	*Situation*	*No. of bolts and washers*	*Length of bolts*
1.	At horizontal laps of sheets. At eaves when fill pieces are used.	Twice the number of sheets in one horizontal course.	Depth of purlin plus 90 mm
2.	At eaves when filler pieces are not used.	Twice the number of sheets in one horizontal course	Depth of purlin + 75 mm
3.	At intermediate purlins where horizontal laps do not occur.	Twice the number of sheets in one horizontal course.	Depth of purlin + 75 mm

Holes for fixing the sheets shall be drilled in the centre of end lap of the sheets. The diameter of the holes shall be 2 mm more than the diameter of the fixing bolt.

Wind Ties. As for CCI sheet roofing.

3.10.13. AC Corrugated Sheet Roofing

Laying and fixing. Same as for AC corrugated sheet roofing Sheets shall be laid with smooth side upwards. The end marked 'Top' on the smooth side shall point towards the ridge.

Laps

End lap. As for ACC sheets.

Side lap. One corrugation on the left hand small corrugation of each sheet shall be covered by the right hand large corrugation.

For fixing ACC sheets bolts and washers shall be as given in Table 3.19.

Table 3.19. Bolts and Washers

S. No.	*Situation*	*No. of bolts and washers*	*Length of bolts*
1.	At horizontal (End) laps of sheets. At eaves when filler pieces are used.	Short bolts. Number of sheets in one horizontal course plus two.	Depth of purlin plus 75 mm.
2.	At eaves when filler pieces are not used. At redge when sheets and ridge pieces are not secured by the same bolt.	Twice the number of sheets in one horizontal course plus one.	Depth of purlin plus 75 mm.
3.	At intermediate purlins where horizontal laps do not occur.	Number of sheets in one horizontal course plus one.	Depth of purlin plus 75 mm.

Ridges. Ridges shall be laid as per manufacturer's instructions. In the case of adjustable ridge, with the rolls of two wings fitting closely and with serration of serrated ridges registering correctly with the sheets underneath.

Hips. While laying hip pieces, serrations to suit the corrugations of the sheets below shall be cut in them so that they will snug fit over the sheets.

Other accessories. Other accessories such as louvers etc. shall be laid and secured with the same GI hook bolt to secure the sheets to the roof or with separate GI hook bolts, nuts and washers to the sheeting generally.

Gutters. Gutters shall be laid in such a way that a minimum fall of 1 in 120 is provided. Where possible steeper fall may be provided.

Gutters shall be true to line and slope. They shall be laid with the connected accessories such as drop ends, stop ends, nozzles, angles and union clips etc.

Spigot and socket ends of gutters shall be connected together at their laps with one row of GI 8 mm dia. bolts.

The number of jointing material per joint of different types and sizes of gutters are given in Table 3.20.

Table 3.20. Jointing Materials for Gutters

S. No.	*Type of gutters*	*Normal size in mm*	*Required per joint*			
			Plastic roofing compound	*8 mm dia GI bolt*	*Washer 25 mm No.*	*Bitumen Washer 25 mm Dia Nos.*
1.	Socketed	125	170 G	1 No. 45 mm long	2	2
2.	Socketed	200	255 G	3 Nos. 45 mm long	6	6
3.	Socketed half round	150	170 G	1 No. 45 mm long	2	2
4.	Socketed half round	250	567 G	3 Nos. 45 mm long	6	6
5.	Socketed half round	300	709 G	3 No. 45 mm long	6	6
6.	Plain ended boundry wall or eaves	275 × 125 × 175	737 G	8 No. 40 mm long	16	16
7.	Plain ended boundry wall or eaves	300 × 150 × 225	850 G	8 No. 50 mm long	16	16
8.	Plain ended boundry well or eaves	450 × 150 × 300	1020 G	8 No. 50 mm long	16	16
9.	Plain ended boundry well or eaves	500 × 150 × 125	1049 G	10 No. 50 mm long	20	20
10.	Plain ended valley	400 × 125 × 130	850 G	8 No. 50 mm long	16	16
11.	Plain ended valley	450 × 125 × 150	850 G	8 No. 50 mm long	16	16
12.	Plain ended valley	600 × 150 × 225	1105 C	8 No. 50 mm long	16	16
13.	Plain ended valley	900 × 200 × 225	1531 G	12 No. 50 mm long	24	24

3.10.14. Red and White Sand Stone Rooting

Stone slabs of specified thickness shall be placed over joists or beams.

The maximum spacing of RCC battens or beams shall not exceed shall not exceed the spacing given in Table 3.21.

Table 3.21. Spacing of Rafters

Thickness of slab	*Maximum spacing of rafters centre to centre cm*
40 mm	52.5
45 mm	60
50 mm	68

The bearing of the slabs over the joists shall not be less than 25 mm.

The slabs and the joists shall be kept wet during the progress of the work for a period of seven days.

3.10.15. Jack Arch Roof

Jack Arch roofing shall consist of bricks of specified class in lime or cement mortar, laid on edge, springing from and supported on RS Joists.

The span of the arch varies from 1.3 to 2 metres and its rise is about 1/8th of its span. Minimum thickness of the arch is kept as 100 mm.

The bricks for the springing course shall be cut to template on the ground in sufficient number before the commencement of the arch.

The rods of specified size shall fee provided in end arches of the roof. The spacing of the rods (ties) which shall be not less than 12 mm in diameter, shall be not greater than 20 times the width of the joist. These rods shall be placed not less than 75 mm from the bottom of the joists.

A layer of at least 60 mm thick concrete shall be placed over the bricks at the crown. Haunches shall be filled to make the top surface sloping suitable for draining water. Minimum specified slope is 1 in 60.

The work shall be kept wet for a period of fourteen days after completion.

3.10.15.1. Terraced Brick on Edge Roofing. Terrace shall consist of a course of thoroughly burnt terrace bricks in lime mortar. The bricks shall be laid diagonally across the joints. They shall extend at least 150 mm over the wall. Thickness of the joints, shall not exceed 10 mm. The bricks shall be kept immersed in water for 24 hours before laying. After 10 days or when the brick on edge course has set, a layer of lime concrete shall be laid over the brick on edge course. The compacted thickness of this layer shall not be less than 75 mm. During the process of compacting by beating, the surface shall be kept wet by sprinkling lime water over the surface.

Three courses of flat tiles shall be laid, over the lime concrete after six days of completing lime concreting or after lime concrete terracing has hardened. These tiles shall be laid diagonally breaking the joints. The joints of the tiles shall not be more than 6 mm wide.

Before being used the flat tiles shall be kept immersed in water for two hours. The joints of the top layer shall be kept open to afford key for pointing.

The top surface shall be pointed with 1 : 3 cement mortar and the bottom surface shall be plastered with 12 mm, 1 : 3 cement mortar. Roof shall be laid with a slope of 1 in 48.

As the work proceeds, it shall be kept thoroughly wetted until the mortar has set.

3.10.16. Tiled Roofing with Flat and Pan Tiles

The maximum distance between centres of common rafters for the roof shall not exceed 600 mm. The size of reepers shall be 50 mm × 12 mm upto a spacing of 600 mm between centres of rafters. Reepers shall be nailed with wire nails 38 mm long. The length of reepers shall cover at least four rafters.

The joints of two adjacent rows shall come over the same rafter. At eaves there shall be two reepers side by side and the flat tile shall start from the centre of the last but one reeper. The lower reeper shall be of such thickness and shape that the uniformity of the top slope of the roof shall be maintained.

The first layer of pan tiles shall be laid overlapping lengthwise for a little more than half of their length, the concave side being upwards and the second layer shall then be laid with side upwards and covering the joints between the rows of tiles of the previous layer, the lap being two thirds of the length of tiles.

Ridges and hips shall be finished with large semi-circular tiles set in mortar and neatly plastered.

Valleys shall be lined with 1.25 mm thick iron sheeting 12 mm wide, carried 75 mm into the wall top unless flashing is specified.

3.10.17. Tiled Roofing with Mangalore Tiles

The maximum distance between centres of rafters shall not exceed 600 mm. Teak reepers 50 mm × 25 mm shall be nailed to each rafter at central distances suited to the size of the tiles by means of 50 mm long nails. Joints shall come over the rafters. The joints of two adjacent rows of reepers shall not come over the same rafter.

The tiles shall be laid from the eaves towards the ridge after fitting of the reepers. The rebate of the tiles shall rest fully against the reepers.

To prevent the rain from the gutters, sides of the valleys and for, 230 mm on either side of the roof, 12 mm thick cement plaster shall be done.

At the eaves, wind tie shall be placed over the ends of the last tiles and secured by means of GI washers and screws, 25 mm into the rafter, to prevent blowing of the tile.

Two ventilation tiles to every 10 sq. m of the finished surface of the roof shall be provided at suitable places. These tiles shall fit, close and tight with other tiles.

3.10.18. Single Allahabad Tiled Roofing

The tiles shall be supported on wooden battens 25 mm × 50 mm. These battens shall be fixed over common rafters at 300 mm centres.

The battens shall be nailed to rafters at 300 mm centres. The length of battens shall be nailed to rafters with wire nails 70 mm × 25 mm. The length of battens shall be such that it covers at least three rafters. The spacing of rafters for the given size of battens shall not exceed 900 mm.

Single gile shall consist of a layer of trough shaped tile 300 mm × 400 mm in size laid on battens. The edges of every two adjacent tiles shall be covered with semi-cylindrical tile 150 mm × 350 mm in size slightly tapering towards one end.

The flat tile must lap accurately one over the other.

Each semi-cylindrical tile shall fit exactly in its position both on the flat tile under it, and also into and on the next semi-cylindrical tile respectively above and below it.

Eaves tile shall be laid in lime mortar.

Ridges and hips shall be covered by giles specially manufactured to suit their position.

Samples of the tiles shall be got approved by the Engineer-in-charge before they are incorporated in the work.

Valley shall be formed with GI sheets. The tiles which end in valleys shall be set in lime mortar.

The roof on completion shall be true to line and slope and shall be leak proof.

3.10.19. Double Allahabad Tile Roofing

Double Allahabad tile roofing consists of two layers of single tiling with the difference that in the bottom layer semi-hexagonal tiles take the place of semi-cylindrical tiles.

3.10.20. First Class Mud Roofing

The battens of wood or RCC shall have properly finished surface at the top so as to give an even bearing to the tiles. The battens shall be spaced 300 mm apart but no batten shall be placed closer than 75 mm from the wall.

Over the battens a layer of 200 mm × 150 mm × 30 mm tiles shall be laid with joints covering over the centre of the battens.

All vertical joints shall be fine as possible and filled with mortar without leaving any voids.

The second layer of tiles shall then be laid on 12 mm bed of 1 : 4 (Cement : Sand) mortar, breaking joints in both directions with the layer underneath.

The junction of the parapet wall and top tile layer shall be rounded off with a Gola.

The top surface of the tiles shall then be wetted and 6 mm thick coat of plaster in cement mortar 1 : 4 spread over it and carried along the Gola and parapet wall upto the drip course. The thickness of the plaster at the parapet wall shall however be increased to 12 mm. The plaster shall be cured for 10 days and allowed to dry completely. The dried surface shall be treated with two coats of hot bitumen grade 85/25 at the rate of 2.75 kg per sq. m.

25 mm thick layer of mud plaster shall be laid over bitumen coat and over this 100 mm of silty loamy soil shall be laid and well compacted. The roof shall then be finished with another 25 mm thick layer of mud plaster and lepai.

Lepai shall be done before laying the drip course.

In order to prevent scour, platforms or khurras shall be made.

3.10.21. Mud Phuska

The soil shall be stacked in required quantities in about 300 mm high stacks over a level round and top surface divided into suitable compartments by bunding Estimated quantity of water corresponding to optimum moisture content, about 12 hours before use, and allowed to soak.

The stacks of soil shall then be worked up with spade.

Preparation of the Mud Plaster. The dry soil shall be reduced to fine powder and mixed with water in a pit. Fibrous reinforcing material such as chopped not longer than 20 mm in proportion of 30 to 35 kg per cu. m of soil shall be added while mixing. The mixture shall be allowed to mature for a period of not less than seven days. Mud mortar used as bedding for brick tiles shall be prepared in the same manner as for mud plaster but without addition of any reinforcing material.

Leeping plaster. Leeping plaster shall be prepared by mixing soil which is free from coarse sand with equal volume of cowdung and adding the required quantity of water. The mixture shall then be worked to a homogeneous mass.

The prepared soil shall be laid in loose layers of thickness not greater than 15 cm. The surface shall then be allowed to dry for a period of not less than 24 hours.

When the surface of mud plaster has dried, a thin coat of leeping plaster not less than 3 mm thick shall be applied and finished with a trowel.

3.10.22. Paving with Tiled Bricks laid Flat on and Grouted with Cement Mortar over Roofs

The surface shall be hacked, roughened and cleaned thoroughly. It shall then be wetted before applying the mortar. Cement mortar of 1 : 3 mix shall then be spread in 12 mm layers evenly over the surface. Tile bricks which have been soaked in water for at least one hour shall then be laid open jointed. The joints shall however not be wider than 10 mm. Transverse joints in alternate layers shall come directly in line with one another. The open joints shall then be grouted with 1 : 3 cement mortar. The joints shall be finished flush with brick surface.

The tile paving shall be cured for at least seven days.

3.10.23. Gola

The height of Gola at the wall face shall not at any point be less than 75 mm.

The brick face of the parapet and the tile brick face of terrace where the Gola will be formed shall be scrubbed clean of all dust and other foreign material and well wetted. The concrete shall then be laid along the junction of the terrace and parapet and well compacted and formed to shape with wooden thappies until the mortar cream comes to the surface.

The Gola shall then be rounded and finished smooth with the lime plaster of specified mix. The top end of the finished Gola shall end exactly at the junction of the underside of the drip course with the parapet.

The bottom line of the Gola shall be straight and the surface shall be smooth and uniform.

3.10.24. Purnalas

These are shallow channels formed on the face of the wall for the rain water from the roof to run down, by plastering the masonry face to the width of the purnalas with cement mortar of specified mix and 20 mm thickness. The width of the purnala specified, means the width of the channel inclusive of fillets.

The surface shall be plastered 20 mm thick with the specified mortar to the required width of the purnala. When the plaster is still wet two cement mortar fillets of the specified size and section shall be made on two sides of the channel with the same mortar and mix as the blacking plaster.

3.10.25. Paving of Roof with Bitumen

The surface to be pointed shall be cleaned with wire brushes Bitumen of specified grade shall be heated to the specified temperature and poured over the surface at the specified rate.

The coat of bitumen shall be continued at least 15 cm along the vertical surfaces joining the roof. In the parapet wall it shall be continued upto the drip course.

Immediately after painting dry, clean sharp and course sand at the rate of 0.6 cu. m/100 sq. m shall be evenly spread and levelled over the surface when the bitumen is still.

3.10.26. Water Proofing Treatment

Well defined cracks, other than hair cracks in the roof structure shall be to *'V'* section, cleaned and filled up flush with cement sand slurry or with bitumen conforming to IS : 702–1961. The surface to be treated shall have a minimum slope of 1 in 120.

Priming Coat. A priming coat consists of bituminous solution of low viscosity. It shall be applied with brush on the roof and wall surface at specified weight per unit area.

Under layer. Where water proofing greatment is required to be isolated from the roof surface, a layer of bitumen saturated felt (under layer) shall be spread over the roof surface and tucked into the flashing grooves.

Water proofing treatment. Water proofing treatment consists of a four or six course treatments.

The above mentioned four and six course treatments are described below :

A. Four course treatment

A four course treatment is given as 'Normal Treatment' or 'Floating Treatment'. These treatments are described below :

Normal treatment

(*i*) Hot applied bitumen at the rate of 1.2 kg/sq. m 'minimum'.

(*ii*) Hessian base self finished felt type 3 grade 1.

(*iii*) Hot applied bitumen at the rate of 1.2 k/sq. m minimum.

(*iv*) Pea-sized gravel or grit at the rate of 0.006 cu. m/sq. m.

OR

Floating treatment

(*i*) Fibre based bitumen saturated under lay type 1.

(*ii*) Hot applied bitumen at the rate of 1.2 kg/sq. m minimum.

(*iii*) Fibre based self finished felt type 2, grade 1 or 2.

(*iv*) Hessian based self finished type 3 grade 1.

(*v*) Pea sized gravel or grit at the rate of 0.008 cu. m/sq. m.

B. Six course treatment

Six Course treatment consists of the following :

(*i*) Hot applied bitumen at the rate of 1.2 kg/sq. m.

(*ii*) Hessian base self-finished felt type 3 grade 1.

(*iii*) Hot applied bitumen at the rate of 1.2 kg/sq. m minimum.

(*iv*) Hessian based self-finished felt type 3 grade 1.

(*v*) Hot applied bitumen at the rate of 1.2 kg/sq. m minimum.

(*vi*) Pea sized gravel or grit at the rate of 0.006 cu. m/sq. m.

OR

(*i*) Hot applied bitumen at the rate of 1.2 kg/sq. m minimum.

(*ii*) Fine-based self-finished felt type 2 grade 1 or grade 2.

(*iii*) Hot applied bitumen at the rate of 1.2 kg/sq m. minimum.

(*iv*) Fine-based self-finished felt type 2 grade 1 or grade 2.

(*v*) Hot applied bitumen at the rate of 2.5 kg/sq. m minimum.

(*vi*) Pea sized gravel or grit at the rate of 0.008 cu. m/sq. m.

Laying of felt. The self finished felt shall be cut to the required length. It shall be brushed clean to get rid of all dust and dirt. The felt shall be laid in length running at right angles to the direction of the run of gradient.

Each length shall be laid in position and rolled up for a distance of half its length. Hot bonding material shall be poured on to the roof across full width of the felt as the latter is steadily unrolled and pressed down. The excess bonding material which sqeezes out at the ends shall be removed. When the first half of the felt has been bonded to the roof, other half shall be rolled up and then unrolled on the hot bonding material in the same way. Subsequent strips shall be laid in the same manner. Each strip shall overlap the preceeding one by at least 75 mm at the longitudinal edges and 100 mm at the ends.

The third layer of bonding material in four course treatment shall be carried out in the same manner.

In a six course treatment the third and fifth layer of bonding material shall be laid as for four course treatment.

Water proofing treatment shall be carried into the drain pipe or outlets by at least 100 mm.

Flashing. Felts shall be laid as flashings whereever junction of vertical and horizontal surfaces occur.

The lower edge of flashing shall overlap the felt laid on flat portion of the roof and the upper edge of the flashing shall be tucked into the horizontal groove 75 mm thick wide and 65 mm deep, provided at a minimum height of 150 mm from top of the roof surface.

After the top flashing layer has been laid, the penultimate layer of bonding material shall be applied.

Low dividing wall. Where low dividing walls or inverted beams are met with, the same shall be covered with a four or six course treatment.

Expansion joints. Expansion joints shall be provided on as required basis.

Treatment of bubble formation. When bubble forming takes place, the following procedure shall be adopted to rectify the defect.

Remove the gravel from the ballooned surface. Cut open and squeeze out that rapped vapour. Seal the bitumen felt back on the surface by applying additional bitumen.

3.10.27. Water proofing roofs with plastic roofing compound

The roof surface and vertical wall surfaces upto 250 mm from level shall be thoroughly cleaned with wire brushes. All cracks shall be exposed and made into *V*-shape 25 mm wide at top and 12 to 20 mm deep. The surface shall be dusted off and exposed cracks shall be filled with plastic roofing compound "Standard Black" and spread upto 75 mm on either side.

The compound shall be applied when the surface is thoroughly dry. The roof and the wall surface upto 250 mm shall then be painted with cold roofing primer liquid at the rate of 0.24 litre/sq. m. without leaving any blank patches. Plastic roofing compound black shall then be applied over the roofing at the rate of 2.75 kg per sq. m. Coarse sand shall be spread over the roof surface at the rate of 0.006 cu.m per sq. m and rolled with wooden roller so that the sand gets integrated with the compound.

3.10.28. China Mosaic Work

12 mm thick screed of cement lime mortar (1 : 2 : 9) shall be laid on the top of roofing. Before the screed is about to set a floating coat of 3 mm thick cement lime mortar shall be laid on the screed. While the floating coat is still green, broken pieces of tiles thoroughly soaked in water shall be set flat as closely as possible, The surface shall then be rolled lightly with wooden roller to ensure proper setting of the pieces. After a day, the surplus cement grout is cleaned off. The surface shall be kept wet for 10 days.

3.10.29. Rainwater Pipe

The sectional area of rain water pipe shall be at the rate of 1 sq. cm per 0.7 to 0.8 sq. m of the area drained.

Spouts of stone-ware or GI pipes shall be placed at the mouth of Khurras and fixed in cement mortar 1 : 4 with the socket embedded in the masonry and the spigot end projecting outside.

CI rainwater pipes shall be in full length of 1.8 m lengths, unless shorter lengths of pipes are required.

The pipes and the fittings shall be fixed in vertical alignment unless otherwise specified. They shall be fixed to the wall at all junctions with MS holder clamps.

The pipes shall be fixed vertically. The spigot of the upper pipe shall be properly fitted in the socket of the lower pipe.

The spigot end shall butt the shoulder of the socket and leave no gap in between. The annular space between the socket and spigot will be well packed with spun yarn leaving 25 mm from the lip of the socket for the lead. The joint shall then be lead caucked.

The general specifications for the pipe fittings shall conform to the specifications for CI rainwater pipes.

3.11. CEILING AND LINING

3.11.1. Indian Standards to be Followed

The following standards shall be followed :

IS : 287–1972. Moisture content of timber used for different purposes.

IS : 451–1961. Wood screws.

IS : 723–1961. Mild steel wires.

IS : 1331–1971. Cut sizes of Timber.

IS : 3348–1965. Insulation Boards.

IS : 3129–1965. Particle Board for Insulation.

IS : 303–1960. Plywood for general purposes.

IS : 1328–1970. Veneered decorative plywood.

IS : 2098–1964. Asbestos cement building boards.

IS : 702–1961. Industrial bitumen

IS : 3308–1969. Wood wool building.

IS : 3144–1965. Mineral wool thermal insulation material.

IS : 2046–1969. Decorative Thermo-setting resin.

IS : 2547–1963. Gypsum building plaster.

IS : 2818 (Part I)–1967. Indian Hessian.

IS : 749–1955. Handloom Dungri cloth.

3.11.2. Materials

3.11.2.1. Timber Boards and Battens. Timber boards and battens shall conform to the respective standards.

3.11.2.2. Insulation Boards. Insulation boards shall follow the respective standards given under 16.9.0.

3.11.2.3. Fibre hard board. Fibre hard boards shall conform to the respective standard.

3.11.2.4. Wood particle board. Wood particle board shall conform to the respective standard.

3.11.2.5. Veneered particle board. Veneered particle board shall conform to the relevant standard.

3.11.2.6. Block Board. Block Board shall conform to the relevant standard.

3.11.2.7. Ply wood and veneered decorative board. Ply wood and veneered decorative board shall conform to relevant, standard.

3.11.2.8. Expanded or Foamed polystyrene boards and tiles. These shall be of approved material and conform to the specifications indicated.

3.11.2.9. Asbestos cement boards. Asbestos cement boards shall conform to the relevant standards.

3.11.2.10. Wood wool slab. Wood wool slab shall conform to the relevant standard.

3.11.2.11. Mineral wool insulation Blanket. The thickness of insulation wool blankets shall be as under (See Table 3.22).

Table 3.22. Thickness of Insulation Wool Blankets

Temperature range °C	*Thickness (mm)*
–10 to 0	50
0 to 10	40
10 to 20	30
20 to 30	30
30 to 40	40
30 to 50	50

3.11.2.12. Hollow glass bricks. Hollow glass wall bricks shall be of size 200 mm × 200 mm × 100 mm with tolerance of 3 mm (plus or minus).

3.11.2.13. Plaster of Paris. Plaster of Paris shall conform to the relevant standard.

3.11.2.14. Hessian or Textile cloth. Hessian or Textile cloth shall conform to the relevant standard.

3.11.3. Workmanship

3.11.3.1. Timber Planking. Timber planks shall be sawn in the direction of the grain or cut square and straight.

Each groove shall have tongued and grooved jointing. In the case of skirting, however, butt jointing shall be permitted.

Framework shall be of Teak wood or any other hard wood specified.

The countersunk wood screw holes shall be carefully filled with putty conforming to IS : 419–1967.

3.11.3.2. Timber plank ceiling. The frame for supporting the ceiling may be wooden or metal. It shall be treated with wood preservative in the case of wood-work.

Planks of specified timber of required thickness shall be used. The width of planks shall be not more than 100 mm upto 20 mm thick planks and 150 mm for planks above 150 mm thickness. The longitudinal edges of the planks shall be jointed with tongue and grooved joints.

The outer lines of the planks shall be accurately fixed parallel and close to the wall. Each subsequent plank shall be carefully jointed up. The screws shall not be thinner than designation 8 and of a length not less than twice the thickness of the board.

3.11.3.3. Insulating board in wall lining. Fixing. The stud and ground for fixing the boards shall be spaced at 300 mm to 450 mm centres, bothways. The actual spacing shall depend on the width of the cut boards in the panel arrangement.

For grounds on solid walls planed battens 40 mm × 20 mm shall be used.

The nails shall have a shank diameter of 2.5 mm and head diameter of about 8 mm. The length of the nails shall be 30 mm for board thickness of 12 mm while for thicker boards length of nails shall be not less than twice the thickness of the board or 30 mm whichever is longer.

Nails shall be spaced at supports at 100 mm to 150 mm centre to centre and at 75 mm centre-at edges.

3.11.3.4. Insulating boards in ceiling. Fixing. The battens may range from 65 to 75 mm × 40 mm to 50 mm and spacing may range from 450 mm to 600 mm for longitudinal battens and 600 mm to 1200 mm for cross battens depending on the size of the boards.

The boards are first nailed to the intermediate framing member proceeding from centre of the board outwards, the edges being nailed the last.

The screws shall be rustless and greased before fixing. The length of the screws shall be 30 to 35 mm for boards of 12 mm thickness and not less than twic the thickness of the board or 30 mm whichever is more.

3.11.3.5. Fibre hard boards in wall lining. Fixing. The work shall be carried out as for "Insulation boards in lining".

3.11.3.6. Fibre hard board in ceiling. Fixing The work shall be carried out as for "Insulation boards in ceiling".

3.11.3.7. Wood particle board, veneered particle board etc. The work shall be carried out as for "Insulation boards in lining".

3.11.3.8. Wood particle board, veneered particle board etc. Fixing. The work shall be generally carried out as for "Insulation boards in ceiling".

Spacing for boards above 10 mm thickness may be from 600 mm to 900 mm for longitudinal battens and 900 to 1300 mm for cross battens.

3.11.3.9. Plywood, veneered decorative plywood and Block boards in walling. Fixing. The plywood shall be used in the form of panels with stiffened edges by rails, stiles or narrow strips of wood metal or other materials.

The edges of plywood panels shall be protected before sealing with suitable sealer.

While making butt joint in a block board, both edges shall be grooved and a separate tongue glued in.

In the case of decorative boards, the pattern and figure matching shall be decided and put on paper and boards, preferably numbered for these positions.

3.11.3.10. Plywood, decorative plywood and block boards in ceiling. Fixing. The work shall be carried out as for wood particle board, veneered particle board etc.".

Spacing shall vary from 450 mm to 600 mm for boards of thickness varying from 4 mm to 10 mm for longitudinal battens and 600 mm to 1200 mm for cross battens. For boards of thickness greater than 10 mm the spacing for longitudinal battens varies from 600 mm to 900 mm and for cross battens the spacing varies from 900 mm to 1300 mm.

When necessary, plywood may be stiffened along the edges and also in intermediate positions by stiles or narrow strips of wood, metal or other materials.

The screws shall be fixed starting from one corner and extending to both sides to fix the boards flat and level.

The length of the screws shall be 25 mm for boards upto 7 mm thickness, 35 mm for boards between 7 mm and 12 mm in thickness and thickness plus 20 mm for boards of above 12 mm thickness. Screws shall be rustless and greased before fixing.

3.11.3.11. Expanded or foamed polystyrene boards and tiles in lining. Fixing. The work shall be carried but as for "Insulation boards in lining"

3.11.3.12. Expanded or foamed polystyrene boards and tiles in ceiling. Fixing. The work shall be carried out as for "Insulation boards in ceiling".

3.11.3.13. Wooden cover fillets (Beading). Beadings shall be of specified wood and size.

The overlap of the beadings shall be equal on either side of the plank.

Beading shall be placed true of all exposed faces and on the rear face. It shall be fixed centrally over the butt joints between the two boards.

The junction of the beading shall be mitred.

3.11.3.14. Asbestos cement board in lining. Fixing. The work shall be carried out as for "Fibre Hard Board in wall lining".

Care shall be taken to avoid rigid fixing as it may cause cracking if the supporting structure expands or shrinks.

The boards shall be fixed either with wooden cover fillets or asbestos strips.

3.11.3.15. Asbestos cement board in ceiling. Fixing. The work shall be carried out as for "Fibre hard board in ceiling".

The spacing of screws shall depend on the size and height of asbestos boards and as specified by the manufacturers.

3.11.3.16. Wood wool and Mineral wool Blanket work in lining. Fixing. The work shall be carried out as for "Insulating board in wall lining."

Bitumen of grade 85/25 shall be heated to the required temperature and applied hot at the rate of 2.2 kg/m^2.

3.11.3.17. Wood wool and Mineral wool blanket in ceiling. Fixing. The work shall be carried out as for "Insulating board in ceiling. Decorative laminates shall be fixed to the frame/base with approved adhesive as per instructions of the manufacturers.

3.11.3.18. Hollow glass block in walls. A fairly dry and fatty mortar 1 : 4 (1 white cement : 4 white sand) shall be used as the blocks are non-observant. The joints shall not be less than 6.4 mm nor more than 10 mm in width.

Before laying the bottom course, the sill shall be coated with emulsion of bitumen and then bedded with the specified mortar.

Every third course shall be provided with reinforcing strips 65 mm wide of non-rust in open mesh. These strips shall be secured to the main structure by embedding for a horizontal distance of 200 mm and then turning it vertically for a length of 75 mm in case of end supports.

In case of intermediate supports, the horizontal distance shall be half the width of then support.

Intermediate supports shall be provided in the panels where the height is more than 5 metres or area is more than 10 m^2. 10 mm thick clearance joints shall be provided on both the sides and top in all cases and clearance shall be filled with a cushioning material like putty.

In external panels recess must be provided into which the top and sides are built free of the main structure, except where dimensions of the panel do not exceed 2 m^2.

Where intermediate panels are provided, it is not necessary to provide recesses in them.

3.11.3.19. Glass Blocks in ceiling. Fixing. The glass blocks shall be arranged such that each block is surrounded and supported by reinforced concrete forming a cellular slab. The timber formwork shall be provided over the whole area. To achieve proper shape pads of three plyboard shall be nailed on the form boarding.

After concrete has been sufficiently set the inside boarding and pads of three ply shall be removed and glass blocks placed in position. The joint between RCC slab and glass blocks shall be as thin as possible. It shall be filled with 1.3 cement sand mortar mixed with water proofing compound. The portion of RCC ribs projecting below glass blocks shall be rendered smooth with 1 : 3 cement : Sand mortar.

3.11.3.20. Plaster of Paris (Gypsum Anhydrous) ceiling over wooden strips. In case of sloping roofs, the battens shall be securely fixed as main supports to the underside of the tie beams of the trusses at the required centres by means of bolts and nuts of proper size.

In case of flat roofs, the battens shall be securely fixed to the walls and pillars by holding down bolts and shall be fastened to the slab above with iron straps or mild steel bars of suitable section anchored therein.

Cross battens of 50 mm × 40 mm sections at about 400 mm centres shall be fixed as right angles to the main battens. Before being covered with ceiling the frame work shall be treated with approved wood reservative. The underside of the frame work shall be true to planes and slopes.

Wooden strips or laths 25 mm × 6 mm of specified wood shall be fixed to the cross battens in parallel rows with gaps of 10 mm in between by means of flat headed nails. The strips shall be butt jointed and not overlapped. The joints shall be staggered. The minimum length of strips to be used shall be 1.5 m depending upon the length of strips required.

Rabbit wire mesh shall then be fixed to the underside of wooden strips at the junction with the battens with nails at pitch of 150 mm to 200 mm.

The plaster of Paris will be mixed with water to a workable consistency and shall be applied to the underside of the laths over the rabbit wire mesh.

The joints shall be finished flush to make the ceiling in one piece.

3.11.3.21. Plaster of Paris (Gypsum Anhydrous) Coiling Tiles. The wooden formwork shall consist of main and cross battens of suitable sections. The width of scantling shall be sufficient to provide a nailing space of minimum 60 mm. The longitudinal and header scantlings shall be so arranged that the tiles can be fixed to form the panel arrangement required and there is supporting scantling under each and every edge of tiles. The frame work shall be treated with preservative before it is covered with tiling.

Tiles of plaster of paris reinforced with hessian cloth shall be prepared in suitable sizes. The maximum size of the tile shall be 750 mm in each direction. Wooden forms of height equal to thickness of tiles shall be placed on a truly level and smooth surface such as glass sheet.

The tiles shall be fixed to the cross battens of the ceiling frame with 40 mm brass screws at a spacing of 150 mm to 200 mm centres on all edges. The line of screws shall be not less than 10 mm away from the edge of the tiles.

3.11.3.22. Cloth Ceiling. Fixing. The cloth shall be fixed either directly to the ceiling or frame work on separate frames not more than 1.5 m × 1.5 m in size with 40 mm × 12 mm wooden corner fillets.

The cloth shall be damped, stretched over frames and fastened with tacks on the outside. The frames shall be screwed to the roof timber or to the ceiling joints and the joints covered with wooden fillets.

3.12. PLASTERING AND POINTING

3.12.1. IS Codes to be Referred to

The following IS Codes shall be referred to :

IS : 369–1967. Ordinary, Rapid hardening and low heat portland cement.

IS : 455–1967. Ordinary, Blast furnace slag cement.

IS : 712–1973. Building Limes.

IS : 1542–1960. Sand for plaster.

IS : 383–1970. Coarse and fine aggregate from natural sources for concrete.

IS : 2394–1965. Application of lime plaster finish.

IS : 1661–1972. Cement lime plaster finishes.

IS : 2402–1963. External rendered finishes.

IS : 1635–1960. Field slaking of and preparation of putty.

IS : 412–1962. Expanded metal sheets.

3.12.2. Materials

3.12.2.1. Class B and C shall be used. Lime putty.

This shall be obtained by slaking lime with fresh water and sifting it. Slaking shall be carried out as per IS : 1635–1960.

3.12.2.2. Neeru. This shall be prepared by mixing putty and sand in equal proportion and chopped jute and 4 kg per cum of mortar. The mixture shall be properly ground to fine paste between two stones.

3.12.2.3. Sand. This shall conform to IS : 1542–1960. Specifications for sand for plaster.

3.12.2.4. Aggregates. Aggregates shall conform to IS : 383–1270. Specifications for coarse and fine aggregates from natural sources for concrete.

3.12.2.5. Pebbles. These shall be either small pebbles or crushed stones of size 10 mm to 20 mm.

3.12.2.6. Water. Potable water is normally suitable.

3.12.2.7. Surkhi. Shall conform to relevant specifications.

3.12.2.8. Stone Marble Dust. Shall conform to standard laid for mortars.

3.12.2.9. Ash. Shall conform to relevant specifications under 'Mortar'.

3.12.2.10. Integral Water Proofing Compound. Shall conform to IS : 2645–1964. Specifications for integral water proofing compound Water proofing liquid shall be 'AZROK' or other equal and approved make.

3.12.2.11. Bitumen Cutback. Shall conform to IS : 217–1961. Specification for cut back-Digboi type.

3.12.2.12. Solid. Shall conform to relevant specification under 'Mortar'. Cholled straw (Bhoosa) for mixing with mud mortar for plastering shall be clean, thin fibres not longer than 20 mm.

3.12.2.13. Wire netting. Wire netting for metal laths shall be galvanised with wire 0.90 mm diameter and of 12.5 mesh.

3.12.2.14. Expanded metal. Expanded metal for metal laths shall be as per IS : 412–1962 specification for Expanded metal steel sheets for general purposes.

3.12.3. Workmanship

3.12.3.1. General

Scaffolding (Staging). Wooden bailies, bamboos, planks, trestles and other scaffolding materials shall be sound and properly examined before use.

The surface to be plastered shall be cleaned and properly prepared.

The first undercoat shall be applied to the ceiling. After ceiling plaster has been completed, scaffolding shall be removed and under coating applied to the walls.

The surface of the first under coat shall be adjusted and screeds laid to serve as guides in bringing the work to an even surface.

After a suitable lapse of time, the finishing coat shall be applied first to the ceiling and then to the walls. Plastering of cornices, decorative features etc. shall be completed before the finishing coat is applied.

3.12.3.2. Lime Plaster. One coat plaster or two coat plaster work shall be carried out as detailed below :

(*i*) ***One coat plaster.*** Plaster about 15 cm × 15 cm shall first be applied horizontally and vertically not more than 2 metres intervals to serve as gauges. The mortar shall then be laid on the wall between the gauges. The thickness of the mortar applied shall be slightly more than the specified thickness so that after being beaten with thapies the required thickness is obtained. The thickness shall finally be checked by placing straight edge between the gauges. Finally the surface shall be finished true with trowel or wooden float. Excessive trowelling or overworking the float shall be avoided. During the process a solution of lime putty shall be applied on the surface to make the surface workable.

At the end of the day's work, the plaster shall be cut clean to line both horizontally and vertically. Before recommencing the plaster, the edge of the old work shall be scraped clean and wetted with lime putty before applying plaster to the adjoining area. Horizontal joints in plaster shall not occur on parapet tops and copings.

Curing of plastered surface shall start after 24 hours of finishing the plaster and the plastered surface shall be kept wet for a period of 7 days. To control period of curing days of plastering shall be marked on various sections of the wall.

(*ii*) ***Two coat plaster.*** The first coat of specified thickness shall be applied in the same way as the one coat plaster.

Before the first coat hardens, its surface shall be beaten up by edges of wooden tapers and close dents shall be made on the surface. After the first coat shall be allowed to set for a period of 3 to 5 days depending upon the weather conditions. During this period the surface shall be kept wet.

The second coat of specified thickness shall be completed in the same manner as the first coat.

Curing for the second coat shall be done in the same way as the first coat.

(*iii*) ***Three coat plaster.*** Tl first two coats shall be applied in the same way as two coat plaster. The third or finishing coat shall be completed to the specified thickness in the same way as the second coat.

Curing shall be done as for the Two Coat plaster.

Lime punning or Neeru finish consists in finishing the interior with a thin (3 mm) coat of fat lime putty mixed with equal amount of sand. Before actual use, putty shall be matured for two or three days.

The mortar for punning shall be applied in 3 mm thin layer just after the under coat has hardened.

Curing of punned surface shall be started as soon as punning has hardened but not earlier than 24 hours after punning has been completed.

3.12.3.3. Cement and Cement Lime Plaster. The plastering work shall be carried out in the same manner as lime plaster with the exception of the following :

(*i*) Beating of thapies shall not be done on the cement plaster.

(*ii*) No lime putty solution shall be applied on the surface while finishing.

Cement lime plaster shall be used within two hours after the addition of water to the cement provided it is kept agitated after every 20 minutes. Cement plaster shall be used within half an hour after addition of water.

Each coat shall be kept continuously damp till the subsequent coat is applied.

For application of floating coat with neat cement slurry adopt the following procedure.

When plaster has been brought to a true surface with the wooden straight edge, it shall be uniformly treated over the entire area with a paste of neat cement and rubbed smooth so that the whole surface is covered with the neat cement coating. The quantity of cement applied for this treatment shall be 1 kg per square metre of the surface.

When water proofing compound treatment is desired, the compound shall be mixed dry in the proportion specified by the manufacturers. Care shall be taken to see that the water proofing compound, mixes thoroughly with the cement and does not run out when water is mixed to the cement compound mix.

When water proofing is desired to be done with liquid type compound, the liquid compound shall be diluted with three parts of water by volume and applied to the surface with an interval of 24 hours between subsequent coats. The surface to be treated shall be thoroughly washed and completely dried before applying the solution.

3.12.3.4. Metal Lathing. Lathing shall be tightly stretched with a long way of mesh across the supports before nailing. This shall be secured with 25 mm galvanised steel staples or nails at 200 mm centres if the studding is of wood and with 0.90 mm iron tying wire if the studding is of steel. Sides of sheets shall be wired together with galvanised wire of diameter not less than 1.25 mm every 100 mm between supports.

Before plastering the surface, the metal lathing shall be brushed over with thin cement slurry or given a protective coat of bitumen oil or paint.

3.12.3.5. Plastering to Lathing. Mortars for the first coat shall be of stiff consistency and applied as evenly as possible to give a good cover to the lathing. Too much pressure shall not be used in applying plaster to lathing.

3.12.3.6. Plaster to Ceiling. The surface shall be cleaned scrubbed clean with wire brushes. Concrete surface shall be pack marked with a pointed tool at a spacing of not more than 50 mm. The packs shall be not less than 3 mm deep. This ensures a proper key for the plaster. The work shall conform to "Cement and cement Lime plaster".

3.12.3.7. Rough Cast Finish. The base surface which is to receive rough cast finish shall be in plastic state. Rough cast mix shall be wetted and shall be dashed on the plaster base by hand scoop so that the mix gets well pitched into the plaster base. The mix shall then be again dashed over the vacant spaces, so that the finishes surface presents a homogeneous surface of sand mixed with gravel.

Curing for the plastered rough cast surface shall be done as for "Cement and Cement Lime Plaster".

3.12.3.8. Pebble Dash Plaster. The specifications shall be same as for Rough Cast Finish except that the aggregates used for dashing *i.e.*, pebble or graded crushed stone shall be well washed and drained and thrown wet on the plaster bays while it is still plastic using strong whipping motion at right angles to the face of the wall pressed flat and filling the uncovered parts by hand so that finished surface presents a homogeneous surface. To ensure good bond finished surface shall be lightly tapped with a trowel.

3.12.3.9. Coloured Plaster. The surface shall be prepared as for "Cement and Cement Lime Plaster".

Finishing coat shall consist of cement marble dust and crushed stone dust in the ratio of 1 : 1 : 3 with red oxide to obtain the required shade. The colour shall be mixed thoroughly with dry cement, then the mortar shall be mixed in the same manner as ordinary cement mortar using the pigment cement and crushed stone dust and marble dust mixture.

3.12.3.10. Mortar Bands. Plain band is a plastic strip of uniform width and of uniform thickness provided for decorative or other purposes flush with, sunk below or projecting beyond wall plaster. Flush band is one where due to difference in mix or shade of the mortar, the band is executed as a separate and distinct operation from the wall plaster.

The thickness of the raised band is the thickness of the projection beyond the planes of the wall plaster, while the thickness of the flush or sunk band thickness will be the thickness of the plaster measured from the untreated wall surface.

3.12.3.11. Pointing. The joints shall be raked to such a depth that the minimum thickness of raking is not less than 10 mm. Mortar shall be flushed into the raked out joint with a pointing trowel according to the pointing specified.

The common varieties of pointing are :

1. **Flush pointing.** The mortar shall be pressed into the joints, it shall be finished flush and levelled.

2. **Ruled pointing.** The joint shall initially flush finished and then while the mortar is still green, a groove of shape and size shall be formed by running a forming tool straight along the centre line of joints till a smooth and hard surface is formed.

3. **Outer weather struck pointing.** The mortar shall first be pressed into joints. The top of horizontal joints shall be neatly pressed back by about 3 mm with the pointing tool so that the joint is sloping from top to bottom. The vertical joint shall be ruled pointed.

4. **Raised and cut pointing.** This type of pointing shall project from the wall facing with edges cut parallel so as to have a uniformly raised band about 6 mm raised and width 10 mm or more as specified.

The surface of pointing shall be kept cured by watering for seven days.

5. **Pointing on brick flooring.** Specifications shall be as for general pointing.

3.13. WHITE WASHING, COLOUR WASHING, DISTEMPERING AND OTHER FINISHES

3.13.1. Indian Standards to be Followed

The following Indian Standards shall be followed :

IS : 47–1950. Colour for paints.

IS : 261–1966. Copper sulphate.

IS : 63–1964. Whiting for paints.

IS : 77–1968. Linseed oil boiled for paints.

IS : 427–1965. Distemper dry, as required.

IS : 428–1969. Distemper, oil Emulsion.

IS : 5410–1969. Cement paints.

IS : 5411–(Part I)–1969. Plastic Emulsion.

3.13.2. Materials

The following materials shall be used :

3.13.2.1. Clearcolle. This shall be made from glue and boiling water. 1 kg of glue shall be added to every 15 litres of water.

3.13.2.2. Lime. Lime for white washing shall be freshly burnt 'C' lime (Fat lime).

3.13.2.3. Water. Portable water is most suitable.

3.13.2.4. Gum. Best quality gum shall be used for this purpose.

3.13.2.5. Ultramarine Blue or Indigo. This shall conform to IS : 55–1970.

3.13.2.6. Pigments. Mineral colours not affected by lime shall be used in preparing colourwash.

3.13.3. Workmanship

3.13.3.1. White Washing with Lime. White washing with lime shall conform to IS : 6278–1971.

3.13.3.2. Scaffolding. No part of scaffolding shall rest against the surface to be white washed or colour washed.

3.13.3.3. Preparation of the Surface. Before white washing, the surface shall be cleaned of all dust, dirt, mortar droppings etc.

Surface already white washed shall be broomed down to remove all dirt, dust, loose scales of lime wash and other foreign matters.

Surface spoiled by smoke soot shall be scraped with steel wire brushes or steel scrapers.

Oil and grease spots shall be removed by a suitable chemical and smooth surface shall be rubbed with wire brushes.

All unsound portions of surface plaster shall be removed to full depth of plaster in rectangular patches and plastered again. Such portions shall be wetted and allowed to dry. They shall then be given one coat of white wash.

All unnecessary nails shall be removed, the holes cracks etc. not exceeding 0.1 sq. m. shall be made good with material similar in composition to the surface to be prepared.

3.13.3.4. Preparation of White Wash. The fat lime shall be slaked at site and shall be mixed and stirred with about 5 litres of water for 1 kg of unslaked lime to make a thin cream. This shall be allowed to stand for 24 hours and then screened through a clean coarse cloth. 4 kg of gum dissolved in hot water shall be added to each cubic metre of lime cream. Small quantity of ultra-marine blue (upto 3 gms per kg of lime) shall be added to last two coats of white wash.

3.13.3.5. Application of White Wash. White wash shall be applied with "MOONG" brush to the specified number of coats. The operation shall consist of a stroke from the brush from top downward and another from down upward followed by one stroke horizontally from right to left and another from left to right. This constitutes one single coat.

Each coat shall be allowed to dry before the next coat is applied.

White washing to ceiling shall be done before the same is done on the walls.

For undercoated surfaces at least two coats shall be applied.

For decorated surfaces, after preparation of the surface, a coat of white wash shall be applied over the patches and repairs. Then one or more coats of white wash shall be applied over the entire surface.

3.13.3.6. Colour Washing. Old colour wash shall be entirely removed, if the new colourwash is different from the old one. The surface shall then be prepared by brushing or scraping or by other suitable mean. Sufficient quantity of colour wash shall then be prepared for the complete job. The colourwash shall be of even tint over the whole surface.

Preparation of colour wash with pigments shall be as under :

(*a*) **With Yellow or Red Ochre.** Solid lump if any shall be powdered and solution in water prepared and added to whitewash sieving through a coarse cloth.

(*b*) **With Blue Vitriol.** Fresh crystals of blue vitriol shall be powdered and added to small quantity of water. Sufficient, quantity of solution shall be strained through a coarse cloth. The filtrate shall be mixed with white wash.

Colour wash from other colouring materials shall be prepared as per manufacturer's instructions.

Colour wash shall be applied in the same manner as white wash.

3.13.3.7. White washing with chalk whiting. 2½ kg of whiting and one litre of double size (prepared from 1/4 kg of glue) shall be mixed together and placed in a covered vessel with enough water to cover the mixture which shall be allowed to cool till it becomes jelly.

3.13.3.8. Hiramchi (Red Ochre) wash. Hiramchi cement and surkhi (100 mesh) and water shall be mixed in the proportion of 3 : 2.5 : 12 : 5 by volume. The powder shall be mixed dry first and then added to water. The mixture shall be applied with brushes.

3.13.3.9. Cement slurry wash. Cement shall be added to water to give the consistency of ready mixed paint. The slurry shall be applied with brushes to form a smooth bidded opaque surface.

3.13.3.10. Cement wash with boiled linseed oil on iron work. Partland Cement and boiled linseed oil shall be mixed together in the following proportion to the consistency of cream.

Cement	6 kg
Boiled linseed oil	5 litres

The iron surface shall be thoroughly cleaned and freed from dirt, dust, etc.

3.13.3.11. Dry Distempering

(*a*) **Undercoated surfaces.** The surface shall be thoroughly cleaned of dirt, dust, etc. New plaster shall be allowed to dry for at least 2 months before applying distemper.

(*b*) **Decorated Surfaces.** All loose particles shall be removed. Where heavy scaling has taken place, the entire surface shall be scraped with wire brushes to remove accumulated distemper clean surface.

(*c*) **Priming coat of whiting shall be applied over the prepared surface in case of new work.** No coat of white washing with lime shall be used as priming coat for distemper.

The treated surface shall be allowed to dry before applying distemper. The dry distemper shall be stirred slowly in clean warm water using 6 decilitre (0.6 litres) of water per kg of distemper. It shall be allowed to stand for atleast 30 minutes before applying. After priming coat has dried, the surface shall -be lightly sand papered taking care not to disturb the priming coat.

Prepared distemper shall then be applied in minimum two coats with proper distemper brushes in horizontal strokes immediately followed by vertical ones which together shall constitute one coat. The subsequent coats over the preceding one shall be applied only when the previous coat has dried.

3.13.3.12. Oil-Bound Distemper. In ease of decorative surfaces already dry distempered and required for application of oil bound distemper, the dry distemper shall be removed completely by washing to the last trace and allowed to dry and sand paper smoothed.

The primer as used on undecorated surface shall be alkali-resistant applied before distempering the walls.

The distemper shall be diluted with water or any other thinner recommended by the manufacturers. Only sufficient quantity of distemper required for the day's work shall be prepared. For undecorated surfaces, after the primer coat has dried for at least 48 hours the surface shall be lightly sand papered to make it smooth for receiving the distemper. Minimum two coats of distemper shall be applied with brushes in horizontal strokes followed by vertical strokes. These two sets of strokes (Horizontal and vertical) form one coat.

15 cm double bristled distemper brushes shall be used.

3.13.3.13. Water Proof Cement Paint. Portland cement paints are made readily by adding paint powder to water and stirring to obtain a thick paint which should then be diluted to a workable consistency. Equal volumes of paint powder and water make a satisfactory paint. The paint shall be made in such quantities as can be used up within an hour of mixing.

No painting shall be done if painted surface is likely to be exposed to temperatures below 7°C within 48 hours after application.

For undecorated surfaces, the surface shall be treated with minimum two coats of water proof cement paint.

Not less than 24 hours shall be allowed between two coats and no subsequent coat shall be applied unless the previous coat has become sufficiently hard to receive the next coat.

Cement paint shall be applied with a brush with relatively short stiff hog or fibre bristles.

Water proof cement paint shall not be applied on surfaces already treated with white wash.

Painted surface shall be sprinkled with water two or three times a day.

3.13.3.14. Wall painting with plastic emulsion paint. The mix shall be prepared as recommended by the manufacturers. The thinning is to be done with water and not with turpentine.

The paint shall be laid evenly and smoothly by means of crossing and laying off.

The crossing and laying off consists of covering the area with paint, brushing the surface hard for the first time over and brushing alternately in opposite directions two or three times and then finally brushing lightly in a direction at right angles to the same. In this process, no brush marks shall be left after the laying off is finished.

The paint dries by evaporation of the water content and as soon as water has evaporated the film gets hard and the next coat can be applied.

For undecorated surfaces, the surface shall be treated with minimum two coats of water proof cement paint.

In preparing walls for plastic emulsion painting no oil base putties shall be used in filling cracks holes etc. Washing of surfaces treated with emulsion paint shall not be done within two to three weeks of application.

No priming coat is required for masonry or plastered surfaces.

3.14. PAINTING AND POLISHING

3.14.1. Indian Standards to be Followed

The following Standards shall be followed :

IS : 75–1967. Linseed oil.

IS : 102–1962. Ready mixed paint.

IS : 2074–1962. Ready mixed paint oxide zinc chrome, painting.

IS : 133–1965. Enamel interior.

IS : 2933–1964. Enamel interior.

IS : 2932–1964. Exterior type under coating.

IS : 113–1950. Ready mixed paint, brushing under coating.

IS : 114–1950. Ready mixed paint, spraying under coating.

IS : 129–1962, Ready made paint brushing, finishing.

IS : 112–1950. Ready mixed paint, spraying under coating etc.

IS : 117–1964. Ready mixed paint, brushing, finishing, semi-gloss.
IS : 118–1962. Yellow and orange brushing, finishing, etc.
IS : 119–1962. Ready mixed paint brushing, finishing, semi-gloss for general purposes.
IS : 120–1962. Brushing, finishing semi-gloss for general purposes.
IS : 121–1962. Brown brushing.
IS : 122–1962. Brown brushing, finishing etc.
IS : 123–1962. Brushing, finishing, semi-gloss for general purposes.
IS : 124–1962. Ready mixed paint, brushing, finishing.
IS : 125–1962. Ready mixed paint, brushing, finishing.
IS : 126–1962. Brushing, finishing, exterior semi-gloss.
IS : 127–1962. Ready mixed paint, brushing, finishing.
IS : 128–1962. Ready mixed paint, brushing, finishing.
IS : 137–1965. Brushing matt or egg shell flat.
IS : 2339–1963. Aluminium paint.
IS : 158–1968. Brushing bituminous paint.
IS : 159–1950. Ready mixed paint, brushing, acid resisting.
IS : 160–1960. Ready mixed paint, spraying acid resisting.
IS : 290–1961. Coal tar black paint.
IS : 341–1952. Black Japan paint.
IS : 158–1968. Brushing bituminous paint.
IS : 2339–1963. Aluminium paint.
IS : 106–1962. Ready mixed paint, brushing white lead.
IS : 345–1962. Ready mixed paint.
IS : 3536–1966. Ready mixed paint, wood primer pink.
IS : 3585–1966. Ready mixed paint, aluminium brushing priming.
IS : 218–1961. Creosote and anthracene oil.
IS : 133–1965. Enamel interior under coating.
IS : 2982–1964. Enamel synthetic.
IS : 2933–1964. Exterior Type 2 undercoating.
IS : 3537–1966. Ready mixed paint, finishing interior.
IS : 3539–1966. Ready mixed paint, under oil finishes.
IS : 113–1950. Ready mixed paint, spraying under coating.
IS : 114–1950. Ready mixed paint, spraying under coating.
IS : 129–1962. Ready mixed paint, oil gloss.
IS : 3631–1966. Ready mixed paint, finishing exterior.
IS : 3539–1966. Ready mixed paint, under oil finishes.
IS : 111–1950. Ready mixed paint, brushing under coating.
IS : 117–1964. Ready mixed paint, semi-gloss.
IS : 112–1950. Ready mixed paint, spraying under coating.
IS : 119–1962. Ready mixed paint, brushing finishing semi-gloss.
IS : 124–1962. Ready mixed paint, brushing finishing semi-gloss.
IS : 125–1962. Ready mixed paint, IS colour No. 106 (Royal blue).

IS : 127–1962. Ready mixed paint, semi-gloss for general purpose.

IS : 128–1962. Ready mixed paint, semi-gloss for general purposes.

IS : 1188–1957. Ready mixed paint, brushing oil gloss genuine zinc oxide.

IS : 133–1965. Enamel interior under painting.

IS : 137–1965. Brushing matt or egg shell flat.

IS : 2338 (Part II)-1967. Finishing of wood and wood base material.

IS : 337–1952. Varnish finish, interior.

IS : 338–1952. Varnish under coating.

IS : 339–1952. Varnish under coating.

IS : 524–1968. Varnish finishing exterior and general purposes.

IS : 525–1968. Varnish finishing exterior and general purposes.

IS : 348–1968. French polish.

IS : 75–1967. Linseed oil raw and refined.

IS : 1504–1968. Commercial Bee's wax.

IS : 290–1961. Coal tar black paint.

IS : 341–1952. Black Japan paint.

IS : 212–1961. Crude oil tar.

IS : 218–1961. Creosote and anthracene.

IS : 109–1968. Ready mixed paint. IS colour No. 361 (light stone).

IS : 156–1850. Floor paint brushing.

IS : 3678–1966. Thick white for lettering.

IS : 347–1952. Shellac varnish.

IS : 164–1951. Road marking paint.

IS : 83–1950. Turpentine for paints.

3.14.2. Workmanship

3.14.3. General

The material required for painting work shall be obtained direct from approved manufacturers.

All materials not in use shall be kept properly protected.

In case thinning is required for any brand of material, only the brand of thinner recommended by the manufacturers shall be used.

The surface to be painted shall be thoroughly cleaned and dusted. The brushing operations shall be adjusted to the spreading capacity advised by the manufacturers.

Every time after the paint has been worked out of the brush bristles, the bristles of the brush shall be opened up by striking the brush against a portion of the unpainted surface with the end of the bristles help at right angles to the surface.

Where so specified the painting shall be done with spray. Spraying shall be done only when dry condition prevails.

Spots that are not accessible to the spray pattern shall be touched up by brush after spraying.

At the end of the operation, the spray gun shall be cleaned thoroughly so as to be free from dirt.

Each coat shall be allowed to dry completely before next is applied.

Each coat except the last one shall be lightly rubbed down with sand paper or pumice stone and cleaned off dust before next coat is applied.

In painting doors and windows, the putty round the glass panes shall also be painted. Brushes used for painting shall conform to the following standards: (See Table 3.23).

Table 3.23. Painting Brushes

IS : No.	*Subject*
384–1961	Specifications for brushes, paints and varnishes.
IS : 486–1954	Specifications for brushes; sash tools for paints and varnishes.
IS : 487–1954	Specifications for brushes, paints and varnishes (I) oval, ferrule bound and (II) round, copper wire bound.

3.14.3.1. Steel and other metal surfaces. Reference shall be made to the following Indian Standards : (See Table 3.24).

Table 3.24. Steel and Other Metal Surface Relevant Standards

IS : No.	*Subject*
2524 (Part I)–1968	Painting of non-ferrous metals in buildings.
2524 (Part II)-1968	Painting of non-ferrous metals in buildings.
1477 (Part I)–1971	Painting of ferrous metals in building.
1477 (Part II)–1963	Painting of ferrous metals in building. Painting and allied finishes.

The surface before cleaning shall be freed of all dust and dirt. Where old paint is not deteriorated the surface shall be rubbed down with sand paper and finally wiped with mineral turpentine to remove grease and perspiration of hand marks.

Where complete removal of old paint is required one of the following methods shall be adopted :

(*i*) **Hand scrapping.** The surface shall be scrapped thoroughly with, hand scrapper followed by wire brushing.

(*ii*) **Flame cleaning.** Flame cleaning is restricted to heavy steel, as it may lead to buckling of light gauge materials.

Before treating with flame oil, grease and other materials shall be removed. Primer coat shall be applied immediately after flame cleaning treatment.

(*iii*) **Paint remover.** Paint remover shall be used as per manufacturer's instructions.

3.14.3.2. Wood and wood based materials. The following Indian Standards shall be followed. (See Table 3.25).

Table 3.25. Wood and Wood Based Materials Relevant Standards

IS. No.	*Subject*
2338–1967 (Part I)	Finishing of wood and wood based materials. Part I operations.
2338–1967 (Part II)	Wood and wood based materials. Part II Schedule.
426–1961	Specifications for paste filler.
110–1968	Ready mixed paint for enamels.

The surface of wood to be painted may be new or old. In the case of new wood the surface shall be dried and freed from dirt or dust.

Any knots, resinous streaks or bluish sapwood shall be treated with two coats of pure shellac knotting applied thinly and extended about 25 mm beyond the actual area requiring treatment.

New wood based materials may further be divided into the following :

(A) **New wood based material.**

(*i*) **Plywood and blockboard.** As for new surface.

(*ii*) **Hard board.** The surface shall be dusted off and treated with a coat of plastic emulsion paint thinned with water.

(*iii*) **Particle board.** The surface shall be filled with a thin brush able thinner.

(*iv*) **Insulation boards.** Two thin coats of water based paints shall be applied by spraying.

(B) **Preparation of previously painted material.**

Firm old paint shall be cleaned down by washing with alkaline soap solution.

(C) **Removal of old paint.**

The old paint film shall be removed by one of the following methods :

(*i*) By using paint remover.

(*ii*) By using blow lamp.

(*iii*) By using caustic soda solution.

Before the application of priming coat, dirt or any other extraneous material is removed from the surface to be painted. In case the surface already finished with primer coat is not satisfactory, the surface shall be run down to bare wood and reprimed.

Painting of the surface may be done either by brushing or by spraying. The brushing operations are to be adjusted to the spreading capacity advised by the manufacturers.

In case of spray painting, spray machine used may be (*a*) high pressure with small air aperture type or (*b*) a low pressure with large air gap type, depending upon the nature and location of the work to be carried out.

Spraying shall be done only when dry conditions prevail.

3.14.3.3. Applying wood preservative. Wood preservative specified shall be applied in two coats. The first coat shall be allowed to dry for 24 hours before the second coat is applied.

3.14.3.4. Varnishing. Surface to be varnished shall be prepared to produce a smooth dry matt surface. Previous coats of paint or stain, if any, shall be allowed to dry and rubbed down lightly, wiped off and allowed to dry.

Varnish shall be applied liberally with a brush over the surface. Once varnish has begun to set, it shall not be retouched.

In case of two coats of varnish work, the first one shall be hard drying undercoating of flatting varnish. This shall be allowed to dry hard and then be flatted down before the finishing coat.

3.14.3.5. Spirit of oil stains. Surface intended for staining shall be prepared scrupulously clean and free from greasy finger marks.

Small cracks or nail holes shall be stopped in case of spirit stains.

Stains shall be applied by brushing and wiping. The stains shall be thinned in such a way that they can be applied without over staining. Spirit stains in particular require careful and quick application.

3.14.3.6. French polish. All unevenness shall be rubbed down to smoothness with sand paper and the surface shall be well dusted.

A pad of woolen cloth covered by a fine cloth shall be used to apply the polish. The pad shall be moistened with polish and rubbed hard on the surface.

To finish off, the pad shall be covered with a fresh piece of clean fine cloth, slightly damped with methylated spirit and rubbed lightly and quickly with circular motion.

3.14.3.7. Linseed oil. The oil shall be applied freely with brushes and spread evenly and smooth till no further oil is absorbed.

3.14.3.8. Bees waxing. Pure bees wax free from parafin or stearine adulterants shall be used.

The polish shall be applied evenly with a clean soft pad of cotton cloth in such a way that the surface is completely and fully covered. Subsequent coat shall be applied after the surface has dried. This surface shall then rubbed with soft flannel until the surface has assumed a uniform gloss.

3.14.3.9. Coal tarring. 200 gms of unslaked lime shall be added to every litre of coal tar and heated till it begins to boil. It shall then be taken off the fire and kerosine oil added slowly at the rate of 1 part kerosine oil to 6 or more parts by volume. Lime is added to prevent the tar from running.

3.14.3.10. Concrete/Masonry/Asbestos cement/Plastered surfaces. Reference shall be made to the following Indian Standards. (See Table 3.26).

Table 3.26. Painting Concrete/Masonry/Plastered Surfaces

IS : Code No.	*Subject*
2338–19	
2395 (Part I)–1966	Code of practice for painting concrete/masonry/plastered surfaces.
2395 (Part I)–1967	Code of practice for painting concrete/masonry/plastered surfaces.
3140–1965	Code of practice for painting concrete/masonry/plastered surfaces.

The surface to be painted shall be allowed to dry for at least three months.

Before painting' the surface shall be thoroughly brushed to remove all dirt.

In case of previously treated surfaces the old paint shall be removed by rubbing with pumice stone and then by washing with soap arid water.

If the old paint is badly blistered and flaked, it shall be completely scraped off and the surface coated with a suitable scaler.

3.14.3.11. Floor painting. In the case of new surface the floor shall be cleaned off all dirt and dust. The floor shall be rinsed thoroughly with water and dried. Painting with floor paints shall not be done over concrete surfaces less than two years old.

In case of previously painted surfaces the flooring shall not be brought into use for a week after final coat.

3.14.3.12. Wax polish. This shall be done as for Bees wax.

3.14.3.13. Lettering with paint. The letters and figures shall be as specified. These shall be stenciled and drawn in pencil and got approved before painting. They shall be of uniform size and finished neatly. The edges shall be straight or in pleasant smooth curves.

Iron and Steel Work. The priming coat shall have dried up completely before painting is started All dust and dirt shall be carefully and thoroughly wiped away.

The ready mixed paints of approved brand and manufacture and of the required shades shall be used. They shall conform in all respects to the relevant IS Specifications.

Distemper, Oil Bound. Oil emulsion distemper (See IS : 428–1969 latest edition) of approved brand and manufacture shall be used. The primer when used as on new work shall be cement primer or distemper primer as specified. These shall be of the same manufacture as distemper. The distemper shall be diluted with water or any other prescribed thinner in a manner recommended by the manufacture. Only sufficient quantity of distemper required for the days work shall be prepared.

For new work the surface shall be thoroughly cleaned of dust, old white or colour wash by washing and scrubbing. The surface shall then be allowed to dry for at least 48 hours. It shall then be sand papered to give a smooth and even surface.

In case of old work, all loose pieces and scales shall be removed by sand papering.

Printing Coat. The priming coat shall be with distemper primer or cement primer as specified.

Oil bound distemper is not recommended to be applied, with in six months of the completion of wall plaster.

Distemper Coat. For new work, after the primer coat has dried for at least 48 hours, the surface shall be lightly sand papered to make it smooth for receiving the distemper, taking care not to rule out the priming coat.

Subsequent coats shall be applied in the same way. Two or more coats of distemper as are found necessary shall be applied over the primer coats to obtain an even shade.

Painting, Cement Paint, Material. The cement paint shall be (conforming to IS : 5410–1969) of approved brand and manufacture and shade as given by the Architect.

Preparation of Surface. The surface shall be thoroughly cleaned of all mortar dropping, dirt, dust, algae, grease and other foreign matter by brushing and washing. The surface shall be thoroughly wetted with clean water before the cement paint is applied.

Preparation mix. Cement paint shall be mixed in such quantities as can be used up within an hour of its mixing as otherwise the mixture will met and thicken, affecting flow and finish. Cement paint shall be mixed with water in two stages. The first stage shall comprise of 2 parts of cement paint and one part of water stirred thoroughly and allowed to stand for 5 minutes. Care shall be taken to add the cement paint gradually to the water and not vice versa. The second stage shall comprise of adding further one part of water to the mix and stirring thoroughly to obtain a liquid of workable and uniform consistency. In all cases the manufacturer's instruction shall be followed meticulously.

The lids of cement paint drums shall be kept tightly closed when not in use, as by exposure to atmosphere the cement paint rapidly becomes air set due to its hygroscopic qualities.

Application. The solution shall be applied on the clean and wetted surface with brushes or spraying machine. The solution shall be kept well stirred during the period of application. It shall be applied on the surface which is on the shady side of the building so that the direct heat of the sun on the surface is avoided. The method of application of cement paint shall be as per manufacturer's specification. The completed surface shall be watered after the day's work.

3.15. DRAINAGE, SANITATION AND WATER SUPPLY

General. The work shall be carried out, complying in all respects with the requirements of relevant bye-laws of the local body in whose jurisdiction the work is situated.

For items pertaining to the building work, the specifications detailed under relevant sub-heads for building work shall be followed.

Any damage caused to the building, or to electric, sanitary, water supply or other installations etc. therein, either due to negligence on the part of the contractor, or due to actual requirements of the work, shall be made good and the building or the installation shall be restored to its original condition by the contractor. Nothing extra shall be paid for it, except where otherwise specified.

For making good the damage to the under mentioned items of work, the specifications as given in the following paras shall be used unless directed otherwise.

(*a*) **Masonry work.** Masonry work shall be made good by using the same class of bricks, tiles or stones as was damaged during the execution of the work. The mortar used shall be cement mortar 1 : 5 (1 cement : 5 fine sand) or as directed by the Engineer-in-Charge.

(*b*) *Concrete work for sub-grade of the flooring, foundations and other plain concrete works*. Cement concrete 1 : 5 : 10 (1 cement : 5 coarse sand : 10 graded stone) aggregate 40 mm nominal size) shall be used, after applying a coat of neat cement slurry at the junction with old work.

(*c*) *Cement concrete in floors and in R.C.C. work*. Cement concrete 1 : 2 : 4 (1 cement : 2 coarse sand : 4 graded stone aggregate 20 mm nominal size) shall be used after applying a coat of neat cement slurry at the junction with old work, and the surface finished to match with the surrounding surface.

(*d*) *Plastering*. Cement plaster 1 : 4 mix (1 cement : 4 sand) shall be used. Sand shall be fine or coarse as used in the original work. The surface shall be finished with two or more coats of white wash, colour wash distemper or painting as required but where the surface is not to be white washed, colour washed distempered or painted, it shall be finished smooth with a floating coat of neat cement as required, to match with the surrounding surface.

(*e*) *Other items*. Damage to any other item shall be made good as directed by the Engineer-in-Charge. All sanitary appliances including sanitary fittings, fixtures, toilet requisites, shall be of size, make and design as specified in the item of work as per sample approved by the Engineer-in-Charge.

All exposed G.I., C.I. or lead pipes and fittings shall be painted with approved quality of paint and shade as specified. The painting work shall conform to specifications described under S.H. "Painting".

All sanitary and plumbing work shall be carried out through licensed plumbers. On completion of the work, the site shall be cleaned and all rubbish disposed off as directed by the Engineer-in-Charge.

Installation

General. All pipelines, locations of fittings and fixtures etc. shall be as specified or as directed-by the Engineer. Correctness of lines, plumb, orientation, symmetry and levels shall be strictly ensured. All items shall be fully secured against movement in any direction and so located as to allow easy maintenance where desired by the Engineer, suitable workers to be provided for underground and concealed pipelines and other items.

All pipelines and fittings fixtures shall be installed leakproof. When the workers under scope of this specification connect with others, the connections shall be such as to prevent any splashing of spilling or emission of foul odour and gases.

Water Storage Tanks. The tanks shall be made form best quality M.S. sheet of gauges as specified. In case of tank of capacity (net) of 540 or 1080 litres the gauges (thickness) shall be 2.80 m. The sheets shall be welded to form the tank as per standard practice of welding as laid down by I.S. code (latest). Each tank shall be provided with 40 mm dia G.I. scour pipe which shall terminate into a socket and a plug, 25 mm CI. over flow pipe with fittings and brass mosquito proof coupling conforming to the municipal design and approved by the Engineer-in-Charge with sieve No. 725 dia perforations and ball valve with copper or plastic float of specified size and pressure. Every ball to be so adjusted that the top level of water in the tank its 25 mm below the tip of the overflow pipe.

Each tank shall be provided with 40 cm dia standard mosquito proof C.I. hinged cover with locking arrangement.

A priming coat of red lead to be applied both internal and external surfaces. The inside surface to be painted with two coats of bitumastic paint and external surface to be painted with two coats of paint of approved make and shade. The tank shall be erected as directed by the Engineer-in-Charge.

Soil and Drainage Pipe

Gradients. The gradients of the pipes shall be as specified in the drawing for drainage or as specified by the Engineer-in-Charge.

Relation with water supply pipelines. Under no circumstances unless specifically cleared by the Engineer-in-Charge special drainage and soil pipes shall be allowed to come to close to water supply pipelines.

Laying. Each separate pipe shall be individually set for line, level, plumb, etc. Where lengths of sewer of drain pipes are laid in trench, properly painted sight-rails shall be fixed across the trench at the height, equal to length of the boning rod to be used, above the required invert level of the drain or sewer at the point where the sight is fixed. More sight rails shall be required at manholes, change of gradient and intermediate positions if the distance for sighting is too far, which shall not be more than 15 m apart. The excavation shall be boned in atleast once in every 2 m. The foot of the boning rod shall be set on block of wood of the exact thickness of the wall of the pipe. Each pipe shall be separately and accurately boned between sight rails.

For water pipelines, meticulous care shall be taken to avoid chances of airlock and water hammer. The layout of pipe work shall be such that there is no possibility of backflow towards the source of supply form any cistern appliances whether by siphonage or otherwise. Where desired by the Engineer, pipes shall be concealed in masonry or concrete of the structure. Chases, openings, conduits as necessary shall be cut or left in the masonry on concrete. Clamps and fittings shall be as per the standard practice and approved by the Engineer.

Support and Protection to Pipelines. All drainage and sewer pipes shall be laid with sockets leading uphill. Preferably the pipes shall rest on solid and even foundations for the full length of the barrel. However, the pipe manufacturer's instruction as approved by the Engineer shall be followed in the matter of support and jointing.

Entry into Structures. For entry of the pipelines into any building or structure suitable conduits under the structure or sleeves shall be used. The conduits and sleeves shall be such as to allow easy repairs and replacement of the pipes. When openings or chases are required to be made in the structure for entry of pipelines, locations and sizes shall be marked and checked by the Engineer. After laying of the pipeline the openings and chases shall be mended.

Traps and Ventilating Pipes. Pipes for carrying off the waste from water closets and waste water and overflow water from baths, wash basins, sinks to drains shall be trapped immediately beneath such fixtures. Traps shall have minimum water seal of 50 mm and shall be ventilated whenever such ventilation is necessary to maintain water seal of the trap. Ventilating pipes shall be carried up vertically form the drain to a height of at least 600 mm above the outer covering of the roof of the building or as shown on drawings. All vertical ventilating, anti-syphonage and similar pipe shall be covered on top with a cowl. The cowl shall be made of C.I. unless desired otherwise by the Engineer.

Manhole and Inspection Chambers. The maximum distance between manholes shall be 15 metre unless otherwise mentioned. In addition, at every change of alignment gradient or diameter there shall be manhole or inspection chamber. The distance between manhole or inspection chamber and gully chamber shall not exceed 6 metre unless desired otherwise. Manhole shall be constructed so as to be watertight under test. The benching at the sides shall be carried out in such a manner as to provide no lodgement for any splashings in case of accidental flashing of the chamber. The channel or drain at the bottom of chamber shall be plastered with 1:2 cement, sand mortar and finished smooth to the grade. The channels and drains shall be shaped and laid to provide smooth flow.

Connection to existing sewer lines shall be through a manhole. Manholes shall be provided with standard covers, usually C.I. or as desired by the Engineer. The covers shall be close fitting so as to prevent gases from coming out.

Jointing. Jointing of laid pipes shall be so planned as to avoid completely any movement or strain to the joints already made. If any joint is suspected to be damaged it shall be opened out and redone. All joints between pipes, pipes and fittings and manholes shall be gastight when above ground and watertight when underground. Method of jointing shall be as per instruction of the pipe and fittings manufacturer and as approved by the Engineer. However, in the absence of any instructions available from the manufacturer the methods as detailed hereunder shall be used.

(*a*) **Cast Iron Pipes.** Socket and spigot pipes be joined by cast lead shall joints. The spigot shall be centred in the socket of the next pipe by tightly caulking in sufficient turns of tarred gasket or hemp yarn to have unfilled half depth of socket. When the gasket or hamp yarn has been caulked tightly a jointing ring shall be placed round the barrel and tightened against the face of the socket to prevent airlock. Molten lead shall then be poured into fill the remainder of the socket and caulked with suitable tools right round the joint to make up for shrinkage of the molten metal on cooling and shall be finished 3 mm behind the socket face.

In special cases if flanged joints are accepted by the Engineer the joints shall be made leakproof by inserting approved type of rubber or other gaskets not less than 1.5 mm thick. The bolts shall be secured in stages to avoid uneven strain. Damaged gaskets shall be replaced.

(*b*) **Glazed Stoneware Pipes.** Tarred gasket or hemp yarn soaked in thick cement slurry shall first be placed round the spigot of each pipe and the spigot shall then be placed into the socket of the pipe previously laid. The pipe then shall be adjusted and fixed in the correct position and the gasket caulked tightly so as not to fill more than ¼ of the total depth of the socket. The remainder of the socket shall be filled with a stiff mixture of cement mortar of 1 : 1 proportion. When the socket is filled, a fillet shall be formed round the joint with a trowel, forming an angle of 45° with the barrel of the pipe. The newly made joints shall be protected, until set, from use and rain and shall be covered with damp sacking or other suitable materials.

(*c*) **GI Pipes.** Threads shall be cut with sharp tools, and before jointing all scales shall be removed from pipes by suitable means. The screwer threads of the pipe shall be cleaned out and the joints mode by screwing the fittings after treating the thread with approved pipe jointing compound. Once a joint has been screwed up it shall not be backed off unless the threads are recleaned and new compound applied.

(*d*) **Jointing Cast Iron Pipes with Stoneware Pipes.** Where any cast iron soil pipe, ventilating pipe or trap is connected with a stoneware or semi-vertified waste pipe or drain communicating with a sewer, the beaded spigot and of such cast iron soil pipe, waste or ventilating or trap shall be inserted into a socket of such stoneware pipe or drain and the joint made with mortar consisting of one part of cement and one part of clean, sharp, and after placing a tarred gasket or hemp yarn soaked in neat cement slurry found the joint and inserted in it by means of a caulking tool.

(*e*) **Jointing Stoneware with Cast Iron Pipes.** Where any water closet pan or earthenware trap connected to such a pan is to be jointed with a cast iron soil pipe, the joint between the stoneware spigot and the cast iron socket shall always be of a flexible nature, such joint shall be made with a mixture of bitumen and chopped asbestos fire.

Trenches and other Excavation. Width of the trench at the bottom shall be such as to provide 200 mm clearance on either side of the pipe for facility of laying and jointing.

Excavated material shall be stacked sufficiently away from the edge of the trench and the side of the soil bank shall not be allowed to become such as to endanger the stability of the excavation. Soil may be carted away and used for filling the trench behind the work. All excavations shall be properly timbered, where necessary. Efficient arrangements for dewatering during excavation and keeping it dry till backfilling done shall be made to the satisfaction of the Engineer. Sumps for the dewatering shall be located clear of the pipe layout.

Special care shall be taken not to damage underground services, cables etc. These when exposed shall be kept adequately supported till the trench is backfilled.

The backfilling shall be done only after the pipeline has been tested and approved by the Engineer. Special care shall be taken to pack under and side of the pipes hand-packed thoroughly with selected material. At least 300 mm over the pipe shall also be filled with soft earth or sand. Consolidation shall be done in 150 mm layers. The surface water shall be prevented from getting into the filled up trench. Traffic shall not be inconvenienced by heaping up unduly the backfilling material to compensate future settlement. All future settlements shall be made good regularly to minimise inconvenience of traffic where applicable.

Toilet fixtures and accessories. All sanitary fittings such as water closet (pedestal or squatting) type urinal, partition for urinals, cisterns, brackets, lavatory basins, sinks, toilet paper holders, mirror, glass-plates, bib cocks, etc. shall be of approved quality and types manufactured by well known manufacturer's such as Hindustan Sanitary Ware, etc. as per the latest I.S. Standard. The fixing of the items shall be as per standard, practice followed by Central Public Works Department following its latest specifications.

Measurement. Assembly of sanitary fittings or single sanitary fitting together with the fixing shall be enumerated. The method shall be as adopted in the Central Public Works Department following the latest Schedule and Specifications.

Rate. The rate shall include the cost of all materials and labour involved in all operations for any relevant item of work.

3.16. INTERNAL ELECTRIFICATION SPECIFICATIONS

General. The material workmanship and the installation as a whole will be generally governed by relevant I.S. Specification and will be covered under Indian Electricity Rules as amended. The specifications given hereinafter and in modifications to the above referred specification are to be strictly followed.

Items of work of the contract are deemed to cover internally all allied minor items of physical and electrical works so as to make the installation in each building or part thereof completed as for switching on electric supply and taking into use the installation.

Particular attention is drawn to the neatness in appearance which is to be achieved by judicious planning of the runs of the cables, the location of the light fittings, fans, switches, socket outlets, main the switches and to the reinstalment of any surfaces frame work, painting etc. damaged in the process of execution of electrical installations.

Due regard shall be given to the door and window openings, the layout of furniture, locations of water taps, sink etc. in fixing the runs of cables and positions of fittings and control switches and outlet points. The installation shall strictly comply with the provisions contained in the latest edition of the Indian Electricity Rules and latest Editions of Indian Standard Specification as applicable to these works, except where such regulations and rules are modified by the Technical Specifications.

All electrical works shall be executed by properly skilled licensed supervisors and workmen of the contractor.

"Looping" in system of wiring shall generally be used throughout installation. Connectors may, however, be used where looping is not practicable, if approved by the Engineer-in-Charge.

Diagonal runs shall not be permitted. All branches shall be taken off at right angles. Cables shall be kept clear off hot water or stream pipes etc.

All wiring of this work shall be carried out in steel surface conduits.

Scope of work. Supply and fixing of internal electrical installation commencing from and including Main and Sub-main Board located in the main building to all light-fittings, fans and other outlet points.

Supply and fixing main earthing to the building.

Supply and fixing fans and light fixtures complete with regulators including sign lighting.

Details of supplies to be made by the contractor should be as per Bill of Materials attached. Any other item of supplies for successful completion of the work shall be provided by the contractor without any extra cost.

Materials and Samples. All items shall conform to relevant IS. Specifications.

Conduits. Steel conduits tubing used for wiring shall conform to IS : 732. The diameter of the conduits will depend on the number of conductors to be drawn to each conduit. All conduit pipes shall be of approved gauge and the work shall be carried out as per specification of Central Public Works Department.

Cables. All cables used on the work shall be of reputed make and should have proper approval of the Engineer-in-Charge. The cables shall be rated at 250 volts for single phase wiring and 660 volts for three phase wiring and shall conform to IS : 434.

Switches. All switches used shall be reputed make and must have the prior approval of the Engineer-in-Charge. These piano key switches shall conform to the latest I.S. Specifications.

Socket outlets. All socket outlets both for 5 amp as well as 15 amp should be of three pins with combine piano key switches. This should be of reputed make conforming to relevant I.S. Specifications and have the prior approval of the Engineer-in-Charge.

Ceiling roses. All ceiling roses shall be of bakelite and conform to relevant I.S. Specifications.

Porcelain connectors. These shall be provided inside the teakwood round block/terminal conduit boxes. The wiring shall be done in such a way that wire from the connector to the fan/fluorescent tube are not visible.

Main Board of incoming and outgoing switches will be double metal clad type of reputed makes like Standard, L.T.-Siemens etc. These switches will be suitable for heavy conduit operations and should conform to the relevant I.S. Specifications.

Distributors boards. The main distribution boards and sub-distribution boards both for power and light shall be fabricated as per the drawings. The overall dimensions of the distribution boards/sub-distribution boards shall be approved by the Engineer-in-Charge after the makes of the switches are finalised. The location of these boards shall be as indicated on the drawing.

Testing. All the electrical installation shall be tested on completion of work for the following :

Insulation resistance test. The insulation resistance of entire, installation shall not be less than one mega ohm. It shall be not less than 50 divided by the number of points on each circuit.

Earth continuity test. This shall not exceed one ohm from any point of the installation.

Earth resistance test. This shall not exceed 5 ohms.

Polarity test single pole switches. The face conductor shall be connected to the incoming terminal with a single pole switch in 'OFF' position there shall be no live conductor at the outlet point controlled by the switch.

Working test. This shall be a test with supply switched on all appliances fixed and connected for checking the actual working of the installation.

4

Methods of Measurements

4.1. INTRODUCTION

Measurement is an important step in the estimating and payment of any civil engineering work. Methods of measurements are not uniform in all the construction agencies and Public Works Departments. Hence many variations can be seen in these methods.

All works shall be measured in decimal system.

(*a*) Linear dimensions shall be measured to the nearest to 1 cm.

(*b*) Areas shall be worked out to two places of decimal.

(*c*) Cubical contents shall be worked out to the nearest 0.01 m^3.

Methods of measurements in respect of the various categories of works are given in the following articles.

4.2. CARRIAGE OF MATERIALS

Earth, lime, stone, metal, steam coal, sand and such similar materials shall be stacked properly.

Length, breadth and height of stacks shall be measured correct to 1 cm. The quantity shall be worked out in cubic metres correct to two places of decimal. The volume of stacks shall be reduced by percentages as shown against each for looseness in stacking to arrive at a net quantity for payment.

Earth

1. In loose stacks such as cart load, lorry loads etc.	20%
2. In consolidated fills	10%
3. In fills consolidated by heavy machinery but not under O.M.C.	5%
4. In fills consolidated by heavy mechanical machinery at O.M.C.	Nil
5. Consolidated fills in confined situation such as under floor etc.	Nil
6. Manure	8%
7. Sand, moorum, building rubbish and lime	Nil
8. Excavated rocks	50%
9. Soting Stone Boulder 100 mm and above	15%
10. Stone metal 40 mm gauge and above	7.5%
11. Coarse aggregate/Stone metal below 40 mm gauge	Nil

No reduction shall be made in respect of articles or materials for which mode of payment is by length or weight or number.

4.3. EARTH-WORK

(*a*) **Surface Excavation.** The length, breadth and depth shall be measured correct to the nearest cm in case the measurements are taken with tape. If measurements are taken with staff and level, the level shall be recorded correct to 5 mm, the cubical contents shall be worked out to the nearest two places of decimal in cubic metres.

Where excavation is in trenches or from borrow pits, the measurements of cutting the trenches or borrow pits shall be made in uniform grounds.

Where the ground is not uniform or where the site is required to be levelled, levels shall be taken before the start and after the completion of the work and the quantity of excavation in cutting computed from these levels.

Where ordinary rock and hard rock is mixed, the measurement of the excavation shall be made by the methods as described above. The two kinds of rock shall be stacked separately and measured in stacks. The net quantity of the two kinds of rocks shall be arrived at by applying deduction of 50% for looseness in stacks. If the sum of net quantity of two kinds of rocks exceeds the total quantity of the excavated material, then the quantity for each type of rock shall be worked out from the total quantity in the ratio of net quantities in measurements of the two types of rocks.

Where soil, ordinary rock and hard rock are mixed, the measurements for the entire excavation shall be made as explained above. Excavated material from 'hard rock', and 'ordinary rock' shall be stacked separately, measured and each reduced by 50% to allow for voids to arrive at the quantity payable under 'hard rock' and 'ordinary rock' the difference between the entire excavation and the sum of the quantity payable under 'hard rock' and 'ordinary rock' shall be paid for as excavation in soil.

Where it is not possible to take measurements from borrow pits or cutting, excavation shall be worked out from filling. The actual measurements or fill shall be calculated by taking levels of the original ground before start of the work after site clearance and after compaction of the fill at suitable intervals and the quantity of earth work so computed shall be reduced by 10% in case of consolidated fill.

(*b*) Excavation in foundation, trenches, or drains. Same as specified above.

(*c*) Filling in trenches, under floors etc.

1. **Filling Sides of Foundation.** The cubical contents of foundation concrete and masonry in foundation upto ground level shall be worked out and the same deducted from the cubical contents of earthwork in excavation for foundations to arrive at the quantity for filling sides of foundation.

2. **Filling in Plinth and under Floors.** Depth of consolidated earth filling shall be measured for the purpose of payments. The dimension of the filling shall be on the basis of pre-measurement correct to the nearest cm and cubical contents worked out in cubic metre correct to two places of decimal.

3. **Sand Filling in Plinth.** Volume of consolidated filling shall be measured. The dimensions shall be measured correct to the nearest cm and cubical contents worked out in cubic metre correct to two places of decimal.

(*d*) **Surface Dressing.** Surface dressing shall include removing vegetation, cutting and filling upto 15 cm and dressing the area. Area of the ground dressed shall be measured. Length and breadth shall be measured correct to the nearest centimetre and area worked out in square metres correct to two places of decimal.

(*e*) **Jungle Clearance.** Only the area over which the jungle cutting has been done shall be measured. The length and width shall be measured correct to the nearest cm and area worked out in square metres correct to two places of decimal. Cutting of trees less than 30 cm in girth shall be considered incidental to the clearing and grubbing operations.

(*f*) **Felling Trees.** Cutting of trees above 30 cm in girth (measured at a height of one metre above ground level) shall be paid for in terms of numbers, according to the sizes given below :

1. Beyond 30 cm girth, upto and including 60 cm girth.
2. Beyond 60 cm girth, upto and including 120 cm girth.
3. Beyond 120 cm girth, upto and including 240 cm girth.
4. Above 240 cm girth.

(*g*) **Anti termite Treatment.** The measurements shall be made in sq m on the basis of plinth area of the building at ground floor only.

1. **Treatment along outside of foundations.** The measurements shall be made in running metres taking length along the plinth of the building.

2. **Treatment of soil under floors.** The measurement shall be made in sq m inside clear dimensions of rooms, verandah etc. shall be taken.

3. **Treatment to voids in masonry.** The measurements shall be made in running metres along the plinth of the building.

4. **Treatment to wood work.** The measurements shall be made in running metres, for choakhats, joints, purlins, beams etc.

(*h*) **Planking and strutting.** The dimensions shall be measured correct to the nearest cm and the area of the face supported shall be worked out correct to two places of decimal (*i*) Depth not exceeding 1.5 m (*ii*) Depth exceeding 1.5 m in stages of 1.5 m.

4.4. CONCRETE WORK

(*a*) The aggregate shall be measured in stacks and paid for after making a deduction of 7.5% of the gross measurements of stacks in respect of aggregates of nominal size 40 mm and above.

(*b*) **Lime concrete.** Length and breadth shall be measured correct to a cm. The thickness of slab, partitions etc. and cross-sectional dimensions in case of posts, columns, beams and the like shall be measured correct to the nearest 5 mm. The consolidated cubic contents of lime concrete shall be calculated net to the nearest 0.01 cubic metre concrete laid in excess of the sections shown in the drawing, shall not be measured.

No deduction shall be made for

1. Ends of dissimilar materials (*e.g.* joists, beams, posts, girder, rafters, purlin, trusses, corbels, steps etc.) upto 500 sq m in section.

2. Opening upto 100 cm^2.

3. Volume occupied by pipes, conduits, sheathing etc. not exceeding 100 cm^2 each in cross-sectional area.

4. Small voids not exceeding 100 cm^2 in area each.

(*c*) Cement concrete (same as lime concrete) and for present work as under—

1. Wall panel, floor/roof slab	in square metres stating the thickness.
2. String or lacing courses copings, bed plates, anchor block, plain window sill, shelves, louvers, steps, stair cases etc.	in cubic metres.

3. Kerbs, edgings etc. in cubic metres.
4. Solid block work in cubic/sq metres.
5. Hollow block work in cubic/sq metres.
6. Light weight partitions in square metres stating the thickness.

(*d*) **Damp Proof Course.** The length and breadth shall be measured correct to a cm, and its area shall be calculated in square metres correct to two places of decimal. The depth shall not be less than the specified thickness at any section.

4.5. REINFORCED CEMENT CONCRETE WORK

(*a*) **Form work.** Measurement shall be taken of the area of shuttering in contact with the concrete surface. Dimensions of form work shall be measured correct to a cm. No deductions from the shuttering due to the openings/obstructions shall be made if area of such openings/obstructions does not exceed 0.1 sq metre. Nothing extra shall be paid for forming such openings.

(*b*) **Reinforcement.** Reinforcement including authorised spacer bars and lappages shall be measured in length of different diameters, as actually used in the work nearest to a centimetre and their weight calculated on the basis of standard tables. Wastages shall not be paid.

(*c*) **Concreting.** Dimensions shall be measured nearest to 1 cm except for the thickness of slab, which shall be measured to nearest 0.5 cm. The areas shall be worked out in nearest 0.01 sq metre. The cubical contents shall be worked out to nearest 0.01 cubic metre. No deductions shall be made for the following.

1. Ends of dissimilar materials (*e.g.* joists, beams, posts, girders, rafters, purlins, trusses, corbels, steps, etc.) upto 500 sq cm in cross-section.
2. Opening upto 0.1 sq m.
3. The volume occupied by reinforcement.
4. The volume occupied by water pipes, conduits etc. not exceeding 25 sq cm each in cross-sectional area.

4.6. BRICK-WORK

Dimensions shall be measured correct to a cm. Areas shall be worked out in sq m correct to two places of decimal. Cubic contents shall be worked out in cum correct to two places of decimal. No deduction shall be made for the following :

1. Ends of dissimilar materials (*i.e.* joists, beams, posts, girders, rafters, purlins, trusses, steps, etc.) each 500 sq m in section.
2. Opening each upto 0.1 sq m.
3. Wall plates and bed plates, bearings of slabs, chajjas and the like.
4. Drainage holes and recesses for cement concrete blocks to embed for doors, windows etc.
5. Holes etc. for iron fixtures, pipes upto 300 mm dia.
6. Forming chases in masonry each upto section of 350 sq m.
7. Corbels, string courses, projecting plasters, aprons, sills, cornices, over-sailing courses and other projections etc. of sprayed bullnosed or any other type of projection with made or cut bricks, shall be measured separately in running metres stating dimensions of each projections.
8. Walls of half brick thickness or less shall each be measured separately and shall be given in square metres stating the wall thickness.

9. Brick work in backing to stone or other type of facing shall be measured separately.

10. Masonry in chimney breasts, chimney stacks, smoke or air flues upto 0.25 sq m sectional area, shall be measured as solid and no extra payment shall be made for pargeting and coring such flues.

11. Apertures for fireplaces shall not be deducted.

12. Square or rectangular pillars shall be measured as walls.

13. Circular pillars shall be measured net as per actual dimensions.

14. Brickwork in cavity walls shall be included with general brickwork. The width of the cavity shall not be measured. The forming of the cavity shall be given in square metres, stating the width of the cavity and shall include the ties and their number per square metre.

15. **Brickwork in arches.** The length of the arch shall be measured as the mean of the extrados and intrados of the arch correct to a cm. The thickness of the arch shall be measured in multiples of half brick. The cubical contents shall be calculated in cubic metre, correct to two places of decimal.

16. **Half brick masonry.** The length and the height of the wall shall be measured correct to a cm. The area shall be calculated in sq m.

17. **Honeycomb brickwork.** The length and height shall be measured correct to a cm. Area shall be calculated in square metres correct to two places of decimal. Honeycomb openings shall not be deducted.

18. **Joining old brickwork with new brickwork.** The height and thickness shall be measured, nearest to a cm. The vertical face of the new work at the junction shall be measured nearest to 1 cm. The area shall be calculated in square metres, nearest to two places of decimal.

4.7. STONE WORK

The length, height and thickness shall be measured correct to a cm. The thickness of wall shall be measured at joints, excluding the bushings. The quantity shall be calculated in cubic metre nearest to two places of decimal.

No deduction shall be made for the following :

1. Ends of dissimilar materials upto 0.1 sq m in section.
2. Openings each upto 0.1 sq m in area.
3. Bearings of RCC slabs, chajja.
4. Drain holes, recesses, iron fixtures, pipes upto 300 mm dia forming chases each upto section of 350 sq m.

4.8. WOOD WORK

(*a*) **Door window frames.** Wood work wrought and framed shall be measured for finished dimensions. No allowance shall be made for wastage. Length of each piece shall be measured over all nearest to a cm, so as to include projections for tenons, scarves or mitres, width and shrickness shall be measured to the nearest mm. Cubical contents shall be worked out in units of 10 cubic decimetre in whole numbers. In case of mouldings, roundways, rebates, circular and varying sections, the sectional area of the piece shall be taken as the area of the least square or rectangle from which such a section can be cut.

(*b*) **Trusses.** Wood work shall be measured for finished dimensions, no allowances shall be made for dimensions, supplied beyond those specified. Length of each piece shall be measured overall, nearest to a cm, so as to include projections for tenons, scarves or mitres, width and thickness shall be measured to the nearest mm. Cubical contents can be worked out in units of 10 cubic decimetre in whole number.

(*c*) **Shutters.** Length and width of the shutters shall be measured to the nearest cm in closed position covering the rebates of the frame but excluding the gap between the shutter and the frame overlap of two shutters shall not be measured. All work shall be measured net as fixed. The area within the rebates of the frame shall be calculated in square metres nearest to two places of decimal. No extra payment shall be made for shape, joints, etc. except for circular or segmental portions which shall be measured separately.

4.9. STEEL WORK

(*a*) **Steel work in single sections.** The work as fixed in place shall be measured in running metres correct to a millimetre and their weights calculated on the basis of standard tables. Weight of cleats, brackets, packing pieces, bolts, nuts, washers, distance pieces, separators, diaphragm gussets (taking over all square dimensions) fish plates, etc. shall be added to the weight of respective items. In riveted work, allowance is to be made for weight of rivet heads. An addition of 2.5% of the weight of structure shall be made for shop and site rivet heads in riveted steel structures.

No deduction shall be made for rivet/or bolt holes the weight of steel sheet, plate and strip shall be taken from relevant Indian standards based on 7.85 kg/m^2 for every millimetre sheet thickness.

(*b*) **Steel work in built up sections.** The work as fixed in place shall be measured in running metres correct to a millimetre and their weights calculated on the basis of standard tables correct to the nearest kilogram. Weight of cleats, brackets, packing pieces, bolts, nuts, washers, distance pieces, separator, diaphragm gussets taking overall square dimensions, fish plates etc. shall be added to the weight of respective items. No deduction shall be made for skew cuts, in rivetted works, allowance is to be made for the weight or rivet heads, (2.5%) in case of welding, the weight of welding material shall not be added in the weight of members for payment.

(*c*) **Steel doors, windows, gates, etc.** The height and the width shall be measured correct to a cm and its area for payment shall be calculated in square metres correct to two places of decimal.

(*d*) **Fan clamps.** The M.S. clamps and rings shall be counted in numbers.

4.10. FLOORING

(*a*) **Cement concrete floor.** Length and breadth shall be measured correct to a cm and its area as laid shall be calculated in sq m correct to two places of decimal. No deduction shall be made for any opening of area upto 0.10 sq m.

(*b*) **Terrazo (marble chips) flooring.** Length and breadth shall be measured correct to a cm before laying skirting, dado or wall plaster. The area as laid shall be calculated in sq m, correct to two places of decimal. No deduction shall be made for any opening in floor area upto 0.1 sq m (10 dm^2) dividing strips of metals inserted in terrazo to form bays, patterns shall be measured in running metres.

4.11. ROOFING

(*a*) **Corrugated galvanised steel sheet roofing.** The length and breadth shall be measured correct to 1 cm. Area shall be worked out in sq m correct to two places of decimal. The superficial area of roof coverings shall be measured on the flat without allowance for laps and corrugations. No deduction in measurement shall be made for openings upto 0.4 sq m. For valley, ridges and hips, the measurement shall be taken for the finished work in length along the centre line of ridge or hips etc., correct to a cm. The laps shall not be measured.

(*b*) **Asbestos cement corrugated sheet roofing.** Length and breadth shall be measured correct to a cm and its area shall be calculated in square metres correct to two places of decimal. The superficial area of roof coverings shall be measured on the flat without allowance for laps and corrugations.

No deduction in measurements shall be made for opening upto 0.4 sq m. For ridges, hips, '*S*' types, louver, valleys, apron finishing pieces, eaves filler pieces, north light and ventilator curves, borge boards and expansion joints for sheets, shall be measured for the finished work, along the centre line, in length correct to a cm. Laps between adjacent pieces shall not be measured. For ridge finials, cowl type ventilators, curved board for north light, curves, roof light, expansion joints for ridge and expansion joints for northlight curve, shall be measured and paid for in numbers.

(*c*) **Mud phuska terracing with brick paving.** Length and breadth shall be measured correct to a cm. The measurements shall be taken for finished work over the filled surface, in superficial area. No deductions shall be made for openings or recesses of areas up to 0.40 sq m such as chimney stacks, roof lights or khuras.

4.12. FINISHING

(*a*) **Plaster.** Length and breadth shall be measured correct to a cm and its area shall be calculated in square metres correct to two places of decimals.

A coefficient of 1.63 shall be adopted for the measurement of one side plastering on honey comb work having 6 × 10 cm opening.

Deductions in measurements, for the openings etc. shall be as under :

(*i*) No deductions shall be made for openings or ends of joists, beams, columns, posts, girders, steps, etc. upto 0.5 sq m in area; no addition shall be made either, for the jambs, soffits and sills of such openings. The above procedure will apply to both faces of wall.

(*ii*) Deductions for openings exceeding 0.5 sq m but not exceeding 3 sq m each, shall be made for reveals, jambs, soffits, sills, etc. of these openings. When both faces of the walls are plastered with same plaster, deduction shall be made for one face only; and when two faces of the walls are plastered with different types of plaster or if one face is plastered and other is pointed, or one face is plastered and other is unplastered, deduction will be made from the plaster or pointing on the side of the frame for the doors, windows etc. on which width or reveal is less than that on the other side but no deduction shall be made on the other side. Where width of reveals on both faces of wall is equal, deduction of 50% of area of opening on each face shall be made from area of plaster and/or pointing as the case may be.

(*iii*) For opening having door frame equal to or projecting beyond thickness of wall, full deduction for opening shall be made from each plastered face of wall.

(*iv*) For openings exceeding 3 sq m in area, deduction will be made in the measurements for the full opening of the wall treatments on both faces, while at the same time, jambs, sills and soffits will be measured for payment.

In measuring jambs, sills and soffits, deduction shall not be made for the area in contact with the frame of doors, windows etc.

Note. The above rules also apply to pointing work.

(*b*) **White washing colour washing and distempering.** Length and breadth shall be measured correct to a cm and area shall be calculated in sq m correct to two places of decimals.

Measurements for jambs, soffits and sills etc. for opening shall be as described in 'Plaster'.

Corrugated surfaces shall be measured flat as fixed and the area so measured shall be increased by 20% for each face.

(*c*) **Painting, polishing and varnishing.** The length and breadth shall be measured correct to a cm. The area shall be calculated in sq metres correct to two place of decimal. Trusses, girders etc. shall be measured in sq metres.

4.13. DISMANTLING AND DEMOLITIONS

(*a*) **Fixing doors, windows and chowkhats in existing openings.** Measurement shall be made in numbers.

(*b*) **Making opening in the masonry construction and fixing chowkhats for doors and window.** Measurements shall be made in numbers.

(*c*) **Renewing glass panes.** Measurement shall be made by measuring the area of glass in sq metres.

Note. *Dismantling and demolitions.* All work shall be measured net in the decimal system, as fixed in its place, subject to the following limits :

(*i*) Dimensions shall be measured correct to a cm.

(*ii*) Areas shall be worked out to two places of decimal.

(*iii*) Cubic contents shall be worked out correct to the nearest 0.01 m^3.

(*d*) **Walls and piers.** Shall be measured in cubic metres.

(*e*) **R.C.C. Work and R.B. Work.** Shall be measured in cubic metres.

(*f*) **Roofs.** Shall be measured in square metres.

(*g*) **Floors.** Shall be measured in cubic metres.

(*h*) **Wood Work.** Shall be measured in square metres.

(*i*) **Steel and Iron Works.** Shall be measured in kilograms.

(*j*) **Water Pipe Lines and Sewer Lines.** Shall be described by their internal diameter and length and measured in running metres inclusive of joints.

The following coefficient shall applied to the areas measured flat and not girthed.

Coefficient of Measurements

Table 4.1

S. No.	*Description of Work*	*Multiplying coefficients*
	I Wood Work	
1.	Panelled or framed and braced or ledged and battened or ledged and; battened and braced; doors and windows etc.	1.30 (for each side)
2.	Flush door etc.	1.20 (for each side)
3.	Part panelled and part glazed or gauzed doors windows etc.	1.00 (for each side)
4.	Fully glazed or gauzed doors, windows etc.	0.80 (for each side)
5.	Fully venetioned or lovered doors, windows etc.	1.80 (for each side)
6.	Trellis (or jaffri) work one way or two way.	2.00 (for painting all over)
7.	Carved or enriched work.	2.00 (for each side)
8.	Weather boarding.	1.20 (for each side)
9.	Wood shingle roofing	1.10 (for each side)
10.	Boarding with cover fillets and match boarding	1.05 (for each side)
11.	Tile and slate battening	0.80 (for painting all over)

(*Contd.*)

	II Steel Work Doors Windows etc.	
12.	Plain sheeted steel doors or windows	1.10 (for each side)
13.	Fully glazed or gauzed steel doors and windows	0.50 (for each side)
14.	Partly panelled and partly glazed or gauzed doors and windows	0.80 (for each side)
15.	Corrugated sheeted steel doors or windows	1.25 (for each side)
16.	Collapsible gates	1.50 (for painting all over)
17.	Rolling shutters of interlocked laths	1.10 (for each side)
	III General	
18.	Expanded metal, hard drawn steel wire fabric of approved quality, grill works and gratings in guard bars, balustrades, railings, partitions and M.S. bars in window frames, open palisade fencing and gates including standards, braces, rails stays etc. in timber or steel	1.00 (for paint all over)
19.	Corrugated iron sheeting in roofs, side clading etc.	1.14 (for each side)
20.	A.C. corrugated sheeting in roofs, side clading etc.	1.20 (for each side)
21.	A.C. semicorrugated sheeting in roofs, side clading etc. or Nainital pattern using plain sheets	1.10 (for each side)
22.	Wire gauze shutters including painting of wired gauze	1.00 (for each side)
23.	Rain water pipes, fixtures and fittings	Running metres

4.14. WELL FOUNDATIONS

(*a*) **Sinking of Well.** Shall be measured in running metres stating the shape and cross-section of the well.

(*b*) **Concrete Wells.** Shall be measured in cubic metres. Measurements for reinforcement shall be made in kilograms.

4.15. PILING

(*a*) **Precast Reinforced Concrete Pipes.** The cement concrete in piles shall be measured in cubic metres. The reinforcement shall be measured in kilograms.

Driving piles shall be measured in running metres.

(*b*) **Timber Piles.** Timber piles shall be measured in running metre stating size of the pile. Drawing timber piles shall be measured in running metres.

(*c*) **Steel Sheet Piles.** Sheet piles shall be measured by weight. Drawing sheet pile shall be measured in square metres.

(*d*) **Cast in Situ Driven Concrete Piles.** Forming pile and drawing casings shall be measured in running metres. Reinforcement and concrete shall be measured in kilograms and in cubic metres.

4.16. TUNNELING

(*a*) **Tunnel in Hard Rock Not Requiring Support.** The quantity of excavation shall be measured in cubic metres and shall be the volume of the tunnel measured in solid contained within hypothetical line a (also known as '*B*' line or pay line) over breaks extending beyond '*B*' line shall be measured separately.

(*b*) **Method of Measurement of Support.** The measurement of temporary and permanent supports shall be done by weight, in kilograms, which shall include the total weight of steel sections including the lagging if any, butt plates, feather plates, bolts and nuts and tie rods etc. When timber is used as temporary supports, it shall be measured separately. Grouting behind the supports and concrete lining shall be measured separately in terms of number of 50 kg cement bags stating the material used. The drilling of the hole shall be measured separately in running metres of the hole drilled.

(*c*) **Concrete Lining.** Measurement for the concrete lining shall be made of the quantity of concrete placed between the formwork or the outside surface of the steel snell when used and the payline, which shall be 'B' line or payline adopted for excavation at the place. No deduction shall be made for the volume of the reinforcement, but the volume of permanent steel supports, where provided shall be deducted from the total volume of concrete lining.

4.17. WATER SUPPLY AND SANITATION WATER LINES

(*a*) **Water Lines.** Pipes shall be described by their internal diameter and length, unless otherwise stated and measured in running metres inclusive of joints (the measurement shall be taken along the centre line of pipes and fittings or specials) fittings and specials shall be enumerated 'extra over' pipes.

(*b*) **Excavations of Trenches.** Method of measurement for excavation for trenches for laying pipe lines and other allied works and filling the trenches etc. shall be as in earth work.

(*c*) **Testing.** The measurement for testing of the pipe lines shall be in running metres.

(*d*) **Miscellaneous Works.** The value, cistern, public fountain platform, fire hydrants etc. shall be described in detail and enumerated.

4.18. SEWER LINES

(*a*) **Sewer Lines.** Sewer lines shall be described by their internal diameter and length unless otherwise stated and measured in running metres inclusive of joints (the measurement shall be taken along the central line of pipes and fittings) fittings and specials shall be enumerated 'extra over' pipes.

(*b*) **Manholes.** Manholes and inspection chambers shall be fully described and enumerated. They shall be classified into different groups depending upon the depth, such as, upto half metre depth, half to one metre depth, one to two, two to three metre depth and so on. The depth of the manhole shall be the distance between the top of the manhole cover and the inverted level of the main drain.

(*c*) **Appurtenant Items.** Ventilating shafts, gully traps, flushing cisterns and other appurtenant items of work shall be enumerated. The items of the work shall be described in detail and the type of designs showing all the dimensions shall be given.

4.19. WATER SUPPLY, PLUMBING, DRAINS AND SANITARY FITTINGS

(*a*) All pipes and fittings shall be classified according to their diameters, method of jointing and fixing, substance, quality and finish. The diameter shall be the nominal diameter of the material bore.

(*b*) In the case of fittings of unequal bore, the largest bore shall be measured.

(*c*) All pipes shall be measured net, length as laid or fixed shall be measured over all fittings, like bends, junctions etc. (which shall not be measured separately), in running metres. The length shall be taken along the centre line of the pipes and fittings.

(*d*) The method of laying and jointing pipes and fittings shall be fully described.

(*e*) The testing of plumbing and sanitary works shall be included in the description of the item.

(*f*) Lead caulked joints shall be enumerated separately.

(*g*) Caps, collars, plugs, stopped ends etc. shall be described and enumerated.

(*h*) Sluice valves, hydrants, stop cock covers, surface boxes and water meters shall be described and enumerated and each shall be measured separately according to the diameter. The joining to pipes on either shall be described.

(*i*) The connection with the water main shall be described and enumerated.

(*j*) Boilers, cisterns and cylinders shall be enumerated stating the size, location and method of fixing.

(*k*) **Plumbing Brass Work.** Bibcocks, (plug or screw down) pillar cocks, stop cocks, ball valves, boiler or cisterns screws, caps and linings also cleaning eyes with screw caps, ferrules, sleeve pieces, thimbles, unions, waste washers, perforated gratings and like shall be described and enumerated. The joints and the fixing shall also be described and included in the item.

(*l*) **Soil Waste and Vent Pipes.** Bends, branches inspection or access doors, swan necks, enlarged sockets, etc. shall be enumerated as extra over. Wire guards and ventilating cowls over tops of pipes shall be described and enumerated and measured separately, according to the bore of the pipe. Stack clamps, shall be described and enumerated stating the length of stay and the method fixing to wall or roof. Lead pipes shall be classified according to their size and weight per running metre and shall be measured in running metres. Traps shall be enumerated and joints at both ends shall be measured separately.

(*m*) **Drains.** The pipes shall be described and each type measured separately. All fittings, specials etc. being enumerated as extra over. Concrete beds, haunching and coverings, including any formwork required, shall be described and measured in running metres stating the size of pipe, the dimensions and mix of concrete. Gullies, syphons, intercepting traps, together with their setting, concrete bedding and connections to drains shall be described and enumerated.

(*n*) **Sanitary Fittings.** Closet pans, urinals, partitions for closet and urinals, water waste preventors, flushing pipes, brackets, lavatory basins, baths, mixing valves, shower roses, sinks, levelling tanks, holders for toilet papers, glass shelves and other fittings together with the fixing of the same shall be enumerated and fully described.

4.20. ROAD WORK INCLUDING AIR FIELD PAVEMENTS

(*a*) Measurements shall be taken in bottom less boxes or measuring boxes or in closely packed stacks prepared on level ground and measured in cubic metres.

(*b*) Where thickness is measured, it shall be the minimum thickness after compaction.

(*c*) All road work shall be measured in square metres, except where otherwise stated. In case of soling, sub-bases, etc., the measurement shall be done in square metres or cubic metres.

(*d*) Excavation and earth work necessary to bring the road alignment to proper levels shall be measured in accordance with the provisions given in 'earth work'.

(*e*) Rolling and watering formations, when required, may be either included with the item or measured separately in square metres.

(*f*) Soling shall be described stating the thickness. The description shall include fitting of interstices with spalls.

(*g*) Sub-bases of clinker, ashes, shingle, gravel, brick ballast, moorum, bajri, etc. shall be measured separately.

4.21. TAR AND BITUMEN ROADS

(*a*) Work carried out with different types of bitumen shall be measured separately.

(*b*) Priming surfaces of W.B.M. Road shall be measured in square metres.

(*c*) Edging shall be measured in running metres.

4.22. CEMENT CONCRETE ROADS AND BASES

(*a*) Work shall be measured either in square metres or cubic metres.

(*b*) Concrete required to be spread and consolidated by mechanical spreaders and vibratory compacting equipment shall be measured separately.

(*c*) If concrete is reinforced with bars or fabric reinforcement, it shall be measured separately.

(*d*) Formwork for pavings shall be measured separately.

(*e*) Expansion and dummy joints shall be described and measured separately in running metres, stating the thickness and depth of the joints.

4.23. MISCELLANEOUS

(*a*) ***Screening.*** Total quantity of road metal, stone chips, etc. required to be screened shall be measured in cubic metres.

(*b*) ***Breaking.*** Breaking stone, brick or other road material into required sizes shall be measured in cubic metres of stacked materials after breaking.

(*c*) ***Scarifying.*** Scarifying shall be measured in square metres stating the depth scarified and the type of surface.

(*d*) ***Berms.*** Preparation of berms shall be measured in running metres stating the average filling and width.

4.24. ELECTRICAL WORK

Wiring

(*a*) Wiring in different systems, such as T.R.S. on battens, VIR in casing and capping, VIR in conduit etc. shall be fully described and measured separately, in running metres. It shall be further classified according to the sizes of cables used.

(*b*) Concealed conduit work and surface conduit work shall also be classified separately.

(*c*) Distribution board, wood blocks, lamp holders, socket outlet, brackets, shades, regulators, fuses and call bell/buzzer shall be measured separately in numbers.

4.25. POINTS

(*a*) Fan and light points, light point controlled by two-way switches, two-pin socket outlet points, three pin socket outlet points, circuit points, etc. shall be measured in numbers.

(*b*) Earthing of electric installation shall be fully described and measured separately.

(*c*) Joints or junction boxes shall be included in the description and shall not be paid separately.

4.26. PLINTH, CARPET AND RENTABLE AREAS AND CUBICAL CONTENTS IN BUILDINGS

1. Terminology

(*a*) **Plinth area.** Shall mean the built up covered area measured at the floor level of the basement or of any storey.

(*b*) **Carpet area.** Shall mean the covered area of the usable rooms at any floor level.

(*c*) **Rentable area.** Shall mean the usable carpet area at any floor level.

(*d*) **Balcony.** A horizontal projection with a hand-rail, balustrade or a parapet, to serve as passage or sitting out place.

(*e*) **Mezzanine floor.** An intermediate floor in between two main floors, having minimum height of 2.2 m from the floor and having a proper access to it.

(*f*) **Stair cover (Mumty).** It is a space having a roof over a stair case and its landing, built to enclose only the stairs for the purpose of providing protection from weather and not used for human habitation.

(*g*) **Loft.** An intermediate storage area in between two main floors.

(*h*) **Porch.** It is a covered surface supported on pillars or otherwise for the purpose of pedestrian or vehicular approach to a building.

(*i*) **Circulating area.** Shall mean the floor area of verandahs, balconies, passages and stair case, etc., which are used for movement of persons using the building at any floor level.

4.27. MEASUREMENT OF PLINTH AREA

For the purpose of plinth area, following shall be included :

(*a*) Area of the wall at the floor level excluding plinth offsets, if any;

(*b*) Internal shaft for sanitary installations and garbage, provided these do not exceed 2 m^2 in area, vertical duct for air conditioning, lift well including landing.

(*c*) Stair cover (mumty); (*d*) Machine rooms; and (*e*) Porch.

The following shall not be included in the plinth area :

(*a*) Additional floor for seating in assembly building/theatres and auditorium etc.

(*b*) Cantilevered porch.

(*c*) Balcony. (*d*) Area of loft.

(*e*) Internal sanitary shaft provided these are more than 2 m^2 in area.

(*f*) Area of architectural band, cornice, etc.

(*g*) Area of vertical sun breaker; or box, loaver projecting out and other architectural features, for example slabs projection for flower pot, etc.

(*h*) Open platform. (*i*) Terrace at floor one.

(*j*) Spiral stair case including landing; and

(*k*) Towers, turrets, domes projecting above the terrace level at terrace.

4.28. MEASUREMENT OF CARPET AREA

(*a*) From the plinth area as worked out, the area of the wall shall be deducted. Thickness of wall shall be inclusive of finishing and dado if the height of such finish is more than 1 m from floor finish.

The following shall be included in the wall area :

(*a*) Door and other openings in the wall.

(*b*) Intermediate pillars, supports or any other such obstruction within the plinth area.

(*c*) Pilaster along wall exceeding 300 cm^2 in area.

(*d*) Flues which are within the wall.

(*e*) Built in cup board, almirah and shaft appearing within a height of 2.2 m from floor, and

(*f*) Fire places projecting beyond the face of the wall in living or bed room.

The following shall be excluded from the wall area :

(*a*) Pilaster along wall not exceeding 300 cm^2 in area; and

(*b*) Chullah platform projecting beyond the face or the wall.

The carpet area shall be the plinth area worked out as above, excluding the area of the following portions :

(*a*) Verandah.
(*b*) Corridor and passage.
(*c*) Entrance hall and porch.
(*d*) Stair case and mumty.
(*e*) Shaft and machine room for lift.
(*f*) Bath room and lavatory.
(*g*) Kitchen and pantry.
(*h*) Store.
(*i*) Canteen.
(*j*) Air-conditioning duct and plant room; and
(*k*) Shaft for sanitary piping.

4.29. MEASUREMENT OF RENTABLE AREA

Residential Buildings

The rentable area shall be the carpet area as worked out, but shall further include the following :

(*a*) The carpet area of kitchen, pantry, store, lavatory, bath room; and

(*b*) Fifty percent of carpet area of unglazed and 100 percent of glazed verandah.

It shall, however, exclude the carpet area of the following :

(*a*) Covered portion of the building within portions as specified above, such as storage space on top, landings of stair case, under and first landing and waist slab on floor one.

(*b*) Fifty per cent of the carpet area of balcony.

Non-Residential Buildings. The rentable area shall be the carpet area as worked out above, but shall further include the carpet area of the canteen including store, kitchen and pantry attached to it.

It shall however, not include carpet area of bath room and lavatory.

4.30. MEASUREMENT OF CIRCULATING AREA

The circulating area of any floor shall comprise of the following :

(*a*) Verandahs and balconies.
(*b*) Passages and corridors.
(*c*) Entrance halls.
(*d*) Stair cases and mumties; and
(*e*) Shafts for lift.`

4.31. MEASUREMENT OF CUBICAL CONTENTS

The cubical contents of basement or any storey shall be worked out by multiplying the plinth area of the basement or the storey by the height between the floor level of the basement or the storey and the next higher floor, or the top or the roof in case no higher floor exists.

5

Measurement of Works

Measurement of work occupies a very important place in the planning and execution of any civil engineering project from the time of first estimates to final completion and settlement of payments. Methods followed for the measurement are not uniform, and considerable differences exist between the practices followed by different construction agencies and also between various Central and State Government Departments. While it is recognised that each system of measurement has to be specifically related to administrative and financial organization with departments responsible for the work, a unification of the various systems at the technical level has been accepted as very desirable, specially as it permits a wider circle of operation for civil engineering contractors, and eliminates ambiguities and misunderstandings arising out of inadequate information and knowledge of various systems followed.

5.1. ROUNDING OFF VALUES

5.1.1. Introduction

This prescribes rules for rounding off numerical values for the purpose of reporting results of a test, an analysis, a measurement or a calculation. It also makes recommendations as to the number of figures that should be retained in course of computation.

Number of Decimal Places. A value is said to have as many decimal places as there are number of figures in the value, counting from the first figure after the decimal point and ending with the last figure on the right.

Examples : *Value*	*Decimal Places*
0.029 50	5
21.029 5	4
2 000.000 001	6
291.00	2
10.32×10^3	2

Number of Significant Figures. A value is said to have as many significant figures as there are number of significant *digits* in the value, counting from the left-most *non*-zero digit and ending with the right-most digit in the value.

Examples : *Value*	*Significant Figures*
0.029 500	5
0.029 5	3
10.029 5	6
2 000.000 001	10
5 677.0	5
567 700	6
56.77×10^2	4
0 056.770	5
3 900	4

Note : [Any of the digits, 1, 2, 3,....., 9 occurring in a value shall be a significant digit (s); and zero shall be a significant digit only when it is preceded by some other digit (excepting zeros) on its left. When appearing in the power of 10 to indicate the magnitude of the unit in the expression of a value, zero shall not be a significant digit. With a view to removing any ambiguity regarding the significance of the zeros at the end in a value like 3 900, it would be always desirable to write the value in the power-of-ten notation. For example, 3 900 may be written as 3.9×10^3, 3.90×10^3 or 3.900×10^3 depending upon the last figure(s) in the value to which it is desired to impart significance.

Fineness of Rounding. The unit to which a value is rounded off. For example, a value may be rounded to the nearest 0.000 01, 0.000 2, 0.000 5, 0.001, 0.002 5, 0.005, 0.01, 0.07, 1, 2.5, 10, 20, 50, 100 or any other unit depending on the fineness desired.

5.1.2. Rules for Rounding off Values

The rule usually followed in rounding off a value to unit fineness of rounding is to keep unchanged the last figure retained when the figure next beyond is less than 5 and to increase by 1 the last figure retained when the figure next beyond is more than 5. There is diversity of practice when the figure next beyond the last figure retained is 5. In such cases, some computers 'round up', that is, increase by 1, the last figure retained; others 'round down', that is, discard everything beyond the last figure retained. Obviously, if the retained value is always 'rounded up' or always 'rounded down', the sum and the average of a series of values so rounded will be larger or smaller than the corresponding sum or average of the unrounded values.

Rounding Off to Unit Fineness. In case the fineness of rounding is unity in the last place retained, the following rules shall be followed :

Rule I—When the figure next beyond the last figure or place to be retained is less than 5, the figure in the last place retained shall be left unchanged.

Rule II—When the figure next beyond the last figure or place to be retained is more than 5 or is 5 followed by any figures other than zeros, the figure in the last place retained shall be increased by 1.

Rule III—When the figure next beyond the last figure or place to be retained is 5 alone or 5 followed by zeros only, the figure in the last place retained shall be (*a*) increased by 1 if it is odd and (*b*) left unchanged if even (zero would be regarded as an even number for this purpose).

Some examples illustrating the application of Rules I to III are given in Table 5.1.

Table 5.1. Examples of Rounding Off Values to Unit Fineness

Value	*FINENESS OF ROUNDING*							
	1		0.1		0.01		0001	
	Rounded Value	*Rule*	*Rounded Value*	*Rule*	*Rounded Value*	*Rule*	*Rounded Value*	*Rule*
7.260 4	7	I	7.3	II	7.26	I	7.260	I
14.725	15	II	14.7	I	14.72	III(*b*)	14.725	—
3.455	3	I	3.5	II	3.46	III(*a*)	3.455	—
13.545 001	14	II	13.5	I	13.55	II	13.545	I
8.725	9	II	8.7	I	8.72	III(*b*)	8.725	—
19.205	19	I	19.2	I	19.20	III(*b*)	19.205	—
0.549 9	1	II	0.5	I	0.55	II	0.550	II
0.650 1	1	II	0.7	II	0.65	I	0.650	I
0.049 50	0	I	0.0	I	0.05	II	0.050	III (*a*)

The rules for rounding laid down as above may be extended to apply when the fineness of rounding is 0.10, 10, 100, 1 000, etc. For example, 2.43 when rounded to fineness 0.10

becomes 2.40. Similarly, 712 and 715 when rounded to the fineness 10 become 710 and 720, respectively.

Rounding off to Fineness Other than Unity. In case the fineness of rounding is not unity, but, say, it is n, the given value shall be rounded off according to the following rule :

Rule IV—When rounding to a fineness n, other than unity, the given value shall be divided by n. The quotient shall be rounded off to the nearest whole number in accordance with the rules discussed above for unit fineness of rounding. The number so obtained, that is, the rounded quotient, shall then be multiplied by n to get the final rounded value. Some examples illustrating the application of Rule IV are given in Table 5.2.

Note 4—The rules for rounding off a value to any fineness of rounding, n, may also be stated in line with those lor unit fineness of rounding as follows :

Divide the given value by n so that an integral quotient and a remainder are obtained. Round off the value in the following manner :

(*a*) If the remainder is less than $n/2$, the value shall be rounded down such that the rounded value is an integral multiple of n.

(*b*) If the remainder is greater than $n/2$, the value shall be rounded up such that the rounded value is an integral multiple of n.

(*c*) If the remainder is exactly equal to $n/2$, that rounded value shall be chosen which is an integral multiple of $2n$.

Table 5.2. Examples of Rounding Off Values to Fineness other than Unit

Value	*Fineness of Rounded, n*	*Quotient*	*Rounded Quotient*	*Final Rounded Value*
(1)	*(2)*	*(3) = (1)/(2)*	*(4)*	*(5) = (2) × (4)*
1.6478	0.2	8.239	8	1.6
2.70	0.2	13.5	14	2.8
2.496 8	0.3	8.322 7	8	2.4
1.75	0.5	3.5	4	2.0
0.687 21	0.07	9.817 3	10	0.70
0.875	0.07	12.5	12	0.84
325	50	6.5	6	3×10^2
1 025	50	20.5	20	10×10^2

Fineness of rounding other than 2 and 5 is seldom called for in practice. For these cases, the rules for rounding may be stated in simpler form as follows :

(*a*) Rounding off to fineness 50, 5, 0.5, 0.05, 0.005, etc.

Rule V—When rounding to 5 units, the given value shall be doubled and rounded off to twice the required fineness of rounding. The value thus obtained shall be halved to get the final rounded value.

For example, in rounding off 975 to the nearest 50, 975 is doubled giving 1950 which becomes 2000 when rounded off to the nearest 100; when 2000 is divided by 2, the resulting number 1000 is the rounded value of 975.

(*b*) Rounding off to fineness 20, 2, 0.2, 0.02, 0.002, etc.

Rule VI—When rounding to 2 units, the given value shall be halved and rounded off to half the required fineness of rounding. The value thus obtained shall then be doubled to get the final rounded value. For example, in rounding off 2.70 to the nearest 0.2, 2.70 is halved giving 1.35 which becomes 1.4 when rounded off to the nearest 0.1 ; when 1.4 is doubled, the resulting number 2.8 is the rounded value.

Successive Rounding. The final rounded value shall be obtained from the most precise value available in one step only and not from a series of successive roundings. For example, the value 0.549 9, when rounded to one significant figure, shall be written as 0.5 and not as 0.6 which is obtained as a result of successive roundings to 0.550, 0.55, and 0.6. It is obvious that the most precise value available is nearer to 0.5 and not to 0.6 and that the error involved is less in the former case. Similarly, 0.650 1 shall be rounded off to 0.7 in one step and not successively to 0.650, 0.65 and 0.6, since the most precise value available here is nearer to 0.7 than to 0.6 (*see also* Table 5.1).

In those cases where a final rounded value terminates with 5 and it is intended to use it in further computation, it may be helpful to use a '+' or '–' sign after the final 5 to indicate whether a subsequent rounding should be up or down. Thus 3.214 7 may be written as 3.215— when rounded to a fineness of rounding 0.001. If further rounding to three significant figures is desired, this number would be rounded down and written as 3.21 which is in error by *less* than half a unit in the last place otherwise, rounding off 3.215 would have yielded 3.22 which is in error by *more* than half a unit in the last place. Similarly, 3.205 4 could be written as 3.205 + when rounded to 4 significant figures. Further rounding to 3 significant figures would yield the value as 3.21.

In case the final 5 is obtained exactly, it would be indicated by leaving the 5 as such without using '+' or '–' sign. In subsequent rounding the 5 would then be treated in accordance with Rule III.

5.1.3. Number of Figures to be Retained

Pertinent to the application of the rules for rounding off is the underlying decision as to the number of figures that should be retained in a given problem. The original values requiring to be rounded off may arise as a result of a test, an analysis or a measurement, in other words, experimental results, or they may arise from computations involving several steps.

Experimental Results. The number of figures to be retained in an experimental result, either for the purpose of reporting or for guiding the formulation of specifications will depend on the significance of the figures in the value.

Computations. In computations involving values of different accuracies, the problem as to how many figures should be retained at various steps assumes a special significance as it would affect the accuracy of the final result. The rounding off error will, in fact, be injected into computation every time an arithmetical operation is performed. It is, therefore, necessary to carry out the computation in such a manner as would obtain accurate results consistent with the accuracy of the data in hand.

While it is not possible to prescribe details which may be followed in computations of various types, certain basic rules may be recommended for single arithmetical operations which, when followed, will save labour and at the same time enable accuracy of original data to be normally maintained in the final answers.

As a guide to the number of places or figures to be retained in the calculations involving arithmetical operations with rounded or approximate values, the following procedures are recommended :

(*a*) ***Addition***—The more accurate values shall be rounded off so as to retain *one more place* than the last significant figure in the least accurate value. The resulting sum shall then be rounded off to the last significant place in the least accurate value.

(*b*) ***Subtraction***—The more accurate value (of the two given values) shall be rounded off, before subtraction, to the *same place* as the last significant figure in less accurate value; and the result shall be reported as such.

(c) ***Multiplication and division***—The number of *significant figures* retained in the more accurate values shall be kept *one more* than that in the least accurate value. The result shall then be rounded off to the same number of significant figures as in the least accurate value.

(d) When a long computation is carried out in several steps, the intermediate results shall be properly rounded at the end of each step so as to avoid the accumulation of rounding errors in such cases. It is recommended that, at the end of each step, one more significant figure may be retained than is required under (a), (b) and (c) (see also note 7).

[The loss of the significant figures in the subtraction of two nearly equal values is the greatest source of inaccuracy in most computations, and it forms the weakest link in a chain computation where it occurs. Thus, if the values 0.169 52 and 0.168 71 are each correct to five significant figures, their difference 0.000 81, which has only two significant figures, is quite likely to introduce inaccuracy in subsequent computation.

If, however, the difference of two values is desired to be correct to k significant figures and if it is known, beforehand that the first m significant figures at the left will disappear by subtraction, then the number of significant figures to be retained in each of the values shall be $m + k$ (see Example 4).

To ensure a greater degree of accuracy in the computations, it is also desirable to avoid or defer as long as possible certain approximation operations like that of the division or square root. For example, in the determination of sucrose by volumetric method, the expression $\frac{20w_1}{w_2}\left(\frac{f_2}{v_2} - \frac{f_1}{v_1}\right)$ may be better evaluated by taking its calculational form as $20w_1 (f_2v_1 - f_1v_2)/w_2v_1v_2$ which would defer the division until the last operation of the calculation.]

EXAMPLES

Example 5.1. *Required to find the sum of the rounded off values 461.32, 381.6, 76.854 and 4.746 2.*

Since the least accurate value 381.6 is known only to the first decimal place, all other values shall be rounded off to one more place, that is, to two decimal places and then added as shown below :

461.32
381.6
76.85
4.75

924.52

The resulting sum shall then be reported to the same decimal place as in the least accurate value, that is, as 924.5.

Example 5.2. *Required to find the sum of the values 28 490, 894, 657.32, 39 500, and 76939, assuming that the value 39500 is known to the nearest hundred only.*

Since one of the values is known only to the nearest hundred, the other values shall be rounded off to the nearest ten and then added as shown below :

2 849 × 10
89 × 10
66 × 10
3 950 × 10
7 694 × 10

14 648 × 10

The sum shall then be reported to the nearest hundred as 1 465 × 100 or even as 1.465×10^5.

Example 5.3. *Required to find the difference of 679.8 and 76.365, assuming that each number is known to its last figure but no farther.*

Since one of the values is known to the first decimal place only, the other value shall also be rounded off to the first decimal place and then the difference shall be found.

$$\begin{array}{r} 679.8 \\ 76.4 \\ \hline 603.4 \end{array}$$

The difference, 603.4 shall be reported as such.

Example 5.4. *Required to evaluate* $\sqrt{2.52} - \sqrt{2.49}$ *correct to five significant figures.*

Since $\sqrt{2.52} = 1.587\ 450\ 79$

$\sqrt{2.49} = 1.577\ 973\ 38$

and three significant figures at the left will disappear on subtraction, the number of significant figures retained in each value shall be 8 as shown below :

$$\begin{array}{r} 1.587\ 450\ 8 \\ 1.577\ 973\ 4 \\ \hline 0.009\ 477\ 4 \end{array}$$

The result, 0.009 477 4, shall be reported as such (or as $9.477\ 4 \times 10^{-3}$).

Example 5.5. *Required to evaluate* $35.2/\sqrt{2}$ *given that the numerator is correct to its last figure.*

Since the numerator here is correct to three significant figures, the denominator shall be taken as $\sqrt{2} = 1.414$. Then,

$$\frac{35.2}{1.414} = 24.89$$

and the result shall be reported as 24.9.

Example 5.6. *Required to evaluate* $3.78\,\pi/5.6$, *assuming that the denominator is true to only two significant figures.*

Since the denominator here is correct to two significant figures, each number in the numerator would be taken up to three significant figures. Thus,

$$\frac{3.78 \times 3.14}{5.7} = 2.08.$$

The result shall, however, be reported as 2.1.

5.2. MATERIALS

Description of Item. Description of each item shall, unless otherwise stated, include wherever necessary, conveyance and delivery, handling, unloading, storing, etc.

Limits of Measurement. Dimensions shall be measured net in decimal system to the nearest 0.01 m, area to nearest 0.01 m^2, volume to nearest 0.01 m^3, weight to nearest 1 kg, unless otherwise stated in the relevant Indian Standard(s) on the specification of materials.

5.2.1. Method of Measurement of Materials

Various types of materials shall be measured as mentioned in Table 5.3.

Table 5.3. Measurement of Materials

Name of Material	*How Measured*
Aggregates	
Brick/stone of 40 mm nominal size and above	In m^3 after making a deduction of 7.5 percent from stack measurements and as per type
Brick/stone aggregates of less than 40 mm size cinder, sand, *moorum*, fly ash, pozzolana, stone, stone dust	In m^3 of gross stack measurements according to nominal size and type
Aluminium Flats	In kg, stating size
Aluminium Strip and Edging	In running metre stating size
Asbestos Cement Products	
Barge boards	Enumerated, stating size
Ridge	In pairs, according to size and type
Gutters	Enumerated, stating size, type and length
Roof lights, north light curves	Enumerated, stating size and type
Sheets	Enumerated, stating type, size and length
Ventilators, eaves fillers, apron pieces, louvers, cowls, ridge finials, septic tanks	Enumerated and described
Bitumen Products	
Bitumen felt	In m^2, stating type, grade and width
Bitumen hot sealing compound	By weight, in kg, stating grade and type
Bitumen road tar	In tonnes, stating type
Joint filler (sealing compound)	In kg
Boards	
Plywood, etc.	In m^2, stating type and thickness
Brick/Brick Tiles	Enumerated, stating class and size
Blocks Building (Clay, Cement, Stone, etc.)	Enumerated stating size, type and grade, if any
Cement/Lime Pozzolana Mixture	In kg, stating type
Distemper	In kg
Doors/Windows/Ventilator Frames	In linear metre and described (outside dimensions measured)
Doors/Windows/Ventilators (Excluding Fittings and Finishes)	In m^2 and described
Fibre Glass Felt	In m^2 stating thickness and grade
Filler Fibrous/Non Fibrous	In m^2 and described
Fittings for Doors and Windows	Enumerated
Galvanized Steel Barbed Wire	In kg, stating type and size
Galvanized Steel Sheets (Corrugated/Plain)	In quintals or enumerated, stating type and size
Glass Sheets (Plain/Pin Head/Frosted/Wired/ Splinter Proof)	In m^2, stating type, thickness and size
Glass Strips	In running metres, stating thickness and width
Jali (Cement Concrete/Clay)	In m^2, stating thickness and type
Lead for Caulking	In kg
Lime	In kg, stating class
Marble Chips	In quintal, stating size and described

Marble Dust	In kg
Marble Pieces	In kg, stating colour
Marble Slab	In m^2, stating thickness and type
Metal Beading	In running metres, stating type and size
Paints, Emulsions and Thinners	In litres, stating type and class
Paint (Stiff) and Pigment	In kg, stating type and class
Pipes and Accessories	
Pipe fittings	Enumerated and described
Pipes (except mild steel)	In running metres and described
Precast Units for Flooring	Enumerated and described
Rope Manila	In kg and described
Rubber Rings for Pipes	Enumerated and described
Steel	
Mild steel sheets	In tonnes, stating size and thickness
Mild steel expanded metal	In m^2 and described
Wire fabric/chain fabric	In m^2 and described
Hoop iron/bolts/rivets/bars/structural sections/ rails/mild steel pipes	In kg or tonnes and described
Stone	
Boundary stone/kilometre stone	Enumerated, stating size and type
Kerb stone	Enumerated, stating size
Floor stone slabs	In m^2 and described
Soling stone, boulders, rubble	In m^2, after making a deduction of 15 percent from gross stack measurements, stating nominal size and type
Sanitary Fittings	
Cisterns/clamps/cocks/ferrules/footrests/ gratings/hydrants/traps/bath tubs/urinal/ valves/wash basins/WC pans/showers/towel rails/bidets	Enumerated and described
Tiles	Enumerated, stating type and size
Timber	
Blocks/baulks	Enumerated, stating type and size
Ballies	Enumerated, specifying diameter and described (diameter shall be measured at 1.5 from the thick end)
Bamboos	Enumerated and described
Scantlings/planks/battens	In m^3, stating size and type
Tiles (Other than sanitary)	In m^2, stating size and type
Wall Tiles/False Ceiling Tiles/Roofing Tiles	Enumerated, stating type and size
Water Proofing Compound	In kg
Water Proofing Paste/Emulsion/Liquid	In litres
Wire	In kg and described
Wire Rope	In running metre and described

5.3. EARTHWORK

5.3.1. Measurements

Unless otherwise stated, hereinafter all work shall be measured net in decimal system, as fixed in position as given below :

(*a*) Each dimension shall be measured to the nearest 0.01 m, where any dimension is more than 25 m it should be measured to the nearest 0.1 m ;

(*b*) Areas shall be worked out to the nearest 0.01 m^2 ; and

(*c*) Cubical contents shall be worked out to the nearest 0.01 m^3.

The following works shall not be measured separately and allowance for the same shall be deemed to have been made in the description of main item :

(*a*) Setting out works, profiles, etc ;

(*b*) Site clearance, such as cleaning grass and vegetation ;

(*c*) Unauthorised bettering or benching of excavation ;

(*d*) Forming (or leaving) 'dead men' or 'tell-tales' in borrow pits and their removal after measurements ;

(*e*) Forming (or leaving) steps in sides of deep excavation and their removal after measurements ;

(*f*) Excavation for insertion of planking and strutting ;

(*g*) Unless otherwise specified, removing slips or falls in excavations ;

(*h*) Bailing out or pumping of water in excavation from rains ;

(*i*) Bailing out or pumping of water in excavation from sub-soil

(*j*) Slinging or supporting pipes, electric cables, etc. met during excavation.

Special pumping other than what is included in (*h* and *i* above stated) and well point dewatering where resorted to, shall each be measured separately for all stages of pumping, including, intermediate stages unless otherwise stated, in kWh against separate specific provisions made for the purpose.

5.3.2. Classification

The materials to be excavated shall be classified as follows unless otherwise specified :

(*a*) *Soft/Loose Soil*—Generally any soil which yields to the ordinary application of pick and shovel, or to *phawra*, rake or other ordinary digging implement ; such as vegetable or organic soil, turf, gravel, sand, silt, loom, clay peat, etc.

(*b*) *Hard/Dense Soil*—Generally any soil which requires the close application of picks, or jumpers or sacrifiers to loosen ; such as stiff clay, gravel and cobblestone.

(*c*) *Mud*—A mixture of soil and water in fluid or weak solid state.

(*d*) *Soft/Disintegrated Rock* (*not Requiring Blasting*)—Rock or boulders which may be quarried or split with crowbars. This will also include laterite and hard conglomerate.

(*e*) *Hard Rock* (*Requiring Blasting*)—Any rock or boulder for the excavation of which blasting is required.

(*f*) *Hard Rock* (*Blasting Prohibited*)—Hard rock requiring blasting as described under (*e*) but where blasting is prohibited for any reason and excavation has to be carried out by chiselling, wedging or any other agreed method.

Note : A broad classification of soil and rock for earthwork suitable for conditions generally occurring in practice has been provided where necessary, further sub-classification may be done to suit individual cases depending on the properties of the substrata.

5.3.3. Method of Measurement of Various Types of Excavation

The measurement of earthwork shall be done in cubic metres, unless otherwise mentioned. The measurements to be taken shall be those of the authorised dimensions from which soil has been taken out and shall be measured without allowance for increase in bulk.

Excavation in Earthwork Including Rock Cutting. The measurement of excavation in earthwork including rock cutting shall be made as follows :

(*a*) Where the excavation is in trenches or from borrow pits in fairly uniform ground, the measurements of cutting in trenches or borrow pits shall be made. 'Dead men' or 'tell-tales' may be left at suitable intervals to determine the average depth of excavation.

(*b*) Where the ground is not uniform levels shall be taken before the start, after site clearance and after the completion of the work and the quantity of excavation in cutting computed from these levels.

(*c*) Where soft/disintegrated rock and hard rock are mixed the measurement for the total quantity shall be made by method (*a*) and/or (*b*) given above. The hard rock excavated shall be stacked and measured in stack. The quantity of the hard rock excavated shall be arrived at by applying pre-accepted deductions (stated as a percentage) for voids. From the total quantity of the mixture the quantity of hard rock excavated thus arrived at shall be deducted to work out the quantity of the soft, disintegrated rock excavated.

(*d*) Where hard/dense soil, soft/disintegrated rock and hard rock are mixed, the measurement for the total quantity shall be made by methods (*a*) and/or (*b*) given above. If possible after the removal of the hard/dense soil the levels of the exposed rock surface shall be taken and the quantity of the hard/dense soil removed, worked out from the difference between the original levels and the new levels. If this is not possible the excavation shall be completed leaving tell-tales and from the cross-section of these tell-tales, the area of the hard/dense soil excavated shall be worked out and then the volume of the hard/dense soil excavated arrived at. Quantity of hard/dense soil shall then be deducted from the total quantities of excavation done. The balance shall then be treated as total quantity of hard rock and soft/disintegrated rock. The quantities of hard rock and soft/disintegrated rock shall then be separated as in (*c*) above by stacking the hard rock separately.

(*e*) Where soft/loose soil, hard/dense soil, soft/disintegrated rock and hard rock are mixed, the measurements of the entire quantity shall be made by methods (*a*) and/or (*b*) given above. The separate quantities of soft/loose soil and hard/dense soil shall be worked out from the cross-section based on dead men or tell-tales as mentioned in (*d*) in case of hard/dense soil. The total quantity of soft/loose and hard/dense soil shall then be deducted from the total excavation to arrive at the total quantity of rock excavated. The quantities of soft/disintegrated rock and hard rock excavated be worked out separately as in case of (*c*) above.

Wherever it is not possible or convenient to take measurements from borrow pits or cutting, excavation shall be worked out from 'filling'.

Dressing or trimming sides of excavations and levelling or grading and ramming of bottoms shall be described with the item of excavation except in the case of rough excavation.

All excavation shall be measured in successive stages of 1.5 m stating the commencing level. This shall not apply to cases where no lift is involved as in hillside cutting.

All excavation shall generally be described as 'excavate and get out'. Getting out shall include throwing the excavated earth at least one metre or 1/3 depth (*see* Note) of excavation whichever is more clear of the edge of excavation. The subsequent disposal of the surplus excavated material shall either be stated as a separate item or included with the item of excavation stating the lead.

[**Note :** In special cases where the disposal area is limited or where the application of this requirement if impracticable person in-charge may adopt a berm of reduced which in any case not less than one metre provided the material being excavated is sufficiently stable and shoring is designed to carry the additional loads.]

In case of the following works, authorised quantities (calculated on the basis of authorised working space) or those actually excavated, whichever are less, shall be measured :

(*a*) In work which requires form work ;

(*b*) In work which will be covered externally with a damp proof covering ;

(*c*) In work which will be covered externally with protective masonry work of brick, stone, precast concrete, etc ;

(*d*) Trenches which are to receive post tensioned concrete ground beams ;

(*e*) Special works like guniting, etc ; and

(*f*) In work which requires workmen to operate from the outside.

Authorised working space shall be specified in each case (Relevant Indian Standards, if any, may be consulted for guidance). Where authorised working space is not so specified the following shall apply :

'60 cm measured from the face of structure (including protective measures, if any) at lowest level, where extra working space is required. In addition, for item (*d*) the extra length at each end shall be 1.5 m.'

Battering and benching shall be specified and measured along with main item of excavation.

5.3.4. Filling

The actual measurement of the fill shall be calculated by taking levels of the original ground before start of the work after site clearance and after compaction of the fill at suitable intervals and the quantity of fill computed from these levels. The deductions shall be made from actual measurements in all cases of fills except for floors to arrive a net measurement of filling based on pre-accepted or specified deduction (stated as percentage) for voids. If the fillings is obtained from the borrow pits it shall be measured from the borrow pits as 'excavation'.

Surface Dressing. Trimming of natural ground, excavated surface and filled up area to remove vegetation and/or small inequalities not exceeding 15 cm deep shall be described as surface dressing and measured in square metres.

Rough Excavation. Excavation not requiring dressing of sides and bottom and reduction to exact levels, such as winning earth from borrow pits, hillside cutting, etc, shall be described as rough excavation and measured in cubic metres.

Surface Excavation. Excavation exceeding 1.5 m in width as well as 10 m^2 on plan but not exceeding 30 cm in depth shall be described as 'surface excavation' and measured in square metres.

Excavation Over Area. Excavation exceeding 1.5 m in width as well as 10 m^2 on plan, and 30 cm in depth shall be described as excavation over areas and measured in cubic metres.

Excavation in Trenches for Foundations and for Pipes, Cables, etc. Excavation in trenches for foundations and for pipes, cables, etc, not exceeding 1.5 m in width and for shafts, wells, cesspits and the like not exceeding 10 m^2 on plan shall be so described and measured in cubic metres.

The authorised quantities (calculated on the basis of authorised width) or those excavated whichever are less shall be measured in case of excavation for pipes, cables, etc. For purpose of calculating the contents, cross-sections shall be taken at suitable intervals. The authorised width shall be specified in each case. (Relevant Indian Standards, if any, may be consulted for guidance)'. Excavation trenches for foundation : for depth exceeding 1 m, an allowance of 5 cm/m depth for each side of trench shall be added to the specified width.

Post Holes. Independent post holes (or similar holes), each not exceeding 0.5 m^3, shall be enumerated and the description shall include return, fill and ram and removal of surplus spoil.

Return, Fill and Ram. Returning, filling and ramming of excavated earth where not described with the item of excavation shall be measured in cubic metres and shall include spreading in layers not exceeding 20 cm in depth, watering, well ramming and levelling.

Embankments. Forming embankments and filling to make up levels shall be measured in cubic metres and shall include the formation of slopes. If the material is to be deposited in layers this shall be described stating the thickness of such layers. The method of consolidation shall be described. The measurement shall be taken in successive stages of 1.5 m stating commencing level. Filling under floors shall be measured in cubic metres and shall include spreading in layers not exceeding 20 cm in depth watering, well ramming and levelling.

5.3.5. Lead and Lift

Lead. The distance for removal shall be measured over the shortest practicable route and not necessarily the route actually taken. Distances not exceeding 250 m shall be measured in units of 50 m. Distance exceeding 250 m and not exceeding 500 m shall be measured as a separate item. Leads beyond 500 m shall be measured in units of 500 m, that is, there will be one item for lead exceeding 500 m and not exceeding 1 000 m, another item for lead exceeding 1 000 m and not exceeding 1 500 m and so on up to 5 km. Where the lead exceeds 5 km, it will be measured in units of 1 km, half kilometre and above be reckoned as one and less than half kilometre shall be ignored.

The description of items shall include loading and unloading. If spoil heaps requiring re-handling have become consolidated due to passage of time or any other reason, it shall be so stated and such heaps shall be measured separately. For the purpose of measurements of lead, the area excavated shall be divided into suitable blocks and for each block the distance from the centre of the block to centre of placed earth pertaining to this block shall be taken as lead.

Lift. Lift shall be measured from ground level. Excavation upto 1.5 m depth below ground level and depositing excavated-material on the ground shall be included in the item of earthwork for various kinds of soil. Extra lift shall be measured in unit of 1.5 m or part thereof. Obvious lift shall only be measured ; that is lifts inherent in the lead due to ground slope shall not be measured except for lead up to 2.50 m.

When earth has to be carried over a bank/obstruction and dumped beyond it, the lift shall be difference in level between the centre of gravity of the excavated earth and the top of bank/construction.

5.3.6. Planking and Strutting

The planking and strutting required to uphold the face of excavated earth etc. shall be measured in square metres of face supported, and grouped ; separately in stages of 1.5 m.

The description shall include use and waste of all necessary timber work, including wales, struts and open or close poling boards, their fixing and subsequent removal.

Planking and strutting to the following shall be measured separately :

(*a*) Trenches ;

(*b*) Areas (the description shall include use and waste of raking shores) ; and

(*c*) Shafts, wells, cesspits, manholes and the like.

Where tightly driven close butt jointed sheeting is necessary as in the case of running sand, the item shall be measured separately and the packing of cavities behind sheeting with suitable material shall be included in description of the item. Planking and strutting required to be left permanently in position shall be measured separately.

5.3.7. Removing Trees and Hedges

Clearing of shrubs, brushwood, small trees not exceeding 30 cm girth shall be measured in square metres, and shall deem to include removal and disposal.

Cutting down hedges and removal of fences shall be fully described and measured in running metres and shall deem to include removal and disposal.

Cutting down trees of 30 cm girth and over up to 100 cm girth shall be enumerated as one item. The cutting down of trees exceeding 100 cm girth shall be enumerated stating the girth. The girth shall be measured at one metre above ground level. The item shall include lopping of branches and removal and disposal.

Digging out of roots including stacking shall be measured separately and enumerated.

5.4. FOUNDATIONS—PILE AND WELL

Description of Items. The description of each item shall, unless otherwise stated, be held to include where necessary, conveyance and delivery, handling, unloading, storing, fabrication, hoisting, all labour for finishing to required shape and size, setting, fitting and fixing in position, straight cutting and waste, return of packings, etc.

Measurements. All work shall be measured net in decimal system as fixed in its place as given below :

(*a*) Linear dimensions shall be measured to the nearest 0.01 m,

(*b*) Areas shall be worked out to the nearest 0.01 m^2, and

(*c*) Cubic contents shall be worked to the nearest 0.01 m^3.

A general description of the nature of the site shall be stated. The available information as to the strata through which the piles are to be driven shall be stated or reference showing records of bores be given. If piles are to be provided from any level other than ground level, it shall be stated. If the piling frame is to be lowered or raised, the exact height and nature of the working shall be described, separate items shall be provided for driving raker/ in groups/ isolated/lengthened/trial piles.

Items shall include any extra excavation filling and/or ramming required at the time of construction for the movement of piling frame for executing piling work. Bringing plant to the site and erecting it and dismantling and taking it back, shall be measured separately as lump sum items.

[**Note :** Shifting of plant at site of work shall be included in the item of piles.]

If load testing is to be done, the provision for such test shall be specified and measured separately.

5.4.1. Method of Measurement of Precast Reinforced Concrete Piles

The precast reinforced concrete piles shall be described according to grade of concrete, section and length, the extra strength of the heads being stated. Any requisite mould shall be included in the description as also the necessary strapping, bolts and lifting holes.

The cement concrete in piles shall be measured in cubic metres, arrived at by multiplying the cross-section area of the pile by the length of the pile as cast from the head of the pile to the tip of shoes. No deduction shall be made for chamfers, tapered points or the volume of reinforcement or holes for lifting piles.

The formwork, links and sleeves shall be included in the description of the item. The reinforcement shall be measured separately. The shoes for each size shall be enumerated separately stating the approximate mass.

Driving piles to a given level and redriving of lengthened piles shall be measured in running metres, separate measurements being made for piles of 5 m length and less and subsequently for every 1 m length range. The driving of piles shall be measured from the tip of the shoes to the ground level as shown in the drawings or as found at site at the time of driving. The raker piles shall be measured along the axis of the pile.

The measurement of handling transporting and pitching of piles shall be enumerated for each occasion. For stripping the heads of the piles, the length to be stripped shall be stated and measured per linear metre.

Stripping off the head of the piles for bond length shall be enumerated. When concrete piles are lengthened in position, after they have been lowered, the cement concrete when used for lengthening shall be measured as a separate item. This item should include the extra labour involved in stripping the exposed end to form connection of new with old work, and any excavation, if required.

5.4.2. Method of Measurement of Timber Piles

Timber piles shall be described and measured in running metre stating the species of timber and size of the pile. If over 5 m in length, the length extra over 5 m shall be measured in stages of one metre.

The diameter of the pile shall be arrived at by measuring girth at two metres below the large end of the piles. Any tolerance on the cross-sectional dimensions of the timber in permitting above or below those shown in drawings shall be specified. Shaping and shoeing of pile shall be enumerated stating the approximate weight of the shoe and size of the pile.

Handling, transporting and pitching of piles shall be enumerated for each occasion. Driving timber piles shall be measured from the tip of the shoe to ground level as shown in the drawings or as found at site at the time of driving. This item shall also include cutting the top of the pile and dressing it for fixing mild steel ring against splitting during driving. The supply and fixing of iron rings to the pile head before driving and also the labour involved in cutting off the ringed portion or any portion damaged in driving shall be included in the description of the item.

Joints in piles shall be described and enumerated.

5.4.3. Method of Measurement of Steel Sheet Piles (Permanent)

Supply only of sheet piles shall be measured by weight. The description of the item shall include the cross-sectional shape, nomenclature of manufacture, specification of material, details of fabrication such as lengthening by means of welding, riveting, drilling or burning holes, joining or fixing of structural rolled steel sections, handling and transportation to the site and the like. Piles exceeding 12 m long shall be described separately stating the lengths in further stages of 3 m. All struts, anchor bolts, anchor plates, turn buckles, waling etc. shall be measured separately.

When sheet piles are to be painted prior to driving, such painting shall be measured in square metres obtained by multiplying the length by the perimeter of the fabricated sheet pile measured along the profile. Description of the item shall include the method of preparation of surface, number of coats, mode of painting and the like.

Lifting, handling, pitching, engaging through interlocks or clutches of an adjacent sheet piles and driving shall be measured separately for each type in square metres obtained by multiplying the length of the embedded portion of the pile in soil and half of the perimeter as defined in IS : 2314—1963. The length of the embedded portion shall be obtained by measuring from the level of the ground where the tip of the sheet pile first touches before driving, to the ultimate level of the tip of the piles after driving.

Wherever sheet piles are to be driven under/in water necessitating use of special hammers and/or loader frames such piles shall be described and measured separately. Driving corner piles and junction piles shall be measured in running metres representing the length of embedment.

Cutting or bunring through steel piles shall be measured in running metres as extra over the pile. The disposal of cut length shall be described.

Extraction of piles shall be measured separately in square metres obtained by multiplying the embedded length in soil by the nominal width of piles from centre to centre of clutches. Operations such as lifting, handling and removing from site shall be described and included in the item.

5.4.4. Method of Measurement of Cast In-Situ Driven Concrete Piles

The description of the pile shall state the nominal diameter, grade of concrete, reinforcing bars, length of the cage.

Forming pile shafts including concrete, and driving casings to a given level shall be measured as one item in running metres.

Reinforcement including bars to be left in the pile cap for embedding shall be measured separately. The length of the cast in-situ piles shall be measured from the toe of the pile to the pile cut off level. The description of the pile shall state the diameter and type of casing, the grade of concrete, details of reinforcement of the core, and whether the casing is to be withdrawn or left in. The provision of pile shoes and the forming of enlarged bases shall be included in the item.

Empty boring shall be measured separately in running metres and the length shall be from working ground level to the cut off level of the pile. The type of the filling shall be stated.

5.4.5. Method of Measurement of Cast In-Situ Bored Reinforced Concrete Piles

Empty boring shall be measured separately in running metres and the length shall be from working level to the cut off level of the pile. The type of filling shall be stated. Concrete shall be measured separately in cubic metres from founding level to cut off level of the pile.

The boring through boulders and rock strata except in respect of isolated boulders not exceeding the diameter of the pile shaft shall be measured extra over. Reinforcement in pile including bars to be left in the pile cap for embedment shall be measured separately.

The description of the pile shall state the nominal diameter, grade of concrete, size of aggregate, the reinforcing bars, the length of cage, the provision of liners, if any. Permanent mild steel liners if provided shall be measured separately in weight. In case of under-reamed or bulb-based piles, the bulbs shall be measured and enumerated. The description of piles shall state the diameter of the bulb.

5.4.6. Method of Measurement of Reinforced Cement Concrete Sheet Piles

The reinforced cement concrete sheet piles shall be measured in cubic metres arrived at by multiplying the cross-section area of the pile by the length of the pile as cast from the head of the pile to the tip of the shoes.

The description of the item shall include the cross-sectional shape, grade of concrete, extra strength of the head. Any requisite mould shall be included in the description as also necessary strapping, holds and lifting holes.

Lifting, handling, pitching engaging through adjacent piles and driving shall be measured separately for each type in square metres obtained by multiplying the length of the embedded portion of the pile and half the parameter of the section. The length of the embedded portion shall be obtained by measuring from the level of the ground where the tip of the pile first touches before driving to the ultimate level of the tip of the piles after driving.

Wherever sheet piles are to be driven under/in water necessitating use of special hammers and/or loader frames such piles shall be described by measuring separately. Driving corner piles and junction piles shall be measured separately. Cutting piles shall be measured in running metres as extra over. The disposal of cut length shall be described. The extraction of piles other than due to defective driving shall be measured separately in square metres.

5.4.7. Method of Measurement of Timber Sheet Piles

The timber sheet piles shall be described and measured in running metres stating the species of timber and cross-section. Handling, transporting and pitching of piles shall be enumerated for each occasion.

Driving timber sheet piles shall be measured in square metres obtained by multiplying the length of the embedded portion of the pile in soil and half the parameter of the construction.

Whenever sheet piles are to be driven under/in water necessitating use of special hammers and/or loader frames such piles shall be described and measured separately.

The corner and junction piles shall be measured separately.

Cutting pile shall be measured in running metres as extra over. The disposal of cut length shall be described.

The extraction of piles other than due to defective driving shall be measured separately.

5.4.8. Method of Measurement of Board Precast Concrete Piles

The precast reinforced concrete piles shall be described according to grade of concrete, section and length, the extra strength of the heads being stated. Any requisite mould shall be included in the description as also the necessary strapping, bolts and lifting holes.

The cement concrete shall be measured separately in cubic metres arrived at multiplying the cross-sectional area of the pile by the length of pile as cast from head of the pile to the tip. No deduction shall be made for chamfers, tapered points or the volume of reinforcement on holes for lifting piles.

The formwork, links and sleeves should be included in description of the item. The reinforcement shall be measured separately. Placing pile shaft shall be measured in running metres from founding level to working level of the pile.

Empty boring shall be measured separately in running metres and the length shall be from working ground level to the cut off level of the pile. The boring through boulders and rock strata except in respect of isolated boulders not exceeding diameter of the pile shaft shall be made measured as extra over.

The measurement of handling, transporting and pitching of piles shall be enumerated for each occasion. For strapping the heads of the pile, the length to be stripped shall be stated and measured in running metres. Stripping off the heads of the pile for bond length shall be enumerated. Grouting shall be measured in cubic metre describing fully type and method.

5.5. WELL FOUNDATION

Description of Items. The description of each item shall, unless otherwise stated, be held to include where necessary, conveyance and delivery, handling, loading, unloading, storing, fabrication, hoisting, all labour for finishing to required shape and size, setting, fitting and fixing in position, straight cutting and waste.

Measurement. All work shall be measured net in decimal system as fixed in its place as given below :

(*a*) Linear dimensions shall be measured to the nearest 0.01 m,

(*b*) Areas shall be worked out to the nearest 0.01 m^2, and

(*c*) Cubic contents shall be worked to the nearest 0.01 m^3.

Removal of obstructions other than those requiring use of one-tonne-chisel for 24 hours during sinking operations shall be measured separately on the basis of quantum merit.

5.5.1. Well Sinking

The item of well sinking shall include use of kentiledge to the extent required for sinking and correcting the well in position. The provision of island, if required, shall be measured separately.

The sinking shall be measured in running metres stating the shape and size. For this purpose, the measurement shall be taken from the level at which the cutting edge is pitched to the level at which it rests finally.

[**Note :** The level of cutting edge shall be plane joining the lower most portion of the well curb, which cuts into the soil during sinking or acts as a penetration face.]

5.5.2. Steining and Curb

Concrete/brick work/stone masonry in the steining and concrete in top plug and curb shall be described and measured in cubic metres. The formwork shall be included in the item.

Concrete in the bottom plug including sump, if any, shall be measured on the basis of cement bags consumed. The filling in the well shall be measured in cubic metres stating the type of filling. Measurement for the reinforcement including mild steel bars, steel links, binders and steel plates shall be made separately.

Measurement for the steel cutting edge and steel armouring (if done) shall be made separately. Cutting off the extra height of steining where required shall be measured in cubic metres.

5.5.3. Pneumatic Sinking

Work executed under different working pressure range shall be measured separately. Pneumatic sinking shall be measured in running metres stating the size and shape. The depth of sinking shall be measured from the level at which air is introduced to the level at which air is stopped.

The following shall be measured separately :

(*a*) Bringing of and removing the pneumatic sinking plant from the site ;

(*b*) Use of this plant when fitted on well/when not fitted on well (to be measured separately) ;

(*c*) Fixing and removing of adopter and airlock ;

(*d*) Corbel slab ; and

(*e*) Keeping the well under pressure during plugging, guniting, repairing, inspection, testing but excluding sinking.

5.6. CONCRETE WORKS

Description of Items. The description of each item shall, unless otherwise stated, be held to include where necessary, conveyance and delivery, handling, unloading, storing, fabrication, lowering, hoisting, all labour for finishing to required shape and size, setting, fitting and fixing in position, straight cutting and waste, disposal of packing, etc.

Dimensions. Unless otherwise stated all work shall be measured net in decimal system as fixed in its place. Any work done extra over the specified dimensions shall be ignored. Dimensions shall be measured to nearest 0.01 m except for the thickness of slab which shall be measured to nearest 0.005 m.

Areas shall be worked out to nearest 0.01 m^3. Cubic contents shall be worked out to nearest 0.01 m^3. Cubic contents shall be worked out to nearest 0.01 m^3.

5.6.1. Lime Concrete and Mud Concrete

Works of lime concrete and mud concrete shall be fully described and measured in cubic metres.

5.6.2. Cement Concrete Works

Concrete works shall be measured under the following categories. Works in plain/reinforced/prestressed concrete shall each be measured separately. Works in precast and cast *in-situ* concrete shall be kept separate :

(*a*) Bridges ; (*b*) Dams and spillways ;

(*c*) Barrages and weirs ; (*d*) Canal works ;

(*e*) Tunnels and shafts ; (*f*) Harbour, docks and marine works ;

(*g*) Special structures, such as power house, overhead water reservoir, chimneys and shafts, towers, silos and similar other structures ;

(*h*) Buildings.

Units of Measurement—Unless otherwise stated all concrete work shall be measured in cubic metres.

Formwork—Unless otherwise stated formwork shall be measured separately in accordance with Section 8.

Finishes—Fair finishing of exposed surfaces, of concrete including backing or roughening surfaces of concrete shall be included in the description. Special finishes other than those obtained through formwork shall be so described and measured separately in square metres.

Reinforcement—Unless otherwise stated reinforcement shall be measured separately. Where concrete and reinforcement are measured as a composite item they shall be fully described indicating that supply of reinforcement is included in the item ; in such cases items identical in other respects but varying in reinforcement shall be measured separately.

Special Concrete—Concrete processed in special manner, such as cooled, heated, cellular, expansive and heat resisting shall be fully described and measured separately.

All plain, rebated, grooved, locking and tongued joints shall be included in the description.

No deductions shall be made for the following :

(*a*) Ends of dissimilar materials, for example, beams, posts, girders, rafters, purlins, trusses, corbels and steps up to 500 cm^2 in cross-section ;

(*b*) Opening up to 0.1 m^2 or as specified ;

(*c*) Volume occupied by reinforcement ;

(*d*) Volume occupied by pipes, conduits, sheathing, etc., not exceeding 100 cm^2 each in cross-sectional area or as specified ;

(*e*) Small voids, such as the shaded portions in Fig. 5.1, when these do not exceed 40 cm^2 each in cross-section ;

(*f*) Moulds, drip moulding, chamfers, splays rounded or covered angles, beds, grooves and rebates up to 10 cm in girth ; and

(g) Stops, mitres, returns, rounded ends, junctions, dishings, etc. in connection with linear or super labours.

[**Note :** In calculating area of an opening, the thickness of any separate lintel or sill shall be included in the height. No extra labour for forming such openings or voids shall be measured.]

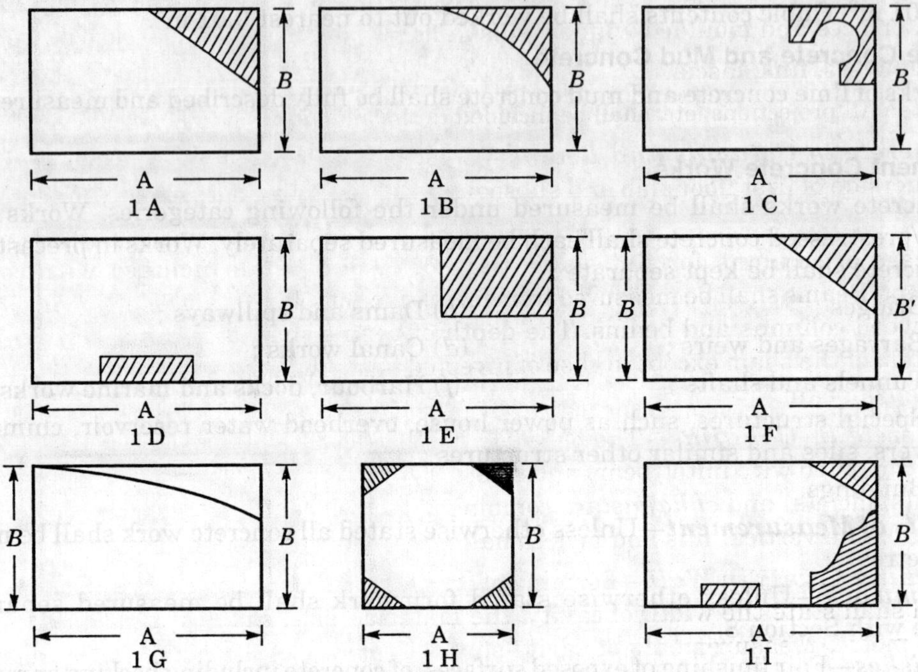

Fig. 5.1. Shaded Portion Showing Small Voids.

5.6.3. Reinforced/Plain Cement Concrete (Cast *In-Situ*)

Concrete cast *in-situ* shall be classified as follows :

(a) Foundations, footings, bases for columns ;

(b) Walls (any thickness) including attached pilasters, buttresses, plinth and string courses, fillets, etc ;

(c) Slabs, supported on wall/beams/columns, landings, balconies, canopies, bridge slabs ;

(d) Slabs other than those specified in (c) ;

(e) *Chhajjas* including portions bearing on the wall ;

(f) Lintels, shelves, beams and bressumers ;

(g) Columns, piers, abutments, pillars, posts and struts ;

(h) Staircase including stringer beams but excluding landings ;

(i) Balustrades, newels and railing ;

(j) Spiral staircases (including landing) ;

(k) Arches ;

(l) Domes, vaults ;

(m) Shell roof, arch rib and folded plates ;

(n) Chimneys and shafts ;

(o) Canal lining ;

(*p*) Ballast walls, retaining walls, return walls ;

(*q*) Concrete filling to precast components ;

(*r*) Kerbs, steps and the like ;

(*s*) String or lacing courses, parapets, copings, bed block, anchor blocks, plain, window sills and the like ;

(*t*) Cornices and moulded window sills ; and

(*u*) Louvers, fins, fascia.

[**Note :** All projections, etc. shall be included in the main items.]

Concrete in Columns and Beams—Columns shall be measured from top of column base to underside of first floor slab and subsequently from top of floor slab to underside of floor slab above.

In case of columns for flat slabs, flare of column shall included with column for measurement. Beams shall be measured from face to face of columns and shall include haunches, if any, between columns and beams. The depth of beams shall be measured from bottom of slab to bottom of the beam except in case of inverted beam where it shall be measured from top of slab to top of beam.

Concrete in Chhajjas—The *chhajjas* shall be measured inclusive of bearing. When *chhajjas* is combined with lintel, beam and slab, it shall be measured as clear portion. Whenever vertical fin(s)/facia(s) and *chhajjas* are combined, *chhajjas* shall be measured clear between fin(s)/facia(s). The vertical fins and facies shall be measured through.

Forming Cavity in Wall—Forming of cavity shall be measured in square metres. The description shall state the width of cavity, the material, size, shape of tics and their number per square metre. Measurements of cavity shall be taken along a plane at centre of cavity ; deduction being made for all openings and solid portion of walls.

Labour and material for closing cavities at the jambs, sills and heads of openings shall be described and measured separately in running metres. Items shall include use of cores for keeping cavity clear, uniform, and forming the requisite weep and vent holes.

Concrete Casing to Beams and Steel Stanchions—Concrete casing to steel joists or beams, steel stanchions, etc., shall be measured in cubic metres. Volume occupied by joists shall not be deducted except in the case of boxed stanchions or girders, in which case boxed portion only shall be deducted.

Surface Channels—Concrete in channel shall be measured in cubic metres. Volume of channel shall be deducted from the concrete. Where shape of cross-section is round, elliptical or oval ; area of section shall be taken as three-fourth of the width at top, multiplied by average depth at centre.

Forming channels in concrete shall be measured in running metres and inner girth stated. Channel, finished fair or formed in spade finish to receive lining of brick, concrete or stone, etc., shall be measured separately.

Reinforced/Plain Concrete—Precast. Precast concrete works shall include use of mould, finishing face and supply of reinforcement as described. Mix and ingredients of setting mortar, providing and fixing inserts, if required, for fixing at site and finishing shall be stated. Alternatively, reinforcement may be measured separately. Unless otherwise stated hoisting and setting in position shall be included in item. The work shall be classified and measured as indicated in Table 5.4. Each item of work shall be fully described.

Table 5.4. Measurement Reinforced/Plain Concrete—Precast Component

S. No.	*Classification*	*Method of Measurement*
1.	Wall panel, floor/roof slabs	In square metres
2.	Beams unit and columns, trusses etc.	In running metres or numbers
3.	Channel unit and purlins	In running metres or numbers
4.	String or lacing courses, copings, bed plates, anchor blocks, plain window sills, shelves louvers, steps, staircases, etc.	In running metres or numbers
5.	Kerbs edgings, etc.	In running metres or numbers
6.	Solid blockwork	In cubic metres or square metres
7.	Hollow blockwork	In cubic metres or square metres
8.	Light weight partitions	In square metres stating the thickness
9.	Door/window frames	In running metres stating the size
10.	Waffle units	In square metres or numbers
11.	Water tank	In numbers
12.	*Jallies*	In square metres of opening fitted stating thickness
13.	Fencing posts	In numbers or cubic metres
14.	Folded slab	In cubic metres.

Plain and moulded work shall be measured separately. Any finishing work on precast component shall be fully described and measured separately in square metres.

Fencing Posts—Concrete fencing posts, corner posts straining or terminal posts and struts shall be classified according to size as follows :

(*a*) Those having an average sectional area not exceeding 100 cm^2,

(*b*) Those having an average sectional area exceeding 100 cm^2 but not exceeding 250 cm^2, and

(*c*) Those of an average area over 250 cm^2.

The item shall include forming of chamfered or rounded angles, and flat splayed, rounded or mitred tops. Holes for wire or nails and/or building in fastenings shall also be included.

Prestressed Concrete—*Cast In-Situ*. Prestressed concrete work cast *in-situ* shall be fully described. Concrete in structural members, such as columns, beams and slabs shall each be measured separately.

Members cast in sections (that is not in one continuous operation) shall be fully described. Forming and grouting or sealing ducts or grooves shall be measured in running metres fully describing size and other particulars of sleeves (or sheating), temporary supports required in formation of ducts and composition of grout.

Forming and grouting the air-holes at ends middle or sides or any other position of ducts shall be included in the description of item. Filling in the jacking or anchoring recesses shall be described stating finish to exposed surface or filling and measured separately in cubic metres.

Supplying, fixing and tensioning steel wire/strands/or cables (measured between anchorages) shall be measured in kilograms stating ultimate strength and proof stress and size of wire or cable. Each size shall be measured separately. No allowance shall be made for extra lengths in anchorages or elsewhere. The number of stands in each cable, type of central core, and type of sheathing, if any, on wires shall be stated. Degreasings, straightening, cutting to lengths and assembling wires and cables, cones, wedges anchor-plates, spacers, distance pieces and other expandable items shall be deemed to be included with main item.

Prestressed Concrete—Precast. Prestressed concrete precast works shall be fully described. Formwork or moulds for precast units and for forming anchorage pockets shall be deemed to be included with items.

Precast units shall be enumerated stating number, size, length, method of fixing and bedding. Unless otherwise stated, hoisting, transportation, assembly and setting in position shall be included in item. The classification shall be as follows :

(*a*) Pre-tensioned in the mould ;

(*b*) Post-tensioned on ground after casting ;

(*c*) Cast in section, assembled and post-tensioned before erection ;

(*d*) Post-tensioned after hoisting but capable of self-support ;

(*e*) Cast in sections for assembly *in-situ* and post-tensioned after erection ; and

(*f*) Post-tensioned after hoisting but requiring support until tensioning is completed.

Cores, wires, strands and cables for post-tension members shall be measured as above. In case of pre-tension members, these items shall be included in the main item.

5.6.4. Miscellaneous Items

Expansion Joints—Expansions joints in floors, roofs and walls shall be described as including all formwork and labour necessary to form joint and shall be measured in running metres stating depth and width of joint. Alternatively, these may be measured in square metre stating the width of the joint.

Material used in filling and or for covering shall be fully described and measured separately in running metres. Where sheet of copper, brass, aluminium or of any other material is used, it shall be fully described and measured in running metres.

Damp-proof course in concrete shall be described and measured in square metres stating thickness. Item shall include formwork and fair finish to edges and also levelling and preparing of brickwork or stone masonry to receive damp-proof course. Horizontal and vertical damp-proof courses shall each be measured separately.

Waterproofing Concrete—Waterproofing material used for waterproofing of concrete shall be described stating quantity of material to be used and measured separately in litres or kilograms. Surface treatment of concrete shall be measured in square metres stating number of coats or dressings and proportion of waterproofing material to water.

Guniting—Guniting shall be fully described and finished surface measured in square metres.

Pack/Pressure Grouting

Grout holes—The length of grout holes drilled either for pack grouting or pressure grouting through concrete shall be measured in running metres. Grout holes drilled through plate steel liners shall, however, be enumerated separately.

Grout pipes and fittings—Grout pipes and fittings provided for grouting shall be meas-ured in kilograms and weight of all pipes and fittings shall be derived either by actual weighment or from known weights and lengths.

Water pressure testing—Measurement for water pressure testing shall, where necessary, be made separately for each hole and enumerated. Measurement for grouting shall be made on basis of the weight of cement in grout actually forced into holes. Stone dust and other additions, if used, shall be measured separately in loose dry state before mixing and shall be measured by boxes of approved size and design.

Grouting Stanchion Bases—Cement grouting under plates of stanchion or precast con-crete column or steel grillages shall be measured in square metres and its mix stated.

Holding Down Bolts—Grouting in of holding down bolts and the temporary boxings or wedges to form holes for the same shall be enumerated. Depth and height of the hole and mix shall be stated and grouting included in description.

Cutting in Concrete—Work involving cutting, or sinking into existing concrete shall be classified as follows :

(*a*) Grooves, chases and like shall he measured in running metres stating girth ; and

(*b*) Holes, mortices and openings shall be measured per centimetre of depth of cutting and shall be classified as follows :

(1) Up to 250 cm^2 in area, and

(2) Exceeding 250 cm^2 and up to and including 0.1 m^2 area.

[**Note :** Area shall be reckoned as the net area required and not necessarily the area actually cut.]

Cutting opening exceeding 0.1 m^2 in area shall be measured in cubic metre and items shall include provision for fixing and removal of existing support and temporary support. Cutting of existing reinforced cement concrete surfaces and exposing reinforcement without damaging the same shall be measured in square metres stating depth.

Toothing and Bonding—Where new concrete walls are bonded to existing walls an item of labour and material in cutting, toothing and bonding shall be measured in square metres.

5.7. BRICK WORK

Measurement. All work shall be measured net in the decimal system, as fixed in place, as given below :

(*a*) Dimension shall be measured to the metres 0.01 m,

(*b*) Areas shall be worked out to the nearest 0.01 m^2, and

(*c*) Cubic contents shall be worked out to the nearest 0.01 m^3.

Description of Item. Description of each item shall, unless otherwise stated, be held to include, where necessary, conveyance, delivery, handling, unloading, storing, waste, return of packings, necessary scaffolding, tools and tackle.

Waste. All measurements of cuttings shall, unless otherwise stated, be deemed to include consequent waste.

Deduction. Where minimum area is defined for deduction of an opening, void or both, such area shall refer only to opening or void within the space measured.

5.7.1. Brickwork—General

Bricks and mortar to be used for brickwork shall be fully described. Where it is proposed to specify a bond other than English bond, it shall be so stated. The item of general brickwork, shall be deemed to include the following :

(*a*) Raking out joints for plastering or for pointing done as a separate process or finishing joints flush as work proceeds ;

(*b*) Preparing tops of existing walls and the like for raising ;

(*c*) Rough cutting and waste for forming gables, cores of arches, splays at eaves and the like and all rough cutting in the body of brickwork, unless otherwise stated ;

(*d*) Plumbing to angles ;

(*e*) Forming reveals to jambs where fair cutting on exposed faces is not involved ;

(*f*) Leaving holes for pipes, etc ;

(*g*) Building-in holdfasts, air bricks, fixing bricks, etc. ;

(*h*) Building-in ends of beams, joists, slabs, lintels, sills, trusses, etc.

(*i*) Forming openings and flues for which no deduction is made.

(*j*) Bedding wall plates, lintels, sills, roof tiles, corrugated sheets, etc. in or on walls, if not covered in respective trade, and

(*k*) Leaving chases of section not exceeding 50 cm in girth.

Following categories of brickwork shall be included with general brickwork.

(*a*) Footings ;

(*b*) Battered (measured net). Battered surfaces shall, however, be measured separately in square metres as an extra-over ;

(*c*) Eaves or beam fillings, no deduction being made for joists, etc ;

(*d*) Brickwork (excluding refractory brickwork) in chimney breasts, chimney stacks, smoke or air flues (except independent chimney shaft as in factories for steam boilers) ; and

(*e*) Pilasters, plain copings and sills.

[**Note :** In the case of receding courses of panels, recess shall not be deducted.]

5.7.2. Measurement

Brickwork shall generally be measured in cubic metres, unless otherwise stated. Walls one brick thick and less shall each be measured separately in square metres stating thickness.

Walls exceeding one brick thick but not exceeding three bricks in thickness shall be measured in multiples of half-brick which shall be deemed to be inclusive of mortar joints. Where fractions of half-brick occur due to architectural or other reasons, measurement shall be taken as follows :

(*a*) Up to ¼ brick—actual measurement, and

(*b*) Exceeding ¼ brick—full half-brick.

For walling which is more than three bricks in thickness actual thickness of wall shall be measured. No deductions or additions shall be made on any account for the following :

(*a*) Ends of dissimilar materials (that is, joists, beams, lintels, posts, girders, rafters, purlins, trusses, corbels, steps, etc.) ; up to 0.1 m^2 in section ;

(*b*) Opening up to 0.1 m^2 in area (see Note) ;

(*c*) Wall plates, bed plates, and bearing of slabs, *chhajjas* and the like, where thickness does not exceed 10 cm and bearing does not extend over the full thickness of wall ;

(*d*) Cement concrete blocks as for holdfasts and holding down bolts ;

(*e*) Iron fixtures, such as wall ties, pipes up to 300 mm diameter and holdfasts for doors and windows ; and

(*f*) Chases of section not exceeding 50 cm in girth.

[**Note :** In calculating area of an opening, any separate lintel or sills shall be included with the size of the opening but end portions of lintel shall be excluded and extra width of rebated reveals, if any, shall also be excluded.]

Fireplaces, Chimneys, etc.—Brickwork (excluding, refractory brickwork) in chimney breasts, chimney stacks, smoke or air flues not exceeding 0.2 m^2 in sectional area shall be measured as solid, and no extra measurement shall be made for pargetting and coring such flues. Where flues exceed 0.2 m^2 in sectional area, deduction shall be made for the same, and pargetting and coring flues measured in running metres, stating size of flue. Apertures for fireplaces, shall not be deducted and no extra labour shall be measured for splaying of jambs and throating.

Pillars /Columns—Pillars, shall be fully described and measured in cubic metres. Where pillars of different sections and shapes are involved their numbers shall be stated in addition in each case. Pillars shall be measured and kept separate as under :

(*a*) Rectangular or polygonal on plan,

(*b*) Curved on plan to any radius, and

(*c*) Any other type.

[**Note :** Rectangular pillar/column shall mean a detached masonry portion such that its breadth does not exceed 3 times its thickness and thickness itself does not exceed 3-brick lengths.]

5.7.3. Circular Brickwork

Brickwork circular on plan to a mean radius not exceeding 6 m shall be measured separately and shall include all cutting and waste and templates. Brickwork circular on plan to a mean radius exceeding 6 m shall be measured separately and included with general brickwork.

5.7.4. Backing to Masonry

Brickwork in backing to masonry shall be measured separately stating average thickness ; description shall include all cutting and waste for bonding.

5.7.5. Honeycomb Brickwork

Honeycomb brick walling shall be measured in square metres stating thickness and pattern of honeycombing. Honeycomb opening shall not be deducted.

5.7.6. Independent Chimney Shafts

Brickwork in independent chimney shafts (as for large steam boilers) shall be measured not inclusive of all cutting, waste and templates and kept under the following categories :

(*a*) Rectangular on plan,

(*b*) Polygonal on plan, and

(*c*) Curved on plan to any radius.

Height of chimney from ground/datum line shall be stated.

5.7.7. Cavity Walls

Forming of cavity shall be measured in square metres stating-width of cavity and shall include ties and their number per square metre. Material, size and shape of ties shall be described. Measurement of cavity shall be taken along a plane at centre of cavity, deduction being made for all openings and solid portions of walls.

Labour and material for closing cavities at jambs, sills and heads of openings shall be described and measured separately in running metres. Use of cores for keeping cavity clear and forming requisite weep and vent holes shall be described.

5.7.8. Reinforced Brickwork

Reinforced brickwork shall be measured and kept separate from general brickwork and unless otherwise stated, reinforcement shall be measured separately.

5.7.9. Brick Nogging

Brickwork above one brick in thickness shall be included with general brickwork, brickwork one brick and less in thickness shall be measured. Dimensions shall be measured overall. Timber work shall be measured separately.

5.7.10. Brickwork with Fair Face or Architectural Appearance

Brickwork with fair face or architectural appearance shall be measured separately.

5.7.11. Brickwork in Arches, Vaults or Staircases

Brickwork in arches, vaults or staircases shall be measured separately ; work in selected uncut bricks and in purpose made or fair cut and rubbed bricks shall be so described and measured separately and shall include centering for spans up to 2 m. For spans exceeding 2 m, centering shall be measured separately. Cutting to skews shall be included in the description.

5.7.12. Underpinning

Brickwork in underpinning shall be measured separately and an item for extra labour and material in wedging up on top of underpinning shall be measured in square metres as length multiplied by width of top course.

5.7.13. Fair Cutting of Brickwork

Fair cutting exceeding 10 cm in width or in girth in splayed angles weatherings, cornices, quoins, etc. (where purpose-made bricks are not used), shall be measured separately in square metres. Fair cutting not exceeding 10 cm in width or girth, such as in splays and chamfers, shall be measured in running metres, stating width/ girth. Circular fair cutting shall be measured separately in square metres.

5.7.14. Brick Edgings

Brick edgings, as to roads and the like, shall be described and measured in running metres.

5.7.15. Filleting

Filleting in Mortar, as in flashings on roofs, shall be described and measured in running metres stating shape and sectional area of fillets.

5.7.16. Broken Glass Coping

Broken glass coping laid along with brickwork shall be measured in square metres and described stating thickness of mortar and weight of broken glass per square metre of coping.

5.7.17. Damp-Proof Courses

Damp-proof course shall be described and measured in square metres stating thickness. Description shall include levelling up and/or preparing brickwork to receive the treatment and use and waste of form work, if required. Vertical and horizontal damp-proof courses shall be measured separately.

5.7.18. Brickwork Around Steel Joists (Encasing)

Encasing brickwork to steel joists or beams, steel stanchions, etc. shall be measured in cubic metres. Volume occupied by joists shall not be deducted except in case of boxed stanchions or girders in which case box portion only shall be deducted. Extra labour in cutting and fitting brickwork around steel joists, stanchions, girders, etc., shall be measured separately in square metres of finished surfaces.

5.7.19. Sills, Cornices, etc.

Plain corbels, string courses, aprons, friezes, sills, cornices, drip courses, oversailing courses, and other projections, etc. of splayed, bullnosed or any other type of purpose-made or cut bricks shall be fully described and measured in running metres stating depth and width of projection. No deduction shall be made from masonry of wall for the bearing portion of drip course, bearing of moulding and cornice.

5.7.20. Brick Tile Work

Brick tile work shall be measured separately and the rules for measuring ordinary brickwork shall be followed.

5.7.21. Chases, Rebates, etc.

Cutting chases, rebates, throatings, grooves, etc., in brickwork shall be measured in running metres stating girth and classified as follows :

(*a*) Not exceeding 10 cm in girth, and

(*b*) Exceeding 10 cm but not exceeding 20 cm in girth.

Chases, rebates, etc. exceeding 20 cm in girth shall be measured in square metres (girth × length).

5.7.22. Cutting Holes

Cutting holes through brickwork including making good shall be measured per centimetre of depth of cutting and shall be classified as follows :

(*a*) Holes not exceeding 400 cm^2 in area, and

(*b*) Holes exceeding 100 cm^2 and not exceeding 0.1 m^2 in area.

5.7.23. Cutting Openings

Cutting openings exceeding 0.1 m^2 in area in walls one brick thick and less shall be measured in square metres and in walls exceeding one brick thick shall be measured in cubic metres.

5.7.24. Toothing and Bonding

Where new walls are bonded to existing walls, an item of labour and material in cutting, toothing and bonding shall be measured in square metres of vertical face in contact with new work only.

5.8. STONE MASONRY

Measurements. All work shall be measured net in decimal system, as fixed in its place, unless otherwise stated herein as given below :

(*a*) Dimensions shall be measured to the nearest 0.01 m,

(*b*) Areas shall be worked out to the nearest 0.01 m^2, and

(*c*) Cubic contents shall be worked out to the nearest 0.01 m^3.

Description of Item. Description of each item shall, unless otherwise stated, be held to include, conveyance, delivery, handling, unloading, storing, waste, return of packings, scaffolding, tools and tackle, as necessary.

Waste. All measurements of cutting shall, unless otherwise stated, be deemed to include consequent waste.

Deduction. Where minimum area is defined for deduction of an opening, void, or both, such area shall refer only to opening or void within the space measured.

5.8.1. Walling

Type of stone, kind of walling and mix of mortar shall be described. Item of general walling shall be deemed to include the following :

(*a*) Bond stones ;

(*b*) Raking out joints for plastering or for pointing, done as a separate process or finishing joints flush as work proceeds ;

(*c*) Preparing top of existing wall and the like for raising ;

(*d*) Rough cutting and waste for forming gables, cores of arches, splays at eaves and the like and all rough cutting in the body of walling ;

(*e*) Leaving holes for pipes and similar items ;

(*f*) Building-in holdfasts, air bricks, fixing bricks, etc. ;

(*g*) Bedding wall plates, lintels, sills, roof tiles, corrugated sheets, etc., in or on walls, if not covered in respective trade ;

(*h*) Building-in-ends of joists, beams, lintels, etc., and making good ; and

(*i*) Forming openings and flues for which no deduction is made.

Random or uncoursed rubble walling brought up to courses shall be measured separately stating minimum and maximum heights of courses. In case of coursed work, height of course shall be stated, if regularly diminished, it shall be so described stating maximum and minimum heights of courses.

Stone walling circular on plan to a mean radius not exceeding 6 m shall be measured separately and shall include all cutting and waste and templates. Stone walling circular on plan to a mean radius exceeding 6 m shall be measured net and included with general walling. The following classes of work shall be included with general walling :

(*a*) Footings ;

(*b*) Battered stone masonry (measured net). Battered surfaces shall, however, be measured separately in square metres as an extra over.

(*c*) Eaves or beam filling, no deduction being made for joists, rafters, etc. ;

(*d*) Stone walling in chimney breasts, chimney stacks ; smoke or air flues ; and

(*e*) Plasters.

5.8.2. Measurement

Except where otherwise stated, stone masonry generally shall be measured in cubic metres and face work in square metres. No deduction or addition shall be made for the following :

(*a*) Ends of dissimilar materials (that is, joists, beams, lintels, posts, girders, rafters, purlins, trusses, corbels, steps, etc.) up to 0.1 m^2 in section ;

(*b*) Openings up to 0.1 m^2 in area (*see* Note) ;

(*c*) Wall plates, bed plates, and bearing of slabs, *chhajjas* and the like, where thickness does not exceed 10 cm and bearing does not extend over the full thickness of wall ;

(*d*) Cement concrete blocks for holdfasts, holding-down bolts and the like ; and

(*e*) Iron fixtures, such as wall ties, pipes up to 300 mm diameter and holdfasts for doors and windows.

[**Note :** In calculating area of an opening, any separate lintel or sill shall be included with the size of the opening but end portions of lintel shall be excluded and extra width of rebated reveals, if any, shall also be excluded.]

Fireplaces, Chimneys etc.—Stone walling in chimney breasts, chimney stacks, with smoke or air flue(s) not exceeding 0.20 m^2 each in sectional area shall be measured as solid, and no extra measurement shall be taken for pargetting and coring such flue(s). Where flue(s) exceed 0.20 m^2 in sectional area, deduction shall be made for the same and pargetting and coring flue(s) shall be measured in running metres stating size(s) of flue(s). Aperture for fireplace shall not be deducted and no extra labour shall be measured for splaying of jambs and throating.

Pillars/Columns. Pillars/columns shall be fully described and measured in cubic metres. These shall be measured in the following categories :

(*a*) Rectangular or polygonal on plan,

(*b*) Curved on plan to any radius, and

(*c*) Any other type.

[**Note :** Rectangular pillar/column shall mean a detached masonry portion such that its breadth does not exceed 3 times its thickness and thickness itself does not exceed 60 cm.]

5.8.3. Stone Nogging

Stone nogging shall be measured in square metres, stating thickness of wall and shall include face work to both sides. Dimensions shall be measured overall.

5.8.4. Stone Masonry in Arches and Vaults

Stone work in rough arches and vaults shall be described and measured separately and shall include centering for spans up to 2 m. For spans exceeding 2 m, centering shall be measured separately. Facings to arches shall be measured separately.

5.8.5. Underpinning

Stone walling in underpinning shall be measured separately and an item for extra labour and material in wedging up on top of underpinning with thin slabs or slates shall be measured in square metres (as length multiplied by width of top course).

5.8.6. Levelling Up

Levelling up of uncoursed random walling for damp-proof courses, band courses, and the like shall be measured separately in square metres and the material, such as concrete or mortar to be used in levelling up shall be described.

5.8.7. Facings

If facing stones are the same as those used in body of walling, additional work involved in dressing stones shall be described as 'extra over' walling. If stones are to be dressed on beds and joints, it shall be so stated. If facing stones are different from those used in body of walling, facings may be stated as 'stone and labour in facing'. Type of such facing and average bed shall be described, and bonders, if any, shall also be described and number per square metre stated. Bonding to stone walling and to brick work shall be measured separately. In case of circular facings, not exceeding 6 m radius on plan, radius shall be stated. Circular facing exceeding 6 m radius on plan shall be included with general facing.

5.8.8. Arches in Facings

Dressing to arches in faced work shall be measured in square metres, measured on face and exposed soffit ; rise of arch and width of soffit shall be stated and joints described. In case of arches in random rubble, cutting of skewbacks and over and under a arches shall be included with the item. Cutting over arches, skewbacks, etc., in superior type of facework shall be measured separately in running metres.

5.8.9. Angles in Facings

External angles in facings shall be measured in running metres and if quoin stones are larger than general facing stones, their average size shall be stated. If edge margins of quoin stones are drafted, this shall be described stating width of drafting. Squints, birds-mouths, splayed or rounded angles and the like shall each be measured separately in running metres stating width of splay or girth of rounded angle. Squints, birds-mouths and external and internal angles to battered facings shall each be measured separately in running metres ; if quoin stones to battered facings have horizontal joints, these shall be so described.

5.8.10. Chases, Rebates, etc.

Cutting chases, rebates, throatings, grooves, etc., in walling shall be measured in running metres stating girth and classified according to girth as follows except in case of throating which shall be measured separately :

(*a*) Not exceeding 10 cm in girth, and

(*b*) Exceeding 10 cm but not exceeding 20 cm in girth.

Chases, rebate, etc. exceeding 20 cm in girth, shall be measured in square metres (girth multiplied by length).

5.8.11. Cutting Holes

Cutting holes through walling and making good shall be measured per centimetre of depth of cutting and shall be classified as follows :

(*a*) Holes not exceeding 400 cm^2 in area, and

(*b*) Holes exceeding 400 cm^2 and not exceeding 0.1 m^2 in area.

5.8.12. Cutting Openings

Cutting openings exceeding 0.1 m^2 in area shall be measured in cubic metres.

5.8.13. Toothing and Bonding

Where new walls are bonded to existing walls, an item of labour and material in cutting, toothing and bonding shall be measured in square metres of surface in contact with new work only. Spacing and size of toothings required to be cut in the existing work shall be described.

5.8.14. Dressed Stonework

Stonework as in sills, steps, string courses, cornices, columns, caps, copings, lintels, etc. shall each be measured in cubic metres. Type of dressing shall be described and measured in square metres as extra over. Dressed stonework as in *chhajjas, jallies*, shelves and the like shall be described as measured in square metres (inclusive of bearing). Each stone shall be measured as smallest rectangular block from which finished dressed stone can be worked.

5.8.15. Additional Labour in Dressed Stonework

The following labours shall be measured separately in square metres when exceeding 10 cm in girth or width and in running metres if not exceeding 10 cm in girth or width, unless included in the main item :

(*a*) Sunk work to faces, beds and joints as in arches, voussoirs and key blocks, splays, batters, weatherings, etc.; and

(*b*) Moulded work as in cornices (girth of moulding measured).

The following labours shall be measured separately in running metres, when not exceeding 10 cm in width or girth, unless included in the main item :

(*a*) Chamfers, arises, or splays not exceeding 1.5 cm in width ;

(*b*) Chamfers, arises, or splays exceeding 1.5 cm but not exceeding 10 cm in width ;

(*c*) Rounded bullnoze-angles or mouldings or hollow angles ;

(*d*) Rebates, grooves (square, hollow or dove-tailed) in facework ;

(*e*) Rebates, grooves (square, hollow or dove-tailed) for joints, tongues of sills, etc. ; and

(*f*) Cutting chisel drafted margin.

Drilling or cutting holes shall be enumerated stating diameter of hole and its depth. Cutting rectangular or dove-tailed mortice in dressed stones shall be enumerated stating size in cubic centimetres ; and running with cement or lead shall be described.

5.8.16. Stops, Mitres, etc.

Stops, mitres and returned ends shall be described and enumerated.

5.8.17. Figures, Letters, etc.

Curved figures, letters, etc. shall be described and enumerated stating dimensions.

5.8.18. Boulder Work

Boulder work shall be measured in cubic metres stating size of boulders and classified as follows :

(*a*) Boulder filling dry hand-packed,

(*b*) Boulder walling dry, and

(*c*) Boulder walling in mortar stating mix of mortar.

5.9. FORMWORK

Description of Items. The description of each item shall, unless stated otherwise, be held to include where necessary, conveyance and delivery, handling, loading, unloading, storing, fabrication, hoisting, lowering all labour for finishing to required shape and size, and levels of striking and removal.

Measurements. All works shall be measured net in decimal system, as fixed in its place as given below :

(*a*) Dimensions shall be measured to the nearest 0.01 m.

(*b*) Areas shall be worked out to the nearest 0.01 m^2.

5.9.1. Description of Formwork

The formwork shall include the following :

(*a*) Splayed edges, notchings, allowance for overlaps and passings at angles, sheathing battens, strutting, bolting, nailing, wedging, casing, striking and removal ;

(*b*) All supports, struts, braces, wedges as well as mud sills, piles or other suitable arrangements to support the formwork ;

(*c*) Bolts, wire ties, clamps, spreaders, nails or any other items to hold the sheathing together ;

(*d*) Working, scaffolds, ladder, gangways, and similar items ;

(*e*) Filleting to form stop-chamfered edge or splayed external angles not exceeding 20 mm wide to beams, columns and the like ;

(*f*) If required, temporary opening in the forms for pouring concrete, inserting vibrators, and cleaning holes for moving rubbish from the interior of the sheathing before pouring concrete ;

(*g*) Dressing with oil to prevent adhesion ; and

(*h*) Raking of circular cutting.

5.9.2. Type of Formwork

Separate items shall be provided for formwork with type of contact surface, such as :

(*a*) wrought formwork (that i3, sheathing having planed surface or sawn timber) ;

(*b*) sheathing formed from tongued and grooved boards ;

(*c*) sheathing having plywood lining ;

(*d*) sheathing having special lining or any other arrangement to give extra smooth finish or texture or decorative surface for architectural concrete ;

(*e*) sheathing of steel sheeting, tubing or other varieties ; and

(*f*) slip from technique extrusion process.

5.9.3. Classification

Formwork shall be generally classified as follows and measured separately, unless specified otherwise :

(*a*) Foundation, footings, bases of columns, etc. ; and mass concrete ;

(*b*) Flat surfaces, such as soffits of floors, roofs landing and the like ; where floors exceed 200 mm in thickness the formwork shall be measured separately stating the thickness ;

(*c*) Vertical surfaces, such as walls, partitions and the like, including attached pilasters, butteresses, plinth and string courses and the like, etc. ;

(*d*) Sloping or battering surfaces, including folded plates ;

(*i*) Where inclination to horizontal plane does not exceed 30° (requiring shuttering only on the underside) ;

(*ii*) Where inclination to horizontal plane exceeds 30° (where shuttering may be provided both on underside and upperside, if required) (only underside area to be measured) ;

(*e*) *Arches* (*i*) up to 6 m span (*ii*) above 6 m span

(*f*) *Cylindrical Shells (Area of Underside to be Measured)*

(*i*) Radius less than 3 m (*ii*) Radius above 3 m

(*g*) Wafle or ribbed slabs where shuttering is required for bottom inclined surface ;

(*h*) Dormer vaults and shell roofs having curved surfaces in both directions (only the area of underside shall be measured) ;

(*i*) Sides and soffits of beams, beam haunchings, cantilevers, griders, bressumers and lintels ; beams and girders 1 m deep and over shall be measured separately ;

(*j*) Sides of columns, piers, pillars, posts and stanchions and struts (square/rectangular/polygonal/circular/curved to be measured separately) ;

(*k*) Edges of slabs and breaks in floors and walls (to be measured in running metres where under 200 mm width or thickness) ;

(*l*) Cornices and mouldings ;

(*m*) Small surfaces, such as cantilever ends, brackets and ends of steps, caps and bases to pilasters and columns and the like ;

(*n*) *Chullah* hoods, weather shades, *chhajjas*, corbels, etc. including edges ;

(*o*) Staircases with sloping or stepped soffits, including risers and stringers, excluding landing ;

(*p*) Spiral staircases ;

(*q*) Chimneys and shafts ;

(*r*) Elevated water reservoirs ;

(*s*) Well steining ; and

(*t*) Fins.

5.9.4. Method of Measurement

Formwork shall be measured in square metres as the actual surfaces in contact with the concrete or any other material requiring formwork. Formwork to small features, shall be enumerated. Formwork left in shall be so described.

Where formwork is required to be lined with wallboard, hardboard, polyethylene sheet or paper lining or to be coated with mould liquid or limewhite, such formwork shall be so described and measured separately. Where lining of wallboard, asbestos, cork slab and the like is of a permanent character and is to be left in, such lining shall be measured separately the description shall include any necessary fixing to the concrete.

No deductions shall be made for opening up to 0.4 m^2. No deduction shall be made for any opening/cutouts when slip form technique is used. Raking of circular cutting and rounded or moulded edges shall be measured in running metres. Moulded stoppings shall be enumerated. Formwork to secondary beams shall be measured up to the sides of main beams, but no deduction shall be made from the formwork of the main beam where the secondary beam intersects it. Formwork to beam shall be measured up to sides of column, but no deduction shall be made from the formwork to stanchion or column casings at intersections of beam.

5.10. WOODWORK AND JOINERY

Description of Items. The description of each item shall, unless otherwise stated, be held to include where necessary, conveyance and delivery, handling, unloading, storing, fabrication, hoisting, all labour for finishing to required shape and size, setting, fitting and fixing in position, and straight cutting waste.

Measurements. Unless otherwise stated all works shall be measured net in decimal system, as fixed in position as given below :

(*a*) Length and width shall be measured to the nearest 0.01 m. Width of single or detached planks shall, however, be measured to the nearest 2 mm. Thickness shall be measured to the nearest 2 mm.

(*b*) Scantlings, battens, and baulks shall, however, be measured to the nearest 2 mm in each cross-sectional dimension.

Areas shall be worked out to the nearest 0.01 m^2. Cubical contents shall be worked out to the nearest 0.001 m^3.

5.10.1. General

The description and type of the wood to be used shall be stated ; each kind of wood shall be measured separately. The work shall be measured in cubic metres unless otherwise stated hereinafter. The work shall be measured separately for 'fixed' and 'framed and fixed'. 'Framed and fixed' work shall be that which involve mortice and tenon or dove-tailed joints.

All work shall include nails. Work 'secret fixed', fixed with screws' or 'fixed with screws and cups' or 'fixed with bolts and washers' shall be so described and measured separately. If screws are of other than ordinary steel, they shall be so described. Screws used for fixing builders hardware shall be measured along with the hardware.

All work shall be measured net as fixed, that is, no extra measurement shall be made for shape, joints, etc. except given below :

(*i*) Scantlings, battens, etc. in sections other than rectangular shall be measured as the least rectangle from which the section can be obtained.

(*ii*) In case of scantlings, battens, etc. with varying sections, largest section shall be measured.

(*iii*) Mitred pieces shall be measured along longest length.

(*iv*) Circular or segmental portions shall be measured net separately.

The description of items shall include all the necessary keys, wedges, dowels, wood or bamboo pins to tenoned joints and clenching of nail heads. In measuring framed timber, length of tenons and scarfs shall be added to site length of framed member. Extra lengths where required to be embedded in walls/floors shall be added to site lengths.

Unless specifically mentioned a tolerance of 1.5 mm shall be allowed for each wrought face. Items of plain woodwork exceeding 20 cm in width, if required in one width, shall be so described and measured separately. All lineal labours, such as rebates (straight or splayed) beads and chambers shall be described and included with the item.

Plugging to walls for planks, etc. shall be described and measured in running metres per row stating the spacing of plugs. Plugging to walls for fittings or detached work, etc. shall be described and enumerated.

Wrought timber shall be so described and measured separately except where planing is measured separately.

[**Note :** The term 'wrought' carries the same meaning as 'planed'.]

Planing shall be measured in square metres for all wrought surfaces, unless timber has been described as wrought. The following labours shall be measured separately in square metres when the timbers measured in cubic metres and in running metres stating the thickness when timber is measured in square metres :

(*a*) Scribing,

(*b*) Notching exceeding 15 cm each in girth, and

(*c*) Circular cutting.

Unless included in the description of main item the following labours shall be measured separately in running metres stating width or girth, and include all mitres and stops :

(*a*) Rebates, tongues and grooves ;

(*b*) Beads, staff beads and flutes ; and

(*c*) Mouldings.

The following labours shall be measured separately in numbers :

(*a*) Ends, splayed or rounded and wrought ;

(*b*) Wrought and pointed or rounded ends to posts, etc. including mitred intersections where necessary ;

(*c*) Rafter feet projecting with splayed or moulded ends ;

(*d*) Notches not exceeding 15 cm each in girth stating thickness ;

(*e*) Boring holes (other than for bolt), stating diameter and depth of holes ; and

(*f*) Cutting holes square in section, stating size and depth of holes.

5.10.2. Types of Work

Doors and windows leaves shall be described, method of fixing indicated and measured in square metres. Each type shall be measured separately.

[**Note :** Where there is a combination of two or more types of doors or windows, it shall either be measured as clubbed item or the different portions measured separately, the dividing line being the centre of the rail separating the different portions.]

No extra width or labour shall be measured for rebated and/or splayed meeting stiles of doors and windows. Boarding shall be described and measured in square metres under the following headings stating the finished thickness in each case :

(*a*) Roof boarding ;
(*b*) Ceiling ;
(*c*) Floors ;
(*d*) Panelling ;
(*e*) Weather boarding ; and
(*f*) Shelves, fittings racks, bins, almirah linings and the like.

Description shall include all straight and raking cutting and waste and heading joints where required. Side joints shall be described and work with different kinds of joints shall be measured separately. In the case of rebated, tongued and grooved, grooved and fillered and secret jointed boarding and weather boarding the measurement shall be net as fixed, extra width of rebates, tongues, etc., being ignored.

Boarding fixed to curved surfaces in narrow widths shall be measured separately and shall include shooting the joints to proper splay. In case of boarded floors the width of boards, the method of jointing and nailing shall be described ; if floors are to be traversed or finished for polishing, it shall be so stated.

In case of weather boarding, width and thickness of boards and lap shall be stated. In case of feather-edged boarding, thickness shall be the maximum thickness. All chamfering, rebating, etc. to edges of weather boarding shall be described.

Batten work shall be described and measured in running metres. Trellis work shall be measured in square metres stating size of laths and spacing. One-way and two-way trellis work shall each be measured separately.

Posts, rails, stiles, braces and other supports for trellis work and for doors and windows frames in trellis work shall be measured separately. Doors and windows formed in trellis work shall be measured along with trellis work.

Shoring and Strutting. Shoring and strutting timbers (use and waste) shall be measured in cubic metres and shall include necessary bolts, wedges, dog-spikes, nails, putting together, erecting maintaining in position for the required period, striking and removal.

Bally Work. Bally work shall be measured in running metres stating mean diameter.

(**Note :** Mean diameter shall be the average of diameters at the ends.)

Staircases. Work to staircases shall be measured under a separate heading and measured in detail as given below. Where detailed working drawings are available staircases may be measured as an omnibus item fully described stating the tread area in square metres.

(*i*) Landings including bearers shall be measured as for boarded floors.

(*ii*) Treads and risers shall be measured in square metres, the area being obtained by multiplying the length of tread by the exposed width of tread plus the rise from step to step. Winders and risers shall be included with the item.

(*iii*) Housing of treads risers, fliers and winders shall be included in the description, as also all labours, such as cross-tonguing, cross-grooving, cross-rebating, framing and gluing, wedging and blocking.

(*iv*) Carriages, if provided, shall be measured separately.

(*v*) Returned ends to treads with shaped brackets under a rounded, quadrant of curtail ends to treads and risers shall be enumerated.

(*vi*) Walls strings shall be measured in running metres stating the width and thickness and shall include plugging to wall and housing for treads and risers.

(*vii*) Outer strings shall be measured in for wall strings and shall include housing for treads and risers, tenoning or notching at ends to fit newel posts, landings, etc.

(*viii*) Cut strings shall be measured as for outer strings and shall include cutting of upper edge for treads.

(*ix*) Ramped, circular and wreathed portion shall be measured separately and so described.

(*x*) Hand-rails shall be measured in running metres along top centre line stating extreme section of straight portions and whether rounded or moulded.

(*xi*) Circular level, ramped and wreathed hand-rails shall be measured separately. Quadrants, short ramps and wreaths and scroll ends shall be enumerated.

(*xii*) Mitres, housing joints and hand-rail screws and dowels at junction of circular part with straight one shall be enumerated.

(*xiii*) Balusters shall be described and enumerated stating size and shall include framings or housing at ends.

(*xiv*) Newels shall be described and measured in running, metres stating the section, and if turned the length of turning shall be stated.

(*xv*) Sunk panels and mouldings planted-on housed-in to newels shall be stated.

(*xvi*) Newel caps and pendants shall be described and enumerated.

Cased Frames of Vertical Sliding Windows. Cased frames of vertical sliding windows shall be described and measured in running metres, along the outer edge.

Skirtings, Cornices, Picture and Dado Rails, etc. Skirtings, cornices, picture rails, dado rails and similar mouldings shall be described including method of fixing and measured in running metres.

Trap Doors. Trap doors shall be described and enumerated as 'extra over' relevant item. Pelmet boxes shall be described and measured in running metres along the sides and face planking.

Turned Work. Turned work shall be measured in running metres stating the girth.

Sundries. The following types of work shall be fully described and enumerated :

(*a*) Wardrobes and cupboards ; (*b*) Draining boards ;

(*c*) Plate racks ; (*d*) Curtain brackets ;

(*e*) Towel rails ; (*f*) Toilet fixtures ;

(*g*) Back boards to cisterns ; and

(*h*) Small fittings, such as door and window stops.

5.11. STEEL WORK AND IRON WORK

Description of Items. The description of each item which covers both fabrication and erection shall include conveyance and delivery, handling, unloading, storing, hoisting and all labour for finishing to required shape and size. Alternatively, in each item of work fabrication or erection shall be described and measured separately.

Dimensions. Unless otherwise stated all work shall be measured net in decimal system, as fixed in its place as given below :

(*i*) Dimensions excepting cross-section and thickness of plate shall be measured to nearest 0.001 m except for reinforcement which shall be measured to nearest 0.005 m.

(*ii*) Areas excluding cross-sectional measurement shall be worked out to nearest 0.001 m^2.

(*iii*) Weights shall be worked out to nearest 1 kg.

Mill tolerance shall be ignored when the weight is determined by calculation. The priming coat shall be described and included in item of fabrication. The weight of steel sheet, plate and strip ; rolled steel sections, steel rods, and steel strips ; forged steel, steel castings and steel tubes shall be taken from relevant Indian Standards.

Unless otherwise specified, an addition of 2.5 percent of the weight of structure shall be made for shop and site rivet heads in riveted steel structures. Unless otherwise specified, in the case of welded steel structures no allowance shall be made for the weld metal. Wedging-up, under stanchion bases or steel grillages shall be described and enumerated.

5.11.1. Steel Work

Various items of steelwork shall be classified and measured separately under following categories. Work in each classification shall be described. Bolted, riveted and welded structures shall be described as such and measured separately :

(*a*) Rolled sections (joist, channel, angle or tee) fixed independently without connecting plates.

(*b*) Rolled sections fixed with connecting plate or angle clears as in main and cross-beams, hip and jack rafters, purlins connected to common rafters and the like.

(*c*) Rolled joists, with or without stiffeners in grillages (thc weight of stiffeners shall he added to the weight of joists).

(*d*) Compound girders.

(*e*) Plate girders (stating type and overall height of girder).

(*f*) Lattice girders, aerial masts, tank staging and like (stating details of members and overall height of structure).

(*g*) Single stanchions composod of rolled joists or channels with caps, bases, splices, angle brackets, etc.

(*h*) Compound stanchions with caps, bases, splices, angle brackets, etc.

(*i*) Trusses and trussed purlins (stating spans and overall heights).

(*j*) Framing of cladding and glazing.

(*k*) Crane gantry rails including fastenings.

(*l*) Staircases including stringers, treads, landings, handrails, etc.

(*m*) Plates (plain or chequered), square cut or notched, holed (ordinary or countersunk) without any attachments.

(*n*) Plates of classification (*m*) above with riveted, bolted or welded attachments.

(*o*) Running rails and girders for sliding doors.

(*p*) Platework with or without stiffeners for :

(1) Bunkers, (2) Chutes, (3) Chimneys including ladders,

(4) Tanks with or without covers including stays but excluding stagings,

(5) Gutters and downpipes, and (6) Furnace shell.

(*q*) Anchor bolts, holding down bolts including all fittings and sag rods ;

(*r*) Wind ties to roofs, strakes for wooden bridges, cores for hand rails (straight portion), running bars for doors and fencing posts and struts ;

(*s*) Framed work, such as grills, gratings, framed guard bars, ladders, walk ways, railings, brackets and similar work ;

(*t*) Straps, hooks, clamps, holdfasts, well ties, inserts, knee pieces, and similar work ;

(*u*) Ornamental work as in grills, balustrades, and curved, ramped and scroll portion of cores for hand-rails ; and

(*v*) Steelwork for :

(1) doors, (2) hydraulic gates, and (3) cassions and well curbs.

[**Note 1 :** In composite construction shear connectors, if any, will form part of structural steelwork.

Note 2 : The above classification with suffix *B*, *R* or *W* shall be indicated in bills of quantities to denote bolted, riveted or welded construction respectively.]

The steelwork shall be measured by weight except otherwise mentioned. Unless otherwise specified, weight of cleats, brackets, packing pieces, bolts, nuts, washers, distance pieces, separators, diaphragm, gussets (taking overall rectangular dimensions), fish plates, etc. shall be added to the weight of respective items. In riveted work, allowance is to be made for weight of rivet heads. No deduction shall be made for rivet or bolt holes (excluding holes for anchor or holding down bolts). Deduction in case of rivet or bolt hole shall however be made if its area exceeds 0.02 m^2 and for notch if its area exceeds 0.5 m^2. For other type of openings like holes for service pipe, etc. deduction shall be made if its area exceeds 0.1 m^2.

5.11.2. Tubular Structures

The tubular structures shall be described and measured by weight.

5.11.3. Cables/Guy Wires

The cables and guy wires shall be described and measured in running metres stating the diameter or by mass.

5.11.4. Bearings

These shall be classified as roller, rocker, sliding, etc. and fully described and enumerated.

5.11.5. Pipes for Flues

Flue pipes of steel sheeting shall be measured overall in funning metres and described as including all short lengths, cutting and waste. The method of joining and fixing shall be described. Supports shall be measured separately. The diameter of pipes, thickness of sheeting and whether black or galvanized shall be stated. In case of galvanized steel pipes, class of galvanization shall be stated. Bends, elbows, cowls, tapered pipes to fit outlets of ranges, and roofs plates with sleeve shall be enumerated and measured as extra over.

5.11.6. Duct Work

The duct metal work shall be described and measured in square metres on basis of surface area. Supports shall be measured separately.

5.11.7. Expanded-Metal Work and Weld Meshwork

Expanded-metal work and weld meshwork shall be described including laps, meshes, weight, strands and method of fixing and measured in square metres. Openings exceeding 0.2 m^2 shall be deducted. Raking or circular cutting and waste shall be included in the description.

5.11.8. Steel Reinforcement

Bar reinforcement shall be measured by weight in kilograms and shall include cutting to lengths, hooked ends, cranking or bending (straight or spiral). Authorized overlaps, chairs/separators shall be measured. When welding of joints is authorised same shall be described; joints, butt welded shall be measured in numbers and lap welded shall be measured in running metres of the length welded.

Fabric reinforcement shall be described (including meshes and strands) and measured in square metres. Authorised lap shall be measured. Wire netting used as encasement shall be described (including meshes and wires) and shall be measured in square metres. Authorised laps shall be measured. Raking or circular cutting and waste shall be included in description.

Binding wire for reinforcement shall not be measured, but shall be included in description of item.

[**Note :** Term 'binding wire' is reserved for wire binding together reinforcement in contact.]

Hoop iron shall be fully described and measured in running metres.

5.11.9. Miscellaneous Work

Bolts including nuts and washers shall he described and measured by weight in kilograms. Plain or barbed wire fencing shall be fully described and each line or wire shall be measured in running metres. Patent plain wire fencing shall be fully described and measured in square metres. Wire mattresses, nets shall be fully described including method of tying and measured in square metres. Authorised laps shall be measured.

Collapsible gates shall be described and measured in square metres as fixed stating size of gate opening, pickets, pivoted flat bars and size of meshes formed by them when fully extended. Top and bottom runners, pulleys, locking lugs and handles shall be described and included with item. Description shall also include erection in position and securing runners with holdfasts and brackets.

Steel rolling shutters/grills shall be described and measured in square metres. The width shall be measured as the outer distance between the backs of the two guide channels of the rolling shutters and the height shall be the distance between the sill and the centre of the hood cover.

Gauge and type of the shutter/grills, distance between centres of interlock and bridge depth shall be stated. Description shall include spring winding mechanism operated mechanically or manually, jamb guides, bottom rail, locking and door operating arrangements. Where a wicket gate has to be provided it shall be described. Any protective treatment required to be applied at manufacturer's works, such as painting or hot dip galvanizing shall be described.

Unless otherwise stated, steel doors, windows ventilators and glazing frames shall be measured in square metres as fixed stating type given in relevant Indian Standard. Method of fixing and hanging and fastenings shall be included with item.

Gates for Compound Walls and Railing. Gates shall be described and enumerated or measured in square metres ; hangings, guide rails and fastenings shall be described and included with item.

Steel Louvre. Louvres shall be described and measured in square metres on the basis of opening covered.

Slotted Pipes. Site-perforated pipes shall be described and measured by mass in kilogram. Deductions for perforations/slots shall, however, be made if its area exceeds 0.02 m^2. The manufactured perforated pipe shall, however, be described and measured in running metres.

5.11.10. Cast Ironwork

Cast iron flue (smoke) pipes shall be measured overall in running metres and described as including all short length, cutting and waste. Method of jointing and fixing shall be described, and diameter of pipes and mass per standard length stated. Bends, inspection doors and cowls shall be enumerated and measured as extra over.

Spiral Staircases. Spiral staircases shall be enumerated, stating overall diameter and height, total number of treads, riser and sleeves in one piece, central shaft or poles including base plate and other attachment handrail and balusters. Exit landings shall be described and enumerated. Stays, if required, shall be stated.

Stanchions, Columns and Lamp Posts. These shall be described and measured in numbers specifying mass. Grid flooring and grills shall be described including size and weight of each piece and measured in square metres on the basis of overall area. Except as hereinbefore described, cast ironwork shall be measured by mass and classified under the following headings :

(*a*) ***Unmachined***—such as brackets, frames, gully, tops, manhole covers, gratings, fire doors, soot doors and frames ; and balls and stop cock boxes.

(*b*) ***Machine turned***—such as pulleys and similar work.

5.12. HARDWARE

Description of Item. The description of each item shall, unless otherwise stated, be held to include, wherever necessary, conveyance and delivery, handling, unloading, storing and all labour for fitting and fixing in position, cutting and waste, return of packing, etc.

Limits of Measurement. The dimensions shall be measured net in decimal system nearest to 0.01 m.

Mode of Measurements. The various kinds of builders hardware shall be described and measured separately according to the material, finish, size pattern and method of fixing. All builders hardware shall be fully described and enumerated except the following which shall be measured in running metres :

(*a*) Curtain rods or poles, stating the outer diameter ;

(*b*) Curtain Rails—Curtain runners, brackets and stops shall be described and included with the item stating the number per metre of rail ;

(*c*) Rails for sliding sashes stating the size of the rail ; and

(*d*) Sash Lines—The girth or diameter shall be stated.

Fixing of hardware items shall include all fittings, cutting, sinking, boring and morticing, the supply of screws (or bolts, nuts and washers in the case of hardware made for fixing with bolts), to match. Hardware fixed to wood and metal shall each be measured separately. Hardware fixed flush shall be so described.

5.12.1. Measurement of Sizes of Hardware

The sizes of the hardware articles shall be measured as indicated in Table 5.5.

Table 5.5 Measurement of Sizes of Hardware

S. No.	*Name of Article*	*How Measured*
1.	Bolts	(*a*) The length of face plate in flush bolts (*b*) The length of shoots (bolt) in other bolts
2.	Hinges	(*a*) The length of the joint or knuckle of butt hinges (*b*) The width between flanges and also the height of parliament hinges (*c*) The length of the leaf (that is, from the joint or knuckle to the point), in case of tee and strap hinges (*d*) The length of the spring cylinder for regulating spring of butt hinges (*e*) The length of joint in case of back flap hinges
3.	Latches (Suffolk or Norfolk)	The dimensions of the plate (having the bow handle) and the size number
4.	Latches, rim (Night)	
5.	Locks, rim	
6.	Locks, mortice	The horizontal length of face across the body excluding the box staple or striking plate
7.	Locks, cabinet or cup board	
8.	Locks drawer	
9.	Locks furniture	The maximum diameter of the knob
10.	Cleats belaying	Straight distance between two ends of cleat
11.	Catches spring (for fanlight)	The flat overall size in elevation of the plate with spring catch excluding the striking plate
12.	Fasteners, cockspur	The length of handle from the centre of pivot or hinged joint
13.	Fasteners and stays (casement)	Extreme length including thickness of back plate
14.	Pivots and sockets	The dimensions of each plate
15.	Stays, quadrant (for fanlight)	The shortest straight length between the extreme ends of the quadrant stay
16.	Brackets for shelving	The extreme width and height
17.	Door handles	Grip length
18.	Hat pegs	Extreme length including thickness of plate
19.	Hat and coat hooks	Measured diagonally from extreme top of fixing plate to the extreme top of knob
20.	Wardrobe hooks	Measured diagonally from extreme top of fixing plate to the extreme top of knob

(Contd.)

21.	Screw hooks dresser or cup pattern	Straight length excluding screwed end
22.	Cabin or casement hook with two eyes on plate	Straight length between centre of two eyes when fixed
23.	Wire hooks with two screwed eyes	The overall length of the hook excluding the screwed eye The diameter of wire shall be stated
24.	Knob	The maximum diameter of the knob
25.	Hasp and staples :	
	(*a*) Wire type	The overall length of hasp including the hinged plate
	(*b*) Plate type	The length measured from the centre of the hinge to the end of the hasp excluding the hinged plate
26.	Ships, rat-tail including friction plate	Length measured from the centre of the spindle to the centre of the roller
27.	Springs, patent helical	
28.	Screwed eyes	The overall length of the screwed eye and diameter of wire shall be stated
29.	Door closer (hydraulically regulated)	The weight and the width of the door to which it is intended to be fitted shall be stated
30.	Finger plates	The length, width and thickness of the plates
31.	Sliding door bolt (Aldrop)	Length of the bolt
32.	Floor door stopper with plate	Length of its plate
33.	Hooks and eyes	Length of the hook measured out to out

5.13. GLAZING

Description of Items. The description of each item shall, unless stated otherwise, be held to include where necessary, conveyance and delivery, handling, loading, unloading, storing and waste.

Measurements. All works shall be measured net in decimal system as fixed in its place as given below :

(*i*) Dimensions shall be measured to the nearest 0.01 m.

(*ii*) Areas shall be worked out to the nearest 0.01 m^2.

The various kinds of sheets for glazing like glass and other materials shall be described and shall be measured separately. In the case of wired glass, design or pattern of reinforcement shall be described and in case of frosted glass it shall be stated whether it is on one or both sides. Work in wood, metal concrete and the like shall be measured separately. The method of glazing shall be described and measured separately under the following classification. The type and putty shall also be described ;

(*a*) Front and back putty and sprigged or fixed with glazing pins ;

(*b*) Bedded in putty and fixed with beads ; and

(*c*) Bedded in rubber or velvet and fixed with beads (wherever required).

Method of Measurement. Work shall be measured in square metres stating the thickness. The dimensions of each pane shall be clear dimensions of opening plus width of rebates of structural member of window/door. The pane other than rectangular or square shall be measured as the smallest rectangular area from which pane can be cut. Straight cutting shall be deemed to be included in the item.

Circular cutting shall be measured as extra over in running metres. The term circular shall be deemed to include any form of curve. Glass and sheet louvers shall be described and enumerated. Hacking-out old broken glass and preparing for new glass shall be measured in square metres.

Holes drilled in work shall be enumerated stating diameter of the hole, type and thickness of the glass/sheet and size of the pane. Grinding, polishing and rounding off edges of glass or glazing sheet shall be described and measured in running metres.

5.14. PAVING, FLOOR FINISHES, DADO AND SKIRTING

Description of Items. The description of each item shall, unless otherwise stated, be held to include wherever necessary conveyance and delivery, handling, unloading, storing, fabrication hoisting, all labour for finishing to required shape and size, setting, fitting and fixing in position, straight cutting and waste, return of packings, and other incidental operations.

Dimension. All work shall be measured net, as laid, in the decimal system as under, unless otherwise stated hereinafter :

(*a*) Dimensions shall be measured to the nearest 0.01 m, and

(*b*) Areas shall be worked out to nearest 0.01 m^2.

Cuttings. All cuttings shall unless otherwise stated be held to include the consequent waste.

Mode of Measurement. All work shall be measured in square metres unless otherwise stated. Deductions for ends of dissimilar materials or other articles embedded shall not be made for areas not exceeding 0.1 m^2. Work in isolated width not matching with the general finish shall be measured as below :

(*a*) Width 30 cm and below in running metres (the description to include for cutting to edges if any), and

(*b*) Width above 30 cm in square metres.

Expansion and dummy joints shall be described and measured separately in running metres stating depth and width of joints. The filler shall be described and included in the description of item. Work in repairs shall be so described and preparation of old surfaces to receive such work shall be included in the description.

Work in isolated areas not exceeding 1 m^2 each shall be so described stating the nature thereof. Work to a pattern or in more than one colour shall be so described stating the nature thereof. Curved work, conical work and spherical work shall be described separately stating the radius. Labour in such works shall be so described and measured separately.

5.14.1. In Situ Finishes

In situ finishes shall be classified according to the kind of material (for example, granolithic, terrazzo, mosaic ; etc.) and measured separately. The following particulars shall be given for each classification :

(*a*) Composition and mix ;

(*b*) Thickness, which shall be exclusive of keys, grooves and open joints ;

(*c*) Number of coats ;

(*d*) Nature of surface treatment (for example, steel trowelled, wood floated, polished, sprinkled with carborundum powder, etc.) ;

(*e*) Nature of base and any special treatment to the same ; and

(*f*) Situations, for example, whether in flooring or in dado/skirting.

Work executed to imitate stone slab, or stone blocks shall be so described stating the average size of the slabs or blocks, the surface finish (for example, plain, rough, etc.) Work to floors laid in bays and work to floors laid in panels between dividing strips shall be so described stating the size of bay or area of panel or bay. The dividing strip shall be measured separately.

Work in floors laid in one operation with the base concrete shall be so described. No deduction shall be made for voids not exceeding 0.2 m^2. Work in treads, risers and edges of landings shall be measured in square metres. Work in landings shall be included in the main item. Work to wall strings and open strings shall be measured in square metres. Ends, angles, ramps and wreathed corners shall be included with the item.

Moulded nosings shall be measured in running metres ; returned moulded ends and angles to mouldings shall be included in the description. Dados (including raking dados) shall be measured in square metres. Skirting (including raking skirting) shall be measured in running metres stating the height. Mitres, stops, returned ends and the like shall be included with the item.

Work to kerbs shall be measured in running metres stating the girth on face. Raking kerbs and vertical kerbs shall each be so described. Arises, rounded edges and coves shall be included in the description. Angles and intersections shall be enumerated separately. Forming channels shall be measured in running metres as extra over the finishings in which they occur stating the girth on face. Arrises shall be included in the description. Ends, angles, intersections and outlets shall each be enumerated separately.

Lining to channels shall be measured in running metres stating the girth on face. Arrises and coves shall be included in the description. Ends, angles, intersections and outlets shall each be enumerated separately. Dividing strips shall be described stating size and thickness and measured separately in running metres. Description shall include for ends, angles and intersections and method of fixing, embedding, etc.

5.14.2. Tile, Slab or Block Finishes

Particulars of the following shall be given

(*a*) Kind of tile, slab or block units (for example, precast concrete, precast terrazzo, brick, natural stone, cast stone, slate, marble, wood-blocks, cork, rubber, etc.) ;

(**Note** : In case of precast concrete work, the mix to be stated.)

(*b*) Thickness and size of tile, slab or block units ;

(*c*) Shape of units where other than rectangular ;

(*d*) Nature of surface finish (for example, glazed, rubbed, polished, type of dressing in case of stone, etc.) ;

(*e*) Bedding or other method of fixing units ;

(*f*) Grouting, pointing or other finish to joints ;

(*g*) Nature of base (for example ; wood, screeded bed, concrete, brickwork, etc.) ;

(*h*) Situations, for example, whether in flooring or in dado/skirting ; and

(*i*) Layout of joints.

Temporary moulds for precast tile, slab or block units shall be deemed to be included with the item. No deduction shall be made for voids not exceeding 0.2 m^2. Square cutting at joint and at boundaries shall be deemed to be included with the items except as provided below. Raking, cutting and curved cutting shall each be measured separately in running metres except where occurring within a pattern. In case of work laid to diagonal patterns, straight cutting at boundary (measured around the perimeter of each area) shall be measured in running metres.

Fair edges, rebated edges, rounded edges, chamfered edges, splayed edges, bevelled edges and the like shall be measured separately in running metres including ends, angles, metres, intersections, etc. Moulded edges, grooves, flutes and the like shall each be measured separately in running metres. Ends, angles and intersections shall each be enumerated separately.

Cutting and fitting around steel stanchions and the like (grouped together) shall be described and enumerated. Cutting and fitting around pipes, tubes, bars, cables, conduits and the like shall be described and enumerated. Cutting and fitting around profile of steps shall be enumerated. Cutting and fitting around ducting brackets, newels, WC pedestals, vents, sootdoors and the like (grouped together) shall be enumerated stating the size in stages of 25 cm girth.

Dividing strips shall be described stating size and thickness and measured separately in running metres. Description shall include for ends, angles and intersections and method of fixing, embedding, etc.

Dados (including raking dados) shall be measured in square metres. Skirting (including raking skirting) shall be measured in running metres stating the height. Mitres, stops, returned ends and the like shall be included with the item.

Channels and lining to channels shall each be measured separately in running metres describing the section and average depth. Channels to falls shall be so described. Rounded edges shall be included in the description. Ends, angles, intersections and outlets shall each be enumerated separately.

Kerbs shall be measured in running metres describing the section and shall include rounded edges coves, etc. Special tiles and special slabs to form coved internal angles of any radius, rounded external angles, architraves, mouldings, ceiling ribs, cornices and the like shall each be measured in running metres separately according to size and shape.

Work to treads, risers and edges of landings shall be measured separately in square metres. Work in landings shall be included in the main item.

5.14.3. Sheet Finishes

Particulars of the following shall be given :

(*a*) Kind of sheeting (linoleum, cork, rubber, etc.) ;

(*b*) Thickness and quality of sheeting ;

(*c*) Method of fixing and joining ; and

(*d*) Nature of base.

Laps and seams shall be included in the description stating the lap and type of seam and shall not be measured separately. Sheet finishes to vertical inclined and horizontal surfaces shall be measured separately. No deduction shall be made for voids not exceeding 0.2 m^2.

Raking cutting and curved cutting shall each be measured separately in running metres except where occurring within a pattern. Forming rounded external angles and coved internal angles shall each be measured separately in running metres stating the girth.

Cover strips over joints of finishes shall be described stating the size and measured in running metres. Description shall include for ends, angles and intersections. Cutting and fitting around steel stanchions and the like (grouped together) shall be described and enumerated. Cutting and fitting around pipes, tubes, bars, cables, conduits and the like shall be described and enumerated.

Cutting and fitting around profile of steps shall be enumerated. Cutting and fitting around ducting brackets newels, WC pedestals, vents, soot-doors and the like (grouped together) shall be enumerated stating the size in stages of 25 cm girth.

5.14.4. Bedding and Backings

Particulars of the following shall be given :

(*a*) Composition and mix ;

(*b*) Thickness which shall be exclusive of keys, grooves, open joints ; and

(*c*) Nature of base and any treatment of the same.

Screeded beds for all floor finishes shall be described and measured. No deduction shall be made for voids not exceeding 0.2 m^2. Bedding and backing laid in bays or laid in panels between dividing strips shall be so described stating the size of bay or area of panel or bay.

Bedding and backing in treads, risers and edges of landings shall each be measured separately in square metres. Work in landings shall be included in the main item. Bedding and backing in skirtings and dados shall be measured separately.

Forming channels in beds shall be measured in running metres as extra over the beads in which they occur stating the girth on face. Arrises, rounded edges, coves, ends, angles, intersections, outlets and the like shall be included with the items.

5.15. ROOF COVERING

Description of Items. The description of each item shall, unless otherwise stated, be held to include, where necessary, conveyance and delivery, handling, unloading, storing fabrication, hoisting, all labour for finishing to required shape and size.

Measurements. Unless otherwise stated hereinafter all works shall be measured net in decimal system, as fixed in its place as given below.

(*i*) Dimensions shall be measured to the nearest 0.01 m.

(*ii*) Areas shall be worked out to the nearest 0.01 m^2.

Work executed in the snow shall be measured separately.

Bills of Quantities. The bills of quantities shall fully describe the materials and workmanship and accurately represent the work to be executed.

The superficial area of roof coverings and cladding as laid shall be measured on the flat in square metres without allowance for laps and corrugations, if any.

Portions of roof covering overlapped by ridge or hip, etc. shall be included in the measurements of the roof except where otherwise stated.

Any opening not exceeding 0.4 m^2 shall not be deducted and forming such openings requiring cutting shall be enumerated.

Any opening exceeding 0.4 m^2 shall be deducted and cutting required shall be measured in running metres.

Cutting across corrugations shall be measured on the flat and not girthed.

No additions shall be made for laps cut through.

Sheeting curved or bent to curvature shall be measured separately.

The woodwork and steelwok shall be measured separately under the relevant sections.

The type of sheeting shall be described stating the thickness. The side and end laps shall be stated.

If the side and end laps are bolted or riveted, it shall be so stated specifying the spacing of the bolts or rivets.

Nainital pattern sheet-roofing shall be fully described and measured separately and shall include all rolls, clips, etc. Measurements shall be taken on the flat and not girthed.

Ridges, hips and valleys shall be measured along the central line in running metres stating the girth and flashings in square metres. The laps, passings and method of fixing shall be described.

The laps along the length of the ridge, hips, valleys or flashing pieces shall not be measured separately.

5.15.1. Asbestos Cement Sheet Roofing

The type of sheeting shall be described, stating the thickness. The side and end laps shall be stated and the method of fixing described. If required to be fixed in accordance with maker's instructions, it shall so be stated.

Ridges and hips shall be described stating the laps and measured in running metres along the central line; where in two pieces, these shall be measured as one length.

Ridge finials, cowl type ventilators, curved barge boards for northlight curves, roof lights, expansion joints for ridges and expansion joints for northlight curves shall be described and enumerated. Ridge finials where in two interlocking pieces, shall be measured as one number.

Eaves filler pieces, aprons, barge boards, corner pieces, flashings, louvers, northlight and ventilator curves, expansion joints for sheets and other similar specials shall he described and measured for the finished work in running metres stating the laps and the method of fixing.

Ventilator sheets and other sheeting of dissimilar material shall be described and enumerated as 'extra over' on ordinary sheeting. Eaves and valley gutters shall be described and measured in running metres along the central line. Accessories, such as drop ends, stop ends, nozzles and angles shall be described and enumerated as 'extra over' gutters. Union clips (loose sockets) shall not be measured separately.

5.15.2. Roof Sheeting Other than Metal and Asbestos Cement

The method of measurement given in 4 shall also be applicable to roof sheeting of plastic, fibre glass, etc.

5.15.3. Cladding (Plain, Corrugated or Semi-Corrugated)

The type of sheeting shall be described stating the thickness. The side and end laps shall be stated and method of fixing described. If the side and end laps are bolted or riveted it shall be so stated specifying the spacing of bolts or rivets.

5.15.4. Roof Tiling

The description shall state the kind, pattern quality and size of the tiles, the gauge to which they are to be laid and the method of laying. Single and double tiling shall each be measured separately. Ridges, hips and valleys, shall be measured in running metres. If set in mortar, it shall be so stated specifying the mortar.

Special ridge and hip tiles shall be described stating the kind, pattern, quality and size as also the mortar in which bedded and pointed. Coloured mortar (to match the coloured tiling, if required to be used for pointing) shall be described. Hip hooks shall be enumerated stating the size and whether black or galvanized. Eaves tiles bedded in mortar on walls shall be measured in running metres as extra for eaves describing the motor and width of bedding.

Filling ends and spaces between tiles at caves with mortar shall be measured in running metres and described stating the depth of filling. Filling to single and double tiling shall be measured separately. Screwing eaves tiles to battens shall be measured in running metres stating type, size, spacing of screws and washers. Drilling holes in the tiles shall be included in the description.

Half tiles or one and a half tiles at verges shall not be measured separately, but straight cutting and waste at verges shall be allowed for the full length of the verge and measured in running metres. Tiles at verges bedded in mortar on walls shall be measured in running metres as 'extra over' for verges describing the mortar and width of the bedding. Country tiling shall be described as including all cutting and waste. Special ventilating tiles and glass tiles shall be enumerated as 'extra over' only over roof tiling.

5.15.5. Roof Shingles

Wood shingles to roof shall be measured in the same way as in the case of roof tiling.

5.15.6. Roof Slating

Slate roofs shall be measured in the same way as in the case of roof tiling.

5.15.7. Terraced Roofing

The size and quality of burnt bricks, brick tiles, stone slabs and similar materials for terraced roofing, method of laying, jointing, pointing and mix and type of mortar shall be described, stating the number of layers of bricks tiles, etc.

Madras terrace roofing shall be fully described and plaster finish on the top and underside included in the item. Flat brick tile roofing shall be fully described stating the thickness and number of layers. Hollow roof with brick on edge bridging courses in between two layers of tiles shall be fully described and measured separately.

Flush pointing to tiles on top and underside of roof shall be described and included in the item of roofing. Tiles laid in *Chhajjas* and sun shades shall be measured separately.

The type of stone, quality and its dressing for stone slab roofing shall be described stating the thickness of slabs and spacing of battens or joists. If the size of slabs is required to be uniform, it shall be so stated.

Jack arch roofing including provision of centering shall be measured flat overall in square metres. The clear span, rise and thickness of arch, method of laying, joining and pointing shall be described. The finish to top and underside shall also he stated and included in the description.

5.15.8. Roof Treatment

Lime concrete in terracing shall be described and measured in square metres stating consolidated average thickness. Mud terraced roof shall be described stating average consolidated thickness.

Each type of waterproofing treatment shall be fully described (including type, quality and quantity of materials, side and end laps, where necessary) and shall be measured in square metres. All cutting, waste, forming of openings and wedging and pointing edges in masonry work shall be included in the description. Turn-ups and turn-downs at eaves, verges, abutment, etc. shall be measured along with waterproofing treatment.

The primer where provided shall also be measured separately. The waterproofing treatment in flashings, aprons, gutters, hips, ridges, valleys, etc. shall be fully described and measured net separately in square metres.

The waterproofing treatment between laps of corrugated sheeting shall be fully-described including the method of securing and measured in running metres stating the width.

5.15.9. Thatching, Matting and Bamboo Work

The materials shall be described stating the kind of fibre or straw and the finished thickness. The description shall include bamboo or wood securing fillers, tying string and trimming to eaves and verges.

Thatched capping to ridges and hips shall be described and measured along central line in running metres stating the girth. Matting, material, number of layers, laps and the method of fixing shall be described and all cutting and waste shall be included. Cover strips and cross-bracings of split bamboos or wooden laths shall be measured in square metres as 'extra over' matting and the method of fixing shall be described.

Bamboos laid one-way or two-way *Jaffri* work shall each be measured separately in square metres stating the size of bamboos and their spacing. Framing shall be included with the item. Split bamboo work and whole bamboo work shall be measured separately.

Whole bamboos fixed independently as support to matting shall be measured in running metres stating the mean girth. The description shall state the method of fixing and application of preservatives, if required.

5.15.10. Rain Water Goods

Gutters and pipes shall be described and measured in running metres including all short lengths, cutting and waste. The material, protective coating, if any, the pattern, the method of jointing and fixing shall be described. The length shall be measured along the central line. The length of all fittings, such as bends, junctions angles and the like shall be included.

Brackets for gutters shall be measured separately under the relevant section. Angles (internal or external), drop ends and stopped ends shall be enumerated as 'extra over' the length of gutters and shall include extra joints, cutting and waste.

Pipe rails, distance pieces and holder bats shall be described and included with the fixing of the pipes. Bends, elbows, offsets, shoes, branches, swan necks and heads shall be enumerated as 'extra over' the length of pipe and shall include for extra joints, cutting and waste.

5.16. CEILING AND LINING

Description of Items. The description of each item shall, unless otherwise stated, be held to include where necessary, conveyance and delivery, handling, unloading, storing, fabrication, hoisting, all labour for finishing to required shape and size.

Measurements. Unless otherwise stated here-in-after all works shall be measured net in decimal system, as fixed in its place, as given below.

(*i*) Dimension shall be measured to the nearest 0.01 m.

(*ii*) Areas shall be worked out to the nearest 0.01 m^2.

Each type of work in ceiling and lining shall be measured separately.

5.16.1. Measurements

The materials, its thickness and method of fixing, shall be described. Supporting members shall be measured separately in the relevant section, unless otherwise specified.

If work is to be formed to any specific pattern, it shall be so stated.

Work formed to circular surfaces shall be measured separately; if fixed with screws, it shall be so stated. All straight and raking cutting and waste shall be included with the item concerned.

All work unless otherwise described shall be measured as flat in square metres.

No deduction in measurement shall be made for openings not exceeding 0.4 m^2 and no extra measurement shall be made for forming such openings. For any opening exceeding 0.4 m^2 in area, deductions in measurements for the full openings shall be made and in such cases any labour involved in marking these openings shall be measured separately. Boarding fixed to curved surfaces in width not exceeding 15 cm shall be measured separately and shall include shooting the edges to proper splays.

Circular cutting and waste shall be measured in running metres stating the thickness and type of material. Cover fillets over joints shall be measured separately in running metres stating the material width and thickness of fillet. If the edges of fillets are chamfered, rounded or moulded, this shall be stated. Mitring at junctions shall be included in the description.

Sealing joints of plaster or fibre boards shall be measured in running metres. The method of sealing shall be described. Chamfering or rounding edges of fibre boarding and cutting V-groove in the same shall be measured in running metres.

Insulation boards and slabs fixed to surfaces shall be measured in square metres stating type, the number of layers, thickness of each layer and the method of fixing. Hollow insulation blocks shall be measured in square metres specifying the thickness. The method of setting and the type of mortar shall be described.

5.17. PLASTERING AND POINTING

Description of Items. Description of each item shall, unless otherwise stated, be held to include, wherever necessary, conveyance; delivery; handling; unloading; storing; necessary scaffolding; protective cover; cleaning stains from floors, walls, return of packings, etc. and other incidental changes.

Dimensions. All work shall be measured net as executed in the decimal system, as given below:

(*a*) Dimensions shall be measured to the nearest 0.01 m, and

(*b*) Areas shall worked out to the nearest 0.1 m^2.

Preparatory Work. Preparatory work, such as raking out joints, scarifying and cleaning, shall be included in the description of item unless otherwise specified.

5.17.1. Plastering. Plaster work shall be classified according to the material used and each classification shall be measured separately. The following particulars shall be given for each classification:

(*a*) Mix of mortar ;

(*b*) Number of coats and thickness of each coat ;

(*c*) Nature of surface treatment ;

(*d*) Nature of base ;

(*e*) Curved work, conical work, spherical work and eliptical work stating the radius ; and

(*f*) Any special treatment of base.

Description shall include arises, internal rounded angles, external chamfers and/or rounded angles not exceeding 80 mm in girth. In case of fibrous plaster, particulars of methods of application and of treatment of joints shall also be given. Work in repairs shall be so described stating thickness of dubbing, if any. Plastering on roofs, ceilings and walls shall be measured separately.

Removing plaster by scraping or otherwise shall be measured separately in square metres. Plastering in isolated widths or in widths not forming part of general plastering work (as in bands, cornices, sunk, panels etc.) and in chamfers, rounded angles exceeding 80 mm in girth shall be measured as below:

(*a*) 30 cm or below in width/girth, in running metres; and

(*b*) Width/girth above 30 cm in square metres.

Plastering at a height greater than 10 m above ground/datum level shall be measured separately in stages of 5 m height except interior plastering in case of building which shall be measured separately for each storey. All plastering shall be measured in square metres unless otherwise described. Cutting to edges shall be measured separately in running metres or alternatively described and included in the item.

5.17.2. Deductions

For jambs, soffits, sills, etc. for openings not exceeding 0.5 m^2 each in area, for ends of joists, beams, posts, girders, steps, etc. not exceeding 0.5 m^2 each in area, and for openings exceeding 0.5 m^2 and not exceeding 3 m^2 in each area, deductions and additions shall be made in the following manner:

(*a*) No deduction shall be made for ends of joists, beams, posts, etc. and openings not exceeding 0.5 m^2 each and no addition shall be made for reveals, jambs, soffits, etc. of these openings nor for finish to plaster around ends of joists, beams, posts, etc.

(*b*) Deductions for openings exceeding 0.5 m^2 but not exceeding 3 m^2 each shall be made as follows and no addition shall be made for reveals, jambs, soffits, sill, etc. of these openings :

(1) When both faces of wall are plastered with same plaster, deduction shall be made for one face only.

(2) When two faces of wall are plastered with different types of plaster or if one face is plastered and the other pointed, deduction shall be made from the plaster or pointing on the side on which width of reveals is less than that on the other side but no deduction shall be made on the other side. Where widths of reveals on both faces of wall are equal, deduction of 50 percent of area of opening on each face shall be made from areas of plaster and/or pointing as the case may be.

(3) When only one face is plastered and the other face is not, full deduction shall be made from plaster if width of reveal on plastered side is less than that on unplastered side but if widths of reveal on both sides are equal or width of reveal on plastered side is more, no deduction shall be made.

(4) When width of door frame is equal to thickness of wall or is projecting beyond thickness of wall, full deduction for opening shall be made from each plastered face of the wall.

In case of openings of area above 3 m^2 each, deduction shall be made for opening on each face but jambs, soffits and sills shall be measured.

(**Note :** In calculating areas of openings, the extra width of rebated reveals, if any, shall be excluded.)

Ceilings shall be measured between walls or partitions and dimensions before plastering shall be taken. Width covered by cornices or coves, if any shall be deducted. Soffits of stairs shall be measured as plastering on ceilings. Flewing soffits shall be measured separately.

Ribs and mouldings on ceilings shall be measured as for cornices, deduction being made from plastering if width/girth exceeds 15 cm. Measurement of wall plastering shall be taken between walls or partitions (dimensions before plastering being taken) for length and from top of floor or skirting to ceiling for height. Depth of cornices or coves, if any, shall be deducted.

Sides of pilasters, projections, etc. shall be added to plaster on walls. Mouldings, architraves, ceiling ribs, cornices and the like on pilasters and around openings, etc. shall be measured separately.

Length shall be measured in running metres at the centre of girth. Girth shall be measured along curve of moulding. Moulded cornices and coves shall be measured in square metres, the area being arrived at by multiplying length by girth.

Forming letters or figures in plaster shall be enumerated stating the height. Plastering on lathing shall be measured separately stating the number of coats and thickness of each coat.

Lathing shall be fully described and measured net : wood and steel lathing shall be measured separately. Laps, gauge and mesh of steel lathing shall be stated, no allowance being made for laps or cutting.

Size of laths, their distance apart and the kind of timber shall be stated in the case of wood lathing. Connector lathing shall be measured separately. Plastering on honeycomb work shall be described and measured in square metres on the basis of overall superficial area without deducting openings.

5.17.3. Pointing

Proportions of materials shall be described. Various types of pointing shall be measured separately. Pointing of different types of walls, floors, roofs, etc. shall be measured separately. Type and material of surface to be pointed shall be described.

Pointing in single detached joints as for flashings shall be measured in running metres. Pointing brick and tile work with mortars of matching shades shall be measured separately. Pointing shall be measured in square metres. Removing pointing by raking or otherwise shall be measured in square metres.

5.17.4. Deductions

For jambs, soffits, sills, etc. for openings not exceeding 0.5 m^2 each in area; for ends of joists, beams, posts, girders, steps, etc. not exceeding 0.5 m^2 each in area; and for openings exceeding 0.5 m^2 and not exceeding 3 m^2 each, deductions and additions shall be made in the following manner:

(*a*) No deduction shall be made for ends of joists, beams, posts, etc. and openings not exceeding 0.5 m^2 each, and no addition shall be made for reveals, jambs, soffits, sills, etc. of these openings nor for finish around ends of joists, beams posts, etc.

(*b*) Deductions for openings exceeding 0.5 m^2 but not exceeding 3 m^2 each shall be made as follows and no addition shall be made for reveals, jambs, soffits, sills, etc. of these openings:

(1) When both faces of wall are pointed with the same type of pointing, deduction shall be made for one face only.

(2) When two faces of wall are pointed with different types of pointing or if one face is plastered and the other pointed, deduction shall be made in the plaster or pointing on the side on which the width of reveals is less than that on the other side, but no deduction shall be made from plaster or pointing on the other side. Where widths of reveals on both faces of wall are equal, deduction of 50 percent of area of opening on each face shall be made from areas of plastering and/or pointing as the case may be.

(3) When width of door frame is equal to thickness of wall or is projecting beyond thickness of wall, full deduction for opening shall be made from each pointed face of the wall.

(4) When only one face is pointed and the other face is not pointed, full deduction shall be made from pointing if width of reveal on the pointed side is less than that on unpointed side, but if widths of the reveals on both sides are equal or width of reveal on pointed side nor any addition shall be made for reveals, jambs, soffits, sills, etc. In case of openings of area above 3 m^2 each, deduction shall be made for opening on each face but jambs, soffits and sills shall be measured.

(**Note :** In calculating areas of openings, extra width of rebated reveal, if any, shall be excluded.)

Racking-out joints shall be measured in square metres of alternatively included in description of item. Raking-out single detached joint shall be measured separately in running metres. Pointing on honey-comb work shall be described and measured in square metres on the basis of overall superficial area without deducting openings.

5.18. WHITE-WASHING, COLOUR WASHING, DISTEMPERING AND OTHER FINISHES

Description of Items. Description of each item shall, unless otherwise stated, be held to include, where necessary, conveyance; delivery handling; unloading; storing; waste; return of packings, necessary scaffolding; protective cover; and cleaning stains from floors, walls, glass panes, etc.

Number of Coats. Decorative treatment shall be fully described stating the number of coats in each case.

Preparatory Work. Preparatory work, such as brooming down, steel wire brushing, scrapping washing and rubbing down, shall be described and included in the main item. Preparatory work on new surfaces and primary coats, if any, shall be described and included in the main item. Preparatory work on old treated surfaces shall be described and included in the main item.

Classification. Various decorative treatments shall be measured separately under the various classifications as given below and materials and type of surfaces to be treated shall be fully described:

(*a*) Whitewash, colour wash, etc;
(*b*) Non-washable distemper;
(*c*) Washable distemper;
(*d*) Waterproof paint (colour/colourless);
(*e*) Chalk whiting to cloth or hessian surface;
(*f*) Linseed oil and cement to steel and iron work; and
(*g*) Cement slurry wash.

Priming and alkali neutralizing treatments, scraping of surface, washing surfaces spoilt by smoke soot, removal of oil and grease spots, treatment for disinfection with efflorescence moulds moss, fungi algae and litchen shall be measured separately and materials described.

Walls, Ceilings, etc. Work on walls, ceilings and sloping roofs shall each be measured separately.

Old Treated Surfaces. Work on old treated surfaces shall be measured separately and so described.

Measurement. All work shall be measured net in the decimal system as executed and as given below:

(*a*) Dimensions shall be measured to the nearest 0.01 m, and

(*b*) Areas of individual items shall be worked out to the nearest 0.01 m^2.

Whitewashing, colour washing, and distempering, except where otherwise stated, shall be measured in square metres.

Deductions. For jambs, soffits, sills, etc. for openings not exceeding 0.5 m^2 each in area; for ends of joists beams, posts, girders, steps, etc. not exceeding 0.5 m^2 each in area; and for openings exceeding 0.5 m^2 and not exceeding 3 m^2 each in area, deductions and additions shall be made in the following manner:

(*a*) No deduction shall be made for ends of joists, beams posts, etc. and openings not exceeding 0.5 m^2 each and no addition shall be made for reveals, jambs, soffits, sill of these openings nor for finish around ends of joists, beams, posts, etc.

(*b*) Deduction for openings exceeding 0.5 m^2 but not exceeding 3 m^2 each shall be made as follows and no addition shall be made for reveals, jambs, soffits, sills, etc. of these openings :

(1) When both faces of wall are provided with the same finish, deduction shall be made for one face only.

(2) When each face of wall is provided with a different finish, deduction shall be made for that side on which width of reveal is less than that of the other side but no deduction shall

be made on the other side; where widths of reveals on both faces of wall are equal, deduction of 50 percent of area of opening on each face shall be made from area of finish.

(3) When only one face is treated and other face is not treated, full deduction shall be made if width of reveal on the treated side is less than that on the untreated side, but if width of reveal is equal or more than that on the untreated side, neither deduction for the opening nor addition for reveals, jambs, soffits, sills, etc. shall be made.

(4) When the width of door frame is equal to thickness of wall or is projecting beyond the thickness of wall, full deduction for opening shall be made from each face of wall.

(5) When the reveal is only one side, full deduction for the face having no reveal shall be made and for the face having reveal, deduction of 50 percent of the opening shall be made.

In case of opening of areas above 3 m^2 each, deductions shall be made for openings, but jambs, soffits and reveals shall be measured.

No deduction shall be made for attachments, such as casings, conduits, pipes, electric wiring and the like.

Corrugated surfaces shall be measured flat as fixed and not girthed. Quantities so measured shall be increased by the following percentages and the resultant shall be included in general areas:

(*a*) Corrugated steel sheets	14 percent
(*b*) Corrugated asbestos cement sheets	20 percent
(*c*) Semi-corrugated asbestos cement sheets	10 percent
(*d*) Nainital pattern roofs (plain sheeting with rolls)	10 percent
(*e*) Nainital pattern roofs with corrugated sheets	25 percent

Cornices and other wall features, when not picked out in a different finish/colour, shall be girthed and included in general area. The painting for building surfaces shall be kept separate and the surfaces to be painted shall be described. It shall be stated whether measurements are flat or girthed. Alternatively different surfaces may be grouped into one general item, areas of uneven surfaces be converted into equivalent plain areas as under:

(*a*) External walls of plain brick work faced with recessed, raised or weather stuck pointing — 20 percent

(*b*) Sand faced plaster width up to 4 mm size — 50 percent

(*c*) Rough cast plaster with stone aggregate up to 10 mm — 100 percent

(*d*) Pebble dash finish — 275 percent

RCC Jallies up to 50 mm thick, the quantity shall be increased by 50 percent if painted on one side and 70 percent if painted on both sides; when thicker than 50 mm the quantity shall be based on actual area painted.

5.19. PAINTING, POLISHING, VARNISHING, ETC.

Description of Item. Description of each item shall, unless otherwise stated, be held to include, where necessary, conveyance; delivery; handling; unloading; storing; waste; return of packings; necessary scaffolding; protective cover; and cleaning stains from floors, walls, glass panes, etc.

Measurement. All work shall be measured net in the decimal system, as executed and as given below:

(*a*) Dimensions shall be measured to the nearest 0.01 m, and

(*b*) Areas shall be worked out to the nearest 0.01 m^2.

Bill of Quantities. Items of works shall fully describe materials and truly represent the work to be executed.

Preparatory work, such as knotting, priming, stopping and rubbing down, burning off or stripping shall be described and the number of coats shall be stated. Work on surfaces previously painted shall be measured separately. Where special colours or other special finishes are required, it shall be so stated.

Work on different surfaces shall be measured separately classified as follows and the preparatory work shall be described and included in the items:

(*a*) Non-absorbent surfaces, such as on steel and other metals; and

(*b*) Semi-absorbent surfaces, such as wood, fibre-board.

5.19.1. Measurement of Painting

Painting, except where otherwise stated, shall be measured in square metres.

No deduction shall be made for openings not exceeding 0.5 m^2 each, and no addition shall be made for painting to beading, moulding, edges, jambs, soffits, sills, etc. of such openings.

In case of fabricated structural steel and iron work, priming coat of paint shall be included with fabrication. Subsequent coats of paint shall be measured separately on the basis of weight of steel work and iron work or in square metres. The weight/area of steel sheet, plate and strip; rolled steel sections, steel rods and steel strips forged steel, steel castings and steel tubes shall be taken from relevant Indian Standard. If rivet heads, bolt heads (with or without washers), nuts (with or without washers and including projecting portion of shank) are picked out in a tint different from that of adjacent work, these shall be enumerated and measured as extra over.

(**Note :** No addition shall be made to the weight calculated for the purpose of measurement of steel and iron work for the paint applied either in shop or at site.)

Painting upto 10 cm in width or in girth and not in conjunction with similar painted work shall be measured in running metres and shall include cutting to line where so required. Cutting to line, where not included in the item, shall be measured separately in running metres. Small articles up to 0.1 m of painted surface, where not in conjunction with similar painted work, shall be enumerated.

Painting on different types of work shall be kept separate and surfaces to be painted shall be described. It shall be stated whether measurements are flat or girthed. Alternatively, different surfaces may be grouped a into one general item, areas of uneven surfaces being converted into equivalent plain areas in accordance with Table 5.6.

Corrugated sheet surfaces and Nainital pattern roof surfaces shall be included with plain surfaces after increasing their areas by the following percentages:

(*a*) Corrugated sheets	14 percent
(*b*) Nainital pattern roof (plain sheets with rolls)	10 percent
(*c*) Nainital pattern roof with corrugated sheets	25 percent
(*d*) Asbestos cement sheets, corrugated	20 percent
(*e*) Asbestos cement sheets, semi-corrugated	10 percent

Painting on eaves-gutters, rain-water pipes, soil and ventilating pipes and steel poles shall be measured in running metres stating the size or girth. Fittings, such as bends, shoes, branches, heads, etc. shall be included in the length.

Table 5.6. Equivalent Plain Areas of Uneven Surfaces

S. No.	*Description of Work*	*How Measured*	*Multiplying Factor*
1.	Panelled or framed and braced or ledged and battened or ledged, batten-battened and braced joinery	Measured flat (not girthed) including *CHOWKHAT* or frame, Edges, chocks, cleats, etc. shall be deemed to be included in the item	1.3 (for each side)
2.	Flush joinery	Measured flat (not girthed) including *CHOWKHAT* or frame. Edges, chocks, cleats, etc. shall be deemed to be included in the item	1.20 (for each side)
3.	Flush shutter	Measured flat overall	1.20 (for each side)
4.	Fully glazed or gauzed joinery	Measured flat (not girthed) including *CHOWKHAT* or frame. Edges, chocks, cleats, etc. shall be deemed to be included in the item	0.80 (for each side)
5.	Partly panelled and partly glazed or gauzed joinery	Measured flat (not girthed) including *CHOWKHAT* or frame. Edges, chocks, cleats, etc. shall be deemed to be included in the item	1 (for each side)
6.	Fully venetianed or louvred joinery	Measured flat (not girthed) including *CHUWKHAT* or frame. Edges, chocks, cleats, etc. shall be deemed to be included in the item	1.80 (for each side)
7.	Weather boarding	Measured flat (not girthed) supporting framework shall not be measured separately	1.20 (for each side)
8.	Wood shingle roofing	Measured flat (not girthed)	1.10 (for each side)
9.	Boarding with cover fillets and match boarding	Measured flat (not girthed)	1.05 (for each side)
10.	Tile and slate battening	Measured flat overall; no deduction shall be made for open spaces	0.80 (for painting all over)
11.	Trellis (or *JAFFRI*) work one-way or two-way	Measured flat overall; no deduction shall be made for open space ; supporting members shall not be measured separately	2 (for painting all over)
12.	Guard bars, balus-trades, gates, gratings, grills, expanded metal and railings	Measured flat overall; no deduction shall be made for open spaces; supporting members shall not be measured separately	1 (for painting all over)
13.	Gates and open palisade fancing including standards, braces, rails, stays, etc	Measured flat overall; no deduction shall be made for open spaces; supporting members shall not be measured separately (*see* Note 1)	1 (for painting all over)
14.	Carved or enriched work	Measured flat	2 (for each side)

15.	Steel roller shutters	Measured flat (size of opening) overall; jamb guides, bottom rails and locking arrangement, etc, shall be included in the item (top cover shall be measured separately)	1.10 (for each side)
16.	Plain sheet steel doors and windows	Measured flat (not girthed) including frame, edges, etc	1.10 (for each side)
17.	Fully glazed or gauzed steel doors and windows	Measured flat (not girthed) including frame, edges, etc	0.50 (for each side)
18.	Partly panelled and partly glazed or gauzed steel doors	Measured flat (not girthed) including frame, edges, etc	0.80 (for each side)
19.	Collapsible gate	Measured flat (size of opening)	1.50 (for painting all over)

Note 1–The height shall be taken from bottom of lowest rail, if palisades do not go below it or from lower end of palisades, if they project below lowest rail, up to top of palisades, but not up to top of standards if they are higher than palisades.

Note 2–Where doors, windows, etc. are of composite types other than those included in this table, different portions shall be measured separately with their appropriate coefficients, centre line of common rail being taken as the dividing line between the two portions.

Note 3–Measurement of painting doors, windows, collapsible gates, rolling shutters, etc. as given in this table shall be deemed to include painting, if required, of all iron fittings in the same shade.

Note 4–When two faces of a door, window, etc. are to be treated with different specified finishes, measurable under separate items, edges of frames and shutters shall be treated with the one or the other type of finish and measurement thereof shall be deemed to be included in the measurement of the face treated with that finish.

Note 5–In case where shutters are fixed on both faces of a frame, measurement for the door frame and shutter on one face shall be taken in the manner already described, while the additional shutter on the other face shall be measured exclusive of the frame.

Note 6–Where shutter is provided with clearance exceeding 15 cm at top and/or at bottom, such openings shall be deducted from the overall measurement and relevant coefficients applied.

Painting on small articles, such as gate and turn straps, metal ceiling/roses, metal switch-blocks, heads and nuts or bolts, articles of builder's hardware and the like when picked out in different tint or not in conjunction with similar painted work shall be enumerated.

Flag staffs, chimneys, aerial masts (not latticed), water tanks, flood light towers, overhead electric masts, spires and the like requiring special scaffolding shall be measured separately stating the size, height and average girth.

Painting in repair work up to 1 m^2 shall be enumerated in the following categories:

(*a*) Not exceeding 0.1 m^2,

(*b*) Exceeding 0.1 m^2 and not exceeding 0.5 m^2, and

(*c*) Exceeding 0.5 m^2 and not exceeding 1 m^2.

5.19.2. Varnishing

Application of sizing, staining and varnishing on wood-work shall be measured in accordance with the work provisions described in 5.19.1.

Polishing. Polishing on wood work shall be described as including all preparatory work and bodying-in and shall be measured in square metres in accordance with the provisions contained in 5.19.1. Alternatively, articles shall be described and enumerated.

5.19.3. Preservative Treatment

Surface application of wood preservatives shall be measured in square metres irrespective of girth or size, and the provisions contained in 5.19.1 shall be followed.

5.19.4. Tarring

Tarring shall be measured as for painting in accordance with the provisions contained in 5.19.1.

5.19.5. Writing Letters and Figures

Letters, figures and similar items shall be enumerated stating height and form or style, namely, block, italics, etc. stops, commas, hyphens and the like shall be deemed to be included in the item.

5.20. DEMOLITION AND DISMANTLING

Measurements. Measurement of all work, except hidden work, shall be taken before demolition or dismantling and no allowance for increase in bulk shall be made.

All work shall be measured net in the decimal system as fixed in its place, as given below.

(*i*) Dimensions shall be measured to the nearest 0.01 m.

(*ii*) Areas shall be worked out to the nearest 0.01 m^2.

(*iii*) Cubic contents shall be worked out to the nearest 0.01 m^3.

Precautions. Attention shall be drawn to any necessary precaution that may be taken for the protection of the public and the owner's property.

Temporary shoring for the safety of portions not required to be pulled down or of adjoining property, and temporary enclosures or partitions shall be included in the main item.

If precautions are required to be taken to keep down dust, nuisance, etc. it shall be so stated.

Demolition and Dismantling. Works required to be demolished and those required to be dismantled shall each be measured separately.

Lead. The description shall include separation of serviceable material from the unserviceable, stacking within 100 m and disposal of debris. Removal of material beyond 100 m shall be measured separately. The distance for removal shall be measured over the shortest practicable route and not necessarily the route actually taken. Distances exceeding 100 m and upto 1 km shall be measured in units of 100 m and those exceeding 1 km in units of 500 m. Works laid dry and with mortar shall be measured separately and the type of mortar shall be stated. Framed and unframed works shall be measured separately.

Disconnecting/Maintaining of Services. Attention shall be directed to any necessary disconnecting or maintaining of services, whether temporary or permanent; and an item shall be provided for making good if required.

5.20.1. Walls and Piers

Walls, independent piers, columns and their footing and foundation of brick, stone or concrete shall be described and measured in cubic metres. All copings, corbels, cornices and other projections shall be included with the wall measurements. In measuring the thickness of plastered walls, the thickness of the plaster shall be excluded.

Ashlar face stones, dressed stone work, precast concrete articles, etc. if required to be taken down in tact, shall be so stated and measured separately in cubic metres. Honeycomb work and hollow block walling of bricks, stone or concrete shall be measured as solid. Cleaning of bricks and stacking them for measurement, including all extra handling and removal and disposal of rubbish as stated, shall be enumerated in thousands of cleaned bricks.

Cleaning of stone obtained from demolished/dismantled stone masonry of any description including ashlar facing, dressed stonework, stone slabs or flagging and precast concrete blocks including all extra handling and disposal of rubbish as stated shall be measured in cubic metres of cleaned stone.

5.20.2. Reinforced Concrete and Reinforced Brick Work

Reinforced concrete structures and reinforced brick roofs and walls with their footing and foundation shall be measured in cubic metres and if reinforcement is required to be cut, it shall be so stated.

Where reinforcement is required to be separated, scraped and cleaned, the work shall be stated separately and measured in kilograms of salvaged steel.

5.20.3. Roof coverings generally including battens, boarding matts, bamboo *jaffari*, other subsidiary support, shall be measured in square metres stating the thickness and size or gauge. Ridges, hips and valleys shall be girthed and included with the roof area. Corrugated and semicorrugated surfaces shall be measured flat and not girthed. Mud on roofs shall be measured in cubic metres. Lead sheets in roofs shall be measured in kilograms and hips valleys, flashings, linings to gutters, etc. shall be included in this weight. Supporting members, such as rafters, purlins, beams, joists and trusses, where of wood, shall be measured in cubic metres and where of steel or iron sections, in kilograms. If the span exceeds 10 m, it shall be so stated.

5.20.4. Ceilings

Stripping of ceiling shall be measured in square metres and described. Supporting joists, beams, etc. shall be measured in cubic metres or in kilograms.

5.20.5. Concrete and Brick Roofs and Floors

Concrete and brick roofs and floors shall be measured in cubic metres. Beams, cantilevers and other supports of similar material shall be included in the item.

5.20.6. Floors and Pavings

Floors and pavings except concrete pavings, shall be measured in cubic metres and mode of fixing shall be described. Concrete pavings shall be measured in square metres stating their thickness.

5.20.7. Partitions, Trellis Work (*JAFFARI*), etc.

Partitions or light walls of lath and plaster, trellis work (*jaffari*), expanded metal, thin concrete or terra-cotta slabs and other similar materials, including framework, if any, shall be measured in square metres stating the thickness.

5.20.8. Woodwork

Ballies shall be measured in running metres. All other woodwork under 40 cm^2 in section shall be measured in running metres and average 40 cm^2 and over in cubic metres. Boarding including wooden *chhajjas* and sunshades with supports shall be measured in square metres stating the thickness.

5.20.9. Steel and Iron Work

All steel and iron work shall be measured in kilograms. The weight shall be computed from standard tables unless the actual weight can be readily determined. Riveted work, where rivets are required to be cut, shall be measured separately. Structural steel required to be re-erected shall be measured separately.

In framed steel gates the weight of any covering material or filling, such as iron sheets and expanded metal, shall be added to the weight of the main article if such covering is not ordered to bo taken out separately.

5.20.10. Doors and Windows

Doors, windows, clear storey windows, ventilators, etc. (wood or steel) whether to be removed while dismantling of walls or by making recesses in walls, when the walls are not to be dismantled, shall be enumerated. Those exceeding 3 m^2 in the size of openings shall be measured separately. Removal of *chowkhats*, architraves, holdfasts and other attachments shall be included in the item.

5.20.11. Posts or Struts

Posts or struts (wood, steel or R.C.C.) any section including taking out embedded portion shall be measured in running metres.

5.20.12. Fencing Wire Mesh

Fencing wire mesh of any type with framework shall be measured in square metres. If the framework is required to be separated and wire mesh put into rolls, it shall be so stated.

Taking out any description of serviceable glass, except polished plate, from old sashes, skylights, etc. (any thickness, weight or size) raking out old putty, etc. shall be measured in square metres. Irregular or circular plans shall be measured as rectangular or square.

5.20.13. Water Pipe Lines and Sewer Lines

Water pipe lines including rain water pipes with clamps and specials, sewer lines (salt glazed ware or concrete), etc. shall be described by their internal diameter and length and measured in running metres inclusive of joint (the measurement shall be taken along the centre line of pipe and fittings). If the joints, specials and fittings, etc. are required to be separated, it shall be so stated and enumerated. Pucca drains shall be measured in cubic metres and described. Valve, cisterns, public foundation platforms, fire hydrants, etc. shall be enumerated.

Manholes and inspection chambers shall be enumerated stating the size and depth of manhole/inspection chamber. They shall be classified into different groups depending upon the depth, such as upto half metre depth, half to one metre, one to two metres depth and so on. The depth of manhole shall be the distance between the top of manhole cover and invert level of the drain. Ventilating shafts, gulley traps, flushing cisterns and other appurtenant items of work shall be enumerated.

5.20.14. Road Work

Different types of road surfaces shall be measured separately. Road paving shall be measured in square metres and described. Concrete paving shall he measured as in 5.20.6. If concrete is reinforced with bars or fabric reinforcement, it shall be so stated and measured separately. Soling and sub-bases shall be measured in cubic metres separately for each type of material.

5.21. WATER SUPPLY, PLUMBING AND DRAINS

Description of Items. The description of each item shall, unless otherwise stated, be held to include, wherever necessary, conveyance and delivery, handling, loading, unloading, storing, fabrication, hoisting, all labour for finishing to required shape and size, setting, fitting and fixing in position, straight cutting and waste, return of packings, and other incidental operations.

Dimensions. All work shall be measured net as fixed, to the nearest 0.01 metre unless otherwise stated hereinafter.

All pipes and fittings shall be classified according to their nominal diameter, king of material, quality and the method of jointing and shall be measured in running metres unless otherwise specified. The method of laying jointing and fixing shall be fully described. The item shall include all cutting and waste of pipes and also cutting threads where necessary. In the case of fittings of unequal diameter, it shall be designated by largest diameter. The testing of water supply drains and plumbing shall be included in the description of the item. Lead caulked joints shall be enumerated separately.

Pipes laid or fixed in ducts, chases, trenches, embedded in floor, fixed to walls, ceilings, etc. with supports shall be measured separately. The method of measurement for excavation of trenches for laying pipelines and other allied works and refilling of the trenches, etc. shall be in accordance with Section 3. Concrete beds, haunchings and coverings, including any formwork required, shall be described and measured in running metres stating size of the pipe, dimensions and mix of concrete.

Cutting through walls, floors, etc. and making good shall be included with the item. This shall, however, not include concealed pipe work in which case the cutting of chase and making good shall be measured separately in running metres.

Lengths of pipes not exceeding one metre, other than running lengths, shall be measured separately in running metres and described as in short length.

5.21.1. Water Supply

Standard fittings like elbows, bends, tees, connectors, unions, diminishing sockets shall be included along with the pipes. Caps, collers, plugs, stopped ends and similar items of the pipe shall be described and enumerated.

Sluice valves, hydrants, stop-cocks, covers, surface boxes and water meters shall be described and enumerated and shall be measured separately according to the diameter. The jointing to pipe on either side shall be described. The connection to the water main shall be described and enumerated.

Boilers, Cisterns and Cylinders. Boilers, cisterns and cylinders shall be enumerated stating the type, size, location, method of fixing, working and test pressure and the type and size of the connections for pipes. Perforations for connections shall be enumerated.

Insulating Coverings to Boilers, Pipes, etc—Insulating coverings shall be fully described and measured in square metres in the case of boilers, cylinders and tanks and in running metres in the case of pipes stating the diameter. No deduction shall be made for manholes, hands, holes, pipes, etc. passing through insulation, nor shall any extra be measured for finishing insulations around such openings. Insulation to bends, elbows, tees, valves and the like shall be enumerated as extra over.

5.21.2. Plumbing

Plumber's Work. Locks, taps, valves, pillar-cock, stop-cock, ball valves, caps and linings, also cleaning, eyes with screw caps, ferrules, thimbles, unions, waste washers, perforated gratings and the like shall be described and enumerated. The joints and the fixing shall also be described and included in the item.

Benels, elbows, tees, branches, inspection or access doors, swan necks, enlarged sockets, etc. for soil waste and bent pipes shall be enumerated as extra over. Wire guards and ventilating cowls over tops of pipes shall be described and enumerated and measured separately according to the bore of the pipe.

Stack clamps shall be described and enumerated stating the length of stay and the method of fixing to wall or roof. Brass pipes shall be classified according to their external diameter and thickness of metal. The description shall state the method of jointing and fixing. Standard fittings like elbows, bends, tees, connectors, unions and diminishing sockets shall be enumerated.

Traps shall be described and enumerated. Joints at both ends shall be included in the item. Water closets, washdown type/squating type/siphonic washdown type wash basins, laboratory sinks, urinals, bowl type/half stall type/squatting plate type partition slabs, siphonic toilets, foot rests, shower roses, traps for squatting pans, universal water closets, flushing cisterns for urinals, automatic type, flushing cisterns for water closets and urinals, siphonic type, brackets and supports, bath tubs, cast iron gratings for drainage purposes, mixing valves, water closets, seats, self-closing taps, kitchen sinks, water spreaders for urinals, half round channels, foot rests, traps for squatting pans, waste fittings for wash basins and sinks, waste plugs and accessories for sinks and wash basins and other similar fittings together with fixing of the same shall be enumerated and fully, described.

5.21.3. Drain Pipes

The pipes shall be classified according to their nominal diameter, the quality of pipe, kind of material and the method of jointing and shall be measured in running metres, inclusive of all joints. The measurement shall be taken along the central line of the pipes and fittings or specials. All fittings or specials shall be enumerated separately as extra over the pipes. Cutting and jointing the pipes to such fittings or specials shall be deemed to be included with the item of fittings or specials.

Alternatively, the pipes shall be classified according to the nominal diameter, quality, kind of material and shall be measured in running metres. The measurement shall be taken along the central line of the pipes and in between the fittings or specials. All joints, fittings or specials shall be described and enumerated separately. Cutting of pipes for jointing to such fittings or specials shall be deemed to be included with the item of fittings or specials. The manholes and inspection chamber shall be measured in detail as per relevant Sections.

Alternatively the manholes and inspection chambers shall be described and enumerated. They shall be classified into different groups depending upon the depth, such as upto half metre depth, half to one, one to two, two to three and so on. The depth of the manhole shall be the distance between the top of the manhole cover and the invert of the main drain.

5.22. WATER AND SEWER-LINES

Description of Items. The description of each item shall, unless otherwise stated, be held to include wherever necessary conveyance and delivery, handling, unloading, storing, fabrication, hoisting, all labour for finishing to the required shape and size, setting, fitting and fixing in position, straight cutting and waste, and other incidental operations.

Dimensions. All work shall be measured net as fixed, to the nearest 0.01 metre, unless otherwise stated hereinafter.

Excavation and Earthwork. Method of measurement for excavation and earthwork for laying pipelines and other allied works shall be as given in Article 5.3.

Bed, Benchings and Covering. Method of measurement for beds, benchings and covering shall be as given in Article 21.3.

5.22.1. Method of Measurement of Water Lines

Pipes shall be classified according to their diameter, length of each pipe, kind of material, the quality of pipe and the method of jointing, and shall be measured in running metres inclusive of all joints. The measurement shall be taken along the central line of the pipes and fittings or specials. All fittings or specials shall be enumerated separately as extra over the pipes. Cutting and jointing the pipes to such fittings or specials shall be deemed to be included with the item of fittings or specials.

Alternatively, pipes shall be classified according to their diameter, kind of material quality of the pipe and shall be measured in running metres. The measurement shall be taken along the central line of the pipes and in between the fittings or specials. All joints, fittings or specials shall be fully described and enumerated separately. Cutting of pipes for jointing to such fittings or specials shall be deemed to be included with the item of fittings or specials.

Suspended pipes and vertical pipes shall be so described and the supports and other fixing arrangement measured separately.

Testing. The measurement for testing of the pipelines shall be in running metres, unless otherwise stated.

Miscellaneous Works. The valve cistern, public fountain platforms, fire hydrants, etc. shall be fully described and enumerated. All other miscellaneous works, such as supports like hangers, pillars, crossing of railway lines and culverts, cutting and reconditioning of pavements, deviation of pipelines and cables, dismantling and reconstruction of masonry works shall be measured as given in relevant Sections.

5.22.2. Method of Measurement of Sewer Lines

Sewer lines shall be classified according to their diameter, length of each pipe, kind of material, the quality of pipe and the method of jointing, and shall be measured in running metres inclusive of all joints. The measurement shall be taken along the central line of the sewers and fittings or specials. All fittings or specials shall be enumerated separately as 'extra over' the sewers. Cutting and jointing the sewers to such fittings or specials shall be deemed to be included with the item of fittings or specials.

Alternatively, sewers shall be classified according to their diameter, kind of material, quality of the pipe and shall be measured in running metres. The measurement shall be taken along the central line of the sewers and in between the fittings or specials. All joints, fittings or specials shall be fully described and enumerated separately. Cutting and jointing of sewers to such fittings or specials shall be deemed to be included with the item of fittings or specials.

Manholes. The manholes and the inspection chambers shall be measured in detail in accordance with the relevant section.

Alternatively, the manholes and inspection chambers shall be described and enumerated. They shall be classified into different groups depending upon the depth, such as, up to half metre depth, half to one, one to two, two to three and so on. The depth of the manhole shall be the distance between the top of the manhole cover and the invert of the main drain.

Appurtenant Items. Ventilating shafts, pumping mains and other appurtenant items of work shall be described and enumerated. Alternatively, these items shall be measured in detail as recommended in relevant Sections.

Testing. Measurement for testing of sewers shall be in running metres between manholes.

5.23. ROADWORK INCLUDING AIRFIELD PAVEMENT

Measurements. All work shall be measured net in the decimal system, fixed in its place, subject to the following limits, unless otherwise stated:

(*a*) Length and width shall be measured to the nearest 0.01 m the thickness shall be measured to nearest 0.005 m or nearest to specified tolerance whichever is less;

(*b*) Areas shall be worked out to the nearest 0.01 m^2; and

(*c*) Cubic contents shall be worked out to the nearest 0.01 m^3.

Bills of Quantities. The bills of quantities shall describe the materials and workmanship, and accurately represent the work to be executed.

The levels shall be taken before and after construction, at a grid of points 5 m centre to centre longitudinally in straight reaches and at 2.5 m on curves. On 2 lane roads, the levels shall be taken at four positions from transversely at 0.75 m and 2.75 m from either edge of the carriage way, and single lane roads at two positions transversely at 1.25 m from either edge of the carriage way, and also at the crown and edges. The reference for the transverse grid line shall be left in the form of embedded reference points on either ends so as to locate the grid points from level measurement after each successive course is laid. However, for pavement courses laid on widening portions at least one line of level shall be taken on each strip of the widening. The thickness of the pavement at these points shall be the difference of levels before and after construction falling in that area.

All work shall be measured in square metres, except where otherwise stated. The length shall be measured between the end of the pavement and the central line of the expansion joint or between the central line of consecutive expansion joint; the width shall be between the edge of a pavement and the central line of the construction joint or between the central line of construction and expansion joint or between the central line of consecutive construction joints.

Excavation and earthwork necessary to bring the road alignment to proper levels making embankment, drains and site clearance shall be measured in accordance with the provisions given in Article 20.3. Rolling and watering formations, when required, may be either included with the item or measured separately in square metres. The method of measurement for the materials for the roadwork shall be as given in Article 20.

Works involved in the preparation of cut formation shall be measured in units indicated below:

(*i*) Loosening and recompacting of subgrade level	square metre
(*ii*) Removal of unsuitable material	cubic metre
(*iii*) Replacement with suitable material in lieu of unsuitable material removed	cubic metre
(*iv*) Preparing rocky subgrade	square metre

Stripping including storing and re-application of top soil shall be measured in cubic metres.

5.23.1. Roadwork Generally

Soiling and sub-bases shall be described stating the thickness. Levelling course shall be measured as volume compacted in position in cubic metres. The volume shall be worked out as product of surface area and average thickness using prismoidal formulae.

Stripping including storing and re-application of top soil shall be measured as volume in cubic metres. Works involving loosening and recompacting of original ground shall be measured in square metres. Removal of unsuitable material at embankment foundation and replacement with suitable material shall be measured as in cubic metres.

5.23.2. Tar and Bitumen Roads

Binder. Tar or bitumen, hereinafter referred to as 'binder' shall be described stating type, grade and penetration value. Work carried out with different types of binders, shall be measured separately.

Priming. Priming surfaces of water-bound macadam prior to surface dressing shall be measured separately stating the type and quantity of primer per square metre.

Edging. Edging shall be measured in running metres describing the material and method of placing.

The excavation required to be done shall be included in the description of item and shall not be measured separately.

Tack Coat. Tack coat shall be measured in terms of surface area of application in square metres depending upon the rate of spread specified.

Bituminous Macadam Base in Binder Course. Bituminous macadam with binder course shall be measured as finished work in cubic metres.

The work of filling potholes not exceeding 0.005 m^3 shall included in the description of item and shall not be measured separately.

Bituminous Penetration Macadam Base in Binder Course. Penetration macadam base with binder course shall be measured as finished work in square metres.

Built Up Spray Gourt Rase Course. Built up spray grout shall be measured as finished work in square metres.

Surface Dressing. Each coat of surface dressing shall be measured as finished work in square metres.

Open Graded Premix Carpet. Open-graded premix carpet shall be measured as finished work in square metres.

Mix Seal Surfacing. Mix seal surfacing shall be measured as finished work in square metres.

Semi Dense Carpet. The semi-dense carpet shall be measured as finished work in cubic metres.

Asphaltic Concrete. Asphaltic concrete shall be measured as finished work in cubic metres.

Seal Coat. Seal coat shall be measured as finished work in square metres.

Pre-Fabricated Bitumenized Surfacing. The work shall be described and work in single layer and double layer shall each be measured separately in square metres.

5.23.3. Miscellaneous

Screening. Total quantity of rod metal, stone chips, etc. required to be screened shall be measured in cubic metres.

Breaking. Breaking stone, brick or other road materials into required sizes be measured in cubic metres of stacked materials after breaking, stating the size before and after breaking, and shall include tracking.

Scarifying. Scarifying shall be measured in square metres stating the depth scarified and the type of surface. Hand and machine scarifying shall each be measured separately.

Berms. Preparation of berms shall be measured in running metres stating the average filling and width.

Sub-bases, Bases and Shoulders. Granular sub-base shall be measured as finished work in position in cubic metres. Stabilized soil sub-base shall be measured as finished work in position in cubic metres. Water bound macadam base and sub-base course shall be measured as finished work in position in cubic metres.

Potholes. Potholes exceeding 0.005 m^3 shall be measured in cubic metres.

Shoulder. Shoulder construction shall be measured as finished work in position in cubic metres.

Pre-splitting Rock Excavation Slopes. The area of presplitting shall be measured as square metres of specified presplit slope surface.

Turfing with Sods. Turfing with sods shall measured as finished work in square metres.

Seeding and Mulching. Seeding and mulching shall be measured as finished work in square metres.

Drain. Pipe for sub-surface drain shall be measured in linear metres between extreme ends of the installation is complete. Jointing of pipes including the provision of hessian wrappings at open joints, plugging the upgrade end of pipe, providing grating/screen at the outlet end and providing impervious clay covering where required shall be included in the description and shall not be measured separately. Backfill material and aggregates for aggregate drains shall be measured as laid in position in cubic metres. Removal of unsuitable material and its replacement with suitable material in the trench bed shall be measured in volume of suitable material laid in position in cubic metres.

Culverts. RCC pipe culverts shall be measured along their centre between the inlet and the outlet ends in running metres. The concrete bedding shall be measured as per Article 21.23.

5.23.4. Cement Concrete Pavements

The strength of cement concrete to be used shall be described and the work shall be measured either in cubic metres or square metres. Concrete required to be spread and consolidated by mechanical spreaders and vibratory compacting equipment shall be measured separately and so described.

If concrete is reinforced with bars or fabric reinforcement, it shall be so stated and measured separately. Reinforcement shall be measured separately. Formwork for pavings shall be measured separately. Special surface finishes shall be described and measured separately in square metres or alternatively included with the main item itself.

Construction and dummy joints shall be described and measured separately if not included in the main item in running metres stating the thickness and depth of joint. The expansion joints shall be measured in running metres stating the thickness and depth of joint. Steel bowel bars including ferrules shall be described stating the length and diameter or bars and enumerated.

Steel plate reinforcement to the joints shall be described as including the metal sheath stating the thickness and width of the plate and the gauge of the metal sheath and measured in running metres of the joint. Forming tongued and groved longitudinal butt-joints shall be measured in running metres.

6

Analysis of Rates

6.1. INTRODUCTION

The rate per unit of any item of works, depends upon the cost of material, cost of labour, and other miscellaneous expenses, such as sundries, contractor's profit and overhead expenditures.

The quantity of material, may vary, according to their physical properties etc. The rates of material may also vary from place to place and similarly the labour cost also vary in plain and hilly areas. Hence, it is clear that the rate for any item of work is not constant and varies from one place to another place.

While working out the rates, for any item of the work, the following considerations must be made :

1. Specification of work, drawings of particular item that is shape and size; quantity and quality of material required ; availability of material, operations required while using the material, and rates of material at actual site of work.

2. Types of labour required ; availability of labour at the site of work ; facilities to labour ; local rates of labour ; any special type of labour needed.

3. Different types of machines needed for the operations and completion of jobs or items of works.

4. Source of water ; expenditure on water ; profit and overhead expenditure expected.

Sundries. Sundries, covers the expenditure towards the purchase of tools etc, required for the operations for the item of work and generally this expenditure does not exceed above 1% of the total rate of item.

Contractor's profit and overhead expenditure. Profit is required on the money which is spent on the work and to cover the overhead expenditure to maintain office and supervisory staff etc. For this 10% amount is added on the material and labour cost.

Hence for calculating the rate for any item of work, it is essential to know

(*a*) Quantity of material.

(*b*) Rate of material at site.

(*c*) Number of labourers needed (Task work).

(*d*) Wages of the labourers (Local rates/Contractor's rate).

(*e*) Water charges.

(*f*) Sundries.

(*g*) Contractor's profit and overhead expenditure.

6.2. FACTORS AFFECTING THE RATES

The following factors govern the rate :

(*a*) Specification of item.

(*b*) Specification of material.

(*c*) Cost of material at site.

(*d*) Transportation of material.

(*e*) Labour wages.

(*f*) Miscellaneous expenditure, such as rent, taxes, establishment, stationery, telephone etc. and supervision, repairs, depreciation, amenities to labourers, compensation, insurance, interest on investments and losses on advances etc.

6.3. BASIC RATES OF MATERIALS

Table 6.1. Materials for Building Work and Road Work

Note : These rates are exclusive of contractor's profit, overheads and carriage but include octroi, royalty, sales tax etc. These rates vary from place to place and at the same place from department to department and time to time as per Cost Index. It is, therefore, essential to refer rates prevailing at the area/jurisdiction under consideration.

S. No.	*Description*	*Unit*	*Rate ₹*
	6.1.1. A-Adhesive (rubber base)	kilogram	100.00
	Aggregate :		
	(1) Brick Aggregate (Single size) :		
1 A	63 mm nominal size	cum	155.00
1 B	50 mm nominal size	cum	160.00
1 C	40 mm nominal size	cum	165.00
1 D	25 mm nominal size	cum	170.00
1 E	20 mm nominal size	cum	180.00
	(2) Over Burnt (Jhama) Brick Aggregate :		
1 F	120 mm to 40 mm size	cum	150.00
1 G	90 mm to 40 mm size	cum	175.00
	(3) Stone Aggregate (Single size) :		
1 H	75 mm nominal size	cum	220.00
1 I	63 mm nominal size	cum	225.00
1 J	50 mm nominal size	cum	225.00
1 K	40 mm nominal size	cum	230.00
1 L	25 mm nominal size	cum	240.00
1 M	20 mm nominal size	cum	265.00
1 N	12.5 mm nominal size	cum	270.00
1 O	10 mm nominal size	cum	270.00
1 P	6 mm nominal size	cum	280.00
1 Q	100 mm nominal size	cum	225.00
1 R	80 mm nominal size	cum	220.00
	(4) Stone Chippings/Screenings :		
1 S	12.5/13.2 mm nominal size	cum	265.00
1 T	10/11.2 mm nominal size	cum	265.00
1 U	4.75 mm nominal size	cum	270.00
1 V	150 micron nominal size	cum	280.00

S. No.	Description	Unit	Rate ₹
	6.1.2. Aluminium sheet 24 gauge :	sq m	160.00
	Aluminium Strips		
2 A	Aluminium strip 40 mm wide and 2 mm thick	kilogram	115.00
2 B	Aluminium plain strip edging 57 × 12 × 3 mm	metre	70.00
2 C	Aluminium Plain Strip edging 38 × 12 × 3 mm	metre	50.00
2 D	Aluminium Strip 10 mm	kilogram	115.00
2 E	Aluminium Strip 25 mm	kilogram	115.00
2 F	Aluminium strip 38 mm wide and 1.6 mm thick	kilogram	115.00
	6.1.3. Asbestos Cement Products except pipes :		
3 A	Apron flashing pieces	each	82.00
	(1) Angles for plain ended eaves or boundary wall gutters :		
3 B	275 × 125 × 175 mm/279.4 × 127.0 × 177.8 mm nominal size	each	195.00
3 C	300 × 150 × 225 mm/304.8 × 152.4 × 228.6 mm nominal size	each	277.00
3 D	450 × 150 × 300 mm/457.2 × 152.4 × 304.8 mm nominal size	each	382.00
3 E	500 × 150 × 250 mm/508.0 × 152.4 × 254.0 mm nominal size	each	434.00
3 F	Barge Board 2.44 metre long	each	197.00
3 G	Barge Board 1.83 metre long	each	148.00
3 H	Curved barge board	each	85.00
3 I	Close fittings adjustable ridge 1.10 m long	pair	135.00
	(2) A.C. Drop end for socketed half round gutter :		
3 J	150/152.4 mm nominal size with 100/101.6 mm dia drain outlet	each	44.00
3 K	250/254 mm nominal size with 100/101.6 mm and 150/152.4 mm dia drain outlet	each	75.00
3 L	300/304.8 mm nominal size with 100/101.6 mm and 150/152.4 mm dia drain outlet	each	115.00
	(3) Drop end for plain ended eaves for boundary wall gutter :		
3 M	275 × 125 × 175 mm/279.4 × 127.0 × 177.8 mm nominal size with 100/101.6 mm and 150/152.4 mm dia outlet	each	74.00
3 N	300 × 150 × 225 mm/304.8 × 152.4 × 228.6 mm nominal size with 100/101.6 mm and 150/152.4 mm dia outlet	each	123.00
3 O	450 × 150 × 300 mm/457.2 × 152.4 × 304.8 mm nominal size with 100/101.6 mm and 150/152.4 mm dia outlet	each	133.00
	(4) Drop end for plain ended valley gutter :		
3 P	500 × 150 × 250 mm/508.0 × 152.4 × 254.0 mm nominal size with 100/101.6 mm and 150/152.4 mm dia outlet	each	141.00
3 Q	400 × 125 × 250 mm/406.4 × 127.0 × 254.0 mm nominal size with 100/101.6 mm and 150/152.4 mm dia outlet	each	98.00

(Contd.)

S. No.	Description	Unit	Rate ₹
3 R	450 × 125 × 150 mm/457.2 × 127.0 × 152.4 mm nominal size with 100/101.6 mm and 150/152.4 mm dia outlet	each	97.00
3 S	600 × 150 × 225 mm/609.6 × 152.4 × 228.6 mm nominal size with 100/101.6 mm and 150/152.4 mm dia outlet	each	154.00
3 T	900 × 200 × 225 mm/914.4 × 203.2 × 228.6 mm nominal size with 100/101.6 mm and 150/152.4 mm dia outlet	each	167.00
3 U	Eaves filler pieces	each	61.00
3 V	Expansion joint for North light curves	each	86.00
3 W	Expansion joint for ridges	each pair	160.00
3 X	Louvers 'S' type (1.75 m)	each	64.00
3 Y	North light adjustable ridge 1.22 mm long	pair	109.00
	(5) Nozzle for socketed half round eaves gutters :		
3 Z	150/152.4 mm nominal size	each	51.00
3 AA	250/254.0 mm nominal size	each	78.00
3 BB	300/304.8 mm nominal size	each	117.00
	(6) Nozzle for plain ended eaves or boundary wall gutters :		
3 CC	275 × 125 × 175 mm/279.4 × 127.0 × 177.8 mm nominal size	each	67.00
3 DD	300 × 150 × 225 mm/304.8 × 152.4 × 228.6 mm nominal size	each	108.00
3 EE	450 × 150 × 300 mm/457.2 × 152.4 × 304.8 mm nominal size	each	118.00
3 FF	500 × 150 × 250 mm/508.0 × 152.4 × 254.0 mm nominal size	each	128.00
	(7) Nozzle for plain ended valley gutters :		
3 GG	450 × 125 × 150 mm/457.2 × 127.0 × 152.4 mm nominal size	each	118.00
3 HH	600 × 150 × 225 mm/609.6 × 152.4 × 228.6 mm nominal size	each	119.00
3 II	900 × 200 × 225 mm/914.4 × 203.2 × 228.6 mm nominal size	each	157.00
3 JJ	400 × 125 × 250 mm/406.4 × 127 × 254 mm nominal size :	each	117.00
3 KK	North light ventilator curves	each	146.00
3 LL	One piece plain angular ridge 1.22 metres long	each	86.00
	(8) Plain ended eaves or boundary wall gutters :		
3 MM	275 × 125 × 175/279.4 × 127.0 × 177.8 mm nominal size	each	216.00
3 NN	300 × 150 × 225 mm/304.8 × 152.4 × 228.6 mm nominal size	each	310.00
3 OO	450 × 150 × 300 mm/457.2 × 152.4 × 304.8 mm nominal size	each	435.00
3 PP	500 × 150 × 250 mm/508.0 × 152.4 × 254.0 mm nominal size	each	485.00
	(9) Plain ended valley gutters :		
3 QQ	400 × 125 × 250 mm/406.4 × 127.0 × 254.0 mm nominal size	each	362.00
3 RR	450 × 125 × 150 mm/457.2 × 127.0 × 152.4 mm nominal size	each	318.00
3 SS	600 × 150 × 225 mm/609.6 × 152.4 × 228.6 mm nominal size	each	425.00
3 TT	900 × 200 × 225 mm/914.4 × 203.2 × 228.6 mm nominal size	each	619.00
3 UU	Ridge finials	pair	54.00
3 VV	Roof light (1.82 metre long)	each	638.00
3 WW	Serrated or plain wing Adjustable Ridge 1.22 m long	pair	117.00
3 XX	Sheets 6 mm thick (corrugated)	sq m	130.00
3 YY	Sheets plain 6 mm thick	sq m	118.00
3 ZZ	Sheets plain 4 mm thick	sq m	82.00

S. No.	Description	Unit	Rate ₹
	(10) Socketed half round gutter :		
3 AAA	150/152.4 mm nominal size	each	147.00
3 BBB	250/254.0 mm nominal size	each	203.00
3 CCC	300/304.8 mm nominal size	each	347.00
	(11) Stop end for socketed half round eaves gutter :		
3 DDD	150/152.4 mm nominal size	each	18.00
3 EEE	250/254.0 mm nominal size	each	25.00
3 FFF	300/304.8 mm nominal size	each	35.00
	(12) Stop end for plain ended eaves or boundary wall gutters :		
3 GGG	275 × 125 × 175 mm/279.4 × 127.0 × 177.8 mm nominal size	each	32.00
3 HHH	300 × 150 × 225 mm/304.8 × 152.4 × 228.6 mm nominal size	each	50.00
3 III	450 × 150 × 300 mm/457.2 × 152.4 × 304.8 mm nominal size	each	58.00
3 JJJ	500 × 150 × 250 mm/508.0 × 152.4 × 254.0 mm nominal size	each	61.00
	(13) Stop end for plain ended valley gutters :		
3 KKK	400 × 125 × 250 mm/406.4 × 127.0 × 254.0 mm nominal size	each	49.00
3 LLL	450 × 125 × 150 mm/457.2 × 127 × 152.4 mm nominal size	each	57.00
3 MMM	600 × 150 × 225 mm/609.6 × 152.4 × 228.6 mm nominal size	each	61.00
3 NNN	900 × 200 × 225 mm/914.4 × 203.2 × 228.6 mm nominal size	each	102.00
3 OOO	Unserrated adjustable ridge for hips	pair	118.00
3 PPP	Bajri	cum	214.00
3 QQQ	Bhusa	quintal	134.00
	6.1.4. Bitumen felt fibre base (vegetable or animal) :		
4 A	Type 2 grade I	sq m	43.00
4 B	Type 2 grade II	sq m	43.00
4 C	Bitumen felt, glass fibre base, type 2 grade 1	sq m	82.00
	6.1.5. Bitumen hot sealing compound :		
5 A	Grade A	kilogram	12.00
5 B	Bitumen solution primer of approved quality	litre	13.00
5 C	Premoulded joint filler 12 mm thick	sq m	227.00
	6.1.6. Bitumen and Coal Tar :		
6 A	Blown type petroleum bitumen of penetration 85/25 approved quality	tonne	7800.00
6 B	Coal Tar	litre	9.00
6 C	Paving bitumen S-90 of approved quality	tonne	8220.00
6 D	Paving Asphalt 30/40 Penetration	tonne	8220.00
6 E	Paving Asphalt 80/100 Penetration	tonne	6500.00
6 F	Solvent	kilogram	7.00

(Contd.)

S. No.	Description	Unit	Rate ₹
6 G	Blasting Powder	kilogram	18.00
6 H	Blasting fuse (fuse wire)	each	7.00
	6.1.7. Boards :		
	Flame retardant face insulating board :		
7 A	12 mm thick	sq m	175.00
7 B	18 mm thick	sq m	240.00
7 C	25 mm thick	sq m	325.00
7 D	Impregnated fibre board 12 mm thick	sq m	195.00
	6.1.8. Flat pressed 3 layer particle board (medium density) Grade I :		
8 A	6 mm thick	sq m	136.00
8 B	12 mm thick	sq m	195.00
8 C	18 mm thick	sq m	255.00
8 D	25 mm thick	sq m	340.00
	6.1.9. Natural colour insulating board :		
9 A	12 mm thick	sq m	129.00
9 B	18 mm thick	sq m	196.00
9 C	25 mm thick	sq m	274.00
	6.1.10. White face insulating board :		
10 A	12 mm thick	sq m	165.00
10 B	18 mm thick	sq m	250.00
10 C	25 mm thick	sq m	320.00
	6.1.11. Extra for veneered particle board with :		
11 A	Commercial veneering on both sides	sq m	64.00
11 B	Teak veneering on both sides	sq m	345.00
11 C	Teak veneering on one side and commercial veneering on other side	sq m	224.00
	6.1.12. Brackets :		
12 A	Brass brackets	each	90.00
12 B	C.P. Brass brackets	each	112.00
	6.1.13. Bricks :		
13 A	F.P.S. bricks class designation 75	thousand	1150.00
13 B	F.P.S. bricks class designation 50	thousand	1050.00
13 C	F.P.S. bricks class designation 35	thousand	800.00
13 D	F.P.S. brick tiles class designation 100	thousand	1250.00
13 E	F.P.S. brick tiles class designation 75	thousand	1150.00
13 F	Modular bricks class designation 75	thousand	1500.00
13 G	F.P.S. over burnt bricks	thousand	963.00
13 H	Brick bats	cum	150.00
13 I	Fire clay bricks	100 Nos.	1200.00
13 J	F.P.S. Clay fly ash bricks class designation 75	thousand	700.00
	6.1.14. Brushes :		
14 A	Wire brush	each	8.00
14 B	Soft brush	each	6.00
	6.1.15. Cement :		
15 A	Portland Cement	tonne	2525.00
15 B	White Cement	tonne	8000.00

S. No.	Description	Unit	Rate ₹
	6.1.16. Chemicals :		
16 A	Ammonium chloride	kilogram	7.50
16 B	Caustic soda	kilogram	20.00
16 C	Copper accetate	kilogram	130.00
16 D	Copper chloride	kilogram	140.00
16 E	Copper Nitrate	kilogram	128.00
16 F	Hydrochloric Acid	kilogram	15.00
16 G	Circular C.I. box for ceiling fan	each	22.00
16 H	Coal (Steam)	quintal	161.00
16 I	Coconut	kilogram	75.00
16 J	Concrete block (Foam)	cum	2106.00
16 K	Cotton string 6 mm dia. (machine made)	metre	2.00
16 L	Cramp Gun metal 25 × 6 × 300 mm	each	50.00
16 M	Cramp Gun metal 15 × 6 × 165 mm	each	20.00
16 N	Dahi (Curd)	kilogram	20.00
	6.1.17. Distemper :		
17 A	Dry	kilogram	19.00
17 B	Oil bound washable	kilogram	35.00
17 C	Fire clay	quintal	40.00
	FITTINGS :		
	6.1.18. Anodised Aluminium fittings		
	(1) Butt Hinges :		
18 A	125 × 75 × 4 mm	ten	330.00
18 B	125 × 63 × 4 mm	ten	310.00
18 C	100 × 75 × 4 mm	ten	290.00
18 D	100 × 63 × 3.2 mm	ten	280.00
18 E	100 × 63 × 4 mm	ten	290.00
18 F	75 × 63 × 4 mm	ten	180.00
18 G	75 × 63 × 3.2 mm	ten	150.00
18 H	75 × 45 × 3.2 mm	ten	66.00
18 I	50 × 35 × 3.2 mm	ten	50.00
18 J	Casement stay 250 mm	each	30.00
	(2) Flush bolt :		
18 K	250 mm size	each	45.00
18 L	150 mm size	each	32.00
18 M	100 mm size	each	21.00
	(3) Handles :		
18 N	125 mm with plate 175 × 32 mm	ten	270.00
18 O	100 mm with plate 150 × 32 mm	ten	174.00
18 P	75 mm with plate 125 × 32 mm	ten	156.00
18 Q	Hanging type door stopper	each	10.00
18 R	Kicking plate 50 cm long 100 × 3.15 mm	each	80.00
18 S	Piano hinges	metre	22.00
18 T	Pull bolt lock (locking bolt) of size 85 mm × 42 mm with screws, bolts, nuts and washers complete	each	20.00

(Contd.)

S. No.	Description	Unit	Rate ₹
	(4) Screws :		
18 U	50 mm	cent	28.00
18 V	40 mm	cent	24.00
18 W	30 mm	cent	21.00
18 X	25 mm	cent	19.00
18 Y	20 mm	cent	15.00
	6.1.19. Sliding door bolt :		
19 A	300 × 16 mm	each	85.00
19 B	250 × 16 mm	each	82.00
	6.1.20. Tower bolt (barrel type) :		
20 A	300 × 10 mm	ten	322.00
20 B	250 × 10 mm	ten	288.00
20 C	200 × 10 mm	ten	257.00
20 D	150 × 10 mm	ten	190.00
20 E	100 × 10 mm	ten	150.00
20 F	Pair of Anodised Aluminium lever handles for 100 mm mortice latch and lock	each	148.00
	6.1.21. Brass Fittings :		
21 A	Ball catcher 10 mm diameter	each	6.00
21 B	Brackets (curtain rods) 20 mm	each	18.00
21 C	Casement window fastener	each	22.00
	6.1.22. Casement stays (straight peg type) :		
22 A	300 mm weighing not less than 0.33 kg	each	48.00
22 B	250 mm weighing not less than 0.28 kg	each	42.00
22 C	200 mm weighing not less than 0.24 kg	each	36.00
22 D	Chain with hook for fan light catch	each	9.00
22 E	Cupboard knob or ward robe knob 50 mm	each	13.00
22 F	Curtain rails with roller stop ends and brackets	metre	78.00
22 G	Curtain rod 12 mm dia 1.25 mm thick	metre	48.00
22 H	Curtain rod 20 mm dia 1.25 mm thick	metre	52.00
22 I	Curtain rod 25 mm dia 1.25 mm thick	metre	67.00
	6.1.23. Cupboard lock 6 levers (best make of approved quality) :		
23 A	40 mm size	each	22.00
23 B	50 mm size	each	30.00
23 C	65 mm size	each	38.00
23 D	75 mm size	each	45.00
	6.1.24. Door latch :		
24 A	300 × 16 × 5 mm (0.380 Kg)	each	57.00
24 B	250 × 16 × 5 mm (0.350 Kg)	each	53.00
24 C	150 mm floor door stopper (0.357 Kg)	each	86.00
24 D	Fanlight catch	ten	90.00
24 E	Fanlight pivot	ten	102.00
24 F	Finger plate 30 cm long 65 × 1.6 mm (0.350 Kg)	each	50.00
	6.1.25. Flush bolts :		
25 A	250 mm	each	65.00
25 B	150 mm	each	45.00

S. No.	Description	Unit	Rate ₹
25 C	100 mm	each	30.00
25 D	Indicating Bolt (vacant/engaged)	each	70.00
25 E	Furniture handles (cupboard handle)	each	10.00
	6.1.26. Handles :		
26 A	125 mm with plate 175 × 32 mm	each	65.00
26 B	100 mm with plate 150 × 32 mm	each	55.00
26 C	75 mm with plate 125 × 32 mm	each	40.00
26 D	Hanging type door stopper 150 mm	each	25.00
26 E	Hydraulic door closer with necessary accessories and screws complete	each	280.00
	6.1.27. Hard drawn hooks and eyes :		
27A	300 mm	ten	350.00
27 B	250 mm	ten	320.00
27 C	200 mm	ten	300.00
27 D	150 mm	ten	275.00
27 E	100 mm	ten	220.00
	6.1.28. Hasps and Staples (Safety type) :		
28 A	300 mm	ten	385.00
28 B	115 mm	ten	320.00
28 C	90 mm	ten	255.00
28 D	Helical Spring 150 mm	each	140.00
	6.1.29. Hinges :		
	(1) Butt hinges (light/Ordinary type) :		
29 A	125 × 70 × 4 mm	ten	320.00
29 B	100 × 70 × 4 mm	ten	190.00
29 C	75 × 40 × 2.5 mm	ten	100.00
29 D	50 × 40 × 2.5 mm	ten	55.00
	(2) Butt hinges (heavy type) :		
29 E	125 × 85 × 5.5 mm (0.70 kg)	ten	1140.00
29 F	100 × 85 × 5.5 mm (0.56 kg)	ten	960.00
29 G	75 × 65 × 4.0 mm (0.20 kg)	ten	325.00
	(3) Double acting Spring Hinges :		
29 H	150 mm	each	241.00
29 I	125 mm	each	162.00
29 J	100 mm	each	134.00
	(4) Parliamentary hinges :		
29 K	150 × 125 × 27 × 5 mm	ten	1252.00
29 L	125 × 125 × 27 × 5 mm	ten	1059.00
29 M	100 × 125 × 27 × 5 mm	ten	867.00
29 N	75 × 100 × 20 × 3.2 mm	ten	674.00
	(5) Single acting spring hinges :		
29 O	150 mm	each	157.00
29 P	125 mm	each	125.00
29 Q	100 mm	each	80.00
29 R	Kicking plate 50 cm long 100 × 3.15 mm	each	205.00
29 S	Mortice latch and lock 100 × 65 mm with 6 levers and a pair of brass lever handles	each	210.00
29 T	Mortice latch 100 mm × 65 mm with a pair of brass lever handles	each	180.00
29 U	Night latch	each	250.00

(Contd.)

S. No.	Description	Unit	Rate ₹
29 V	Lock bolts	each	20.00
29 W	Peeping plate 70 × 50 mm	each	45.00
29 X	Piano hinges	metre	80.00
29 Y	Pull bolt (locking bolt) of size 85 mm × 42 mm with screws, bolts, nuts and washers complete	each	105.00
29 Z	Quadrant stays 300 mm	each	52.00
29 AA	Rim latch and lock 100 mm	each	125.00
29 BB	Rim latch 100 mm	each	120.00
29 CC	100 mm mortice latch and lock with 6 levers without pair of handles	each	125.00
	6.1.30. Sliding Door Bolts :		
30 A	300 × 16 mm	each	145.00
30 B	250 × 16 mm	each	134.00
	6.1.31. Screws :		
31 A	50 mm	cent	125.00
31 B	40 mm	cent	125.00
31 C	30 mm	cent	75.00
31 D	25 mm	cent	42.00
31 E	20 mm	cent	30.00
31 F	20 mm × 6 gauge of good quality	cent	80.00
	6.1.32. Tower bolts (barrel type) :		
32 A	250 × 10 mm	each	96.00
32 B	200 × 10 mm	each	77.00
32 C	150 × 10 mm	each	58.00
32 D	100 × 10 mm	each	38.00
	6.1.33. CHROMIUM PLATED FITTINGS (BRASS) :		
	Casement stays (straight peg type) :		
33 A	300 mm weighing not less than 0.33 Kg.	each	58.00
33 B	250 mm weighing not less than 0.28 Kg.	each	52.00
33 C	200 mm weighing not less than 0.24 Kg	each	42.00
33 D	Casement window fastner	each	41.00
33 E	Cupboard lock (six levers) 65 × 35 mm	each	41.00
33 F	Chain with hook for fanlight catch	each	10.00
	6.1.34. Cupboard lock (Nickled) :		
34 A	40 mm size	each	25.00
34 B	50 mm size	each	34.00
34 C	65 mm size	each	43.00
34 D	75 mm size	each	50.00
	6.1.35. Door latch :		
35 A	300 × 16 × 5 mm (380 gms)	each	69.00
35 B	250 × 16 × 5 mm (350 gms)	each	64.00
	6.1.36. Flush Bolts :		
36 A	250 mm	each	80.00
36 B	150 mm	each	50.00
36 C	100 mm	each	35.00
36 D	Fanlight catch	ten	182.00
36 E	Fanlight pivot	ten	165.00
36 F	Floor door stopper 150 mm (350 gms)	each	82.00

S. No.	Description	Unit	Rate ₹
	6.1.37. Handles :		
37 A	125 mm with plate 175 × 32 mm	each	72.00
37 B	100 mm with plate 150 × 32 mm	each	57.00
37 C	75 mm with plate 125 × 32 mm	each	49.00
37 D	Hanging type door stopper	each	27.00
	6.1.38. Hard drawn hooks and eyes :		
38 A	300 mm	ten	465.00
38 B	250 mm	ten	425.00
38 C	200 mm	ten	412.00
38 D	150 mm	ten	375.00
38 E	100 mm	ten	320.00
	6.1.39. Hasps and staples (safety type) :		
39 A	150 mm	ten	455.00
39 B	115 mm	ten	348.00
39 C	90 mm	ten	294.00
39 D	Helical door spring 150 mm	each	150.00
	6.1.40. Hinges :		
	(1) Butt hinges (Heavy type) :		
40 A	125 × 85 × 5.5 mm (750 gms)	ten	1260.00
40 B	110 × 70 × 5.5 mm (560 gms)	ten	1034.00
40 C	75 × 65 × 4 mm (200 gms)	ten	380.00
	(2) Butt hinges (Light/Ordinary type) :		
40 D	125 × 70 × 4 mm	ten	380.00
40 E	100 × 70 × 4 mm	ten	341.00
40 F	75 × 40 × 2.5 mm	ten	115.00
40 G	50 × 40 × 2.5 mm	ten	89.00
	(3) Double acting spring hinges :		
40 H	150 mm	each	240.00
40 I	125 mm	each	166.00
40 J	100 mm	each	110.00
	(4) Parliamentary hinges :		
40 K	150 × 125 × 27 × 5 mm	ten	1315.00
40 L	125 × 125 × 27 × 5 mm	ten	1112.00
40 M	100 × 125 × 27 × 5 mm	ten	910.00
40 N	75 × 100 × 20 × 3.2 mm	ten	708.00
	(5) Single acting spring hinges :		
40 O	150 mm	each	153.00
40 P	125 mm	each	104.00
40 Q	100 mm	each	85.00
40 R	Indicating bolt (Vacant/engaged)	each	140.00
40 S	Finger plate 30 cm long 65 × 1.6 mm	each	150.00
40 T	Kicking plate 50 cm long 100 × 3.15 mm	each	175.00
40 U	Lock bolts	each	19.00
40 V	Mortice latch and lock 100 mm × 65 mm with 6 levers and a pair of brass lever and a pair of brass handles	each	240.00
40 W	Mortice latch 100 mm × 65 mm with a pair of brass lever handles	each	225.00
40 X	Night latch	each	285.00

(Contd.)

S. No.	Description	Unit	Rate ₹
40 Y	Peeping plate 70 × 50 mm	each	50.00
40 Z	Pull bolt lock (locking bolt) of size 85 mm × 42 mm with screws, bolts, nuts and washers complete	each	90.00
40 AA	Quadrant stay 300 mm	each	51.00
40 BB	Rim latch and lock 100 mm	each	348.00
40 CC	Rim latch 100 mm	each	260.00
	6.1.41. Rods (Curtain rods of 1.25 mm thick) :		
41 A	12 mm diameter	metre	89.00
41 B	20 mm diameter	metre	129.00
41 C	25 mm diameter	metre	168.00
	6.1.42. Screws :		
42 A	50 mm	cent	145.00
42 B	40 mm	cent	116.00
42 C	30 mm	cent	84.00
42 D	25 mm	cent	57.00
42 E	20 mm	cent	45.00
	6.1.43. Sliding door bolts :		
43 A	300 × 16 mm	each	155.00
43 B	250 × 16 mm	each	140.00
	6.1.44. Tower bolts (barrel type) :		
44 A	250 × 10 mm	each	59.00
44 B	200 × 10 mm	each	47.00
44 C	150 × 10 mm	each	35.00
44 D	100 × 10 mm	each	26.00
44 E	Wardrobe Knob 50 mm	each	20.00
	6.1.45. COPPER OXIDISED FITTINGS (BRASS) :		
	(1) Casement stays (straight type) :		
45 A	300 mm weighing not less than 0.33 kg	each	61.00
45 B	250 mm weighing not less than 0.28 kg	each	52.00
45 C	200 mm weighing not less than 0.24 kg	each	44.00
45 D	Casement window fastener	each	42.00
45 E	Chain with hook for fanlight catch	each	11.00
	(2) Door latch :		
45 F	300 × 16 × 5 mm (380 gms)	each	62.00
45 G	250 × 16 × 5 mm (350 gms)	each	58.00
45 H	Fanlight catch	ten	178.00
45 I	Fanlight pivot	ten	155.00
45 J	Finger plate 30 cm long 65 × 1.6 mm	each	45.00
45 K	Floor door stopper 150 mm (350 gms)	each	80.00
	(3) Flush Bolts :		
45 L	250 mm	each	76.00
45 M	150 mm	each	50.00
45 N	100 mm	each	35.00
	(4) Handles :		
45 O	125 mm with plate 175 × 32 mm	each	72.00
45 P	100 mm with plate 150 × 32 mm	each	60.00
45 Q	75 mm with plate 125 × 32 mm	each	50.00
	(5) Hasps and staples (safety type) :		
45 R	150 mm	ten	475.00
45 S	115 mm	ten	360.00
45 T	90 mm	ten	340.00

S. No.	Description	Unit	Rate ₹
	(6) Hard drawn hooks and eyes :		
45 U	300 mm	ten	460.00
45 V	250 mm	ten	410.00
45 W	200 mm	ten	395.00
45 X	150 mm	ten	360.00
45 Y	100 mm	ten	299.00
	6.1.46. Hinges :		
	(1) Butt hinges (Heavy type) :		
46 A	125 × 85 × 5.5 mm	ten	1250.00
46 B	100 × 85 × 5.5 mm	ten	1020.00
46 C	75 × 65 × 4 mm	ten	365.00
	(2) Butt hinges (Light/Ordinary type) :		
46 D	125 × 70 × 4 mm	ten	450.00
46 E	100 × 70 × 4 mm	ten	350.00
46 F	75 × 40 × 2.5 mm	ten	135.00
46 G	50 × 40 × 2.5 mm	ten	100.00
	(3) Double acting spring hinges :		
46 H	150 mm	each	275.00
46 I	125 mm	each	200.00
46 J	100 mm	each	140.00
	(4) Parliamentary hinges :		
46 K	150 × 125 × 27 × 5 mm	ten	1440.00
46 L	125 × 125 × 27 × 5 mm	ten	1250.00
46 M	100 × 125 × 27 × 5 mm	ten	1060.00
46 N	75 × 100 × 20 × 3.2 mm	ten	850.00
	(5) Single acting hinges :		
46 O	150 mm	each	172.00
46 P	125 mm	each	138.00
46 Q	100 mm	each	84.00
46 R	Kicking plate 50 cm long 100 × 3.15 mm	each	210.00
46 S	Mortice latch and lock 100 mm × 65 mm with 6 levers and a pair of brass lever handles	each	230.00
46 T	Mortice latch 100 mm × 65 mm with a pair of brass lever handles	each	230.00
46 U	Night catch	each	249.00
46 V	Peeping plate 70 × 50 mm	each	45.00
46 W	Pull bolt (locking bolt) of size 85 mm × 42 mm with screws, bolts, nuts and washers complete	each	197.00
46 X	Quadrant stays 300 mm	each	49.00
46 Y	Rim latch and lock 100 mm	each	173.00
46 Z	Rim latch 100 mm	each	163.00
46 AA	Indicating Bolt (vacant/engaged)	each	150.00
46 BB	Cupboard lock (6 levers) 65 × 35 mm size	each	50.00
	6.1.47. Screws :		
47 A	50 mm	cent	100.00
47 B	40 mm	cent	86.00
47 C	30 mm	cent	60.00
47 D	25 mm	cent	40.00
47 E	20 mm	cent	30.00

(Contd.)

S. No.	Description	Unit	Rate ₹
	6.1.48. Sliding door bolts :		
48 A	300 × 16 mm	each	152.00
48 B	250 × 16 mm	each	139.00
	6.1.49. Tower bolts (barrel type) :		
49 A	250 × 10 mm	each	95.00
49 B	200 × 10 mm	each	74.00
49 C	150 × 10 mm	each	56.00
49 D	100 × 10 mm	each	38.00
	6.1.50. OXIDISED MILD STEEL FITTINGS :		
50 A	Chain with hook for fan light catch 300 mm	each	4.00
	(1) Door latch :		
50 B	300 × 20 × 6 mm	each	15.00
50 C	250 × 20 × 6 mm	each	15.00
50 D	Fan light catch	ten	32.00
50 E	Fan light pivot	ten	40.00
	(2) Handles :		
50 F	125 mm	each	3.00
50 G	100 mm	each	2.00
50 H	75 mm	each	1.00
50 I	Pull bolt lock of size 85 mm × 42 mm with bolts and nuts complete	each	19.00
	(3) Hasps and staples (safety type) :		
50 J	150 mm	ten	42.00
50 K	115 mm	ten	35.00
50 L	90 mm	ten	30.00
	6.1.51. Hinges :		
	(1) Butt hinges :		
51 A	125 × 65 × 2.12 mm	ten	73.00
51 B	100 × 58 × 1.90 mm	ten	39.00
51 C	75 × 47 × 1.70 mm	ten	20.00
51 D	50 × 37 × 1.50 mm	ten	16.00
	(2) Double acting spring hinges :		
51 E	150 mm	each	55.00
51 F	125 mm	each	45.00
51 G	100 mm	each	30.00
	(3) Parliamentary hinges :		
51 H	150 × 125 × 27 × 2.80 mm	ten	207.00
51 I	125 × 125 × 27 × 2.80 mm	ten	163.00
51 J	100 × 125 × 27 × 2.80 mm	ten	130.00
51 K	75 × 100 × 20 × 2.24 mm	ten	98.00
	(4) Single acting spring hinges :		
51 L	150 mm	each	55.00
51 M	125 mm	each	50.00
51 N	100 mm	each	35.00
	(5) Piano hinges :		
51 O	1 mm thick 35 mm wide finished with nickle plating	metre	14.00
51 P	1 mm thick 35 mm wide finished with brass plating	metre	16.00

S. No.	Description	Unit	Rate ₹
	(6) Tee hinges :		
51 Q	300 × 115 × 2.24 mm	ten	104.00
51 R	250 × 100 × 2.24 mm	ten	96.00
	6.1.52. Hooks and Eyes :		
52 A	300 mm	ten	60.00
52 B	250 mm	ten	45.00
52 C	200 mm	ten	40.00
52 D	150 mm	ten	30.00
52 E	100 mm	ten	20.00
	6.1.53. Screws :		
53 A	50 mm	cent	26.00
53 B	40 mm	cent	23.00
53 C	30 mm	cent	14.00
53 D	25 mm	cent	11.00
53 E	20 mm	cent	9.00
	6.1.54. Sliding door bolts :		
54 A	300 × 16 mm	each	25.00
54 B	250 × 16 mm	each	22.00
	6.1.55. Tower bolts (barrel type) :		
55 A	250 × 10 mm	each	15.00
55 B	200 × 10 mm	each	12.00
55 C	150 × 10 mm	each	9.00
55 D	100 × 10 mm	each	6.00
	6.1.56. MILD STEEL FITTINGS BRIGHT FINISHED OR BLACK ENAMELLED :		
56 A	Bolts and nuts 50 × 6 mm	each	2.00
56 B	Chain with hook for fan light catch 300 mm long	each	3.00
	(1) Door latch :		
56 C	300 × 20 × 6 mm	each	16.00
56 D	250 × 20 × 6 mm	each	13.00
56 E	Fan light catch	ten	30.00
56 F	Fan light pivot	ten	25.00
	(2) Handles :		
56 G	125 mm	each	4.00
56 H	100 mm	each	3.00
56 I	75 mm	each	2.00
	(3) Hasps and staples (safety type) :		
56 J	150 mm	ten	38.00
56 K	115 mm	ten	32.00
56 L	90 mm	ten	26.00
56 M	Helical door spring 150 mm	each	26.00
	6.1.57. Hinges :		
	(1) Butt hinges :		
57 A	125 × 65 × 2.12 mm	ten	65.00
57 B	100 × 58 × 1.90 mm	ten	35.00
57 C	75 × 47 × 1.70 mm	ten	18.00
57 D	50 × 37 × 1.50 mm	ten	14.00
	(2) Double acting spring hinges :		
57 E	150 mm	each	50.00

(Contd.)

S. No.	Description	Unit	Rate ₹
57 F	125 mm	each	41.00
57 G	100 mm	each	26.00
	(3) Parliamentary hinges :		
57 H	150 × 125 × 27 × 2.80 mm	ten	145.00
57 I	125 × 125 × 27 × 2.80 mm	ten	128.00
57 J	100 × 125 × 27 × 2.80 mm	ten	88.00
57 K	75 × 100 × 20 × 2.24 mm	ten	68.00
	(4) Piano hinges :		
57 L	1 mm thick 35 mm wide finished with nickle plating	metre	14.00
57 M	1 mm thick 35 mm wide finished with brass plating	metre	16.00
	(5) Single acting spring hinges :		
57 N	150 mm	each	45.00
57 O	125 mm	each	40.00
57 P	100 mm	each	35.00
	(6) Tee hinges bright finished or/and black enamelled :		
57 Q	300 × 115 × 2.24 mm	ten	110.00
57 R	250 × 100 × 2.24 mm	ten	100.00
	6.1.58. Hooks and Eyes :		
58 A	300 mm	ten	50.00
58 B	250 mm	ten	40.00
58 C	200 mm	ten	35.00
58 D	150 mm	ten	25.00
58 E	100 mm	ten	18.00
	6.1.59. Screws :		
59 A	50 mm	cent	24.00
59 B	45 mm	cent	20.00
59 C	40 mm	cent	16.00
59 D	30 mm	cent	13.00
59 E	25 mm	cent	10.00
59 F	20 mm	cent	8.00
	6.1.60. Sliding door bolts bright finished or/and enamelled :		
60 A	300 × 16 mm	each	22.00
60 B	250 × 16 mm	each	20.00
	6.1.61. Tower bolts (barrel type) :		
61 A	250 × 10 mm	each	12.00
61 B	200 × 10 mm	each	10.00
61 C	150 × 10 mm	each	8.00
61 D	100 × 10 mm	each	5.00
	6.1.62. Flush doors :		
	(1) Block Board Construction Teak wood ply on both faces :		
62 A	40 mm thick	sq m	825.00
62 B	35 mm thick	sq m	800.00
62 C	30 mm thick	sq m	765.00
62 D	25 mm thick	sq m	730.00
	(2) Commercial ply on both faces :		
62 E	40 mm thick	sq m	500.00

S. No.	Description	Unit	Rate ₹
62 F	35 mm thick	sq m	480.00
62 G	30 mm thick	sq m	460.00
62 H	25 mm thick	sq m	430.00
	(3) Commercial ply on one face :		
62 I	40 mm thick	sq m	720.00
62 J	35 mm thick	sq m	690.00
62 K	30 mm thick	sq m	660.00
62 L	25 mm thick	sq m	625.00
62 M	Lipping	sq m of door area	100.00
	(4) Louvers :		
62 N	Decorative type	sq m of door area	150.00
62 O	Rebate cutting	sq m of door area	25.00
	(5) Vision Panel :		
62 P	Square	sq m of door area	76.00
62 Q	Circular	sq m of door area	82.00
62 R	Fuel wood	quintal	250.00
62 S	Flyash cum	cum	Free
62 T	Galvanised steel barbed wire	quintal	2325.00
	6.1.63. Galvanised Steel Bolts and Nuts :		
63 A	Galvanised steel bolts and nuts 6 mm dia. and 25 mm long round head with slots	ten	4.00
63 B	Galvanised steel bolts and nuts 10 mm dia. and 125 mm long	each	5.00
63 C	Galvanised steel turn buckles	each	5.00
63 D	Galvanised steel bolts 10 mm dia 27 cm long both sides threaded with 4 galvanised steel nuts	each	8.00
63 E	Galvanised steel bolts 10 mm dia 7 cm long with nuts	each	4.00
63 F	Galvanised steel bolts and nuts 8 mm dia.	each	2.00
63 G	Galvanised steel J or L hooks 8 mm dia.	ten	30.00
63 H	Galvanised steel corrugated sheets	quintal	2700.00
63 I	Galvanised steel plain sheets	quintal	2725.00
63 J	Glass block 20 × 20 × 10 cm	each	98.00
63 K	Glass sheet of nominal thickness 3 mm (weighing not less than 7.5 kg/sq m)	sq m	142.00
63 L	Glass sheet of nominal thickness 4 mm (weighing not less than 10 kg/sq m)	sq m	175.00
63 M	Glass sheet of nominal thickness 5.5 mm (weighing not less than 13.50 kg/sq m)	sqm	250.00
63 N	Glass sheet frosted of nominal thickness 3 mm (weighing not less than 7.5 kg/sq m)	sq m	172.00
63 O	Glass sheet (pin head) 3 mm thick	sq m	98.00
63 P	Glass sheet (wired) 6 mm thick	sq m	310.00
63 Q	Glass strips 4 mm thick 40 mm deep	metre	4.00
63 R	Glass strips 6 mm thick 40 mm deep	metre	7.00

(Contd.)

S. No.	Description	Unit	Rate ₹
63 S	Glass strips 25 mm wide and 4 mm thick	metre	3.00
63 T	Glass strips 50 mm wide and 4 mm thick	metre	6.00
63 U	Glass strips 78 mm wide and 4 mm thick	metre	9.00
63 V	Glass strips 52 mm wide and 4 mm thick	metre	7.00
63 W	Glass strips 62 mm wide and 4 mm thick	metre	8.00
63 X	Glue	kilogram	35.00
63 Y	Hessian cloth	sq m	6.00
63 Z	Hiramachi	quintal	220.00
63 AA	Hooks (for Brass cleats) 7 to 10 cm size	each	23.00
63 BB	Iron pintels including welded pin	each	18.00
	6.1.64. Jali (cement concrete) :		
64 A	50 mm thick	sq m	150.00
64 B	40 mm thick	sq m	120.00
64 C	25 mm thick	sq m	90.00
64 D	Khas (unwashed)	quintal	1000.00
	6.1.65. Linoleum :		
65 A	Jaspe linoleum 2.00 mm thick	sq m	198.00
65 B	Jaspe linoleum 1.65 mm thick	sq m	144.00
65 C	Marble type linoleum 3.3 to 4.5 mm thick	sq m	304.00
65 D	Marble type linoleum 3.2 mm thick	sq m	289.00
65 E	Plain linoleum 4.5 mm thick	sq m	265.00
65 F	Plain linoleum 3.2 mm thick	sq m	209.00
	6.1.66. Lime :		
66 A	Dehradun white lime	quintal	250.00
66 B	Dry hydrated lime (factory made)	quintal	135.00
66 C	Satna lime	quintal	135.00
66 D	Unslaked lime	quintal	230.00
	6.1.67. Marble chips upto 4 mm and down size :		
67 A	Baroda green	quintal	90.00
67 B	Chocolate, grey or yellow	quintal	90.00
67 C	White and black	quintal	90.00
67 D	Large size above 4 mm, white and black	quintal	90.00
67 E	Marble dust/powder	cum	700.00
67 F	Marble pieces	quintal	100.00
	6.1.68. MARBLE SLABS :		
	(A) BLACK MARBLE		
	(1) Abu Zebra :		
68 A	20 mm thick	sq m	700.00
	(2) Bhainslana Zebra :		
68 B	20 mm thick	sq m	640.00
	(3) Kishangarh Zebra :		
68 C	20 mm thick	sq m	590.00
	(4) Makrana Dhobi Doongri Zebra :		
68 D	20 mm thick	sq m	400.00
	(5) Narnaul Zebra :		
68 E	20 mm thick	sq m	535.00

S. No.	Description	Unit	Rate ₹
	(6) Plain :		
68 F	20 mm thick	sq m	600.00
	(B) BROWN MARBLE :		
	(1) Bar :		
68 G	20 mm thick	sq m	540.00
	(2) Narnaul :		
68 H	20 mm thick	sq m	440.00
	(C) GREEN MARBLE :		
	(1) Abu :		
68 I	20 mm thick	sq m	710.00
	(2) Baroda :		
68 J	20 mm thick	sq m	650.00
	(3) Bundi :		
68 K	20 mm thick	sq m	590.00
	(4) Falna :		
68 L	20 mm thick	sq m	750.00
	(D) GREY MARBLE :		
	(1) Bundi :		
68 M	20 mm thick	sq m	540.00
	(2) Kumari :		
68 N	20 mm thick	sq m	480.00
	(E) PINK MARBLE :		
	(1) Bundi Adanga :		
68 O	20 mm thick	sq m	365.00
	(2) Makrana Adanga :		
68 P	20 mm thick	sq m	600.00
	(3) Plain :		
68 Q	20 mm thick	sq m	430.00
	(F) WHITE MARBLE :		
	(1) Abu plain :		
68 R	20 mm thick	sq m	1700.00
	(2) Abu panther :		
68 S	20 mm thick	sq m	675.00
	(3) Abu veined :		
68 T	20 mm thick	sq m	860.00
	(G) Makrana chalk doongri veined :		
68 U	20 mm thick	sq m	590.00
	(H) Makrana Doongri adanga veined :		
68 V	20 mm thick	sq m	485.00
	(I) Makrana first quality plain :		
68 W	20 mm thick	sq m	3660.00
	(J) Makrana second quality plain veined :		
68 X	20 mm thick	sq m	1560.00
68 Y	Marble stone pieces for crazy flooring	quintal	100.00

(Contd.)

S. No.	Description	Unit	Rate ₹
	6.1.69. Metallic floor hardener :	quintal	120.00
	6.1.70. MARBLE BLOCK :		
	(1) WHITE MARBLE :		
70 A	White makrana first quality plain	10 cu dm	933.00
70 B	White makrana second quality plain	10 cu dm	333.00
70 C	Abu plain	10 cu dm	480.00
70 D	Abu panther	10 cu dm	225.00
70 E	Makrana Doongri Adanga veined	10 cu dm	162.00
70 F	Makrana chalk Doongri veined	10 cu dm	196.00
70 G	Abu veined	10 cu dm	287.00
	(2) PINK MARBLE :		
70 H	Plain	10 cu dm	143.00
70 I	Makrana Adanga	10 cu dm	200.00
70 J	Bundi Adanga	10 cu dm	122.00
	(3) GREEN MARBLE :		
70 K	Baroda	10 cu dm	217.00
70 L	Abu	10 cu dm	237.00
70 M	Falna	10 cu dm	180.00
70 N	Bundi	10 cu dm	150.00
	(4) BLACK MARBLE :		
70 O	Plain	10 cu dm	143.00
70 P	Bhainslana Zebra	10 cu dm	160.00
70 Q	Kishangarh Zebra	10 cu dm	127.00
70 R	Abu Zebra	10 cu dm	180.00
70 S	Narnaul Zebra	10 cu dm	147.00
70 T	Makrana Dhobi Doongri Zebra	10 cu dm	133.00
	(5) GREY MARBLE :		
70 U	Kumari	10 cu dm	117.00
70 V	Bundi	10 cu dm	145.00
	(6) BROWN MARBLE :		
70 W	Bar	10 cu dm	180.00
70 X	Narnaul	10 cu dm	147.00
	6.1.71. Metal Beading :		
71 A	Steel	metre	11.00
71 B	Aluminium	metre	25.00
71 C	Misri	kilogram	30.00
71 D	Moorum	cum	190.00
71 E	Mud (dry)	cum	7.00
	6.1.72. Muslin cloth :		
72 A	For lining	metre	16.00
72 B	For sarkanda chicks	metre	19.00
72 C	Munj or ban	kilogram	20.00
72 D	Niwar (cotton)	metre	3.00
	6.1.73. OIL :		
73 A	Crude oil of specific weight 881 kg/cum	tonne	5500.00
73 B	Diesel oil	litre	8.00

S. No.	Description	Unit	Rate ₹
73 C	Kerosene oil	litre	7.50
73 D	Linseed oil (raw)	litre	50.00
73 E	Linseed oil (double boiled)	litre	68.00
73 F	Mobil oil	litre	56.00
73 G	Petrol	litre	21.00
73 H	Turpentine oil	litre	20.00
	6.1.74. Paints :		
74 A	Acid proof paint (chocolate or black)	litre	71.00
74 B	Aluminium paint	litre	91.00
74 C	Anticorrosive bituminous paint (black)	litre	47.00
74 D	Black Japan	litre	52.00
74 E	Enamel paint	litre	90.00
74 F	Flat wall paint	litre	92.00
74 G	Floor enamel paint in all shades except green	litre	75.00
74 H	Floor enamel paint in green shade	litre	80.00
74 I	Oil type wood preservative	litre	42.00
74 J	Paint remover	litre	64.00
74 K	Plastic emulsion paint	litre	130.00
74 L	Plastic emulsion sealer	litre	90.00
74 M	Ready mixed paint for steel work in all shades except white or green	litre	68.00
74 N	Ready mixed paint for steel work	litre	71.00
74 O	Red oxide	litre	64.00
74 P	Roofing paint for iron sheets in white, grey or green shade	litre	67.00
74 Q	Roofing paint for iron sheets in red colour	litre	66.00
74 R	Synthetic enamel paint black or chocolate shade	litre	90.00
74 S	Synthetic enamel paint in all shades except black or chocolate	litre	100.00
74 T	Water proofing cement paint	kilogram	21.00
74 U	White lead (ready mixed)	litre	45.00
74 V	White lead	kilogram	42.00
	6.1.75. Pegs :		
75 A	Chromium plated brass	each	22.00
75 B	Pig lead	kilogram	40.00
	6.1.76. Pigments :		
76 A	Black colour dark shade	kilogram	32.00
76 B	Green or blue medium shade	kilogram	36.00
76 C	Red, chocolate, orange, buff or yellow (red oxide of iron) light shade	kilogram	48.00
	6.1.77. Pins-Copper pins 6 mm dia 7.5 cm long :	each	12.00
	6.1.78. Pipes and accessories :		
	(A) Asbestos Cement Pipes and Accessories :		
	(1) Asbestos cement bends :		
78 A	50/50.8 mm dia without door	each	13.00
78 B	50/50.8 mm dia with door	each	16.00

(Contd.)

S. No.	Description	Unit	Rate ₹
78 C	80/76.2 mm dia without door	each	16.00
78 D	80/76.2 mm dia with door	each	19.00
78 E	100/101.6 mm dia without door	each	19.00
78 F	100/101.6 mm dia with door	each	22.00
	(2) Asbestos cement hexagonal rain water head :		
78 G	250 × 200/241.3 × 203.2 mm dia and 100/101.6 mm dia	each	25.00
78 H	300 × 250 mm and 100 mm dia	each	28.00
78 I	400 × 300 mm and 100 mm dia	each	45.00
	(B) Asbestos cement junction equal double 92.5 and 112.5 degree :		
78 J	50/50.8 mm dia without door	each	28.00
78 K	50/50.8 mm dia with door	each	35.00
78 L	80/76.2 mm dia without door	each	38.00
78 M	80/76.2 mm dia with door	each	40.00
78 N	100/101.6 mm dia without door	each	45.00
78 O	100/101.6 mm dia with door	each	50.00
	(C) Asbestos cement junction equal single 92.5 and 112.5 degree :		
78 P	50/50.8 mm dia without door	each	27.00
78 Q	50/50.8 mm dia with door	each	30.00
78 R	80/76.2 mm dia without door	each	22.00
78 S	80/76.2 mm dia with door	each	34.00
78 T	100/101.6 mm dia without door	each	30.00
78 U	100/101.6 mm dia with door	each	40.00
78 V	Asbestos cement pentagonal rain water head 230 × 200 mm and 80 mm dia or 100 mm dia	each	30.00
	(D) Asbestos cement rain water pipes :		
78 W	50/50.8 mm dia and 2 meters long	each	17.00
78 X	80/76.2 mm dia and 2 meters long	each	26.00
78 Y	100/101.6 mm dia and 2 meters long	each	34.00
78 Z	150/152.4 mm dia and 2 meters long	each	58.00
	(E) Standard holdar bat clamps for A.C. pipes :		
78 AA	50/50.8 mm dia	each	9.00
78 BB	80/76.2 mm dia	each	10.00
78 CC	100/101.6 mm dia	each	11.00
	(F) Standard holdar bat clamps for sand cast iron or cast iron pipes :		
78 DD	50 mm dia	each	10.00
78 EE	75 mm dia	each	11.00
78 FF	100 mm dia	each	15.00
78 GG	150 mm dia	each	20.00
	(G) Asbestos cement Standard Shoe :		
78 HH	50/50.8 mm dia	each	16.00
78 II	80/76.2 mm dia	each	20.00
78 JJ	100/101.6 mm dia	each	26.00
	(H) Asbestos cement offsets :		
	50/50.2 mm projection		
78 KK	50/50.8 mm dia	each	22.00
78 LL	80/76.2 mm dia	each	28.00
78 MM	100/101.6 mm dia	each	45.00

S. No.	Description	Unit	Rate ₹
	6.1.79. CAST IRON PIPES AND ACCESSORIES :		
	(1) Cast iron branches (plain) :		
79 A	75 mm dia single branch	each	70.00
79 B	100 mm dia single branch	each	105.00
79 C	150 mm dia single branch	each	280.00
79 D	75 mm dia double branch	each	130.00
79 E	100 mm dia double branch	each	160.00
	(2) Cast iron flat head or corner type bend :		
79 F	75 mm dia (inner)	each	60.00
79 G	100 mm dia (inner)	each	72.00
79 H	150 mm dia (inner)	each	120.00
	(3) Cast iron rain water pipes :		
79 I	75 mm dia and 1.80 metre long	each	215.00
79 J	100 mm dia and 1.80 metre long	each	270.00
79 K	150 mm dia and 1.80 metre long	each	525.00
	(4) Cast iron plain bend :		
79 L	75 mm dia (inner)	each	50.00
79 M	100 mm dia (inner)	each	65.00
79 N	150 mm dia (inner)	each	130.00
	(5) Cast iron plain shoe :		
79 O	75 mm dia (inner)	each	50.00
79 P	100 mm dia (inner)	each	65.00
79 Q	150 mm dia (inner)	each	130.00
	(6) Cast iron offsets (plain) :		
79 R	75 mm dia 55 mm projection	each	90.00
79 S	75 mm dia 75 mm projection	each	75.00
79 T	100 mm dia 55 mm projection	each	90.00
79 U	100 mm dia 75 mm projection	each	100.00
	SAND CAST IRON PIPES AND ACCESSORIES :		
	(1) Sand cast iron plain bend :		
79 V	75 mm dia	each	68.00
79 W	100 mm dia	each	82.00
79 X	150 mm dia	each	203.00
	(2) Sand cast iron plain shoe :		
79 Y	75 mm dia	each	50.00
79 Z	100 mm dia	each	70.00
79 AA	150 mm dia	each	130.00
	(3) Sand cast iron rain water pipes :		
79 BB	75 mm dia and 1.80 metre long	each	264.00
79 CC	100 mm dia and 1.80 metre long	each	300.00
79 DD	150 mm dia and 1.80 metre long	each	570.00
	6.1.80. Plate - Copper :	kilogram	160.00
	(1) Pulleys :		
80 A	38 mm dia	each	12.00
80 B	25 mm dia	each	12.00
80 C	40 mm dia	each	12.00

(Contd.)

S. No.	Description	Unit	Rate ₹
	6.1.81. Plastic roofing compound :	kilogram	30.00
	6.1.82. Plaster of Paris :	kilogram	5.00
	6.1.83. Plug :	each	4.00
	6.1.84. Primers :		
84 A	Aluminium primer	litre	62.00
84 B	Cement primer	litre	62.00
84 C	Distemper primer	litre	60.00
84 D	Pink primer (for wood)	litre	55.00
84 E	Red oxide zinc chromate primer	litre	60.00
	6.1.85. Polish :		
85 A	French spirit polish	litre	102.00
85 B	Wax polish (ready made)	kilogram	112.00
85 C	Putty for steel work	kilogram	37.00
85 D	Putty for wood work	kilogram	23.00
	6.1.86. PVC Sheets :		
86 A	Polyvinyl chloride sheet 1.5 mm thick	sq m	214.00
86 B	Polyvinyl chloride sheet 2.0 mm thick	sq m	247.00
86 C	Polyvinyl chloride sheet 3.0 mm thick	sq m	414.00
86 D	Polyvinyl chloride sheet 400 micron thick	sq m	42.00
	6.1.87. Rivets :	quintal	2300.00
	6.1.88. Road reflector :	each	400.00
	6.1.89. Rolling shutters and its parts :		
89 A	Rolling shutter made of 80 × 1.25 mm machine rolled laths	sq m	480.00
89 B	Top cover for rolling shutters	metre	200.00
89 C	27.5 cm long wire spring grade no. 2 for rolling shutters	each	125.00
89 D	Ball bearing for rolling shutters	each	125.00
	(1) Extra for mechanical devices chain and cranked operation for operating rolling shutters :		
89 E	Exceeding 10.00 sq m and upto 16.80 sq m area of door	sq m	175.00
89 F	Exceeding 16.80 sq m area of door	sq m	180.00
89 G	Royalty for good earth	cum	5.00
89 H	Royalty for sludge (from okhla)	cum	33.00
89 I	Rubber sheet 3.2 mm thick	sq m	147.00
89 J	Rubber sheet 4.8 mm thick	sq m	202.00
89 K	Rubber sheet 6.4 mm thick	sq m	274.00
89 L	Rubbing compound	kilogram	100.00
89 M	Selkhari	kilogram	5.00
	6.1.90. Sand :		
90 A	Coarse sand (zone III)	cum	315.00
90 B	Fine sand (zone IV)	cum	175.00
90 C	Sand-zone V (Jamuna)	cum	105.00
90 D	Sarkand	quintal	300.00
90 E	Sealing compound	kilogram	12.00
90 F	Seam bolts nuts 6 mm dia and 25 mm long	ten	16.00
90 G	Shellac	kilogram	50.00
90 H	Spirit	litre	20.00
90 I	Spunyarn	kilogram	20.00

S. No.	Description	Unit	Rate ₹
90 J	Standard quality hard board sheet 3 mm thick	sq m	70.00
90 K	Standard quality hard board sheet 4 mm thick	sq m	81.00
90 L	Standard quality hard board sheet 4.5 mm thick	sq m	89.00
	6.1.91. Steel doors and windows :		
91 A	Pressed steel door frames (mild steel sheet 1.25 mm) profile 'A'	metre	80.00
91 B	Pressed steel door frames (mild steel sheet 1.25 mm) profile 'B'	metre	90.00
91 C	Pressed steel door frames (mild steel sheet 1.25 mm) profile 'C'	metre	105.00
91 D	Ready made steel door with necessary hinges, lugs and glazing clips excluding other fittings and their fixing	sq m	570.00
91 E	Ready made steel window (fixed) with lugs and glazing clips excluding other fittings and their fixing	sq m	270.00
91 F	Ready made steel window (side hung) with lugs, hinges and glazing clips excluding other fittings and their fixing	sq m	530.00
91 G	Ready made steel ventilator (top hung) with lugs, hinges and glazing clips excluding other fittings and their fixing	sq m	530.00
91 H	Ready made steel ventilator (central hung) with pivots, lugs, glazing clips excluding other fittings and their fixing	sq m	530.00
	6.1.92. Steel :		
92 A	Mild steel barbed wire	quintal	2140.00
92 B	Mild steel bolts 6 mm dia and 25 mm long with hexagonal head	ten	5.00
92 C	Bolts and nuts upto 300 mm in length	quintal	2800.00
92 D	Bolts and nuts above 300 mm in length	quintal	2800.00
92 E	20 × 6 mm mild steel clamps 15 cm long (for securing chicks)	each	10.00
92 F	Mild steel sheets for tanks	quintal	1750.00
92 G	Mild steel expanded metal 20 × 60 mm strands	sq m	100.00
92 H	Flats upto 10 mm in thickness	quintal	1425.00
92 I	Flats exceeding 10 mm in thickness	quintal	1425.00
92 J	Mild steel flat angle iron clamp 50 × 6 mm and 50 cm long including bolts and nuts	each	40.00
92 K	Hard drawn steel wire fabric	sq m	150.00
92 L	Mild steel hooks	each	10.00
92 M	Hoop iron 30 mm × 25 mm × 1.6 mm	quintal	1530.00
92 N	Hard drawn steel wire	quintal	2200.00
92 O	20 mm dia holding down bolts	quintal	2140.00
92 P	Mild steel ring 40 mm dia 6 mm round bar	each	5.00
92 Q	Mild steel rivets	quintal	2200.00
92 R	Mild steel plates	quintal	1710.00
92 S	Mild steel round bar 12 mm dia and below	quintal	1435.00
92 T	Mild steel round bar above 12 mm dia	quintal	1430.00
92 U	Average rate of Mild steel round bars for reinforcement	quintal	1432.00
92 V	Mild steel square bars	quintal	1500.00

(Contd.)

S. No.	Description	Unit	Rate ₹
92 W	Twisted steel/deformed bars	quintal	1450.00
92 X	Straining bolts	each	28.00
92 Y	Structural such as tees, angles, channels and R.S. Joists	quintal	1470.00
92 Z	"U" shape mild steel clamps	each	17.00
92 AA	Pull bolt (locking bolt) with screws complete	each	25.00
92 BB	Mild steel sheets with bolts and puts to rest on pintels	each	56.00
92 CC	Mild steel flat strap fitting	quintal	1425.00
92 DD	Mild steel tubes, hot finished welded type	kilogram	25.00
92 EE	Mild steel tubes, hot finished seamless type	kilogram	34.00
92 FF	Mild steel tubes, electric resistant or induction butt welded.	kilogram	30.00
	6.1.93. Stones and stone tiles :		
93 A	Boundry stone top chisel dressed 15 × 15 × 90 cm	each	34.00
93 B	Carborundum stone 100 × 50 × 50 mm	ten	380.00
93 C	Through and bond stone	cent	800.00
93 D	Crushed stone 2.36 mm to 12.5 mm size	cum	450.00
93 E	Kerb stone 30 × 20 cm	metre	70.00
93 F	Kerb stone 30 × 10	metre	60.00
93 G	Kilometre stone top chisel dressed 22.5 × 10 × 75 cm	each	60.00
93 H	Kota stone slab 20 mm to 25 mm thick (semi-polished)	sq m	180.00
93 I	25 mm thick Kota stone slabs (rough chiselled)	sq m	95.00
93 J	Kota stone slab 30 mm to 40 mm thick (semi-polished)	sq m	190.00
93 K	Kota stone slab 45 mm to 50 mm thick (semi-polished)	sq m	200.00
93 L	Red sand stone slab 45 mm and 50 mm thick (un-polished)	sq m	151.00
93 M	Red sand stone slab 75 mm thick (un-polished and unchiselled)	sq m	270.00
93 N	White sand stone slab 75 mm thick (un-polished)	sq m	320.00
93 O	Red sand stone slab 40 mm thick	sq m	129.00
93 P	White sand stone slab 40 mm thick	sq m	150.00
93 Q	Red sand stone slab 30 mm thick	sq m	100.00
93 R	White sand stone slab 30 mm thick	sq m	120.00
93 S	Soling stone	cum	150.00
93 T	Red sand stone block	10 cu dm	45.00
93 U	White sand stone block	10 cu dm	50.00
93 V	Stone dust	cum	470.00
93 W	Stone for masonry work	cum	270.00
93 X	Stone for pitching 15 cm × 22.5 cm	cum	180.00
93 Y	Stoneware spouts 100 mm dia 60 cm long	each	22.00
93 Z	Stone grit 6 mm and down size or pea sized gravel	cum	395.00
93 AA	White sand stone slab 45 mm and 50 mm thick (un-polished)	sq m	215.00
93 BB	Cutting marble or sand stone slab upto 50 mm thick by mechanical device	metre	4.00
93 CC	8 mm thick granite stone tiles (mirror polished of all shades)	sq m	400.00
93 DD	8 mm thick marble tiles (polished) Raj Nagar	sq m	200.00
93 EE	18 to 20 mm (average) thick Doongri-Adanga marble tiles (polished)	sq m	200.00

S. No.	Description	Unit	Rate ₹
93 FF	7.3 mm thick ceramic tiles of all shades (as per manufacturer's specification)	sq m	185.00
93 GG	Chequered terrazo tiles 22 mm thick (medium shade)	sq m	131.00
93 HH	Chequered terrazo tiles 22 mm thick (dark shade)	sq m	116.00
93 II	Chequered terrazo tiles 30 mm thick (light shade)	sq m	136.00
93 JJ	Chequered terrazo tiles 30 mm thick (medium shade)	sq m	148.00
93 KK	Chequered terrazo tiles 30 mm thick (dark shade)	sq m	123.00
93 LL	Decorated white background glazed tiles 152 mm × 152 mm	ten	63.00
93 MM	Decorated coloured background glazed tiles 152 mm × 152 mm	ten	66.00
93 NN	White glazed tiles 152 mm × 152 mm	ten	46.00
93 OO	Glazed colour tiles 152 mm × 152 mm	ten	46.00
93 PP	Polyvinyl chloride tiles 1.5 mm thick	sq m	280.00
93 QQ	Polyvinyl chloride tiles 2.0 mm thick	sq m	315.00
93 RR	Polyvinyl chloride tiles 3.0 mm thick	sq m	435.00
93 SS	Precast terrazo tiles 20 mm thick (light shade)	sq m	144.00
93 TT	Precast terrazo tiles 20 mm thick (medium shade)	sq m	125.00
93 UU	Precast terrazo tiles 20 mm thick (dark shade)	sq m	108.00
93 VV	Strips-Aluminium fluted 3.15 mm thick and 150 mm wide	metre	140.00
93 WW	Surkhi	cum	300.00
93 XX	Sundries L.S. provision	1 time	**Prevailing C. I. based on 1.1.92.** 100
	6.1.94. Timber :		
	(A) BALLIES :		
	(1) Hollock Ballies :		
94 A	Hollock ballies 80 mm diameter	metre	18.00
94 B	Hollock ballies 100 mm diameter	metre	22.00
94 C	Hollock ballies 125 mm diameter	metre	25.00
94 D	Hollock ballies 150 mm diameter	metre	30.00
	(2) Safeda Bailies :		
94 E	Safeda ballies 80 mm diameter	metre	8.00
94 F	Safeda ballies 100 mm diameter	metre	12.00
94 G	Safeda ballies 125 mm diameter	metre	17.00
94 H	Safeda ballies 150 mm diameter	metre	21.00
	(B) BAMBOO :		
94 I	Bamboo 25 mm dia 2.5 metre long	score	120.00
94 J	Bamboo 25 mm dia 3.0 metre long	score	140.00
94 K	Commercial plywood 4 mm	sq m	110.00
94 L	Decorative plywood 4 mm	sq m	210.00
94 M	First class deodar wood in scantling	10 cu dm	265.00
94 N	First class deodar wood in planks	10 cu dm	285.00
94 O	Second class deodar wood in scantling	10 cu dm	244.00
94 P	Second class deodar wood in planks	10 cu dm	254.00
94 Q	Hollock wood in scantling	10 cu dm	168.00

(Contd.)

S. No.	*Description*	*Unit*	*Rate ₹*
94 R	Hollock wood in planks	10 cu dm	188.00
94 S	First class kail wood in scantling	10 cu dm	115.00
94 T	First class kail wood in planks	10 cu dm	145.00
94 U	Second class kail wood in scantling	10 cu dm	100.00
94 V	Second class kail wood in planks	10 cu dm	120.00
94 W	Mango wood in scantling	10 cu dm	50.00
94 X	Mango wood in planks	10 cu dm	60.00
94 Y	Sal wood in scantling	10 cu dm	178.00
94 Z	Sal wood in planks	10 cu dm	188.00
94 AA	Superior class teak wood such as Dandeli, Balarshah or Malabar in scantling	10 cu dm	600.00
94 BB	Superior class teak wood such as Dandeli, Balarshah or Malabar in planks	10 cu dm	610.00
94 CC	First class teak wood in scantling	10 cu dm	354.00
94 DD	First class teak wood in planks	10 cu dm	365.00
94 EE	Second class teak wood in scantling	10 cu dm	297.00
94 FF	Second class teak wood in planks	10 cu dm	310.00
94 GG	Extra for selected planks of superior teak wood	10 cu dm	50.00
94 HH	Extra for selected planks of first class teak wood	10 cu dm	50.00
94 II	Extra for selected planks of second class teak wood	10 cu dm	50.00
94 JJ	Extra for selected planks of first class deodar wood	10 cu dm	40.00
94 KK	Extra for selected planks of second class deodar wood	10 cu dm	40.00
94 LL	Extra for selected planks of first class kail wood	10 cu dm	25.00
94 MM	Extra for selected planks of second class kail wood	10 cu dm	25.00
94 NN	Kiln seasoning of timber	cum	400.00
	(C) PANELS :		
94 OO	Ply wood 3 ply with teak ply on one face and commercial ply on another face 3 mm thick	sq m	175.00
94 PP	Ply wood 3 ply with teak ply on one face and commercial ply on another face 4 mm thick	sq m	226.00
94 QQ	Ply wood 5 ply with commercial ply on both faces 6 mm thick	sq m	175.00
94 RR	Ply wood 5 ply with commercial ply on both faces 8 mm thick	sq m	199.00
94 SS	Ply wood 5 ply with teak ply on both faces 9 mm thick	sq m	360.00
94 TT	Ply wood 5 ply with teak ply on one face and commercial ply on another face 6 mm thick	sq m	310.00
94 UU	Ply wood 5 ply with teak ply on one face and commercial ply on another face 9 mm thick	sq m	360.00
94 VV	Ply wood 7 ply with teak ply on both faces 19 mm thick	sq m	366.00
94 WW	Ply wood 7 ply with teak ply on one face and commercial ply on another face 9 mm thick	sq m	401.00
94 XX	Ply wood 7 ply with teak ply on one face and commercial ply on another face 19 mm thick	sq m	538.00

S. No.	Description	Unit	Rate ₹
94 YY	Ply wood 9 ply with commercial ply on both faces 13 mm thick	sq m	277.00
94 ZZ	Ply wood 9 ply with commercial ply on both faces 16 mm thick	sq m	362.00
94 AAA	Ply wood 9 ply with commercial ply on both faces 19 mm thick	sq m	414.00
94 BBB	Ply wood 9 ply with teak ply on both faces 13 mm thick	sq m	555.00
94 CCC	Ply wood 9 ply with teak ply on one face and commercial ply another face 13 mm thick	sq m	485.00
	(D) Varnishes :		
93 DDD	Ordinary varnish	litre	30.00
93 EEE	Superior copal varnish	litre	68.00
93 FFF	Superior spar varnish	litre	72.00
93 GGG	Water proofing materials	kilogram	12.00
	(E) Washers :		
93 HHH	G.I. limpet washer	cent	15.00
93 III	Bitumen washer	cent	15.00
93 JJJ	G.I. plain washer thick	cent	24.00
93 KKK	G.I. plain washer thin	cent	15.00
93 LLL	G.I. plain washer for seam bolts	cent	15.00
93 MMM	G.I. plain washer for ornamental gutter	cent	17.00
93 NNN	Mild steel washer	quintal	1700.00
	6.1.95. Wax-Bee's commercial :	kilogram	100.00
	(1) Welding :		
95 A	By gas plant	cm.	0.60
95 B	By electric plant	cm.	0.50
	Whiting :	quintal	250.00
95 C	Wire mesh (Rabbit)	sq m	25.00
95 D	Wire nails	kilogram	19.00
	(2) Gypsum board ceiling :		
95 E	Gypsum board	sq m	122.00
95 F	Ceiling sections	metre	31.00
95 G	Perimetre channel	metre	19.00
95 H	Intermediate channel	metre	33.00
95 I	Ceiling angle	metre	14.00
95 J	Connecting clips	each	4.00
95 K	Soffit cleat	each	2.00
95 L	Joint filler	kilogram	16.00
95 M	Joint finisher	kilogram	18.00
95 N	Joint tape	roll	100.00
95 O	Dash fastener	each	6.40
95 P	Drive all screws	100	33.00
95 Q	Primer	litre	60.00
95 R	Chloropyriphos 20% E.C.	litre	95.00
95 S	Chromium plated brackets (Curtain rod)	each	4.00

(Contd.)

Table 6.2. BASIC RATES LABOUR

Note : These rates are exclusive of contractor's profit and overheads and are inclusive of wages for weekly day of rest

S. No.	*Description*	*Unit*	*Rate* ₹
1.	Bandhani	per day	75.00
2.	Bhishti	per day	71.00
3.	Blacksmith 1st class	per day	110.00
4.	Blacksmith 2nd class	per day	90.00
5.	Bullockman with single bullock	per day	130.00
6.	Carpenter 1st class	per day	110.00
7.	Carpenter 2nd class	per day	90.00
8.	Chowkidar	per day	65.00
9.	Beldar	per day	65.00
10.	Coolie	per day	65.00
11.	Fitter (Grade 1)	per day	110.00
12.	Assistant Fitter or 2nd class Fitter	per day	90.00
13.	Frash	per day	65.00
14.	Glazier	per day	90.00
15.	Khalasi	per day	65.00
16.	Mason (for plaster of paris work) 1st class	per day	110.00
17.	Mason (for brick work) 1st class	per day	110.00
18.	Mason (for brick work) 2nd class	per day	90.00
19.	Mason (for plain stone work) 2nd class	per day	90.00
20.	Mason (for ornamental stone work) 1st class	per day	110.00
21.	Driver for Road Roller, Concrete Mixer, Truck etc.	per day	110.00
22.	Mate	per day	71.00
23.	Mali	per day	65.00
24.	Mistry	per day	110.00
25.	Painter	per day	90.00
26.	Rock Excavator	per day	65.00
27.	Rock Breaker	per day	65.00
28.	Rock Hole Driller	per day	65.00
29.	Stone Chiseller	per day	75.00
30.	Sewerman	per day	75.00
31.	Sweeper	per day	70.00
32.	Sprayman (for bitumen, tar etc.)	per day	70.00
33.	Skilled Beldar (for floor rubbing etc.)/Grinder	per day	70.00
34.	White Washer	per day	70.00
35.	Upholster 1st class	per day	130.00
36.	Upholster 2nd class	per day	110.00
37.	Welder	per day	100.00

S. No.	Description	Unit	Rate ₹
38.	Well Sinker	per day	90.00
39.	Assistant Artist Painter	per day	110.00
40.	Stone Cutter 1st class	per day	110.00
41.	Stone Cutter 2nd class	per day	100.00
42.	Mason (average)	per day	100.00
43.	Carpenter (average)	per day	100.00
44.	Operator (Pile)	per day	130.00
45.	Mechanic (Pile)	per day	100.00

*These rates are average of 1st class and 2nd class categories. This is for use in the analysis of rate only.

Table 6.3. BASIC RATES CHARGES OF PLANTS

S. No.	Description	Unit	Rate ₹
1.	Coaltar Boiler 900 to 1400 litres	per day	250.00
2.	Concrete Mixer 0.14 cubic metre	per day	200.00
3.	Diesel Road Roller - 8 to 10 tonne	per day	800.00
4.	Diesel Truck - 7 to 10 tonne capacity	per day	800.00
5.	Coaltar Sprayer	per day	150.00
6.	Barber green, drying, mixing and Asphalt Plant, with accessories, capacity 30/45 tonne	per day	7000.00
7.	Derrick monkey rope	per day	472.00
8.	Pumpset for pumping water @ 3636.8 litres/hour	per day	150.00
9.	Vibrator (Needle type 40 mm)	per day	150.00
10.	Machine for rubbing of floors	per day	110.00
11.	Front end loader	per day	400.00
12.	Dozer	per day	500.00
13.	Mastic Cooker	per day	400.00
14.	Tipper	per day	800.00
15.	Loader	per day	500.00
16.	Hand Grinder for mirror polish	per day	200.00
17.	Spray unit	per day	150.00
18.	Pin Vibrator	per day	200.00
19.	Surface Vibrator	per day	250.00
20.	Bitumen Mixer	per day	400.00

Note : Above hire-charges include cost of services of operating staff and supply of lubricating oil.

Table 6.4. BASIC RATES MATERIALS FOR SERVICES

S. No.	*Description*	*Unit*	*Rate* ₹
	Note: These rates are exclusive of contractor's profit, overheads and carriage but include octroi, royalty, sales tax, etc.		
1.	**Bleaching powder**	quintal	580.00
	Board Draining :		
2.	600 × 450 × 25 mm thick teakwood with skirting and beading	each	342.00
3.	750 × 450 × 25 mm thick teakwood with skirting and beading	each	390.00
	Bolts and Nuts :		
4.	16 mm dia. 60 mm long	each	6.00
5.	16 mm dia. 65 mm long	each	6.00
6.	20 mm dia. 65 mm long	each	8.50
7.	20 mm dia. 70 mm long	each	11.00
8.	20 mm dia. 75 mm long	each	11.50
9.	20 mm dia. 80 mm long	each	12.00
10.	24 mm dia. 85 mm long	each	25.00
11.	24 mm dia. 90 mm long	each	28.00
12.	27 mm dia. 100 mm long	each	32.00
	Box (Surface) :		
13.	For stop cock	each	50.00
14.	For sluice valve	each	96.00
15.	For fire hydrant	each	228.00
16.	For water meter	each	139.00
	Bracket - C.I. :		
17.	For flushing cistern	pair	22.00
18.	For wash basin and sinks	pair	28.00
19.	Brass fisher Union 32 mm	each	43.00
20.	Brass fisher Union 40 mm	each	52.00
	Cap (Brass) perforated for :		
21.	15 mm dia pipe	each	5.00
22.	20 mm dia pipe	each	6.00
23.	25 mm dia pipe	each	12.00
	Chain :		
24.	G.I. chain with G.I. pull	each	7.50
25.	C.P. brass chain with 32 mm dia rubber plug	each	13.00
26.	C.P. brass chain with 40 mm dia rubber plug	each	15.00
	Channel S.W. (60 cm long) :		
27.	100 mm dia.	each	18.00
28.	150 mm dia.	each	30.00
29.	250 mm dia.	each	52.00

S. No.	Description	Unit	Rate ₹
	Channel - Vitreous China :		
30.	Without stop end with outlet 100 × 300 mm	each	72.00
31.	Without stop end without outlet 100 × 300 mm	each	70.00
32.	Without outlet 100 × 300 mm	each	74.00
33.	Without outlet 100 × 600 mm	each	140.00
	Cistern :		
	Low level :		
34.	10 litres without fittings (vitreous china)	each	615.00
35.	10 litres with fittings (vitreous china)	each	1215.00
	Automatic C.I. flushing Cistern :		
36.	5 litres with fittings	each	125.00
37.	10 litres with fittings	each	140.00
38.	15 litres with fittings	each	171.00
	High level :		
39.	10 litres C.I. flushing cistern with fittings and C.I. chain and pull	each	375.00
	Clamps :		
40.	Holder bat clamp 32 mm	each	5.00
41.	Clamps and M.S. stays including bolts and nuts for 100 mm pipe	each	13.00
	M.S. Holder bat clamp of approved Design for :		
42.	100 mm S.C.I. pipe	each	7.00
43.	75 mm S.C.I. pipe	each	7.00
44.	50 mm S.C.I. pipe	each	6.00
45.	Clamps and M.S. stays including bolts and nuts for 50 mm pipe	each	12.00
46.	Clamps and M.S. stays including bolts and nuts for 75 mm pipe	each	13.00
	Clearing eye with chain and lid		
47.	100 mm dia	each	22.00
48.	150 mm dia	each	25.00
49.	250 mm dia	each	30.00
	Cocks :		
	Brass bib cock :		
50.	15 mm dia	each	65.00
51.	20 mm dia	each	80.00
52.	25 mm dia	each	124.00
	Brass stop cock :		
53.	15 mm dia	each	72.00
54.	20 mm dia	each	80.00
55.	25 mm dia	each	122.00
56.	32 mm dia	each	140.00
57.	40 mm dia	each	190.00
58.	50 mm dia	each	280.00

(Contd.)

S. No.	*Description*	*Unit*	*Rate* ₹
	Container for liquid soap with C.P. brass lid and brackets :		
59.	Glass	each	37.00
60.	Plastic	each	24.00
61.	Coupling (Mosquito Proof) of approved design	each	12.00
	Covers :		
62.	C.I. mosquito proof 40 cm dia. and frame with locking arrangement	each	135.00
63.	C.I. cover and frame 350 × 300 mm inside	each	90.00
64.	C.I. cover without frame 300 × 300 mm inside cover of 4.50 kg	each	70.00
	L.D. Rectangular :		
65.	455 × 610 mm with frame	each	460.00
66.	455 × 610 mm without frame	each	280.00
	M.D. 500 mm dia :		
67.	With frame	each	1100.00
68.	Without frame	each	800.00
	H.D. 560 mm dia :		
69.	With frame	each	2250.00
70.	Without frame	each	1200.00
	Ferrule Brass, C.I. Mouth :		
71.	15 mm dia	each	50.00
72.	20 mm dia	each	84.00
73.	25 mm dia	each	120.00
	Foot Rests :		
74.	Vitreous china 250 × 130 × 30 mm	pair	69.00
75.	Vitreous china 250 × 125 × 25 mm	pair	60.00
	Grating (C.I.) :		
76.	100 × 100 mm	each	6.00
77.	125 × 125 mm	each	7.00
78.	150 × 150 mm	each	10.00
79.	180 × 180 mm	each	15.00
80.	Grating (Gully) C.I. with frame 500 × 450 mm	each	380.00
	Grating (S.C.I.) for gully or Nahni :		
81.	100 mm dia	each	6.00
82.	150 mm dia	each	8.50
83.	Hydrant (Fire)	each	1200.00
	Insertions of Rubber for pipe joints :		
84.	For 50 mm dia pipe joints	each	6.00
85.	For 80 mm dia pipe joints	each	7.00
86.	For 100 mm dia pipe joints	each	9.00
87.	For 125 mm dia pipe joints	each	10.00
88.	For 150 mm dia pipe joints	each	13.00
89.	For 200 mm dia pipe joints	each	17.00

S. No.	Description	Unit	Rate ₹
	Container for liquid soap with		
90.	For 250 mm dia pipe joints	each	22.00
91.	For 300 mm dia pipe joints	each	29.00
92.	For 350 mm dia pipe joints	each	35.00
93.	For 400 mm dia pipe joints	each	55.00
94.	For 450 mm dia pipe joints	each	65.00
95.	For 500 mm dia pipe joints	each	80.00
96.	For 600 mm dia pipe joints	each	90.00
	C.I. detachable joints for A.C. pressure pipes :		
97.	80 mm dia	each	65.00
98.	100 mm dia	each	80.00
99.	125 mm dia	each	100.00
100.	150 mm dia	each	125.00
101.	200 mm dia	each	200.00
102.	250 mm dia	each	250.00
103.	300 mm dia	each	300.00
104.	Mirror of superior make glass 60 × 45 cm	each	180.00
105.	Single matting	each	10.00
106.	C.P. brass overflow 32 mm dia	each	132.00
107.	C.P. brass overflow 40 mm dia	each	144.00
108.	Pads for inlet and outlet	each	6.00
109.	Vitreous china pedestal for wash basin	each	435.00
110.	Pig lead	kilogram	40.00
	PIPES :		
	ASBESTOS CEMENT PRESSURE PIPES (CLASS 15)		
111.	80 mm dia	metre	96.00
112.	100 mm dia	metre	117.00
113.	125 mm dia	metre	140.00
114.	150 mm dia	metre	170.00
115.	200 mm dia	metre	280.00
116.	250 mm dia	metre	360.00
117.	300 mm dia	metre	490.00
	CAST IRON PIPES AND SPECIALS :		
118.	Centrifugally cast (spun) iron S & S pipes (class LA)	quintal	1500.00
119.	S & S C.I. standard specials upto 300 mm dia (heavy class)	quintal	1370.00
120.	S & S C.I. non-standard specials upto 300 mm dia (heavy class)	quintal	1363.00
121.	S & S C.I. standard specials over 300 mm dia (heavy class)	quintal	1540.00
122.	S & S C.I. non-standard specials over 300 mm dia (heavy class)	quintal	1510.00
123.	Flanged C.I. standard specials upto 300 mm dia (heavy class)	quintal	1482.00
124.	Flanged C.I. non-standard specials upto 300 mm dia (heavy class)	quintal	1465.00

(*Contd.*)

S. No.	Description	Unit	Rate ₹
	Container for liquid soap with		
125.	Flanged C.I. standard specials over 300 mm dia (heavy class)	quintal	1650.00
126.	Flanged C.I. non-standard specials over 300 mm dia (heavy class)	quintal	1620.00
127.	Casing pipe 100 mm dia	metre	180.00
	C.I. specials plain ended for A.C. pressure pipes		
	Plain ended C.I. bends 80 mm dia :		
128.	90 degree	each	105.00
129.	45 detree	each	80.00
130.	22.50 degree	each	68.00
131.	11.25 degree	each	55.00
	Plain ended C.I. bends 100 mm dia :		
132.	90 degree	each	165.00
133.	45 degree	each	115.00
134.	22.50 degree	each	75.00
135.	11.25 degree	each	96.00
	Plain ended C.I. bends 125 mm dia :		
136.	90 degree	each	232.00
137.	45 degree	each	222.00
138.	22.50 degree	each	159.00
139.	11.25 degree	each	125.00
	Plain ended C.I. bends 150 mm dia :		
140.	90 degree	each	315.00
141.	45 degree	each	290.00
142.	22.50 degree	each	204.00
143.	11.25 degree	each	145.00
	Plain ended C.I. bends 200 mm dia :		
144.	90 degree	each	505.00
145.	45 degree	each	441.00
146.	22.50 degree	each	298.00
	Plain ended C.I. bends 250 mm dia :		
147.	90 degree bends	each	837.00
148.	45 degree bends	each	718.00
149.	22.50 degree	each	512.00
	Plain ended C.I. Tees :		
150.	80 × 80 mm dia	each	152.00
151.	100 × 80 mm dia	each	198.00
152.	100 × 100 mm dia	each	215.00
153.	125 × 125 mm dia	each	315.00
154.	150 × 80 mm dia	each	368.00
155.	150 × 100 mm dia	each	381.00
156.	150 × 125 mm dia	each	409.00
157.	150 × 150 mm dia	each	431.00
158.	200 × 80 mm dia	each	587.00
159.	200 × 100 mm dia	each	600.00

S. No.	Description	Unit	Rate ₹
160.	200 × 125 mm dia	each	626.00
161.	200 × 200 mm dia	each	713.00
162.	250 × 250 mm dia	each	1150.00
163.	300 × 100 mm dia	each	1210.00
164.	300 × 200 mm dia	each	1300.00
	Plain ended C.I. crosses :		
165.	80 × 80 mm dia	each	191.00
166.	100 × 80 mm dia	each	232.00
167.	100 × 100 mm dia	each	271.00
168.	125 × 125 mm dia	each	388.00
169.	150 × 80 mm dia	each	426.00
	Plain ended C.I. caps :		
170.	80 mm dia	each	102.00
171.	100 mm dia	each	132.00
172.	150 mm dia	each	219.00
173.	200 mm dia	each	363.00
174.	250 mm dia	each	497.00
	Plain ended C.I. flange adopters :		
175.	80 mm dia	each	116.00
176.	100 mm dia	each	143.00
177.	150 mm dia	each	230.00
178.	250 mm dia	each	428.00
	Plain ended C.I. reducers :		
179.	100 × 80 mm dia	each	132.00
180.	125 × 80 mm dia	each	151.00
181.	125 × 100 mm dia	each	176.00
182.	150 × 80 mm dia	each	188.00
183.	150 × 100 mm dia	each	207.00
184.	200 × 150 mm dia	each	308.00
185.	250 × 125 mm dia	each	398.00
186.	300 × 200 mm dia	each	588.00
	CENTRIFUGALLY CAST (SPUN) IRON SOIL WASTE VENT PIPES AND FITTINGS :		
	S & S Pipe 1.75 metres long :		
187.	100 mm dia	each	300.00
188.	75 mm dia	each	259.00
189.	50 mm dia	each	197.00
	Bends :		
	With access doors :		
190.	100 mm dia	each	82.00
191.	75 mm dia	each	68.00
192.	50 mm dia	each	65.00
	Plain :		
193.	100 mm dia	each	82.00

(Contd.)

S. No.	Description	Unit	Rate ₹
194.	75 mm dia	each	68.00
195.	50 mm dia	each	54.00
	Heal rest sanitary bends :		
196.	100 mm dia	each	90.00
197.	75 mm dia	each	80.00
198.	50 mm dia	each	65.00
	Double equal junction :		
	With access door :		
199.	100 × 100 × 100 × 100 mm	each	191.00
200.	75 × 75 × 75 × 75 mm	each	144.00
201.	50 × 50 × 50 × 50 mm	each	96.00
	Plain :		
202.	100 × 100 × 100 × 100 mm	each	173.00
203.	75 × 75 × 75 × 75 mm	each	123.00
204.	50 × 50 × 50 × 50 mm	each	78.00
	Single equal Junctions :		
	With access door :		
205.	100 × 100 × 100 mm	each	149.00
206.	75 × 75 × 75 mm	each	111.00
207.	50 × 50 × 50 mm	each	95.00
	Plain :		
208.	100 × 100 × 100 mm	each	133.00
209.	75 × 75 × 75 mm	each	95.00
210.	50 × 50 × 50 mm	each	71.00
	Double unequal junction :		
	With access door :		
211.	100 × 100 × 75 × 75 mm	each	179.00
212.	100 × 100 × 50 × 50 mm	each	150.00
	Plain :		
213.	100 × 100 × 75 × 75 mm	each	167.00
214.	100 × 100 × 50 × 50 mm	each	150.00
	Single unequal Junctions :		
	With access door :		
215.	100 × 100 × 75 mm	each	146.00
216.	100 × 100 × 50 mm	each	146.00
217.	75 × 75 × 50 mm	each	110.00
	Plain :		
218.	100 × 100 × 75 mm	each	131.00
219.	100 × 100 × 50 mm	each	131.00
220.	75 × 75 × 50 mm	each	100.00
	Single unequal invert branch of required degree :		
221.	100 × 100 × 75 mm	each	140.00

S. No.	Description	Unit	Rate ₹
222.	100 × 100 × 50 mm	each	140.00
	CENTRIFUGALLY CAST (SPUN) IRON S & S :		
	Offsets :		
	75 mm Offset for :		
223.	75 mm dia. pipe	each	81.00
224.	100 mm dia. pipe	each	115.00
	150 mm Offset for :		
225.	50 mm dia. pipe	each	95.00
226.	75 mm dia. pipe	each	106.00
227.	100 mm dia. pipe	each	133.00
	Centrifugally cast (spun) iron door pieces :		
228.	100 mm	each	122.00
229.	75 mm	each	99.00
	Slotted Cowl (Terminal Guard) :		
230.	100 mm	each	68.00
231.	75 mm	each	56.00
232.	50 mm	each	45.00
	Centrifugally cast (spun) iron collars :		
233.	100 mm	each	47.00
234.	75 mm	each	40.00
235.	50 mm	each	32.00
	Centrifugally cast (spun) iron pass over pipe :		
236.	50 mm	each	115.00
	Flush pipe :		
	Flush pipe with union spreaders and clamps all in C.P. Brass for :		
237.	Single stall	each	350.00
238.	Double stall	each	550.00
239.	Range of three stall	each	725.00
240.	Range of four stall	each	900.00
	Flush pipe and spreaders G.I. for single lipped urinal :		
241.	Single lipped urinal	each	150.00
242.	Range of two lipped urinals	each	300.00
243.	Range of three lipped urinals	each	450.00
244.	Range of four lipped urinals	each	575.00
	Flush pipe (G.I.) and spreaders for squatting plate urinal :		
245.	Single set of one plate	each	205.00
246.	Range of two plates	each	275.00
247.	Range of three plates	each	340.00
248.	Range of four plates	each	415.00
249.	Galvanised iron telescopic flush pipe with brass union (32 mm) dia	each	180.00

(Contd.)

S. No.	Description	Unit	Rate ₹
	G.I. Pipes and Fittings :		
	G.I. Pipes :		
250.	15 mm dia	metre	34.00
251.	20 mm dia	metre	40.00
252.	25 mm dia	metre	56.00
253.	32 mm dia	metre	72.00
254.	40 mm dia	metre	81.00
255.	50 mm dia	metre	112.00
256.	65 mm dia	metre	140.00
257.	80 mm dia	metre	190.00
	G.I. back (Jam) nuts :		
258.	15 mm dia	each	5.00
259.	20 mm dia	each	6.00
260.	25 mm dia	each	10.00
261.	32 mm dia	each	13.00
262.	40 mm dia	each	15.00
263.	50 mm dia	each	18.00
264.	65 mm dia	each	20.00
265.	80 mm dia	each	28.00
	G.I. bend 90 degree :		
266.	15 mm dia	each	5.00
267.	20 mm dia	each	8.00
268.	25 mm dia	each	13.00
269.	32 mm dia	each	21.00
270.	40 mm dia	each	28.00
271.	50 mm dia	each	44.00
272.	65 mm dia	each	79.00
273.	80 mm dia	each	117.00
	G.I. crosses :		
274.	15 mm dia	each	14.00
275.	20 mm dia	each	20.00
276.	25 mm dia	each	31.00
277.	32 mm dia	each	50.00
278.	40 mm dia	each	68.00
279.	50 mm dia	each	102.00
280.	65 mm dia	each	163.00
281.	80 mm dia	each	218.00
	G.I. elbows :		
282.	15 mm dia	each	6.00
283.	20 mm dia	each	11.00
284.	25 mm dia	each	13.00
285.	32 mm dia	each	16.00
286.	40 mm dia	each	22.00
287.	50 mm dia	each	35.00
288.	65 mm dia	each	65.00
289.	80 mm dia	each	90.00

S. No.	Description	Unit	Rate ₹
	G.I. nipples :		
290.	15 mm dia	each	10.00
291.	20 mm dia	each	12.00
292.	25 mm dia	each	21.00
293.	32 mm dia	each	25.00
294.	40 mm dia	each	28.00
295.	50 mm dia	each	31.00
296.	65 mm dia	each	37.00
297.	80 mm dia	each	47.00
	G.I. plugs :		
298.	15 mm dia	each	2.00
299.	20 mm dia	each	3.00
300.	25 mm dia	each	5.00
301.	32 mm dia	each	8.00
302.	40 mm dia	each	17.00
303.	50 mm dia	each	24.00
304.	65 mm dia	each	26.00
305.	80 mm dia	each	31.00
	G.I. sockets (reducing) :		
306.	20 mm to 15 mm	each	8.00
307.	25 mm to any smaller size	each	12.00
308.	32 mm to any smaller size	each	18.00
309.	40 mm to any smaller size	each	20.00
310.	50 mm to any smaller size	each	28.00
	G.I. Tees (equal) :		
311.	15 mm	each	6.50
312.	20 mm	each	10.00
313.	25 mm	each	15.50
314.	32 mm	each	25.00
315.	40 mm	each	25.00
316.	50 mm	each	29.00
317.	65 mm	each	54.00
318.	80 mm	each	64.00
319.	G.I. inlet connection :	each	45.00
	G.I. Unions :		
320.	15 mm nominal bore	each	13.00
321.	20 mm nominal bore	each	18.00
322.	25 mm nominal bore	each	23.00
323.	32 mm nominal bore	each	28.00
324.	40 mm nominal bore	each	38.00
325.	50 mm nominal bore	each	64.00
326.	65 mm nominal bore	each	95.00
327.	80 mm nominal bore	each	121.00
328.	S.C.I. pipe 100 mm	metre	185.00
329.	S.C.I. pipe 150 mm	metre	314.00

(Contd.)

S. No.	Description	Unit	Rate ₹
	SAND CAST IRON SOIL, WASTE AND VENT PIPES AND FITTINGS :		
	Single socketed pipe 1.80 metres long :		
330.	50 mm	each	202.00
331.	75 mm	each	237.00
332.	100 mm	each	289.00
333.	150 mm	each	575.00
	Bend :		
	Plain :		
334.	50 mm	each	51.00
335.	75 mm	each	68.00
336.	100 mm	each	82.00
337.	150 mm	each	203.00
	With access door :		
338.	50 mm	each	62.00
339.	75 mm	each	79.00
340.	100 mm	each	95.00
341.	150 mm	each	235.00
	Single equal junctions Plain :		
342.	50 × 50 × 50 mm dia	each	70.00
343.	75 × 75 × 75 mm dia	each	83.00
344.	100 × 100 × 100 mm dia	each	132.00
	With access door :		
345.	50 × 50 × 50 mm dia	each	76.00
346.	75 × 75 × 75 mm dia	each	110.00
347.	100 × 100 × 100 mm dia	each	148.00
	Double equal junctions Plain :		
348.	50 × 50 × 50 × 50 mm dia	each	105.00
349.	75 × 75 × 75 × 75 mm dia	each	136.00
350.	100 × 100 × 100 × 100 mm dia	each	183.00
	With access door :		
351.	50 × 50 × 50 × 50 mm dia	each	130.00
352.	75 × 75 × 75 × 75 mm dia	each	157.00
353.	100 × 100 × 100 × 100 mm dia	each	203.00
	Slotted Cowl (terminal guard) :		
354.	50 mm dia	each	38.00
355.	75 mm dia	each	48.00
356.	100 mm dia	each	59.00
	SAND CAST IRON S & S :		
	Off Sets :		
	76 mm Offset for :		
357.	50 mm dia pipe	each	91.00

S. No.	Description	Unit	Rate ₹
358.	75 mm dia pipe	each	103.00
359.	100 mm dia pipe	each	139.00
	114 mm Offset for :		
360.	50 mm dia pipe	each	97.00
361.	75 mm dia pipe	each	105.00
362.	100 mm dia pipe	each	135.00
	152 mm Offset for :		
363.	50 mm dia pipe	each	78.00
364.	75 mm dia pipe	each	105.00
365.	100 mm dia pipe	each	132.00
	Single unequal junctions :		
	Plain :		
366.	100 × 100 × 75 mm dia	each	131.00
367.	100 × 100 × 50 mm dia	each	131.00
368.	75 × 75 × 50 mm dia	each	94.00
	With access door		
369.	100 × 100 × 75 mm dia	each	146.00
370.	100 × 100 × 50 mm dia	each	146.00
371.	75 × 75 × 50 mm dia	each	110.00
	Double unequal junctions :		
	Plain :		
372.	100 × 100 × 75 × 75 mm dia	each	129.00
373.	100 × 100 × 50 × 50 mm dia	each	129.00
374.	75 × 75 × 50 × 50 mm dia	each	104.00
	With access door :		
375.	100 × 100 × 75 × 75 mm dia	each	134.00
376.	100 × 100 × 50 × 50 mm dia	each	160.00
377.	75 × 75 × 50 × 50 mm dia	each	134.00
	Heal rest Bend :		
378.	50 mm dia	each	64.00
379.	75 mm dia	each	79.00
380.	100 mm dia	each	95.00
	Single equal invert branch of required degree :		
381.	50 × 50 × 50 mm dia	each	88.00
382.	75 × 75 × 75 mm dia	each	112.00
383.	100 × 100 × 100 mm dia	each	154.00
	Double equal invert branch of required degree :		
384.	50 × 50 × 50 × 50 mm dia	each	118.00
385.	75 × 75 × 75 × 75 mm dia	each	139.00
386.	100 × 100 × 100 × 100 mm dia	each	182.00
	Single unequal invert branch of required degree :		
387.	100 × 100 × 75 mm dia	each	139.00

(*Contd.*)

S. No.	Description	Unit	Rate ₹
388.	100 × 100 × 50 mm dia	each	137.00
389.	75 × 75 × 50 mm dia	each	100.00
	Double unequal invert branch of required degree :		
390.	100 × 100 × 75 × 75 mm dia	each	200.00
391.	100 × 100 × 50 × 50 mm dia	each	200.00
392.	75 × 75 × 50 × 50 mm dia	each	170.00
393.	Sand cast iron pass over pipe 50 mm dia	each	115.00
	Sand cast iron door pieces :		
394.	50 mm dia	each	77.00
395.	75 mm dia	each	98.00
396.	100 mm dia	each	121.00
	Collar :		
397.	50 mm dia	each	32.00
398.	75 mm dia	each	40.00
399.	100 mm dia	each	47.00
	Unplasticised P.V.C. connection pipe with brass		
	Union :		
	30 cm long :		
400.	15 mm bore	each	13.00
401.	20 mm bore	each	19.00
	45 cm long		
402.	15 mm bore	each	18.00
403.	20 mm bore	each	26.00
	Tee (S.C.I.) :		
404.	100 mm dia	each	95.00
405.	150 mm dia	each	320.00
406.	Hand pump	each	300.00
	Polyethene pipes :		
407.	15 mm dia	metre	10.00
408.	20 mm dia	metre	19.00
409.	25 mm dia	metre	26.00
410.	32 mm dia	metre	42.00
411.	40 mm dia	metre	51.00
412.	50 mm dia	metre	70.00
	R.C.C. Pipes and collars :		
	NP 2 Class pipe :		
413.	100 mm dia	metre	90.00
414.	150 mm dia	metre	100.00
415.	250 mm dia	metre	125.00
416.	300 mm dia	metre	171.00
417.	450 mm dia	metre	268.00
418.	500 mm dia	metre	321.00
419.	600 mm dia	metre	428.00
420.	700 mm dia	metre	492.00

S. No.	Description	Unit	Rate ₹
421.	750 mm dia	metre	580.00
422.	800 mm dia	metre	640.00
423.	900 mm dia	metre	770.00
424.	1000 mm dia	metre	960.00
425.	1100 mm dia	metre	1177.00
426.	1200 mm dia	metre	1260.00
	NP 2 Class Collars :		
427.	100 mm dia	each	12.00
428.	150 mm dia	each	19.00
429.	250 mm dia	each	18.00
430.	300 mm dia	each	28.00
431.	450 mm dia	each	44.00
432.	500 mm dia	each	48.00
433.	600 mm dia	each	61.00
434.	700 mm dia	each	78.00
435.	750 mm dia	each	90.00
436.	800 mm dia	each	100.00
437.	900 mm dia	each	120.00
438.	1000 mm dia	each	150.00
439.	1100 mm dia	each	182.00
440.	1200 mm dia	each	195.00
	P1 Class R.C.C. Pipe :		
441.	100 mm dia	metre	106.00
442.	150 mm dia	metre	126.00
443.	250 mm dia	metre	156.00
444.	300 mm dia	metre	224.00
445.	450 mm dia	metre	427.00
446.	500 mm dia	metre	.480.00
447.	600 mm dia	metre	508.00
448.	700 mm dia	metre	630.00
	P1 Class R.C.C. Collars :		
449.	100 mm dia	each	17.00
450.	150 mm dia	each	18.00
451.	250 mm dia	each	22.00
452.	300 mm dia	each	31.00
453.	450 mm dia	each	44.00
454.	500 mm dia	each	58.00
455.	600 mm dia	each	88.00
456.	700 mm dia	each	92.00
	P2 Class R.C.C. Pipes :		
457.	100 mm dia	metre	136.00
458.	150 mm dia	metre	169.00
459.	250 mm dia	metre	225.00
460.	300 mm dia	metre	348.00
461.	450 mm dia	metre	599.00
462.	500 mm dia	metre	685.00
463.	600 mm dia	metre	962.00

(*Contd.*)

S. No.	Description	Unit	Rate ₹
	P2 Class R.C.C. Collars :		
464.	100 mm dia	each	16.00
465.	150 mm dia	each	18.00
466.	250 mm dia	each	26.00
467.	300 mm dia	each	35.00
468.	450 mm dia	each	74.00
469.	500 mm dia	each	115.00
470.	600 mm dia	each	120.00
	P3 Class R.C.C. Pipes :		
471.	100 mm dia	metre	135.00
472.	150 mm dia	metre	145.00
473.	250 mm dia	metre	251.00
474.	300 mm dia	metre	392.00
475.	80 mm dia	metre	102.00
476.	350 mm dia	metre	295.00
477.	400 mm dia	metre	425.00
	P3 Class R.C.C. Collars :		
478.	100 mm dia	each	21.00
479.	150 mm dia	each	23.00
480.	250 mm dia	each	35.00
481.	300 mm dia	each	45.00
	STONEWARE PIPES GRADE A (60 CM LONG) :		
482.	100 mm dia	each	25.00
483.	150 mm dia	each	35.00
484.	200 mm dia	each	50.00
485.	230 mm dia	each	57.00
486.	250 mm dia	each	65.00
487.	300 mm dia	each	90.00
488.	380 mm dia	each	115.00
489.	450 mm dia	each	150.00
490.	350 mm dia	each	110.00
491.	400 mm dia	each	130.00
492.	Stone ware pipe 100 mm dia	metre	34.00
493.	Rubber plug each	each	4.00
	Sinks :		
	Kitchen Sink (Fire clay) :		
494.	600 × 450 × 150 mm	each	800.00
495.	600 × 450 × 250 mm	each	1035.00
496.	750 × 450 × 250 mm	each	1252.00
	Marble chips kitchen sink :		
497.	600 × 450 × 150 mm	each	140.00
498.	600 × 450 × 250 mm	each	185.00
499.	750 × 450 × 250 mm	each	400.00
	White vitreous china kitchen sink :		
500.	600 × 450 × 150 mm	each	780.00
501.	600 × 450 × 250 mm	each	1235.00

S. No.	Description	Unit	Rate ₹
	White vitreous china laboratory sink :		
502.	450 × 300 × 150 mm	each	482.00
503.	600 × 450 × 200 mm	each	1200.00
	Seats :		
504.	Seat teakwood polished or mahogany finished complete with lid C.P. brass hinges and rubber buffers	each	105.00
505.	Seat teakwood polished or mahogany finished complete without lid with C.P. brass hinges and rubber buffers	each	71.00
506.	White plastic seat (solid) with lid C.P. brass hinges and rubber buffers	each	200.00
507.	Black plastic seat (solid) with lid C.P. brass hinges and rubber buffers	each	180.00
508.	600 × 120 mm glass shelf with anodised aluminium angle frame, C.P. brass brackets and guard rail of standard size	each	58.00
	Shower rose (C.P. brass) for 15 to 20 mm inlet		
509.	100 mm dia	each	15.00
510.	150 mm dia	each	25.00
511.	Soap dish (C.P. brass) with bracket	each	50.00
512.	Spun yarn	kilogram	20.00
513.	Strainer brass 40 mm dia 1.5 metre long	each	300.00
	Tank :		
514.	Polyethylene water storage tank with cover and suitable locking arrangement	per litre capacity	3.40
	R.C.C. circular tank with cover and necessary holes but without fittings :		
515.	270 litres	each	650.00
516.	540 litres	each	1080.00
517.	15 mm C.P. brass tap	each	75.00
518.	20 mm C.P. brass tap	each	91.00
	Towel Rails :		
519.	Towel rail C.P. brass 750 × 20 mm together with a pair of C.P. brass brackets to fit the size of towel rail	each	74.00
520.	Towel rail C.P. brass 600 × 20 mm together with a pair of C.P. brass brackets to fit the size of towel rail	each	67.00
521.	750 × 20 mm anodised aluminium towel rail alongwith a pair of anodised aluminium brackets	each	50.00
522.	600 × 20 mm anodised aluminium towel rail alongwith a pair of anodised aluminium brackets	each	43.00
	Toilet paper holder of standard size :		
523.	C.P. brass	each	28.00
524.	Vitreous china	each	55.00

(Contd.)

S. No.	Description	Unit	Rate ₹
	Traps :		
	Trap (C.I.) for standard urinal with vent arm with operating and other couplings in C.P. Brass :		
525.	50 mm dia	each	90.00
526.	65 mm dia	each	105.00
527.	80 mm dia	each	112.00
	Trap (CP. brass) :		
528.	32 mm dia	each	60.00
529.	40 mm dia	each	77.00
	Trap (Sand cast iron) :		
530.	100 mm S.C.I. trap with vent hole	each	150.00
531.	100 mm S.C.I. trap with 100 mm inlet and 100 mm outlet	each	120.00
532.	100 mm S.C.I. trap with 100 mm inlet and 75 mm outlet	each	90.00
533.	100 mm S.C.I. trap with 100 mm inlet and 50 mm outlet	each	75.00
	S.W. Gully Traps		
	P Type :		
534.	100 × 100 mm	each	35.00
535.	125 × 100 mm	each	45.00
536.	150 × 100 mm	each	48.00
537.	180 × 100 mm	each	70.00
538.	180 × 150 mm	each	90.00
	Q Type :		
539.	125 × 100 mm	each	34.00
	S Type :		
540.	125 × 100 mm	each	86.00
	C.P. Brass union		
541.	150 × 100 mm	each	93.00
542.	32 mm	each	31.00
543.	40 mm	each	43.00
	Urinals :		
544.	Vitreous china lipped front urinal	each	220.00
545.	Fire clay stall urinal	each	2260.00
546.	Vitreous china squatting plate urinal	each	385.00
	Valve :		
	Ball valve :		
	H.P. with Copper Floats :		
547.	15 mm dia	each	150.00
548.	20 mm dia	each	250.00
549.	25 mm dia	each	300.00
	H.P. or L.P. with Polyethene Floats :		
550.	15 mm dia	each	80.00

S. No.	*Description*	*Unit*	*Rate* ₹
551.	20 mm dia	each	135.00
552.	25 mm dia	each	150.00
	Brass full way valve with C.I. wheel (screwed end) :		
553.	15 mm dia	each	60.00
554.	20 mm dia	each	80.00
555.	25 mm dia	each	130.00
556.	32 mm dia	each	180.00
557.	40 mm dia	each	220.00
558.	50 mm dia	each	350.00
559.	65 mm dia	each	454.00
560.	80 mm dia	each	714.00
	Gun metal non-return valve-horizontal (screwed end) :		
561.	25 mm dia	each	150.00
562.	32 mm dia	each	254.00
563.	40 mm dia	each	346.00
564.	50 mm dia	each	518.00
565.	65 mm dia	each	871.00
566.	80 mm dia	each	1196.00
	Gun metal non return valve-vertical (Screwed end) :		
567.	25 mm dia	each	118.00
568.	32 mm dia	each	154.00
569.	40 mm dia	each	199.00
570.	50 mm dia	each	268.00
571.	65 mm dia	each	698.00
572.	80 mm dia	each	945.00
	Sluice valve (with Caps) C.I. :		
	Class I :		
573.	80 mm dia	each	1100.00
574.	100 mm dia	each	1450.00
575.	125 mm dia	each	1800.00
576.	150 mm dia	each	2200.00
577.	200 mm dia	each	3900.00
578.	250 mm dia	each	5834.00
579.	300 mm dia	each	7356.00
	Class II :		
580.	80 mm dia	each	1210.00
581.	100 mm dia	each	1595.00
582.	125 mm dia	each	1980.00
583.	150 mm dia	each	2420.00
584.	200 mm dia	each	4290.00
585.	250 mm dia	each	5417.00
586.	300 mm dia	each	8092.00
	Wash Basins		
	Flat back wash basin (vitreous china) :		
587.	630 × 450 mm	each	458.00

(Contd.)

S. No.	Description	Unit	Rate ₹
588.	550 × 400 mm	each	324.00
589.	450 × 300 mm	each	225.00
	Angle back wash basin (vitreous China) :		
590.	600 × 480 mm	each	395.00
591.	400 × 400 mm	each	280.00
592.	Surgeon type wash basin (vitreous China) of size 600 × 460 mm	each	670.00
593.	C.P. brass waste 32 mm	each	35.00
594.	C.P. brass waste 40 mm	each	41.00
	Water closet :		
595.	Vitreous China Indian type w.c. pan size 580 mm	each	213.00
596.	Vitreous China Orissa type w.c. pan size 580 mm	each	560.00
597.	Vitreous China pedestal type water closet	each	421.00
598.	White vitreous China dual purpose closet (Anglo Indian W.C.) suitable for use as squatting pan or European type water closet as per manufacturer's specifications	each	480.00

Table 6.5. BASIC RATES ADDITIONAL MATERIALS

S. No.	Description	Unit	Rate ₹
1.	Acid Proof cement	tonne	6428.00
2.	M.S. Butt hinges 100 × 58 × 2.5 mm	ten	70.00
3.	M.S. Butt hinges 125 × 90 × 4 mm	ten	110.00
4.	Galvanised wire mesh of average width of aperture 1.4 mm and nominal dia. of wire 0.63 mm	sq m	126.00
5.	Galvanised wire mesh of average width of aperture 1.18 mm nominal dia wire 0.556 mm	sq m	139.00
6.	Galvanised wire mesh of average width of aperture 1.00 mm nominal dia. of wire 0.50 mm	sq m	86.00
7.	Frosted glass sheet of nominal thickness 4 mm (weighing not less than 10 kg/sq m)	sq m	120.00
8.	Nickle plated M.S. pipe 20 mm dia.	metre	45.00
9.	Nickle plated M.S. Brackets for curtain rod 20 mm	each	1.50
10.	Nickle plated M.S. Brackets for curtain rod 25 mm	each	2.50
11.	Brass screws 35 mm	cent	70.00
12.	Chromium plated brass screws 35 mm	cent	56.00
13.	Copper oxidised brass screws 35 mm	cent	48.00
14.	Oxidised mild steel screws 35 mm	cent	24.00
15.	Mild steel screws 35 mm	cent	25.00
16.	Mild steel conduit pipe (heavy type) ISI marked-20 mm dia.	metre	30.00
17.	Mild steel conduit pipe (heavy type) ISI marked-25 mm dia.	metre	32.00

S. No.	Description	Unit	Rate ₹
18.	Rolling shutters of 80 × 0.90 mm laths	sq m	350.00
19.	Rolling shutters of 80 × 1.2 mm laths	sq m	375.00
20.	Top cover of Rolling shutters 0.90 mm thick	metre	115.00
21.	Top cover of Rolling shutters 1.20 mm thick	metre	131.00
22.	Rawl plug 50 mm (designation 10 no.)	each	6.50
23.	Teak wood lipping of size 25 × 3 mm in pelmets	metre	6.00
24.	Flat pressed 3 layer and graded particle board (medium density) Grade 1 conforming to IS : 3087 – 18 mm thick	sq m	255.00
25.	Aluminium tee channel (heavy duty) with rollers and stop end	metre	20.00
26.	Hydraulic door closer sleek design type	each	482.00
27.	Hydraulic door closer hidden design type	each	669.00
28.	Aluminium hanging floor door stopper with twin rubber and stopper	each	36.50
	Oxidised M.S. casement stay (straight peg type) :		
29.	300 mm not less than 0.33 kg.	each	9.00
30.	250 mm not less than 0.28 kg.	each	8.50
31.	200 mm not less than 0.24 kg.	each	8.00
	M.S. handle for steel windows including bolts, nuts and washers :		
32.	100 mm	each	4.50
33.	150 mm	each	5.50
34.	Extra for providing grilled rolling shutters with 8 mm dia. M.S.	sq m	100.00
35.	M.S. sheet circular or hexagonal box for fan clamp including top and bottom lid.	each	15.00
36.	Chequerred precast cement concrete tiles 22 mm thick using marble chips of size 6 mm - Light shade using white cement	sq m	377.00
37.	White marble Raj nagar plain - 20 mm thick (slab area 0.10 m^2 to 0.20 m^2)	sq m	482.00
	Single fired ceramic tiles 8 mm thick with matt finish		
38.	150 × 150 mm size	10 Nos.	70.00
39.	200 × 200 mm size	10 Nos.	70.00
40.	White/off white glazed screen printed tiles of minimum thickness 5 mm (150 × 150 mm size)	10 Nos.	50.00
41.	Acid and alkali resistant tiles size 300 × 300 mm 10 mm thick	10 Nos.	330.00
42.	Araldite GY 257	kilogram	360.00
43.	Hardner HY 850	kilogram	298.00
44.	Hardner HY 825	kilogram	257.00
45.	Hardner HY 830	kilogram	298.00
46.	Flow control agent	litre	210.00
47.	Acrosil D.T. 0.75	litre	36.00
48.	Quartz sand No. 10	kilogram	2.50

(Contd.)

S. No.	Description	Unit	Rate ₹
49.	C.I. grating 125 × 100 mm	each	130.00
50.	S.C.I. Tee 150 mm	each	335.00
51.	Bath tub (Gel coated glass fibre reinforced polyster resin)	each	2300.00
52.	Zinc chromate yellow primer	litre	45.00
53.	Expanded polystyrene type N-Normal	sq m	79.00
54.	Expanded polystyrene type-SE	sq m	105.00
	Stainless steel kitchen sink-with drain board		
55.	510 × 1040 bowl depth 178 mm	each	1624.00
56.	400 × 915 bowl depth 160 mm	each	1036.00
57.	500 × 1000 bowl depth 178 mm	each	1512.00
	Stainless steel kitchen sink-without drain board :		
58.	610 × 510 bowl depth 200 mm	each	980.00
59.	535 × 460 bowl depth 178 mm	each	924.00
60.	510 × 432 bowl depth 172 mm	each	812.00
61.	Coloured Orissa pattern W.C. pan 580 × 440 mm	each	868.00
62.	Coloured Pedestal type W.C. pan (European type)	each	635.00
63.	Coloured low level flushing cistern 10 litres (Vitreous China)	each	770.00
64.	Coloured (other than black) solid P.V.C. plastic seat in European W.C. pan	each	300.00
65.	Stainless steel grating 75 mm dia	each	11.00
66.	Stainless steel grating 100 mm dia	each	12.00
	Plastic moulded jali of required colour and shade for floor/nahani trap :		
67.	Circular type (100 mm dia)	each	36.00
68.	Rectangular with openable circular lid	each	45.00
	Mirror with white plastic moulded frame :		
69.	Circular shape 450 mm dia.	each	150.00
70.	Rectangular shape 453 × 357 mm	each	118.00
71.	Oval shape 450 × 350 mm (outer dimensions)	each	139.00
72.	Rectangular shape 1500 × 450 mm	each	505.00
73.	Hard board 6 mm thick	sq m	126.00
	PVC waste pipe for sink and wash basin including PVC waste fittings		
	Semi Rigid pipes with fittings :		
74.	32 mm dia. with length not less than 700 mm	each	10.00
75.	40 mm dia. with length not less than 700 mm	each	12.00
	Flexible pipe (Coil Shaped) with fittings :		
76.	32 mm dia. with length not less than 700 mm	each	14.00
77.	40 mm dia. with length not less than 700 mm	each	14.00
	Controlled low level flushing cistern with fittings-High density polythylene/poly propylene :		
78.	10 lit. (full flush) capacity-white	each	525.00
79.	10 lit. (full flush) capacity-coloured	each	625.00

S. No.	Description	Unit	Rate ₹
80.	8 lit. (full flush) capacity-white	each	500.00
81.	8 lit. (full flush) capacity-coloured	each	800.00
	Controlled low level flushing cistern with all fittings-vitreous china :		
82.	10 lit. (full flush) capacity-white	each	773.00
83.	10 lit. (full flush) cpacity-coloured	each	1198.00
	S.W. Intercepting trap :		
84.	100 mm dia. meter	each	100.00
85.	150 mm dia.	each	160.00
	Precast reinforced cement concrete manhole cover with frame		
	L.D-25 :		
86.	Rectangular shape 600 × 450	each	532.00
87.	Square shape 350 mm × 350 mm	each	800.00
88.	Circular shape 450 mm dia.	each	950.00
	MD-10 :		
89.	Rectangular shape 500 × 500 mm	each	605.00
90.	Circular shape 500 mm dia.	each	1275.00
	HD-20 :		
91.	Circular shape 560 mm dia.	each	1650.00
	EHD 35 :		
92.	Circular shape 560 mm dia.	each	2000.00
	FACTORY MADE SHUTTERS :		
	Laminated veneer lumber styles rails as per TADS IS : 1995 and panels of		
	12 mm thick plain type 1. medium density flat pressed three layer, graded particle board (FPT-I) as per IS : 3087-1985 bonded with BWP type synthetic resin adhesive, as per IS : 848-1974.		
93.	35 mm thick shutters	sq m	700.00
94.	40 mm thick shutters	sq m	775.00
	12 mm thick both sides prelaminated type-I, medium density flat pressed three layer, graded particle board (FPTI) as per IS : 3087-1985 bonded with BWP type synthetic resin adhesive as per IS : 848-1974 :		
95.	35 mm thick shutter	sq m	1050.00
96.	40 mm thick shutter	sq m	1125.00
	12 mm thick exterior grade, plain medium density fibre board as per IS : 12406-1986 :		
97.	35 mm thick shutters	sq m	750.00
98.	40 mm thick shutters	sq m	825.00
	12 mm thick one side prelaminated type I, other side balancing lamination, medium density, flat pressed three layer, graded particle board (FPT-I) as per IS : 3087, bonded with BWP type synthetic resin as per IS : 848-1974.		

(Contd.)

S. No.	Description	Unit	Rate ₹
99.	35 mm thick shutters	sq m	950.00
100.	40 mm thick shutters	sq m	1025.00
	12 mm thick exterior grade, both side prelaminated medium density fibre board as per IS : 12406-1988 :		
101.	35 mm thick shutters	sq m	1100.00
102.	40 mm thick shutters	sq m	1175.00
	12 mm thick exterior grade one side prelaminated other side balancing lamination medium density fibre board as per IS : 12406-1988 :		
103.	35 mm thick shutters	sq m	1000.00
104.	40 mm thick shutters	sq m	1075.00
	Sheet glass using 10 kg/sq m glass panes :		
105.	40 mm thick shutters	sq m	830.00
106.	35 mm thick shutters	sq m	755.00
107.	30 mm thick shutters	sq m	675.00
	Using galvanised wire gauge with average width of aperture 1.4 mm on both direction with wire of dia. 0.63 mm :		
108.	40 mm thick shutters	sq m	800.00
109.	35 mm thick shutters	sq m	725.00
110.	30 mm thick shutters	sq m	650.00
111.	Laminated veneer lumber conforming to TADS IS : 1995 manufactured in factory in frames of door, windows	10 cu dm	230.00
	Factory made shutters with, kiln seasoned eucalyptus wood and treated by ammoniacal copper arsanite treatment styles rails as per TADS 5 : 1994 and panel inserts of 12 mm thick plain type I, medium density flat pressed layer, graded particle board (FPT-I) as per IS : 3087-1985 bonded with BWP type synthetic resin adhesive as per IS : 848-1974 :		
112.	35 mm thick shutter	sq m	981.00
113.	40 mm thick shutter	sq m	1017.00
	12 mm thick both sides prelaminated type-I medium density flat pressed three layer, graded particle board (FPT-I) as per IS : 3087-1985 bonded with BWP type synthetic resin adhesive as per IS : 848-1974 :		
114.	35 mm thick shutter	sq m	1611.00
115.	40 mm thick shutter	sq m	1773.00
	12 mm thick one side prelaminated type-I, other side balancing lamination medium density flat pressed three layer, graded particle board (FPT-I) as per IS : 3087-1905, bonded with BWP type synthetic resin adhesive as per IS : 848-1974.		
116.	35 mm thick shutter	sq m	1296.00
117.	40 mm thick shutter	sq m	1395.00
	Sheet glass using 10 kg/sq m glass panes :		

S. No.	Description	Unit	Rate ₹
118.	40 mm thick shutter	sq m	981.00
119.	35 mm thick shutter	sq m	1017.00
120.	30 mm thick shutter	sq m	1053.00
	Using galvanised wire gauge with average width of aperture 1.4 mm on both directions with wire of dia. 0.63 mm :		
121.	40 mm thick shutter	sq m	936.00
122.	35 mm thick shutter	sq m	954.00
123.	30 mm thick shutter	sq m	972.00
124.	Eucalyptus wood kiln seasoned and treated by ammoniacal copper arsanite treatment as per FRI Dehradun technology conforming to TADS 5-1994		
	Eucalyptus wood scantling	10 cu dm	230.00
125.	C.I. pile shoe	kilogram	8.00
126.	M.S. pile shoe	kilogram	12.00
127.	Bentonite	tonne	3000.00
128.	Oxidised M.S. safety chain (weighing not less than 450 gms) for door	each	21.00
129.	Coloured glazed tiles 5 mm thick	sq m	253.00
130.	Factory printed glazed tiles 5 mm thick	sq m	260.00
131.	C.I. grating 150 mm dia. (Weighing not less than 440 gm)	each	12.00
	U-PVC pipes (working pressure 4 kg/cm^2) :		
132.	Single socketed pipe 75 mm dia.	metre	68.00
133.	Single socketed pipe 110 mm dia.	metre	133.00
134.	Rubber (Seal) Ring 75 mm dia.	metre	10.00
135.	Rubber (Seal) Ring 110 mm dia.	metre	11.00
136.	UPVC coupler for UPVC drainage pipes 75 mm	each	32.00
137.	UPVC coupler for UPVC drainage pipes 110 mm	each	48.00
138.	UPVC pusufit coupler (single) 75 mm thick	each	33.00
139.	UPVC pusufit coupler (single) 110 mm thick	each	57.50
	UPVC single equal Tee (with door) :		
140.	75 × 75 × 75 mm	each	53.50
141.	110 × 110 × 110 mm	each	97.50
	UPVC single equal Tee (with door) :		
142.	75 × 75 × 75 mm	each	63.00
143.	110 × 110 × 110 mm	each	112.00
	UPVC double equal door Tee :		
144.	75 × 75 × 75 × 75 mm	each	174.00
145.	110 × 110 × 110 × 110 mm	each	277.00
	UPVC single equal Y with door :		
146.	75 × 75 × 75 mm	each	84.50
147.	110 × 110 × 110 mm	each	149.00
	UPVC single equal Y without door :		
148.	75 × 75 × 75 mm	each	65.50
149.	110 × 110 × 110 mm	each	121.50
	UPVC double equal Y with door :		

(Contd.)

S. No.	Description	Unit	Rate ₹
150.	75 × 75 × 75 × 75 mm	each	137.00
151.	110 × 110 × 110 × 110 mm	each	190.00
	UPVC bend 87.5° :		
152.	75 mm bend	each	42.50
153.	110 mm bend	each	73.00
	UPVC bend 45° :		
154.	75 mm bend	each	36.00
155.	110 mm bend	each	61.50
	UPVC plain shoe :		
156.	75 mm bend	each	90.00
157.	110 mm bend	each	173.00
	UPVC pipe clip :		
158.	75 mm bend	each	9.50
159.	110 mm bend	each	25.75
	Cellular concrete blocks of average size (50 cm × 25 cm)		
	Grade A-light wt. :		
160.	8.5 cm thick	sq m	140.00
161.	10 cm thick	sq m	165.00
162.	15 cm thick	sq m	247.00
163.	25 cm thick	sq m	412.00
164.	40 cm thick	sq m	660.00
	Grade B-Medium wt. :		
165.	8.5 cm thick	sq m	162.00
166.	10 cm thick	sq m	190.00
167.	15 cm thick	sq m	285.00
168.	25 cm thick	sq m	475.00
169.	40 cm thick	sq m	760.00
	Heavy Grade-Heavy wt. :		
170.	8.5 cm thick	sq m	174.00
171.	10 cm thick	sq m	205.00
172.	15 cm thick	sq m	308.00
173.	25 cm thick	sq m	513.00
174.	40 cm thick	sq m	820.00
175.	Bonded mineral wool roll, 50 mm thick	sq m	78.75
176.	Fibre glass tissue reinforcement	sq m	22.00
177.	Bitumen primer	kilogram	13.00
178.	Pea size gravel	cum	395.00
	Precast chequered cement tiles 22 mm thick :		
179.	Dark shade using ordinary cement	sq m	250.00
180.	Medium shade using 50% white cement and 50% grey cement	sq m	325.00
181.	Epoxy paint	litre	206.00
182.	Fire retardant paint	litre	225.00
183.	Melamine polish	litre	161.50

S. No.	Description	Unit	Rate ₹
184.	Silicon water repellent	litre	185.00
	Table rubbed polished stone 25 mm thick (105 × 60 cm) :		
185.	Kota stone	sq m	700.00
186.	Raj Nagar Marble stone-25 mm thick	sq m	1700.00
187.	Granite stone-25 mm thick	sq m	2200.00
	Tests		
	Verticle load testing (INITIAL) of piles in accordance with IS : 2911 (Part-IV) including installation of loading platform and preparation of pile head or construction of test cap and dismantling of test cap after test etc. complete as per specification and direction of Engineer-in-charge Single Pile :		
188.	Upto 50 tonne capacity pile	per test	17200.00
189.	Above 50 tonne and upto 100 tonne capacity piles	per test	25800.00
	Group of two or more piles :		
190.	Upto 50 tonne capacity each	per test	34400.00
	Cyclic vertical load testing of piles in accordance with IS : 2911 part IV including preparation of pile head etc. for Single piles :		
191.	Upto 50 tonne capacity tonne	per test	10300.00
192.	Above 50 tonne capacity pile and upto 100 tonne capacity piles	per test	15450.00
	Group of two piles		
193.	Upto 50 tonne capacity each	per test	20600.00
	Lateral load testing of single pile in accordance with IS: 2911 part-IV for determining safe allowable lateral load on pile.		
194.	Upto 50 tonne capacity pile	per test	10000.00
195.	Above 50 tonne capacity pile and upto 100 tonne capacity piles	per test	15000.00
196.	Hard crete	litre	250.00
197.	Road marking paint (spirit based)	litre	75.00
198.	Superior quality road rnarking paint equivalent to Goodlass Nerolac brand no. 452/002	litre	129.00
199.	C.P. Brass bibcock 15 mm	each	145.00
200.	C.P. Brass long nose bibcock 15 mm	each	168.00
201.	C.P. Brass long body bibcock 15 mm	each	194.00
202.	C.P. Brass stop cock (concealed) 15 mm	each	177.00
203.	C.P. Brass angle valve 15 mm	each	130.00
204.	C.P. Brass basin Mixer pillar tap 15 mm	each	533.00
205.	PVC bibcock 15 mm	each	20.00
206.	PVC stop cock 15 mm	each	20.00
207.	PVC stop cock 20 mm	each	20.00
208.	Pressed clay tiles	1000 nos.	8000.00

(Contd.)

S. No.	Description	Unit	Rate ₹
209.	Plain ceiling tiles (BWP type phenol formaldehyde synthetic resin bonded) (600 × 600 × 12 mm)	each	60.00
210.	Semi perforated ceiling tiles (600 × 600 × 12 mm)	each	60.00
211.	25 mm thick particle board	sq m	340.00
212.	30 mm thick prelaminated flush door shutter	sq m	350.00
213.	IInd class teak wood lipping 25 mm wide × 12 mm thick	metre	15.00
214.	25 mm thick melamine faced prelaminated three layer particle board	sq m	465.00
215.	White Marble Raj Nagar plain-30 mm thick	sq m	1500.00
	20 mm thick marble slab, areawise :		
216.	Abu plain white marble		
217.	Above 0.10 sq m upto 0.2 sq m	sq m	1326.00
218.	Above 0.2 sq m upto 0.5 sq m	sq m	2109.00
219.	Above 0.5 sq m upto 1.0 sq m	sq m	3000.00
220.	Above 1.0 sq m upto 2.0 sq m	sq m	3300.00
	Makrana Dongri Adanga marble :		
221.	Above 0.10 sq m upto 0.2 sq m	sq m	550.00
222.	Above 0.2 sq m upto 0.5 sq m	sq m	600.00
223.	Above 0.5 sq m upto 1.0 sq m	sq m	650.00
224.	Above 1.0 sq m upto 2.0 sq m	sq m	700.00
	Raj Nagar Plain white marble :		
225.	Above 0.10 sq m upto 0.2 sq m	sq m	482.00
226.	Above 0.2 sq m upto 0.5 sq m	sq m	603.00
227.	Above 0.5 sq m upto 1.0 sq m	sq m	904.00
228.	Above 1.0 sq m upto 2.0 sq m	sq m	1024.00
	Udaipur green marble :		
229.	Above 0.10 sq m upto 0.2 sq m	sq m	386.00
230.	Above 0.2 sq m upto 0.5 sq m	sq m	542.00
231.	Above 0.5 sq m upto 1.0 sq m	sq m	700.00
232.	Above 1.0 sq m upto 2.0 sq m	sq m	750.00
	Kishangarh Zebra Black marble :		
233.	Above 0.10 sq m upto 0.2 sq m	sq m	580.00
234.	Above 0.2 sq m upto 0.5 sq m	sq m	600.00
235.	Above 0.5 sq m upto 1.0 sq m	sq m	625.00
236.	Above 1.0 sq m upto 2.0 sq m	sq m	650.00
	Granite Black :		
237.	Above 0.10 sq m upto 0.2 sq m	sq m	1627.00
238.	Above 0.2 sq m upto 0.5 sq m	sq m	1747.00
239.	Above 0.5 sq m upto 1.0 sq m	sq m	1928.00
240.	Above 1.0 sq m upto 2.0 sq m	sq m	1928.00
	Granite pink :		1000.00
241.	Above 0.10 sq m upto 0.2 sq m	sq m	
242.	Above 0.2 sq m upto 0.5 sq m	sq m	1125.00
243.	Above 0.5 sq m upto 1.0 sq m	sq m	1250.00
244.	Above 1.0 sq m upto 2.0 sq m	sq m	1400.00
	Granite grey :		
245.	Above 0.10 sq m upto 0.2 sq m	sq m	1250.00
246.	Above 0.2 sq m upto 0.5 sq m	sq m	1450.00
247.	Above 0.5 sq m upto 1.0 sq m	sq m	1600.00
248.	Above 1.0 sq m upto 2.0 sq m	sq m	1800.00
249.	Aluminium T or L sections	kilogram	115.00

S. No.	Description	Unit	Rate ₹
	For flush door shutters :		
250.	Extra for providing teak veneering on one side instead of commercial veneering	sq m	136.00
251	Extra for providing teak veneering on both sides instead of commercial veneering	sq m	272.00
252.	Paving Asphalt 60/70 penetration	tonne	9415.00
	Expandable fastner with plastic sleeve and M.S. Screws.		
253.	25 mm long	each	5.00
254.	32 mm long	each	5.50
255.	40 mm long	each	7.00
256.	50 mm long	each	8.50
257.	Accelerating admixture	kilogram	20.00
258.	Retarding admixture	kilogram	45.00
259.	Plasticiser/super plasticizer	kilogram	35.00
260.	Wall form panel 1250 × 500 mm	each	797.50
261.	Tie bolt 12 mm dia 100 mm length	each	22.00
262.	Tie bolt 12 mm dia 150 mm length	each	24.00
263.	Tie bolt 20 mm dia 150 mm length	each	44.00
264.	Tie bolt 20 mm dia 225 mm length	each	55.00
265.	Spring coil 12 mm	each	6.00
266.	Plastic cone 12 mm dia	each	8.00
267.	Corner angle 45 × 45 × 5 mm 1.50 m long	each	220.00
268.	100 mm channel shoulder 2.5 m long	each	825.00
269.	Double clip (bridge clip)	each	55.00
270.	Single clip	each	46.00
271.	M.S. tube 40 mm dia	metre	192.50
272.	Wall form panel 1250 × 450 mm	each	759.00
273.	Corner angle 45 × 45 × 5 m 2.50 m long	each	200.00
274.	Column clamp 450 × 1070 m	each	935.00
275.	Prop 2 m (2-3.5 m)	each	654.00
276.	Binding wire	kilogram	19.00
277.	Gun metal cramp	kilogram	40.00
278.	Stainless steel cramp	kilogram	2.00
279.	Adjustable span ESO + SI (2.35-3.40)	each	1204.50
280.	Adjustable telescopic prop 3 m (2.02-3.75 m)	each	731.00
281.	Beam clamp 300-380 mm (450-1070 mm)	each set	275.00
282.	Prop 4 m	each	19.00
283.	Double coupler	each	33.00
284.	Cadmium plated full threaded steel screws (30 × 4 mm dia.)	cent	14.00
285.	Aluminium washer 2 mm thick 15 mm dia	cent	4.00
286.	12 mm M.S. 'U' beading	metre	2.00
	M.S. tower bolt-bright finished/black stove enamelled.		
287.	250 × 10 mm	each	18.00
288.	200 × 10 mm	each	18.00
289.	150 × 10 mm	each	16.00
290.	100 × 10 mm	each	12.00

(Contd.)

S. No.	Description	Unit	Rate ₹
291.	Plastic encapsuled M.S. foot rest 30 × 20 × 15 cm	each	65.00
292.	R.C.C. vent shaft 9.10 m long of standard design	each	4000.00
	G.I. pipe (Class-B) :		
293.	100 mm nominal bore	metre	315.00
294.	150 mm nominal bore	metre	495.00
	Flushing Cistern :		
295.	P.V.C. 10 lts capacity (low level) (White) (with fittings, accessories and flush pipe)	each	400.00
296.	P.V.C. automatic flushing cistern 5 lts capacity	each	425.00
297.	P.V.C. automatic flushing cistern 7.5 lts capacity	each	640.00
298.	P.V.C. automatic flushing cistern 10 lts capacity	each	850.00
299.	P.V.C. automatic flushing cistern 15 lts capacity	each	1000.00
300.	15 mm C.P. brass tap with elbow operation lever	each	222.00
	Draining Board		
301.	White glazed fire clay draining board 600 × 450 × 25 mm	each	422.00
302.	Raj Nagar Marble stone draining board 600 × 450 × 25 mm	each	350.00
303.	Glass reinforced Gypsum (GRG) board 8.5 mm thick	sq m	179.00
	Galvanised M.S. sheet 0.5 mm thick pressed channel section of size :		
304.	50 × 32 mm	metre	31.00
305.	72 × 32 mm	metre	37.00
	Galvanised M.S. sheet 0.50 mm thick pressed stud.		
306.	48 × 34 × 36 mm	metre	38.00
307.	70 × 34 × 36 mm	metre	44.00
	Copper oxidised (black finish) mild steel Tower bolt :		
308.	250 × 10 mm	ten	110.00
309.	200 × 10 mm	ten	70.00
310.	150 × 10 mm	ten	68.00
311.	100 × 10 mm	ten	40.00
	G.I. flush pipe and C.P. brass spreader including C.P. connecting pipe :		
312.	Single lipped urinal	each	246.00
313.	Range of two lipped urinals	each	591.00
314.	Range of three lipped urinals	each	739.00
315.	Range of four lipped urinals	each	1056.00
316.	White vitreous china clay half stall urinal flat back 580 × 380 × 350 mm or angle back 450 × 375 × 350 mm with waste fittings as per IS : 2556	each	860.00
	Precast R.C.C. grating with frame :		
317.	500 × 450 mm horizontal grating	each	484.00
318.	450 × 100 mm vertical grating	each	250.00
319.	RC-3 (Rapid curing) bitumen conforming to IS 217	tonne	13363.00
320.	G.I. Tee 100 mm dia	each	200.00

S. No.	Description	Unit	Rate ₹
321.	G.I. Tee 150 mm dia	each	250.00
322.	3 mm thick translucent white acrylic plastic sheet	sq m	395.00
323.	12 thick particle board ceiling tile	sq m	78.00
324.	Cadmium plated steel screws 20 mm	cent	95.00
325.	Dash hold fastener 12.5 mm dia, 40 mm long with 6 mm dia bolt	each	26.00
326.	Anodising 15 microns on aluminium sections	kilogram	25.00
327.	Neoprin/EPDM rubber gasket	metre	14.00
328.	Double action hydraulic floor spring	each	750.00
329.	6 mm dia. M.S. adjustable hangers including clips (upto 1.2 m length)	each	18.00
330.	G.I. Check nut 125 mm	each	30.00
331.	G.I. union 100 mm dia.	each	240.00
332.	G.I. union 150 mm dia.	each	810.00
	PTMT FITTINGS :		
333.	15 mm PTMT bib cock	each	72.00
334.	15 mm PTMT bib cock with flange (fancy)	each	88.00
335.	15 mm PTMT bib cock long body with flange	each	102.00
336.	15 mm dia PTMT stop cock (male thread)	each	72.00
337.	15 mm dia (F/T) stop cock (female thread)	each	72.00
338.	20 mm dia. PTMT stop cock	each	81.00
339.	PTMT pillar cock	each	108.00
340.	PTMT push cock 15 mm dia.	each	63.00
341.	PTMT push cock 12 mm dia. 20 mm BSP	each	52.00
342.	PTMT grating 100 mm dia.	each	20.00
343.	125 mm grating	each	27.00
344.	125 mm grating with waste hole	each	27.00
	Rectangular type with openable circular lid :		
345.	150 mm size 18 mm high with 100 mm dia. (110 gm)	each	30.00
346.	150 mm size 18 mm high with 31 mm waste (100 gms)	each	25.00
347.	Double acting air valve 50 mm	each	2500.00
348.	Double acting air valve 80 mm	each	3500.00
349.	Double acting air valve 100 mm	each	4200.00
350.	Water meter (including testing charges) 80 mm	each	1330.00
351.	Water meter (including testing charges) 100 mm	each	2016.00
352.	Water meter (including testing charges) 150 mm	each	2706.00
353.	Water meter (including testing charges) 200 mm	each	3670.00
354.	Dirt box srainer 80 mm	each	2015.00
355.	Dirt box srainer 100 mm	each	3055.00
356.	Dirt box srainer 150 mm	each	4100.00
357.	Dirt box srainer 200 mm	each	5560.00
358.	Cat's eye	each	250.00
	Water stops :		
359.	Serrated with central bulb (225 mm wide, 8-11 mm thick)	metre	252.00
360.	Dumb bell with central bulb	metre	227.00
361.	Kicers	metre	400.00

(Contd.)

S. No.	Description	Unit	Rate ₹
	Wedge expansion hold fastner :		
362.	1/4″ or 6 mm	each	6.50
363.	3/8″ or 10 mm	each	10.00
364.	1/2″ or 12 mm	each	21.50
365.	Gun metal non return valve horizontal type 100 mm dia.	each	1250.00
366.	Gun metal non return valve verticle type 100 mm dia. Test	each	1145.00
	Verticle routine test of piles in accordance with IS : 2911 (Part-IV) including installation of loading platform and preparation of pile head or construction of test cap and dismantling of test cap after test etc. complete as per specification and direction of Engineer-in-charge		
	Single Pile :		
367.	Upto 50 tonne capacity pile	per test	10300.00
368.	Above 50 tonne and upto 100 tonne capacity piles	per test	15450.00
	Group of two or more piles :		
369.	Upto 50 tonne capacity each	per test	20600.00
	8 mm thick (mirror polished tiles machine cut edge) :		
370.	Granite brown	sq m	400.00
371.	Raj Nagar white	sq m	200.00
372.	Banswara white	sq m	200.00
373.	Wheel 40 mm dia. 40 mm wide	each	25.00
374.	Wheel 75 mm dia. 40 mm wide	each	45.00
375.	Aluminium single cleat of size 30 × 32 × 3	each	4.50
376.	Aluminium grip strip of size 50 × 12 × 2	each	2.50
377.	25 mm prelaminated flush door both side decorative	sq m	612.00
378.	30 mm prelaminated flush door both side decorative	sq m	780.00
379.	20 mm prelaminated flush door both side decorative	sq m	350.00
380.	20 mm prelaminated flush door one side decorative other white balancing	sq m	475.00
381.	Aluminium U beading	kilogram	125.00
382.	Heptachlor	lit	95.00
383.	Glass sheet (Pin headed) 4 mm thick	sq m	160.00
	Raj Nagar plain-white marble (table rubbed and polished 20 mm thick) :		
384.	Above 0.10 sq m upto 0.20 sq m	sq m	400.00
385.	Above 0.20 sq m upto 0.50 sq m	sq m	550.00
	30 mm thick		
386.	Above 0.10 sq m upto 0.20 sq m	sq m	1000.00
387.	Above 0.20 sq m upto 0.50 sq m	sq m	1200.00
	Marble 20 mm thick mirror polished machine cut upto 0.10 sq m :		
388.	Abu plain white marble	sq m	1200.00
389.	Makrana Doongri Adanga, veined white marble	sq m	480.00
390.	Raj Nagar plain white marble	sq m	403.00
391.	Udaipur Green marble	sq m	350.00

S. No.	Description	Unit	Rate ₹
392.	Kishangarh Zebra black marble	sq m	550.00
393.	Granite black	sq m	1520.00
394.	Granite pink	sq m	900.00
395.	Granite grey	sq m	1100.00
396.	Strip-Aluminium fluted 3.15 mm thick and 200 mm wide	metre	185.00
397.	Second class deodar teak wood lipping 30 mm width	metre	15.00
398.	× 12 mm Chlordane emulsifiable concentrate	litre	240.00
	Veneered particle board with commercial veneering on both sides :		
399.	12 mm thick	sq m	257.00
400.	18 mm thick	sq m	320.00
401.	25 mm thick	sq m	434.00
	Veneered particle board with one side teak veneering and other side commercial veneering :		
402.	12 mm thick	sq m	407.00
403.	18 mm thick	sq m	490.00
404.	25 mm thick	sq m	558.00
	Veneered particle board with teak veneering on both sides :		
405.	12 mm thick	sq m	529.00
406.	18 mm thick	sq m	611.00
407.	25 mm thick	sq m	682.00
	Prelaminated particle board with one side decorative and other side balancing lamination, flat pressed 3 layer and graded (medium density) Grade I, Type II conforming to IS : 12823 (exterior grade :		
408.	12 mm thick	sq m	412.00
409.	18 mm thick	sq m	477.00
410.	25 mm thick	sq m	541.00
	Prelaminated particle board with both sides decorative lamination, flat pressed 3 layer and graded (medium density) Grade I, Type II conforming to IS : 12823 (exterior grade) :		
411.	12 mm thick	sq m	477.00
412.	18 mm thick	sq m	553.00
413.	25 mm thick	sq m	612.00
	Oxidised M.S. piano hinges finished with brass plating :		
414.	50 mm (Over all width)	metre	18.00
415.	65 mm (Over all width)	metre	20.00
	Oxidised M.S. hinges finished with nickel plating :		
416.	50 mm (Over all width)	metre	16.00
417.	65 mm (Over all width)	metre	18.00
	M.S. piano hinges finished with nickel plating :		
418.	50 mm (Over all width)	metre	16.00
419.	65 mm (Over all width)	metre	18.00
420.	Acid resistant tiles 10 mm thick 300 × 300 mm size	ten	330.00
421.	Alkali resistant tiles 10 mm thick 300 × 300 mm size	ten	330.00

Table 6.6. (Carriage by Mechanical Transport including loading, Unloading and stacking)

N.B. : These rates are exclusive of 10% contractor's profit and over head charges.

S. No.	*Description*	*Unit*	*Rate* ₹
1.	Steam coal	tonne	45.75
2.	Bricks	1000 nos.	179.44
3.	Stone aggregate below 40 mm nominal size	cum	84.61
4.	Coarse sand	cum	110.05
5.	Timber	cum	50.32
6.	Steel	tonne	54.51
7.	Stone aggregate 40 mm nominal size and above	cum	91.57
8.	Brick tiles	1000 nos.	112.15
9.	Lime	cum	41.93
10.	Cement	tonne	35.94
11.	C.I. pipes 100 mm dia	100 metre	85.93
12.	Tar bitumen	tonne	55.91
13.	C.I. pipes 150 mm dia	100 metre	137.49
14.	Soling stone and masonary stone	cum	99.54
15.	Stone blocks white and red sand stone and Kota Stone slab	tonne	35.94
16.	C.I. pipes 200 mm dia	100 metre	229.14
17.	C.I. pipes 250 mm dia	100 metre	312.47
18.	C.I. pipes 300 mm dia	100 metre	404.37
19.	C.I. pipes 350 mm dia	100 metre	572.86
20.	C.I. pipes 400 mm dia	100 metre	763.81
21.	C.I. pipes 450 mm dia	100 metre	982.05
22.	C.I. pipes 600, 700, 750 and 800 mm dia	100 metre	1374.86
23.	S.W. pipes 100 mm dia	100 metre	52.42
24.	S.W. pipes 150 mm dia	100 metre	104.83
25.	S.W. pipes 200 mm dia	100 metre	186.37
26.	S.W. pipes 230 mm dia	100 metre	239.62
27.	S.W. pipes 250 mm dia	100 metre	299.52
28.	S.W. pipes 300 mm dia	100 metre	381.21
29.	S.W. pipes 350 mm dia	100 metre	524.17
30.	S.W. pipes 400 mm dia	100 metre	762.42
31.	S.W. pipes 450 mm dia	100 metre	931.85
32.	S.W. pipes 500 mm dia	100 metre	1048.33
33.	S.W. pipes 600 mm dia	100 metre	1397.78
34.	R.C.C. circular tank 270 litres	each	146.97
35.	R.C.C. circular tank 540 litres	each	244.95
36.	Steel cylinder R.C. pipes 900 mm dia	100 metre	2291.44
37.	Steel cylinder R.C. pipes 1100 mm dia	100 metre	3437.16
38.	Steel cylinder R.C. bench	tonne	35.94
39.	C.I. pipes 125 mm dia	100 metre	114.57
40.	Good earth	cum	36.05
41.	Dump manure	cum	31.35
42.	A.C. pipes 100 mm dia	100 metre	85.93
43.	A.C. pipes 125 mm dia	100 metre	114.57
44.	A.C. pipes 150 mm dia	100 metre	137.49
45.	A.C. pipes 200 mm dia	100 metre	229.14
46.	A.C. pipes 250 mm dia	100 metre	404.37

S. No.	Description	Unit	Rate ₹
47.	A.C. pipes 300 mm dia	100 metre	404.37
48.	Brick aggregate	cum	71.76
49.	Fine sand (1 part Badarpur sand : 2 parts Jamuna sand)	cum	70.23
50.	Rubbish	cum	41.93
51.	Moorum	cum	41.93
52.	Surkhi	cum	71.76
53.	Stone dust	cum	84.61
54.	Marble dust and marble chips	cum	50.32
55.	Lime pozzolana mixture L.P. 40	tonne	35.94
56.	High alumina cement	tonne	35.94
57.	G.I. pipes below 100 mm dia	tonne	35.94
58.	C.I. pipes below 100 mm dia	tonne	35.94
59.	A.C. sheet and accessories	tonne	35.94
60.	C.C. pipes below 100 mm dia and other heavy materials	tonne	35.94
61.	R.C.C. pipes 100 mm dia	100 metre	85.93
62.	Steel cylinder R.C. pipes 100 mm dia	100 metre	85.93
63.	Unreinforced cement pipes 100 mm dia	100 metre	85.93
64.	R.C.C. pipes 125 mm dia	100 metre	114.57
65.	Steel cylinder R.C. pipes 125 mm dia	100 metre	114.57
66.	Unreinforced cement pipes 125 mm dia	100 metre	114.57
67.	R.C.C. pipes 150 mm dia	100 metre	137.49
68.	Steel cylinder R.C. pipes 150 mm dia	100 metre	137.49
69.	Unreinforced cement pipes 150 mm dia	100 metre	137.49
70.	R.C.C. pipes 200 mm dia	100 metre	229.14
71.	Steel cylinder R.C. pipes 200 mm dia	100 metre	229.14
72.	Unreinforced cement pipes 200 mm dia	100 metre	229.14
73.	R.C.C. pipes 250 mm dia	100 metre	312.47
74.	Steel cylinder R.C. pipes 250 mm dia	100 metre	312.47
75.	Unreinforced cement pipes 250 mm dia	100 metre	312.47
76.	R.C.C. pipes 300 mm dia	100 metre	404.37
77.	Steel cylinder R.C. pipes 300 mm dia	100 metre	404.37
78.	Unreinforced cement pipes 300 mm dia	100 metre	404.37
79.	R.C.C. pipes 350 mm dia	100 metre	572.86
80.	Steel cylinder R.C. pipes 350 mm dia	100 metre	572.86
81.	Unreinforced cement pipes 350 mm dia	100 metre	572.86
82.	R.C.C. pipes 400 mm dia	100 metre	763.81
83.	Steel cylinder R.C. pipes 400 mm dia	100 metre	763.81
84.	Unreinforced cement pipes 400 mm dia	100 metre	763.81
85.	R.C.C. pipes 450 and 500 mm dia	100 metre	982.05
86.	Steel cylinder R.C. pipes 450 and 500 mm dia	100 metre	982.05
87.	Unreinforced cement pipes 450 and 500 mm dia	100 metre	952.05

(*Contd.*)

S. No.	Description	Unit	Rate ₹
88.	G.I. sheet and accessories	tonne	35.94
89.	R.C.C. pipes 600, 700, 750 and 800 mm dia	100 metre	1374.86
90.	Steel cylinder R.C. pipes 600, 700, 750 and 800 mm dia	100 metre	1374.66
91.	Unreinforced cement pipes 600, 700, 750 and 800 mm dia	100 metre	1374.86
92.	Marble slab	tonne	35.94
93.	Bamboo including poolas	tonne	41.93
94.	Plaster of paris	tonne	35.94
95.	Cast iron fittings	tonne	35.94
96.	A.C. pipes below 100 mm dia	tonne	35.94
97.	Red bajri	cum	50.32
98.	Kerb stone blocks	tonne	60.40
99.	Channel stone blocks	tonne	60.40
100.	Barbed wire	tonne	35.94
101.	Premoulded joint filler	tonne	55.91
102.	Sealing compound	tonne	55.91
103.	Sludge	cum	31.35
104.	Spun iron S & S pipes 80 mm dia	100 metre	35.94
105.	Spun iron S & S pipes 100 mm dia	100 metre	85.93
106.	Spun iron S & S pipes 125 mm dia	100 metre	114.57
107.	Spun iron S & S pipes 150 mm dia	100 metre	137.49
108.	Spun iron S & S pipes 200 mm dia	100 metre	229.14
109.	Spun iron S & S pipes 250 mm dia	100 metre	312.47
110.	Spun iron S & S pipes 300 mm dia	100 metre	404.37
111.	Spun iron S & S pipes 350 mm dia	100 metre	572.86
112.	Spun iron S & S pipes 400 mm dia	100 metre	763.81
113.	Spun iron S & S pipes 450 mm dia	100 metre	982.05
114.	Spun iron S & S pipes 500 mm dia	100 metre	982.05
115.	Spun iron S & S pipes 600 mm dia	100 metre	1374.86
116.	C.I. pipes 500 mm dia	100 metre	982.05
117.	R.C.C. pipes 900 mm dia	100 metre	2291.44
118.	R.C.C. pipes 1000 mm dia	100 metre	3437.16
119.	R.C.C. pipes 1100 mm dia	100 metre	3437.16
120.	R.C.C. pipes 1200 mm dia	100 metre	3437.16
121.	Jamuna sand	cum	50.32
122.	Pig lead	tonne	35.94
123.	Solvent/Diesel	quintal	5.59

Table 6.7. Carriage of Materials

A-By Mechanical Transport including Loading, Unloading and Stacking

	Materials	Unit	Rate								Remarks
			1 Km.	*2 Km.*	*3 Km.*	*4 Km.*	*5 Km.*	*Beyond 5 Km. upto 10 Km. per Km.*	*Beyond 10 Km. upto 20 Km. per Km.*	*Beyond 20 Km. per Km.*	
1	(A) Lime, moorum, building rubbish, earth, manure or sludge and excavated rock :										The rates will be applicable to net quantities after deduction of prescribed percentage for viods mentioned in the specification under subhead "Carriage of Materials". They also charge from place to place and also depend upon diesel prices.
	(*i*) Lime, moorum, buliding rubbish	cum	31.72	35.48	39.17	42.71	46.12	2.99	2.35	1.82	
	(*ii*) Earth	cum	39.66	44.34	48.96	55.38	57.66	3.72	2.95	2.27	
	(*iii*) Manure or sludge	cum	34.94	38.56	42.58	46.42	50.14	3.26	2.56	1.97	
	(*iv*) Excavated rock	cum	63.45	70.95	78.35	85.42	92.26	5.48	4.71	3.62	
2	(B) Sand, stone aggregate and soiling stone										
	(*i*) Sand, stone aggregate below 40 mm nominal size	cum	38.07	42.57	47.00	51.25	55.35	3.59	2.83	2.17	
	(*ii*) Stone aggregate 40 mm nominal size and above	cum	41.21	46.07	50.88	55.46	59.91	3.88	3.06	2.35	
	(*iii*) Soiling stone	cum	44.79	50.08	35.91	60.29	65.12	4.22	3.32	2.55	
3	Bricks	1000 Nos.	95.18	106.43	117.52	128.13	138.38	8.98	7.06	5.43	
4	Brick	Tiles 1000 Nos.	59.49	66.52	73.45	80.08	86.49	5.61	4.41	3.39	

(*Contd.*)

5	Cement, stone blocks, G.I., C.I., A.C. & C.C. pipes below 100 mm dia and other heavy materials	tonne	27.19	30.40	53.57	36.61	39.53	2.56	2.01	1.55	
6	Steel	tonne	47.62	50.83	54.01	57.04	59.96	2.56	2.01	1.55	
7	Timber	cum	38.07	42.57	47.00	51.25	55.35	3.59	2.83	2.17	
8	Tar Bitumen	tonne	42.31	47.30	52.23	56.95	61.50	3.99	3.14	2.41	
9	Solvent	qtl.	4.24	4.73	5.23	5.70	6.15	0.40	0.32	0.24	
10	Steam coal	tonne	34.61	38.70	42.74	46.60	30.33	3.27	2.56	1.97	
11	S.W. Pipes										
	(*a*) 100 mm dia	100 m	39.66	44.34	48.96	53.38	57.66	3.74	2.95	2.27	
	(*b*) 150 mm dia	100 m	79.31	88.68	97.63	106.78	115.31	7.48	5.89	4.52	
	(*c*) 200 mm dia	100 m	141.01	157.66	174.10	189.82	205.01	13.30	10.46	8.04	
	(*d*) 230 mm dia	100 m	181.29	202.71	223.85	244.06	263.85	17.09	13.45	10.34	
	(*e*) 250 mm dia	100 m	226.11	253.39	279.81	305.06	321.47	21.37	16.82	12.93	
	(*f*) 300 mm dia	100 m	288.42	322.49	356.11	388.27	419.33	27.20	21.40	16.45	
	(*g*) 350 mm dia	100 m	396.57	443.41	489.67	533.86	576.59	37.40	29.43	22.62	
	(*h*) 400 mm dia	100 m	576.83	644.96	712.23	771.53	838.66	54.40	42.80	32.90	
	(*i*) 450 mm dia	100 m	705.02	788.29	870.51	949.09	1025.03	66.48	52.32	40.22	
	(*j*) 500 mm dia	100 m	793.14	836.83	979.32	1067.74	1153.16	74.80	58.65	45.24	
	(*k*) 600 mm dia	100 m	1057.53	1182.43	1305.77	1423.04	1537.56	99.74	78.46	60.31	

12	R.C.C. Pipes, A.C. Pipes, Steel cylinder, R.C. Pipes, C.I. Pipes and unreinforced cement pipes										
	(*a*) 100 mm dia	100 m	65.01	72.69	80.27	87.52	94.52	6.13	4.83	3.71	
	(*b*) 125 mm dia	100 m	86.68	96.62	107.03	116.69	126.03	8.17	6.44	4.94	
	(*c*) 150 mm dia	100 m	104.02	116.30	128.44	140.03	151.24	9.81	7.72	5.93	
	(*d*) 200 mm dia	100 m	173.36	193.84	214.06	233.39	252.05	16.35	121.86	9.89	
	(*e*) 250 mm dia	100 m	236.41	264.33	291.90	318.25	343.72	22.30	17.55	13.49	
	(*f*) 300 mm dia	100 m	365.94	342.08	377.75	411.85	444.81	28.85	22.70	17.45	
	(*g*) 350 mm dia	100 m	433.41	484.61	535.15	583.46	630.15	40.88	32.15	24.72	
	(*h*) 400 mm dia	100 m	577.89	646.14	713.53	777.95	840.19	54.49	42.88	32.96	
	(*i*) 450 mm & 500 mm dia	100 m	743.00	830.75	917.40	1000.22	1080.26	70.07	55.13	42.37	
	(*j*) 600, 700, 750 & 800 mm dia	100 m	1040.19	1163.05	1284.36	1400.31	1512.35	98.10	77.18	59.32	
	(*k*) 900 mm dia	100 m	1733.66	1938.42	2140.59	2333.85	2520.58	163.49	128.63	98.88	
	(*l*) 1000, 1100 & 1200 mm dia	100 m	2600.48	2907.64	3210.89	3500.76	3780.88	245.25	192.95	148.32	

Table 6.7 (*a*) Labour output constants are given in Table

S. No.	*Description of Work*	*Unit*	*Labour*	*Recommended constant in days*	*Remarks*
1.	**Excavation and Earthwork**				
	(*a*) Excavation over areas (Hard/Dense soil) depth up to 1.5 m and removal	cum	Mate	0.06	
			Mazdoor	0.62	
	(*b*) Excavation in trenches (Soft/Loose soil for foundations depth up to 1.5 m and removal (up to one metre away from edge)				Extra for refilling in layers etc. Mate 0.02 Mazdoor 0.25
		cum	Mate	0.05	Bhisti 0.02
			Mazdoor	0.50	
2.	**Concrete**				
	(*a*) Hand mixed cement concrete in foundations including mixing, pouring, consolidating and curing	cum	Mason	0.10	
			Mazdoor	2.13	
			Bhisti	0.70	
	(*b*) Hand mixed line concrete in foundations	cum	Mason	0.10	
			Mazdoor	2.65	
			Bhisti	0.80	
			Bullock with Driver	0.15	
	(*c*) R.C.C. work in situ in roofs. Excluding formwork, and reinforcement	cum	Mason	0.24	
			Mazdoor	2.50	
			Bhisti	0.90	
			Mixer Operator	0.07	
			Mixer	0.07	
			Vibration	0.07	
3.	**Mortars**				
	(*a*) Mixing by hand, cement mortar of any mix/proportions	cum	Mazdoor	0.75	
			Bhisti	0.07	
	(*b*) Mixing by hand cement lime sand of any proportions	cum	Mazdoor	1.33	
			Bhisti	0.10	
			Bullock with Driver	0.33	
4.	**Brick work (walls)**				
	(*a*) Exceeding one brick thick, in cement/lime mortar	cum	Mason	0.94	Labour for mixing mortar will be extra in all types of brick-work
			Mazdoor	1.80	
	(*b*) One brick thick, in cement/lime mortar	sq m	Bhisti	0.20	
			Mason	0.25	
	(*c*) Half brick thick, in cement mortar	sq m	Mazdoor	0.40	
	(*d*) Tile work in superstructure in cement mortar	sq m	Bhisti	0.10	
			Mason	0.12	
			Mazdoor	0.20	
			Bhisti	0.07	
			Mason	1.80	
			Mazdoor	1.80	
			Bhisti	0.20	

S. No.	Description of Work	Unit	Labour	Recommended constant in days	Remarks
5.	**Form work**				
	(a) Fabrication and erection with all supports, struts, braces, etc. complete				
	(i) Columns and walls	cum	Carpenter	0.25	
			Mazdoor	0.20	
	(ii) Suspended floors/roofs	sq m	Carpenter	0.23	
			Mazdoor	0.20	
	(iii) Sides and soffits of beams	sq m	Carpenter	0.30	
			Mazdoor	0.20	
6.	**Reinforcement**				
	Bar, Reinforcement including cutting, bending and bending in position complete	Quintal	Bar Bender	1.00	
			Mazdoor	1.00	
7.	**Plastering and Pointing**				
	(a) 15 mm thick cement plaster including mixing of mortar	sq m	Mason	0.08	
			Mazdoor	0.10	
			Bhisti	0.10	
	(b) Struck pointing to brick work in cement mortar including mixing mortar	sq m	Mason	0.08	
			Mazdoor	0.10	
			Bhisti	0.10	
8.	**Paving and Floor Finish**				
	(a) 40 mm thick P.C.C. floor finished smooth	sq m	Mason	0.08	Labour for mixing concrete will be extra for (a) and (b)
			Mazdoor	0.12	
			Bhisti	0.10	
	(b) 40 mm thick terrazo flooring				
	(i) Laying	sq m	Mason	0.22	
			Mazdoor	0.22	
			Bhisti	0.10	
	(ii) Cutting, grinding and polishing	sq m	Mazdoor	0.50	
			Machine	0.40	
9.	**Damp-Proof Course**				
	(a) 40 mm thick P.C.C. damp proof course including formwork	sq m	Mason	0.10	
			Mazdoor	0.10	
			Bhisti	0.01	
	(b) 20 mm thick cement mortar D.P.C. including form work	sq m	Mason	0.10	
			Mazdoor	0.10	
			Bhisti	0.01	
10.	**Joinery**				
	(a) Door and window chokhats of wood	cum	Carpenter	20.00	
			Mazdoor	2.00	
	(b) 40 mm thick door and window shutters of any type	sq m	Carpenter	0.90	
			Mazdoor	0.10	
	(c) Fixing of ready made shutters to frames including fixing of fittings	sq m	Carpenter	0.25	
			Mazdoor	0.25	

(Contd.)

S. No.	*Description of Work*	*Unit*	*Labour*	*Recom-mended constant in days*	*Remarks*
11.	**Glazing**				
	Fixing glass panes on steel or wood work bedded with putty	sq m	Glazier Mazdoor	0.20 0.01	
12.	**Painting and Polishing**				
	French polishing complete on new work	sq m	Painter	0.35	
13.	**White Washing and Colour Washing**				
	(*a*) White washing with lime 3 coats new surface	sq m	Washer Mazdoor	0.02 0.01	
	(*b*) Two coat of colour washing over an under coat of whitewash on new work	sq m	Washer Mazdoor	0.03 0.01	
	(*c*) White wash one coat on old or new work with lime or cement	sq m	Washer	0.02	
	(*d*) Distempering with dry distemper 3 coats on new surface including a primary coat	sq m	Painter Mazdoor	0.08 0.04	
14.	**Terraced Roofing**				
	(*a*) 10 cm thick mud phuska complete with one layer of tile brick etc. finished with cement rounting including Gobri leeping	sq m	Mason Mazdoor Bhisti	0.13 0.36 0.11	
	(*b*) 10 cm thick lime concrete terracing complete	sq m	Mason Mazdoor Bhisti	0.10 0.37 0.15	

Table 6.7 (*b*) Quantity of Work in per day

S. No.	*Description of Item*	*Quantity of work per day*	*Remarks*
1.	**Mason**		
	1. Lime Concrete	10 cum	
	2. Cement Concrete 1 : 5 : 10 mix.	10 cum	
	3. Cement Concrete 1 : 2 : 4 mix. in R.C.C. work	3 cum	or 20 to 30 sq m
	4. Brickwork in foundations	2 cum	
	5. Brickwork in superstructure	1.5 cum	
	6. Brickwork in arches	1 cum	
	7. Half brickwork in partitions	8 sq m	
	8. Tile work in super structure	0.5 cum	
	9. 40 mm thick D.P.C.	10 sq m	
	10. Stone work ashlar type	0.25 cum	
	11. Stone work random rubble	1 cum	
	12. Marble work	0.05 cum	
	13. Brick flooring	15 sq m	
	14. P.C.C. flooring	8 to 10 sq m	

	15. Terrazo flooring	4 to 5 sq m	
	16. Marble flooring	1 to 2 sq m	
	17. Stone flooring	4 to 5 sq m	
	18. Mud phuska	8 sq m	
	19. Lime concrete terracing	10 sq m	
	20. (*a*) 15 mm thick plaster	10 sq m	(*b*) 6 mm thick 15 sq m
	21. (*b*) Pointing	10 sq m	
	22. Punning	20 sq m	
	23. R.B. work	4 to 5 sq m	
	24. Tile roofing	5 sq m	or 1 cum
	25. Three coat white or colour washing on new surface	50 sq m	
	26. Two coat white-washing on old surface	100 sq m	
2.	**Carpenter**		
	1. Timbering in trenches open type	300 to 400 sq m	
	2. Centring and shuttering	4 to 8 sq m	
	3. Door and window chokhats	0.05 cum	
	4. Doors and window shutters	1 sq m	
	5. Jaffri work	1 sq m	
	6. Pelmets	5 m	
	7. Jali work	5 sq m	
	8. Wooden floors	0.5 sq m	
	9. A.C. sheet roof	8 sq m	
	10. Ceiling work	2 sq m	
	11. Fixing shutters	4 sq m	
	12. Fixing glass panes	5 sq m	
	13. Wooden marking	2 to 4 sq m	
3.	**Painter**		
	1. Distempering on new surface including priming coat and preparation of surface	20 sq m	
	2. Wood preservative on new wood work	50 sq m	
	3. Painting wood work with priming coat	20 sq m	
	4. Painting new wood work with two coats along with priming coat	10 sq m	
	5. Painting old wood work with one coat	30 sq m	
	6. Varnishing new wood work complete	20 sq m	
	7. Polishing new wood work complete	5 sq m	
	8. Applying a coat of hot bitumen on DPC, proof etc.	50 sq m	
4.	**Blacksmith**		
	1. M.S. bars, bending, binding and placing in position	100 kg	
	2. Structural steel work, in trusses, columns, etc.	200 kg	
5.	**Mazdoor**		
	1. Earth work in trenches	2 to 3 cum	
	2. Earth work in filling	5 to 10 cum	
	3. Concrete work in foundations	0.4 cum	
	4. Concrete work in R.C.C. slabs etc.	0.3 cum	
	5. Mixing cement mortar	3 cum	
	6. Delivering bricks	4000 Nos.	
	7. Breaking of brick ballast 25 mm size	0.8 cum	
	8. Breaking of stone ballast 40 mm size	0.5 cum	
	9. Excavation in rock	1 cum	
	10. Delivering mortar	5 cum	

Quantities of Materials

Quantities of material required for different items of work are given in Table 6.8.

Table 6.8 (*a*) Lime Mortar (Unit 1 cum)

S. No.	Description	Lime putty cum	Sand cum	Surkhi cum	Ash cum	Remarks
1.	Lime mortar 1 : 1 (Lime putty : 1 sand)	0.7 (426 kg)	0.7	—	—	(*a*) For 1 cum of motar; 1.42 cum of dry material is required.
2.	Lime mortar 1 : 1 : 1 (Lime putty : 1 surkhi : 1 sand)	0.473 (284 kg)	0.473	0.473	—	(*b*) 1 cum lime putty is equal to 600 kg of unslaked lime.
3.	Lime mortar 1 : 1 : 1 (Lime putty : 1 Ash : 1 sand)	0.473 (284 kg)	0.473		0.473	(*c*) Material is calculated according to proportions.

Table 6.8 (*b*) Cement Mortar (Unit 1 cum)

S. No.	Description	Cement cum	Sand cum	Remarks
1.	Cement mortar 1 : 1 (1 cement : 2 sand)	0.71 (21.3 Bags)	0.71	(*a*) For 1 cum of mortar of 1 : 1, 1 : 2 and 1 : 3; 1.42 cum of dry material is required.
2.	Cement mortar 1 : 2 (1 cement : 2 sand)	0.473 (14.2 Bags)		
3.	Cement mortar 1 : 3 (1 cement : 3 sand)	0.355 (10.6 Bags)	0.946	(*b*) For 1 cum of mortar of 1 : 4, 1 : 5, 1 : 6; 1.3 cum of dry material is required.
4.	Cement mortar 1 : 4 (1 cement : 4 sand)	0.26 (7.8 Bags)	1.04	(*c*) 1 cum cement is equal to 30 bags (1430 kg).
5.	Cement mortar 1 : 5 (1 cement : 5 sand)	0.217 (6.5 Bags)	1.08	(*d*) Material is calculated according to proportions.
6.	Cement mortar 1 : 6 (1 cement : 6 sand)	0.176 (5.0 Bags)	1.05	

Table 6.8 (*c*) Cement Lime Mortar (Unit 1 cum)

S. No.	Description	Cement cum	Lime putty cum	Sand cum	Remarks
1.	Cement lime mortar 1 : 1 : 6 (1) cement : 1 lime putty : 6 (sand)	0.177 (5.3 Bags)	0.177 (106 kg)	1.06	1. For 1 cum of mortar 1.42 cum of dry material is required.
2.	Cement mortar 1 : 1 : 7 (1) cement : 1 lime putty : 6 (sand)	0.158 (4.7 Bags)	0.158 (95 kg)	1.10	2. Material is calculated according to proportions.
3.	Cement mortar 1 :1 : 8 (1) cement : 1 lime putty : 8 (sand)	0.142 (4.2 Bags)	0.142 (85 kg)	1.13	

Note : 1. For 1 cum of mud mortar, 1.10 cum of dry mud is required.

2. For blasting 10 cum of hard rock 6.42 kg of powder and 7 No. of fuses are required (7 Nos. of holes are drilled).

3. Wooden materials, are used for 16 No. of operations (or 16 times) in trenches for timbering for their useful life.

Table 6.8 (*d*) Lime Concrete (Unit 1 cum)

S. No.	Description	Lime putty cum	Sand cum	Coarse Aggregate cum	Ash or Surkhi cum	Remarks
1.	Lime concrete 1 : 3 mix. (1 lime putty : sand)	0.142 (85 kg)	0.426	1.00	—	(*i*) 40% lime mortar is used.
2.	Lime concrete 1 : 1 : 1 mix. (1 lime putty : 1 ash : 1 sand)	0.19 (114 kg)	0.19	1.00	0.19	(*ii*) 1 cum of coarse aggregate is used.

Table 6.8 (*e*) Cement Concrete (Unit 1 cum)

S. No.	Description	Cement cum	Sand cum	Coarse Aggregate cum	Remarks
1.	Cement concrete 1 : 2 : 4 mix (1 cement : 2 sand : 4 coarse aggregate)	0.22 (6.6 Bags)	0.44	0.88	For 1 cum of finished concrete, 1.54 cum of dry material is required in their proportions.
2.	Cement concrete 1 : 3 : 6 mix	0.154 (4.6 Bags)	0.462	0.924	
3.	Cement concrete 1 : 4 : 8 mix	0.118 (3.5 Bags)	0.72	0.944	
4.	Cement concrete 1 : 5 : 10 mix	0.096 (2.8 Bags)	0.480	0.960	
5.	Cement concrete 1 : 6 : 12 mix	0.08 (2.4 Bags)	0.48	0.96	

Note : 1. The timber will become unserviceable, after being used 16 times in centring and shuttering for R.C.C. work.

2. D.P.C. 40 mm thick, with cement concrete 1 : 2 : 4 mix, for 100 sq. m, 24.32 bags of cement are required.

3. R.C.C. work 1 : 1 ½ : 3 mix, for 1 cum of concrete 8 bags or cement are required.

4. R.C.C. work 1 : 1 : 2 mix, for 1 cum of concrete 12.8 bags of cement are required.

5. For cement slurry on R.C.C. slab, 2.75 kg per sq. m of cement is required.

6. Rendering smooth the tops of suspended floors with cement mortar 1 : 2 mix ; including floating coat of neat cement, 8 bags of cement are required for 100 sq m of surface area.

Table 6.8 (*f*) Brickwork (Unit 1 cum)

S. No.	Description	Brick No.	Cement Bags	Sand cum	Remarks
1.	Brick work 1 : 3 mix (1 cement : 3 sand)	500 Nos.	2.60	0.25	By volume 25% of cement mortar is used.
2.	Brickwork 1 : 4 mix	500 Nos.	1.95	0.25	
3.	Brickwork 1 : 5 mix	500 Nos.	1.60	0.25	
4.	Brickwork 1 : 6 mix	500 Nos.	1.30	0.25	
5.	Half brick masonry 1 : 3 (1 cement : 3 sand) unit sq m	55 Nos.	0.26	0.025	
6.	Brick tile masonry 1 : 6 (1 cement : 6 sand)	950 Nos.	1.60	0.32	By volume 30% of cement mortar is used.
7.	R.B. work in roofs, 1 : 2 mix (1 cement : 2 sand)	420 Nos.	6.40	0.43	By volume 45% of cement mortar is used.

Note : 1. Honeycomb brick work in cement mortal 1 : 4 : 11 bags of cement are required 100 sq m.

2. Joining old brickwork with new brickwork, in cement mortar 1 : 3 : 4 bags of cement are required for 100 sq m.

3. Tile brickwork 5 cm thick in cement mortal' 1 : 3 : 7 bags of cement are required for 100 sq m.

Table 6.8 (g) Stone Work (Unit 1 cum)

S. No.	Description	Stone cum	Cement Bags	Sand cum	Remarks
1.	Random rubble masonry in cement mortar 1 : 6 (1 cement : 6 sand)	1 cum	0.86	0.37	By volume 35% cement mortar is used.
2.	Coarsed rubble masonry in cement mortar 1 : 6 (1 cement : 6 sand)	1.6 cum	1.60	0.32	By volume 30% cement mortar is used.
3.	Stone work in plain Ashlar in cement mortar 1 : 6 (1 cement : 6 sand)	1.3 cum	1.00	0.20	By volume 20% cement mortar is used.
4.	Stone work for wall lining etc. (veneer work) 60 mm thick in cement mortar 1 : 3 (1 cement : 3 sand) Unit sq m.	1 sq m 80 cum	0.20	0.02	By volume 5% cement mortar is used.

Note : 1. Marble work in steps, in cement mortar 1 : 4 : 1.5 bags of cement are required for 1 sq m.

2. Marble work for wall lining, 4 cm thick, in cement mortar 1 : 3 : 20.5 bags of cement are required for 100 sq m.

3. Fixing 4 cm thick jali, in cement mortar 1 : 2 : 7 bags of cement are required for 100 sq m.

4. 50 × 50 × 50 mm wood plugs, fixing in cement mortar 1 : 3 : 0.02 bag of cement is required for 100 Nos.

5. Fixing standard steel door and window frames, in concrete blocks ; 2060 bags of cement are required for 100 sq m.

6. Fixing 20 × 6 mm, mild steel 15 cm. long clamps, for securing chick tops ; 0.1 bag of cement is required for 100 Nos.

Table 6.8 (h) Flooring (Unit 1 sq m)

S. No.	Description	Brick No.	Cement Bags	Sand cum	Coarse Aggregate 20 mm Size	Marble chips 4 mm Size	Remarks
1.	Brick flooring in cement mortar 1 : 6	50	0.15	0.030	–	–	
2.	40 mm thick cement concrete flooring 1 : 2 : 4, finished with a floating coat of neat cement	–	0.30	0.018	0.35	–	
3.	40 mm thick marble chips flooring, under layer 31 mm thick cement concrete 1 : 2 : 4 and top layer 9 mm thick marble chips mortar	–	0.30	0.014	0.028	14 kg	Marble powder 2 kg

Note : 1. 20 mm cement plaster skirting upto 30 cm height with cement mortar 1 : 3, finished with a floating coat of neat cement, 28 bags of cement are required for 100 sq m.

2. Marble chips skirting upto 30 cm height, top layer 6 mm thick marble chips ; 29 bags of cement are required for 100 sq m.

3. Marble stone slab flooring, 25 mm thick, over 20 mm thick base of cement mortar 1 : 4 : 27 bags of cement are required for 100 sq m.

4. Kota stone slab flooring, 25 mm thick, 30 bags of cement are required for 100 sq m laid over 20 mm base of cement mortar 1 : 4.

5. 40 mm sand stone flooring, over 20 mm thick base, of cement mortar 1 : 5 : 15 bags of cement are required for 100 sq m.

6. Floating coat of neat cement, 202 kg of cement is required for 1 sq m.

6.4. I Finishing Work

(i) Roofing

Note : 1. 50 mm thick stone slab roofing, laid in cement mortar 1 : 4, 1.40 bags are required for 100 sq m.

2. 10 cm thick mud phuska ; covered with flat tiles bricks grouped with cement mortar 1 : 3 :; and cement pointing on top with cement mortar 1 : 3 ; 7.60 bags of cement are required for 100 sq. m.

Table 6.8 (i) Finishing (Unit 100 sq m)

S. No.	*Description*	*Cement Bags*	*Sand cum*	*Remarks*
1.	6 mm thick cement plaster 1 : 3 (1 cement : 3 sand)	7.40	0.74	0.70 cum of mortar.
2.	12 mm thick cement plaster 1 : 6	7.20	1.44	1.44 cum of mortar
3.	20 mm thick cement plaster 1 : 6	11.20	2.24	2.2 cum of mortar
4.	Neat cement punning	4.40	—	
5.	Brick pointing on stone work with cement mortar 1 : 3	3.00	0.30	0.30 cum of mortar
6.	Flush pointing on brick work with cement mortar 1 : 6	1.00	0.20	0.20 cum of mortar
7.	18 mm plaster with terrazo finish under layer 12 mm cement plaster 1 : 3 and top layer 6 mm marble chips mortar	23.30	1.47	2.16 cum of mortar

Table 6.8 (j) Miscellaneous Building Works

S. No.	*Description of Item*	*Unit*	*Cement Bags*	*Remarks cum*
1.	Repair to plaster with cement mortar 1 : 4	100 sq m	14.00	
2.	Fixing door chowkhats in openings	each	0.24	
3.	Regarding terracing of mud phuska	100 sq m	11.40	
4.	Fixing M.S. fan clamps	each	0.03	
5.	Rough cast or pebble dash plaster	100 sq m	19.20	
6.	Making plinth protection	100 sq m	17.20	
7.	Laying kerb stone 30 × 20 cm	100 m	3.00	
8.	Fixing R.C.C. posts in concrete	100 Nos.	130.00	
9.	Fixing road signs	each	1.00	
10.	Cement concrete 1 : 2 : 4 (Coarse Aggregate 40 mm side) in pavements, roads, taxi tracks, etc.	cum	6.60	
11.	Fixing India w.c. complete	each	0.10	
12.	Fixing flat back or wall corner type urinal	each	0.10	
13.	Jointing S.W. pipe 100 mm dia	100 m	0.05	
14.	Laying cement concrete 1 : 5 : 10 alround S.W. pipe including bed concrete, for 100 mm dia	each	4.30	
15.	Fixing S.W. gully trap	100 m	4.30	
16.	Constructing brick masonry manhole inside size 90 × 80 cm 60 cm deep	each	0.50	
17.	Constructing circular manhole 1.4 m internal diameter, 2.45 m deep	each	4.40	
18.	Constructing brick masonry open surface drain 10 cm 20 cm depth	each 100 m	9.20 3.45	
19.	Cutting holes upto 30 × 30 cm and making good	100 No.	4.96	
20.	Making chases upto 7.5 × 7.5 cm and making good	100 m	1.76	

Table 6.8 (*k*) Finishing Work (White Washing, Distempering and Painting etc.)

S. No.	*Description of Item*	*Material*	*Unit*	*Quantity*	*Remarks*
1.	White washing on new work (3 coats)	1 Lime	1 sq m	3 kg	
2.	White washing on old work (2 coats)	1 Lime	1 sq m	2 kg	
3.	White washing on old work (1 coat)	1 Lime	1 sq m	1 kg	
4.	Distemper on new work	(*i*) whiting (*ii*) distemper	1 sq m 1 sq m	0.10 kg 0.15 kg	
5.	Distemper on old work	1 Distemper	1 sq m	0.10 kg	
6.	Cement paint on new work (3 coats)	1 Distemper	1 sq m	0.50 kg	
7.	Cement paint on old work	1 Cement paint	1 sq m	0.20 kg	
8.	Painting with oil type wood preservative on old work	1 Oil type wood preservative	1 sq m	0.10 litre	
9.	Painting with oil type wood preservative on old work	1 Old type wood preservative	1 sq m	0.08 litre	
10.	Priming coat on wood work	1 Ready mixed primer	1 sq m	0.08 litre	
11.	Priming coat on steel work	1 Ready mixed primer	1 sq m	0.05 litre	
12	Priming coat on plastered surface	1 Ready mixed primer	1 sq m	0.10 liter	
13.	Painting on new work (2 coats)	1 Ready mixed paint	1 sq m	0.12 litre	
14.	Painting on old work	1 Ready mixed paint	1 sq m	0.06 litre	
15.	Varnishing on new work (2 coats)	1 Flatting varnish 2 Copal varnish	1 sq m 1 sq m	0.08 litre 0.12 litre	
16.	Varnishing on old work	1 Copal varnish	1 sq m	0.08 litre	
17.	Polishing with wax polish on new work	1 Wax polish	1 sq m	0.05 kg	
18.	Polishing with wax polish on old work	1 Wax polish	1 sq m	0.02 kg	
19.	French spirit polishing on new work	1 Spirit 2 Shellac	1 sq m 1 sq m	0.15 litre 0.02 kg	
20.	French spirit polishing on old work	1 Spirit 2 Shellac	1 sq m 1 sq m	0.08 litre 0.01 kg	
21.	Painting on G.I. sheets or new work	Ready mixed paint	1 sq m	0.08 litre	
22.	Painting on G.I. sheets on old work	Ready mixed paint	1 sq m	0.04 litre	

6.5. ANALYSIS OF RATES FOR DIFFERENT ITEMS OF BUILDING WORK

Analysis of rates for different item of work is given below.

Rates are based mostly on DSR-1997. However where such rates are not available local market rates have been adopted. Rates prevailing at places under consideration should be referred. Rates should be calculated taking rates of items like material, labour etc. prevailing theirin *i.e.* place under consideration. DSR rates can also be considered if required or market rates be adopted.

Earthwork

1. Earthwork in excavation over areas including disposal of excavated earth lead upto 50 m and lift upto 1.5 m, disposed earth to be levelled neatly and dressed.

Table 6.9. Ordinary Soil (Unit 1 cum)

S. No.	*Description*	*Unit*	*Qty.*	*Rate* ₹	*Cost* ₹	*Remarks*
1.	(*a*) **Material**					
	(*b*) **Labour**				Nil	
	1. Mates	each	0.06 No.	71.00	4.26	
	2. Mazdoors	each	0.62 No.	65.00	40.30	
	(*c*) **Misc.**					
	1. Add for water charges @ 1.5				44.56	
					0.67	
	2. Add for sundries L.S.				45.23	
					0.60	
	3. Add for contractor's profit and overheads @ 10%				45.83	
					4.58	
	= ₹ 50.40 per cum				50.41	
				Say	50.40	

2. Earthwork in excavation over areas including disposal of excavated earth lead upto 50 m and lift upto 1.5 m. disposed soil to be levelled neatly and dressed.

Table 6.10. Hard Rock Requiring Blasting (Unit 1 cum)

S. No.	*Description*	*Unit*	*Qty.*	*Rate* ₹	*Cost* ₹	*Remarks*
2.	(*a*) **Material**					
	1. Powder	kg	0.7 kg	18.00	12.60	
	2. Fuse	each	1 No.	7.00	7.00	
	(*b*) **Labour**					
	1. Excavators	each	0.2 No.	65.00	13.00	
	2. Breakers	each	0.5 No.	65.00	32.50	
	3. Hole-drillers	each	0.2 No.	65.00	13.00	
	4. Mazdoors	each	0.8 No.	65.00	52.00	
	(*c*) **Misc.**					
	1. Add for water charges @ 1 ½ %				130.10	
					1.95	
	2. Add for sundries L.S.				132.05	
					1.95	
	3. Add for contractor's profit and overhead @ 10%				134.00	
					13.40	
	= ₹ 147.40 per cum				147.40	

3. Earthwork in excavation in foundation trenches or drains, including dressing of sides and ramming the bottom, lift upto 1.5 m and lead upto 50 m.

Table 6.11. Ordinary Soil (Unit 1 cum)

S. No.	Description	Unit	Qty.	Rate ₹	Cost ₹	Remarks
3.	(*a*) **Material**				Nil	
	(*b*) **Labour**					
	1. Mate	each	0.05 Nos.	71.00	3.55	
	2. Mazdoor	each	0.50 Nos.	65.00	32.50	
	(*c*) **Misc.**				36.05	
	1. Add for water charges @ 1½%				0.54	
					36.59	
	2. Add for sundries L.S.				0.41	
					37.00	
	3. Add for contractor's profit and overhead @ 10%				3.70	
	= ₹ 40.70 per cum				40.70	

4. Filling available excavated earth in trenches, plinth, sides of foundations etc. In layers not exceeding 20 cm in depth, consolidating each deposited layer by ramming and watering, lead upto 50 m and lift upto 1.5 m.

Table 6.12. Ordinary Earth (Unit 1 cum)

S. No.	Description	Unit	Qty.	Rate ₹	Cost ₹	Remarks
4.	(*a*) **Material**	—	—	—	Nil	
	(*b*) **Labour**					
	1. Mate	each	0.02	71.00	1.42	
	2. Mazdoor	each	0.25	65.00	16.25	
	3. Bhisti	each	0.02	71.00	1.42	
					19.09	
	(*c*) **Misc.**					
	1. Add for water charges @ 1 ½%	–	–	–	0.28	
					19.37	
	2. Add for sundries L.S.	–	–	–	0.13	
					19.50	
	3. Add for contractor's profit and overhead @ 10%	–	–	–	1.95	
	= ₹ 21.45 per cum				21.45	

5. Complete rate excavation in trenches and filling excavated earth.

Excavation ; as per item No. 3 = ₹ 40.70

Filling ; as per item No. 4 = ₹ 21.45

Total = ₹ 62.15

Say ₹ 62.00 per cum.

6. Open timbering in trenches including strutting and shoring complete. (Measurements to be taken of the face area timbered).

Table 6.13 (Unit 1 sq m)

S. No.		Description	Unit	Qty.	Rate ₹	Cost ₹	Remarks
5.	(a)	**Material** Depth not exceeding 1.5 m. Details of cost for a trench of length 30 m and 1.5 m deep surface area = 2 × 30 × 1.5 = 90 sq m **Materials (Soft wood)** Polling Board 1.5 × 0.25 m × 0.038 m 2 × 40 × 1.5 × 0.25 × 0.38 = 1.14 cum	cum	1.14 cum	115.00	13110.00	
		Walling 100 mm × 100 mm 4 × 30 × 0.1 × 0.1 = 1.20 cum	cum	1.20 cum	115.00	13800.00	
		Ballies sepelts (100 mm dia and 1.5 m long) 2 × 17 × 1.5 = 51 m	m	51 m	12.00	612.00	
						27522.00	
		This can be used for sixteen times on the work. Therefore cost for using once	$= \frac{27522}{16}$	= ₹ 1720.12			
	(b)	**Labour**				1720.12	
		1. Carpenter 100	each	0.25 Nos.	100.00	25.00	
		2. Mazdoor	each	0.50 Nos.	65.00	32.50	
						1777.62	
	(c)	**Misc.**				26.66	
		1. Add for water charges @ 1½%				1804.28	
		2. Add for sundries L.S.				1.72	
		3. Add for contractor's profit and overhead @ 10%				1806.00 180.60	
						1986.60	
		Cost for 90 sq m = ₹ 1986.60 Cost per sq m = ₹ $\frac{1986.60}{90}$ = ₹ 22.07 Say ₹ 22.05 per sq m.					

7. **Filling in plinth with sand under floors including watering. Ramming, consolidating and dressing complete.**

Table 6.14 (Unit 1 cum)

S. No.		Description	Unit	Qty.	Rate ₹	Cost ₹	Remarks
6.	(a)	**Material**					
		(1) Fine sand	cum	1.00	175.00	175.00	
	(b)	**Labour**					
		1. Mate	each	0.02	71.00	1.42	
		2. Mazdoor	each	0.25	65.00	16.25	
		3. Bhisti	each	0.02	71.00	1.42	
						194.09	
	(c)	**Misc.**					
		1. Add for water charges @ 1½%				2.91	
						197.00	
		2. Add for sundries L.S.				1.00	
						198.00	
		3. Add for contractor's profit and overhead @ 10%				19.80	
		= ₹ 217.80 per cum				217.80	

Concrete Work

8. Providing and laying in foundations mud concrete with graded brick aggregate 40 mm nominal size, excluding cost of centring and shuttering.

Table 6.15 (Unit 1 cum)

S. No.	Description	Unit	Qty.	Rate ₹	Cost ₹	Remarks
7.	(*a*) **Material**					
	1. 40 mm brick aggregate	cum	1.00 cum	165.00	165.00	
	2. 40% mortar of mud	cum	0.48 cum	50.00	24.00	$\frac{0.40 \times 120}{100}$ = 0.48 cum
					189.00	
	(*b*) **Labour**					
	1. Mate	each	0.10 No.	71.00	7.10	
	2. Mazdoor	each	2.00 No.	65.00	130.00	
	3. Bhisti	each	0.10 No.	71.00	7.10	
					333.20	
	(*c*) **Misc.**					
	1. Add for water charges @ 1½%				5.00	
					338.20	
	2. Add for sundries L.S.				1.80	
					340.00	
	3. Add for contractor's profit and overhead @ 10%				34.00	
	= ₹ 374.0 per cum				374.00	

9. Providing and laying in foundations and plinth lime concrete with graded brick aggregate 40 mm. Nominal size and 40% mortar comprising of 1 lime putty : 1 ash : 1 fine sand excluding cost of centring and shuttering.

Table 3.16. (Unit 1 cum)

S. No.	Description	Unit	Qty.	Rate ₹	Cost ₹	Remarks
8.	(*a*) **Material**					
	1. Lime (Fat)	kg	114 kg	1.50	171.00	
	2. Ash	cum	0.19 cum	60.00	11.40	
	3. Fine sand	cum	0.19 cum	115.00	33.25	
	4. Brick aggregate 40 mm size	cum	1.00 cum	165.00	165.00	
					380.65	
	(*b*) **Labour**					
	1. Mason	each	0.10 No.	110.00	11.00	
	2. Mazdoor	each	2.65 No.	65.00	172.25	
	3. Bhisti	each	0.80 No.	71.00	56.80	
	4. Bullock with Driver	each	0.15 No.	130.00	19.50	
					640.20	
	(*c*) **Misc.**					
	1. Add for water charges @ 1 ½%				9.60	
					649.80	
	2. Add for sundries L.S.				1.20	
					651.00	
	3. Add for contractor's profit and overhead @ 10%				65.10	
	= ₹ 716.10 per cum				716.10	

10. Providing and laying on terrace lime concrete with graded brick aggregate 25 mm nominal size and 50% mortar compressing of 1 lime putty : 2 surkhi.

Table 6.17 (Unit 1 cum)

S. No.	*Description*	*Unit*	*Qty.*	*Rate* ₹	*Cost* ₹	*Remarks*
9.	(*a*) **Material**					
	1. Lime (Fat)	kg.	142 kg	1.35	191.70	
	2. Surkhi	cum	0.467 cum	300.00	140.10	
	3. Brick aggregate 25 mm size	cum	1.00 cum	170.00	170.00	
					501.80	
	(*b*) **Labour**					
	1. Mason	each	1.00 Nos.	110.00	110.00	
	2. Mazdoor	each	3.70 Nos.	65.00	240.50	
	3. Bhisti	each	1.50 Nos.	71.00	106.50	
	4. Concrete mixer with operator	each day	0.05 Nos.	310.00	15.50	
					974.30	
	(*c*) **Misc.**					
	1. Add for water charges ® 1½%				14.61	
					988.91	
	2. Add for sundries L.S.				2.09	
					991.00	
	3. Add for contractor's profit and overhead @ 10%				99.10	
	= ₹ 1090.10 per cum				1090.10	

11. Providing and laying cement concrete 1 : 5 : 10 (1 cement : 5 fine sand : 10 graded stone aggregate 40 mm nominal size) excluding cost of centring and shuttering in foundations and plinth.

Table 6.18 (Unit 1 cum)

S. No.	*Description*	*Unit*	*Qty.*	*Rate* ₹	*Cost* ₹	*Remarks*
10.	(*a*) **Material**					
	1. Cement	per bag	2.0 bag	128.63	257.26	
	2. Fine sand cum	0.48 cum	175	84.00		
	3. Stone aggregate 40 mm size	cum	0.96 cum	165.00	158.40	
					499.66	
	(*b*) **Labour**					
	1. Mason	each	0.10 No.	110.00	11.00	
	2. Mazdoor	each	2.13 No	65.00	138.45	
	3. Bhisti	each	0.70 No.	71.00	49.70	
	4. Concrete mixer with operator	each day	0.05 No.	310.00	15.50	
					714.31	
	(c) **Misc.**					
	1. Add for water charges @ 1½%				10.71	
					725.02	
					4.98	
	2. Add for sundries L.S.				730.00	
	3. Add for contractor's profit and overhead @ 10%				73.00	
	= ₹ 803.00 per cum				803.00	

12. Providing and laying cement concrete 1 : 2 : 4 (1 cement : 2 coarse sand : 4 graded stone aggregate 20 mm nominal size) excluding cost of centring and shuttering in foundations and plinth.

Table 6.19 (Unit 1 cum)

S. No.	*Description*	*Unit*	*Qty.*	*Rate* ₹	*Cost* ₹	*Remarks*
11.	(*a*) **Material**					
	1. Cement	per bag	6.6 bags	128.63	848.96	
	2. Coarse sand	cum	044. cum	315.00	138.60	
	3. Stone aggregate 20 mm size	cum	0.88 cum	265.00	233.20	
				202.40	1220.76	
	(*b*) **Labour**					
	1. Mason	each	0.24 No.	110.00	26.40	
	2. Mazdoor	each	2.80 No.	65.00	82.00	
	3. Bhisti	each	0.90 No.	71.00	63.90	
	4. Concrete mixer with operator	each day	0.14 No.	310.00	43.40	
	5. Vibrator with operator	each day	0.70 No.	(110 + 110 = 220)	154.00	
					1690.46	
	(*c*) **Misc.**					
	1. Add for water charges @ 1 ½%				25.35	
					1715.81	
	2. Add for sundries L.S.				4.19	
					1720.00	
	3. Add for contractor's profit overhead @ 10%				172.00	
	= ₹ 1892.00 per cum				1892.00	

13. Centring and shuttering including strutting, propping etc. and removal of form work for foundations and plinth.

Table 6.20 (Unit 1 sq m)

S. No.	*Description*	*Unit*	*Qty.*	*Rate* ₹	*Cost* ₹	*Remarks*
12.	(*a*) **Material**					
	Detail of cost for 10 sq m of area of contact with-concrete (2.5 m × 2.5 m and 1 m high)—					
	(*i*) 50 ft wood planks 38 mm thick (four faces)					
	2 × 2.576 × 1.000 = 5.152 sq m					
	2 × 2.500 × 1.000 = 5.000 sq m					
	10.152 sq m					
	Wastage 5 % 00.508 sq m					
	10.660 sq m					
	10.660 × 0.038 = 0.4051 cum	cum	0.4051 cum	11500.00	4658.65	
	2. Ballies 100 mm dia. 1.5 m long for strutting, two nos. on each face (four faces)					
	4 × 2 × 1.50 = 12.00 m	per m	12 m	12.00	144.00	
					4802.65	

	This can be used for sixteen times on the work. Therefore cost for using once	$= ₹ \frac{4802.65}{16} = ₹ 300.16$				
	(b) **Labour**					
	1. Carpenter	each	1.25 No.	100.00	125.00	
	2. Mazdoor	each	1.25 No.	65.00	81.25	
					506.41	
	(c) **Misc.**					
	1. Add for water charges @ 1½%				7.60	
					514.01	
	2. Add for sundries L.S.				1.09	
					515.10	
	3. Add for contractor's profit and overhead @ 10%				51.51	
	Cost of 10 sq m				566.61	
	Cost per sq m = $₹ \frac{566.61}{10} = ₹ 56.66$ = ₹ 56.65 per sq m					

Damp-Proof Course

14. Providing and laying D.P.C. 50 mm thick with cement concrete 1 : 2 : 4 (1 cement : 2 coarse sand : 4 graded stone aggregate 20 mm nominal size).

Table 6.21 (Unit 1 sq m)

S. No.	*Description*	*Unit*	*Qty.*	*Rate* ₹	*Cost* ₹	*Remarks*
13.	(a) **Material**					
	Detail of cost of 10 sq m cement concrete 1 : 2 : 4 = 10 × 0.05 = 0.5 cum					
	1. Cement	per day	3.3 bags	128.63	424.48	
	2. Coarse sand	cum	0.22 cum	31.50	69.30	
	3. Stone aggregate 20 mm size	cum	0.44 cum	265.00	116.60	
					610.38	
	(b) **Labour**					
	1. Mason	each	1 No.	110.00	110.00	
	2. Mazdoor	each	1 No.	65.00	65.00	
	3. Bhisti	each	0.1 No.	71.00	7.10	
					792.48	
	(c) **Misc.**					
	1. Add for water charges @ 1½%				11.88	
					804.36	
	2. Add for sundries L.S.				2.64	
					807.00	
	3. Add for contractor's profit and overhead @ 10%				80.70	
	Cost of 10 sq m				887.70	
	Cost of 1 sq m = $₹ \frac{887.70}{10} = ₹ 88.77 = ₹ 88.75$ per sq m					

15. Providing and laying D.P.C. 20 mm thick with cement mortar 1 : 0 (1 cement : 3 coarse sand)

Table 6.22 (Unit 1 sq m)

S. No.	Description	Unit	Qty.	Rate ₹	Cost ₹	Remarks
14.	(*a*) **Material**					
	Detail of cost of 10 sq m cement mortar 1 : 3 = 10 × 0.02 = 0.2 cum					
	1. Cement	per bag	2.12 bag	128.63	272.70	
	2. Coarse sand	cum	0.21 cum	315.00	66.15	
					338.85	
	(*b*) **Labour**					
	1. Mason	each	1 No.	110.00	110.00	
	2. Mazdoor	each	1 No.	65.00	165.00	
	3. Bhisti	each	0.1 No.	71.00	7.10	
					320.95	
	(*c*) **Misc.**					
	1. Add for water charges @ 1½%				9.31	
					630.26	
	2. Add for sundries L.S.				2.84	
					633.10	
	3. Add for contractor's profit and overhead @ 10%				63.31	
	Cost of 10 sq m				696.41	
	Coat of 1 sq m = ₹ $\frac{696.41}{10}$ = ₹ 69.64 = ₹ 69.65 per sq m					

16. Applying a coat of hot bitumen (maxphalte 80/100) using 2.0 kg per sq m on D.P.C. after cleaning the surface with brushes and finally with a piece of cloth soaked in kerosene oil.

Table 6.23 (Unit 1 sq m)

S. No.	Description	Unit	Qty.	Rate ₹	Cost ₹	Remarks
15.	(*a*) **Material**					
	Details of cost of 10 sq m					
	1. Maxphalte 80/100	kg	20 kg	6.50	130.00	
	2. Kerosene oil	litre	2 litre	7.50	15.00	
	3. Fuel for heating	quintal	0.04 quintal	250.00	10.00	
					155.00	
	(*b*) **Labour**					
	1. Painter	each	0.20 No.	90.00	18.00	
	2. Mazdoor	each	0.20 No.	65.00	13.00	
					186.00	
	(*c*) **Misc.**					
	1. Add for water charges @ 1½%				2.79	
					188.79	
	2. Add for sundries L.S.				1.21	
					190.00	
	3. Add for contractor's profit and overhead @ 10%				19.00	
	Cost of 10 sq m				209.00	
	Cost of 1 sq m = ₹ $\frac{209}{10}$ = ₹ 20.90 = ₹ 20.90 per sq m.					

Reinforced Cement Concrete

17. R.C.C. work 1 : 2 : 4 (1 cement : 2 coarse sand : 4 graded stone aggregate 20 mm nominal size) in roofs, lintels, beams, etc. including finishing and plastering the ceiling with cement mortar 1 : 3 (1 cement : 3 fine sand) of thickness not exceeding 6 mm to give a smooth and even surface but excluding cost of centring, shuttering and reinforcement.

Table 6.24 (Unit 1 cum)

S. No.	Description	Unit	Qty.	Rate ₹	Cost ₹	Remarks
16.	(a) **Material**					
	Concrete 1 : 2 : 4 = 1 cum					
	1. Cement	per bag	6.6 bags	128.63	848.96	
	2. Coarse sand	cum	0.44 cum	315.00	138.60	
	3. Stone aggregate 20 mm size	cum	0.88 cum	265.00	233,20	
	Cement mortar 1 : 3					
	Covering 10 sq m					
	= 10 × 0.006 = 0.06 cum					
	1. Cement	per bag	0.64 bag	128.63	82.32	
	2. Fine sand	cum	0.064 cum	175.00	11.62	
					1314.70	
	(b) **Labour**					
	For concrete work					
	1. Mason	each	0.24 No.	110.00	26.40	
	2. Mazdoor	each	2.50 No.	65.00	162.50	
	3. Bhisti	each	0.90 No.	7.00	63.90	
	4. Concrete mixer with operator	each day	0.14 No.	310.00	43.40	
	5. Vibrator with operator	each day	0.07 No.	220.00	15.40	
	For plastering					
	1. Mason	each	0.65 No.	110.00	71.50	
	2. Mazdoor	each	0.65 No.	65.00	42.25	
	3. Bhisti	each	0.65 No.	71.00	46.15	
					1786.20	
	(c) **Misc.**					
	1. Add for water changes @ 1½%				26.79	
					1812.99	
	2. Add for sundries L.S.				5.01	
					1818.00	
	3. Add for contractor's profit and overhead @ 10%				181.80	
	= ₹ 1999.80 per cum				1999.80	

18. Centring and shuttering including strutting, propping etc, and removal of form work for roofs etc.

Table 6.25 (Unit 1 sq m)

S. No.	Description	Unit	Qty.	Rate ₹	Cost ₹	Remarks
17.	(a) **Material**					
	Details of cost for a room :					
	3 × 3 = 9 sq m height 3.0 m					
	soft wood centring					

		Description	Unit	Qty.	Rate	Cost	Remarks
		1. Battens 75 mm × 100 mm : 5 × 3.00 × 0.75 × 0.10 = 0.112 cum	cum	0.112 cum	11500.00	1288.00	
		2. Plants 38 mm : 3.00 × 3.00 × 0.038 = 0.342 cum	cum	0.342 cum	11500.00	3933.00	
		3. Sal ballies 100 mm dia : 15 × 3.00 = 45 m	per m	45 m	12.00	540.00	
						5861.00	
		This can be used for sixteen times on the work. Therefore, cost for using once		$\frac{5861.0}{16}$		= ₹ 366.31	
	(*b*)	**Labour**					
		1. Carpenter	each	2.07 Nos.	100.00	207.00	
		2. Mazdoor	each	1.80 Nos.	65.00	117.00	
	(*c*)	**Misc.**				690.31	
		1. Add for water charges @ 1½%				10.35	
						700.66	
		2. Add for sundries L.S.				7.34	
						708.00	
		3. Add for contractor's profit and overhead @ 10%				70.80	
						778.80	
		Cost of 1 sq m = ₹ $\frac{778.80}{9}$ = ₹ 86.53					
		Cost of 1 sq m = ₹ 86.50 per sq m					

19. Mild steel reinforcement for R.C.C. work including bending, binding and placing in position complete.

Table 6.26 (Unit 1 kg)

S. No.		Description	Unit	Qty.	Rate ₹	Cost ₹	Remarks
18.	(*a*)	**Material** Details of cost for 1 quintal					
		1. Mild steel bars 1.00 q Wastage 5% 0.05 q 1.05 q	quintal	01.05 q	1432.00	1503.60	
	(*b*)	**Labour**					
		1. Black smith	each	1 No.	110.00	110.00	
		2. Mazdoor	each	1 No.	65.00	65.00	
						1678.60	
	(c)	**Misc.**					
		1. Add for water charges @ 1½%				25.18	
						1703.78	
		2. Add for sundries L.S.				7.22	
						1711.00	
		3. Add for contractor's profit and overhead @ 10%				171.10	
		Cost of 100 kg				1882.10	
		Cost of 1 kg = ₹ $\frac{1882.10}{100}$ = ₹ 18.82 = ₹ 18.82 per kg					

Brickwork

20. Second class brickwork in lime mortar 1 : 1 : (1 lime putty : 1 ash : 1 fine sand).

Table 6.27 (Unit 1 cum)

S. No.	Description	Unit	Qty.	Rate ₹	Cost ₹	Remarks
19.	(a) **Material**					By volume 25% mortar is used
	1. Second class bricks	1000 No.	500 Nos.	1050.00	525.00	
	2. Lime putty	kg	71 kg	2.30	163.30	
	3. Ash	cum	0.118 cum	60.00	7.08	
	4. Fine sand	cum	0.118 cum	175.00	20.65	
					716.03	
	(b) **Labour**					
	1. Mason	each	0.94 No.	110.00	103.40	
	2. Mazdoor	each	1.80 No.	65.00	117.00	
	3. Bhisti	each	0.20 No.	71.00	14.20	
					950.63	
	(c) **Misc.**					
	1. Add for water charges @ 1½%				14.26	
					964.89	
	2. Add for sundries L.S.				6.11	
					971.00	
	3. Add for contractor's profit and overhead @ 10%				97.10	
	= ₹ 1068.10 per cum				1068.10	

21. Second class brickwork in cement mortar 1 : 6 (1 cement : 6 fine sand).

Table 6.28 (Unit 1 cum)

S. No.	Description	Unit	Qty.	Rate ₹	Cost ₹	Remarks
20.	(a) **Material**					By volume 25% mortar is used
	1. Second class brick	% 1000 Nos.	500 No.	1050.00	525.00	
	2. Cement	per bag	1.30 ba	125.00	167.22	
	3. Five sand	cum	0.25 cum	175.00	43.75	
					735.97	
	(b) **Labour**					
	1. Mason	each	0.94 No.	110.00	103.40	
	2. Mazdoor	each	1.80 No.	65.00	117.00	
	3. Bhisti	each	0.20 No.	71.00	14.20	
					970.57	
	(c) **Misc.**					
	1. Add for water charges @ 1½%				14.56	
					985.13	
	2. Add for sundries L.S.				4.87	
					990.00	
	3. Add for contractor's profit and overhead @ 10%				99.00	
					1089.00	
	= ₹ 1089.00 per cum					

22. Second class brickwork in mud mortar.

Table 6.29 (Unit 1 cum)

S. No.	Description	Unit	Qty.	Rate ₹	Cost ₹	Remarks
21.	(*a*) **Material**					By volume 30% mortar is used
	1. Second class bricks	1000 No.	500 Nos.	1050.00	525.00	
	2. Dry mud	cum	0.36 cum	7.00	2.52	
					527.52	
	(*b*) **Labour**					
	1. Mason	each	0.94 No.	110.00	103.40	
	2. Mazdoor	each	0.80 No.	65.00	52.00	
	3. Bhisti	each	1.30 No.	71.00	92.30	
					775.22	
	(*c*) **Misc.**					
	1. Add for water charges @ 1½%				11.63	
					786.85	
	2. Add for sundries L.S.				2.15	
					789.00	
	3. Add for contractor's profit and overhead @ 10%				78.90	
	= ₹ 867.90 per cum				867.90	

23. Half brick masonry (second class) in cement mortar 1 : 3 (1 cement : 3 coarse sand).

Table 6.30 (Unit 1 sq m)

S. No.	Description	Unit	Qty.	Rate ₹	Cost ₹	Remarks
22.	(*a*) **Material**					By volume 25% mortar is used
	1. Second class bricks	1000 Nos.	50 No.	1050.00	52.50	
	2. Cement	per bag	0.26 kg	128.63	33.44	
	3. Coarse sand	cum	0.025 kg	315.00	7.87	
					93.81	
	(*b*) **Labour**					
	1. Mason	each	0.12 No.	110.00	13.20	
	2. Mazdoor	each	0.20 No.	65.00	13.00	
	3. Bhisti	each	0.07 No.	71.00	4.97	
					124.98	
	(*c*) **Misc.**					
	1. Add for water charges @ 1½%				1.87	
					126.85	
	2. Add for sundries L.S.				1.15	
					128.00	
	3. Add for contractor's profit and overhead @ 10%				12.80	
					130.80	
	= ₹ 130.80 per sq m					

24. Brick tile masonry in cement mortar 1 : 6 (1 cement : 6 fine sand)

Table 6.31 (Unit 1 cum)

S. No.		Description	Unit	Qty.	Rate ₹	Cost ₹	Remarks
23.	(a)	**Material**					By volume 30% mortar is used
		1. Brick tile	1000 Nos.	950 Nos.	1250.00	1187.50	
		2. Cement	per bag	1.60 bag	128.03	205.80	
		3. Fine sand	cum	0.32 cum	175.00	56.00	
						1448.30	
	(b)	**Labour**					
		1. Mason	each	1.80 No.	110.00	198.00	
		2. Mazdoor	each	1.80 No.	65.00	117.00	
		3. Bhisti	each	0.20 No.	71.00	14.20	
						1777.30	
	(c)	**Misc.**					
		1. Add for water charges @ 1½%				26.66	
						1803.96	
		2. Add for sundries L.S.				7.04	
						1811.00	
		3. Add for contractor's profit and overhead @ 10%				181.10	
		= ₹ 1992.10 per cum				1992.10	

25. First class reinforced brickwork in roofs, in cement mortar 1 : 2 (1 cement : 2 coarse sand).

Table 6.32 (Unit 1 cum)

S. No.		Description	Unit	Qty.	Rate ₹	Cost ₹	Remarks
24.	(a)	**Material**					By volume 45% mortar is used
		1. First class bricks	1000 No.	420 No.	1150.00	483.00	
		2. Cement	per bag	6.40 bag	128.63	823.23	
		3. Coarse sand	cum	0.43 cum	315.00	135.45	
						1341.68	
	(b)	**Labour**					
		1. Mason	each	1.00 No.	110.00	110.00	
		2. Mazdoor	each	2.00 No.	65.00	130.00	
		3. Bhisti	each	0.40 No.	71.00	28.40	
						1610.08	
	(c)	**Misc.**					
		1. Add for water charges @ 1½%				24.15	
						1634.23	
		2. Add for sundries L.S.				8.77	
						1643.00	
		3. Add for contractor's profit and overhead @ 10%				164.30	
						1807.30	
		= ₹ 1807.30 per cum					

Stone Work

26. Random Rubble masonry with hard stone in foundations and plinth in cement mortar 1 : 6 (1 cement : 6 fine sand).

Table 6.33 (Unit 1 cum)

S. No.	Description	Unit	Qty.	Rate ₹	Cost ₹	Remarks
25.	(a) **Material**					By volume 33% mortar is used
	1. Stone	cum	1 cum	270.00	270.00	
	2. Cement	per bag	1.77 bags	128.63	227.67	
	3. Fine sand	cum	0.35 cum	175.00	61.25	
					557.92	
	(b) **Labour**					
	1. Mason	each	1.00 No.	110.00	110.00	
	2. Mazdoor	each	2.00 No.	65.00	130.00	
	3. Bhisti	each	0.20 No.	71.00	14.20	
					812.12	
	(c) **Misc.**					
	1. Add for water charges @ 1½%				12.18	
					824.30	
	2. Add for sundries L.S.				5.70	
					830.00	
	3. Add for contractor's profit and overhead @10%				83.00	
	= ₹ 913.00 per cum				913.00	

27. Coursed rubble masonry with hard stone in foundation and plinth in cement mortar 1 : 6 (1 cement : 6 fine sand)

Table 6.34 (Unit 1 cum)

S. No.	Description	Unit	Qty.	Rate ₹	Cost ₹	Remarks
26.	(a) **Material**					
	1. Stone	cum	1.20 cum	270.00	324.00	By volume 30% mortar is used
	2. Cement	per bag	1.60 bag	128.63	205.80	
	3. Fine sand	cum	0.32 cum	175.00	56.00	
					585.80	
	(b) **Labour**					
	1. Mason	each	1.80 Nos.	110.00	198.00	
	2. Mazdoor	each	2.50 Nos.	65.00	162.50	
	3. Bhisti	each	0.20 Nos.	71.00	14.20	
					960.50	
	(c) **Misc.**					
	1. Add for water charges ® 1½%				14.40	
					974.90	
	2. Add for sundaries L.S.				5.10	
					980.00	
	3. Add for contractor's profit and overhead @ 10%.				98.00	
	= ₹ 1078.00 per cum				1078.00	

28. Stone work in plain ashlar cyclopean in superstructure in cement mortar 1 : 6 (1 cement : 6 course sand)

Table 6.35 (Unit 1 cum)

S. No.	Description	Unit	Qty.	Rate ₹	Cost ₹	Remarks
27.	(a) **Material**					By volume 10% mortar is used
	1. Stone (red or white)	cum	1.33 cum	270.00	359.10	
	2. Cement	per bag	0.53 bags	128.63	68.17	
	3. Coarse sand	cum	0.10 cum	315.00	31.50	
					458.77	
	(b) **Labour**					
	1. Mason	each	4.00 Nos.	110.00	440.00	
	2. Mazdoor	each	4.00 Nos.	65.00	260.00	
	3. Bhisti	each	1.00 Nos.	71.00	71.00	
					1229.77	
	(c) **Misc.**					
	1. Add for water charges @ 1½%				18.45	
					1248.22	
	2. Add for sundaries L.S.				8.78	
					1257.00	
	3. Add for contractor's profit and overhead @ 10%				125.70	
					1382.70	
	= ₹ 1382.70 per cum					

29. Stone work for wall lining etc. (veneer work) 55 mm thick in cement mortar 1 : 6 (1 cement : 6 coarse sand)

Table 6.36 (Unit 1 sq m)

S. No.	Description	Unit	Qty.	Rate ₹	Cost ₹	Remarks
28.	(a) **Material**					
	1. Stone (red or white)	sq m	1 sq m	270.00	270.00	
	2. Cement	per bag	0.05 bag	128.63	6.43	
	3. Coarse sand	cum	0.01 cum	315.00	3.15	
					279.58	
	(b) **Labour**					
	1. Mason	each	0.20 No.	110.00	22.00	
	2. Mazdoor	each	0.10 No.	65.00	6.50	
	3. Bhisti	each	0.05 No.	71.00	3.55	
					311.63	
	(c) **Misc.**					
	1. Add for water charges @ 1½%				4.67	
					316.30	
	2. Add for sundries L.S.				1.70	
					318.00	
	3. Add for contractor's profit and overhead @ 10%				31.80	
					349.80	
	= ₹ 349.80 per cum					

30. Marble work (Table rubbed and polished) for wall lining (veneer work) 2.5 cm thick in cement mortar 1 : 3 (1 cement : 3 coarse sand).

Table 6.37 (Unit 1 sq m)

S. No.	Description	Unit	Qty.	Rate ₹	Cost ₹	Remarks
29.	(a) **Material**					
	1. White marble	sq m	1 sq m	365.00	365.00	
	2. Cement	per bag	0.10 bag	128.63	12.86	
	3. Coarse sand	cum	0.01 cum	315.00	3.15	
					381.01	
	(b) **Labour** (Special)					
	1. Mason for marble work	each	1 No.	110.00	110.00	
	2. Mazdoor	each	0.2 No.	65.00	13.00	
	3. Bhisti	each	0.05 No.	71.00	3.55	
					507.56	
	(c) **Misc.**					
	1. Add for water charges @ 1½%				7.61	
					515.17	
	2. Add for sundries L.S.				4.83	
					520.00	
	3. Add for contractor's profit and overhead @ 10%				52.00	
					572.00	
	= ₹ 572.00.per sq m					

Wood Work

31. Providing wood work in frames of doors, windows, and other frames, wrought, framed and fixed in position of second class kail wood.

Table 6.38 (Unit 1 cum)

S. No.	Description	Unit	Qty.	Rate ₹	Cost ₹	Remarks
30.	(a) **Material**					
	Details of cost for chowkhat of a door					
	206.75 × 117.5 cm					
	2 × 206.75 × 9.5 × 7.0 cm = 0.028 cum					
	1 × 117.5 × 9.5 × 7.0 cm = 0.008 cum					
	= 0.036 cum					
	Add for wastage @ 5% = 0.002 cum					
	Grand Total = 0.038 cum					
	Kail wood	cum	0.038 cum	11500.00	437.00	
	(b) **Labour**					
	1. Carpenter	each	20 × 0.038 No	100.00	76.00	
	2. Mazdoor	each	2 × 0.038 No	65.00	49.40	
					562.40	
	(c) **Misc.**					
	1. Add for sundries L.S.				1.60	
					564.00	
	2. Add for contractor's profit and overhead @ 10%				56.40	
					620.40	
	Cost per cum = ₹ $\frac{620.40}{0.038}$ = ₹ 16326.30					
	= ₹ 16326.30 per cum					

32. Providing and fixing 3.3 mm thick shutters for doors and windows of kail wood.

Table 6.39 (Unit 1 sq m)

S. No.	Description	Unit	Qty.	Rate ₹	Cost ₹	Remarks
31.	(*a*) **Material**					
	Details of cost for shutters of a door (half glazed and half panelled) 200 × 108 cm = 2.16 sq m					
	Styles—4 × 200 × 9.5 × 3.5 cm = 0.027 cum					
	Rails—2 × 110.5 × 19.7 × 3.5 cm = 0.015 cum					
	1 × 110.5 × 9.5 × 3.5 cm = 0.004 cum					
	Panels—2 × 48 × 41 × 1.6 cm = 0.006 cum					
	Sash bars—2 × 114 × 3.8 × 3.5 cm = 0.003 cum					
	6 × 48 × 3.8 × 3.5 cm = 0.004 cum					
	Beadings—16 × 92 × 1.9 × 1.2 cm = 0.003 cum					
	Total 0.062 cum					
	Add wastage 10% 0.006 cum					
	Grand Total 0.068 cum					
	Kail wood	cum	0.068 cum	11500.00	782.00	
	(*b*) **Labour**					
	1. Carpenter	each	2.16 × 0.90 No.	100.00	194.40	
	2. Mazdoor	each	2.16 × 0.10 No.	65.00	14.04	
					990.44	
	(*c*) **Misc.**					
	1. Add for sundries L.S.				8.56	
					999.00	
	2. Add for contractor's profit and over head @ 10%				99.90	
					1088.90	
	Cost per sq m = ₹ $\frac{1088.90}{2.16}$ = ₹ 504.12					
	= ₹ 504.10 per sq m					

33. **Fixing of ready made shutters to frames including fixing of fittings.**

Table 6.40 (Unit 1 sq m)

S. No.	Description	Unit	Qty.	Rate ₹	Cost ₹	Remarks
32.	(*a*) **Labour**					
	1. Carpenter	each	0.25 No.	100.00	25.00	
	2. Mazdoor	each	0.25 No.	71.00	17.75	
					42.75	
	(*b*) **Misc.**					
	1. Add for sundries L.S.				1.25	
					44.00	
	2. Add for contractor's profit and overhead @ 10%				4.40	
	= ₹ 48.40 per sq m				48.40	

34. Fixing glass panes on steel or wood work bedded with putty.

Table 6.41 (Unit 1 sq m)

S. No.	Description	Unit	Qty.	Rate ₹	Cost ₹	Remarks
33.	(a) **Labour**					
	1. Carpenter	each	0.20 No.	100.00	20.00	
	2. Mazdoor	each	0.01 No.	65.00	0.65	
					20.65	
	(b) **Misc.**					
	1. Add for sundries L.S.				0.35	
					21.00	
	2. Add for contractor's profit and overhead @ 10%				2.10	
					23.10	
	= ₹ 23.10 per sq m					

Steel Work

25. Steel work welded or riveted or bolted, in built up sections, trusses and framed work, including cutting, hoisting, fixing in position, in joists, trees, angles, flats and channels.

Table 6.42 (Unit per quintal)

S. No.	Description	Unit	Qty.	Rate ₹	Cost ₹	Remarks
34.	(a) **Material**					
	1. Steel 1.00 q					
	Wastage @ 5% 0.05 q					
	Total 1.05 q	quintal	1.05 q	1432.00	1503.60	
	2. Weld etc. L.S.				20.00	
					1523.60	
	(b) **Labour**					
	1. Welder	each	0.50	100.00	50.00	
	2. Blacksmith	each	1.00	110.00	110.00	
	3. Bandhani	each	0.50	75.00	37.50	
	4. Mazdoor	each	0.50	65.00	32.50	
					1783.60	
	(c) **Misc.**					
	1. Add for sundries L.S.				16.40	
					1800.00	
	2. Add for contractor's profit and overhead @ 10%				180.00	
					1980.00	
	= ₹ 1980.0 per quintal					

Flooring

36. 2nd class brick flooring in cement mortar 1 : 6 (1 cement : 6 fine sand)

Table 6.43 (Unit 1 sq m)

S. No.	Description	Unit	Qty.	Rate ₹	Cost ₹	Remarks
35.	(a) **Material**					
	1. 2nd class bricks	1000 Nos.	50 Nos.	1050.00	52.50	By volume 30% mortar is used.
	2. Cement	per bag	0.15 bag	128.63	20.58	
	3. Fine sand	cum	0.03 cum	175.00	5.25	
					78.33	
	(b) **Labour**					
	1. Mason	each	0.10 No.	110.00	11.00	
	2. Mazdoor	each	0.15 No.	65.00	9.75	
	3. Bhisti	each	0.05 No.	71.00	3.55	
					102.63	
	(c) **Misc.**					
	1. Add for water charges @ 1½%				1.54	
					104.17	
	2. Add for sundries L.S.				1.83	
					606.00	
	3. Add for contractor's profit and over head @ 10%				10.60	
	= ₹ 116.60 per sq m				116.60	

37. 2nd class dry brick flooring including filling joints with fine sand.

Table 6.44 (Unit 1 sq m)

S. No.	Description	Unit	Qty.	Rate ₹	Cost ₹	Remarks
36.	(a) **Material**					
	1. 2nd class bricks	1000 Nos.	50 Nos.	1050.00	52.50	
	2. Fine sand	cum	0.015 cum	175.00	2.62	
					55.12	
	(b) **Labour**					
	1. Mason	each	0.08	110.00	8.80	
	2. Mazdoor	each	0.12	65.00	8.16	
	3. Bhisti	each	0.05	71.00	3.55	
					75.63	
	(c) **Misc.**					
	1. Add for water charges @ 1½%				1.13	
					76.76	
	2. Add for sundries L.S				1.24	
					78.00	
	3. Add for contractor's profit and overhead @ 10%				7.80	
	= ₹ 85.80 per sq m				85.80	

38. 40 mm thick cement concrete flooring 1 : 2 : 4 (1 cement : 2 coarse and : 4 graded stone) aggregate 20 mm normal size finished with a floating coat of neat cement.

Table 6.45 (Unit 1 sq m)

S. No.		*Description*	*Unit*	*Qty.*	*Rate* ₹	*Cost* ₹	*Remarks*
37.	(*a*)	**Material**					
		1. Cement	per bag	0.30 No.	128.63	38.59	
		2. Coarse sand	cum	0.018 cum	315.00	5.67	
		3. Stone ballast 20 mm gauge	cum	0.035 cum	265.00	9.28	
						53.54	
	(*b*)	**Labour**					
		1. Mason	each	0.08 No.	110.00	8.80	
		2. Mazdoor	each	0.12 No.	65.00	7.80	
		3. Bhisti	each	0.10 No.	71.00	7.10	
						77.24	
	(*c*)	**Misc.**					
		1. Add for water charges @ 1½%				1.16	
						78.40	
		2. Add for sundries L.S.				0.60	
						79.00	
		3. Add for contractor's profit and overhead @ 10%				7.90	
		= ₹ 87.90 per sq m				87.90	

39. 20 mm thick cement mortar skirting with cement mortar 1 : 3 (1 cement : 3 coarse sand) finished with a floating coat of next cement including rounding of junctions with floor.

Table 6.46 (Unit 1 sq m)

S. No.		*Description*	*Unit*	*Qty.*	*Rate* ₹	*Cost* ₹	*Remarks*
38.	(*a*)	**Material**					
		1. Cement	per bag	0.28 No.	128.63	36.02	
		2. Coarse sand	cum	0.03 cum	315.00	9.45	
						45.47	
	(*b*)	**Labour**					
		1. Mason	each	0.20 No.	110.00	22.00	
		2. Mazdoor	each	0.30	65.00	19.50	
		3. Bhisti	each	0.10	71.00	7.10	
						94.07	
	(*c*)	**Misc.**					
		1. Add for water charges @ 1½%				1.41	
						95.48	
		2. Add for sundries L.S.				0.52	
						96.00	
		3. Add for contractor's profit and overhead @ 10%				9.60	
		= ₹ 105.60 per sq m				105.60	

40. 40 mm thick marble chips flooring rubbed and polished to granolithic finish, under layer 31 mm thick cement concrete 1 : 2 : 4 (1 cement; 2 coarse sand : 4 graded stone aggregate 12.5 mm nominal size) and top layer 9 mm thick with white black marble chips of size from 1 to 4 mm nominal size laid in cement marble powder mix 3 : 1 (3 cement : 1 marble powder) by weight in proportion of 4 : 7 (4 cement marble powder mix : 7 marble chips) by volume.

Table 6.47 (Unit 1 sq m)

S. No.	*Description*	*Unit*	*Qty.*	*Rate* ₹	*Cost* ₹	*Remarks*
39.	(*a*) **Material**					
	1. Cement	per bag	0.32 No.	128.63	41.16	
	2. Coarse sand	cum	0.014 cum	315.00	4.41	
	3. Stone balast 12.5 mm size	cum	0.028 cum	450.00	12.60	
	4. Marble chips 1 to 4 mm size	kg	14 kg	0.90	12.60	
	5. Marble powder	kg	2 kg cum	0.50	1.00	
					71.77	
	(*b*) **Labour**					
	(*i*) For laying					
	1. Mason	each	0.22 No.	110.00	24.20	
	2. Mazdoor	each	0.22 No.	65.00	14.30	
	3. Bhisti	each	0.10 No.	71.00	7.10	
					117.37	
	(*ii*) For cutting, grinding and polishing					
	1. Mazdoor	each	0.50 No.	65.00	32.50	
	2. Machine	each day	0.40 day	110.00	44.00	
					193.87	
	(c) **Misc.**					
	1. Add for water charges @ 1½%				2.90	
					196.77	
	2. Add for sundries L.S.				1.23	
					198.00	
	3. Add for contractor's profit and overhead @ 10%				19.80	
	= ₹ 117.80 per sq m				117.80	

41. 18 mm thick marble chips skirting with under layer 12 mm thick in cement plaster 1 : 3 (1 cement : 3 coarse sand), rubbed and polished 15 granolithic finish top layer 6 mm thick with white, black marble chips of size from smallest : 4 mm nominal size laid in cement marble powder mix 3 : 1 (3 cement : 1 marble powder) by weight in proportion of 4 : 7 (4 cement marble powder mix : 7 marble chips) by volume.

Table 6.48 (Unit 1 sq m)

S. No.	*Description*	*Unit*	*Qty.*	*Rate* ₹	*Cost* ₹	*Remarks*
40.	(*a*) **Material**					
	1. Cement	per bag	0.23 bag	128.63	29.58	

	2. Coarse sand	cum	0.014 cum	315.00	4.41
	3. Marble chips	kg	9 kg	0.50	4.50
	4. Marble dus.	kg	1.4 kg	0.50	0.70
					39.19
	(*b*) **Labour**				
	(*i*) For laying				
	1. Manson	each	0.30 No.	110.00	33.00
	2. Mazdoor	each	0.30 No.	65.00	19.50
	3. Bhisti	each	0.10 No.	71.00	7.10
					98.79
	(*ii*) For cutting, grinding and polishing				
	1. Mazdoor	each	0.70	65.00	45.50
					144.29
	(*c*) **Misc.**				
	1. Add for water charges @ 1½%				2.16
					146.45
	2. Add for sundries L.S.				0.55
					147.00
	3. Add for contractor's profit and overhead @ 10%				14.70
	= ₹ 161.70 per sq m				161.70

42. Precast terrazzo tiles 20 mm thick with white, black marble chips of sizes upto 6 mm, laid in floors, on 25 mm thick bed of lime mortar 1 : 1 : 1 (1 lime putty : 1 surkhi : 1 coarse sand) jointed with neat cement slurry mixed with pigment to match the shade of the tiles including rubbing and polishing complete with precast tiles of dark shades using ordinary cement.

Table 6.49 (Unit 1 sq m)

S. No.	*Description*	*Unit*	*Qty.*	*Rate* ₹	*Cost* ₹	*Remarks*
41.	(*a*) **Material**					
	1. Terrazzo tiles including 10% wastage	sq m	1.10 sq m	116.00	127.60	
	2. Cement	per bag	0.05 bag	128.63	6.43	
	3. Lime putty	kg	3.00 kg	2.30	6.90	
	4. Surkhi	cum	0.01 cum	300.00	30.00	
	5. Coarse sand	cum	0.01 cum	315.00	3.15	
					174.08	

	(b) **Labour**					
	(i) For laying					
	1. Mason	each	0.12 No.	110.00	13.20	
	2. Mazdoor	each	0.20 No.	65.00	13.20	
	3. Bhisti	each	0.10 No.	71.00	0.71	
	(ii) For cutting, grinding and polishing					
	1. Mazdoor	each	0.50 No.	65.00	32.50	
	2. Machine	each day	0.40 day	110.00	44.00	
					201.19	
	(c) **Misc.**					
	1. Add for water charges @ 1½%				3.02	
					204.21	
	2. Add for sundries S.L.				1.79	
					206.00	
	3. Add for contractor's profit and overhead @ 10%				20.60	
	= ₹ 226.60 sq m				226.60	

43. Marble stone flooring over 25 mm thick base of lime mortar 1 : 1 : 1 (1 lime putty : 1 surkhi : 1 coarse sand) laid and jointed with gray coment slurry including rubbing and polishing complete with white Makrana marble 25 mm thick.

Table 6.50 (Unit 1 sq m)

S. No.	Description	Unit	Qty.	Rate ₹	Cost ₹	Remarks
42.	(a) **Material**					
	1. Marble Stone	sq m	1.00 sq m	600.00	600.00	
	2. Cement	per bag	0.05 bag	128.63	6.48	
	3. Lime putty	kg	3.00 kg	2.30	6.90	
	4. Surkhi	cum	0.01 cum	300.00	3.00	
	5. Coarse sand	cum	0.01 cum	315.00	3.15	
					619.53	
	(b) **Labour**					
	(i) For laying					
	1. Mason	each	0.50 no.	110.00	55.00	
	2. Mazdoor	each	0.50 no.	65.00	32.50	
	3. Bhisti	each	0.01 no.	71.00	0.71	
	(ii) For cutting, grinding and polishing					
	1. Mazdoor	each	0.70 no.	65.00	45.50	
					753.24	
	(c) **Misc.**					
	1. Add for water charges @ 1½%				11.30	
					764.54	
	2. Add for sundries L.S.				3.46	
					768.00	
	3. Add for contractor's profit and overhead @ 10%				76.80	
	= ₹ 844.80 per sq m				844.80	

44. 40 mm thick Kota stone slab flooring over 25 mm thick base of lime mortar 1 : 1 : 1 (1 lime putty : 1 surkhi : 1 coarse sand) laid over and jointed with grey cement slurry mixed with pigment to match the shade of the slab including rubbing and polishing complete.

Table 6.51 (Unit 1 sq m)

S. No.	*Description*	*Unit*	*Qty.*	*Rate* ₹	*Cost* ₹	*Remarks*
43.	(*a*) **Material**					
	1. Kota stone	sq m	1.00 sq m	180.00	180.00	
	2. Cement	per bag	0.05 bag	128.63	6.43	
	3. Lime putty	kg	3.00 kg	2.30	6.90	
	4. Surkhi	cum	0.01 cum	300.00	3.00	
	5. Coarse sand	cum	0.01 cum	315.00	3.15	
					199.48	
	(*b*) **Labour**					
	(*i*) For laying					
	1. Mason	each	0.25	110.00	27.50	
	2. Mazdoor	each	0.25	65.00	16.25	
	3. Bhisti	each	0.10	71.00	7.10	
	(*ii*) For cutting, grinding and polishing					
	1. Mazdoor	each	0.50	65.00	32.50	
					282.83	
	(*c*) **Misc.**					
	1. Add for water charges @ 1½%				4.24	
					287.07	
	2. Add for sundries L.S.				2.93	
					290.00	
	3. Add for contractor's profit and overhead @ 10%				29.00	
	= ₹ 319.00 per sq m				319.00	

45. 40 mm thick fine dressed stone flooring over 25 mm thick base of lime mortar 1 : 1 : 1 (1 lime putty : 1 surkhi : 1 coarse sand) with joints finished flush (Red sand stone).

Table 6.52 (Unit 1 sq m)

S. No.	*Description*	*Unit*	*Qty.*	*Rate* ₹	*Cost* ₹	*Remarks*
44.	(*a*) **Material**					
	1. Red sand stone	sq m	1.00 sq m	151.00	151.00	
	2. Cement	per bag	0.05 bag	128.63	6.43	
	3. Lime putty	kg	3.00 kg	2.30	6.90	
	4. Surkhi	cum	0.01 cum	300.00	3.00	
	5. Coarse sand	cum	0.01 cum	315.00	3.15	
					170.48	
	(*b*) **Labour**					
	1. Mason	each	0.20 No.	110.00	22.00	
	2. Mazdoor	each	0.20 No.	65.00	13.00	
	3. Bhisti	each	0.10 No.	71.00	7.10	
					212.58	

	Description	Unit	Qty.	Rate	Cost	Remarks
	(c) **Misc.**				212.58	
	1. Add for water charges @ 1 ½%				3.19	
					215.77	
	2. Add for sundries L.S.				1.23	
					217.00	
	Add for contractor's profit and overhead @ 10%				21.70	
	= ₹ 238.70 per sq m				238.70	

46. First class Indian teak wood, 25 mm wooden flanking, tongued and grooved in flooring including fixing with iron screws complete.

Table 6.53 (Unit 1 sq m)

S. No.	Description	Unit	Qty.	Rate ₹	Cost ₹	Remarks
45.	(a) **Material**					
	1. 1st class teak wood $1 \times \frac{2.5}{100} = 0.025$ cum					
	Add 20% for joints and wastage = 0.005 cum					
	Total 0.003 cum	cum	0.03 cum	11500.00	345.00	
	2. Screws L.S.				5.00	
					350.00	
	(b) **Labour**					
	1. Carpenter	each	0.50 No.	100.00	50.00	
	2. Mazdoor	each	0.50 No.	65.00	32.50	
					432.50	
	(c) **Misc.**					
	1. Add for sundries L.S.				5.50	
					438.00	
	2. Add for contractor's profit and overhead @ 10%				43.80	
	= ₹ 481.80 per sq m				481.80	

Roofing

47. Providing corrugated G.I. sheet roofing, 0.80 mm thick, fixed with galvanised iron J or L hooks, bolts and nets, 8 mm diameter with bitumen and G.I limpet washers or with G.I. limpet washers filled with white lead complete, excluding the cost of purlins, rafters and trusses.

Table 6.54 (Unit 1 sq m)

S. No.	Description	Unit	Qty.	Rate ₹	Cost ₹	Remarks
46.	(a) **Material**					
	1. G.I. sheet 0.1 mm thick = 1.00 sq m					
	Add 15%' for laps and wastages = 0.15 sq m					

	Description	Unit	Qty.	Rate	Cost	Remarks
	Total = 1.15 sq m	sq m	1.15 sq m	175.00	201.25	
	2. G.I.L., Hooks with washers etc.	each	5 No.	10.00	50.00	
					251.25	
	(b) **Labour**					
	1. Carpenter	each	0.08 No.	100.00	8.00	
	2. Mazdoor	each	0.16 No.	65.00	10.40	
					269.65	
	(c) **Misc.**					
	1. Add for sundries L.S.				1.35	
					271.00	
	2. Add for contractor's profit and overhead @ 10%				27.10	
	= ₹ 298.10 per sq m				298.10	

48. Providing asbestos cement sheets roofing fixed with galvanised iron J or L hooks, bolts and nuts 5 mm dia G.I. plain and bitumen washers complete, excluding the cost of purlins, rafters, and trusses, 7 mm thick.

Table 6.55 (Unit 1 sq m)

S. No.	Description	Unit	Qty.	Rate ₹	Cost ₹	Remarks
47.	(a) **Material**					
	1. A.C. sheet 7 mm thick = 1.00 sq m Add 15% for laps and wastage = 0.15 sq m Total = 1.15 sq m	sq m	1.15 sq m	175.00	201.25	
	2. G.I.L. Hooks	each	5 No.	10.00	50.00	
					251.25	
	(b) **Labour**					
	1. Carpenter	each	0.08 No.	100.00	8.00	
	2. Mazdoor	each	0.16 No.	65.00	10.40	
					269.65	
	(c) **Misc.**					
	1. Add for sundries L.S.				1.35	
					271.00	
	2. Add for contractor's profit and overhead @10%				27.10	
	= ₹ 298.10 per sq m				298.10	

49. Providing mangalore tile roofing, fixed with wooden battens, excluding the cost of battens.

Table 6.56 (Unit 1 sq m)

S. No.	*Description*	*Unit*	*Qty.*	*Rate* ₹	*Cost* ₹	*Remarks*
48.	(*a*) **Material**					
	Tile (20 cm × 30 cm) = 16 No.					
	Add 6% wastage = 1 No.					
	17 No.	100 No.	17 No.	125.00	21.25	
	(*b*) **Labour**					
	1. Mason	each	0.10 No.	110.00	11.00	
	2. Mazdoor	each	0.20 No.	28.00	5.60	
					37.85	
	(*c*) **Misc.**					
	1. Add for sundries L.S.				1.15	
					39.00	
	2. Add for contractor's profit and overhead @ 10%				3.90	
	= ₹ 42.90 per sq m				42.90	

50. Providing Allahabad tile roofing, fixed with wooden battens, excluding the cost of battens.

Table 6.57 (Unit 1 sq m)

S. No.	*Description*	*Unit*	*Qty.*	*Rate* ₹	*Cost* ₹	*Remarks*
49.	(*a*) **Material**					
	1. Flat tiles 11 No. Add wastage 1 No. } = 12 No.	% No.	12 No.	115.00	13.80	
	2. Half round tiles 11 No. Add wastage 1 No. } = 12 No	% No.	12.No.	130.00	15.60	
	3. Cement	per bag	0.50 No.	128.63	64.32	
	4. Fine sand	cum	0.10 cum	175.00	17.50	
					111.22	
	(*b*) **Labour**					
	1. Mason	each	0.10 No.	110.00	11.00	
	2. Mazdoor	each	0.20 No.	65.00	13.00	
	3. Bhisti	each	0.10 No.	71.00	7.10	
					129.32	
	(*c*) **Misc.**					
	1. Add for water charges @ 1½%				1.94	
					131.26	
	2. Add for sundries L.S.				1.74	
					133.00	
	3. Add for contractor's profit and overhead @ 10%				13.20	
	= ₹ 146.20 per sq m				146.20	

51. 50 mm thick, red stone slab roofing and laying in cement mortar 1 : 4 (1 cement : 4 coarse sand) over karries, including painting and excluding the cost of karries.

Table 6.58 (Unit 1 sq m)

S. No.	Description		Unit	Qty.	Rate ₹	Cost ₹	Remarks
50.	(a) **Material**						
	1. 50 mm thick red stone slab	1.00 sq m					
	Add 10% wastage	0.10 sq m					
	Total	1.10 sq m	sq m	1.10 sq m	151.00	166.10	
	2. Cement		per bag	0.14 bag	128.63	18.00	
	3. Coarse sand		cum	0.02 cum	315.00	6.30	
						190.40	
	(b) **Labour**						
	1. Mason		each	0.12 No.	110.00	13.20	
	2. Mazdoor		each	0.25 No.	65.00	16.25	
	3. Bhisti		each	0.06 No.	71.00	4.26	
						224.11	
	(c) **Misc.**						
	1. Add for water charges @ 1½%					3.44	
						227.55	
	2. Add for sundries L.S.					1.45	
						229.00	
	3. Add for contractor's profit and overhead @ 10%					22.90	
	= ₹ 251.90 per sq m					251.90	

52. Providing thatcher roofing 15 cm thick in two layers, each 75 mm thick with poolas, half split bamboo fillet and tying string complete.

Table 6.59 (Unit 1 sq m)

S. No.	Description	Unit	Qty.	Rate ₹	Cost ₹	Remarks
51.	(a) **Material**					
	1. Grass poolas	cent	18 No.	60.00	10.80	
	2. Bamboo 25 mm dia.	score	5 No.	50.00	1.74	
	3. Moonj string	kg	1 kg	9.00	9.00	
					21.54	
	(b) **Labour**					
	1. Thatcher	each	0.30 No.	70.00	21.00	
	2. Mazdoor	each	0.30 No.	65.00	19.50	
					62.04	
	(c) **Misc.**					
	1. Add for sundries L.S.				0.96	
					63.00	
	2. Add for contractor's profit and overhead @ 10%				6.30	
	= ₹ 69.30 per sq m				69.30	

53. Providing 150 mm diameter, fixing and hoisting in position sal bailies in trusses including cost of iron nails and spikes required and applying wood preservative on all exposed surfaces.

Table 6.60 (Unit per metre)

S. No.	Description	Unit	Qty.	Rate ₹	Cost ₹	Remarks
52.	(*a*) **Material**					
	1. 50 mm dia sal bailies For a truss 6 mm clear span ; king post 1.5 mm high. Tie beam 1 × 6.9 m = 6.9 m Principal raften 2 × 3.76 = 7.52 m King post 1 × 1.5 = 1.50 m Struts 2 × 1.13 = 2.26 m Total = 18.18 m Add 10% wastage = 1.82 m Grand total = 20.00 m	per metre	20.00 m	30.00	600.00	
	2. Nails, spikes and wood preservative L.S.			50		
				650.00		
	(*b*) **Labour**					
	1. Carpenter	each	1 No.	100.00	100.00	
	2. Mazdoor	each	1 No.	65.00	65.00	
	3. Bandhani	each	0.25 No.	70.00	17.50	
						832.50
	(*c*) **Misc.**					
	1. Add for sundries L.S.					5.50
						838.00
	2. Add for contractor's profit and overhead @ 10%					83.80
	Cost = $\frac{921.80}{18.18}$ = ₹ 49.03					921.80
	= ₹ 50.70 per metre					

54. Providing and fixing 20 mm thick wooden planks ceiling excluding framework M.S. screws.

Table 6.61 (Unit 1 sq m)

S. No.	Description	Unit	Qty.	Rate ₹	Cost ₹	Remarks
53.	(*a*) **Material**					
	1. 2nd class teak wood planks = 1.00 sq m Add 5% wastage = 0.05 sq m = 1.05 × 0.02 cum = 0.021 cum	cum	0.02	36500.00	730.00	
	2. M.S. screw 40 mm long	% No.	70 No.	20.00	14.00	
					87.00	
	(*b*) **Labour**					
	1. Carpenter	each	0.15 No.	100.00	15.00	
	2. Mazdoor	each	0.03 No.	65.00	1.95	
					103.95	
	(*c*) **Misc.**					
	1. Add for sundries L.S.				1.05	
					105.00	
	2. Add for contractor's profit and overhead @ 10%				10.50	
	= ₹ 115.50 per sq m				115.50	

55. 10 m thick mud phuska of damped brick earth on roofs, laid to slope consolidated and plastcred with 25 mm thick mud mortar mixed with phuska at 35 kg per cum of earth and gobri leaping with mix 1 : 1 (1 clay : 1 cow dung) and covered with flat tile bricks grouted with cement mortar 1 : 3 (1 cement : 3 fine sand) and finished neat.

Table 6.62 (Unit 1 sq m)

S. No.	Description	Unit	Qty.	Rate ₹	Cost ₹	Remarks
54.	(*a*) **Material**					
	1. Mud l × $\frac{10}{100}$ = 0.10 cum					
	Add 20% wastage = 0.02 cum					
	Total = 0.12 cum	cum	0.12 cum	7.00	0.84	
	2. Mud mortar 25 mm thick = 0.06 cum	cum	0.026 cum	50.00	1.30	
	3. Bhusa 0.026 × 35 = 0.91					
	Add 5% wastage = 0.05					
	0.96 kg	kg	0.96 kg	1.34	1.29	
	4. Cow dung L.S.				1.00	
	5. Mud mortar for gobry laying L.S.				10.00	
	6. Tile 20 × 20 × 5 cm	100 %	38 No.	125.00	47.50	
	7. Cement	per bag	0.17 bag	128.63	21.87	
	8. Fine sand	cum	0.017 cum	165.00	2.80	
					86.60	
	(*b*) **Labour**					
	1. Mason	each	0.20 No.	110.00	22.00	
	2. Mazdoor	each	0.40 No.	65.00	26.00	
	3. Bhisti	each	0.10 No.	71.00	7.10	
					141.70	
	(*c*) **Misc.**					
	1. Add for water charges @ 1 ½%				21.25	
					162.95	
	2. Add for sundries L.S.				1.05	
					164.00	
	3. Add for contractor's profit and overhead @ 10%				16.40	
	= ₹ 180.40 per sq m				180.40	

56. Painting top of roofs with bitumen of approved quality at 2 kg sq per sq m. Impregnated with a coat of coarse sand including cleaning the slab surface with brushes and finally with a piece with a piece of cloth lightly soaked in kerosene oil complete.

Table 6.63 (Unit 1 Sq m)

S. No.		Description	Unit	Qty.	Rate ₹	Cost ₹	Remarks
55.	(a)	**Material**					
		1. Maxphalte 80/100	kg	2 kg	6.50	13.00	
		2. Coarse sand L.S.				1.50	
		3. Kerosene oil L.S.				1.00	
		4. Fuel for heating L.S.				1.00	
						16.50	
	(b)	**Labour**				**B/F**	
		1. Painter	each	0.02 No.	90.00	1.80	
		2. Mazdoor	each	0.02 No.	65.00	1.30	
						19.60	
	(c)	**Misc.**					
		1. Add for sundries L.S.				0.40	
						20.00	
		2. Add for contractor's profit and overhead @ 10%				2.00	
		= ₹ 22.00 per sq m				22.00	

57. Labour rates for rain water pipes fixing.
(1) 100 mm diameter C.I. rain water pipe = ₹ 5.0 per m
(2) 100 mm diameter M.S. holder bat clamps = ₹ 3.00 each
(3) 100 mm diameter C.I. plain bend = ₹ 3.00 each
(4) 100 mm diameter C.I. head flat = ₹ 3.00 each
(5) 100 mm diameter C.I. plan shoe = ₹ 3.00 each
(6) For 100 mm diameter pipe lead caulked joint = ₹ 5.0 each

Finishing

58. 12 mm Lime plaster 1 : 1 : 1 (1 lime putty : 1 surkhi : 1 fine sand)

Table 6.64 (Unit 1 sq m)

S. No.		Description	Unit	Qty.	Rate ₹	Cost ₹	Remarks
56.	(a)	**Material**					Add 20% for joints
		1. Lime putty	kg	4.1 kg	2.30	9.43	
		2. Surkhi	cum	0.01 cum	300.00	3.00	*i.e.* $\frac{12}{1000}$ + 20%
		3. Fine sand	cum	0.01 cum	175.00	1.75	
						14.18	of $\frac{12}{1000}$
							= 0.0144 cum
	(b)	**Labour**					
		1. Mason	each	0.08 No.	110.00	8.80	Mortar
		2. Mazdoor	each	0.10 No.	65.00	6.50	0.0144
		3. Bhisti	each	0.10 No.	71.00	7.10	cum
						22.40	
	(c)	**Misc.**					
		1. Add for water charge @ 1½%				0.34	
						22.74	
		2. Add for sundries L.S.				.26	
						23.00	
		3. Add for contractor's profit and overhead @ 10%				2.30	
		= ₹ 25.30 per sq m				25.30	

59. 12 mm cement lime plaster 1 : 1 : 6 (1 cement : 1 lime putty : 6 fine sand)

Table 6.65 (Unit 1 sq m)

S. No.	Description	Unit	Qty.	Rate ₹	Cost ₹	Remarks
57.	(*a*) **Material**					
	1. Cement	per bag	0.07 bag	128.63	9.00	Mortar
	2. Lime putty	kg	1.50 kg	2.30	3.45	0.0144
	3. Fine sand	cum	0.015 cum	175.00	2.63	cum
					15.08	
	(*b*) **Labour**					
	1. Mason	each	0.08 No.	110.00	8.80	
	2. Mazdoor	each	0.10 No.	65.00	6.50	
	3. Bhisti	each	0.10 No.	71.00	7.10	
					37.48	
	(*c*) **Misc.**					
	1. Add for water charges @ 1½%				0.56	
					38.04	
	2. Add for sundries L.S.				0.96	
					39.00	
	3. Add for contractor's profit and overhead @ 10%				3.90	
	= ₹ 42.90 per sq m				42.90	

60. 12 mm cement plaster 1 : 6 (cement : 6 find sand)

Table 6.66 (Unit 1 sq m)

S. No.	Description	Unit	Qty.	Rate ₹	Cost ₹	Remarks
58.	(*a*) **Material**					0.0144 cum of mortar.
	1. Cement	per bag	0.07	128.63	9.00	
	2. Fine sand	cum	0.015 cum	175.00	2.63	
					11.63	
	(*b*) **Labour**					
	1. Mason	each	0.08 No.	110.00	8.80	
	2. Mazdoor	each	0.10 No.	65.00	6.50	
	3. Bhisti	each	0.10 No.	71.00	7.10	
					34.03	
					0.51	
	(*c*) **Misc.**					
	1. Add for water charges @ 1½%					
					34.54	
					0.46	
	2. Add for sundries L.S.				35.00	
	3. Add for contractor's profit and overhead @ 10%				3.50	
	= ₹ 38.50 per sq m				38.50	

61. 12 mm cement plaster 1 : 6 (1 cement : 6 coarse sand)

Table 6.67 (Unit 1 sq m)

S. No.	*Description*	*Unit*	*Qty.*	*Rate* ₹	*Cost* ₹	*Remarks*
59.	(*a*) **Material**					0.0144 cum of mortar
	1. Cement	per bag	0.07 bag	128.63	9.00	
	2. Coarse sand	cum	0.015 cum	315.00	4.73	
					13.73	
	(*b*) **Labour**					
	1. Mason	each	0.08 No.	110.00	8.80	
	2. Mazdoor	each	0.10 No.	65.00	6.50	
	3. Bhisti	each	0.10 No.	71.00	7.10	
					36.16	
	(*c*) **Misc.**					
	1. Add for water charge @ 1½%				0.54	
					36.70	
	2. Add for sundries L.S.				0.30	
					37.00	
	3. Add for contractor's profit and overhead @ 10%				3.70	
	= ₹ 40.70 per sq m				40.70	

62. Flush pointing with cement mortar 1 : 6 (1 cement : 6 fine sand)

Table 6.68 (Unit 1 sq m)

S. No.	*Description*	*Unit*	*Qty.*	*Rate* ₹	*Cost* ₹	*Remarks*
						0.002 cum of mortar
60.	(*a*) **Material**					
	1. Cement	per bag	0.01 bag	128.63	1.28	
	2. Fine sand	cum	0.002 cum	175.00	0.35	
					1.63	
	(*b*) **Labour**					
	1. Mason	each	0.08 No.	110.00	8.80	
	2. Mazdoor	each	0.10 No.	65.00	6.50	
	3. Bhisti	each	0.10 No.	71.00	7.10	
					24.03	
	(*c*) **Misc.**					
	1. Add for water charges @ 1½%				0.36	
					24.39	
	2. Add for sundries L.S.				0.11	
					24.50	
	3. Add for contractor's profit and overhead @ 10%				2.45	
	= ₹ 26.95 per sq m				26.95	

White WashingColour Washing and Distempering

63. White washing with lime on new work (three or more costs)

Table 6.69 (Unit 1 sq m)

S. No.	Description	Unit	Qty.	Rate ₹	Cost ₹	Remarks
61.	(*a*) **Material**					
	Detail of cost of 10 sq m					
	1. Lime	kg	30 kg	2.50	75.00	
	2. Indigo, gum etc.	L.S.			5.00	
					80.00	
	(*b*) **Labour**					
	1. Washer	each	0.20 No.	70.00	14.00	
	2. Mazdoor	each	0.10 No.	65.00	6.50	
					104.50	
	(*c*) **Misc.**					
	1. Add for water charges @ 1½%				1.57	
					106.07	
	2. Add for sundries L.S.				0.93	
					107.00	
	3. Add for contractor's profit and overhead @ 10%				10.70	
					117.70	
	Cost per sq m = $\frac{117.70}{10}$ = 11.77 = 11.75 per sq m					

Note 1. For colour washing, add in lump sum for colouring stuff, in the cost of material.
2. Labour for 10 sq m, (*a*) Washer 0.30 No. (*b*) Mazdoor 0.10 No.

64. White washing with lime on old work (Two or more coats) to give an even shade.

Table 6.70 (Unit 1 sq m)

S. No.	Description	Unit	Qty.	Rate ₹	Cost ₹	Remarks
62.	(*a*) **Material**					
	Detail of cost of 10 sq m					
	1. Lime	kg	20 kg	2.50	50.00	
	2. Indigo, gum etc.	L.S.	–	–	3.00	
					53.00	
	(*b*) **Labour**					
	1. Washer	each	0.10 No.	70.00	7.00	
	2. Mazdoor	each	0.15 No.	65.00	9.75	
					69.75	
	(*c*) **Misc.**					
	1. Add for water charges @ 1½%				1.05	
					70.80	
	2. Add for sundries L.S.				0.20	
					71.00	
	3. Add for contractor's profit and overhead @ 10%				7.10	
					78.10	
	Cost per sq m = $\frac{78.10}{10}$ = ₹ 7.81 = ₹ 7.80 per sq m					

65. White washing with lime on old work to given an even shade.

Table 6.71 (Unit 1 sq m)

S. No.	*Description*	*Unit*	*Qty.*	*Rate* ₹	*Cost* ₹	*Remarks*
63.	(*a*) **Material**					
	Detail of cost of 10 sq m					
	1. Lime	kg	10 kg	2.50	25.00	
	2. Indigo, gum etc.	L.S.			2.00	
					27.00	
	(*b*) **Labour**					
	1. Washer	each	0.05 No.	70.00	3.50	
	2. Mazdoor	each	0.05 No.	65.00	3.25	
					33.75	
	(*c*) **Misc.**					
	1. Add for water charges © 1½%				0.50	
					34.25	
	2. Add for sundries L.S.				0.75	
					35.00	
	3. Add for contractor's profit and overhead @ 10%				3.50	
					38.50	
	Cost per sq m = $\frac{38.50}{10}$ = ₹ 3.85					
	= 3.85 per sq m					

66. Distempering with dry distemper (Two or more coats) on new work, over and including priming coat of whiting to give an even shade.

Table 6.72 (Unit 1 sq m)

S. No.	*Description*	*Unit*	*Qty.*	*Rate* ₹	*Cost* ₹	*Remarks*
64.	(*a*) **Material**					
	For priming coat					
	1. Whiting	kg	0.1 kg	2.50	2.50	
	2. Putty, blue etc.	L.S.	0.15 kg	230.00	3.45	
	For final coats					
	3. Dry distemper	kg	0.08 kg	19.00	1.52	
					7.47	
	(*b*) **Labour**					
	1. Painter	each	90	90.00	3.60	
	2. Mazdoor	each	.01	65.00	6.65	
	3. Brushes, sandpaper etc. L.S.			1.00	1.00	
					12.72	
	(*c*) **Misc.**					
	1. Add for water charges @ 10%				0.19	
					12.91	
	2. Add for sundries L.S.				0.07	
					12.98	
	3. Add for contractor's profit and overhead @ 10%				1.29	
					14.27	
	= ₹ 14.25 per sq m			say	14.25	

67. Distempering with dry distemper (Two or more coats) on old work to give an even shade.

Table 6.73 (Unit 1 sq m)

S. No.	*Description*	*Unit*	*Qty.*	*Rate* ₹	*Cost* ₹	*Remarks*
65.	(*a*) **Material**					
	1. Dry distemper	kg	0.10 kg	19	1.90	
	2. Brushes, sand paper etc.	L.S.			0.20	
					2.10	
	(*b*) **Labour**					
	1. Painter	each	0.02 No.	90.00	18.00	
	2. Mazdoor	each	0.01 No.	65.00	0.65	
					20.75	
	(*c*) **Misc.**					
	1. Add for water charges @ 1½%				0.31	
					21.06	
	2. Add for sundries L.S.				0.94	
					22.00	
	3. Add for contractor's profit and overhead @ 10%				2.20	
	= ₹ 24.20 per sq m				24.20	

Painting Varnishing and Polishing

68. Finishing walls with water proofing cement paint, on new work (Three or more coats) to give an even shade.

Table 6.74 (Unit 1 sq m)

S. No.	*Description*	*Unit*	*Qty.*	*Rate* ₹	*Cost* ₹	*Remarks*
66.	(*a*) **Material**					
	1. Water proofing cement paint	kg	0.5 kg	21.00	10.50	
	2. Brushes, sand paper etc.	L.S.			0.50	
					11.00	
	(*b*) **Labour**					
	1. Painter	each	0.15 No.	90.00	13.50	
	2. Mazdoor	each	0.01 No.	65.00	0.65	
	3. Bhisti	each	0.10 No.	71.00	7.10	
					32.25	
	(*c*) **Misc.**					
	1. Add for water charges @ 1½%				0.48	
					32.73	
	2. Add for sundries L.S.				0.27	
					33.00	
	3. Add for contractor's profit and overhead @ 10%				3.30	
	= ₹ 36.30 per sq m				36.30	

69. Finishing walls with water proofing cement paint on old work (one or more coats) to give an even shade.

Table 6.75 (Unit 1 sq m)

S. No.	*Description*	*Unit*	*Qty.*	*Rate* ₹	*Cost* ₹	*Remarks*
67.	(*a*) **Material**					
	1. Water proofing cement paint	kg	0.2 kg	21.00	4.20	
	2. Brushes, sand paper etc.	L.S.			0.10	
					4.30	
	(*b*) **Labour**					
	1. Painter	each	0.05 No.	90.00	4.50	
	2. Mazdoor	each	0.05 No.	65.00	3.25	
	3. Bhisti	each	0.05 No.	71.80	3.60	
					15.65	
	(*c*) **Misc.**					
	1. Add for water charges @ 1½ %				0.23	
					15.88	
	2. Add for sundries L.S.				0.12	
					16.00	
	3. Add for contractors profit and overhead @ 10%				1.60	
	= ₹ 17.60 sq m				17.60	

70. Painting two coats with oil type wood preservative on new work.

Table 6.76 (Unit 1 sq m)

S. No.	*Description*	*Unit*	*Qty.*	*Rate* ₹	*Cost* ₹	*Remarks*
68.	(*a*) **Material**					
	1. Oil type wood preservative	Litre	0.10 litre	42.00	4.20	
	2. Brushes, sand paper	L.S.			0.80	
					5.00	
	(*b*) **Labour**					
	1. Painter	each	0.02 No.	90.00	1.80	
	2. Mazdoor	each	0.01 No.	65.00	0.65	
					7.45	
	(*c*) **Misc.**					
	1. Add for sundries L.S.				0.35	
					7.80	
	2. Add for contractor's profit and overhead @ 10%				0.78	
					8.58	
	= ₹ 8.58 per sq m					

71. Painting one coat with oil type wood preservative on old work.

Table 6.77 (Unit 1 sq m)

S. No.		*Description*	*Unit*	*Qty.*	*Rate* ₹	*Cost* ₹	*Remarks*
69.	(*a*)	**Material**					
		1. Oil type wood preservative	Litre	0.08 liter	42.00	3.36	
		2. Brushes sand paper etc.	L.S.			1.64	
						5.00	
	(*b*)	**Labour**					
		1. Painter	each	0.01 No.	90.00	0.90	
		2. Mazdoor	each	0.005 No.	28.00	0.14	
						6.04	
	(*c*)	**Misc.**					
		1. Add for sundries L.S.				0.06	
						6.70	
		2. Add for contractor profit and over head @ 10%				0.67	
						7.37	
		= ₹ 7.35 per sq m			say	7.35	

72. Applying priming coat with ready mixed primer on wood work complete.

Table 6.78 (Unit 1 sq m)

S. No.		*Description*	*Unit*	*Qty.*	*Rate* ₹	*Cost* ₹	*Remarks*
70.	(*a*)	**Material**					
		1. Ready mixed primer	litre	0.08 litre	71.00	5.68	
		2. Putty, sand paper, brushes etc.	L.S.			1.32	
						7.00	
	(*b*)	**Labour**					
		1. Painter	each	0.02 No.	90.00	1.80	
		2. Mazdoor	each	0.01 No.	65.00	0.65	
						9.45	
	(*c*)	**Misc.**					
		1. Add for sundries L.S.				0.55	
						10.00	
		2. Add for contractor's profit and overhead @ 10%				1.00	
		= ₹ 11.00 per sq m.				11.00	

73. Applying priming coat with ready mixed primer on steel work complete.

Table 6.79 (Unit 1 sq m)

Item No.	*Description*	*Unit*	*Qty.*	*Rate* ₹	*Cost* ₹	*Remarks*
71.	(*a*) **Material**					
	1. Readymixed primer	litre	0.05 litre	71.00	3.55	
	2. Sand paper, brushes etc.	L.S.			0.45	
					4.00	
	(*b*) **Labour**					
	1. Painter	each	0.02 No.	90.00	1.80	
	2. Mazdoor	each	0.01 No.	65.00	0.65	
					6.45	
	(*c*) **Misc.**					
	1. Add for sundries L.S.				0.55	
					7.00	
	2. Add for contractor's profit and overhead @ 10%				0.70	
	= ₹ 7.70 per sq m				7.70	

74. Applying priming coat with ready mixed primer on plastered surface.

Table 6.80 (Unit 1 sq m)

S. No.	*Description*	*Unit*	*Qty.*	*Rate* ₹	*Cost* ₹	*Remarks*
72.	(*a*) **Material**					
	1. Ready-mixed primer	litre	0.10 litre	710.00	7.10	
	2. Putty, plaster of paris, sand paper and brushes etc.	L.S.			0.90	
					8.00	
	(*b*) **Labour**					
	1. Painter	each	0.03 No.	90.00	2.70	
	2. Mazdoor	each	0.02 No.	65.00	1.30	
					12.00	
	(*c*) **Misc.**					
	1. Add for sundries L.S.				0.50	
					12.50	
	2. Add for contractor's profit and overhead @ 10%				1.25	
	= ₹ 13.75 per sq m				13.75	

75. Painting two or more coate (excluding priming primint coat) with ready mixed paint on new work to give an even shede.

Table 6.81 (Unit 1 sq m)

S. No.	*Description*	*Unit*	*Qty.*	*Rate* ₹	*Cost* ₹	*Remarks*
73.	(*a*) **Material**					
	1. Readymixed paint	litre	0.12 litre	71.00	8.52	
	2. Brushes, sand paper etc.	L.S.			0.48	
					9.00	
	(*b*) **Labour**					
	1. Painter	each	0.05 No.	90.00	4.50	
	2. Mazdoor	each	0.01 No.	65.00	0.65	
					14.15	
	(*c*) **Misc.**					
	1. Add for sundries L.S.				0.85	
					15.00	
	2. Add for contractor's profit and overhead @ 10%				1.50	
	= ₹ 16.50 per sq m				16.50	

76. Painting one or more coats with ready-mixed paint on old work to give an even shade.

Table 6.82 (Unit 1 sq m)

S. No.	*Description*	*Unit*	*Qty.*	*Rate* ₹	*Cost* ₹	*Remarks*
74.	(*a*) **Material**					
	1. Readymixed paint	litre	0.06 litre	71.00	4.26	
	2. Brushes, sand paper etc.	L.S.			0.24	
					14.50	
	(*b*) **Labour**					
	1. Painter	each	0.03 No.	90.00	2.70	
	2. Mazdoor	each	0.015 No.	650.00	0.98	
					18.08	
	(*c*) **Misc.**					
	1. Add for sundries L.S.				1.81	
					19.99	
	2. Add for contractor's profit and overhead @ 10%				1.99	
					21.98	
	= ₹ 22.00 per sq m			say	22.00	

77. Varnishing (Two or more coats) with Copal varnish on new work including an under coat of flatting varnish with glue sizing.

Table 6.83 (Unit 1 sq m)

S. No.	*Description*	*Unit*	*Qty.*	*Rate* ₹	*Cost* ₹	*Remarks*
75.	(*a*) **Material**					
	1. Flatting varnish	litre	0.08 litre	30.00	2.40	
	2. Glue for sizing	kg	0.01 kg	20.00	0.20	
	3. Copal varnish	litre	0.12 litre	65.00	8.16	
	4. Putty, brushes sand paper etc.	L.S.			1.50	
					12.26	
	(*b*) **Labour**					
	1. Painter	each	0.10 No.	90.00	9.00	
	2. Mazdoor	each	0.02 No.	65.00	1.30	
					22.56	
	(*c*) **Misc.**					
	1. Add for sundries L.S.				0.44	
					23.00	
	2. Add for contractor's profit and overhead @ 10%				2.30	
	= ₹ 25.30 per sq m				25.30	

78. Varnishing (One or more coats) with Copal varnish on old work.

Table 6.84 (Unit 1 sq m)

S. No.	*Description*	*Unit*	*Qty.*	*Rate* ₹	*Cost* ₹	*Remarks*
76.	(*a*) **Material**					
	1. Copal varnish	litre	0.08 litre	68.00	5.44	
	2. Repair to surface	L.S.			0.56	
					6.00	
	(*b*) **Labour**					
	1. Painter	each	0.03 No.	90.00	2.70	
	2. Mazdoor	each	0.01 No.	65.00	0.65	
					9.35	
	(*c*) **Misc.**					
	1. Add for sundries L.S.				0.35	
					9.70	
	2. Add for contractor's profit and overhead @ 10%				0.97	
					10.67	
	= ₹ 10.65 per sq m			say	10.65	

79. Polishing on wood work with ready made wax polish on new work.

Table 6.85 (Unit 1 sq m)

S. No.	*Description*	*Unit*	*Qty.*	*Rate* ₹	*Cost* ₹	*Remarks*
77.	(*a*) **Material**					
	1. Readymade wax polish	kg	0.05 kg	71.00	3.55	
	2. Soap, brushes, cloth etc.	L.S.			0.45	
					4.00	
	(*b*) **Labour**					
	1. Painter	each	0.08 No.	90.00	7.20	
	2. Mazdoor	each	0.02 No.	65.00	1.30	
					12.50	
	(*c*) **Misc.**					
	1. Add for sundries L.S.				0.50	
					13.00	
	2. Add for contractor's profit and overhead @ 10%				1.30	
	= ₹ 14.30 per sq m				14.30	

80. Polishing on wood work with ready made wax polish on old work.

Table 6.86 (Unit 1 sq m)

S. No.	*Description*	*Unit*	*Qty.*	*Rate* ₹	*Cost* ₹	*Remarks*
78.	(*a*) **Material**					
	1. Readymade wax polish	kg	0.02 kg	71.00	1.42	
	2. Soap, brushes, cloth etc.	L.S.			0.28	
					1.70	
	(*b*) **Labour**					
	1. Painter	each	0.04 No.	90.60	3.60	
	2. Mazdoor	each	0.01 No.	65.00	0.65	
					5.95	
	(*c*) **Misc.**					
	1. Add for sundries L.S.				0.15	
					6.10	
	2. Add for contractor's profit and overhead @ 10%				0.61	
					6.70	
	= ₹ 6.70 sq m			say	6.70	

81. French spirit polishing (two or more coats) including a coat of wood filler on new work.

Table 6.87 (Unit 1 sq m)

S. No.	Description	Unit	Qty.	Rate ₹	Cost ₹	Remarks
79.	(*a*) Material					
	1. Spirit	litre	0.15 litre	21.00	3.15	
	2. Pigment	L.S.			1.00	
	3. Shellac	kg	0.02 kg	50.00	1.00	
	4. Turpentine oil, linseed oil, woollen cloth, Putty, sand paper, cotton etc.		L.S.		1.50	
					6.65	
	(*b*) **Labour**					
	1. Painter	each	0.35 No.	90.00	31.50	
	2. Mazdoor	each	0.05 No.	65.00	3.25	
					41.40	
	(*c*) **Misc.**					
	1. Add for sundries L.S.				0.50	
					41.90	
	2. Add for contractor's profit and overhead @ 10%				4.19	
					46.09	
	= ₹ 46.10 per sq m			say	46.10	

82. French spirit polishing (one or more coats) on old work.

Table 6.88 (Unit 1 sq m)

S. No.	Description	Unit	Qty.	Rate ₹	Cost ₹	Remarks
80.	(*a*) **Material**					
	1. Spirit	litre	0.08	21.00	1.68	
	2. Shellac	kg	0.01	50.00	0.50	
	3. Turpintine oil, linseed oil, woollen cloth, sand paper, cotton etc.	L.S.			1.50	
					3.88	
	(*b*) **Labour**					
	1. Painter	each	0.15	90.00	13.50	
	2. Mazdoor	each	0.02	65.00	1.30	
					18.63	
	(*c*) **Misc.**					
	1. Add for sundries L.S.				0.32	
					19.00	
	2, Add for contractor's profit and overhead @ 10%				1.90	
	= ₹ 20.90 per sq m				20.90	

Brick Moulding and Burning (in Delhi)

83. Mixed Class Burnt Bricks

Table 6.89 (Unit 1000 Nos)

S. No.		Description	Unit	Qty.	Rate ₹	Cost ₹	Remarks
81.	(a)	**Material**					
		1. Mud	cum	2.00 cum	7.00	14.00	
		2. Fine sand	cum	0.10 cum	175.00	17.50	
		3. Coal	tonne	0.20 tonne	161.00	22.00	
						53.50	
	(b)	**Labour**					
		1. Mistry	each	0.10 No.	110.00	11.00	
		2. Moulder	each	1 No.	90.00	90.00	
		3. Mazdoor for dissing, pussing and carrying mud.	%	9.50 No.	65.00	6.17	
		4. Mazdoor for drying and loading kiln with bricks	each	1 No.	65.00	65.00	
		5. Mazdoor for burning the bricks	each	0.50 No.	65.00	35.00	
		6. Mazdoor for unloading, shorting and stacking bricks		1.00 No.	65.00	65.00	
		7. Bhisti	each	0.20 No.	71.00	14.20	
						339.87	
	(c)	**Misc.**					
		1. Add for chimney, dampers, moulds, etc.	L.S.			4.13	
						344.00	
		2. Add for water charges @ 1½%				5.16	
						349.16	
		3. Add for sundries L.S.				2.84	
						352.00	
		4. Add for contractor's profit and overhead @ 10%				35.20	
		= ₹ 387.20 per 1000 No.				387.20	

Note. First Class 60% ; 2nd Class 20% : 3rd Class 10% and overburnt etc. 10%.

84. Satna lime burning.

Table 6.90 (Unit 1 cum) weight 600 kg : Slaked lime

S. No.		Description	Unit	Qty.	Rate ₹	Cost ₹	Remarks
82.	(a)	**Material**					
		1. Lime stone	cum	0.75 cum	150.00	112.50	
		2. Coal	tonne	0.10 tonne	161.00	16.10	
		3. Dried wood etc.	L.S.			20.00	
						148.60	

Description	Unit	Quantity	Rate	Amount
(*b*) **Labour**			BF	148.60
1. Lime burner	each	0.5 No.	900.00	45.00
2. Mazdoor for breaking and loading	each	2 No.	65.00	130.00
3. Mazdoor for unloading and preparing lime	each	2 No.	65.00	130.00
4. Bhisti	each	1 No.	71.00	71.00
				524.60
(*c*) **Misc.**				
1. Add for water charges @ 1½%				7.87
				532.47
2. Add for sundries L.S.				2.53
				535.00
3. Add for contractor's profit and overhead @ 10%				53.50
= ₹ 588.50 per cum (600 kg)				588.50

Note. Unslaked stone lime increases 105 times in bulk when slaked and yields 1.5 times in bulk of pure lime.

Repair to Buildings

Table 6.91

S. No.	*Description*	*Unit*	*Labour required*	*Remarks*
1.	Repair to plaster in patches with cement mortar	1 sq m	1. Mason—0.12 No. 2. Mazdoor—0.18 No. 3. Bhisti—0.03 No.	
2.	Fixing door chowkhat in existing opening	one No.	1. Mason—0.50 2. Mazdoor—0.75 No.	
3.	Fixing window chowkhat in existing opening	one No.	1. Mason—0.33 No. 2. Mazdoor—0.50 No.	
4.	Fixing glass panes	1 sq m	1. Glazier—0.20 No. 2. Mazdoor—0.01 No.	
5.	Regarding terracing of mud phuska covered with tiles	1 sq m	1. Mason—0.12 No. 2. Mazdoor—0.12 No. 3. Bhisti—0.02 No.	
6.	Dismantling old plaster and raking out joint sand cleaning the surface.	1 sq m	1. Mazdoor—0.05 2. Bhisti—0.01	
7.	Fixing M.S. fan clamps of standard shape and size	one no	1. Mason—0.12 No. 2. Mazdoor—0.25 No.	

Note : 1. Add for sundries

2. Add for contractor's profit and overhead @ 10%

3. Work out the cost of item.

Dismantling and Demolishing

Table 6.92

S. No.	Description	Unit	Labour required	Remark
1.	Demolishing lime concrete and disposal of material.	1 cum	1. Mazdoor—0.80 No.	
2.	Demolishing cement concrete 1 : 4 : 8 mix or leaner mix.	1 cum	1. Mazdoor—1.40 No.	
3.	Demolishing R.C.C. work including stacking of steel.	1 cum	1. Mazdoor—2.40 No.	
4.	Demolishing R.B. work including stacking of steel.	1 cum	1. Mazdoor—3.00 No.	
5.	Demolishing brick work in mud mortar including stacking of serviceable material.	1 cum	1. Mazdoor—0.7 No.	
6.	Demolishing brick work in lime mortar with old mughal bricks including stacking of material.	1 cum	1. Mazdoor—1.70 No.	
7.	Demolishing brick work in lime mortar including stacking of serviceable material.	1 cum	1. Mazdoor—0.8 No.	
8.	Demolishing brick work in cement mortar including stacking of serviceable material.	1 cum	1. Mazdoor—2.00 No.	
9.	Demolishing stone rubble masonry in lime mortar including stacking of material.	1 cum	1. Mazdoor—1.10 No.	
10.	Demolishing stone rubble masonry in cement mortar including stacking of material.	1 cum	1. Mazdoor—2.33 No.	
11.	Dismantling doors, windows shutters including chowkhat etc. and stacking of material.	each	1. Mason—0.10 No. 2. Mazdoor—0.02 No.	
12.	Dismantling wood work in frames, trusses, joists, etc. and stacking of material.	per metre	1. Carpenter—0.008 No. 2. Mazdoor—0.003 No.	
13.	Dismantling steel work in sections in R.S. joists etc. including stacking of material.	100 kg	1. Black smith—0.05 No. 2. Bandhani—0.10 No. 3. Mazdoor—0.15 No.	
14.	Demolishing mud phuska, brick tile covering in terracing and disposal of material.	1 sq m	1. Mason—0.06 No. 2. Mazdoor—0.12 No.	
15.	Dismantling G.I. sheets roofing etc. including stacking of material.	1 sq m	1. Carpenter—0.05 No. 2. Mazdoor—0.10 No.	

S. No.	Description	Unit	Labour required	Remark
16.	Dismantling asbestos sheet roofing etc. including stacking of material.	1 sq m	1. Carpenter—0.02 No. 2. Mazdoor—0.04 No.	
17.	Dismantling stone slab roofing including stacking of serviceable material.	1 cum	1. Mazdoor—2.50 No.	
18.	Dismantling jack arch roofing and floors including stacking of material.	1 sq m	1. Mazdoor—0.25 No.	
19.	Dismantling barbed wire in fencing including making rolls.	100 kg	1. Mazdoor—3.50 No.	
20.	Dismantling fencing posts including earthwork and concrete.	each	1. Mazdoor—0.33 No.	

Note : 1. Add for sundries
2. Add for contractor's profit and overhead @ 10%
3. Work out the cost of item.

Miscellaneous Building Work

Table 6.93

S. No.	Description	Unit	Labour required	Remark
1.	Rough cast plaster with natural cement finishing.	1 sq m	1. Mason—0.1 No. 2. Mazdoor—0.1 No. 3. Bhisti—0.1 No.	
2.	Pebble dash plaster with natural cement.	1 sq m	1. Mason—0.15 No. 2. Mazdoor—0.15 No. 3. Bhisti—0.15 No.	
3.	Making plinth protection, 50 mm pick cement concrete finished with neat cement.	1 sq m	1. Mason—0.2 No. 2. Mazdoor—0.4 No. 3. Bhisti—0.1 No.	
4.	Brick edging including grouting with cement mortar.	1 sq m	1. Mason—0.01 2. Mazdoor—0.01 3. Bhisti—0.05	
5.	Masonry in fire clay refractory bricks.	1 sq m	1. Mason—0.80 No. 2. Mazdoor—1.20 No.	
6.	Cutting chases in walls, for conduct pipe and filling the same.	per metre	1. Mason—0.05 No. 2. Mazdoor—0.05 No.	

Note : 1. Add for sundries
2. Add for contractor's profit and overhead @ 10%
3. Work out the cost of item.

Sanitary Installations (Internal)

Table 6.94

S. No.	*Description*	*Unit*	*Labour required*
1.	Fixing white water closet (W.C.) squatting pan (Indian type w.c. pan) size 580 mm, with 100 mm sand cast iron P or S trap, 12.5 litre high level C.I. flushing cistern with fittings R.S. brackets; 32 mm diameter alvanised steel telescopic flush pipe with fittings and clamps 25 mm G.I. overflow pipe (1.8 m) with specials and mosquito proof coupling and G.I. chain and pull complete including painting of cistern and fittings, cutting and making good the walls and floors where required.	each	1. Fitter—1.25 No. 2. Mason—0.50 No. 3. Mazdoor—1.00 No.
2.	Fixing white glazed fire clay single stall urinal with 5 litres C.I. automatic flushing cistern with fittings, R.S. brackets, standard size C.P. brass flush pipe spreaders with unions, and clamps (all in C.P. brass) C.I. trap with outlet grating and other couplings in C.P. brass including painting of cistern and fittings, cutting and making good the walls and floors where required.	each	1. Fitter—1.75 No. 2. Mason—1.75 No. 3. Mazdoor—4 No.
3.	Fixing, white wash basin size 630 × 450 mm with a pair of 15 mm C.P. brass pillar taps; R.S. brackets painted white, C.P. brass chain with rubber plug 32 mm C.P. brass waste 32 mm diameter C.P. brass trap and union complete including cutting and making good the walls where required.	each	1. Fitter—0.30 No. 2. Mason—0.30 No. 3. Mazdoor—0.60 No.
4.	Fixing kitchen sink size 600 × 450 × 150 mm with R.S. brackets, C.P. brass chain with rubber plug 40 mm; C.P brass waste and 40 mm C.P. brass trap with necessary unions complete, including painting the fittings, cutting and making good the walls where required.	each	1. Fitter—0.20 No. 2. Mason—0.30 No. 3. Mazdoor—0.50 No.
5.	Fixing teak wood draining board size 600 × 450 × 25 mm with 65 to 75 mm high skirting and beading, wax polished, supported on a pair of R.S. brackets painted complete.	each	1. Fitter—0.05 No. 2. Mason—0.15 No. 3. Mazdoor—0.20 No.
6.	Fixing one piece construction cast iron bath tub size 1700 mm × 740 mm × 440 mm, white vitreous enamelled inside and painted with enamel paint outside including integral over flow and with detachable feet, a pair of 120 mm C.P. brass pillar traps, 40 mm C.P. brass waste, 32 mm C.P. brass over flow, C.P. brass chain with rubber plug; 40 mm C.P. brass trap with union complete.	each	1. Fitter—0.50 No. 2. Mazdoor—1.00 No.
7.	Fixing 600 × 450 mm bevelled edge mirror of supperior glass complete with 6 mm thick asbestos sheet ground fixed to wooden cleat with C.P. brass screws and washers.	each	1. Carpenter—0.30 No. 2. Mazdoor—0.30 No.

S. No.	Description	Unit	Labour required
8.	Fixing 600 × 120 mm glass shelf with C.P. brass brackets and guard rail complete, fixed to wooden cleats with C.P. brass screws.	each	1. Carpenter—0.20 No 2. Mazdoor—0.20 No.
9.	Fixing C.P. brass towel rail complete with C.P. brass brackets fixed to wooden cleats with C.P. brass screws 600 × 20 mm size.	each	1. Carpenter—0.15 No. 2. Mazdoor—0.15 No.
10.	Fixing liquid soap glass container with C.P. brass led and brackets fixed to wooden cleats with C.P. brass screws.	each	1. Carpenter—0.10 No. 2. Mazdoor—0.10 No.
11.	Fixing sand cast iron soil, waste and vent pipes, 100 mm dia.	metre	1. Fitter—0.02 No. 2. Bandhani—0.01 No. 3. Mazdoor—0.04 No.
12.	Fixing M.S. holder bat clamps for 100 mm dia pipe.	each	1. Fitter—0.01 No. 2. Mazdoor—0.01 No.
13.	Fixing sand iron bend of required degree with access door insertion rubber washer 3 mm thick, bolts and nuts complete, 100 mm.	each	1. Fitter—0.01 No. 2. Mazdoor—0.01 No.
14.	Fixing sand cast iron plain bend of required degree, 100 mm.	each	1. Fitter—0.01 No. 2. Mazdoor—0.01 No.
15.	Fixing sand cast iron heel rest sanitary bend.	each	1. Fitter—0.01 No. 2. Mazdoor—0.01 No.
16.	Fixing sand cast iron single equal plain junction of required degree with access door, insertion rubber washer 3 mm thick, bolts and nuts complete, 100 × 100 × 100 mm.	each	1. Fitter—0.01 No. 2. Mazdoor—0.01 No.
17.	Fixing sand cast iron single equal plain junction of required degree, 100 × 100 × 100 mm	each	1. Fitter—0.01 No. 2. Mozdoor—0.01 No.
18.	Fixing sand cast iron off-sets, 100 mm with 100 mm projection.	each	1. Fitter—0.01 No. 2. Mazdoor—0.01 No.
19.	Fixing sand cast iron door piece, insertion rubber washer 3 mm thick, bolts and nuts complete, 100 mm	each	1. Fitter—0.01 No. 2. Mazdoor—0.01 No.
20.	Fixing sand cast iron terminal guard, 100 mm.	each	1. Fitter—0.01 No. 2. Mazdoor—0.01 No.
21.	Fixing sand cast iron collar 100 mm.	each	1. Fitter—0.01 No. 2. Mazdoor—0.01 No.
22.	Making lead caulked joints in sand cast iron pipes and fittings of 100 mm dia.	each	1. Fitter—0.10 No. 2. Mazdoor—0.01 No.
23.	Fixing M.S. stays and clamps for sand cast iron pipes of 100 mm dia.	each	1. Fitter—0.01 No. 2. Mazdoor—0.01 No.
24.	Fixing sand cast iron trap of self-cleansing design with sand cast iron screwed down or each hinged grating with or without vent iron complete including cutting and making good the walls and floors; 100 mm inlet and 100 mm outlet.	each	1. Mason—0.50 No. 2. Mazdoor—0.50 No.

Sanitary Installation (External)

Table 6.95

S. No.	*Description*	*Unit*	*Labour required*
1.	Laying and jointing glazed stoneware pipes wite stiff mixture of cement mortar in proportions of 1 : 1 (1 cement : 1 fine sand) including testing of joint etc. complete, 100 mm diameter.	metre	1. Mason—0.5 No. 2. Mazdoor—0.10 No. 3. Bhisti—0.02 No.
2.	Laying cement concrete 1 : 5 : 10 (1 cement : 5 fine sand : to graded stone aggregate 40 mm nominal size) alround S.W. pipes including bed concrete 15 cm thick. For 100 mm dia. S.W. pipe.	metre	1. Mason—0.02 No. 2. Mazdoor—0.04 No. 3. Bhisti—0.10 No.
3.	Fixing square-mouth S.W. gully trap complete with C.I. grating brick masonry chamber and water-light C.I. cover with frame of 300 × 300 mm size (inside) for 100 × 100 mm size-P type.	each	1. Mason—0.50 No. 2. Mazdoor—0.50 No. 3. Bhisti—0.10 No.
4.	Constructing brick masonry manhole with second class bricks in cement mortar 1 : 5 (1 cement : 5 fine sand) R.C.C. top slab inside plaster, making channels, and in finished with neat cement complete, inside size 90 × 80 cm and 60 cm deep, including C.I. cover with frame 455 × 610 mm. Internal dimensions.	each	1. Mason—1.5 No. 2. Mazdoor—3.0 No. 3. Bhisti—1.0 No.
5.	Constructing brick masonry circular type manhole 1.4 mm internal diameter with second class bricks in cement mortar 1 : 5; inside cement plaster with a floating coat of neat cement, R.C.C. top slab, making channels, nearly finished complete, 2.45 m deep with C.I. cover and frame.	each	1. Mason—2.0 No. 2. Mack smith—4.0 No. 3. Mazdoor—1.0 No.
6.	M.S. foot rests fixing in manholes with 20 × 20 × 10 cm cement concrete, with 20 mm diameter round bar.	each	1. Mason—0.10 No. 2. Mack smith—0.10 No. 3. Mazdoor—0.20 No.
7.	Making connection of drain or sewer line with existing manhole including breaking into and making good the walls, floors, etc.	each	1. Mason—0.15 No. 2. Mazdoor—0.15 No.
8.	Fixing R.C.C. spun iron shaft with cowl 140 mm and 200 mm internal and external dia. respectively at top, 300 and 450 mm internal and external dia, at the bottom and 9.10 m overall length, bottom 1.25 below ground level, fixed in a pit 90 × 90 cm × 1.5 m with cement concrete 1 : 4 : 8 mix, 25 cm in bed, and 20 cm alround, with top with in cement concrete 1 : 2 : 4 mix; including making connection with sewer manhole, complete.	each	1. Mason—2.00 No. 2. Bandhani—2.00 No. 3. Mazdoor—4.00 No. 4. Bhisti—1.00 No.
9.	Constructing brick masonry road gully chamber 50 × 45 × 60 cm including 500 × 450 mm C.I. horizontal grating with frame complete.	each	1. Mason—1.00 No. 2. Mazdoor—2.00 No. 3. Bhisti—0.50 No.
10.	Laying spun iron pipes (Class LA) for drainage.	metre	1. Fitter—0.10 No. 2. Mazdoor—0.10 No.

S. No.	Description	Unit	Labour required
11.	Constructing second class brick masonry open surface drain. In cement mortar 1 : 4 mix; including earth excavation, 10 cm thick bed concrete 1 : 5 : 10, and 25 mm thick cement concrete 1 : 2 : 4, for filling haunches, including 12 mm thick cement plaster with a floating coat of neat cement inside the drain complete 10 cm drain 20 cm average depth.	metre	1. Mason—1.00 No. 2. Mazdoor—1.50 No. 3. Bhisti—0.50 No.
12.	Cutting holes upto 30 × 30 cm in walls including making good the same.	each	1. Mason—0.50 No. 3. Mazdoor—1.50 No.
13.	Making soak pit 1.20 × 1.20 × 1.20 m, filled with brick bats including S.W. drain pipe 100 mm diameter and 1.20 m long complete.	each	1. Mazdoor—2.50 No. 2. Mason—0.50 No.
14.	Labour for cutting C.I. pipe with steel saw 100 mm dia. C.I. pipe	each cut	1. Fitter—0.05 No. 2. Mazdoor—0.05 No.

Water Supply (Internal)

Table 6.96

S. No.	Description	Unit	Labour required
1.	Fixing G.I. pipes complete with G.I. fittings and clamps including cutting and making good the walls etc. 15 mm nominal bore.	metre	1. Fitter—0.10 No. 2. Mazdoor—0.05 No.
2.	Fixing G.I. pipes complete with G.I, fittings including trenching and refilling etc. 15 mm nominal bore.	metre	1. Fitter—0.10 No. 2. Mazdoor—0.15 No.
3.	Making connection of G.I. distribution branch with G.I. main 25 mm to 40 mm nominal bore by fixing etc., including cutting and treading the pipe etc. complete.	each	1. Fitter—0.30 No. 2. Mazdoor—0.30 No.
4.	Fixing water meter and stop cock in G.I. pipe line including cutting and threading the pipe and making long screws etc. complete.	each	1. Fitter—0.30 No. 2. Mazdoor—0.30 No.
5.	Fixing brass bib cock, 15 mm nominal size.	each	1. Fitter—0.01 No. 2. Mazdoor—0.01 No.
6.	Fixing brass stop cock 15 mm nominal size.	each	1. Fitter—0.01 No. 2. Mazdoor—0.01 No.
7.	Fixing ball valves (brass) with copper floats 15 mm nominal size.	each	1. Fitter—0.01 No. 2. Mazdoor—0.10 No.
8.	Fixing brass ferrule C.I. mouth cover including boring and tapping the main 15 mm nominal size.	each	1. Fitter—0.10 No. 2. Mazdoor—0.10 No.
9.	Fixing lead connection pipe with brass unions, 30 mm tong, 15 mm nominal size.	each	1. Fitter—0.01 No. 2. Mazdoor—0.01 No.
10.	Fixing C.P. brass shower rose with 15 mm inlet, 100 mm diameter.	each	1. Fitter—0.01 No. 2. Mazdoor—0.01 No.
11.	Placing on terrace R.C.C. circular tank as per designs with covers and necessary holes, 270 litres capacity.	each	1. Bandhani—2.00 No. 2. Mazdoor—3.00 No.

S. No.	Description	Unit	Labour required
12.	Boring with 100 mm diameter casting pipe for tube well in all soils including removing the casting pipe after the tube well is lowered and tested.		
	(*i*) upto 6 m depth	metre	1. Fitter—0.10 No. 2. Mazdoor—0.01 No.
	(*ii*) beyond 6 m and upto 12 m depth	metre	1. Fitter—0.10 No. 2. Mazdoor—0.60 No.
	(*iii*) beyond 12 m and upto 18 m depth	metre	1. Fitter—0.15 No. 2. Mazdoor—0.10 No.
13.	Fixing hand pump in position, for 40 mm diameter G.I. pipe complete.	each	1. Fitter—0.10 No. 2. Mazdoor—0.10 No.
14.	Making chases upto 7.5 cm in walls including making good after housing G.I. pipe etc.	metre	1. Mason—0.10 No. 2. Mazdoor—0.20 No.

Water Supply (External)

Table 6.97

S. No.	Description	Unit	Labour required
1.	Excavating trenches of required width for pipes, including excavation for sockets, and dressing of sides, ramming of bottom, depth upto 1.5 metre, including getting out the excavated soil, and then returning the soil as required, in layers not exceeding 20 cm depth, including consolidating each deposited layer by ramming watering etc. and disposing off. Surplus excavated soil within a load of 50 m. In ordinary soil, pipes upto 300 mm dia.	metre	1. Mate—0.05 No. 2. Mazdoor—1.00 No. 3. Bhisti—0.05 No.
2.	Filling in trenches with sand including watering, ramming, consolidating and dressing complete.	cum	1. Mazdoor—0.20 No. 2. Bhisti—0.05 No.
3.	Laying in position centrifugally cast (spun) iron or vertically cast iron, S and S or flanged pipes.	quintal	1. Fitter—0.10 No. 2. Mazdoor—0.30 No.
4.	Laying in Position S and S or flanged C.I. special such as tees, bends, collars, tappers and caps etc.	quintal	1. Fitter—0.25 No. 2. Mazdoor—0.40 No.
5.	Fixing C.I. sluice valves class I (with caps) complete with bolts, nuts, rubber insertions etc. upto 300 mm dia.	each	1. Fitter—0.50 No. 2. Fitter—0.50 No.
6.	Fixing spindle fire hydrant with 65 mm outlet complete with bolts, nuts and rubber insertions etc.	each	1. Fitter—0.30 No. 2. Mazdoor—0.40 No.
7.	Constructing masonry chamber 60 × 60 × 75 cm inside with second class brickwork in cement mortar 1 : 5 mix for sluice valves or for fire Hydrants complete.	each	1. Mason—1.50 No. 2. Mazdoor—3.00 No. 3. Bhisti—0.50 No.
8.	Making lead caulked joints to span iron or C.I. pipes and special including testing of the joints upto 300 mm dia.	each	1. Fitter—0.10 No. 2. Mazdoor—0.10 No.
9.	Disinfecting C.I. water mains by flushing with water containing bleaching powder at 0.5 cm per litre of water and cleaning the same with fresh water, operation to be repeated three times upto 300 mm diameter C.I. pipe.	100 m	
10.	Fixing air relief valve complete with bolts, nuts and rubber insertion etc.	each	1. Fitter—1.00 No. 2. Mazdoor—1.00 No.

Road Work

Table 6.98

S. No.	Description	Unit	Labour required
1.	Preparation of sub-grade by excavating earth to an average of 30 cm depth, dressing to camber and consolidating with road roller including making good the undulation etc. and disposal of surplus earth lead upto 50 metres.	100 sq m	1. Mate—0.20 No. 2. Mazdoor—20.00 No. 3. Hire charges of road roller—0.06 day
2.	Consolidation of sub-grade with road roller including making good the undulation etc. with earth and resolving the subgrade.	100 sq m	1. Hire charges of road roller—0.06 day
3.	Stacking of stone for soling at site of work.	cum	1. Mazdoor—0.40 No.
4.	Laying stone soling including pacting with smaller stones and consolidation with road roller including spreading and consolidation of blinding material moorum or earth etc.	cum	1. Mazdoor—0.70 No. 2. Bhisti—0.20 No. 3. Hire charges of road rollar—0.006 day
5.	Stacking of moorum at site.	cum m	1. Mazdoor—0.40 No.
6.	Stacking stone aggregate 50 mm nominal size.	cum	1. Mazdoor—0.40 No.
7.	Stacking stone aggregate 63 mm nominal size.	cum	1. Mazdoor—0.40 No.
8.	Stacking of Red Bajri at site.	cum	1. Mazdoor—0.40 No.
9.	Laying wearing course with stone aggregate including screening, sorting, spreading to template and consolidation with road roller, complete including spreading and consolidation of blinding material.	cum	1. Mazdoor—0.50 No. 2. Bhisti—0.25 No. 3. Hire charges of road roller—0.033 day
10.	Second class brick edging in full brick width and half brick depth including excavation, refilling and disposal of surplus earth 1ead upto 50 metres.	metre	1. Mason—0.02 No. 2. Mozdoor—0.02 No.
11.	Scarifying metalled (water-bound) road surface including disposal of rubbish load upto 50 m and consolidation with road roller of the aggregate received from scarifying.	100 sq m	1. Mazdoor—2.50 No.
12.	Painting one coat with paving bitumen S-90, using 2.25 kg of bitumen per sq m with 1.65 cum of stone aggregate 12 mm nominal size per 100 sq m of road surface complete.	sq m	1. Mate—0.002 No. 2. Mazdoor—0.05 No. 3. Mistry—0.001 No. 4. Spray man—0.001 No. 5. Bhisti—0.001 No. 6. Hire charges of road rollar ; Boiler and Tar sprayer unit 0.001 each day
13.	Painting two coats with paving bitumen S-90, 2 kg of bitumen per sq m with 1.5 cum of stone aggregate 12 mm nominal size per 100 sq m of road surface, for first coat, and 1 kg of bitumen per sq m with 0.9 cum of stone aggregate 10 mm nominal size per 100 sq m of road surface for second coat complete.	sq m sq m sq m cum	1. Mate—0.002 No. 2. Mazdoor—0.08 No. 3. Mistry—0.002 No. 4. Bhisti—0.001 No. 5. Spray man—0.001 No. 6. Hire charges of road roller, Boiler and Tar spray unit 0.0015 each day

S. No.	Description	Unit	Labour required
14.	2.5 cm premix carpet surfacing with 3 cum of stone aggregate 10 mm nominal size per 100 sq m and bitumen emulsion using 96 kg per cum of aggregate including a tack coat of 1 kg bitumen emulsion per sq of road surface complete.	sq m	1. Mate—0.001 No. 2. Mazdoor—0.10 No. 3. Mistry—0.002 No. 4. Bhisti—0.001 No. 5. Hire charges (*i*) Road roller—0.001 day (*ii*) Boiler—0.0015 day (*iii*) Mixer—0.0005 day
15.	Seal coat, with paving bitument S-90, using 1.5 kg of bitumen per sq m with 1.05 cum of stone aggregate 10 mm nominal size per 100 sq m of road surface.	sq m	1. Mate—0.001 No. 2. Mazdoor—0.04 No. 3. Mistry—0.001 No. 4. Bhisti—0.001 No. 5. Spray man—0.005 No. 6. Hire charges (*i*) Road roller—0.005 day (*ii*) Tar spray unit—0.005 day
16.	Cement concrete 1 : 2 : 4 (1 cement : 2 coarse sand : 4 graded stone aggregate 40 mm nominal size) in pavements, roads, taxitracks and runway, laid to required slope and camber including consolidation, finishing and tamping complete.	cum	1. Mason—0.50 No. 2. Carpenter—0.25 No. 3. Mazdoor—3.00 No. 4. Bhisti—0.50 No.

Notes : 1. For calculating the cost of the item of work ; add, cost of material, labour charges, sundries, water charges, and contractor's profit and over head @ 10%.

2. One roller does 1860 sq m of consolidation per day of 8 hours and using 18 litres diesel of sub-grade.

3. One roller, does 170 cum consolidation per day of 8 hours and uses 18 litres of diesel of soling course.

4. The depth of soling layer, reduces by 25% after consolidation.

5. One roller does 30 cum consolidation per day of 8 hours and uses 18 litres of diesel of wearing course.

6. Steam coal for heating bitumen @ 2 quintal per tonne of bitumen.

7. One roller does 100 sq m consolidation per day of 8 hours and uses 18 litres of diesel of one coat painting.

8. One roller does 1000 sq m consolidation per day of 8 hours and uses 18 litres of diesel of first coat, and does 1600 sq m of second coat, in two coat painting.

7

Building Estimates

7.1. INTRODUCTION

In preparing the estimate of building normally following items of works are involved :

1. Earth work
2. Concrete work
3. Brick work upto plinth level
4. Damp, proof, course (D.P.C.)
5. Brick work in super structure
6. Doors and windows (wood work)
7. Roofing
8. Flooring
9. Finishing
10. Miscellaneous.

In each case the quantity of item is calculated with the help of given drawings. Few examples are given below.

Example 7.1. *Work out the quantities of* :

(*i*) *Earth work* (*ii*) *Cement concrete and* (*iii*) *Brick work*

From the given plan and section of a wall. (Refer Fig. 7.1)

Table 7.1. Details of Measurements

S. No.	*Description of item*	*No.*	*Length L*	*Breadth B*	*Depth or height D/H*	*Content*	*Remark*
1.	Earth work in excavation in foundation trenches in ordinary soil, lift upto 1.5 m						
	Wall	1	10.30	0.50	0.60	3.09	
				Total		3.09 cum	
2.	Cement concrete 1 : 5 : 10 mix in foundation						
	Wall	1	10.30	0.50	0.20	1.03	
				Total		1.03 cum	
3.	Second class brickwork in foundation and plinth in cement mortar 1 : 6 mix						
	Wall 1st Step	1	10.10	0.30	0.20	0.606	
	2nd Step	1	10.00	0.20	0.50	1.000	
				Total		1.606 cum	

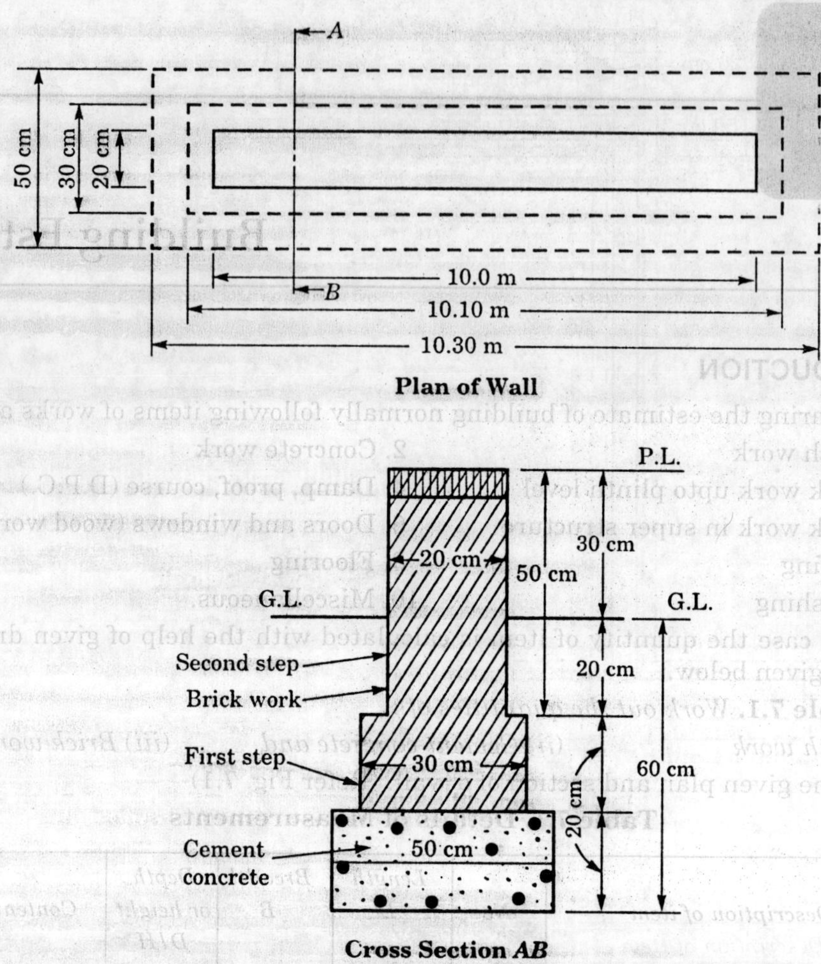

Fig. 7.1

Table 7.2. Abstract of Quantities

S. No.	Description of Item	Quantity	Remark
1.	Earth work in excavation in foundation trenches including dressing of sides and ramming of bottom, lift upto 1.5 m and include lead upto 50 m	3.09 cum	
2.	Laying cement concrete 1 : 5 : 10 (1 cement : 5 fine sand 10 graded stone agregate 40 mm nominal size)	1.03 cum	
3.	Second class brick in foundation and plinth in cement mortar 1 : 6 (1 cement : 6 find sand)	1.606 cum	

Example 7.2. *Calculate the quantities of the following items.*

(i) Earth work *(ii) Cement concrete* *(iii) Brick work.*

From the given plan and section of a wall. (Ref. Fig. 7.2)

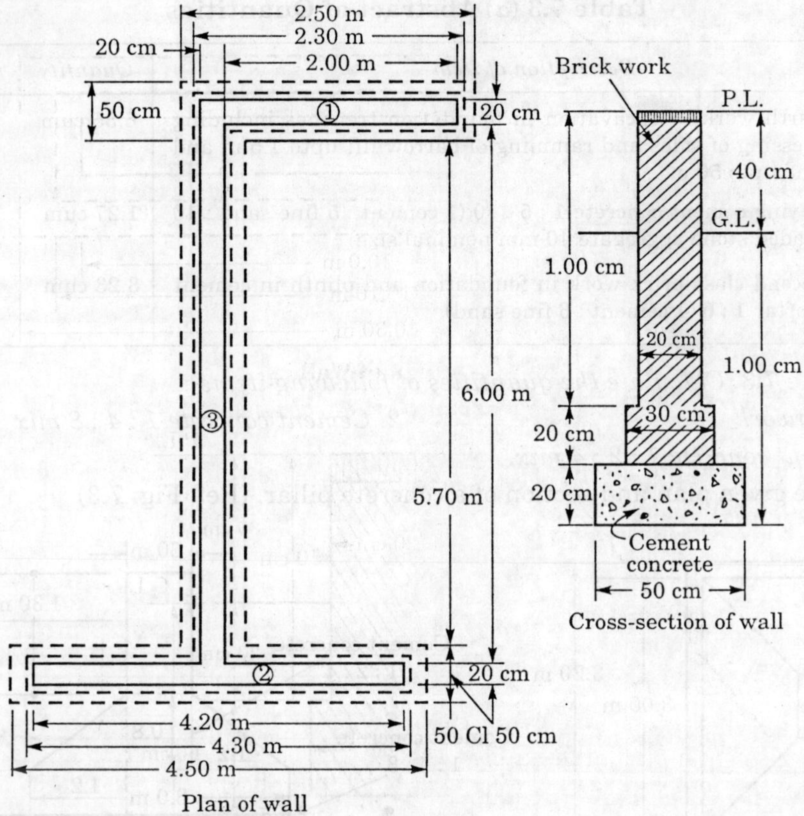

Fig. 7.2

Table 7.3. Abstract of Quantities

S. No.	*Description of Item*	*No.*	*L*	*B*	*D/H*	*Content*	*Remark*
1.	Earth work in excavation in foundation trenches in ordinary soil, lift upto 1.5 m						
	Wall No. 1	1	2.50	0.50	1.00	1.25	
	Wall No. 2	1	4.50	0.50	1.00	2.25	
	Wall No. 3	1	5.70	0.50	1.00	2.85	
					Total	6.35 cum	
2.	Cement concrete 1 : 5 : 10 mix in foundation						
	Wall No. 1	1	2.50	0.50	0.20	0.25	
	Wall No. 2	1	4.50	0.50	0.20	0.45	
	Wall No. 3	1	5.70	0.50	0.20	0.57	
					Total	1.27 cum	
3.	Second class brick work in foundation and plinth in cement mortar 1 : 6 mix						
	Wall No. 1 1st Step	1	2.30	0.30	0.20	0.138	
	2nd Step	1	2.20	0.20	1.00	0.440	
	Wall No. 2 1st Step	1	4.30	0.30	0.20	0.258	
	2nd Step	1	4.20	0.20	1.00	0.840	
	Wall No. 3 1st Step	1	5.90	0.30	0.20	0.354	
	2nd Step	1	6.00	0.20	1.00	1.200	
					Total	3.230 cum	

Table 7.3 (*a*) Abstract of Quantities

S. No.	*Description of Item*	*Quantity*	*Remark*
1.	Earth work in excavation in foundation trenches including dressing of sides and ramming of barrow lift upto 1.5 m and lead upto 50 m	6.35 cum	
2.	Laying cement concrete 1 : 5 : 10 (1 cement : 5 fine sand : 10 graded stone aggregate 40 mm nominal size)	1.27 cum	
3.	Second class brick work in foundation and plinth in cement mortar 1 : 6 (1 cement : 6 fine sand)	3.23 cum	

Example 7.3. *Calculate the quantities of following items :*

1. Earthwork *2. Cement concrete 1 : 4 : 8 mix*

3. Cement concrete 1 : 2 : 4 mix.

From the given plan and section of a concrete pillar. (Ref. Fig. 7.3)

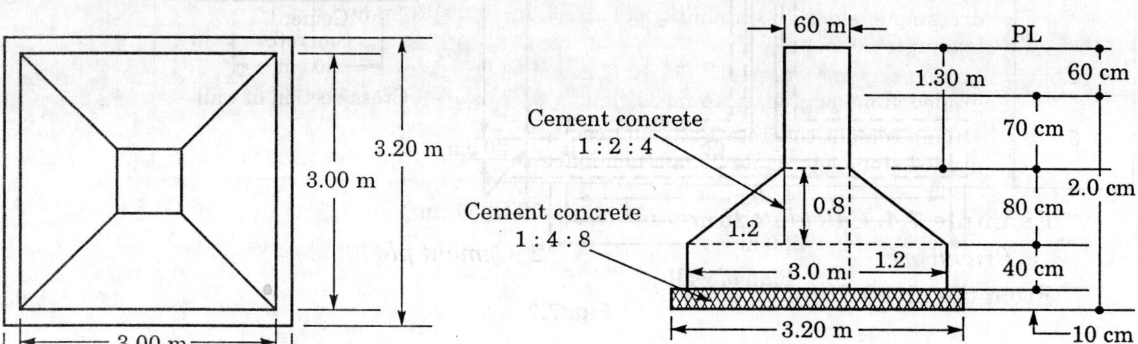

Fig. 7.3

Table 7.4. Details of Measurements

S. No.	*Description of item*	*No.*	*L*	*B*	*D/H*	*Content*	*Remark*
1.	Earth work in excavation in foundation trenches in ordinary soil; Lift upto 1.5 m						
	Pillar	1	3.20	3.20	2.00	20.48	
	Total					20.48 cum	
2.	Cement concrete 1 : 5 : 10 mix in foundation						
	Pillar Base	1	3.20	3.20	0.10	1.024	
	Total					1.024 cum	

S. No.	Description	No.	L	B	H	Quantity	Remarks
3.	Cement concrete 1 : 2 : 4 mix. in foundation and Plinth.						
	Pillar Base	1	3.00	3.00	0.40	3.60	
	Frustom of pyramid $= \frac{h}{6}(A_1 + A_2 + 4A_m)$ $= \frac{0.80}{6}\{3 \times 3 + 0.6 \times 0.6 + 4 \times \left(\frac{3+0.6}{2}\right) \times \left(\frac{3+0.6}{2}\right)\}$	1				2.976	
	Square Pillar	1	0.60	0.60	1.30	0.468	
	Total					7.044 cum	

Table 7.5. Abstract of Quantities

S. No.	*Description of Item*	*Quantity*	*Remark*
1.	Earthwork in excavation in foundation trenches including dressing of sides and ramming of bottom, lift upto 1.5 m and lead upto 50 m.	20.48 cum	
2.	Laying cement concrete 1 : 5 : 10 (1 cement : 5 fine sand : 10 graded stone aggregate 40 mm nominal size)	1.024 cum	
3.	Laying cement concrete 1 : 2 : 4 (1 cement : 2 coarse sand : 4 graded stone aggregate 20 mm nominal size)	7.044 cum	

Example 7.4. *Calculate the quantities of following items :*

1. *Brickwork*
2. *Cement plaster*

From the given drawing of steps.

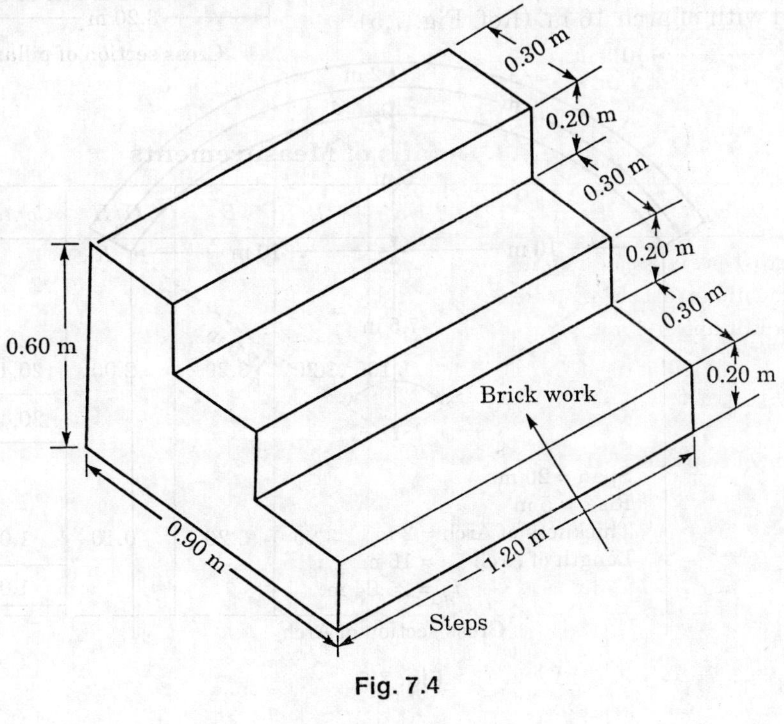

Fig. 7.4

Table 7.6. Details of Measurements

S. No.	*Description of Item*	*No.*	*L*	*B*	*D/H*	*Content*	*Remark*
1.	Second class brick work in steps in cement mortar 1 : 6 mix						
	1st Step	1	1.20	0.30	0.20	0.072	
	2nd Step	1	1.20	0.30	0.40	0.144	
	3rd Step	1	1.20	0.30	0.60	0.216	
	Total					0.432 cum	
2.	12 mm cement plaster 1 : 3 (1 cement : 3 fine sand)						
	Steps front vertical surfaces	3	1.20	0.20		0.72	
	Horizontal surfaces	3	1.20	0.30		1.08	
	Back vertical surface	1	1.20	0.60		0.72	
	Side surfaces 1st Step	2	0.30	0.20		0.12	
	2nd Step	2	0.30	0.40		0.24	
	3rd Step	2	0.30	0.60		0.36	
	Total					3.24 m^2	

Table 7.7. Abstract of Quantities

S. No.	*Description of Item*	*Quantity*	*Remark*
1.	Second class brick work in steps in cement mortar 1 : 6 (1 cement : 6 coarse sand)	0.432 cum	
2.	12 mm cement plaster 1 : 3 (1 cement : 3 fine sand)	3.24 sq m	

Example 7.5. *Calculate the quantities of the following items :*

1. *Brick work* 2. *Plaster on intrados.*

From the given drawing of a bridge arch 20 m. span, with rise 1/4th of span, thickness of arch 2 m. and with of arch 16 m. (Ref. Fig. 7.5)

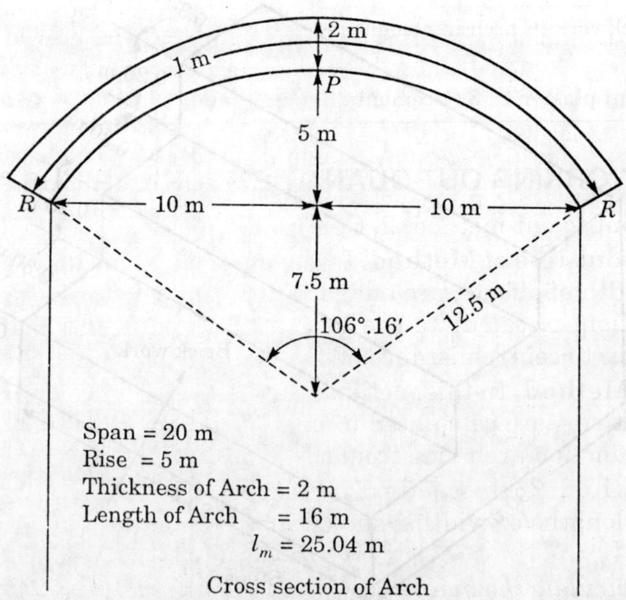

Fig. 7.5

Table 7.8. Details of Measurements

S. No.	*Description of Item*	*No.*	*L*	*B*	*D/H*	*Content*	*Remark*
1.	1st class brick work in arch in cement mortar 1 : 3 mix.						
	Radius of arch = OP						
	$(10 \times 10) = [5 \times (2\,OP—5)]$						
	$OP' = 12.5$ m						
	$OR = (12.5 + 1.0) = 13.5$ m						
	Mean length $= lm$						
	Angle at centre = 106° 16′						
	(Calculated with natural tangents)						
	$\dfrac{lm}{106° - 16'} = \dfrac{2\pi R}{360°}$						
	$lm = \dfrac{2 \times \pi \times 13.5 \times 106° 16'}{360°}$ m						
	= 25.04 m	1	25.04	16.00	2.00	801.28	
	Total					801.28 cum	
2.	12 mm cement plaster 1 : 3 mix.						
	Width = 1						
	$\dfrac{2\pi \times 12.5 \times 106° 16'}{360°} = 23.18$ m						
		1	23.18	16.00		370.88	
	Total					370.88 sq m	

Table 7.9. Abstract of Quantities

S. No.	*Description of Item*	*Quantity*	*Remark*
1.	Ist class brickwork in arch in cement mortar 1 : 3 (1 cement : 3 coarse sand)	801.28 cum	
2.	12 mm cement plaster 1 : 3 (1 cement : 3 coarse sand)	370.88 sq m	

7.2. METHODS OF WORKING OUT QUANTITIES FOR VARIOUS ITEMS OF WORKS

1. In-to-in and out to out method. 2. Centre line method. 3. Crossing method.

1. **In-to-in and out-to-out Method.** In this method, to calculate the length of the wall in one direction, the width of offsets, are added in the centre to centre distance, of that wall; and in the other direction, to calculate the length of the wall, the width of the offsets are deducted from the centre to centre distance of that wall. This method is largely used.

2. **Centre line Method.** In this method, the centre to centre distances of the walls, in one and the other directions, are calculated to find out the quantities, and reductions for the half width, for each T-junction are made from the worked out centre to centre distance.

3. **Crossing method.** In this method the lengths of the walls in both the directions are taken according to the lengths/or widths; shown in the plan of the building, to calculate the quantities.

Example 7.6. *Calculate the quantities of the following items :*

1. *Earthwork.* 2. *Concrete work* 3. *Brickwork.*

From the given plan and section of the wall by using all the three methods of working out quantities of a room. (Ref. Fig. 7-6)

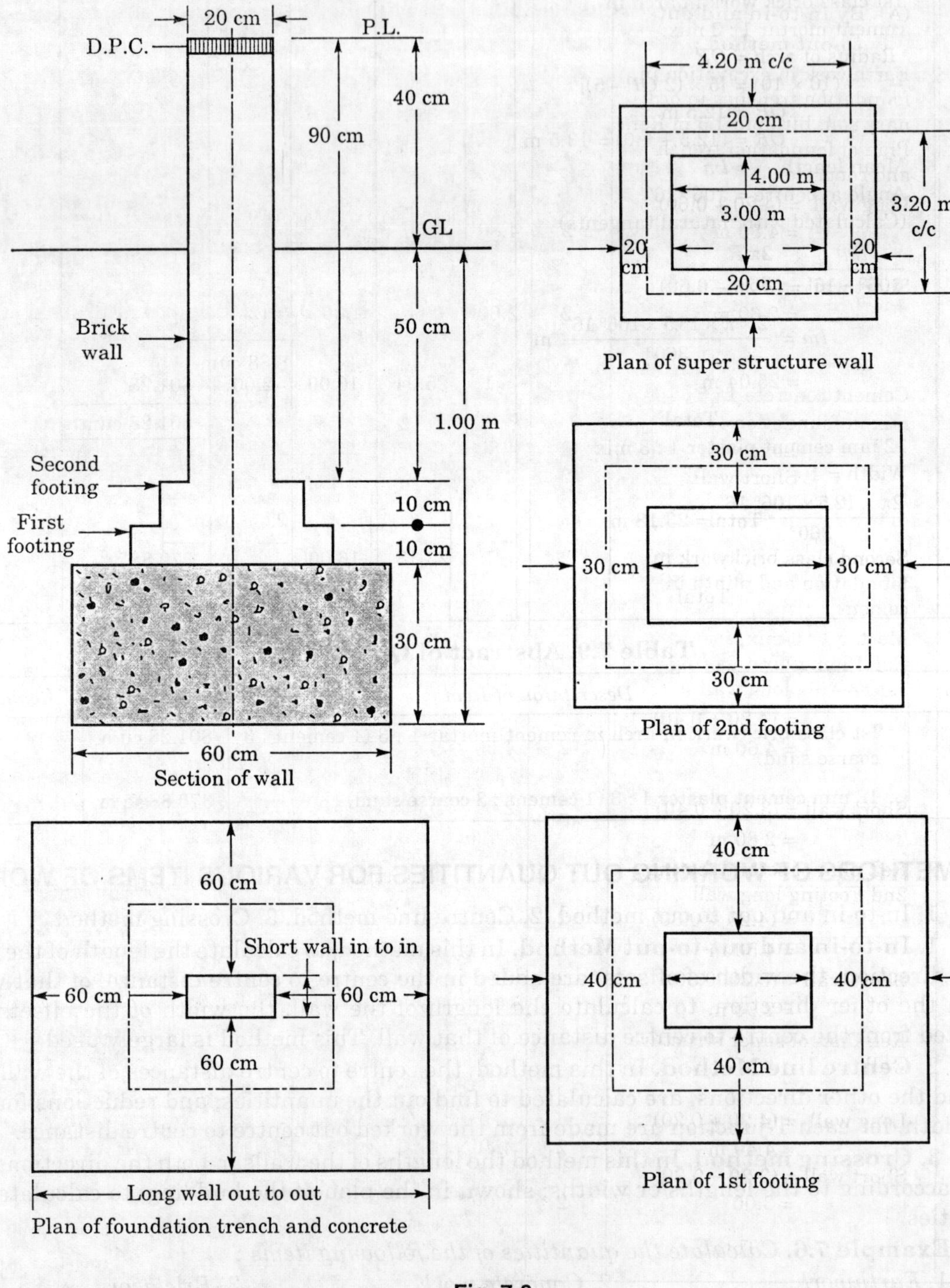

Fig. 7.6

Table 7.10. Detailed of Measurements

S. No.	Description of Item	No.	L	W	H/D	Contents	Remark
	(A) By in-to-in and out-to-out method :						
1.	Earthwork in excavation in foundation trenches in ordinary soil, lift upto 1.5 m Ref. Plan of foundation trench and concrete.						
	Long wall = (4.20 + 0.60) = 4.80 m	2	4.80	0.60	1.00	5.76	c/c distance = 4.20 width =0.60 m
	Short wall = (3.20 – 0.60) = 2.60 m	2	2.60	0.60	1.00	3.12	c/c distance = 3.20 m width = 0.60 m
	Total					8.88 cum	
2.	Cement concrete 1 : 5 : 10 mix in foundation						
	Long wall	2	4.80	0.60	0.30	1.728	
	Short wall	2	2.60	0.60	0.30	0.935	
	Total					2.664 cum	
3.	Second class brickwork in foundation and plinth in cement Mortar 1 : 6 mix Ref. Plan of first footing 1st Footing long wall = (4.20 + 0.40) = 4.60 m	2	4.60	0.40	0.10	0.368	c/c distance = 4.20 m width = 0.40 m
	Short wall = (3.20 – 0.40) = 2.80 m	2	2.80	0.40	0.10	0.224	c/c distance = 3.20 m width = 0.40 m
	Ref. plan of second footing 2nd Footing long wall = (4.20 + 0.30) = 4.50 m	2	4.50	0.30	0.10	0.270	c/c distance = 4.20 m width = 0.30 m
	Short wall = (3.20. 0.30) = 2.90 m	2	2.90	0.30	0.10	0.174	c/c distance = 3.20 m width = 0.30 m
	Ref. Plan of super structure wall						c/c distance = 4.20 m width = 0.20 m
	Long wall = (4.20 + 0.20) = 4.40 m	2	4.40	0.20	0.90	1.584	c/c distance = 3.20 m width = 0.20 m
	Short wall = (3.20 – 0.20) = 3.00	2	3.00	0.20	0.90	1.080	
	Total					3.70 cum	

(Contd.)

S. No.	Description of Item	No.	L	W	H/D	Contents	Remark
	(B) By centre line method :						
1.	Earthwork in excavation, in foundation trenches in ordinary soil, lift upto 1.5 m.						
	Long wall	2	4.20	0.60	1.00	5.04	c/c distance = 4.20 m
	Short wall	2	3.20	0.60	1.00	3.84	c/c distance = 3.20 m
	Total					8.88 cum	
2.	Cement concrete 1 : 5 : 10 mix in foundation						
	Long wall	2	4.20	0.60	0.30	1.512	
	Short wall	2	3.20	0.60	0.30	1.152	
	Total					2.664 cum	
3.	Second class brickwork in foundation and plinth in cement mortar 1 : 6 mix.						
	1st Footing Long wall	2	4.20	0.40	0.10	0.336	
	Short wall	2	3.20	0.40	0.10	0.256	
	2nd Footing Long wall	2	4.20	0.30	0.10	0.252	
	Short wall	2	3.20	0.30	0.10	0.192	
	Super structure wall						
	Long wall	2	4.20	0.20	0.90	1.512	
	Short wall	2	3.20	0.20	0.90	1.152	
	Total					3.700 cum	
	(C) By crossing method :						
1.	Earthwork in excavation, in foundation trenches, in ordinary soil, lift upto 1.5 m						
	Long wall (4.00 + 0.20 + 0.20)	2	4.40	0.60	1.00	5.28	
	Short wall	2	3.00	0.60	1.00	3.60	Ref. plan of super-structure
	Total					8.88 cum	
2.	Cement concrete 1 : 5 : 10 mix in foundation						
	Long wall	2	4.40	0.60	0.30	1.584	
	Short wall	2	3.00	0.60	0.30	1.080	
	Total					2.664 cum	
3.	Second class brick work in foundation and plinth, in cement mortar 1 : 6 mix						
	1st Footing Long wall	2	4.40	0.40	0.10	0.352	
	Short wall	2	3.00	0.40	0.10	0.240	
	2nd Footing Long wall	2	4.40	0.30	0.10	0.264	
	Short wall	2	3.00	0.30	0.10	0.180	
	Super structure wall						
	Long wall	2	4.40	0.20	0.90	1.584	
	Short wall	2	3.00	0.20	0.90	1.080	
	Total					3.700 cum	

Table 7.10 (a) Abstract of Quantities

S. No.	Description of Item	Quantity by in-to-in and out-to-out method	Quantity by centre line method	Quantity by crossing method
1.	Earthwork in excavation in foundation trenches including dressing of sides and ramming of bottom, lift upto 1.5 m and lead upto 50 m	8.88 cum	8.88 cum	8.88 cum
2.	Laying cement concrete 1 : 5 : 10 (1 cement : 5 fine sand : 10 graded stone 40 mm nominal size.)	2.664 cum	2.664 cum	2.664 cum
3.	Second class brick work in foundation and plinth in cement mortar 1 : 6 (1 cement : 6 fine sand)	3.70 cum	3.70 cum	3.70 cum

Example 7.7. *Calculate the quantities of the following items :*

(1) Earthwork. *(2) Concrete work,* *(3) Brickwork,*

From the given plan and section of the wall by using all the three methods of working out quantities of a room. (Ref. Fig. 7.7)

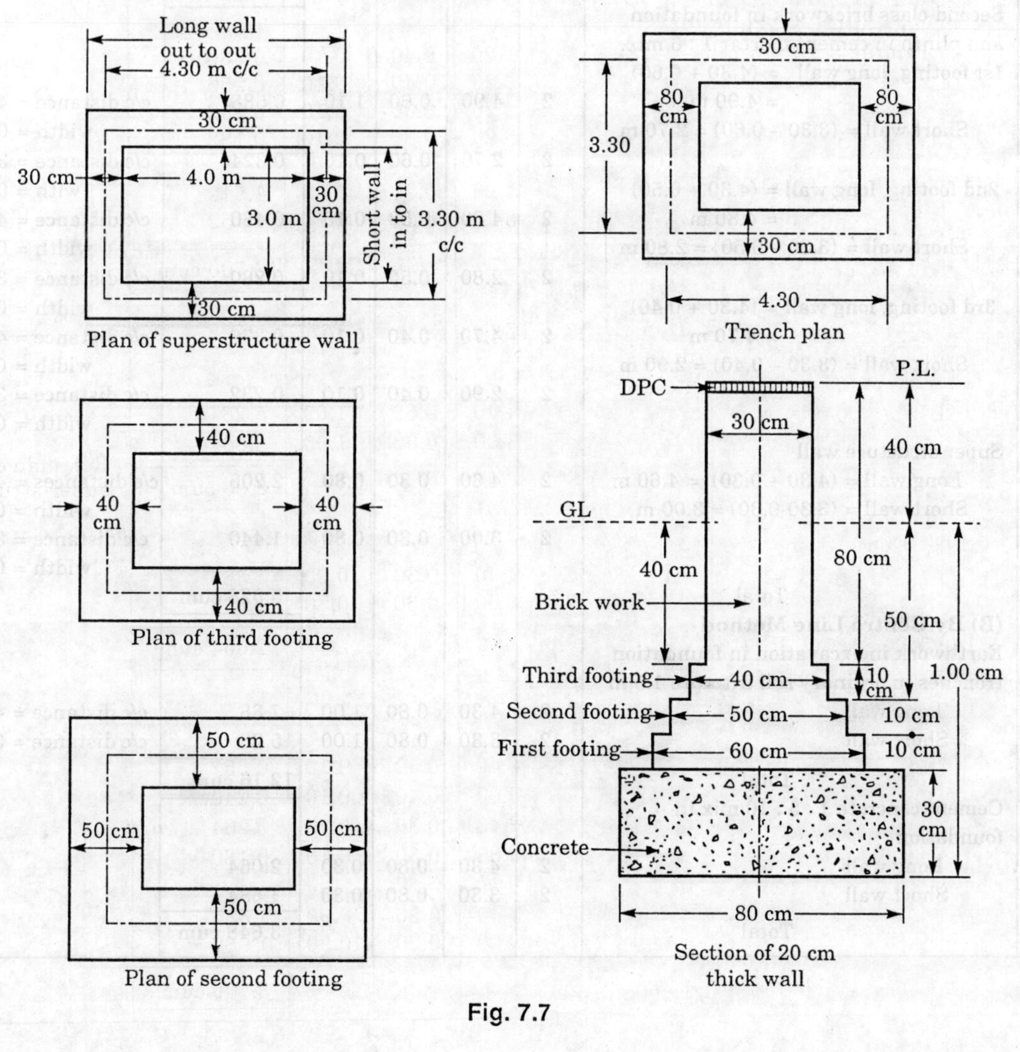

Fig. 7.7

Table 7.11. Details of Measurements

S. No.	*Description*	*No.*	*L*	*W*	*H/D*	*Contents*	*Remark*
	(A) By in-to-in and out-to-out method						
1.	Earthwork in excavation in foundation trenches in ordinary soil, lift upto 1.5 m						
	Long wall = (4.30 + 0.80) = 5.10 m	2	5.10	0.80	1.00	8.16	c/c distance = 4.30 m width = 0.80 m
	Short wall = (3.30 – 0.80) = 2.50 m	2	2.50	0.80	1.00	4.00	c/c distance = 3.30 m width = 0.80 m
	Total					12.16 cum	
2.	Cement concrete 1 : 5 : 10 mix in foundation						
	Long wall	2	5.10	0.80	0.30	2.448	
	Short wall	2	2.50	0.80	0.30	1.200	
	Total					3.648 cum	
3.	Second class brickwork in foundation and plinth in cement mortar 1 : 6 mix.						
	1st footing, long wall = (4.30 + 0.60) = 4.90 m	2	4.90	0.60	1.10	0.588	c/c distance = 4.30 m width = 0.60 m
	Short wall = (3.30 – 0.60) = 2.70 m	2	2.70	0.60	0.10	0.324	c/c distance = 3.30 m with = 0.60 m
	2nd footing, long wall = (4.30 + 0.50) = 4.80 m	2	4.80	0.50	0.10	0.480	c/c distance = 4.30 m width = 0.50 m
	Short wall = (3.30 – 0.50) = 2.80 m	2	2.80	0.50	0.10	0.280	c/c distance = 3.30 m width = 0.50 m
	3rd footing, long wall = (4.30 + 0.40) = 4.70 m	2	4.70	0.40	0.10	0.376	c/c distance = 4.30 m width = 0.40 m
	Short wall = (3.30 – 0.40) = 2.90 m	2	2.90	0.40	0.10	0.232	c/c distance = 3.30 m width = 0.40 m
	Super structure wall						
	Long wall = (4.30 + 0.30) = 4.60 m	2	4.60	0.30	0.80	2.208	c/c distances = 4.30 m width = 0.30 m
	Short wall = (3.30-0.30) = 3.00 m	2	3.00	0.30	0.80	1.440	c/c distance = 3.30 m width = 0.30 m
	Total					5.928 cum	
	(B) By Centre Line Method						
1.	Earthwork in excavation in foundation trenches in ordinary soil lift upto 1.5 m						
	Long wall	2	4.30	0.80	1.00	7.88	c/c distance = 4.30 m
	Short wall	2	3.30	0.80	1.00	5.28	c/c distance = 3.30 m
	Total					12.16 cum	
2.	Cement concrete 1 : 5 : 10 mix in foundation						
	Long wall	2	4.30	0.80	0.30	2.064	
	Short wall	2	3.30	0.80	0.30	1.584	
	Total					3.648 cum	

3.	Second class brick work in foundation and plinth in cement mortar 1 : 6 mix						
	1st footing Long wall	2	4.30	0.60	0.10	0.516	
	Short wall	2	3.30	0.60	0.10	0.396	
	2nd footing Long wall	2	4.30	0.50	0.10	0.430	
	Short wall	2	3.30	0.50	0.10	0.330	
	3rd footing Long wall	2	4.30	0.40	0.10	0.344	
	Short wall	2	3.30	0.40	0.10	0.264	
	Super structure wall						
	Long wall	2	4.30	0.30	0.80	2.064	
	Short wall	2	3.30	0.30	0.80	1.584	
	Total					5.928 cum	
	(C) By Crossing Method						
1.	Earthwork in excavation in foundation trenches in ordinary soil lift upto 1.5 m						
	Long wall	2	4.60	0.80	1.00	7.36	
	Short wall	2	3.00	0.80	1.00	4.80	
	Total					12.16 cum	
2.	Cement concrete 1 : 5 : 10 mix in foundation						
	Long wall	2	4.60	0.80	0.30	2.208	
	Short wall	2	3.00	0.80	0.30	1.440	
	Total					3.648 cum	
3.	Second class brick work in foundation and plinth in cement mortar 1 : 6 mix						
	1st footing Long wall	2	4.60	0.60	0.10	0.552	
	Short wall	2	3.00	0.60	0.10	0.360	
	2nd footing Long wall	2	4.60	0.50	0.10	0.460	
	Short wall	2	3.00	0.50	0.10	0.300	
	3rd footing Long wall	2	4.60	0.40	0.10	0.368	
	Short wall	2	3.00	0.40	0.10	0.240	
	Super structure wall						
	Long wall	2	4.60	0.30	0.80	2.208	
	Short wall	2	3.00	0.30	0.80	1.440	
	Total					5.928 cum	

Table 7.12. Abstract of Quantities

S. No.	*Description of Item*	*Quantity by in-to-in and out-to-out method*	*Quantity by centre line method*	*Quantity by crossing method*
1.	Earthwork in excavation in foundation trenches including dressing of sides and ramming of bottom, lift upto 1.5 m and lead upto 50 m	12.16 cum	2.16 cum	12.16 cum
2.	Laying cement concrete 1 : 5 : 10 (1 cement : 5 fine sand : 10 graded stone aggregate 40 mm nominal size)	3.648 cum	3.648 cum	3.648 cum
3.	Second class brick work in foundation and plinth in cement mortar 1 : 6 (1 cement : 6 fine sand)	5.928 cum	5.928 cum	5.928 cum

Example 7.8. *Calculate the quantities of the following items :*

(*1*) *Earthwork* (*2*) *Concrete work* (*3*) *Brick work*

from the given plan and section of 20 cm thick wall as in example 7.6, by using all the three methods of working out quantities of the rooms. (Ref. Fig. 7.8)

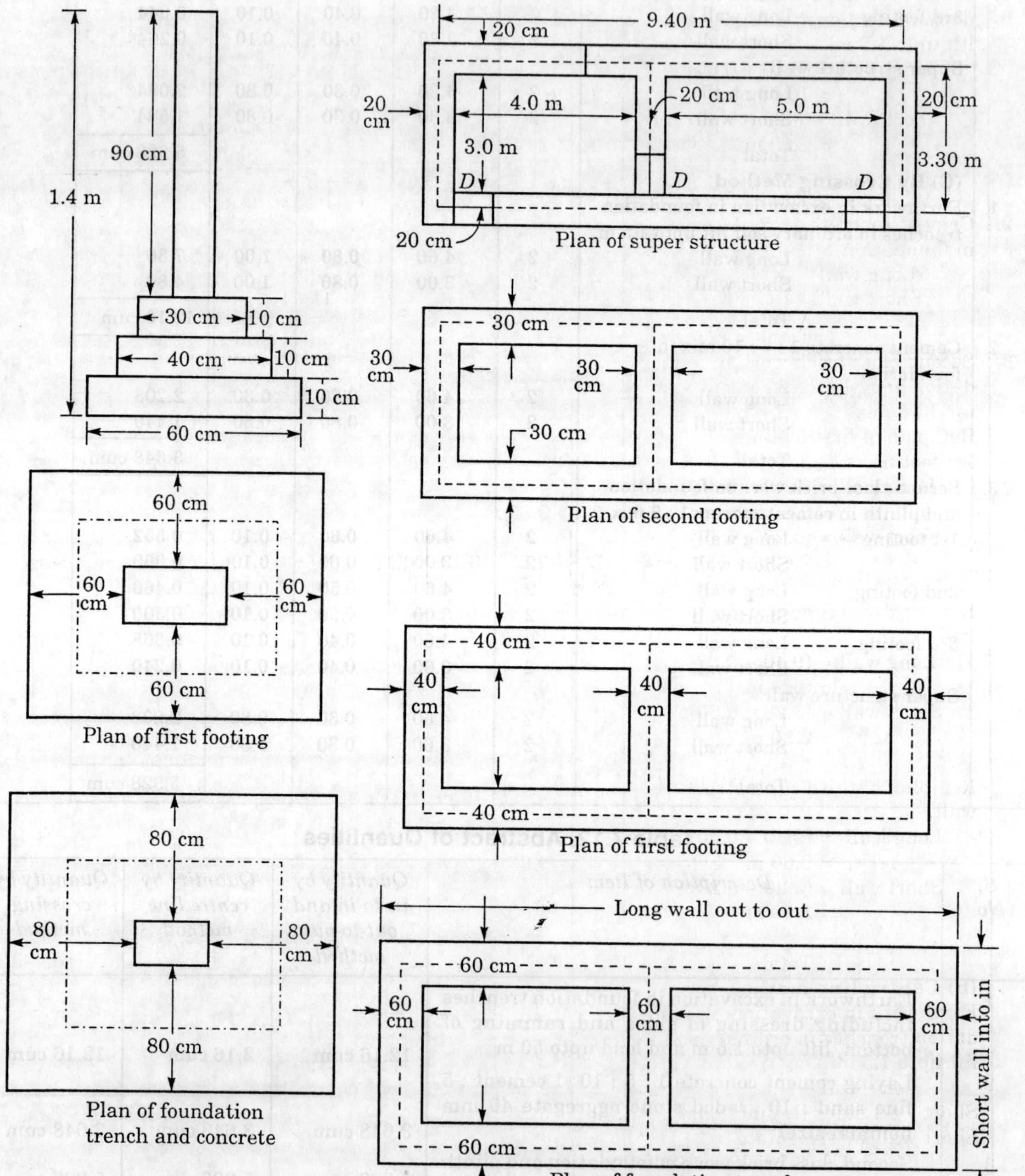

Fig. 7.8

Table 7.13. Details of Measurements

S. No.	Description of Item	No.	L	W	H/D	Content	Remarks
	(a) By into-in and out to out method						
1.	Earthwork in excavation in foundation trenches in ordinary soil, lift upto 1.5 m.						
	Long wall = (9.40 + 0.60) = 10.00 m	2	10.00	0.60	1.00	12.00	c/c distance = 9.40 m width = 0.60 m
	Short wall = (3.20 – 0.60) = 2.60 m	3	2.60	0.60	1.00	4.68	c/c distance = 3.20 m width = 0.60 m
	Total					17.68 cum	
2.	Cement concrete 1 : 5 : 10 mix in foundation						
	Long wall	2	10.00	0.60	0.30	3.600	
	Short wall	3	2.60	0.60	0.30	1.404	
	Total					5.004 cum	
3.	Second class brick work in foundation and plinth in cement mortar 1 : 6 mix.						
	Ref. plan of first footing						
	1st footing,						
	Long wall = (9.40 + 0.40) = 9.80 m	2	9.80	0.40	0.10	0.784	c/c distance = 9.40 m width = 0.40 m
	Short wall = (3.20 – 0.40) = 2.80 m	3	2.80	0.40	0.10	0.336	c/c distance = 3.20 m width = 0.40 m
	Ref. plan of second footing						
	2nd footing,						
	Long wall = (9.40 + 0.30) = 9.70 m	2	9.70	0.30	0.10	0.582	c/c distance = 9.40 m width = 0.30 m
	Short wall = (3.20 – 0.30) = 2.90 m	3	2.90	0.30	0.10	0.261	c/c distance = 3.20 m width = 0.30 m
	Ref. plan of third superstructure wall.						
	Long wall = (9.40 + 0.20) = 9.60 m	2	9.60	0.20	0.90	3.456	c/c distance = 9.40 m width = 0.20 m
	Short wall = (3.20 – 0.20) = 3.00 m	3	3.00	0.20	0.90	1.620	c/c distance = 3.20 m width = 0.20 m
	Total					7.039 cum	
	(b) Centre line method						
	Earthwork in excavation, in foundation trenches in ordinary soil, lift upto 1.5 m.						
	Long wall	2	9.40	0.60	1.00	11.280	c/c distance = 9.40 m
	Short wall Sides (L-junctions)	2	3.20	0.60	1.00	3.840	c/c distance = 3.20 m
	Short wall Intermediate = (3.20 – 2 × 0.30) = 2.60 (T-junction)	1	2.60	0.60	1.00	1.560	for each T-junction deduct 1/2 width. *i.e.* 0.60 × 1/2 = 0.30 m
	Total					17.68 cum	

(Contd.)

2.	Cement concrete 1 : 5 : 10 mix in foundation.						
	Long wall	2	9.40	0.60	0.30	3.384	
	Short wall	2	3.20	0.60	0.30	1.152	
	Short wall	1	2.60	0.60	0.30	0.468	
	Total					5.004 cum	
3.	Second class brick work in foundation and plinth in cement mortar 1 : 6 mix						
	1st footing.						
	Long wall	2	9.40	0.40	0.10	0.752	Deduct for 2 No. of T-junctions = 1/2 width of footing.
	Short wall	2	3.20	0.40	0.10	0.256	
	Short wall	1	2.80	0.40	0.10	0.112	
	(3.20 – 2 × 0.20) = 2.80 m						
	2nd footing						
	Long wall	2	9.40	0.30	0.10	0.564	Deduct for 2 No. of T-junctions.
	Short wall	2	3.20	0.30	0.10	0.192	
	Short wall	1	2.90	0.30	0.10	0.087	
	(3.20 – 2 × 0.15) = 2.90 m						
	Superstructure wall						
	Long wall	2	9.40	0.20	0.90	3.384	Deduct for 2 No. of T-junctions.
	Short wall	2	3.20	0.20	0.90	1.152	
	Short wall	1	3.00	0.20	0.90	0.540	
	(3.20 – 2 × 0.10) = 3.00 m						
	Total					7.039 cum	
	(c) By crossing method						
1.	Earthwork in excavation, in foundation trenches in ordinary soil, lift upto 1.5 m						
	Long wall = (4.00 + 5.00 + 0.20 + 0.20 + 20) = 9.60 m	2	9.60	0.60	1.00	11.52	
	Short wall	3	3.00	0.60	1.00	5.40	
	Total					16.92 cum	
2.	Cement concrete 1 : 5 : 10 mix in foundation						
	Long wall	2	9.60	0.60	0.30	3.456	
	Short wall	3	3.00	0.60	0.30	1.08	
	Total					4.536 cum	
3.	Second class brickwork in foundation and plinth in cement mortar 1 : 6 mix						
	1st footing						
	Long wall	2	9.60	0.40	0.10	0.768	
	Short wall	3	3.00	0.40	0.10	0.360	
	2nd footing						
	Long wall	2	9.60	0.30	0.10	0.576	
	Short wall	3	3.00	0.30	0.10	0.270	
	Superstructure wall						
	Long wall	2	9.60	0.20	0.90	3.456	
	Short wall	3	3.00	0.20	0.90	1.620	
	Total					7.050 cum	

Table 7.14. Abstract of Quantitites

S. No.	*Description of Item*	*Quantity by in-to-in and out-to-out method*	*Quantity by centre line method*	*Quantity by crossing method*
1.	Earthwork in excavation in foundation trenches including dressing of sides and ramming of bottom, lift upto 1.5 m and lead upto 50 m.	16.68 cum	16.68 cum	16.92 cum
2.	Laying cement concrete 1 : 5 : 10 (1 cement : 5 fine sand : 10 graded stone aggregate 40 mm nominal size).	5.004 cum	5.004 cum	4.536 cum
3.	Second class brickwork in foundation and plinth in cement mortar 1 : 6 (1 cement : 6 fine sand)	7.039 cum	7.039 cum	7.050 cum

Example 7.9. *Calculate the quantities of the following items :*

1. Earthwork. *2. Concrete work.*
3. Brickwork in foundation and plinth. *4. D.P.C.*
5. Brick work in superstructure. *6. Concrete coping.*
7. Cement pointing.

From the given plan and cross-sections of a compound wall. (Ref. Fig. 7.9)

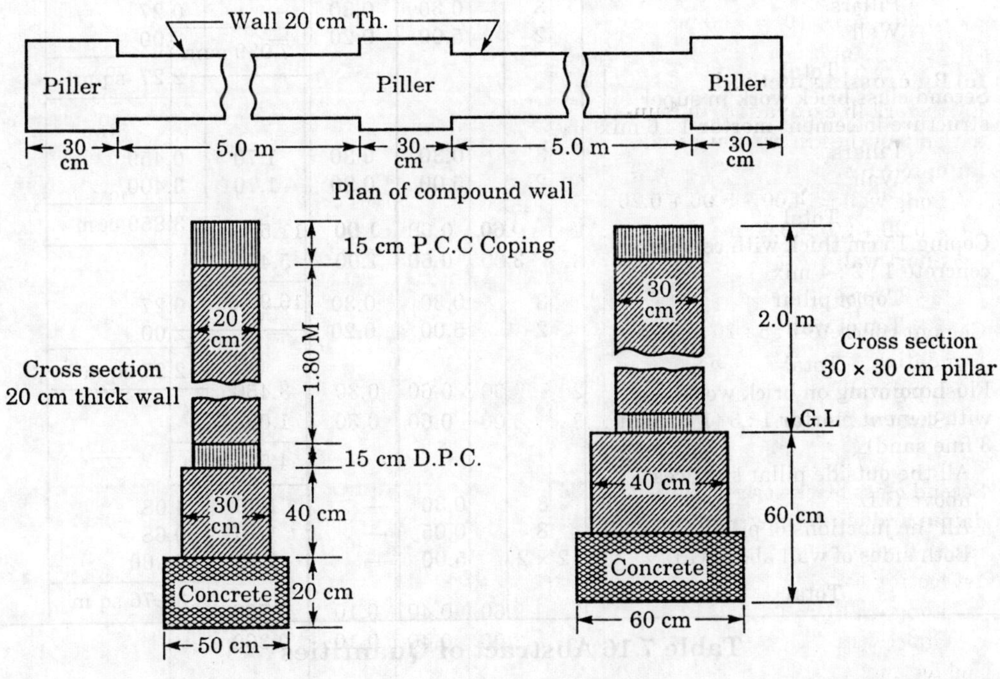

Fig. 7.9

Table 7.15. Details of Measurements

S. No.	Description of Item	No.	L	W	H/D	Content	Remark
1.	Earthwork in excavation in foundation trenches in ordinary soil, lift upto 1.5 m						
	Pillars	3	0.60	0.60	0.60	0.648	
	Wall between Pillars (5.00–0.15–0.15) = 4.70 m	2	4.70	0.50	0.60	2.820	
	Total					3.468 cum	
2.	Cement concrete 1 : 5 : 10 mix in foundation						
	Pillars	3	0.60	0.60	0.20	0.1944	
	Wall	2	4.70	0.50	0.20	0.8460	
	Total					1.0404 cum	
3.	Second class brickwork in foundation and plinth in cement mortar 1 : 6 mix						
	Pillars	3	0.40	0.40	0.40	0.192	
	Wall	2	4.80	0.30	0.40	1.152	
	Total					1.344 cum	
4.	Damp proof course 50 mm thick with cement concrete 1 : 2 : 4 mix						
	Pillars	3	0.30	0.30	—	0.27	
	Wall	2	5.00	0.20	—	2.00	
	Total					2.27 sq m	
5.	Second class brick work in super structure in cement mortar 1 : 6 mix						
	Pillars	3	0.30	0.30	1.70	0.459	
	Wall	2	5.00	0.20	1.70	3.400	
	Total					3.859 cum	
6.	Coping 15 cm thick with cement concrete 1 : 2 : 4 mix						
	Top of pillar	3	0.30	0.30	—	0.27	
	Top of wall	2	5.00	0.20	—	2.00	
	Total					2.27 sq m	
7.	Flush pointing on brick work with cement mortar 1 : 3 (1 cement : 3 fine sand)						
	All the outside pillar surfaces above G.L.	8	0.30	—	1.70	4.08	
	All the junctions of pillar and wall	8	0.05	—	1.70	0.68	
	Both sides of wall above G.L.	2 × 2	5.00	—	1.70	34.00	
	Total					38.76 sq m	

Table 7.16 Abstract of Quantities

S. No.	Description of Item	Quantity	Remark
1.	Earthwork in excavation in foundation trenches including dressing of sides and ramming of bottom, lift upto 1.5 m and lead upto 50 m	3.468 cum	
2.	Laying cement concrete 1 : 5 : 10 (1 cement : 5 fine sand : 10 graded stone aggregate 40 mm nomiiial size)	1.0404 cum	

3.	Second class brick work in foundation and plinth in cement mortar 1 : 6 (1 cement : 6 fine sand)	1.344 cum	
4.	Laying damp proof course 50 mm thick with cement concrete 1 : 2 : 4 (1 cement : 2 coarse sand : 4 graded stone aggregate 20 mm nominal size)	2.27 sq m	
5.	Second class brick work in superstructure in cement mortar 1 : 6 (1 cement : 6 fine sand)	3.859 cum	
6.	Laying coping 15 cm thick with cement concrete 1 : 2 : 4 (1 cement: 2 corse sand : 4 graded stone aggregate 20 mm nominal size) finished with a coat of neat cement	2.27 sq m	
7.	Flush pointing on brick work with cement mortar 1 : 3 (1 cement : 3 fine sand)	38.76 sq m	

General cross-section of 20 cm thick wall from foundation to the top of roof.

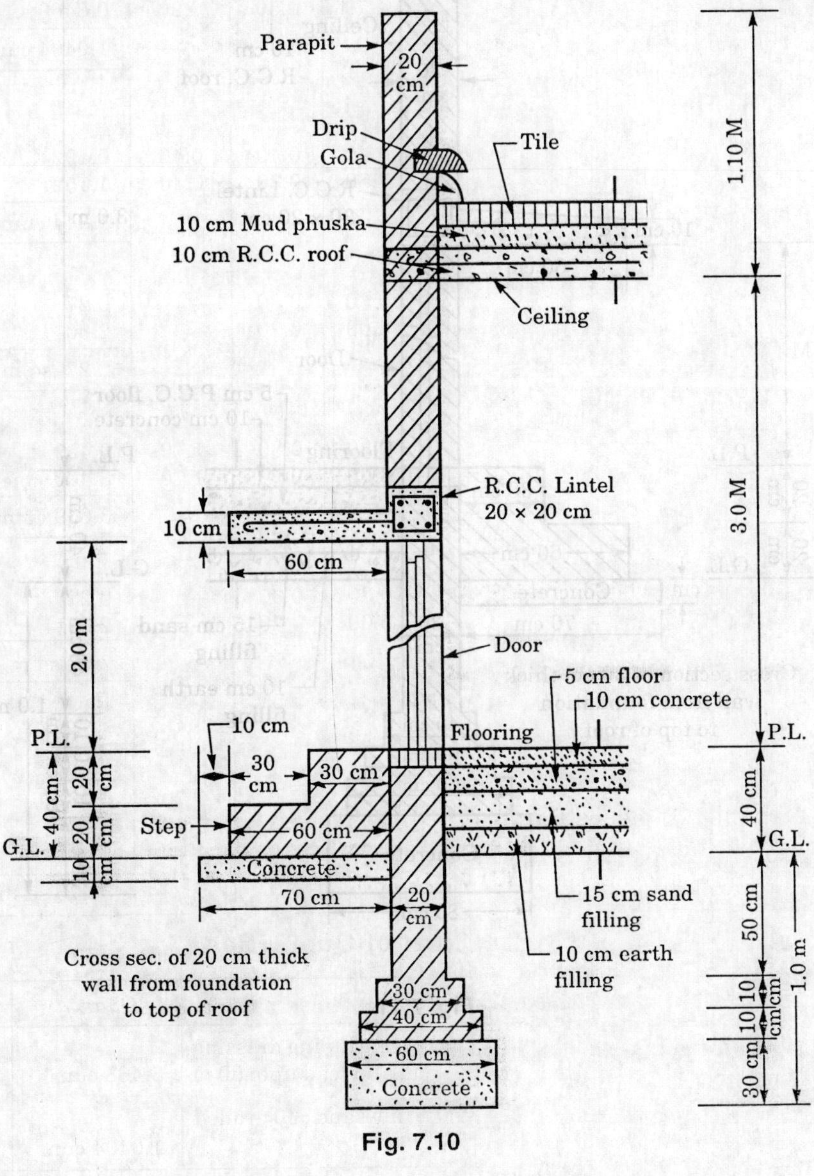

Fig. 7.10

General cross-section of 30 cm thick wall from foundation to the top of roof.

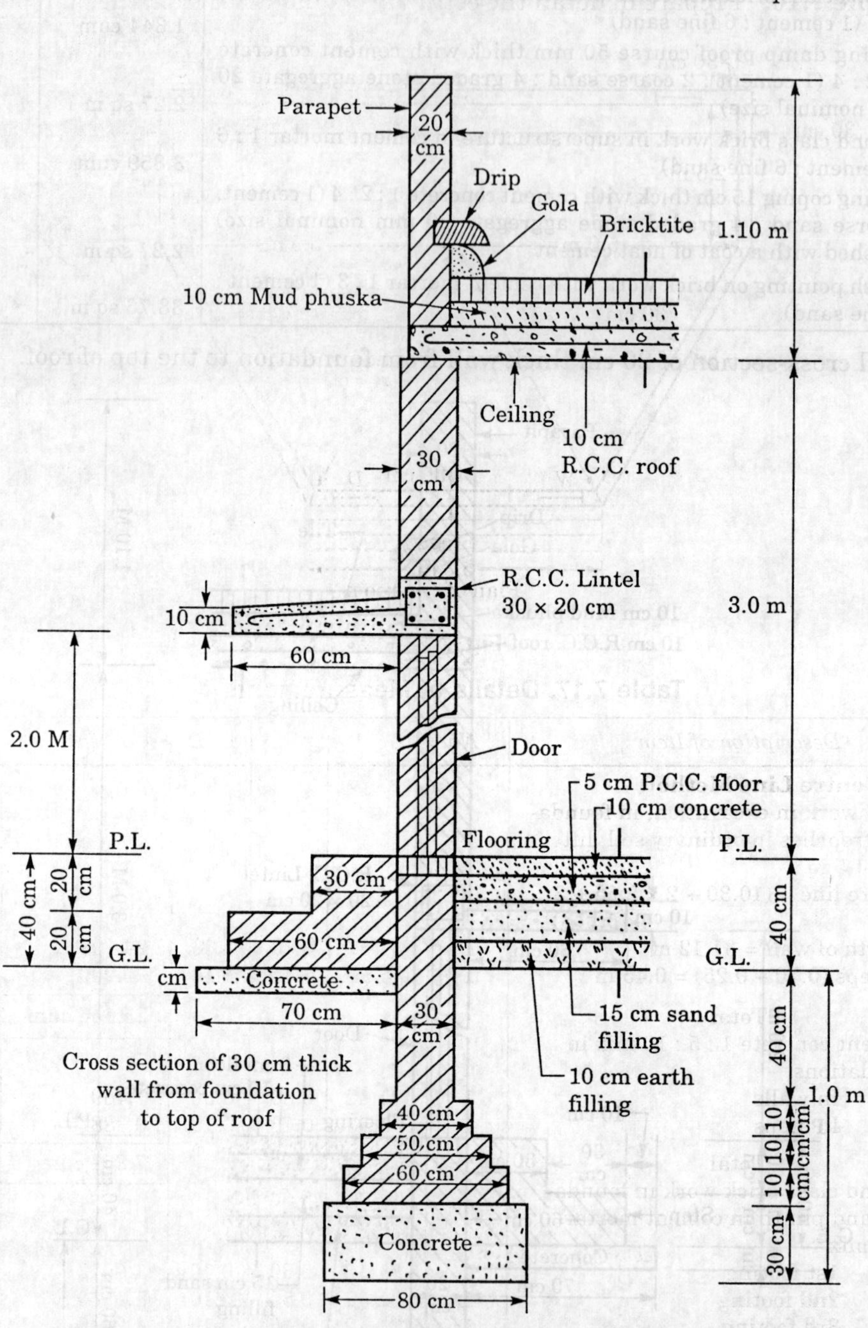

Fig. 7.11

Example 7.10. Prepare in detail the estimate of quantities from the plan of one room.

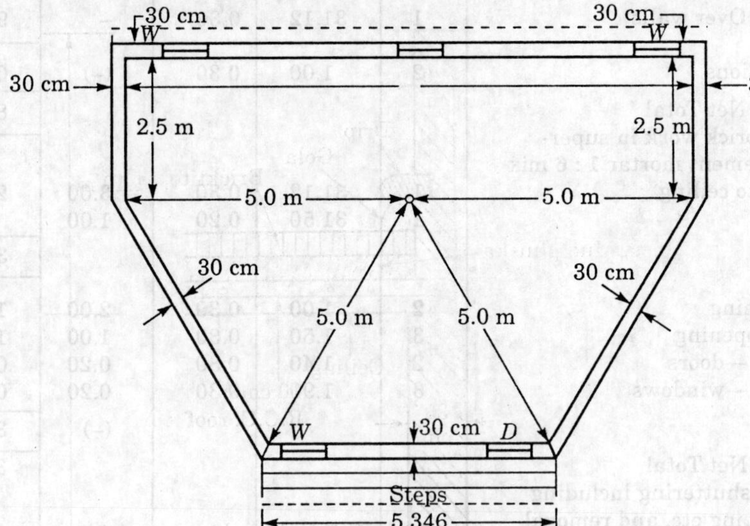

Plan of one room

Fig. 7.12

Table 7.17. Details of Measurements

S. No.	*Description of Item*	*No.*	*L*	*W*	*H/D*	*Content*	*Remarks*
	By Centre Line Method						
1.	Earthwork in excavation, in foundation trenches in ordinary soil, lift upto 1.5 m						
	Centre line = (10.30 + 2 × 2.65 + 3 × 5.173)						
	Length of wall = 31.12 m	1	31.12	0.80	1.00	24.896	
	In steps (0.70 – 0.25) = 0.45 m	1	5.55	0.45	1.10	0.250	
	Total					25.146 cum	
2.	Cement concrete 1 : 5 : 10 mix in foundations						
	In walls	1	31.12	0.80	0.30	7.469	
	In steps	1	5.55	0.70	0.10	0.388	
	Total					7.857 cum	
3.	Second class brick work in foundation and plinth in cement mortar 1 : 6 mix						
	1st footing	1	31.12	0.60	0.10	1.8672	
	2nd footing	1	31.12	0.50	0.10	1.5560	
	3rd footing	1	31.12	0.40	0.10	1.2448	
	Wall upto P.L.	1	31.12	0.30	0.80	7.4688	
	In steps : 1st step	1	5.35	0.60	0.20	0.6420	
	2nd step	1	5.35	0.30	0.20	0.3210	
	Total					13.0998 cum	
	Say					13.10 cum	

(*Contd.*)

4.	50 mm thick D.P.C. with cement concrete 1 : 2 : 4 mix.					
	Over walls	1	31.12	0.30	–	9.336
	Deduct					
	Door portions	2	1.00	0.30	(–)	0.600
	Net Total					8.736 sq m
5.	Second class brick work in super-structure in cement mortar 1 : 6 mix					
	Walls upto ceiling	1	31.12	0.30	3.00	28.008
	Parapit	1	31.50	0.20	1.00	7.300
						34.308 cum
	Deductions					
	Door opening	2	1.00	0.30	2.00	1.200
	Window opening	3	1.50	0.30	1.00	1.350
	Lintels over —doors	2	1.40	0.30	0.20	0.168
	—windows	3	1.90	0.30	0.20	0.342
					(–)	3.06 cum
	Net Total					31.248 cum
6.	Centring and shuttering including strutting, proping etc. and removal of form work for					
	Lintels Door bottom	2	1.00	0.30	–	0.600
	Sides	2 × 2	1.40	0.20	–	1.120
	Windows bottom	3	1.50	0.30	–	1.350
	Sides	3 × 2	1.90	0.20	–	2.280
	Sun shed Front side Bottom	1	5.35	0.60	–	3.210
	Face	1	5.35	0.10	–	0.535
	Sides	2	0.60	0.10	–	0.120
	Back side Bottom	1	10.60	0.60	–	7.360
	Face	1	10.60	0.10	–	1.060
	Sides	2	0.60	0.10	–	0.120
	Roof Bottom	1	10.00	2.50	–	25.000
	Botttom	1	$\left(\frac{10 \times 5}{2}\right) \times 2.16$		–	17.200
	Side faces	1	32.25	0.20	–	7.450
	Total					64.405 sq m
7.	R.C.C. work 1 : 2 : 4 mix in Lintels					
	Door	2	1.40	0.30	0.20	0.168
	Windows	3	1.90	0.30	0.20	0.168
	Sun shed Front side	1	5.35	0.60	0.10	0.321
	Back side	1	10.60	0.60	0.10	0.636
	Roof	1	10.60	2.80	0.20	5.936
		1	$\left(\frac{10.60 + 5.35}{2}\right) \times 2.40 \times 0.20 = 3.828$			
	Total					11.057 cum
8.	Mild steel reinforcement for R.C.C. work including bending binding and placing in position complete					
	Reinforcement @1½% of total quantity of R.C.C. work					
	$= \frac{11.047 \times 1.5}{100} \times 7840$ kg/cum					1300 kg
	Total					1300 kg

9.	Providing wood work in frames of doors, windows and other frames, wrought, framed and fixed in position Second class Indian teakwood					
	Doors (1.20 + 2 × 2.10) = 5.40	2	5.40	0.10	0.15	0.162
	Windows (2 × 1.70 + 2 × 1.00) = 5.40	3	5.40	0.10	0.15	0.243
	Total					0.405 cum
10.	Providing and fixing 40 mm thick panelled, glazed shutters for doors and windows including necessary iron fittings of second class Indian teak wood					
	Doors	2	0.82	—	1.90	3.116
	Windows	3	1.32	—	0.82	3.247
	Total					6.363 sq m
11.	Providing and fixing M.S. hold fasts 20 cm × 50 mm × 5 mm					
	Doors	2 × 3				6 No
	Windows	3 × 2				6 No
	Total					12 No
12.	Filling in plinth with Jamna sand under floors, including watering ramming consolidating and dressing complete					
	Room	1	10.00	2.50	0.15	3.750
		1	$\left(\frac{10+5}{2}\right)$	× 2.16	0.15	2.430
	Total					6-18 cum
13.	Laying in foundations and plinth lime concrete with graded brick aggregate 40 mm nominal size					
	Room	1	10.00	2.50	0.10	2.50
		1	$\left(\frac{10+5}{2}\right)$	× 2.16	0.10	1.62
	Total					4.12 cum
14.	50 mm thick cement concrete flooring 1 : 2 : 4 mix					
	In room	1	10.00	2.50	—	25.00
		1	$\left(\frac{10+5}{2}\right)$	× 2.16	—	16.20
	On steps	2	5.35	0.30	—	3.210
	On door sills	2	1.00	0.30	—	0.600
	Total					45.01 sq m

(*Contd.*)

15.	20 mm thick cement plaster skirting with cement mortar 1 : 3 mix					
	In room (10 + 2 × 2.5 + 3 × 5) = 30 m	1	30.00	—	0.20	6.00
	Step faces	2	5.35	—	0.20	2.14
	sides	2	0.60	—	0.20	0.24
		2	0.30	—	0.20	0.12
					(–)	8.50 sq m
	Deductions					
	For door openings	2	1.00	—	0.20	(–)0.40
						7.10 sq m
	Add for jambs	2 × 2	0.30	—	0.20	0.24
	Net total					7.34 sq m
16.	12 mm thick cement plaster 1 : 6 (1 cement : 6 fine sand)					
	In Side Walls Room					
	(*a*) Room (10 + 2 × 2.5 + 3 × 5) = 30 m	1	30.00	—	2.80	84.00
	Deduct					
	Windows openings	3	1.50	—	1.00	(–)4.50
	Net total					79.50 sq m
	(*b*) **Outside Walls**					
	(10.60 + 2 × 2.80 + 3 × 5.35) = 32.25 m	1	32.25	—	4.80	154.80
	Top of parapit	1	31.50	—	0.20	6.30
	Inside parapit	1	30.75	—	1.00	30.75
	Deduct					
						191.85 sq m
	Door openings	2	1.00	—	2.00	4.000
	Face of step	1	5.35	—	0.70	3.745
					(–)	7.745
	Net total					184.105 sq m
	Total quantity = (*a*) + (*b*)					263.605 sq m
17.	6 mm thick cement plaster to ceiling 1 : 3 (1 cement : 3 fine sand)					
	Room	1	10.00	2.50	—	25.00
		1	$\left(\frac{10 \times 5}{2}\right)$	× 216	—	17.20
	Sun shed Front top and bottom	1 × 2	5.35	0.60	—	6.42
	Face	1	5.35	0.10	—	0.535
	Ends	2	0.60	0.10	—	0.120
	Back side	1	10.60	1.30	—	13.78
	(60 + 60 + 10 = 1.30					
	Ends	2	0.60	0.10	—	0.12
	Total					62.175 sq m
18.	Applying priming coat with ready mixed primer of approved brand on wood work complete					
	Door panelled 2	2 × 1.3	1.00	—	2.00	10.40
	Windows glazed 2	3 × 0.8	1.50	—	1.00	7.20

30 cm Belows G.L.

19.	Painting two or more coats with superior ready mixed paint on new wood work						
	Door panelled 2	2 × 1.3	1.00	—	2.00	10.20	
	Windows glazed 2	3 × 0.8	1.50	—	1.00	7.40	
	Total					17.60 sq m	
20.	White washing with lime on new work (three or more coats) to give an even shade						
	Same as item 16 (*a*)					79.500	
	Same as item 17					62.175	
	Total					141.675 sq m	
21.	Colour washing on new work (two or more coats) to give an even shade						
	Same as item 16 (*b*)					184.105	
	Total					184.105 sq m	
22.	Painting top of roof with bitumen of approved quality						
	Over roof	1	10.20	2.60	—	27.52	
		1	$\left(\frac{10.20 \times 5.10}{2}\right) \times 2.20$			17.83	
	Total					43.35 sq m	
23.	10 cm thick mud phuska, covered with flat tile bricks						
	Over roof	1	10.20	2.60	—	27.52	
		1	$\left(\frac{10.20 \times 5.10}{2}\right) \times 2.20$			17.83	
	Total					43.35 sq m	
24.	Providing 10 cm thick 2nd class brick drip course at junctions of roof and walls in cement mortar 1 : 6 (1 cement : 6 fine sand)						
	At roof junction with parapet	1	30.75	—	—	30.75	
	Total					30.75 m	

Table 7.18. Abstract of Quantities

S. No.	*Description of Item*	*Quantities*	*Remark*
1.	Earth work in excavation in foundation trenches including dressing of sides and ramming of bottom lift upto 1.5 m and lead upto 50 m.	25.146 cum	
2.	Laying cement concrete 1 : 5 : 10 (1 cement : 5 fine sand : 10 graded stone aggregate 40 mm nominal size)	7.857 cum	
3.	Second class brick work in foundation and plinth in cement mortar 1 : 6 (1 cement : 6 fine sand)	13.10 cum	

(*Contd.*)

4.	Laying damp proof course 50 mm thick with cement concrete 1 : 2 : 4 (1 cement : 2 coarse sand : 4 graded stone aggregate 20 mm nominal size)	8.736 sq m	
5.	Second class brick work in superstructure in cement mortar 1 : 6 (1 cement : 6 fine sand)	31.248 cum	
6.	Centring and shuttering including strutting, propping etc. and removal of form work etc. for R.C.C. work.	64.405 sq m	
7.	Reinforced cement concrete work 1 : 2 : 4 (1 cement : 2 coarse sand : 4 graded stone aggregate 20 mm nominal size) excluding cost of centring, shuttering and reinforcement.	11.047 cum	
8.	Mild steel reinforcement for R.C.C. work including bending, binding and placing in position complete.	1300 kg	
9.	Providing wood work in frames of doors, windows and other frames, wrought, framed and fixed in position of second class Indian teak wood.	0.405 cum	
10.	Providing and fixing 40 mm thick panelled, glazed; shutters for doors and windows including necessary iron fittings of second class Indian teak wood.	6.363 sq m	
11.	Providing and fixing M.S. holdfasts 20 cm × 50 mm × 5 mm size.	12 Nos.	
12.	Filling in plinth with Jamna sand under floors, including watering, ramming, consolidating and dressing complete.	6.18 cum	
13.	Providing and laying under floors, lime concrete with graded brick aggregate 40 mm nominal size and 40% mortar comprising of 1 lime putty : 1 ash : 1 fine sand.	4.12 cum	
14.	50 mm thick cement concrete flooring 1 : 2 : 4 (1 cement : 2 coarse sand : 4 graded stone aggregate 20 mm nominal size) finished with a floating coat of neat cement.	45.01 sq m	
15.	20 mm thick cement plaster skirting with cement mortar 1 3 (1 cement : 3 coarse sand) finished with a floating coat of neat cement, including rounding of junctions with floor.	7.34 sq m	
16.	12 mm thick cement plaster 1 : 6. (1 cement : 6 fine sand)	263.605 sq m	
17.	6 mm thick cement plaster to ceiling 1 : 3 (1 cement : 3 fine sand)	62.175 sq m	
18.	Applying priming coat with ready mixed primer of approved brand on new wood work complete.	17.60 sq m	
19.	Painting two or more coats with superior quality ready mixed paint for wood work of approved brand on new work to give an even shade.	17.60 m	
20.	White washing with lime on new work to give an even shade.	141.675 sq m	
21.	Colour washing on new work (two or more coats) to give an even shade.	184.105 sq m	
22.	Painting top of roofs with bitumen @ 20 kg per 10 m^2 impregnated with a coat of coarse sand at 60 dm^3 per 10 m^2 including cleaning of surface complete.	43.35 sq m	
23.	10 cm thick mud phuska of damped brick earth on roofs laid to slope, consolidated and plastered with 25 mm thick mud mortar mixed with bhusa at 35 kg per cum of earth and gobri leaping with mix 1 : 1 (1 clay : 1 cowdung) and covered with a flat tile bricks grouted with cement mortar 1 : 3 (1 cement : 3 fine sand) and finished neat.	43.35 sq m	
24.	Providing 10 cm thick 2nd class brick drip course at junctions of roof and wall in cement mortar 1 : 6 (1 cement : 6 fine sand)	30.75 metre	

Example 7.11. *Prepare in detail the estimate of quantities of two rooms with the help of the given plan.*

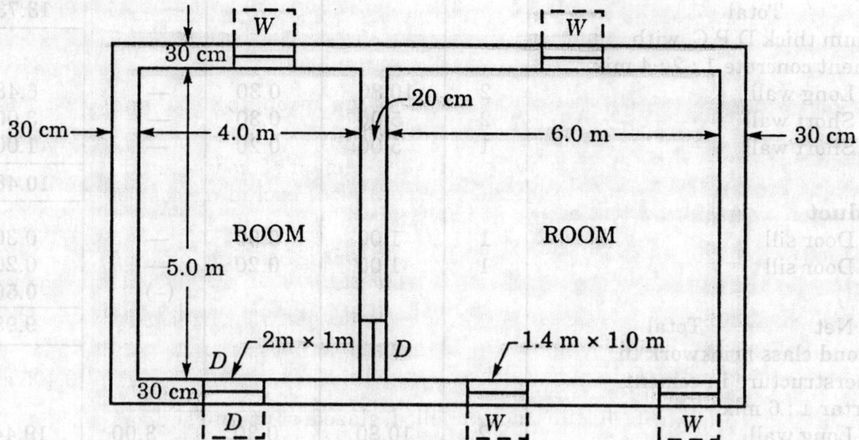

Plan of two rooms

Fig. 7.13

Table 7.19. Details of Measurements (Refer Figs. 7.10 and 7.11)

S. No.	*Description of Item*	*No.*	*L*	*W*	*H/D*	*Content*	*Remark*
	By in-to-in and out-to-out method						
1.	Earth work in excavation, in foundation trenches in ordinary soil, lift upto 1.5 m						
	Long wall	2	11.3	0.80	1.00	18.080	c/c 10.50 m
	Short wall	2	4.50	0.80	1.00	7.200	c/c 5.30 m
	Short wall (20 cm)	1	4.50	0.60	1.00	2.700	c/c 5.30 m
	In step	1	1.20	0.45	0.10	0.054	
	Total					28.034 cum	
2.	Cement concrete 1 : 5 : 10 mix in foundations						
	Long wall	2	11.30	0.80	0.30	5.424	
	Short wall	2	4.50	0.80	0.30	2.160	
	Short wall	1	4.50	0.60	0.30	0.810	
	In steps	1	1.20	0.70	0.10	0.084	
	Total					8.478 cum	
3.	Second class brickwork in foundation and plinth in cement mortar 1 : 6 mix						
	Long wall 1st footing	2	11.10	0.60	0.10	1.332	
	2nd footing	2	11.00	0.50	0.10	1.100	
	3rd footing	2	10.90	0.40	0.10	0.872	
	Wall upto P.L.	2	10.80	0.30	0.80	5.184	
	Short wall 1st footing	2	4.70	0.60	0.10	0.564	
	2nd footing	2	4.80	0.50	0.10	0.480	
	3rd footing	2	4.90	0.40	0.10	0.392	
	Wall upto P.L.	2	5.00	0.30	0.80	2.400	
	Short wall (20 m) 1st footing	1	4.70	0.40	0.10	0.188	
	2nd footing	1	4.80	0.30	0.10	0.144	
	3rd course	1	4.90	0.20	0.10	0.098	
	Wall upto P.L.	1	5.00	0.20	0.80	0.800	

(Contd.)

	In steps 1st step	1	1.00	0.60	0.20	0.120	
	2nd step	1	1.00	0.30	0.20	0.060	
	Total					13.734 cum	
4.	50 mm thick D.P.C. with cement concrete 1 : 2 : 4 mix						
	Long wall	2	10.80	0.30	—	6.480	
	Short wall	2	5.00	0.30	—	3.000	
	Short wall	1	5.00	0.20	—	1.000	
						10.480	
	Deduct						
	Door sill	1	1.00	0.30		0.30	
	Door sill	1	1.00	0.20	—	0.20	
					(−)	0.500	
	Net Total					9.980 sq m	
5.	Second class brickwork in superstructure in cement mortar 1 : 6 mix						
	Long wall	2	10.80	0.30	3.00	19.44	
	Short wall	2	5.00	0.30	3.00	9.00	
	Short wall	1	5.00	0.20	3.00	3.00	
	Parapet (10.80 + 10.80 + 2 × 5.20 = 32 m)	1	32.00	0.20	1.00	6.40	
						37.84	
	Deductions						
	Door opening	1	1.00	0.30	2.00	0.600	
	Door opening	1	1.00	0.20	2.00	0.400	
	Lintels Over door	1	1.40	0.30	0.20	0.084	
	Door	1	1.40	0.20	0.20	0.056	
	Over windows	4	1.90	0.30	0.20	0.456	
						1.596	
	Net Total					36.244 cum	
6.	Centring and shuttering for R.C.C. work						
	Lintels Door Bottom	1	1.00	0.30	—	0.300	
	Sides	2	1.40	0.20	—	0.560	
	Door Bottom	1	1.00	0.20	—	0.200	
	Sides	2	1.40	0.20	—	0.560	
	Windows Bottom	4	1.50	0.30	—	1.800	
	Sides	4 × 2	1.90	0.20	—	3.040	
	Sunshades Bottom windows	4	1.50	0.60	—	3.600	
	Door	1	1.00	0.60	—	0.600	
	Face window	4	1.50	0.10	—	0.600	
	Door	1	1.90	0.60	—	0.600	
	Sides	5 × 2	0.60	0.10	—	0.600	
	Roof Room	1	5.00	4.00		20.000	
	Room	1	7.00	5.00		30.000	
	Side faces	2	10.80	0.10	—	2.160	
	Side faces	2	5.60	0.10	—	10.20	
	Total					65.640 sq m	
7.	R.C.C. work 1 : 2 : 4 mix in						
	Lintels Door	1	1.40	0.30	0.20	0.084	
	Door	1	1.40	0.20	0.20	0.056	
	Window	4	1.90	0.30	0.20	0.456	
	Sun shades Doors	1	1.00	0.60	0.10	0.060	
	Window	4	1.50	0.60	0.10	0.360	
	Roof Over rooms	1	10.80	5.60	0.10	6.048	
	Total					7.064 cum	

Item	Particulars	No.	L	B	H/D	Quantity
8.	Mild steel reinforcement for R.C.C. work					
	Reinforcement @1½% or total quantity of R.C.C. work					
	$= \frac{7.064 \times 1.5}{100}$					
	× @ 7840 kg/cm = 831 kg					
	Total = 831 kg					
9.	Providing wood work in frames of doors and windows					
	Doors	2	5.40	0.10	0.15	0.162
	Windows	4	5.40	0.10	0.15	0.324
	Total					4.486 cum
10.	Providing and fixing 40 mm thick panelled, glazed shutters for doors and windows of 2nd class teak wood					
	Doors	2	0.82	—	1.90	3.116
	Windows	4	1.2	—	0.82	4.329
	Total					7.445 sq m
11.	Providing and fixing M.S. holdfasts					
	Doors	2 × 3				6
	Windows	4 × 2				8
	Total					14 Nos.
12.	Pilling in plinth with Jamna sand under floors					
	Room	1	4.00	5.00	0.15	3.00
	Room	1	6.00	5.00	0.15	4.50
	Total					7.50 cum
13.	Laying in foundations and plinth lime concrete (under floors)					
	Room	1	4.00	5.00	0.10	2.00
	Room	1	6.00	5.00	0.10	3.00
	Total					5.00 cum
14.	50 mm thick cement concrete flooring 1 : 2 : 4 mix					
	In Room	1	4.00	5.00	—	20.00
	Room	1	6.00	5.00	—	30.00
	On steps	2	1.00	0.30	—	0.60
	On door sills	1	1.00	0.30	—	0.30
		1	1.00	0.20	—	0.20
	Total					51.10 sq m

(Contd.)

15.	20 mm thick cement plaster skirting with cement mortar 1 : 3 mix						
	In Room	1	18.00	—	0.20	3.60	
	Room	1	22.00	—	0.20	4.40	
	Step Faces	2	1.00	—	0.20	0.40	
	Sides	2	0.60	—	0.20	0.24	
	Deduct	2	0.30	—	0.20	0.12	
					(+)	8.76	
	Door opening	1	1.00	—	0.20	0.20	
	Door	1 × 2	1.00	—	0.20	0.40	
					(–)	0.60	
	Add for Door jambs	1 × 2	0.20	—	0.20	0.08	
		1 × 2	0.30	—	0.20	0.12	
	Net Total				(+)	0.20	
						8.56 sq m	
16.	12 mm thick cement plaster 1 : 6 mix in side rooms A						
	Room	1	18.00	—	2.80	50.40	
	Room	1	22.00	—	2.80	61.60	
						112.00	
	Deduct						
	Door opening	1	1.00	—	1.80	1.80	
	Windows	4	1.50	—	1.00	6.00	
					(–)	7.80	
	Net Total A					104.20 sq m	
	Outside walls B (2 × 10.80 + 2 × 5.60)						
	= 32.80 m	1	32.80	—	4.80	157.44	30 cm
	Top of parapet	1	32.00	—	0.20	7.40	below
	Inside parapet	1	31.20	—	1.00	31.20	G.L.
						195.04	
	Deduct						
	Door opening	1	1.00	—	2.00	2.00	
	Face or step	1	1.00	—	0.70	0.70	
					(–)	2.70	
	Net Total B					192.34 sq m	
	Total (A + B)					296.54 sq m	
17.	6 mm thick cement plaster to ceiling 1 : 3 mix						
	Rooms	1	4.00	5.00	—	20.00	
	Sunshades Door	1	6.00	5.00	—	30.00	
	Face	1 × 2	1.00	0.60	—	1.20	
	Sides	1	1.00	0.10	—	0.10	
	Windows	1 × 2	0.60	0.10	—	0.12	
	Face	4 × 2	1.50	0.60	—	7.20	
	Sides	1	1.50	0.10	—	0.15	
		4 × 2	0.60	0.10	—	0.48	
	Total					59.25 sq m	

18.	Applying priming coat on wood work					
	Door panelled	2 × 2 × 1.3	1.00	—	2.00	10.40
	Windows glazed	4 × 2 × 8	1.50	—	1.00	9.60
	Total					20.00 sq m
19.	Painting two or more coats on new wood work					
	Door panelled	2 × 2 × 1.3	1.00	—	2.00	10.40
	Window glazed	4×2×8	1.50	—	1.00	9.60
	Total					20 sq m
20.	White washing with lime on new work					
	Same as item 16 A			104.20		
	Same as item 17			59.25		
	Total					163.45 sq m
21.	Colour washing on new work					
	Same as item No. 16 B			192.34		
	Total					192.34 sq m
22.	Painting top of roof with bitumen					
	Over Roof	1	10.40	5.20	—	54.08
	Total					54.08 sq m
23.	10 cm thick mud phuska covered with flat tile bricks					
	Over Roof	1	10.40	5.20	—	54.08
	Total					54.08 sq m
24.	Providing 10 cm thick 2nd class brick drip course					
	At roof junction	2	10.40	—	—	20.80
	With parapet	2	5.20	—	—	10.40
	Total					31.20 m

Table 7.20. Abstract of Quantities

S. No.	*Description of Item*	*Quantity*	*Remark*
1.	Earth work in excavation in foundation trenches including dressing of sides and ramming of bottom lift upto 1.5 m and lead upto 50 m.	28.034 cum	
2.	Laying cement concrete 1 : 5 : 10 (1 cement : 5 fine sand : 10 graded stone aggregate 40 mm nominal size).	8.478 cum	
3.	Second class brick work in foundation and plinth in cement mortar 1 : 6 (1 cement : 6 fine sand).	13.734 cum	
4.	Laying damp proof course 50 mm thick with cement concrete 1 : 2 : 4 (1 cement : 2 coarse sand : 4 graded stone aggregate 20 mm nominal size).	9.980 sq m	
5.	Second class brickwork in superstructure in cement mortar 1 : 6 (1 cement : 6 fine sand).	36.244 cum	
6.	Centring and shuttering including strutting, propping etc. and removal of formwork etc. for R.C.C. work.	65.640 sq m	

(*Contd.*)

7.	Reinforced cement concrete work 1 : 2 : 4 (1 cement : 2 coarse sand : 4 graded stone aggregate 20 mm nominal size) excluding cost of centring shuttering and reinforcement.	7.064 cum	
8.	Mild steel reinforcement for R.C.C. work including bending, binding and placing in position complete.	831 kg	
9.	Providing wood work in frames of doors, windows, and other frames, wrought, framed and fixed in position of second class Indian teak wood.	0.486 cum	
10.	Providing and fixing 40 mm thick panelled, glazed ; shutters for doors and windows including necessary iron fittings of second class Indian wood.	7.445 sq m	
11.	Providing and fixing M.S. holdfasts 20 cm × 50 mm × 5 mm size.	14 No	
12.	Filling in plinth with Jamna sand under floors, including watering, ramming, consolidating and dressing complete.	7.50 cum	
13.	Providing and laying under floors, lime concrete with graded brick aggregate 40 mm normal size and 40% mortar comprising of 1 lime putty : 1 ash : 1 fine sand.	5.00 sq m	
14.	50 mm thick cement concrete flooring 1 : 2 : 4 (1 cement : 2 coarse sand : 4 graded stone aggregate 20 mm nominal size) finished with a floating coat of neat cement.	51.10 sq m	
15.	20 mm thick cement plaster skirting with cement mortar 1 : 3(1 cement : 3 coarse sand) finished with floating coat of neat cement, including rounding of junctions with floor.	8.36 sq m	
16.	12 mm thick cement plasters 1 : 6 (1 cement : 6 fine sand).	296.54 sq m	
17.	6 mm thick cement plaster to ceiling 1 : 3 (1 cement : 3 fine sand).	59.25 sq m	
18.	Applying priming coat with a ready mixed primer of approved brand on new wood work complete.	20 sq m	
19.	Painting two or more coats with superior quality ready mixed paint for work of approved brand on new work to a give an even shade.	20 sq m	
20.	White-washing with line one new work to give an even shade.	163.45 sq m	
21.	Colour washing on new work (two or more coats) to give an even shade.	192.34 sq m	
22.	Painting for proof with bitumen 20 kg per 10 m^2 impregnated with a coat of coarse sand at 60 cm^3 per 10 m^2 including cleaning of surface complete.	54.08 sq m	
23.	10 cm thicks mud phuska of damped brick earth on proofs laid to slope, consolidated and plastered with 25 mm thick mud mortar mixed with bhusa at 35 kg per cum of earth and gobri leaping with mix 1 : 1 (1 clay : 1 cowdung) and covered with a flat tile bricks grouted with cement mortar 1 : 3 (1 cement : 3 fine sand) and finished neat.	54.08 sq m	
24.	Providing 10 cm thick 2nd class brick drip course at junctions or proof and wall in cement mortar 1 : 5 (1 cement : 6 fine sand).	31.20 sq m	

Example 7.12. *Prepare in detail the estimate of quantities of a house with the help of the given plan.*

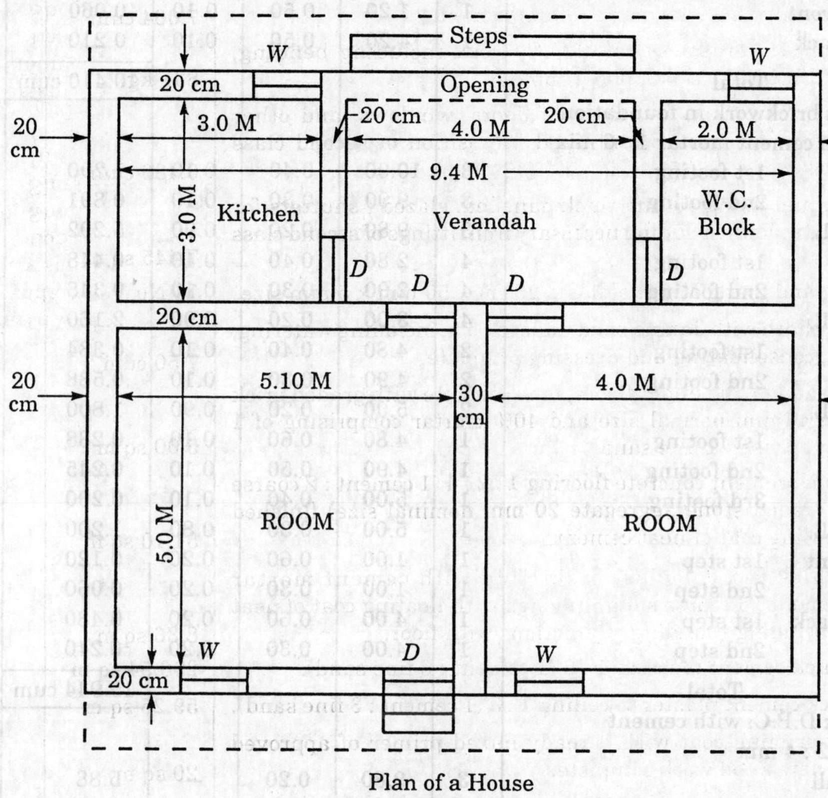

Fig. 7.14

Note. Refer Figs. 7.10, 7.11 for cross-section.

Table 7.21. Details of Measurements

S. No.	*Description of Items*	*No.*	*L*	*W*	*H/D*	*Content*	*Remark*
	By in-to-in and out-to-out method.						
1.	Earth work in excavation, in foundation trenches, in ordinary soil, lift upto 1.5 m						
	Long wall	3	10.20	0.60	1.00	18.36	c/c 9.60
	Short wall	4	2.60	0.60	1.00	6.24	c/c 3.20
	Short wall	2	4.60	0.60	1.00	5.52	c/c 5.20
	Short wall (30 cm)	1	4.60	0.80	1.00	3.68	c/c 5.20
	In steps Front	1	1.20	0.50	0.10	0.060	
	Back	1	4.20	0.50	0.10	0.210	
	Total					34.07 cum	
2.	Cement of concrete 1 : 5 : 10 mix in foundations						
	Long wall	3	10.20	0.60	0.30	5.508	
	Short wall	4	2.60	0.60	0.30	1.872	

(*Contd.*)

	Short wall	2	4.60	0.60	0.30	1.656	
	Short wall	1	4.60	0.80	0.30	1.104	
	In steps Front	1	1.20	0.50	0.10	0.060	
	Back	1	4.20	0.50	0.10	0.210	
	Total					10.410 cum	
3.	Second class brickwork in foundation and plinth in cement mortar 1 : 6 mix						
	Long wall 1st footing	3	10.00	0.40	0.10	1.200	
	2nd footing	3	9.90	0.30	0.10	0.891	
	wall upto P.L.	3	9.80	0.20	0.90	5.292	
	Short wall 1st footing	4	2.80	0.40	0.10	0.448	
	2nd footing	4	2.90	0.30	0.10	0.348	
	wall upto P.L.	4	3.00	0.20	0.90	2.160	
	Short wall 1st footing	2	4.80	0.40	0.10	0.384	
	2nd footing	2	4.90	0.30	0.10	0.588	
	wall upto P.L.	2	5.00	0.20	0.90	1.800	
	Short wall 1st footing	1	4.80	0.60	0.10	0.288	
	2nd footing	1	4.90	0.50	0.10	0.245	
	3rd footing	1	5.00	0.40	0.10	0.200	
	wall upto P.L.	1	5.00	0.30	0.80	1.200	
	In steps Front 1st step	1	1.00	0.60	0.20	0.120	
	2nd step	1	1.00	0.30	0.20	0.060	
	Back 1st step	1	4.00	0.60	0.20	0.480	
	2nd step	1	4.00	0.30	0.20	0.240	
	Total					15.944 cum	
4.	50 mm thick D.P.C. with cement concrete 1 : 2 : 4 mix						
	Long wall	3	9.80	0.20	—	5.88	
	Short wall	4	3.00	0.20	—	2.40	
	Short wall	2	5.00	0.20	—	2.00	
	Short wall	1	5.00	0.30	—	1.50	
						11.78	
	Deductions						
	Door sill	5	1.00	0.20	—	1.00	
	Ver. opening	1	4.00	0.20	—	0.80	
					(–)	1.80 sq m	
	Net Total					9.98 sq m	
5.	Second class brick work in superstructure in cement mortar 1 : 6 mix						
	Long wall	3	9.80	0.20	3.00	17.64	
	Short wall	4	3.00	0.20	3.00	7.20	
	Short wall	2	5.00	0.20	3.00	6.00	
	Short wall	1	5.00	0.30	3.00	4.50	
	Parapet (9.80 + 9.80 + 8.20 + 8.20) = 36 m	1	36.00	0.20	1.00	7.20	
						42.54	
	Deduction						
	Door openings	5	1.00	0.20	2.00	2.00	
	Window openings	4	1.50	0.20	1.00	1.20	
	Ver. opening	1	4.00	0.20	2.00	1.60	

Item	Particulars		No.	L	B	H	Quantity	
	Lintel Over door		5	1.40	0.20	0.20	0.28	
	Over window		4	1.90	0.20	0.20	0.304	
	Beam Over verandah opening		1	4.80	0.20	0.40	0.388	
						(–)	5.772	
	Net Total						37.768	
6.	Centring and shuttering for R.C.C. work.							
	Lintels	Door Bottom	5	1.00	0.20	—	1.00	
		Side	5 × 2	1.40	0.20	—	2.80	
	Windows	Bottom	4	1.50	0.20	—	1.20	
		Side	4 × 2	1.90	0.20	—	3.04	
	Sunshades	Bottom	2	9.80	0.60	—	11.76	
		Face	2	9.80	0.60	—	11.76	
		Sides	2 × 2	0.60	0.10	—	0.24	
	Roof	Room	1	5.10	5.00	—	25.50	
		Room	1	4.00	5.00	—	20.00	
		Kitchen	1	3.00	3.00	—	9.00	
		Verandah	1	4.00	3.00	—	12.00	
		W.C. Block	1	2.00	3.00	—	6.00	
	Side faces		2	9.80	0.10	—	1.96	
			2	8.60	0.10	—	1.72	
	Total						107.98 sq m	
7.	R.C.C. work 1 : 2 : 4 mix in							
	Lintels	Doors	5	1.40	0.20	0.20	0.280	
		Windows	4	1.90	0.20	0.20	0.304	
	Beam	Ver. opening	1	4.80	0.20	0.40	0.384	
	Sunshade		2	9.80	0.60	0.10	1.176	
	Roof		1	9.80	8.60	0.10	8.428	
	Total						10.572 cum	
8.	Mild steel reinforcement for R.C.C. work Reinforcement @ 1½% of total quantity of R.C.C. work							
	$= \dfrac{10.572 \times 1.5}{100} \times$ @ 7.840 kg/cum							
	= 1244						1244 kg	
	Total						1244 kg	
9.	Providing wood work in frames of doors and windows.							
	Doors		5	5.40	0.10	0.15	0.405	
	Windows		4	5.40	0.10	0.15	0.344	
	Total						0.749 cum	
10.	Providing and fixing 40 mm thick panelled, glazed shutters for doors and windows of 2nd class Indian teak wood.							
	Doors		5	0.82	—	1.90	7.7900	
	Windows		4	1.32	—	0.82	4.3296	
	Total						12.1196 sq m	

(Contd.)

11.	Providing and fixing M.S. holdfasts.				say	12.12 sq m	
	Doors	5×3				15	
	Windows	4×2				8	
	Total					23 Nos.	
12.	Filling plinth with Jamna sand under floors.						
	Room	1	5.10	5.00	0.15	3.825	
	Room	1	4.00	5.00	0.15	3.000	
	Kitchen	1	3.00	3.00	0.15	1.350	
	Verandah	1	4.00	3.00	0.15	1.800	
	W.C.	1	2.00	3.00	0.15	0.900	
	Total					10.875 cum	
13.	Laying in foundations and plinth lime concrete (under floor).						
	Room	1	5.10	5.00	0.10	2.55	
	Room	1	4.00	5.00	0.10	2.00	
	Kit.	1	3.00	3.00	0.10	0.90	
	Ver.	1	4.00	3.00	0.10	1.20	
	W.C.	1	2.00	3.00	0.10	0.60	
	Total					7.25 cum	
14.	50 mm thick cement concrete flooring 1 : 2 : 4 mix.						
	Room	1	5.10	5.00	—	25.50	
	Room	1	4.00	5.00	—	20.00	
	Door sill	3	1.00	0.20	—	0.60	
	On step	1×2	1.00	0.30	—	0.60	
	Total					47.70 sq m	
15.	20 mm thick cement plaster skirting with cement mortar 1 : 3 mix.						
	Room	1	20.20	—	0.20	4.04	
	Room	1	18.00	—	0.20	3.60	
	Step	2	1.00	—	0.20	0.40	
	Door opening	2	0.60	—	0.20	0.24	
						8.28	
	Deduct	3	1.00	—	0.20	(–)0.60	
	Add Door Jambs	3×2	0.20	—	0.20	(–)0.24	
	Total					7.92 sq m	
16.	Providing and fixing glass strips 50 mm wide and 3 mm thick in joints of terrazo floor.						
	Kit.	4×2	3.00	—	—	24	
	Ver.	4	4.00	—	—	16	
	Ver.	4	3.00	—	—	12	
	W.C.	2×3	2.00	—	—	12	
	Total					64 m	

17.	50 mm thick marble chips flooring in dark shade pigment with ordinary cement.						
	Kit.	1	3.00	3.00	—	9.00	
	Ver.	1	4.00	3.00	—	12.00	
	W.C.	1	2.00	3.00	—	7.00	
	Sills of door	2	1.00	0.20	—	0.40	
	On step	2	4.00	0.30	—	2.40	
	Sills of opening	1	4.00	0.20	—	0.80	
	Total					30.60 sq m	
18.	20 mm thick marble chips skirting in dark shade pigment with ordinary cement.						
	Kit.	1	12.00	—	1.00	12.00	
	Ver.	1	10.40	—	0.20	2.08	
	W.C.	1	10.00	—	1.00	10.00	
	Add Jambs of Doors	(2×2)	0.20	—	1.00	0.80	
						24.88	
	Deduct Door opening	2	1.00	—	1.00	2.00	
	Door opening Ver.	4	1.00	—	0.20	0.80	
					(–)	2.80	
	Net Total					22.08 sq m	
19.	12 mm thick cement plaster 1 : 6 mix. **Inside** (*A*)						
	Room	1	20.20	—	2.80	56.56	
	Room	1	18.00	—	2.80	50.40	
	Kit.	1	12.00	—	2.00	24.00	
	Ver.	1	14.00	—	2.80	39.20	
	W.C.	1	10.00	—	2.00	20.00	
						190.16	
	Deduct Door Openings	4	1.00	—	1.80	7.20	
	Window	4	1.50	—	1.00	6.00	
	Ver. Opening	1	4.00	—	2.00	8.00	
					(–)	21.20	
	Add Jambs of Door	(1×2)	0.20	—	1.80	0.72	
	Soffit of Beam	1	4.00	—	0.20	0.80	
					(+)	1.52	
	Net Total (*A*)					170.48 sq m	
	Outside (*B*) (2 × 9.80 + 2 × 8.60) = 36.80 m	1	36.80	—	4.80	176.64	30 cm Belows G.L.
	Top of parapet	1	36.00	—	0.20	7.20	
	Inside parapet	1	35.20	—	1.00	35.20	
						219.04	
	Deductions						
	Door opening	1	1.00	—	2.00	2.00	
	Ver. opening	1	4.00	—	2.00	8.00	
	Face of step	1	1.00	—	0.70	0.70	
		1	4.00	—	0.70	2.80	
					(–)	13.50	
	Net Total (*B*)					205.54 sq m	
	Total (*A* + *B*)					376.02 sq m	

(*Contd.*)

20.	6 mm thick cement plaster to ceiling 1 : 3 mix.						
	Room	1	5.10	5.00	—	25.50	
	Room	1	4.00	5.00	—	20.00	
	Kit.	1	3.00	3.00	—	9.00	
	Ver.	1	4.00	3.00	—	12.00	
	W.C.	1	2.00	3.00	—	6.00	
	Sunshades Top and bottom	2×2	9.80	0.60	—	23.52	
	Face	2	9.80	0.10	—	1.96	
	Sides	2×2	0.60	0.10	—	0.24	
	Total					98.22 sq m	
21.	Applying priming coat on wood work.						
	Door panelled	2 × 5 × 1.3	1.00		2.00	26.0	
	Window glazed	2 × 4 × 0.8	1.50	—	1.00	9.6	
	Total					35.60 sq m	
22.	Painting two or more coats on new wood work.						
	Door panelled	2 × 5 × 1.3	1.50		2.00	26.0	
	Window glazed	2 × 4 × 8	1.00	—	1.00	9.60	
	Total					35.60 sq m	
23.	White washing with lime on new work.						
	Same as item 19 (*A*)					170.48	
	Same as item 20					52.72	
	Total					223.20 sq m	
24.	Colour washing on new work.						
	Same as item 19 (B)					205.54	
	Total					205.54 sq m	
25.	Painting top of roof with bitumen						
	Over roof	1	9.40	8.20	—	77.08	
	Total					77.28 sq m	
26.	10 cm thick mud phuska covered with flat tile bricks.						
	Over roof	1	9.40	8.20	—	77.08	
	Total					77.08 sq m	
27.	Providing 10 cm thick 2nd class brick drip course.						
	At junction with parapet	2	9.40	—		18.80	
		2	8.20	—		16.40	
	Total					35.20 m	

Table 7.22 Abstract of Quantities

S. No.	Description of Item	Quantity	Remark
1.	Earthwork in excavation in foundation trenches including dressing of sides and ramming of bottom lift upto 1.5 m and lead upto 50 m.	34.07 cum	
2.	Laying cement concrete 1 : 5 : 10 (1 cement: 5 fine sand : 10 graded stone aggregate 40 mm nominal size)	10.41 cum	
3.	Second class brickwork in foundation and plinth in cement mortar 1 : 6 (1 cement : 6 fine sand)	15.944 cum	
4.	Laying damp proof course 50 mm thick with cement concrete 1 : 2 : 4 (1 cement : 2 coarse sand : 4 graded stone aggregate 20 mm nominal size)	9.98 cum	
5.	Second class brick work in superstructure in cement mortar 1 : 6 (1 cement : 6 fine sand)	36.768 cum	
6.	Centring and shuttering including strutting, proping etc. and removal of formwork etc. for R.C.C. work.	107.98 sq m	
7.	Reinforced cement concrete work 1 : 2 : 4 (1 cement : 2 coarse sand : 4 graded stone aggregate 20 mm nominal size) excluding cost of centring shuttering and reinforcement.	10.572 cum	
8.	Mild steel reinforcement for R.C.C. work including bending, binding and placing in position complete.	1244 kg	
9.	Providing wood work in frames of doors, windows, and other frames, wrought, framed and fixed in position of second class Indian teak wood.	0.749 cum	
10.	Providing and fixing 40 mm thick panelled, glazed, shutters for doors and windows including necessary iron fittings, of second class Indian teak wood.	12.12 sq m	
11.	Providing and fixing M.S. holdfasts 20 cm × 50 mm × 5 mm size.	23 No.	
12.	Filling in plinth with Jamna sand, under floors, including watering, ramming consolidating and dressing complete.	10.875 cum	
13.	Providing and laying under floors, lime concrete with graded brick aggregate 40 mm nominal size and 40% mortar comprising of 1 lime putty : 1 ash : 1 fine sand.	7.25 cum	
14.	50 mm thick cement concrete flooring 1 : 2 : 4(1 cement : 2 coarse sand : 4 graded stone aggregate 20 mm nominal size) finished with a floating coat of neat cement.	46.70 sq m	
15.	20 mm thick cement plaster skirting with cement mortar 1 : 3 (1 cement : 3 coarse sand) finished with a floating coat of neat cement, including rounding of junctions with floor.	7.92 sq m	
16.	Providing and fixing class strips, 50 mm wide and 3 mm thick in joints of terrazzo floor.	64 metre	

(Contd.)

17.	50 mm thick marble chips flooring rubbed and polished to granolithic finish, under layer 40 mm thick cement concrete 1 : 2 : 4 (1 cement : 2 coarse sand : 4 graded stone aggregate 12.5 mm nominal size) and top layer 10 mm thick with white and black marble chips of sizes 1 mm to 4 mm nominal size, laid in cement marble powder mix 3 : 1 (3 cement : 1 marble powder) by weight in proportion of 4 : 7 (4 cement marble powder mix : 7 marble chips, by volume in dark shade pigment with ordinary cement.	30.60 sq m	
18.	20 mm thick marble chips skirting, rubbed and polished to granolithic finish, top layer 10 mm thick with white and black marble chips of sizes from smallest to 4 mm nominal size, laid in cement marble power mix 3 : 1 (3 cement : 1 marble powder) by weight in proportion of 4 : 7 (4 cement marble powder mix : 7 marble chips) by volume, with under layer 10 mm thick in cement plaster 1 : 3 (1 cement : 3 coarse sand) in dark shade pigment with ordinary cement.	22.08 sq m	
19.	12 mm thick cement plaster 1 : 6 (1 cement : 6 fine sand)	376.02 sq m	
20.	6 mm thick cement plaster to ceiling 1 : 3 (1 cement : 3 fine sand)	52.72 sq m	
21.	Applying priming coat with a ready mixed primer or approved brand on new wood work complete	35.60 sq m	
22.	Painting two or more coats with superior quality ready mixed paint for wood work of approved brand on new work to give an even shade.	35.60 sq m	
23.	White-washing with lime on new work to give an even shade.	223.20 sq m	
24.	Colour washing on new work (two or more coats) to give an even shade.	205.54 sq m	
25.	Painting top of roof with bitumen @ 20 kg. per 10 m^2 impregnated with a coat of coarse sand at 60 dm^3 per 10 m^2 including cleaning of surface complete.	77.08 sq m	
26.	10 cm thick mud phuska of damped brick earth on roofs laid to slope, consolidated and plastered with 25 mm thick mud mortar mixed with bhusa at 35 kg. per cum of earth and gobri leaping with mix 1 : 1 (1 clay : 1 cow-dung) and covered with a flat tile bricks, grouted with cement mortar 1 : 3 : 1 cement : 3 fine sand) and finished heat.	77.08 sq m	
27.	Providing 10 cm thick 2nd class brick drip course at junctions of roof and wall in cement mortar 1 : 6 (1 cement : 6 fine sand)	35.20 metre	

Part II

Different Types of Roof

Estimate of various types of roof is given in examples 7.13 to 7.19.

Example 7.13. *Calculate the quantities of*

1. *First class brick work in jack arch in 1 : 4 mix.*
2. *Lime concrete in haunch filling.*
3. *Steel work.*
4. *Cement plaster 1 : 3 mix.*
5. *Centring and shuttering.*
6. *Lime terracing.*

With the help of given plan and cross-section of jack arch roof over a room 900 m × 7-00 m arch span 1.80 m.

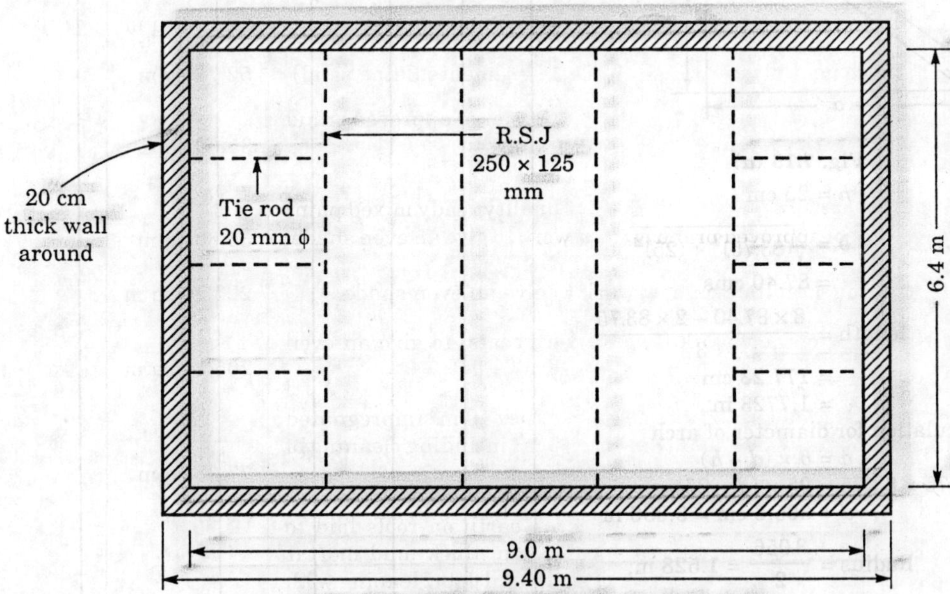

Line plan (Jack arch roof) (40 cm thick walls)

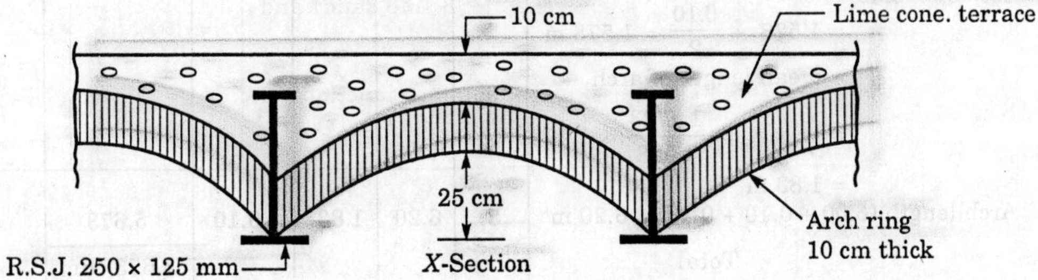

X-Section

Fig. 7.15

Table 7.23. Details of Measurements

S. No.	*Description of Item*	*No.*	*L*	*W*	*H/D*	*Content*	*Remark*
1.	First class brick work in arches 1 : 4 mix Length of an arch "*L*" is given by $= \frac{8b - 2a}{3}$ where $b = \sqrt{a^2 + b^2}$ $a = \frac{180}{2} - \frac{12.5}{2} = 83.75$ 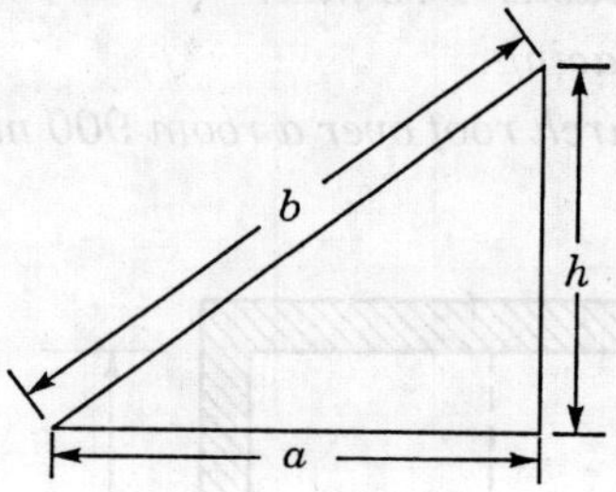 **Fig. 7.15 (*a*)** $h = 25$ cm *i.e.* $b = \sqrt{(83.75)^2 + (25)^2}$ $= 87.40$ cms *i.e.* length $= \frac{8 \times 87.40 - 2 \times 83.75}{3}$ $= 177.23$ cm $= 1.7723$ m Calculation for diameter of arch $a \times a = b \times (d - h)$ $83.75 \times 83.75 = 25 \times (d - 25)$ or $d = 305.6$ cm $= 3.056$ m or Radius $= \frac{3.056}{2} = 1.528$ m. r_m = mean radius $= 1.528 + \frac{0.10}{2} = 1.578$ m l_m = mean length of arch $= \frac{L}{r} \times r_m = \frac{1.7723}{1.528} \times 1.578$ $= 1.83$ m						
	Arch length (6.00 + 0.10 + 0.10) = 6.20 m	5	6.20	1.83	0.10	5.673	
	Total					5.673 cum	
2.	Providing and laying on terrace lime concrete in haunch						

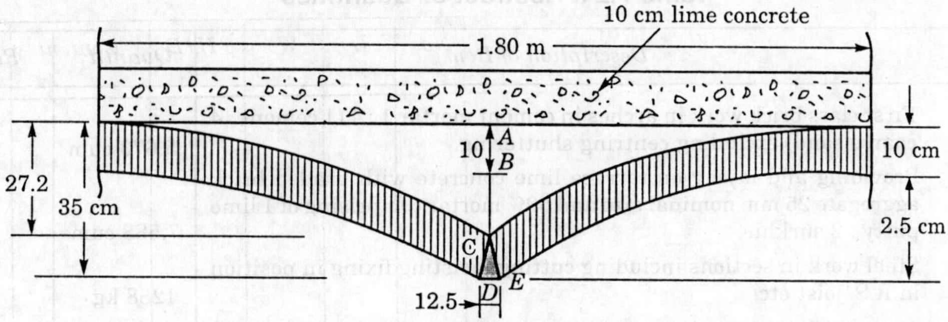

Fig. 7.15 (*b*)

Calculations

Thickness of concrete at the spandrill excluding 10 cm thick lime terracing

$= AC = AD - CD$ cm

$= (25 + 10) - CD$ cm

$= 35 - CD$

$$CD = \sqrt{CE^2 - DE^2}$$

$$= \sqrt{(10)^2 - (6.25)^2}$$

$= 7.8$ cm

i.e. $AC = 35 - 7.8$ cm $= 27.2$ m

S.No.	Description	No.	L	B	H	Quantity	Remarks
	Lime concrete in haunches	10	6.20	$\frac{0.90 \times 0.272}{2}$	=	7.588	
	Total					7.588 cum	
	(Lime concrete is not a triangle but it is curved triangle. Therefore factor of 10.9 is taken for area)						
	Total						
3.	Steel work in sections R.S. Joist						
	R.S.J. 250 × 125 @ 47.55 kg/m	4	6.60	@	47.55	1255.32	
	Tie Rods 20 mmϕ @ 2.47 kg/m	6	2.20	@	2.47	32.60	
	Total					1287.92 kg	
4.	6 mm thick cement plaster 1 : 3 mix						
	In soffit of arches	5	6.00	1.772	—	53.16	
	Total					53.16 sq m	
5.	Centring and shuttering for arch work						
	For arches	5	6.00	1.783	—	53.16	
	Total					53.16 sq m	
6.	10 cm thick lime terrace over jack arch roof	1	9.40	6.40	—	60.16	
	Total					60.16 sq m	

Table 7.24. Abstract of Quantities

S. No.	Description of Item	Quantity	Remark
1.	First class brick work in arches in cement mortar 1 : 4 (1 cement : 4 coarse sand) excluding centring shuttering.	5.673 cum	
2.	Providing and laying on terrace lime concrete with graded brick aggregate 25 mm nominal size and 50% mortar comprising of 1 lime putty : 2 surkhi.	7.588 cum	
3.	Steel work in sections including cutting, hoisting fixing in position in R.S. joist etc.	1288 kg	
4.	6 mm thick cement plaster to ceiling 1 : 3 (1 cement : 3 fine sand).	53.16 sq m	
5.	Centring and shuttering including strutting, proping etc. and removal of form work etc; for jack arch roofing.	53.16 sq m	
6.	Lime concrete terracing on roofs, average thickness 10 cm laid to fall with 25 mm nominal size brick aggregate, and 50% lime mortar 1 : 2 (1 lime putty : 2 surkhi) rammed and finished with gur and belgiri treatment complete, including rounding of junctions with parapet wall complete.	60.16 sq m	

Example 7.14. *Calculate the quantities of :*

1. Wood work in beams. *2. Wood work in joists.*

3. 50 mm thick red stone slab roofing. *4. Painting top of roof with bitumen.*

5. Lime concrete terracing covered with flat brick tiles.

With the help of given plan and cross-section of wooden roof over a room 7.00 m × 9.09 m.

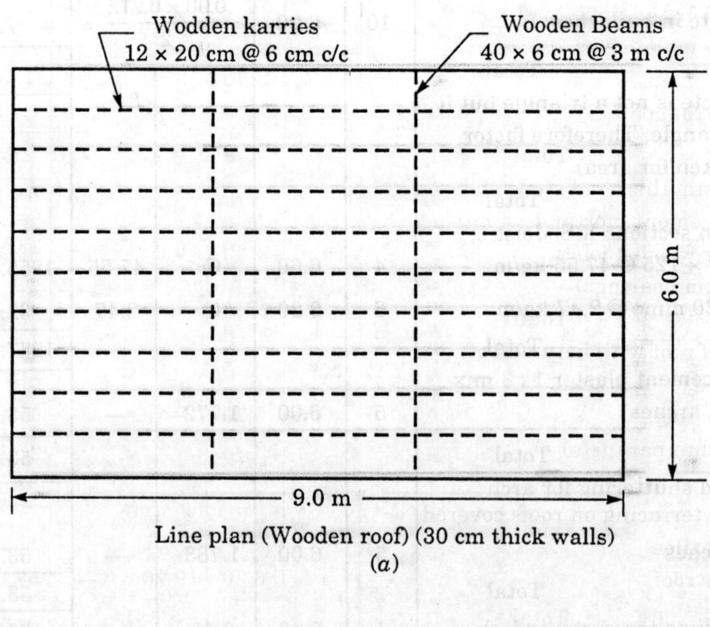

Line plan (Wooden roof) (30 cm thick walls)

(*a*)

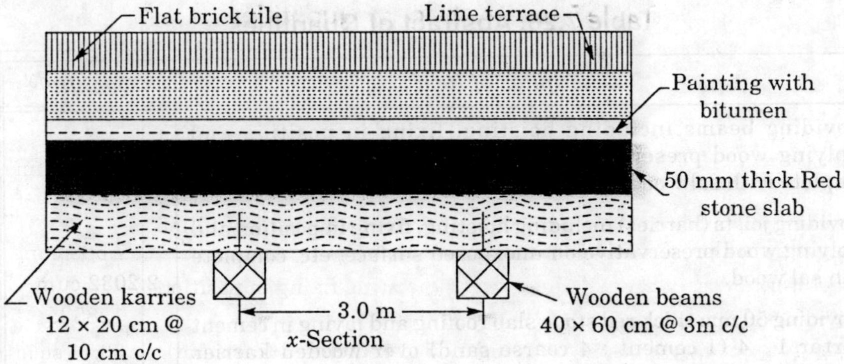

(b)

Fig. 7.16

Table 7.25. Details of Measurements

S. No.	*Description*	*No.*	*L*	*W*	*H/D*	*Content*	*Remark*
1.	Providing beams including hoisting, fixing in position and applying wood preservative complete of sal wood						
	Wooden beams (30 thick walls)	2	6.40	0.40	0.60	3.072	
	Total					3.072 cum	
2.	Providing joists (karries) including hoisting, fixing in position and applying wood preservative complete with sal wood						
	End spans	2 × 9	3.40	0.12	0.20	1.4688	
	Central span	1 × 9	3.40	0.12	0.20	0.7344	
	Total					2.2032 cum	
3.	Providing 50 mm thick red stone slab roofing and laying in cement mortar 1 : 4 mix						
	Over wooden joists (20 cm bearings)	1	6.40	9.40	—	60.16	
	Total					60.16 sq m	
4.	Painting top of roof with betumen of approved quality						
	Over roof (Within parapets)	1	6.20	9.20	—	57.04	
	Total					57.04 sq m	
5.	Lime concrete terracing on roofs covered with flat brick tiles						
	Over roof	1	6.20	9.20	—	57.04	
	Total					57.04 sq m	

Table 7.26. Abstract of Quantities

S. No.	*Description of Item*	*Quantity*	*Remark*
1.	Providing beams including hoisting, fixing in position and applying wood preservative for the unexposed surfaces etc. complete with sal wood.	3.072 cum	
2.	Providing joists (karries) including hoisting, fixing in position and applying wood preservative on unexposed surface, etc. complete with sal wood.	2.2032 cum	
3.	Providing 50 mm thick red stone slab roofing and laying in cement mortar 1 : 4 (1 cement : 4 coarse sand) over wooden karries including painting the exposed joints with the same mortar complete	60.16 sq m	
4.	Painting top of roofs with bitumen of approved quality at 20 kg per 10 m^2 impregnated with a coat of coarse sand at 60 dm^3 per 10 m^2 of surface complete	57.04 sq m	
5.	Lime concrete terracing on roofs, average thicness 10 cm laid to fall with 25 mm nominal size brick aggregate and 50% line mortar 1 : 2 line putty : 2 surkhi) rammed and finished with gur and belgiri treatment complete and covered with flat brick tiles grouted with cement mortar 1 : 3 (1 cement : 3 fine sand) over 12 mm layer of cement mortar 1 : 3 (1 cement : 3 fine sand) over 12 mm layer of cement mortar 1 : 3 fine sand) and finished neat.	57.04 sq m	

Example 7.15. *Calculate the quantities of :*

1. Corbels. *2. Sal wood work.* *3. A.C. sheet roofing.*

4. A.C. roofing accessories. *5. Wind tiles.*

with the help of given plan and cross-section of lean-to-roof covered with A.C. sheet over a verandah 2.00 m wide and 10 m long.

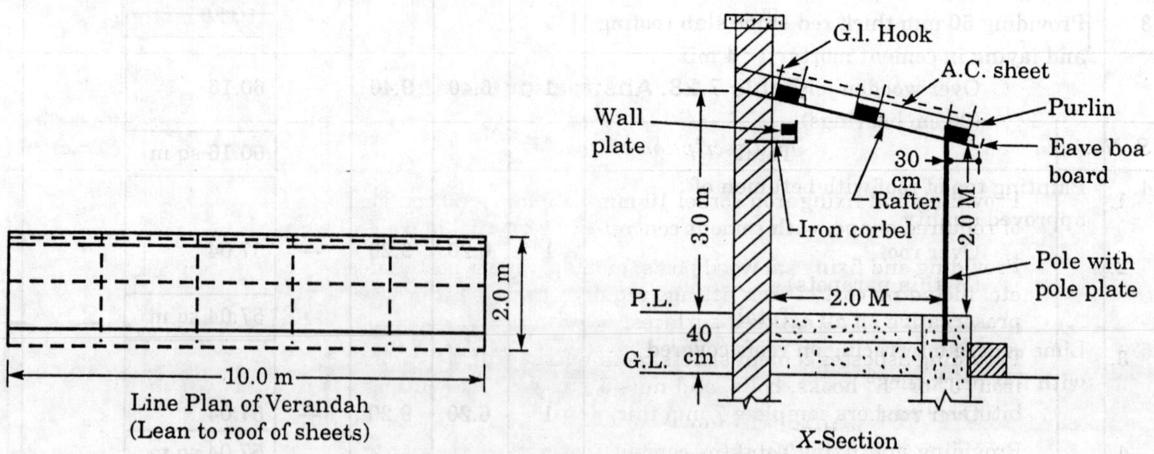

Fig. 7.17

Table 7.27. Details of Measurements

S. No.	*Description of Item*	*No.*	*L*	*W*	*H/D*	*Content*	*Remark*
1.	Providing and fixing iron corbels in wall						
	To support wall plate	6				6 Nos.	
	Total					6 Nos.	
2.	Providing and fixing sal wood in poles, purlins, rafters, etc.						
	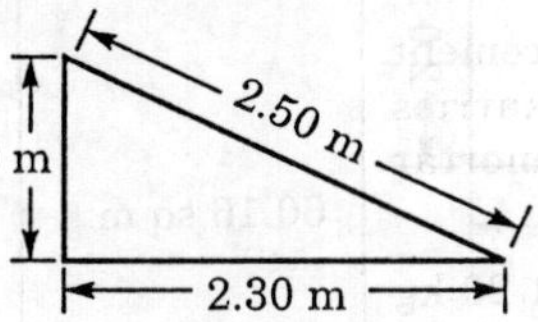 Poles	6	2.60	0.15	0.15	0.351	
	Pole plate	1	10.20	0.10	0.15	0.153	
	Wall plate	1	10.20	0.10	0.15	0.153	
	Purlins	3	10.20	0.10	0.15	0.459	
	Rafter	6	2.50	0.15	0.20	0.450	
	Fig. 7.17 (*a*) Cleats	6×3	0.30	0.15	0.10	0.270	
						1.836 cum	
3.	Providing A.C. sheets roofing fixed with G.I. "J" or "L" hooks; 7 mm thick						
	A.C. sheet roof over verandah	1	10.20	2.30	—	27.52	
	Total					27.52 sq m	
4.	Providing and fixing asbestos cement roofing accessories with G.I. "J" or "L" hooks						
	Eave's filler pieces	1	10.20	—	—	10.20	
	Barge board	2	2.60	—	—	5.20	
	Total					15.40 metre	
5.	Providing and fixing wind tiles of 40 × 6 mm flat iron section						
	At lower end	1	10.20	—	—	10.20	
	Total					10.20 metre	

Table 7.28. Abstract of Quantities

S. No.	*Description of Item*	*Quantity*	*Remark*
1.	Providing and fixing iron corbel 10 mm × 60 mm × 30 cm. long of required shape, with cement concrete 1 : 2 : 4 mix, in wall.	6 No.	
2.	Providing and fixing sal wood posts; purlins, rafters post plates etc. including cost of iron fittings required and applying wood preservative on all exposed surfaces.	1.836 cum	
3.	Providing asbestos cement sheets roofing fixed with galvanized iron "J" or "L" hooks, bolts, and nuts 5 mm dia. G.I. plain and bitumen washers complete 7 mm thick.	26.52 sq m	
4.	Providing and fixing asbestos cement roofing accessories with G.I. "J" or "L" hooks, bolts and nuts and G.L seam bolts and nuts, G.I. plain and bitumen washes etc, complete.	15.40 metre	
5.	Providing and fixing wind tiles of 40 × 6 mm flat iron section.	10.20 metre	

Example 7.16. *Calculate the Quantities of :*

1. M.S. round holding down bolts. *2. Wood work in rafters and battens.*

3. Tile work.

with the help of given plan and cross-section of lean-to-roof covered with Mangalore tiles over a verandah 2.00 m wide and 6 m long.

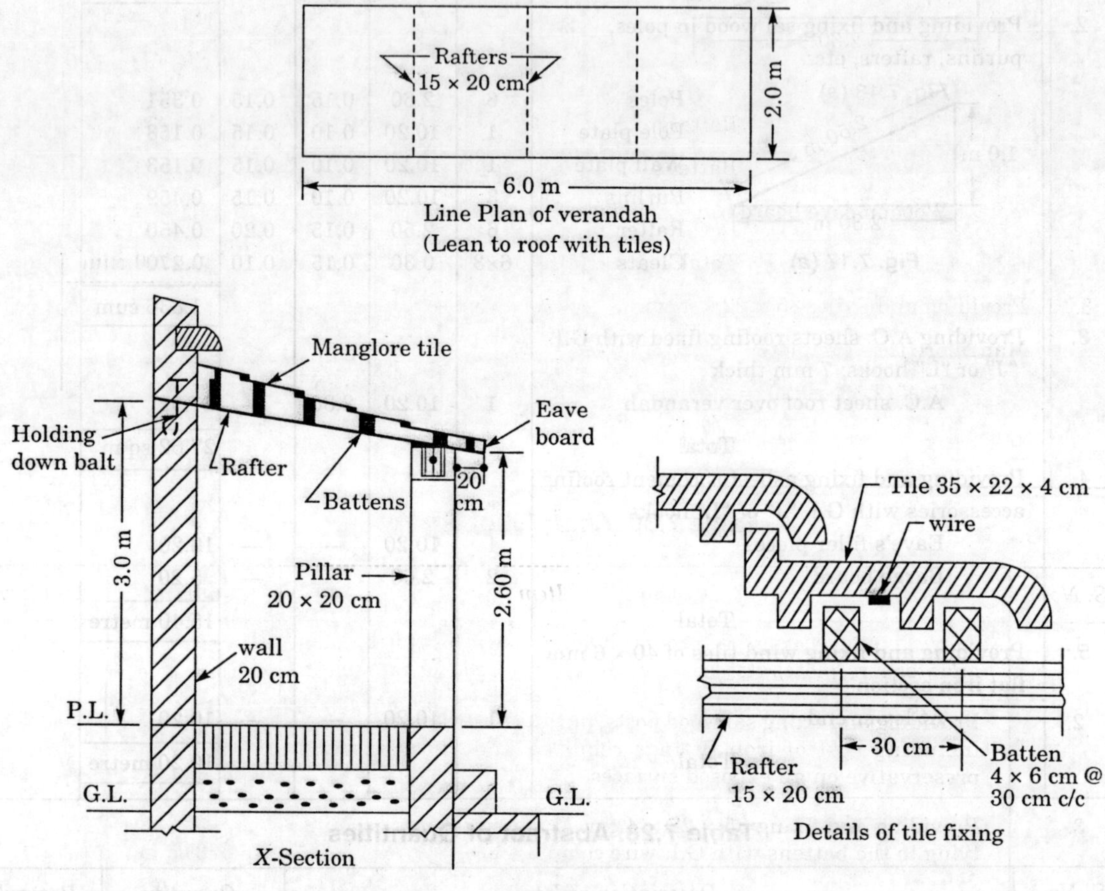

Fig. 7.18

Table 7.29. Details of Measurements

S. No.	*Description of Item*	*No.*	*L*	*W*	*H/D*	*Content*	*Remark*
1.	Providing and fixing M.S. round holding down bolts with nuts and washers, plates, size 20 mm dia and 60 cm. long complete.						
	To secure Rafters	2 × 3	—	—			6 Nos.
	Total					6 Nos.	

2.	Providing and fixing sal wood posts, purlins, rafters etc. 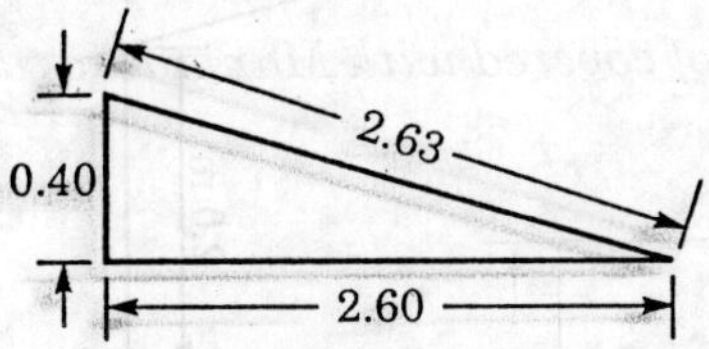 Fig. 7.18 (*a*)						
	Rafters	3	2.63	0.15	0.20	0.2360	
	Battens	8	6.20	0.04	0.60	0.1190	
	Wooden eave board	1	6.00	0.05	0.15	0.0450	
	Total					0.4000 cum	
3.	Providing and fixing 35 × 22 × 4 cm. Mangalore tiles complete.						
	Roof (2.63 – 0.20) = 2.43 m	1	2.43	6.20	—	15.066	
	Total					15.066 sq m	

Table 7.30. Abstract of Quantities

S. No.	*Description of Item*	*Quantity*	*Remark*
1.	Providing and fixing M.S. round holding down bolts with nuts and washers, plates etc. size 20 mm dia. and 60 cm. long complete.	6 Nos.	
2.	Providing and fixing sal wood posts, purlins, rafters battens, etc. including cost of iron fittings required and applying wood preservative on all exposed surfaces.	0.40 cum	
3.	Providing and fixing 35 × 22 × 4 cm. Mangalore tiles including tying to the battens with G.I. wire complete.	15.066 sq m	

Example 7.17. *Calculate the Quantities of* :

1. M.S. round holding down bolts. *2. Wood work in purlin.*

3. Providing bamboo's below thatch roof. *4. Thatch roofing.*

with the help of given plan and cross-section of thatch roof over a room 4.00 m × 300 m.

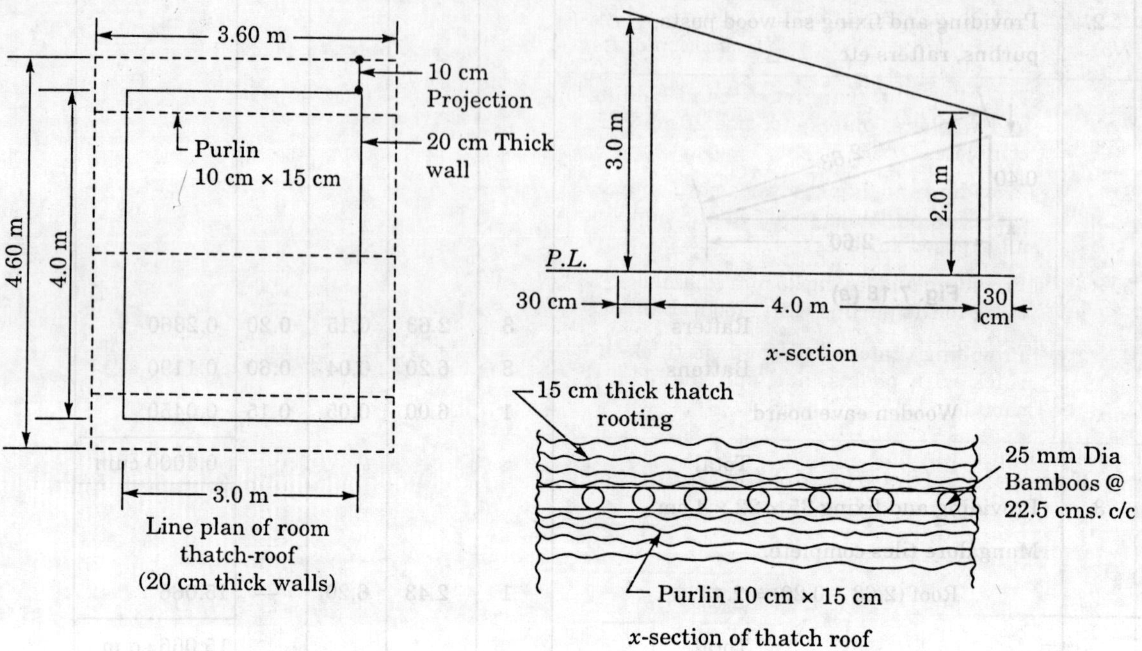

Fig. 7.19

Table 7.31. Details of Measurements

S. No.	*Description of Item*	*No.*	*L*	*W*	*H/D*	*Content*	*Remark*
1.	Providing and fixing m.s. round holding down bolts.						
	To secure purlins	3 × 2	—	—	—	6	
				Total		6 Nos.	
2.	Providing and fixing sal wood posts, purlins etc. Purlin	3	3.60	0.10	0.15	0.162	
				Total		0.162 cum	
3.	Providing and laying 25 mm diameter bamboos 22.5 cm apart						
	Below thatch roof	1	4.71	3.60	—	79.86	
				Total		79.86 sq m	
	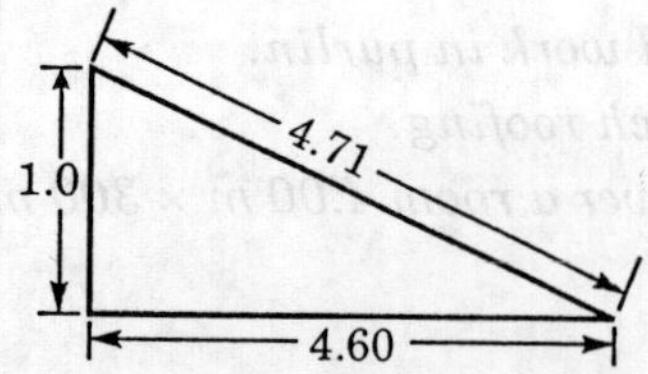 Fig. 7.19(*a*)						
4.	Providing thatch roof 15 cm thick in two layers each 75 mm thick						
	Thatch roof	1	4.71	3.60	—	79.86	
				Total		79.86 sq m	

Table 7.32. Abstract of Quantities

S. No.	Description of Item	Quantity	Remark
1.	Providing and fixing m.s. round holding down bolts with nuts and washers, plates etc. size 20 mm diameter and 60 cm long complete.	6 No.	
2.	Providing and fixing salwood posts, purlins, rafters, etc. including cost of iron fittings required and applying wood preservative on all exposed surfaces.	0.162 cum	
3.	Providing and laying 25 mm ϕ bamboos, 22.5 cm aparts including tying to the purlins with Moonj, Ban, or string complete.	79.86 sq m	
4.	Providing thatch roofing 15 cm thick in two layers each 75 mm thick with poolas, half split bamboo fillet and tying strings complete.	79.86 sq m	

Example 7.18. *Calculate the Quantities of :*

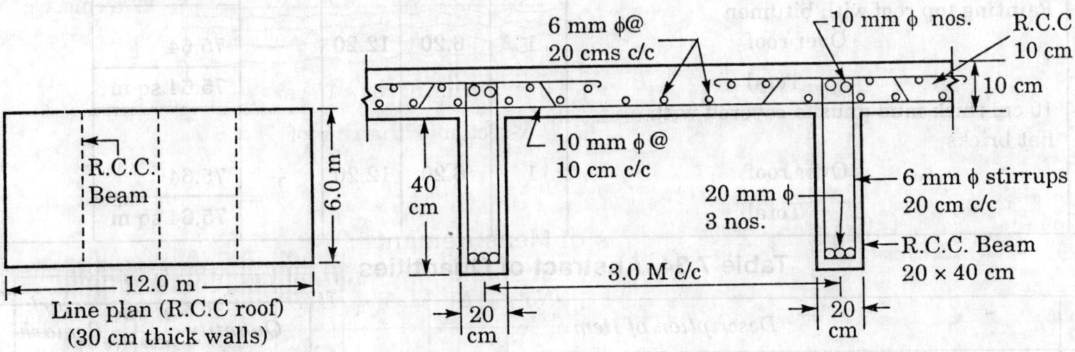

Fig. 7.20

1. *Centring and shuttering.*
2. *Cement concrete 1 : 2 : 4 mix.*
3. *M.S. Bars.*
4. *6 mm thick cement plaster.*
5. *Painting top of roof.*
6. *10 cm thick mud phuska with tile bricks.*

with the help of given plan and cross-section of R.C.C. roof over a hall 6.00 m × 12.00

Table 7.33. Details of Measurements

S. No.	Description of Item		No.	L	W	H/D	Content	Remark
1.	Centring and shuttering for R.C.C. work							
	Beam	Bottom	3	6.00	0.20	—	3.60	
		Sides						
	Slab	Bottom	3 × 2	6.00	0.40		14.40	
		(12.00 – 3 × 0.20) = 11.40 m	1	11.40	6.00	—	68.40	
		Sides	2	6.60	0.10	—	1.32	
			2	12.60	0.10	—	2.52	
		Total					90.24 sq m	

(*Contd.*)

2.	Cement concrete 1 : 2 : 4 mix for R.C.C. work					
	Beams	3	6.60	0.20	0.40	1.584
	Slab	1	12.60	6.60	0.10	8.316
	Total					9.900 cum
3.	Providing and fixing M.S. bars for R.C.C. work					
	m.s. bars @ 1.5% = $\frac{9.90 \times 1.15}{100}$					
	× @ 7840 per cm = 1165					1165 kg
	Total					11650 N
4.	6 mm thick cement plaster to ceiling 1 : 3 mix					
	Beams	3	6.00	1.00	—	18.00
	(40 + 20 + 40) = 100 cm = 1 m	1	11.40	6.00	—	68.40
	Slab					
	Total					86.40 sq m
	Painting top roof with bitumen					
	Over roof	1	6.20	12.20	—	75.64
	Total					75.64 sq m
5.	10 cm thick mud phuska covered with fiat bricks					
	Over roof	1	6.20	12.20	—	75.64
	Total					75.64 sq m

Table 7.34. Abstract of Quantities

S. No.	*Description of Item*	*Quantity*	*Remark*
1.	Centring and shuttering including strutting, proping etc. and removal of formwork etc. for R.C.C. work.	90.24 sq m	
2.	Reinforced cement concrete work 1 : 2 : 4 (1 cement : 2 coarse sand : 4 graded stone aggregate 20 mm nominal size) excluding cost of centring shuttering and reinforcement.	9.90 cum	
3.	Mild steel reinforcement for R.C.C. work including bending, binding and placing in position complete.	1165 kg	
4.	6 mm thick cement plaster to ceiling 1 : 3 (1 cement : 3 fine sand).	86.40 sq m	
5.	Painting top of roof with bitumen @ 20 kg per 10 m^2 impregnated with a cost of coarse sand at 60 dm^3 per 10 m^2 including cleaning of surface complete.	75.64 sq m	
6.	10 cm thick mud phuska of damped brick earth on roof laid to slope, consolidated and plastered with 25 mm thick mud mortar mixed with bhusa at 35 kg per cum of earth and gobri leaping with mix 1 : 1 (1 clay : 1 cowdung) and covered with a flat tile bricks, grouted with cement mortar 1 : 3 (1 cement : 3 find sand) and finished neat.	75.64 sq m	

Example 7.19. *(A) Fig. 7.21 (a) and calculate the lengths of(i) hip rafter (OA) ; (ii) Jack rafter (BC) and (iii) rafter (OD). (All dimensions are centre to centre).*

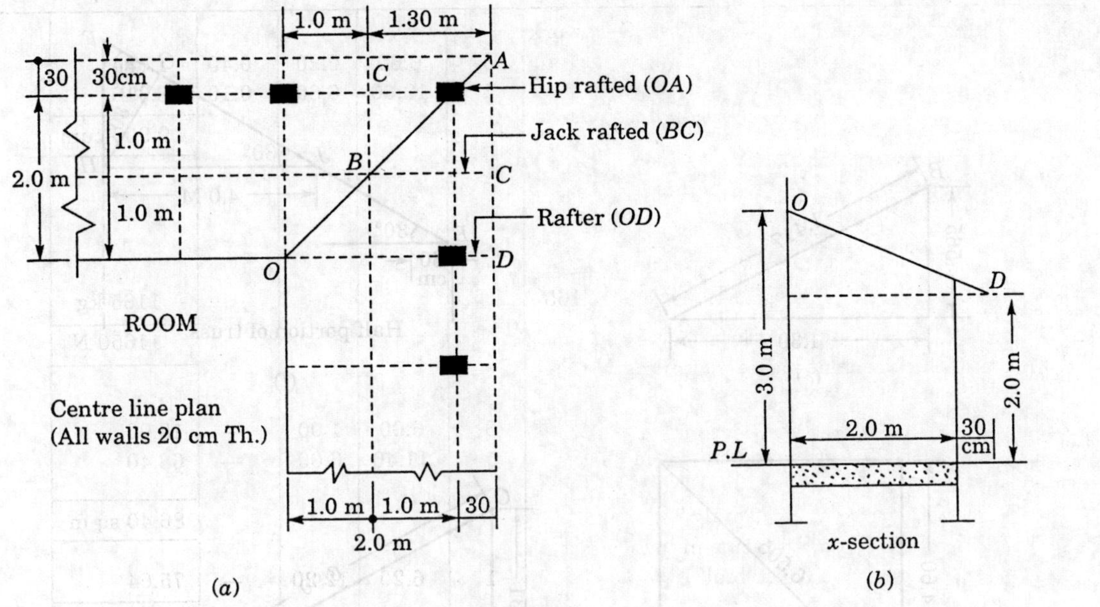

Fig. 7.21

(B) Fig. 7.21 (b) and calculate the length of (i) hip rafter (OA) (ii) jack rafter (BC) and (ii) rafter (OD).

Also calculate the lengths of different members of truss (all dimensions are centre to centre).

Calculations—Part (A). Length of rafter = *OD*

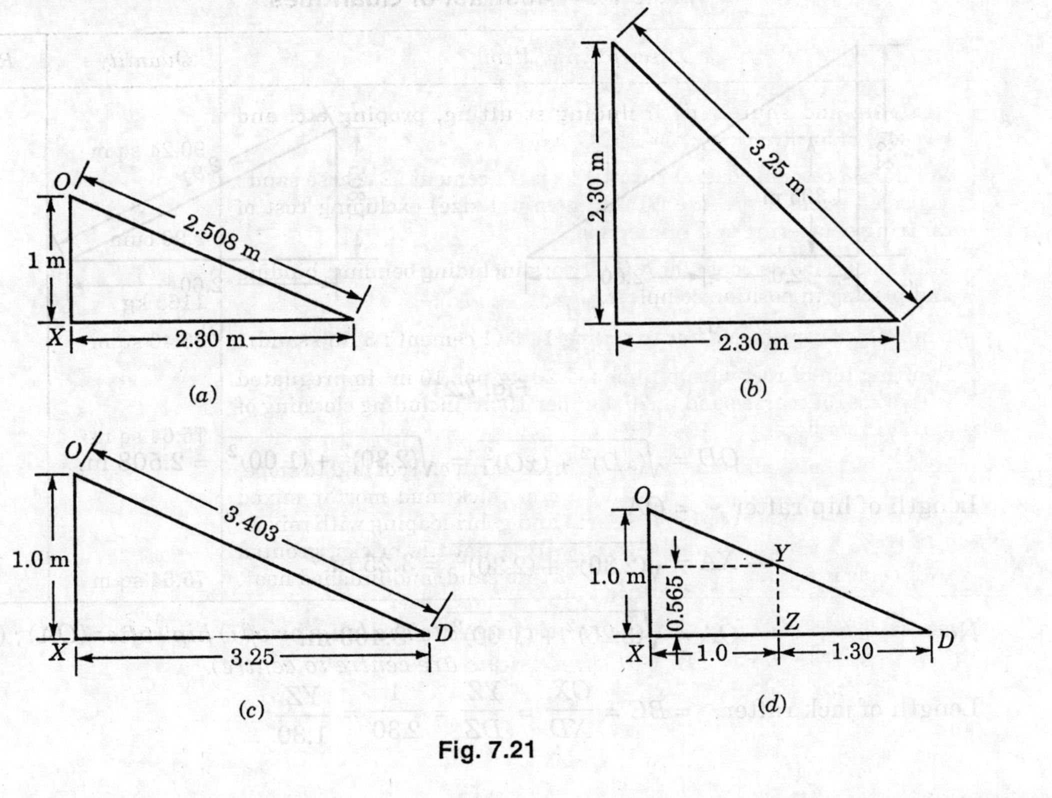

Fig. 7.21

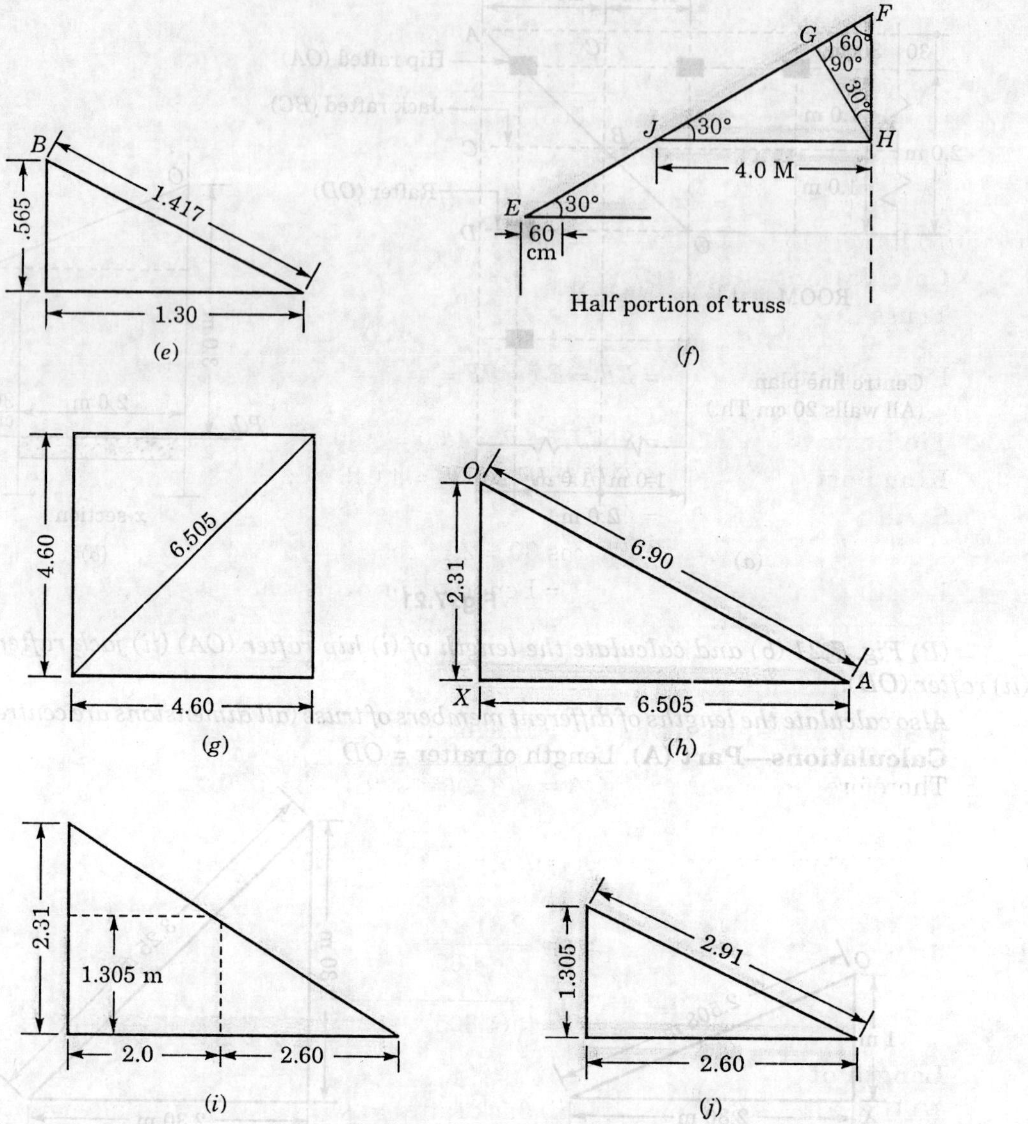

Fig. 7.21

$$OD = \sqrt{(xD)^2 + (xO)^2} = \sqrt{(2.30)^2 + (1.00)^2} = 2.508 \text{ m.}$$

Length of hip rafter $= OA$

$$XA = \sqrt{(2.30)^2 + (2.30)^2} = 3.25 \text{ m.}$$

Now $$OA = \sqrt{(3.25)^2 + (1.00)^2} = 3.403 \text{ m.}$$

Length of jack rafter $= BC = \dfrac{OX}{XD} = \dfrac{YZ}{DZ} = \dfrac{1}{2.30} = \dfrac{YZ}{1.30}$

$$YZ = \frac{1.30}{2.30} = 0.565 \text{ m}$$

$$BC = \sqrt{(0.565)^2 + (1.30)^2} = 1.417 \text{ m.}$$

Length of :

(*i*) Hip rafter OA = 3.403 m (*ii*) Jack rafter BC = 1.417 m

(*iii*) Rafter OB = 2.508 m.

Calculations—Part (B)

Truss

Principal rafter $= EF = EJ + JF = \frac{0.60}{\cos 30} + \frac{4.00}{\cos 30} = 0.693 + 4.619 = 5.312$ m.

Tie Beam $= 2 \times JH = 2 \times 4.00 = 8.00$ m.

King post $= F.H = JF \sin 30 = 4.619 \times ½ = 2.31$ m.

Strut $= GH$

$= FH \cos 30 = 2.31 \cos 30 = 2.00$ m.

Length of rafter = Length of principal rafter = 5.312 m.

Length of hip rafter $= OA = 5.312$ m.

Horizontal projection or $OA = \sqrt{(4.60)^2 + (4.60)^2} = 7.505$ m.

Height of ridge above wall = Height of king post = 2.31 m.

Therefore $OA = \sqrt{(6.505)^2 + (2.31)^2} = 6.90$ m.

Length of jack rafter $= BC = \frac{2.31}{4.60} = \frac{xy}{2.60}$

i.e. $$xy = \frac{2.31 \times 2.60}{4.60} = 1.305 \text{ m.}$$

$$BC = \sqrt{(1.305)^2 + (2.60)^2} = 2.91 \text{ m.}$$

Length of

(*i*) Hip rafter = 6.90 m (*ii*) Jack rafter = 2.91 m (*iii*) Rafter = 5.312 m.

Length of truss members

1. Tie beam = 8.00 m
2. King post = 2.31 m
3. Principal rafter = 5.312 m
4. Strut = 2.00 m.

Example 7.20. *Calculate the quantities of :*

1. M.S. round holding down bolts

2. Salwood work in truss etc.

3. A.C. sheet rooting

4. A.C. roofing accessories

5. A.C. ridges and hips

6. M.S. wind ties.

with the help of given plan and cross-section of pitched roof for a hall 6.00 m × 9.00 m.

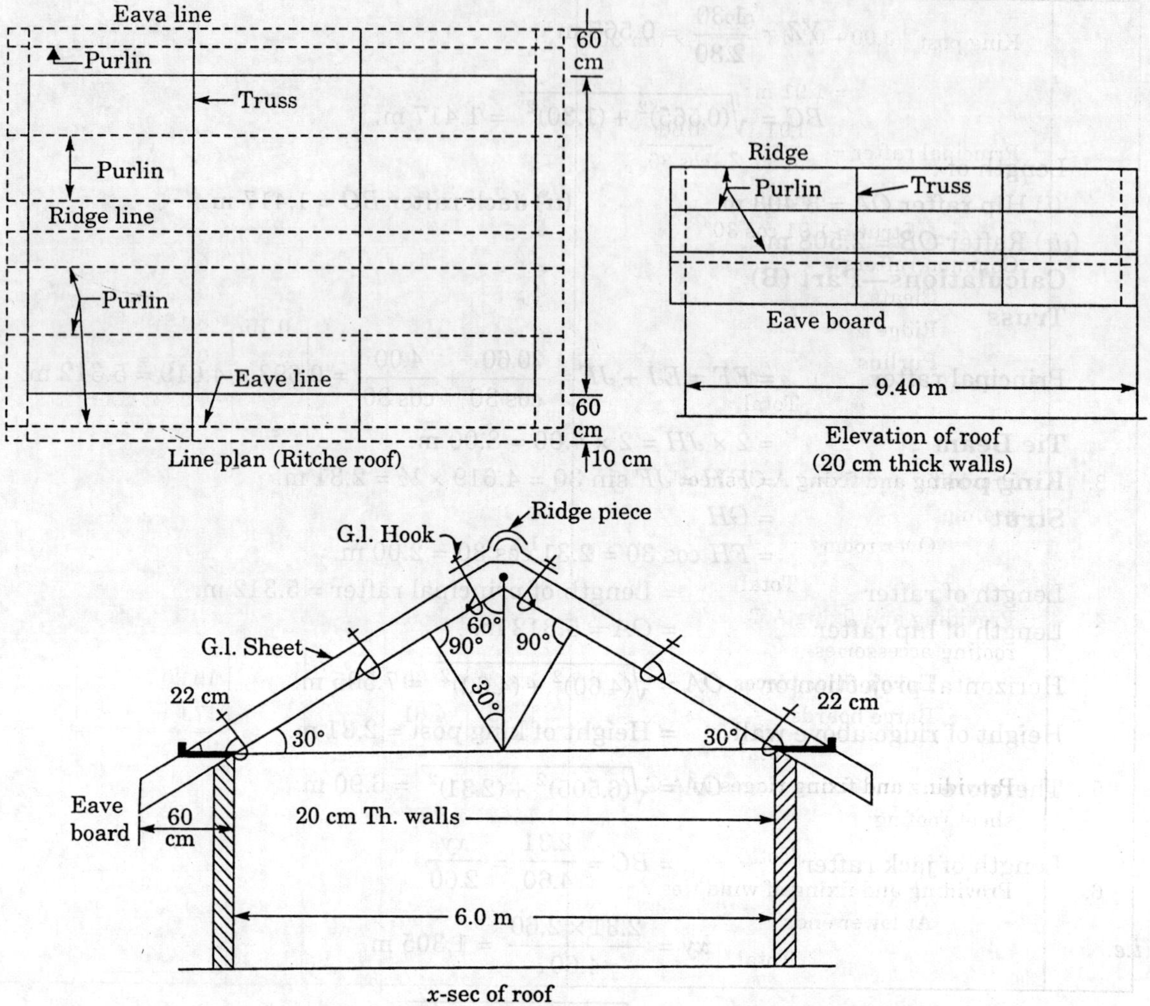

Fig. 7.22

Table 7.35

S. No.	*Description of Item*	*No.*	*L*	*W*	*H/D*	*Content*	*Remark*
1.	Providing and fixing M.S. holding down bolts						
	For truss	2 × 2	—	—	—	4	
	For rafter over end walls	2 × 2	—	—	—	4	
	Total					8 Nos.	
2.	Providing and fixing sal wood in truss, rafter, purlins etc.						
	In truss						
	2. Nos. Tie beam						
	(6.00 + 2 × 0.20 + 2 × 0.22) = 6.84 m	2	6.84	0.15	0.30	0.6156	

	King post $\left(3.00 + 0.20 + \frac{0.22}{2}\right) \times \tan 30°$						
	= 1.91 m	2	1.91	0.15	0.15	0.8595	
	Principal rafter = $\frac{1.91}{\sin 30} + \frac{0.60}{\cos 30}$						
	= 4.51 m	2 × 2	4.51	0.15	0.22	0.5953	
	Strut = 1.91 cos 30°	2 × 2	1.654	0.15	0.15	0.1488	
	Common rafters	4	4.51	0.15	0.22	0.5953	
	Cleats	4 × 6	0.30	0.15	0.10	0.1080	
	Ridge	1	9.60	0.10	0.15	0.1440	
	Purlins	2 × 3	9.60	0.10	0.15	0.8640	
	Total					3.9305 cum	
					say	3.931 cum	
3.	Providing and fixing A.C. sheet roofing						
	Over room	1 × 2	9.60	4.61	—	88.512	
	Total					88.512 sq m	
4.	Providing and fixing A.C. roofing accessories						
	Eave's filler pieces	1 × 2	9.60	—	—	19.20	
	Barge boards	1 × 2	4.61	—	—	17.64	
	Total					37.84 m	
5.	Providing and fixing ridges in A.C. sheet roofing	1 × 2	9.60	—	—	19.20	
	Total					19.20 m	
6.	Providing and fixing of wind ties						
	At lower ends	1 × 2	9.60	—	—	19.20	
	Total					19.20 m	

Table 7.36. Abstract of Quantities

S. No.	*Description of Item*	*Quantity*	*Remark*
1.	Providing and fixing M.S. round holding down bolts with nuts and washers, plate etc. size 20 mm diameter and 60 cm long complete.	8 Nos.	
2.	Providing and fixing sal wood truss, purlins, rafters etc. including cost of iron fittings required and applying wood preservative on all exposed surfaces.	3.931 cum	
3.	Providing asbestos cement sheet roofing fixed with galvanized iron 'J' or 'L' hooks, bolts and nuts, 5 mm diameter G.I. plain and bitumen washers complete.	88.512 sq m	
4.	Providing and fixing asbestos cement roofing accessories with G.I. 'J' or 'L' hooks, bolts and nuts and G.I. seam bolts and nuts, G.I. plain and bitumen washers etc. complete.	36.84 metre	
5.	Providing and fixing ridge in asbestos cement sheets rooting with G.I. 'J' or 'L' hooks, bolts and nuts 8 mm diameter G.I. plain and bitumen washers complete.	19.20 metre	
6.	Providing and fixing wind ties of 40 × 6 mm flat iron section.	19.20 metre	

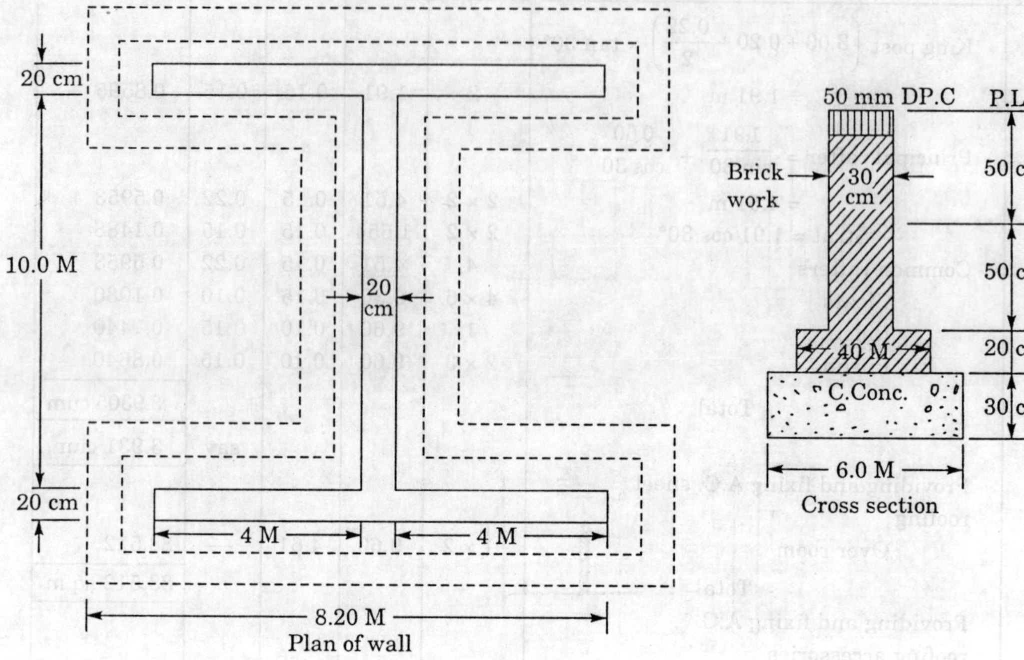

Fig. 7.23

Example 7.21. *Double storeyed building. (Ground Floor) (see figure 7.24 A)*

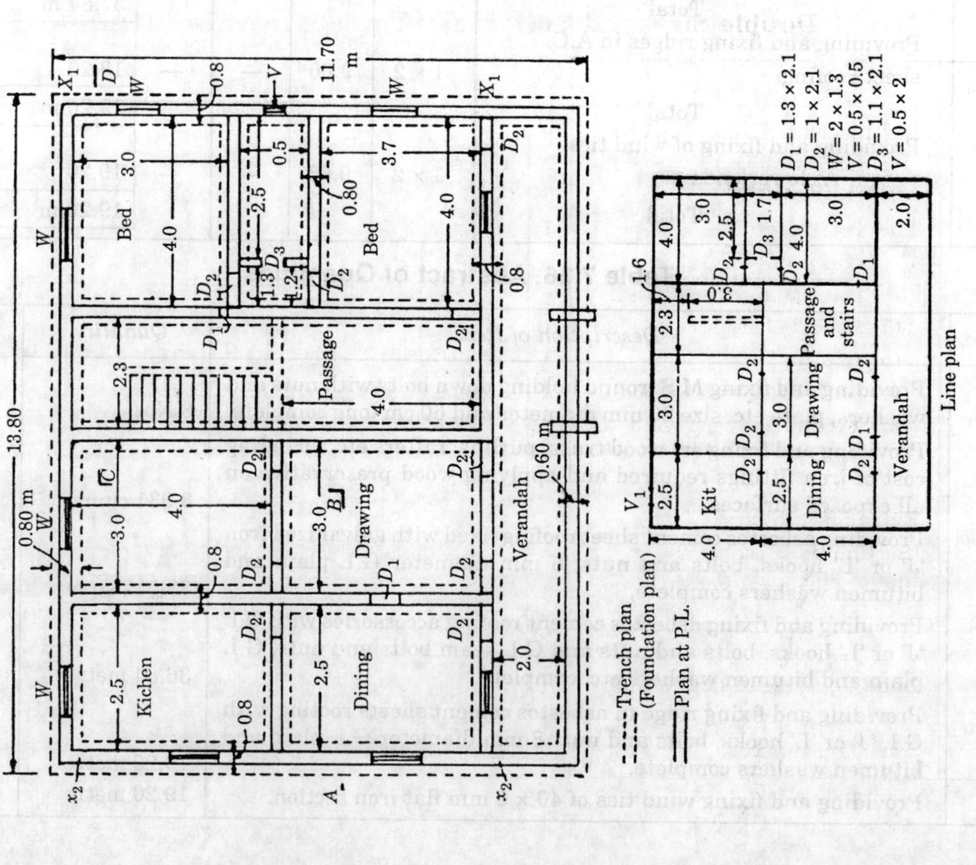

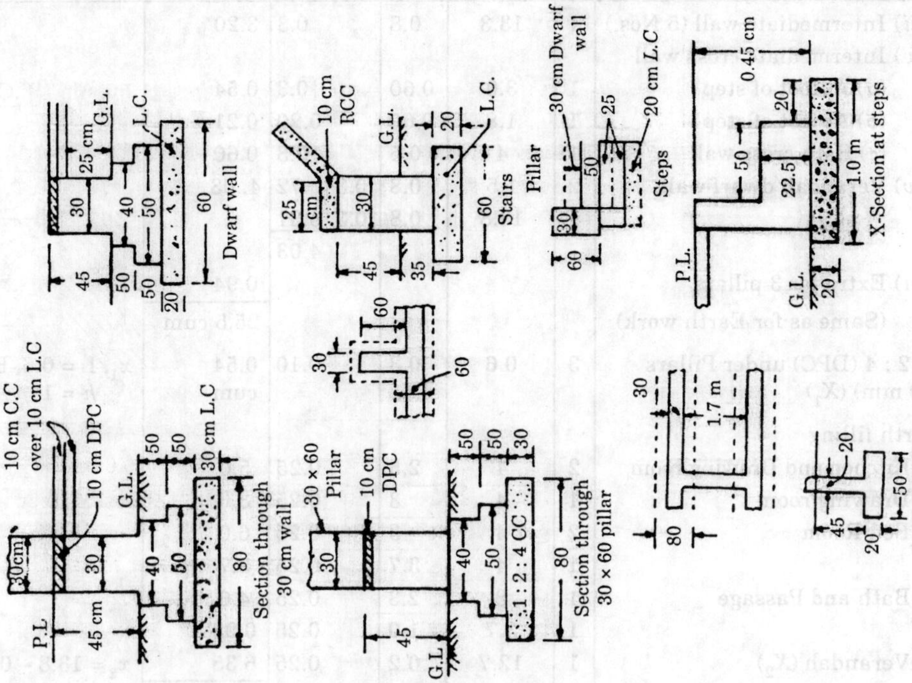

Fig. 7.24 A. Double Storeyed Building. (Ground Floor)

Double Storeyed Building. (Ground Floor) (see figure)

S. No.	*Particular of Item*	No	L	B	H/D	Qnty.	Remarks
1.	Earthwork in Excavation						
	(*i*) Long wall (x_1)	2	138(x_1)	0.8	13.00	28.70	
	(*ii*) Cross wall (x_2)	5	7.8(x_2)	0.8	1.30	40.56	$x_1 = 25 + 3 + 2.3 + 4 + 5$
	(*iii*) Intermediate cross wall (SN)x_3	1	13.3(x_3)	0.8	1.30	13.83	$\times 9 + 0.5 = 138$
	(*iv*) Intermediate cross wall						$x_2 = 83 - \frac{0.8-3}{2} \times 2$
	(*a*) At foot of steps (x_4)	1	30.00	0.6	0.60	1.08	
	(*b*) At stair	1	1.80	0.8	1.30	1.87	$= 8.3 - 0.5 = 7.8$
	(*v*) Bath cross wall (5 Nos.)	1	0.04	0.5	1.30	2.60	$x_3 = (2.5 - 0.5) + 3 - 0.5$
	(*vi*) Verandah dwarf wall	2	1.50	0.8	1.3} 3.12	17.47	$+ (2.3 - 0.5) + 2(4 - 5).$
		1	13.80	0.8	1.3} 14.35	cum	$= 2 + 2.5 + 1.8 + 7 = 13.3$
					17.47		x_4 = L = 30, B = 0.6,
	Extra for 3 Pillars						$h = 0.6$
	(Section up PL same as	3	.3	.8	1.3	0.94	At stair 2.3 − 0.5 = 15,
	that of 30 cm wall)					cum	B = 0.8, h = 1.3
						107.05	
						un	
2.	Lime Concrete in Foundation						
	(*i*) Long wall	2	13.8	0.80	0.3	6.62	
	(*ii*) Cross wall	5	7.8	0.8	0.3	9.36	

(*Contd.*)

	(*iii*) Intermediate wall (5 Nos.)	1	13.3	0.8		0.3	3.20	
	(*iv*) Intermediate cross wall							
	(*a*) At foot of step	1	3.0	0.60		0.3	0.54	
	(*b*) At foot of step	1	1.8	0.60		0.20	0.21	
	(c) Bath cross wall	1	4	0.5		0.3	0.60	
	(*v*) Verandah dwarf wall	2	1.5	0.8	0.3 }	.72	4..03	
		1	13.8	0.8	0.3 }	3.31		
						4.03		
	(*vi*) Extra for 3 pillars						0.94	
	(Same as for Earth work)						25.5 cum	
3.	1 : 2 : 4 (DPC) under Pillars (10 mm) (X_1)	3	0.6	0.3		0.10	0.54 cum	x_1, L = 0.6, B = 0.3, h = 1
4.	Earth filling							
	(*i*) Kitchen and Drawing room	2	4	2.5		0.25	5.0	
	(*ii*) Drawing room	1	4	3		0.25	3.6	
	(*iii*) Bed Room	2	4	3		0.25	6.0	
		1	4	3.7		0.25	3.7	
	(*iv*) Bath and Passage	1	8	2.3		0.25	4.6	
		1	3.7	1.0		0.25	0.92	
	(*v*) Verandah (X_2)	1	12.7	0.2		0.25	6.35	x_2 = 13.8 – 0.6 – 0.5
							29.57 cum	= 12.7
5.	Brick work 1 : 6 C.C.							x_1 = 2.5 + 3 + 2.3 + 4
	on foundation G.L.							+ 0.3 × 0.5 – 0.5 = 13.3
	(*a*) First Footing							x_2 = 8 + 0.3 – 0.3 = 8
	(*i*) Long wall (x_1)	2	13.30	0.5		0.50	6.65	
	(*ii*) Cross wall (x_2)	5	8	0.5		0.50	10.60	
	(*iii*) Intermediate wall	2	(2.5 – .1)	0.5		0.50	0.60 }	
		2	(4–.1)	0.5		0.50	0.97 } 2.12	
		1	(23–.1)	0.5		0.50	0.55 } cum	
	(*iv*) Verandah dwarf wall	1	13.80	0.5		0.50	3.45 }	
		1	18.50	0.5		0.50	0.92 } 4.37	
	Extra of 3 Pillar	3	0.50	0.5		0.50	0.37 cum	
	(*v*) Intermediate cross wall							
	(*i*) At foot of staircase	1	2.10	.30		0.45	0.28 } 1.2	x_3 = 2.3 – .2 = 2.1
		1	0.60	.20		0.70	0.84 }	
	(*ii*) 20 cm wall along staircase	2	1.00	.20		2.00	0.8 cum	
							26.03 cum	
	(*b*) Second Footing							
	(*i*) Long wall (x_1)	2	12.00	0.4		0.50	4.80	x_1 = 12.8 – (8 – .4)
	(*ii*) Cross wall (x_2)	5	8.00	0.4		0.40	6.40	× 2 = 12
	(*iii*) Intermediate wall	2	(3 –.3)	0.4		0.50	1.08 }	x_2 = 8
		2	(4 –.3)	0.4		0.50	1.48 } 2.9	
		1	(2 –.3)	0.4		0.50	0.34 }	

	(*iv*) Extra for 3 pillar	3	.305	0.4	0.50	0.18 cum	
	(*v*) Verandah dwarf wall	1	.80	0.4	0.50	2.76 } 3.14	
		2	(2 –.1) = 1.9	0.4	0.50	0.76 }	
	(*vi*) Intermediate wall						
	(*a*) At first of step		Include in 1st footing			—	
	(*b*) Stair					17.80 + 26.03 = 43.83	
6.	25 mm 1 : 2 : 4 cement concrete						
	(*i*) Long wall	2	12.00	3.00	0.10	0.72	
	(*ii*) Cross wall	5	7.80	0.30	0.10	1.17	
	(*iii*) Internal cross wall	2	2.70	0.40	0.10	0.20 }	
		2	3.70	0.50	0.10	0.37 } 0.65	
		1	(1.70 × 1.40)	0.50	0.10	0.08 }	
	(*iv*) (*a*) Top of stair	1	2.20	0.30	0.10	0.06	
	(*b*) Top of step	2	0.60	0.20	0.10	0.02	
	(*v*) Verandah dwarf wall	1	13.80	0.30	0.10	0.41 } 0.46	
		2	1.85	0.30	0.10	0.05 }	
						3.32 cum	
7.	BW 1 : 6 between CL and PL						
	(*i*) Long wall	1	12.60	0.30	0.45	3.4	
	(*ii*) Cross over	5	7.80	0.30	0.45	0.54	
	(*iii*) Internal intermediate wall	1	15.30	0.30	0.45	2.06	2.5 × 2 + 2.3 + 2 × 4 = 15.3
	(*iv*) Intermediate cross wall						
	(*a*) Stairs	1	2.30	0.60	0.45	0.62	
	(*b*) Steps	2	6.00	0.20	0.225	.054	
		1	2.30	0.50	0.225	0.26	
	Stairs, side wall	2	0.60	0.20	0.45	0.108	
	(*vi*) Bath room cross wall	1	1.00	0.30	0.45	0.13	
	Verandah dwarf wall	2	12.80	0.30	0.45	0.54	
		1	0.20	0.30	0.45	1.73 } 2.27	
	Add for 3 Pillars	3	0.60	0.30	0.45	0.24 }	
						7.62 cum	
8.	BW in Superstructure 1 : 6 (cement : sand)						r_1 = 13.3 – (.8 – .3) × 2 = 12.3
	(*i*) Long wall	2	12.30	0.30	3.00	22.14	
	(*ii*) Cross wall	5	7.80	0.30	3.00	35.10	
	Intermediate wall	1	15.30	0.30	3.00	13.72	
	Verandah Pillar	3	0.60	0.30	3.00	1.62	
						72.58	
	Deduct for door, windows, ventilators D_1	2	1.30	0.30	2.10	2.34	
		5	1.00	0.30	2.10	3.15	
	W	7	2.30	0.30	1.30	5.46	
	V	1	0.50	0.30	0.50	0.08	
						11.03	
						(72.58 – 11.03) = 61.55 cum	

(*Contd.*)

S. No.	Description		No.	L	B	H	Quantity	Remarks
9.	RCC. 1 : 2.4 on slab lintel excluding reinforcement put including shuttering and centring							L = 2.5 + 3 + 2.3 + 4 = 11.5 + 0.3 × 3 + 0.2 × 2 = 13.1 } 2.27
	(*i*) 10 cm		1	13.10	11.70	0.10	15.33	
	(*ii*) Verandah front		2	13.10	1.20	0.30	0.79	(20 cm over each end)
	"	side	2	1.60	0.30	0.30	0.29	$L = \sqrt{2.5^2 + 15^2} = 292$
	(*iii*) Lintels	D_1	2	1.60	0.30	0.10	0.09	3 ÷ 0.15 = 20
		D_2	5	1.30	0.30	0.10	0.20	
		W	7	1.10	0.30	0.10	0.23	
		V	1	0.80	0.30	0.10	0.02	
	(*iv*) Staircase wall		2	2.92	1.00	0.20	1.16	
	Stain Step		20	1.00	0.20	0.50	2.00	
			1	2.30	—	0.30	0.69	
			1	2.30	0.30	0.30	0.20	
							21.60 cum	
10.	Cement sand 12 mm thick plaster on wall inside							
	(*i*) Bedroom	Long wall	3 × 2	4.00	3.00	—	72.33 sq m	
		Short wall	3 × 2	3.00	3.00	—	54.00 sq m	
		Bed room	1 × 2	3.70	3.00	—	22.20 sq m	
	(*ii*) Drawing room							
		Long wall	2	4.00	3.00	—	24.00 sq m	
		Short wall	2	3.00	3.00	—	18.00 sq m	
	(*iii*) Kitchen							
		Long wall	2	4.00	3.00	—	24.00 sq m	
		Short wall	2	2.50	3.00	—	15.00 sq m	
	(*iv*) Dining room							
		Long wall	2	4.00	3.00	—	24.00 sq m	
		Short wall	2	3.00	3.00	—	18.00 sq m	
	(*v*) Verandah							
		Long wall	1	13.30	3.00	—	39.90 sq m	2.5 + 3 + 2.3 + 4 + 1.5 = 13.3
		Short wall	2	1.85	3.00	—	11.10 sq m	
	(*vi*) Bath and Passage							2.0 – 0.15 = 1.85
		Long wall	2	3.70	3.00	—	22.80 sq m	
		Short wall	4	1.00	3.00	—	12.00 sq m	
	(*vii*) Extra for Pillar		3 × 2 × 2	0.30	3.00	—	10.80 sq m	
	(*viii*) Stair case and Passage		2	8.00	3.00	—	48.00 sq m	
							453.10	
	Deduct :	D_1	2	1.30	2.10	—	5.46	
		D_2	5	1.00	2.10	—	10.50	
		W	7	2.00	1.30		18.20	
							34.16	
							453.10	
							34.16	
	Wall above staircase						418.94 cum	
			2	1.00	2.00	4	4	
							422.94 cum	

11.	1 : 4.6 mm ceiling plaster						
	(*i*) Bed room	3	4.00	3.00	—	36.00	
		1	4.00	3.70	—	14.80	
	(*ii*) Drawing room	1	4.00	3.00	—	12.00	
	(*iii*) Kitchen	1	4.00	2.50	—	10.00	
	(*iv*) Dining room	—	4.00	2.50	—	10.00	
	(*v*) Bath and Passage	4.10	1.10	1.00	—	4.00	
	(*vi*) Verandah	1	11.90	2.00	—	23.80	– 0.11+ 3.3 = 11.9
	(*vii*) Passage and stair	1	8.30	2.30	—	19.09	
	Water slab	2	9.20	1.00	—	18.40	
						147.69	
12.	1 : 2 : 4 cement concrete 25 mm thick floor						
	(*i*) Bed room	3	4	3.00	—	36.99	
		1	4	3.70	—	14.80	
	(*ii*) Drawing room	1	4	3.00	—	12.00	
	(*iii*) Dressing room	1	4	2.50	—	10.00	
	(*iv*) Kitchen	1	4	2.50	—	10.00	
	(*v*) Bath and Passage	1	3.70	1.00	—	3.70	
	(*vi*) Verandah	1	11.90	2.00	—	2.38	
	Passage and stairs	1	8.30	2.30	—	19.01	
						132.81	
	Deduct Pillar inside verandah	0.10	0.30	0.30	—	0.27	
						132.54	
13.	M.S. Railing of stair case	2	2.92	—	—	5.84 m	Length of railing shall be equal to waste slab (assumed as 100 N/m)
14.	4 cm thick RCC Precast jali work including fixing on internal wall	1	2.00	2.30	—	4.60 m^2	
15.	Three coat white washing (**)		(10 + 11) 339.23 + 110.16			449.39 m^2	The quantity shall be equal to used plaster and plastic
16.	Colour wash (***) two coats one coat white washing		(10 + 11)			449.39 m^2	
17.	M.S. (****) reinforcement on slab and level including bend as placing on		(1% of door 9) = .1926×78.9			15.11 q	(****) Quantity equal to 1% of RCC work in item 9 Qnty. on earth $\frac{P}{100}$ × 785q. Density of stair = 78.59 cm

(*Contd.*)

18.	Salwood in chaukhat						
	Doors	2	5.30	0.12	0.07	0.08	
		5	5.00	0.12	0.07	0.22	
	Windows	7	9.20	0.12	0.07	0.54	
	Ventilator	1	2.00	0.12	0.07	0.02	
						.85 cum	
19.	30 mm thick Deodar wood in doors, windows, shutters including M.S. Steel fill up						
	D_1	2	1.80	—	1.93	6.95	
	D_2	5	0.88	—	1.93	8.50	
	W	7 × 2	0.40	—	1.18	6.60	
		7 × 2	0.82	—	1.18	13.50	
						35.55 m^3	
20.	30 mm thick glazed ventilator (Deodar wood)	1	0.35	—	0.38	0.14 m^2	
21.	Painting door and windows two coats over one coat of primary						
	D_1	2	2.60	1.30	—	6.76	
	D_2	5	2.60	1.00	—	13.00	
	Windows	7	2.60	2.00	—	36.40	
	Ventilator	1	2.00	0.50	0.50	1.00	
	M.S. ventilator and windows grafter	1	0.40	1.18	—	0.48	
		7	0.82	1.18	—	6.80	
						64.44	
22.	M.S. work on doors, windows, ventilators						
	Door	8 × 7	—	—	—	56 Nos.	
	Window	7 × 4	—	—	—	28.00	
	Ventilator	1 × 2	—	—	—	2.00	
						86 @ 860 N	10 Nos. each (86 kg)
	16 mm round bar in window @ 1.50 N/m	7	9.00	2.00	—	126.00 m	
		1	2.00	5.00	—	1.00 m	
						127 m	@ 1.58 N/m = 200.64 kg
						86.00 kg +	200 kg = 286.6 kg
						say	287 kg
						2.87 q	= 2.87 quintals
23.	Coal taring two coats using 0.16 and 0.12 litre coal tar per sqm in first and second coat respectively						
	D	2	5.30	0.12		1.28	
		5	5.00	0.12	—	3.00	
	Window	7	9.20	0.12	—	7.73	
	Verandah	1	2.00	0.12	—	0.24	
						12.25 m^2	

Double Storeyed Building (First Floor)

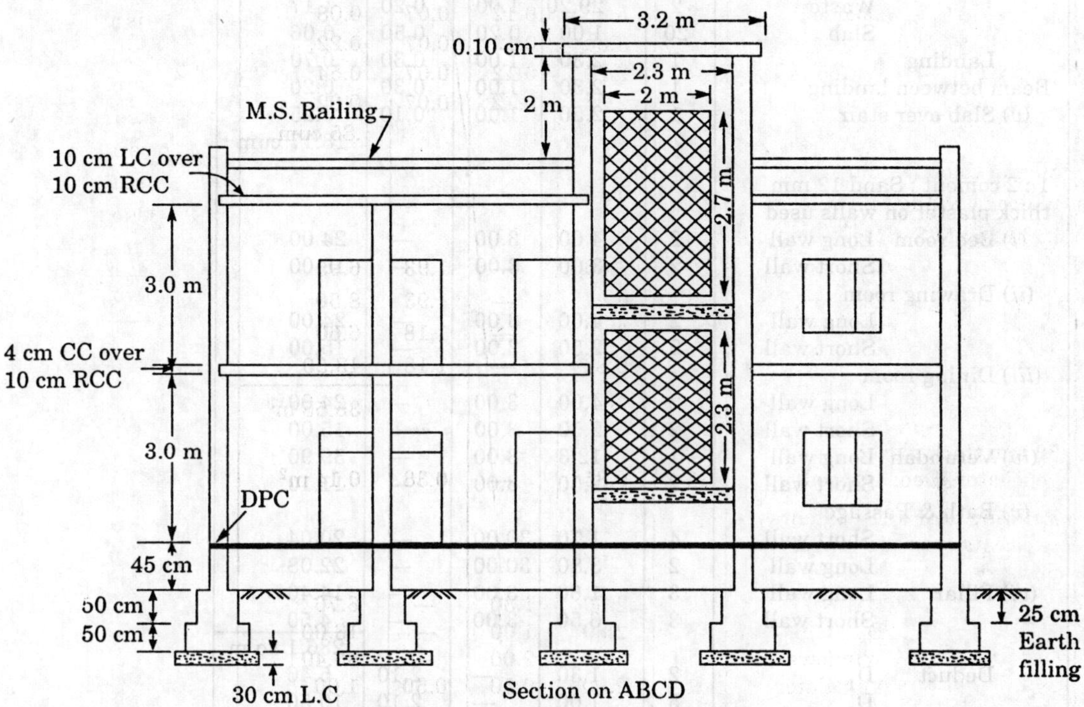

Fig. 7.24 B. Double Storeyed Building.

D. S. Building (First Floor)

S. No.	*Particular of Item*	No.	L	B	H/D	Qnty.	Remarks
1.	BW on 1 : 6 cement mortar (Superstructure)						n_1 2.5 + 3 + 2.3 + 4.0 + 5 × 4 = 13.8 – 5 = 13.3
	(*i*) Long wall	2	13.30	0.30	0.30	23.94	
	(*ii*) Cross wall	5	8.30	0.30	0.30	37.35	
	(*iii*) Internal wall	1	13.50	0.20	3.00	8.10	
	(*iv*) Bath—cross wall	1	1.70	0.20	3.00	1.02	
	(*v*) Verandah pillar	3	0.60	0.30	3.24	1.74	
						72.15	
	Deduct for door, window & lintel as per item 8 of G.F.		72.50–11.03		=	61.12	
	(*vi*) Wall above staircase	2	1.00	1.00	2	4.00	
						65.12	
2.	RCC work 1: 2 : 4 in slabs and lintels including reinforcement						
	(*i*) 10 cm slab	1	13.1	11.0	0.10	14.41	
	(*ii*) Verandah beam						
	Front	1	13.1	0.20	0.30	11.40	
	Side	1	2.40	0.20	0.30	0.14	
	(*iii*) Lintels D_1	2	1.60	0.20	0.30	0.10	
	D_2	5	1.30	0.30	0.10	0.12	
	W	7	1.10	0.30	0.10	0.23	
	V	1	0.80	0.30	0.10	0.02	

(*Contd.*)

	(*iv*) Stair case						
	Waste	2	29.20	1.00	0.20	1.17	
	Slab	20	1.00	0.20	0.50	0.06	
	Landing	1	2.30	1.00	0.30	0.70	
	Beam between landing	1	2.30	1.00	0.30	0.20	
	(*v*) Slab over stair	1	2.50	1.00	0.10	0.25	
						18.17 cum	
3.	1 : 2 cement : Sand 12 mm thick plaster on walls used						
	(*i*) Bed room Long wall	2	4.00	3.00	—	24.00	
	Short wall	2	3.00	3.00	—	18.00	
	(*ii*) Drawing room						
	Long wall	2	4.00	3.00	—	24.00	
	Short wall	2	2.50	3.00	—	15.00	
	(*iii*) Dining room						
	Long wall	2	4.00	3.00	—	24.00	
	Short wall	2	2.50	3.00	—	15.00	
	(*iv*) Verandah Long wall	1	12.3	3.00	—	39.90	
	Short wall	2	2.50	3.00	—	11.10	
	(*v*) Bath & Passage						
	Short wall	4	1.70	30.00	—	20.04	
	Long wall	2	3.80	30.00	—	22.08	
	(*vi*) Pillar Long wall	3	1.60	3.00	—	14.40	
	Short wall	3	6.50	3.00	—	4.50	
						236.1 sq m	
	Deduct D_1	2	1.30	—	2.10	5.46	
	D_2	5	1.00	—	2.10	10.50	
	W	7	2.00		0.30	4.20	
						20.16	
						(236 – 20.16) = 215.94	
						215.94	
	(*vii*) Wall above staircase	2	2.50	—	2.00	10.00	
						225.94 sq m	
4.	1 : 4 – 6 mm thick ceiling Plaster						
	(*i*) Bed room	3	4.00	3.00	—	36.00	
		1	4.00	3.70	—	14.80	
	(*ii*) Drawing room	1	4.00	3.00	—	12.00	
	(*iii*) Kitchen	1	4.00	2.50	—	10.00	
	(*iv*) Dining room	1	4.00	2.50	—	10.00	
	(*v*) Bath & passage	1	3.70	1.70	—	6.29	
	(*vi*) Verandah	1	11.90	2.60	—	23.80	
	(*vii*) Passage & stairs	1	8.30	2.30	—	19.80	
	waste slab	1	9.20	10.00	—	9.02	
	(*viii*) Bath & slab above stairs	1	2.50	1.00	—	2.50	
						143.68 sq m	
5.	1 : 2 : 4 cement concrete 25 mm thick flooring						
	(*i*) Bed room	3	4.00	3.00	—	36.6	
	(*ii*) Drawing room	1	4.00	3.70	—	14.8	

	(*iii*) Kitchen	1	4.00	3.00	—	12.6	
	(*iv*) Dining room	1	4.00	2.50	—	10.0	
	(*v*) Bath & passage	1	3.70	1.70	—	6.29	
	(*vi*) Verandah	1	11.90	2.00	—	23.8	
						112.88	
	Deduct for pillar inside verandah	3	0.30	0.30	—	0.27	
						112.61	
	Passage & stairs	1	8.30	2.30	—	19.09	
						131.70	
6.	M.S. railing of stair*(x_1)	2	2.92	—	—	5.84	x_1 Length of railing shall be equal to waist of slab @ 100 N/m
7.	4 cm thick precast jali work including fixing in external wall	1	2.00	2.70	—	5.40	
8.	Three coats white washing (x_2)	225.94 + 143.68 = 369.62				369.62 m	This shall be equal to item (3 and 9)
9.	Colour washing (x_3)	(item 3 & 4) 225.94 143.68 369.62				369.62 m²	x_3, quantity shall be equal to used plaster
10.	M.S. reinforement 1% of item $18.17 \times \frac{1}{100} = .181$ cum® 785%					15.1 quintal	
11.	Sal wood work (x_4)					0.85 cm	x_4 As per item 18 of GF
12.	30 mm thick deodar wood in doors & windows shutter					35.55	x_5 As per item 19 of GF
13.	30 mm thick (x_6) glazed ventilator					0.14 m²	x_6 As per item 21 of GF
14.	Painting doors & windows x_7					64.44 m²	x_7 As per item 21 of GF
15.	MS work (x_8) on doors and windows					2.87 q	x_8 As per item 22 of GF
16.	Coal tarring two coats using 0.16 and 0.12 thick of coaltar per sq.m in first and second coal respectively					12.25 m	x^9 As per item 23 of GF

Double Storey Building Abstract of Quantity

S. No.	*Particular of items*	*Work*	*G.F.*	*F.F.*	*Total*	*Remark*
1.	EW in excavation	cm	107.05	—	107.05 cum	
2.	L.C. in Foundation	"	25.50	—	25.50	
3.	1 : 2 : 4 cement concrete (DPC)	"	0.54	—	0.54	
4.	Earth filling	"	29.57	—	29.57	
5.	BW in 1 : 6 c.c. in Foundation	"	43.80	—	43.80	
6.	25 mm 1 : 2 : 4 c.c.	"	3.32	—	3.32	
7.	BW 1 : 6 between GL & PL	"	7.21	—	7.21	
8.	BW in superstructure 1 : 4	"	61.55	65.12	126.67	
9.	RCC 1 : 2 : 4 in slab	"	0.21	18.18	39.18	
10.	1 : 2 cement : sand 12 m plaster	sq m	422.94 sq	225.94	648.85	
11.	1 : 4-6 mm ceiling plaster	"	147.69	143.68	291.37	
12.	1 : 2 : 4 c.c. 25 mm thick flooring	sq m	132.54	131.70	264.24	
13.	MS Railing for staircase	"	5.84	5.84	11.68	
14.	4 cm thick RCC precast Jali	m^2	4.60	5.40	10.00	
15.	Three coat white-wash		449.39	386.19	835.58	
16.	MS reinforcement on slab and lintels	q	15.11	15.11	30.22	
17.	Sal wood chaukhat	cum	0.85	0.85	1.70	
18.	30 mm thick deodar wood in doors & windows	"	35.55	35.55	71.10	
19.	30 mm thick glazed ventilator	m^2	0.14	0.14	0.28	
20.	Painting doors & windows two coats and one coat primary	m^2	64.44	64.41	128.84	
21.	MS work in doors, windows & ventilators	q	2.87	2.87	5.74	
22.	Coal tar work two coats	m^2	12.28	12.28	24.56	

Double Storeyed Building

Earthwork

1. Earthwork in Excavation

(*v*) Bathroom cross wall

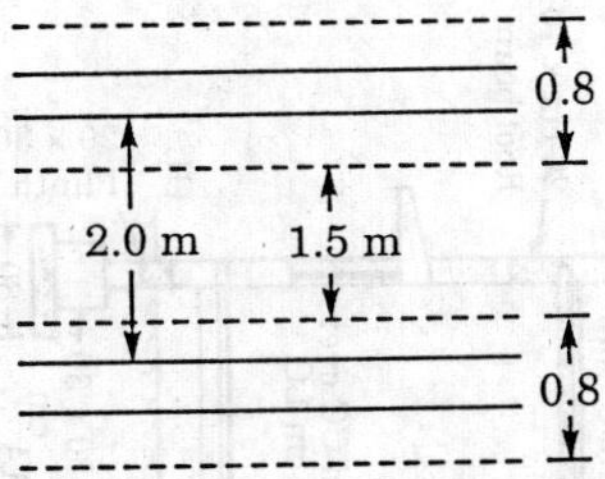

(*vi*) Verandah dwarf wall

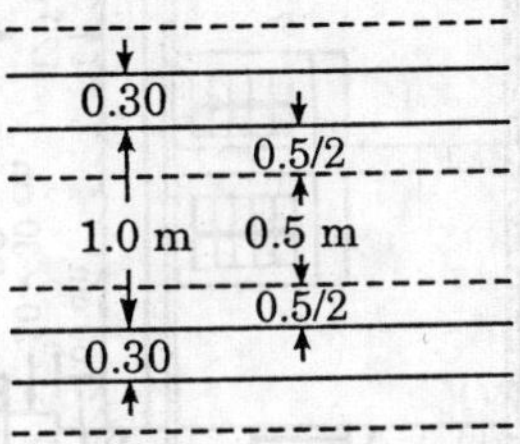

(*vii*) Extra for Pillar

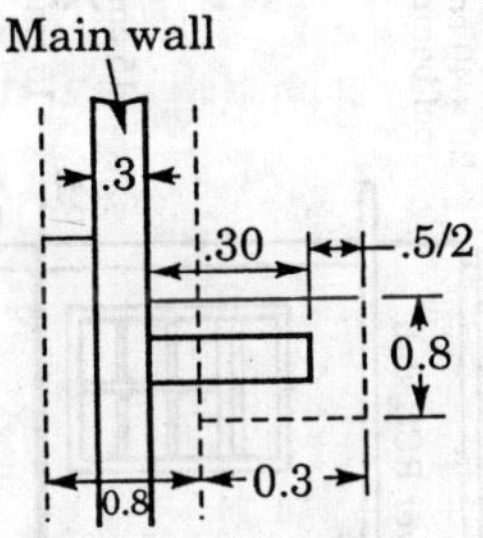

2. Lime concrete in foundation

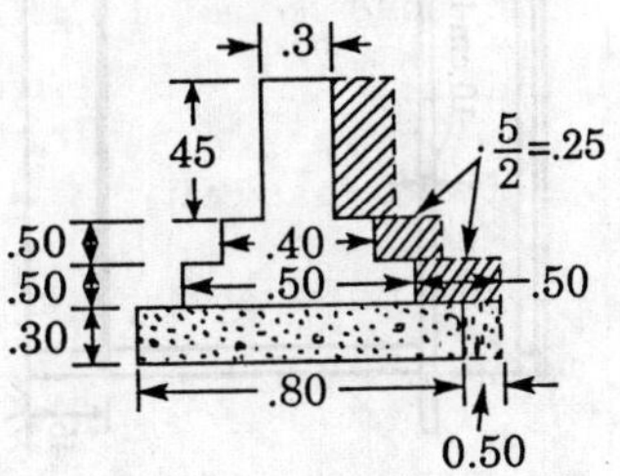

3. Brickwork 1 : 6 CC on foundation upon G.L.

First Floor

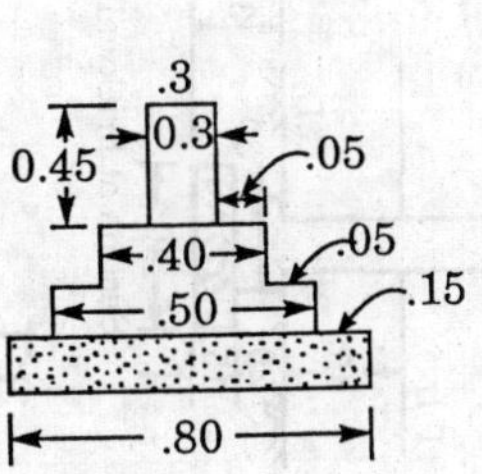

Fig. 7.25

Example 7.22. *RCC Framed Structures (See Fig. 7.26)*

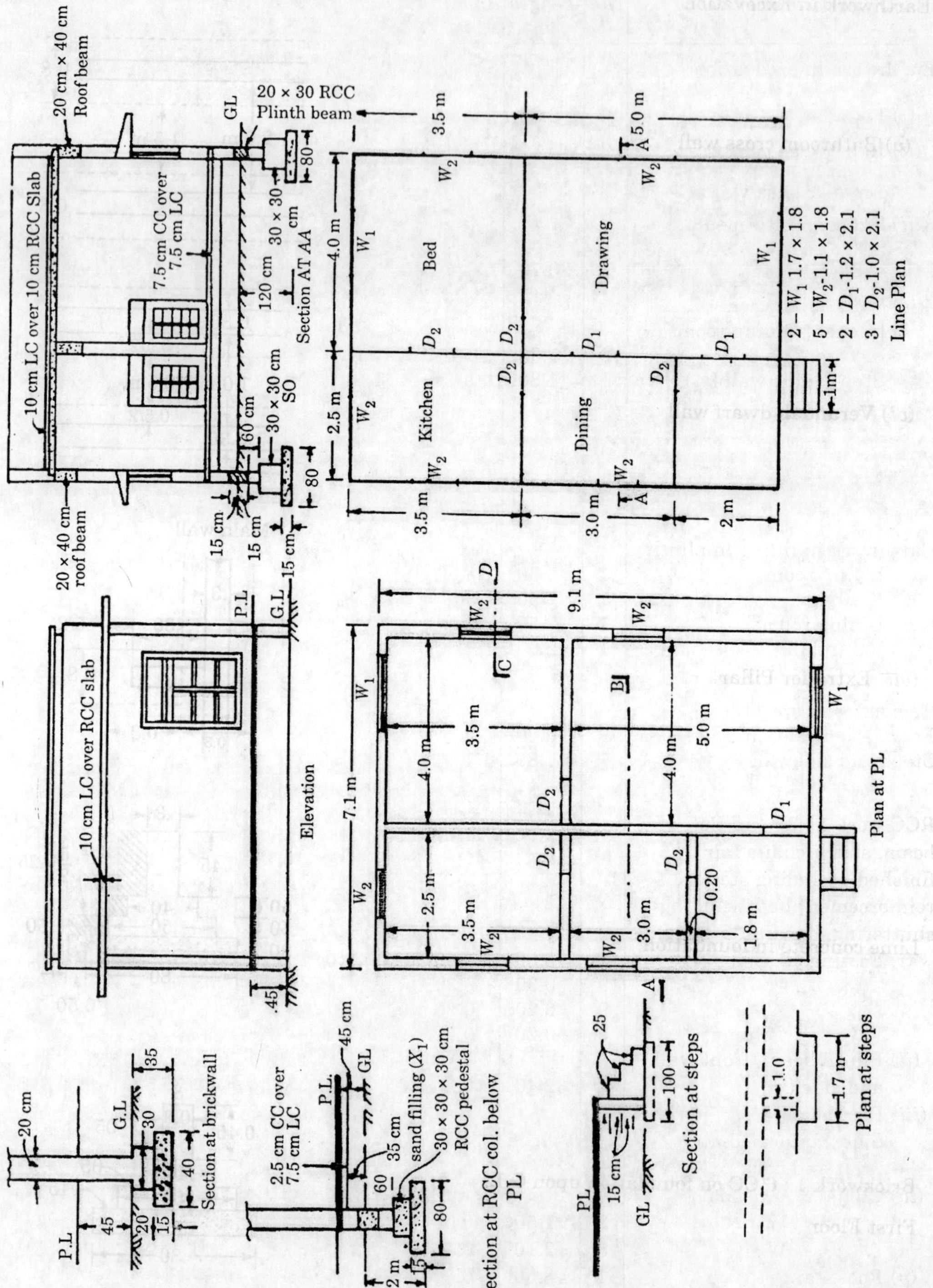

Fig. 7.26

Example 7.23. *RCC Framed Structures (See Fig. 7.26)*

S. No.	*Particular of item*	*No.*	*Length m*	*Breadth m*	*H/D m*	*Quantity*	*Remarks*
1.	Earthwork in excavation						
	(*i*) Foundation (col)	9	0.80	0.80	1.20	6.91	$x_1 = 25 + 4 - \left(\frac{8-2}{2}\right)$
	(*ii*) In between cols. (x_1)	2	5.30	0.40	0.35	1.48	$\times 4 = 5.3$
	Front & back walls						$x_2 = [8.5 -]\frac{8-2}{2} \times 6$
	(*iii*) Side and intermediate						$= \{8.5 - [1.8]\} \times .2$
	wall (x_2)	1	20.70	0.40	0.35	2.90	$+ 8.5 - \left(\frac{0.8-2}{2} \times 4\right)$
	(*iv*) Wall in between kitchen, Dining room						$= (6.7 \times 2) + (8.5) - 1.2$
	& Verandah (x_3)	2	1.30	0.40	0.35	0.36	$= 134 + 7.3 = 207$
	Step & side wall (x_4)	1	1.80	1.05	0.15	0.28	$x_3 = 2.5 - 1.2 = 1.3$
						11.93 cum	x_4 = steps included side walls and 10 cm project-steps extended part.
2.	Earthwork in filling in plinth						
	Living room	1	5.00	3.00	0.35	4.80	
	Kitchen	1	2.50	3.00	0.35	2.63	
	Dining room	1	2.50	3.00	0.35	2.63	
	Verandah	1	2.00	2.00	0.35	1.40	
						11.46 cum	
3.	Cement concrete 1 : 3 : 6						
	Foundation column base	9	0.80	0.80	0.15	0.86	
	Steps and sidewall	1	1.80	1.05	0.15	0.28	
						1.14 cum	
4.	RCC work 1 : 2 : 4 in Col. beam, slab + chajja fair finished excluding steel reinforcement but including shuttering, bending & bending						
	(*i*) Footings & Col.	9	0.80	0.80	0.15	0.86 } 1.34	$x_1 = (8.5 + 0.6) \times 2$
		9	0.30	0.30	0.30	0.24	$+ (6.5 + 0.6) \times 2$
		9	0.20	0.20	0.75	0.27	$= 9.1 \times 2 + 7.1 \times 2$
	Columns	9	0.20	0.20	0.36	1.30	$= 32.4$
	(*ii*) Plinth beam, front wall and side (x_1)	1	32.40	0.20	0.30	1.94	$x_2 = (65 + 2 + 6.5 - 5.6)$
	(*iii*) Roof beam						$= 13 + 7.1 = 20.1$
	Sides, intermediate front and back (x_2)	1	20.10	0.20	0.40	1.60	
	(*iv*) Chajja & sunshed						
	W_1	2	1.50	0.56	0.05	0.084	
	W_2	3	2.10	0.50	0.05	0.16	
	(*v*) Roof stain	1	8.50	6.50	0.10	5.52	
						6.42	

(*Contd.*)

5.	M.S. steel including binding in RCC						
	(*i*) RCC footing @ 0.5%	–	1.34 × .5/100	= 0.67/106		1.52 +1.25	+ 1.97 + 3.44 = 8.7 q
	(*ii*) RCC col @ 1.5%	–	1.30 × 1.5/100	= 1.90/160			
	(*iii*) Beam 1%	–	1.6 × 1/100	= .25/106		8.7 q	
	(*iv*) Chajja 0.15%	–	1.08 × .15/100	= 4.42/106			
	(*v*) Roof stain .8%	–	5.52 × .8/100				
6.	First class Brick 1 : 6 cement : Sand						$x_1 = 2.60 + .45 = 3.15$
	Kitchen & Dining	3	2.5	0.20	3.05(x_1)	4.58	
	Living & Drawing	2	8.5	0.20	3.05	10.37	
	Left side wall	1	8.5	0.20	3.05	5.19	
	Walls in bed and Drawing	2	40	0.20	3.05	4.88	
	Walls in between Drawing	1	4.0	0.10	3.05	2.44	
	Plinth wall under 10 m						
	Partition wall	1	5.0	0.10	.45	1.53	
	Wall under Verandah						
	Front parapet	1	2.5	0.20	.45	0.23	
	Wall under Verandah						
	Side parapet	1	1.6	0.20	0.45	0.14	
	Steps	1	1.70	0.75	0.15	0.19	
		1	1.4	0.5	0.15	0.10	
		1	1.0	0.25	0.15	0.04	
	Parapet wall over roof slab						
	Front & back	2	6.2	0.2	0.70	1.74	
	Side	2	8.9	0.2	0.70	25.0	
						33.98 cum	8.5 + 0.40 = 8.9
	Deduct opening						
	Door	1	1.2	2.1	—	2.52	33.24 S.m × 0.20
		4	1.0	2.1	—	8.4	= 6.65
	Window	2	1.1	1.8	—	3.96	
		3	1.7	1.8	—	9.15	
						(33.98 – 6.65) = 27.33 cam	
7.	10 cm lime concrete in roof terrace (Lime Puly : 2 Surkh)				1	7.7	8.9 — 68.53 m^2
8.	Teak wood work framed and fixed in door windows Chaukhat						x_1 = 2 va = 2.14, 5.25 1No. 1.0
	Door 100 × 200	3	5.28(x_1)	0.12	0.08	0.15 cum	x_2 = 2 va 2.64 = 5.28 2 Hr. 1.2 = 2.4
	Door with fan light 1.2 × 2.6	1	7.68(x_2)	0.12	0.08	0.07 cum	7.68
	Window 1.7 × 1.8	2	14.0(x_3)	0.12	0.08	0.27	x_3 4Hr. 1.8 × 4 = 7.2 4 Hr 1.7 × 4 = 6.8 14
	Window 1.10 × 1.8	5	21(x_4)	0.12	0.08	1.00	x_4 = 6 ver = 1.8 × 6 = 10.8
						1.49 cum	6 Hr. = 1.7 × 6 = 10.2 21

9.	Door Shutters 4 cm thick panelled of Teak wood (second class)	4	0.87	—	2.03(x_1)	7.06	x_1 = Height 210 – 8
	100 × 210	1	1.67	—	2.08	3.39	+ 1.5 – 0.5
						10.45 sq m	202 + 1
							= 203 mm = 2.03 m
10.	Window shutters 4 cm thick, glazed of teak wood 170 × 180	2	1.47	—	1.62	4.76	
	Window 110 × 180	5	0.97	—	1.62	7.86	
						12.62 sq m	
11.	Iron work in hold fast in windows & doors						
	Door 120 × 210	1 × 8	—	—	—	8 Nos.	4 on each side
	" 100 × 210	4 × 6	—	—	—	24 Nos.	3 " "
	Windows 5 Nos.	5 × 6	—	—	—	30 Nos.	3 " "
						62 Nos.	
12.	Window bars (10 cm centre approx.)						
	Window 170 × 180	2 × 15	1.30	—	—	39.00 m.	
	Fan light	2 × 2	1.70	—	—	68.00 m	
	Windows	5 × 8	1.30	—	—	7.54 m	
	Fan light	3 × 2	1.30	—	—	7.80 m	
						61.14 m	
13.	Flat bars 25 mm × 6 mm Horizontally at middle of	2 × 1	1.70	—	—	5.10 m	
	windows 3 × 1	1.00	—		3.0 m		
						8.10 m	
14.	12 mm plaster in 1 : 6 cement mortar						
	Bed & Dining	2	8.50	—	2.60	44.2 sq m	
		2	5.00	—	2.60	26 sq m	
		4	4.00	—	2.60	41.60	
	Kitchen	2	3.50	—	2.6	18.20	
	Dining room & Ver.	5	2.50	—	2.60	32.50 sq m	
						162.50 sq m	
	Deduct openings						
	Door 1.2 × 2.1	1	2.10	2.10	—	2.52	
	1 × 2.1	4	1.00	2.10	—	8.40 sq m	22.98 sq m
	Windows 1.7 × 1.8	2	1.70	1.80	—	6.12	to be deducted
	1.1 × 1.8	3	1.80	—	—	5.94	
	12 mm cement plater 1 : 6 cement : Sand Motar						
	Brick wall	1	7.20	3.05	—	21.96	(x_1) 2.5 + 4 + 0.7 = 7.2
	Right outer side	1	5.90	3.05	—	18.00	
	Living Verandah					14.64	
	Left outer side of kitchen and dining	1	8.6(x_2)	3.05	—	26.23	(x_2) = 4 + 4 + 0.2 + 0.2
	Verandah parapet	1	2.30	—	1.15	2.64	+ 0.3 = 8.6
	Front	1	2.00	—	1.15	2.30	

(*Contd.*)

	Side wall step						
	Outer side	2	0.60	—	0.6	0.72	$(x_3) = 2.5 + 4 + 0.3 = 6.8$
	Inner side	2	0.60	—	0.3	0.36	
	Top side	2	0.60	—	0.3	0.36	
	Parapet above roof beam						
	Inner face front beam	2	6.8(x_3)	—	0.6	8.16	
	Inner face side	2	65.00	—	0.6	7.80	
	Top side	2	7.20	—	0.2	2.88	
		2	6.50	—	0.2	2.60	
	Outer face of front and back including groove 5 cm × 5 cm	2	7.2	—	0.2	2.88	$x_3 = 2.5 + 4 + 0.3 = 6.8$
	Groove side	2	6.9	—	0.2	2.76	
						276.79–22.98 = 253.81	
15.	15 mm thick plaster in 1 : 4 (Cement : coarse sand) walls finished neat cement flooring						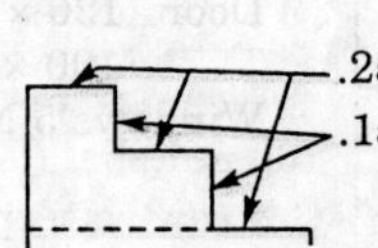
	Tread wall	1	1.4	1.05	1.47		0.25 × 0.3 + 0.15 × 2 – 0.7 + 0.30 = 1.05
16.	2.5 C.C. 1 : 2 : 4 over and including 7.5 lime concrete fair finished wall neat cement floor						
	Living room	1	4.00	3.50	—	14.00 sq m	
	Kitchen	1	2.50	4.00	—	10.00	
	Drawing room	1	5.00	4.00	—	2.00	
	Verandah	1	2.50	1.80	—	4.50	
	Dining room	1	2.50	3.00	—	7.50	
						38.00 sq m	
17.	White-washing 3 coats inside (x_1)					253.81 sq m	x_1 = same item plaster in term 14
18.	Colour washing 2 coats Over one coat white washing (outside wall)	Same as for outside plaster under item 14					
						253.81 sq m	
19.	Painting doors and windows two coats over one primary coat						
	Panelled door	1 × 2¼	1.20	—	2.10	5.67	
	" "	3 × 2½	1.00	—	2.10	14.18	
	Glazed fan light over door	1 × 1	1.20		0.50	0.60	
	Glazed window	2 × 1	1.70	—	1.80	6.12	
	Bars & fan light	5 × 1	1.10		1.80	9.90	
	over door	1 × 1	1.04	—	0.42	1.08	
						37.55 sq m	

20.	Coal tar two coats using .16 and .12 liter coal tar 128 sq m in first and second coat respectively						$x_1 = 2.1 + 2 + 1.2 = 5.4$ x_2 Fan light $(0.5 + 0.5) + 1.2 = 2.2$
	Door 1.20 × 2.1	1	5.4(x_1)	0.12	0.21	1.78	$x_3 = 2.1 \times 2 + 1.0$ $= 4.2 + 1 = 5.2$
	Extra for fan light	1	2.2(x_2)	0.12	0.50	0.13	$x_4 = 1.7 \times 2 + 5 \times 2$ $+ 1.7 \times 2$
	Door	4	5.20(x_3)	0.12	0.21	6.86	$= 3.4 + 1.0 + 3.4$ $= 6.8 + 1.0 = 7.8$
	Windows wall fan light 1.7 × (2.1 + 0.5)	1	7.80(x_4)	0.12	—	0.94 sq m	$x_5 = 1.1 \times 2 + (1.8 + 0.5)$ $= 2.1 + 2.6 = 4.7$
	Windows 1.1 × 1.8	4	4.70(x_5)	0.12	—	2.25	
						11.96 sq m	
21.	100 mm dia. C.I. raw waterpipe painted and filled	2	10			2m	

RCC Framed Structure

Abstract of Quantities

S.No.	*Particular of item*	*Unit*	*Quantity*	*Remarks*
1.	Earthwork in Excavation	cum	11.93 cum	
2.	Excavation filled & plaster	"	11.46 cum	
3.	Cement concrete 1 : 3 : 6 Foundation Col. + Base : steps	"	1.14	
4.	RCC work 1 : 2 : 4	"	6.42 cum	
5.	M.S. steel including binding	quintal	8.7 q	
6.	First class BN in 1 : 6 cement : sand	cum	27.23	
7.	10 cm lime concrete in roof	sq m	68.53	
8.	Teak wood, wrought framed and fixed	cum	1.49	
9.	Door shutter 4 cm thick	sq m	10.45	
10.	Window shutter 4 cm thick	"	12.62	
11.	Iron work or hold face	No.	62	
12.	Window bars 1 (0 cm centre)	m	61.14 kg	
13.	Flat bar 25 mm × 6 mm	m	8.1	
14.	12 mm plaster 1 : 6 cement mortor	sq m	253.81	
15.	15 mm thick plaster 1 : 4 finished with neat concrete		1.47	
16.	25 cu cc 1 : 2 : 4	"	380	
17.	White washing 3 coats		253.81	
18.	Colour washing 2 coats		253.81	
19.	Painting doors & windows		37.55	
20.	Coal tarring two coats		11.96	
21.	100 mm dia. C.I. raw water pipe painted	m	2 m	

Exercise 1

Work out the quantities of

(*i*) Earth work (*ii*) Cement concrete

(*iii*) Brick work (*iv*) D.P.C.

From the given plan and section of a wall. (Fig. 7.24)

Exercise 2

Calculate the quantities of the following items :

1. Earthwork
2. Cement concrete 1 : 4 : 8 mix
3. Cement concrete 1 : 2 : 4 mix
4. Area of centring and shuttering.

From given plan and section of a concrete pillar. (Refer Fig. 7.27)

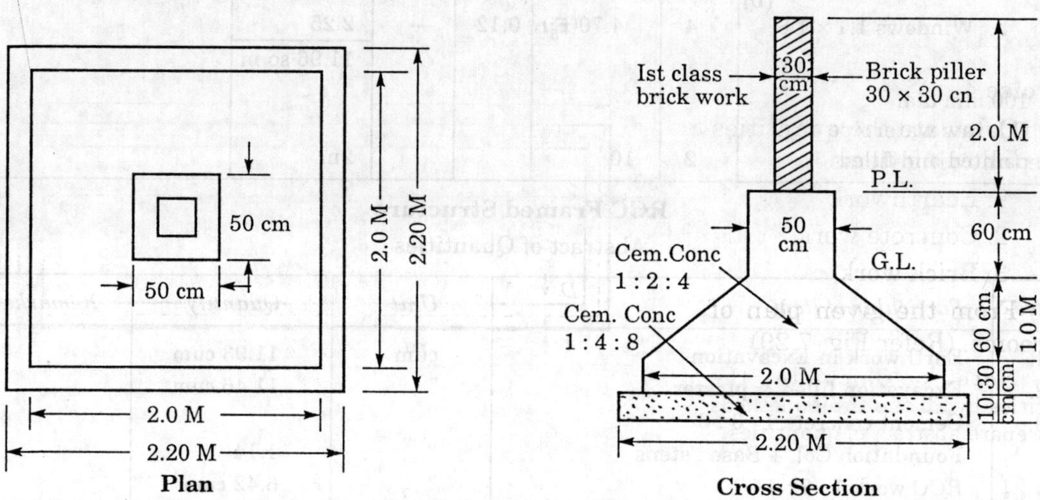

Fig. 7.27

Excercise 3

Calculate the quantities of the following items :

1. Brick work
2. Cement plaster

From the given drawing of steps. (Refer Fig. 7.28)

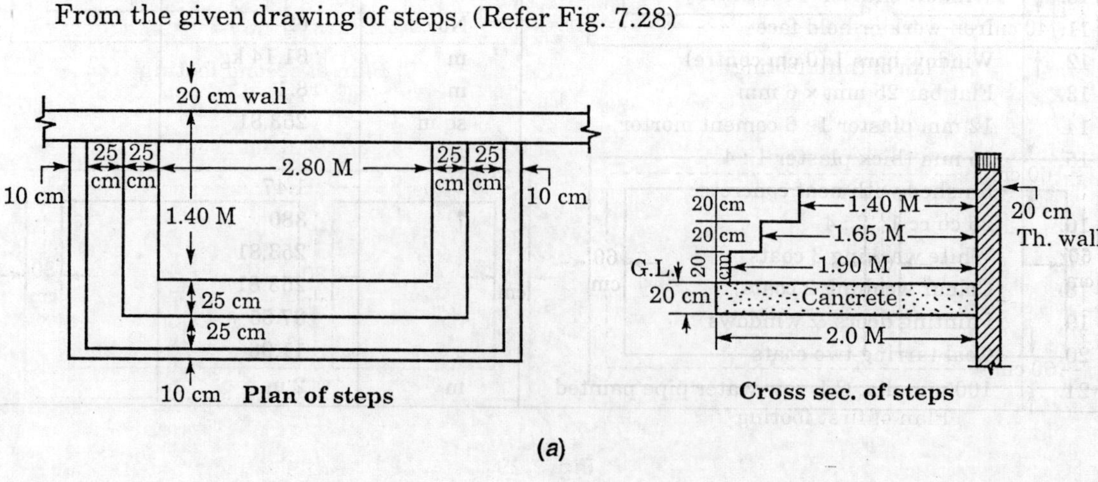

(*a*)

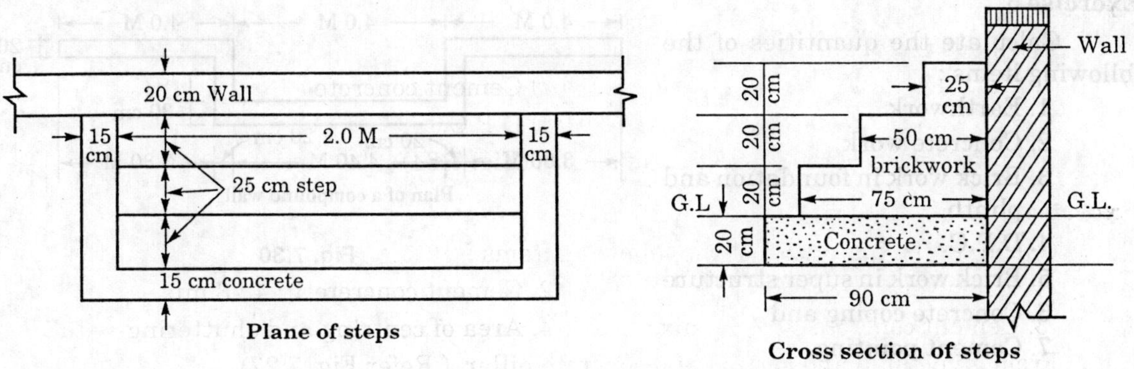

(b) (c)

Fig. 7.28

Exercise 4

Calculate the quantities of the following items :

1. Eearthwork
2. Concrete work
3. Brick work

From the given plan of two rooms. (Refer Fig. 7.29)

Note : Calculate the quantities by all the three methods and prepare abstract of quantities.

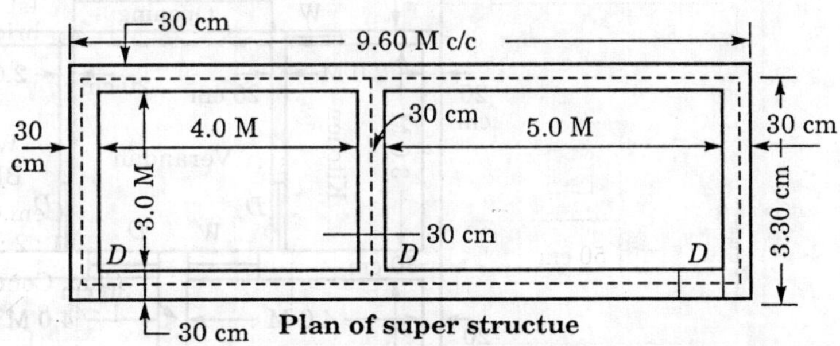

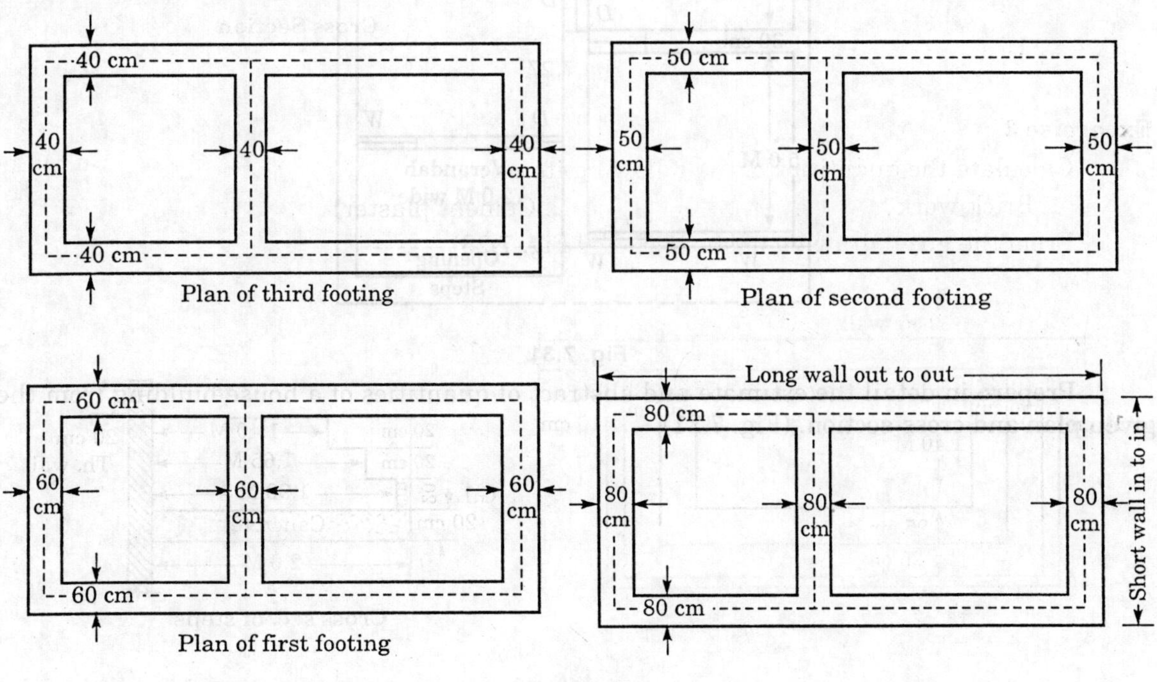

Fig. 7.29

Exercise 5

Calculate the quantities of the following items :

1. Earthwork
2. Concrete work
3. Brick work in foundation and plinth
4. D.P.C.
5. Brick work in super structure
6. Concrete coping and
7. Cement pointing.

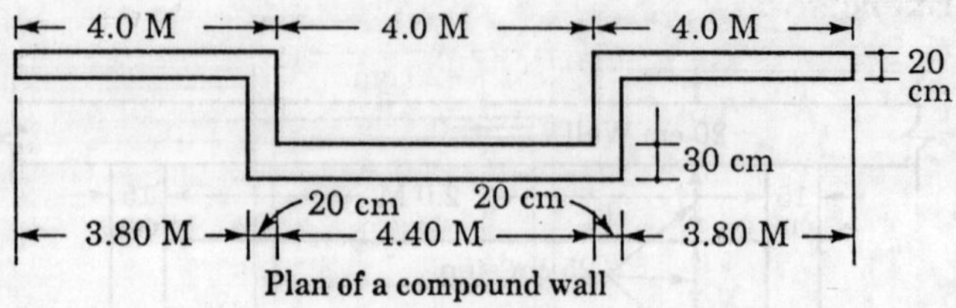

Fig. 7.30

Exercise 6

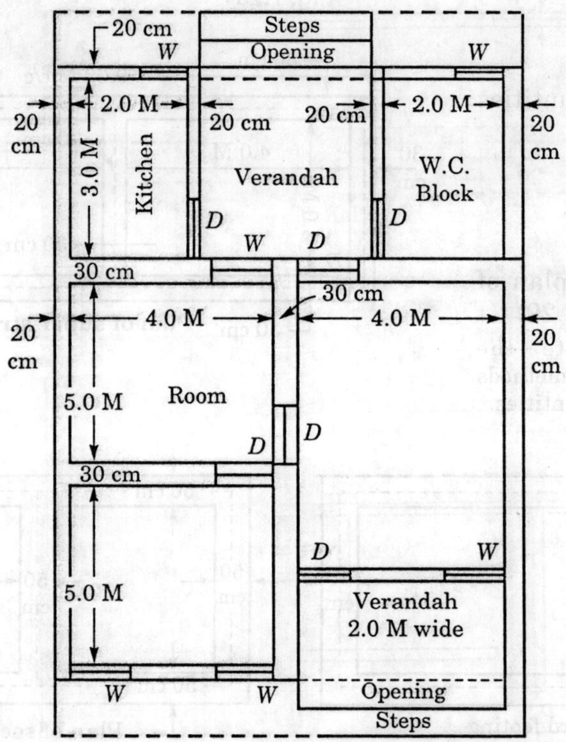

Fig. 7.31

Prepare in detail the estimate and abstract of quantities of a house building from the given plan and cross-section. (Fig. 7.31)

Exercise 7

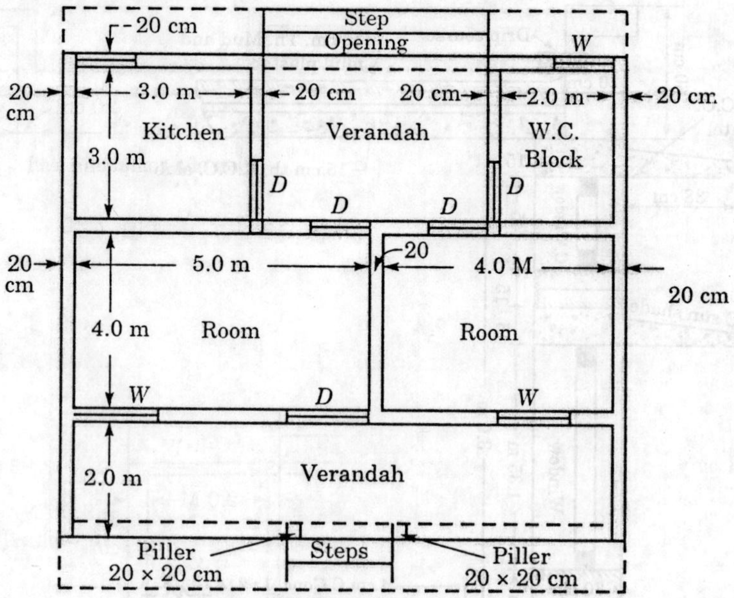

Plan of a house

Fig. 7.32

Prepare in detail the estimate and abstract of quantities of a house building from the given plan and cross-section. (Fig. 7.32)

Exercise 8

Prepare in detail the estimate and abstract of quantities of a house building from the given plan and cross-section. (Fig. 7.33)

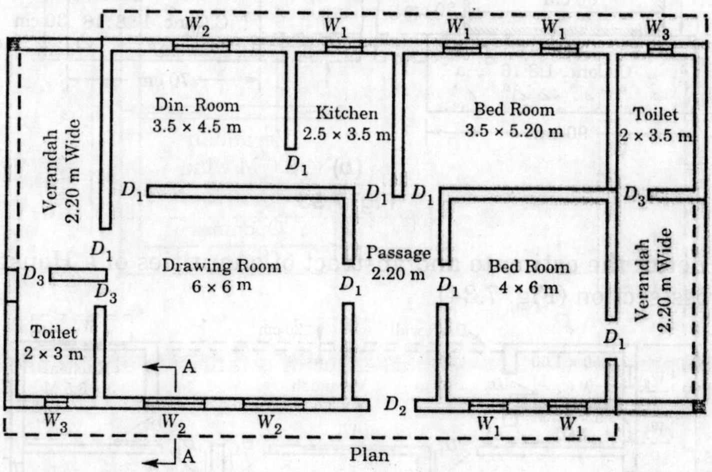

Plan

(a)

D_1 = Door 1.00 × 2.00
D_2 = Door 1.70 × 2.00
D_3 = Door 0.70 × 200
C_5 = Window 0.80 × 0.45

W_1 = Window 1.00 × 1.35
W_2 = Window 1.50 × 1.35
W_3 = Window 0.60 × 1.35

1. External Walls 30 cm 1 inch

2. Internal Wall 20 cm 1 inch

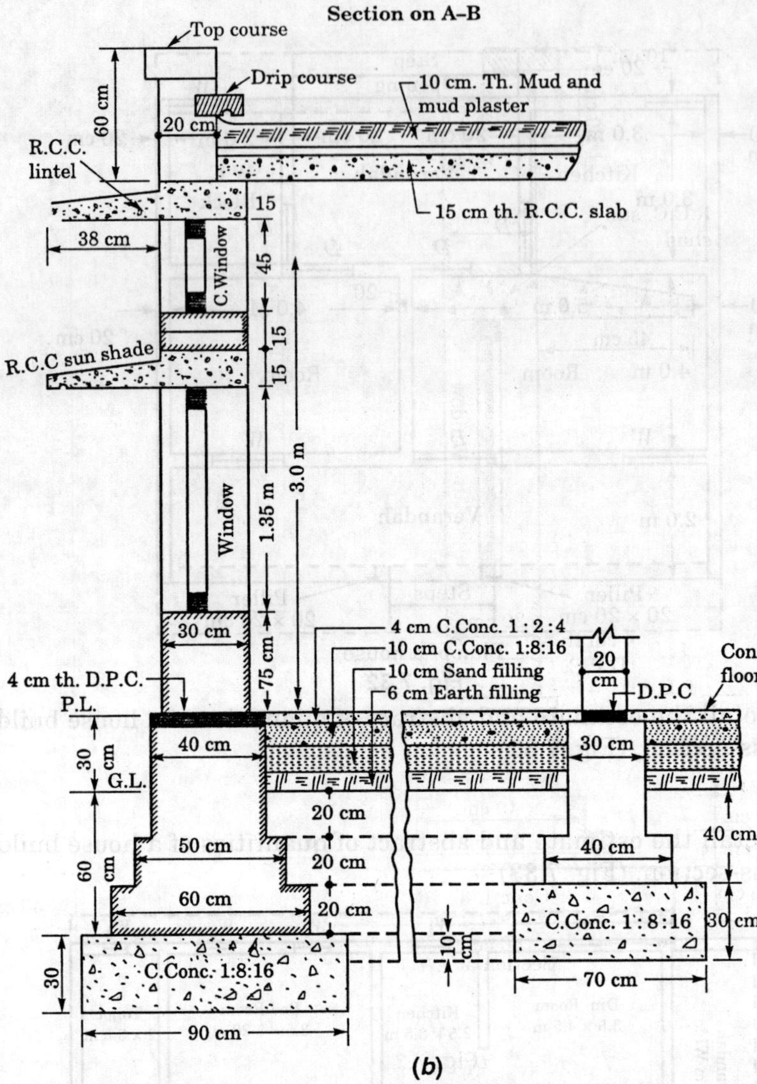

(*b*)

Fig. 7.33

Exercise 9

Prepare in detail the estimate and abstract of quantities of a House Building from the given plan and cross-section (Fig. 7.34)

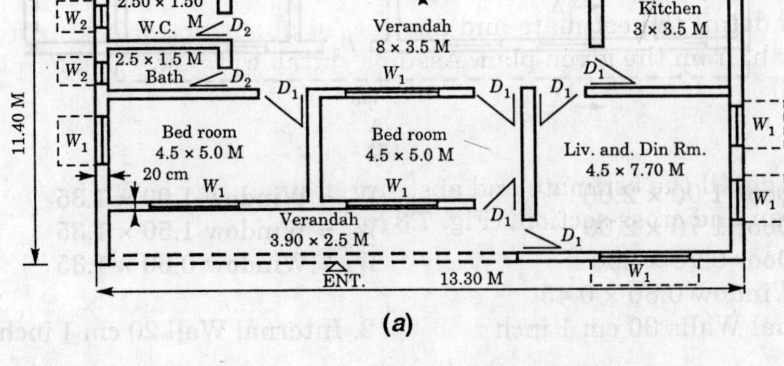

(*a*)

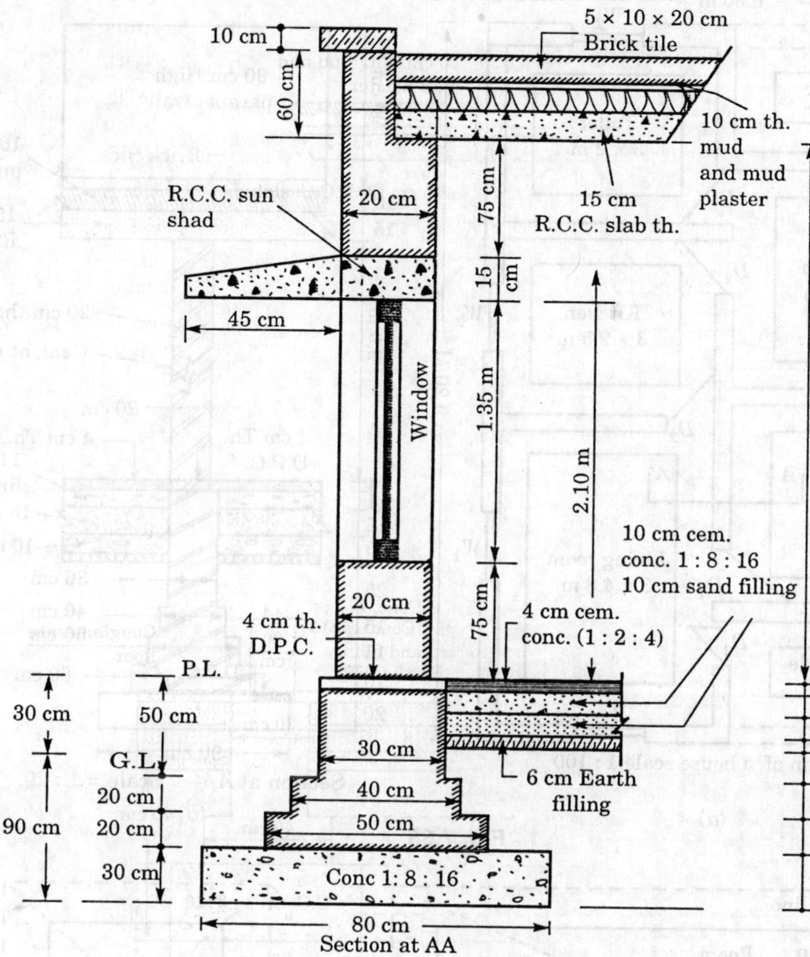

Section at AA

(b)

Fig. 7.34

Exercise 10

Prepare in detail the estimate and abstract of quantities of a house building from the given plan cross-section.

Exercise 11

Prepare in detail the estimate and abstract of quantities of pitched roof to cover two halls and verandah, from the given plan. Assume suitable cross-section for pitched and lean-to-roof. (Fig. 7.36)

Exercise 12

Prepare in detail the estimate and abstract of quantities of pitched roof to cover a half from the given plan and cross-section. (Fig. 7.37)

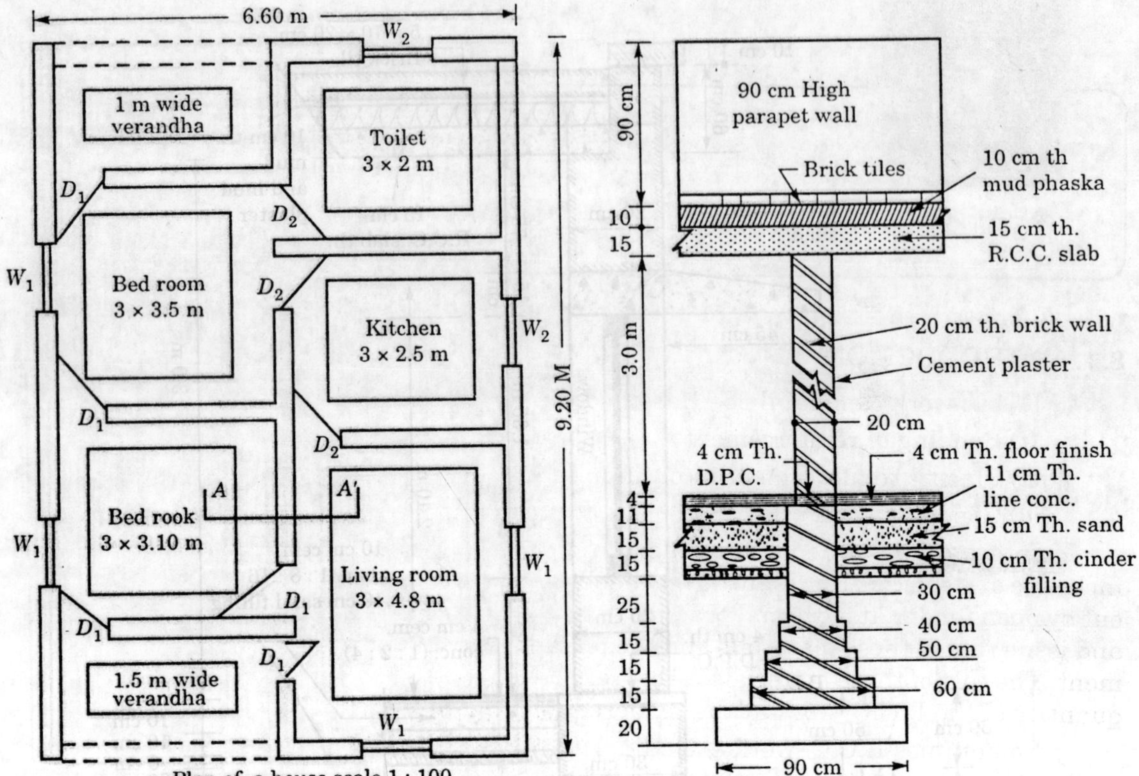

Plan of a house scale 1 : 100

(*a*)

Section at AA' Scale = 1 : 20

(*b*)

Fig. 7.35

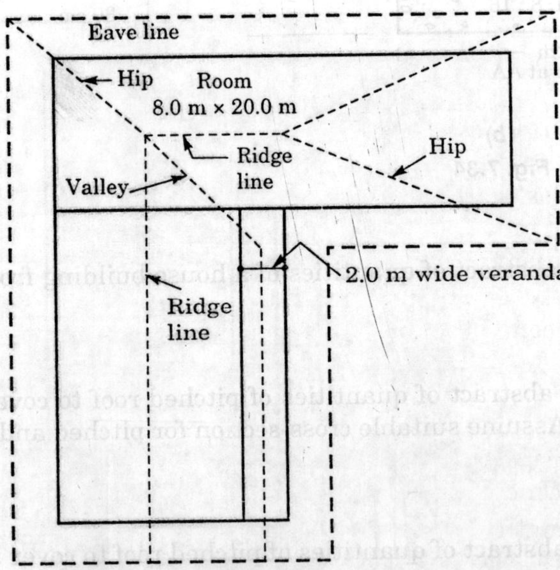

Line plan (Pitched Roof)

Fig. 7.36

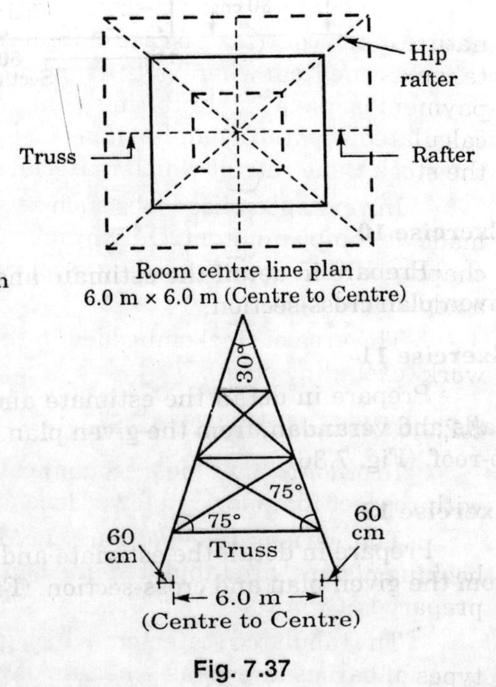

Fig. 7.37

8

Estimate of R.C.C. Works and Steel Structures

8.1. INTRODUCTION

R.C.C. work can mainly be classified under the following :

(*i*) Bending of reinforcement. (*ii*) Centring and shuttering work.

(*iii*) Placing reinforcement in position including, binding of steel.

(*iv*) Concrete work.

In some departments the schedule of rates specified includes complete R.C.C. item inclusive of steel, centring, shuttering, bending and binding. In such cases, if the work is given out by open tender, it is normal practice to issue cement and steel from the departmental store and issue rate of these materials and the place of delivery are mentioned in the contract document. The cost of these materials is recovered from the contractor who is paid according to the quantity of the R.C.C. work at the tendered rate.

Some times R.C.C. work excluding steel but inclusive of bending, and binding of steel and centring and shuttering is estimated as one item and steel work is worked out separately.

Sometimes, specially in the case of complicated centring and shuttering work, the area of centring and shuttering is estimated separately.

As far as payment to the contractor for the work done is concerned, it depends upon the nature of the contract. In case of item rate contract R.C.C. work (usually of 1 : 2 : 4 concrete) is taken as one item where in the work is measured in terms of its cubical contents and no extra payment is made for shuttering, centring or bending or binding of steel. Reinforcement steel is calculated separately and paid as a separate item at the specified rate. This rate may not be the stock issue rate at which material is made available to the contractor.

In very specialised jobs such as silos, water tanks etc. the payment for complete unit is made as lump sum item. Only number of units are entered in the measurement book. In this chapter, R.C.C. work including steel reinforcement is taken as one item and steel is taken as a additional item.

The area of steel embedded in the concrete is normally ignored while calculating R.C.C. work (excluding steel).

8.2. SCHEDULE OF BARS

In order to have most economical use of steel not any proper quantity but also its position with respect to upper and lower face of concrete as well as bending of the bars is required.

The various types of bars, *i.e.* length, diameter, position of bend, angle of bend and booking of bars, are tabulated and separate benches of proper bending of each type of bar are prepared at work site.

The tabulated statement which gives above details along with detailed drawing of various types of bars is known as schedule of reinforcement or schedule of bars.

Table 8.1 gives a typical reinforcement schedule in respect of straight, cranked or bent up, and overlapping bars.

Table 8.1. Typical Schedule of Reinforcement

S. No.	*Description of bar*	*Details of Reinforcement*	*Position of bar*	*Spacing of bar*	*No. of bar*	*Remark*
1.	Straight bar	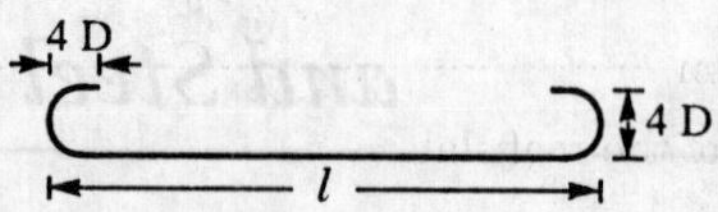	Bottom of slab allowed for cover	20 cm (say)	20 (say)	l = length of slab or beam less two end cover. Total length of bar $= L + 18D$, D = Dia of bar
2.	Cranked bar	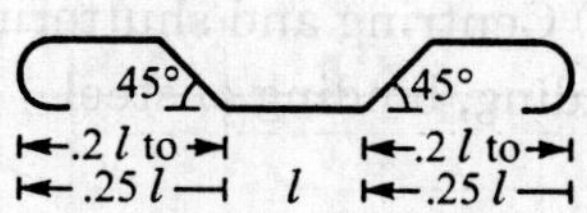	Alternate bent	20 cm (say)	Governed by dimension of the number	Alternate bars bent up at both ends to take care of end moments.
3.	Bent up bar	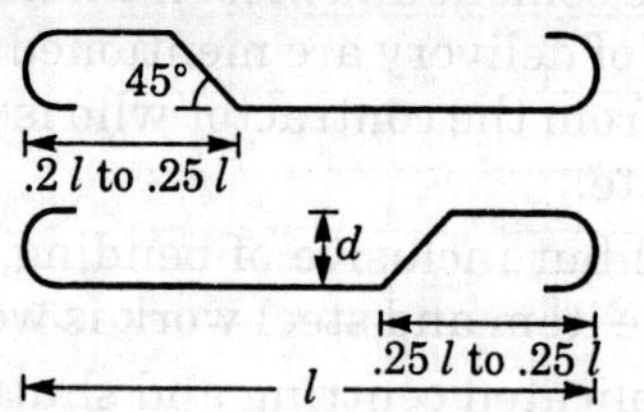		15 cm (say)	Governed by requirement	Extra length due to one band $= \frac{d}{\sin 45 \phi d} - d$ $= 0.47\,d$ say $0.5\,p$ here d is the vertical distance between centres of bar d is equal to depth of the slab erasmic top and bottom cover from top and bottom reinforcement respectively.
4.	Overlapping	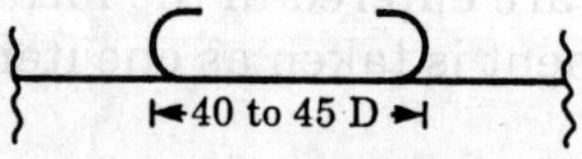				

8.3. ESTIMATE OF A R.C.C. ROOF SLAB

Fig. 8.1 gives details of a R.C.C. slab roof 9 m × 3 m (clear). Estimate the R.C.C. work for this slab.

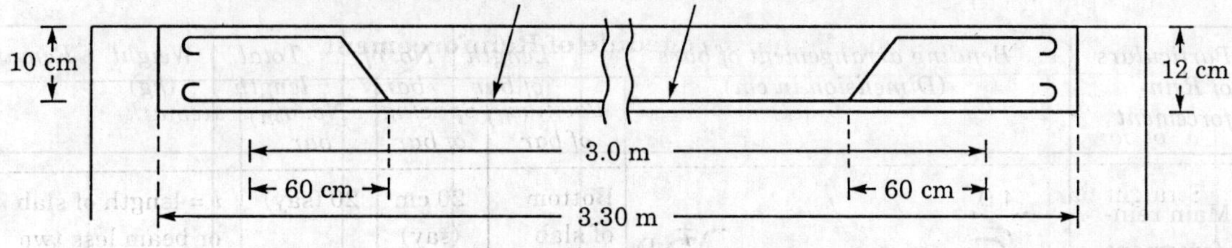

(*a*) Cross-section of the roof slab

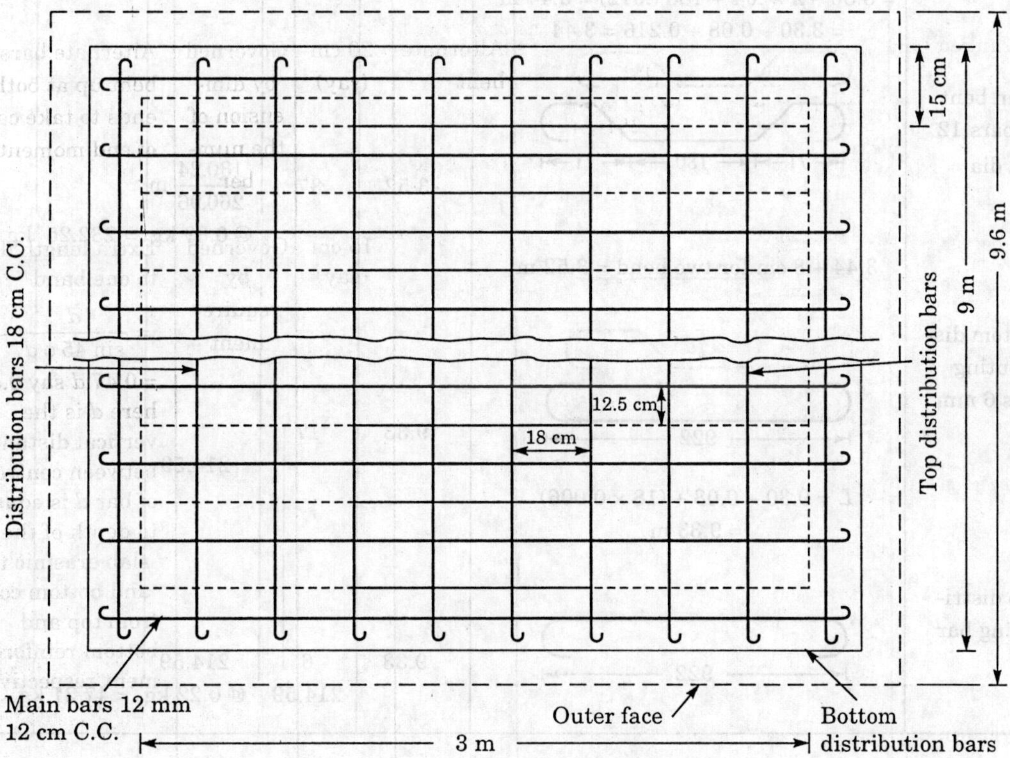

(*b*) Part plan showing details of reinforcement

Fig. 8.1

Table 8.2. Schedule of Reinforcement–R.C.C. Slab

Particulars of Rein-forcement	*Bending arrangement of bars (Dimension in cm)*	*Length of bar (m)*	*No. of bars*	*Total length (m)*	*Weight (kg)*	*Remark*
Main rein-forcement 12 mm dia	 322 **L = 3.30 – side cover + 2 hooks)** **= 3.30 – 2 × .04 + 180 (.012) = 3.44 m** **= 3.30 – 0.08 + 0.216 = 3.44**	**3.44**	**38**	**130.72**		
Main bent up bars 12 mm dia	 71 — 180 — 71 **3.44 + 8 cm for two bend = 3.52 m**	**3.52**	**37**	**130.24** **260.96 m** **@ 0.89 kg**	**= 232.25 kg**	
Bottom dis-tributing bars 6 mm dia	 922 **L = 9.30 – 0.08 + (18 × 0.006)** **= 9.33 m**	**9.33**	**17** }	**214.59**		
Top distri-buting bar	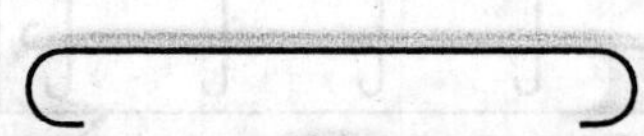 922	**9.33**	**6** } **214.59**	**214.59** **@ 0.22 kg**	**= 47.21 kg**	

The details of measurements and calculation of quantities are shown in Table 8.3.

Table 8.3. Details of Measurements and Calculation of Quantities. (R.C.C. Roof Slab)

S. No.	*Particulars of item of work*	*No.*	*Length*	*Breadth*	*Height Depth*	*Quantity*	*Remarks*
1.	R.C.C. work 1 : 2 : 4 excluding steel but inclusive of centring and shuttering and bending and binding of steel.	1	9.3	3	0.12	3.683 cum	No deduction is made in volume of concrete work for steel bars
2.	M.S. steel reinforcement in R.C. slab.						
	(*a*) Main bars 12 mm dia @ 0.89 kg/m						
	(*i*) Straight bar 25 cm c.c.						
	No. = $\frac{9.30 - 0.08}{0.25} + 1 = 38$	38	3.44				
	(*ii*) Bent up bars 25 cm c.c.						
	No. = $\frac{9.30 - 0.08}{0.25} + 1 = 37$	37	3.52				
		Total 260.94 m @ 0.89 kg/m = 232.25 kg					
	(*b*) Distribution bars 6 mm dia @ 0.22 kg/m						
	(*i*) Bottom bars central portion 18 cm c.c.						
	$\frac{180}{18} + 1$	11	9.33				
	(*ii*) Bottom bars two sides	2 × 3	9.33				
	(*iii*) Top bars	2 × 3	9.33				
		214.5 m @ 0.22 kg/m 47.21 kg					
3.	Centring shuttering.	1	0.9	3	27	279.46 kg	

The abstract of cost of R.C.C. roof slab is given in Table 8.4.

Table 8.4. Abstract of Cost of R.C.C. Slab Roof
(Based on CPWD SR—1997)

S. No.	*Particulars of item of work*	*Quantity*	*Unit*	*Rate*	*Cost*	*Remark*
1.	R.C.C. work 1 : 2 : 4 excluding steel and including inclusive of centring and shuttering and bending and binding of steel	3.683 cum	cum			
2.	Mild steel reinforcement in R.C.C. work.	279.46 kg	kg			
3.	Centring and shuttering.	27 m^2	sq m			
				Total		
	Add 1½% for water charges					
	Add 10% for contractor's profit					
		Grand Total		Say ₹		

8.4. ESTIMATE OF A R.C.C. BEAM (R.C.C. WORK)

Fig. 8.2 gives details of a R.C.C. beam of 9 metre clear span and 80 cm × 40 cm section. Estimate the R.C.C. work for this beam.

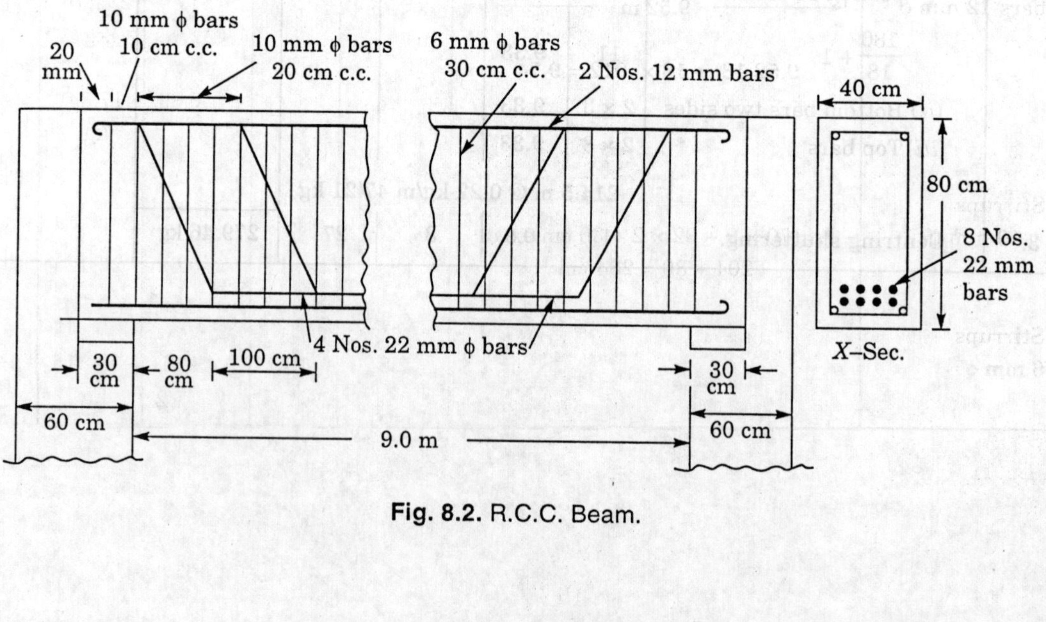

Fig. 8.2. R.C.C. Beam.

Table 8.5 gives schedule of reinforcement.

Table 8.5. Schedule of Bars R.C.C. Beam

Particulars of reinforcement	*Bending arrangement of bar*	*Length of bar (m)*	*No. of bars*	*Total length (m)*	*Weight (kg)*	*Remark*
Main straight bars 22 mm ϕ	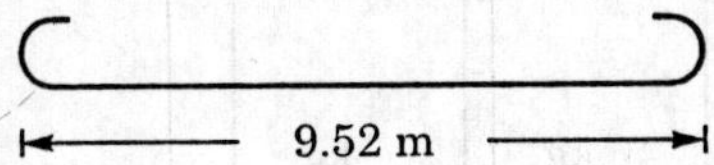 $L = 9.52 + 18 \times 22 = 9.92$	9.92	2	39.68		
Main bent up bars 22 mm ϕ	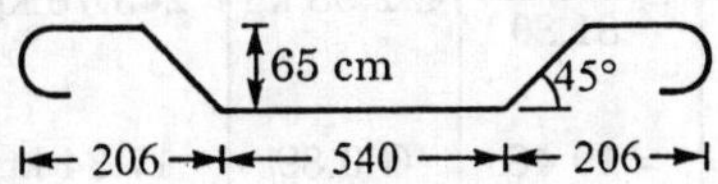 9.52 + 18 × .02 + 65 cm = 10.53	10.53	2	21.06		
Main bent up bars 22 mm ϕ	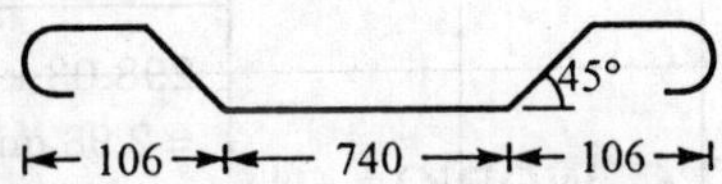	10.53	× 2	21.06		
Top straight bars 12 mm ϕ	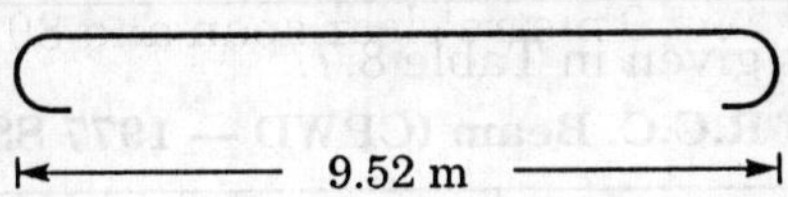 9.52 18. + 18 × .012 = 9.74	9.74	2	81.8 @ 2.98 14.48 @ 0.89	234.76 kg 17.34 kg	
Stirrups 10 mm ϕ	L = 70 × 2 + 32 × 2 + 30 cm extra 204 + 30 = 234 cm	2.34	18	42.12 @ 0.62	26.12 kg	
Stirrups 6 mm ϕ		2.34	21	49.15 @ 0.22	10.81 kg	

The details of measurement and calculation of quantity are shown in Table 8.6.

Table 8.6. Details of Measurements and Calculations of Quantity (R.C.C. Beam)

S. No.	Particulars of item of work	No.	Length	Breadth	Height Depth	Quantity	Remark
1.	R.C.C. work 1 : 2 : 4 excluding steel but inclusive of shuttering and bending and binding of steel	1	9.6 m	0.4 m	0.80 m	3.07 cum	No deduction is made for steel bars
2.	M.S. steel reinforcement						
	(*a*) Main bars						
	(*i*) 22 mm dia straight bars	4	9.92	= 39.68 m			
	(*ii*) 22 mm φ bent up bars	4	10.53	$= \frac{42.12}{81.80}$	@ 2.98 kg	243.76 kg	
	(*iii*) 12 mm dia top bars	2	9.74	= 19.48	@ 0.89	17.34 kg	
	(*b*) Stirrups						
	(*i*) 10.8 mm dia steel stirrups	18	2.34	= 42.12 m	@ 0.66	26.12 kg	
	(*ii*) 6 mm dia side stirrups	21	2.34	49.15	@ 0.22	10.81 kg	
						298.03 kg = 2.98 qnt	
3.	Centring and shuttering	1	9	0.40	—	3.60 m^2	

The abstract of cost of R.C.C. beam is given in Table 8.7.

Table 8.7. Abstract of Cost of R.C.C. Beam (CPWD — 1977 SSR)

S. No.	Particulars of item of work	Quantity	Unit	Rate	Cost	Remark
1.	R.C.C. work 1 : 2 : 4 excluding steel centring and shuttering and bending and binding of steel	3.07	cum			
2.	Mild steel reinforcement in R.C.C. work	298 kg	kg			
3.	Shuttering	3.60	sq m			
				Total		
	Add 1½% for water charges					
	Add 10% for contractor's profit					
			Grand Total			
				Say ₹		

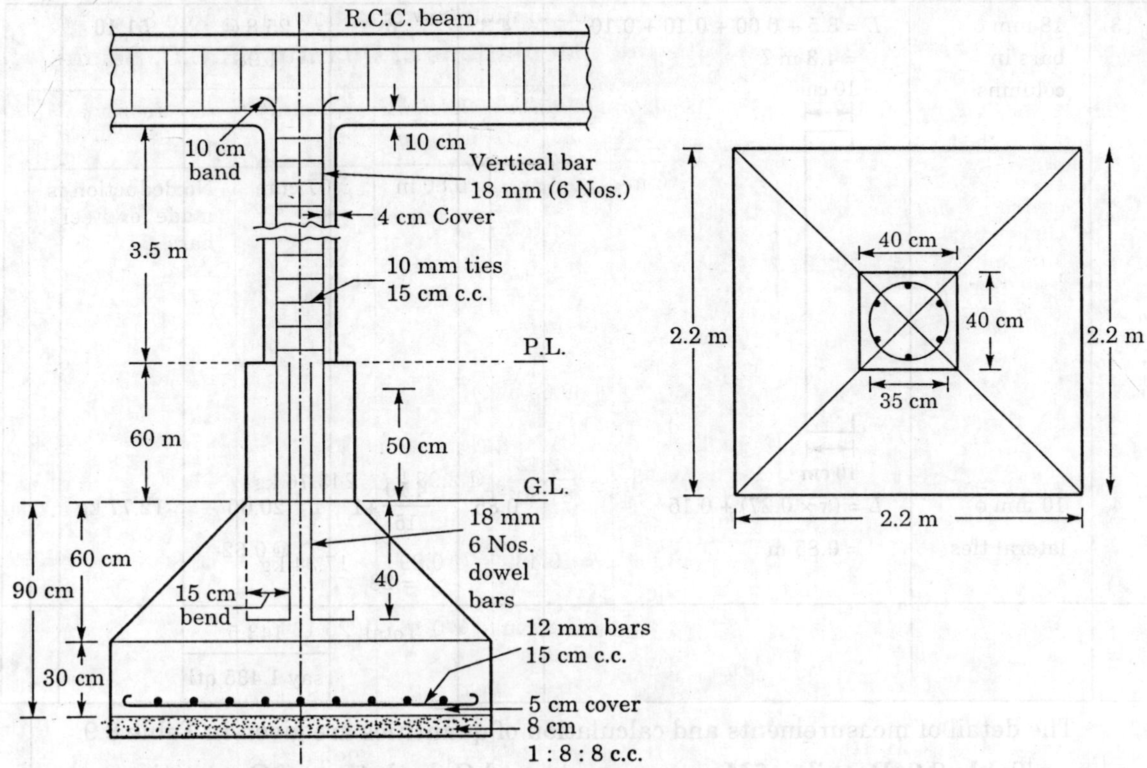

Fig. 8.3

8.5. ESTIMATE OF A R.C.C. COLUMN FOUNDATIONS

Fig. 8.3 gives details of a RCC column with footing foundation. Prepare a detailed estimate for the work.

Table 8.8 gives schedule of reinforcement.

Table 8.8. Schedule of Reinforcement

S. No.	*Particulars of Reinforcement*	*Bending Arrangement of Bars*	*Length of bar (m)*	*No. of bar*	*Total length*	*Weight kg*	*Remark*
1.	12 mm φ bars in base footing	l $L = 220 - 2 \times 4 + 18 \times 1.2$ $= 2.34$ m	2.34	$\frac{220-8}{15}+1$ $= 15$ one way	$2 \times 15 \times 2.34$ 70.20 @ 0.89	62.30 kg	
2.	18 mm φ dowel bars	15 cm $L = 0.50 + 0.90 -$ cover + bend $= 1.40 - 0.09 + 0.15 = 1.46$ m	1.46	6	8.76 @ 1.98	17.34 kg	

(*Contd.*)

3.	18 mm ϕ bars in columns	$L = 3.5 + 0.60 + 0.10 + 0.10$ $= 4.3$ m ? 	4.3	6	25.8 @ 1.98	51.10
4.	10 mm ϕ lateral ties	$L = (\pi \times 0.27) + 0.15$ $= 0.85$ m	0.85	$\frac{4.10}{15} + 1$ $= 28$	20.60 @ 0.62	12.77 kg
				Total	143.5	
					say 1.435 qtl	

The detail of measurements and calculation of quantities are given in Table 8.9.

Table 8.9. Details of Measurements and Calculation of Quantities (RCC Column)

S. No.	Particulars of Item of Work	No.	Length (m)	Breadth (m)	Height Depth (m)	Quantity	Remark
1.	Earthwork in excavation in foundation	1	2.20	2.20	0.98	4.74 cum	
2.	1 : 4 : 8 cement concrete (base)	1	2.20	2.20	0.08	0.39 cum	
3.	1 : 2 : 4 RCC work in footing (excluding steel but including centring and shuttering)						
	(*i*) Bottom square portion	1	2.20	2.20	0.30	1.452	
	(*ii*) Trapezoidal portion	1	$\left[\frac{(2.2)^2 + (0.40)^2}{2}\right]$ $= 2.5$ sq m		0.60	1.5 cum	
						2.96 cum	
4.	1 : 2 : 4 RCC work in column above G.L.						
	(*i*) Square portion upto plinth	1	0.40	0.40	0.60	0.096 cum	
	(*ii*) Circular portion above plinth	1×	$\left[\frac{\pi \times (0.35)^2}{4}\right]$		3.50	0.39 cum	
	Total					0.486 cum	

5.	M.S. steel reinforcement					
	(i) 12 mm φ bars in base footing	30	2.34	—	60.20	@ 0.89 = 53.58 kg
	(ii) 18 mm φ dowel bars	6	1.46	—	876	@ 1.98 = 17.34 kg
	(iii) 18 mm φ bars in column	6	4.3	—	25.8	@ 1.98 = 51.10 kg
	(iv) 10 mm φ laterals	28	0.85	—	20.60	@ 0.62 = 12.77 kg
	Total					134.79
					say	1.35 qtl.
6.	Centring and shuttering		0.6 × 1.6 =			0 96 m^2
			3.5 × π × 0.35 =			3.85 m^2
						4.81 m^2

The abstract of RCC columm given in Table 8.10.

Table 8.10. Abstract of Cost of RCC Column (Based on CPWD—SSR 1977)

S. No.	*Particulars of Item of Work*	*Quantity*	*Until*	*Rate*	*Cost*	*Remark*
1.	Earthwork in Excavation in foundation	4.74	cum	65.55	310.71	
2.	1 : 4 : 8 cement concrete (base)	0.39	cum	1158.65	451.87	
3.	1 : 2 : 4 RCC work in footing	2.96	cum	1740.90	5153.06	
4.	1 : 2 : 4 RCC work in column	0.48	cum	1907.65	915.67	
5.	M.S. steel reinforcement	1.35	quintal	2010.00	2713.50	
6.	Centring and shuttering	4.81	m^2	53.65	258.06	
			Total		9802.87	
	Add 1½% for water charge				147.04	
					9949.91	
	Add 10% for contractor's profit				994.49	
			Grand Total		10944.40	
				Say ₹	10944.0	

8.6. ESTIMATE OF A R.C.C. RETAINING WALL

Fig. 8.4 gives detail of a R.C.C. retaining wall 25 m long. Prepare a detail estimate for the work.

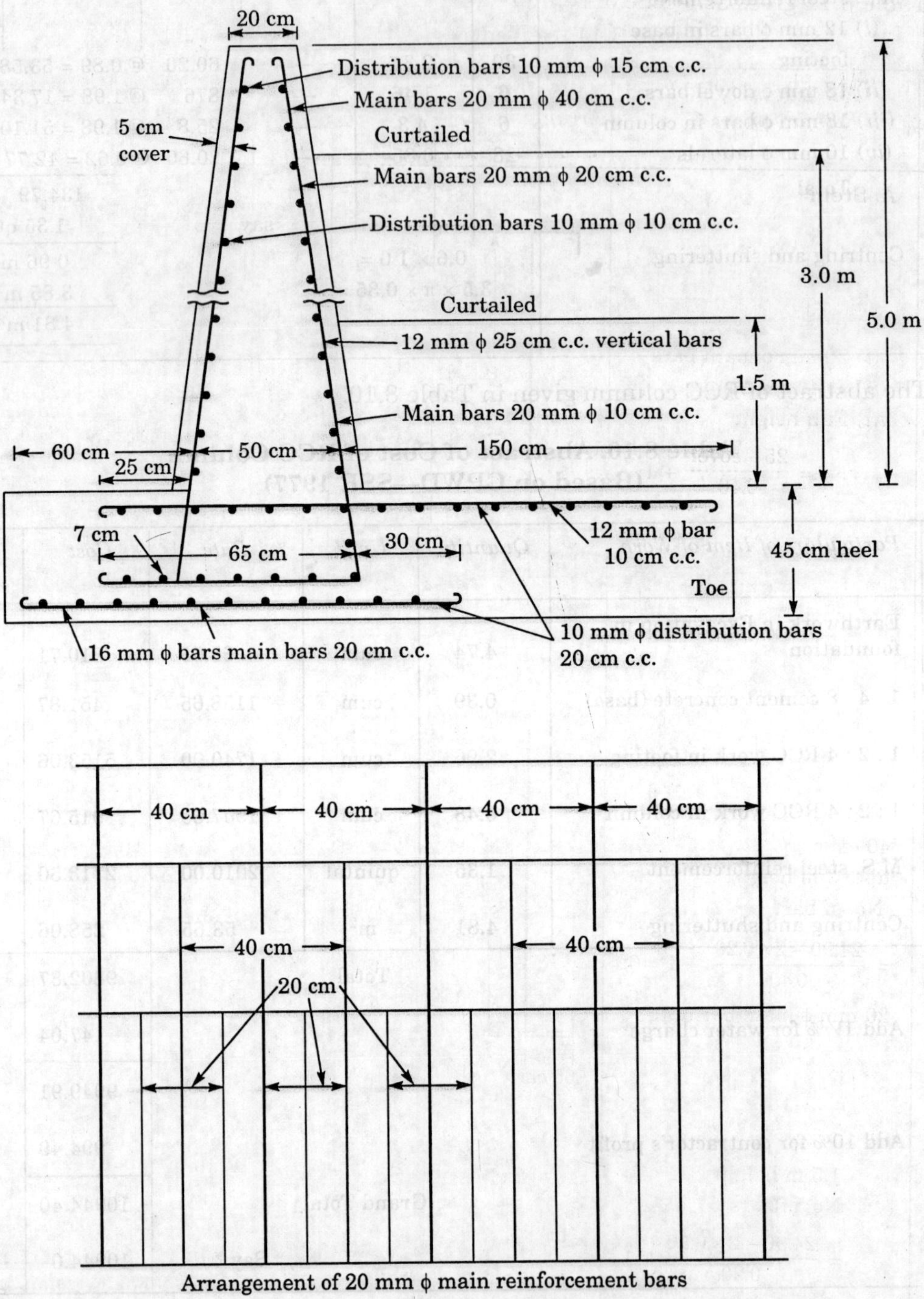

Fig. 8.4. R.C.C. Retaining wall.

Table 8.11 gives schedule of reinforcement.

Table 8.11. Schedule of Reinforcement

S. No.	*Particulars of Reinforcement*	*Bending Arrangement*	*Length of bar m*	*No. of bars*	*Total Length m*	*Weight kg*	*Remarks*
	A. Stem						
1.	(*i*) 20 mm φ main bars (*ii*) at 40 cm c.c. (*iii*) Full height No.= $\frac{25 - cover}{0.40} + 1$ $= \frac{24.90}{0.40} + 1 = 63$	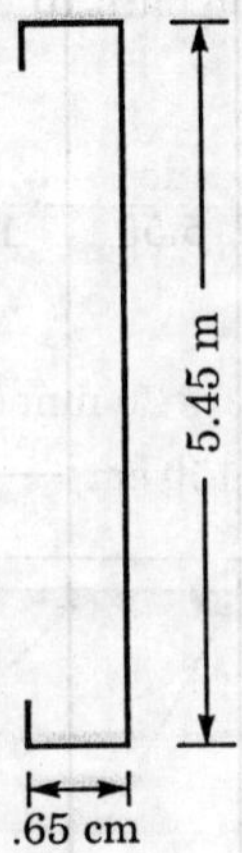	6.34	63	394.42		L= 5.45–top cover – bottom cover + 2 hooks + 0.65 = 5.45 – 0.05 – 0.07 + (18 × 0.020) + 0.65 = 6.34
2.	20 mm φ main bar 40 cm c.c. upto 3 m heights. No. of bar $= \frac{24.90 - 2 \times 0.20}{0.40} + 1 = 62$ 20 mm φ main bar upto	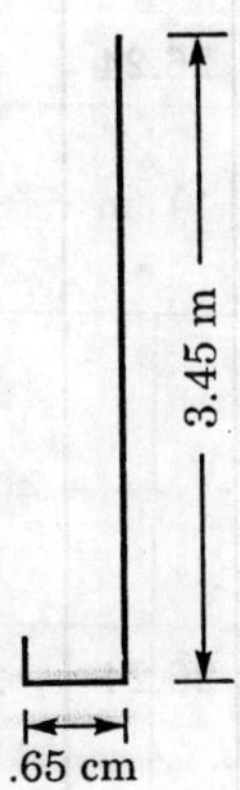	4.34	62	269.08		L = 6.34 – 20 = 4.34
3.	1.5 m height No. of bars $= \frac{24.90 - 2 \times 0.10}{0.20} + 1$ = 125		2.8	125	350		L = 6.34–3.50 = 2.80

Total 20 mm φ bar for stem 1013.50 m @ 2.47 kg = 2503.35 kg

(*Contd.*)

							L = 4.45 – (top + bottom) cover 2 hole = 5.45 – 0.07 – 0.5 + 15 (.012) = 5.55 m
4.	12 mm φ vertical bar left side of stem @ 25 cm c.c. No. = $\dfrac{5.45 - 0.05 - 0.07}{15} + 1$ = 101	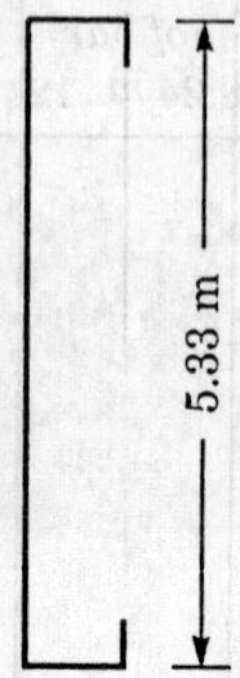	5.55	101	560.55 @ 0.89	497.89 kg	
5.	10 mm φ distribution bar right side 15 cm c.c. No. = $\dfrac{5.45 - 0.05 - 0.07}{15} + 1$ = 36 + 1 = 37 L = 25 – 2 cover + 20 overlaps + 6 hooks = 25 – 0.10 + (2 × 40 × 0.010) + 6 × 9 × 0.010 = 25 – 0.10 + 0.80 + 0.54 = 26.24 m (Assuming two joints)	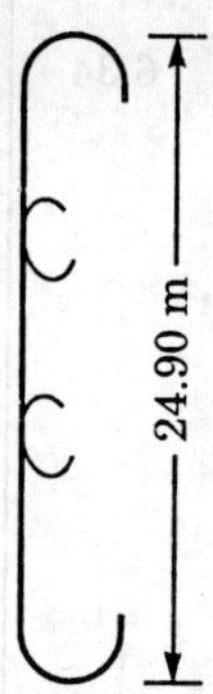	26.24	37	970.88 m @ 0.62 kg	623.04 kg	
6.	10 mm φ distribution bars left side 20 cm c.c. No.= $\dfrac{5.45 - 0.05 - 0.07}{0.20} + 1$ = 28 L = 25.60 – 2 cover + 2 overlap + 6 holes		26.24	28	734.72 @ 0.62	455.50	L = 25 + 10 + (2 × 40 × 0 + 6 × 9 × .011 = 26.24 m Assuming join
	(B) Base Slab						
7.	10 mm φ distribution bar at bottom (toe) at 20 cm c.c. No. = $\dfrac{0.60 + 0.50 + 0.30 - 0.05}{0.20} + 1 = 8$ L = 25–2 cover + 2 over laps + 6 hooks = 25–0.10 + (2 × 40 + 0.01) + (6 × 9 × 0.01) = 26.24 (Assuming two joints)		26.24	8	209.92		

8.	10 mm dia distributing bar top (heel) @ 20 cm c.c. No. = $\frac{1.50 + 0.50 + 0.25 - 0.05}{0.20} + 1 = 12$		26.24	12	314.88 524.80 @ 0.62 kg	325.38 kg	Length same as for bottom distribution bar
9.	16 mm φ bar at bottom (toe) at 20 cm c.c. No. = $\frac{25 - 0.10}{0.20} + 1$ $L = 0.60 + 0.50 + 0.30 - 0.05 + 18 \times 0.016 = 1.64$ m	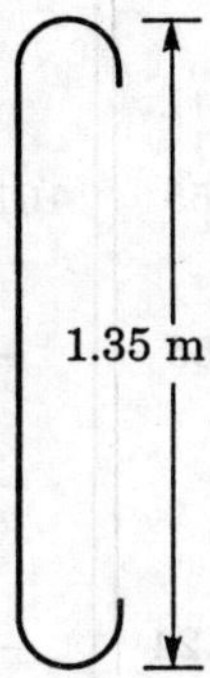	1.64	126	195.65 m @ 1.58	310.17 kg	
10.	12 mm φ bar at top (heel) at 10 cm c.c. No. = $\frac{25.00 - 0.10}{0.1} + 1$ 249 + 1 = 250 $L = 1.50 + 0.50 + 0.30 - 0.05 + (18 \times 0.012) = 2.47$ m	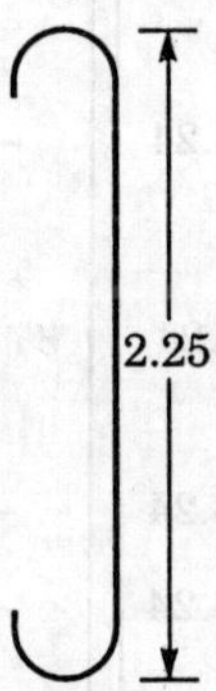	2.47	250	517.50 m @ 0.89 kg	460.58 5176.45 kg 51.76 Quintal	

The details of measurement and calculation of quantities are given in Table 8.12.

Table 8.12. Details of Measurements and Calculation of Quantities (R.C.C. Retaining Wall)

S. No.	*Particular of Item of bars*	*No*	*Length m*	*Breadth m*	*Height/ Depth m*	*Quantity*	*Remark*
1.	R.C.C. work 1 : 2 : 4 including steel but winding coils and shuttering						
	(*i*) Stem	1	25	$\frac{0.5 - 0.2}{2}$	5	43.75 cum	
	(*ii*) Base slab (Toe and heel)	1	25	2.6	0.45	33.75 cum	

(*Contd.*)

2.	Steel bars in reinforcement						
	A. Stem						
	(*i*) 20 mm φ bars @40 cm c.c. full height	63	6.34	—	—	394.42 m	
	(*ii*) " " upto 3 m height	62	4.34	—	—	269.08 m	
	(*iii*) " " upto 1.5 m height	125	2.8	—	—	350.00 m	
						1013.50 m @ 2.47 kg = 2503.35 kg	
	(*iv*) 12 mm φ vertical bars	101	5.55	—	—	560.55 m @ .89 m = 497.89 kg	
	(*v*) 10 mm φ distribute bars right side	37	26.24	—	—	970.88 m @ 0.62 kg = 623.04 kg	
	(*vi*) 10 mm left side	28	26.24	—	—	734.72 @ .62 kg = 455.50	
	B. Base Slab						
	(*i*) 10 mm φ distribution bars at bottom	8	28.24	—	—	209.92	
	(*ii*) 10 mm φ distribution brass at top	12	26.24	—	—	314.38	
						524.80 m @ 0.62 kg = 325.3 kg	
	(*iii*) 16 mm φ bars at bottom (Toe)	126	1.64	—	—	196.65 m @ 1.58 kg = 310.71 kg	
	(*iv*) 12 mm φ bars at top (Heel)	250	2.47	—	—	517.50 @ 0.89 kg = 460.58 kg	
	Total reinforcement					5176.45 kg 51.76 quintal	
3.	Centring and shuttering	2	25	5.0	—	275 m	

The abstract of cost of R.C.C. retaining wall given in Table 7.13.

Table 8.13. Abstract of Cost of R.C.C. Retaining Wall (CPWD—SSR—1977)

S. No.	*Particulars of item of work*	*Quantity*	*Unit*	*Rate*	*Cost*	*Remark*
1.	R.C.C. work 1 : 2 : 4 excluding steel but inclusive of centring and shuttering	33.74 cum	cum	1740.80	58734.59	
2.	M.S. steel reinforcement	51.76 q	kg	20.10	104037.6	
3.	Centring and shuttering	250	sq m	89.55	22387.50	
	Add 1½% for water charges			Total	185159.69	
					2777.39	
	Add 10% for contractor's Profit				18793.71	
					1819.37	
					20613.08	
				Say	20613.00	

Fig. 8.5 shows details of a steel roof truss having a span of 10.00 m. Estimate the quantity of steel work required for complete fabrication of one truss.

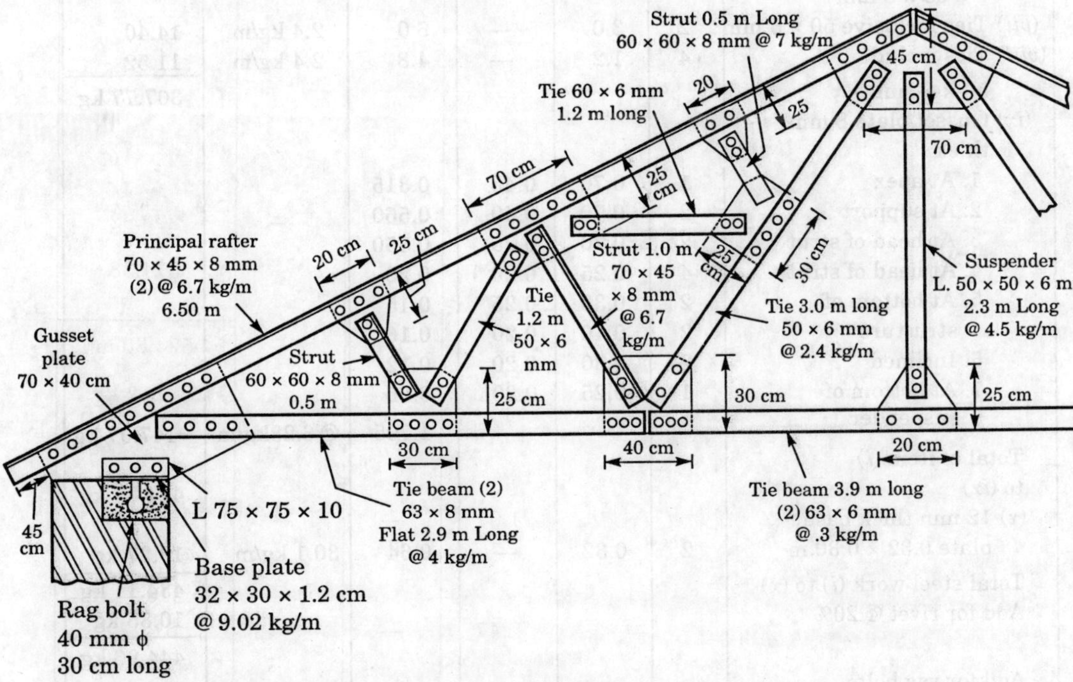

Fig. 8.5

1. Principal Rafter 2 × 70 × 45 × 8 mm @ 6.7 kg/m

Length of the rafter, assuming 1/2 : 1 slope of the truss

Half the horizontal length : 5.0 (clear span) + 0.40 = 5.40

Horizontal inclined length = 1.1 × 5.5 = 6.05 m

Add inclined clearance 45 cm = 6.05 + 0.45 = 6.50 m

In tie beam 2 × 80 × 6 mm F.B.

Details of measurements and calculation of quantities are given in Table 8.14.

Table 8.14. Details of Measurements and Calculation of Quantities of Steel Work in a Roof Truss

S. No.	Particulars of item of work	No.	Length (m)	Breadth (m)	Quantity or content (m)	Weight per unit	Total quantity of weight	Remark
1.	**Steel work**							
	(i) Principal Rafters 70 × 45 × 8 mm (2)	2 × 2	6.50	—	26 m	6.7 kg	174.20	
	(ii) Strut 60 × 60 × 8 mm	4	0.50	—	2.0	7 kg/m	14.00	
	(iii) Strut 70 × 45 × 8 mm	2	1.0	—	2.0	6.7 kg/m	13.40	
	(iv) Central suspended 50 × 50 × 64 mm	1	2.3	—	2.3	4.5 kg/m	10.35	
	(v) Ties main 2 × 63 × 6 mm flat	2	3.9	—	7.8	3.0 kg/m	23.40	
	(vi) Ties sides 2 × 63 × 8 mm	2 × 2	2.9	—	11.6	4 kg/m	46.40	
	(vii) Ties inclusive 50 × 6 mm	2	3.0	—	6.0	2.4 kg/m	14.40	
	(viii) Ties include 50 × 6 mm	4	1.2	—	4.8	2.4 kg/m	11.52	
							307.77 kg	
	(ix) Gusset plate 8 mm thick							
	1. At apex	1	0.70	0.45	0.315			
	2. At support	2	0.70	0.40	0.560			
	3. At head of strut	2	0.70	0.25	0.350			
	4. At head of strut	4	0.25	0.20	0.20			
	5. At bottom of structure	2	0.30	0.25	0.15			
		2	0.40	0.20	0.16			
	6. Inclined	2	0.30	0.20	0.12			
	7. At bottom of suspender	1	0.25	0.20	0.05			
					1.705	@ 6.28kg/m^2	=147.07 kg	
	Total of item (i) to (ix)						414.84 kg	
	(x) 12 mm thick base plate 0.32 × 0.30 m	2	0.32	—	0.64	30.1 kg/m	19.27 kg	
	Total steel work (i) to (x)						434.11 kg	
	Add for rivet @ 20%						10.85 kg	
							444.96 kg	
	Add for rag bolts 40 mm dia 30 cm lay @ 5 kg	4	—	—	4	25 kg	20.00 kg	
							464.96 kg	
						Say	465 kg	

Table 8.15 gives abstract of cost for steel work for steel roof truss.

Table 8.15. Abstract of Cost of Steel Roof Truss

S. No.	*Particulars of item of work*	*Quantity*	*Unit*	*Rate* ₹	*Cost* ₹	*Remark*
1.	Steel work	465 kg	*q*	1967.00	9146.55	
				Total	9146.55	
	Add 10% for				914.65	
	contractor's profit				10,161.20	
	Grand Total			Say ₹	10,161.00	

8.7. ESTIMATE OF A STEEL COLUMN

Figure 8.6 gives details of a steel column. Estimate the quantities of steel work.

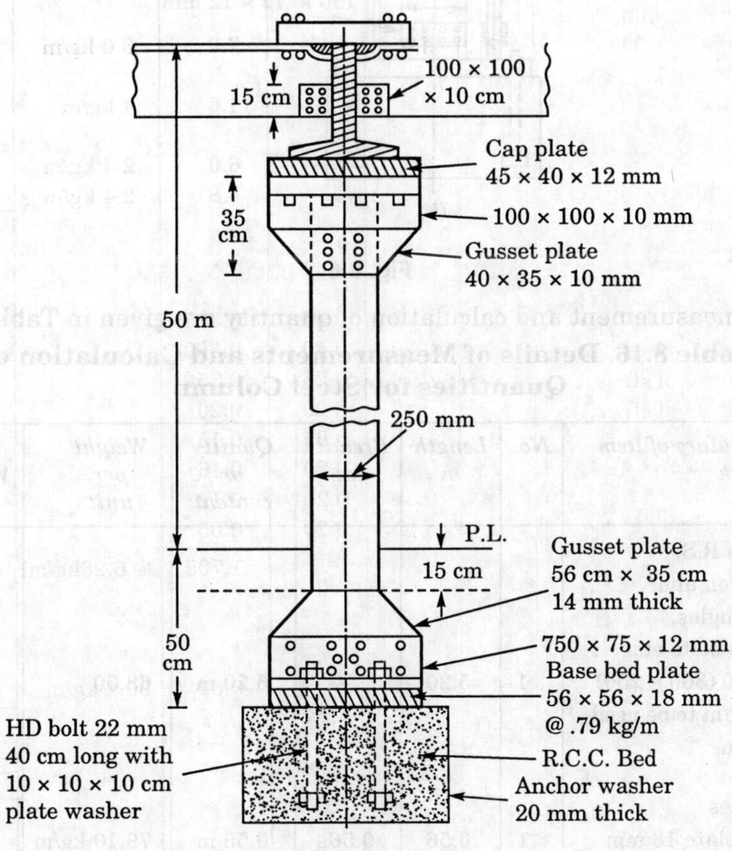

(*a*)

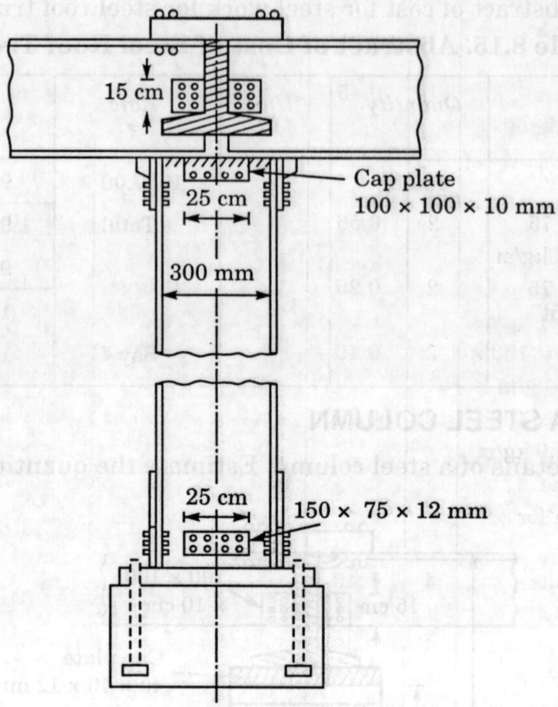

(b)

Fig. 8.6

Details of measurement and calculation of quantity are given in Table 8.16.

Table 8.16. Details of Measurements and Calculation of Quantities for Steel Column

S. No.	Particulars of item of work	No.	Length m	Breadth m	Quality or content	Weight per unit	Total Weight	Remark
1.	Steel work in R.S. joints, I-section and connecting angles, plates, rivets bolts etc.							
	(i) ISHB-300 (300 × 250) @ 63.0 kg/m to be used as column	1	5.20	—	5.20 m	63.00	327.60	
							327.60 kg	
	(ii) M.S. plates							
	1. Base plate 18 mm thick at 79.1 kg/m	1	0.56	0.56	0.56 m	79.10 kg/m	44.24 kg	
2.	Gusset plate at base 14 mm @ 6.15 kg/m (as rectangle)	2	0.56	0.35	0.56 m	61.50 kg/m	21.53 kg	

	3. Gusset-plate at top 40 × 35 × 10 mm @ 31.4 kg/m	2	0.40	0.35	0.35 m	31.50 kg/m	21.98 kg
	4. Cap plate 12 mm 44 × 40 @ 42.4 kg/m	1	0.45	0.40	0.40 m	42.40 kg/m	16.96 kg
							104.70 kg
	(*iii*) Angle iron cleats						
	1. At base 750 × 75 × l2mm @ 20.l kg/m	2	0.56	—	1.12 m	20.10 kg/m	22.50 kg
	2. At base 153 × 75 × 12 mm @ 20.1 kg/m	2	0.25	—	0.50 m	20.10 kg/m	10.05 kg
	3. Cap plate 100 × 100 × 10 mm @ 14.9 kg/m	2	0.40	—	0.80 m	14.90 kg/m	11.92 kg
	4. Cap plate 100 × 100 × 10 mm @ 14.9 kg/m	2	0.25	—	0.50 m	14.9 kg/m	7.45 kg
							51.92 kg
	(*iv*) Rivets @ 5% of the weight of column for rivets						
	(*v*) Holding down bolts 22 mm ϕ 40 cm by	4	0.40	—	1.6 m	2.98 kg/m	4.77 kg
	Head and nut	4	0.40	—	1.6 m	0.20 kg/m	0.32 kg
	100 mm anchor was 20 mm thick @ 15.7 kg/m	4	0.10	0.10	0.10 m	15.70 kg/m	1.57 kg
							6.66 kg
	Total steel weight						490.26 kg
						Say	4.90 quintal

Abstract of cost of steel work for steel column is given in Table 8.17.

Table 8.17. Abstract of Cost of Steel Column

S. No.	*Particulars of item of work*	*Quantity*	*Unit*	*Rate*	*Cost* ₹	*Remarks*
1.	Steel work of steel column	4..90	quintal	1967.00	9638.30	
				Total	9638.30	
	Add 10% for contractor's Profit				963.83	
					10602.10	
				Say ₹	10602.00	

9

Earth-Work

9.1. DEFINITION OF EARTHWORK

The term "earthwork" in its widest sense comprehends excavation in rock as well as in the looser materials of the earth's crust. It also includes embanking and puddling.

9.2. METHOD OF MEASUREMENTS OF EARTHWORK

The work shall be measured as given below :

(*i*) Each dimension shall be measured nearest to 0.01 m.

(*ii*) Area shall be worked out nearest to 0.01 sq m.

(*iii*) Volume shall be worked out nearest to 0.01 cum.

9.3. LEAD AND LIFT

Lift is the vertical distance through which the excavated soil is lifted beyond a certain specified depth.

Lead is the crow flying horizontal distance from the centre of borrow pit to the centre of the earthwork at site, *i.e.* centre of the area of excavation to the centre of placed earth.

(A) AREAS

9.4. CALCULATIONS OF AREAS

To calculate the quantities of earthwork it is necessary to know the methods of calculating of areas.

Areas from offsets to a base line :

Offsets at regular' intervals.

The area may be calculated by the following rules :

1. **Mid-ordinate rule.** In this method it is assumed that the earth surface is straight between the extremities of the ordinates. The area is divided into a number of divisions of equal distance and the ordinates are measured at the mid portion of each division.

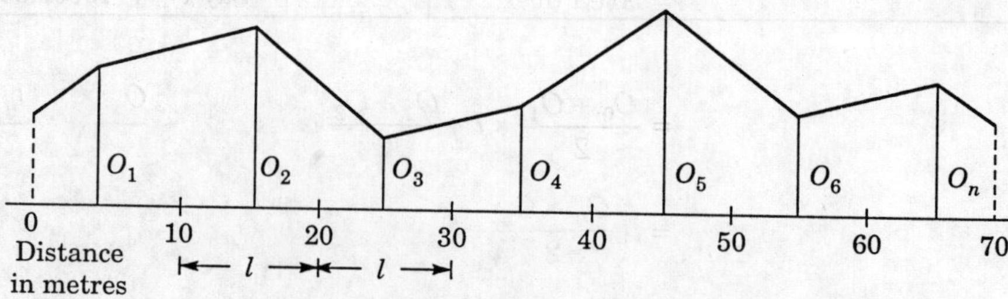

Fig. 9.1

Calculation of area

Area of one division = Distance × Ordinate = $l \times O_1$

Area of second division = $l \times O_2$

∴ Total area $= lO_1 + lO_2 + lO_3 + \ldots\ldots lO_n = l(O_1 + O_2 + O_3 + \ldots\ldots O_n) = l\Sigma O$

= Distance of each division × Sum of the mid ordinate.

2. **Average ordinate rule.** In this method it is assumed that the earth surface is straight between the extremities of the ordinates. The area is divided into a number of divisions of equal distance and the ordinates are measured to each of the point of the division of the base line.

Area = Average ordinate × Total length

$$= \left\{\frac{O_0 + O_1 + O_2 + \ldots + O_n}{n+1}\right\} \times nl = \frac{\Sigma O \times nl}{(n+1)}$$

$$= \frac{\text{(Sum of all the ordinates)} \times \text{(Total length)}}{\text{(No. of ordinate)}}$$

3. **Trapezoidal rule**

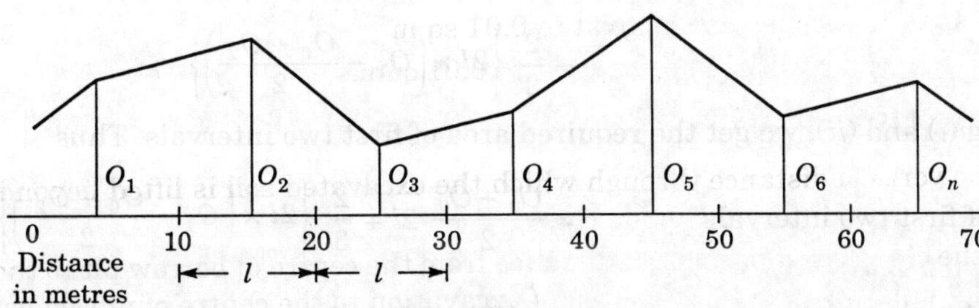

Fig. 9.2

Area of first trapezoid $= \dfrac{O_0 + O_1}{2} \times l$

Area of second trapezoid $= \dfrac{O_1 + O_2}{2} \times l$

Similarly area of the last (*nth*)

Trapezoid $= \dfrac{O_n - 1 + O_n}{2} \times l$

Hence the total area of the figure

= Area of first trapezoid + Area of second trapezoid + ... Area of last trapezoid

$$= \frac{O_0 + O_1}{2} \times l + \frac{O_1 + O_2}{2} \times l + \ldots\ldots + \frac{O_{n-1} + O_n}{2} \times l$$

$$= l\left(\frac{O_0 + O_n}{2} + O_1 + O_2 + \ldots\ldots O_{n-1}\right)$$

$$\text{Area} = \begin{pmatrix}\text{Distance between}\\ \text{each division}\end{pmatrix}\left\{\frac{\text{First ord.} + \text{Last ord.}}{2} + \text{(Sum of remaining ords.)}\right\}$$

Area = Add the average of the end ordinate to the sum of the intermediate ordinates and multiply this total sum by the common distance between the ordinates.

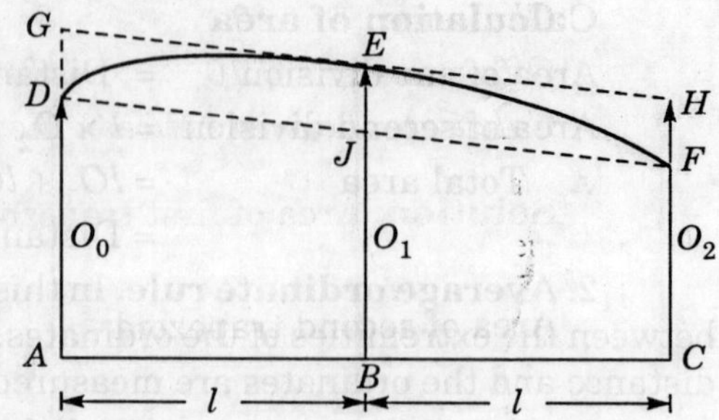

Fig. 9.3

4. **Simpson's one-third Rule.** In this method it is assumed that the earth surface is parabolic between the ordinates.

Calculations

Area of *ABCD* + area of *BCFE*

= Area of trapezoid *ACFJD* + Area of segment *DJFE*

Hence Area of trapezoid *ACFJD* $= \frac{O_0 + O_2}{2} \times 2l$ ...(*i*)

Area of segment *DJFE* $= \frac{2}{3} \times \{AC \times JE\} = 2/3\ \{AC \times (BE - BJ)\}$

$$= \frac{2}{3}\left\{2l \times \left(O_1 - \frac{O_0 + O_2}{2}\right)\right\} \quad ...(ii)$$

Adding (*i*) and (*ii*), we get the required area of first two intervals. Thus

Area of first two intervals $= \frac{O_0 + O_2}{2}\ 2l + \frac{2}{3}\left\{2l \times \left(O_1 - \frac{O_0 + O_2}{2}\right)\right\}$

$$= \frac{l}{3}(O_0 + 4O_1 + O_2) \quad ...(iii)$$

Similarly the area of next two intervals

$$= \frac{l}{3}(O_2 + 4O_3 + O_4) \quad ...(iv)$$

The area of the last two intervals $= \frac{l}{3}\ (O_{n-2} + 4O_{n-1} + O_n)$

Therefore, the total area $= \frac{l}{3}\ \{(O_0 + O_n) + 4(O_1 + O_3 + ... + O_{n-1})$

$+ 2(O_2 + O_3 + ...O_{n-2})\} + 2$

= One-third of the common interval × {(sum of the two end ordinates) + 4 (sum of the even intermediate ordinates) + 2 (the sum of odd intermediates ordinates)}

Note : This is applicable when the number of divisions of the area are even, *i.e.* the total numbers of ordinate are odd.

If there are odd numbers of division, *i.e.* even numbers of ordinate, the area of the last division is calculated separately and added to get the total area.

The result obtained by this rule are more accurate.

Example 9.1. *The following perpendicular offsets were taken from a chain line to an irregular boundary :*

Chainage	*0*	*8*	*20*	*30*	*36*	*40 m*
Offset	*6.10*	*4.30*	*3.90*	*7.00*	*4.60*	*5.00 m*

Calculate the area between the chain line, the boundary and the end offsets.

Solution. Area of first trapezoid $= (8 - 0)\left\{\frac{6.10 + 4.30}{2}\right\} = 41.60$ sq m $= 8 \times \left\{\frac{6.1 + 4.3}{2}\right\}$

Area of second trapezoid $= (20 - 8)\left\{\frac{4.30 + 3.90}{2}\right\} = 49.20$ sq m

Area of third trapezoid $= (30 - 20)\left\{\frac{3.90 + 7.00}{2}\right\} = 54.50$ sq m

Area of fourth trapezoid $= (36 - 30)\left\{\frac{7.00 + 4.60}{2}\right\} = 34.80$ sq m

Area of fifth trapezoid $= (40 - 36(\left\{\frac{4.60 + 5.00}{2}\right\} = 19.20$ sq m

Total area = 41.60 + 49.20 + 54.50 + 34.80 + 19.20 = 199.3 sq m.

Example 9.2. *The following perpendicular offsets were taken at 20 m intervals from a survey line to an irregular boundary line :*

3.75, 4.15, 5.70, 4.95, 6.00, 5.35, 4.95.

Calculate the area enclosed between the survey line, the irregular boundary line and the first and last offsets, by application of (*a*) *average ordinate rule,* (*b*) *trapezoidal rule and* (*c*) *Simpson's rule.*

Solution. (*a*) By average ordinate rule

$$\text{Area} = \frac{\Sigma O \times nl}{(n+1)} = \frac{(\text{Sum of all ordinates}) \times (\text{Total distance})}{(\text{No. of ordinate})}$$

$\Sigma O = 3.75 + 4.15 + 5.70 + 4.95 + 6.00 + 5.35 + 4.95 = 34.85$ m (sum of ords.)

$nl = 6 \times 20 = 120$ m (Total length)

$n + 1 = 6 + 1 = 7$ No. of ordinate.

$$\text{Area} = \frac{34.85 \times 120}{7} = 597.43 \text{ sq m.}$$

(*b*) By trapezoidal rule

$$\text{Area} = l(\frac{O_0 + O_n}{2} + O_1 + O_2 + \ldots\ldots + O_{n-1})$$

$$= \left(\begin{array}{c}\text{Distance between}\\ \text{each division}\end{array}\right)\left\{\frac{\text{First ord.} + \text{Last ord.}}{2} + (\text{Sum of remaining ords.})\right\}$$

$$= 20\left\{\frac{3.75 + 4.95}{2} + (4.15 + 5.70 + 4.95 + 6.00 + 5.35)\right\}$$

$$= 20\{4.35 + (26.15)\} = 20 \times 30.50 = 610 \text{ sq m.}$$

(*c*) By Simpson's rule

$$= \frac{l}{3}\{(O_0 + O_n) + 4(O_1 + O_3 + O_n) + 2(O_3 + O_4 + \ldots + O_{n-2})\}$$

$$= \frac{\text{Common distance}}{3}\left\{\left(\begin{array}{c}\text{Sum of two}\\ \text{end ords.}\end{array}\right) + 4\left(\begin{array}{c}\text{Sum of even}\\ \text{int. ords.}\end{array}\right) + 2\left(\begin{array}{c}\text{Sum of odd}\\ \text{int. ords.}\end{array}\right)\right\}$$

$$= \frac{20}{3}\{(3.75 + 4.95) + 4(4.15 + 4.95 + 5.35) + 2(5.70 + 6.00)\}$$

$$= \frac{20}{3}\{(8.70) + (57.80) + (23.40)\} = \frac{20}{3} \times 89.90 = 599.33 \text{ sq m.}$$

Example 9.3. *A series of offsets were taken from a chain line to a curved boundary line at intervals of 20 metres in the following order :*

0, 1.60, 2.30, 3.30, 4.50, 3.80, 2.10, 1.40, 1.00, 0 m.

Compute the area between the chain line, the curved boundary and the end offsets by (a) average ordinate rule, (b) trapezoidal rule, and (c) Simpson's rule.

Solution. (*a*) By average ordinate rule

$$\text{Area} = \frac{\Sigma O \times nl}{(n+1)}$$

$$\Sigma O = 0 + 1.60 + 2.30 + 3.30 + 4.50 + 3.80 + 2.10 + 1.40 + 1.00 + 0 = 20.00 \text{ m.}$$

$$nl = 9 \times 20 = 180 \text{ m.} \quad n + 1 = (9 + 1) = 10 \text{ No.}$$

$$\text{Area} = \frac{20 \times 180}{10} = 360 \text{ sq m}$$

(*b*) By trapezoidal rule

$$\text{Area} = l\left\{\frac{O_0 + O_n}{2} + O_1 + O_2 + \ldots\ldots O_{n-1}\right\}$$

$$= 20\left\{\frac{O + O}{2} + 1.60 + 2.30 + 3.30 + 4.50 + 3.80 + 2.10 + 1.40 + 1.00\right\}$$

$$= 20 \times 20 = 400 \text{ sq m.}$$

(*c*) By Simpson's rule.

(**Note.** Taking 9 No. of odd ordinates for Simpson's rule and adding the area of last two ordinates.

$$\text{Area} = \frac{l}{3}\{(O_0 + O_{n-1}) + 4(O_1 + O_2 + \ldots O_{n-1}) + 2(O_2 + O_4 + \ldots\ O_{n-2})\} + \left\{\frac{O_{n-1} + O_n}{2}\right\} \times l$$

$$= \frac{20}{3}\{(0 + 1.00) + 4(1.60 + 3.30 + 3.80 + 1.40) + 2(2.30 + 4.50 + 2.10)\} + \left\{\frac{1.00 + 0}{2}\right\} \times 20$$

$$= \frac{20}{3}\{1.00 + 40.40 + 17.80\} + \frac{1}{2} \times 20 = \frac{20}{3} \times 59.20 + 10$$

$$= 394.66 + 10 = 404.66 \text{ sq m.}$$

EXERCISES

Exercise 9.1. The following perpendicular offsets were taken from a chain line to a hedge

Chainage	0	20	40	60	80	120	160	200	250	300
Offsets	3.70	4.10	5.60	3.70	3.00	6.10	5.60	4.30	3.70	4.50

Calculate the area between the survey line, the hedge and the end offsets by (*a*) average ordinate rule (*b*) trapezoidal rule and (*c*) Simpson's rule.

Exercise 9.2. The following offsets were taken from a chain line to a hedge

Distance in m	0	20	60	100	110	120	130
Offsets in m	2.0	4.0	3.0	7.0	6.0	4.0	1.0

Calculate the area enclosed between the chain line, the hedge and the end offsets.

Exercise 9.3. Plot the following details of a field and calculate its area. All measurements being in metres.

Left offset	Chainage	Right offset
	J	
	100	
	92	16 H
K 20	80	22 G
L 18	60	42 F
	46	10 E
M 22	26	36 D
		12 C
	16	
		20 B
N 12	10	
5		
	0	
	A	

(B) VOLUMES

General. Three methods are adopted for the calculation of volumes. They are :

(*i*) From cross-sections. (*ii*) From spot level. (*iii*) From contours.

The first two methods are used for the measurements of earthwork while the third method is used for the calculation of reservoir etc. capacities.

Calculations from cross-sections. This method is widely adopted for the calculations of earthworks in engineering works. The total volume is divided into a series of solid portions, by the planes of cross-sections. The solids are in the form of prisms, wedge and prismoid. Cross-sections are taken according to the character of the ground and the accuracy needed. The areas along the cross-sections are worked out and then the volumes are calculated either by Trapezoidal formula or by Prismoidal formula.

(*a*) *Level section.* In this case the ground is level transversly.

$$\text{Area} = A = Bd + Sd^2$$

and

$$\text{volume} = V = l\{Bd + Sd^2\}$$

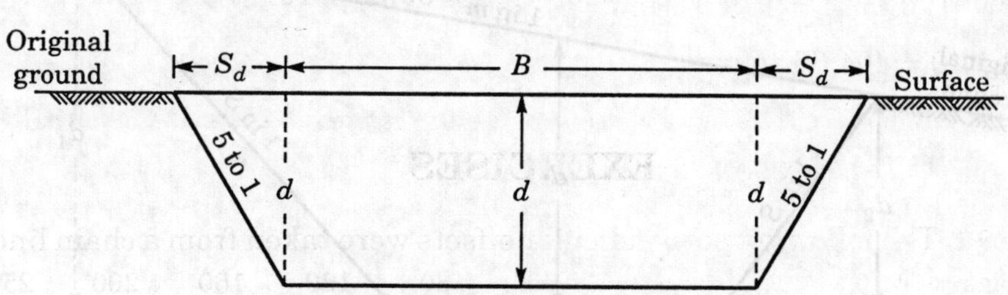

Fig. 9.4

(b) *Two-level section*. In this case the ground slope crosses the formation level.

$$W_1 = \frac{B}{2} + Sd_1 = \frac{B}{2} + \frac{mS}{m-S}\left(d + \frac{B}{2m}\right)$$

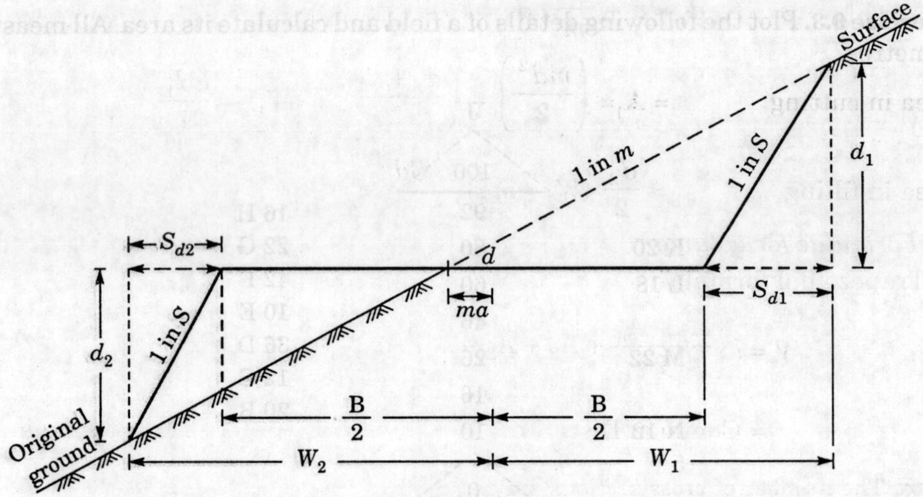

Fig. 9.5

$$W_2 = \frac{B}{2} + Sd_2 = \frac{B}{2} + \frac{mS}{m-S}\left(d - \frac{B}{2m}\right)$$

$$d_1 = d + \frac{W_1}{m},\ d_2 = d - \frac{W_2}{m}$$

$$A = \text{Area} = \left\{\left(\frac{d_1 + d_2}{2}\right) \times (W_1 + W_2)\right\} - \frac{Sd_1^2}{2} - \frac{Sd_2^2}{2}.$$

(c) *Side-hill two-level section*. In this case the ground is sloping transversely, but the slope of the ground intersects the formation level, such that the area is formed in cutting and in filling *i.e.* partially in cutting and partially in filling.

$$W_1 = \frac{B}{2} + Sd_1 = \frac{B}{2} + \frac{mS}{m-S}\left(d + \frac{B}{2m}\right)$$

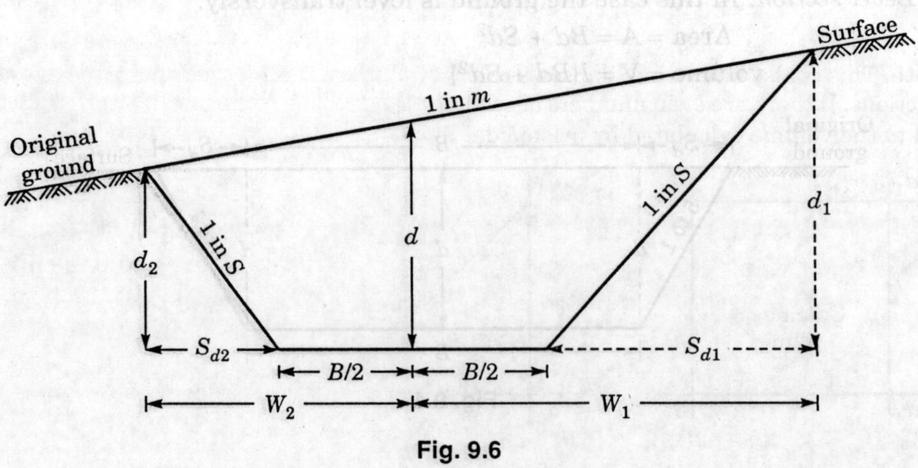

Fig. 9.6

$$W_2 = \frac{B}{2} + Sd_2 = \frac{B}{2} + \frac{mS}{m-S}\left(\frac{B}{2m} - d\right)$$

$$d_1 = d + \frac{W_1}{m},\ d_2 = d - \frac{W_2}{m}$$

Area in cutting $= A_1 = \left(\frac{md^2}{2}\right) + \left(\frac{d_1 + d_1}{2}\right) \times (W_1) - \frac{Sd_1^2}{2}$

Area in filling $= \frac{d_2}{2}\,(W_2 - md) - \frac{Sd_2^2}{2}$.

(*d*) *Formulae for volume*

(*i*) Trapezoidal formula

$$V = l\left\{\frac{A_1 + A_n}{2} + A_2 + A_3 + \ldots + A_{n-1}\right\}$$

$$= \text{Common Distance}\left\{\frac{\text{1st Area} + \text{Last Area}}{2} + \text{Sum of remaining area}\right\}$$

Note. The number of cross-sections may be even or odd. It is also known as average end area formula.

(*ii*) Prismoidal formula

$$V = \frac{l}{6}(A_1 + A_2 + 4A_m)$$

where l = Length of the prismoid measured perpendicular to the two end parallel planes.

A_1 = Area of cross-section of one end plane.

A_2 = Area of cross-section of the other end plane.

A_m = Mid area = Area of the plane midway between the end planes and parallel to lines.

Also $V = \frac{l}{3}\{(A_1 + A_n) + 4(A_2 + A_4 + \ldots + A_{n-1}) + 2(A_3 + A_5 + \ldots + A_{n-2})\}$

$= \frac{\text{Common Distance}}{3}$ {(1st Area + Last Area) + 4 (Sum of even areas) + 2(Sum of remaining odd areas)}

Note. This is also known as Simpson's rule for volumes. It is also necessary to have odd numbers of cross-sections. If there are even numbers of sections, the area of end strip will be calculated separately and added to the volume calculated by prismoidal formula.

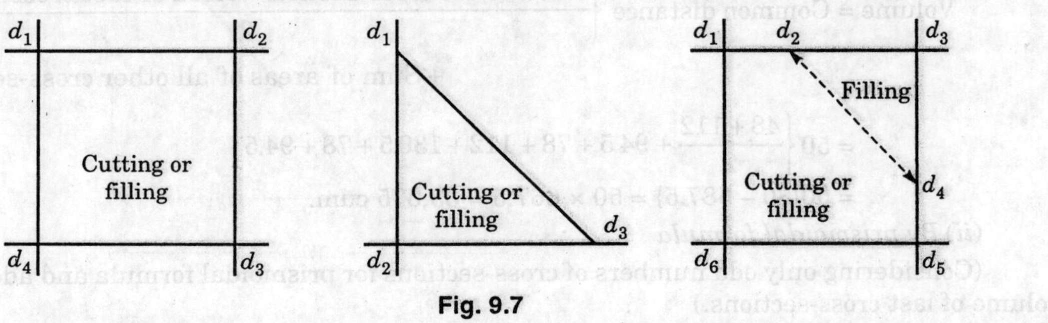

Fig. 9.7

(*e*) *Measurement of volumes from spot levels*. This method is used to calculate the quantities of earthwork in cutting or in filling in large areas for general levelling and dressing for development works. The entire area is divided into a number of equal triangles, squares or rectangles. The original surface levels or natural surface levels before earthwork and the new finished surface levels, after earthwork are recorded by spot levelling and the earthwork is calculated. The depth of earthwork are marked at the corners of the squares etc. into which the ground is divided. The volume of each division is calculated by the following formulae :

$$\text{Volume of truncated triangular prism} = A\left(\frac{d_1 + d_2 + d_3}{3}\right)$$

$$\text{Volume of truncated rectangular prism} = A\left(\frac{d_1 + d_2 + d_3 + d_4}{4}\right)$$

In one truncated rectangular prism.

$$\text{Volume of cutting} \quad = A\left(\frac{d_1 + d_2 + d_4 + d_5 + d_6}{5}\right)$$

$$\text{and volume of filling} \quad = A\left(\frac{d_2 + d_3 + d_4}{3}\right)$$

where A = Horizontal area of the cross-section d_1, d_2, d_3,...etc. Depth of cutting or filling at corners.

Example 9.4. *A road embankment is 20 m wide with side slopes 2 : 1. The ground is level in the transverse direction to the centre line. Calculate the volume contained in a length of 350 metres. The central height at 50 m intervals being 2.0, 3.5, 3.0, 4.0, 4.5, 3.0, 3.5 and 4.0 m respectively.*

Solution. Area in level section

$$A = Bd + Sd^2 \,;\, B = 20 \text{ m} \,;\, S = 2$$

$$A_0 = [20 \times 2.0 + 2 \times (2.0)^2] = 48 \text{ sq m}$$

$$A_{50} = [20 \times 3.5 + 2 \times (3.5)^2] = 94.5 \text{ sq m}$$

$$A_{100} = [20 \times 3.0 + 2 \times (3.0)^2] = 78 \text{ sq m}$$

$$A_{150} = [20 \times 4.0 + 2 \times (4.0)^2] = 112 \text{ sq m}$$

$$A_{200} = [20 \times 4.5 + 2 \times (4.5)^2] = 130.5 \text{ sq m}$$

$$A_{250} = [20 \times 3.0 + 2 \times (3.0)^2] = 78 \text{ sq m}$$

$$A_{300} = [20 \times 3.5 + 2 \times (3.5)^2] = 94.5 \text{ sq m}$$

$$A_{350} = [20 \times 4.0 + 2 \times (4.0)^2] = 112 \text{ sq m.}$$

(*i*) *By trapezoidal formula*

$$\text{Volume} = \text{Common distance}\left\{\frac{\text{Area of 1st cross-section} + \text{Area of last cross-section}}{2} + \text{Sum of areas of all other cross-sections}\right\}$$

$$= 50\left\{\frac{48 + 112}{2} + 94.5 + 78 + 112 + 130.5 + 78 + 94.5\right\}$$

$$= 50\{80 - 587.5\} = 50 \times 667.5 = 33{,}375 \text{ cum.}$$

(*ii*) *By prismoidal formula*

(Considering only odd numbers of cross-sections for prismoidal formula and adding the volume of last cross-sections.)

$$\text{Volume} = \frac{\text{Common distance}}{3} \{(\text{1st area + last area}) + 4\,(\text{Sum of even areas}) + 2\,(\text{Sum of remaining odd areas})\}$$

$$= \frac{50}{3} \times \{48 + 94.5) + 4(94.5 + 112 + 78) + 2(78 + 130.5)\}$$

$$= \frac{50}{3} \times \{(142.5) + 4(284.5) + 2(208.5)\}$$

$$= \frac{50}{3} \times \{142.5 + 1138.0 + 417.0\}$$

$$= \frac{50}{3} \times 1697.5 = 28291.6 \text{ cum.}$$

∴ *Add.* The volume of last strip

$$\text{Volume} = 50\left(\frac{94.5 + 112}{2}\right) = 5162.5 \text{ cum.}$$

∴ Total volume = 33,454.1 cum.

Example 9.5. *Estimate the quantity of earthwork in excavation for a road in cutting in hilly tract between 1500 to 1600 metres. The cross-sections are taken at 50 m intervals. The relevant data for the cross-sections is given below :*

Cross-section at RD	*Depth of cutting in the centre in metres*	*Cross-shape of the ground*
1500th m	4.0	1 in 10θ (V in H)
1550th m	3.0	1 in 20θ (V in H)
1600th m	4.0	1 in 20θ (V in H)

The side slopes of the cutting are 1 : 1 and the formation width of the road is 10 m.

Solution. Cross-section at *RD* 1500.

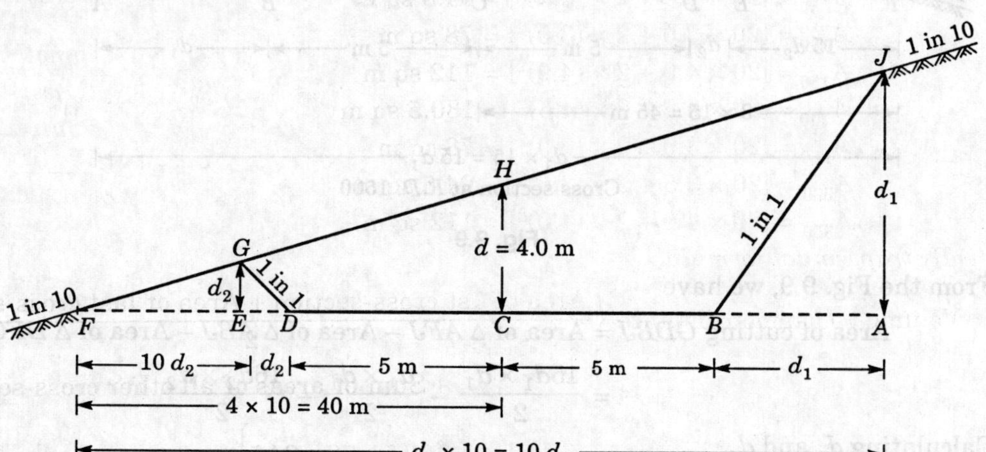

Cross-section at *R.D.* 1500

Fig. 9.8

From Fig. 9-8, we have

Area of cutting $GDBJ$ = Area of $\Delta\, AFJ$ – Area of $\Delta\, ABJ$ – Area of $\Delta\, DFG$

$$= \frac{10d_1 \times d_1}{2} - \frac{d_1 \times d_1}{2} - \frac{11d_2 \times d_2}{2}$$

Calculating d_1 and d_2

$10\, d_1 = 40 + 5 + d_1$	$10d_2 - d_2 + 5 = 40$
or $10d_1 - d_1 = 45$	or $11d_2 = 40 - 5$
or $9d_1 = 45$	$d_2 = \frac{35}{11}$
or $d_1 = 5$	

Now area of cutting $GDBJ = \frac{10d_1 \times d_1}{2} - \frac{d_1 \times d_1}{2} - \frac{11d_2 \times d_2}{2}$

$$= \frac{10 \times 5 \times 5}{2} - \frac{5 \times 5}{2} - 11 \times \frac{35}{11} \times \frac{35}{11} \times \frac{1}{2}$$

$$= 125 - 12.5 - 55.68 = 56.82 \text{ sq m.}$$

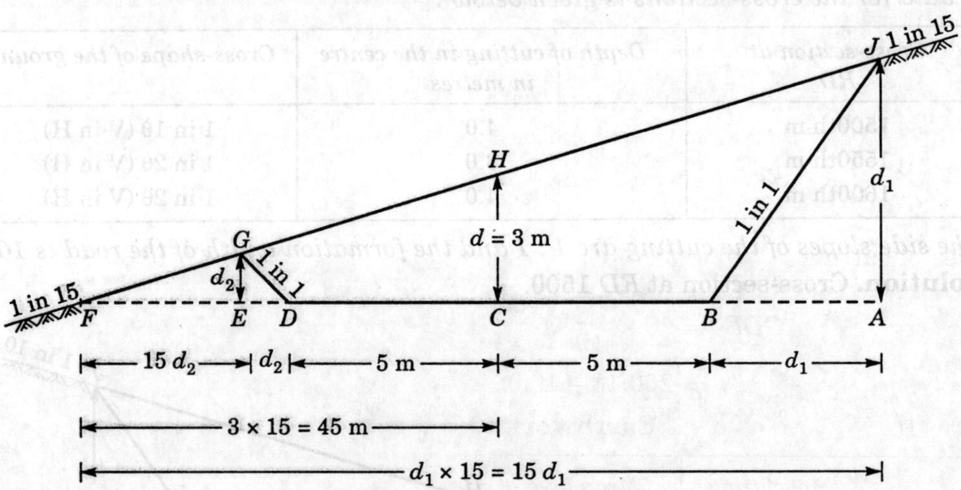

Cross-section at *R.D.* 1500

Fig. 9.9

From the Fig. 9.9, we have

Area of cutting $GDBJ$ = Area of $\Delta\, AFJ$ – Area of $\Delta\, ABJ$ – Area of $\Delta\, DFG$

$$= \frac{15d_1 \times d_1}{2} - \frac{d_1 \times d_1}{2} - \frac{16d_2 \times d_2}{2}$$

Calculating d_1 and d_2

$15d_1 = 45 + 5 + d_1$	$15d_1 + d_2 + 5 = 45$
$14d_1 = 50$	$16d_2 = 45 - 5$
$d_1 = \frac{50}{14}$	$d_2 = \frac{40}{16}$

$$\text{Area of cutting } GDBJ = 15 \times \frac{50}{14} \times \frac{50}{14} \times \frac{1}{2} - \frac{50}{14} \times \frac{50}{14} \times \frac{1}{2} - 16 \times \frac{40}{16} \times \frac{40}{16} \times \frac{1}{2}$$

$$= 95.66 - 6.37 - 50 = 39.29 \text{ sq m.}$$

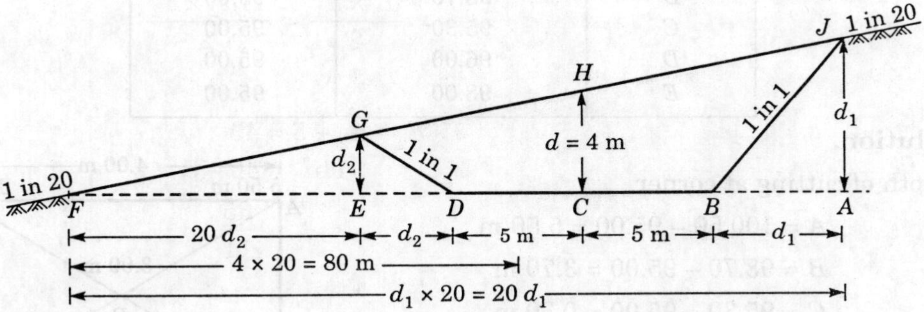

Fig. 9.10

From the Fig. 9.10, we have

$$\text{Area of cutting } GDBJ = \text{Area of } \Delta AFJ - \text{Area of } \Delta ABJ - \text{Area of } \Delta DFG$$

$$= \frac{20\, d_1 \times d_1}{2} - \frac{d_1 \times d_1}{2} - \frac{21\, d_2 \times d_2}{2}$$

Calculating d_1 and d_2

$$20\, d_1 = 80 + 5 + d_1$$

$$19\, d_1 = 85$$

$$d_1 = \frac{85}{19}$$

$$20\, d_2 + d_2 + 5 = 80$$

$$21\, d_2 = 80 - 5$$

$$d_2 = \frac{75}{21}$$

Area of cutting

$$GDBJ = 20 \times \frac{85}{19} \times \frac{85}{19} \times \frac{1}{2} - \frac{85}{19} \times \frac{85}{19} \times \frac{1}{2} - 21 \times \frac{75}{21} \times \frac{75}{21} \times \frac{1}{2}$$

$$= 200.13 - 10.00 - 133.92 = 56.21 \text{ sq m.}$$

Earthwork Calculations

R.D. *m*	*Area of cutting* *sq m*	*Mean area of cutting* *sq m*	*Length* *m*	*Quantity of earthwork* *cum*
1500	56.82	—		
1550	39.29	48.055	50	2402.75
1600	56.21	47.750	50	2387.50
			Total	4790.25 cum.

Example 9.6. *A rectangle ABCD 400 m × 200 m forms the plan of part of an excavation. AB and CD are the longer sides, and E is the point of intersection of the diagonals. From the following original surface levels and final excavated levels, calculate the volume of earthwork in excavation within ABCD.*

Point	*Original level*	*Final level*
A	100.50	95.00
B	98.70	95.00
C	95.30	95.00
D	96.00	95.00
E	98.00	95.00

Solution.

Depth of cutting at corner

$A = 100.50 - 95.00 = 5.50$ m

$B = 98.70 - 95.00 = 3.70$ m

$C = 95.30 - 95.00 = 0.30$ m

$D = 96.00 - 95.00 = 1.00$ m.

$E = 98.00 - 95.00 = 3.00$ m.

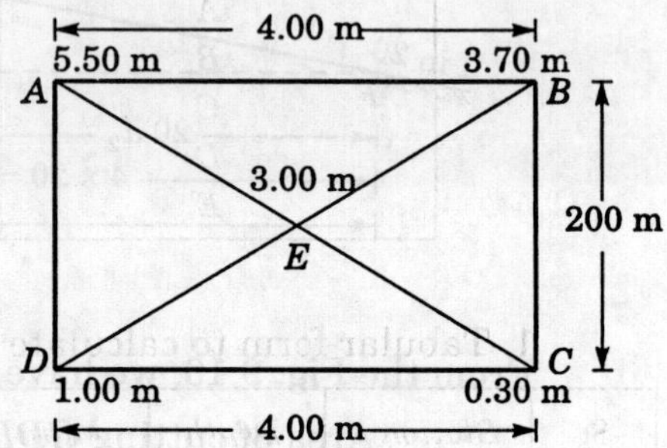

Fig. 9.11

$$V = A\left(\frac{d_1 + d_2 + d_3}{3}\right) \text{ cum.}$$

$$\text{Volume of } AED = 200 \times \frac{400}{2} \times \frac{1}{2}\left(\frac{5.50 + 3.00 + 1.00}{3}\right) = 63333.33 \text{ cum}$$

$$\text{Volume of } BEC = 200 \times \frac{400}{2} \times \frac{1}{2}\left(\frac{3.70 + 3.00 + 0.30}{3}\right) = 46666.66 \text{ cum}$$

$$\text{Volume of } ABE = 400 \times \frac{200}{2} \times \frac{1}{2}\left(\frac{5.50 + 3.00 + 3.70}{3}\right) = 81333.33 \text{ cum}$$

$$\text{Volume of } DEC = 400 \times \frac{200}{4} \times \frac{1}{2}\left(\frac{1.00 + 3.00 + 0.30}{3}\right) = 28666.66 \text{ cum}$$

Total volume = 63333.33 + 46666.66 + 81333.33 + 28666.66 = 220,000 cum.

Exercise 9.4. A road embankment is 15 m wide with side slopes 2 : 1. The ground is level in the transverse direction to the centre line. Calculate the volume contained in the length of 200 metres. The central height at 20 m intervals being 3.4, 2.7, 4.2, 5.6, 3.2, 3.9, 4.1, 4.6, 5.2, 5.4 and 2.6 m.

Exercise 9.5. Estimate the quantity of earthwork in excavation for a hilly road in cutting between 100 to 200 metres. The cross-sections are taken at 20 m intervals the relevant data for the cross-sections is given below :

Cross-section at, R.D.	*Depth of cutting in the Centre in metres*	*Cross-slope of the ground*
100	2.00	1 in 10
120	3.00	1 in 12
140	4.00	1 in 15
160	3.50	1 in 18
180	2.50	1 in 20
200	1.00	1 in 15

The side slopes of the cutting are 1 : 1 and the formation width of the road is 12 m.

Exercise 9.6. A rectangle *ABCD* 300 m × 150 m. From the plan of parts of an excavation, *AB* and *CD* are the longer sides and *E* is the point of intersection of the diagonals. From the following original surface levels and final excavated levels, calculate the volume of earthwork in excavation within *ABCD*.

Point	*Original level*	*Final level*
A	200.00	195.00
B	198.00	195.00
C	196.00	195.00
D	201.00	195.00
E	197.00	195.00

Tabular Forms

1. Tabular form to calculate the quantity of earthwork.

S. No.	*Station or Chainage or R.D.*	*Depth or height*	*Main depth or height* d^2	*Area of central portion* Bd	*Area of sides* Sd^2	*Total Sectional area* $Bd + Sd^2$	*Distance between stations* l	*Quantity* $(Bd + Sd^2) \times l$	
								Filling	*Cutting*

2. Tabular form for area of sides.

S. No.	*Station or R.D.*	*Depth or height*	*Mean depth or height*	*Breadth of side slopes* $= d\sqrt{S^2+1}$	*Length between stations* l	*Total area of both side slopes* $2ld\sqrt{S^2+1}$

Part II

9.5. EARTHWORK IN LEVELLING AND DRESSING OR LARGE AREAS

In large areas, for general levelling and dressing for development works, the entire area is divided into a number of squares or rectangles. The length and width is decided according to the topography of the area. Spot levels, before and after the earthwork are recorded and the earthwork is calculated. The earthwork may be either cutting/filling or in cutting and partly in filling.

1. Earthwork Fully in Cutting

Example 9.7. *Calculate the quantity of earthwork, in an area, for general levelling and dressing from the following data shown in Fig. 9.12.*

Solution. Volume = Area $\left(\dfrac{d_1 + d_2 + d_3 + d_4}{4}\right)$ cum

Calculating d_1, d_2, d_3 and d_4 for each square we have :

$$V_A = 50 \times 50 \left(\frac{0+1+3+2}{4}\right) = 3750 \text{ cum}$$

$$V_B = 50 \times 50 \left(\frac{1+2+3+3}{4}\right) = 5625 \text{ cum}$$

$$V_C = 50 \times 50 \left(\frac{2+1+2+3}{4}\right) = 5000 \text{ cum}$$

$$V_D = 50 \times 50 \left(\frac{2+3+4+3}{4}\right) = 7500 \text{ cum}$$

$$V_E = 50 \times 50 \left(\frac{3+3+4+4}{4}\right) = 8750 \text{ cum}$$

$$V_F = 50 \times 50 \left(\frac{3+2+3+4}{4}\right) = 7500 \text{ cum}$$

$$V_G = 50 \times 50 \left(\frac{3+4+5+4}{4}\right) = 10000 \text{ cum}$$

$$V_H = 50 \times 50 \left(\frac{4+4+6+5}{4}\right) = 11875 \text{ cum}$$

$$V_J = 50 \times 50 \left(\frac{4+3+7+6}{4}\right) = 12500 \text{ cum.}$$

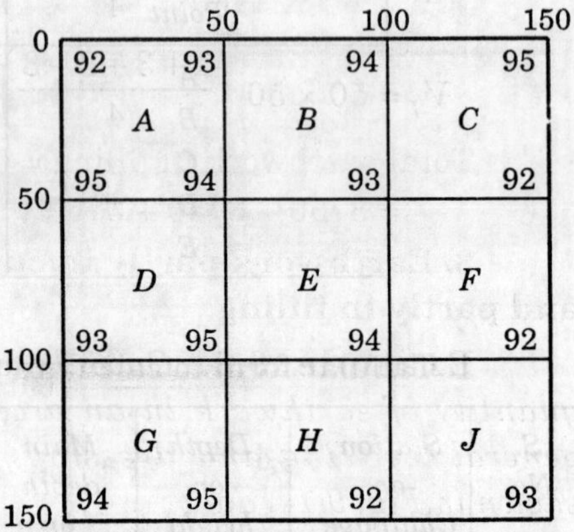

Fig. 9.12

Total earthwork in cutting = $(V_A + V_B + V_C + V_D + V_E + V_F + V_G + V_H + V_J)$

= 3750 + 5625 + 5000 + 7500 + 8750 + 7500 + 10000 + 11875 + 12500 = 72,500 cum

2. Earthwork in Fully Filling

Example 9.8. *Calculate the quantity of earthwork in an area, for general levelling and dressing, from data shown in Fig. 9.13.*

Solution. Volume = Area $\left(\dfrac{d_1 + d_2 + d_3 + d_4}{4}\right)$ cum

Calculating d_1, d_2, d_3 and d_4 for each square, we have

$$V_A = 50 \times 50 \left(\frac{3+2+1+0}{4}\right) = 3750 \text{ cum}$$

$$V_B = 50 \times 50 \left(\frac{2+1+2+1}{4}\right) = 3750 \text{ cum}$$

$$V_C = 50 \times 50 \left(\frac{1+0+3+2}{4}\right) = 3750 \text{ cum}$$

$$V_D = 50 \times 50 \left(\frac{0+1+0+2}{4}\right) = 1875 \text{ cum}$$

$$V_E = 50 \times 50 \left(\frac{1+2+1+0}{4}\right) = 2500 \text{ cum}$$

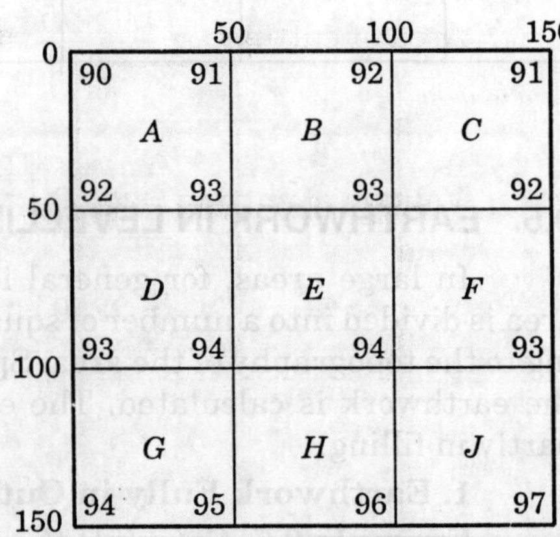

Fig. 9.13

$$V_F = 50 \times 50 \left(\frac{2+3+3+1}{4}\right) = 5625 \text{ cum}$$

$$V_G = 50 \times 50 \left(\frac{2+0+0+1}{4}\right) = 1875 \text{ cum}$$

$$V_H = 50 \times 50 \left(\frac{0+1+3+0}{4}\right) = 2500 \text{ cum}$$

$$V_J = 50 \times 50 \left(\frac{1+3+2+3}{4}\right) = 5625 \text{ cum.}$$

Total earthwork in filling = $(V_A + V_B + V_C + V_D + V_E + V_F + V_G + V_H - V_J)$

= 3750 + 3750 + 3750 + 1875 + 2500 + 5625 + 1875 + 2500 + 5625 = 31250 cum.

3. Earthwork partly in cutting and partly in filling

Example 9.9. *Calculate the quantity of earthwork in an area, for general levelling and dressing, from shown in Fig. 9.14, data :*

Solution. Volume = Area (Av. depth.) cum.

Calculating depth of cutting or height of filling for each square and the distances where the finished level of surface is 10000 within the square. Area of filling and cutting is marked by dotted lines within each square. We have :

Plan Showing Natural Surface Level

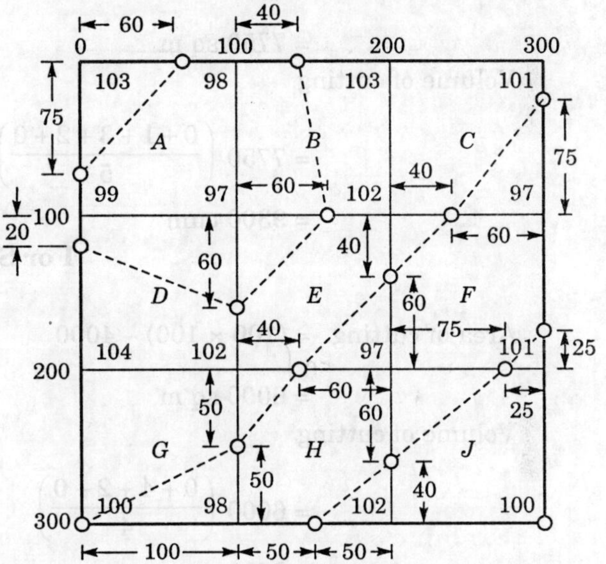

Fig. 9.14

For Square A

Area of cutting $= \dfrac{60 \times 75}{2} = 2250$ sq m

Volume of cutting $= 2250 \left(\dfrac{3+0+0}{3}\right)$

= 2250 cum

Area of filling = (100 × 100) – 2250

= 7750 sq m

Volume of filling

$= 7750 \left(\dfrac{0+2+3+1+1}{5}\right)$

= 9300 cum

For Square B

Area of cutting $= (100 \times 100) - 5000$

$= 5000$ sq m

Volume of cutting

$= 5000 \left(\dfrac{0+3+2+0}{4}\right)$

$= 6250$ cum

Area of filling $= 100\left(\dfrac{40+60}{5}\right)$

$= 5000$ sq m

Volume of filling

$= 5000 \left(\dfrac{0+2+3+0}{4}\right)$

$= 6250$ cum

For Square C

Area of cutting $= (100 \times 100) - 2250$

$= 7750$ sq m

Volume of cutting

$= 7750 \left(\dfrac{0+1+3+2+0}{5}\right)$

$= 9300$ cum

Area of filling $= \dfrac{60 \times 75}{2}$

$= 2250$ sq m

Volume of filling

$= 2250 \left(\dfrac{0+3+0}{3}\right)$

$= 2250$ cum

For Square D

Area of cutting $= (100 \times 100) - 4000$

$= 6000$ sq m

Volume of cutting

$= 6000 \left(\dfrac{0+4+2+0}{4}\right)$

$= 9000$ cum

Area of filling $= 100 \times \left(\dfrac{20+60}{2}\right)$

$= 4000$ sq m

Volume of filling

$= 4000 \left(\dfrac{0+1+3+0}{4}\right) = 4000$ cum

For Square E

Area of cutting

$= (100 \times 100) - 3600 = 6400$ sq m

Volume of cutting

$= 6400 \left(\dfrac{0+0+2+0+0+2}{6}\right)$

$= 4266.66$ cum

Area of filling $= \dfrac{60 \times 60}{2} + \dfrac{60 \times 60}{2}$

$= 1800 + 1800 = 3600$ sq m

Volume of filling

$= 1800 \left(\dfrac{0+3+0}{3}\right) + 1800 \left(\dfrac{0+3+0}{3}\right)$

$= 1800 + 1800 = 3600$ cum

For Square F

Area of cutting $= \dfrac{40 \times 40}{2} + \dfrac{25 \times 25}{2}$

$= 800 + 312.50 = 1112.50$ sq m

Area of filling

$= (100 \times 100) - 1112.5 = 8887.5$ sq m

Volume of cutting

$$= 800\left(\frac{0+2+0}{3}\right) + 312.5\left(\frac{0+1+0}{3}\right)$$

$$= 533.30 + 104.17 = 607.47 \text{ cum}$$

Volume of filling

$$= 8887.5\left(\frac{0+0+3+0+0+3}{6}\right)$$

$$= 8887.50 \text{ cum}$$

For Square G

Area of cutting

$$= (100 \times 100) - 2500 = 7500 \text{ sq m}$$

Volume of cutting

$$= 7500\left(\frac{0+4+2+0}{4}\right) = 11250 \text{ cum}$$

Area of filling

$$= \frac{100 \times 50}{2} = 2500 \text{ sq m}$$

Volume of filling

$$= 2500\left(\frac{0+2+0}{3}\right) = 1666.66 \text{ cum}$$

For Square H

Area of cutting

$$= \frac{40 \times 50}{2} + \frac{40 \times 50}{2}$$

$$= 1000 + 1000 = 2000 \text{ sq}$$

Volume of cutting

$$= 1000\left(\frac{0+2+0}{3}\right) + 1000\left(\frac{0+2+0}{3}\right)$$

$$= 666.66 + 666.66 = 1333.32 \text{ cum}$$

Area of filling

$$= (100 \times 100) - 2000 = 8000 \text{ sq m}$$

Volume of filling

$$= 8000\left(\frac{0+0+3+0+0+2}{6}\right)$$

$$= 6666.66 \text{ cum}$$

For Square I

Area of cutting

$$= (100 \times 100) - 2250 = 7750 \text{ sq m}$$

Volume of cutting

$$= 7750\left(\frac{0+2+0+1+0}{5}\right) = 4650 \text{ cum}$$

Area of filling

$$= \frac{60 \times 75}{2} = 2250 \text{ sq m}$$

Volume of filling

$$= 2250\left(\frac{0+3+0}{8}\right) = 2250 \text{ cum}$$

Plan Showing Natural Surface Level (N.S.L)

	A 0	20	40	60	80	100	120	140	160	180	200	
CS at 0	30.00	30.10	30.25	30.50	30.70	30.85	31.00	30.90	30.85	31.00	31.15	A_1
CS at B 20	30.15	30.20	30.35	30.50	30.70	31.00	31.10	31.20	31.10	30.20	30.40	B_1
CS at C 40	30.35	30.60	30.70	31.00	31.05	30.90	31.00	31.10	31.00	30.40	30.60	C_1
CS at D 60	30.45	30.75	30.90	31.15	31.20	31.00	31.20	30.90	31.00	30.60	30.80	D_1
CS at D 80	30.50	30.60	30.70	30.90	31.00	30.80	31.80	30.80	31.00	30.80	31.00	E_1
CS at F 100	30.75	31.00	31.90	31.00	31.10	30.90	31.00	31.70	30.90	31.00	31.00	F_1

Fig. 9.15

Total volume of earth work in cutting = 48,907.45 cum
Total volume of earth work in filling = 44,870.82 cum

EXERCISES

Exercise 9.7. Calculate the quantity of earth work in an area, for general levelling and dressing from the following data. (Ref. Fig. 9.15)

Exercise 9.8. Calculate the quantity of earth work in an area, for general levelling and dressing from the following data. (Ref. Fig. 9.16)

Plan Showing Natural Surface Level (N.S.L)

		0	20	40	60	80	100	120	140	160	180	200	
CS at *A*	0	28.50	28.70	28.60	28.90	29.55	29.50	29.00	29.10	28.75	28.60	28.50	A_1
CS at *B*	20	28.10	28.20	29.00	28.75	29.00	29.50	29.00	29.60	28.75	29.00	29.00	B_1
CS at *C*	40	28.20	29.00	28.75	29.00	29.60	29.10	29.60	30.00	29.60	29.40	29.00	C_1
CS at *D*	60	28.15	29.15	29.00	29.15	29.20	29.70	30.00	29.75	29.00	29.20	29.70	D_1
CS at *E*	80	28.95	29.00	29.70	29.30	29.60	29.00	29.50	29.60	29.30	29.10	29.60	E_1
CS at *F*	100	29.00	29.60	30.00	29.70	30.00	29.60	29.80	29.70	30.00	29.00	29.70	F_1

Fig. 9.16

Exercise 9.9. Calculate the quantity of earth work in an area, for general levelling and dressing from the following data. (Ref. Fig. 9.17)

Plan Showing Natural Surface Level (N.S.L)

		0	20	40	60	80	100	120	140	160	180	200	
CS at *A*	0	40.00	40.70	41.20	41.80	42.00	42.70	43.70	43.50	42.70	42.00	43.00	A_1
CS at B	20	41.20	41.00	42.00	42.80	41.60	43.00	43.60	44.00	43.00	44.00	43.10	B_1
CS at *C*	40	42.00	41.80	42.00	42.60	42.00	43.10	43.90	44.00	43.70	42.00	43.20	C_1
CS at *D*	60	42.60	42.00	41.70	42.80	42.80	43.20	44.00	43.70	43.10	42.60	43.00	D_1
CS at *E*	80	43.60	42.00	43.00	42.00	44.00	43.10	44.00	43.00	42.10	43.10	43.40	E_1
CS at *F*	100	44.00	43.70	44.00	43.00	43.60	44.00	43.60	43.10	42.00	43.00	44.00	F_1

Fig. 9.17

4. Earth Work in Canals

There are three types of canal sections. The shape is generally trapezoid. They are :

1. Fully in cutting
2. Fully in filling
3. Partly in cutting and partly in filling.

Economical depth or balancing depth. At any section, if the quantity of earth work in cutting is equal to the quantity of earth in filling, the depth of such a cross-section is known as "economical depth".

Calculation of earth work. The quantity of earth work = Area × Length

$= (Bd + Sd^2) \times \text{Length} \quad V = l\{Bd + Sd^2\}$

1. Earth Work for Canal in Fully Cutting

Example 9.10. *Calculate the quantity of earth work of an irrigation channel, with the following data :*

R.D.	*N.S.L.*	*Proposed Bed Level*
0	240.00	239.00
500	239.70	
1000	239.40	
1500	239.10	
2000	238.80	

Bed width 5 metres, side slope in cutting 1 to 1 and in filling V½ to 1, bank width 2.0 m both sides. Full supply depth = 1.00 m, free board 0.40 m, bed slope 1 in 5000.

Solution.

R.D.	*N.S.L*	*R.L. of Bed*	*Cutting*
0	240.00	239.00	1.00
500	239.70	238.90	0.80
1000	239.40	238.80	0.60
1500	239.10	238.70	0.40
2000	238.80	238.60	0.20

F.S.D.= 1000 m Area = $(Bd + Sd^2)$ Free Board = 0.40 m

Total = 1.40 m cross-section at R.D. 0 (Ref. Fig. 9.18)

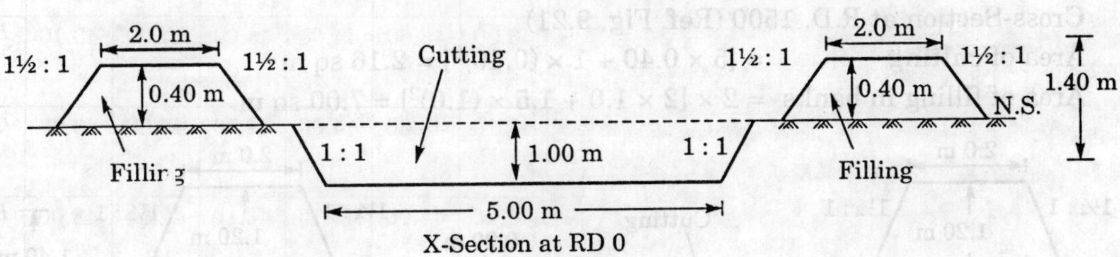

Fig. 9.18

Area of cutting $= [5 \times 1.00 + 1 \times (1.00)^2] = 6.00$ sq m

Area of filling in banks $= 2 \times [2 \times 0.40 + 1.5 \times (0.40)^2] = 2.08$ sq m

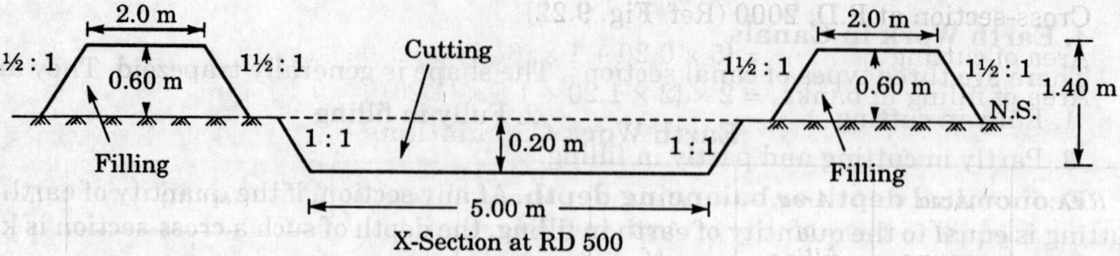

Fig. 9.19

Cross-section at R.D. 500. (Ref. Fig. 9.19)

Area of cutting $= [5 \times 0.80 + 1 \times (0.80)^2] = 4.64$ sq m

Area of filling in banks $= 2 \times [2 \times 0.60 + 1.5 \times (0.60)^2] = 3.32$ sq m.

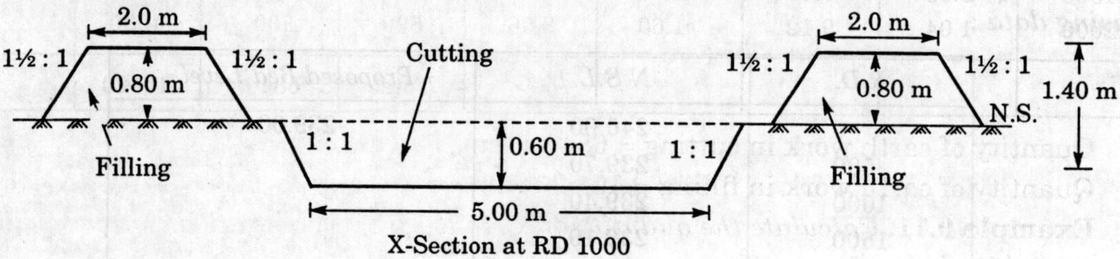

Fig. 9.20

Cross-Section at R.D. 1000 (Ref. Fig. 9.20)

Area of cutting $= [5 \times 0.60 + 1 \times (0.60)^2] = 3.36$ sq m

Area of filling in banks $= 2 \times [2 \times 0.80 + 1.5 \times (0.80)^2] = 5.12$ sq m

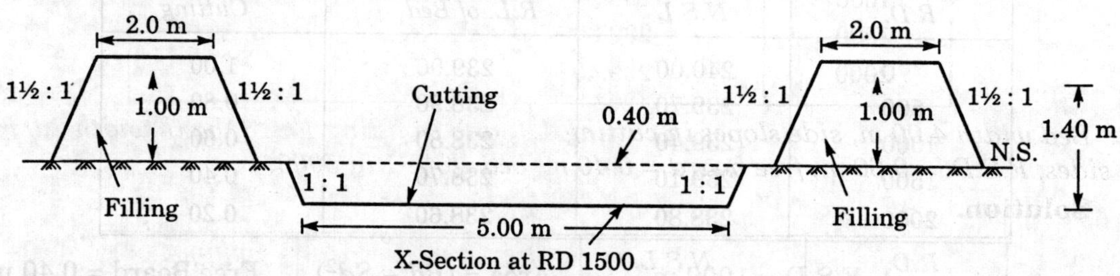

Fig. 9.21

Cross-Section at R.D. 1500 (Ref. Fig. 9.21)

Area of cutting $= [5 \times 0.40 + 1 \times (0.40)^2] = 2.16$ sq m

Area of filling in banks $= 2 \times [2 \times 1.0 + 1.5 \times (1.0)^2] = 7.00$ sq m.

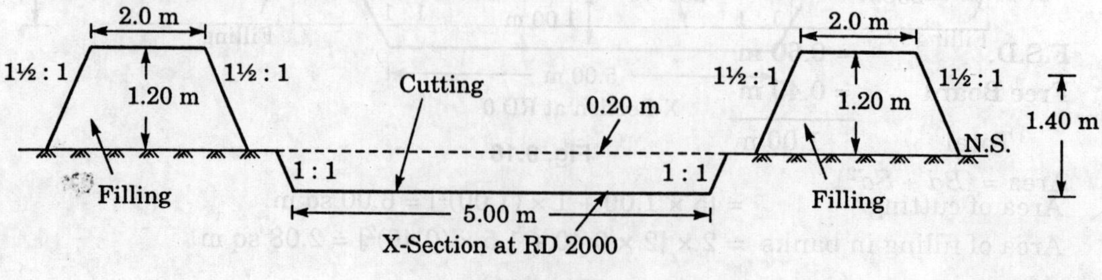

Fig. 9.22

Cross-section at R.D. 2000 (Ref. Fig. 9.22)

Area of cutting = $[5 \times 0.20 + 1 \times (0.20)^2] = 1.04$ sq m

Area of filling in banks = $2 \times [2 \times 1.20 + 1.5 \times (1.20)^2] = 9.12$ sq m.

Earth Work Calculations

R.D.	*Area of cutting*	*Area of filling*	*Mean Area of cutting*	*Mean Area of filling*	*Length*	*Quantity*		*Remark*
						Cutting	*Filling*	
0	6.00	2.08	—	—	—			
500	4.64	3.32	5.32	2.70	500	2660	1350	
1000	3.36	5.12	4.00	4.22	500	2000	2110	
1500	2.16	7.00	2.76	6.06	500	1380	3030	
2000	1.04	9.12	1.60	8.06	500	800	4030	
					Total	6840	10520	

Quantity of earth work in cutting = 6840 cum

Quantity of earth work in filling = 10,520 cum.

Example 9.11. *Calculate the quantity of earth work of an irrigation channel, with the following data :*

R.D.	*N.S.L.*	*Proposed Bed Level*
0	239.00	240.00
500	239.10	
1000	239.20	
1500	239.30	
2000	239.40	

Bed width 4.00 m, side slopes in cutting 1:1, and in filling 1½ : 1, bank width 2.0 metre both sides, F.S.D. = 0.60 m, free board = 0.40 m, bed slope 1 in 5000.

Solution.

R.D.	*N.S.L.*	*R.L. of Bed*	*Filling*
0	239.00	240.00	1.00
500	239.10	239.90	0.80
1000	239.20	239.80	0.60
1500	239.30	239.70	0.40
2000	239.40	239.60	0.20

F.S.D. = 0.60 m

Free Board = 0.40 m

Total 1.00 m

Area = $(Bd + Sd^2)$

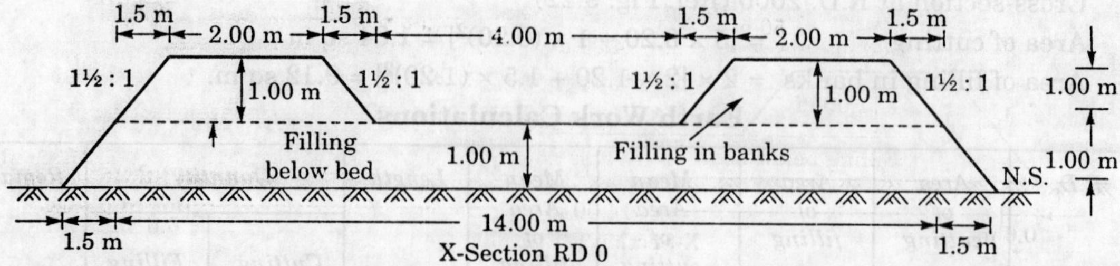

Fig. 9.23

Cross-section at R.D. 0 (Ref. Fig. 9.23)

Area of filling below bed $= [14 \times 1.0 + 1.5 \times (1.0)^2] = 15.50$ sq m

Area of filling in banks $= 2 \times [2 \times 1.0 + 1.5 \times (1.0)^2] = 7.00$ sq m

Total 22.50 sq m

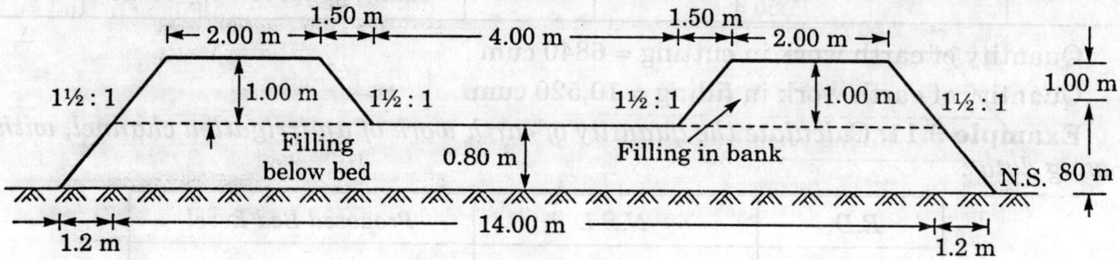

Fig. 9.24

Cross-section at R.D. 500 (Ref. Fig. 9.24)

Area of filling below bed $= [14 \times 0.80 + 1.5 \times (0.80)^2] = 12.16$ sq m

Area of filling in banks $= 2 \times [2 \times 1.0 + 1.5 \times (10)^2] = 7.00$ sq m

Total 19.16 sq m

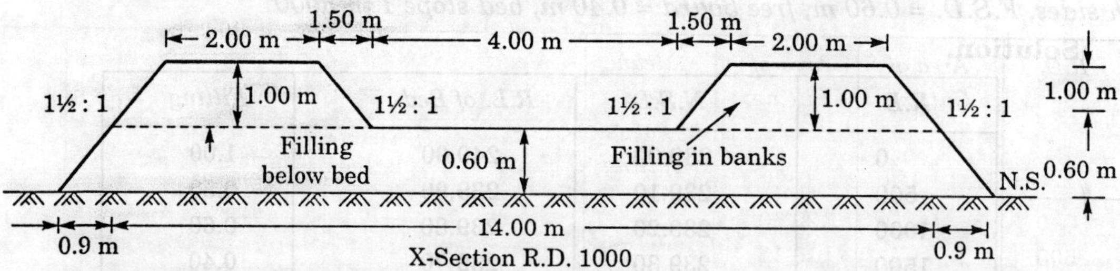

Fig. 9.25

Cross-section at R.D. 1000 (Ref. Fig. 9.25)

Area of filling below bed $= [14 \times 0.60 + 1.5 \times (0.60)^2] = 8.94$

Area of filling in banks $= 2 \times [2 \times 1.0 + 1.5 \times (1.0)^2] = 7.00$ sq m

Total 15.94 sq m

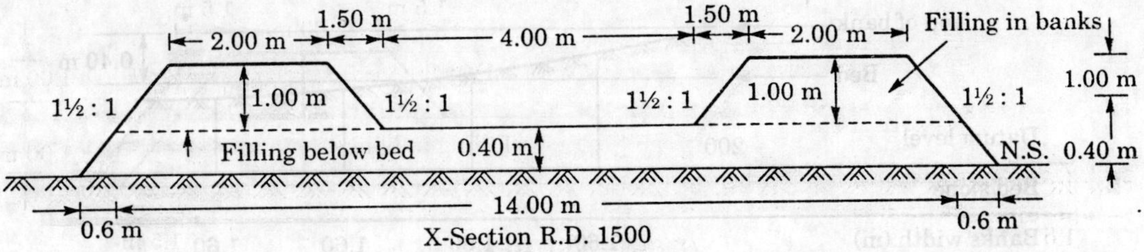

Fig. 9.26

Cross-section at R.D. 1500 (Ref. Fig. 9.26)

Area of filling below bed = [14 × 0.40 + 1.5 × $(0.40)^2$] – 5.84

Area of filling banks = 0.2 × [2 × 1.0 + 1.5 × $(1.0)^2$] = 7.00 sq m

Total 12.84 sq m

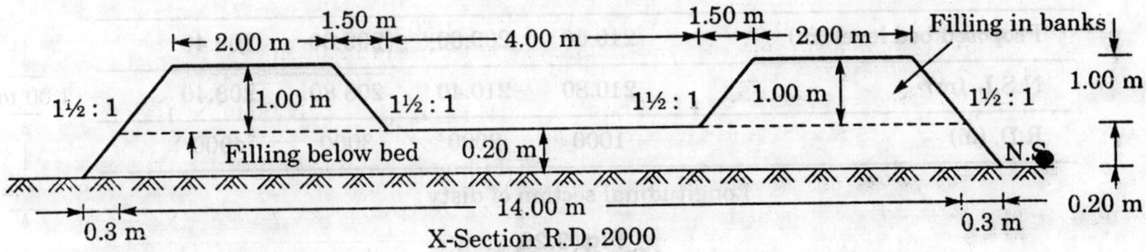

Fig. 9.27

Cross-section at R.D. 2000 (Ref. Fig. 9.27)

Area of filling below bed = [14 × 0.20 + 1.5 × $(0.20)^2$] = 2.86 sq m

Area of filling in banks = 2 × [2 × 1.0 + 1.5 × $1.0)^2$] = 7.00 sq m

Total 9.86 sq m

Earth-Work Calculations

R.D.	*Area of Cutting*	*Area of Filling*	*Mean Area of Cutting*	*Mean Area of Filling*	*Length*	*Quantity*		*Remark*
						Cutting	*Filling*	
0	—	22.50	—	—	—		—	
500	—	19.16	—	20.83	500		10,415	
1000	—	15.94	—	17.55	500	—	8,775	
1500	—	12.84	—	14.39	500		7195	
2000	—	9.86	—	11.35	500	—	5675	
					Total	—	32,060	

Quantity of earth work in filling = 32,060 cum.

Example 9.12. *Calculate the quantity of earth work for a portion of distributory partly in cutting and partly in filling from the longitudinal section given below. Side slope in cutting 1 : 1 and in filling 1½ : 1. (Ref. Fig. 9.28).*

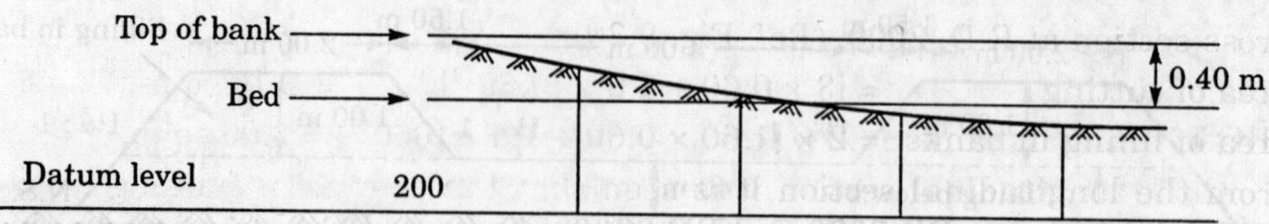

Bed slope				
Banks width (m)	1.60	1.60	1.60	1.60
Free board (m)	0.40	0.40	0.40	0.40
F.S.D. (m)	0.80	0.80	0.80	0.80
Bed width (m)	3.00	3.00	3.00	3.00
Depth of filling (m)	—	—	0.80	1.00
Depth of cutting (m)	0.80	0.60	—	—
Proposed bed level (m)	210.00	209.80	209.60	209.40
N.S.L. (m)	210.80	210.40	208.80	208.40
R.D. (m)	1000	2000	3000	4000

Longitudinal section of disty

Fig. 9.28

Solution. F.S.D. = 0.80 m

Free Board = 0.40 m

Total 1.20 m.

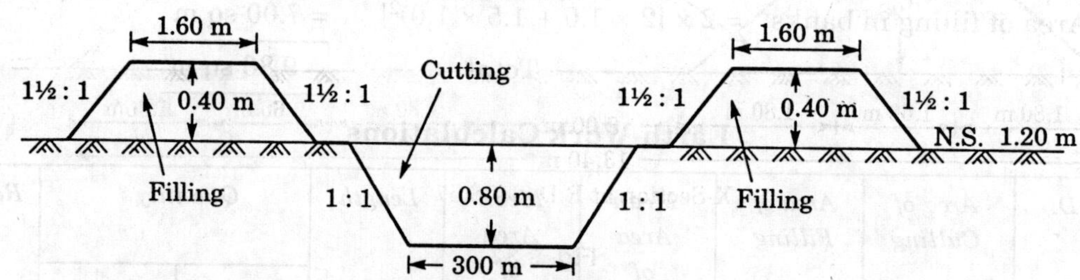

X-Section at R.D. 1000

Fig. 9.29

Cross-section at R.D. 1000 (Ref. Fig. 9-29)

Area of cutting = $[3 \times 0.80 + 1.0 \times (0.80)^2]$ = 3.04 sq m

Area of filling in banks = $2 \times [1.60 \times 0.40 + 1.5 \times (0.40)^2]$ sq m = 1.76 sq m

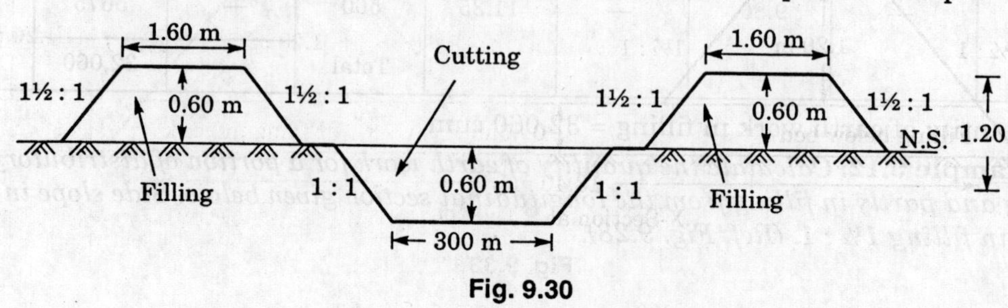

Fig. 9.30

Cross-section at R.D. 2000. (Ref. Fig. 9.30)

Area of cutting = $[3 \times 0.60 + 1.0 \times (0.60)^2]$ = 2.16 sq m

Area of filling in banks = $2 \times [1.60 \times 0.60 + 1.5 \times (060)^2]$ = 3.00 sq m.

From the longitudinal section it is seen that the channel is passing from cutting to filling, at a point between RD 2000 and RD 3000. The exact RD is calculated as below : (Ref. Fig. 9.31)

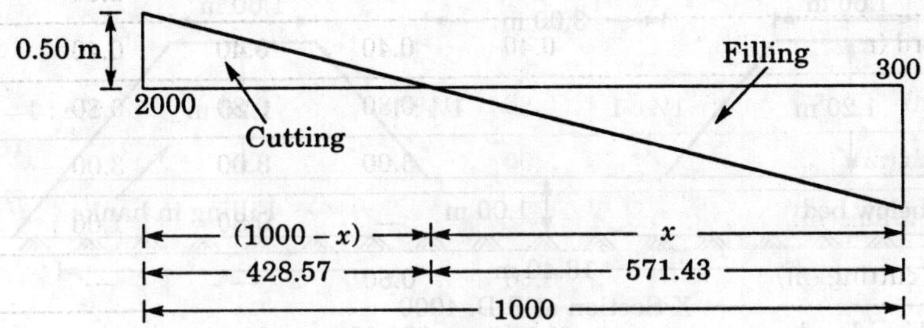

Fig. 9.31

$$\frac{1000 - x}{0.60} = \frac{x}{0.80} \quad \text{or} \quad x = 571.43 \text{ m}$$

or $(1000 - x) = 428.57$ m

Therefore exact RD = 2428.57 m.

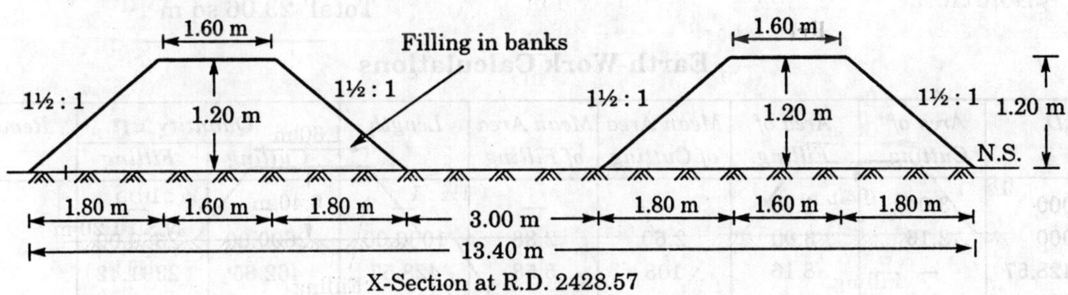

X-Section at R.D. 2428.57

Fig. 9.32

Cross-section at R.D. 2428.57 (Ref. Fig. 9.32)

Area of cutting = 0

Area of filling in banks = $2 \times [1.6 \times 1.20 + 1.5 \times (1.20)^2]$ = 8.16

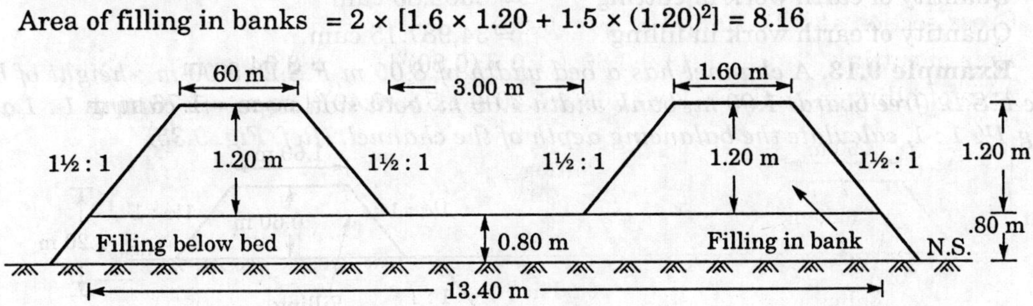

X-Section at R.D. 3000

Fig. 9.33

Cross-section at RD 3000 (Ref. Fig. 8.33)

Area of cutting = 0

Area of filling below bed = $[13.40 \times 0.80 - 1.5 \times (0.80)^2]$ = 12.68 sq m

Area of filling in banks = $2 \times [1.6 \times 1.2 + 1.5 \times (1.20)^2]$ = 8.16 sq m

Total 20.84 sq m

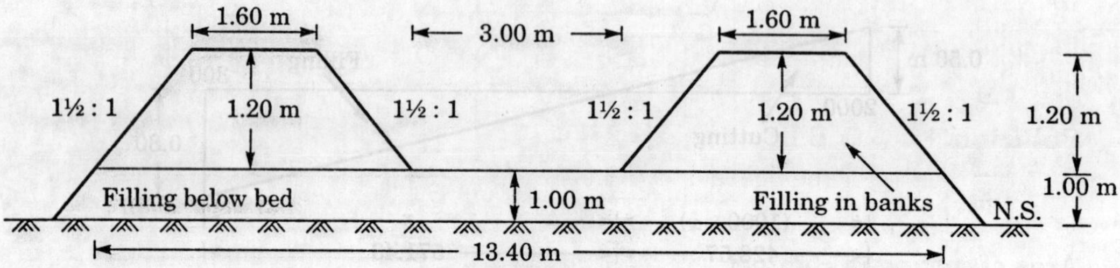

X-Section at R.D. 4000

Fig. 9.34

Cross-section at R.D. 4000 (Ref. Fig. 9.34)

Area of cutting = 0

Area of filling below bed = $[13.40 \times 1.0 + 1.5 \times (1.0)^2]$ = 14.90 sq m

Area of filling in banks = $2 \times [1.6 \times 1.2 + 1.5 \times (1.20)^2]$ = 8.16 sq m

Total 23.06 sq m

Earth-Work Calculations

R.D.	*Area of Cutting*	*Area of Filling*	*Mean Area of Cutting*	*Mean Area of Filling*	*Length*	*Quantity*		*Remark*
						Cutting	*Filling*	
1000	3.04	1.76	—	—	—	—	—	
2000	2.16	3.00	2.60	2.38	1000.00	2600.00	2380.00	
2428.57	—	8.16	108	5.58	428.57	462.85	2391.42	
3000	—	20.84	—	14.50	571.43	—	8285.73	
4000	—	23.06	—	21.95	1000.00	—	21950.00	
					Total	3062.85	34987.15	

Quantity of earth work in cutting = 3062.85 cum

Quantity of earth work in filling = 34,987.15 cum.

Example 9.13. *A channel has a bed width of 8.00 m F.S.D. 3.00 m ; height of banks above F.S.L. (free board) 1.00 m, bank width 4.00 m, both side slope—in cutting 1 : 1 and in filling 1½ 1 : 1, calculate the balancing depth of the channel. (Ref. Fig. 9.35)*

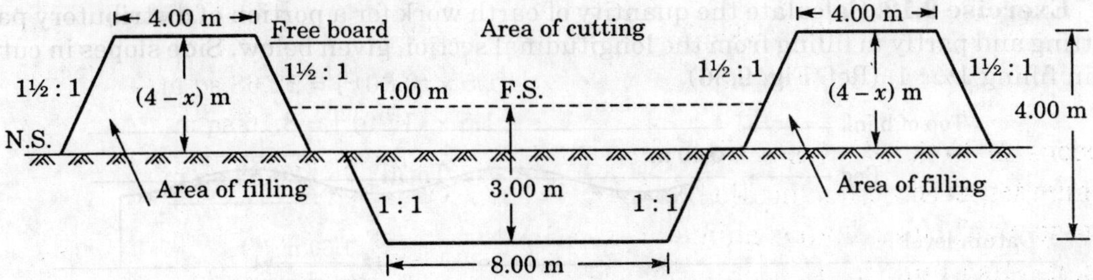

Fig. 9.35

Solution. F.S.D = 3.00

Free board = 1.00

Total 4.00

Area of cutting in channel

$= (8.00 \times x + 100 \times x^2)$

Area of filling in banks $= 2 \times [4.00 \times (4 - x) + 1.5 \times (4 - x)^2]$

Equating both we have

$$(8.00 \times x + 1.0 \times x^2) = 2[4.00(4 - x) + 1.5(4 - x^2)]$$

$$x^2 + 8x = 32 - 8x + 32 + 2x^2 - 16x$$

$$64 - 24x + 2x^2 - x^2 - 8x = 0 \quad \text{or} \quad x^2 - 32x + 64 = 0$$

$$x = 2.144 \text{ m.}$$

Hence balancing depth of channel = 2.144 m.

Exercise 9.10. Calculate the quantity of earth work of an irrigation channel, with the following data :

R.D.	*N.S.L.*	*Proposed bed level*
0	21000	209.80
500	210.60	
1000	211.00	
1500	211.50	
2000	212.20	

Bed width 4.00 m, side slope in cutting 1 : 1, and in filling 1½ : 1, bank width 200 m. Both sides, F.S.D. 1.20 m, free board 0.40 m, bed slope 1 in 5000.

Exercise 9.11. Calculate the quantity of earth work of an irrigation channel, with the following data :

R.D.	*N.S.L.*	*Proposed bed level*
0	241.60	242.00
500	241.60	
1000	241.40	
1500	241.30	
2000	241.00	

Bed width 4.00 m, side slope in cutting 1 : 1 and in filling 1½ : 1, bank width 2.00 m both sides, F.S.D. 0.80 m, free board 0.40 m, bed slope 1 in 5000.

Exercise 9.12. Calculate the quantity of earth work for a portion of distributory partly in cutting and partly in filling from the longitudinal section given below. Side slopes in cutting 1 : 1 in filling 1½ : 1. (Ref. Fig. 9.36)

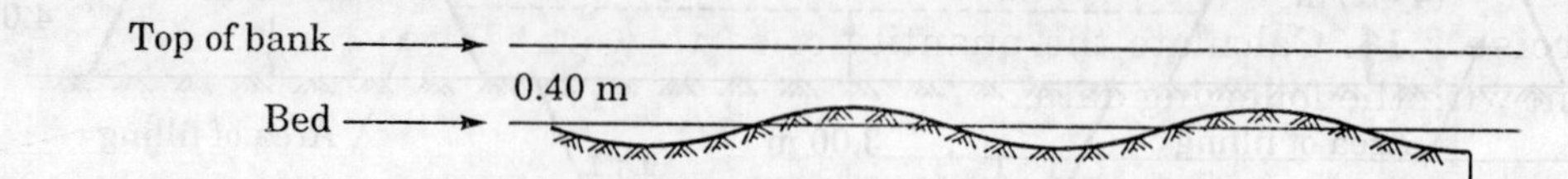

Datum level					
Free board (m)	0.40	0.40 m	0.40 m	0.40 m	0.40 m
Bed slope	←		1 in 5000		→
Banks width (m)	2.00 m	2.00 m	2.00 m	2.00 m	2.00 m
F.S.D. (m)	1.60 m	1.60 m	1.60 m	1.60 m	1.60 m
Bed width (m)	4.00 m	4.00 m	4.00 m	4.00 m	4.00 m
Depth of filling (m)	1.00	—	1.20	—	0.40 m
Depth of cutting (m)	—	020 m	—	0.40 m	—
Proposed bed level (m)	202.00 m	201.80 m	201.60 m	201.40 m	201.20 m
N.S.L. (m)	201.00 m	202.00 m	200.40 m	201.80 m	200.80 m
R.D. (m)	1000	2000	3000	4000	5000

Longitudinal - Section of distributery

Fig. 9.36

Exercise 9.13. Calculate the quantity of earth work of an irrigation channel, with the following data :

R.D.	*N.S.L.*	*Proposed bed level*
0	240.00	239.00
500	239.00	
1000	238.00	
1500	239.00	
2000	239.00	

Exercise 9.14. Calculate the quantity of earth work of an irrigation channel, with the following data :

R.D. (m)	*N.S.L. (m)*	*Proposed bed level*
1000	240.00	239.00 m
2000	240.00	
3000	238.00	
4000	237.00	
5000	239.00	

Bed width 5.00 m, side slope in cutting 1 : 1, and in filling 1½ : 1 bank with 2.00 m both sides ; F.S.D. 1.60 m, free board 0.40 m, bed slope 1 in 5000.

Exercise 9.15. A channel has a bed width of 10.00 ; F.S.D. = 3.00 m ; free board = 1.00 m, bank width 4.00 m, both sides, side slope in cutting 1 : 1 and in filling 1½%. ; Calculate the balancing depth of the channel.

Exercise 9.16. Calculate the quantity of earth work for the construction of a flood embankment with the following data :

R.D. (m)	*N.S.L. (m)*	*Bank level (m)*	*Height (m)*	*Top width of bank (m)*	*Side slope*	*Remark*
1000	200.00	205.00	5.00	10.00	3 : 1	
2000	199.00	205.00	5.00	10.00	3 : 1	
3000	198.00	205.00	7.00	10.00	3 : 1	
4000	197.00	205.00	8.00	10.00	3 : 1	

Earth Work in Ramp and Railway Embankments—Examples

Example 9.14. *Calculate the quantity of earth work in a ramp for a road-railway crossing, with the following data :*

Width of road embankment = 10.00 m

Height of railway embankment = 2.00 m

Side slope in filling 1 in 3

Gradient of ramp 1 in 30

Assume that the ground is level across the road.

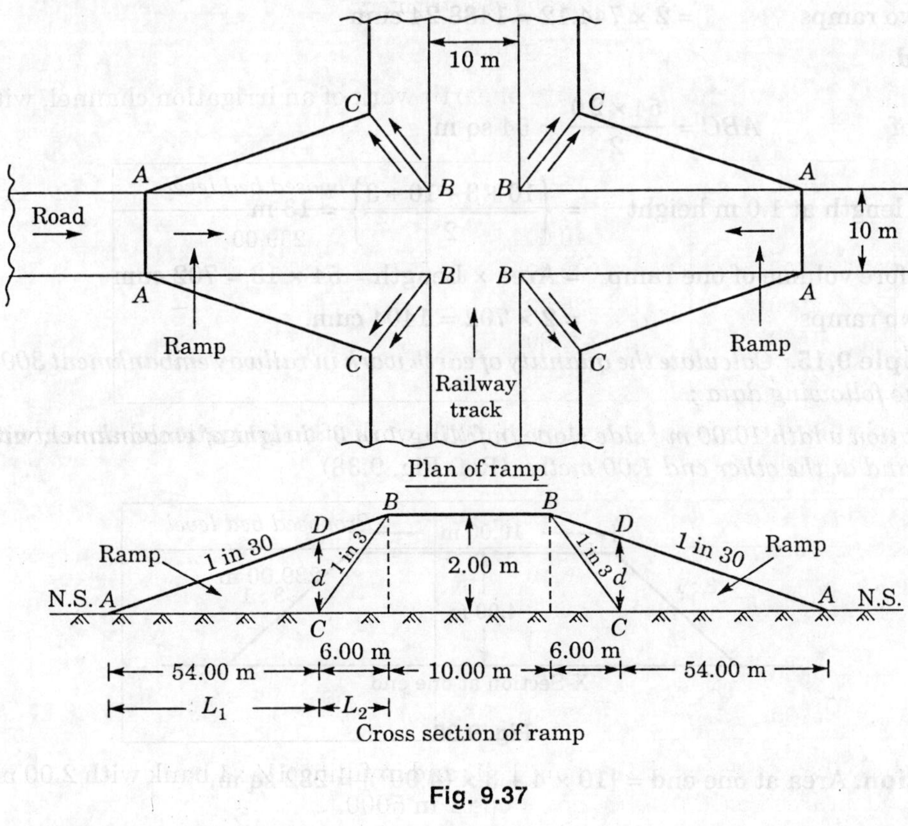

Fig. 9.37

Solution. (Ref. Fig. 9.37)

Height of filling of the junction of railway and road embankment for ramp

$$= \frac{2}{60} = \frac{d}{54} \quad \text{or} \quad d = \frac{2 \times 54}{60} = 1.80 \text{ m}$$

Using Prismoidal Formula

Area of cross-section of ramp at AA = 0.

Area of cross-section of ramp at BB = 0.

Area of ramp at middle point *i.e.* at 27 m.

where height of filling $= \frac{1.80}{2} = 0.90 = A_m$

or $A_m = (Bd + Sd^2) = [10 \times 0.9 + 3 \times (0.9)^2] = 11.43$ sq m

Area of ramp at the junction marked

$C = [10 \times 1.8 + 3 \times (1.8)^2] = 27.72$ sq m

Calculation of Volume

For one ramp $= \frac{L_1}{6}(A_{AA} + 4\,A_m + A_{CC}) + L_2\left(\frac{A_{CC} - A_{BB}}{2}\right)$

$= \frac{54}{6}(0 + 4 \times 11.43 + 27.72) + 6\left(\frac{27.72 + 0}{2}\right)$

$= 660.96 + 83.16 = 744.12$ cum

For two ramps $= 2 \times 744.12 = 1488.24$ cum

2nd Method

Area of $ABC = \frac{54 \times 2.0}{2} = 54$ sq m

Mean length at 1.0 m height $= \left\{\frac{10 + 3 + 10 + 3}{2}\right\} = 13$ m

Therefore volume of one ramp = Area × Length = 54 × 13 = 702 cum

For two ramps = 2 × 702 = 1404 cum.

Example 9.15. *Calculate the quantity of earth work in railway embankment 3000 metres long, with the following data :*

Formation width 10.00 m ; side slope in filling 1 in 3 : height of embankment at one end 4.00 metres and at the other end 1.00 metre. (Ref. Fig. 9.38)

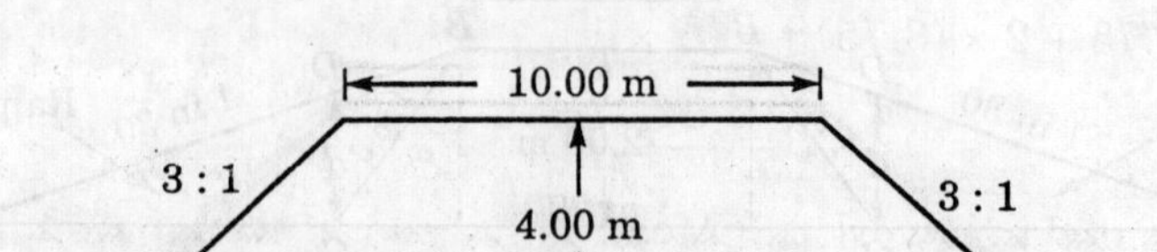

Fig. 9.38

Solution. Area at one end = [10 × 4 + 3 × (4.00³)] = 232 sq m.

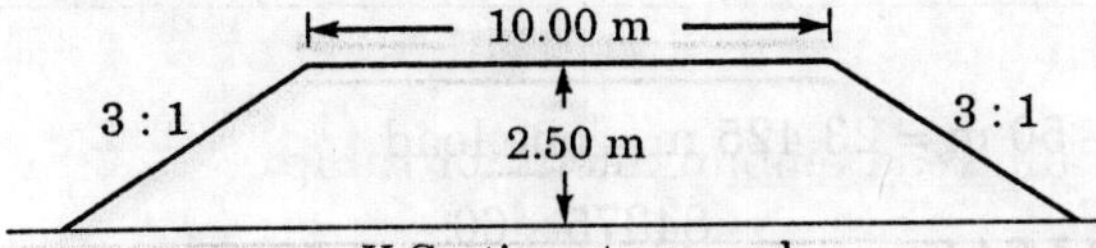

X-Section at one end

Fig. 9.39

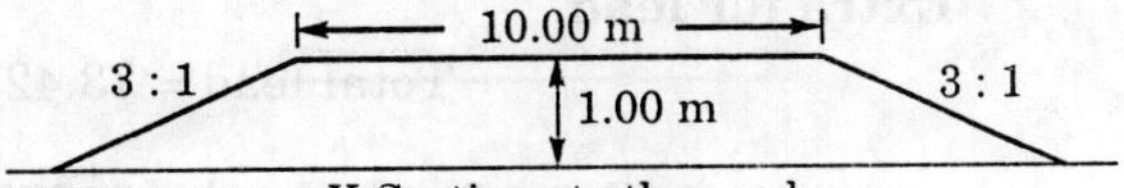

X-Section at other end

Fig. 9.40

Area at middle $= [10 \times 2.5 + 3 \times (2.5)^2] = 71.875$ sq m. (Ref. Fig. 9.39)

Area at other end $= [10 \times 1 + 3 \times (1.0)^2] = 13$ sq m. (Ref. Fig. 9.40).

Volume of earth $= \dfrac{3000}{6}\{232 + 4 \times 71.875 + 13\}$

Earth work $= 266250$ cum.

Example 9.16. *Calculate the quantity of earth work for a portion of railway embankment fully in filling with the following data :*

Length	*Central height at mid length*	*Formation width*
1000 m	3.75 m	15.00 m

Side slope 1 in 2. Also work out the cost of earth work at the rate of ₹ 300 per % cum for a lead upto 50 m with 1.5 m lift. Extra cost for every additional 1.5 m lift or part thereof at the rate of ₹ 40 per % cum and for every additional lead of 50 m or part thereof at the rate of ₹ 60 per % cum ; leaving a dlear distance of 30 m from the toe ; depth of borrow pit = 1.5 m side slope in cutting 1 in 1. (Ref. Fig. 9.41)

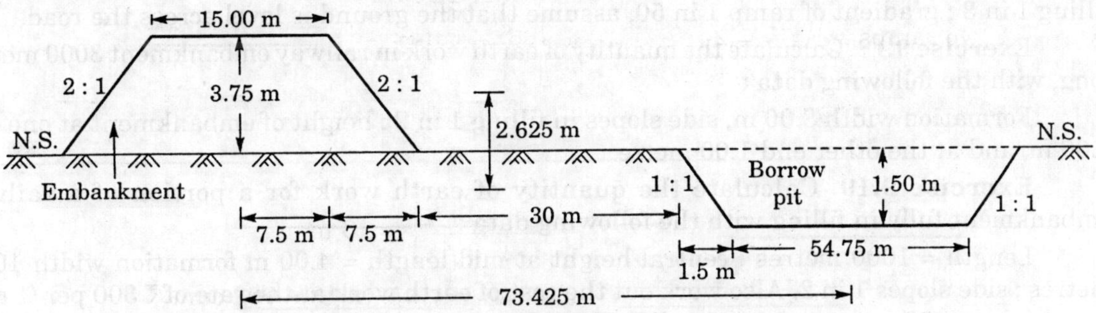

X-Section at mid length of railway embankment

Fig. 9.41

Solution.

Calculations for the width of bottom pit (B)

Area of embankment at mild length = Area of borrow pit at mid length

$$[15 \times 3.75 + 2 \times (3.75)^2] = [B \times 1.5 + 1 \times (1.5)^2] \quad \text{or} \quad 84.375 = 1.5\,B + 2.25$$

$$B = \frac{84.375 - 2.25}{1.5} = 54.75 \text{ m}$$

Total quantity of earth work = Mean area × Length = 84.375 × 100 = **84,375 cum**

Costing

Cost of earth work (lift 1.5 m and lead upto 50 m)

= 84,375 cum @ ₹ 300 % cum

$$= \frac{84{,}375 \times 300}{100} = ₹\ 2{,}53{,}125$$

Extra for lead

Total lead = 73.425 – 50 m = 23.425 m = one lead.

Cost of extra lead = 84375 @ ₹ 64 % cum = $\frac{84375 \times 60}{100}$ = ₹ 50625

Extra for lift

Total average lift = $\frac{3.75 + 1.50}{2}$ = ₹ 2.625 m

Extra lift = (2.625 – 150) = 1.25 m = (one lift)

Cost of extra lift = 84,375 cum @ ₹ 40% cum

= ₹ 33,750

Total cost of the earth work = ₹ 2,53,125

+ ₹ 50,625

+ ₹ 33,750

₹ 3,37,500

Allowing for increase in cost for 1977–97 = 3,37,500

Exercise 9.17. Calculate the quantity of earth work in a ramp for a road railway crossing, with the following data :

Width of embankment 8.00 m, height of railway embankment 3.00 m, side slopes in filling 1 in 3 ; gradient of ramp 1 in 50, assume that the ground is level across the road.

Exercise 9.18. Calculate the quantity of earth work in railway embankment 3000 metres long, with the following data :

Formation width 8.00 m, side slopes in filling 1 in 2 ; height of embankment at one end 3.00 m, and at the other end 1.00 metre.

Exercise 9.19. Calculate the quantity of earth work for a portion of a railway embankment fully in filling with the following data :

Length = 1000 metres ; central height at mid length = 4.00 m formation width 10.00 metres ; side slopes 1 in 2. Also work out the cost of earth work at the rate of ₹ 300 per % cum for a lead upto 50 metres with 1.5 m lift. Extra for every additional lead of 50 m or part thereof at the rate of ₹ 60 per % cum and every additional 1.5 m lift or part thereof at the rate of ₹ 40 per % cum : depth of borrow pit 2.00 m ; leaving a clear distance of 25 m. From the toe of the embankment side slope in cutting 1 : 1.

Earth Work in Roads

Example 9.17. *Calculate the quantity of earth work for the road embankment with the following data :*

Length of road = 300 metre, height of embankment at one end 1.00 m and at other end 1.50 metre ; formation width 10.00 metre, side slope in filling 1½ : 1, no transverse slope.

Solution. Area = $(B + d + Sd^2)$

Method I

Quantity of earth work = Length × Mean sectional area (A_m)

Mean height = $\frac{1.00 + 1.60}{2} = \frac{2.60}{2}$ = 1.30 m

$\therefore$ Quantity = 300 × [10 × 1.3 + 1.5 × (1.3)²] = 300 × 15.535

= **4660.5 cum**

Method II

$$\text{Quantity of earth work} = \text{Length} \times \text{Average area} \left(\frac{A_1 + A_2}{2}\right)$$

Area at one end (A_1) = (10 × 1 + 21.5 × 1²) = 11.5 sq m

Area at other end (A_2) = [10 × 1.6 + 1.5 × (1.6)²] = 19.84 sq m

$$\text{Average area} = \frac{11.50 + 19.84}{2} = 15.67 \text{ sq m}$$

Quantity = 300 × 15.67 = **4701 cum**

Method III

By prismoidal formula.

$$\text{Quantity of earth work} = \frac{l}{6}\{A_1 + 4A_m + A_2\} = \frac{300}{6}\{11.50 + 4 \times 15.535 + 19.84\}$$

$$= \frac{300}{6} \times 93.48 = \mathbf{46.4\ cum}$$

Note. Earth work calculated by prismoidal formula is more correct than those calculated by other formula method.

Example 9.18. *Calculate the quantity of earth work for the road with the following ddta :*

R.D.	*N.S.L.*	*Formation Level*
0	202.00	203.00
20	203.20	
40	203.50	
60	204.00	
80	205.40	
100	206.60	

The road formation has a upward gradient of 1 in 20. Formation width 10 metre, side slope in filling 1 in 2.

Solution.

R.D.	*N.S.L.*	*Formation Level*	*Height of filling*
0	202.00	203.00	1.00
20	203.20	204.00	0.80
40	203.50	205.00	1.50
60	204.00	206.00	2.00
80	205.40	207.00	1.60
100	206.60	208.00	1.40

Note. Draw cross-section at every R.D.

Area = [$Bd - Sd^2$)

Area at R.D. 0 = [10 × 1 + 2 × (1.00)²] = 12 sq m

Area at R.D. 20 = [10 × 0.80 + 2 × (0.80)²] = 9.28 sq m

Area at R.D. 40 = $[10 \times 1.50 + 2 \times (1.5)^2] = 19.50$ sq m

Area at R.D. 60 = $[10 \times 2 + 2 \times (2.00)^2] = 28$ sq m

Area at R.D. 80 = $[10 \times 1.60 + 2 \times (1.60)^2] = 21.12$ sq m

Area at R.D. 100 = $[10 \times 1.40 \times 2 \times (1.40)^2] = 17.92$ sq m

Earth Work Calculations

R.D.	*Area of filling*	*Mean Area of filling*	*Length*	*Quantity of Filling*	*Remark*
0	12.00	—	—	—	
20	9.28	10.64	20	212.8	
40	19.50	14.39	20	287.8	
60	28.00	23.75	20	475.0	
80	21.12	24.56	20	491.2	
100	17.92	19.52	20	390.4	
			Total	1857.2 cum	

Earth work in filling = 1,857.2 cum.

Example 9.19. *Calculate the quantity of earth work for the road with the following data :*

R.D.	*N.S.L.*	*Formation Level*
0	201.80	200.00
100	201.00	
200	200.20	
300	199.60	
400	199.00	

The road formation has a downward gradient of 1 in 100. Formation width = 12-00 m; side slope in cutting 1 in 1.

Solution.

R.D.	*N.S.L.*	*Formation Level*	*Depth of cutting*
0	201.80	200.00	1.80
100	201.00	199.50	1.50
200	200.20	199.00	1.20
300	199.60	198.50	1.10
400	199.00	198.00	1.00

Area = $(Bd + Sd^2)$

Note. Draw cross-sections at every R.D.

Area at R.D. 0 = $[12 \times 1.80 + 1 \times (1.80)^2] = 24.84$ sq m

Area at R.D. 100 = $[12 \times 1.50 + 1 \times (1.50)^2] = 20.25$ sq m

Area at R.D. 200 = $[12 \times 1.20 + 1 \times (1.20)^2] = 15.84$ sq m

Area at R.D. 300 = $[12 \times 1.10 + 1 \times (1.10)^2] = 14.41$ sq m

Area at R.D. 400 = $[12 \times 1 + 1 \times (1.0)^2] = 13$ sq m

Earth-Work Calculations

R.D.	Area of cutting	Mean Area of cutting	Length	Quantity of Cutting	Remark
0	24.84	—	—	—	
100	20.25	22.545	100	2254.5	
200	15.84	18.045	100	1804.5	
300	14.41	15.125	100	1512.2	
400	13.00	13.705	100	1370.5	
			Total	6942.0 cum	

Earth work in cutting = 6942.0 cum

Example 9.20. *Calculate the quantity of earth work for the road with the following data : Formation width = 10.00 m, side slope in cutting 1 : 1 and in filling 2:1.*

Solution.

R.D.	N.S.L.	Formation Level	Height of filling	Depth of cutting	Remark
0	208.00	206.00	—	2.00	R.D. where height of filling and depth of cutting is zero = 157.90 (see calculations)
100	207.70	205.00	—	2.20	
200	203.40	205.00	1.60	—	
300	203.10	204.50	1.40	—	

Calculations for the R.D. between 100 and 200 ; where height of filling and depth of cutting is zero.

Let the distance = x m from R.D. 100 (Draw figure)

$$\therefore \quad \frac{2.20}{x} = \frac{1.60}{(100 - x)}$$

or $$1.60x = 2.20 \times 100 - 2.20x \quad \text{or} \quad 3.80x = 220$$

$$x = \frac{200}{3.80} = 57.90 \text{ m}$$

$\therefore$ R.D. = 157.90 m

Earth Work Calculations in Tabular Form
Given B = 10.00 m ; S in cutting = 1; S in Filling = 2

R.D.	Height or depth	Mean height or depth	Area of central portion	Area of side slopes	Total Area	Distance between stations	Quantity $l \times (Bd + Sd^2)$		Remark
							Cutting	Filling	
			$B \times d$	Sd^2	$(Bd + Sd^2)$	l	(–)	(+)	
Cutting									
0	–2.00	–	–	–	–	–	–	–	
100	–2.20	–2.10	–21.10	–4.41	–25.41	100	2541	–	
157.90	0.00	–1.10	–11.0	–1.21	–12.21	57.90	707	–	
Filling									
200	1.60	0.80	8.0	1.28	9.28	42.10	–	390.7	
300	1.40	1.50	15.0	4.50	19.50	100	–	1950.0	
						Total	3248	2340.7 cum	

Earth work in cutting = 3248 cum

Earth work in filling = 2340.7 cum.

Example 9.21. *Calculate the quantity of earth work for the road, party in cutting and partly in filling, from the longitudinal section given below. Side slopes in cutting and filling are 1. in 1. The formation width is 10.00 metre. (Ref. Fig. 9.42)*

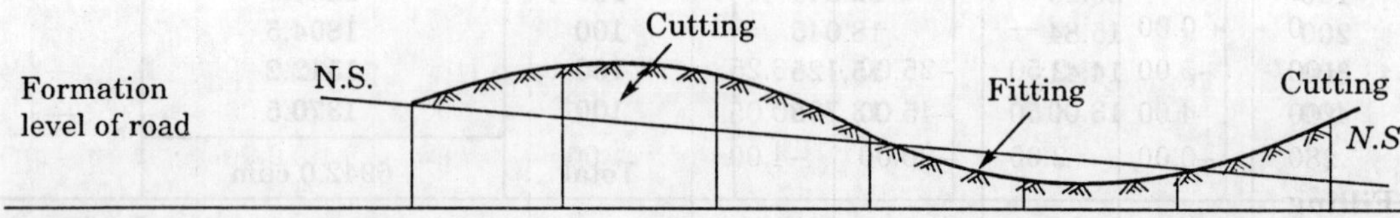

Datum level	210.00						
Width of formation (m)	——— 10.00 m ——— 10.00 m ——— 10.00 m ———						
Side slopes	——— 1 in 1 ——— 1 in 1 ——— 1 in 1 ———						
Formation slope	——— 1 in 100 fall ———						
Depth of cutting (m)	0.00	5.00	4.00	—	—	—	1.00
Height of filling (m)	—	—	—	1.00	2.50	3.00	—
Formation level (m)	220.00	219.00	218.00	217.00	216.00	215.00	214.00
N.S.L. (m)	220.00	224.00	222.00	216.00	213.50	212.00	215.00
R.D. (m)	0	100	200	300	400	500	600

Fig. 9.42

Solution. (*i*) Calculations for the R.D. between 200 and 300; where the depth of cutting and height of filling is zero. Let the distance = x from R.D. 200 (draw figure).

or
$$\frac{4}{x} = \frac{1}{(100 - x)}$$

$$x = 80 \text{ m}$$

$\therefore$ D.R.= 280.

(*ii*) Calculations for the R.D. between 500 and 600; where the height of filling and depth of cutting is zero. Let the distance = x from R.D. 500. (draw figure)

or
$$\frac{4}{x} = \frac{1}{(100 - x)}$$

$$x = 75 \text{ m}$$

$\therefore$ R.D. = 575.00

Earth work calculations in tabular form,

Given $B = 10.00$ m, S in cutting = 1

S in filling = 1.00

R.D.	Height or depth	Mean height or depth	Area of central position	Area of side slopes	Total area	Distance between stations	Quantity $l \times (Bd - Sd^2)$ Cutting	Filling	Remark
			$B \times d$	Sd^2	$Bd + Sd^2$	l	(–)	(+)	
Cutting									
0	+ 0.00	—	—	—	—	—	—	—	
100	–5.00	–2.50	–25.00	–6.25	–31.25	100	3125.00	—	
200	–4.00	–4.50	–45.00	–20.05	–65.25	100	6525.00	—	
280	–0.00	–2.00	–20.00	–4.00	–24.00	80	1920.00	—	
Filling									
300	1.00	0.50	5.00	0.25	5.25	20	—	105.00	
400	2.50	1.75	17.50	3.0625	20.5625	100	—	2056.25	
500	3.00	2.75	27.50	7.5625	35.0625	100	—	3506.25	
575	0.00	1.50	15.00	2.25	17.25	75	—	1293.75	
Cutting									
600	–1.00	–0.50	–5.00	–0.25	–5.25	25	131.25	—	
						Total	11701.25	6961.25	

Earth work in cutting = 11,701.25 cum
Earth work in filling = 6961.25 cum.

EXERCISES

Exercise 9.20. Calculate the quantity of earth work for the read with the following data :

R.D.	M.S.L.	Formation level
0	206.00	201.00
100	205.00	
200	204.00	
300	203.00	
400	201.00	
500	200.00	
600	204.00	

The road formation has a upward gradient of 1 in 100; formation width 12.00 m, side slope in cutting and in filling 1 : 1.

Exercise 9.21. Calculate the quantity of earth work for the road with the following data :

R.D.	M.S.L.	Formation level
0	198.00	200.00
20	199.00	199.00
40	200.00	198.00
60	201.00	199.00
80	202.00	200.00
100	203.00	201.00

Formation width = 8.00 m, side slope in cutting 1 : 1 ; side slope in filling 1 : 1.

Exercise 9.22. Calculate the quantity of earth work for the road with the following data :

R.D. (m)	*Depth of cutting (m)*	*Height of filling (m)*	*Remark*
0	1.00	—	
100		1.00	Draw figures to calculate
200	3.00	—	the R.D. of zero cutting
300		2.00	and filling.
400	0.50	—	

Formation width = 10.00 m, side slope in cutting 1 : 1 and side slope in filling 1½ : 1.

Earth Work in Hill Roads

Example 9.22. *Calculate the quantity of earth work for a Hill-road with the following data :*

Formation width 8.00 m; side slop e in cutting transverse slope of ground 1 in 8.

R.D. (m)	*N.S.L. (m)*	*Formation Level (m)*	*Cutting*	*Remark*
0	305.00	300.00	5.00	
100	306.00	302.00	4.00	
200	307.00	304.00	3.00	
300	308.00	306.00	2.00	
400	309.00	308.00	1.00	

Solution. Cross-section at R.D. 0. (Ref. Fig. 9.43)

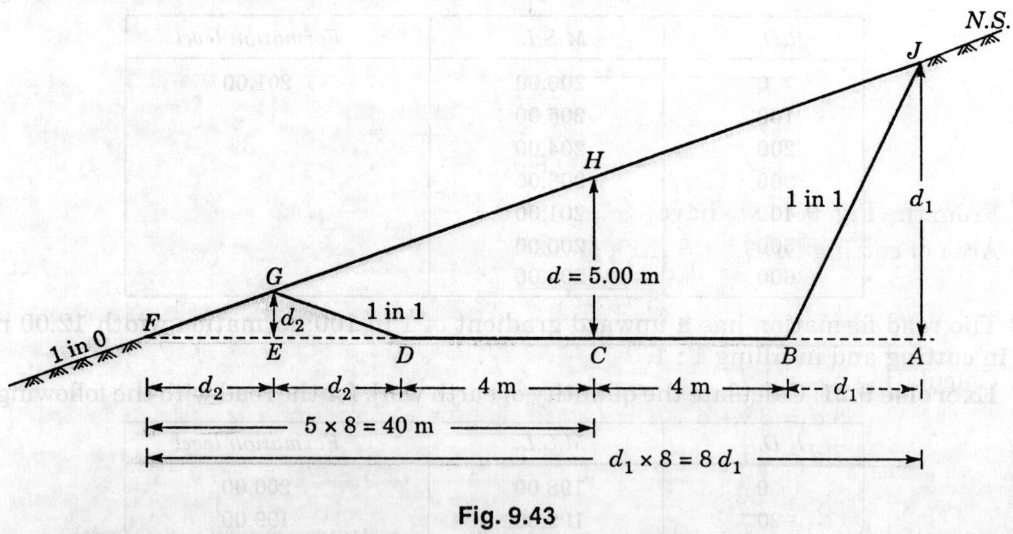

Fig. 9.43

From the Fig. 9.43 we have,

Area of cutting *GDBJ* = Area of Δ*AFJ*–Area of Δ*ABJ*–Area of Δ*DFG*

$$= \frac{8\,d_1 \times d_1}{2} - \frac{d_1 \times d_1}{2} - \frac{9\,d_2 \times d_2}{2}$$

Calculation d_1 and d_2

$8\,d_1 = 40 + 4 + d_1$	$8\,d_2 + d_2 + 4 = 40$
$7\,d_1 = 44$	$9\,d_2 = 36$
$d_1 = \dfrac{44}{7}$	$d_2 = 4$

$$\text{Now area of cutting } GDBJ = \frac{8\,d_1 \times d_1}{2} - \frac{d_1 \times d_1}{2} - \frac{9\,d_2 \times d_2}{2}$$

$$= 8 \times \frac{44}{7} \times \frac{44}{7} \times \frac{1}{2} - \frac{44}{7} \times \frac{44}{7} \times \frac{1}{2} - \frac{9 \times 4 \times 4}{2}$$

$$= 158.04 - 19.76 - 72 = 66.28 \text{ sq m}$$

Cross-section at R.D. 100 (Ref. Fig. 9.44)

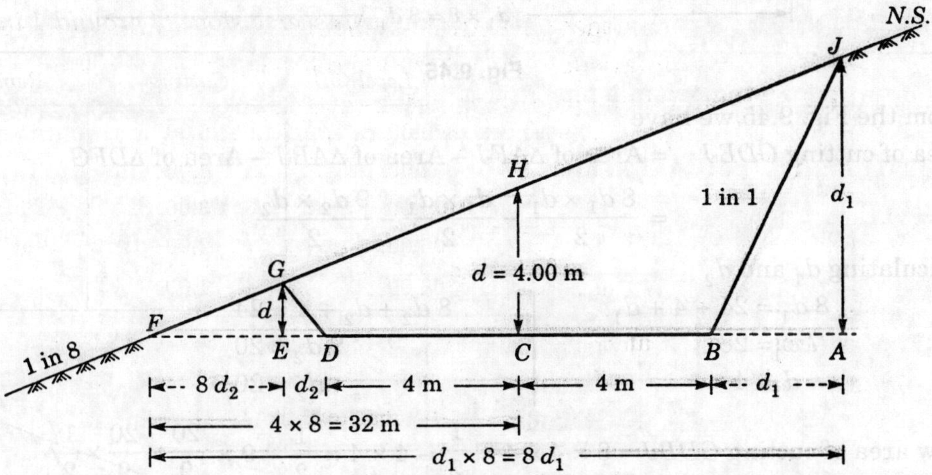

Cross-section at R.D. 100

Fig. 9.44

From the Fig. 9.44 we have

Area of cutting $GDBJ$ = Area of ΔAFJ – Area of ΔABJ – Area of ΔDFG

$$= \frac{8\,d_1 \times d_1}{2} - \frac{d_1 \times d_1}{2} - \frac{9\,d_2 \times d_2}{2}$$

Calculating d_1 and d_2

$8\,d_1 = 32 + 4 + d_1$	$8\,d_2 + d_2 + 4 = 32$
$7\,d_1 = 36$	$9\,d_2 = 28$
$d_1 = \dfrac{36}{7}$	$d_2 = \dfrac{28}{9}$

$$\text{Now area of cutting } GDBJ = 8 \times \frac{36}{7} \times \frac{36}{7} \times \frac{1}{2} - \frac{36}{7} \times \frac{36}{7} \times \frac{1}{2} - 9 \times \frac{28}{7} \times \frac{28}{9} \times \frac{1}{2}$$

$$= 105.79 - 13.22 - 43.55 = 49.02 \text{ sq m}$$

Cross-section at R.D. 200 (Ref. Fig. 9.45)

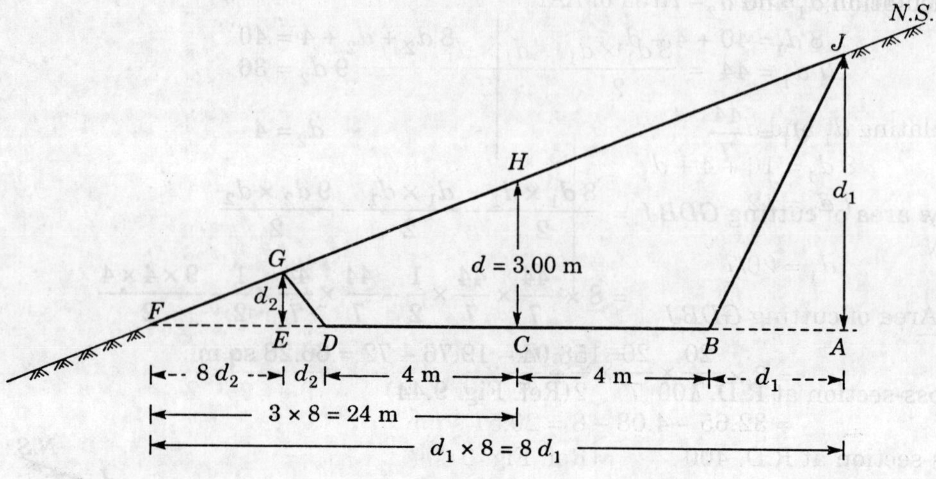

Fig. 9.45

From the Fig. 9.45 we have

Area of cutting $GDBJ$ = Area of ΔAFJ – Area of ΔABJ – Area of ΔDFG

$$= \frac{8\,d_1 \times d_1}{2} - \frac{d_1 \times d_1}{2} - \frac{9\,d_2 \times d_2}{2}$$

Calculating d_1 and d_2

$$8\,d_1 = 24 + 4 + d_1 \qquad\qquad 8\,d_2 + d_2 + 4 = 24$$

$$7\,d_1 = 28 \qquad\qquad 9\,d_2 = 20$$

$$d_1 = 4 \qquad\qquad d_2 = 20/9$$

Now area of cutting $GDBJ = 8 \times 4 \times 4 \times \frac{1}{2} - 4 \times 4 \times \frac{1}{2} - 9 \times \frac{20}{9} \times \frac{20}{9} \times \frac{1}{2}$

$$= 64 - 8 - 22.22 = 33.78 \text{ sq m}$$

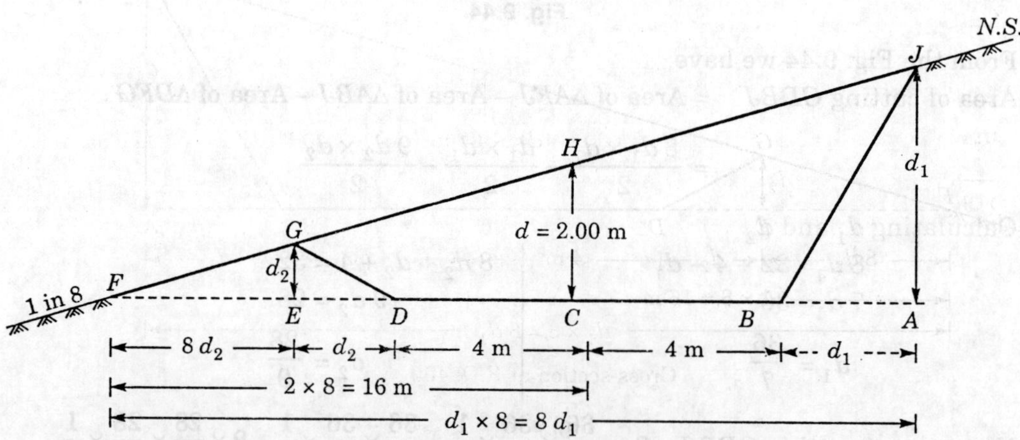

Fig. 9.46

Cross-section at R.D. 300 (Ref. Fig. 9.46)

From Fig. 9.46 we have

Area of cutting $GDBJ$ = Area of ΔAFJ – Area of ΔABJ – Area of ΔDFG

$$= \frac{8\,d_1 \times d_1}{2} - \frac{d_1 \times d_1}{2} - \frac{9\,d_2 - d_2}{2}$$

Calculating d_1 and d_2

$8\,d_1 = 16 + 4 + d_1$	$8\,d_2 + d_2 + 4 = 16$
$7\,d_1 = 12$	$9\,d_2 = 12$
$d_1 = 20/7$	$d_2 = \frac{12}{9}$

Now Area of cutting $GDBJ$

$$= 8 \times \frac{20}{7} \times \frac{20}{7} \times \frac{1}{2} - \frac{20}{7} \times \frac{20}{7} \times \frac{1}{2} - 9 \times \frac{12}{9} \times \frac{12}{9} \times \frac{1}{2}$$

$$= 32.65 - 4.08 - 8 = 20.57 \text{ sq m}$$

Cross-section at R.D. 400 (Ref. Fig. 9.47)

From the Fig. 9.47, we have

Area of cutting $GDBJ$ = Area of ΔAFJ – Area of ΔABJ – Area of ΔDFG

$$= \frac{8\,d_1 \times d_1}{2} - \frac{d_1 \times d_1}{2} - \frac{9\,d_2 \times d_2}{2}$$

Calculating d_1 and d_2

$8\,d_1 = 8 + 4 + d_1$	$8\,d_2 + d_2 + 4 = 8$
$7\,d_1 = 12$	$9\,d_2 = 4$
$d_1 = \frac{12}{7}$	$d_2 = \frac{4}{9}$

Refer Cross-section at R.D. 400 (Ref. Fig. 9.47)

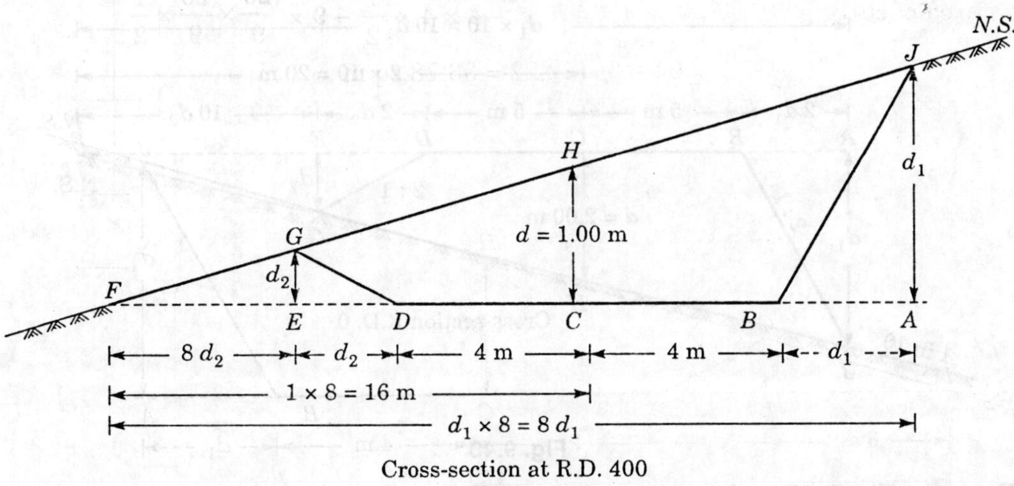

Cross-section at R.D. 400

Fig. 9.47

$$\text{Now area of cutting } GDBJ = 8 \times \frac{12}{7} \times \frac{12}{7} \times \frac{1}{2} - \frac{12}{7} \times \frac{12}{7} \times \frac{1}{2} - 9 \times \frac{4}{9} \times \frac{4}{9} \times \frac{1}{2}$$

$$= 11.75 - 1.46 - 0.88 = 9.41 \text{ sq m}$$

Earth Work Calculations

R.D. (m)	*Area of cutting (sq m)*	*Mean area of cutting (sq m)*	*Length (m)*	*Quantity of earth work (cum)*
0	66.28	—	—	—
100	49.02	57.65	100	5765
200	33.78	41.40	100	4140
300	20.57	27.17	100	2717
400	9.41	14.99	100	1499
			Total	14,121 cum

Example 9.23. *Calculate the quantity of earth work for a hill road with the following data :*

Formation width 10.00 m; side slope in filling 2 : 1; transverse slope of ground 1 in 10.

R.D. (m)	*N.S.L. (m)*	*Formation Level (m)*	*Filling (m)*	*Remark*
0	310.00	312.00	2.00	
100	309.40	311.00	1.60	
200	309.00	310.00	1.00	
300	307.80	109.00	1.20	
400	306.60	308.00	1.40	

Solution.

Cross-section at R.D. 0 (Ref. Fig. 9.48)

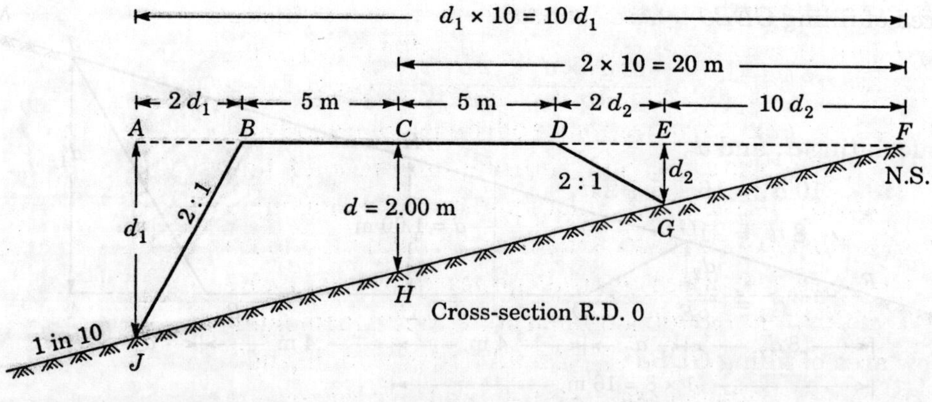

Fig. 9.48

From the Fig. 9.48 we have

Area of filling $GDBJ$ = Area of ΔAFJ – Area of ΔABJ – Area of ΔDFG

$$= \frac{10\,d_1 \times d_1}{2} - \frac{2\,d_1 \times d_1}{2} - \frac{12\,d_2 \times d_2}{2}$$

Calculating d_1 and d_2

$$10\,d_1 = 20 + 5 + 2\,d_1 \qquad 10\,d_2 + 2\,d_2 + 5 = 20$$
$$8\,d_1 = 25 \qquad 12\,d_2 = 15$$
$$d_1 = \frac{25}{8} \qquad d_2 = \frac{15}{12}$$

Now area of filling *GDBJ*

$$= 10 \times \frac{25}{8} \times \frac{25}{8} \times \frac{1}{2} - 2 \times \frac{25}{8} \times \frac{25}{8} \times \frac{1}{2} - 12 \times \frac{15}{12} \times \frac{15}{12} \times \frac{1}{2}$$

$$= 48.82 - 9.76 - 1.56 = 37.50 \text{ sq m}$$

Cross-section at R.D. 100. (Ref. Fig. 9.49)

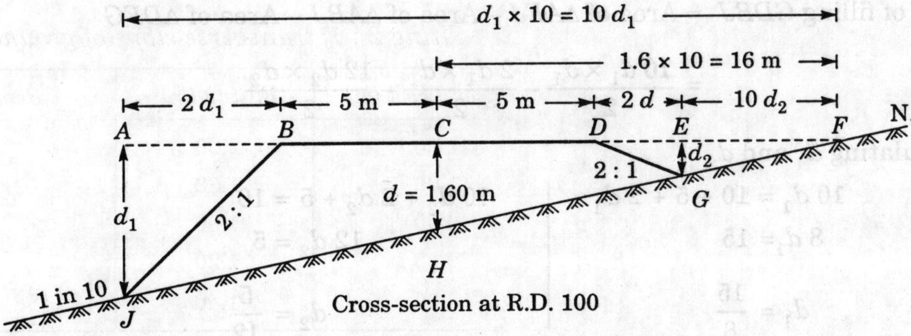

Fig. 9.49

From the Fig. 9.49 we have

Area of filling *GDBJ* = Area of ΔAFJ – Area of ΔABJ – Area of ΔDFG

$$= \frac{10\,d_1 \times d_1}{2} - \frac{2\,d_1 \times d_1}{2} - \frac{12\,d_2 \times d_2}{2}$$

Calculating d_1 and d_2

$$10\,d_1 = 16 + 5 + 2\,d_1 \qquad 10\,d_2 + d_2 + 5 = 16$$
$$8\,d_1 = 21 \qquad 12\,d_2 = 11$$
$$d_1 = \frac{21}{8} \qquad d_2 = \frac{11}{12}$$

Now area of filling *GDBJ*

$$= 10 \times \frac{21}{8} \times \frac{21}{8} \times \frac{1}{2} - 2 \times \frac{21}{8} \times \frac{21}{8} \times \frac{1}{2} - 12 \times \frac{11}{12} \times \frac{11}{12} \times \frac{1}{2}$$

$$= 34.45 - 6.89 - 5.04 = 22.52 \text{ sq m}$$

Cross-section at R.D. 200 (Ref. Fig. 9.50)

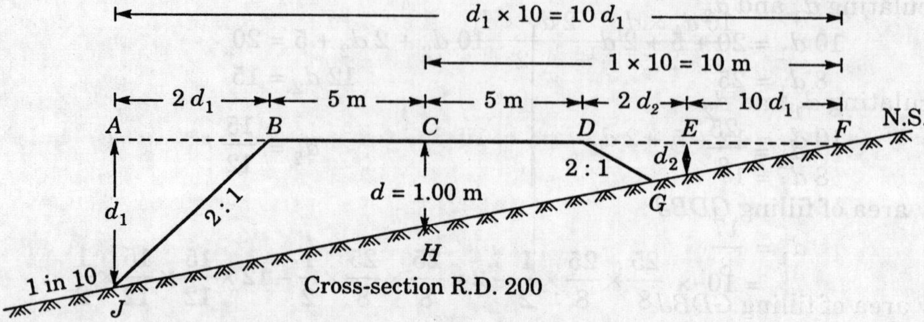

Fig. 9.50

From the Fig. 9.50, we have

Area of filling $GDBJ$ = Area of ΔAFJ – Area of ΔABJ – Area of ΔDFG

$$= \frac{10\, d_1 \times d_1}{2} - \frac{2\, d_1 \times d_1}{2} - \frac{12\, d_2 \times d_2}{2}$$

Calculating d_1 and d_2

$10\, d_1 = 10 + 5 + 2\, d_1$	$10\, d_2 + 2\, d_2 + 5 = 10$
$8\, d_1 = 15$	$12\, d_2 = 5$
$d_1 = \frac{15}{8}$	$d_2 = \frac{5}{12}$

Now area of filling $GDBJ$

$$= 10 \times \frac{15}{8} \times \frac{15}{8} \times \frac{1}{2} - 2 \times \frac{15}{8} \times \frac{15}{8} \times \frac{1}{2} - 12 \times \frac{5}{12} \times \frac{5}{12} \times \frac{1}{2}$$

$$= 17.57 - 3.51 - 1.04 = 13.02 \text{ sq m}$$

Cross-section at R.D. 300 (Ref. Fig. 9.51).

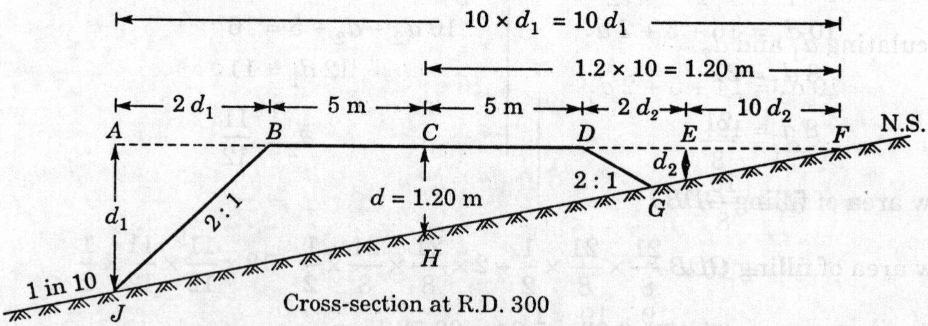

Fig. 9.51

From the Fig. 9.51 we have

Area of filling $GDBJ$ = Area of ΔAFJ – Area of ΔABJ – Area of ΔDFG

$$= \frac{10\, d_1 \times d_1}{2} - \frac{2\, d_1 \times d_1}{2} - \frac{12\, d_2 \times d_2}{2}$$

Calculating d_1 and d_2

$10\, d_1 = 12 + 5 + 2\, d_1$	$10\, d_2 + 2\, d_2 + 5 = 12$
$8\, d_1 = 17$	$12\, d_2 = 7$
$d_1 = \frac{17}{8}$	$d_2 = \frac{7}{12}$

Now area of filling *GDBJ*

$$= 10 \times \frac{17}{8} \times \frac{17}{8} \times \frac{1}{2} - 2 \times \frac{17}{8} \times \frac{17}{8} \times \frac{1}{2} - 12 \times \frac{7}{12} \times \frac{7}{12} \times \frac{1}{2}$$

$$= 22.57 - 4.51 - 2.04 = 16.02 \text{ sq m}$$

Cross-section at R.D. 400 (Ref. Fig. 9.52)

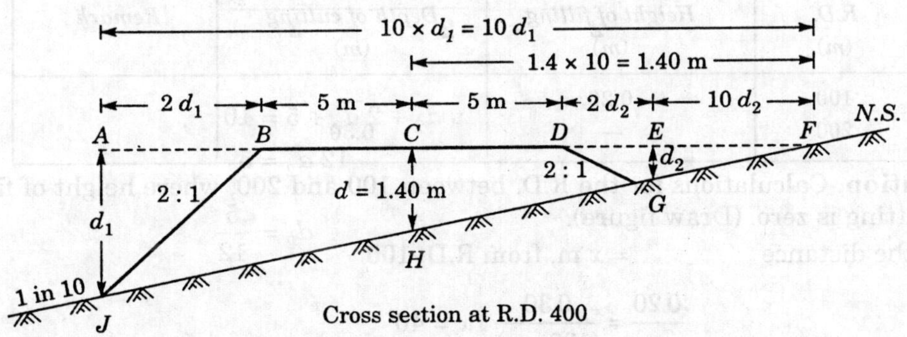

Fig. 9.52

Area of filling *GDBJ* = Area of ΔAFJ – Area of ΔABJ – Area of ΔDFG

$$= \frac{10\, d_1 \times d_1}{2} - \frac{2\, d_1 \times d_1}{2} - \frac{12\, d_2 \times d_2}{2}$$

Calculating d_1 and d_2

$10\, d_1 = 14 + 5 + 2\, d_1$	$10\, d_1 + 2\, d_2 + 5 = 14$
$8\, d_1 = 19$	$12\, d_2 = 9$
$d_1 = \frac{19}{8}$	$d_2 = \frac{9}{12}$

Now area of filling *GDBJ*

$$= 10 \times \frac{19}{8} \times \frac{19}{8} \times \frac{1}{2} - 2 \times \frac{19}{8} \times \frac{19}{8} \times \frac{1}{2} - 12 \times \frac{19}{12} \times \frac{19}{12} \times \frac{1}{2}$$

$$= 28.20 - 5.64 - 3.37 = 19.19 \text{ sq m}$$

Earth-Work Calculations

R.D. (m)	*Area of filling (sq m)*	*Mean area or filling (sq m)*	*Length (m)*	*Quantity of earth work (cum)*
0	37.50			
100	22.52	30.01	100	3001
200	13.02	17.17	100	1717
300	16.02	14.52	100	1452
400	19.19	17.60	100	1760
			Total	7930 cum

Example 9.24. *Calculate the quantity of earth work for a hill road with the following data :*

Formation width 10.00 m, side slope in filling 2 : 1, side slope in cutting 1 : 1, transverse slope of ground 1 in 10.

R.D. (m)	*Height of filling (m)*	*Depth of cutting (m)*	*Remark*
100	0.20	—	
200	—	0.30	

Solution. Calculations for the R.D. between 100 and 200, where height of filling and depth of cutting is zero. (Draw figure).

Let the distance = x m, from R.D. 100

$$\frac{0.20}{x} = \frac{0.30}{(100 - x)}, \; x = 40$$

i.e. R.D.= 140

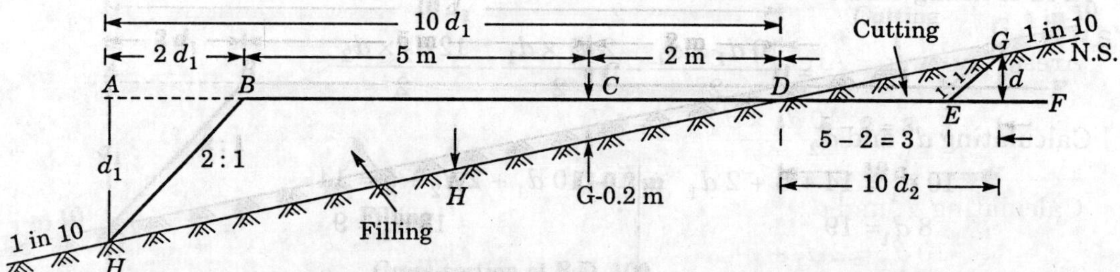

Cross-section at R.D. 100

Fig. 9.53

From the Fig. 9.53, we have

Area of filling = Area of ADH – Area of ΔABH

$$= \frac{10\,d_1 \times d_1}{2} - \frac{2\,d_1 \times d_1}{2} = 4\,d_1 \times d_1$$

Area of cutting = Area of ΔDGF – Area of ΔGFE

$$= \frac{10\,d_2 \times d_2}{2} - \frac{d_2 \times d_2}{2} = 4.5\,d_2 \times d_2$$

Calculating d_1 and d_2

$10d_1 = 2d_1 + 5 + 2$ | $10\,d_2 = 3 + d_2$

$8d_1 = 7$ | $9\,d_2 = 3$

$d_1 = 7/8$ | $d_2 = 3/9$

Area of filling = $4\,d_1 \times d_1 = 4 \times 7/8 \times 7/8 = 3.86$ sq m

Area of cutting = $4.5 \times d_2 \times d_2 = 4.5 \times 3/9 \times 3/9 = 0.50$ sq m

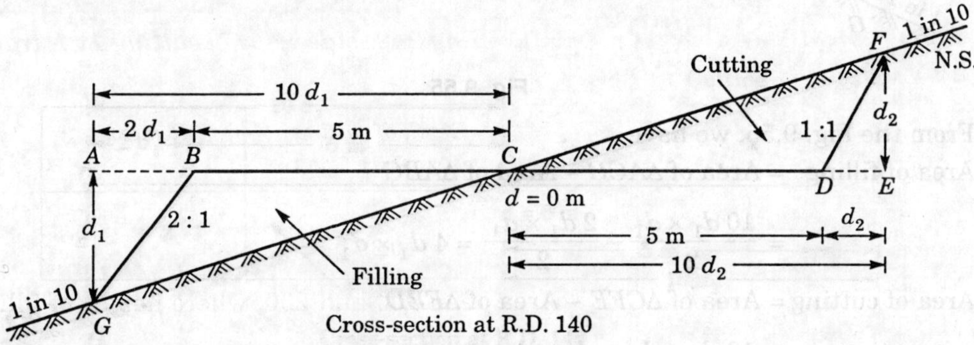

Cross-section at R.D. 140

Fig. 9.54

From the Fig. 9.54, we have

Area of filling = Area of ΔACG–Area of ΔABG

$$= \frac{10\,d_1 \times d_1}{2} - \frac{2\,d_1 \times d_1}{2} = 4\,d_1 \times d_1$$

Area of cutting = Area of ΔCFE – Area of ΔFED

$$= \frac{10\,d_2 \times d_2}{2} - \frac{d_2 \times d_2}{2} = 4.5\,d_2 \times d$$

Calculating d_1 and d_2

$10\,d_1 = 2\,d_1 + 5$ | $10\,d_2 = 5 + d_2$

$8\,d_1 = 5$ | $9\,d_2 = 5$

$d_1 = 5/8$ | $d_2 = 5/9$

Area of filling $= 4d_1 \times d_1 = 4 \times \frac{5}{8} \times \frac{5}{8} \times = 1.56$ sq m

Area of cutting $= 4.5\,d_2 \times d_2 = 4.5 \times \frac{5}{9} \times \frac{5}{9} = 1.38$ sq m

Cross-section at R.D. 200 (Ref. Fig. 9.55)

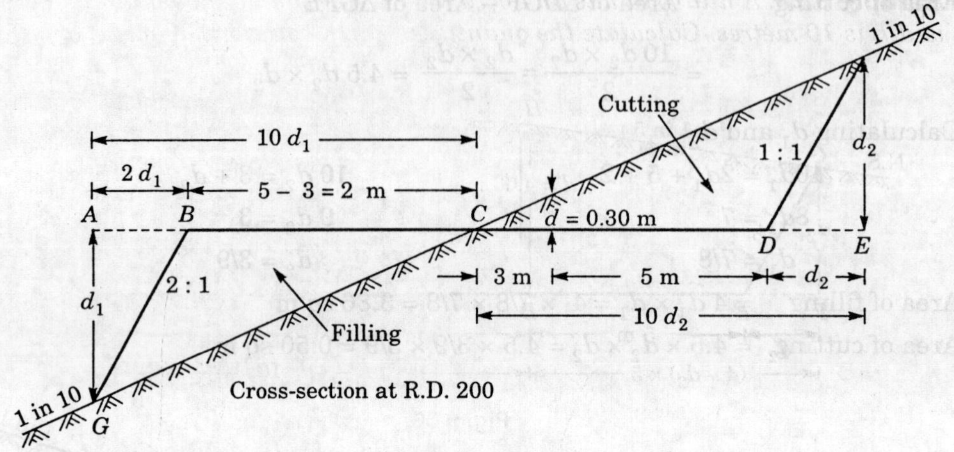

Fig. 9.55

From the Fig. 9.55, we have

Area of filling $= \text{Area of } \Delta ACG - \text{Area of } \Delta ABG$

$$= \frac{10\,d_1 \times d_1}{2} - \frac{2\,d_1 \times d_1}{2} = 4\,d_1 \times d_1$$

Area of cutting $= \text{Area of } \Delta CFE - \text{Area of } \Delta FED$

$$= \frac{10\,d_2 \times d_2}{2} - \frac{d_2 \times d_2}{2} = 4.5\,d_2 \times d_2$$

Calculating d_1 and d_2

$$10\,d_1 = 2d_1 + 2 \qquad\qquad 10\,d_2 = d_2 + 5 + 3$$
$$8\,d_1 = 2 \qquad\qquad 9\,d_2 = 8$$
$$d_1 = 2/8 \qquad\qquad d_2 = 8/9$$

Area of filling $= 4d_1 \times d_1 = 4 \times \frac{2}{8} \times \frac{2}{8} = 0.25$ sq m

Area of cutting $= 4.5\,d_2 \times d_2 = 4.5 \times \frac{8}{9} \times \frac{8}{9} = 3.55$ sq m

Earth Work Calculations

R.D.	*Area of filling*	*Area of cutting*	*Mean area of filling*	*Mean area of cutting*	*Length*	*Quantity Filling*	*Quantity Cutting*	*Remark*
100	3.06	0.50	–	–	–	–	–	
140	1.56	1.38	2.31	0.94	40	92.40	37.60	
200	0.25	3.55	0.90	2.46	60	54.00	147.60	
					Total	146.40	185.20 cum	

Quantity of earth work

In filling = 146.40 cum

In cutting = 185.20 cum

Example 9.25. *A hill road has an average cross-section as shown in Fig. 9.56. The formation width is 10 metres. Calculate the quantity of earthwork for 100 metre length of road.*

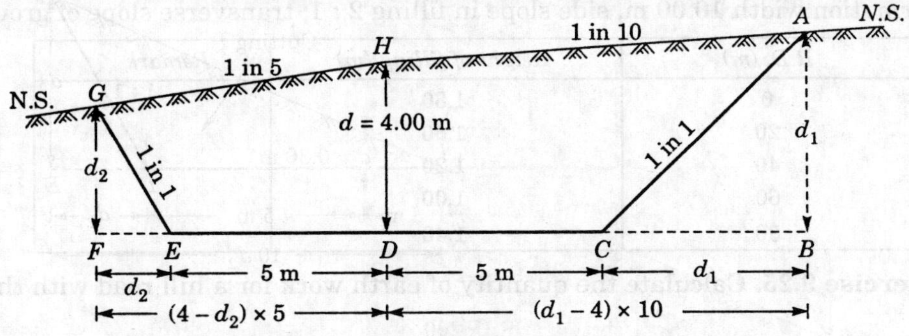

Fig. 9.56

From the Fig. 9.56, we have

Area of cutting = Area of Fig. *GHDF* – Area of ΔGEF + Area of Fig. *HABD* – Area of ΔABC

$$= \left\{\left(\frac{d_2 + d}{2}\right) \times (d_2 + 5) - \frac{d_2 \times d_2}{2}\right\} + \left\{\left(\frac{d + d_1}{2}\right) \times (5 + d_1) - \frac{d_1 \times d_1}{2}\right\}$$

Calculating d_1 and d_2

$5 + d_1 = (d_1 - 4) \times 10$	$d_2 + 5 = (4 + d_2) \times 5$
$5 + d_1 = 10\, d_1 - 40$	$d_2 + 5 = 20 - 5\, d_2$
$9\, d_1 = 45$	$6\, d_2 = 15$
$d_1 = 5$	$d_2 = 2.5$

$$d = 4.0 \text{ (From the Fig.)}$$

$$\text{Area of cutting} = \left\{\left(\frac{2.5 + 4.0}{2}\right) \times (2.5 + 5) - \frac{2.5 \times 2.5}{2}\right\} + \left\{\left(\frac{4.0 + 5}{2}\right) \times (5 + 5) - \frac{5 \times 5}{2}\right\}$$

$$= \left\{\left(\frac{6.5}{2} \times 7.5\right) - \frac{6.25}{2}\right\} + \left\{\left(\frac{9.0}{2} \times 10\right) - \frac{25}{2}\right\}$$

$$= 21.250 + 32.50 = 53.75 \text{ sq m.}$$

Quantity of earth work = Area × Length = 53.75 × 100 = 5375 cum.

EXERCISES

Exercise 9.23. Calculate the quantity of earth work for a hill road with the following data :

Formation width 8.00 m, side slope in cutting 1:1, transverse slope of ground 1 in 8.

R.D. (m)	*Depth of cutting (m)*	*Remark*
0	1.20	
20	2.40	
40	3.00	
60	2.80	
80	2.20	

Exercise 9.24. Calculate the quantity of earth work for a hill road with the following data :

Formation width 10.00 m, side slope in filling 2 : 1; transverse slope of ground 1 in 10.

R.D. (m)	*Height of filling (m)*	*Remark*
0	1.80	
20	1.60	
40	1.20	
60	1.00	
80	1.40	

Exercise 9.25. Calculate the quantity of earth work for a hill road with the following data :

Formation width 12.00 m side slope in filling 2 : 1; side slope in cutting 1 : 1.

R.D. (m)	*Depth of cutting m*	*Height of filling (m)*	*Transverse slope of ground*	*Remark*
100	1.20	—	1 in 10	
120	—	1.10	1 in 15	
140	1.30	—	1 in 20	
160	—	1.50	1 in 25	
180	1.70	—	1 in 30	
200	—	1.90	1 in 10	

Exercise 9.26. A hill road has an average cross-section as shown in one Fig. 9.57. The formation width is 12 metres. Calculate the quantity of earth work for 100 metre length of road.

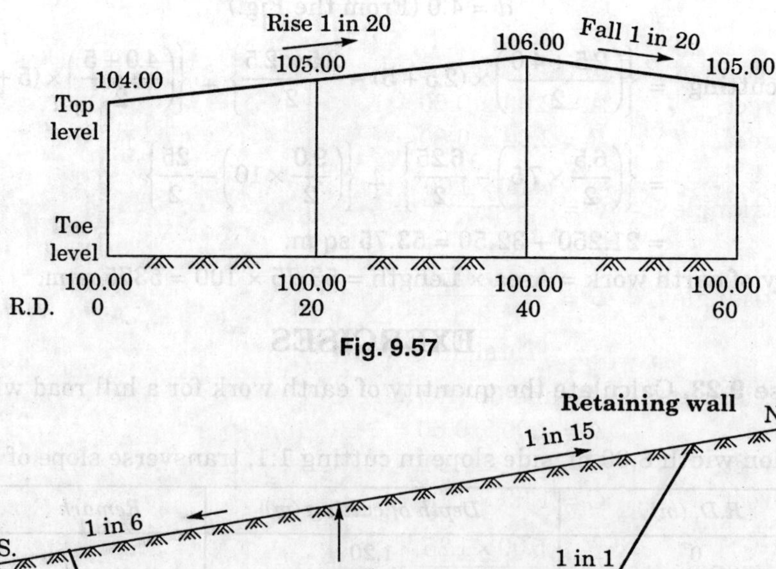

Fig. 9.57

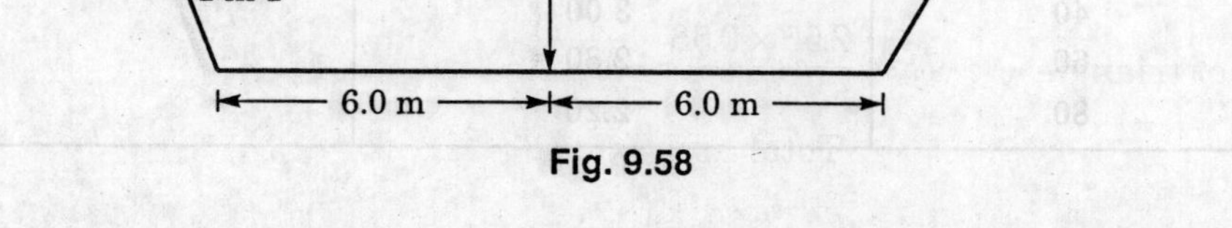

Fig. 9.58

Retaining walls are constructed to resist the pressure of earth filling and the traffic load on the road. It is generally built up in hill roads, with day stone masonry. The top width is generally kept of 60 cm width, and front face better varying from 1 : 4 (H : V) to 1 : 3 (H.V.)

Example 9.26. *Find out the quantity of dry stone masonry for the construction of a retaining wall shown in the longitudinal section Fig. 9.58 with the following data :*

Top width 60 cm, face batter 1 : 4 (H : V) ; Back vertical with offsets, 20 cm at 2 m, 4 m, 6 m from the top. Foundation to be at right angle to the face. Top of the wall rises at 1 in 20 from R.D. 0 to R.D. 40 ; Falls at 1 in 20 from R.D. 40 to R.D. 60. To the toe level of the wall at each R.D. is 100.00 and the top level of the wall at R.D. 0 is 104.00.

Solution. From the longitudinal section, the cross-sections as every R.D.s are drawn and the area is calculated.

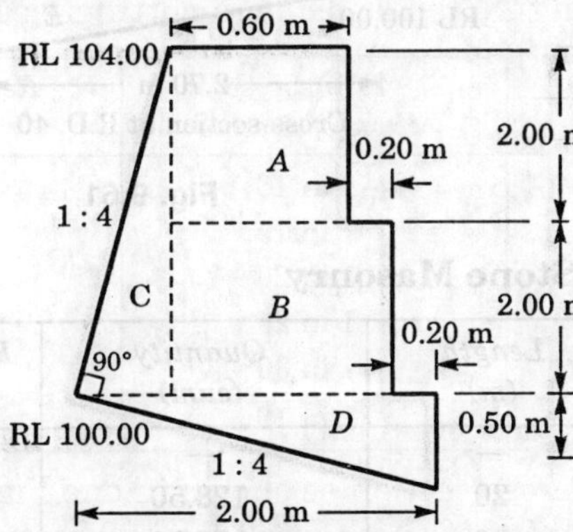

Cross-section at R.D. 0

Fig. 9.59

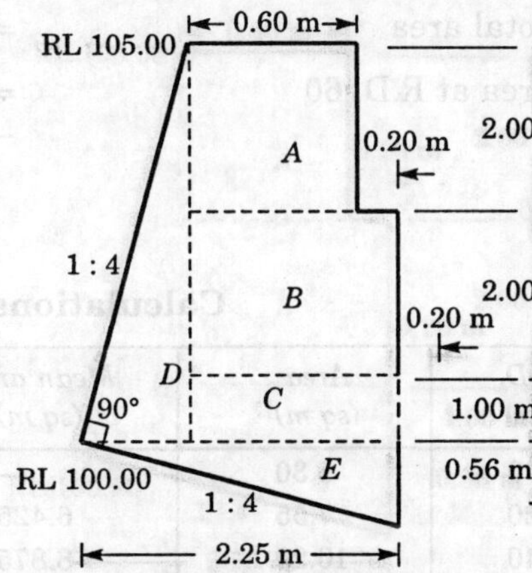

Cross-section at R.D. 20 and 60

Fig. 9.60

Cross-section at R.D. 0 (Ref. Fig. 9.59)

Area of rect. $A = 2.00 \times 0.60 = 1.20$ sq m

Area of rect. $B = 2.00 \times 0.80 = 1.60$ sq m

Area of triangle $C = \dfrac{4.00 \times 1.00}{2} = 2.00$ sq m

Area of triangle $D = \dfrac{2.00 \times 0.50}{2} = 0.50$ sq m

Total area = 5.30 sq m

Cross-section at R.D. 20 and 60 (Ref. Fig. 9.60)

Area of rect. $A = 2.00 \times 0.60 = 1.20$ sq m

Area of rect. $B = 200 \times 0.80 = 1.60$ sq m

Area of rect. $C = 1.00 \times 1.00 = 1.00$ sq m

Area of triangle $D = \dfrac{5.00 \times 1.25}{2} = 3.12$ sq m

Area of triangle $E = \dfrac{2.55 \times 0.56}{2} = 0.63$ sq m

Total area = 7.55 sq m

Cross-section at R.D. 40 (Ref. Fig. 9.61)

Area of react. $A = 2.00 \times 0.60 = 1.20$ sq m

Area of react. $B = 2.00 \times 0.80 = 1.60$ sq m

Area of triangle $C = 2.00 \times 1.00 = 2.00$ sq m

Area of triangle $D = \frac{6.00 \times 1.50}{2} = 4.50$ sq m

Area of triangle $E = \frac{2.70 \times 0.67}{2} = 0.90$ sq m

Total area = 10.20 sq m

Area at R.D. 60 = 7.55 sq m

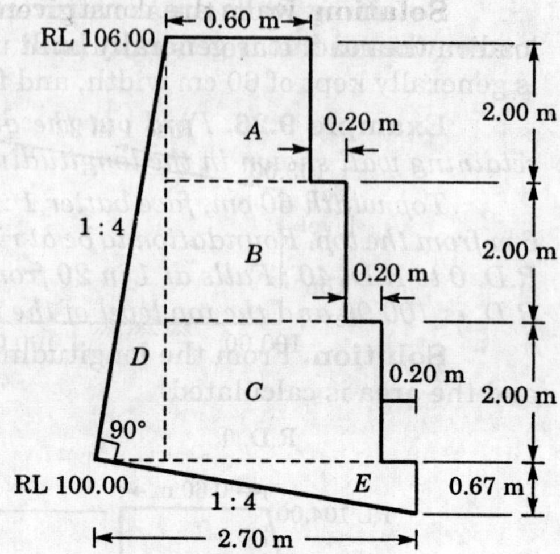

Cross-section at R.D. 40

Fig. 9.61

Calculations of Dry Stone Masonry

R.D. (m)	*Area (sq m)*	*Mean area (sq m)*	*Length (m)*	*Quantity (cum)*	*Remark*
0	5.30	—	—	—	
20	7.55	6.425	20	128.50	
40	10.20	8.875	20	177.50	
60	7.55	8.875	20	177.50	
			Total	483.50 cum	

Example 9.27. *Calculate the quantity of dry stone masonry for the construction of a Retaining wall of the following data :*

The top width of the wall = 1.00 m

Face batter = 1 : 3 (H : V)

Back face vertical with offsets of 20 cm at, 3 m from the top ;

The foundation will be at right angles to the face ;

Top of the wall rises at 1 in 20 from RD 0 to RD 20;

Falls at 1 in 20 from R.D. 40 to RD 60, and at level between RD 20 and RD 40;

R.L. of top of the wall at R.D. 0 = 103.00;

Toe levels of the wall are given below.

R.D.	*Toe Levels*
0	100.00
20	100.00
40	99.50
	99.50
	100.50
60	100.500

Solution. From the above given data, the longitudinal and cross-sections at every R.D's are drawn and the area is calculated.

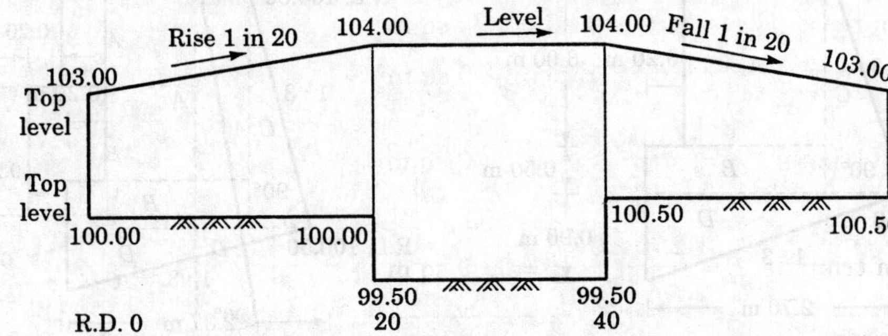

Fig. 9.62

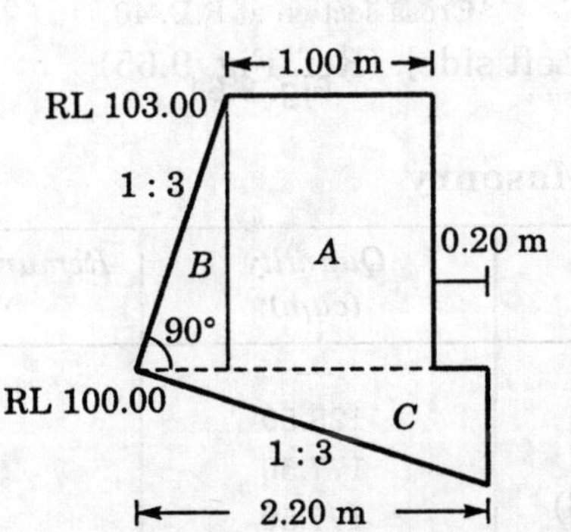

Fig. 9.63

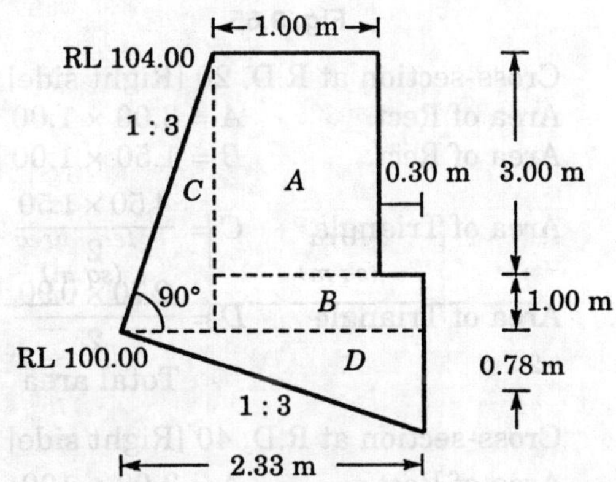

Fig. 9.64

Cross-section at R.D. 0. (Ref. Fig. 9.63)

Area of Rect. $A = 3.00 \times 1.00 = 3.00$ sq m

Area of Triangle $B = \dfrac{3.00 \times 1.00}{2} = 1.50$ sq m

Area of Triangle $C = \dfrac{2.20 \times 0.73}{2} = 0.80$ sq m

Total area 5.30 sq m

Cross-section at R.D. 20 [Left side] (Ref. Fig. 9.64)

Area of Rect. $A = 3.00 \times 1.00 = 3.00$ sq m

Area of Rect. $B = 1.00 \times 1.00 = 1.00$ sq m

Area of Triangle $C = \dfrac{4.00 \times 1.33}{2} = 2.66$ sq m

Area of Triangle $D = \dfrac{2.33 \times 0.78}{2} = 0.90$ sq m

Total area 7.56 sq m

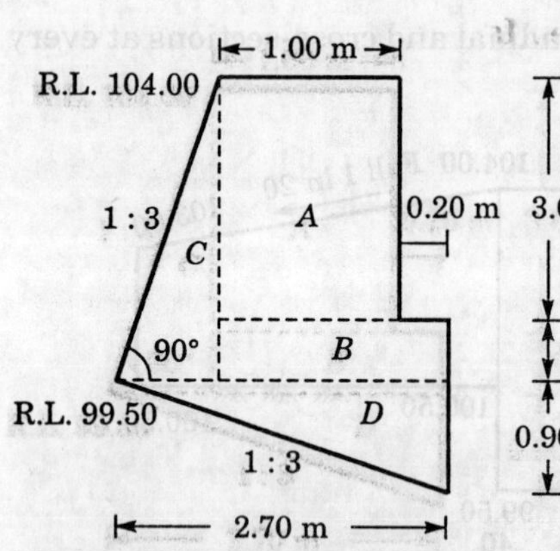

Cross-section at R.D. 20 (Right side) and R.D. 40 (Left side)

Fig. 9.65

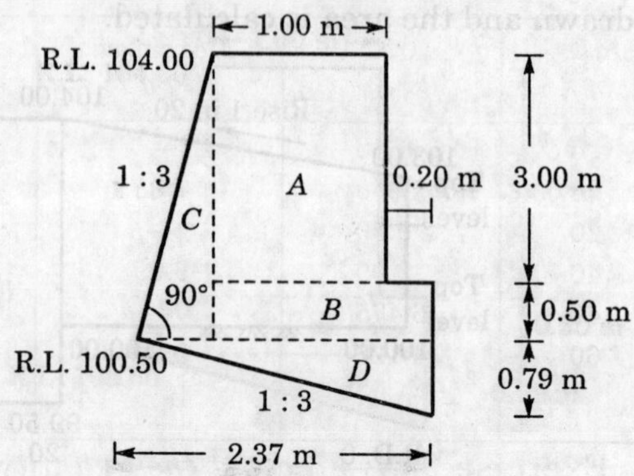

Cross-section at R.D. 40 (Right side)

Fig. 9.66

Cross-section at R.D. 20 [Right side] and R.D. 40 [Left side]. (Ref. Fig. 9.65)

Area of Rect. $A = 3.00 \times 1.00 = 3.00$ sq m

Area of Rect. $B = 1.50 \times 1.00 = 1.50$ sq m

Area of Triangle $C = \dfrac{4.50 \times 1.50}{2} = 3.37$ sq m

Area of Triangle $D = \dfrac{2.70 \times 0.90}{2} = 1.22$ sq m

Total area 9.09 sq m

Cross-section at R.D. 40 [Right side] (Ref. Fig. 9.66)

Area of Rect. $A = 3.00 \times 100 = 3.00$ sq m

Area of Rect. $B = 0.50 \times 1.00 = 0.50$ sq m

Area of Triangle $C = \dfrac{3.50 \times 1.17}{2} = 2.04$ sq m

Area of Triangle $D = \dfrac{2.37 \times 0.79}{2} = 0.935$ sq m

Total area 6.475 sq m

Cross-section at R.D. 60 (Ref. Fig. 9.67)

Area of Rect. $A = 2.50 \times 1.00 = 2.500$ sq m

Area of Triangle $B = \dfrac{2.50 \times 0.83}{2} = 1.035$ sq m

Area of Triangle $C = \dfrac{2.03 \times 0.68}{2} = 0.690$ sq m

Total area 4.225 sq m

(–) **Deduct**

= 4.225 sq m

(–) Area of Rect. $D = 0.20 \times 0.50 = (–)0.100$ sq m

Net area 4.125 sq m

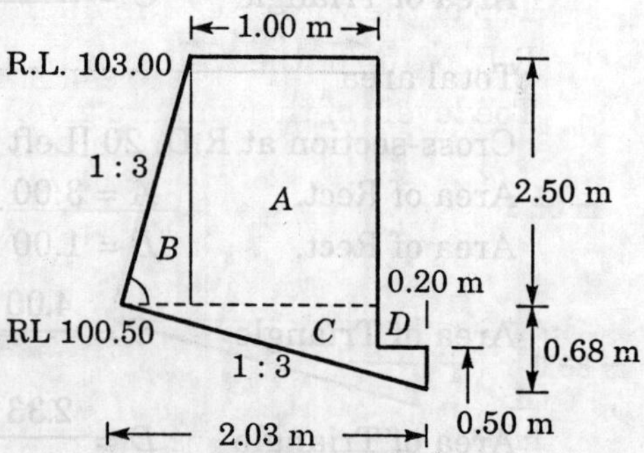

Cross-section at R.D. 60

Fig. 9.67

Calculations of Dry Stone Masonry

R.D. (m)	*Area (sq m)*	*Mean area (sq m)*	*Length (m)*	*Quantity (cum)*	*Remark*
0	5.30	—	—	—	—
20	7.56	7.93	20	158.6	Left side
20	9.09	—	—	—	Right side
40	9.09	9.09	20	181.8	Left side
40	6.475	—	—	—	Right side
60	4.125	5.30	20	106.0	
			Total	446.4 cum	

Exercise 9.27. *Find out the quantity of dry stone masonry for the construction of a retaining wall of the following data :*

The top width of the wall = 1.00 m

Face batter 1 : 4 (H : V)

Back face vertical with offsets of 20 cm at 2 m, and 4 m, from the top ;

The foundation will be at right angles to the face ;

Top of the wall rises 1 in 30 from R.D. 0 to 30 ; and falls at 1 in 20 from R.D. 30 to 50;

R.L. of top of the wall at R.D. 0 = 104.00

Toe levels of the wall are given below :

R.D.	*Toe level*
0	100.00
30	100.00
50	100.00

Exercise 9.28. *Find out the quantity of dry stone masonry for the construction of a retaining wall of the following data :*

The top width of the wall = 1.20 m.

Face batter 1 : 3 (H : V)

Back face vertical with offsets of 0.30 m at 3 m and 6 m from the top ;

The foundation will be at right angles to the top ;

Top of the wall rises 1 in 40 from R.D. 0 to 40 ; and falls at 1 in 10, from R.D. 40 to 70;

R.L. of top of the wall at R.D. 70 = 104.00.

Toe levels of the wall are given below :

R.D.	*Toe levels*
0	100.00
	100.00
40	99.00
70	99.00

10

Culverts

10.1. INTRODUCTION

Culvert is a small bridge. The span in generally upto 4 metres. The main components of the culvert, are (*i*) abutments to support the arch or slab, (*ii*) wing walls to retain the earth in embankment with or without returns and (*iii*) the arch or slab.

10.2. GENERAL SPECIFICATIONS

Earthwork. Foundations are taken generally 1.00 m below the bed level of drain.

Foundations. Cement concrete 1 : 4 : 8 (1 cement : 4 coarse sand : 8 stone or brick aggregate (40 mm nominal size is generally used).

Brick work. 1st class brick work in cement mortar 1 : 3 (1 cement : 3 coarse sand is generally used). Arch or slab : As per design.

Flooring. Dry brick pitching is generally done.

Finishing. Inside the culvert 20 mm thick cement plaster 1 : 3 (1 cement : 3 coarse sand) finished with a floating coat of neat cement. Outside the culvert on all faces cement pointing 1 : 3 (1 cement : 3 coarse sand) is generally done. At the top of parapet wall, cement concrete coping is also provided.

10.3. DESIGN FEATURES

The common types of culvert are :

1. Arch culvert 2. Slab culvert 3. Pipe culvert 4. Box culvert.

The main components of the culvert (see article 9.1 also) are briefly described below :

(*i*) **Abutments.** These are end supports of culverts. They retain earth on their back and stream water on the front faces. The height of the abutment is kept about 1.00 metre to 1.50 metre above H.F.L. of the stream. The length of the abutment is kept according to the formation width of the road. The water face is kept vertical. The back face retaining earth is provided with steps or footing or a batter upto 1 : 5. The top width of the abutment for slab culvert is kept 50 cm for spans of 3 to 6 metres. In case of arch culvert the top width is calculated as :

$$B = \frac{R}{5} + \frac{r}{10} + 0.6 \text{ metre}$$

where B = Width at the springing level in metres

R = Radius of the soffit in metres

r = Rise of the arch in metres.

The base width of the abutment at the top of the concrete course will be 0.4 to 0.45 times the height between the top of concrete in foundation and the road level.

(*ii*) **Wing walls.** These are the walls constructed at the two ends of the abutment to retain the earth in the embankment and also to protect them from the stream water. These may be as (*a*) return wing wall, constructed at right angle to the abutment and (*b*) splayed wing wall, constructed at 45° with the abutment.

The top width of the wing wall is kept 30 to 40 cm. The width of the wing wall at the bottom is kept 0.30 to 0.40 times the height between road level and top of the concrete course in the foundation. The length of the wing wall is kept as 1.5 to 2 times the height. Front face batter varies from 1 : 10 to 1 : 20 and back face batter varies from 1 : 5 to 1 : 10.

(*iii*) **Arch.** In arch culvert, segmental arch is generally provided. The rise is kept 1/3 to 1/4 of span. The thickness of arch ring may be, as per Rankine's formula

$$T = 0.12\,R$$

where T = Thickness of arch

R = Radius of the soffit.

(*iv*) **Parapet.** The height of parapet varies from 30 to 100 cm and thickness of parapet wall is generally 20 to 30 cm.

10.4. MISCELLANEOUS DATA IN RESPECT OF ARCHED CULVERT

(*a*) **Circle and its properties**

1. The circumference of a circle = $\pi d = \pi 2r$; d = diameter, r = radius.

2. Length of the arc = $\dfrac{\pi d n}{360}$; n = number of degree in the arc.

Also length of arc $= \dfrac{4\sqrt{(\text{Length of the chord})^2 + 4\,(\text{Rise})^2} - \text{Length of the chord}}{3}$

3. Area of sector $= \dfrac{\text{Area of circle} \times n}{360}$

Also area of sector $= \dfrac{\text{Length of arc} \times \text{Radius}}{2}$

(*b*) Area of segment (app.)

= 2/3 × Span × Rise

Also area of segment = Area of sector – Area of the triangle formed by radii and chord.

(*c*)

Degree	*Sin*	*Cos*	*Tan*
30°	$\frac{1}{2}$	$\frac{\sqrt{3}}{2}$	$\frac{1}{\sqrt{3}}$
45°	$\frac{2}{\sqrt{2}}$	$\frac{1}{\sqrt{2}}$	1
60°	$\frac{\sqrt{3}}{2}$	$\frac{1}{2}$	$\sqrt{3}$

(*d*) **Calculations for the Radius of Arch**

$$\frac{\text{Span}}{2} \times \frac{\text{Span}}{2} = (\text{Dia} - \text{Rise}) \times \text{Rise}$$

Calculate diameter and hence calculate the radius of arch.

Example 10.1. *Estimate the quantities of different items of works for an abutment with wing walls of culvert.*

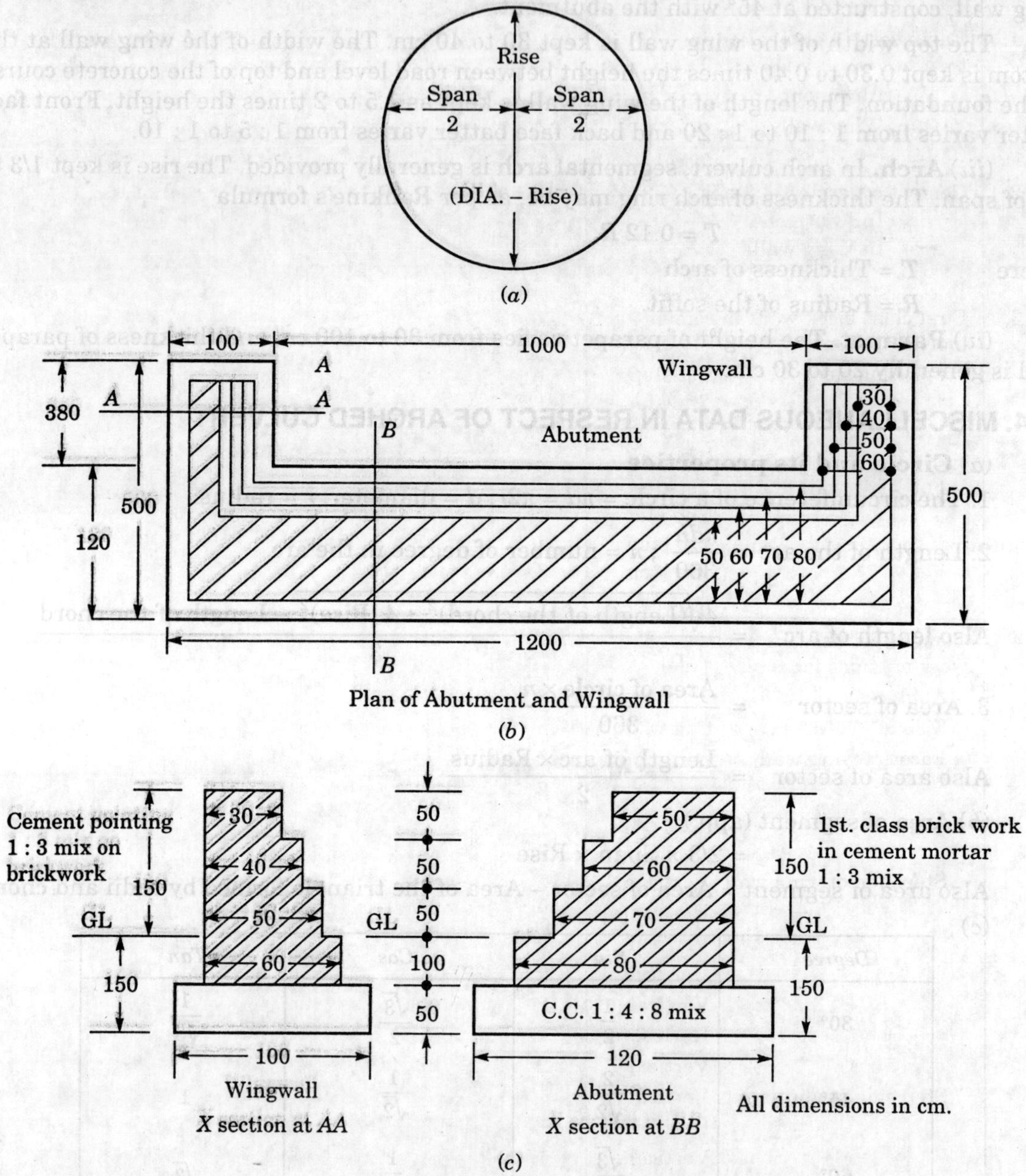

Fig. 10.1

Table 10.1. Details of Measurements

S.No.	Description of Item		No.	L	W	H/D	Content	Remark
1.	Earthwork in excavation in trenches							
	Abutment		1	12.00	1.20	1.50	21.60	
	Wing walls		2	3.80	1.00	1.50	11.40	
		Total					33.00 cum	
2.	Cement concrete 1:4:8 mix							
	In Abutment		1	12.00	1.20	0.50	7.20	
	In Wing walls		2	3.80	1.00	0.50	3.80	
		Total					11.00 cum	
3.	First class brick work in cement mortar 1 : 3 mix							
	For Abutment	1st step	1	11.60	0.80	1.00	9.28	
		2nd step	1	11.60	0.70	0.50	4.06	
		3rd step	1	11.60	0.60	0.50	3.48	
		4th step	1	11.60	0.50	0.50	2.90	
	For Wing wall	1st step	2	3.80	0.60	1.00	4.56	
		2nd step	2	3.90	0.50	0.50	1.95	
		3rd step	2	4.00	0.40	0.50	1.60	
		4th step	2	4.10	0.30	0.50	1.23	
		Total					29.06 cum	
4.	Cement pointing 1 : 3 mix on brick work outsides faces of							
	Abutment		1	11.60	—	2.50	29.00	
	Side of abutment and wing wall		2	4.60	—	2.50	23.00	
	Faces of wing wall		2	0.30	—	0.50	0.30	
			2	0.40	—	0.50	0.40	
			2	0.50	—	0.50	0.50	
			2	0.60		1.00	1.20	
	Step side of wing wall	Vertical	2	4.10	—	0.50	4.10	
		Horizontal	2	4.10	0.10	—	0.82	
		Vertical	2	4.00	—	0.50	4.00	
		Horizontal	2	4.00	0.10	—	0.80	
		Vertical	2	3.90	—	0.50	3.90	
		Horizontal	2	3.90	0.10	—	0.78	
		Vertical	2	3.80	—	1.00	7.60	
	Step side of abutment	Vertical	1	11.00	—	0.50	5.50	
		Horizontal	1	10.80	0.10	—	1.08	
		Vertical	1	10.80	—	0.50	5.40	
		Horizontal	1	10.60	0.10	—	1.06	
		Vertical	1	10.60	—	0.50	5.30	
		Horizontal	1	10.40	0.10	—	1.04	
		Vertical	1	10.40	—	1.00	10.40	
	Top of wing wall		2	4.10	0.30	—	2.46	
	Top of abutment		1	11.60	0.50	—	5.80	
		Total					114.44 sq m	

Table 10.2. Abstract of Quantities

S. No.	Description of item	Quantity	Remark
1.	Earthwork in excavation in foundation trenches including dressing of sides and ramming of bottoms, left upto 1.5 m and lead upto 50 m.	33 cum	
2.	Providing and laying cement concrete 1 : 4 : 8 (1 cement: 4 coarse sand : 8 graded stone aggregate 40 mm nominal size).	11 cum	
3.	First class brickwork in cement mortar 1: 3 (1 cement: 3 coarse sand)	29.06 cum	
4.	Cement pointing 1 : 3 (1 cement : 3 coarse sand).	114.44 sq m	

Example 10.2. *Estimate the quantities of different items of works for an abutment with wing wall, of culvert.*

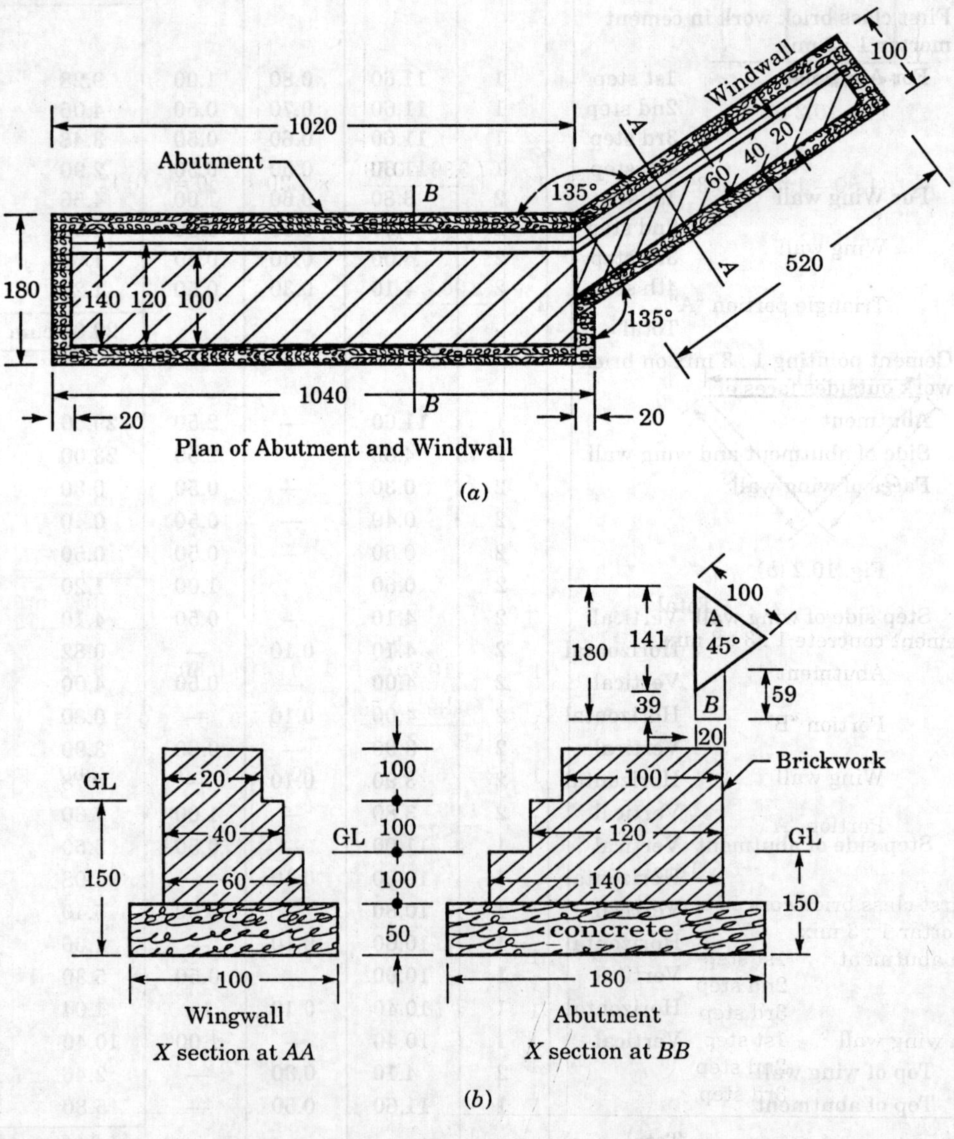

Fig. 10.2

Table 10.3. Details of Measurements

S. No.	Description of Item	No.	L	W	H/D	Content	Remark
1.	Earth work in excavation in foundation trenches						
	Abutment	1	10.20	1.80	1.50	27.54	
	Portion "B" of abutment						
	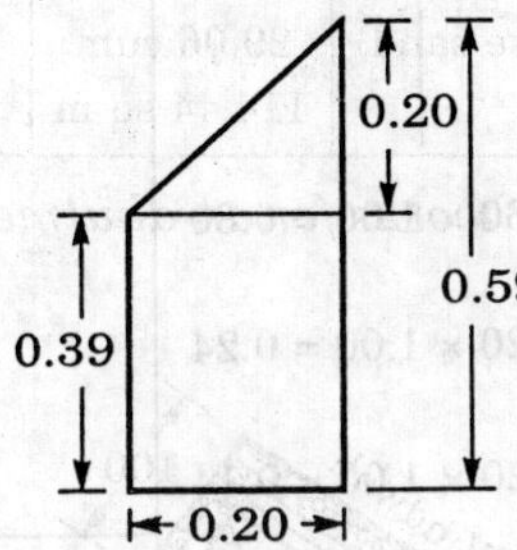 Fig. 10.2 (*a*)						
	(1.80 – 1.41) = 0.39	1	$\left(\frac{0.39+0.59}{2}\right)$ × 0.20 × 1.50 = 0.0147				
	Wing wall	1	5.30 1.00	1.50	7.30		
	Triangle portion "A"	1	$\frac{1.00 \times 1.00}{2}$	1.50	0.75		
	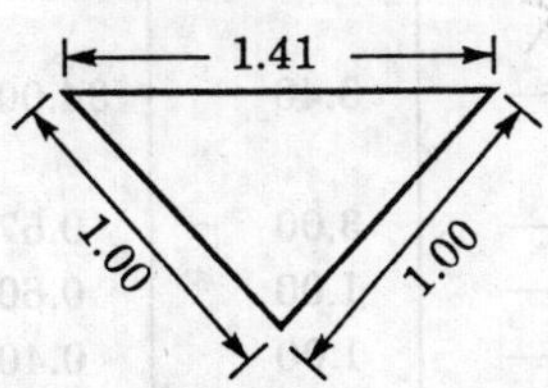 Fig. 10.2 (*b*)						
	Total					36.105 cum	
2.	Cement concrete 1 : 3 : 8 mix						
	Abutment	1	10.20	1.80	0.50	9.18	
	Portion "B"	1	$\left(\frac{0.39+0.59}{2}\right)$ × 0.20 × 0.50 = 0.005				
	Wing wall	1	5.20	1.00	0.50	2.60	
	Portion "A"	1	$\frac{1.00 \times 1.00}{2}$		0.50	0.25	
	Total					12.035 cum	
3.	First class brickwork in cement mortar 1 : 3 mix						
	In abutment 1st step	1	10.00	1.40	1.00	14.00	
	2nd step	1	10.00	1.20	1.00	12.00	
	3rd step	1	10.00	1.00	1.00	10.00	
	In wing wall 1st step	1	5.00	0.60	1.00	3.00	
	2nd step	1	5.00	0.40	1.00	2..00	
	3rd step	1	5.00	0.20	1.00	1.00	

(*Contd.*)

Portion "A"

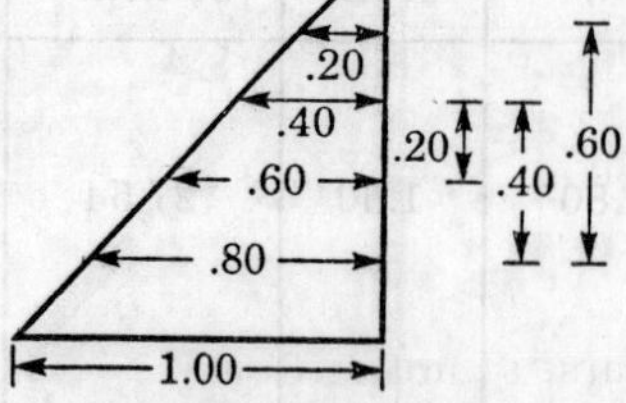

Fig. 10.2 (*c*)

S.No.	Description		No.	L	W	H	Quantity
	In portion "A"	1st step	1	$= \frac{0.80 + 0.20}{2} \times 0.60 \times 1.00 = 0.30$			
		2nd step	1	$= \frac{0.80 + 0.40}{2} \times 0.20 \times 1.00 = 0.24$			
		3rd step	1	$= \frac{0.80 + 0.60}{2} \times 0.20 \times 1.00 = 0.14$			
		Total					42.68 cum
4.	Cement pointing 1 : 3 mix on brick work on exposed surface						
	Abutment	End face	1	1.40	—	1.00	1.40
			1	1.20	—	1.00	1.20
			1	1.00	—	1.00	1.00
		Front face	1	10.00	—	3.00	30.00
		Top	1	10.00	1.00	—	10.00
	Step face (1.00 + 0.20 + 1.00 + 0.20 + 1.00) = 3.40		1	10.00	—	3.40	34.00
	Portion "B" (0.39–0.20) = 0.19		1	0.19	—	3.00	0.57
	Wing wall	End face	1	0.60	—	1.00	0.60
			1	0.40	—	1.00	0.40
			1	0.20	—	1.00	0.20
		From face	1	5.00	—	3.00	15.00
		Top	1	5.00	0.20	—	1.00
	Step face (1.00+0.20+1.00+ 0.20 + 1.00) = 340		1	5.00	—	3.40	17.00
	Portion "A"	Front	1	0.80	—	3.00	2.40
		Top	1	$\frac{0.80 + 0.60}{2} \times 0.20$			0.14
		Step side	1	0.60	—	1.00	0.60
			1	0.40	—	1.00	0.40
			1	0.20	—	1.00	0.20
			1	$\frac{0.60 + 0.40}{2} \times 0.20$			0.10
			1	$\frac{0.40 + 0.20}{2} \times 0.20$			0.06
		Total					116.27 sq m

Table 10.4. Abstract of Quantities

S. No.	Description of item	Quantity	Remark
1.	Earthwork in excavation in foundation trenches including dressing of sides and ramming of bottom, lift upto 1.5 m and lead upto 50 m.	36.105 cum	
2.	Providing and laying cement concrete 1 : 4 : 8 (1 cement : 4 coarse sand : 8 graded stone aggregate 40 mm nominal size).	12.035 cum	
3.	First class brickwork in cement mortar 1 : 3 (1 cement : 3 coarse sand)	42.68 cum	
4.	Cement pointing 1 : 3 (1 cement : 3 coarse sand).	116.27 sq m	

Example 10.3. *Estimate the quantities of different items of works for an abutment, wing wall with return of culvert.*

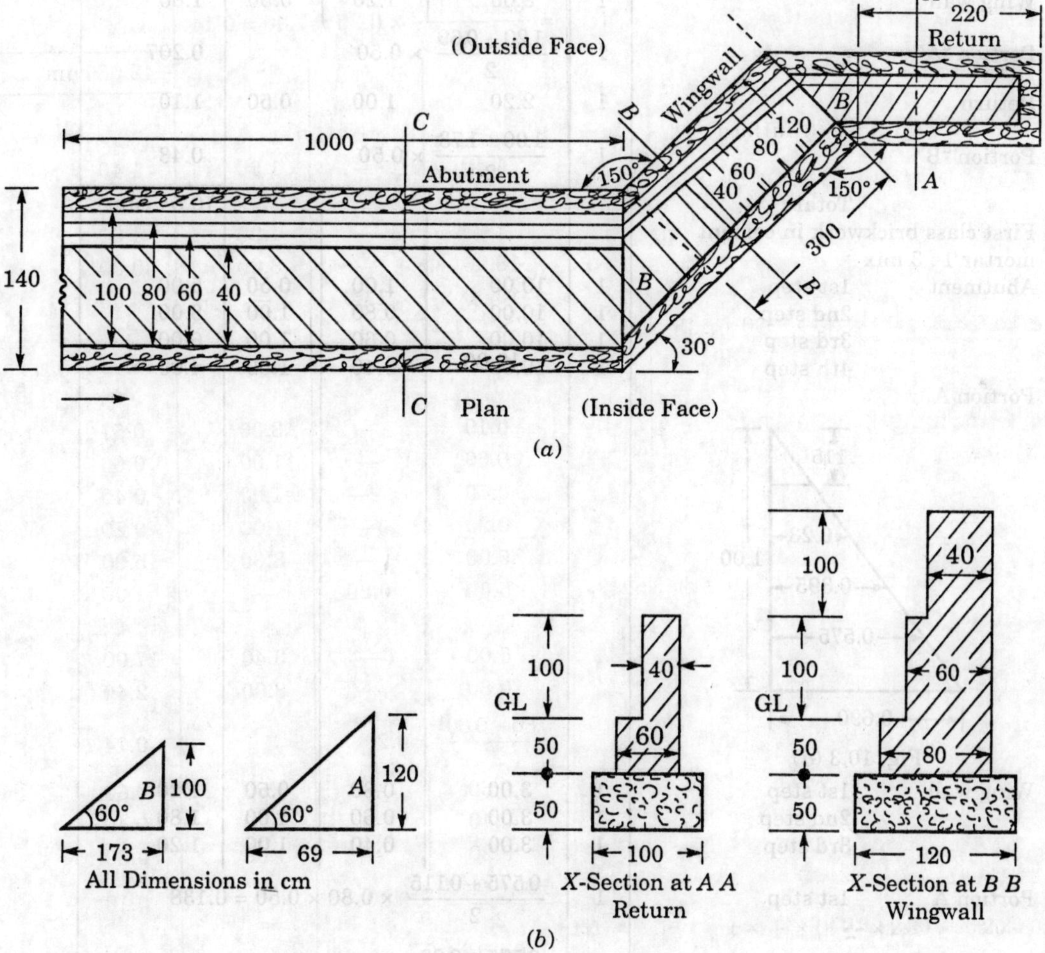

Fig. 10.3

Table 10.5. Details of Measurements

S. No.	*Description of item*		*No.*	*L*	*W*	*H/D*	*Contents*	*Remark*
1.	**Earthwork in excavation in trenches**							
	Abutment		1	10.00	1.40	1.00	14.000	
	Wing wall		1	3.00	1.20	1.00	3.600	
	Triangular portion "A"		1	$\frac{1.20+0.69}{2} \times 1.00$			0.414	
	Return		1	2.20	1.00	1.00	2.200	
	Triangular portion "B"		1	$\frac{1.00+1.73}{2} \times 1.00$			0.865	
		Total					21.079 cum	
2.	**Cement concrete 1 : 4 : 8 mix**							
	Abutment		1	10.00	1.40	0.50	7.00	
	Wing wall		1	3.00	1.20	0.50	1.80	
	Portion "A"		1	$\frac{1.20+0.69}{2} \times 0.50$			0.207	
	Return		1	2.20	1.00	0.50	1.10	
	Portion "B"		1	$\frac{1.00+1.73}{2} \times 0.50$			0.43	
		Total					10.54 cum	
3.	**First class brickwork in cement mortar 1 : 3 mix**							
	Abutment	**1st step**	1	10.00	1.00	0.50	5.00	
		2nd step	1	10.00	0.80	1.00	8.00	
		3rd step	1	10.00	0.60	1.00	6.00	
		4th step	1	10.00	0.40	1.00	4.00	
	Portion A							
	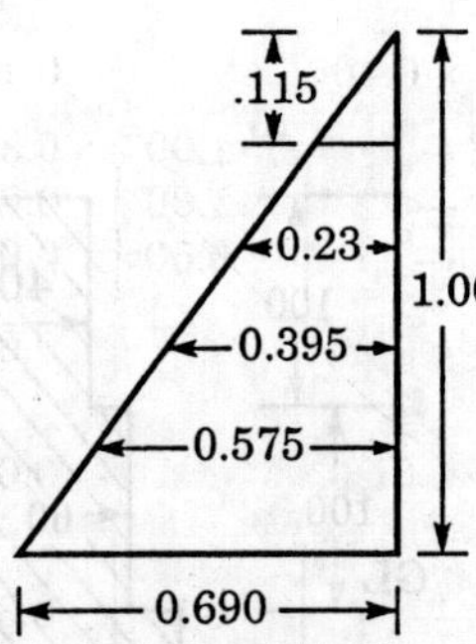 Fig. 10.3 (*a*)							
	Wing wall	**1st step**	1	3.00	0.80	0.50	1.20	
		2nd step	1	3.00	0.60	1.00	1.80	
		3rd step	1	3.00	0.40	1.00	1.20	
	Portion A	**1st step**	1	$\frac{0.575+0.115}{2} \times 0.80 \times 0.50 = 0.138$				
		2nd step	1	$\frac{0.575+0.23}{2} \times 0.60 \times 1.00 = 0.242$				
		3rd step	1	$\frac{0.575+0.345}{2} \times 0.40 \times 1.00 = 0.184$				

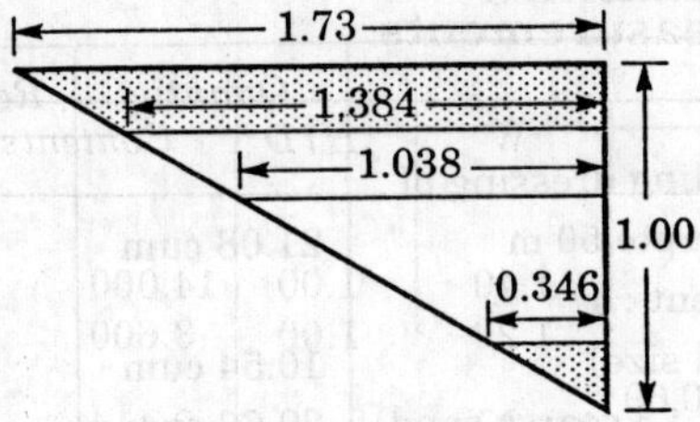

Fig. 10.3 (*b*)

Item No.	Description	No.	L	B	H	Quantity
	Return Portion B 1st step	1	2.00	0.60	0.50	0.60
	2nd step	1	2.00	0.40	1.00	0.80
	1st step	1	$\frac{1.384 + 0.346}{2} \times 0.60 \times 0.50 = 0.26$			
	2nd step	1	$\frac{1.038 + 0.346}{2} \times 0.40 \times 1.00 = 0.277$			
	Total					29.66 cum
4.	Cement pointing 1 : 3 mix on brick work on exposed surfaces					
	Abutment	1	10.00	—	3.50	35.00
	Front face	1	10.00	0.40	—	4.00
	Top					
	Step face (1.00 + 0.20 + 1.00 + 0.20 + 1.00 + 0.20 + 0.50) = 4.10	1	10.00	—	4.10	41.00
	Wing wall					
	Front face	1	3.00	—	2.50	7.50
	Top	1	3.00	0.40	—	1.20
	Step face (1.00 + 0.20 + 1.00 + 0.20 + 0.50) = 2.90	1	3.00	—	2.90	8.70
	Portion A					
	Front	1	0.575	—	2.50	1.437
	Top	1	$\frac{0.50 + 0.345}{2} \times 0.40$			0.184
		1	0.345	—	1.00	0.345
		1	0.23	—	1.00	0.230
		1	0.115	—	0.50	0.038
		1	$\frac{0.345 + 0.23}{2} \times 0.20$			0.057
		1	$\frac{0.23 + 0.115}{2} \times 0.20$			0.034
	Return					
	End side	1	0.60	—	0.50	0.30
		1	0.40	—	1.00	0.40
	Front face	1	2.00	—	1.50	3.00
	Top	1	2.00	0.40	—	0.80
	Step side (1.00 + 0.20 + 0.50) = 170	1	2.00	—	1.70	3.40
	Portion B					
	Face	1	0.346	—	1.50	0.519
	Top	1	$\frac{0.346 + 1.038}{2} \times 0.40$			0.290
	Steps	1	1.038	—	1.00	1.038
		1	1.384	—	0.50	0.692
		1	$\frac{1.038 + 1.384}{2} \times 0.20$			0.242
	Total					110.43 sq m

Table 10.6. Abstract of Quantities

S. No.	*Description of item*	*Quantity*	*Remark*
1.	Earthwork in excavation in foundation trenches including dressing of sides and ramming of bottom, lift upto 1.5 m and lead upto 50 m	21.08 cum	
2.	Provinding and laying cement concrete 1 : 4 : 8 (1 cement : 4 coarse sand : 8 graded stone aggragate 40 mm nominal size)	10.54 cum	
3.	First class brick work in cement mortar 1 : 3 (1 cement : 3 coarse sand)	29.66 cum	
4.	Cement pointing 1 : 3 (1 cement : 3 coarse sand)	110.43 sq m	

Example 10.4. *Estimate the quantities of different items of works for an abutment wing wall with return of culvert.*

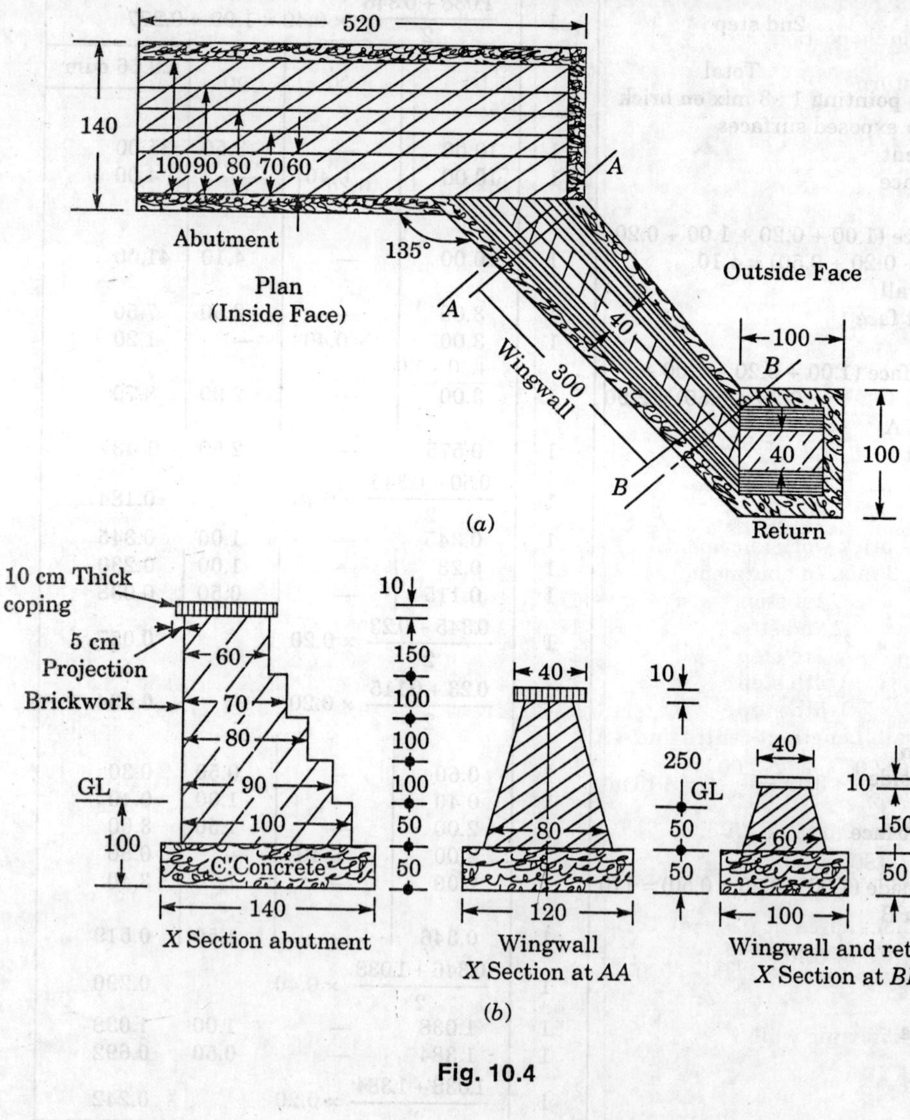

Fig. 10.4

Table 10.7. Details of Measurements

S. No.	*Description of item*	*No.*	*L*	*W*	*H/D*	*Content*	*Remark*
1.	Earthwork in excavation in trenches	1	5.20	1.40	1.00	7.28	
	Abutment	1	0.20	0.20	1.00	0.04	
						7.32	
	Deduct. Portion common with Wing wall (–)	1	1.70	0.20	1.00	0.34	
	Net Total					6.98	
	Add. Wing wall						
	Triangular portion A	1	$\frac{1.20 \times 1.20}{2} \times 1.00$			0.72	
	Triangular portion B	1	$\frac{1.00 \times 1.00}{2} \times 1.00$			0.50	
	Middle portion	1	3.00	$\left(\frac{1.20 + 1.00}{2}\right)$	× 1.00	3.30	
	Add. Return	1	1.00	1.00	1.00	1.00	
	Total					12.50 cum	
2.	Cement concrete 1 : 4 : 8 mix Abutment	1	5.20	1.40	0.50	3.64	
		1	0.20	0.20	0.50	0.02	
						3.66	
	Deduct. Common portion (–)	1	1.70	0.20	0.50	0.17	
						3.49	
	Add. Wing wall	1	$\frac{1.20 \times 1.20}{2} \times 0.50$			0.36	
		1	$\frac{1.00 \times 1.00}{2} \times 0.50$			0.25	
		1	3.00	$\left(\frac{1.20 + 1.00}{2}\right)$	0.50	1.65	
	Return	1	1.00	1.00	0.50	0.50	
	Total					6.25 cum	
3.	First class brick work in cement mortar 1 : 3 mix. In abutment						
	1st step	1	5.00	1.00	0.50	2.50	
	2nd step	1	5.00	0.90	1.00	4.50	
	3rd step	1	5.00	0.80	1.00	4.00	
	4th step	1	5.00	0.70	1.00	3.50	
	5th step	1	5.00	0.60	1.50	4.50	
	In wing wall. Length at centre line $= \left(\frac{1.20}{2} + 3.00 + \frac{1.00}{2}\right) = 4.10$ m						
	Cross-sectional area at *AA* end $= \left(\frac{0.80 + 0.40}{2} \times 3.00\right) = 1.80$						
	Cross-sectional area at *BB* end $= \left(\frac{0.60 + 0.40}{2} \times 1.50\right) = 0.75$						
	Brick work in wing wall	1	4.10	$\left\{\frac{1.80 + 0.75}{2}\right\}$ =		5.22	
	In return	1	0.80	$\left\{\frac{0.60 + 0.40}{2}\right\}$ 1.50 =		0.60	
	Total					24.82 cum	

(Contd.)

S.No.	Description	No.	L	B	H	Quantity	Remarks
4.	10 cm thick cement concrete coping						
	Over abutment	1	5.00	0.70	—	3.50	
	Over wing wall	1	$\sqrt{\{(3.00-1.50)^2+(4.10)^2\}}$ $= 43.65 \times 0.50 =$			2.18	
	Over return	1	0.80	0.50	—	0.40	
	Total					6.08 sq m	
5.	20 mm thick cement plaster 1 : 3 mix.						
	Abutment Inside face	1	5.00	5.00	—	25.00	
	Deduct portion covered with wing wall	1	$\left\{\frac{1.13+0.56}{2}\right\}$			2.10 = 1.77	
	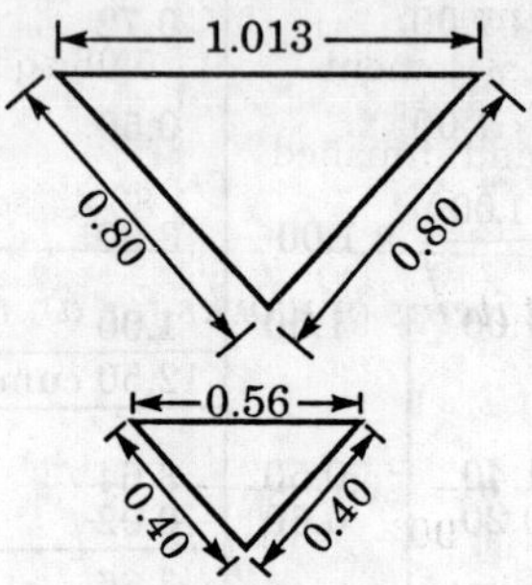 Fig. 10.4 (a)						
	Outside face (0.50 + 0.10 + 1.00 + 0.10 + 1.00 + 0.10 + 1.00 + 0.10 + 1.50) = 5.40 m	1	5.00	5.40	—	27.00	
		2	0.60	1.50	—	1.80	
	End faces	2	0.70	1.00	—	1.40	
		2	0.80	1.00	—	1.60	
		2	0.90	1.00	—	1.80	
		2	1.00	0.50	—	1.00	
	Wing wall. Inside face Central portion (0.60 + 3.00 + 0.50) = 4.10		$1 \times 4.10 \times \frac{\sqrt{\{(3.0)^2+(0.20)^2\}}+\sqrt{\{(1.50)^2+(0.10)^2\}}}{2}$ $= 1 \times 4.10 \times \frac{3.006+1.503}{2}$			= 9.24	
	Triangular portion A	1	$\frac{0.80+0}{2} \times 3.006$			= 1.20	
	Triangular portion B	1	$\frac{0.60+0}{2} \times 1.503$			= 0.45	
	Outside face (3.00 + 0.20 + 0.20)		$3.40 \times \frac{3.006+1.503}{2}$			= 7.66	
	Triangular portion A	1	$\frac{(0.20+0)}{2} \times 3.006$			= 0.30	
	Triangular portion B	1	$\left(\frac{0.10+0}{2}\right) \times 1.503$			= 0.07	
	Return Inside and outside faces		$0.80\sqrt{(0.10)^2+(1.50)^2}$			= 2.40	
	End face	1	$\left(\frac{0.60+0.40}{2}\right) \times 1.50$			= 0.75	
	Total					83.44 sq m	

Table 10.8. Abstract of Quantities

S. No.	*Description of item*	*Quantity*	*Remark*
1.	Earthwork in excavation in foundation trenches including dressing of sides and ramming of bottom, lift upto 1.5 m and lead upto 50 m.	12.50 cum	
2.	Providing and laying cement concrete 1 : 4 : 8 (1 cement : 4 coarse sand : 8 graded stone aggregate 40 mm nominal size)	6.25 cum	
3.	First class brick work in cement mortar 1 : 3 (1 cement : 3 coarse sand)	24.82 cum	
4.	Providing and laying 10 cm thick coping in cement concrete 1 : 2 : 4 (1 cement : 2 coarse sand : 4 graded stone aggregate 20 mm nominal size) including finished with floating coat of neat cement	6.08 sq m	
5.	20 mm thick cement plaster 1 : 3 (1 cement : 3 coarse sand) finished with floating coat of neat cement.	83.44 sq m	

Example 10.5. *Estimate the quantities of different items of works for an abutment with wing wall of culvert.*

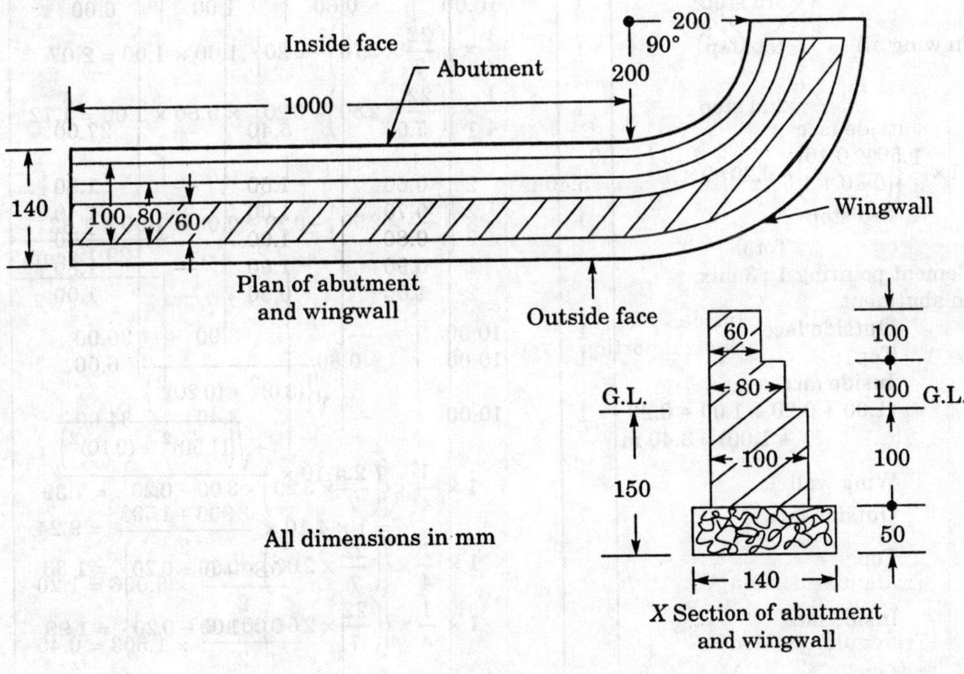

Fig. 10.5

Table 10.9. Details of Measurements

S. No.	*Description of item*	*No.*	*L*	*W*	*H/D*	*Content*	*Remark*
1.	Earthwork in excavation in trenches						
	In abutment	1	10.00	1.40	1.50	21.00	
	In wing wall	1	$\frac{1}{4}\times\left\{\left(\frac{22}{7}\times\frac{(3.40)^2}{4}\right)-\left(\frac{22}{7}\times\frac{(2.00)^2}{4}\right)\right\}$ 1.50 = 2.22				
	Total					23.22 cum	
2.	Cement concrete 1 : 4 : 8 mix.						
	In abutment	1	10.00	1.40	0.50	7.00	
	In wing wall	1	$\frac{1}{4}\times\left\{\left(\frac{22}{7}\times\frac{(3.40)^2}{4}\right)-\left(\frac{22}{7}\times\frac{(2.00)^2}{4}\right)\right\}$ 0.50 = 0.74				
	Total					7.74 cum	
3.	First class brickwork in cement mortar 1 : 3 mix						
	In abutment 1st step	1	10.00	1.00	1.00	10.00	
	2nd step	1	10.00	0.80	1.00	8.00	
	3rd step	1	10.00	0.60	1.00	6.00	
	In wing all 1st step	1	$\frac{1}{4}\times\left\{\left(\frac{22}{7}\times 2.70\right)-0.20\right\}$ 1.00 × 1.00 = 2.07				
	2nd step	1	$\frac{1}{4}\times\left\{\left(\frac{22}{7}\times 2.80\right)-0.20\right\}$ × 0.80 × 1.00 = 1.72				
	$\left[1\times\frac{1}{4}\left\{\left(\frac{22}{7}\times\ldots\right)-0.20\right\}0\times\ldots\right]$ 3rd step	1	$\frac{1}{4}\times\left\{\left(\frac{22}{7}\times 2.90\right)-0.20\right\}$ 0.06 × 1.00 = 1.33				
	Total					29.12 cum	
4.	Cement pointing 1 : 3 mix.						
	In abutment						
	Outside face	1	10.00	—	3.00	30.00	
	Top	1	10.00	0.60	—	6.00	
	Inside face (1.00 + 0.20 + 1.00 + 0.20 + 1.00) = 3.40 m	1	10.00	—	3.40	34.00	
	Wing wall Outside face		$1\times\frac{1}{4}\times\left\{\left(\frac{22}{7}\times 3.20\right)\times 3.00-0.20\right\}$ = 7.39				
	Top		$1\times\frac{1}{4}\times\left\{\left(\frac{22}{7}\times 2.00\right)\times 0.60-0.20\right\}$ = 1.33				
	Inside face		$1\times\frac{1}{4}\times\left\{\left(\frac{22}{7}\times 2.60\right)\times 1.00-0.20\right\}$ = 1.99				
	$\left[1\times\frac{1}{4}\left\{\left(\frac{22}{7}\times\ldots\right)-0.20\right\}\times\ldots\right]$		$1\times\frac{1}{4}\times\left\{\left(\frac{22}{7}\times 2.50\right)\times 0.20-0.20\right\}$ = 0.38				
			$1\times\frac{1}{4}\times\left\{\left(\frac{22}{7}\times 2.40\right)\times 1.00-1.20\right\}$ = 1.83				
			$1\times\frac{1}{4}\times\left\{\left(\frac{22}{7}\times 2.30\right)\times 0.20-0.20\right\}$ = 0.35				
	End face		$1\times\frac{1}{4}\times\left\{\left(\frac{22}{7}\times 2.20\right)\times 1.0-0.20\right\}$ = 1.67				
		1	1.00	—	1.00	1.00	
		1	0.80	—	1.00	0.80	
		1	0.60	—	1.00	0.60	
	Total					87.34 sq m	

Table 10.10. Abstract of Quantities

S. No.	Description of item	Quantity	Remark
1.	Earth work in excavation in foundation trenches including dressing of sides and ramming of bottom, lift upto 1 : 5 m and lead upto 50 m.	23.22 cum	
2.	Providing and laying cement concrete 1 : 4 : 8 (1 cement : 4 coarse sand : 8 graded stone aggregate 40 mm nominal sand)	7.74 cum	
3.	First class brick work in cement mortar 1 : 3 (1 cement : 3 coarse sand)	29.12 cum	
4.	Cement pointing 1 : 3 (1 cement : 3 (coarse sand).	87.34 sq m	

Example 10.6. *Estimate the quantities of different items of works of the culvert with the help of given drawings.*

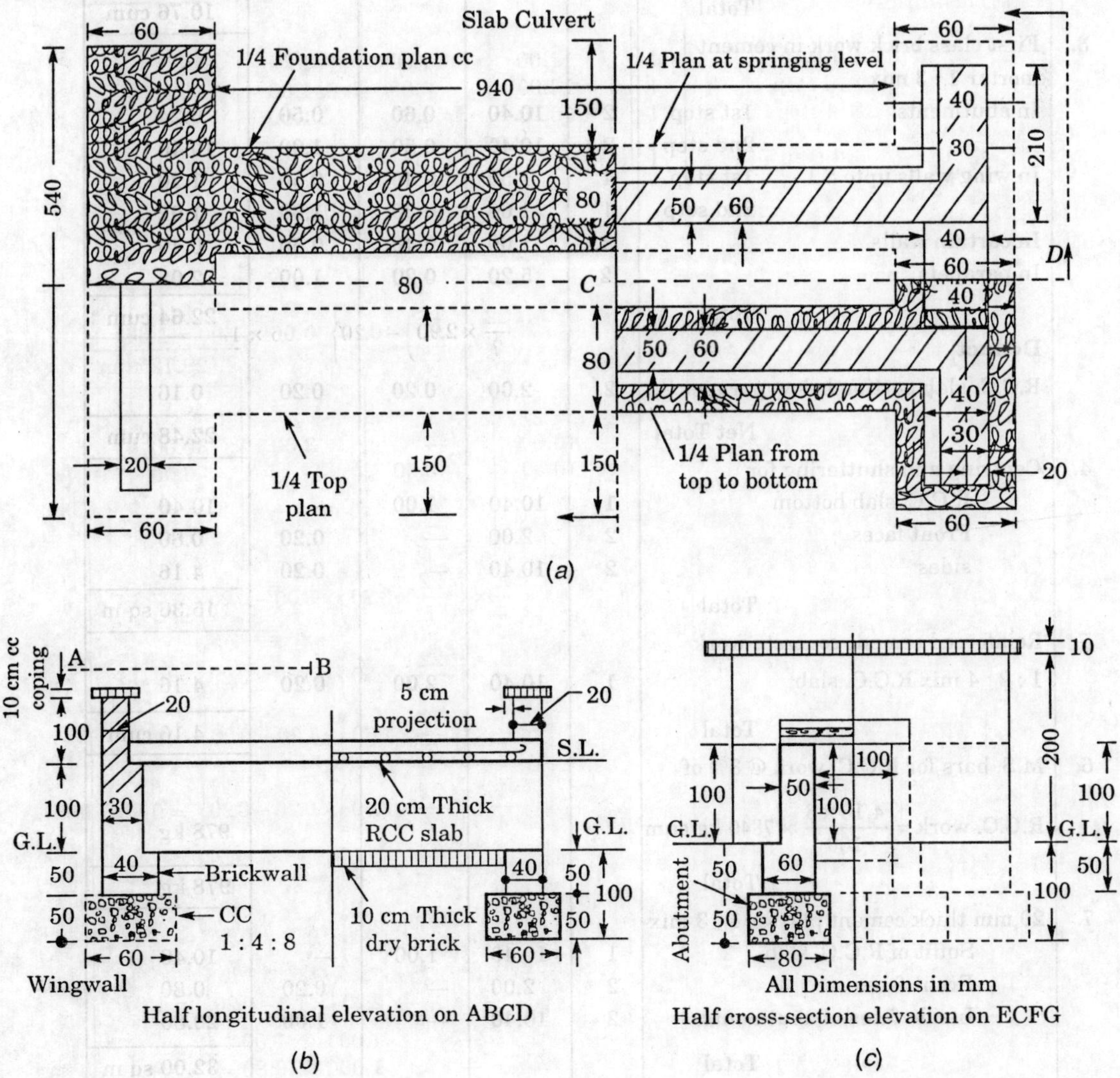

Fig. 10.6

Table 10.11. Details of Measurements

S. No.	Description of item		No.	L	W	H/D	Content	Remark
1.	Earth work in excavation in							
	In abutments		2	10.60	0.80	1.00	16.96	
	In wing walls		4	1.50	0.60	1.00	3.60	
	In curtain walls		2	0.80	0.60	1.00	0.96	
	For dry brick pitching		1	9.40	0.60	0.10	0.564	
		Total					22.084 cum	
2.	Cement concrete 1 : 4 : 8 mix							
	In abutments		2	10.60	0.80	0.50	8.48	
	In wing walls		4	1.50	0.60	0.50	1.80	
	In curtain walls		2	0.80	0.60	0.50	0.48	
		Total					10.76 cum	
3.	First class brick work in cement mortar 1 : 3 mix							
	In abutments	1st step	2	10.40	0.60	0.50	6.24	
		2nd step	2	10.40	0.50	1.00	10.40	
	In wing walls upto S.L.	1st step	4	1.50	0.40	0.50	1.20	
		2nd setp	4	1.60	0.30	1.00	1.92	
	In curtain walls		2	1.00	0.40	0.50	0.40	
	In parapets		2	5.20	0.20	1.00	2.08	
		Total					22.64 cum	
	Deduct							
	R.C.C. slab portion below parapet (–)		2	2.00	0.20	0.20	0.16	
		Net Total					22.48 cum	
4.	Centring and shuttering for							
	R.C.C. slab bottom		1	10.40	1.00	—	10.40	
	Front faces		2	2.00	—	0.20	0.80	
	sides		2	10.40	—	0.20	4.16	
		Total					15.36 sq m	
5.	Reinforced cement concrete work							
	1 : 2 : 4 mix R.C.C. slab		1	10.40	2.00	0.20	4.16	
		Total					4.16 cum	
6.	M.S. bars for R.C.C. work @ 3% of							
	R.C.C. work = $\frac{4.16 \times 3}{100} \times 7840$ kg/cum						978 kg	
		Total					978 kg	
7.	20 mm thick cement plaster 1 : 3 mix							
	Soffit of R.C.C. slab		1	10.40	1.00	—	10.40	
	Front faces		2	2.00	—	0.20	0.80	
	Inside faces of abutments		2	10.40	—	1.00	20.80	
		Total					32.00 sq m	

8.	Cement pointing 1 : 3 mix						
	Curtain wall outsides	2	1.00	—	0.50	1.00	
	Over brick pitching and top of curtain wall	1	10.40	1.00	—	10.40	
	Front faces of wing walls and abutments upto S.L	4	2.10	—	1.50	12.60	
	Parapets inside and outside	2 × 2	5.20	—	1.00	20.80	
	Total					44.80 sq m	
	Deduct						
	R.C.C. slab portions (–)	2 × 2	2.00	—	0.20	1.60	
						43.20 sq m	
	Add						
	Wing walls end faces	4	0.40	—	0.50	0.80	
		4	0.30	—	1.00	1.20	
		4	0.20	—	1.00	0.80	
	Wing walls step sides. 1st step	4	1.50	—	0.50	3.00	
		4	1.50	0.10	—	0.60	
	2nd step	4	1.60	—	1.00	6.40	
		4	1.60	0.10	—	0.64	
	Abutments step sides						
	(10.40–0.40–0.40)	2	9.60	—	0.50	9.60	
	1st step = 9.60 m	2	9.80	0.10	—	0.19	
	2nd step = (10.40–0.30–0.30)						
	= 9.80 m	2	9.60	—	1.00	19.60	
	Total					86.03 sq m	
9.	Dry brick pitching						
	For drain bed	1	9.60	1.00	—	9.60	
	Total					9.60 sq m	
10.	10 cm thick cement concrete coping on the top of parapet	2	5.30	0.30	—	3.18	
	Length = (5.20 + 0.05 + 0.05) = 5.30 m						
	Width = (0.20 + 0.05 + 0.05) = 0.30 m						
	Total					3.18 sq m	

Table 10.12. Abstract of Quantities

S. No.	Description of item	Quantity	Remark
1.	Earthwork in excavation in foundation trenches including dressing of sides and ramming of bottom, lift upto 1.5 m and lead upto 50 m.	22.08 cum	
2.	Providing and laying cement concrete 1 : 4 : 8 (1 cement : 4 coarse sand : 8 graded stone aggregate 40 mm nominal size)	10.76 cum	
3.	First class brick work in cement mortar 1 : 3 (1 cement : 3 coarse sand)	22.48 cum	
4.	Centring and shuttering including strutting proping etc. and removal of form work for R.C.C. work	15.36 sq m	
5.	Reinforced cement concrete work 1 : 2 : 4 (1 cement : 2 coarse sand : 4 graded stone aggregate 20 mm nominal size) in slab etc. excluding the cost of centring shuttering and reinforcement	4.16 cum	
6.	Mild steel reinforcement for R.C.C. work including bending, binding and placing in position complete	978 kg	
7.	20 mm thick cement plaster 1 : 3 (1 cement : 3 coarse sand) finished with floating coat of neat cement	32.00 sq m	
8.	Cement pointing 1 : 3 (1 cement : 3 coarse sand)	86.03 kg	
9.	Dry brick pitching, half brick thick, with second class bricks, including filling of joints with fine sand	9.60 sq m	
10.	Providing and laying 10 cm thick coping in cement concrete 1 : 2 : 4 (1 cement : 2 coarse sand : 4 graded stone aggregate 20 mm nominal size) including finished with floating coat of neat cement	3.18 sq m	

Example 10.7. Estimate the quantities of different items of works of the culvert with the help of given drawings.

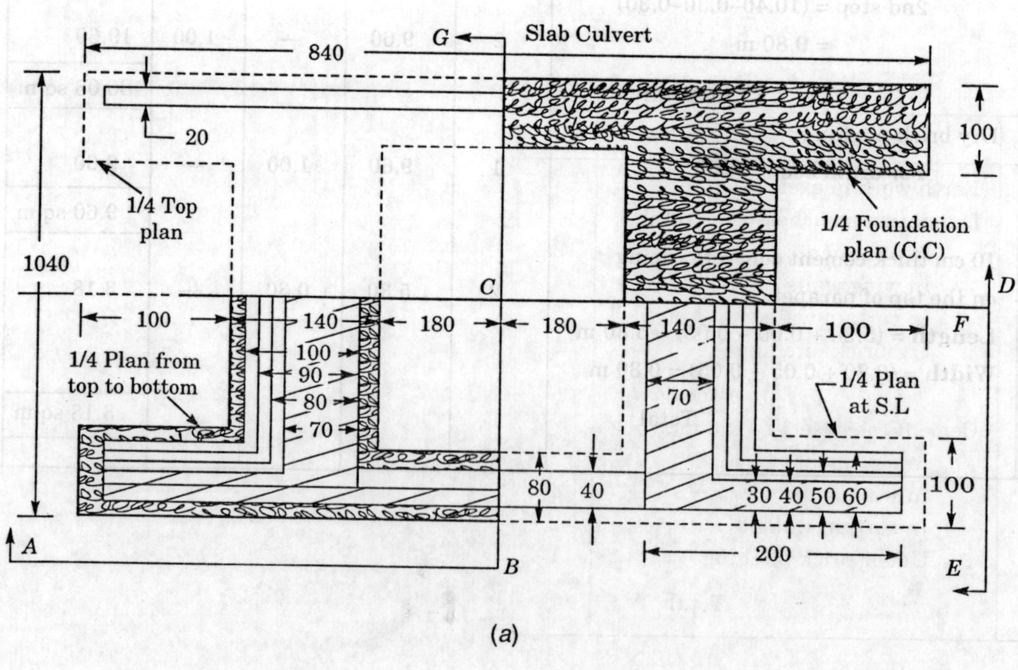

(*a*)

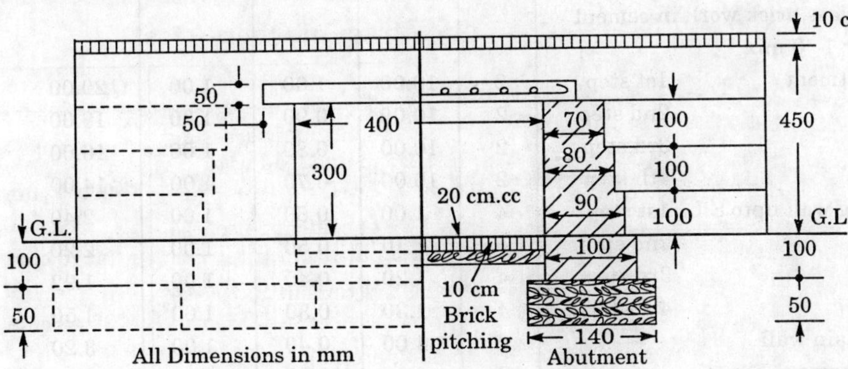

Cross-sectional elevation on ABCD

(b)

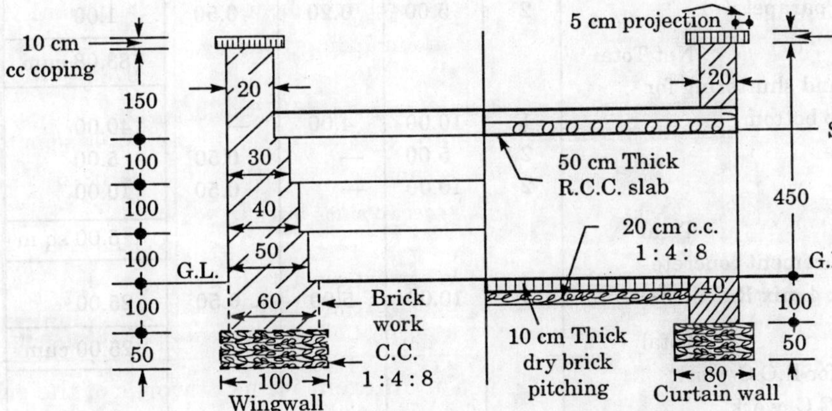

Half longitudinal elevation on EFCG.

(c)

Table 10.13. Details of Measurements

S. No.	Description of item	No.	L	W	H/D	Content	Remark
1.	Earth work in excavation in foundation trenches						
	In abutments	2	10.40	1.40	1.50	43.68	
	In wing walls	4	1.00	1.00	1.50	6.00	
	In curtain walls	2	3.60	0.80	1.50	8.64	
	For brick pitching	1	8.80	3.60	0.30	9.50	
	Total					67.82 cum	
2.	Cement concrete 1 : 4 : 8 mix						
	In abutments	2	10.40	1.40	0.50	14.56	
	In wing walls	4	1.00	1.00	0.50	2.00	
	In curtain walls	2	3.60	0.80	0.50	2.88	
	Under brick pitching	1	9.20	4.00	0.20	7.36	
	Total					26.80 cum	

(Contd.)

3.	First class brick work in cement mortar 1 : 3 mix					
	In abutment 1st step	2	10.00	1.00	1.00	20.00
	2nd step	2	10.00	0.90	1.00	18.00
	3rd step	2	10.00	0.80	1.00	16.00
	4th step	2	10.00	0.70	1.00	14.00
	In wing wall upto S.L. 1st step	4	1.00	0.60	1.00	2.40
	2nd step	4	1.10	0.50	1.00	2.20
	3rd step	4	1.20	0.40	1.00	1.92
	4th step	4	1.30	0.30	1.00	1.56
	In curtain wall	2	4.00	0.40	1.00	3.20
	In parapets	2	8.00	0.20	1.50	4.80
						84.08
	Deduct R.C.C. slab portion below parapet (–)	2	5.00	0.20	0.50	1.00
	Net Total					83.08 cum
4.	Centring and shuttering for R.C.C. slab bottom	1	10.00	4.00	—	40.00
	Front faces	2	5.00	—	0.50	5.00
	Sides	2	10.00	—	0.50	10.00
	Total					5.00 sq m
5.	Reinforced cement concrete work 1 : 2 : 4 mix R.C.C. slab	1	10.00	5.00	0.50	25.00
	Total					25.00 cum
6.	M.S. bars for R.C.C. work @ 3% of R.C.C. work					
	$= \dfrac{25 \times 3}{100} \times 7840$ kg/cum					5880 kg
	Total					5880 kg
7.	20 cm thick cement plaster 1 : 3 mix					
	Soffit of R.C.C. slab	1	10.00	4.00	—	40.00
	Front faces	2	5.00	—	0.50	5.00
	Inside faces of abutments	2	5.00	—	3.00	60.00
	Total					105.00 sq m
8.	Cement pointing 1 : 3 mix					
	Curtain walls outsides	2	4.00	—	1.00	8.00
	Over brick pitching and top of curtain walls	1	10.00	4.00	—	40.00
	Front faces of wing walls and abutments upto S.L.	4	2.00	—	4.00	32.00
	Parapets inside and outside	2 × 2	8.00	—	1.50	48.00
						128.00
	Deduct. R.C.C. slab portions	2 × 2	5.00	—	0.50	10.00
						118.00

S. No.	Particulars	No.	L	B	H	Quantity	Remarks
	Add. Wing walls end faces	4	0.60	—	1.00	2.40	
		4	0.50	—	1.00	2.00	
		4	0.40	—	1.00	1.60	
		4	0.30	—	1.00	1.20	
		4	0.20	—	1.50	1.20	
	Wing walls step sides 1st step	4	1.00	—	1.00	4.00	
		4	1.00	0.10	—	4.00	
	2nd step	4	1.10	—	1.00	4.40	
		4	1.10	0.10	—	0.44	
	3rd step	4	1.20	—	1.00	4.80	
		4	1.20	0.10	—	0.48	
	4th step	4	1.30	—	1.00	5.20	
		4	1.30	0.10	—	0.52	
	Abutments, step sides						
	1st step (10 – 0.60 – 0.60) = 8.80 m	2	8.80	—	1.00	17.60	
		2	9.00	0.10	—	1.80	
	2nd step (10 – 0.50 – 0.50) = 9.00 m	2	9.00	—	1.00	18.00	
		2	9.20	0.10	—	1.84	
	3rd step (10 – 0.40 – 0.40) = 9.20 m	2	9.20	—	1.00	18.40	
		2	9.40	0.10	—	1.88	
	4th step (10 – 0.30 – 0.30) = 9.40 m	2	9.40	—	1.00	18.80	
	Top of abutments	2	9.60	0.20	—	3.84	
	Total					232.50 sq m	
9.	Dry brick pitching For drain bed	1	9.20	4.00	—	36.80	
	Total					36.80 sq m	
10.	10 cm thick cement concrete coping On the top of parapets	2	8.10	0.30	–	4.86	
	Total					4.86 sq m	

Table 10.14. Abstract of Quantities

S. No.	*Description of Item*	*Quantity*	*Remark*
1.	Earth work in excavation in foundation trenches including dressing of sides and ramming of bottom, lift upto 1.5 m and lead upto 50 m.	67.82 cum	
2.	Providing and laying cement concrete 1 : 4 : 8 (1 cement: 4 coarse sand : 8 graded stone aggregate 40 mm nominal size)	26.80 cum	
3.	First class brick work in cement mortar 1 : 3 (1 cement : 3 coarse sand)	83.08 cum	
4.	Centring and shuttering including strutting, proping etc. and removal of form work for R.C.C. work.	55.00 sq m	
5.	Reinforced cement concrete work 1 : 2 : 4 (1 cement : 2 coarse sand : 4 graded stone aggregate 20 mm nominal size) in slab etc. excluding the cost of centring shuttering and reinforcement	25 cum	
6.	Mild steel reinforcement for R.C.C. work, including bending, binding and placing in position complete.	5880 kg	

(Contd.)

7.	20 mm thick cement plaster 1 : 3 (1 cement : 3 coarse sand) finished with floating coat of neat cement.	105.00 sq m	
8.	Cement pointing 1 : 3 (1 cement : 3 coarse sand)	232.50 sq m	
9.	Brick pitching, half brick thick, with second class bricks, including filling of joints with cement mortar 1 : 6 (1 cement : 6 fine sand)	36.80 sq m	
10.	Providing and laying 10 cm thick coping in cement concrete 1 : 2 : 4 (1 cement: 2 coarse sand : 4 graded stone aggregate 20 mm nominal size) including finished with floating coat of neat cement	4.86 sq m	

Example 10.8. *Estimate the quantities of different items of works of the culvert with the help of given drawings.*

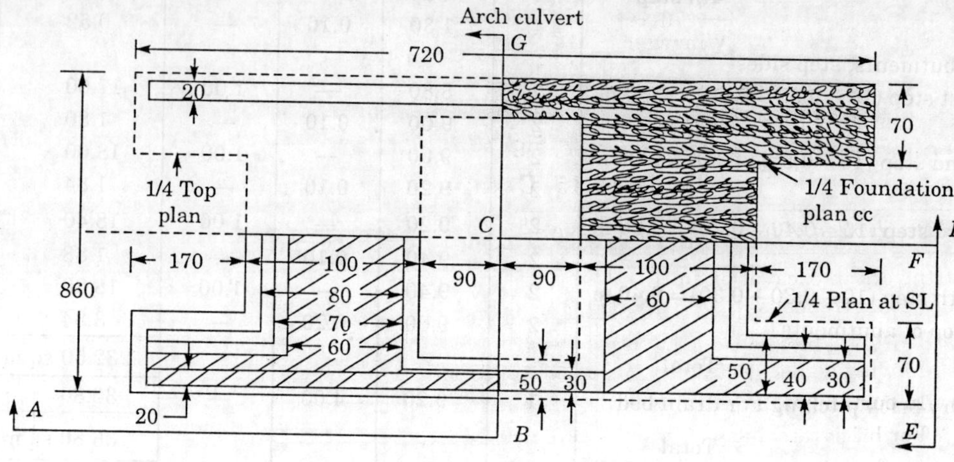

(*a*)

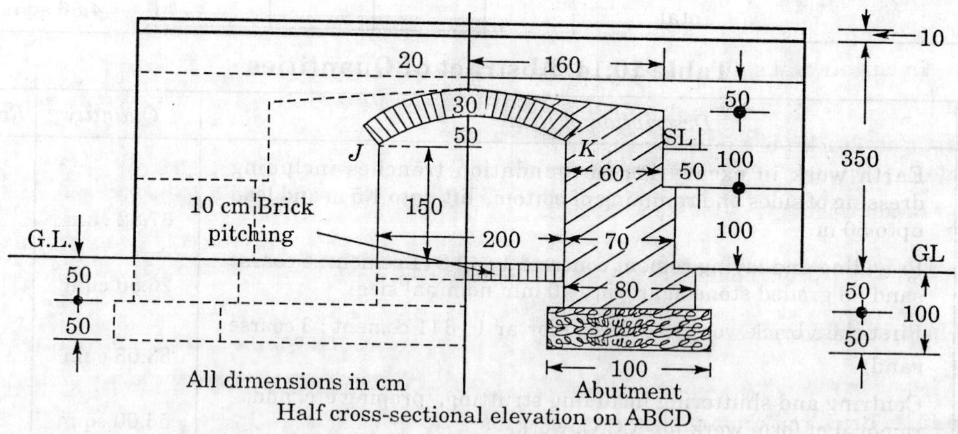

(*b*)

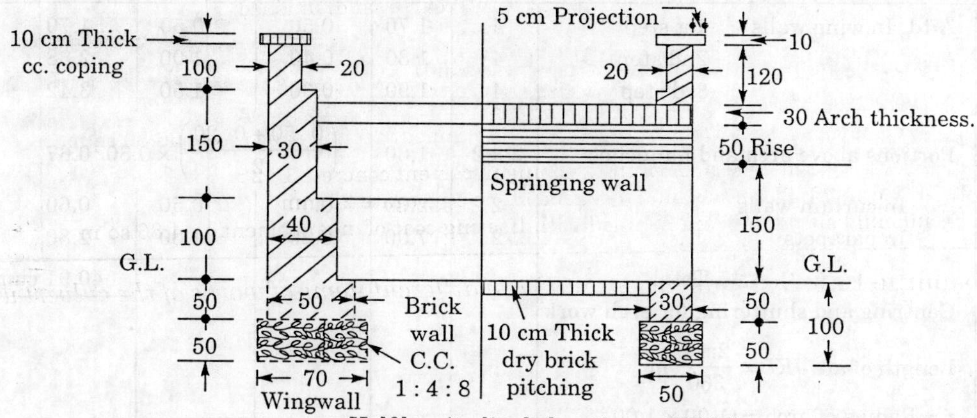

Half longitudinal elevation on EFCG

(*c*)

Fig. 10.8

Table 10.15. Details of Measurements

S. No.	*Description of item*	*No.*	*L*	*W*	*H/D*	*Content*	*Remark*
1.	Earthwork in excavation in foundation trenches						
	In abutments	2	8.60	1.00	1.00	17.20	
	In wing walls	4	1.70	0.70	1.00	4.76	
	In curtain walls	2	1.80	0.60	1.00	1.80	
	For brick pitching	1	7.60	1.80	0.10	1.37	
	Total					25.13 cum	
2.	Cement concrete 1 : 4 : 8 mix						
	In abutments	2	8.60	1.00	0.50	8.60	
	In wing walls	4	1.70	0.70	0.50	2.38	
	In curtain walls	2	1.80	0.50	0.50	0.90	
	Total					11.88 cum	
3.	First class brick work in cement mortar 1 : 3 mix						
	In abutment 1st step	2	8.40	0.80	0.50	6.72	
	2nd step	2	8.40	0.70	1.00	11.76	
	3rd step upto S.L.	2	8.40	0.60	0.50	5.04	
	In haunches above S.L. and crown	2	8.40	$\left(\frac{0.50+0.80}{2}\right)$	1.60 =	17.47	
						40.99 cum	
	Deduct. Brick work in arch as per item No. 5 (–)	–	–	–	(–)	6.55	
	Volume of segment *JKL*						
	Area = $\left(\frac{2}{3}\times \text{Span} \times \text{Rise}\right)$ (–)	1	$8.40 \times \frac{2}{3} \times 2.00 \times 0.50$		(–)	5.60	
						28.84 cum	

(*Contd.*)

	Add. In wing walls 1st step	4	1.70	0.50	0.50	1.70	
	2nd step	4	1.80	0.40	1.00	2.88	
	3rd step	4	1.90	0.30	1.50	3.42	
	Portions above arch and haunches	2 × 2	1.60	$\left(\frac{0.50+0.20}{2}\right)$ × 0.80		0.67	
	In curtain walls	2	2.00	0.30	0.50	0.60	
	In parapets	2	7.00	0.20	1.00	2.80	
	Total					40.91 cum	
4.	Centring and shuttering for arch work						
	Length of arc $JKL = \frac{2\pi r\theta}{360}$ m						
	r = Radius of arch = (1.00 × 1.00						
	= (2r – 0.50) × 0.50						
	or r = 1.25 m						
	θ = number of degree in the arch						
	$\tan\frac{\theta}{2} = \frac{1.00}{(1.25-0.50)} = \frac{1.00}{0.75} = 53.13°$						
	0 = 53.13° × 2 = 106.26°						
	or Arc length $JKL = 2 \times \frac{22}{7} \times 1.25$						
	$\times \frac{106.26}{360} = 2.32$ m						
	Centring	1	8.40	2.32	–	19.49	
	Total					19.49 sq m	
5.	First class brick work in cement mortar 1 : 2 mix						
	In arch						
	Mean length of arc of arch						
	$= \frac{2\pi r\theta}{360} = 2 \times \frac{22}{7} \times \left(1.25 + \frac{0.30}{2}\right)$						
	$\times \frac{106.26}{360} = 2.60$ m						
	Arch work	1	8.40	2.60	0.30	6.552	
	Total					6.552 cum	
6.	20 cm thick cement plaster 1 : 3 mix						
	Soffit of arch	1	8.40	2.32	–	19.49	
	Inside faces of abutments	2	8.40	–	1.50	25.20	
	Top of abutments and hanches	2	8.40	$\sqrt{(1.60)^2 + (0.30)^2}$		= 27.38	
	Total					72.07 sq m	
7.	Cement pointing 1 : 3 mix						
	Curtain wall outside faces	2	1.00	–	0.50	1.00	
	Over brick pitching and top of curtain walls	1	8.40	1.00	–	8.40	
	Front faces of wing walls and abutments upto S.L.	4	2.50	–	2.00	20.00	

S. No.	Description	No.	L	B	H	Quantity	Remarks
	Parapets inside and outside faces above S.L.	2 × 2	7.00	–	2.00	56.00	
	Parapets inside faces	2	7.00	0.10	–	1.40	
	(–)						
	(–)					86.80 sq m	
	Deduct. Segmental portion outside	2	$2/3 \times 2.00 \times 0.50$			1.33	
	Inside arch portion etc. *JKL*	2 × 2	1.60	$\left(\dfrac{0.80+0.50}{2}\right)$		4.16	
						81.31	
	Add. Wing wall end faces	4	0.50	–	0.50	1.00	
		4	0.40	–	1.00	1.60	
		4	0.30	–	1.50	1.80	
		4	0.20	–	1.00	0.80	
	Wing walls steps sides 1st step	4	1.70	–	0.50	3.40	
		4	1.70	0.10	–	0.68	
	2nd step	4	1.80	–	1.00	7.20	
		4	1.80	0.10	–	0.72	
	3rd step	4	1.90	–	0.50	3.80	
	Abutments step sides 1st step	2	7.40	–	0.50	7.40	
		2	7.60	0.10	–	1.52	
	2nd step	2	7.60	–	1.00	15.20	
		2	7.80	1.10	–	1.56	
	3rd step	2	7.80	–	1.00	15.60	
	Total					143.59 sq m	
8.	Dry brick pitching for drain bed	1	7.80	2.00	–	15.60	
	Total					15.60 sq m	
9.	10 cm thick cement concrete coping On the top of parapets	2	7.10	0.30	–	4.26	
	Total					4.26 sq m	

Table 10.16. Abstract of Quantities

S. No.	*Description of Item*	*Quantity*	*Remark*
1.	Earth work in excavation in the foundation trenches including dressing of sides and ramming of bottom, lift upto 1.5 m and lead upto 50 m.	25.13 cum	
2.	Providing and laying cement concrete 1 : 4 : 8 (1 cement: 4 coarse sand : 8 graded stone aggregate 40 mm nominal size)	11.88 cum	
3.	First class brick work in cement mortar 1 : 3 (1 cement : 3 coarse sand)	40.91 cum	
4.	Centring and shuttering including strutting, proping etc. and removal of form work for brick arch.		
5.	First class brick work in cement mortar 1 : 2 (1 cement : 2 coarse sand) in arches.	19.49 sq m	
6.	20 mm thick cement plaster 1 : 3 (1 cement : 3 coarse sand) finished with floating coat of neat cement.	72.07 sq m	
7.	Cement pointing 1 : 3 (1 cement : 3 coarse sand)	143.59 sq m	
8.	Dry brick pitching, half brick thick, with second class bricks, including filling of joints with fine sand.	15.60 sq m	
9.	Providing and laying 10 cm. thick coping in cement concrete 1 : 2 : 4 (1 cement: 2 coarse . sand : 4 graded stone aggregate 20 mm nominal size) including finished with floating coat of neat cement.	4.26 sq m	

Example 10.9. *Estimate the quantities different items of work of the culvert with the help of given drawings.*

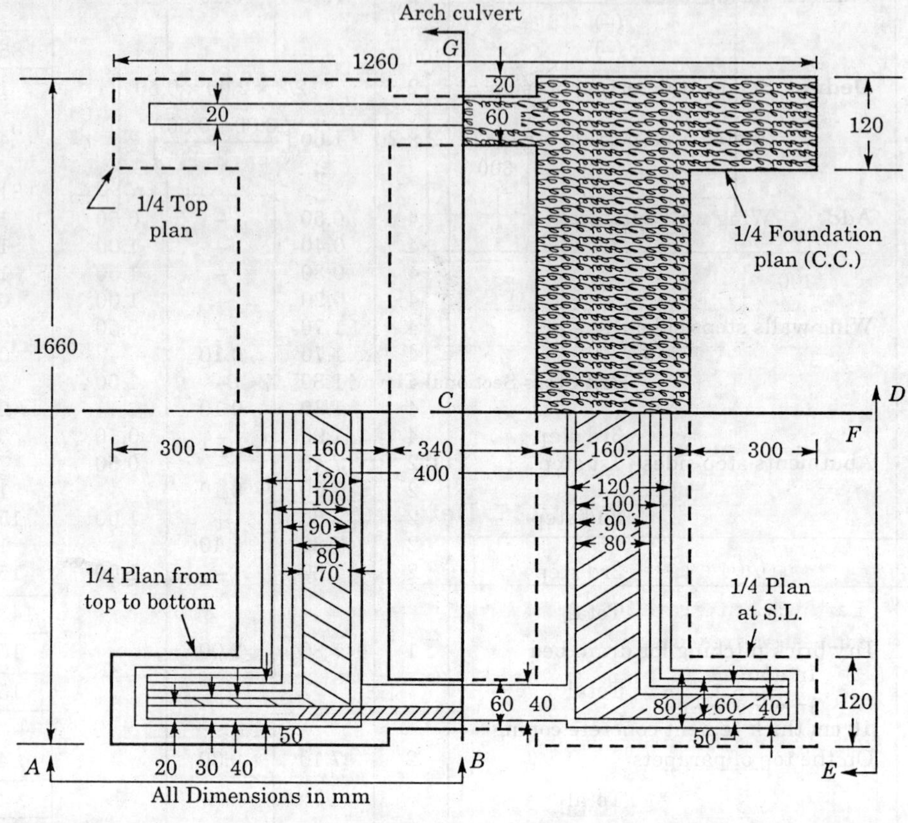

(a)

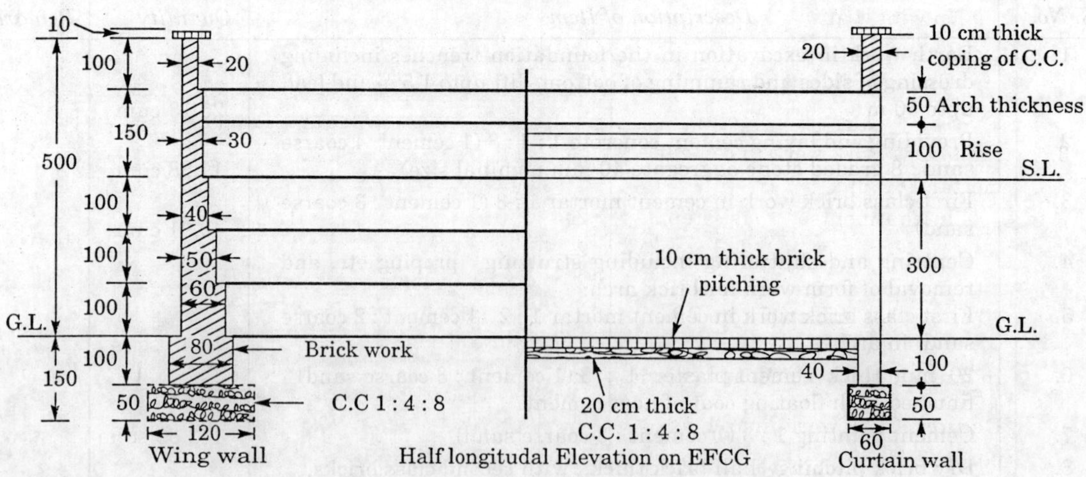

(b)

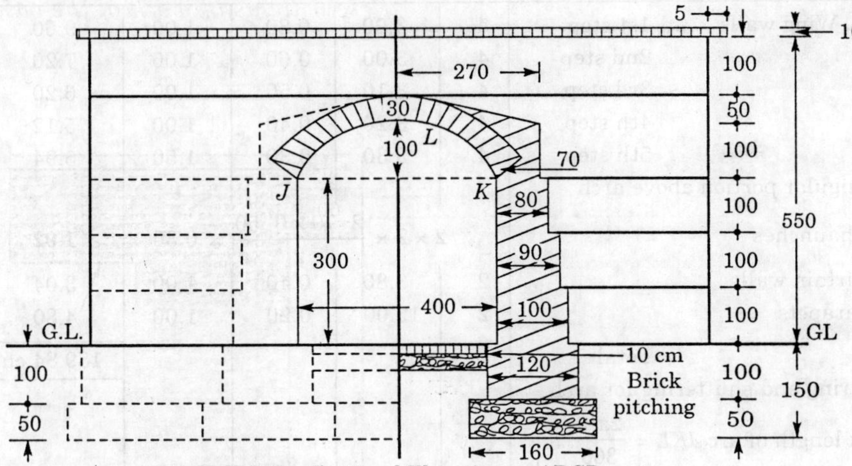

Half Cross-Sectional Elevation on ABCD

(*c*)

Fig. 10.9

Table 10.17. Details of Measurements

S. No.	*Description of Item*	*No.*	*L*	*W*	*H/D*	*Content*	*Remark*
1.	Earthwork in excavation in foundation trenches						
	In abutments	2	16.60	1.60	1.50	79.68	
	In wing walls	4	3.00	1.20	1.50	21.60	
	In curtain walls	2	3.40	0.60	1.50	6.12	
	For brick pitching	1	15.00	3.40	0.30	15.30	
	Total					122.70 cum	
2.	Cement concrete 1 : 4 : 8 mix						
	In abutments	2	16.60	1.60	0.50	26.56	
	In wing walls	4	3.00	1.20	0.50	7.20	
	In curtain walls	2	3.40	0.60	0.50	2.04	
	Under brick pitching	1	15.20	3.80	0.20	11.55	
	Total					47.35 cum	
3.	First class brick work in cement mortar 1 : 3 mix						
	In abutments 1st step	2	16.20	1.20	1.00	38.88	
	2nd step	2	16.00	1.00	1.00	32.00	
	3rd step	2	16.00	0.90	1.00	28.80	
	4th step upto S.L.	2	16.00	0.80	1.00	25.60	
	In haunches above S.L. and crown	2	16.00 $\left(\dfrac{1.00+1.50}{2}\right) \times 2.70 = 108.00$				233.28	
	Deduct. Brick work in arch as per item No. 5						
	volume of segment *JKL* (–)	—	—	—	(–)	41.60	
	Area = (2/3 × Span × Rise) (–)	16.00 × 2/3 × 4.00 × 1.00 =				42.66	
	Total					149.02 cum	

S. No.	Description	No.	L	B	H	Quantity	Remarks
	Add. Wing walls 1st step	4	3.00	0.80	1.00	9.60	
	2nd step	4	3.00	0.60	1.00	7.20	
	3rd step	4	3.10	0.50	1.00	6.20	
	4th step	4	3.20	0.40	1.00	5.12	
	5th step	4	3.30	0.30	1.50	5.94	
	Triangular portion above arch and haunches		$2 \times 2 \times \frac{2.70 \times 0.50}{2} \times 0.30$			1.92	
	In curtain walls	2	3.80	0.40	1.00	3.04	
	In parapets	2	12.00	0.20	1.00	4.80	
	Total					189.84 cum	
4.	Centring and shuttering for arch work length of arc $JKL = \frac{2\pi r\theta}{360}$ m r = radius of earth = [(2.00 × 2.00) = (2r – 1.00) × 1.00] m = 2.5 m $\tan\frac{\theta}{2} \frac{2.00}{(2.5-1.00)} = \frac{2.00}{1.50} = 53.13°$ $\theta = 53.13° \times 2 = 106.26°$ Arc length $= 2 \times \frac{22}{7} \times 2.5 \times \frac{106.26}{360}$ = 4.64 m						
	Centring	1	16.00	4.64	–	74.24	
	Total					74.24 sq m	
5.	First class brick work in cement mortar 1 : 2 mix In arch Mean length of arc of arch $= \frac{2r\pi\theta}{360} = 2 \times \frac{22}{7}\left(2.50 + \frac{0.50}{2}\right)$ $\times \frac{106.26}{360}$ = 5.20 m	1	16.00	5.20	0.50	41.60	
	Total					41.60 cum	
6.	20 cm thick cement plaster 1 : 3 mix						
	Soffit of arch	1	16.00	4.64	–	74.24	
	Inside faces of abutments	2	16.00		3.00	96.00	
	Top of abutments and haunches	2	$16.00\sqrt{(2.70)^2 + (0.50)^2}$ =			87.87	
	Total					258.11 sq m	
7.	Cement pointing 1 : 3 mix						
	Curtain wall outside faces	2	3.80	–	1.00	7.60	
	Over brick pitching and top of curtain walls	1	16.00	4.00	–	64.00	
	Front faces of wing walls and abutments upto G.L. (12.60–3.80						

	– 0.20–0.20) = 8.40/2						
	= 4.20 + 0.10 = 4.30 m	4	4.30	—	1.00	17.20	
	Above G.L. and upto S.L.	4	4.00	—	3.00	48.00	
	Above S.L. and upto the top of parapet	2	12.00	—	2.50	60.00	
	Inside parapet face	2	12.00	—	1.00	24.00	
						220.80	
	Deduct. Segmental portion *JKL* (–)	2 ×	2/3 × 4.00	× 1.00		5.33	
						215.47 sq m	
	Add. Wing wall end faces	4	0.80	—	1.00	3.20	
		4	0.60	—	1.00	2.40	
		4	0.50	—	1.00	2.00	
		4	0.40	—	1.00	1.60	
		4	0.30	—	1.50	1.80	
		4	0.20	—	1.00	0.80	
	Wing walls step sides 1st step	4	3.00	—	1.00	12.00	
		4	3.00	0.10	—	2.40	
	2nd step	4	3.00	—	1.00	12.00	
		4	3.00	0.10	—	1.20	
	3rd step	4	3.10	—	1.00	12.40	
		4	3.10	0.10	—	1.24	
	4th step	4	3.20	—	1.00	12.80	
		4	3.20	0.10	—	1.28	
	5th step	4	3.30	—	1.50	19.80	
		4	3.30	0.10	—	1.32	
	Triangular portions	4	$= \frac{2.70 \times 0.50}{2}$		—	2.70	
		4	2.70	0.10	—	1.08	
	Abutments step sides 1st step	2	14.60	—	1.00	29.20	
		2	14.80	0.10	—	2.96	
	2nd step	2	14.80	—	1.00	29.60	
		2	15.00	0.10	—	3.00	
	3rd step	2	15.00	—	1.00	30.00	
		2	15.20	0.10	—	3.04	
	4th step	2	15.20	—	1.00	30.40	
		2	15.40	0.10	—	3.08	
	5th step	2	15.40	—	1.00	30.80	
	Total					469.57 sq m	
8.	Brick pitching for drain bed	1	15.20	3.80	—	57.76	
	Total					57.76 sq m	
9.	10 cm thick cement concrete coping						
	On the top of parapets	2	12.10	0.30	—	7.26	
	Total					7.26 sq m	

Table 10.18. Abstract of Quantities

S. No.	Description of Item	Quantity	Remark
1.	Earthwork in excavation in foundation trenches including dressing of sides and ramming of bottom, lift upto 1.5 m and lead upto 50 m.	122.70 cum	
2.	Providing and laying cement concrete 1 : 4 : 8 (1 cement: 4 coarse sand : 8 graded stone aggregate 40 mm nominal size)	47.35 cum	
3.	First class brick work in cement mortar 1 : 3 (1 cement : 3 coarse sand)	189.84 cum	
4.	Centring and shuttering including strutting, proping etc. and removal of form work for brick arch.	74.24 sq m	
5.	First class brick work in cement mortar 1 : 2 (1 cement : 2 coarse sand) in arches.	41.60 cum	
6.	20 mm thick cement plaster 1 : 3 (1 cement : 3 coarse sand) finished with floating coat of neat cement.	258.11 sq m	
7.	Cement pointing 1 : 3 (1 cement : 3 coarse sand)	469.57 sq m	
8.	Brick pitching, half brick thick, with second class bricks, including filling of joints with cement mortar 1 : 6 (1 cement: 6 fine sand)	57.76 sq m	
9.	Providing and laying 10 cm thick coping in cement concrete 1 : 2 : 4 (1 cement: 2 coarse sand : 4 graded stone aggregate 20 mm nominal size) including finished with floating coat of neat cement.	7.26 sq m	

Example 10.10. *Estimate the quantities of different items of works of the culvert with the help of given drawings*

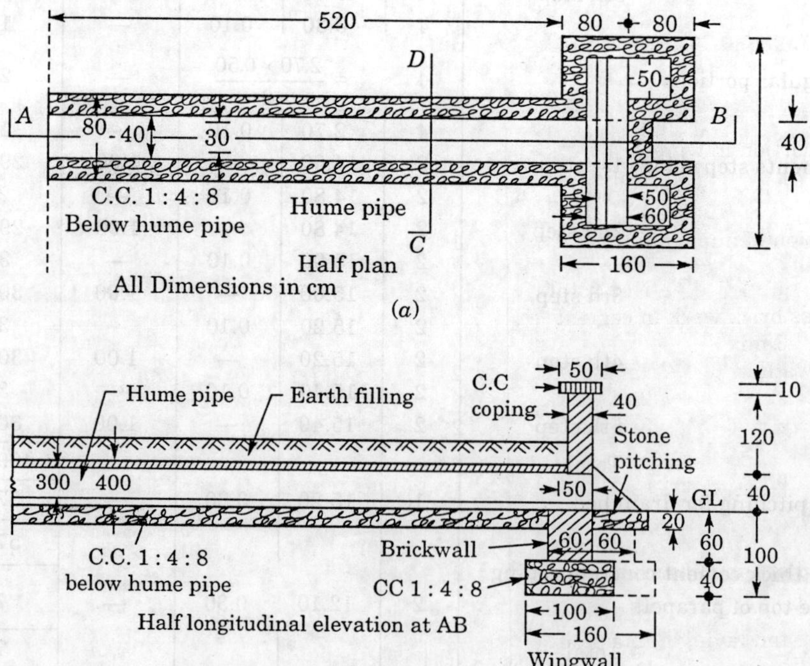

(a)

(b)

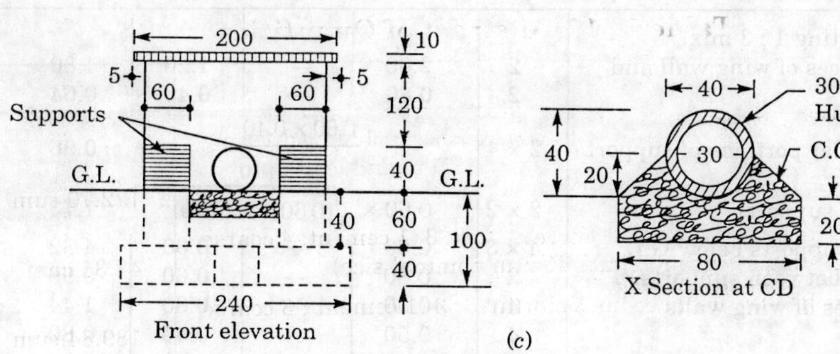

(c)

Fig. 10.10

Table 10.19. Details of Measurements

S. No.	Description of Item	No.	L	W	H/D	Content	Remark
1.	Earthwork in excavation in foundation trenches						
	In wing walls	2	2.40	1.60	1.00	7.68	
	For hume pipe concrete	1	10.40	0.80	0.20	1.66	
	Deduct.						
	Square portion in wing					9.34	
	walls (–)	2	0.40	0.40	1.00	0.32	
	Net Total					9.02 cum	
2.	Cement concrete 1 : 4 : 8 mix						
	In wing walls	2	2.40	1.60	0.40	3.07	
	Under hume pipe	1	10.80	0.80	0.20	1.72	
	(10.40 + 0.20 + 0.20) = 10.80	1	10.80	$\left(\frac{0.80 + 0.40}{2}\right)$	0.20 = 1.29		
						5.08	
	Deduct.						
	Square portion in wing						
	walls (–)	2	0.40	0.40	0.40	0.128	
	Half section of hume pipe (–)	1	$\frac{22}{7} \times \frac{(0.40)^2}{8} \times 10.80$			0.678	
	Net Total					4.37 cum	
3.	First class brick work in cement mortar 1 : 3 mix						
	In wing walls 1st step	2	2.00	0.60	0.60	1.44	
	2nd step	2	2.00	0.50	0.40	0.80	
	3rd step	2	2.00	0.40	1.20	1.92	
	In supports	2 × 2	0.60	0.60	0.60	0.86	
		2 × 2	$0.60 \times \frac{0.60 \times 0.40}{2}$			0.23	
	Deduct. Portion of hume pipe (–)	2	0.50	$\frac{22}{7} \times \frac{(0.40)^2}{4}$		0.126	
	Net Total					5.12 cum	
4.	Providing and laying hume pipe 300 mm dia	1	12.00	—	—	12.00	
	Total					12 metre	

(Contd.)

5.	Cement pointing 1 : 3 mix						
	Front faces of wing wall and	2	2.00	—	1.20	4.80	
	parapet	2	0.80	—	0.40	0.64	
	Triangular portions of support	2 × 4		$\frac{0.60 \times 0.40}{2}$	—	0.96	
	Faces of supports	2 × 2	0.60 ×	$\sqrt{(0.60)^2 + (0.40)^2}$		1.73	
	Side of supports below G.L.	4 × 3	0.60	—	0.60	4.32	
	Portion between supports	2	0.80	—	0.60	0.96	
	End faces of wing walls	4	0.60	—	0.60	1.44	
		4	0.50	—	0.40	0.80	
		4	0.40	—	1.20	1.92	
	Inside faces of wing walls and	2	2.00	—	1.20	4.80	
	parapet	2	2.00	0.10	—	0.40	
		2	2.00		0.40	1.60	
		2	2.00	0.10	—	0.40	
		2	2.00	—	0.60	2.40	
						27.17	
	Deduct. Openings of hume pipe (–)	2 × 2		$\frac{22}{7} \times \frac{(0.40)^2}{8}$		– 0.50	
	Net Total					26.67 sq m	
6.	Dry stone pitching						
	Between supports	2	0.80	0.80	—	1.28	
	Total					1.28 sq m	
7.	10 cm thick cement concrete coping						
	On the top of parapets	2	2.10	0.50	—	2.10	
	Total					2.10 sq m	

Table 10.20. Abstract of Quantities

S. No.	*Description of Item*	*Quantity*	*Remark*
1.	Earthwork in excavation in foundation trenches including dressing of sides and ramming of bottom, lift upto 1.5 m and lead upto 50 m.	9.02 cum	
2.	Providing and laying cement concrete 1 : 4 : 8 (1 cement : 4 coarse sand : 8 graded stone aggregate 40 mm nominal size)	4.37 cum	
3.	First class brick work in cement mortar 1 : 3 (1 cement : 3 coarse sand)	5.12 cum	
4.	Providing and laying hume pipe, jointed with stiff mixture of cement mortar in the proportion of 1 : 2 (1 cement: 2 fine sand) including testing of joints complete 300 mm dia C.C. pipe.	12 metre	
5.	Cement pointing 1 : 3 (1 cement : 3 coarse sand)	26.67 sq m	
6.	Dry stone pitching, 20 cm. thick including supplying of stone and preparing surface complete.	1.28 sq m	
7.	Providing and laying 10 cm thick coping in cement concrete 1 : 2 : 4 (1 cement : 2 coarse sand : 4 graded stone aggregate 20 mm nominal size) including finished with floating coat neat cement.	2.10 sq m	

EXERCISE 10.1

Estimate the quantities of—

1. Earthwork (2) Cement concrete work (3) First class brick work (4) Centring and shuttering work (5) R.C.C. work (6) M.S. bars for R.C.C. work (7) Cement plaster work (8) Cement pointing (9) Dry brick pitching and (10) C.C. coping.

Of the slab culvert with the help of Fig. 10.11.

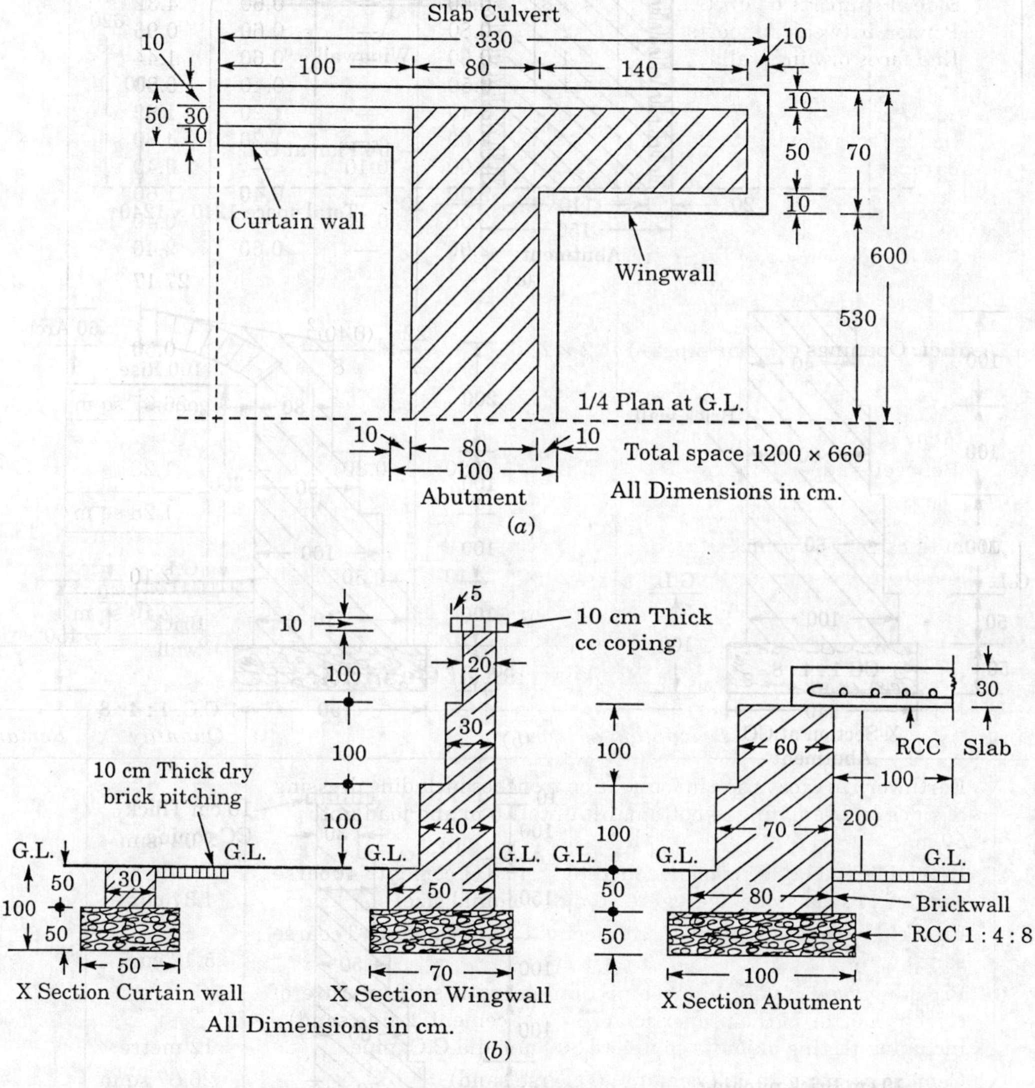

Fig. 10.11

EXERCISE 10.2

Estimate the quantities of—

1. Earthwork, (2) Cement concrete work, (3) First class brick work, (4) Centring and shuttering work, (5) Brick work in arch, (6) Cement plaster, (7) Cement pointing, (8) Brick pitching and (9) C.C. coping.

Of the arch culvert with the help of Fig. 10.12.

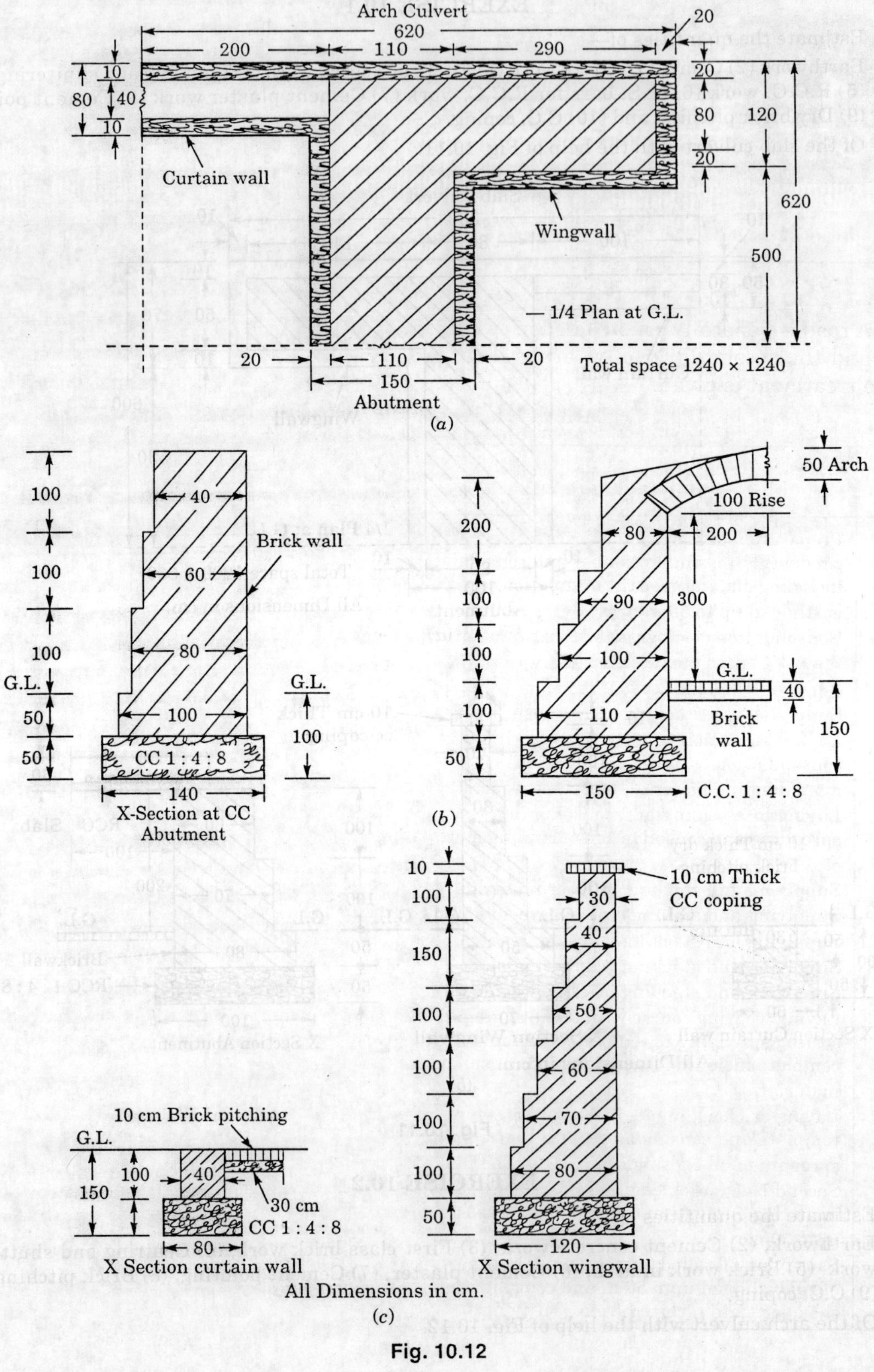

Arch Culvert
620
200
110
290
20
10
80
40
10
20
80
120
20
620
500
Curtain wall
Wingwall
— 1/4 Plan at G.L.
20
110
20
150
Abutment
Total space 1240 × 1240
(a)
100
40
Brick wall
100
60
100
80
G.L.
50
100
50
CC 1 : 4 : 8
140
G.L.
100
X-Section at CC Abutment
200
100
100
100
50
80
90
100
110
150
50 Arch
100 Rise
200
300
G.L.
40
Brick wall
150
C.C. 1 : 4 : 8
(b)
10 cm Brick pitching
G.L.
100
40
150
30 cm
CC 1 : 4 : 8
80
X Section curtain wall
10
100
150
100
100
100
100
50
10 cm Thick CC coping
30
40
50
60
70
80
120
X Section wingwall
All Dimensions in cm.
(c)

Fig. 10.12

11

Roads

A road is generally constructed in two layers. One layer of soling coat about 20 to 30 cm thick, and the second layer of wearing coat about 15 to 20 cm thick over the wearing coat surface treatment is given.

Table 11.1. Road Work Items

S. No.	*Description*	*Unit*	*Rate*	*Remark*
1.	Preparation of subgrade by excavating earth to an average of 30 cm depth, dressing to camber and consolidating with road roller, including making good the undulations etc. and disposal of surplus earth load up to 50 metres.	100 sq m		
2.	Consolidation of subgrade with road roller including making good the undulation etc. with earth and resoling the subgrade.	100 sq m		
3.	Supplying and stacking of stone for soling at site.	cum		
4.	Supplying and stacking of overburnt bricks for soling at site.	1000 No.		
5.	Laying stone soling including packing with smaller stones and consolidation with road roller including spreading and consolidation of binding material, moorum or earth etc.	cum		
6.	Laying brick soling and consolidation with road roller including spreading and consolidation of binding material moorum or earth etc.	cum		
7.	Supplying and stacking of moorum at site.	cum		
8.	Supplying and staking stone aggregate 50 mm nominal size.	cum		
9.	Supplying and stacking stone aggregate 63 mm nominal size.	cum		
10.	Supplying and stacking red bajri at site.	cum		
11.	Supplying and stacking brick aggregate 50 mm nominal size.	cum		
12.	Laying wearing course with stone aggregate including screening, sorting spreading to template and consolidation with road roller, complete including spreading and consolidation of binding material.	cum		
13.	Laying brick aggregate including screening, sorting, spreading to template and consolidation with road roller complete including spreading and consolidation of binding material.	cum		
14.	Second class brick edging laid lengthwise with half brick depth, including excavation, refilling and disposal of surplus earth lead upto 50 m.	metre		
15.	Sacrifying metalled (water bound) road surface including disposal of rubbish lead upto 50 m and consolidation with road roller of the aggregate received from sacrifying.	100 sq m		

(Contd.)

16.	Painting one coat with paving bitumen S-90 of approved quality using 2 kg of bitumen per sq m with 1.50 cum of stone aggregate 10 mm nominal size per 100 sq m of road surface complete.	sq m		
17.	Painting two coats with paving bitumen S-90 of approved quality using 2 kg of bitumen per sq m with 1.50 cum of stone aggregate 10 mm nominal size per 100 sq m of road surface, for first coat and 1 kg of bitumen per sq m with 0.8 cum of stone aggregate 6 mm nominal size per 100 sq m of road surface for second coat complete.	sq m		
18.	25 mm premix carpet surfacing with 3 cum of stone aggregate 10 mm nominal size per 100 sq m and 100 kg of hot bitumen of approved quality per cum of stone aggregate including a tack coat with hot bitumen at 1 kg per sq m of road surface complete.	sq m		
19.	Providing seal coat of premixed sand with hot bitumen using 130 kg of bitumen per cum of sand and 0.80 cum coarse sand per 100 sq m of road surface complete.	sq m		
20.	Cement concrete 1 : 2 : 4 (1 cement : 2 coarse sand : 4 graded stone aggregate 40 mm nominal size) in pavements, roads, taxi, tracks and run ways, laid to required slope and camber including consolidation, finishing and tamping complete.	cum		

Example 11.1. *Prepare the estimate for the construction of a macadam road for one kilometre length having the following specifications :*

Formation width of the road = *12.00 metre*

Average height of bank = *0.60 metre*

Side slopes 2 : 1 (H : V)

Metalled width of road = *3.8 metre*

Soling coat of hard stone 63 mm size, 20 cm thick, sides shall be provided with brick edging, wearing coats in two layers, each layer 10 cm thick of stone aggregate 50 mm nominal size.

Solution.

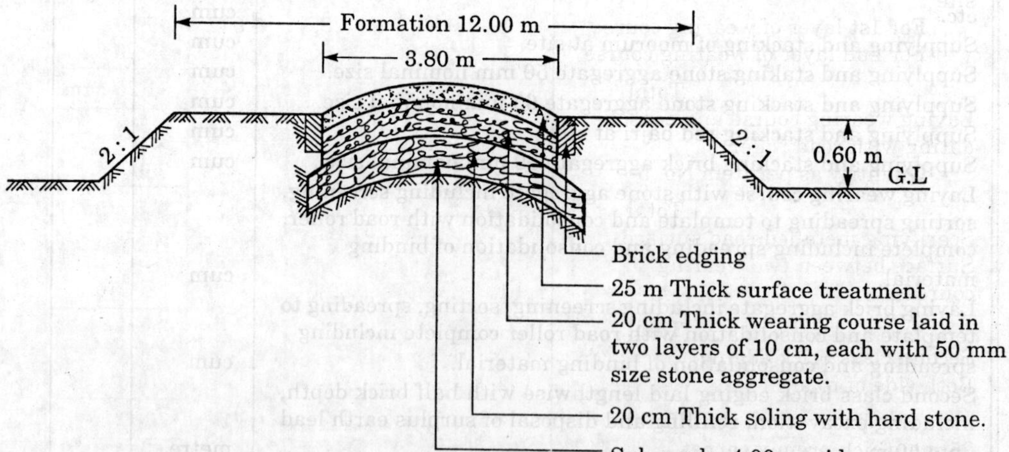

Cross-section of road structure

Fig. 11.1

Table 11.2. Details of Measurements

S. No.	Description	No.	L	W	H/D	Content	Remark
1.	Earthwork in filling $= (Bd + Sd^2) \times$ Length $= [12 \times 0.60 + 2 \times (0.60)^2] \times 1000$ = 7920 cum						
	Total	—	—	—	—	7920 cum	
2.	Preparation of sub-grade For road 1 km length and 4.00 metre wide	1	1000	4.00		4000	
	Total					4000 sq m	
3.	Supplying and stacking of stone for soling For soling coat	1	1000	4.00	0.20	800	
	Total					800 cum	
4.	Laying stone soling and consolidating with road roller quantity as per Item No. 3	—	—	—	—	800	
	Total					800 cum	
5.	Supplying and stacking stone aggregate 50 mm nominal size or wearing coarse in two layers total 20 cm thick	1	1000	3.80	0.20	760	
	Total					760 cum	
6.	Supplying and stacking red bajri at site For 1st layer of wearing course	1	1000	3.80	0.006	22.80	
	For 2nd layer of wearing course	1	1000	3.80	0.006	22.80	
	Total					45.60 cum	
7.	Supplying and stacking moorum at site For 1st layer of wearing course	1	1000	3.80	0.012	45.60	
	For 2nd layer of wearing course	1	1000	3.80	0.012	45.60	
	Total					91.20 cum	
8.	Laying wearing course and consolidating with road roller Quantity as per item No. 5	—	—	—	—	760	
	Total					760 cum	
9.	Scarifying metalled road surface Surface between two wearing courses	1	1000	3.80	—	3800	
	Total					3800 sq m	
10.	Second class brick edging Both side of road	2	1000	—		2000	
	Total					2000 sq m	
11.	25 mm thick premix carpet surfacing Over road surface	1	1000	3.80	—	3800	
	Total					3800 sq m	

Table 11.3. Abstract of Quantities

S. No.	Description of Item	Quantity	Remark
1.	Earthwork in excavation, banking excavated earth in layers not exceeding 20 cm. in depth, breaking clods, watering, rolling each layer complete, lead upto 50 m and left upto 1.5 m.	7920 cum	
2.	Preparation of subgrade by excavating earth to an average of 30 cm. depth, dressing to camber and consolidating with road roller, including making good the undulations etc. and disposal of surplus earth lead upto 50 metres.	4000 sq m	
3.	Supplying and stacking of stone for soling at site.	800 cum	
4.	Laying stone soling including packing with smaller stones and consolidation with road roller including spreading and consolidation of binding material moorum or earth etc.	800 cum	
5.	Supplying and stacking stone aggregate 50 mm nominal size.	760 cum	
6.	Supplying and stacking red bajri at site.	45.60 cum	
7.	Supplying and stacking moorum at site.	91.20 cum	
8.	Laying wearing course with stone aggregate including screening, sorting, spreading to template and consolidation with road roller complete, including spreading and consolidation of binding material.	760 cum	
9.	Scarifying metalled (water bond) road surface including disposal of rubbish lead upto 50 m and consolidation with road roller of the aggregate received from scarifying.	3800 sq m	
10.	Second class brick edging laid lengthwise with half brick depth, including excavation, refilling and disposal of surplus earth lead upto 50 m.	2000 metre	
11.	25 mm premix carpet surfacing with 3 cum of stone aggregate 10 mm nominal size per 100 kg of hot bitumen of approved quality per cum of stone aggregate including a tack coat with hot bitumen at 1 kg per sq m of road surface complete.	3800 sq m	

EXERCISES

Exercise 1. Prepare a detailed estimate for the construction of a service lane with the following data :

Length of service lane= 1000 metre
Metal width of service lane = 2.80 metre
Brick soling = 10 cm. thick
Wearing course = 10 cm. thick
Surface treatment = Painting one coat with bitumen side shall be provided with brick edging.

Exercise 2. Calculate the quantity of materials required for one kilometre length of the road with the following specifications :

1. Brick on edge lengthwise
2. Metalled width 7.00 metre
3. Soling, 20 cm. thick compacted
4. Wearing course in two layers, each layer 10 cm thick compacted.
5. Painting two coats with hot bitumen.

Notes : 1. Moorum layer 12 mm thick. 2. Bajri 6 mm thick.
3. Volume of loose netal gets reduced 3/4th on compaction.

12

Water Supply and Sanitary Works

12.1. INTRODUCTION

(A) Water Supply. Water supply works consist of the following :

(*a*) Head works consisting of the intake works, treatment works and the pumping installation work.

(*b*) Rising mains consisting of the layout of pipe lines from pumping plant to the service reservoir.

(*c*) Service reservoir for storage of water supplied through the rising main.

(*d*) Distribution system consisting of the net work of pipes from the service reservoir upto the house connection.

(*e*) House connection from the nearest service line to the consumer system including the various house connections.

For purpose of estimation, the head works are divided into civil works consisting of the structural details of the complex and mechanical works consisting of the mechanical installation.

The rising mains are estimated as per running metre basis for different diameter and then supply and fixing in position inclusive of digging, laying, refilling and jointing etc. is considered as one item as "Supply and fixing". These pipes may be G.I. (Galvanised iron), C.I. (Cast iron), Steel, R.C.C. (Humpe Pipe), Hume Steel (Cement lined steel) etc. Fittings such as sluice valves, air valves, stop valve etc. are estimated as numbers according to their sizes.

The main pipe lines from the service reservoir upto the house connection are also estimated on running metre basis.

G.I. pipes are normally used for service connection and internal connection.

(B) Sanitary Works. Sanitary works start where the water supply ends. They are classified as under :

(*a*) House connection and fittings of wash-hand basins, sinks, bath tubes, urinals, flushing cistern, flushing pipes etc. The fittings are estimated as per number for complete work according to their sizes. Fill up such as Cowl, Gully trap. Master trap, Mica Valve etc. are also estimated as numbers and the item consists of supply and fittings. In some of the departments (such as M.E.S.) separate item of work exist for supply only, supply and fixing and framing.

(*b*) The sewer line from the manhole of the house connection to the public sewer line is estimated as per running metre according to diameter.

(*c*) Masonry construction such as inspection chambers and manholes are estimated as per numbers of different size including supply and fixing of C.I. manhole covers. Sometimes, in case of large projects, these structures are estimated on the basis of items of work involved.

(*d*) Latrine seat, siphon, flushing cistern, flushing pipes, foot-rests etc. are taken as numbers and estimated as supply only or supply and fixed complete.

(*e*) Where public sewage disposal do not exist such as in isolated farm houses or in small towns the disposal of night soil is satisfactorily done by means of *Septic Tank*. The capacity of the septic tank is such that sewage is retained in the tank for 24 hours. During this period certain decompositions by the action of *anaerobic* bacteria take place thereby breaking and liquifying the night soil thereby leading a small quantity of solid which settles at the bottom of the tank and the effluent which comes out from the septic tank is discharged into a soakage pit. Sometimes the discharge from the septic tank may be let off into a drain after treating it with chlorine or bleaching powder. Where night soil is discharged into septic tank, domestic waste water consisting of kitchen water and surface water should be disposed off separately.

The various elements of the septic tank complex are :

1. The Septic Tank 2. Soakage Pit.

12.2. ESTIMATE OF A SEPTIC TANK

Main features of the septic tank as per recommendation IS : 2470 (Part II) 1971 in respect of residential housing, colonies, hostels and boarding schools where number of users ranges from 50 to 300 are given below :

The septic tank or septicization is a natural biological process in which bacteria and other microscopic and sub-microscopic forms of life acting in the absence of oxygen, reduce organic substances to lower oxidised forms, some dissolved solids. Gases principally carbon dioxide, methane, small amounts of hydrogen sulphide and others are given off.

The biological process in the septic tank represents that portion of the cycle of life and death in which complex organic compounds are reduced to a simple condition to be a available as food for low forms or low forms of plant life.

The principal advantage of septic action in sewage treatment is the relatively small. Amount of sludge that must be cared for, as compared to other processes of sewage treatment. The sludge from the septic tank may be 25 to 30% or 40% less in weight and 75 to 80% less in volume than the sludge from sedimentation tank. Other advantages are less cost and skilled attendance is not required.

A septic tank is a horizontal continuous flow, one storey sedimentation tank through which sewage is allowed to flow slowly to permit the settlement of matter, to settle to the bottom, where it is retained until anaerobic decomposition is established. The suspended organic matter changes into liquid and gaseous substances and the quantity of sludge to be disposed of is reduced considerably.

The purpose of septic tank is to store the sludge, to be disposed off, for such a period of time that partial liquefaction of the sludge may take place, and thus minimise the difficulty of sludge disposal. Therefore, the capacity of the sludge tank is greater than that of the sedimentation tank. The rate of flow of the effluent must be equal to the rate of inflow at all times.

Tanks holding stagnant household sewage are called cesspools.

Design features of Septic tank

The following factors should be taken into consideration :

(*i*) Material used should be water-proof and corrosion resistant.

(*ii*) Natural ventilation provided should be adequate.

(*iii*) A manhole should be provided to permit inspection and cleaning.

(*iv*) Baffles should be limited to one at the inlet and one at the outlet.

(*v*) The escape of gas and sludge to effluent pipe should be avoided.

The following constructional details should be followed in the construction of a septic tank.

1. The shape should be rectangular, the length being 2 to 4 times the breadth.
2. The depth should be 90 to 180 cm plus a free board of 30 to 45 cm.
3. Inlet should be T-shaped pipe. The pipe should be submerged to a depth of 15 to 22.5 cm below the liquid level.
4. The outlet should be T-shaped pipe located at a depth of 15 cm below the liquid level.
5. The inlet baffle is placed 30 cm from inlet pipe. In large tank baffle walls are constructed to prevent short circuiting at l/3rd the length from inlet. The tank is divided into two compartments. The first one serves as the stilling compartment and the second one as settling compartment with a smooth exit of settled sewage.
6. The roof consists of R.C.C. slab with manhole cover in each compartment.
7. The ventilation is provided by a pipe 4 to 5 cm in diameter. It is taken 2.5 metres above the ground level so that the gases of digestion escape about the roof level.
8. The floor is provided with all sides sloping (1 in 7) towards one point.
9. The desludging pipe consists of 10 to 15 cm diameter pipe. It is controlled by a sluice device.

The design of septic tank consists of providing chamber for :

1. Settling of incoming sewage.
2. Storage of digested sludge till it is taken out for further disposal.

Space for the following should be provided for

1. Space for Settling. This can be obtained by determining the average flow and the detention period. Very large capacity is required to accumulate fluctuating flow on the basis of average flow. A detention period of 24 hours is provided.

If the latrines are connected average flow per capita per day may be taken as 45 litres. If waste water is also to be treated, the average flow may range from 90 to 115 litres.

2. Space for Digestion. Per capita provision of 42.5 litres or 0.0425 m^3 is made. There is no mixing, heating etc. in this space and operation goes in natural way.

3. Space for Digested Sludge. The quantity of digested sludge produced in septic tank is about 0.213 litres/capita/day. In 6 months the quantity of digested sludge per capita = $6 \times 30 \times 0.213 = 38.3$ litres or 28 litres compacted. Table 12.1 gives period of sludging and storage capacity.

Table 12.1

Period of sludging	*Storage capacity*
6 month	28 litres
1 year	50 litres
2 year	70 litres
3 year	85 litres

Cleaning period is not intended beyond three years because :

1. Storage of large amount of sludge increases the cost as larger volume is required.
2. The sludge becomes hard and difference to clean.
3. Care should be taken that while cleaning the septic tank some old sludge is left for seeding purpose.

The capacity varies from 110 to 200 litres/capita for smaller tanks depending upon :

1. The water supply
2. Waste water admitted
3. Detention period given
4. Cleaning interval.

Tables 12.2 and 12.3 give recommended capacities and size of septic tanks for housing colonies and hostel/boarding house respectively. [Based on IS : 2470 (Part II) 1971]

Table 12.2. Recommended Capacities and Sizes of Septic Tank for Housing Colonies

No. of users	*Length L (m)*	*Breadth B (m)*	*Liquid Dept. (D) for stated interval of sludge withdrawal*		*Liquid capacities for stated interval of sludge withdrawal*		*Distance of partition wall from the inlet end (m)*
			Once in a year or less (m)	*Once in 2 years (m)*	*Once in a year or less (m^3)*	*Once in 2 years (m^3)*	
100	8.0	2.8	1	1.04	22.4	23.3	5.3
150	10.6	2.7	1	1.15	28.6	32.9	7.1
200	12.4	3.1	1	1.15	38.5	44.2	8.3
300	14.6	3.9	1	1.15	56.9	65.5	9.7

The details of measurements and calculation of quantities are given in Table 12.3.

Table 12.3. Details of Measurement and Calculation of Quantities (Septic Tank)

S. No.	*Particular of work*	*No.*	*Length (m)*	*Breadth (m)*	*Height Depth (m)*	*Quantity*	*Remark*
1.	Earthwork in excavation						Height
	(*i*) Septic tank	1	3.05	1.75	2.05	11.03 cm	$= 1.5 + 0.3 + \frac{20+30}{2}$
	(*ii*) Soakage pit						$= 2.05$
	(1) Excavation upto 3 m depth						
		1	2.1	—	3.00	9.42	$\frac{**\pi \times (2.0)^2}{4}$
						20.45	
	(2) Excavation beyond 3 m depth						
		1	1.54***	—	0.20	0.31	$\frac{***\pi \times (1.4)^2}{4}$
						20.76 cm	
2.	1 : 3 : 6 cement concrete in foundation	1	3.05	1.75	0.20	1.07 cum	
	-do- sloping portion	1	2.25	0.95	0.05**	0.11 cum	$\frac{**0+10}{2} = 5$ cm
						0.11 cum	Average thickness
3.	First class brick work 1 : 5 in cement mortar in septic tank						

	(*i*) Long wall						
	1st step	2	2.85	0.30	0.60	1.03 cum	
	2nd step	2	2.65	0.20	1.25	1.33 cum	
	(*ii*) Short wall						
	1st step	2	0.90	0.30	0.60	0.34 cum	
	2nd step	2	0.90	0.20	1.25	0.47 cum	
						3.17 cum	
4.	2nd class brick work in 1 : 6 cm in soak pits						
	(*i*) Upper portion	1	$\pi \times 1.20^{**} \times 0.20$		0.50	0.38 cum	**L = Average
	(*ii*) Lower portion	1	$(\pi \times 1.20)^{**} \times 0.20$		0.20	0.15 cum	circumference
						0.53 cum	$\frac{1+1.4}{2} = 1.20$ m
5.	2nd class dry brick work (Soakage pits)	1	$(\pi \times 1.20) \times 0.20$		3.00	2.2 cum	
6.	R.C.C. work (precast) 1 : 2 : 4 cement concrete						
	(*i*) Roof cover slab of septic tank	1	2.65	1.35	0.08	0.29 cum	Thickness
	(*ii*) Slab once soak pits	1	$\frac{\pi + (1.4)^2}{4}$	×	0.08	0.128 cum	8 cm
	(*iii*) Baffle wall in septic tank	1	1.20	0.5	0.45	0.027 cum	
						0.445 cum	
7.	1 : 2 cement plaster 12 mm thick with approved water-proofing compound						
	Long wall	2	2.25	—	1.80	8.10	
	Short wall	2	0.90	—	1.80	3.24	
						11.34 sq m	
8.	1 : 2 cement plaster 20 cm thick with approved water-proofing compound (Flooring)	1	2.25	0.95	—	2.14 sq m	
9.	Coarse sand filing or out side of soak pit	1	π(2.00)	0.20*	3.0	3.80 cum	*Mean dia × 1.8 + $\frac{0.4}{2}$ = 2 m
10.	5 cm size brick aggregate out-side of soak pit		π(1.60)	0.20*	3.00	3.02 cum	
	5 cm size brick aggregate at the bottom of the pit	1	$\frac{\pi \times 4^2}{4}$	—	0.20	0.16 cum	
						3.18 cum	
11.	Supply and fix 10 cm dia S.W. pipe and jointing with 1 : 1 cement mortar						
	(*i*) From latrine to septic tank	1	3.5 m (say)	—	—	3.5 m	
	(*ii*) From septic tank to soak pit	1	3.5	—	—	3.5 m	
						7.0 m (running)	

(*Contd.*)

12.	10 cm dia S.W. Bend	1	—	—		1 No.	
13.	10 cm dia S.W. Tee	1		—		1 No.	
14.	Iron foot rest made for 16 mm φ bar	4				4 No.	
15.	5 cm dia C.I. cowl	1				1 No.	
16.	5 cm dia C.I. ventilating pipe	1	2	—	—	2 metre (running)	

Table 12.4. Recommended Capacities and Sizes of Septic Tanks for Hostels and Boarding Schools

No. of users	*Length L (m)*	*Width B (m)*	*Liquid depth (D) for stated intervals of sludge withdrawal*		*Liquid capacities for stated interval of sludge withdrawal*		*Distance of partition wall from inlet end (m)*
			Once in a year (m)	*Once in 2 years (m)*	*Once in a year (m^3)*	*Once in 2 years (m^3)*	
50	5.0	1.6	1.3	1.4	10.4	11.2	3.3
100	5.7	2.1	1.4	1.7	16.8	20.4	3.8
150	5.7	2.4	1.4	1.7	25.8	31.4	5.2
200	8.9	2.7	1.4	1.7	33.6	41.0	6.0
300	10.7	3.3	1.4	1.7	49.5	60.0	7.2

A typical design of septic tank for large installation is given in Fig. 12.1.

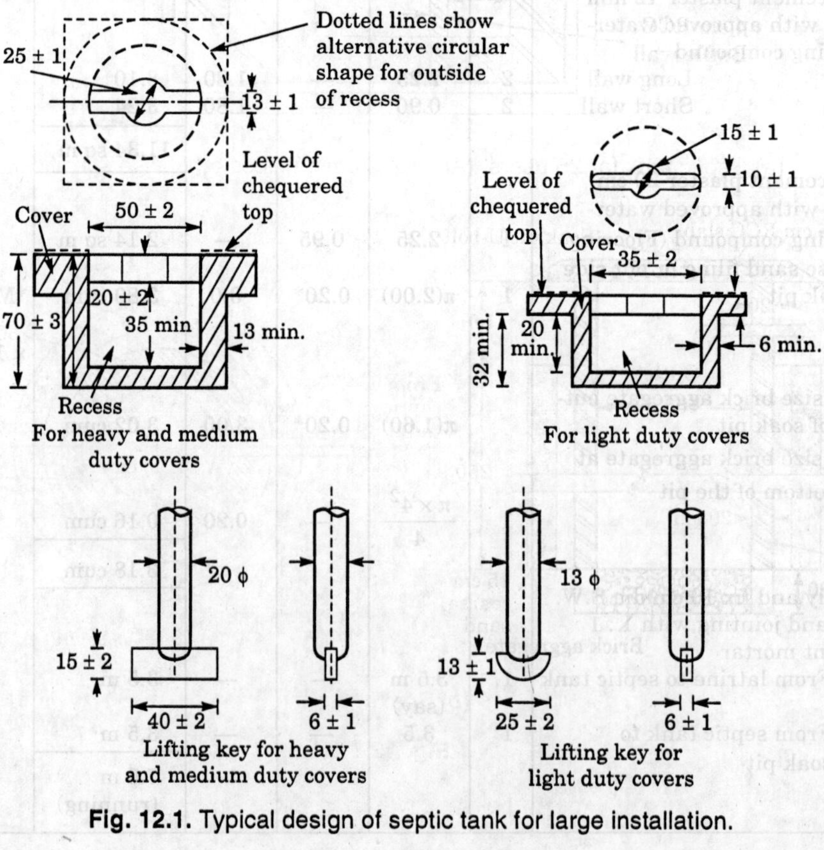

Fig. 12.1. Typical design of septic tank for large installation.

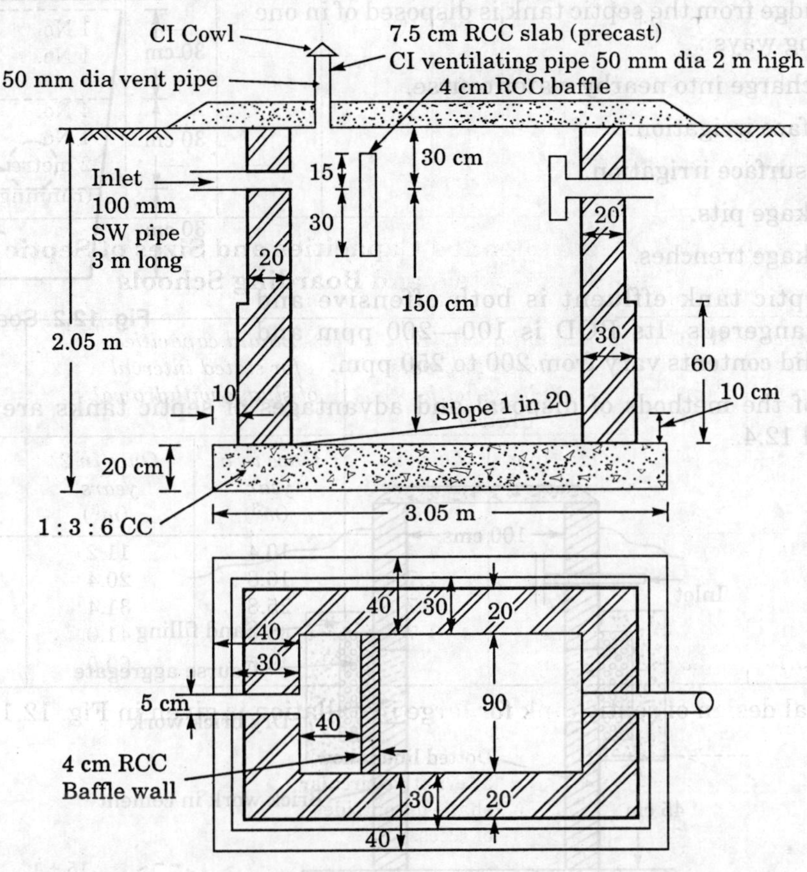

(*a*) Septic tank for 25 users. (All dia. in cms, unless otherwise specific)

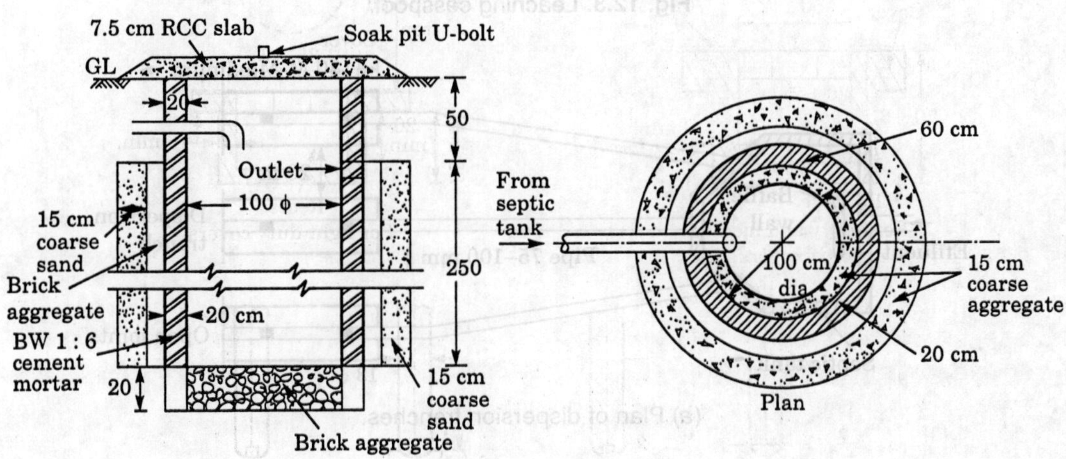

(*b*) Soakage.

Fig. 12.1

The sludge from the septic tank is disposed of in one of the following ways :

1. Discharge into nearby water course.
2. Surface irrigation.
3. Subsurface irrigation.
4. Soakage pits.
5. Soakage trenches.

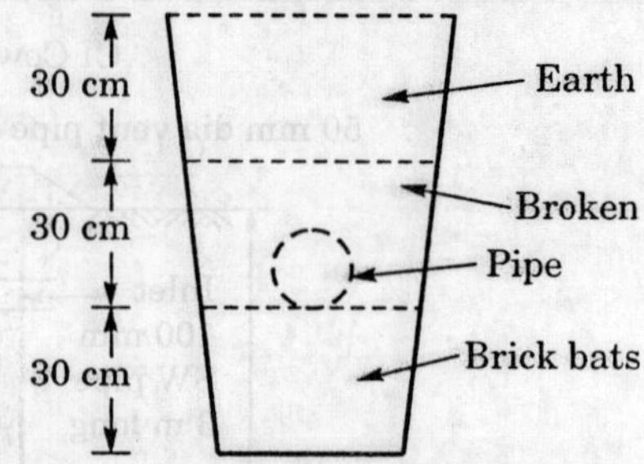

Fig. 12.2. Soakage pits.

The septic tank effluent is both offensive and potentially dangerous. Its BOD is 100—200 ppm and suspended solid contents vary from 200 to 250 ppm.

Some of the methods of disposal and advantages of septic tanks are illustrated in Figs. 12.3 and 12.4.

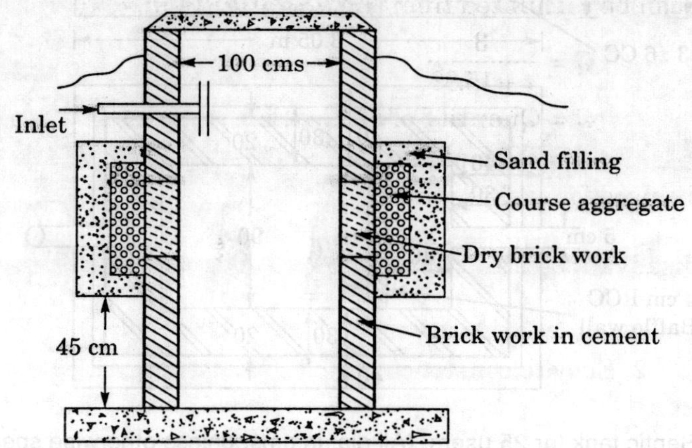

Fig. 12.3. Leaching cesspool.

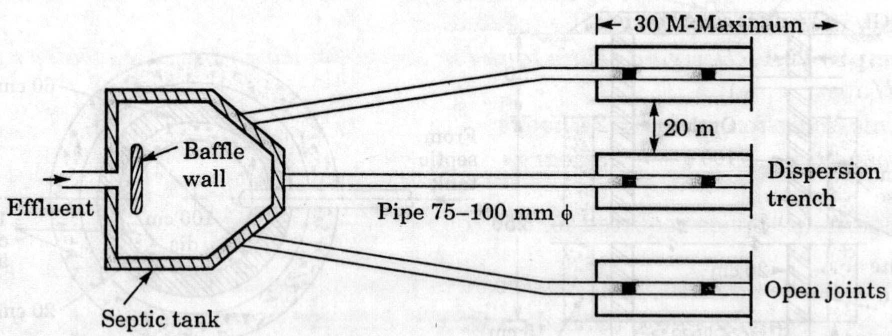

(*a*) Plan of dispersion trenches.

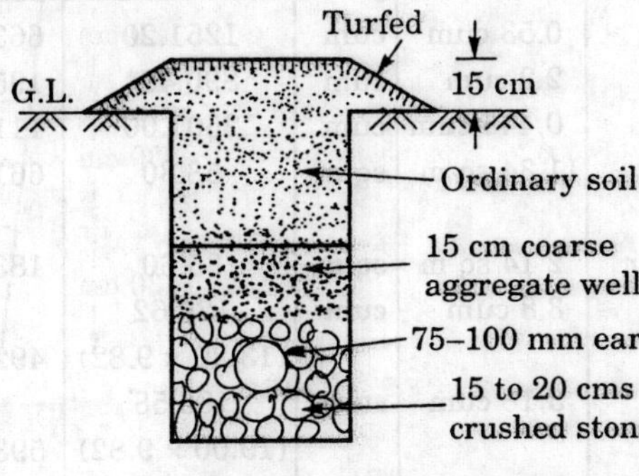

(*b*) Section of dispersion trench.

Fig. 12.4

Soakage area can be calculated from the quantity of effluent which is given by

$$Q = \frac{3}{t + 15.88}$$

where Q = Quantity of effluent m^3/m^2/per day.

t = Time of percolation.

Cesspool can be used for soaking the effluent of septic tanks. It has a water tight bottom and porous sides.

Advantages, disadvantages and limitations of septic tank treatment of sewage are given below :

Advantages

1. Cheap 2. Easy to construct 3. No attendance is required.

Disadvantages

1. Foul smell 2. Effluent is septic and difficult to dispose.

Limitations

1. The usefulness of the system is limited to small number of users.
2. Only domestic sewage can be treated.

Example 12.1. *Design a septic tank for 100 users, assuming rated water supply as 50 litres/head/day.*

Assume detention period = 24 hours

Cleaning time = 3 years.

Solution. (*a*) Space required for setting $= \frac{50 \times 100}{1000} = 5\ m^3$

Table 12.5. Abstract of Cost of Septic Tank

(Based on CPWD SSR 1997)

S. No.	*Particulars of item of work*	*Quantity*	*Unit*	*Rate*	*Cost*	*Remark*
1.	Earthwork in excavation					
	(*i*) Below 3 m depth	20.45 cum	cum	64.10	1249.50	
	(*ii*) Above 3 m depth	6.34 cum	cum	183.57	1160.2	Add 15% to 1 (*i*)
2.	1 : 3 : 6 cement concrete	1.18 cum	cum	1392.80	1643.50	
3.	1 B.W. m 1 : 5 CM.	3.17 cum	cum	1297.43*	1530.97	*Avg. 1 : 4 & 1 : 6

(*Contd.*)

4.	II B.W. m 1 : 6 CM.	0.53 cum	cum	1251.20	663.14	
5.	II B.W. Dry	2.2 cum	cum	890.48*	1959.08	
6.	1 : 2 : 4 Precast RCC work	0.445 cum	cum	2501.00	1113.40	
7.	12 mm thick 1 : 3 (outside-dust) cement plaster	11.34 sq m	sq m	58.30	661.12	
8.	20 mm thick 1:2 cement plaster	2.14 sq m	sq m	85.60	183.18	
9.	Coarse sand filling brick	3.8 cum	cum	129.62		
				(13.20 × 9.82)	492.68	
10.	5 cm size aggregate filling	3.18 cum	cum	186.58		
				(19.00 × 9.82)	593.82	
11.	Supply and fix 10 cm dia C.I. pipe	7.0 m	m	36.40	254.80	
12.	Supply and fix 10 cm dia C.I. bend	1 No.	No.	99.30	99.30	Prime cost
13.	Supply and fix 10 cm dia C.I. tee	1 No.	No.	124.81		
				(12.71 × 9.82)	124.81	
14.	Supply and fix 16 mm ϕ M.S. and iron fort rest	4 No.	No.	51.26		
				(5.22 × 9.82)	205.04	
15.	Supply and fix 5 cm dia cowl	1 No.	No.	98.4 (9.82)	98.2	Prime cost
16.	Supply and fix 5 cm dia C.I. ventilating pipe	metre	2 m	137.70	274.40	
				Total	12561.86	
	Add $1\frac{1}{2}$% for water charges				188.43	
					12750.29	
	Add 10% for contractor's profit				1275.02	
					14025.31	
					1402.	
				Grand Total	15427.81	
				Say	15428.0	

2. Space required for digestion

$$= 100 \times 0.0425 \text{ m}^3 \} \; 0.0425 \text{ m}^3\text{/capita} = 425 \text{ m}^3$$

3. Space required for storage of sludge

$$= 100 \times 0.085 \text{ m}^3 = 8.5 \text{ m}^3.$$

The abstract of cost of septic tank is given in Table 12.5.

12.3. ESTIMATE OF A MANHOLE

Manhole in a sewage disposal scheme is provided for the following :

(*i*) To provide junction for two or more sewer lines

(*ii*) To facilitate provision of bends

(*iii*) For inspection (*iv*) For flushing (*v*) For cleaning.

Along straight sewer lines manholes are provided for cleaning, inspection and flushing. The spacing in such cases varies from 40 to 90 metre depending upon the size of the sewer varying from 15 to 40 cm diameter.

The essential components of a manhole are :

(*i*) Working chamber which may be rectangular or square with provision for inlet, outlet and connecting pipes.

Small size manholes such as 100 × 100 cm may have a single R.C.C. cover where working chamber and access shaft are common. In the case of comparatively deep manholes say above 2.5 m in depth with internal size of 1 m × 2 m the access chamber and working chamber may be separate units.

Example 12.2. *Fig. 12.5 shows detailed estimate of a manhole. Prepare a detailed estimate of the work.*

Total space required $= (5 + 4.25 + 8.5)\ m^3$

$= 17.75\ m^3$.

Allowing 30 cm free board provide following dimensions for septic tank :

Depth $= 1.70 + 30\ cm = 2\ m$

Breadth $= 2\ m$

Length $= 5.5\ m$

Space provided $= 5.5 \times 2 \times 2\ m^3 = 22\ m^3$.

Note. The following values have been assumed :

Setting $= 50$ litres/capita/day

Digestion $= 0.0425\ m^3$/capita

Storage $= 0.049\ m^3$ (1 year)

$= 0.078\ m^3$ (2 years)

$= 0.085\ m^3$ (3 years).

Alternately from Table 12.2 for cleaning once in 2 years.

$$\left.\begin{array}{l} L = 8.0\ m \\ B = 2.8\ m \\ D = 1.04\ m \end{array}\right\}\ \text{Liquid capacity} = 23.3\ m^3 \text{ may be adopted.}$$

Estimate of a Septic Tank

Example 12.3. *Fig. 12.6 gives details of a septic tank. Prepare a detailed estimate of the work.*

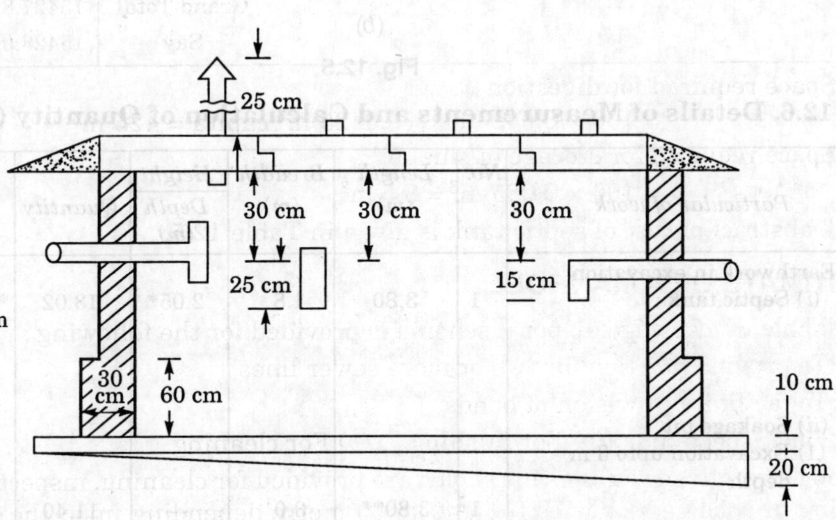

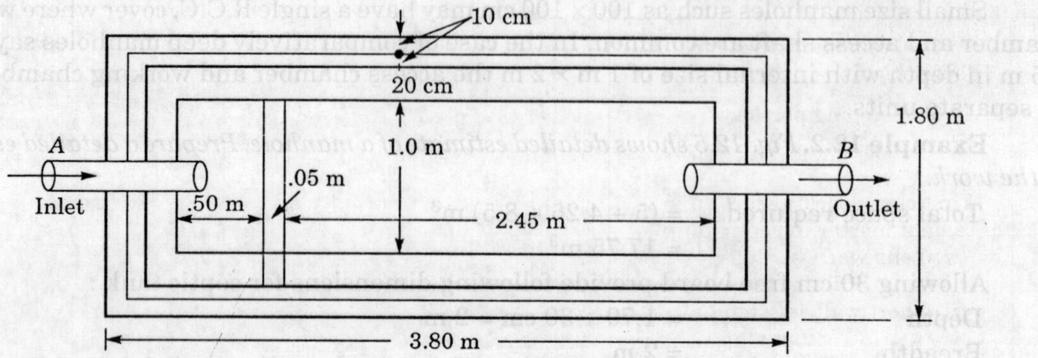

(a)

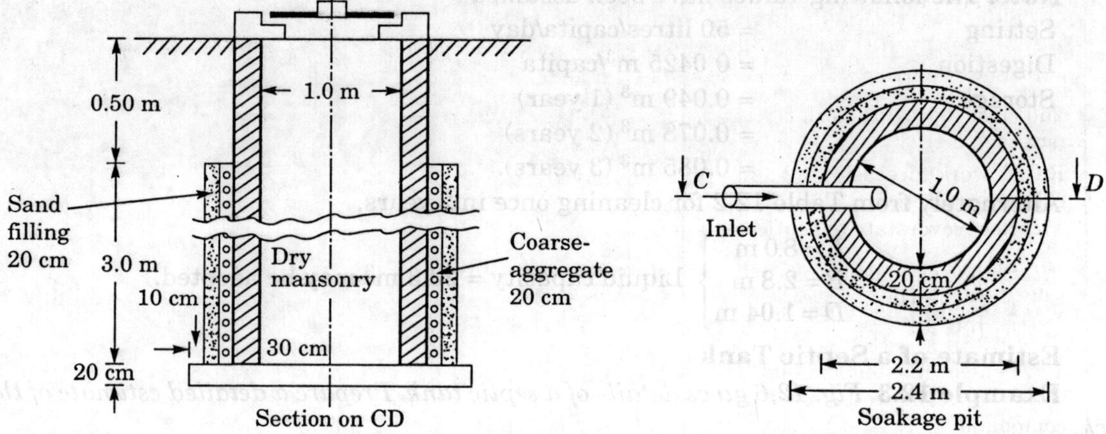

(b)

Fig. 12.5

Table 12.6. Details of Measurements and Calculation of Quantity (Septic Tank)

S. No.	*Particular of work*	*No.*	*Length (m)*	*Breadth (m)*	*Height Depth (m)*	*Quantity*	*Remark*
1.	Earthwork in excavation						
	(*i*) Septic tank	1	3.80	1.8	2.05*	13.02	*Height = 1.5 + 0.3 + $\frac{0.3+0.2}{2}$ = 2.05 m
	(*ii*) Soakage pit						
	(1) Excavation upto 3 m depth	1	3.80**	3.0	—	11.40	$\frac{**\pi \times (2.2)^2}{4}$ = 3.80 m^2
						24.42 m^2	
	(2) Excavation beyond 3 m	1	3.80 (area)	—	0.70	2.66 m^3	

2.	1 : 3 : 6 cement concrete in foundation	1	3.8	1.8	0.20	1.37	
	1 : 3 : 6 sloping portion	1	3.8	1.0	0.50***	0.19	$\frac{**0+10}{2} = 5$ cm
						1.56 m^3	Average thickness
3.	First class brick work 1 : 5 in cement mortar in septic tank						
	(*i*) Long wall 1st step	2	3.6	0.30	0.60	1.30	
	2nd step	2	3.4	0.20	1.20	16.03	
	(*ii*) Short wall 1st step	2	1.0	0.30	0.60	0.36	
	2nd step	2	1.0	0.20	1.20	0.48	
						18.17 m^3	
4.	2nd class B.W. in 1 : 6 cm in soak pit						
	(*i*) Upper portion	1	$\pi \times 1.20$*	0.20	0.50	0.38 cum	*Average circumference
	(*ii*) Lower portion	1	$\pi \times 1.2$*	0.20	0.20	0.15 cum	$= \frac{1+1.4}{2} \times \pi$
5.	2nd class dry brick work (soakage pit)	1	$(\pi \times 1.2)$	0.20	2.8	0.53 cum	
6.	R.C.C. work (precast) 1 : 2 : 4 cement concrete					2.07 cum	
	(*i*) Roof coverstate of septic tank	1	3.4	1.4	0.08	0.38	
	(*ii*) Slab over soakage pit	1	$\frac{\pi \times (0.4)^2}{4}$	—	0.075	0.01	
	(*iii*) Baffle wall in septic tank	1	1.20	0.05	0.40	0.02	
						0.41	
7.	1 : 2 cement plaster 12 mm thick water approved water proofing compound						
	(*i*) Long wall	2	3.0	—	1.8	10.8	
	(*ii*) Short wall	2	1.0	—	1.8	3.6	
						14.4	
8.	1 : 2 cement plaster 20 mm thick with approved water-proofing compound (flooring)	1	3	1	—	3.0	
9.	Coarse sand filling on outside of soak pit	1	$\pi \times 2.00$*	0.20	3	3.8 cum	*Mean dia $= 1.8 + \frac{0.4}{2} = 2\pi$
10.	5 cm size brick aggregate outside of soak pit	1	$\pi(1.60)$	0.20	3.0	3.02 cum	
	5 cm size brick aggregate at bottom of pit	1	$\frac{\pi \times 1^2}{4}$	—	20	1.60 cum	
						4.62 m^3	
11.	S and F 10 cm dia S.W. pipe jointing with 1 : 1 cement mortar						
	(*i*) From latrine to septic tank	1	3.5 m (say)	—	—	3.5 m	
	(*ii*) From septic tank to soak pit	1	3.5 m	—	—	3.5 m	
						7 m running	
12.	10 cm dia SW bed	1	—	—	—	1 No.	
13.	10 cm dia SW tee	1	—	—	—	1 No.	

(*Contd.*)

14.	Iron foot-restmade from 16 mm and bar	4	—	—	—	4 No.	
15.	5 cm dia CI cowl	1	—	—	—	1 No.	
16.	5 cm dia CI ventilation pipe	1	2	—	—	2 m running	
17.	Centring and shuttering roof slab	1	3.4	1.4	—	4.76	
	Slab over soak pit	1	$\frac{\pi \times (0.4)^2}{4}$		—	0.13	
	Baffle wall	2	1.20	—	0.40	0.96	
						5.85	

Table 12.7 gives the abstract of cost of septic tank

Table 12.7. Abstracts of Cost of Septic Tank

S. No.	*Particulars of item of work*	*Quantity*	*Unit*	*Rate*	*Cost*	*Remark*
1.	Earthwork in excavation					
	(*i*) Excavation upto 3 m	24.42	cum	64.10	1565.32	
	(*ii*) Excavation beyond 3 m	2.66	cum	183.37	487.76	
2.	1 : 3 : 6 cement concrete in foundation	1.56 m^3	cum	1433.80	2236.73	
3.	First class B.W. 1 : 6	18.17 m^3	cum	1297.43	23574.30	
4.	Second class B.W. 1 : 6	0.53 m^3	cum	1251.20	663.14	
5.	Second class B.W. dry	2.07 m^3	cum	890.48	1843.13	
6.	R.C.C. work	0.41 m^3	cum	1740.90	717.50	Assuming
	add 1% reinforcement	31.98 kg	kg	18.07	642.80	1% reinforcement
7.	1 : 2 cement plaster 12 mm thick (cement : stone dust)	14.4 m^2	sq m	58.36	20.10	$= \frac{(41 \times 1000)}{100} \times 7.8$
8.	1 : 2 cement plaster 20 mm thick	3.0 m^2	sq. m	85.60	839.52	= 31.98 kg.
9.	Coarse sand filling	3.8 m^3	cum	129.62	492.56	
10.	5 cm brick aggregate filling	4.62 m^2	cum	186.33	662.00	
11.	S & F 10 cm dia C.I. Pipe	7 m	m	36.40	254.80	
12.	10 cm Dia C.I. Bend	1 No.	each	201.30	99.30	
13.	10 cm dia C.I. Tee	1 No.	each	124.81	124.80	
14.	Iron foot rest made for 16 mm φ bar	4 No.	each	51.26	204.80 Provisional item	
15.	S & F 5 cm dia C.I. cool	1	No.	98.40	98.40	
16.	S & F 5 cm dia C.I. vent pipe	2 m	m	137.20	274.40	
17.	Centring and Shuttering	5.85	m^2	53.65	313.85	
					35626.71	
	Add for water charges 1½%				534.39	
					36161.10	
	Add for contractor's profit 10%				3616.11	
					39777.21	
	Say				39777.00	

12.4. ESTIMATE OF A MANHOLE

Manhole is one of the essential ancillary structures in any sewage system. This is provided at every change of alignment or change of gradient of sewer. They are also provided at the junction of two or more sewers starting points of sewers or branches and whenever there is a change in size of the sewer. Depending upon the size of the sewer manholes are otherwise provided as per spacing shown in Table 12.8.

Table 12.8. Spacing of Manholes

Pipe dia mm.	*Spacing m*
Upto 30	45
301 to 500	75
501 to 900	90
Beyond 900	Any interval depending upon local condition and as approved by the engineer incharge.

SI : 4111 (Part I)—1967 covers the requirements for design consideration construction safety measures to be adopted for manholes and types of manholes. The minimum size of rectangular shallow manholes in which a man can work efficiency is 1200 mm along the line and 750 mm across. For circular chamber the diameter should not be less than 1200 mm.

Access to shaft should have a minimum internal diameter of 700 mm. When depth of the shaft exceeds 3 m suitable dimensions should be provided to facilitate cleaning and maintenance. The access shaft when built of brickwork should be corbelled on three sides to reduce it to the size of opening in the cover frame, and to provide easy access on the fourth side to step irons or ladder (see Fig. 12.6).

Fig. 12.7 shows a typical R.C.C. Manhole.

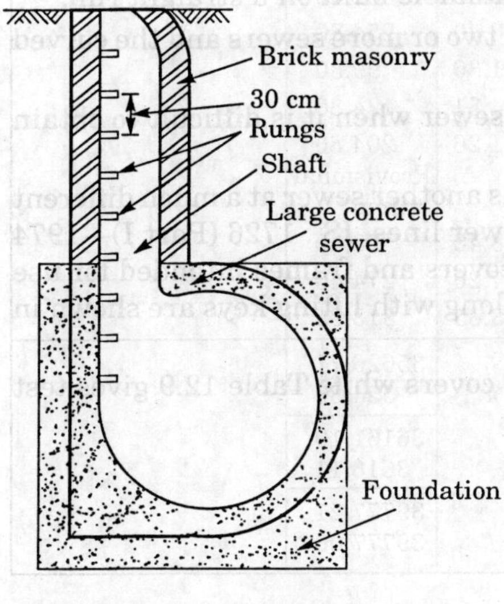

Fig. 12.6. Access to sewers by shaft.

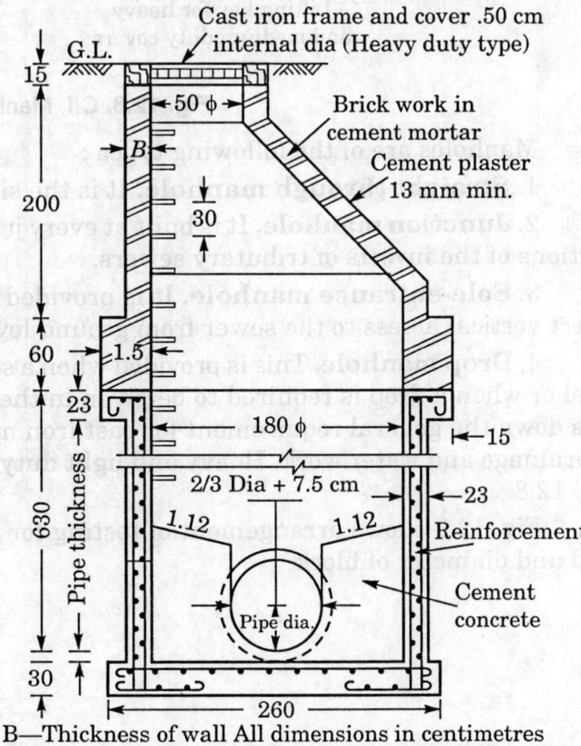

Fig. 12.7. Typical R.C.C. manhole.

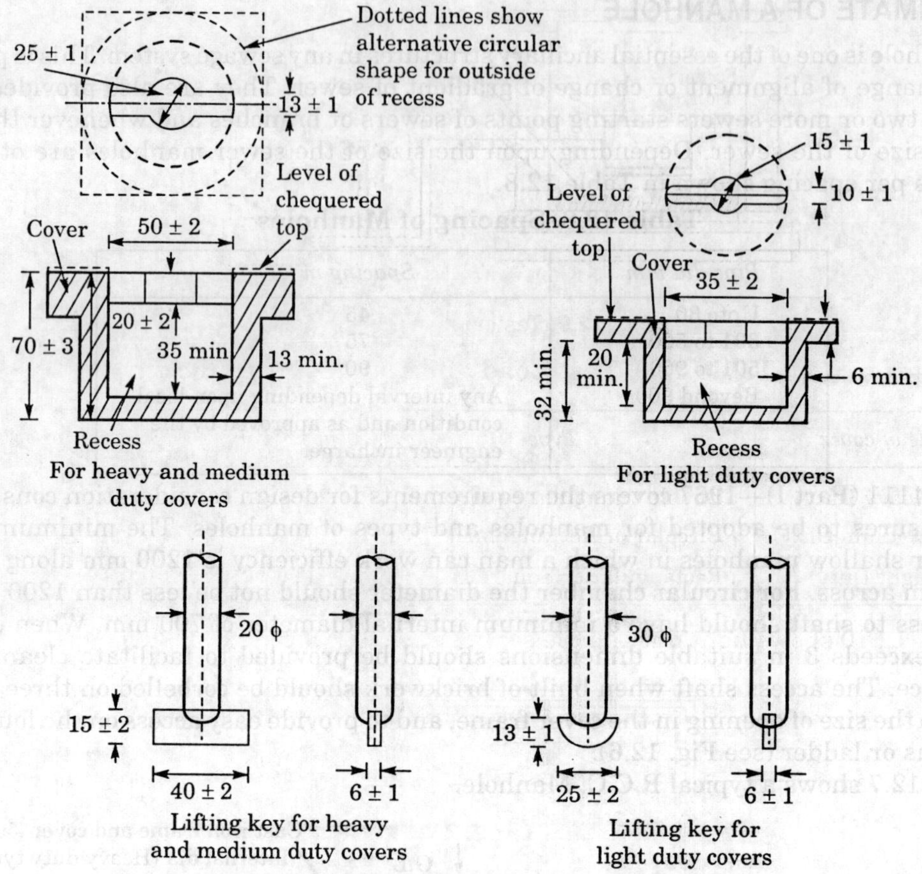

Fig. 12.8. C.I. Manhole covers.

Manholes are of the following types :

1. **Straight through manhole.** It is the simplest manhole built on a straight run.

2. **Junction manhole.** It is built at every junction of two or more sewers and the curved portions of the inverts of tributary sewers.

3. **Sole-entrance manhole.** It is provided in large sewer when it is difficult to obtain direct vertical access to the sewer from ground level.

4. **Drop manhole.** This is provided when a sewer joins another sewer at a much different level or when a drop is required to be given in the same sewer lines. IS : 1726 (Part I)—1974 lays down the general requirement for cast iron manhole covers and frames intended for use in drainage and water work. Heavy and light duty covers along with lifting keys are shown in Fig. 12.8.

Fig. 12.9 shows arrangement of testing for manhole covers while Table 12.9 gives test load and diameter of block.

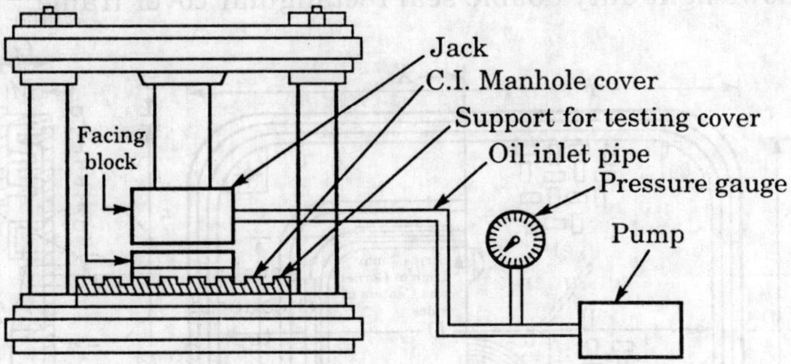

Fig. 12.9. Testing manhole covers.

Table 12.9. Test Load and Diameter of Block

Grade of cover	*Type*	*Load in Tonnes*	*Diameter of block in mm.*
H.D. (Heavy Duty)	Double triangular or Circular	35	300
M.D. (Medium Duty)	Circular or Rectangular	5	100
L.D. (Light Duty)	Rectangular or Square	1	300

Fig. 12.10 shows light duty single seal rectangular cover and frame.

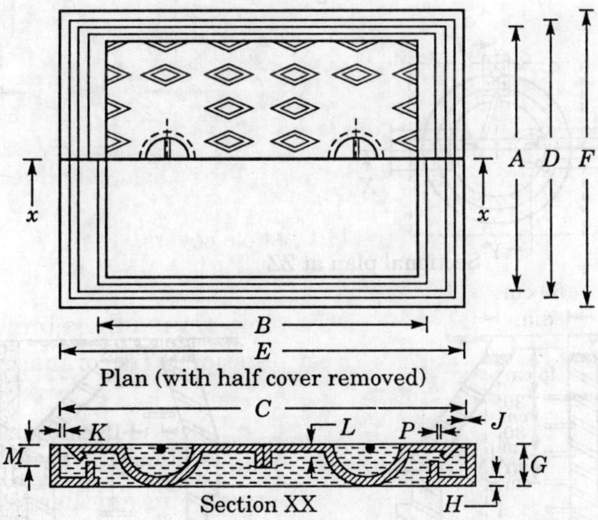

Fig. 12.10. Light duty single seal rectangular cover and frame.

Fig. 12.11 shows light duty double seal rectangular cover frame.

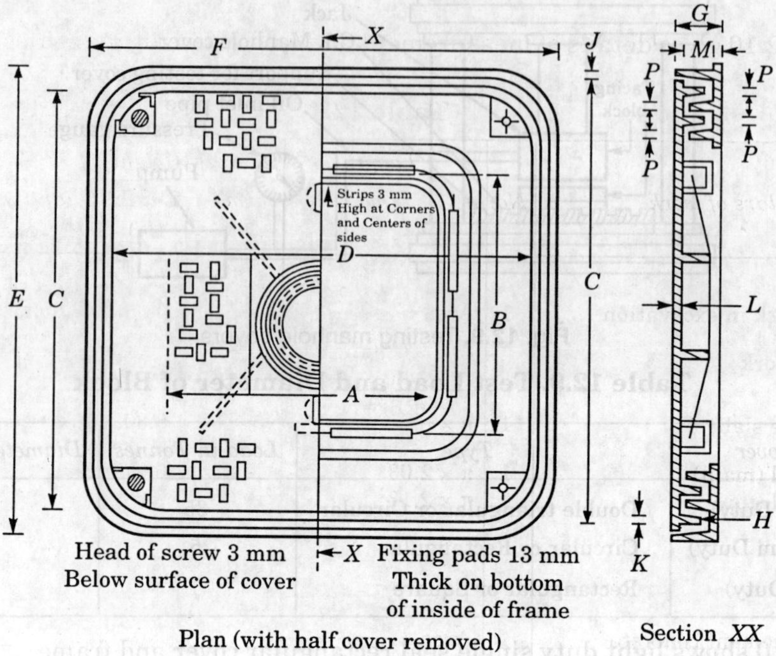

Fig. 12.11

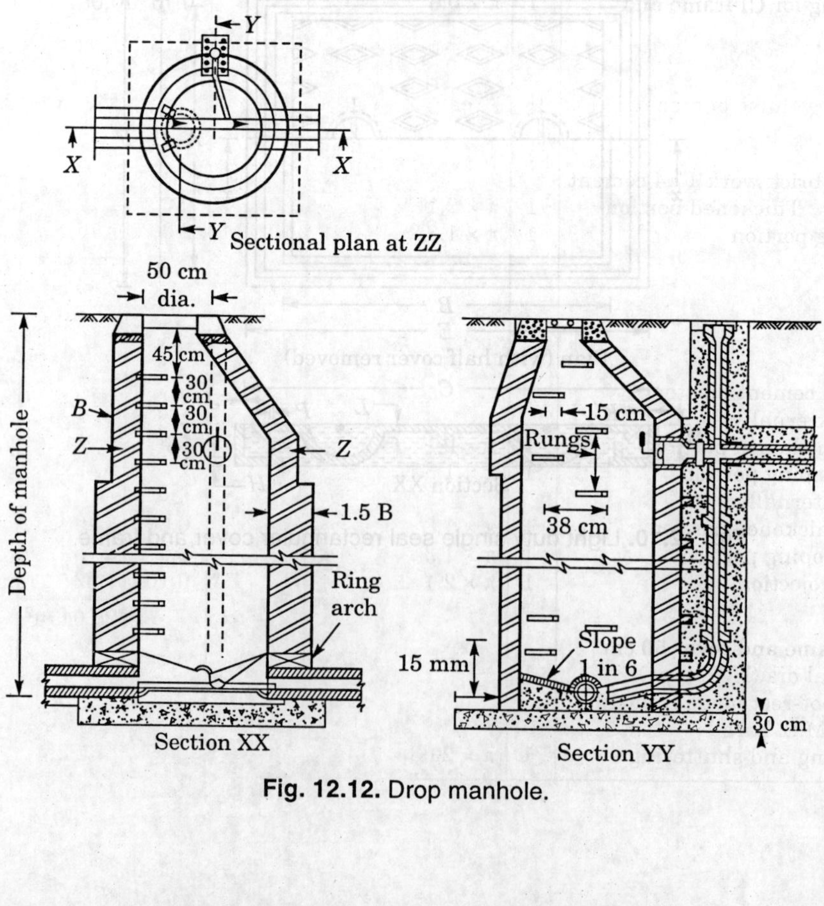

Fig. 12.12. Drop manhole.

Example 12.4. *Fig. 12.7 shows a typical R.C.C. manhole. Prepare a detailed estimate of this work.*

Table 12.10 gives details of measurement and calculation of quantities of a R.C.C. manhole.

Table 12.10

S. No.	Particulars of work	No.	Length (m)	Breadth (m)	Height Depth (m)	Quantity	Remark
1.	Earthwork in excavation	1	Area = $\frac{\pi \times 2.6^2}{4}$	—	9.35	49.65 m^3	
2.	R.C.C. work						
	(i) Base slab	1	$\pi \times \frac{(2.6)^2}{4}$	—	0.30	1.59	
	(ii) Wall (main)	1	π × 2.03*	0.23	6.07*	8.92	
	Wall (top)	1	π × 2.18	0.38	0.23	0.60	*Mean circumference
						11.11 m^3	
3.	1 : 2 : 4 cement concrete	1	Area = $\frac{\pi \times (1.8)^2}{4}$		3.08	7.82	Heights = $\frac{630}{2}$ 315–7 = 308
	Bedding for CI frame and cover	1	π × 0.6	0.20	0.15	0.06	Deduct for ramp
						7.88	
	Deduct volume of pipe	1	Area = $\pi \times \frac{(0.5)^2}{4}$	1.80		0.34	0.5 m average dia
						7.54 m^3	
4.	I class brick work 1 : 4 cement mortar : Thickened portion	1	π × 2.1	0.3	0.60	1.19 m^3	2.1 m average dia
	Sloping portion	1	π × 1.35	0.20	2.00	1.70	$\frac{0.7 \times 2.0}{2}$ = 1.35 m average dia
						2.89 m^3	
5.	13 mm cement plaster						
	(a) Externally						
	Thickened portion	1	π × 2.1		0.60	3.96	
	Sloping portion	1	π × 1.35		2.0	8.48	
	(b) Internally						
	Thickened portion	1	π × 1.8		0.60	3.40	
	Sloping portion	1	π × 1.35		2.0	8.48	
	(c) Projection	1	π × 2.1		0.10	1.32	
						25.64 m^2	
6.	C.I. frame and cover 50 cm internal dia (H.D. type)	1				1 No.	
7.	Iron foot-rest made from 16 mm φ M.S. bars	10				10 No.	
8.	Centring and shuttering	1	π × 2.03	—	6.07	38.67 m^2	

Table 12.11 gives abstracts of cost of a R.C.C. manhole.

Table 12.11

S. No.	Particular of item of work	Quantity	Unit	Rate	Cost	Remark
1.	Earthwork in excavation	49.65 m^3	cum	63.53	3155.26	
2.	R.C.C. work 1 : 2 : 4	11.11	cum	1740.90	19341.40	
3.	1 : 2 : 4 cement concrete work	7.54	cum	1687.45	12723.38	Reinforcement $0.01 \times 11.11\ m^3 = 0.11\ m^3$
4.	1% reinforcement	858	kg	20.10	17245.8	weight $= 1000 \times 7.8 \times 0.11 = 110 \times 7.8$ kg $= 858$ kg.
5.	First class B.W. 1 : 4	2.89	cum	1343.15	38831.48	
6.	12 mm cement plaster 1 : 3	25.64	sq m	58.30	1494.80	
7.	CI frame and cover 50 cm internal diameter H.D. Type	1	No.	500	₹ 500.00	
8.	Iron foot-rest	10	each	52	520.0	
9.	Centring and shuttering	36.67	m^2	53.65	1967.35	
					Total	85779.25
					Add 1½ water charges	1286.69
						87055.94
					Add 10% for w.c. contractor's profit	8705.59
						95761.43
					Say ₹	95761.00

12.5. ESTIMATE OF A SANITARY PIT-LATRINE

A sanitary pit latrine is a cheap and at the same time quite hygeinic system for disposal of night-soil. The pit may be directly under the latrine seat or its may be away from the seat. In the latter case, when one pit is filled, the seat may be connected to another pit without changing the seating management, and the accompanying enclosure.

The latrine pan is of pre-cast 1 : 3 cement : coarse sand and is 48 cm in length. The water seal trap is cast separately and filled to the pan before laying the floor.

The pit has the following dimension :

Diameter : 80 cm.

Depth : 2 to 3 metres

Covering : 6 cm R.C.C. slab with 6 mm ϕ bars at 20 cm centres.

The upper portion of the pit is lined with two layers of brick or stone in mud mortar.

The pit works both as septic tank as well as soak pit. The gas generated in the pit due to anaerobic action is absorbed in the soil.

Depending upon the number of users, one pit may last two to five years.

A typical pit is shown in Fig. 12.13.

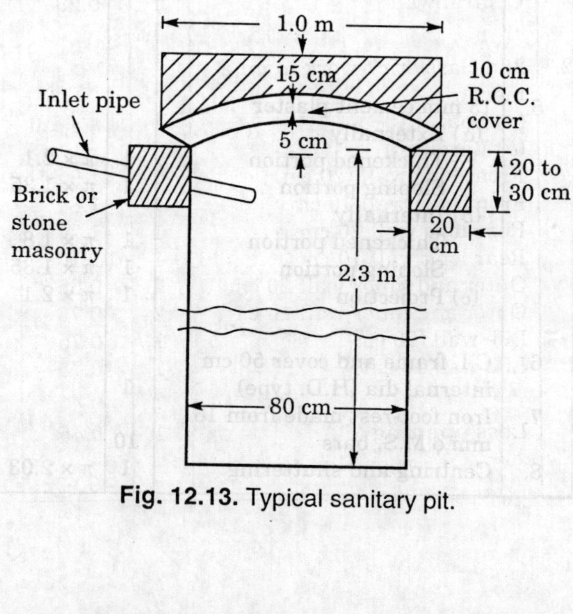

Fig. 12.13. Typical sanitary pit.

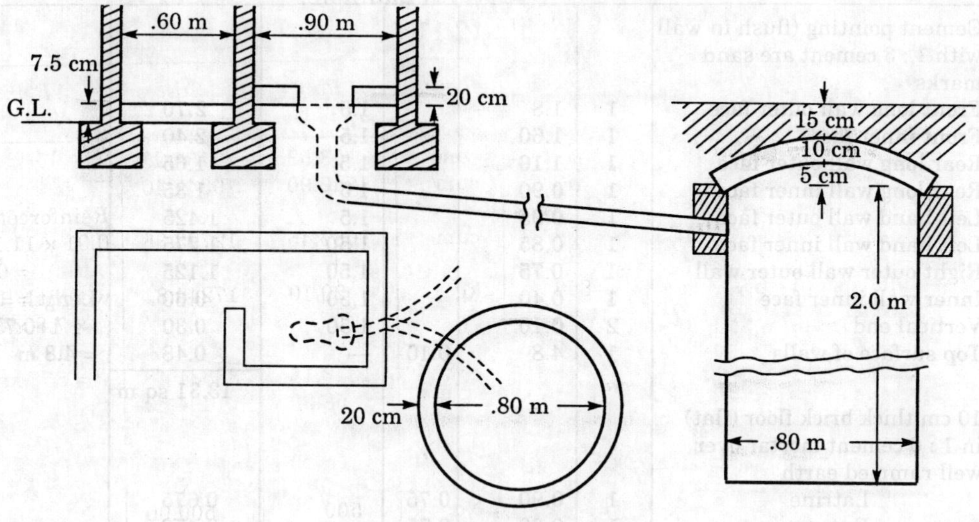

Fig. 12.14. Sanitary pit latrine.

Example 12.5. *Prepare a detailed estimate of a sanitary pit latrine shown in Fig. 12.14.*

Table 12.12 gives details of measurements and calculation of quantities of a sanitary pit latrice.

Table 12.12

S. No.	*Particular of work*	*No.*	*Length (m)*	*Breadth (m)*	*Height Depth (m)*	*Quantity*	*Remark*
1.	Earth work in excavation						
	(*a*) **Soak Pit**	1	$\frac{\pi \times 0.8}{2.51}$	2.1	2.00 cum	10.54 cum	
	(*b*) **Latrine**						
	Front long wall	1	1.9	0.20	0.20	0.076	.018
	Front rear wall	1	1.2	0.20	0.20	0.048	
	Side walls	2	0.65	0.20	0.20	0.052	
	Central wall	1	0.29	0.20	0.20	0.010	
						10.40 cum	
2.	2nd class brick work in mud mortar						
	(*a*) **Soak Pit**	1	π × 1.0	0.20	0.20	0.126	
	(*b*) **Latrine**						
	Front long wall (20 cm)	1	1.9	20	0.20	0.076	
	Front long wall 10 cm	1	1.8	0.10	1.70	0.306	
	Rear long wall 20 cm	1	1.20	0.20	0.20	0.048	
	Rear long wall 10 cm	1	1.10	0.10	1.70	0.187	
	Outer and inner wall 20 cm	2	0.65	0.20	0.20	0.052	
	Outer and inner wall 10 cm	2	0.75	0.10	1.70	0.255	
	Life wall (20 cm)	1	0.75	0.20	0.20	0.030	
	Life wall 10 cm	1	0.75	0.10	1.70	0.125	
						1.205	
	Less opening	1	0.45	0.10	1.70	0.08	
	Net					1.25 cum	

(*Contd.*)

3.	Cement pointing (flush in wall with 1 : 3 cement are sand marks						
	Front long wall outer face	1	1.8		1.5	2.70	
	Front inner face	1	1.60		1.5	2.40	
	Rear long wall outer face	1	1.10		1.5	1.65	
	Rear long wall inner face	1	0.90		1.5	1.35	
	Left hand wall outer face	1	0.95		1.5	1.425	
	Left hand wall inner face	1	0.85		1.50	1.275	
	Right outer wall outer wall	1	0.75		1.50	1.125	
	Inner wall inner face	1	0.40		1.50	0.60	Length = 1.8+0.8
	Vertical end	2	0.10		1.50	0.30	+1.1+0.75+0.3
	Top surface of walls	1	4.8	0.10	—	0.48	= 4.8 m
						13.31 sq m	
4.	10 cm thick brick floor (flat) in 1 : 6 cement mortar over well rammed earth						
	Latrine	1	0.90	0.75		0.675	
	Entrance	1	0.60	0.75		0.450	
						1.125 sq m	
5.	12 mm thick cement plaster over 10 cm thick flat brick flooring 1 : 3	area	same as	SI. 4		1.125 sq m	
6.	For latrine seat foot rest	2 Nos.				2 Nos.	
7.	Precast 1 : 2 : 4 R.C.C. slab cover over pit	1	$\frac{\pi \times (1.0)^2}{4}$	—	0.06	0.047 cum	
	Sanitary Fitting						
8.	Precast latrine pan (cement mortar 1 : 3)	1 No.				1 No.	
9.	Water seal trap	1 No.				1 No.	
10.	Supply and fix 50 mm dia for precast pipe 1 : 3 cement mm	1	2.0 m	—	—	2.0 m	

Table 12.13 gives abstract of cost of sanitary pit latrine.

Table 12.13

S. No.	*Particulars of item of work*	*Quality*	*Unit*	*Rate*	*Cost*	*Remark*
1.	Earth work in excavation	10.54 cum	cum	63.55	664.02	
2.	2nd class B.W. in mud mortar	1.125 cum	cum	906.8	1020.15	
3.	Cement pointing 1 : 3 (flush) cement : sand mortar	13.31 sq m	sq m	24.00	319.44	
4.	10 cm thick brick flooring in 1 : 6 cement mortar	1.125 sq m	sq m	72.00	193.56	
5.	12 mm thick 1 : 3 cement plaster	1.125 sq m	sq m	58.30	65.59	
6.	Latrine seat foot rest	2 Nos.	No.	202.0	404.0	
7.	1 : 2 : 4 precast R.C.C. slab	0.047 cum	cum	1740.90	99.23	0.047 × 0.01 × 1000 × 7.8 kg = 0.47 + 0.01 × 7.8
	(*a*) Reinforcement @ 1%	3.57	kg	20.40	73.14	= 0.47 × 7.8 = 3.57 kg

8.	Precast latrine pan (1 : 3 cement mortar)	1 No.	No.	230.3	230.30	
9.	Waterseal trap	1 No.	No.	200.0	200.0	
10.	Supply and fix 50 mm dia pipe (1 : 3 cement mortar precast)	2 m	m	137.20	274.4	
				Total	3543.83	
		Add water charge 1½%			53.15	
					3596.98	
		Add 10% for contractor's profit			359.69	
					3956.67	
				Grand total say	3956.70	

12.6. ESTIMATE OF SANITARY WORK FROM HOUSE CONNECTION TO PUBLIC SEWER

Example 12.6. *Fig. 12.15 gives a typical part layout of a building complex. Prepare a detailed estimate for sanitary work in respect of the sanitary fittings shown therein.*

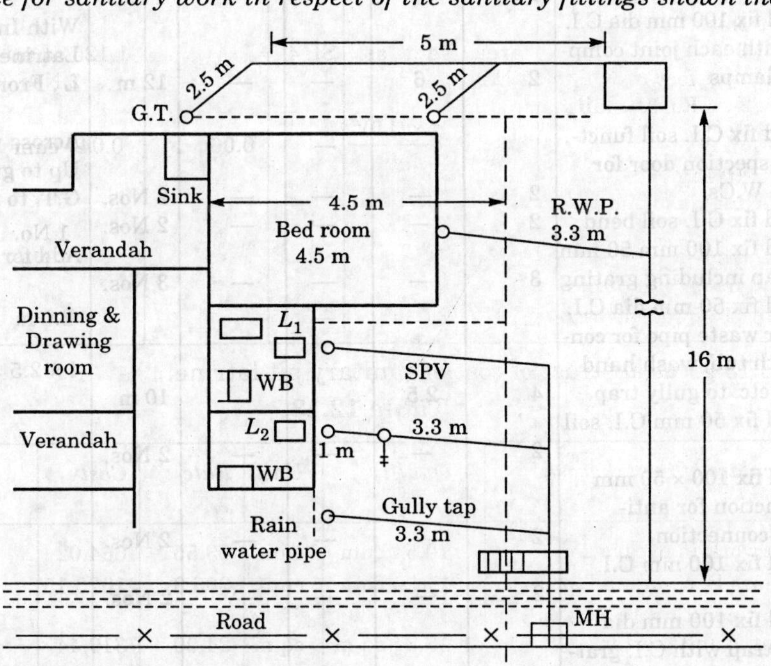

----- : Branch Pipe Line
----- : House Pipe Line
—×— : Public Sewer
M.H. : Man Hole
IT : Intercepting Trap
SPV : Soil Pipe Ventilated
I.C. : Inspection Chamber
L_1 : W.C. European Style
L_2 : W.C. Indian Style

Fig. 12.15. Layout of sewer and water pipe line in a building complex.

Table 12.14 gives details of measurement and calculation of quantities of sanitary works in respect of a building complex.

Table 12.14

S. No.	*No. Particular of work*	*Length (m)*		*Brea-dth (m)*	*Height Depth (m)*	*Quan-tity*	*Remark*
1.	Supply and fix European style W.C. with teak wood cover and seat complete with 14 litres C.I. cistern of standard make complete with fittings and accessories	1	—	—	—	1 No.	
2.	Supply and fix W.C. as in S. No. 1 above but Indian style W.C. (50 cm)	1	—	—	—	1 No.	
3.	Supply and fix foot rests for S. No. 2 above	2 Nos.				2 Nos.	
4.	Supply and fix 100 mm dia P-trap complete with lead joint	1 No.				1 Nos.	
5.	Supply and fix 100 mm dia C.I. soil pipe with each joint complete with clamps	2	6	—	—	12 m	With Indian pattern Latrine seat L : From seat to wall = 0.30 m Across wall = 0.60 m Up to gully trap = 1.8 m G.T. to sewer = 3.4 m = 6.0 m Add for one = 12 m
6.	Supply and fix C.I. soil function with inspection door for connecting W.Cs.	2	—	—	—	2 Nos.	
7.	Supply and fix C.I. soil bend	2	—	—	—	2 Nos.	
8.	Supply and fix 100 mm 50 mm C.I. soil trap including grating	3	—	—	—	3 Nos.	
9.	Supply and fix 50 mm dia C.I. soil pipe for waste pipe for connecting bath tub, wash hand basin sink etc. to gully trap	4	2.5			10 m	4 × 2.5 = 10 m
10.	Supply and fix 50 mm C.I. soil bend	2	—	—	—	2 Nos.	
11.	Supply and fix 100 × 50 mm C.I. soil junction for anti-syphonage connection	2	—	—	—	2 Nos.	
12.	Supply and fix 100 mm C.I. soil cowl	2	—	—		2 Nos.	
13.	Supply and fix 100 mm dia S.W. gully trap with C.I. gratings	4	—	—	—	4 Nos.	G.T. to sewer
14.	Supply and fix 100 mm dia S.W. pipe over 10 cm lime concrete bedding and haunching the pipe and including necessary earth work	1	31.1 m			31.1 m	2 × 2.5 = 5.0 m 2 × 3.3 = 6.6 m I.C. to IT = 16 m I.T. MH = 3.5 m 31.1 m
15.	Supply and fix 10 cm dia S.W. intercepting trap complete	1				1 No.	
16.	Supply and fix 100 mm C.I. mica valve	1				1 No.	

17.	Construction of inspection chamber (90 cm × 120 cm) with 20 cm brick wall in 1 : 6 cement mortar over concrete base inside as per drawings and specifications.	2	—	—	2 Nos.
18.	Construction of Manhole over public Sewer with 30 cm thick wall and 15 cm thick R.C. slab with 60 × 60 cm heavy C.I. hinged type cover	1	—	—	1 No.
19.	Making sewer connections.	1 No.	—	—	1 No.

Table 12.15 gives abstracts of cost of sanitary works in respect of building complex.

Table 12.15

S. No.	*Particulars of item of work*	*Quantity*	*Unit*	*Rate*	*Cost*	*Remark*
1.	Supply and fix European style W.C. with accessories.	1 No.	No.	1562.40	1562.40	
2.	Supply and fix Indian pattern W.C. complete with accessories.	1 No.	No.	1279.75	1279.75	
3.	S & F foot-rest	2 Nos.	No.	105.90	211.80	
4.	S & F 100 mm ϕ P-trap	1 No.	No.	150.0	150.0	*Prime cost
5.	S & F 100 mm ϕ C.I. soil pipe	12 m	m	96.95	2363.40	
6.	S & F C.I. soil junction	2 Nos.	No.	273.8	547.6	
7.	S & F C.I. soil bend	2 Nos.	No.	99.30	198.60	
8.	S & F C.I. soil trap	3 Nos.	No.	388.9	1160.7	
9.	S & F C.I. soil pipe	10 m	m	50.3	503.0	
10.	S & F C.I. 50 mm soil bend	2 Nos.	No.	62.40	124.80	
11.	S & F C.I. 100 x 50 mm C.I. soil junction	2 Nos.	No.	153.75	307.50	
12.	S & F C.I. 100 mm C.I. cowl	2 Nos.	No.	250.0	500.0	Prime cost
13.	S & F C.I. 100 mm S.W. gully trap	4 Nos.	No.	240.0	960	*Prime cost
14.	S & F C.I. 10 mm dia S.W. pipe including laying	31.1 m	m	85.0	1710.50	
15.	S & F S.W. intercepting trap	1 No.	No.	208	208.0	
16.	S & F 100 mm ϕ C.I. mica valve	1 No.	No.	200	200.0	*Prime cost
17.	Construction of inspection chamber complete	2 Nos.	No.	1500	3000.0	L.S
18.	Construction of manhole over public sewer complete	1 No.	No.	2453.95	2453.95	L.S.
19.	Making service connection	1	No.	500	500.0	L.S.
				Total ₹	17942.0	
				Add 1½% of water charges	269.13	
					18211.13	
				Add 10% for contractor's profit	1821.11	
				Grand Total ₹	20032.24	
				Say	20032.0	

12.7. ESTIMATE OF A TYPICAL TUBE-WELL WITH A DEEP HAND PUMP

For construction of a tube-well a casing pipe with a cutter at its end, is dug. During the boring a soil chart is prepared on the basis of soil samples collected during the boring.

The casing pipe is sunk by percussion (for soft soil) or rotary (hard strata) boring when suitable depth has been bored, the strainer which is a perforated or slotted pipe, is lowered followed by lowering of the tube well pipe and the casing pipe is removed simultaneously.

In the case of large diameter tube-well, the pipe is sunk by drilling and sinking. A cutter is attached at the end of the pipe when the desired depth is reached the boring pipe and cutter are replaced by tube-well pipe and the strainer.

Example 12.7. *Fig. 12.16 shows a 75 metre deep tube-well with deep well pump. The tube-well is 50 mm dia. The strainer is made of 3 pieces of 1.5 metre each.*

Prepare a detailed estimate of quantities of item of work assuming suitable data where required.

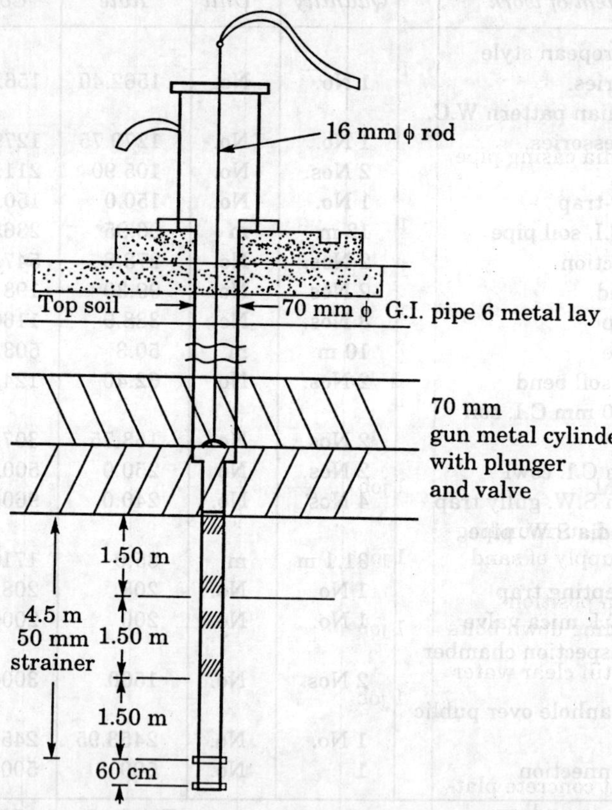

Fig. 12.16. 75 metre tube-well with deep well pump.

Table 12.16 gives details of measurement and calculation of quantity in respect of a 75 metre deep tube well.

Table 12.16

S. No.	Particulars of work	No.	Length (m)	Breadth (m)	Height / Depth (m)	Quantity	Remark
	A. Materials						
1.	50 mm G.I. pipe	1	74.0	—	—	74 m	
2.	70 mm dia. G.I. housing pipe	1	6.0	—	—	60 m	
3.	50 mm dia strainer	3	1.50	—	—	4.5 m	
4.	70 mm dia. metal cylinder with valve and plunger	1	—	—	—	1 No.	
5.	Hand pump with extra length of 16 mm ϕ rod	1	—	—	—	1 No.	
6.	Sockets (extra)	4	—	—	—	4 Nos.	
7.	Bait Plug	1	—	—	—	1 No.	
	B. Sinking						
8.	Boring with 70 mm dia casing pipe (complete operation)						
	(*i*) 0 to 20 m	1	20 m	—	—	20 m	
	(*ii*) 20 to 35 m	1	15 m	—	—	15 m	
	(*iii*) 35 to 50 m	1	15 m	—	—	15 m	
	(*iv*) 50 to 65 m	1	15 m	—	—	15 m	
	(*v*) 65 to 80 m	1	15 m	—	—	15 m	
	C. Labour						
9.	Transport of material	1 job	—	—	—	1 job	
10.	Inserting coarse sand surrounding strainer including supply of sand	1 job	—		—	1 job	
11.	Fixing hand pump in position including S & F holding down bolts	1 job	—	—	—	1 job	
12.	Pumping out water till clear water is obtained	1 job	—	—	—	1 job	
	D. Construction						
13.	Constructing cement concrete platform and foundation including supply of materials	1 job	—			1 job	
14.	Constructing cement concrete drain 3 m in length	1	3 m	—	—	3 m	

Table 12.17 gives abstract of items of work 80 metre tube-well with deep well pump.

Table 12.17

S. No.	*Particulars of item of work*	*Quantity*	*Unit*	*Rate*	*Cost*	*Remark*
	A. Materials					
1.	50 mm C.I. pipe	74 m	m	155.05	11470.00	
2.	70 mm dia C.I. Housing pipe	6 m	m	229.60	1374.00	
3.	50 mm dia strainer	4.5 m	m	500.00	500.00	
4.	70 mm dia metal cylinder with valve and plunger	1	No.	200.00	200.00	
5.	Hand pump with 16 mm ϕ connecting rod	1	No.	1000.00	1000.00	
6.	Sockets	4 Nos	No.	225.60	902.40	
7.	Bait plug	1	No.	50.00	500.00	
	B. Sinking					
8.	Boring with 70 mm dia casing					
	(*i*) 0 to 20 m	20 m	metre	95.35	1907.00	
	(*ii*) 20 to 35 m	15 m	metre	—		
	(*iii*) 35 to 50 m	15 m	metre	134.30	—	
	(*iv*) 50 to 65 m	15 m	metre	per m	8040.00	
	(*v*) 60 to 80 m	15 m	metre	—		
	C. Labour					
9.	Transport of material	1 job	job	—		
10.	Inserting coarse sand	1 job	job	—		
11.	Fixing hand pump	1 job	job	—	2000.0 × 9	
12.	Pumping out water	1 job	job	—		
13.	Constructing cement concrete platform	1 job	job	—		
14.	Constructing cement concrete drains	3 m	m	—		
				Total cost ₹	16423.00	
	Add 5% for contingencies and work charged establishment				821.15	
				Grand Total	17244.15	
				say	17244.00	

12.8. ESTIMATE OF WATER SUPPLY WORK FROM BRANCH SERVICE LINE TO HOUSE CONNECTION

Example 12.8. *Fig 12.15 gives a typical part layout of a building complex. Prepare a detailed estimate for water supply works in respect of fittings and connections shown therein. Assume suitable data where required.*

Table 12.18 gives details of measurements and calculation of quantities for water supply work in a building complex.

Table 12.18

S. No.	Particular of work	No.	Length (m)	Breadth (m)	Height Depth (m)	Quantity	Remark
1.	Supply and fix G.I. tank 150 litre capacity fitted into float valve and accessories	1	—	—	—	1 No.	
2.	Supply and fix C.I. enamelled bath tube complete with accessories 150 × 45 cm.	1	—	—	—	1 No.	
3.	Supply and fix 20 mm dia pipe line complete with sockets, bends and blows and including connection to branch pipe line	1	19.5 m	—	—	19.5 m	Length 15 + 4.5 = 19.5 m
4.	Supply and fix 12 mm C.I. pipe as in sIB above	1	34.1 m	—	—	34.1 m	Length to wash hand basin, sink, bath tub 4 × 3 = 12 m.
5.	S & F 1 mm ϕ brass stop cock heavy type complete		—	—	—	4 Nos.	Connecting pipe 3.3 × 2 + 2.5 = 6.6 + 2.5 = 9.1 m
6.	S & F 12 mm ϕ brass stop cock heavy type complete	5			—	5 Nos.	To overhead tank 1 × 6 = 6 m
7.	S & F C.I. cover for stop cock with chamber and surface block	2	—	—	—	2 Nos.	From overhead tank to flushy cistern 2 × 3.5 = 7 m
8.	Supply and fix 10 mm brass ferrule	1	—	—	—	1 No.	34.1 m
9.	S & F 12 mm lead pipe with double coupling complete	2	—	—	—	2 Nos.	
10.	S & F 12 × 1000 mm shower	1		—	—	1 No.	
11.	S & F 5 cm WHB P or other standard make complete with wall brackets pillar cock and accessories.	2	—	—	—	2 Nos.	
12.	S & F 60 cm × 60 cm sink complete as in Sl. No. 11	1				1 No.	
13.	Cutting holes in walls and making good with cement mortar	6	—	—	—	6 Nos.	

Table 12.19 gives abstract of costs of water supply work in building complex.

Table 12.19

S. No.	*Particulars of item of works*	*Quantity*	*Unit*	*Rate*	*Cost*	*Remark*
1.	S & F G.I. tank 270 litre capacity	1	each	363.92	3639.20	
2.	S & F 150 × 45 cm C.I. enamelled bath tube	1	each	560.00	560.00	
3.	Supply and fix 20 mm φ pipe line	19.5 m	metre	81.75	1594.13	
4.	S & F 15 mm φ C.I. pipe line	34.1 m	metre	62.85	2143.19	
5.	S & F 15 mm φ brass bibcock	4 Nos.	each	94.65	3786.0	
6.	S & F 15 mm φ brass stop cock	5 Nos.	each	84.90	424.5	
7.	S & F.C.I. cover for stop cock wall chamber	2 Nos.	each	1200	240.0	*Prime cost
8.	S & F 10 mm brass ferrule	1 No.	each	80.0	80.0	
9.	S & F 12 mm lead pipe	4 Nos.	each	50.0	200.0	*Prime cost
10.	S & F 10 mm × 100 mm shower	1 No.	each	78.7	78.7	
11.	S & F WHB Parry 630 × 450 mm complete	1 No.	each	1471.10	1471.10	
12.	S & F 600 × 450 × 150 mm sink complete	1 No.	each	3663.0	3663.0	
13.	Cutting holes in walls and making good	6 Nos.	each	20	120.0	*Prime cost
				Total ₹	20159.82	
				Add 1½ % for water charges	302.40	
					20462.22	
				Add 10% for contractor's profit	2046.22	
				Grand Total	22508.44	
				Say ₹	22508.00	

12.9. SOURCES OF WATER SUPPLY

12.9.1. Introduction

All sources of water can be broadly classified under the following two categories :

1. Surface water. 2. Ground water.

The surface water can further be sub-divided into the following categories :

(*i*) Streams (*ii*) Lakes

(*iii*) Ponds (*iv*) Rivers

(*v*) Imponded Reservoir (*vi*) Stored Rain Water.

The ground water is obtained by means of wells and tube wells.

The basic source in both the cases is from the water cycle consisting of Precipitation (Rain), Percolation (Ground water), Run off (River, Sea), evaporation and transpiration (through plants). This endless water cycle does not have any beginning or end.

12.9.2. Rainfall and Run off

When the rain falls, a portion of it percolates in the ground, and a portion evaporates and part of it flows on the ground to join/form stream and river. Some of the water which percolates in the ground comes out in the form of springs etc. and joins the stream. In this way, water reaches the stream from surface run off and from spring or base flow. The total quantity of water which reaches the stream or river, both from surface flow as well as base flow is known as *Run Off*.

The following losses take place during the 'run off' of water :

(*i*) Losses by evaporation (*ii*) Losses by percolation
(*iii*) Losses by absorption.

It may thus be stated that

Rainfall – Losses = Run-off

$$\text{The run-off coefficient (\%)} = \frac{\text{Run-off}}{\text{Rainfall}} \times 100$$

12.9.3. Sources of Water

As already discussed in Article 12.8.1, the basic sources of water are the surface water and ground water. The surface water sources are briefly described below while the ground water source is discussed in the following Articles (12.8.4 and 12.8.5). The surface water sources are discussed with reference to the following impurities :

(*i*) Colour, (*ii*) Odour, (*iii*) Taste,
(*iv*) Physical (*v*) Chemical, (*vi*) Bacterial.

(*i*) **Streams.** The impurities in the stream water are on account of clay, sand, colloidals and minerals. By and large the water is colourless, odourless and tasteless. Depending upon the strata through which water passes, it is likely to have mineral impurities, which may or may not be harmful. Water from stream and springs is the best source of supply.

(*ii*) **Lakes.** Lakes are formed in impervious bed. Since the water is not as free flowing as in the case of stream and springs, it is likely to be affected by bacterial impurities.

Lake water forms a good source of water supply, particularly if the lake is located at high altitude.

(*iii*) **River.** Because of the flowing nature of the water and continuous exposure to heat and light, it has self purification property. It is the major source of water supply for most of the water works in the country.

The water carries sand, silt and clay with it. The intake point should be a good distance upstream from the point at which sewage is discharged into the river.

(*iv*) **Ponds.** Comparatively small quantities of water may be collected from ponds, which are formed by depression in the plain. Because of the stagnant nature of water, it contains physical, chemical and bacterial impurities. It is invariably contaminated and unsuitable for water supply purposes.

(*v*) **Impounded Reservoir.** In most of the rivers in the country there is considerable variation in the discharge between rainy season and dry season. Whereas water during the rains goes waste and occasionally causes flooding, there may be water scarcity or water famine during the summer months.

This difficulty has been partly overcome by storing water by constructing bund, weir or dam across the river. While selecting a suitable site for such a dam, the following factors are taken into consideration :

(*i*) Narrow width so that a comparatively small length would be able to store large quantity.

(*ii*) The quantity of available water. It depends upon the following :

1. Intensity of rainfall. 2. Run-off. 3. Catchment area.

(*iii*) Gravity flow from reservoir to treatment plant.

(*iv*) Near intake point.

(*v*) Impervious soil bed free from porous beds and fissures.

(*vi*) Avoid cultivated area, highway, town and costly estate getting submerged under reservoir water.

(*vii*) Bed soil should be free from soluble salts, minerals etc.

(*viii*) Water shed to be free from swampy areas to avoid bacterial impurities.

12.9.4. Ground Water Flow

The entrance of rain water or melted snow into the ground is known an infiltration. The movement of water from surface to the underground is known as percolation. The quantity of water which percolates from surface to form ground water, depends upon the following factors :

1. **Rainfall characteristics**

(*i*) The quantity of infiltration is moreif the rate of rainfall is slow and without impact.

(*ii*) Heavy rain fall along with impact results in reduced percolation.

2. **Soil characteristics,** *i.e.* porosity of soil and size of the pores.

3. **Soil cover.** This cover protects the soil from getting compacted by rain and detain water for some times depending upon the following :

(*i*) Density of cover

(*ii*) Forest and vegetation on top.

The water which percolated from the surface collects over the impervious strata. This strata which holds water is known as *water bearing startum*. The top of the water level in this stratum is known as *water table*. This level varies throughout the year. During rainy season, the water table is high.

The porosities of common soils are given in Table 12.20.

Table 12.20. Porosities of Common Soils

S. No.	*Type of Soil*	*Porosity*
1.	Sand and gravel moderately compacted	35—40%
2.	Well graded sand and gravel	24—30%
3.	Sand stone	14—30%
4.	Chalk	14—45%
5.	Clay	44—47%
6.	Top soil	37—65%

The various sources of ground water are :

1. Springs. 2. Infiltration Galleries.

3. Porous Pipe Galleries. 4. Wells.

These are briefly described below :

1. **Springs.** Springs are formed under the following conditions.

(*i*) When the surfaces of earth drops sharply below the normal watertable [Fig. 12.17].

(*ii*) When ground water is collected in the form of a reservoir which forces the water to overflow at the surface [Fig. 12.17].

(*iii*) When a fissure in an impervious stratum allows artesian water to flow in the form of springs [Fig. 12.17].

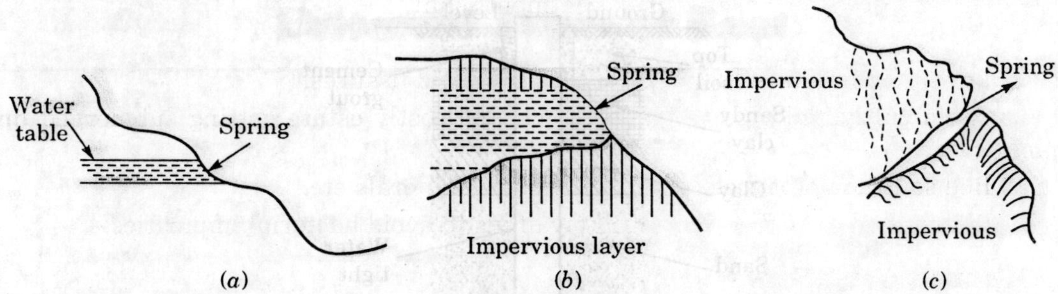

Fig. 12.17

2. **Infiltration Galleries.** These are underground tunnels which are constructed at right angles to the direction of flow of underground water.

3. **Porous Pipe Galleries.** When large quantity of ground water exist over a wide area, it is collected by laying porous pipes or pipes with open joints in the area at some distance as shown in Fig. 12.9. It is also called *Runway water collector.*

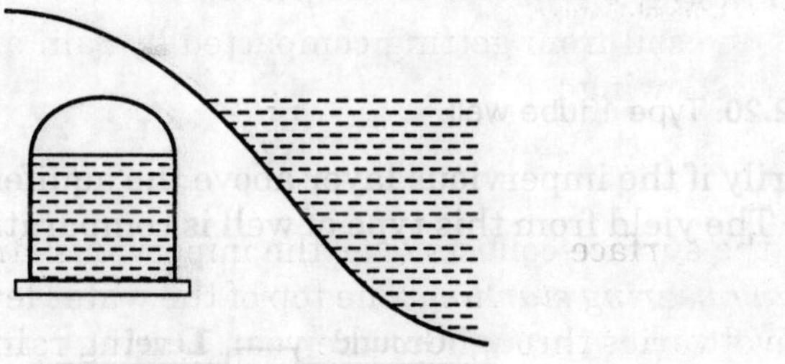

Fig. 12.18

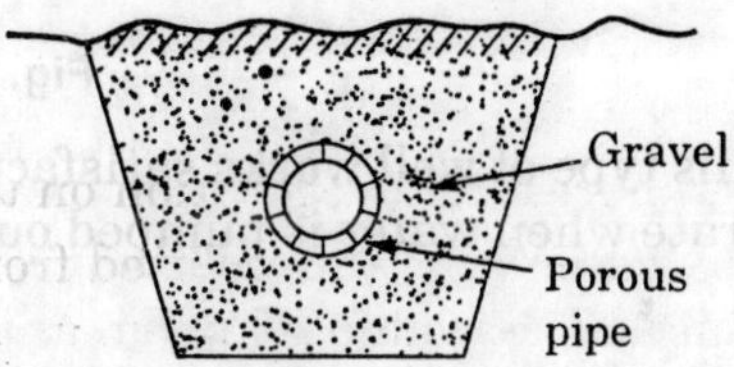

Fig. 12.19

4. **Wells.** Wells may be classified into the following three categories :

(*i*) *Oyen well or Dug well.* These are normally 3 to 5 metre deep and are a normal source of supply for the villages.

(*ii*) *Lined well.* The wells are lined with bricks, stone or concrete.

These wells are 10 to 20 metre deep.

(*iii*) *Deep wells and Tube wells.* These are the normal source of water supply in cities. They are used either alone or to augment the supply from rivers. In remote areas where irrigation facilities are not available, tube wells form the only source of irrigation wells.

Figs. 12.20, 12.21, 12.22, 12.23 and 12.24 illustrate the five types of tube wells.

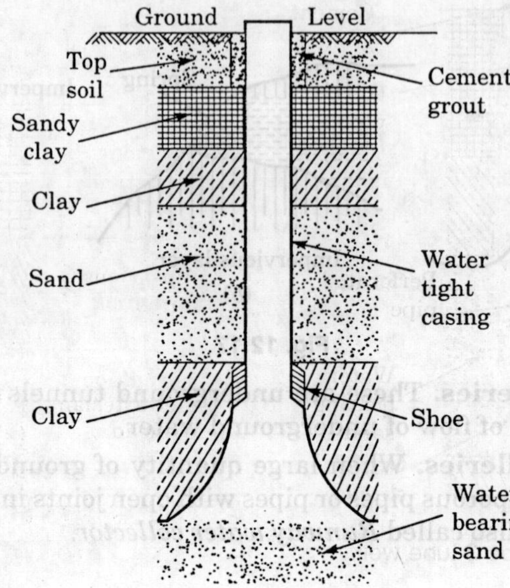

Fig. 12.20. Type 1 tube well.

This type of well works satisfactorily if the impervious layer above the aquifer does not disintegrate when water is pumped out. The yield from this type of well is comparatively less.

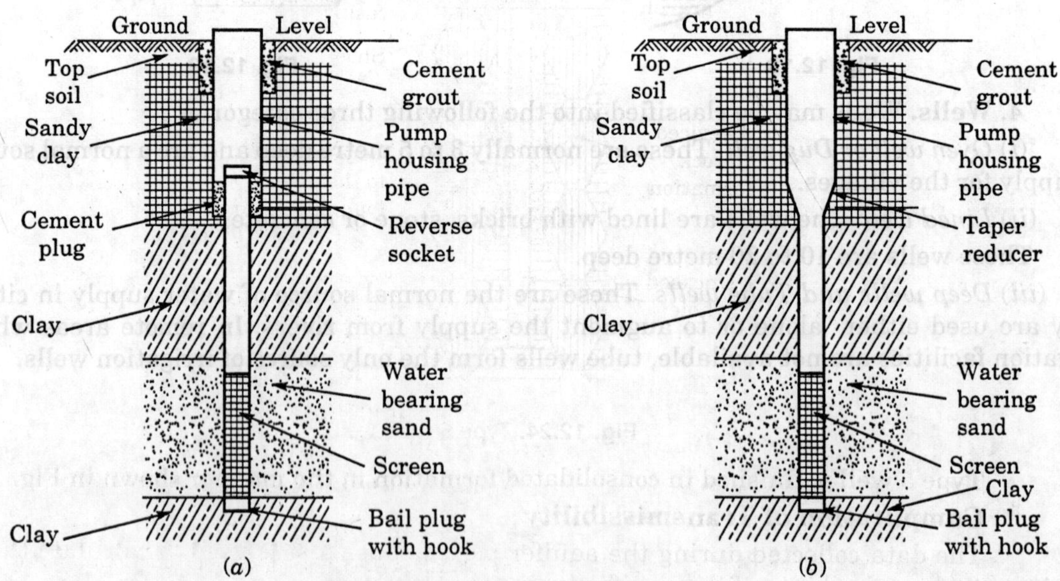

Fig. 12.21. Type 2 tube well.

Types 2 and 3 wells are suitable for unconsolidated formation finished in the manner shown in Figs. 12.21, 12.22.

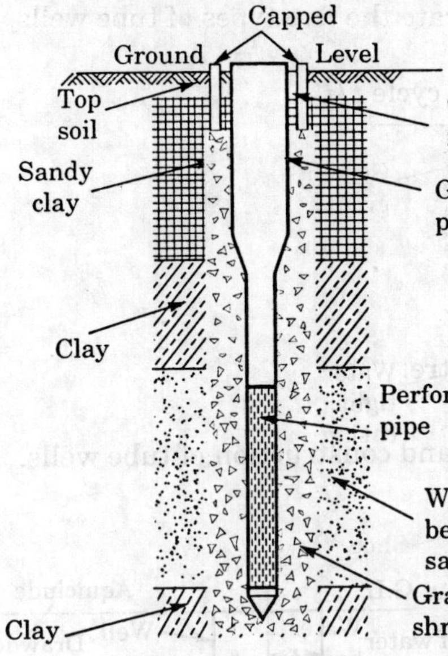

Fig. 12.22. Type 3 tube well.

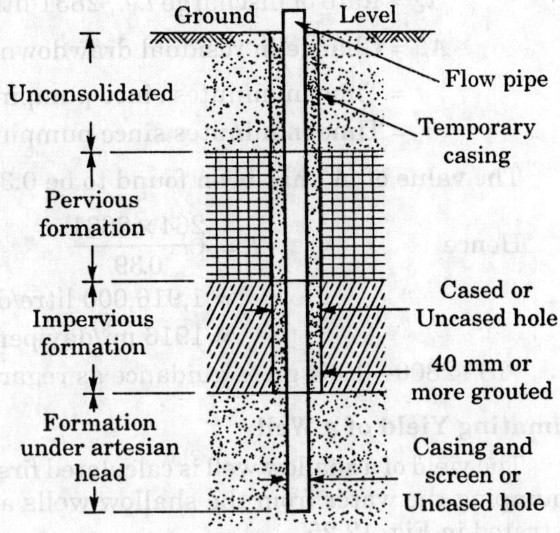

Fig. 12.23. Type 4 tube well.

Type 4 well is finished under artesian condition.

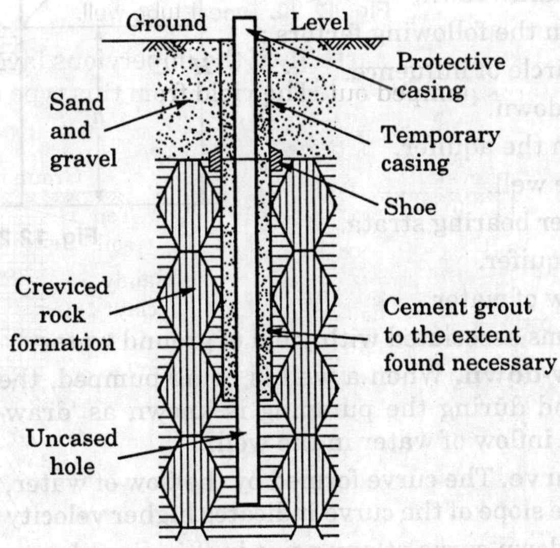

Fig. 12.24. Type 5 tube well.

Type 5 well is finished in consolidated formation in the manner shown in Fig. 12.24.

Computation of Transmissibility

The data collected during the aquifer performance test is used to calculate the coefficient of transmissibility of the aquifers using the equation

$$T = \frac{264 \times Q}{A_s'}$$

where T = Transmissibility in litre/day per metre

Q = Rate of discharge *i.e.*, 2831 litre/min.

A_s' = Charge in residual drawdown over a log cycle t/t'.

t = Time in minutes since pumping started.

t' = Time in minutes since pumping stopped.

The value of A_s' has been found to be 0.39 metre.

$$\text{Hence} \quad T = \frac{264 \times 2831}{0.39}$$

$$= 1{,}916{,}000 \text{ litre/day per metre.}$$

$$= 1916 \text{ m}^3\text{/day per metre.}$$

IS : 2800—1964 gives guidance as regards design and construction of tube wells.

Estimating Yield of a Well

The yield of a shallow well is calculated first by pumping the water from the shallow wells as illustrated in Fig. 12.25.

The discharge is proportional to the draw-down $(H—h) = p$. The yield per unit drawdown or the specific capacity of well is generally expressed in litres/minute/metre of drawdown.

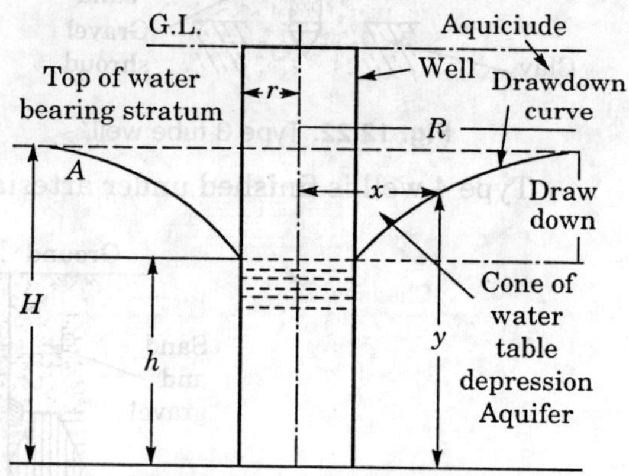

Fig. 12.25. Yield of a well.

Yield depends upon the following factors :

(*i*) Radius of the circle of influence.

(*ii*) Depth of draw-down.

(*iii*) Depth of well in the aquifer.

(*iv*) Diameter of the well.

(*v*) Porosity of water bearing strata.

(*vi*) Inclination of aquifer.

(*vii*) Direction of flow of water.

Explanation of terms associated with yield of ground water.

1. **Depth of Draw-down.** When a well is being pumped, the difference between the levels of water before and during the pumping is known as 'draw-down'. The greater the drawdown, greater is the inflow of water in the well.

2. **Draw-down Curve.** The curve formed by the flow of water, is known as 'draw-down curve'. The increase in the slope of the curve indicates higher velocity of flow and greater flow.

The slope of draw-down curve at any point in it is given by

$$s = \frac{dy}{dx}$$

Since the velocity varies with the slope

$$V \propto \frac{dy}{dx}$$

or $$V = k.s. \text{ (Darcy's Law)}$$

where k = constant, which is termed as transmissibility or transmission constant of the material. It represents the quantity of water, which would flow through a porous medium of a unit cross-section in a unit time, when the hydraulic gradient is unity.

3. **Radius of the Circle of Influence.** When water is drawn from a well, the level of underground water is depressed all-round in the form of an inverted cone. The cone of depression will have a base of radius R, known as the 'Radius of the circle of influence'. The greater the radius of influence, the greater will be the flow of water into the well.

4. **Depth of Well in the Aquifer.** Greater depth of the well in the aquifer represents greater sectional area in the well to allow the water to flow through it.

5. **Diameter of the Well.** Bigger the diameter of the well, greater will be the yield.

Porosity of Water Bearing Stratum. The greater the porosity of the material, more will be inflow into the well.

7. **Inclination of Aquifer.** This influences the flow of underground water from one region to another.

8. **Yield Formula.**

Let H = Depth of water while there is no pumping.

h = Depth of water during pumping.

R = Radius of the circle of influence.

r = Radius of the well.

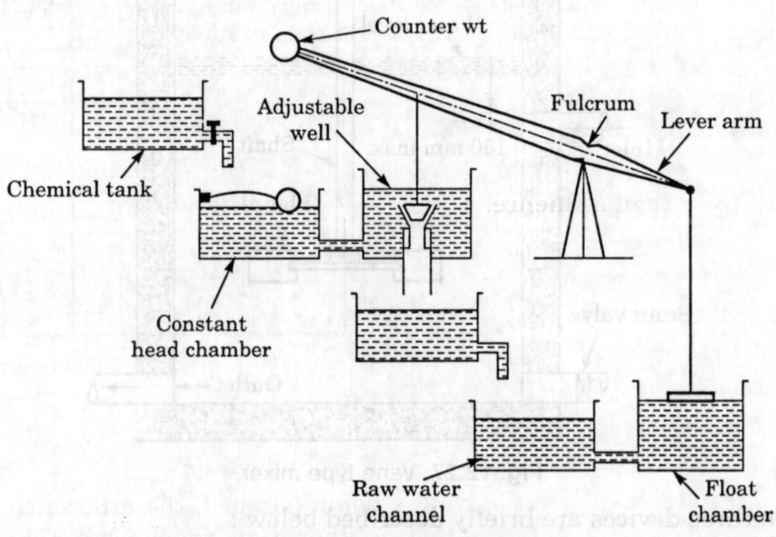

Fig. 12.26. Adjustable weir outlet.

The third is a solution feed device which controls the quantity of solution going in the raw water by means of adjustable weir.

Mixing Devices. In water treatment, rapid mixing of chemical in powder or solution forms with the water to be treated is the perikinetic phase of coagulation. The coagulant is dispersed quickly in the water under treatment giving rise to floccules or nuclei. The main purpose of a proper rapid mixing device is to ensure that all water to be treated receives uniform dosing.

Both mechanical as well as hydraulic mixing devices are used for rapid mixing. However mechanical devices are preferred because they give constant performance over fluctuating flows. Hydraulic devices on the other hand give varying performance depending on the flows. The advantages and disadvantages of hydraulic devices are given below :

Advantages

1. More adaptable to the space available.
2. Less mechanical failure.

Disadvantages

1. Less flexibility in control.   2. Greater loss of head.

The use of hydraulic devices is restricted to design flows of 200 m^3/h. Mechanical device on the other hand may be provided in multiple units for flows exceeding 2000 m^3/h.

IS : 7090—1973 lays down the guide lines for materials, design considerations and method of construction of rapid mixing devices.

Figs. 12.27, 12.28 and 12.29 illustrate the various mechanical mixing devices.

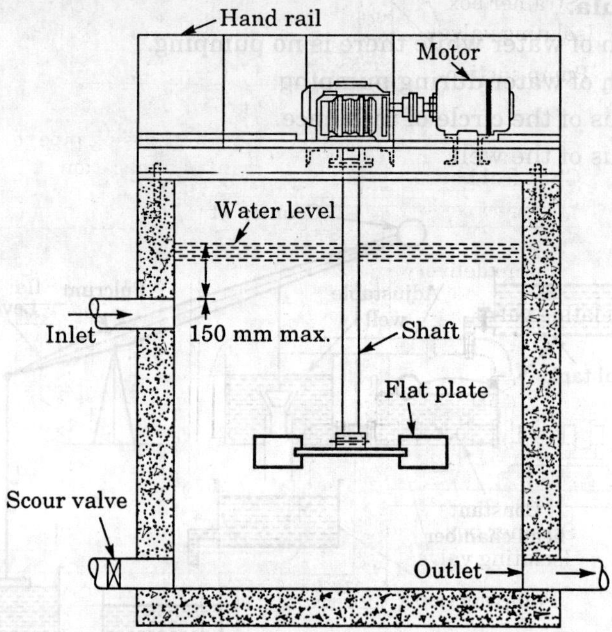

Fig. 12.27. Vane type mixer.

The above three devices are briefly described below :

1. **Vane Type Mixer.** This device consists of an operating mechanism fitted with vane. The vane is installed centrally in a chamber. The water inlet may be from top or bottom (Fig. 12.27). For optimum efficiency the capacity of the motor and the maximum unsupported length of the shaft should be correlated on the lines given in Table 12.21.

Table 12.21. Capacities of Motor and Unsupported Shaft Length for Flow

Flow m^3/H	*Capacity of Motor kW*	*Maximum unsupported length of shaft*
200	0.75	1.5 to 3 m (Not to cause vibration and wobbling).
500	1.25	
1000	2.25	
2000	3.0	
2500	3.75	

2. **Jet Type Mixer.** The jet system of flash mixing produces the agitation in the mixer tank hydraulically. (Fig. 12.28).

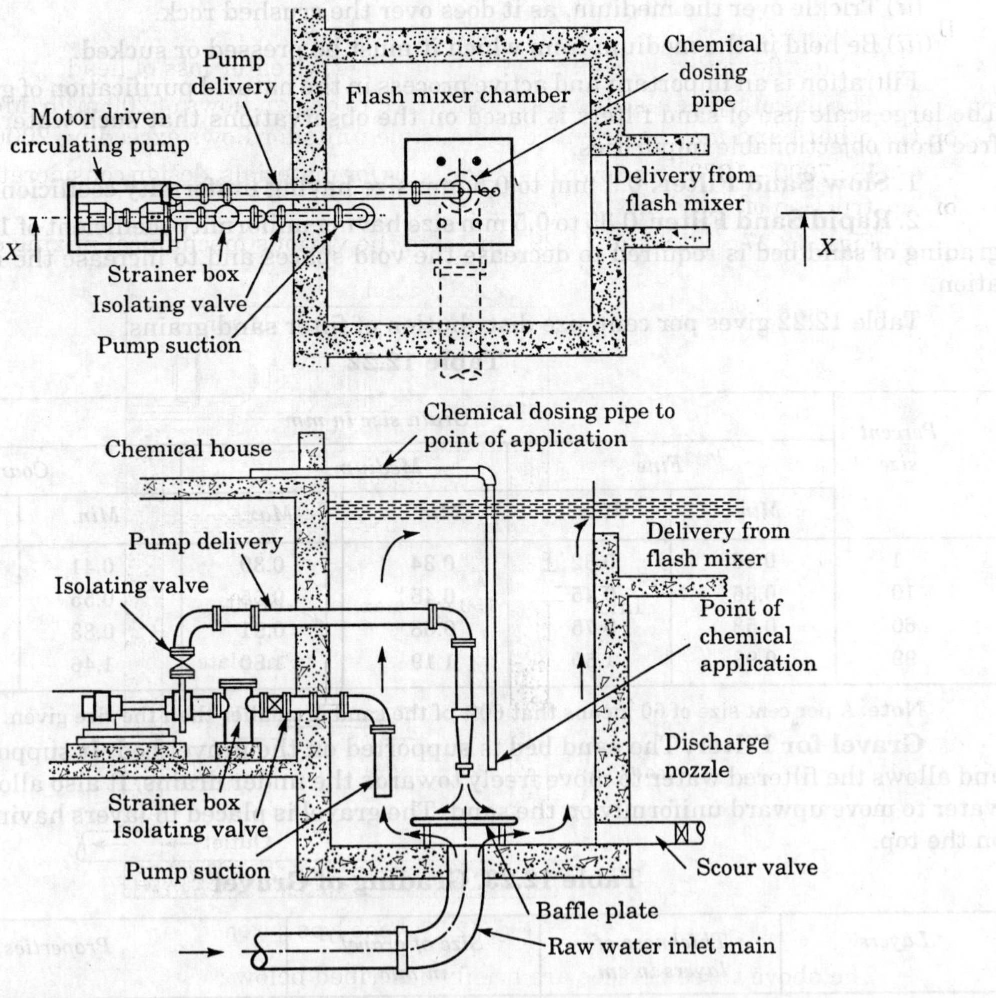

Fig. 12.28. Jet type flash mixer.

3. **High Speed Propeller Mixer.** Blades mounted on a vertical or inclined shaft generate strong currents in axial direction. The propellers have a high rate of flow displacement. The ratio of tank diameter to impeller diameter varies between 6 : 1 to 3 : 1.

Displacement capacity should be about three times the tank volume (Fig. 12.29).

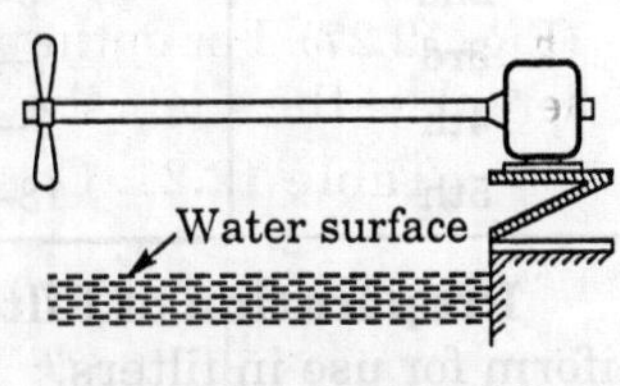

Fig. 12.29. Rapid mixed device.

12.9.5. Filtration

When water flows through a porous, or open-textured medium such as sand, some of the suspended and colloidal impurities in the water are left behind in the pores or openings or upon the medium itself. This process of separating impurities from the carrying liquid is called filtration.

The water may,

(*i*) Fill the pores of the medium, as it does in the sand filters commonly used in water purification.

(*ii*) Trickle over the medium, as it does over the crushed rock.

(*iii*) Be held in the medium from which it must be pressed or sucked.

Filtration is an important and active process in the natural purification of ground water. The large scale use of sand filters is based on the observations that such water is relatively free from objectionable impurities.

1. **Slow Sand Filter.** 0.3 mm to 0.5 mm size having uniformity coefficient of 1.75.

2. **Rapid Sand Filter.** 0.35 to 0.5 mm size having uniformity coefficient of 1.60. Uniform grading of sand bed is required to decrease the void spaces and to increase the rate of filteration.

Table 12.22 gives per cent size distribution of filter sand grains.

Table 12.22

Percent size	*Grain size in mm*					
	Fine		*Medium*		*Coarse*	
	Min.	*Max.*	*Min.*	*Max.*	*Min.*	*Max.*
1	0.26	0.32	0.34	0.39	0.41	0.45
10	0.35	0.45	0.45	0.55	0.55	0.65
60	0.53	0.75	0.68	0.91	0.83	1.08
99	0.93	1.50	1.19	1.80	1.46	2.00

Note. A per cent size of 60 means that 60% of the sand is smaller than the size given.

Gravel for Filter. The sand bed is supported on the gravel bed. It supports the sand and allows the filtered water to move freely towards the under drains. It also allows the wash water to move upward uniformly on the sand. The gravel is placed in layers having finess size on the top.

Table 12.23. Grading of Gravel

Layers	*Thickness of layers in cm*	*Size of gravel in mm*	*Properties*
1st	5—8	4.7— 2.4	Clean, hard, durable, rounded particle free from clay loam, shells. It should not contain flat, thin or long pieces.
2nd	5—8	12.7— 4.7	
3rd	7—13	19.0—12.7	
4th	7—13	38.0—19.0	
5th	13—20	63.0—38.0	

Preparation of Filter Sand. 'Run of Bank' sand may be too coarse, too fine or too non-uniform for use in filters.

Hydraulics of Filtration. The resistance offered by granular materials to the passage of fluids is analogous both to the resistance offered by small pipes to fluids carried by them and to the resistance offered by a fluid to the settling of particles.

Hydraulics of Filter Washing. The burden of suspended matter, collected in filters and on their grains is removed and the bed is restored to capacity either by washing filter material in place or by removing the clogged portions of the bed.

The scouring of granular materials in place is accomplished with the aid of water that rises through the bed and lifts the filter grains into suspension. This is known as *sand expansion*.

Substances that are transferred into the bed during filtration from the water are then flushed upwards through the suspended or expanded bed and washed with the wash water. At the same time substances adhering to the filter grains are dislodged either by the shearing action of the rising water or by the rubbing together of the suspended grains. Scour is important and can be promoted by stirring the expanded filter mechanically with rakes, mechanically with air (either during or before expansion, before expansion being more economical and commonly adopted), or hydraulically with jets of water that are directed into the suspended sand.

As against this, the washing of granular material (after removal from the filter or before placement as a means of cleaning or sizing) is also a kind of differential sedimentation. The relatively coarse and heavy filter grains are allowed to settle against rising water which carries away the dislodged fine and light suspended matter.

12.9.6. Design of Filters

Required Depth of Filters. The various factors which are considered in deciding the depth of filter such that impurities would not be able to penetrate are :

1. Composition, concentration and condition of the impurities required to be removed by filtration from the water to be treated.

2. The reaction of these impurities to be removed to the treatment of filtration.

The reaction is indicated by the following :

(*i*) The rate of filtration.

(*ii*) The size of the filter grains and their variation with depth.

(*iii*) The packing of sand grains or the porosity of the bed.

(*iv*) The temperature of the water.

(*v*) The terminal loss of head or the increase in the loss of head beyond that of the clear bed.

Stanley established the following relationship for the reaction of the floc to unigranular beds of sand :

1. The depth of penetration varies directly with the concentration of iron per unit surface area of bed and establishes as a suitable 'Index of Penetration', the rates of depth of penetration to intensity of surface loading.

2. This ratio becomes large with the increase of

(*i*) Floc concentration (*ii*) Rate of flow and (*iii*) Sand size area.

3. This ratio becomes greater when electrolytes such as NaCl, Na_2SO_4 and $MgSO_4$ are added to the applied water.

4. This ratio decreases as the floc increases in size and as it is subjected to aging.

5. The ratio changes with the change in pH of the applied water and is minimum as the neutral point (pH-7) approaches.

6. Penetration increases further with the increase in viscosity and with the increase in porosity of the bed.

Classification of Filters. Filters are broadly classified under the following categories :

1. **Gravity Filters.** (*a*) Slow sand filters (*b*) Rapid sand filters.

2. **Pressure Filters.** The above filters are described in the following articles (article 12.8.7, 12.8.8, 12.8.10, 12.8.11).

12.9.7. Slow Sand Filters

Construction of Slow Sand Filters. These are shallow tanks 2.5 to 4 m deep having surface area of 100 to 2000 sq. m in plan. These tanks contain 60—90 cm thick bed of sand (Filtering media) supported on 30—50 cm thick gravel bed.

The gravel is supported on a bed of concrete slopping towards a central longitudinal drain, connected by a system of open jointed under-drains.

Inlet. The inlet of slow sand filter consists of a chamber fitted with sluice valve. Normally the inlet pipe is carried vertically into the body of the filter, with the mouth of inlet pipe flush with the water level.

Depth of Water. There is no hard and fast rule for the fixation of water depth. Best results have been obtained by keeping depth of water equal to the thickness of filtering media.

Outlets. After passing through the filter bed, water is collected in the outlet chamber where a regulating arrangement is provided to obtain a regular discharge from the filter. The regulating arrangement may consist of a telescopic pipe or adjustable weir, operated by means of floats so that the depth of mouth of the outlet pipe from the water level inside the outlet chamber is constant.

Operation of Filter. The water from the sedimentation tank outlet enters the slow sand filter through a submersible inlet. This water is uniformly distributed over the sand bed without causing any disturbances. The water passes through the filtering media at an average rate of 2200×10^6 to 3400×10^6 litres/km^2/day.

This rate of filtration is continued until the difference between the water level on the filter and in the outlet chamber is slightly less than the depth of water above the sand. The difference between the water above sand bed and the outlet chamber is called *Loss of head*.

During filtering as the filtering media gets clogged, due to impurities which stay in the pores, the resistance to the passage of water and loss of head also continuously increases. When the loss of head reaches the permissible limit, the working of filter is stopped, and about 2—3 cm sand from the top of bed is scrapped and replaced with clean sand before putting the filter into operation. The scrapped sand is washed with water, dried and stored for return to the filter at the time of the next washing.

12.9.8. Results of Slow Sand Filtration

The main object of slow sand filtration is to remove bacterias and suspended matter from water. In this respect slow sand filters are very efficient. They remove 98 to 99% of bacterias of the raw water and 100% suspended water which cannot be completely removed by sedimentation process. Slow sand filtration also removes odours, tastes and colour from water. Slow sand filtration however, cannot remove pathogenic bacteria. Water treated by filtration has therefore to be disinfected to assure complete safety against water borne diseases. The rate of filtration of these filters is also very slow and requires a large area.

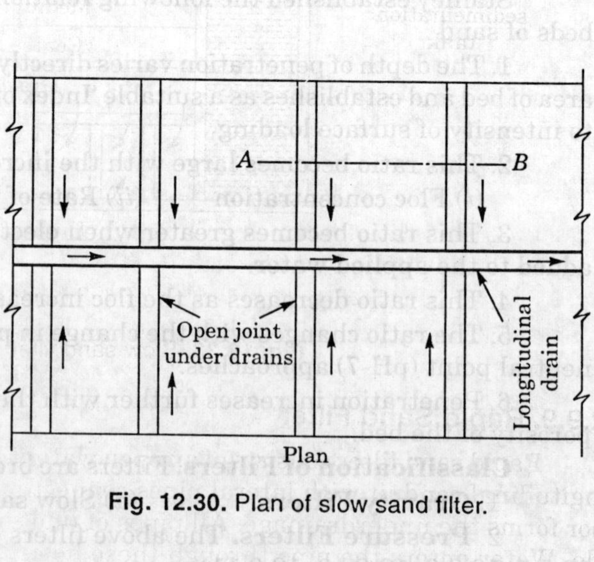

Fig. 12.30. Plan of slow sand filter.

Fig. 12.31 shows details of a typical slow sand filter.

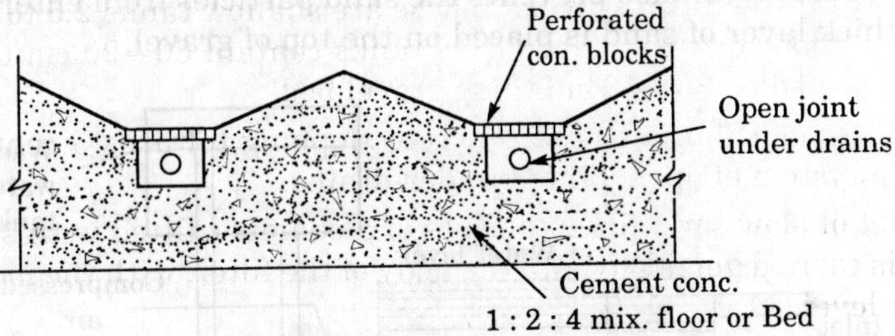

Fig. 12.31. Enlarged section at *AB*.

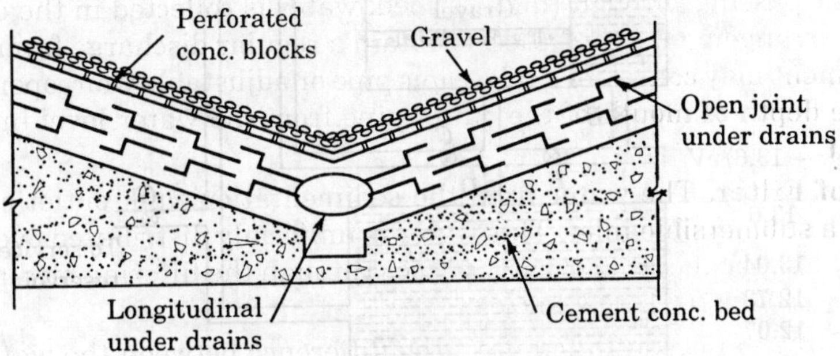

Fig. 12.32. Enlarged section at *CD*.

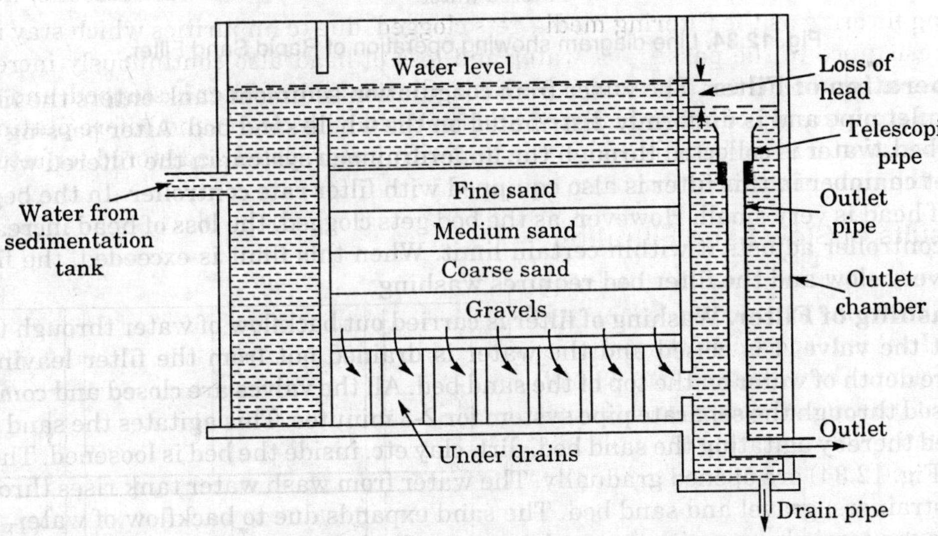

Fig. 12.33. Slow sand filter (sectional elevation).

12.9.9. Rapid Sand Filter

Rapid sand filter consists of an open watertight basin of masonry or concrete. One central longitudinal conduit with lateral pipes connecting from, all sides on sloping brick or concrete floor forms the underdrainage. All pipes of underdrainage system have holes on their bottom side. Water enters the pipe through these holes. This underdrainage system is embedded in

60 cm to 70 cm thick graded gravels. The size of gravel varies from 2.5 cm at the bottom to 0.5 cm at the top. Gravel layer also prevents the sand particles from entering into underdrain pipe. An equally thick layer of sand is placed on the top of gravel.

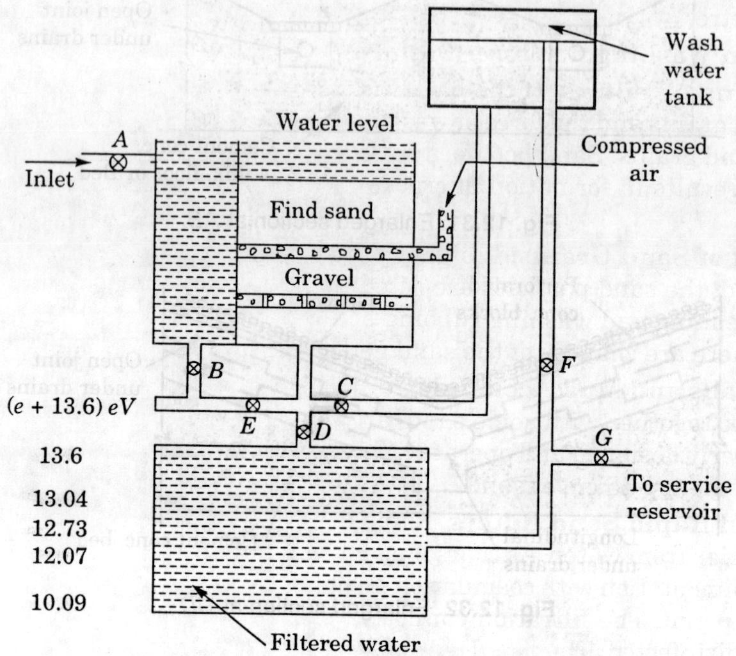

Fig. 12.34. Line diagram showing operation of Rapid Sand Filter.

Operation of Filter. The water from coagulation sediment tank enters the filter unit through inlet pipe and is uniformly distributed on the whole sand bed. After passing through the sand bed, water is collected through the underdrainage system in the filtered water well. The outlet chamber in this filter is also equipped with filter rate controller. In the beginning, the loss of head is very small. However, as the bed gets clogged, the loss of head increases and the rate controller adjusts it within certain limit. When this limit is exceeded, the filtration becomes very slow and the filter bed requires washing.

Washing of Filter. Washing of filter is carried out backflow of water through the sand bed. First the valve *A* is closed and the water is drained out from the filter leaving a few centimetre depth of water on the top of the sand bed. All the valves are closed and compressed air is passed through the separate pipe system for 2-3 minutes. This agitates the sand bed and it is stirred thereby agitating the sand bed, dirt, clay etc. inside the bed is loosened. The valves *C* and *B* (Fig. 12.34) are opened gradually. The water from wash water tank rises through the laterals, strainers, gravel and sand bed. The sand expands due to backflow of water, and the impurities are carried away with the wash water to the drain through the channels, which are meant for this purpose. The washing process is continued till the sand bed appears clearly. The washing of the filters is done generally after 24 hours and it takes about 10 minutes. During backwashing the sand bed expands by about 50%.

Surface Wash. Nowadays the washing of the filter bed is done only at the surface by applying clear water at the rate of 270 litres/m^2/min under the pressure of 0.7 to 1.1 kg/cm^2 through nozzles. These nozzles are kept vertical on the surface of sand bed.

Air-Binding. An excess of negative head causes the dissolved air and gases escape from the water in the form of minute bubbles. These bubbles are retained on the surface of sand grains and also in their voids. This effect is known as 'air binding in a filter'. It causes serious interference with the normal rate of filtration. Negative head is normally not allowed to exceed one metre.

Defects in Washing. Improper washing gives rise to the following defects.

1. **Cracking of Filters.** If the backwashing is not sufficient to produce the required agitation of sand grains and the force of wash water is not adequate, clay and mud remains on the surface of sand grains. Sand bed does not expand uniformly and the particles of sand get cemented. This results in formation of cracks in the sand bed and short-circuiting of water takes place.

2. **Lifting of Sand Grains.** If higher pressure of compressed air and higher velocities of water are used, the sand particles are lifted up without causing them to rub against each other. During cleaning and washing rubbing action is very necessary. If the velocity of wash water is high, there are chances of the sand getting lost.

3. **Mud Balls and Mud Accumulation.** When the washing of the filter is inadequate, turbidity and floc together with some sand, are cemented together to form 'mud balls'. If the filter bed is properly designed and operated, the 'mud balls' should not occupy more than 0.1% of the volume of the top 15 cm of sand.

Results of Rapid Sand Filters. Rapid sand filters remove suspended matter, colour, odour and bacterias from water. As coarser sand is used in Rapid Sand Filters, the water must pass through sedimentation with coagulation processes. The maximum turbidity of water should be less than 40 p.p.m. The filtration cannot remove bacteria completely, and hence filtered water has to be disinfected. The usual rate of filtration is 4500 litres/m^2/hour. The wash water pressure is restricted to 10 metres.

Under Drainage System. In the bottom of the filter under drainage system is laid to collect the filtered water and to distribute wash water uniformly on the filter bed of sand.

The various types of under-drainages are given below :

1. Manifold and Pipe Laterals. 2. Vitrified Tile Blocks.
3. The Wheeler Filter Bottom. 4. The Porous Plate Bottom.

These systems are briefly described below :

1. **The Manifold and Pipe Laterals.** This system is most widely used. It essentially consists of one central C.I. main pipe of about 50 cm diameter. 7.5 to 10 cm diameter laterals are connected on both sides at 15 to 20 cm c.c. spacing. All laterals are of perforated pipes having 6 to 12 mm diameter holes drilled to their bottom at an angle of 30° to 60° with the vertical (Fig. 12.35).

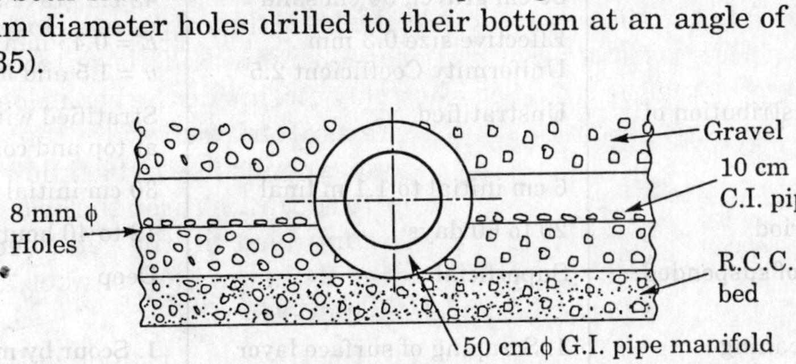

Fig. 12.35. Manifold pipe laterals.

2. Vitrified Tile Blocks. This system is also known as *Leopold Block System*. It consists of vitrified tile blocks having orifices and holes in them for the passage of water. All these tiles are laid in the bottom over which gravel layer is placed (Fig. 12.36).

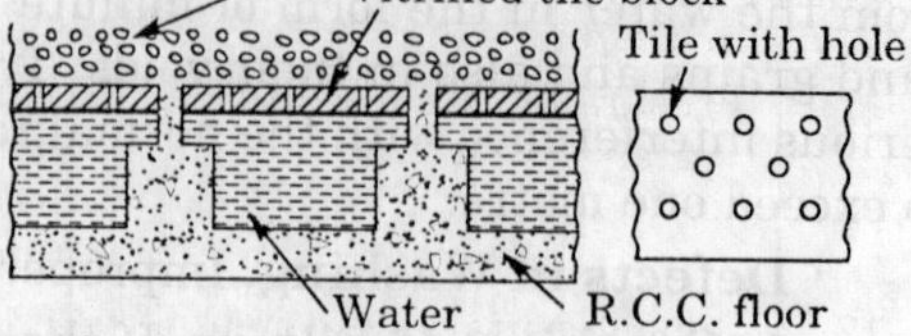

Fig. 12.36. Vitrified tile block.

3. The Wheeler Filter Bottom. This is a very cheap construction. The false bottom is prepared over the real bottom of R.C.C. This false bottom consists of solid inverted, truncated pyramids with water connections at the apex of each pyramid. The pockets are filled with glazed earthenware spheres. (Fig. 12.37).

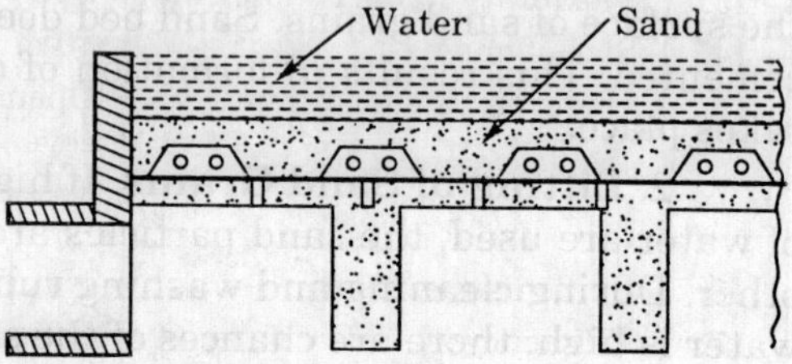

Fig. 12.37. Wheeler filter bottom.

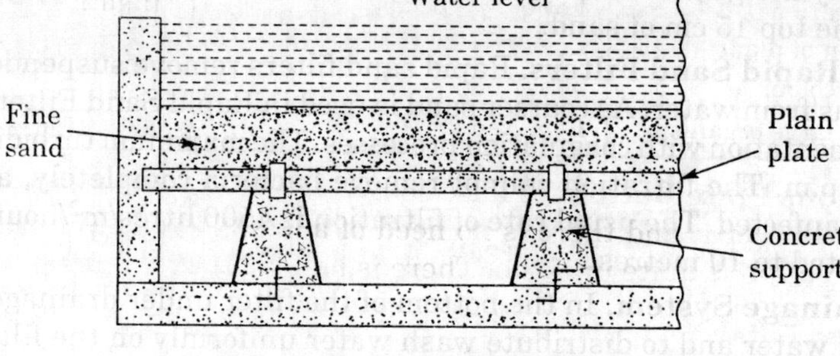

Fig. 12.38. Porous plate bottom.

Table 12.24. Comparison between Rapid Sand Filter and Slow Sand Filter

S. No.	*Item*	*Slow sand filter*	*Rapid gravity filter*
1.	Rate of Filtration	100—180 lit/m²/hour	4000—5000 lit/m²/hour
2.	Area	Requires very large area	Requires very small area
3.	Depth of bed	30 cm gravel, 90 cm sand	45 cm gravel, 70 cm sand
4.	Size of sand	Effective size 0.3 mm Uniformity Coefficient 2.5	E = 0.45 mm and higher u = 1.5 and lower
5.	Grain size distribution of sand filter	Unstratified	Stratified with smallest grains at top and coarsest at bottom
6.	Loss of Head	6 cm initial to 1.1 m final	30 cm initial to 3 m final
7.	Cleaning Period	20 to 60 days	12 to 40 hours
8.	Penetration of suspended matter	Superficial	Deep
9.	Method of cleaning	1. Scraping of surface layer of sand and washing. Removal of sand. 2. Washing surface sand in place by travelling washer.	1. Scour by mechanical rakes, air or water, and removal of dislodged suspended matter by upward flow or back washing which stratifies the bed

10.	Amount of wash water used in cleaning sand	0.2 to 0.6% of water filtered.	1 to 6% of water filtered
11.	Preparatory treatment of water	Generally confined to aeration but could also include flocculation and sedimentation	Flocculation and sedimentation are common
12.	Supplementary treatment of water	In the absence of flocculation, confined to chlorination	Chlorination and other supplementary treatments are common
13.	Flexibility in operation	Not possible	Possible
14.	Size of one unit	30 m × 60 m	6 × 8 m to 8 × 10 m
15.	Under drainage system	Open jointed pipes or drains covered with blocks	1. Manifold and pipe lateral 2. Vitrified tile blocks 3. Wheeler filter bottom 4. Porous plate bottom
16.	Skilled supervision	Not required	Most essential
17.	Efficiency	Efficient in removal of bacteria and suspended matter (98 to 99%)	Cannot remove all bacteria (50–60%) Disinfection is necessary. Removes colour, odour and taste
18.	Cost of construction	Higher	Lower
19.	Cost of operation	Lower	Higher
20.	Depreciation of plant	Lower	Higher
21.	Removal of colour	30%	100%
22.	Removal of large organism	Removed totally	Removed totally

4. **The Porous Plate Bottom.** A false bottom is prepared with porous plates. The sand layer is directly laid over it and there is no need of a gravel layer. The rate of filtration and wash water distribution is quite uniform. There is no fear of corrosion of metal (Fig. 12.38).

12.9.10. Pressure Filter

It is a rapid sand filter placed within a closed water tight steel cylinder. The water passes through the sand bed under a pressure greater than atmospheric. The coagulated water is directly applied to the filter without mixing and flocculation.

The size varies from 2 to 3 m in diameter and length upto 9 metres. The rate of filtration is 6000 to 15,000 litres/hour/m^2.

Cleaning of filter bed is done by backwashing similar to rapid gravity filter. Generally these filters are suitable for small water supply specially in industries. For large water works they are very uneconomical.

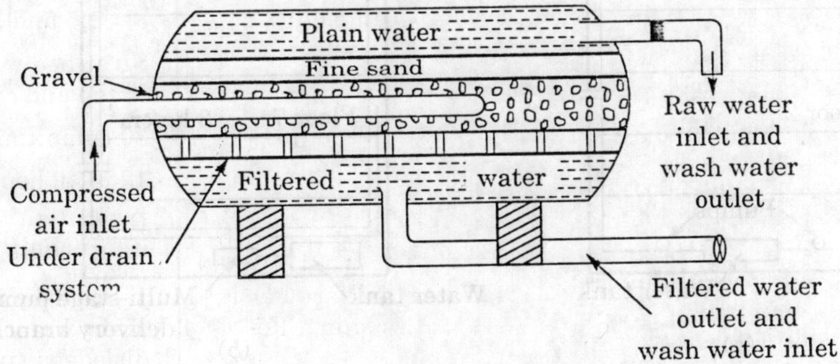

Fig. 12.39. Pressure filter.

Comparison between rapid sand filter and slow sand filter is given in Table 5.5.

12.9.11. Disinfection of Water

The filtration treatments of water described in the preceding articles do not completely eliminate pathogenic bacteria and other potential infective micro-organism.

Post filtration treatment such as boiling of water or chlorination of water, carried out for the sole object of killing infective organism is termed as disinfection of water.

Any disinfectant should meet the following requirements :

1. It must destroy pathogenic organism potentially present in the water.

2. The task should be completed within the time available for disinfection and within the range of water temperatures encountered, and within the fluctuations in composition, concentration, and condition of the water experienced.

3. The disinfectant should not render the water toxic or unpalatable to the consumer or otherwise, objectionable for the purpose that the water is to serve.

4. It should be within reasonable cost, safe and easy to handle and should be conveniently applicable to the water that is to be disinfected.

5. The disinfecting agent should be such that strength or concentration in the treated water, can be quickly determined.

6. The agent should persist within the treated water in sufficient concentration to provide residual protection against recontamination.

Pumps used upto 60 m high buildings should have a rated capacity of 22751/min. The storage tank should have a capacity of more than 2×10^6 litres.

The starting equipment for hydrant pumps should be designed to bring the pumps into operation automatically.

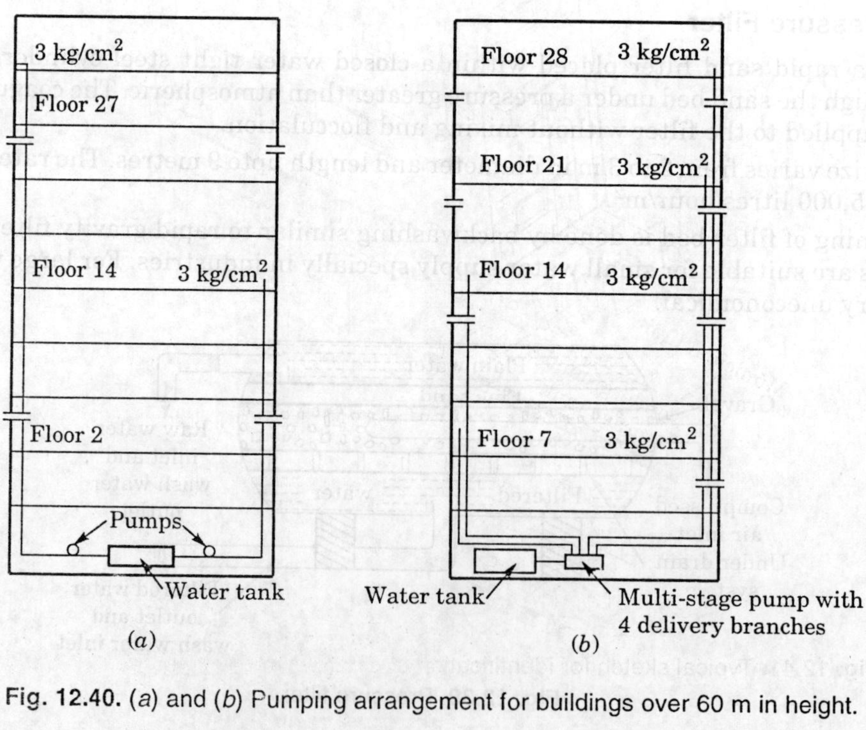

Fig. 12.40. (*a*) and (*b*) Pumping arrangement for buildings over 60 m in height.

12.9.12. Water Supply in Buildings

Many administrative authorities controlling water supply have their own set of bye-laws, rules and regulations for supply of water to suit local condition. While laying pipe lines or plumbing systems, these bye-laws should be strictly conformed.

For intermittent supplies a minimum storage of half day's supply is needed for over-head tanks.

IS : 2065—1972 deals with water supply of buildings and covers general requirements and regulation for water supply, plumbing connected to public water supply, inspection and maintenance of water fittings and appliances.

Fig. 12.41 shows a typical sketch for identification of different types of water supply pipe.

The main features of water supply in buildings are :

1. Obtaining supply from water work.
2. Conveyance and distribution of water within the premises.
3. General requirements for pipe work.
4. Laying of mains and pipes on site.
5. Joining of pipe.
6. Testing of service pipes and fittings.
7. Maintenance.

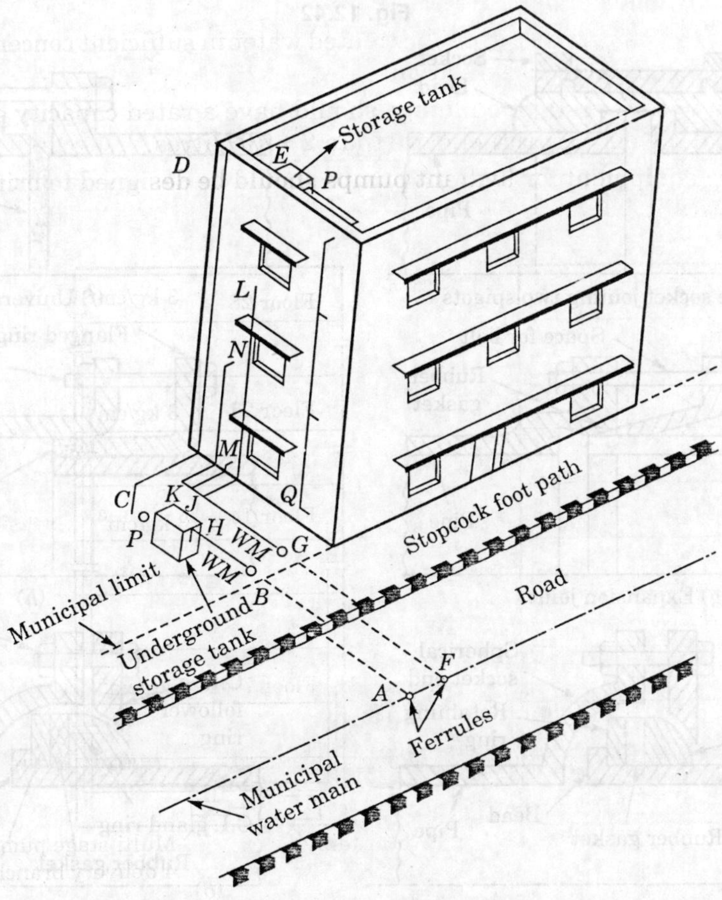

Fig. 12.41. Typical sketch for identification of different types of water supply pipes.

5. Jointing of Pipes

Pipe Joints. Various joints used in water supply are shown in Fig. 12.42.

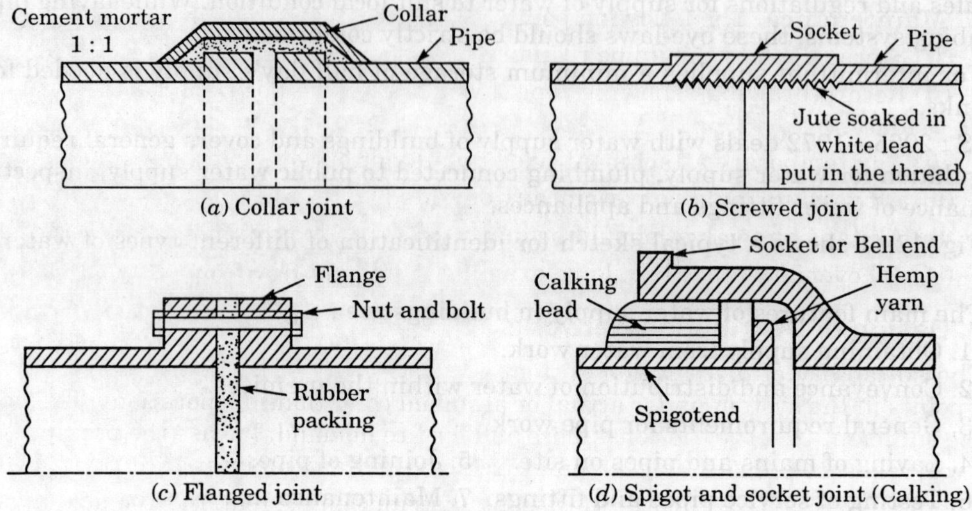

(*a*) Collar joint (*b*) Screwed joint

(*c*) Flanged joint (*d*) Spigot and socket joint (Calking)

Fig. 12.42

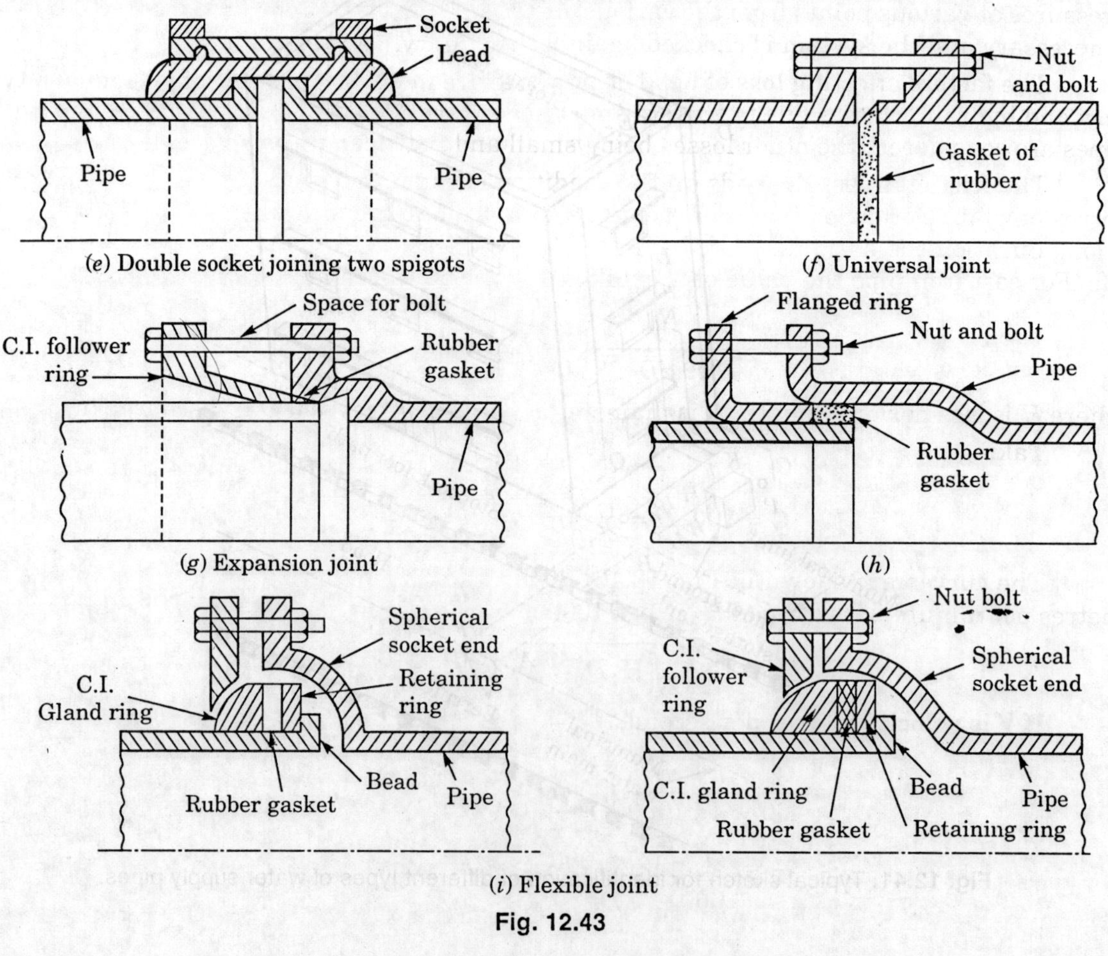

(*e*) Double socket joining two spigots (*f*) Universal joint

(*g*) Expansion joint (*h*)

(*i*) Flexible joint

Fig. 12.43

6. Testing of Service Pipes and Fittings. When the service is completed, it is slowly and carefully charged with water, allowing all air to escape and avoiding all shocks and water hammer. When all drawoff tapes are closed, the service pipe should be absolutely water-tight.

7. Maintenance. The following points should be attended to

(*i*) Storage points should be regularly inspected and cleaned out if necessary.

(*ii*) Record drawings showing pipe layout and valve positions should be kept upto date.

(*iii*) Any temporary attachment fixed to a tap or outlet should never be left as such.

(*iv*) All valves should be periodically operated.

(*v*) All taps and valves should be inspected for water tightness.

(*vi*) All overflow pipes should be examined and kept free from obstruction.

12.9.13. Design of Distribution Networks

The suitability of distribution system is determined from the pressures that exit at various points in the system under actual or assumed conditions of operations. The pressures should be sufficient to serve the consumers and for fire demand. In case the pressures are too high, it will result in unjustifiable expenditure for safety and maintenance.

There is no direct method for designing distribution system and the size of pipes required. In a new system the pipe sizes are assumed, and the system is investigated for the pressures at various points from the various demands on the lines. The pipe sizes are adjusted if necessary and the system is checked again for adequacy.

The factors affecting loss of head or pressure are many such as size of pipe, quantity of flow and hydraulic losses due to friction and other causes. Usually frictional losses in straight pipes are considered, the other losses being small and not clearly known are neglected.

The frictional loss depends on the condition of pipe. The frictional loss increases with corrosion of pipe or deposition that occurs when in use. As the pipe line system is to serve for a long duration the design is to be based on the conditions prevalent at the end of the useful life. For cast iron pipe the value of C is taken 100 in the Hazen and Williams formula

$$H = \frac{1}{0.094\, D^{4.87}} \left(\frac{Q}{C}\right)^{1.85}$$

where H is loss per unit length, D is diameter of pipe in metres and Q is discharge in cumecs.

Taking

$$C = 100,\ H = \frac{Q^{1.85}}{470\, D^{4.87}}$$

The curves are shown in Fig. 12.46. In the monogram, discharge Q_1 is given in cubic metres per minute, loss of head H_1 is per 1000 metres and diameter of pipe D_1 is in mm, then

$$Q_1 = 1.85 \sqrt{\left[H_1 D_1^{4.87} \times 2.2527 \times 10^{-12}\right]}$$

If V is velocity metres per second,

$$\frac{Q_1}{60} = \frac{\pi}{4}\left(\frac{D_1}{1000}\right)^2 \times V$$

$$\therefore \qquad V = \frac{Q_1}{60} \times \frac{(4 \times 1000^2)}{D_1^2\, \pi} = 21220\, \frac{Q_1}{D_1^2}$$

The velocity in the pipe is assumed as 1.0 metre per second for 10 cm diameter pipes varying to 2.0 metres per second for pipes of 50 cm diameter. Distribution pipes are generally 15 cm or more in diameter.

In the pipe network, the following two conditions must be satisfied :

(*a*) The algebraic sum of the pressure drops around a closed loop must be zero.

(*b*) The flow entering a junction must be equal to the flow leaving the same junction.

Based on these principles, the pipe networks are solved by methods of successive approximation. The methods generally employed are :

(1) Hardy cross method

(2) Equivalent pipe method

(3) Construction and analysis of an electrical analogy. The Hardy cross method is relatively simple and accurate, therefore it is used invariably.

Hardy cross method. This is based on the simple fact that the loss of head from one point to another in a distribution system is the same irrespective of the path followed. To arrive at the correct solution of the flow in the pipes of a network, suitable flows are assumed and the head losses between points in the distribution system are computed with the aid of any pipe flow formula generally Hazen Williams formula and monogram. In case the head losses by different paths between two points are not equal with the assumed flows, these are corrected by ΔQ, computed from the expression

$$\Delta Q = \frac{\sum rQ^n}{\sum nrQ^{n-1}}$$

where the numerator is the algebraic sum and the denominator is the arithmetic sum (*i.e.* the sum without regard to signs) r represents the relative resistance and n is the exponent of Q in the formula head loss $H = rQ^n$. In the Hazen and Williams formula

$$r = \frac{K}{C^{1.85}\ d^{4.87}}$$

The analysis is repeated till ΔQ becomes as small as required. The values of r for value of C = 100 are given in Table 12.25.

Table 12.25

Diameter in mm	*r*	*Diameter in mm*	*r*
100	250	400	0.30
150	35	450	0.17
200	8.6	500	0.08
250	2.9	600	0.036
300	1.2	750	0.0138
350	0.56	900	0.0058

The proper assumption of rates of flow in a distribution system may diminish the computations required in the analysis. In case of two pipes from a point carrying Q_1 and Q_2 flows,

$$\frac{Q_1}{Q_1 + Q_2} = \frac{r_2^{1/2}}{r_1^{1/2} + r_2^{1/2}}$$

Similarly for three pipes carrying Q_1, Q_2, Q_3 flows,

$$\frac{Q_1}{Q_1 + Q_2 + Q_3} = \frac{r_2^{1/2}\, r_3^{1/2}}{r_1^{1/2}\, r_2^{1/2} + r_2^{1/2}\, r_3^{1/2} + r_3^{1/2}\, r_1^{1/2}}$$

This is to be applied judiciously taking all other factors into account.

In case H_L is the head loss in length L of a pipe carrying Q discharge $\Delta Q = \dfrac{\Sigma H_L}{n \Sigma \dfrac{H_L}{Q}}$

where numerator is the algebraic sum of the head loss and the denominator is the arithmatic sum (*i.e.* the sum without regard to signs). The value n is taken as 1.85 in Hazen William formula. The corrections are subtracted.

Table 12.24 gives head loss and velocity for smaller diameters and Fig. 12.43 gives the curve. Table 12.25 gives head loss for bigger diameters. Fig. 12.44 gives the curve.

Example 12.9. *Calculate the flows in various pipes for a distribution network shown in Fig. 11.44 (a)*

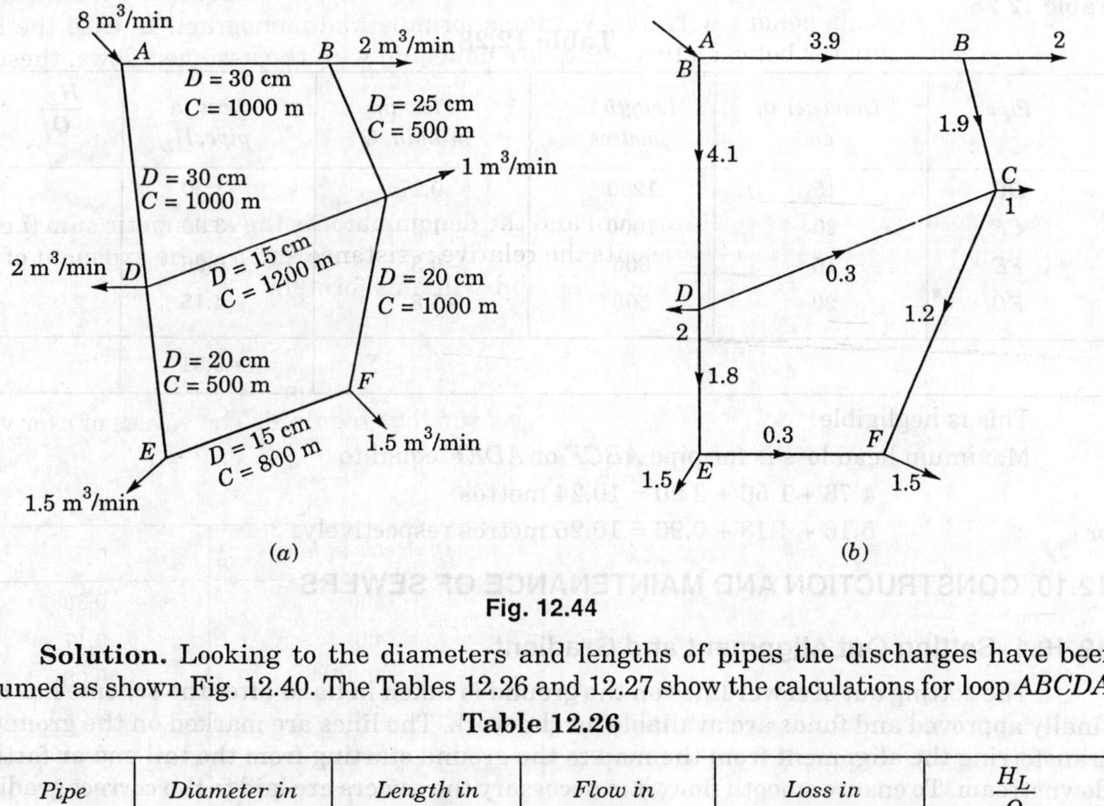

Fig. 12.44

Solution. Looking to the diameters and lengths of pipes the discharges have been assumed as shown Fig. 12.40. The Tables 12.26 and 12.27 show the calculations for loop *ABCDA*.

Table 12.26

Pipe	*Diameter in cm*	*Length in metres*	*Flow in m³/min*	*Loss in pipe, H_L*	$\dfrac{H_L}{Q}$
AB	30	1000	3.9	4.70	1.205
BC	25	500	1.9	1.55	0.816
CD	15	1200	–0.3	–1.44	4.800
DA	30	1000	–4.1	–5.20	1.268
			Σ	–0.39	8.089

$$\frac{\Sigma H_L}{18.5\Sigma \frac{H_L}{Q}} = \frac{-.39}{1.85 \times 8.089} = -0.026$$

Table 12.27

Pipe	*Diameter in cm*	*Length in metres*	*Flow in m³/min*	*Loss in pipe, H_L*	$\frac{H_L}{Q}$
AB	30	1000	3.926	4.78	
BC	25	500	1.926	1.56	
CD	15	1200	– 0.274	– 1.20	
DA	30	1000	– 4.074	– 5.16	
			Σ	– 0.02	

This is a negligible difference. The calculations are carried out for loop *DCFED* in Table 12.28.

Table 12.28

Pipe	*Diameter in cm*	*Length in metres*	*Flow in m³/min, Q*	*Loss in pipe, H_L*	$\frac{H_L}{Q}$
DC	15	1200	0.274	1.20	
CF	20	1000	1.2	3.90	
FE	15	800	– 0.3	– 0.96	
ED	20	500	– 1.8	– 4.13	
			Σ	+ 0.01	

This is negligible.

Maximum head loss is for pipe *ABCF* or *ADEF* equal to

4.78 + 1.56 + 3.90 = 10.24 metres

or 5.16 + 4.13 + 0.96 = 10.25 metres respectively.

12.10. CONSTRUCTION AND MAINTENANCE OF SEWERS

12.10.1. Setting Out Alignment and Gradient

The setting out of sewer lines on the ground is taken in hand after the scheme has been finally approved and funds are available for the work. The lines are marked on the ground by transferring the alignment from the map to the ground starting from the tail end or farthest downstream. To ensure smooth flow, it is necessary the sewers are laid to the correct gradient. For this purpose pegs are fixed at 15 to 20 m intervals and temporary bench marks are established with respect to the GTS bench marks. The setting out is carried out with the help of boning rods, sight rails and levelling instrument.

The boning rod consists of a rectangular timber section (8 cm × 4 cm) of required length along with a *T*-piece (8 cm × 5 cm) joined rigidly by nails.

The sight rail consists of horizontal wooden board of suitable (15 cm × 5 cm) cross-section secured to two vertical posts with the help of steel clamps or nails.

Both the sight rails as well as the boning rods have their centre-lines marked and painted black and white. During setting out of the sewer line to the correct grade at any time at least four sight rails are maintained in the desired level and gradient.

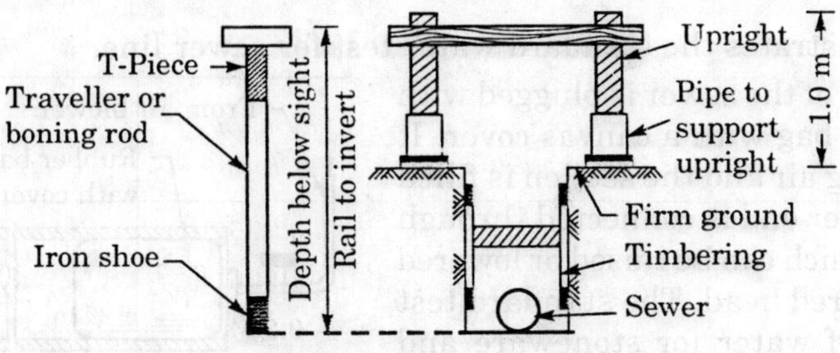

Fig. 12.45. Setting out of sewers.

Fig. 12.45 shows setting out of sewers (using boning rods and sight rails).

Fig. 12.46 illustrates the use of sight rails and boning rod for sewer gradient.

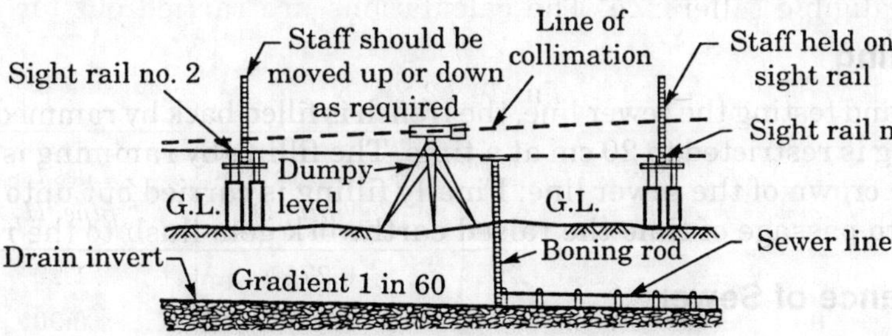

Fig. 12.46. Setting out sewer gradient.

12.10.2. Excavation of Trenches

The profile of the top of excavation is marked on the ground and if necessary traffic diverted. In case of a pavement the same is removed by the available means and excavation is done manually or mechanically as per drawings and specifications. The width of the trench at the bottom in case of large sewers is kept 15 cm more than the external diameter of the sewer. The excavation usually is kept 10 to 15 m ahead of the pipe line work so that trenches do not remain open for long periods.

12.10.3. Laying and Jointing

As already explained in article 12.9.1 boning rods and sight rails are used for trans-ferring centre line and grades from ground to the centre line of sewers. The use of boning rod and sight rails for this purpose is explained in Fig. 12.47.

For ease in joining, the pipes are laid with the socket end up grade (See Fig. 2.3).

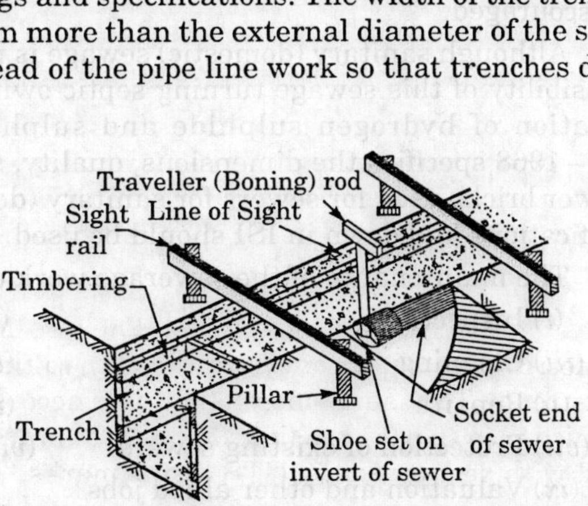

Fig. 12.47. Use of boning rod and sight rails for laying sewer.

The gradient of the sewer, after it is laid in position is checked for level. A straight edge is passed through it and it is made sure that the edge rests squarely upon the level pegs and on the invert of the pipe through its length. Once the level and grades are checked, the pipes are suitably jointed.

12.10.4. Testing

Fig. 12.48 illustrates the standard water test for sewer line.

The lower end of the sewer is plugged with the help of a rubber bag with a canvas cover. It is inflated by blowing air and the section is filled with water. The upper end is connected through a hose by a funnel which can be raised or lowered to maintain the desired head. The standard test pressure is 1.5 m of water for stoneware and concrete pipes and 9 m of water in case of C.I. pipes. The permissible leakage per I.S. specification is 2 litres/cm of diameter/km of sewer line over a period of 10 minutes.

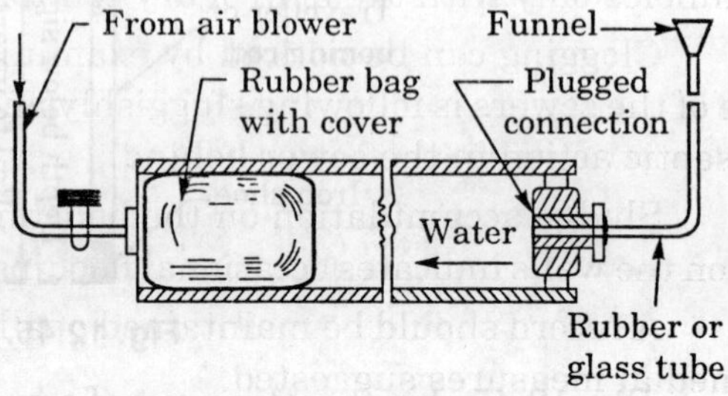

Fig. 12.48. Testing of sewer line.

12.10.5. Back Filling

After laying and testing the sewer line, the trench is filled back by rammed earth. The layer of back fill ramming is restricted to 20 cm at a time. The filling by ramming is done to a height of 45 cm. above the crown of the sewer line. Finally filling is carried out upto 15 cm above the ground level. Due to passage of time the raised earthwork gets flush to the road level.

12.10.6. Maintenance of Sewer

The main object of maintenance of sewers is to keep them clean and free from any obstruction. It is all the more important that a sewer section should be checked for blockade and leakage at regular intervals as the section is not exposed to the surface and is likely to be ignored. It may corrode, erode, clog or otherwise deteriorate. Considerable amount of extra work in maintenance of sewers can be saved if proper sewer bricks are used. The general practice in the country to utilise common building bricks in the construction of sewers should be discouraged.

Although sanitary (domestic) sewage is not corrosive to the brick sewer, there remains a possibility of this sewage turning septic owing to various reasons and thus leading to the formation of hydrogen sulphide and sulphuric acid through biochemical action. IS : 4885—1968 specifies the dimensions, quality, strength and methods of sampling and testing of sewer bricks used for sewers for sanitary (domestic sewage). Only bricks which satisfy the specifications laid down in ISI should be used.

The maintenance of the sewerage work consists of the following :

(*i*) Inspection
(*ii*) Measurement of rate of flow
(*iii*) Cleaning
(*iv*) Flushing
(*v*) Repairs
(*vi*) Supervision of connections
(*vii*) Protection of existing sewers
(*viii*) Prevention of explosives
(*ix*) Valuation and other allied jobs

12.10.7. Inspection of Sewers

Defects in sewers are noticed during the inspection. This type of inspection at regular intervals is part of maintenance programme.

In the case of large size sewers inspection can be carried out by getting down through the manholes and wading or floating through them in boats. This type of inspection includes cleaning of obstacles on the sewer surface. The joints are examined for cracks, loose bricks, deteriorated cement concrete and eroded invert etc. Smaller size sewers are inspected from manholes only with the help of dry cell torches or sunlight reflected by mirrors.

Clogging can be noticed by examining the nature of flow at two adjacent manholes. If one of the sewers is following sluggishly and scum is present it indicates clogging, slow velocity or septic action in the sewer behind.

Sludge accumulation on the benching of manhole or signs of sewage having been high up on the walls indicates occasional flooding of the sewer due to inadequate capacity or clogging.

A record should be maintained of all the inspections made, type of damages noticed and remedial measures suggested.

While inspecting the sewers all the appurtenances should also be inspected. Catch basins may be clogged, flushing tanks may be leaking or not functioning. Automatic regulators and overflows should be inspected for any damage. Inverted siphons should be examined for silting.

The following precautions should be taken while entering sewer :

(*i*) The sewer section to be inspected should be ventilated by keeping a number of manhole covers open on both sides for about an hour prior to the inspection.

Sewers carry all the waste discharges from residential areas and from industries. Some of them purify and consume oxygen from sewers causing breathing difficulties. Due to the interaction of the various discharges and also due to biological decomposition of organic material in them; gases of different nature are produced. Some of these gases are poisonous and toxic while others may be inert but causing physical suffocation.

The presence of toxic or explosive gases such as hydrogen sulphide or gasoline can be found out by the smell of the expelled gases.

In case the explosive gases are absent a light lantern can be lowered down the manhole to test for the presence of oxygen. If the lantern burns brilliantly the sewer can be safe to enter.

In any case, workmen going down for inspection should be tied by means of ropes round their waists. The rope should be held tight by persons on top.

12.10.8. Sewer Cleaning

Cleaning of sewers and removal of blockages are normal items of maintenance. It is desirable to have a regular sewer cleaning programme which will prevent total blocking of the sewer.

In case of small sewers which cannot be entered for cleaning are cleaned by flushing or dragging. These methods are briefly described below :

1. By Flushing

When the sewer is not completely blocked, a flexible fire hose with a 2.5 cm or smaller nozzle is inserted down and water is discharged through this pipe under pressure.

Flushing can also be achieved by tipping large volumes of water into manholes.

Flushing has been found effective upto length of 150 m.

The quantities of water required for flushing of sewers is given in Table 12.29.

Table 12.29. Water for Flushing Sewers m³

Slope of Sewers	*Diameter of Sewers (cm.)*		
	20	*25*	*30*
0.0050	2.264	2.548	2.83
0.0075	1.557	1.840	2.264
0.0100	1.274	1.557	1.981
0.020	0.566	0.760	0.990
0.03	0.424	0.566	0.679

2. **Dragging**

Medium size sewers can be best cleaned by using plows and other scraping devices which are dragged through sewers. A common variety consists of a steel cylinder of 20 to 25 cm in diameter and 60 to 70 cm long with sharp cutting teeth on the open forward end. This is dragged through the sewers by means of 'Pills' which are light floating wooden or rubber balls. It gets stuck up where there is heavy deposit. Due to restricted passage, the velocity of sewage in its neighbourhood increases and the deposited silt gets scoured. Obstruction and blockages in small size sewers can be removed by thrusting.

(*i*) Flexible wooden rods (90 cm by 4 cm dia)
(*ii*) Steel bands fitted with special steel tools to their leading ends.
(*iii*) Turbine sewer cleaner.

12.10.9. Maintenance Equipment

In order that the maintenance of a sewer system is carried out in a satisfactory manner the engineer incharge of maintenances should be in possession of complete and detailed map of the system. He should have at his disposal a truck equipped with the following :

(*i*) Power winch. (*ii*) Flexible wire.
(*iii*) Fire hose. (*iv*) Flexible rods.
(*v*) Interlocking wood rods. (*vi*) Root cutters.
(*vii*) Sewer brushes. (*viii*) Sand buckets, scoops and drags.
(*ix*) Turbine flushing. (*x*) Flash light.
(*xi*) Safety equipment. (*xii*) Gas detectors (H_2S, CH_4, CO).
(*xiii*) Gas masks. (*xiv*) Steel sewer tapes.
(*xv*) Sewer flushing bags. (*xvi*) Rope with block.
(*xvii*) Rain coats. (*xviii*) Tools, hammer, shovels, crowbars, claw bars, wrenches, buckets, rope, ladder, hydrant, wrenches.
(*xix*) Flood lights. (*xx*) Manhole guard rail.
(*xxi*) Traffic signs and red flags.

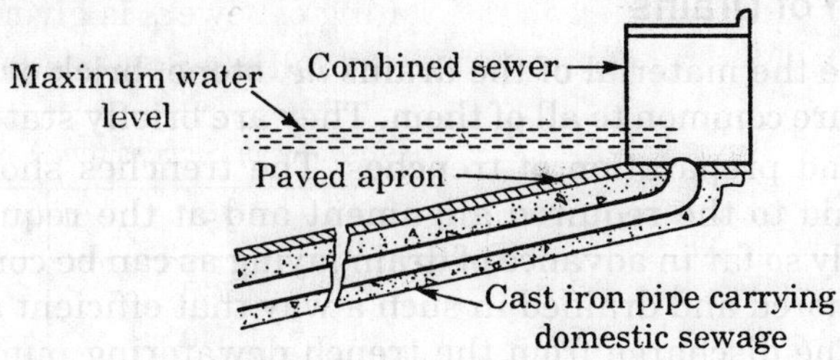

Fig. 12.49. Outlet for a combined sewer.

12.10.10. Tunnelling of a Big Drain

The ability to construct sewers in tunnels has provided a most valuable means of solving drainage services of modern towns and cities.

The size of sewer tunnels range from small heading to accommodate 30 cm pipe to 3.5 metres to 4 metres diameter. In depth they range from a fen metres to 60 metres or more below the ground surface. For this reason, they may be driven through any kind of ground encountered in other forms of tunnelling including hardrode, sandstone, chalk, gravel, sand, ritt, pect etc.

The methods used in constructing sewer tunnels are generally saunter to those employed for other tunnels. The differences lie mainly in practical difficulties of constructing the smaller size. A greater degree of accuracy is necessary for sewage work than is normally required also where sewers run as gravity conduits with variable depths of flow and therefore there is very little choice of position in line or level and must be built to flat and uniform gradients which demand a high degree of precision in setting-out and construction.

The design and operation of sewers has to be carried out with proper regard to the character of the liquids to be handled. Water tightness of sewer tunnels is equally an essential requirement not only to avoid infilterations but more particularly in some case to prevent contamination of underground water supplies.

It is usually satisfactory for the transport of sewage to have a minimum velocity of 75 cm/sec which would imply velocity of 75 cm/sec or more with the sewer flowing at full discharge.

The velocity which will prevent formation of hydrogen sulphide is about 90 cm/sec. Therefore from this complerati velocity of 90 cm/sec should be asined at in temperature countries were than this velocity in warmer countries.

Fen things can be more objectionable or costly than the task of removing deposits from sewers, where sulphide production is aggravated by such deposits, there will be determination in sewer structures.

The choice between open cut and waver and tunnel will depend on several factors. Normally, depth of invert at which tunnelling would be economical will be 6 metres in towns and 8 metres in open country.

12.11. SURFACE AND STORM WATER DRAINS AND THEIR MAINTENANCE

12.11.1. Type of Drains

Surface and storm water drains are provided to carry discharge from used household water as well as flow from catchment areas of the concerned stretches of ground. These drains do not carry discharge from water closet. These drains may be one of the following types :

1. Rectangular. 2. Semicircular. 3. V-shaped.
4. U-shaped. 5. Kerb and channel drains.

12.11.2. Construction of Drains

Whatever may be the material of the drains *i.e.* stone, brick or concrete, the following construction sequence are common to all of them. They are briefly stated and described below.

(*i*) Excavation and preparation of trenches. The trenches should be so dug that the drain section can be laid to the required alignment and at the required depth. The trench should be excavated only so far in advance of drain laying as can be completed in one day. The excavation should be shored and drained in such a way that efficient and safe working of the workmen is assured. The discharge from the trench dewatering pumps should be conveyed either to drainage channels or to natural drains.

The excavation of trench may be carried out manually or with the help of suitable equipment.

The trench should be excavated to the exact gradient specified so that no making of the subgrade by backfilling is required and the concrete bed where required, may be prepared with greatest ease giving a uniform and continuous bearing and support for the trenchs.

The bottom of the trench should be properly trimmed off to present a plain surface and all irregularities should be levelled.

When rock strata has to be excavated and blasting has to be resorted, to prior approval of the competent authority should be obtained and suitable precautions should be taken for the protection of persons and property.

(*ii*) **Bed Concrete.** When the drain is constructed on a soft sori with the maximum watertable laying at the bottom of the drain, a suitable bedding of concrete should be provided. When the maximum watertable is above the bottom of the drain, haunch filling of the section of the drain should be done.

Whenever required, concreting shall be done with 1 : 4 : 8 mass cement concrete or lime concrete.

(*iii*) **Laying.** Laying of the drain shall be carried out according to the drawings specified.

12.11.3. Maintenance of Storm Water Drain

Maintenance of storm water drains consists of the following :

1. Routine inspection of the drain to ensure proper functioning of the same.
2. Rectification of defects noticed during routine inspection.
3. **Cleaning**

(*i*) Cleaning, when required by discharging water from fire hose under high pressure through small nozzle.

(*ii*) Removing obstruction by scrapers.

12.12. SEWAGE PUMPING

12.12.1. Need for Pumping

Sewage and drainage pumps are required under the following situations :

(*i*) When sewage from building is below sewer level. The sewage is taken into a sump and pumped or ejected from there into the sewer.

(*ii*) When the sewer level has gone far down below the ground level. Further deepening of the sewer would be hazardous and uneconomical. In other words, when the flow cannot be taken care of by gravity.

(*iii*) When sewage is required to be carried to disposal works before it gets septic. If not disposed off in time sulphuric acid formation may take place.

(*iv*) When sewage is required to be carried on a ridge.

12.12.2. Problem in Sewage Pumping

The main problems encountered in connection with the sewage pumping are :

(*a*) Special characteristics of the sewage, which may be summarised as :

(*i*) Foul smell of sewage.

(*ii*) Existence of suspended and floating solids which may clog the pumps.

(*iii*) Existence of biological life including the disease germs which are a potential health hazard.

(*b*) Continuously varying incoming sewage which calls for variation in the rate of pumping.

(*c*) The sump wells for collecting sewage from the sewers can not act as balancing tanks because the tank has to be of smaller capacity to avoid longer detention time which may cause a nuisance due to putrefaction and physical chocking of the well. The rate of pumping has therefore to be continuously adjusted to suit the rate of inflow of sewage.

(*d*) The flooding at the sump would not only be a nuisance on account of the foul characteristics of the sewage but would also be a serious health hazard.

12.12.3. Location of Pumping Station [*See IS* : *4111* (*Part IV*) *1968*]

The location of pumping station is governed by the following factors :

(*i*) The area should be free from flooding. The information in respect of the higher recorded flood should be obtained.

(*ii*) When it is not possible to locate the station above the H.F.L. recorded, the layout should be so arranged that the motors are well above the recorded H.F.L. and above the coping of the sump well suction chamber.

(*iii*) The site should be such that in the event of power failure, any overflow into the sump would be diverted into a water course without causing flooding a serious damage to the property. This, however, should not pollute any water course used for drinking water purposes.

12.12.4. General Features of a Pumping Station

1. The pumping station should be far away from residential areas to avoid possibility of complaints for noise or smell.

2. Pumping station should be capable of handling daily and seasonal variation of the inflow.

3. Sewage pumping station includes the following units :

(*i*) Pretreatment of sewage such as screens and grit chambers.

(*ii*) Wet well or sump to receive and hold the sewage until it is pumped.

(*iii*) Dry well for installation of pumps, engines valves and piping.

(*iv*) Pumps to lift sewage.

(*v*) Pipes, valves and controls.

(*vi*) Driving engines to work the pumps.

12.12.5. Pretreatment of Sewage before Pumping

In order to ensure satisfactory operation of the pumps, the following materials which are likely to clog or injure the pumps must be removed :

(*i*) Sticks (*ii*) Leaves (*iii*) Rags

(*iv*) Paper (*v*) Glass (*vi*) Sand

(*vii*) Grit-cinders (*viii*) Other objects which have similar effect on the pumps.

The above materials are removed by

(*i*) Screens (steel set 2.5 × 4 cm)

(*ii*) Grit chamber (30 cm/sec. velocity).

12.12.6. Types of Pumps [*See IS* : *4111* (*Part IV*)- *1968*]

The requirements of a sewage pumps are :

(*i*) It should be reliable

(*ii*) It should be unchokable

(*iii*) It should be accessible for quick maintenance

(*iv*) It should be robust

(*v*) It should be wear resisting.

To secure these requirements some measures of overall efficiency may have to be sacrificed.

The types of pumps available for handling sewage may be divided into the following three groups :

1. Roto Dynamic
2. Reciprocating
3. Pneumatic
4. Centrifugal
5. Airlift

The above pumps are briefly described below :

1. Roto Dynamic Pumps

These pumps are very well suited for pumping sewage. Particular precautions should be taken to see that sewage to be handled does not get septic. The pump should be so located that there is a positive head of sewage above the impeller of the pump on the suction side, when starting up.

2. Reciprocating Pumps

These pumps are recommended for pumping sewage under special circumstances such as in the case of unusually high head. Such pumps are specially designed to run at slow speed for pumping sludge.

The characteristics of a reciprocating pump are :

(*i*) Heavy.

(*ii*) Large dimensions in relation to capacity.

(*iii*) Highly efficient when first installed.

(*iv*) Capable of operating with a suction lift.

(*v*) Can discharge under very high head.

(*vi*) Susceptible to chocking.

(*vii*) Heavy wear and tear.

(*viii*) Valve jamming.

(*ix*) Loss of efficiency through wear.

(*x*) Available as single acting or double acting type.

3. Pneumatic Ejectors

The pneumatic ejector is a simple method of pumping sewage where ease of maintenance and reliability are more important than overall efficiency of the equipment.

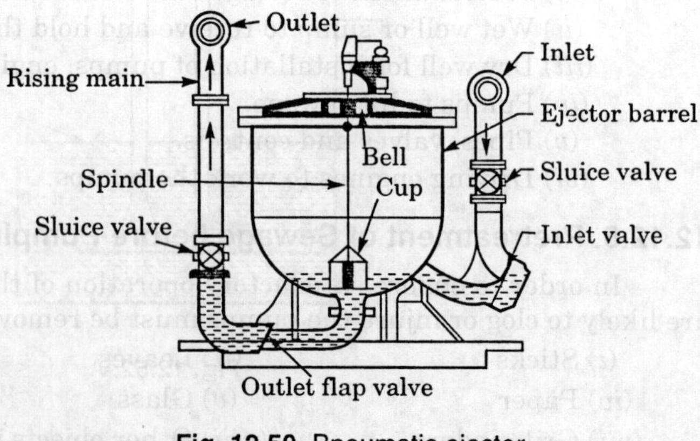

Fig. 12.50. Pneumatic ejector.

The installation consists of an automatic self-starting air compressor, air storage and a set of ejector, the second one as stand by to facilitate repairs. A standby air-compressor is sometimes provided to avoid any breakdown. Several ejector stations may be served by a central air compressing station if the distances are not too great (Fig. 12.50).

4. Centrifugal Pump

These pumps are also well suited for pumping sewage. The main features of this pump are :

(*i*) Can handle solid matter in sewage.

(*ii*) Can be easily installed in sumps.

(*iii*) Axial flow type is non-clogging due to large clearance kept between vanes.

(*iv*) When 'Disintegrating Pump' is used, sewage is disintegrated as it passes through the impeller.

(*v*) The pump may be submerged in the sump or in the dry well. (Fig. 12.51).

5. Air Lift Pump

This system is suitable for pumping sewage having material which is likely to damage or destroy the pump.

When air is ejected into the container, a mixture of air and sewage is formed. This mixture is lighter than sewage and hence sewage is lifted. The system requires compressed air injection and hence it is costly. Fig. 12.52 illustrates the principle of this category of pump.

The various standard systems of installation of pumps are given in Figs. 12.49, 12.50, 12.51 and 12.52, 12.53, 12.54, 12.55, 12.56. (These illustrations are based on IS : 4111 (Part IV)—1968.)

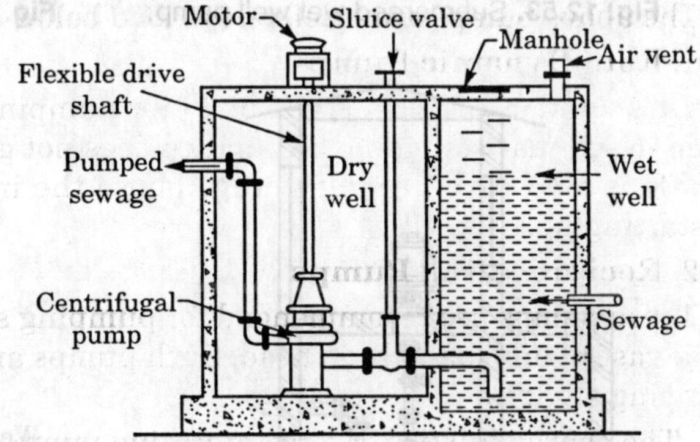

Fig. 12.51. Centrifugal pump, (dry well type).

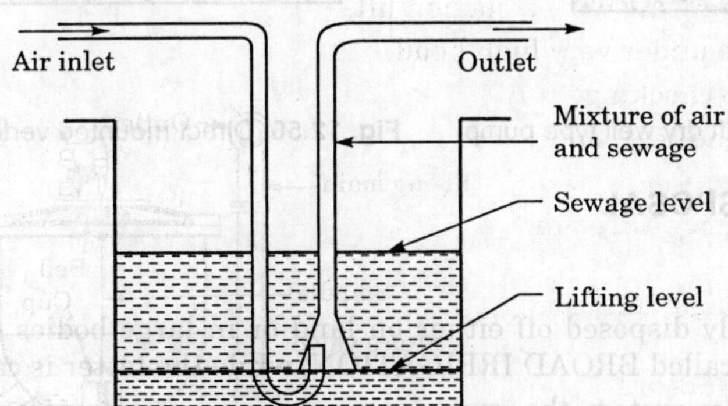

Fig. 12.52. Air lift pump.

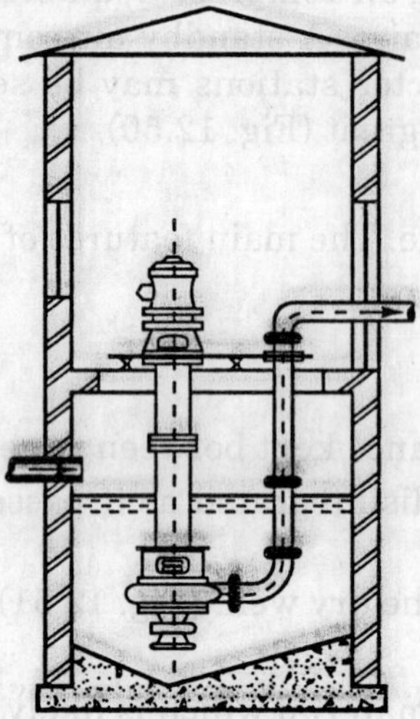

Fig. 12.53. Submerged wet well pump.

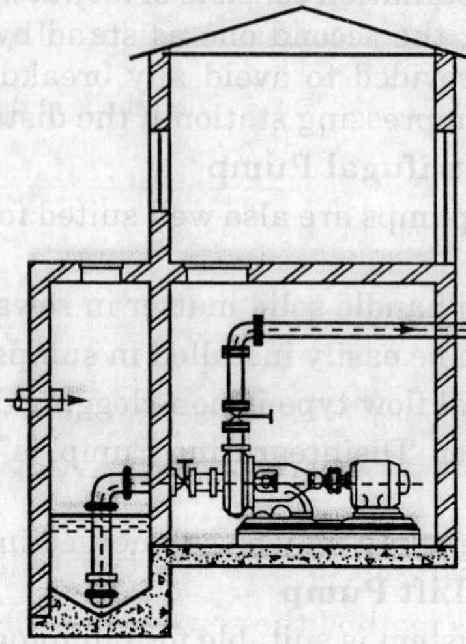

Fig. 12.54. Horizontal shaft dry well type pump.

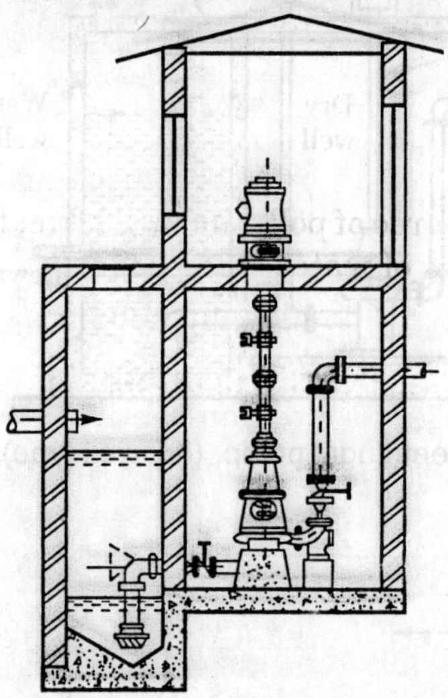

Fig. 12.55. Vertical shaft dry well type pump.

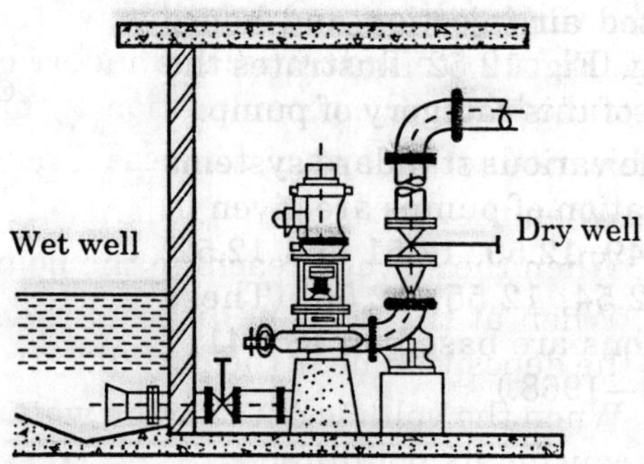

Fig. 12.56. Direct mounted vertical sewage pump.

12.13. SEWAGE DISPOSAL

12.13.1. General

Sewage is finally disposed off either on land or in large bodies of water. The former method of disposal is called BROAD IRRIGATION, while the latter is called the DILUTION.

In broad irrigation system, the sewage is given the primary treatment before disposal, *i.e.*

1. Screening 2. Skimming 3. Plain Settling etc.

In the dilution system only such degree of treatment is given to the sewage as would not cause deterioration of the condition of the body of water (stream, pond or lake etc.) to such an extent as may make the water unfit for normal utility.

12.13.2. Methods of Disposal

The various methods of disposal are illustrated in Fig. 12.57.

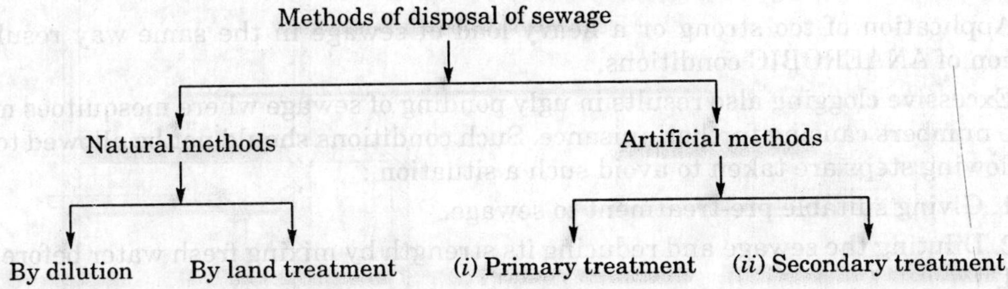

Fig. 12.57. Methods of disposal.

12.13.3. Disposal of Sewage by Dilution

In this method the sewage is discharged into a stream or a large body of water such as lake or sea.

Care should be taken to see that the quality of water in the stream or lake does not deteriorate to the extent of diminishing its normal ability due to addition of sewage. The permissible pollution by sewage depends upon the usage of water and no single standard can be, therefore, laid out. The primary considerations in the formulation of such a standard are :

1. Health. 2. Aesthetics. 3. Economy.

The various purposes for which water charged with sewage may be used are bathing, drinking, fish culture, industrial use and irrigation. The degree of pollution will have, therefore, to be restricted from the consideration of the proposed use of water.

This method of sewage disposal is most suited under the following situations :

1. When the city is located near sea, river or lake.
2. When the sewage reaching the point of disposal is fresh or non-septic.
3. When at the point of disposal the depth of water is sufficient and the current can prevent the deposition near the outfall.
4. When the volume of receiving water is large enough to take the load of sewage safely without causing its pollution.
5. When during flood the receiving water would not cause backward flow in sewers.

At the site of disposal, the following factors should be considered :

1. Putrifying matter does not get deposited at the bottom and start giving offensive odour.
2. Sludge banks are not formed at the top.
3. Unsightly matter does not float on the surface.
4. Acquatic life is not destroyed.

12.13.4. Disposal of Sewage on Land (Irrigation)

When sewage is applied on land, the suspended solids get filtered out.

The volatile organic material in sewage is acted upon by the soil, bacteria and gets mineralised. When the land is sufficiently porous and permeable, natural aeration of its void-spaces takes place and bacteria action remains AEROBIC.

On the other hand, if the land consists of heavy, sticky and fine grained material, it gets choked soon and aeration of voids is not possible. Thus results in ANAEROBIC conditions with associated filthy sight and foul smell.

Application of too strong or a heavy load of sewage in the same way results in the formation of ANAEROBIC conditions.

Excessive clogging also results in ugly ponding of sewage where mosquitoes may breed in large numbers causing further nuisance. Such conditions should not be allowed to develop. The following steps are taken to avoid such a situation :

1. Giving suitable pre-treatment to sewage.

2. Diluting the sewage and reducing its strength by mixing fresh water before applying on land.

3. Limiting the water and organic load (B.O.D.) depending upon the nature of soil and the climatic condition. Table 12.30 gives the limiting value of quantities of sewage that can be applied on land without creating foul conditions.

Table 12.30

S. No.	*Type of Land*	*Quantities of domestic sewage m³/hectare/day after primary treatment that can be applied*	
		Raw sewage	*Pre-treated sewage*
1.	Poor clayey soil	30	60
2.	Average loam	60	120
3.	Good sandy soil	120	180 to 240

Land treatment is suitable under the following situations :

1. When the overall rainfall is very low, the land can be irrigated by sewage.

2. When there is no river or natural water course in which sewage may be discharged.

3. When the quantity of sewage is more, which would pollute river water beyond permissible limits.

4. When rivers usually run dry or have very small flow during summer.

5. When the water table is very deep even during the monsoon and there are no chances of its pollution by land treatment of sewage.

6. When vegetables have good market, land treatment would yield good return.

7. When land is sandy, loamy or alluvial, the porous soil would allow good aeration.

Land treatment consists of broad irrigation or sewage farming.

Broad irrigation is similar to intermittent sand filtration. The land area acts as a crude filter and stabilises sewage by AEROBIC filtration. The character of the water drained from beneath the soil is similar to that from intermittent sand filter.

The under-drains usually consist of 15 to 20 cm diameter porous tile pipes laid open jointed at spacing of 12 to 30 m. The effluent is normally small in volume and well stabilised. It can be disposed off into water courses without causing any nuisance.

The various ways in which land treatment is carried out are :

1. Surface irrigation. (See Fig. 12.58) 2. Sub-soil irrigation. (See Fig. 12.59)

3. Flooding (See Fig. 12.60) 4. Ridge and Furrow (See Fig. 12.61)

5. Spray irrigation. This is carried out with the help of pumping and nozzles.

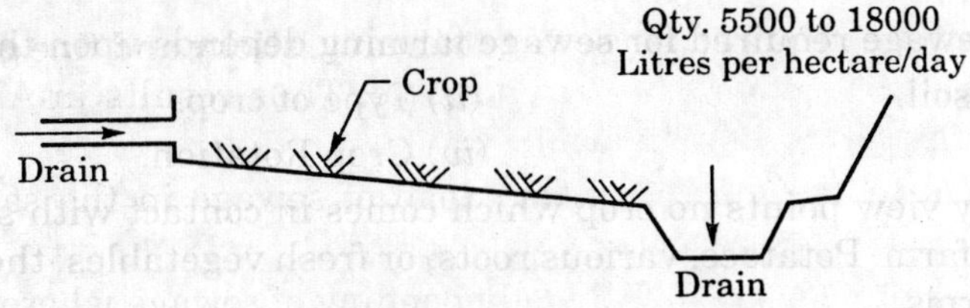

Fig. 12.58. Surface irrigation.

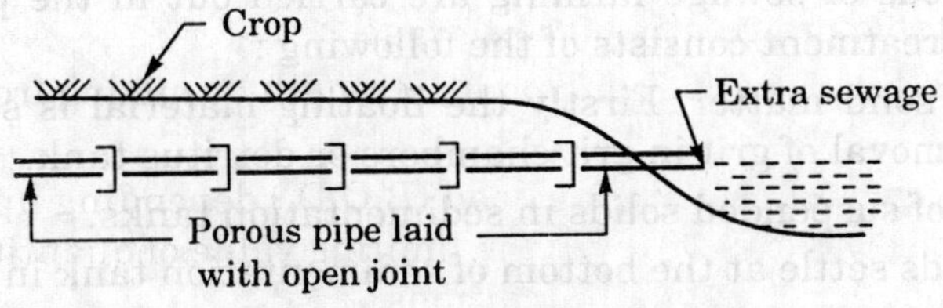

Fig. 12.59. Sub-soil irrigation.

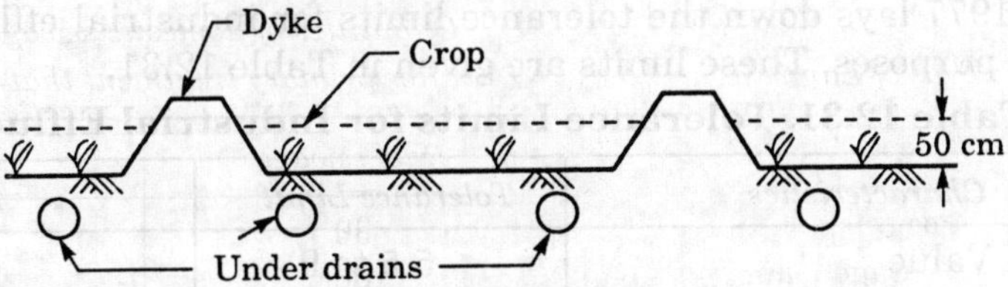

Fig. 12.60. Flooding.

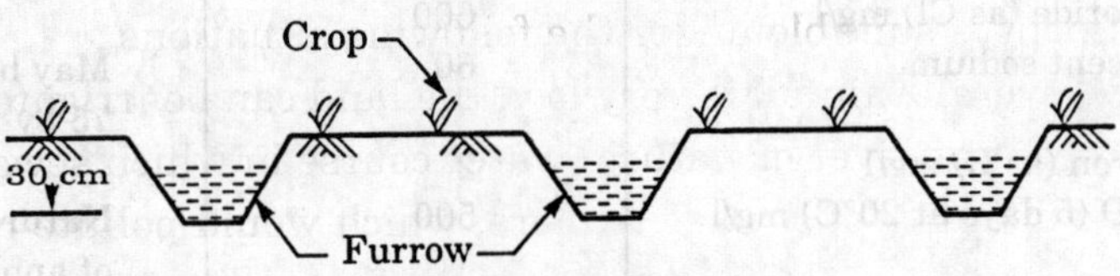

Fig. 12.61. Ridge and furrow.

Sewage Farming. The water and fertilising elements is sewage can be usefully utilised for raising crops. This method of sewage disposal on the land is called "SEWAGE FARMING". In broad irrigation the primary consideration is successful disposal of sewage while in sewage farming the growing of crops gets precedence over method of disposal. Special advantage of sewage farming lies in returning to the land the fertilising constituents which have been drawn from it by way of crops at the same time considerable income is made from the sale of farm products.

Fertilising-Value in Sewage. The common fertilising elements in sewage are :

1. Nitrogen. 2. Phosphorous. 3. Potash.

Raw sewage contains about 20 mg/litre of nitrogen of which 50 per cent is available as plant food.

Normal domestic sewage contains about 10 mg/litre of phosphoric acid and 40 mg/litre of potassium.

Preparation of land for sewage farming consists in constructing drains and dykes. Where required the land is graded to prevent pooling. The land is cleared and underdrains are laid.

Quantity of sewage required for sewage farming depends upon the following :

(*i*) Nature of soil. (*ii*) Type of crop.

(*iii*) Climate. (*iv*) Crop Rotation.

From sanitary view points no crop which comes in contact with sewage should be cultivated on a sewage farm. Potatoes, various roots, or fresh vegetables, therefore, should not be grown on sewage farms.

Grains, fruits and nuts are grown successfully.

Artificial methods of sewage farming are carried out in the primary and secondary stages. The primary treatment consists of the following :

(*i*) Removal of solid matter. Firstly the floating material is separated by screening. This is followed by removal of grit in grit chambers or detritus tank.

(*ii*) Settlement of suspended solids in sedimentation tanks.

Finally the solids settle at the bottom of sedimentation tank in the form of sludge.

In the second stage the effluent of the primary stage is oxidised as explained in article 12.12.5.

IS : 3307—1977 lays down the tolerance limits for industrial effluents discharged on land for irrigation purposes. These limits are given in Table 12.31.

Table 12.31. Tolerance Limits for Industrial Effluent

S. No.	*Characteristics*	*Tolerance Limit*	*Remarks*
1.	*p*H Value	5.5 to 9	
2.	Total dissolved solids	2100	Limit fixed by local authority
3.	Sulphate (as SO_4) mg/l	1000	
4.	Chloride (as Cl) mg/l	600	
5.	Percent sodium	60	May be relaxed upto 75 by local authority
6.	Boron (as B) mg/l	2	
7.	BOD (5 days at 20°C) mg/l	500	Nature of soil and rate of application should also be considered
8.	Oil and grease mg/l	10	
9.	Alpha emitters, μc/ml max.	10^{-9}	
10.	Beta emitters μc/ ml max.	10^{-9}	

When industrial effluents are applied on agricultural land, the hydraulic loadings given in Table 12.32 are generally followed. The nature of the crop, water requirements, climatic conditions and frequency of application should, however, also be taken into consideration.

Table 12.32. Hydraulic Loading Rates

S. No.	*Soil texture classification*	*Recommended Dosage of Settled Industrial Effluent, m^3/ hectare/day*
1.	Sandy	225 to 280
2.	Sandy loam	170 to 225
3.	Loam	110 to 170
4.	Clay loam	55 to 110
5.	Clayey	35 to 55

12.13.5. Oxidation Ponds, Stabilisation Ponds or Lagoons

Oxidation pond is a pool or pond constructed and maintained under conditions (away from the city) for the treatment of sewage.

Treatment in a lagoon is through sunlight, algae, evaporation, percolation, sedimentation and oxidation. It results in the biological stabilisation of the influent.

Advantages and disadvantages of lagoons are given below :

(*a*) **Advantages**

(*i*) Successful disposal of sewage.

(*ii*) Evaporation and percolation of some liquid.

(*iii*) Acts as an equilising basin to the quantity and quality of flow.

(*iv*) Low cost.

(*b*) **Disadvantages**

(*i*) Pollution of surface water.

(*ii*) Silting and over nitrification.

(*iii*) Over growth of Algae, Weed etc.

(*iv*) Breeding of mosquitoes.

(*v*) Putrefactive odour.

The discharge of untreated sewage in water course pollutes the water, affecting quality and public health. The permissible limits of the constituents of sewage effluents discharged into inland surface waters are laid down in IS : 4764—1973. These limits are given in Table 12.33.

Table 12.33. Tolerance Limits for Sewage Effluents Discharged into Surface Waters

S. No.	*Characteristics*	*Tolerance Limits*	*Remarks*
1.	Total suspended solid mg/l max.	30	
2.	B.O.D. for 5 days at 20°C mg/l max.	20	

12.13.6. Sewage Sickness

After continuous application of sewage to land for a long period, the pores in the soil get clogged up by the deposition of solids.

Atmospheric air cannot circulate and the AEROBIC bacteria cannot work upon the solids to bring about their stabilisation. Their place is then taken up by ANAEROBES who do not require the presence of free oxygen.

The mineralisation continues slowly with the production of odourous gases like hydrogen sulphide which are the products of anaerobic decomposition. The land cannot accept any more sewage load and is said to be "SEWAGE SICK."

The sewage sickness can be prevented by the following methods :

(*i*) By giving primary treatment to the sewage. The suspended solids are removed and hence the pores of the soil do not get clogged easily.

(*ii*) By giving rest to the land. This is done by intermittent application of sewage on land. The soil is aerated by ploughing the land.

(*iii*) By crop rotation.

(*iv*) By providing under-drains to collect the excessive quantity of sewage.

(*v*) By frequent ploughing and rotation of soil so as to expose the soil to atmosphere.

12.13.7. Self-purification of Polluted Waters

The self-purification of polluted water is carried out in the following ways :

1. **By Diluting.** When sewage is mixed with large volumes of water it always remains in aerobic condition because dissolved oxygen is always present.

2. **Current.** When sewage is mixed with large volume of water having heavy currents no deposition of sewage takes place.

3. **Sedimentation.** In slow currents sedimentation takes place causing growth of Algae. This results in production of oxygen. Heavier solids settle in stream beds and start anaerobic decomposition. The deposits are washed away during the flood.

4. **Temperature.** At low temperature, the activities of the organism are slow. Due to this the rate of decomposition is also slow. At higher temperature this action is reversed. In summer less time is required but the quantity of dissolved oxygen in cold water is more than in hot water.

5. **Sunlight.** The pathogens are killed when they are exposed to sunlight. Algae also grows in sunlight and this causes production of oxygen. Sunlight, therefore, indirectly helps in the oxidation of unstable matter.

A polluted stream gets divided into the following four different zones :

1. Zone of degration.
2. Zone of active decomposition.
3. Zone of recovery.
4. Zone of cleaner water.

12.13.8. Disposal of Sewage in Sea Water

When sewage is mixed with sea water, the higher specific gravity and low temperature of sea water, causes the lighter and warmer sewage to rise and spread out in a thin film or "SLEEK".

Sewage acts chemically with sea water giving rise to solids of milky appearance which form sludge banks.

The formation of the sludge banks on the shore is avoided by releasing sewage for disposal during low tides only and by taking the sewage far deep into the sea away from the coastal line. The back spreading of the sewage is prevented by constructing thick stone masonry work at the outfall.

Within the estuarine region, the marine area extends upto the low tide level. Water above that point falls in the region of inland surface water. Marine coastal areas extend upto 3 km from the coast lines. Pollution of marine coastal areas with sewage, effluents and wastes from the hinterland is an important problem associated with industrial development.

The following factors have to be taken into consideration for determining sewage disposal operations :

(*a*) Present and future impact on the marine environment, human health, welfare and amenities.

(*b*) Irreversibility of the impact on uncontrolled discharges.

(*c*) Volume and concentration of pollutants.

(*d*) Location of disposal point.

It should be ensured that biological life is fully protected. Many marine organisms breed and spawn in near-shore and seabed areas. IS : 7967-1976 lays down criteria for controlling pollution of marine coastal areas caused by discharge of sewage, effluents and wastes.

The following discharges are prohibited in marine coastal areas except under specified safeguards prescribed by the local authority :

(*a*) Uncontrolled discharge of night soil, sewage and industrial effluents.

(*b*) Solid wastes of domestic or industrial origin.

(*c*) Radio-active effluents and solid wastes.

(*d*) Sand, gravel washings.

(*e*) Unscreened organic suspended solids larger than 3 mm in diameter.

The tolerance limits for water quality after receiving discharges are given in Table 12.34.

Table 12.34. Tolerance Limits for Water Quality after Receiving Discharges

S. No.	*Characteristics*	*Tolerance Limits for*	
		Bathing, recreation shell fish and commercial fish culture and salt manufacture	*Harbour water*
1.	Colour and odour	Not noticeable colour or effensive odour	Not noticeable colour or offensive odour
2.	Floating material	No visible floating matter	No visible floating matter
3.	Suspended solids	No visible suspended solids	—
4.	pH value	6.5 to 8.5	6.5 to 9
5.	Free ammonia (as N) mg/l max	1.2	—
6.	Phenolic compound mg/l max	0.1	—
7.	Dissolved oxygen	40% salinates value or 3 mg/l whichever is high	3 mg/l
8.	Pesticides mg/l	.002	—
9.	Arsenic (as As) mg/1	0.2	—
10.	Mercury (as Hg) mg/l	0.0003	—
11.	Oils and greasy substance mg/1	0.1	10
12.	BOD (5 days at 20°C) mg/l	5	5

IS : 7968-1976 lays down the tolerance limits for industrial effluents discharged into marine coastal area.

Table 12.35 gives tolerance limits for industrial effluents.

Table 12.35

S. No.	*Characteristics*	*Tolerance Limits*
1.	Copper (as Cu) mg/l max	3.0
2.	Lead (as Pb) mg/l max	1.0
3.	Chromium mg/l max	1.0
4.	Cadmium (as Cd) mg/l max	2.0
5.	Mercury (as Hg) mg/l max	0.01
6.	Nickel (as Ni) mg/l max	5.0
7.	Zinc (as Zn) mg/l	5.0
8.	Total suspended solids mg/l max	
	(*a*) For process waste water	100
	(*b*) For cooling water effluent	Total suspended matter content of influent cooling water plus 10 per cent.
9.	Particle size of	
	(*a*) Floatable solids max	3 mm
	(*b*) Settleable solids max	850 microns
10.	pH value	5.5 to 9.0
11.	Temperature max	45°C at point of discharge.
12.	BOD (5 days at 20°C) mg/l max	100
13.	Oils and grease mg/l max	20
14.	Phenolic compounds mg/l max	5.0
15.	Cyanides (as CN) mg/l max	0.2
16.	Sulphides (as S) mg/l max	5.0
17.	Alpha emitters μc/ml max	10^{-8}
18.	Beta emitters μc/ml max	10^{-7}
19.	Residual chlorine mg/l max	1
20.	Arsenic (as As) mg/l max	0.2
21.	Selenium (as Se) mg/l max	0.05
22.	Ammonical nitrogen (as N) mg/l max	50
23.	COD mg/l max	250
24.	Pesticides	
	(*a*) organo-phosphorus compounds (as P) mg/l max	1
	(*b*) chlorinated hydrocarbons (as Cl) mg/l	0.02
25.	Flourides (as F) mg/l max	15

12.14. CANAL HEADWORKS

12.14.1. General

It is necessary to construct canal system in any culturable area where it is required to provide irrigation. The canal system starts with the headworks which may belong to one of the following two types namely :

(1) Diversion work (2) Storage work.

1. **Diversion work.** These works are located across the river near the point of takeoff of the head of the canal system to direct water from the source of supply into the canal.

2. **Storage work.** When the minimum discharge of the water source does not meet the demand during the period of irrigation, reservoir is constructed to meet the fluctuation of water requirement. Sometimes reservoirs are constructed for multi-purpose river valley projects including flood control and hydro-electric power generation.

12.14.2. Objects of Headworks

The primary object of the canal headworks is to direct the water from the river into the canal. The following steps are taken :

1. An obstruction is constructed across the river to serve the following purpose :

(*a*) It prevents the flow of water required for irrigation into the river.

(*b*) It rises the water level in the river locally at the canal take-off point and thus helps in maintaining gravity flow. The excessive cutting of the canal in the head reach is thus reduced.

(*c*) It reduces the fluctuations in the water level of the river.

(*d*) As the flow of water is obstructed, the velocity is reduced and water drops down its silt load before it passes into the canal system.

2. A regulatory structure is constructed at the canal entrance of the take-off point. It provides proper control over the supply to be made. The regulatory structure serves the following purpose :

(*a*) It prevents the river floods entering into the canal.

(*b*) It allows only predetermined discharge to pass into the canal.

(*c*) It prevents the excessive silt entering into the canal.

12.14.3. Selection of Size for Headworks

There are four stages of a river, namely :

1. Mountainous stage
2. Sub-mountainous stage
3. Through stage of river in plains
4. Tidal or delta stage.

As the canal is taken off from the river it is necessary to examine the stage which is suitable for this purpose. These stages are briefly discussed below from the point of view of locating the head works :

1. **Mountainous stage.** Head works should normally not be located in this stage for the following reasons :

(*i*) The construction is expensive.

(*ii*) Area to be cultivated is small.

(*iii*) A number of falls are required to be constructed.

(*iv*) Number of cross drain works are required.

2. **Sub-mountainous stage.** The selection of the headworks may be made in this region. The advantages and disadvantages of locating head works in this region are given below :

(*a*) **Advantages**

(*i*) Construction materials (stone etc.) are locally available as the section of the river is not very wide. Also extensive river training works are not required.

(*ii*) In the initial stage temporary bunds may be constructed for use with locally available materials.

(*iii*) Falls available may be utilised for generation of hydro-electric power.

(*b*) **Disadvantages**

(*i*) Soil in this region is pervious. This increases water losses.

(ii) Greater number of cross-drainage works are required. This increases the cost of the project.

(iii) Area to be cultivated under irrigation is comparatively small.

3. **Through stage**

Headworks may be located in this region. The points in favour and against locating the headworks in this region as given below :

(a) **Points in favour**

(i) The percolation losses in this region are not excessive as in the sub-mountainous stage.

(ii) The demand of water is sufficiently large as compared to other regions.

(iii) Number of cross-drainage works to be constructed are less.

(b) **Points against**

(i) Construction materials may not be available locally.

(ii) As the section is broad, extensive river training is required.

(iii) The initial cost of structure and cost of maintenance is comparatively high.

4. **Delta or Tidal stage.** This region is not suitable for locating the headworks. The surrounding area is not large enough to introduce costly irrigation project.

The site for headworks should be selected after properly considering the following points :

(a) **Economical Consideration**

(i) The material for construction should be available in large quantities in close proximity of the site.

(ii) At the site the river section should be narrow and straight with non-submersible banks. It reduces the cost of training works.

(iii) The cost of connecting the site by rail and roadways should be less.

(iv) The site should be close to the culturable area to reduce the cost of construction of the canal system.

(v) The number of cost drainage works should be as few as possible.

(b) **Functional considerations**

(i) Good command area should be available with moderate height.

(ii) The canal take-off should as far as possible be at right angles to the river. (Fig. 12.62).

(iii) The river reach should have control flow without tendency of scouring or silting.

(iv) The canal should give maximum command.

12.14.4. Constituent Parts of Canal Headworks (Fig. 12.62).

1. Weir
2. Divide wall
3. Under sluices or Scouring sluices
4. Fish ladder
5. Head regulator for the canal
6. Silt exclusion device
7. River training works
8. Guide banks.

12.14.5. Weir or Anicut

The weir provides the obstruction across the river required to raise its water level and direct the water into the canal. It is aligned at right angles to the direction of flow of the river.

Weirs are generally located in alluvial strata or boulder strata of the river. The weir located in alluvial strata is generally preferable except when by its location in the alluvial stage command of the fertile land proposed for irrigation is lost.

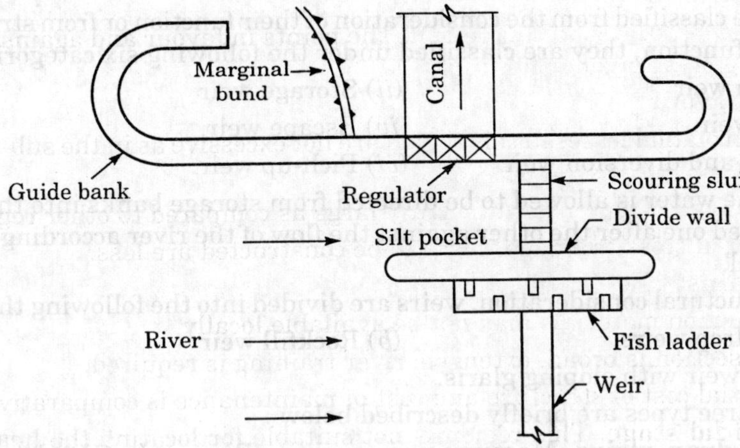

Fig. 12.62. Layout of Headworks.

The following are the advantages of locating a weir in boulder stage in comparison to alluvial stage :

(*a*) **Advantages**

(*i*) The length of the weir is generally shorter in boulder reaches.

(*ii*) Since the silt factor is high in boulder reaches the requirements of cut off and protection works are reduced.

(*iii*) Since high banks are generally available in boulder reaches the cost of training works is reduced.

(*iv*) Construction materials like sand and aggregate are locally available.

(*b*) **Disadvantages**

(*i*) In boulder stage there is excessive loss of water due to sub-soil flow which becomes available in alluvial stage.

(*ii*) From headworks in boulder stage, the canal passes through similar terrain causing excessive absorption losses.

(*iii*) From boulder stage to the ridge the canal usually crosses many drainages.

(*iv*) Demand for irrigation in the area in boulder stage is generally low due to higher rainfall and lesser area for irrigation.

Having decided the location of the weir, the actual construction site is selected from the following considerations :

(*i*) A narrow well-defined channel with high banks is the best.

(*ii*) The canal alignment should enable suitable command and inexcessive digging.

(*iii*) Materials of construction like sand and gravel should be available in the vicinity.

(*iv*) Site should be accessible by rail and road.

From the design consideration, weirs may be classified as :

1. **Gravity weirs.** These weirs have their stability due to the weight of the mass in the body of the weir *i.e.* self weight sufficient to counter all dislodging forces.

2. **Non-gravity weirs.** The structure as a whole is safe and stable against all forces such as concrete weir.

12.14.6. Types of Weirs

Weirs may be classified from the consideration of their function or from structural design. According to their function, they are classified under the following six categories.

(*i*) Diversion weir (*ii*) Storage weir

(*iii*) Pick-up weir (*iv*) Escape weir

(*v*) Stoppage and diversion weir (*vi*) Pich-up weir.

Whenever the water is allowed to be directed from storage banks into the rivers, small weirs are constructed one after the other against the flow of the river according to the location of the take-off canal.

From the structural consideration, weirs are divided into the following three categories.

(*a*) Vertical drop weirs. (*b*) Rockfill weir

(*c*) Concrete weir with sloping glaris.

The above three types are briefly described below :

(*a*) **Vertical drop weirs.** Masonry weir such as *Bhimgoda* (Hardwar), Madhopur, *Rasual*, *Khanki* and *Marala* are examples of this type of construction.

Fig. 12.63 shows details of *Bhimgoda weir* at Hardwar. It is a typical weir of this type.

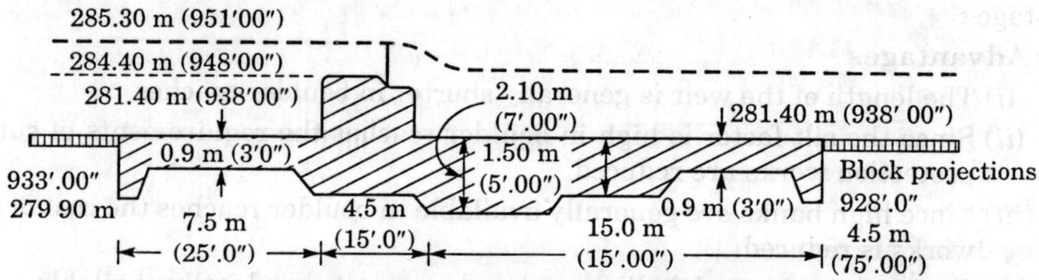

Fig. 12.63. Bhimgoda weir (Vertical drop type).

The main components of this type of weir are :

(*i*) Upstream boulder pitching.

(*ii*) An upstream curtain wall.

(*iii*) Upstream or fore-apron.

(*iv*) Masonry crest with vertical downstream face.

(*v*) Shutter on the crest of the weir.

(*vi*) Downstream flow or rear apron.

(*vii*) Downstream curtain wall.

(*viii*) Downstream rip rap for protection of the channel.

(*b*) **Rockfill weirs.** In this type boulders are laid in the form of glacis on the upstream and downstream with a few intervening walls. The downstream slope is generally made very flat. Its stability or principle of design is not susceptible to exact theoretical treatment.

Large quantities of stone are required both for initial construction as well as for subsequent maintenance. The construction of this type of weir is therefore limited to localities where stones and unskilled labour are available in abundance. Fig. 12.64 gives cross section of Okhla weir (rockfill type).

(*c*) **Concrete weir with sloping glacis.** Weir of this type is of recent origin. Its design is based on Khosla's theory. Piles of sufficient depth are driven at the end of the upstream and downstream aprons. Sometimes an intermediate pile line is also provided. The hydraulic jump is formed on the glacis to dissipate the energy of overflowing water. Fig. 12.65 gives a typical cross-section of this type of weir.

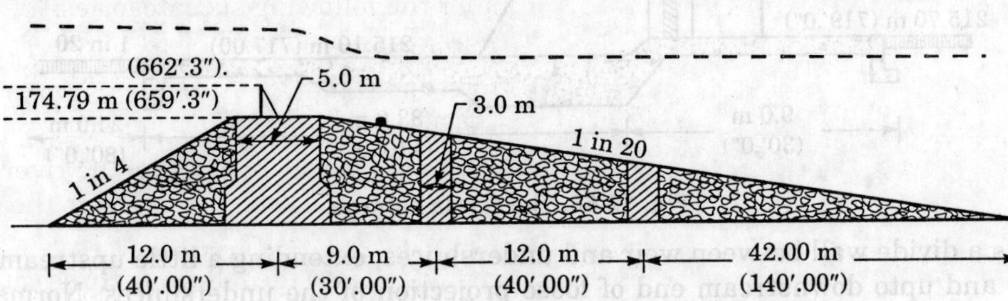

Fig. 12.64. Okhla weir (rockfill type).

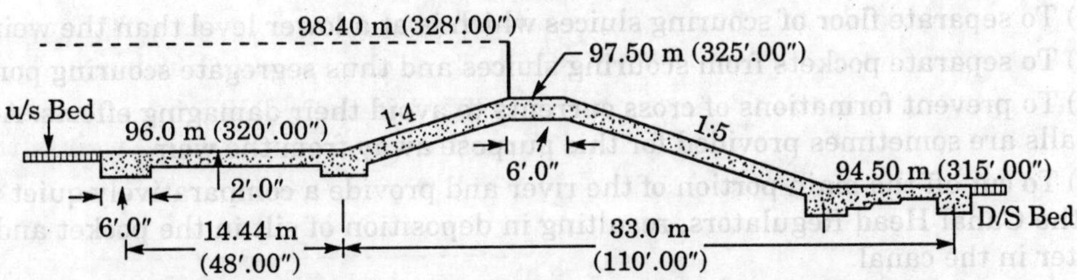

Fig. 12.65. Concrete weir with sloping glacis (The punjab weir).

12.14.7. Barrage

If the difference between the pond level and crest level is within 1½ m, the pond level can be maintained by means of falling shutters. When this difference is more than 1.5 m a gate controller weir is required. This structure is known as a "Barrage". With this type of construction roadway can be constructed across the river at a small additional cost.

The gates of the barrage can be raised clear off the high flood level. This enables the high flood level to be passed with the minimum afflux.

A barrage provides maximum control on the river but it is comparatively more costly. Fig. 12.66 shows the *Sarda Barrage* at *Banbassa* in district Nainital, U.P.

12.14.8. Divide Wall or Groyne

The divide wall is simply a long wall or Groyne (an embankment protected on all sides by stone or concrete blocks) at right angles to the axis of the weir separating the weir from the under sluices. The wall extends upstream to a little distance beyond the beginning of the head regulator and downstream to the end of the loose protection or *Talus* of the undersluices.

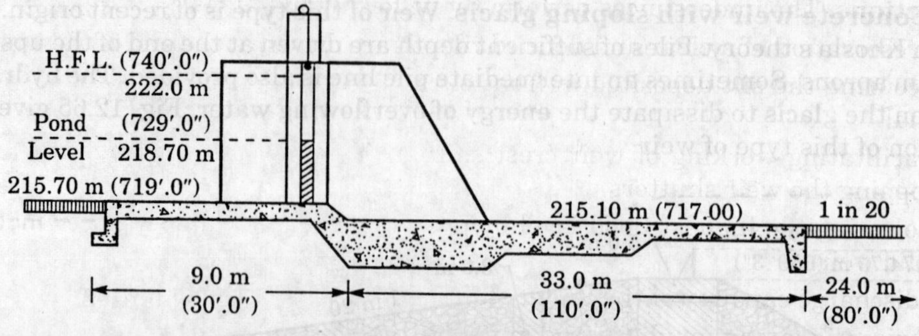

Fig. 12.66. The Sarda barrage.

It is a divide wall between weir and undersluices, extending a little upstream of canal regulator and upto downstream end of loose projection of the undersluices. Normally, it is concrete or masonry structure with top width of 1.5 to 3 m and aligned at right angles to the weir axis. The main functions of the divide wall are :

(*i*) To separate floor of scouring sluices which is at a lower level than the weir proper.

(*ii*) To separate pockets from scouring sluices and thus segregate scouring portion.

(*iii*) To prevent formations of cross currents to avoid their damaging effects. Additional divide walls are sometimes provided for this purpose away from the weir.

(*iv*) To cut off the main portion of the river and provide a comparatively quiet pocket in front of the Canal Head Regulators, resulting in deposition of silt in the pocket and entry of clear water in the canal.

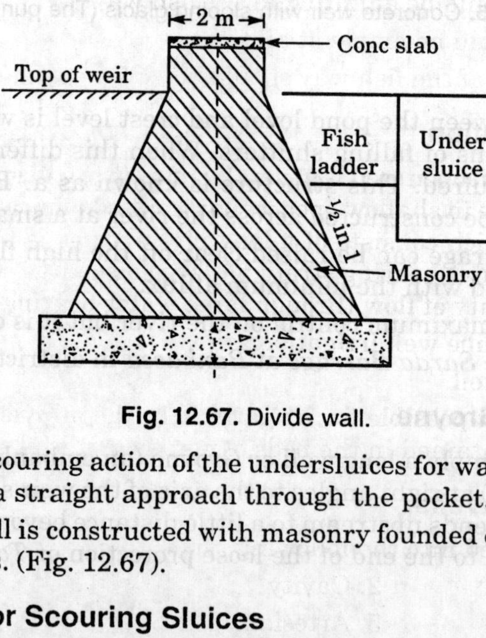

Fig. 12.67. Divide wall.

(*v*) To concentrate scouring action of the undersluices for washing out the silt deposited in the pocket by ensuring a straight approach through the pocket.

Generally divide wall is constructed with masonry founded on a very strong foundation mostly on well foundations. (Fig. 12.67).

12.14.9. Under-Sluices or Scouring Sluices

The undersluices are openings in the weir wall with a crest low level on the canal side. These openings are fully controlled by gates in all types of weir. If two canals take off on either side of the river, it would be necessary to provide two sets of undersluices on either side.

Functions. The undersluices perform the following functions :

(*i*) Preservation of a clear and defined river channel approaching a canal regulator.

(*ii*) Scouring the silt deposited in front of canal regulator and controlling entry of silt into the canal.

(*iii*) Facilitating working of weir crest shutter or gates. The winter floods are passed without dropping the weir shutters.

(*iv*) Lowering the highest flood level by providing greater water way per metre length than the solid weir.

The discharge capacity of the under sluices is greatest of the following :

(*i*) Twice the maximum discharge in the off-take canal.

(*ii*) 20 per cent of the maximum flood discharge.

(*iii*) Maximum winter discharge.

12.14.10. Fish Ladder

In order to enable the fish to ascend the headworks of the rivers and thus reach their spawning grounds for propagation or to follow their migrating habits in search of food. Fish passes or fish ladders are provided on all such works which put an obstruction to their passage.

The general requirements of a fish ladder are :

(*i*) The slope should not be steeper than 1 : 10 so as to ensure a current of velocity not exceeding 2 m per second in any portion of the fish way.

(*ii*) The compartments of bays of the pass must be of such dimensions that the fish do not risk collision with the sides and upper end of each bay when ascending.

(*iii*) Plenty of light should be admitted in the fish way.

(*iv*) Water supply should be ample at all times.

(*v*) The top and sides of the fish way should be above ordinary high water level.

12.14.11. Tube Well Irrigation

The discharge from an open well is generally limited to 5 litres/sec. Mechanical pumping of small discharges available in shallow open wells is not economical. To obtain large discharge mechanically, tube well which consists of a long pipe or tube is bored deep into the ground intercepting one or more water bearing strata : A large discharge compared to an open well is obtained by increased velocity of flow through large water bearing stratum.

Broad categories of tube well irrigation are :

(*i*) Wells in alluvial soil.

(*ii*) Wells in rock, (not possible for irrigation). In the alluvial plains the sub-soil water slowly percolates and is contained in the beds of porous material such as sand and gravel.

12.14.12. Types of Tube Wells

Tube wells are divided into the following types :

1. Strainer
2. Cavity
3. Slotted
4. Radial
5. Artesian.

The above types are briefly described below :

1. Strainer tube well. A higher discharge is obtained from this type as sand is slopped by wire gauge strainers and water from different sand strata are drawn together.

Boring is usually done by a casing pipe 50 to 100 mm larger in diameter than the diameter of the well pipe. After the boring of the well, the pipe assembly which is partly ordinary or blind pipe (resting against clay) and partly strainer (resting against sand) is lowered.

2. **Slotted tube well.** The boring is done for the strainer tube well, but the diameter of the boring pipe has to be large say 40 to 50 cm. The 150 mm slotted tube pipes have slots 50 mm × 3 mm 180 per metre in number (six along the circumference and 80 longitudinally). The development of this well is done gradually after exposing the strata by air compressor pumping water and sand and feeding shingle of 5 mm through the annular space between 40 cm and 15 cm pipe.

3. **Cavity tube well.** A cavity is created at the bottom of the tube well to provide a sufficiently large area of sand to reduce the velocity of water below the critical velocity. The water is supposed to be flowing in it from all directions.

A space of 15 cm to 30 cm in depth in the centre direct under the tube is generally found in such cases. The total quantity of sand taken out is measured and this gives the size of the cavity formed. (See Fig. 12.68).

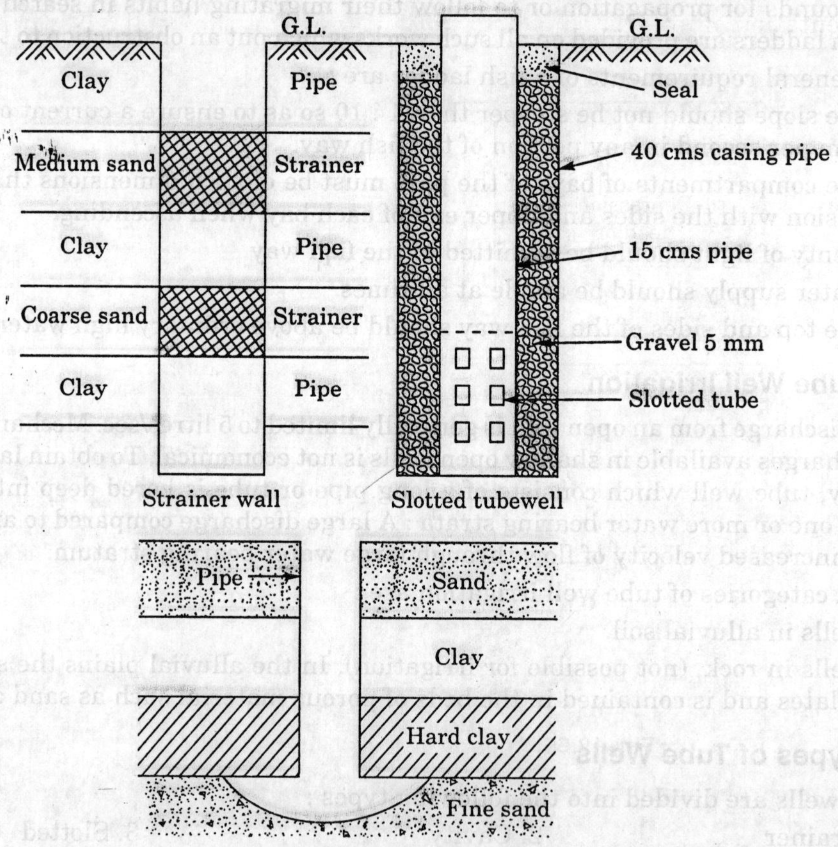

Fig. 12.68. Cavity well.

4. **Radial tube well.** In this type pipe screws are driven horizontally into the Aquifer to facilitate large drafts on subsurface basin. Usually a shaft of 3 to 8 metres in diameter is sunk into the water bearing strata. From special post holes left in the shaft walls, screen pipes are projected out into the strata by power operated hydraulic jacks.

The outer end of each screen pipe is equipped with a perforated boring head which communicates with the removable imperforated inner pipe which extends back into the shaft. A sliding packer maintains a fluid type stoppage in the annular space between the two pipes during the boring operation.

As a matter of fact, conditions in areas where radial wells are proposed, are quite the opposite of those ordinarily considered suitable for stainer wells.

5. **Artesion tube well.** Artesion wells are tube wells which release water under sufficient pressure to rise above the ground surface.

These artesian wells can be formed only where the particular geological formation exists in which an Aquifer is held between the impermeable shape of a basin.

12.14.13. Yield of a Tube Well

Yield of a tube well depends upon :

(*i*) Radius of the centre of influence.
(*ii*) Depth of drawdown.
(*iii*) Depth of well in the Aquifer.
(*iv*) Diameter of the well.
(*v*) Porosity of water bearing strata.
(*vi*) Inclination of the Aquifer.
(*vii*) Orientation of water.
(*viii*) Arrangement of well.

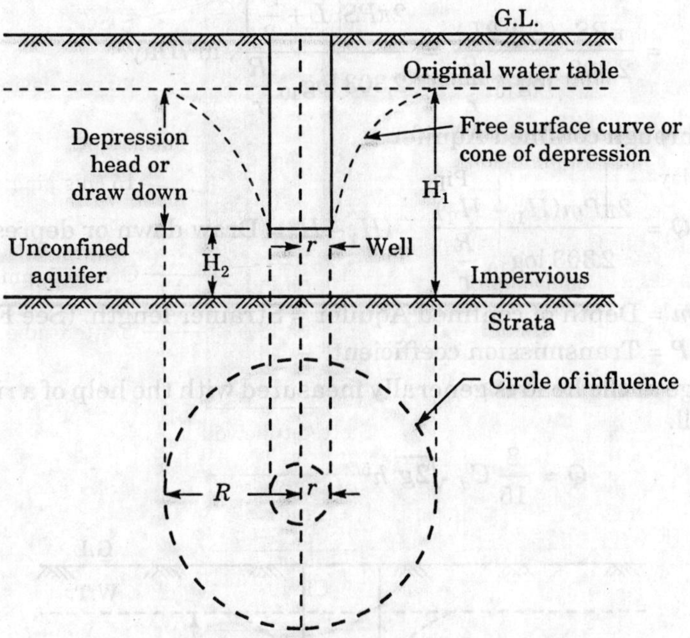

Fig. 12.69. Artesion tube well (unconfined).

Discharge through unconfined Aquifer can be calculated from the formula :

$$Q = \frac{\pi P(H_1^2 - H_2^2)}{2.303 \log_{10} \dfrac{R}{r}}$$

where P = Permeability of the soil (24.80 m/say).

H_1 = Height of water table above impervious layer in m.

H_2 = Height of water level in the tube in metre after depression.

Q = Total discharge of tube well m^3/day.

R = Radius of curve of influence in m.

r = Radius of tube well in m. (See Fig. 12.69).

$S = H_1 - H_2$ (Fig. 12.69).

$$Q = \frac{\pi P(H_1 - H_2)}{2.30 \log_{10} \frac{R}{r}}$$

$S = H_1 - H_2$ = Draw down

$H_1 = S + H_2$

L = Length of strainer

$= H_1 - S = H_2.$

$H_1 + H_2 = (S + 2H_2)$

$$Q = \frac{\pi P(H_1 + H_2)(H_1 - H_2)}{2.303 \log_{10} \frac{R}{r}} = \frac{\pi P(S + 2H_2)S}{2.303 \log_{10} \frac{R}{r}}$$

$$= \frac{\pi PS}{2.303} \frac{(S + 2L)}{\log_{10} \frac{R}{r}} = \frac{2\pi PS\left(L + \frac{S}{2}\right)}{2.303 \log_{10} \frac{R}{r}}, \text{ m}^3\text{/Day}$$

Discharge through confined Aquifer

$$Q = \frac{2\pi Pm(H_1 - H_2)}{2.303 \log_{10} \frac{R}{r}} \quad (H_1 - H_2 = \text{Draw down or depression height}).$$

m = Depth of confined Aquifer = Strainer length. (See Fig. 12.70).

mP = Transmission coefficient.

The discharge at the head is generally measured with the help of a right angled V-notch with a free over fall.

$$Q = \frac{8}{15} C_d \sqrt{2g}\, h^{5/2}$$

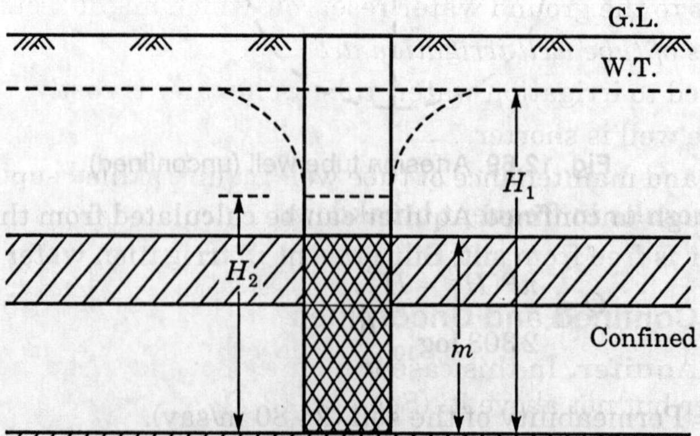

Fig. 12.70. Artesion tube well (confined).

where Q = Discharge in m^3/sec.

C_d = Discharge coefficient 0.62

h = Head over the notch in m.

The specific yield of a tube well is the percentage of water in a given volume of formation that can be recovered in a well as a result of gravity action. If 100 m^3 of saturated formation when drained by gravity, supply 20^3 of water, the specific yield will be 20%.

The percentage of water of a given volume formation, that the formation will not give up against pull of gravity is known as specific retention. This if the specific yield is 20%, the specific retention will be 100 – 20 = 80%.

12.14.14. Tube Well Failures

Failures of tube wells are caused due to the following :

(*i*) Failure due to high rate of pumping or corresponding lower rate of replenishment of the ground water stoppage. This is indicated by persistent and increased fall in the water level and consequent decrease in the discharge from the tube well.

(*ii*) Failure due to faulty construction indicated by mechanical failure of well.

(*iii*) Failure due to screens getting incrusted or corroded. This is indicated by increased depression in the well which results in reduction of discharge and also sometimes in pumping of sand in water.

12.14.15. Tube Well Versus Canal Irrigation

Comparative advantages and disadvantages of tube well as compared to canal irrigation are given below :

Advantages of tube well irrigation are :

(*i*) Isolated piece of land which cannot be served by canals can be easily irrigated by tube well.

(*ii*) Canal irrigation project needs large outlays which is blocked for a considerable period of time before the project is productive whereas tube well may be constructed gradually.

(*iii*) Sale of water from tube wells is on a volumetric basis which results in optimum utilisation of water at the correct time.

(*iv*) Tube well channels are of short length and usually lined. This results in less loss of water than in irrigation system.

(*v*) Pumping from tube well results in lowering of the water table. On the other hand canal irrigation adds to the ground water reservoir which might result in water logging.

Disadvantages of tube well irrigation are :

(*i*) As compared to irrigation water, tube well water is costly.

(*ii*) Life of tube well is shorter.

(*iii*) Operation and maintenance of tube well require skilled supervision. Particularly in isolated places this results in frequent breakdown.

(*iv*) Tube water is free from silt. Silt present in irrigation water helps growth of crop.

12.14.16. Aquifer (Confined and Unconfined)

Unconfined Aquifer. In this case the impervious layer *i.e.* non-water bearing strata lies below the aquifer but not above it. (See Fig. 12.71).

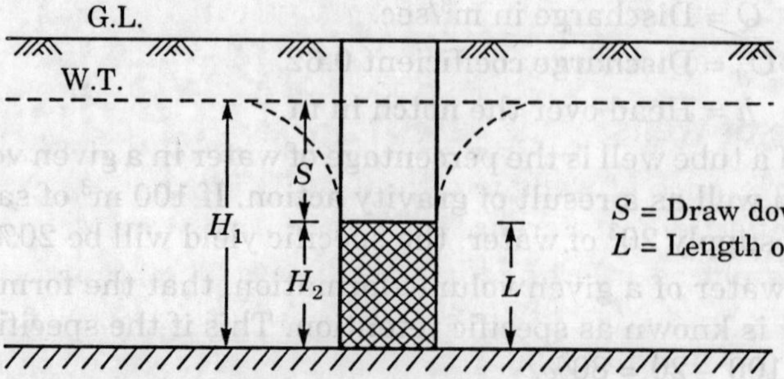

Fig. 12.71. Unconfined aquifer.

The water table in the two dimensional case represents a flow line.

Water actually flows in two directions and does not follow any parabolic form.

Confined Aquifer. It is that aquifer which lies between two impervious strata one at the top and other at the bottom. (See Fig. 12.72).

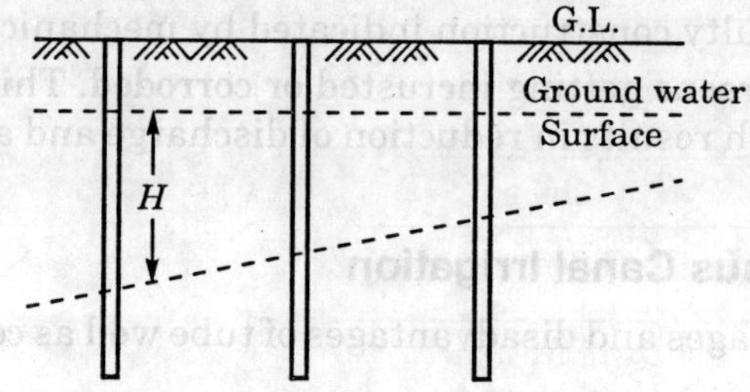

Fig. 12.72. Confined Aquifer.

The head in the case of confined aquifer decreases linearly as shown in Fig. 12.73.

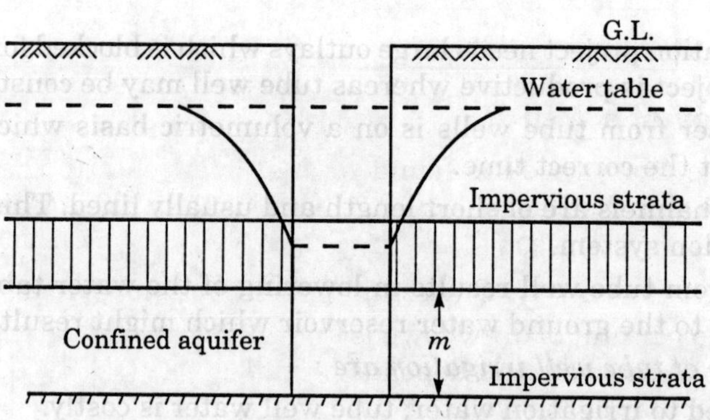

Fig. 12.73. Confined Aquifer.

12.14.17. Well Development

A new deep well is developed to increase its specific capacity, prevent sanding and obtain maximum economic well life.

The various methods used for this are :

(*i*) Pumping

(*ii*) Surging this is created by rapid up and down motion of plunger with a bailer or a circular surge block.

(*iii*) Injection of compressed air

(*iv*) Back washing

(*v*) Addition of solid carbondioxide.

12.14.18. Interference of Wells

The mutual interference of wells is caused when they are located at short distances. Table 12.36 shows the effect of interference in the yield of the wells.

If three wells are placed in a line and equidistant, the reduction in yield is given by Table 12.37.

Table 12.36. Interference of Wells

Distance apart in metres	*Interference percent*
1.5	38.33
3	34.53
30	20.09
60	15.35
120	01.51
300	0.23

Table 12.37. Interference of Well Placed in Line (equidistance)

Distance apart metres	*Interference percent*
1.5	55
3	50.7
30	30.7

12.14.19. Efficiency of a Well

The discharge from a well is found to be proportional to the drawdown. If S be the drawdown and Q be this discharge,

$$S \propto Q$$

or $$S = C_1 Q \text{ (Assuming there are no losses).}$$

The discharge per unit of drawdown is known as specific capacity of the well and depends on the type and other particular of the well.

If a curve is plotted such that the Y ordinate represents the yield and x-ordinate gives drawdown, it is seen that upto certain stage of drawn down the curve is a straight line a certain point and after this, the drawdown is more rapid than the yield. The most efficient performance of the well is then given by the upper end of the straight reach and the percent yield corresponding to this point is a measure of the optimum performance or the efficiency of the well.

The curve thus drawn is known as yield drawdown curve. (See Fig. 12.74).

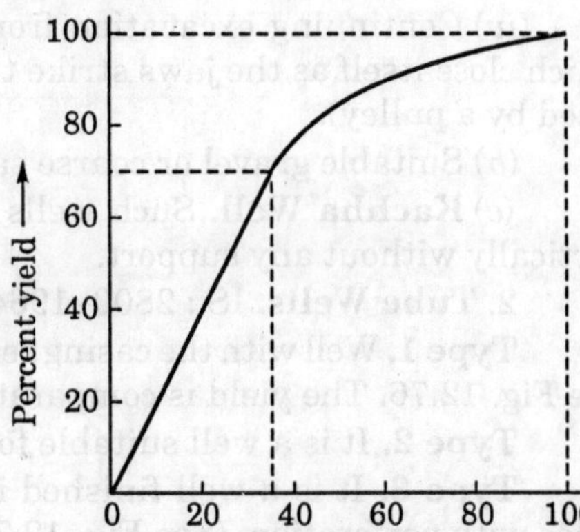

Fig. 12.74. Yield drawdown curve.

12.14.20. Wells and their Construction

Wells are primarily of the following two types :

1. Open well 2. Tube well.

The open wells may be shallow well or deep well. Wells which rest on a pervious stratum and draw their supplies from adjoining area are termed as shallel well. If the well rests on an impervious layer (*Mota* layer) and draws its supply of water from the pervious layer below the impervious strata it is known as deep well. (See Fig. 12.75.)

From the point of view of construction open wells may be classified as :

(*a*) Wells having an impervious lining (masonry) resting on an impervious layer.

(*b*) Wells having a pervious lining (dry brick or stone).

(*c*) Kachha well (without any lining).

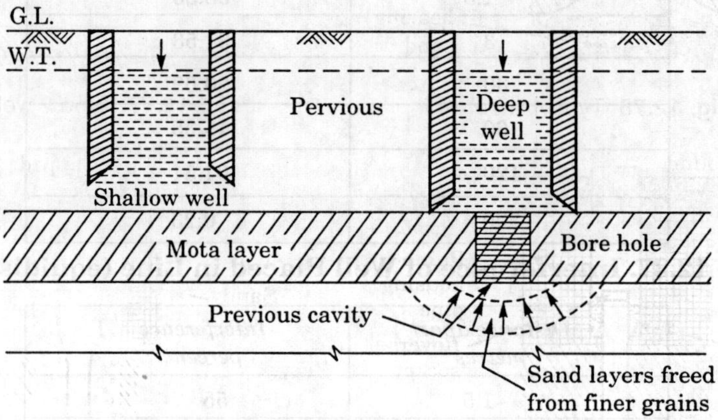

Fig. 12.75. Shallow and deep well.

(*a*) **Well with impervious lining**

Main features of this type of well are :

(*i*) Excavation of pit-by hand tools upto soft strata.

(*ii*) Placing the kerb (circular ring of R.C.C., strata or timber) and building masonry lining upto a few metres above G.L.

(*iii*) Excavating below kerb, loading the staining and sinking the well till water level is reached.

(*iv*) Continuing excavation from the top with the help of *Jhams*. (A jham is a bucket which close itself as the jaws strike the bottom of well) the dislodged material is retained and lifted by a pulley).

(*b*) Suitable gravel or coarse sand strata. Dry brick or stone lining is used on the sides.

(*c*) **Kachha Well.** Such wells are constructed in hard soil where well wall can stand vertically without any support.

2. **Tube Wells.** IS : 2800–1964 classifies tube wells under the following types :

Type 1. Well with the casing resting on a thick, hard, impervious layer above the aquiefer. See Fig. 12.76. The yield is comparatively less.

Type 2. It is a well suitable for unconsolidated formation. (See Fig. 12.77 and 12.78).

Type 3. It is a well finished in unconsolidated formation by use of screens or casing pipes with perforation. (See Fig. 12.79).

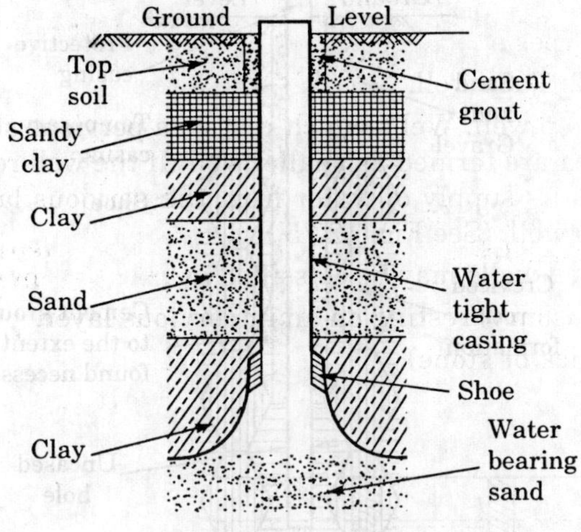

Fig. 12.76. Type 1 tube well.

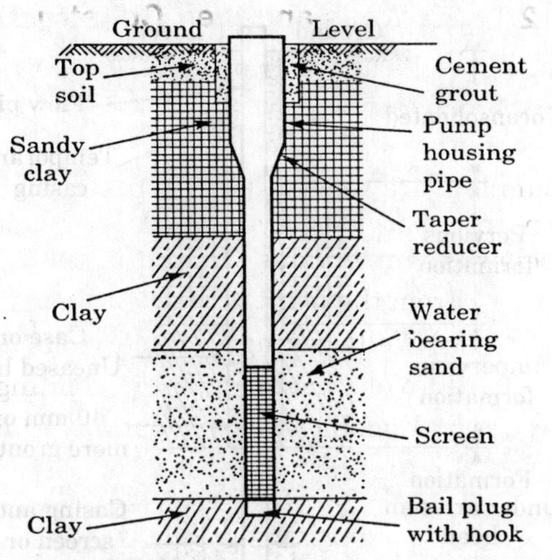

Fig. 12.77. Type 2 well with taper reducer.

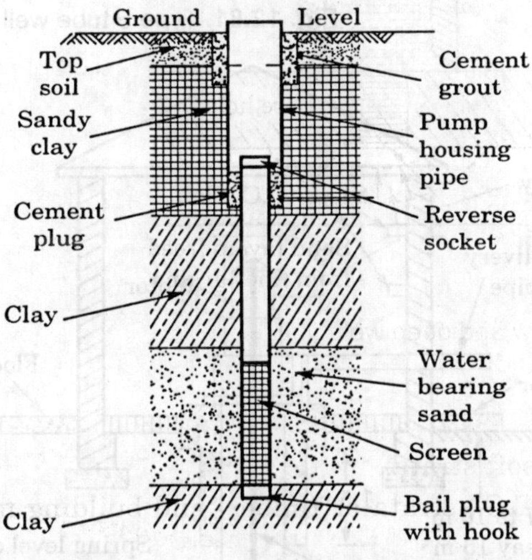

Fig. 12.78. Type 2 well with cement plug.

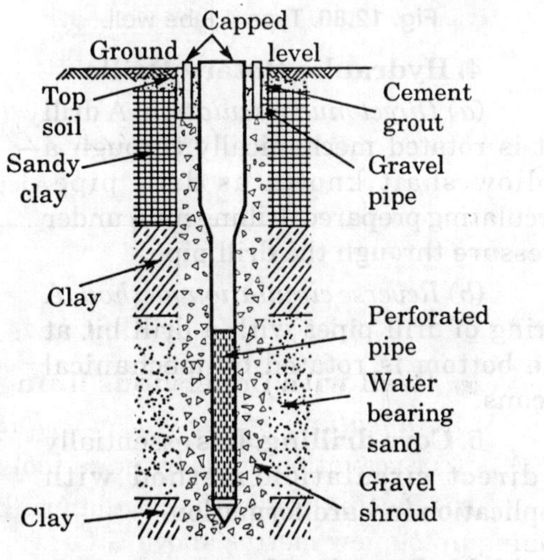

Fig. 12.79. Type 3 tube well.

Type 4. It is a well finished under artesian condition (See Fig. 12.80).

Type 5. It is a well finished in consolidated formation in the manner shown in Fig.12.81.

12.14.21. Methods of Drilling Tube Wells

IS : 2800—1964 gives the following methods of drilling tube wells :

1. **Auger Drilling.** The drilling is done with a claw or spiral auger connected to square rods turned manually with rod letters.

2. **Percussion Drilling.** A heavy drill bit with jar and stem attached to a cable is given spudding motion, up and down, either manually or by power.

3. **Water Jet Boring.** A drill pipe with a drill bit works inside the casing pipes. The drill bit has nozzles through which water ejects below the bottom of the casing pipe.

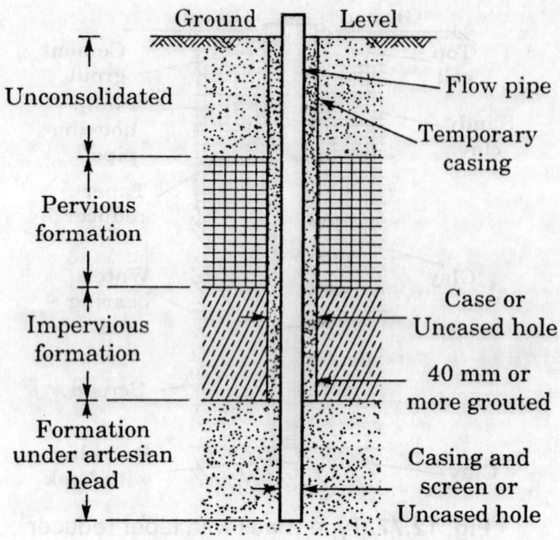

Fig. 12.80. Type 4 tube well.

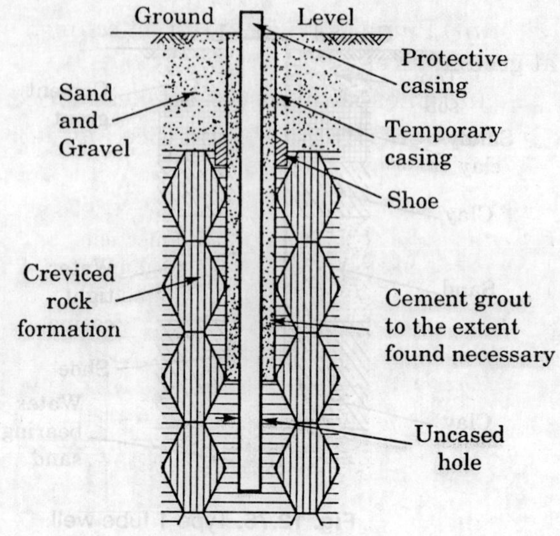

Fig. 12.81. Type 5 tube well.

4. **Hydraulic Rotary Drills**

(*a*) *Direct mud circulation.* A drill bit is rotated mechanically through a hollow shaft known as drill pipe, circulating prepared drilling mud under pressure through the drill pipe.

(*b*) *Reverse circulation method.* A string of drill pipes with a drill bit at the bottom is rotated by mechanical means.

5. **Core drilling.** It is essentially a direct circulation method with application in hard formation.

12.14.22. Pumping Arrangement

The following two types of pumping arrangements are made :

1. Bore Hole and
2. Centrifugal.

1. Bore Hole (See Fig. 12.82).

Fig. 12.80. show a typical Bore Hole Pump. The salient features of the pump are :

(*i*) Small diameter and hence can be lowered in the casing pipe itself.

(*ii*) To accommodate the bump bomb in the casing pipe, the top 20 to 30 m of the bore hole and the casing pipe is kept wider than the remaining normal bore.

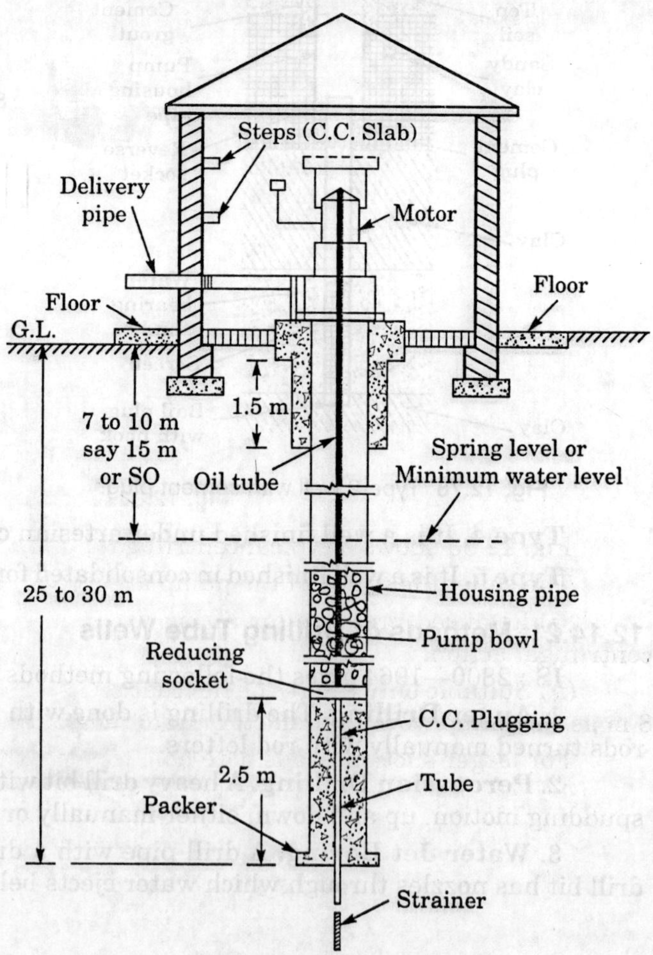

Fig. 12.82. Bore hole pump.

(*iii*) Pump is driven by direct coupled electric motor placed at the top of the line of shaft at ground level.

(*iv*) Cheaper in cost as the need for constructing a sump is avoided.

2. **Centrifugal Pump.** (See Fig. 12.83).

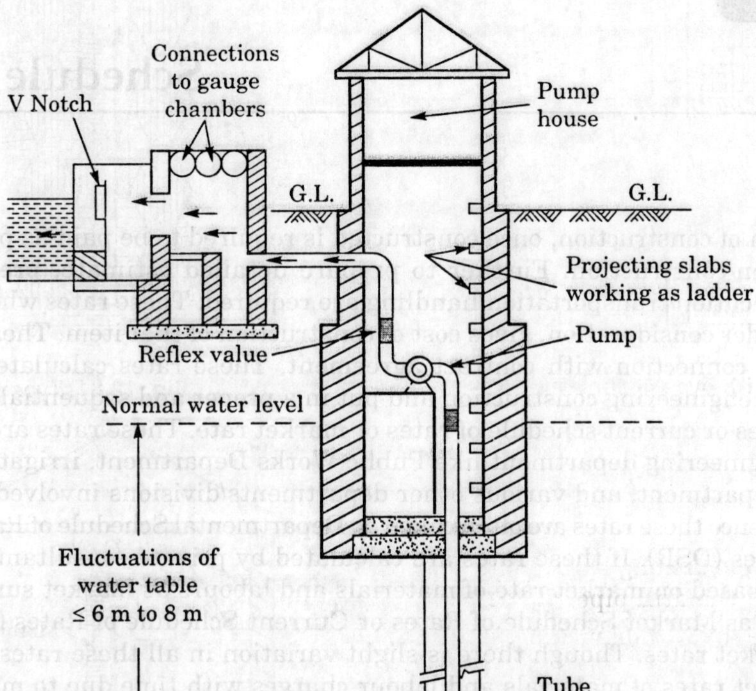

Fig. 12.83. Centrifugal pump.

Fig. 12.83 shows a typical centrifugal pump.

The salient features of the pump are :

(*i*) Required pressure for lifting water from lower level to higher level is created by centrifugal action.

(*ii*) Suitable only where the fluctuation in water table plus the depressed head are below 8 m as the pump works satisfactory upto the maximum suction of 8 m.

For larger suction heads bore hole type pump is recommended.

13

Schedule of Rates

13.1.

Each item of construction, once constructed is required to be paid as per its prevailing rate of execution/construction. Further to prepare detailed estimate, prevailing rates of construction/execution/transportation/handling are required. These rates when multiplied by the quantity under consideration, gives cost of construction of that item. These rates guide in setting rates in connection with contract agreement. These rates calculated for each item involved in civil engineering construction and put in a proper and sequential order are called Schedule of Rates or current schedule of rates or market rate. These rates are also calculated by each civil engineering department like Public Works Department; irrigation department; water supply department, and various other departments/divisions involved in construction or civil works. Hence these rates are often called as Departmental Schedule of Rates or Divisional Schedule of Rates (DSR). If these rates are calculated by private consultants like engineers and architects; based on market rate of materials and labours as market survey. Then these rates are called as Market Schedule of Rates or Current Schedule of Rates (CSR) or current schedule of market rates. Though there is slight variation in all these rates but variation is not large. Market rates of materials and labour charges with time due to many reasons like inflation, demand and supply; wage increments etc. It is therefore essential to department, government agencies to maintain an upto date record of these rates; revised them timely as and when required. Therefore, amendments are made as and when required and published to acquaint contractors, users, with latest rates of construction. These rates are prepared based on rates prevailing in each locality taking into consideration the transportation cost of materials also. These rates include materials cost, labour cost, tools and plants, machineries required if any. Water charges, octroy, taxes, if any, toll, ferry charges, royalties, various types of taxes, if any etc. No extra charges for scaffolding, curing etc. are paid. For finding market rates contractors profit is also taken into consideration. As such schedule of rates consists of

(*a*) Material cost *i.e.* material cost at site therefore includes transportation, sales, royalty etc.

(*b*) Labour cost taking minimum wage into consideration.

(*c*) Tools and plants I/C Machineries, if any

(*d*) Water charges

(*e*) Electrical charges, if any,

(*f*) Contractors profit.

Rates given here are as per old DSR and therefore can not be applied as on today. Users of books and field engineers are required to refer CSR/DSR/Market rate prevailing in that locality under consideration. These rates given here are simply guide various item involved in construction and how rates to be used or referred from DSR.

BUILDING WORK

Table 13.1. EARTH WORK

S. No.	Description	Unit	Rate ₹
1.	Earth work in surface excavation not exceeding 30 cm in depth but exceeding 1.5 m in width as well as 10 sq m on plan including disposal of excavated earth upto 50 m and lift upto 1.5 m, disposed soil to be levelled and neatly dressed :		
	1A All kinds of soil.	cum	63.55
	Earth work in rough excavation, banking excavated earth in layers not exceeding 20 cm in depth, breaking clods watering, rolling each layer with ½ tonne roller or wooden or steel rammers, and rolling every 3rd and top-most layer with power roller of minimum 8 tonnes and dressing up in embankments for roads, flood banks, marginal banks and guide banks or filling up ground depressions, lead upto 50 m and lift upto 1.5 m.		
	1B All kinds of soil.	cum	73.20
	Banking excavated earth in layers not exceeding 20 cm. in depth, breaking clods, watering, rolling each layer with 1/2 tonne roller, or wooden or steel rammers, and rolling every 3rd and top-most layer with power roller of minimum 8 tonnes and dressing up ; in embankments for roads, flood banks, marginal banks, and guide banks etc., lead upto 50 m and lift upto 1.5 m.		
	1C All kinds of soil.	cum	46.10
	Deduct for not rolling with power roller of minimum 8 tones for banking excavated earth in layers not exceeding 20 cm in depth.	cum	1.00
	Deduct for not watering the excavated earth for banking.	cum	1.35
	Earth work in excavation over areas (exceeding 30 cm in depth, 1.5 m in width as well as 10 sq m on plan) including disposal of excavated earth, lead upto 50 m and lift upto 1.5 m; disposed earth to be levelled and neatly dressed :		
	1D All kinds of soil.	cum	64.10
2.	Earth work in excavation over areas (exceeding 30 cm in depth, 1.5 m in width as well as 10 sq m on plan) including disposal of excavated earth, lead upto 50 m and lift upto 1.5 m, disposed earth to be levelled and neatly dressed:		
	2A Ordinary rock	cum	98.35
	2B Hard rock (requiring blasting)	cum	133.50
	2C Hard rock (blasting prohibited)	cum	207.30
3.	Earth work in excavation in foundation trenches or drains (not exceeding 1.5 m in width or 10 sq m on plan) including dressing of sides and ramming of bottoms, lift upto 1.5 m, including getting out the excavated soil and disposal of surplus excavated soil as directed, within a lead of 50 m:		
	3A All kinds of soil.	cum	65.55

(Contd.)

S. No.	Description	Unit	Rate ₹
4.	Excavation work in foundation trenches or drains not exceeding 1.5 m in width or 10 sq m on plan including dressing of sides and ramming of bottoms lift upto 1.5 m, including getting out the excavated soil and disposal of surplus excavated soils as directed, within a lead of 50 m:		
	4A Ordinary rock	cum	108.80
	4B Hard rock (requiring blasting)	cum	149.90
	4C Hard rock (Blasting prohibited)	cum	213.85
5.	Excavating trenches of required width for pipes, cables, etc. including excavation for sockets, and dressing of sides, ramming of bottoms, depth upto 1.5 m including getting out the excavated soil, and then returning the soil as required, in layers not exceeding 20 cm in depth including consolidating each deposited layer by ramming, watering, etc. and disposing of surplus excavated soil as directed, within a lead of 50 m:		
	5A All kinds of soil.		
	5B Pipes, cables etc. not exceeding 80 mm dia.	metre	41.00
	5C Pipes, cables etc. exceeding 80 mm dia. but not exceeding 300 mm dia	metre	76.45
	5D Pipes, cables etc. exceeding 300 mm dia.	metre	103.85
6.	Extra for excavating trenches for pipes, cables etc. in all kinds of soil for depth exceeding 1.5 m, but not exceeding 3 m, (Rate is over corresponding basic item for depth upto 1.5 metre.)	metre	101%
7.	Extra for excavating trenches for pipes, cables, etc., in all kinds of soil for depth exceeding 3 m in depth, but not exceeding 4.5 m. (Rate is over corresponding basic item for depth upto 1.5 metre.)	metre	280%
8.	Excavating trenches of required width for pipes, cables, etc., including excavation for sockets, depth upto 1.5 m including getting out the excavated materials, returning the soil as required in layers not exceeding 20 cm in depth including consolidating each deposited layers by ramming, watering etc. stacking serviceable material for measurements and disposal of unserviceable material as directed, within a lead of 50 m :		
	8A Ordinary rock		
	8B Pipes, cables etc. not exceeding 80 mm dia.	metre	61.90
	8C Pipes, cables etc. exceeding 80 mm dia. but not exceeding 300 mm dia.	metre	154.15
	8D Pipes, cables exceeding 300 mm dia.	metre	177.35
	8E Hard rock (requiring blasting)		
	8F Pipes, cables etc. not exceeding 80 mm dia	metre	81.85
	8G Pipes, cables etc. exceeding 80 mm dia. but not exceeding 300 mm dia.	metre	202.70
	8H Pipes, cables etc. exceeding 300 mm dia.	metre	233.25
	8I Hard rock (blasting prohibited)		
	8J Pipes, cables etc. not exceeding 80 mm dia.	metre	112.05
	8K Pipes, cables etc. exceeding 80 mm dia. but not exceeding 300 mm dia.	metre	277.50
	8L Pipes, cables etc. exceeding 300 mm dia	metre	319.35

S. No.	Description	Unit	Rate ₹
9.	Extra for excavating trenches for pipes, cables, etc. in ordinary/ hard rock exceeding 1.5 m in depth but not exceeding 3 m. (Rate is over corresponding basic item for depth upto 1.5 metre.)	metre	98%
10.	Extra for excavating trenches for pipes, cables, etc. in ordinary/ hard rock exceeding 3 m in depth but not exceeding 4.5 m. (Rate is over corresponding basic item for depth upto 1.5 metre.)	metre	241%
11.	Close timbering in trenches including strutting, shoring and packing cavities (wherever required) complete. (Measurements to be taken of the face area timbered)		
	11A Depth not exceeding 1.5 m.	sq m	43.95
	11B Depth exceeding 1.5 m but not exceeding 3 m.	sq m	45.10
	11C Depth exceeding 3 m but not exceeding 4.5 m	sq m	47.85
12.	Close timbering in case of shafts, wells, cesspits, manholes and the like including strutting, shoring and packing cavities (wherever required) etc. complete. (Measurements to be taken of the face area timbered):		
	12A Depth not exceeding 1.5 m.	sq m	44.85
	12B Depth exceeding 1.5 m but not exceeding 3 m	sq m	47.45
	12C Depth exceeding 3 m but not exceeding 4.5 m	sq m	50.15
13.	Close timbering over areas including strutting, shoring and packing, cavities (wherever required) etc. complete. (Measurements to be taken of the face area timbered):		
	13A Depth not exceeding 1.5 m.	sq m	39.45
	13B Depth exceeding 1.5 m but not exceeding 3 m.	sq m	40.85
	13C Depth exceeding 3 m but not exceeding 4.5 m.	sq m	42.40
14.	Extra for planking, strutting and packing materials for cavities (in close timbering) if required to be left permanently in position (Face area of timber permanently left to be measured).	sq m	583.90
15.	Open timbering in trenches including strutting and shoring complete (Measurements to be taken of the face area timbered):		
	15A Depth not exceeding 1.5 m.	sq m	21.75
	15B Depth exceeding 1.5 m but not exceeding 3 m.	sq m	22.50
	15C Depth exceeding 3 m but not exceeding 4.5 m.	sq m	23.75
16.	Open timbering in case of shafts, wells, cesspits, manholes and the like including strutting and shoring complete (measurements to be taken of the face area timbered):		
	16A Depth not exceeding 1.5 m.	sq m	18.80
	16B Depth exceeding 1.5 m but not exceeding 3 m.	sq m	20.00
	16C Depth exceeding 3 m but not exceeding 4.5 m.	sq m	21.55
17.	Open timbering over areas including strutting, shoring etc. complete. (Measurements to be taken of the face area timbered):		
	17A Depth not exceeding 1.5	sq m	13.45
	17B Depth exceeding 1.5 m but not exceeding 3 m.	sq m	14.35
	17C Depth exceeding 3 m but not exceeding 4.5 m.	sq m	15.70
18.	Extra for planki... .nd strutting in open timbering if required to be left permanently in position (face area of the timber permanently left to be measured).	sq m	287.65

(Contd.)

S. No.	Description	Unit	Rate ₹
19.	Extra rate for quantities of works, executed:		
	19A In or under water and/or liquid mud, including pumping out water as required.	metre depth	20%
	19B In or under foul position, including pumping out water as required.	metre depth	25%
	Note for item no. 13.1.19 : The extra percentage rate is applicable in respect of each item but limited to quantities of work executed in these difficult conditions. The unit, namely, metre depth, to be considered for payment, shall be the depth measured from the sub soil water level upto the centre of gravity of the quantity executed in difficult conditions. The depth shall be reckoned correct to 0.1 metre, 0.05 metre or more shall be taken as 0.1 metre and less than 0.05 metre ignored.		
20.	Filling available excavated earth (excluding rock) in trenches, plinth, sides of foundations etc. in layers not exceeding 20 cm in depth: consolidating each deposited layer by ramming and watering, lead upto 50 m and lift upto 1.5 m.	cum	21.20
21.	Extra for every additional lift of 1.5 m or part thereof in:		
	21A All kinds of soil.	cum	8.75
	21B Ordinary or hard rock.	cum	16.85
22.	Supplying and filling in plinth with Jamuna sand under floors including, watering, ramming consolidating and dressing complete.	cum	189.50
23.	Surface dressing of the ground including removing vegetation and in-equalities not exceeding 15 cm deep and disposal of rubbish, lead upto 50 m and lift upto 1.5 m :		
	23A All kinds of soil	100 sq m	235.40
24.	Ploughing the existing ground to a depth of 15 cm to 25 cm and watering the same:		
	24A All kinds of soil	100 sq m	238.05
25.	Excavating holes upto 0.5 cum including getting out the excavated soil, then returning the soil as required in layers not exceeding 20 cm in depth, including consolidating each deposited layer by ramming, watering etc. disposing of surplus excavated soil; as directed within a lead of 50 m and lift upto 1.5 m:		
	25A All kinds of soil	each	34.15
	25B Ordinary rock	each	55.20
	25C Hard rock (requiring blasting)	each	83.15
	25D Hard rock (blasting prohibited)	each	115.10
26.	Clearing jungle including uprooting of rank vegetation, grass, brush wood, trees and saplings of girth upto 30 cm measured at a height of 1 m above ground level and removal of rubbish upto a distance of 50 m outside the periphery of the area cleared.	100 sq m	121.30
27.	Clearing grass and removal of the rubbish upto a distance of 50 m outside the periphery of the area cleared.	100 sq m	62.50
28.	Felling trees of the girth (measured at a height of 1 m above ground level) including cutting of trunks and branches removing the roots and stacking of serviceable material and disposal of unserviceable material:		

S. No.	Description	Unit	Rate ₹
	28A Beyond 30 cm girth upto and including 60 cm girth	each	37.75
	28B Beyond 60 cm girth upto and including 120 cm girth	each	165.80
	28C Beyond 120 cm girth upto and including 240 cm girth	each	763.15
	28D Above 240 cm girth	each	1532.85
29.	Supplying chemical emulsion in sealed containers including delivery as specified:		
	29A Chlorpyriphos emulsifiable concentrate of 20%	litre	105.60
30.	Diluting and injecting chemical emulsion (to be supplied free of cost at site of work) for PRE-CONSTRUCTIONAL ANTI-termite treatment and creating a continuous chemical barrier under and alround the column pits, wall trenches, basement excavation, top surface of plinth filling, junction of wall and floor, along the external perimeter of building, expansion joints, over the top surface of consolidated earth on which apron is to be laid, surroundings of pipes and conduits etc. complete as per specifications (Plinth area of the building at ground floor only shall be measured for payment):		
	30A Chlorpyriphos Emulsifiable concentrate 20% with 1% concentration	sq m	42.50
31.	Diluting and injecting chemical emulsion for Post-Constructional anti-termite treatment :		
	31A Along external wall where the apron is not provided using chemical imulsion @ 7.5 litres/sq m of the vertical surface of the substructure to a depth of 300 mm including excavation channel along the wall and rodding etc. complete:		
	31B With chlorpyriphos E.C. 20% with 1% concentration.	metre	3.20
	31C Along the external wall below concrete or masonry apron using chemical emulsion @ 2.25 litres per linear metre including drilling and plugging holes etc.		
	31D With chlorpyriphos E.C. 20% with 1% concentration.	metre	5.05
	31E Treatment of soil under existing floors using chemical emulsion @ one litre per hole, 300 mm apart including drilling 12 mm diameter holes and plugging with cement mortar 1 : 2 (1 cement : 2 Coarse sand) to match the existing floor.		
	31F With chlorpyriphos E.C. 20% with 1% concentration.	sq m	24.00
	31G Treatment of existing masonry using chemical emulsion @ one litre per hole at 300 mm interval including drilling holes at 45 degree and plugging them with cement mortar 1 : 2 (1 cement : 2 coarse sand) to the full depth of the hole.		
	31H With chlorpyriphos E.C. 20% with 1% concentration.	metre	3.75
	31I Treatment at points of contact of wood work by chemical emulsion chlorpyriphos. (in oil or kerosene based solution) @ 0.5 litres per hole by drilling 6 mm dia holes at downward angle of 45 degree at 150 mm centre to centre and sealing the same.	metre	31.45
32.	Earth work in excavation by mechanical equipment including disposal of excavated earth, lead upto 50 m and lift upto 5 m, disposed earth to be levelled and neatly dressed.		
	All kinds of soil (excluding ordinary & hard rock)	cum	466.60
	Note for item no 31.32 : This item shall not be operated for general purpose and shall be treated as a provision for special work requirement where the work is to be excuted at a great speed.		

Table 13.2. MORTARS

S. No.	Description	Unit	Rate ₹
	A. LIME MORTAR		
1.	Lime mortar 1 : 1 (1 lime putty : 1 fine sand)	cum	1348.88
2.	Lime mortar 1 : 1 : 1 (1 lime putty : 1 surkhi : 1 fine sand)	cum	1114.26
3.	Lime mortar 1 : 1 : 1 (1 lime putty : 1 surkhi: 1 coarse sand)	cum	1199.67
4.	Lime mortar 1 : 1 : 2 (1 lime putty : 1 surkhi: 2 coarse sand)	cum	1077.18
5.	Lime mortar 1 : 2 (1 lime putty : 2 surkhi)	cum	1174.35
6.	Lime mortar 1 : 3 (1 lime putty : 3 surkhi)	cum	1038.81
7.	Lime mortar 1 : 3 (1 lime putty : 3 coarse sand)	cum	1096.14
8.	Lime mortar 1 : 2 (1 lime putty : 2 fine sand)	cum	1054.15
	B. CEMENT MORTAR		
9.	Cement mortar 1 : 1 (1 cement : 1 fine sand)	cum	2862.69
10.	Cement mortar 1 : 2 (1 cement : 2 fine sand)	cum	2050.21
11.	Cement mortar 1 : 3 (1 cement : 3 fine sand)	cum	1644.28
12.	Cement mortar 1 : 4 (1 cement : 4 fine sand)	cum	1311.36
13.	Cement mortar 1 : 5 (1 cement : 5 fine sand)	cum	1132.09
14.	Cement mortar 1 : 6 (1 cement : 6 fine sand)	cum	978.44
15.	Cement mortar 1 : 2 (1 cement : 2 coarse sand)	cum	2221.04
16.	Cement mortar 1 : 3 (1 cement : 3 coarse sand)	cum	1836.68
17.	Cement mortar 1 : 4 (1 cement : 4 coarse sand)	cum	1503.76
18.	Cement mortar 1 : 5 (1 cement : 5 coarse sand)	cum	1324.49
19.	Cement mortar 1 : 6 (1 cement : 6 coarse sand)	cum	1170.84
20.	Cement mortar 1 : 2 (1 cement : 2 stone dust)	cum	2344.12
21.	Cement mortar 1 : 2 (1 cement : 2 marble dust)	cum	2530.04
22.	Cement mortar 1 : 5 (1 cement : 5 marble dust)	cum	1672.53
23.	Cement mortar 1 : 1 : 3 (1 cement: 1 marble dust: 3 stone dust)	cum	1693.74
24.	White cement Lime mortar 1/4 : 1 : 1 : 1 (1/4 White cement : 1 lime putty : 1 stone dust : 1 marble dust)	cum	2629.24
25.	White cement mortar 1 : 2 (1 White cement : 2 marble dust)	cum	6253.04
26.	White cement mortar 1 : 3 (1 White cement : 3 Marble dust)	cum	4976.97
27.	White cement mortar 1 : 5 (1 White cement : 5 marble dust)	cum	3369.78
	C. CEMENT LIME MORTAR		
28.	Cement lime mortar 1 : 1 : 3 (1 cement : 1 lime putty : 3 fine sand)	cum	1814.06
29.	Cement lime mortar 1 : 1 : 6 (1 cement : 1 lime putty : 6 fine sand)	cum	1296.06
30.	Cement lime mortar 1 : 1 : 7 (1 cement : 1 lime putty : 7 fine sand)	cum	1181.59
31.	Cement lime mortar 1 : 1 : 8 (1 cement : 1 lime putty : 8 fine sand)	cum	1074.02
32.	Cement lime mortar 1 : 2 : 9 (1 cement : 2 lime putty : 9 fine sand)	cum	1180.68

S. No.	Description	Unit	Rate ₹
33.	Cement lime mortar 1 : 1 : 3 (1 cement : 1 lime putty : 3 coarse sand)	cum	1967.85
34.	Cement lime mortar 1 : 1 : 6 (1 cement : 1 lime putty : 6 coarse sand)	cum	1488.46
35.	Cement lime mortar 1 : 3 : 12 (1 cement : 3 lime putty : 12 fine sand)	cum	1122.77
36.	Cement lime mortar 1 : 3 (1 cement: 3 coarse sand with 10% addition of class 'C' lime)	cum	1890.84

Table 13.3. CONCRETE WORK

S. No.	Description	Unit	Rate ₹
	A. LIME CONCRETE		
1.	Providing and laying lime concrete in footings and bases for columns, excluding cost of centring and shuttering:		
	1A With graded stone aggregate 40 mm nominal size and 40% mortar comprising of 1 lime putty : 1 surkhi : 1 fine sand.	cum	1007.20
	1B With graded brick aggregate 40 mm nominal size and 40% mortar comprising of 1 lime putty : 1 surkhi : 1 fine sand.	cum	915.00
2.	Providing and laying on terrace upto floor five level lime concrete with graded brick aggregate 25 mm nominal size and 50% mortar comprising of 1 lime putty : 2 surkhi.	cum	1415.10
3.	Deduct for using 65 mm nominal size graded stone aggregate instead of 40 mm nominal size graded stone aggregate in lime concrete.	cum	3.85
4.	Deduct for using 65 mm nominal size graded brick aggregate instead of 40 mm nominal size graded brick aggregate in lime concrete.	cum	7.70
	B. CEMENT CONCRETE (CAST-IN-SITU)		
5.	Providing and laying in position cement concrete of specified grade excluding the cost of centring and shuttering-All work upto plinth level :		
	5A 1 : 1 : 2 (1 cement : 1 coarse sand : 2 graded stone aggregate 20 mm nominal size)	cum	2487.55
	5B 1 : 1.5 : 3 (1 Cement : 1.5 coarse sand : 3 graded stone aggregate 20 mm nominal size)	cum	1890.45
	5C 1 : 2 : 4 (1 Cement : 2 coarse sand : 4 graded stone aggregate 20 mm nominal size)	cum	1687.45
	5D 1 : 2 : 4 (1 Cement: 2 coarse sand : 4 graded stone aggregate 40 mm nominal size)	cum	1654.65
	5E 1 : 3 : 6 (1 Cement: 3 coarse sand : 6 graded stone aggregate 20 mm nominal size)	cum	1433.80
	5F 1 : 3 : 6 (1 Cement: 3 coarse sand : 6 graded stone aggregate 40 mm nominal size)	cum	1392.80
	5G 1 : 3 : 6 (1 Cement : 3 fine sand : 6 graded stone aggregate 40 mm nominal size)	cum	1298.90
	5H 1 : 4 : 8 (1 Cement: 4 coarse sand : 8 graded stone aggregate 40 mm nominal size)	cum	1250.55

(*Contd.*)

S. No.		Description	Unit	Rate ₹
	5I	1 : 4 : 8 (1 Cement : 4 fine sand : 8 graded stone aggregate 40 mm nominal size)	cum	1156.65
	5J	1 : 5 : 10 (1 Cement : 5 coarse sand : 10 graded stone aggregate 40 mm nominal size)	cum	1137.20
	5K	1 : 5 : 10 (1 cement : 5 fine sand : 10 graded stone aggregate 40 mm nominal size)	cum	1042.85
6.		Providing and laying cement concrete in retaining walls, return walls, walls (any thickness) including attached pilasters, columns, piers, abutments, pillars, posts, struts, buttresses, string or lacing courses, parapets, coping, bed blocks, anchor blocks, plain window sills, fillets etc. upto floor five level, excluding the cost of centring, shuttering and finishing :		
	6A	1 : 1 : 2 (1 Cement : 1 coarse sand : 2 graded stone aggregate 20 mm nominal size)	cum	2644.40
	6B	1 : 1.5 : 3 (1 Cement : 1.5 coarse sand : 3 graded stone aggregate 20 mm nominal size)	cum	2047.30
	6C	1 : 2 : 4 (1 Cement: 2 coarse sand : 4 graded stone aggregate 20 mm nominal size)	cum	1844.30
	6D	1 : 2 : 4 (1 Cement: 2 coarse sand : 4 graded stone aggregate 40 mm nominal size)	cum	1811.50
	6E	1 : 3 : 6 (1 Cement: 3 coarse sand : 6 graded stone aggregate 20 mm nominal size)	cum	1590.65
	6F	1 : 3 : 6 (1 Cement: 3 coarse sand : 6 graded stone aggregate 40 mm nominal size)	cum	1549.65
	6G	1 : 3 : 6 (1 Cement : 3 fine sand : 6 graded stone aggregate 40 mm nominal size)	cum	1455.75
7.		Centring and shuttering including strutting, propping etc. and removal of form work for :		
	7A	Foundations, footings, bases of Columns	sq m	53.65
	7B	Retaining walls, return walls, walls (any thickness) including attached pilasters, buttresses, plinth and string courses fillets etc.	sq m	88.25
	7C	Columns, piers, abutments, pillars, posts and struts.	sq m	114.05
8.		Providing and laying cement concrete in kerbs, steps and the like at or near ground level excluding the cost of centring, shuttering and finishing :		
	8A	1 : 2 : 4 (1 cement : 2 coarse sand : 4 grade stone aggregate 20 mm nominal size)	cum	687.45
	8B	1 : 3 : 6 (1 cement : 3 coarse sand : 6 graded stone aggregate 20 mm nominal size)	cum	1433.75
		C. CEMENT CONCRETE (PRECAST)		
9.		Providing and fixing upto floor five level precast cement concrete string or lacing courses, copings, bed plates, anchor blocks, plain window sills, shelves, louvers, steps, stair cases, etc. including hoisting and setting in position with cement mortar 1 : 3 (1 cement : 3 coarse sand) cost of required centring, shuttering and finishing smooth with 6 mm thick cement plaster 1 : 3 (1 cement : 3 fine sand) on exposed surfaces complete :		

S. No.	Description	Unit	Rate ₹
	9A 1 : 2 : 4 (1 cement : 2 coarse sand : 4 graded stone aggregate 20 mm nominal size)	cum	2502.00
	9B 1 : 3 : 6 (1 cement: 3 coarse sand : 6 graded stone aggregate 20 mm nominal size)	cum	2248.35
10.	Providing and fixing at or near ground level precast cement concrete in kerbs, edgings etc. as per approved pattern and setting in position with cement mortar 1 : 3 (1 cement : 3 coarse sand) including the cost of required centring, shuttering and finishing smooth with 6 mm thick cement plaster 1 : 3 (1 cement : 3 fine sand) on exposed surfaces complete :		
	10A 1 : 2 : 4 (1 cement: 2 coarse sand : 4 graded stone aggregate 20 mm nominal size)	cum	2194.25
11.	Providing and fixing upto floor five level precast cement concrete solid block including hoisting and setting in position with cement mortar 1 : 3 (1 cement : 3 coarse sand), cost of required centring, shuttering and finishing smooth with 6 mm thick cement plaster 1 : 3 (1 cement : 3 fine sand) on exposed surfaces complete :		
	11A 1 : 2 : 4 (1 cement : 2 coarse sand : 4 graded stone aggregate 20 mm nominal size)	cum	2867.50
	11B 1 : 3 : 6 (1 cement : 3 coarse sand : 6 graded stone aggregate 20 mm nominal size)	cum	2696.40
12.	Providing and fixing upto floor five level precast cement concrete hollow block including hoisting and setting in position with cement mortar 1 : 3 (1 cement : 3 coarse sand), cost of required centring, shuttering and finishing smooth with 6 mm thick cement plaster 1 : 3 (1 cement: 3 fine sand) on exposed surfaces complete :		
	12A 1 : 2 : 4 (1 cement : 2 coarse sand : 4 graded stone aggregate 20 mm nominal size)	cum	2498.20
	12B 1 : 3 : 6 (1 cement : 3 coarse sand : 6 graded stone aggregate 20 mm nomial size)	cum	2381.60
13.	Precasting and placing in position 125 mm dia Bollards 600 mm high of required shape including providing M.S. Pipe Sleeve 50 mm dia 300 mm long in the Bollard and M.S. pipe 40 mm dia and 450 mm long with 150 × 150 × 6 mm M.S. plate welded at bottom and embeded 150 mm in cement concrete 1 : 3 : 6 (1 cement : 3 coarse sand : 6 graded stone aggregate 20 mm nominal size) including necessary excavation of size 250 × 250 × 450 mm deep for the same in bitumen/concrete pavement at specified spacing.	each	650.65
	D. DAMP-PROOF COURSE		
14.	Providing and laying damp-proof Course 40 mm thick with cement concrete 1 : 2 : 4 (1 cement : 2 coarse sand : 4 graded stone aggregate 12.5 mm nominal size).	sq m	76.95
15.	Providing and laying damp-proof Course 50 mm thick with cement concrete 1 : 2 : 4 (1 cement : 2 coarse sand : 4 graded stone aggregate 20 mm nominal size).	sq m	94.10
16.	Extra for providing and mixing water proofing material in cement concrete work in the proportion recommended by the manufacturers.	per bag of 50 kg of cement used in the mix.	15.55

(Contd.)

S. No.	Description	Unit	Rate ₹
17.	Applying a coat of residual petroleum bitumen of penetration 80/100 of approved quality using 1.7 kg per square metre on damp proof course after cleaning the surface with brushes and finally with a piece of cloth lightly soaked in kerosene oil.	sq m	22.65
	E. MISCELLANEOUS		
18.	Extra for concrete work in superstructure above floor V level for each four floors or part thereof.	cum	108.35
19.	Extra for laying concrete in or under water and/or liquid mud including cost of pumping or bailing out water and removing slush etc. complete.	per cum per metre depth.	83.65
	Note for item No. 13.3.19 The quantity will be calculated by multiplying the depth measured from the sub-soil water level upto centre of gravity of concrete under sub-soil water level with quantity of concrete in cum executed under sub-soil water. The depth of centre of gravity shall be reckoned correct to 0.1 m, 0.05 m or more shall be taken as 0.1 m and less than 0.05 m ignored.		
20.	Extra for laying concrete in or under foul positions.	cum	33.35
21.	Extra for using 12.5/10 mm nominal size graded/single size stone aggregate instead of 20 mm nominal size graded stone aggregate in cement concrete/reinforced cement concrete 1 : 2 : 4 (1 cement : 2 coarse sand : 4 graded stone aggregate 20 mm nominal size).	cum	3.70

Table 13.4. REINFORCED CEMENT CONCRETE

S. No.	Description	Unit	Rate ₹
	A. CAST-IN-SITU		
1.	Providing and laying in position specified grade of reinforced cement concrete excluding the cost of centring, shuttering, finishing and reinforcement-All work upto plinth level :		
	1A 1 : 1 : 2 (1 cement : 1 coarse sand : 2 graded stone aggregate 20 mm nominal size)	cum	2537.80
	1B 1 : 1.5 : 3 (1 cement : 1.5 coarse sand : 3 graded stone aggregate 20 mm nominal size)	cum	1890.45
	1C 1 : 2 : 4 (1 cement : 2 coarse sand : 4 graded stone aggregate 20 mm nominal size)	cum	1740.90
2.	Reinforced cement concrete work in walls (any thickness), including attached pilasters, buttresses, plinth and string courses, fillets, columns, pillars, piers, abutments, posts and struts, etc. upto floor five level excluding cost of centring, shuttering, finishing and reinforcement :		
	2A 1 : 1 : 2 (1 cement : 1 coarse sand : 2 graded stone aggregate 20 mm nominal size)	cum	2707.75
	2B 1 : 1.5 : 3 (1 cement : 1.5 coarse sand : 3 graded stone aggregate 20 mm nominal size)	cum	2110.65
	2C 1 : 2 : 4 (1 cement : 2 coarse sand : 4 graded stone aggregate 20 mm nominal size)	cum	1907.65

S. No.	Description	Unit	Rate ₹
3.	Reinforced cement concrete work in beams, suspended floors, roofs having slope upto 15°, landings, balconies, shelves, chajjas, lintels, bands, plain window sills, staircases and spiral staircases upto floor five level excluding the cost of centring, shuttering, finishing and reinforcement with 1 : 2 : 4 (1 cement : 2 coarse sand : 4 graded stone aggregate 20 mm nominal size).	cum	1885.15
4.	Providing and laying upto floor five level reinforced cement concrete in kerbs, steps and the like excluding the cost of centring, shuttering, finishing and reinforcement with 1 : 2 : 4 (1 cement : 2 coarse sand : 4 graded stone aggregate 20 mm nominal size).	cum	1804.10
5.	Reinforced cement concrete work in arches, archribs, domes, vaults, shells, folded plate and roofs having slope more than 15° upto floor five level excluding the cost of centring, shuttering, finishing and reinforcement with 1 : 2 : 4 (1 cement : 2 coarse sand : 4 graded stone aggregate 20 mm nominal size).	cum	1832.65
6.	Reinforced cement concrete work in chimneys, shafts, upto floor five level excluding the cost of centring, shuttering, finishing and reinforcement with 1 : 2 : 4 (1 cement: 2 coarse sand : 4 graded stone aggregate 20 mm nominal size).	cum	1914.75
7.	Reinforced cement concrete work in well-steining excluding the cost of centring, shuttering, finishing and reinforcement with 1 : 2 : 4 (1 cement : 2 coarse sand : 4 graded stone aggregate 20 mm nominal size).	cum	1754.60
8.	Reinforced cement concrete work in Vertical and Horizontal fins individually or forming box louvers, facias and eaves boards upto floor five level excluding the cost of centring, shuttering, finishing and reinforcement with 1 : 2 : 4 (1 cement : 2 coarse sand : 4 graded stone aggregate 20 mm nominal size).	cum	1838.45
	B. FORM WORK		
9.	Centring and shuttering including strutting, propping etc. and removal of form for :		
	9A Foundations, footings, bases of columns etc. for mass concrete.	sq m	53.65
	9B Walls (any thickness) including attached pilasters, buttresses, plinth and string courses etc.	sq m	88.30
	9C Suspended floors, roofs, landings, balconies and access platform,	sq m	89.55
	9D Shelves (Cast in situ)	sq m	89.55
	9E Lintels, beams, plinth beams, girders, bressumers and cantilevers.	sq m	71.70
	9F Columns, Pillars, Piers, Abutments, Posts and Struts	sq m	130.65
	9G Stairs, (excluding landings) except spiral-staircases.	sq m	83.80
	9H Spiral staircases (including landing)	sq m	83.35
	9I Arches, domes, vaults upto 6 m span	sq m	301.20
	9J Extra for arches, domes, vaults exceeding 6 m span	sq m	146.65
	9K Chimneys and shafts	sq m	88.30
	9L Well steining	sq m	162.90
	9M Vertical and horizontal fins individually or forming box louvers band, facias and eaves boards	sq m	121.60
	9N Extra for shuttering in circular work (20% of respective centring and shuttering items)	sq m	20%

(Contd.)

S. No.	Description	Unit	Rate ₹
	9O Small lintels not exceeding 1.5 m clear span, moulding as in cornices, window sills, string courses, bands, copings, bed plates, anchor blocks and the like.	sq m	53.65
	9P Edges of slabs and breaks in floors and walls.		
	9Q Under 20 cms wide	metre	23.25
	9R Above 20 cm wide	sq m	6.50
	9S Comics and mouldings	sq m	111.05
	9T Small surfaces such as cantilever ends, brackets and ends of steps, caps and bases to pilasters and columns and the like	sq m	101.05
	9U Weather shade, Chajjas, corbels etc., including edges	sq m	103.50
10.	Providing and fixing tie bolt, spring coil and plastic cone in wall shuttering complete as per the direction of engineer-in-charge :		
	10A 12 mm dia & 100 mm length	each set	56.55
	10B 12 mm dia. & 150 mm length	each set	58.75
	10C 20 mm dia. & 150 mm length	each set	81.00
	10D 20 mm dia. & 225 mm length	each set	93.20
11.	Extra for additional height in centring, shuttering where ever required with adequate bracing, propping etc. including cost of de-shuttering and decentring at all levels, over a height of 3.5 m, for every additional height of 1 metre or part thereof (Plan area to be measured) :		
	11A Suspended floors, roofs, landing, beams and balconies (Plan area to be measured).	sq m	42.40
	C. PRE-CAST R.C.C.		
12.	Providing, hoisting and fixing upto floor five level precast reinforced cement concrete work in string courses, bands, copings, bed plates, anchor blocks, plain window sills and the like including the cost of required centring, shuttering, finishing smooth with 6 mm thick cement plaster 1 : 3 (1 cement: 3 fine sand) on exposed surfaces complete but excluding cost of reinforcement with 1 : 2 : 4 (1 cement : 2 coarse sand : 4 graded stone aggregate 20 mm nominal size).	cum	2537.10
13.	Providing, hoisting and fixing upto floor five level precast reinforced cement concrete in small lintels not exceeding 1.5 m clear span upto floor five level including the cost of required centring, shuttering and finishing smooth with 6 mm thick cement plaster 1 : 3 (1 cement : 3 fine sand) on exposed surfaces but excluding the cost of reinforcement with 1 : 2 : 4 (1 cement : 2 coarse sand : 4 graded stone aggregate 20 mm nominal size).	cum	2648.90
14.	Providing, hoisting and fixing upto floor five level precast reinforced cement concrete in mouldings as in cornices, windows sills etc. including setting in cement mortar 1 : 3 (1 cement: 3 coarse sand) cost of required centring, shuttering and finishing smooth with 6 mm thick cement plaster 1 : 3 (1 cement : 3 fine sand) on exposed surfaces complete but excluding the cost of reinforcement with 1 : 2 : 4 (1 cement : 2 coarse sand : 4 graded stone aggregate 20 mm nominal size).	cum	2820.35

S. No.	Description	Unit	Rate ₹
15.	Providing, hoisting and fixing upto floor five level precast reinforced cement concrete in lintels, beams and bressumers including setting in cement mortar 1 : 3 (1 cement : 3 coarse sand), cost of required centring and shuttering and finishing smooth with 6 mm thick cement plaster 1 : 3 (1 cement: 3 fine sand) on exposed surfaces but excluding the cost of reinforcement with 1 : 2 : 4 (1 cement : 2 coarse sand : 4 graded stone aggregate 20 mm nominal size).	cum	2385.30
16.	Providing, hoisting and fixing upto floor five level precast reinforced cement concrete in shelves including setting in cement mortar 1 : 3 (1 cement : 3 coarse sand), cost of required centring, shuttering and finishing with neat cement punning on exposed surfaces but excluding the cost of reinforcement with 1 : 2 : 4 (1 cement: 2 coarse sand : 4 graded stone aggregate 12.5 mm nominal size).	cum	2354.25
17.	Providing, hoisting and fixing upto floor five level precast reinforced cement concrete in vertical & horizontal fins individually or forming box louvers setting in cement mortar 1 : 2 (1 cement : 2 coarse sand) including the cost of required centring, shuttering and finishing smooth with 6 mm thick cement plaster 1 : 3 (1 cement : 3 fine sand) on exposed surfaces complete but excluding the cost of reinforcement with 1 : 2 : 4 (1 cement : 2 coarse sand : 4 graded stone aggregate 20 mm nominal size).	cum	3657.00
18.	Providing, precast cement concrete Jali 1 : 2 : 4 (1 cement : 2 coarse sand : 4 stone aggregate 6 mm nominal size) reinforced with 1.6 mm dia mild steel wire including centring and shuttering, roughening cleaning, fixing and finishing in cement mortar 1 : 3 (1 cement 3 fine sand) etc. complete excluding plastering of the jambs, sills and soffits :		
	18A 50 mm thick	sq m	268.15
	18B 40 mm thick	sq m	222.90
	18C 25 mm thick	sq m	189.55
	D. ENCASING ROLLED STEEL SECTION		
19.	Encasing rolled steel sections, in beams and columns, with cement concrete 1 : 2 : 4 (1 cement: 2 coarse sand : 4 stone aggregate 12.5 mm nominal size) including centring and shuttering complete but excluding cost of reinforcement.	cum	2750.65
20.	Encasing rolled steel section in grillages with cement concrete 1 : 2 : 4 (1 cement : 2 coarse sand : 4 stone aggregate 12.5 mm nominal size) including centring and shuttering but excluding cost of expanded metal and hangers.	cum	1779.35
21.	Extra for providing and fixing expanded metal mesh of size 20 × 60 mm and strands 3.25 mm wide 1.6 mm thick weighing 3.64 kg. per sq m. for encasing of rolled steel sections in beams, columns and grillages excluding cost of hangers.	sq m	123.15
	E. STEEL REINFORCEMENT		
22.	Reinforcement for R.C.C. work including straightening, cutting, bending, placing in position and binding all complete.		
	22A Mild steel and medium tensile steel bars	kilogram	20.10
	22B Hard drawn steel wire	kilogram	27.85
	22C Cold twisted bars	kilogram	20.30
	22D Hot rolled deformed bars	kilogram	20.30

(Contd.)

S. No.	Description	Unit	Rate ₹
	22E Hard drawn steel wire fabric	kilogram	24.40
	22F Thermo-Mechanically Treated bars.	kilogram	20.30
	F. MISCELLANEOUS		
23.	Extra for RCC work in superstructure above floor V level for each four floors or part thereof.	cum	108.35
24.	Deduct for omitting in R.C.C. work smooth finishing of the exposed surface with 6 mm thick cement mortar 1 : 3 (1 cement : 3 fine sand).	sq m	33.00
25.	Extra for rendering smooth the top of suspended floors, landings and staircases (treads and risers) with cement mortar 1 : 2 (1 cement : 2 coarse sand) including a floating coat of neat cement and protecting the surface with a layer of 7.5 cm of earth laid over 15 mm of fine sand in case of suspended floor and bricks laid in mud mortar in case of landings and steps including subsequent removal and cleaning of the same.	sq m	26.65
26.	Providing and fixing in position copper plate as per design for expansion joints.	kilogram	192.45
27.	Providing and filling in position, blown bitumen in expansion joints.	per cm depth per cm width per 100 m	111.05
28.	Providing and filling in position bitumen mix filler of Proportion 80 kg. of hot bitumen, 1 kg. of cement and 0.25 cubic metre of coarse sand for expansion joints.	per cm depth per cm width per 100 m	39.85
29.	Providing and fixing in position 12 mm thick bitumen impregnated fibre board conforming to IS : 1838 including cost of primer, sealing compound in expansion joints.	per cm depth per 100 m	214.00
30.	Providing and fixing sheet covering over expansion joints with iron screws as per design to match the colour/shade of wall treatment :		
	30A Asbestos sheet 6 mm thick		
	30B 150 mm wide	metre	40.25
	30C 200 mm wide	metre	54.00
	30D Aluminium fluted strips 3.15 mm thick		
	30E 150 mm wide.	metre	169.50
	30F 200 mm wide.	metre	223.75
31.	Add or deduct for plaster drip course/groove in plastered surface or moulding to R.C.C. projections.	metre	6.65
32.	Extra for laying reinforced cement concrete in or under water and/or liquid mud including cost of pumping or bailing out water and removing slush etc., complete.	per cum per metre depth	83.65
	Note For item No. 13.4.32 : The quantity will be calculated by multiplying the depth measured from the subsoil water level upto the centre of gravity of the R.C.C. under subsoil water with the quantity of R.C.C. in cubic metre executed under subsoil water. The depth of centre of gravity shall be reckoned correct to 0.1 m, 0.05 m or more shall be taken as 0.1 m and less than 0.05 m ignored. No extra payment shall be made for placing reinforcement or centring and shuttering under sub-soil water conditions.		
33.	Extra for laying reinforced cement concrete in or under foul positions.	cum	33.35

S. No.	Description	Unit	Rate ₹
	G. DESIGN MIX CONCRETE		
34.	Providing and laying in position machine batched, machine mixed and machine vibrated design mix cement concrete of specified grade for reinforced cement concrete structural elements, excluding the cost of centring, shuttering, finishing and reinforcement—M-20 grade reinforced cement concrete :		
	34A All work upto plinth level	cum	2002.00
	34B All work from plinth level upto floor V level.		
	34C Walls, columns, pillars, posts and struts	cum	2091.60
	34D Beams, plinth beams, girders, bressumers, cantilevers, Suspended floors lintels roofs and staircases including spiral staircases, shelves etc.	cum	2167.80
35.	Extra for R.C.C. work above floor V level for each four floors or part thereof.	cum	108.35
36.	Add or deduct for providing richer or leaner mixes respectively at all floor levels :		
	36A Providing M-25 grade R.C.C. instead of M-20 grade R.C.C.	cum	76.80
	36B Providing M-30 grade R.C.C. instead of M-20 grade R.C.C.	cum	105.30
	36C Providing M-35 grade R.C.C. instead of M-20 grade R.C.C.	cum	128.05
	36D Providing M-15 grade R.C.C. instead of M-20 grade R.C.C.	cum	179.25
37.	Providing and mixing in recommended proportions admixtures (as per IS 9103) to accelerate/retard, setting of concrete, improve workability without impairing strength and durability characteristics of concrete as per manufacturer's specifications and direction of Engineer-in-Charge complete :		
	37A Accelerating admixtures	per bag of 50 kg of cement used in the mix	53.75
	37B Retarding admixtures	-do-	81.55
	37C Water reducing admixtures (Plasticizer/super plasticizer)	-do-	70.45
38.	Providing and placing in position precast reinforced cement concrete waffle units square or rectangular as per design and shape for floors and roofs in 1 : 1½ : 3 (1 cement : 1½ coarse sand : 3 graded stone aggregate 10 mm nominal size) including flush or deep ruled pointing at joints in cement mortar 1 : 2 (1 Cement: 2 Fine sand), making necessary holes of required sizes for carrying through service lines etc., providing steel hooks for lifting etc., form work in precasting, handling, hoisting, centering and erection complete for all floor levels but excluding the cost of reinforcement.	cum	5981.25

Table 13.5. BRICK WORK WITH F.P.S. BRICKS

S. No.	Description	Unit	Rate ₹
	A. BRICK WORK		
1.	Brick work with bricks of class designation 75 in foundation and plinth in :		
	1A Cement lime mortar 1 : 1 : 6 (1 cement: 1 lime putty : 6 fine sand)	cum	1286.00
	1B Cement lime mortar 1 : 2 : 9 (1 cement: 2 lime putty : 9 fine sand)	cum	1253.95
	1C Cement lime mortar 1 : 1 : 6 (1 cement: 1 lime putty : 6 coarse sand)	cum	1339.40
	1D Cement mortar 1 : 4 (1 cement : 4 fine sand)	cum	1290.20
	1E Cement mortar 1 : 6 (1 cement : 6 fine sand)	cum	1197.75
	1F Cement mortar 1 : 4 (1 cement : 4 coarse sand)	cum	1343.65
	1G Cement mortar 1 : 6 (1 cement : 6 coarse sand)	cum	1251.20
2.	Extra for Brick work in superstructure above plinth level upto floor V level.	cum	150.65
3.	Extra for brick work in superstructure above floor V level for each four floors or part thereof.	cum	108.35
4.	Extra for brick work in:		
	4A Square or rectangular pillars.	cum	79.50
5.	Extra for brick work with bricks of class designation 75 curved on plan upto a mean radius not exceeding 6 metres.	cum	120.35
6.	Extra for cutting or chamfering of bricks to required shape in masonry work.	metre	3.65
7.	Constructing tharry with bricks of class designation 75 laid on edge in cement mortar 1 : 4 (1 cement : 4 coarse sand), cement pointing 1 : 2 (1 cement : 2 fine sand) including necessary excavation and 10 cm bed of cement concrete 1 : 5 : 10 (1 cement : 5 fine sand : 10 graded stone aggregate 40 mm nominal size) complete.	sq m	331.95
8.	Extra for forming cavity 5 cm to 7.5 cm wide in cavity walls with necessary weep and vent holes including use of cores and cost of providing and fixing bitumastic coated M.S. ties 300 mm long of 25 mm × 3 mm section at not less than 3 ties per sq m as per approved design.	sq m	24.55
9.	Providing half brick masonry with bricks of class designation 75 in cement mortar 1 : 3 (1 cement : 3 coarse sand) in superstructure for closing cavity 5 to 7.5 cm wide in cavity wall complete with 10 cm/ 11.4 cm wide bitumen felt type 3 grade 1.	metre	56.55
10.	Brick work 7 cm thick with bricks of class designation 75 in cement mortar 1: 3 (1 Cement: 3 coarse sand) in superstructure.	sq m	124.60
11.	Brick work in plain arches in superstructure including centring and shuttering complete for span upto 6 metres with bricks of class designation 75 in cement mortar 1 : 3 (1 cement : 3 coarse sand).	cum	2229.40
12.	Brick work in gauged arches in superstructure in cement mortar 1:3 (1 cement: 3 coarse sand) including centring antishuttering complete, for span upto 6 metres with bricks of class designation 75.	cum	2581.60

S. No.	Description	Unit	Rate ₹
13.	Extra for additional cost of centring for arches exceeding 6 m span including all shuttering, bolting, wedging and removal (Area of the soffit to be measured).	sq m	146.65
	B. HALF BRICK MASONRY		
14.	Half brick masonry with bricks of class designation 75 in foundations and plinth in :		
	14A Cement mortar 1 : 3 (1 cement : 3 coarse sand)	sq m	168.10
	14B Cement mortar 1 : 4 (1 cement : 4 coarse sand)	sq m	157.75
15.	Extra for half Brick masonry in superstructure above plinth level upto floor V level.	sq m	16.70
16.	Extra for half brick masonry in superstructure, above floor V level for every four floors or part thereof.	sq m	12.50
17.	Extra for providing and placing in position 2 Nos. 6 mm dia. M.S. bars at every third course of half brick masonry (with F.P.S. bricks).	sq m	21.25
18.	Providing brick band 10 cm/7.0 cm thick 5 cm/5.7 cm projected from wall face, in bricks of class designation 75 laid in cement mortar 1 : 4 (1 cement : 4 coarse sand).	metre	6.50
	Note For Item No. 13.5.18 : Where modular bricks are used, the thickness of drip course/string coarse/band shall be 10 cm and where 22.9 cm 11.4 cm × 7 cm bricks are used, the thickness shall be 7.0 cm.		
	C. BRICK TILE WORK		
19.	Tile brick masonry with tile bricks of class designation 100 in foundation and plinth in:		
	19A Lime mortar 1 : 1 : 1 (1 lime putty : 1 surkhi : 1 fine sand)	cum	1956.35
	19B Cement lime mortar : 1 : 1 : 6 (1 cement : 1 lime putty : 6 fine sand)	cum	2037.15
	19C Cement lime mortar 1 : 1 : 6 (1 cement : 1 lime putty : 6 coarse sand)	cum	2122.65
	19D Cement mortar 1 : 4 (1 cement : 4 fine sand)	cum	2043.95
	19E Cement mortar 1 : 6 (1 cement : 6 fine sand)	cum	1896.00
	19F Cement mortar 1 : 4 (1 cement : 4 coarse sand)	cum	2129.45
	19G Cement mortar 1 : 6 (1 cement : 6 coarse sand)	cum	1981.50
20.	Extra for tile bricks masonry with tile bricks of class designation 100 in superstructure from plinth level upto floor five level.	cum	165.35
21.	Extra for tile brick masonry with tile bricks of class designation 100 in superstructure above floor five level for every four floors or part thereof.	cum	108.35
22.	Deduct for using tile bricks of class designation 75 instead of tile bricks of class designation 100 in tile brick masonry.	cum	86.30
23.	Extra for tile brick masonry with tile bricks of class designation 100 in square or rectangular pillars.	cum	114.15
24.	Extra for tile brick masonry curved on plan upto a mean radius not exceeding 6 metres.	cum	182.45
25.	Tile brick masonry with tile bricks of class designation 100 in plain arch work in superstructure in cement mortar 1 : 4 (1 cement : 4 coarse sand) including centring and shuttering complete.	cum	2876.20

(*Contd.*)

S. No.	*Description*	*Unit*	*Rate* ₹
26.	Tile brick masonry with tile bricks of class designation 100 in gauged arch work in superstructure in cement mortar 1 : 4 (1 Cement : 4 coarse sand) including centring and shuttering complete.	cum	3208.25
27.	Tile brick masonry work 5 cm thick with tile bricks of class designation 100 in cement mortar 1: 3 (1 cement : 3 coarse sand) in superstructure.	sq m	125.20
	D. HONEY COMB WORK		
28.	Honey-comb brick work 10/11.4 cm thick with bricks of class designation 75 in cement mortar 1 : 4 (1 cement : 4 coarse sand).	sq m	114.85
	E. MOULDING AND CORNICES		
29.	Providing 10 cm/7.0 cm thick and 5 cm/5.7 cm projected string course with bricks of class designation 75 in cement mortar 1 : 4 (1 cement : 4 coarse sand)	metre	6.60
	Note For Item No. 13.5.29 : Where modular bricks are used, the thickness of drip course/string coarse/band shall be 10 cm and where 22.9 cm × 11.4 cm × 7.0 cm bricks are used, the thickness shall be 7.0 cm.		
30.	Moulding and cornices with brick masonry in cement mortar 1 : 4 (1 cement : 4 coarse sand) (girth to be measured in cm and length in running metre.	per metre per cm. girth	0.70
31.	Providing, fixing and embedding in the masonry 150 mm dia asbestos cement pipe flue including fixing and jointing with cement mortar 1 : 2 (1 cement : 2 coarse sand) and hemp etc.	metre	41.70
32.	Extra for laying brick work in or under water and/or liquid mud including cost of pumping or bailing out water and removing slush etc. complete.	per cum per metre depth	83.65
	Note For Item No. 13.5.32 : The quantity will be calculated by multiplying the depth measured from sub-soil water level upto the centre of gravity of brick work under sub-soil water with the quantity of brick work in cum executed under the sub-soil water. The depth of centre of gravity shall be reckoned correct to 0.1 m, 0.05 m or more shall be taken as 0.1 m and less than 0.05 m ignored.		
33.	Extra for laying brick work in or under foul position.	cum	33.35
	F. EXPOSED BRICK WORK		
34.	Brick work with selected bricks of class designation 75 in exposed brick work including making horizontal and vertical grooves 10 mm wide 12 mm deep complete from ground level upto plinth level in cement mortar 1 : 6 (1 cement : 6 fine sand).	cum	1218.25
35.	Brick work with selected bricks of class designation 75 in exposed brick work including making horizontal and vertical grooves 10 mm wide 12 mm deep complete from ground level upto plinth level in cement mortar 1 : 6 (1 cement : 6 coarse sand).	cum	1271.70
36.	Brick work with machine moulded bricks of class designation 75 in exposed brick work including making horizontal and vertical grooves 100 mm wide 12 mm deep complete from ground level upto plinth level in cement mortar 1: 6 (1 cement : 6 fine sand).	cum	1317.50

S. No.	Description	Unit	Rate ₹
37.	Brick work with machine moulded bricks of class designation 75 in exposed brick work including making horizontal and vertical grooves 10 mm wide 12 mm deep complete from ground level upto plinth level in cement mortar 1 : 6 (1 cement : 6 coarse sand).	cum	1364.55
38.	Extra for exposed brick work in superstructure above plinth level and upto floor five level.	cum	193.15
39.	Brick work with clay flyash bricks of class designation 75 in superstructure above plinth level upto floor five level in :		
39A	Cement lime mortar 1 : 1 : 6 (1 cement : 1 lime putty : 6 fine sand)	cum	1428.55
39B	Cement lime mortar 1 : 2 : 9 (1 cement : 2 lime putty : 9 fine sand)	cum	1396.45
39C	Cement lime mortar 1 : 1 : 6 (1 cement : 1 lime putty : 6 coarse sand)	cum	1481.95
39D	Cement mortar 1 : 4 (1 cement : 4 fine sand)	cum	1432.75
39E	Cement mortar 1 : 6 (1 cement : 6 fine sand)	cum	1340.30
39F	Cement mortar 1 : 4 (1 cement : 4 coarse sand)	cum	1486.20
39G	Cement mortar 1 : 6 (1 cement : 6 coarse sand)	cum	1393.75
40.	Extra for Exposed brick work/clay flyash brick work in superstructure above floor five level, for each four floors or part thereof.	cum	108.35

Table 13.6. STONE WORK

S. No.	Description	Unit	Rate ₹
	A. RANDOM RUBBLE MASONRY		
1.	Random rubble masonry with hard stone in foundation and plinth including levelling up with cement concrete 1 : 6 : 12 (1 cement : 6 coarse sand : 12 graded stone aggregate 20 mm nominal size) at plinth level with :		
1A	Cement mortar 1 : 6 (1 cement : 6 coarse sand)	cum	1192.80
1B	Cement mortar 1 : 6 (1 cement : 6 fine sand)	cum	1122.25
1C	Cement lime mortar 1 : 1 : 8 (1 cement: 1 lime putty : 8 fine sand)	cum	1157.30
1D	Lime mortar 1 : 1 : 1 (1 lime putty : 1 surkhi: 1 fine sand)	cum	1172.05
2.	Extra for random rubble masonry with hard stone in superstructure above plinth level and upto floor five level, mcluding levelling up with cement concrete 1 : 6 : 12 (1 cement : 6 coarse sand : 12 graded stone aggregate 20 mm nominal size) at window sills, ceiling level and the like.	cum	183.45
3.	Extra for random rubble masonry with hard stone in superstructure above floor V level for every four floors or part thereof.	cum	144.45
4.	Extra for random rubble masonry with hard stone in :		
4A	Square or rectangular pillars	cum	77.50
4B	Circular pillars.	cum	286.35
5.	Extra for random rubble masonry with hard stone curved on plan for a mean radius not exceeding 6 m.	cum	106.35

(*Contd.*)

S. No.	Description	Unit	Rate ₹
	B. COURSED RUBBLE MASONRY		
6.	Coursed rubble masonry (first sort) with hard stone in foundation and plinth with:		
	6A Cement mortar 1 : 6 (1 cement : 6 coarse sand)	cum	1335.05
	6B Cement mortar 1 : 6 (1 cement : 6 fine sand)	cum	1270.90
	6C Cement lime mortar 1 : 1 : 8 (1 cement: 1 lime putty : 8 fine sand)	cum	1302.75
	6D Lime mortar 1 : 1 : 1 (1 lime putty : 1 surkhi: 1 fine sand)	cum	1316.15
7.	Coursed rubble masonry (second sort) with hard stone in foundation and plinth with :		
	7A Cement mortar 1 : 6 (1 cement : 6 coarse sand)	cum	1253.85
	7B Cement mortar 1 : 6 (1 cement : 6 fine sand)	cum	1189.75
	7C Cement lime mortar 1 : 1 : 8 (1 cement: 1 lime putty : 8 fine sand)	cum	1221.60
	7D Lime mortar 1 : 1 : 1 (1 lime putty : 1 surkhi : 1 fine sand)	cum	1235.00
8.	Extra for coursed rubble masonry with hard stone (first or second sort) in superstructure above plinth level and upto floor five level.	cum	174.25
9.	Extra for coursed rubble masonry with hard stone (first or second sort) in superstructure above floor V level for every four floors or part thereof.	cum	144.45
10.	Extra for coursed rubble masonry with hard stone (first or second sort) in :		
	10A Square or rectangular pillars	cum	86.50
	10B Circular pillars	cum	323.65
11.	Extra for coursed rubble masonry with hard stone (first or second sort) curved on plan for a mean radius not exceeding 6 m.	cum	116.45
	C. ASHLAR MASONRY		
12.	Stone work in plain ashlar in super structure upto floor five level in cement mortar 1 : 6 (1 cement : 6 coarse sand) including pointing with cement mortar 1 : 2 (1 white cement : 2 stone dust) with an admixture of pigment matching the stone shade:		
	12A Red sand stone	cum	10425.00
	12B White sand stone	cum	11165.00
13.	Stone work plain ashlar in arches in cement mortar 1 : 3 (1 cement : 3 coarse sand) including centring, shuttering and pointing with white cement mortar 1 : 2 (1 white cement : 2 stone dust) with an admixture of pigment matching the stone shade :		
	13A Red sand stone	cum	11735.00
	13B White sand stone	cum	12475.00
14.	Stone work plain ashlar in domes in cement mortar 1 : 3 (1 cement : 3 coarse sand) including centring, shuttering and pointing with white cement mortar 1 : 2 (1 white cement : 2 stone dust) with an admixture of pigment matching the stone shade :		
	14A Red sand stone	cum	15960.00
	14B White sand stone	cum	16700.00
15.	Stone work ashlar punched (ordinary) in superstructure upto floor five level in cement mortar 1 : 6 (1 white cement: 6 coarse sand) including pointing with cement mortar 1 : 2 (1 cement : 2 stone dust) with an admixture of pigment matching the stone shade :		

S. No.	Description	Unit	Rate ₹
	15A Red sand stone	cum	10205.00
	15B White sand stone	cum	10945.00
16.	Extra for stone work, plain ashlar or ashlar punched above floor Vth level for every four floors or part thereof.	cum	145.00
17.	Extra for plain ashlar or ashlar punched in :		
	17A Square or rectangular pillars	cum	545.00
	17B Circular pillars	cum	1635.00
18.	Extra for stone work; plain ashlar or ashlar punched curved on plan with a mean radius not exceeding 6 m.	cum	380.00
19.	Extra for additional cost of centring for arches exceeding 6 m span including all strutting, bolting, wedging etc. and removal (area of soffit to be measured).	sq m	146.85
	D. SUNK, MOULDED, CARVED ASHLAR MASONRY		
20.	Stone work sunk or moulded or sunk and moulded upto floor five level in cement mortar 1: 6 (1 cement: 6 coarse sand) including pointing with white cement mortar 1: 2 (1 white cement: 2 stone dust) with an admixture of pigment matching the stone shade :		
	20A Red sand stone	cum	23780.00
	20B White sand stone	cum	24520.00
21.	Extra for stone work sunk or moulded or sunk and moulded or carved in:		
	21A Triangular or square or rectangular pillars	cum	710.00
	21B Circular or polygonal pillars	cum	2010.00
22.	Extra for stone work sunk or moulded in cornices.	per metre per cm girth	4.65
	E. MISCELLANEOUS STONE WORK		
23.	Stone work for wall lining etc. (veneer work) over 12 mm thick bed of cement lime mortar 1 : 1 : 6 (1 cement : 1 lime putty : 6 fine sand) including pointing in white cement mortar 1 : 2 (1 white cement : 2 stone dust) with an admixture of pigment matching the stone shade : (To be secured to the backing by means of cramps which shall be paid for separately) :		
	23A Red sand stone		
	23B 70 mm thick	sq m	882.15
	23C 60 mm thick	sq m	814.25
	23D 50 mm thick	sq m	746.55
	23E 40 mm thick	sq m	678.50
	23F White sand stone		
	23G 70 mm thick	sq m	934.00
	23H 60 mm thick	sq m	858.70
	23I 50 mm thick	sq m	783.60
	23J 40 mm thick	sq m	707.95
24.	Extra for stone work (veneer work) curved on plan with a mean radius not exceeding 6 m.	cum	545.00
25.	Providing and fixing gun metal cramps of required shape for anchoring stone wall lining to the backing or securing adjacent stones in stone wall lining in cement mortar 1 : 2 (1 cement : 2 fine sand) including making the necessary chases :		

(Contd.)

S. No.	*Description*	*Unit*	*Rate* ₹
	25A 25 × 6 mm - 30 cm long	each	61.05
	25B 15 × 6 mm - 16.5 cm long	each	27.75
26.	Providing and fixing stone dowels 10 × 5 × 2.50 cm cut to double wedge shape as per design in cement mortar 1 : 2 (1 cement : 2 fine sand) including making the necessary chases.	each	6.85
27.	Providing and fixing copper pins 7.5 cm long 6 mm diameter for securing adjacent stones in stone wall lining in cement mortar 1 : 2 (1 cement : 2 fine sand) including making the necessary chases.	each	17.25
28.	Providing and fixing sloping chajja of stone 40 mm thick and upto 80 cm wide beyond the wall as measured along the slope in cement mortar 1 : 4 (1 cement : 4 coarse sand) with 12 mm diameter anchoring steel bar 45 cm long fixed in each stone and supported on and including with bricks cove of class designation 75 in cement mortar 1 : 4 (1 cement : 4 coarse sand) including pointing in cement mortar 1 : 2 (1 white cement : 2 stone dust) with an admixture of pigment matching the stone shade:		
	28A Red sand stone:		
	28B With F.P.S. Bricks	sq m	432.75
	28C White sand stone:		
	28D With F.P.S. bricks	sq m	462.70
29.	Providing and fixing horizontal chajja of stone 40 mm thick and upto 80 cm projection in cement mortar 1 : 4 (1 cement : 4 coarse sand) including pointing in white cement mortar 1 : 2 (1 white cement : 2 stone dust) with an admixture of pigment matching the stone shade:		
	29A Red sand stone	sq m	296.15
	29B White sand stone	sq m	324.15
30.	30 mm red sand stone sun-shade (chisel-dressed) supported on red sand stone brackets, fixed in walls with cement mortar 1 : 4 (1 cement : 4 coarse sand) including finishing complete.	sq m	343.55
31.	Providing and fixing red sand stone brackets 55 × 22.5 × 45 cm sunk and moulded including providing and fixing with 4 Nos. gun metal cramp 25 × 6 mm. 30 cm long and dowel bars 7.5 cm long 6 mm dia as per design.	each	990.50
32.	Stone work, plain in copings, cornices, string courses and plinth courses, in cement mortar 1: 6 (1 cement: 6 coarse sand) including pointing with white cement mortar 1 : 2 (1 white cement: 2 stone dust) with an admixture of pigment matching the stone shade :		
	32A Red sand stone	cum	12695.00
	32B White sand stone	cum	13435.00
33.	30 mm thick red sand stone shelves fixed in walls in cement mortar 1 : 3 (1 cement: 3 coarse sand) including finishing complete.	sq m	165.65
34.	30 mm thick red sand stone shelves (chisel dressed) supported on 40 × 40 × 6 mm T or angle iron brackets 0.75 m apart fixed on 15 × 10 × 10 cm blocks of cement concrete 1 : 3 : 6 (1 cement : 3 coarse sand : 6 graded stone aggregate 20 mm nominal size).	sq m	315.95
35.	30 mm thick red sand stone shelves (chisel dressed) supported on precast reinforced cement concrete brackets 1 : 2 : 4 (1 cement : 2 coarse sand : 4 graded stone aggregate 12.5 mm nominal size) fixed 0.75 m apart in walls with cement mortar 1 : 4 (1 cement: 4 coarse sand) with section of the bracket 5 × 10 cm at the wall and tapering to 5 × 5 cm at the free end with a loop reinforcement of one 10 mm diameter bar per bracket.	sq m	231.95

S. No.	Description	Unit	Rate ₹
36.	30 mm red stone shelves (chisel dressed) supported on 5 × 10 cm sal wood brackets 0.75 m apart fixed in walls with cement mortar 1 : 4 (1 cement : 4 coarse sand).	sq m	412.55
37.	Providing and fixing in cement mortar 1 : 6 (1 cement : 6 fine sand) red sand stone slabs 30 mm thick over:		
	37A Drains	sq m	153.55
	37B Flue tops	sq m	153.70
38.	Providing and fixing stone jali 40 mm thick throughout (without sunking or moulding in jali slab) in cement mortar 1 : 3 (1 cement : 3 coarse sand) including pointing in white cement mortar 1 : 2 (1 white cement: 2 stone dust) with an admixture of pigment, matching the stone shade, jali slab without any chamfers etc. :		
	38A Red sand stone	sq m	2090.75
	38B White sand stone	sq m	2116.40
39.	Extra for laying stone work in or under water and/or liquid mud including cost of pumping or bailing out water and removing slush etc. complete.	cum per metre depth	83.65
40.	Extra for laying stone work in or under foul position.	cum	33.35
41.	Wall lining butch work with Dholpur stone 40 mm thick rough facing on the exposed surface with stone strips of minimum length 230 mm and required width including embedding every tenth layer and bottom most layer in masonry or concrete after making necessary chases of size 75 × 75 mm and by providing layer of 75 mm thick strips i/c 12 mm thick bed of cement mortar 1 : 3 (1 cement : 3 coarse sand) i/c ruled pointing in cement mortar 1 : 2 (1 white cement : 2 stone dust) with an admixture of pigment to match the shade of stone complete as per direction of Engineer-in-charge.	sq m	528.00
42.	Stone work for wall lining etc. (Veneer work) over 12 mm thick bed of cement mortar 1 : 3 (1 cement : 3 coarse sand) and jointed with grey cement slurry @ 3.30 kg/sq m. including rubbing and polishing complete. (To be secured to the backing by means of cramps which shall be paid for separately) :		
	42A Kota stone slabs rough chiselled		
	42B 25 mm thick	sq m	698.35
43.	Stone tile work for wall lining with special adhesive like araldite or equivalent over 12 mm thick bed of cement mortar 1 : 3 (1 cement : 3 coarse sand) including pointing in white cement with an admixture of pigment to match the stone shade :		
	43A 8 mm thick (mirror polished and machine cut edge)		
	43B Granite black stone	sq m	673.20
	43C Granite brown stone	sq m	673.20
	43D Raj Nagar white stone	sq m	445.45
	43E Banswara white stone	sq m	445.45

Table 13.7. MARBLE WORK

S. No.	*Description*	*Unit*	*Rate* ₹
1.	Marble work (table rubbed and polished) for wall lining (veneer work) in cement mortar 1 : 3 (1 White cement : 3 coarse sand) including pointing with white cement mortar 1 : 2 (1 white cement : 2 marble dust) with an admixture of pigment to match the marble shade : (To be secured to the backing by means of cramps, which shall be paid for separately).		

RATES PER SQ M

	Type of stone	*Area of slab*		
		0.10 sq m to 0.2 sq m	over 0.2 sq m but upto 0.5 sq m	Over 0.5 sq m but upto 1.0 sq m
1A	White Marble-Raj Nagar Plain			
1B	20 mm thick	196.30	519.30	1657.35
1C	30 mm thick	356.30	1009.90	2453.50

2. Providing and fixing 20 mm thick mirror polished, machine cut for kitchen platforms, vanity counters facias and similar locations of required size of approved shade, colour and texture laid over 20 mm thick base cement mortar 1 : 4 (1 cement: 4 coarse sand) with joints treated with white cement, mixed with matching pigment, epoxy touch ups, including rubbing, curing etc. complete at all levels.

RATES PER SQ M

	Type of stone	*Area of slab*				
		Up to 0.10 sq m	0.10 sq m to 0.2 sq m	over 0.2 sq m but upto 0.5 sq m	Over 0.5 sq m but upto 1.0 sq m	over 1.0 sq m but upto 2.0 sq m
2A	Abu plain white marble	858.50	1863.85	2768.40	3807.75	4160.50
2B	Makrana Doongri Adanga, Veined white marble	876.90	958.60	1008.05	1066.35	1127.45
2C	Rajnagar plain white marble	787.10	879.25	1011.55	1362.65	1505.40
2D	Udaipur Green marble	725.30	767.25	940.40	1124.65	1185.80
2E	Kishangarh Zebra black marble	958.60	993.60	1008.05	1037.20	1069.10
2F	Granite black	2090.10	2214.95	2346.10	2557.20	2559.95
2G	Granite pink	1366.85	1483.50	1620.50	1766.25	1944.05
2H	Granite grey	1600.15	1775.20	1999.60	2174.55	2410.65

S. No.	*Description*	*Unit*	*Rate* ₹
3.	Extra for providing edge moulding to 20 mm thick marble stone counters, Vanities etc. over item no. 8.2 including machine polishing to edge to give high gloss finish etc. complete as per design approved by Engineer-in-Charge :		
3A	Marble work	metre	95.10
3B	Granite work	metre	151.80

S. No.	Description	Unit	Rate ₹
4.	Extra for fixing marble/granite stone over and above corresponding basic item, in facia and drops of width upto 150 mm with expoxy resin based (Araldite or equivalent) adhesive including cleaning etc. complete.	metre	60.25
5.	Extra for providing opening of required size & shape for wash basins/ kitchen sink in kitchen platform, vanity counters and similar location in marble/stone work including necessary holes for pillar taps etc. including rubbing and polishing of cut edges etc. complete.	each opening	19.70
6.	Mirror polishing on marble work/stone work where ever required to give high gloss finish complete.	sq m	81.55
7.	Providing and fixing cramps of required size & shape in RCC/CC backing with cement mortar 1 : 2 (1 cement : 2 fine sand) including drilling necessary hole in stones and embedding the cramp in the hole (fastener to be paid separately) :		
	7A Gunmetal cramps	kg.	129.25
	7B Stainless steel cramps	kg.	235.65
8.	Providing and fixing expansion hold fasteners on CC/R.C.C. surface backing including drilling necessary holes and the cost of bolt etc complete :		
	8A Wedge expansion type		
	8B Fastner with threaded dia. 1/4″ or 6 mm	each	9.95
	8C Fastner with threaded dia. 3/8″ or 10 mm	each	14.55
	8D Fastner with threaded dia. 1/2″ or 12 mm	each	26.95
9.	Providing and fixing gun metal cramps 25 × 6 mm, 30 cm long as per design in cement mortar 1 : 2 (1 cement : 2 fine sand) including making necessary chases.	each	61.05
10.	Providing and fixing gun metal cramps 15 × 6 mm, 16.5 cm long as per design in cement mortar 1 : 2 (1 cement : 2 fine sand) including making necessary chases.	each	27.75
11.	Providing and fixing copper pins 7.5 cm long of 6 mm diameter in cement mortar 1 : 2 (1 cement : 2 fine sand) including making necessary chases.	each	17.25
12.	Providing and fixing stone dowel 10 × 5 × 2.5 cm cut to double wedge shape as per design, in cement mortar 1 : 2 (1 cement : 2 fine sand) including making necessary chases.	each	6.85
13.	Stone tile (polished) work for wall lining over 12 mm thick bed of cement mortor 1 : 3 (1 cement : 3 coarse sand) and cement slurry @ 3.3 kg/sq m including pointing in white cement complete :		
	13A Doongri Adanga marble		
	13B 20 mm thick	sq m	488.05

Table 13.8. WOOD WORK

S. No.	Description	Unit	Rate ₹
	A. FRAMES AND TRUSSES		
1.	Providing wood work in frames of doors, windows, clerestory windows and other frames, wrought framed and fixed in position :		

(Contd.)

S. No.	Description	Unit	Rate ₹
	1A Second class teak wood	cum	37250.00
	1B First class deodar wood	cum	33500.00
	1C Second class deodar wood	cum	31035.00
	1D Sal wood	cum	23295.00
	1E Kiln seasoned and chemically treated hollock wood.	cum	22745.00
2.	Providing laminated veneer lumber conforming to TADS 15 : 1995, manufactured in factories by approved manufacturers, in frames of doors, windows, clerestory windows and other frames, wrought framed and fixed in position as per directions of Engineer-in-charge.	cum	4390.00
3.	Providing eucalyptus wood, kiln seasoned and treated by ammoniacal copper arsenite treatment, as per FRI, Dehradun technology, conforming to TADS 5 : 1994, manufactured in factories under controlled conditions by approved manufacturers, in frames of doors, windows, clerestory windows and other frames, wrought framed and fixed in position as per directions of Engineer-in-charge.	cum	4390.00
4.	Providing wood work in frames of false ceiling, partitions etc. sawn and put up in position :		
	4A First class deodar wood	cum	34620.00
	4B Second class deodar wood	cum	31005.00
	4C Sal wood	cum	23300.00
	4D Mango wood	cum	8360.00
	4E Kiln seasoned and chemically treated hollock wood.	cum	21050.00
5.	Extra for additional labour for circular works, such as in frames of fan light :		
	5A Second class teak wood	cum	3725.00
	5B First class deodar wood	cum	3350.00
	5C Second class deodar wood	cum	3104.00
	5D Sal wood	cum	2330.00
	5E Kiln seasoned and chemically treated hollock wood.	cum	2275.00
6.	Providing and fixing panelled or panelled and glazed shutters for doors, windows and clerestory windows including black enamelled M.S. butt hinges with necessary screws excluding, panelling which will be paid for separately :		

		Rate for thickness of shutters in mm per sq m		
		40	35	30
6A	Second class teak wood	1072.45	960.65	848.85
6B	First class deodar wood	997.85	895.05	792.25
6C	Second class deodar wood	905.40	813.75	722.10
6D	Kiln seasoned and chemically treated hollock wood.	723.00	655.10	587.25

S. No.	Description	Unit	Rate ₹
7.	Providing and fixing laminated veneer lumber door shutter conforming to TADS 15 : 1995, manufactured in factories by approved manufacturers, including black enamelled M.S. butt hinges with necessary screws as per directions of Engineer-in-charge and panelling with panels of.		

S. No.	Description	Unit	Rate ₹
8.	12 mm thick plain Grade-1, medium density flat pressed three layer and graded particle board (FPT-1) conforming to IS : 3087 bonded with BWP type synthetic resin adhesive as per IS : 848 :		
	8A 35 mm thick shutters	sq m	851.90
	8B 40 mm thick shutters	sq m	935.20
9.	12 mm thick prelaminated (with particle board decorative lamination on both sides) Grade-1, medium density flat pressed, three layer and graded (FPT-1) conforming to IS : 3087 bonded with BWP type synthetic resin adhesive as per IS : 848 and prelamination conforming to IS : 12823 Grade 1, Type-II :		
	9A 35 mm thick shutters	sq m	1240.75
	9B 40 mm thick shutters	sq m	1321.05
10.	12 mm thick one side prelaminated (with particle board decorative lamination on other sides) and balancing lamination Grade-1 medium density flat pressed, three layer and graded particle board (FPT-1) conforming to IS : 3087 bonded with PWP type synthetic resin adhesive as per IS : 848 and prelamination conforming to IS : 12823 Grade-1, Type II :		
	10A 35 mm thick shutters	sq m	1129.65
	10B 40 mm thick shutters	sq m	1212.95
11.	Providing and fixing panelled eucalyptus wood door shutter made of kiln seasoned eucalyptus wood and treated by ammoniacal copper arsenite treatment, as per FRI, Dehradun technology conforming to TADS 5 : 1994, manufactured in factories under controlled conditions by approved manufacturers, including black enamelled M.S. butt hinges with necessary screws as per directions of Engineer-in-charge and panelling with panels of.		
12.	12 mm thick plain Grade-1 medium density flat pressed, three layer and graded particle board (FPT-1) conforming to IS : 3087 bonded with BWP type synthetic resin adhesive as per IS : 848 :		
	12A 35 mm thick shutters	sq m	1164.05
	12B 40 mm thick shutters	sq m	1204.05
13.	12 mm thick prelaminated (with decorative lamination on both sides) particle board Grade-1, medium density flat pressed, three layer and graded particle board (FPT-1) conforming to IS : 3087 bonded with BWP type synthetic resin adhesive as per IS : 848 and prelamination conforming to IS : 12823 Grade-1, Type II :		
	13A 35 mm thick shutters	sq m	1850.40
	13B 40 mm thick shutters	sq m	2044.00
14.	12 mm thick prelaminated (with decorative lamination on one side and balancing lamination on other side) particle board Grade-1 medium density flat pressed, three layer and graded particle board (FPT-1) conforming to IS : 3087 bonded with BWP type synthetic resin adhesive as per IS : 848 and prelamination conforming to IS : 12823 Grade-1, Type II :		
	14A 35 mm thick shutters	sq m	1514.05
	14B 40 mm thick shutters	sq m	1624.05

S. No.		Description	Unit	Rate ₹
15.		Providing and fixing panelling or panelling and glazing in panelled or panelled and glazed shutters for doors, windows and clerestory windows (Area of opening for panel inserts excluding portion inside grooves or rebates to be measured). Panelling for panelled or panelled and glazed shutters 25 mm to 40 mm thick :		
	15A	Second class teak wood	sq m	772.15
	15B	First class deodar wood	sq m	718.65
	15C	Second class deodar wood	sq m	652.35
	15D	Kiln seasoned and chemically treated hollock wood	sq m	535.85

		Rate per sq m with		
		Commercial ply on both faces	Teak ply on both faces	Commercial ply on one face and teak ply on other face
		1	2	3
(1)	Ply wood 5 ply			
15E	9 mm thick		587.15	587.15
(2)	Ply wood 7 ply			
15F	9 mm thick			641.55
(3)	Ply wood 9 ply			
15G	12 mm thick	477.05	845.85	753.00

S. No.		Description	Unit	Rate ₹
	(4)	Particle Board 12 mm thick		
	15H	Plain particle board flat pressed, 3 layer and graded (medium density) grade I, conforming to IS : 3087	sq m	368.30
	15I	Veneered particle board with commercial veneering on both sides conforming to IS : 3097	sq m	450.55
	15J	Prelaminated particle board with decorative lamination on one side and balancing lamination on other side, grade I, Type II conforming to IS : 12823.	sq m	656.15
	15K	Prelaminated particle board with decorative lamination on both sides, Grade I, Type II conforming to IS : 12823.	sq m	742.40
16.		Providing and fixing glazed shutters for doors, windows and clerestory windows using 10 kg/square metre (4 mm thick) glass panes including black enamelled M.S. butt hinges with necessary screws :		

		Rate for thickness of shutters in mm per sq m		
		40	35	30
16A	Second class teak wood	1294.85	1199.00	1071.25
16B	First class deodar wood	1212.55	1124.45	1006.95
16C	Second class deodar wood	1110.50	1031.95	927.25
16D	Kiln seasoned and chemically treated hollock wood	908.95	849.55	770.35

(Contd.)

S. No.		Description	Unit	Rate ₹
17.		Providing and fixing glazed laminated veneer lumber shutter conforming to TADS 15 : 1995, manufactured in factories by approved manufacturers, using 10 kg/sq m glass panes for doors, windows and clerestory windows including black enamelled M.S. but hinges with necessary screws as per directions of Engineer-in-charge :		
	17A	40 mm thick shutters	sq m	996.30
	17B	35 mm thick shutters	sq m	913.00
	17C	30 mm thick shutters	sq m	824.10
18.		Providing and fixing glazed eucalyptus wood shutters made of kiln seasoned eucalyptus wood and treated by ammoniacal copper arsenite treatment, as per FRI Dehradun technology conforming to TADS 5 : 1994, manufactured in factories under controlled conditions by approved manufacturers using 10.0 kg/sq m (4 mm thick) glass panes for doors, windows and clerestory windows including black enamelled M.S. butt hinges with necessary screws as per directions of Engineer-in-charge :		
	18A	40 mm thick shutters	sq m	1164.05
	18B	35 mm thick shutters	sq m	1204.05
	18C	30 mm thick shutters	sq m	1244.05
19.		Extra for providing heavy sheet glass panes instead of ordinary glass in glazed doors, windows and clerestory window shutters. (Area of opening for glass panes excluding portion inside rebate shall be measured) :		
	19A	13.75 kg/sq m (5.5 mm thick) instead of 10 kg per sq m (4 mm thick)	sq m	83.35
20.		Extra for providing frosted glass panes 10 kg/sq m (4 mm thick) instead of ordinary glass panes 10 kg/sq m (4 mm thick) in doors, windows and clerestory window shutters. (Area of opening for glass panes excluding portion inside rebate shall be measured).	sq m	126.65
21.		Extra for providing pin headed glass panes instead of ordinary glass panes weighing 10 kg/sq m (4 mm thick) in doors, windows and clerestory windows, shutters (Area of opening for glass panes excluding portion inside rebate shall be measured).	sq m	171.10
22.		Extra for providing anodised aluminium butt hinges instead of black enemelled M.S. butt hinges with necessary screws. (Shutter area to be measured).	sq m	108.65
23.		Deduct if fixed shutters (without hinges) are provided instead of openable shutters for doors, windows or clerestory windows with :		
	23A	Anodised aluminium butt hinges with necessary screws :		
	23B	For IInd class teak wood and other inferior class of wood shutters	sq m	125.15
	23C	Black enamelled M.S. butt hinges with necessary screws.		
	23D	For IInd class teak wood and other inferior class of wood shutters.	sq m	16.50
24.		Providing and fixing 25 mm thick shutters for cup board etc. :		
	24A	Panelled or panelled and glazed shutters :		
	24B	Second class teak wood including anodised aluminium butt hinges with necessary screws.	sq m	958.15
	24C	Glazed shutters :		
	24D	IInd class teak wood including anodised aluminium butt hinges with necessary screws.	sq m	957.40

S. No.	Description	Unit	Rate ₹
25.	Providing and fixing 40 mm thick panelled, glazed or panelled and glazed partitions fixed to frames with iron screws etc. complete (Frames to be paid separately) :		
25A	Second class teak wood	sq m	1199.90
26.	Providing and fixing flat pressed 3 layer particle board (medium density) exterior grade (Grade I) conforming to IS : 3087 to frame, backing or studding with screws etc. complete (Frames, backing or studding to be paid separately) :		
26A	12 mm thick	sq m	254.15
26B	18 mm thick	sq m	324.70
27.	Providing and fixing prelaminated flat pressed 3 layer (medium density) particle board conforming to IS : 3087 with one side decorative and other side balancing lamination Grade I, Type II exterior grade conforming to IS : 12823 in shelves with screws and M.S. or aluminium brackets wherever required, edges to be painted with polyurethene primer (Brackets to be paid separately) :		
27A	18 mm thick	sq m	590.80
27B	25 mm thick	sq m	666.40
28.	Providing brackets fixed in 7.5 × 7.5 × 15 cm blocks of cement concrete 1 : 3 : 6 (1 cement : 3 coarse sand : 6 graded stone aggregate 20 mm nominal size) to support 20 cm wide shelves :		
28A	T or L iron 30 cm long of section 40 × 40 × 6 mm	each	24.85
28B	Aluminium T or L 30 cm long of section 40 × 40 × 4 mm	each	43.60
29.	Extra for using veneered particle exterior grade conforming to IS : 3097 board for fixing to frames, ceiling and shelves etc. :		
29A	Teak ply veneering on one face and commercial ply veneering on other	sq m	402.45
29B	Commercial ply veneering on both faces	sq m	74.65
30.	Providing and fixing 25 mm thick shutters for cupboards etc. including black enamelled M.S. butt hinges with necessary screws :		
30A	Panelled or panelled and glazed shutters-		
30B	Second class teak wood	sq m	905.60
30C	First class deodar wood	sq m	854.15
30D	Second class deodar wood	sq m	790.35
30E	Glazed shutters :		
30F	Second class teak wood	sq m	959.45
30G	First class deodar wood	sq m	904.15
30H	Second class deodar wood	sq m	835.60
31.	Providing and fixing flush door shutters decorative type, core of block board construction with frame of 1st class hard wood and well matched teak 3 ply veneering with vertical grains or cross bands and face veneers on both faces of shutters :		
31A	35 mm thick including anodised aluminium butt hinges with necessary screws.	sq m	1058.80
31B	30 mm thick including anodised aluminium butt hinges with necessary screws.	sq m	1019.90
31C	25 mm thick (for cupboard) including nickle plated bright finished M.S. Piano hinges with necessary screws.	sq m	902.45

S. No.	Description	Unit	Rate ₹
32.	**Providing and fixing flush door shutters non-decorative type, core of block board construction with frame of 1st class hard wood and well matched commercial 3 ply veneering with vertical grains or cross bands and face veneers on both faces of shutters :**		
	32A 35 mm thick including anodised aluminium butt hinges with necessary screws.	sq m	703.25
	32B 30 mm thick including anodised aluminium butt hinges with necessary screws.	sq m	681.05
	32C 25 mm thick (for cupboard) including nickel plated bright finished M.S. piano hinges with necessary screws.	sq m	569.15
33.	**Extra for providing and fixing flush doors with teak veneering :**		
	33A On one side in item no. 9.25	sq m	151.10
34.	**Extra for providing lipping with 2nd class teak wood battens 25 mm minimum depth on all edges of shutters (over all area of door shutter to be measured) Over item no. 9.24 and 9.25.**	sq m	111.10
35.	**Extra for providing vision panel not exceeding 0.1 sq m in all type of flush doors (Cost of glass excluded) (overall area of door shutter to be measured) :**		
	35A Rectangular or square	sq m	84.45
	35B Circular.	sq m	91.10
36.	**Extra if louvers (not exceeding 0.2 sq m) are provided in flush door shutters (overall area of door shutters to be measured) :**		
	36A Decorative type door.	sq m	166.65
37.	**Extra for cutting rebate in flush door shutters (Total area of the shutter to be measured).**	sq m	27.80
38.	**Providing and fixing kiln seasoned and chemically treated hollock wood shutters for semi-circular glazed fan lights including anodised aluminium butt hinges with necessary screws :**		
	38A 40 mm thick	sq m	769.30
39.	**Providing and fixing 40 mm thick louvered shutters with fixed venetians 12 mm thick for windows including bright finished or/and black enamelled M.S. butt hinges with necessary screws :**		
	39A Second class teak wood.	sq m	1353.40
	39B First class deodar wood.	sq m	1160.55
	39C Kiln seasoned and chemically treated Hollock wood	sq m	844.20
40.	**Providing and fixing 40 mm thick wire gauze shutters using galvanised M.S. wire gauze of average width of aperture 1.4 mm with wire of dia. 0.63 mm for doors, windows and clerestory windows including anodised aluminium butt hinges with necessary screws :**		
	40A Second class teak wood.	sq m	1264.55
	40B Kiln seasoned and chemically treated Hollock wood.	sq m	921.15
	40C First class deodar wood.	sq m	1246.15
	40D Second class deodar wood.	sq m	1114.65
41.	**Providing and fixing 40 mm thick wire gauze shutters using galvanised M.S. wire gauze of average width of aperture 1.4 mm with wire of dia. 0.63 mm for doors, windows and clerestory windows including bright finished or/and black enamelled M.S. butt hinges with necessary screws :**		

(Contd.)

S. No.	Description	Unit	Rate ₹
	41A Second class teak wood.	sq m	1201.80
	41B First class deodar wood.	sq m	1049.95
	41C Second class deodar wood.	sq m	959.05
	41D Kiln seasoned and chemically treated Hollock wood	sq m	779.80
42.	Providing and fixing 35 mm thick wire gauze shutters using galvanised M.S. wire gauze of average width of aperture 1.4 mm with wire of dia. 0.63 mm for doors, windows and clerestory windows including anodised aluminium butt hinges with necessary screws :		
	42A Second class teak wood.	sq m	1203.15
	42B Klin seasoned and chemically treated Hollock wood.	sq m	893.75
	42C First class deodar wood	sq m	1137.05
	42D Second class deodar wood	sq m	1055.10
43.	Providing and fixing 35 mm thick wire gauze shutters using galvanised M.S. wire gauze of average width of aperture 1.4 mm with wire of dia. 0.63 mm for doors, windows and clerestory windows including bright finished or/and black enamelled M.S. butt hinges with necessary screws :		
	43A Second class teak wood.	sq m	1094.55
	43B Kiln seasoned and chemically treated Hollock wood.	sq m	785.10
	43C First class deodar wood.	sq m	1028.45
	43D Second class deodar wood.	sq m	946.50
44.	Providing and fixing 30 mm thick wire gauge shutters using galvanised M.S. wire gauge of average width of aperture 1.4 mm with wire of dia. 0.63 mm for doors, windows and clerestory windows including anodised aluminium butt hinges with necessary screws :		
	44A Second class teak wood.	sq m	1019.75
	44B Kiln seasoned and chemically treated Hollock wood.	sq m	755.25
	44C First class deodar wood.	sq m	963.15
	44D Second class deodar wood.	sq m	893.00
45.	Providing and fixing 30 mm thick wire gauze shutters using galvanised M.S. wire gauze of average width of aperture 1.4 mm with wire of dia. 0.63 mm for doors, windows and clerestory windows including bright finished or/and black enamelled M.S. butt hinges with necessary screws :		
	45A Second class teak wood.	sq m	964.10
	45B First class deodar wood.	sq m	835.05
	45C Second class deodar wood.	sq m	764.90
	45D Kiln seasoned and chemically treated Hollock wood.	sq m	627.15
46.	Providing and fixing wire gauze laminated veneer lumber shutters conforming to TADS 15 :1995, manufactured in factories by approved manufacturers using galvanised wire gauze with average width of aperture 1.4 mm in both directions with wire of dia 0.63 mm as per IS : 1568 for doors, windows and clerestory windows including bright finished or/and black enamelled M.S. butt hinges with necessary screws as per directions of Engineer-in-charge :		
	46A 40 mm thick shutters	sq m	963.00
	46B 35 mm thick shutters	sq m	879.65
	46C 30 mm thick shutters	sq m	796.35

S. No.	Description	Unit	Rate ₹
47.	Providing and fixing wire gauze eucalyptus wood shutters made of kiln seasoned eucalyptus wood and treated by ammoniacal copper arsenite treatment, as per FRI, Dehradun technology conforming to TADS 5 : 1994, manufactured in factories under controlled conditions by approved manufacturers using galvanised M.S. wire gauze with average width of aperture 1.4 mm in both directions with wire of dia. 0.63 mm conforming to IS : 1568 for doors, windows and clerestory windows including bright finished or/and black enamelled M.S. butt hinges with necessary screws as per directions of Engineer-in-charge :		
	47A 40 mm thick shutters	sq m	1114.10
	47B 36 mm thick shutters	sq m	1134.05
	47C 30 mm thick shutters	sq m	1154.05
	B. MISCELLANEOUS-WOOD WORK		
48.	Providing 50 × 50 × 50 mm 2nd class teak wood plugs including cutting brick work and fixing in cement mortar 1 : 3 (1 cement : 3 fine sand) and making good the walls etc.	each	6.70
49.	Providing and fixing expandable fastners of specified size with necessary plastic sleeves and galvanised M.S. screws including drilling holes in masonry work/CC/R.C.C. and making good etc. complete :		
	49A 25 mm long	each	6.80
	49B 32 mm long	each	7.70
	49C 40 mm long	each	9.35
	49D 50 mm long	each	9.35
50.	Providing and fixing 2nd class teak wood plain lining tongued and grooved on and including wooden plugs complete with necessary screws and priming coat on unexposed surface :		
	50A 40 mm thick.	sq m	1850.45
	50B 25 mm thick.	sq m	1189.60
51.	Providing and fixing 20 mm thick plain lining tongued and grooved on and including wooden plugs complete with necessary screws and priming coat on unexposed surface with :		
	51A Second class teak wood	sq m	960.35
	51B First class deodar wood	sq m	867.80
52.	Providing and fixing 12 mm thick plain lining tongued and grooved on and including wooden plugs complete with necessary screws and priming coat on unexposed surface with :		
	52A Second class teak wood.	sq m	607.90
	52B First class deodar wood.	sq m	549.55
53.	Providing and fixing in wall lining flat pressed three layer & graded (medium density) particle board prelaminated one side decorative lamination on other side balancing lamination grade I, Type II conforming to IS 12823 including priming coat on unexposed surface, with necessary fixing arrangement and screws etc. complete :		
	53A 12 mm thick	sq m	578.85
	53B 18 mm thick	sq m	658.30
	53C 25 mm thick	sq m	736.50

(Contd.)

S. No.	Description	Unit	Rate ₹
54.	Providing and fixing specified wood frame work consisting of battens 50 × 25 mm fixed with rawl plug and drilling necessary holes for rawl plug etc. including priming coat complete :		
	54A Hollock wood.	cum	29460.00
55.	Providing and fixing 4 mm thick plywood plain lining with necessary screws, priming coat on unexposed surface etc. complete with :		
	55A Teak ply facings of approved manufacture.	sq m	417.50
	55B Commercial ply facings of approved manufacture.	sq m	284.20
56.	Providing and fixing 40 mm thick 2nd class teak wood plain panelling with skirting chair rails, and cornice with necessary screws priming coat on unexposed surface etc. complete :	sq m	2006.35
57.	Providing and fixing skirting of prelaminated with (one side decorative and other side balancing lamination) flat pressed, 3 layer and graded particle board (medium density) Grade I, Type II conforming to IS : 12823, with necessary fixing arrangements and screws including drilling necessary holes for rawl plugs etc. and priming coat on unexposed surface complete :		
	57A 18 mm thick	sq m	636.80
	57B 25 mm thick	sq m	715.05
58.	Providing and fixing wooden moulded beading to door and window frames with iron screws, plugs and priming coat on unexposed surface etc. complete :		
	58A 2nd class teak wood		
	58B 50 × 12 mm	metre	37.75
	58C 50 × 20 mm	metre	40.15
	58D Hollock wood		
	58E 50 × 12 mm	metre	28.80
	58F 50 × 20 mm	metre	38.20
59.	Providing and fixing plain jaffri of 35 × 10 mm laths placed 35 mm apart (frames to be paid separately) including fixing 50 × 12 mm beading complete with :		
	59A Second class teak wood.	sq m	620.15
	59B First class deodar wood.	sq m	579.75
60.	Providing and fixing 18 mm thick, 150 mm wide pelmet of flat pressed 3 layer & graded particle board (medium density) Grade I conforming to IS : 3087) including top cover of 6 mm commercial ply wood, nickel plated M.S. pipe 20 mm dia (heavy type) curtain rod with nickel plated brackets including fixing with 25 × 3 mm M.S. flat 10 cm long and raw plugs 50 mm long (designation 10 no.) etc. all complete.	metre	140.85
61.	Extra for using veneered particle board in item of pelmet 18 mm thick 150 mm wide :		
	61A Commercial veneering on both sides.	metre	11.40
	61B Particle board with teak veneering on both sides.	metre	61.35
	61C Prelaminated particle board with decorative lamination on one side and balancing lamination on the other side, Grade I, Type II conforming to IS : 12823	metre	38.55
62.	Providing and fixing teak wood lipping of size 25 × 3 mm in pelmet.	metre	10.95

S. No.	Description	Unit	Rate ₹
63.	**Providing and fixing curtain rods of 1.25 mm thick chromium plated brass plate, with two chromium plated brass brackets fixed with CP. brass screws and wooden plugs, etc., wherever necessary complete :**		
63A	12 mm dia.	metre	113.05
63B	20 mm dia.	metre	157.45
63C	25 mm dia.	metre	200.80
64.	**Providing and fixing nickel plated M.S. pipe curtain rods with nickel plated brackets :**		
64A	20 mm dia (heavy type)	metre	8.35
64B	25 mm dia (heavy type)	metre	9.00
65.	**Providing and fixing M.S. grills of required pattern in frames of windows etc. with M.S. flats, square or round bars etc. all complete :**		
65A	Fixed to steel windows by welding	kg.	29.10
65B	Fixed to openings/wooden frames with rawl plugs screws etc.	kg.	33.05
66.	**Providing and fixing expanded metal 20 × 60 mm strands 3.25 mm wide and 1.6 mm thick for windows etc. including 62 × 19 mm beading of 2nd class teak wood.**	sq m	300.80
67.	**Providing and fixing hard drawn steel wire fabric 75 × 25 mm mesh of weight not less than 7.75 kg per sq m to window frames etc. including 62 × 19 mm beading of second class teak wood.**	sq m	358.95
68.	**Providing and fixing fly proof galvanised M.S. wire gauze to windows and clerestory windows using galvanised M.S. wire gage with average width of aperture 1.4 mm in both directions with wire of dia. 0.63 mm :**		
68A	With 2nd class teak wood beading 62 × 19 mm	sq m	329.65
68B	With 12 mm mild steel U beading.	sq m	202.50
69.	**Deduct for fixing 75 × 25 mm hard drawn steel wire fabric of weight not less than 7.75 kg. per sq m in panelled and glazed door and window shutter instead of glass sheet 10 Kg./sq m (4 mm thick).**	sq m	27.80
70.	**Providing 40 × 5 mm flat iron hold fast 40 cm long including fixing to frame with 10 mm diameter bolts, nuts and wooden plugs and embeddings in cement concrete block 30 × 10 × 15 cm 1 : 3 : 6 mix (1 cement : 3 coarse sand : 6 graded stone aggregate 20 mm nominal size).**	each	31.20
71.	**Providing beams including hoisting, fixing in position and applying wood preservative for the unexposed surfaces, etc. complete with :**		
71A	Sal wood	cum	21480.00
71B	Hollock wood	cum	20350.00
	C. BRIGHT FINISHED M.S. FITTINGS		
72.	**Providing and fixing M.S. pressed butt hinges bright finished with necessary screws etc. complete :**		
72A	125 × 65 × 2.12 mm	each	11.55
72B	100 × 58 × 1.90 mm	each	7.55
72C	75 × 47 × 1.70 mm	each	5.05
72D	50 × 37 × 1.50 mm	each	2.75
73.	**Providing and fixing M.S. pressed parliamentary hinges bright finished with necessary screws etc. complete :**		
73A	150 × 125 × 27 × 2.80 mm	each	20.45
73B	125 × 125 × 27 × 2.80 mm	each	18.20

(Contd.)

S. No.	Description	Unit	Rate ₹
	73C 100 × 125 × 27 × 2.80 mm	each	13.75
	73D 75 × 100 × 20 × 2.24 mm	each	11.30
74.	**Providing and fixing M.S. single acting spring hinges bright finished with necessary screws etc. complete :**		
	74A 150 mm	each	57.75
	74B 125 mm	each	52.20
	74C 100 mm	each	45.90
75.	**Providing and fixing M.S. double acting spring hinges bright finished with necessary screws etc. complete :**		
	75A 150 mm	each	63.30
	75B 125 mm	each	53.30
	75C 100 mm	each	35.90
76.	**Providing 1 mm thick M.S. Piano hinges finished with nickel plating and fixing with necessary screws :**		
	76A Overall width 35 mm	metre	39.80
	76B Overall width 50 mm	metre	42.05
	76C Overall width 65 mm	metre	44.25
77.	**Providing and fixing M.S. sliding door bolts bright finished or/and black enamelled, with nuts and screws etc. complete :**		
	77A 300 × 16 mm	each	41.10
	77B 250 × 16 mm	each	38.90
78.	**Providing and fixing M.S. tower bolts (barrel type) with necessary screws, etc. complete :**		
	78A Bright satin finished black stove enamelled		
	78B 250 × 10 mm	each	22.65
	78C 200 × 10 mm	each	22.30
	78D 150 × 10 mm	each	19.60
	78E 100 × 10 mm	each	15.15
	78F Copper oxidised (black finish)		
	78G 250 × 10 mm	each	124.90
	78H 200 × 10 mm	each	80.10
	78I 150 × 10 mm	each	77.40
	78J 100 × 10 mm	each	46.25
79.	**Providing and fixing mild steel bright polished nickel plated pull bolt lock conforming to IS : 7534 with necessary nuts and screws etc. complete 85 mm × 42 mm.**	each	30.65
80.	**Providing and fixing M.S. handles conforming to IS : 208 with necessary screws etc. complete:**		
	80A 125 mm	each	5.65
	80B 100 mm	each	4.50
	80C 75 mm	each	3.40
81.	**Providing and fixing M.S. hooks and eyes conforming to IS : 207 :**		
	81A 300 mm	each	6.20
	81B 250 mm	each	5.10
	81C 200 mm	each	4.55
	81D 150 mm	each	3.45
	81E 100 mm	each	2.65

S. No.	Description	Unit	Rate ₹
82.	Providing and fixing M.S. fan light pivots with necessary screws etc. complete.	each	4.35
83.	Providing and fixing M.S. fan light catch with necessary screws etc. complete.	each	4.55
84.	Providing and fixing 300 mm long M.S. chain with hooks for fan light including necessary screws etc. complete.	each	4.85
85.	Providing and fixing M.S. safety hasp and staple conforming to IS : 363 with necessary screws etc. complete :		
85A	150 mm	each	6.00
85B	115 mm	each	5.25
85C	90 mm	each	4.60
86.	Providing and fixing bright finished or/and black enamelled M.S. helical door spring.	each	35.60
87.	Providing and fixing. M.S. handles for steel windows :		
87A	100 mm size weighing not less than 80 gms	each	8.15
87B	150 mm size weighing not less than 100 gms	each	9.25
	D. OXIDISED MILD STEEL FITTINGS		
88.	Providing and fixing oxidised M.S. pressed butt hinges with necessary screws etc. complete :		
88A	125 × 65 × 2.12 mm	each	12.70
88B	100 × 58 × 1.90 mm	each	8.60
88C	75 × 47 × 1.70 mm	each	5.30
88D	50 × 37 × 1.50 mm	each	3.05
89.	Providing and fixing oxidised M.S. pressed parliamentary hinges with necessary screws etc. complete :		
89A	150 × 125 × 27 × 2.80 mm	each	27.60
89B	125 × 125 × 27 × 2.80 mm	each	22.75
89C	100 × 125 × 27 × 2.80 mm	each	19.05
89D	75 × 100 × 20 × 2.24 mm	each	14.40
90.	Providing and fixing oxidised M.S. single acting spring hinges with necessary screws etc. complete :		
90A	150 mm	each	69.05
90B	125 mm	each	63.45
90C	100 mm	each	46.55
91.	Providing and fixing oxidised M.S. double acting spring hinges with necessary screws etc. complete :		
91A	150 mm	each	69.05
91B	125 mm	each	57.90
91C	100 mm	each	41.00
92.	Providing M.S. Piano hinges, finished with brass plating and fixing with necessary screws etc. complete :		
92A	Overall width 35 mm	metre	49.35
92B	Overall width 50 mm	metre	51.60
92C	Overall width 65 mm	metre	53.80
93.	Providing M.S. Piano hinges finished with nickel plating and fixing with necessary screws etc. complete :		

(*Contd.*)

S. No.	Description	Unit	Rate ₹
	93A Overall width 35 mm	metre	40.15
	93B Overall width 50 mm	metre	42.35
	93C Overall width 65 mm	metre	44.60
94.	Providing and fixing oxidised M.S. Tee hinges with necessary screws etc. complete :		
	94A 300 × 115 × 2.24 mm	each	16.70
	94B 250 × 110 × 2.24 mm	each	15.85
95.	Providing and fixing oxidised M.S. sliding door bolts with nuts and screws etc. complete :		
	95A 300 × 16 mm	each	42.75
	95B 250 × 16 mm	each	38.90
96.	Providing and fixing oxidised M.S. tower bolt black finish, (Barrel type) with necessary screws etc. complete :		
	96A 250 × 10 mm	each	19.10
	96B 200 × 10 mm	each	15.75
	96C 150 × 10 mm	each	12.10
	96D 100 × 10 mm	each	8.55
97.	Providing and fixing 85 mm × 42 mm oxidised M.S. pull bolt lock conforming to IS : 7534 with necessary screws bolts, nut and washers etc. complete.	each	24.00
98.	Providing and fixing oxidised M.S. door latches conforming to IS : 5930 with screws etc. complete :		
	98A 300 × 20 × 6 mm	each	19.20
	98B 250 × 20 × 6 mm	each	19.20
99.	Providing and fixing oxidised M.S. handles conforming to IS : 4992 with necessary screws etc. complete :		
	99A 125 mm	each	4.60
	99B 100 mm	each	3.40
	99C 75 mm	each	2.30
100.	Providing and fixing oxidised M.S. fan light pivot with necessary screws etc. complete.	each	6.30
101.	Providing and fixing oxidised M.S. fan light catch with necessary screws etc. complete.	each	4.95
102.	Providing and fixing 300 mm long oxidised M.S. chain with hook for fan light including necessary screws etc. complete.	each	6.00
103.	Providing and fixing oxidised M.S. hasp and staple (Safety type) conforming to IS : 363 with necessary screws etc. complete :		
	103A 150 mm	each	6.55
	103B 115 mm	each	5.65
	103C 90 mm	each	5.10
104.	Providing and fixing oxidised M.S. casement stays (straight peg type) with necessary screws etc. complete :		
	104A 300 mm weighing not less than 200 gms	each	11.70
	104B 250 mm weighing not less than 150 gms	each	11.00
	104C 200 mm weighing not less than 120 gms	each	10.45
105.	Providing and fixing oxidised M.S. Safety chain with necessary fixtures for doors. (Weighing not less than 450 gms)	each	25.10

S. No.	Description	Unit	Rate ₹
	E. BRASS FITTINGS		
106.	**Providing and fixing bright finished brass butt hinges with necessary screws etc. complete :**		
	106A 125 × 85 × 5.5 mm (heavy type)	each	143.20
	106B 125 × 70 × 4 mm (ordinary type)	each	52.10
	106C 100 × 85 × 5.5 mm (heavy type)	each	120.35
	106D 100 × 70 × 4 mm (ordinary type)	each	34.80
	106E 75 × 65 × 4 mm (heavy type)	each	43.70
	106F 75 × 40 × 2.5 mm (ordinary type)	each	18.70
	106G 50 × 40 × 2.5 mm (ordinary type)	each	8.55
107.	**Providing and fixing bright finished brass parliamentary hinges with necessary screws etc. complete :**		
	107A 150 × 125 × 27 × 5 mm	each	153.10
	107B 125 × 125 × 27 × 5 mm	each	131.65
	107C 100 × 125 × 27 × 5 mm	each	110.30
	107D 75 × 100 × 20 × 3.2 mm	each	82.75
108.	**Providing and fixing bright finished brass tower bolts (barrel type) with necessary screws etc. complete :**		
	108A 250 × 10 mm	each	116.50
	108B 200 × 10 mm	each	93.60
	108C 150 × 10 mm	each	72.50
	108D 100 × 10 mm	each	48.60
109.	**Providing and fixing bright finished brass door latch with necessary screws etc. complete :**		
	109A 300 × 16 × 5 mm	each	69.20
	109B 250 × 16 × 5 mm	each	64.75
110.	**Providing and fixing bright finished brass 100 mm nortice latch and lock with 6 levers and a pair of lever handles with necessary screws etc. complete (best make of approved quality).**	each	256.30
111.	**Providing and fixing bright finished brass 100 mm mortice latch with one dead bolt and a pair of lever handles with necessary screws etc. complete (best make of approved quality).**	each	222.95
112.	**Providing and fixing bright finished brass night latch including necessary screws etc. complete (best make of approved quality).**	each	300.75
113.	**Providing and fixing special quality bright finished brass cupboard or wardrobe locks with four levers including necessary screws etc. complete (best make of approved quality) :**		
	113A 40 mm	each	47.45
	113B 50 mm	each	56.30
	113C 65 mm	each	65.20
	113D 75 mm	each	73.00
114.	**Providing and fixing 50 mm bright finished brass cup board or wardrobe knob with necessary screws (best make of approved quality).**	each	16.30
115.	**Providing and fixing bright finished brass handles with screws etc. complete :**		
	115A 125 mm	each	75.00
	115B 100 mm	each	63.75
	115C 75 mm	each	47.10

(Contd.)

S. No.	Description	Unit	Rate ₹
116.	**Providing and fixing bright finished brass hanging type floor door stoper with necessary screws, etc. complete.**	each	29.25
117.	**Providing and fixing bright finished brass hydraulic door closer (Best make of approved quality) with necessary accessories and screws etc. complete.**	each	317.30
118.	**Providing and fixing bright finished brass hydraulic door closer of approved quality with accessories and screws etc. complete :**		
	118A Sleek design type	each	541.55
	118B Hidden type	each	749.30
119.	**Providing and fixing bright finished brass casement window fastener with necessary screws etc. complete.**	each	27.60
120.	**Providing and fixing bright finished brass casement stays (straight peg type) with necessary screws etc. complete :**		
	120A 300 mm weighing not less than 330 gms	each	57.95
	120B 250 mm weighing not less than 280 gms	each	49.80
	120C 200 mm weighing not less than 240 gms	each	43.15
121.	**Providing and fixing bright finished brass fan light catch with necessary screws etc. complete.**	each	15.10
122.	**Providing and fixing bright finished brass hasp and staple (safety type) with necessary screws etc. complete :**		
	122A 150 mm	each	47.60
	122B 115 mm	each	38.95
	122C 90 mm	each	31.75
	F. CHROMIUM PLATED BRASS FITTINGS		
123.	**Providing and fixing chromium plated brass 100 mm mortice latch and lock with 6 levers and a pair of lever handles with necessary screws etc. complete (best make of approved quality).**	each	289.65
124.	**Providing and fixing chromium plated brass night latch including necessary screws etc. complete (Best make of approved quality).**	each	339.65
125.	**Providing and fixing special quality chromium plated brass cupboard locks with six levers including necessary screws etc. complete (Best make of approved quality) of :**		
	125A Size 40 mm	each	50.75
	125B Size 50 mm	each	60.75
	125C Size 65 mm	each	70.75
	125D Size 75 mm	each	78.55
126.	**Providing and fixing chromium plated brass 50 mm cupboard or wardrobe knobs with nuts complete.**	each	24.10
127.	**Providing and fixing chromium plated brass handles with necessary screws etc. complete :**		
	127A 125 mm	each	83.40
	127B 100 mm	each	66.65
	127C 75 mm	each	57.75
128.	**Providing and fixing chromium plated brass casement window fastener with necessary screws etc. complete.**	each	49.35

S. No.		Description	Unit	Rate ₹
129.		Providing and fixing chromium plated brass casement stays (straight peg type) with necessary screws etc. complete :		
	129A	300 mm weighing not less than 330 gms	each	68.25
	129B	250 mm weighing not less than 280 gms	each	61.60
	129C	200 mm weighing not less than 240 gms	each	50.45
		G. ANODISED ALUMINIUM FITTINGS		
130.		Providing and fixing aluminium butt hinges anodised (anodic coating not less than grade AC 10 as per IS : 1868) transparent or dyed to required colour or shade with necessary screws etc. complete :		
	130A	125 × 75 × 4 mm	each	55.35
	130B	125 × 63 × 4 mm	each	53.15
	130C	100 × 75 × 4 mm	each	45.05
	130D	100 × 63 × 4 mm	each	45.05
	130E	100 × 63 × 3.2 mm	each	43.95
	130F	75 × 63 × 4 mm	each	30.20
	130G	75 × 63 × 3.2 mm	each	24.75
	130H	75 × 45 × 3.2 mm	each	15.40
	130I	50 × 45 × 3.2 mm	each	8.60
131.		Providing and fixing aluminium sliding door bolts anodised (anodic coating not less than grade AC 10 as per IS : 1868) transparent or dyed to required colour or shade with nuts and screws etc. complete :		
	131A	300 × 16 mm	each	103.40
	131B	250 × 16 mm	each	100.10
132.		Providing and fixing aluminium tower bolts anodised (anodic coating not less than grade AC 10 as per IS : 1868) transparent or dyed to required colour or shade with necessary screws etc. complete :		
	132A	300 × 10 mm	each	45.05
	132B	250 × 10 mm	each	41.25
	132C	200 × 10 mm	each	37.70
	132D	150 × 10 mm	each	29.70
	132E	100 × 10 mm	each	23.40
133.		Providing and fixing aluminium pull bolt lock anodised (anodic coating not less than grade AC 10 as per IS : 1868) transparent or dyed to required colour and shade with necessary screws etc. complete.	each	25.10
134.		Providing and fixing 50 cm long aluminium kicking plate 100 × 3.15 mm anodised (anodic coating not less than grade AC 10 as per IS : 1868) transparent or dyed to required colour or shade with necessary screws etc. complete.	each	92.95
135.		Providing and fixing aluminium handles anodised (anodic coating not less than grade AC 10 as per IS : 1868) transparent or dyed to required colour or shade with necessary screws etc. complete :		
	135A	125 mm	each	33.45
	135B	100 mm	each	22.70
	135C	75 mm	each	20.20

(Contd.)

S. No.	Description	Unit	Rate ₹
136.	Providing and fixing aluminium hanging floor door stopper anodised (anodic coating not less than grade AC 10 as per IS : 1868) transparent or dyed to required colour and shade with necessary screws etc. complete :		
	136A Single rubber stopper	each	12.90
	136B Twin rubber stopper	each	42.35
137.	Providing and fixing aluminium casement stays anodised (anodic coating not less than grade AC 10 as per IS : 1868) transparent or dyed to required colour and shade with necessary screws etc. complete.	each	37.15
138.	Providing and fixing bright finished brass 100 mm mortice latch and lock with six levers and a pair of anodised (anodic coating not less than grade AC 10 as per IS : 1868) aluminium lever handles with necessary screws etc. complete (Best make of approved quality).	each	326.30
139.	Providing and fixing aluminium tee chanals (heavy duty) with rollers, stop end in pelmets as curtain rod.	metre	23.50
	H. GYPSUM BOARD PARTITIONS		
140.	Providing and fixing partition upto 2.40 m height having composite thickness of 67 mm consisting of frame and double skin 8.5 mm thick Glass Reinforced Gypsum (GRG) board manufactured by spray suction technique with high strength plaster of paris conforming to IS : 8272 and glass fibre of E-glass or A-glass or N-glass in the form of rovings, not less than 2.5% by weight of plaster of paris and conforming to IS : 11320 including providing and fixing of frame work made of special section power pressed from MS sheet and galvanised with Zinc coating of Grade 175 and consisting of floor and ceiling channel 50 mm wide having equal flanges of 32 mm width 0.50 mm thick fixed to floor/ceiling at the spacing of 610 mm centre to centre with dash fastner of 12.5 mm dia. meter 40 mm length and the studs 48 mm wide having one flange of 34 mm and other flange 36 mm and 0.50 mm thick fixed vertically within flanges of floor and ceiling channel and placed at a spacing of 610 mm centre to centre by 6 mm dia bolts and nuts at both ends of partition fixed flush to wall with rawl plugs at the spacing of 450 mm centre to centre and fixing of GRG boards to either side of frame work by 20 mm long drive all screws on studs, floors and ceiling channels at the spacing of 300 mm centre to centre, including jointing and finishing to a flush finish with recommended joint filler, joint paper tape and joint finisher and two coats of primer suitable for GRG board as per manufacturers specifications all complete.	sq m	747.45
141.	Providing and fixing partition above 2.40 m height having composite thickness of 89 mm consisting of frame and double skin 8.5 mm thick Glass Reinforced Gypsum (GRG) board manufactured by spray suction technique with high strength plaster of paris conforming to IS : 8272 and glass fibre of E-glass or A-glass or N-glass in the form of rovings, not less than 2.5% by weight of plaster of paris and conforming to IS : 11320 including providing and fixing frame work made of special section power pressed from MS sheet and galvanised with Zinc coating of Grade 175 and consisting of floor and ceiling channel 72 mm wide having equal flanges of 32 mm width 0.50 mm thick fixed to floor/ceiling at the spacing of 610 mm centre to centre with dash fastner of 12.5 mm dia. meter 40 mm length and the studs 70 mm wide having one flange of 34 mm and other flange 36 mm and		

S. No.	Description	Unit	Rate ₹
	0.50 mm thick fixed vertically within flanges of floor and ceiling channel and placed at a spacing of 610 mm centre to centre by 6 mm dia bolts and nuts and studs at both ends of partition fixed flush to wall with rawl plugs at the spacing of 450 mm centre to centre and fixing of GRG boards to either side of frame work by 20 mm long drive all screws on studs, floors and ceiling channels at the spacing of 300 mm centre to centre, including jointing and finishing to a flush finish with recommended joint filler, joint paper tape and joint finisher and two coats of primer suitable for GRG board as per manufacturers specifications all complete.	sq m	1478.50

Table 13.9. STEEL WORK

S. No.	Description	Unit	Rate ₹
1.	Structural steel work in single section fixed without connecting plate including cutting, hoisting, fixing in position and applying a priming coat of approved steel primer all complete.	kilogram	19.67
2.	Structural steel work in single section fixed with connecting plate including cutting, hoisting, fixing in position and applying a priming coat of approved steel primer all complete.	kilogram	19.54
3.	Structural steel work riveted or bolted in built up sections, trusses and framed work, including cutting, hoisting, fixing in position and applying a priming coat of approved steel primer all complete.	kilogram	20.60
4.	Structural steel work welded in built up sections, trusses and framed work including cutting, hoisting, fixing in position and applying a priming coat of approved steel primer all complete.	kilogram	21.45
5.	Providing and fixing in position collapsible steel shutters with vertical channels 20 × 10 × 2 mm and braced with flat iron diagonals 20 × 5 mm size with top and bottom rail of T-iron 40 × 40 × 6 mm with 40 mm dia. steel pulleys complete with bolts, nuts, locking arrangement, stoppers, handles, including applying a priming coat of approved steel primer.	sq m	1374.40
6.	Providing and fixing 1 mm thick M.S. sheet sliding-shutters with frame and diagonal braces of 40 × 40 × 6 mm angle iron, 3 mm M.S. gusset plates at the junction and corners 25 mm dia pulley, 40 × 40 × 6 mm angle and T-iron guide at the top and bottom respectively including applying a priming coat of approved steel primer.	sq m	1011.40
7.	Providing and fixing 1 mm thick M.S. sheet door with frame of 40 × 40 × 6 mm angle iron and 3 mm M.S. gusset plates at the junctions and corners, all necessary fittings complete, including applying a priming coat of approved steel primer :		
	7A Using M.S. angles 40 × 40 × 6 mm for diagonal braces	sq m	873.50
	7B Using flats 30 × 6 mm for diagonal braces and central cross piece.	sq m	832.55

(Contd.)

S. No.	Description	Unit	Rate ₹
8.	Supplying and fixing rolling shutters of approved make, made of required size M.S. laths interlocked together through their entire length and jointed together at the end by end locks mounted on specially designed pipe shaft with brackets, side guides and arrangements for inside and outside locking with push and pull operation complete including the cost of providing and fixing necessary 27.5 cm long wire springs grade No. 2 and M.S. top cover of required thickness for rolling shutters :		
	8A 80 × 1.25 mm M.S. laths with 1.25 mm thick top cover	sq m	691.95
	8B 80 × 1.20 mm M.S. laths with 1.20 mm thick top cover	sq m	562.55
	8C 80 × 0.90 mm M.S. laths with 0.90 mm thick top cover	sq m	516.05
9.	Providing and fixing ball bearing for rolling shutters.	each	155.20
10.	Extra for providing mechanical device chain and crank operation for operating rolling shutters :		
	10A Exceeding 10.00 sq m and upto 16.80 sq m in the area	sq m	202.60
	10B Exceeding 16.80 sq m in area	sq m	208.20
11.	Extra for providing grilled rolling shutters manufactured out of 8 mm dia. M.S. bar instead of laths as per design approved by Engineer-in-Charge. (area of grill to be measured.)	sq m	111.10
12.	Fixing standard steel glazed doors, windows and ventilators in walls with 15 × 3 mm lugs 10 cm long embedded in cement concrete blocks 15 × 10 × 10 cm of 1 : 3 : 6 (1 cement: 3 coarse sand : 6 graded stone aggregate 20 mm nominal size) or with wooden plugs and screws or rawl plugs and screws or with fixing clips or with bolts and nuts as required, including fixing of glass panes with glazing clips and special metal-sash putty of approved make, or metal beading with screws (only steel windows with lugs, glass panes cut to size and glazing clips or metal beading with screws, shall be supplied by department free of cost.)	sq m	123.50
13.	Providing and fixing steel glazed doors, windows and ventilators of standard rolled steel sections, joints mitred and welded with 15 × 3 mm lugs, 10 cm long, embedded in cement concrete blocks 15 × 10 × 10 cm of 1 : 3 : 6 (1 cement : 3 coarse sand : 6 graded stone aggregate 20 mm nominal size) or with wooden plugs and screws or rawl plugs and screws or with fixing clips or with bolts and nuts as required, including providing and fixing of glass panes with glazing clips and special metal sash putty of approved make complete including applying a priming coat of approved steel primer; excluding the cost of metal beading and other fitting except necessary hinges or pivots as required :		
	13A Doors	sq m	941.40
	13B Windows fixed	sq m	599.90
	13C Windows-side hung	sq m	888.75
	13D Ventilators-top hung	sq m	888.75
	13E Ventilators-centre hung	sq m	888.75
	(1) In composite units of doors, windows and ventilators		
	13F For overall portion treated as fixed.	sq m	599.90
	(2) Extra for side hung portion		

S. No.		*Description*	*Unit*	*Rate* ₹
	13G	Doors	sq m	338.55
	13H	Windows	sq m	288.85
	13I	Extra for top hung portion	sq m	288.85
	13J	Extra for centre hung portion	sq m	288.85
	13K	Extra for providing Vertical Coupling Mullion bar or Horizontal coupling Mullion bar (when openable windows are to be coupled above fixed ones or between two fixed windows) or Horizontal Coupling Mullion bar (where windows are not exposed to weather) (K-11B).	metre	39.60
	13L	Extra for providing Horizontal Coupling Mullion Bar or Weather Bar (Especially used when the coupled unit is exposed to rain) (K-12B)	metre	50.65
14.		Extra for providing and fixing steel beading of approved shape and section with screws instead of glazing clips and metal sash putty in steel doors, windows, ventilators and composite units.	metre	12.50
15.		Providing and fixing T-iron frames for doors, windows and ventilators of mild steel Tee-sections, joints mitred and welded with 15 × 3 mm lugs 10 cm long embedded in cement concrete blocks 15 × 10 × 10 cm of 1 : 3 : 6 (1 cement: 3 coarse sand : 6 graded stone aggregate 20 mm nominal size) or with wooden plugs and screws or rawl plugs and screws or with fixing clips or with bolts and nuts as require including fixing of necessary butt hinges and screws and applying a priming coat of approved steel primer.	kilogram	24.50
16.		Providing and fixing pressed steel door frames manufactured from commercial mild steel sheet of 1.25 mm thickness including hinges jamb, lock jamb, bead and if required angle threshold of mild steel angle of section 50 × 25 mm, or base ties of 1.25 mm pressed mild steel welded or rigidly fixed together by mechanical means, adjustable lugs with split end tail to each jamb including steel butt hinges 2.5 m thick with mortar guards, lock strike-plate and shock absorbers as specified and applying a coat of approved steel primer after pretreatment of the surface as directed by Engineer-in-charge :		
	16A	Profile A	metre	120.85
	16B	Profile B	metre	131.90
	16C	Profile C	metre	148.60
17.		Steel work in built up tubular trusses including cutting, hoisting, fixing in position and applying a priming coat of approved steel primer, welded and bolted including special shaped washers etc. complete :		
	17A	Hot finished welded type tubes	kilogram	35.25
	17B	Hot finished seamless type tubes	kilogram	45.75
	17C	Electric resistance or induction butt welded tubes.	kilogram	41.10
18.		Providing and fixing 20 × 6 mm mild steel 15 cm long clamps for securing chick tops.	each	18.75
19.		Providing and fixing mild-steel rings of 6 mm round bar and 40 mm internal dia for fastening ropes of chicks.	each	13.20
20.		Providing and fixing M.S. fan clamp type I of 16 mm dia M.S. bar bent to shape with hooked ends in R.C.C. slabs during laying including painting the exposed portion of loop, all as per standard design complete.	each	35.00

(Contd.)

S. No.	Description	Unit	Rate ₹
21.	Extra over rate of item No. 10.19 for providing and fixing M.S. fan clamp type II as per design in R.C.C. beams during laying towards the additional height of the clamp due to beam rib.	cm height	0.55
22.	Providing and fixing circular cast iron box for ceiling fan clamp 140 mm internal dia., 73 mm height, 5 mm thick rim, bottom and top lid of 1.5 mm thick M.S. sheet with its top surface hacked for proper bonding top lid shall be screwed into the cast iron box by means of 3.3 mm dia. round headed screws, one lock at the corners. Clamp shall be made of 12 mm dia M.S. bar bent to shape as per standard drawing.	each	43.45
23.	Providing and fixing circular/hexagonal M.S. sheet ceiling fan box with clamp of internal dia 140 mm, 73 mm height, 3 mm thick rim, top and bottom lid of 1.5 mm M.S. sheet. Lids shall be screwed into M.S. box by means of 3 mm round headed screws, clamps shall be made of 12 mm dia M.S. bar bent to shape as per standard drawing with over all length as 80 cm.	each	35.70
24.	Providing and fixing M.S. round holding down bolts with nuts and washer plates complete.	kilogram	31.00
25.	Providing and fixing bolts upto 300 mm in length including nuts and washers complete.	kilogram	38.00
26.	Providing and fixing bolts above 300 mm in length including nuts and washers complete.	kilogram	38.00
27.	Providing and fixing M.S. rivets of sizes in position.	kilogram	41.75
28.	Welding by gas plant including transportation of gas welding plant at site etc. complete.	cm length	0.85
29.	Welding by electric plant including transportation of electric welding plant at site etc. complete.	cm length	0.70
30.	Providing and fixing bright finished brass casement window fasteners of minimum weight 200 grams to side hung steel windows with necessary welding and machine screws etc. complete.	each	32.30
31.	Providing and fixing bright finished brass peg stays 300 mm long of minimum weight 330 grams, to side hung steel windows with necessary welding and machine screws etc. complete.	each	61.15
32.	Providing and fixing bright finished brass peg stays to steel ventilators with necessary welding and machine screws etc. complete :		
	32A 300 mm long of minimum weight of 330 grams.	each	61.15
	32B 250 mm long of minimum weight of 280 grams.	each	54.50
	32C 200 mm long of minimum weight of 240 grams.	each	47.85
33.	Providing and fixing 14 mm bright finished brass spring catch to steel centre hung ventilators with necessary welding and machine screws etc. complete.	each	17.85
34.	Steel work welded in built up sections/framed work including cutting hosting, fixing in position and applying a priming coat of approved steel primer using structural steel etc. as required :		
	34A In stringers, treads, landings etc. of stair cases including use of chequered plate wherever required ; all complete.	kilogram	23.30
	34B In gratings, frames, guard bar, ladders, railings, brackets, gates & similar works.	kilogram	25.15

S. No.	Description	Unit	Rate ₹
35.	Providing and fixing hand rail by welding etc. to steel ladder railing, balcony railing & staircase railing including applying a priming coat of approved steel primer :		
35A	M.S. tube (medium) 40 mm nominal bore	kilogram	36.00
35B	E.R.W. tubes 40 mm nominal dia	kilogram	44.00
35C	G.I. pipes 40 mm nominal bore (class B)	kilogram	33.35

Table 13.10. FLOORING

S. No.	Description	Unit	Rate ₹
	A. FLOORING		
1.	Brick on edge flooring with bricks of class designation 75 including cement slurry etc. complete in cement mortar with F.P.S. bricks :		
1A	1 : 4 (1 cement : 4 coarse sand)	sq m	188.10
1B	1 : 6 (1 cement : 6 coarse sand)	sq m	172.05
2.	Dry brick on edge flooring with bricks of class designation 75 on a bed of 12 mm mud mortar including filling joints with Jamuna sand (with F.P.S. bricks) :	sq m	124.40
3.	Extra for brick flooring laid diagonal herring bone bond or other pattern as specified.	sq m	5.65
4.	Cement concrete flooring 1 : 2 : 4 (1 cement : 2 coarse sand : 4 graded stone aggregate) finished with a floating coat of neat cement including cement slurry, but excluding the cost of nosing of steps etc. complete :		
4A	25 mm thick with 12.5 mm nominal size stone aggregate.	sq m	75.15
4B	40 mm thick with 20 mm nominal size stone aggregate.	sq m	100.45
4C	50 mm thick with 20 mm nominal size stone aggregate.	sq m	118.45
5.	40 mm thick red oxide flooring under layer of 30 mm thick cement concrete 1 : 2 : 4 (1 cement : 2 coarse sand : 4 graded stone aggregate 12.5 mm nominal size) and top layer of 10 mm thick plaster of cement red oxide mix (using 3.5 kg of red oxide of iron per 50 kg of cement) 1 : 3 (1 cement : 3 coarse sand) finished with a floating coat of neat cement red oxide mix of same proportion including cement slurry, but excluding the cost of nosing of steps etc. complete :	sq m	217.80
6.	Add or deduct for using more or less than 3.5 kg of red oxide of iron per 50 kg of cement in 40 mm thick red oxide flooring.	sq m per extra or less kg red oxide of iron used for each 50 kg of cement	8.75
7.	52 mm thick cement concrete flooring with metallic concrete hardener topping under layer 40 mm thick cement concrete 1 : 2 : 4 (1 cement : 2 coarse sand : 4 graded stone aggregate 20 mm nominal size) and top layer 12 mm thick metallic concrete hardener consisting of mix 1 : 2 (1 cement hardener mix : 2 stone aggregate 6 mm nominal size) by volume with which metallic hardening compound of approved quality is mixed in the ratio 4 : 1 (4 parte of cement: 1 part of metallic floor hardening compound of approved quality) by weight including cement slurry, but excluding the cost of nosing of steps etc. complete.	sq m	147.60

(*Contd.*)

S. No.	Description	Unit	Rate ₹
8.	62 mm thick cement concrete flooring with metallic concrete hardener topping under layer 50 mm thick cement concrete 1 : 2 : 4 (1 cement : 2 coarse sand : 4 graded stone aggregate 20 mm nominal size) and top layer 12 mm thick metallic cement hardener consisting of mix 1 : 2 (1 cement hardener mix : 2 stone aggregate 6 mm nominal size) by volume with which metallic hardening compound of approved quality is mixed in the ratio 4 :1 (4 parts of cement: 1 part of metallic floor hardening compound of approved quality) by weight including cement slurry, but excluding the cost of nosing of steps etc complete.	sq m	164.15
9.	Cement plaster skirting (upto 30 cm height) with cement mortar 1 : 3 (1 cement: 3 coarse sand) finished with a floating coat of neat cement :		
	9A 18 mm thick	sq m	91.50
	9B 21 mm thick	sq m	97.60
10.	Red oxide plaster skirting (upto 30 cm height) with top layer of 6 mm thick plaster of cement mortar red oxide mix, using 3.5 kg of red oxide of iron per 50 kg of cement in mortar 1 : 3 (1 cement : 3 coarse sand) finished with a floating coat of cement red oxide mix of same proportion :		
	10A 18 mm thick with under layer 12 mm thick cement plaster 1 : 3 (1 cement : 3 coarse sand)	sq m	111.90
	10B 21 mm thick with under layer 15 mm thick cement plaster 1 : 3 (1 cement : 3 coarse sand)	sq m	117.65
11.	Add or deduct for using more or less than 3.5 kg of red oxide of iron per 50 kg of cement in 18 mm or 21 mm thick red oxide plaster skirting.	sq m per extra or less kg red oxide of iron used for each 50 kg of cement	6.10
12.	Cement concrete pavement with 1 : 2 : 4 (1 cement : 2 coarse sand : 4 graded stone aggregate 20 mm nominal size) including finishing complete :	cum	1908.25
13.	Extra for making chequers of approved pattern on cement concrete floors, steps, landing, pavements etc.	sq m	7.00
	B. TERRAZO FLOORING		
14.	40 mm thick marble chips flooring rubbed and polished to granolithic finish, under layer 34 mm thick cement concrete 1 : 2 : 4 (1 cement : 2 coarse sand : 4 graded stone aggregate 12.5 mm nominal size) and top layer 6 mm thick with white, black, chocolate, grey, yellow or Baroda green marble chips of sizes from 1 mm to 4 mm nominal size laid in cement marble powder mix 3 : 1 (3 cement: 1 marble powder) by weight in proportion of 4 : 7 (4 cement marble powder mix : 7 marble chips) by volume including cement slurry etc. complete :		
	14A Dark shade pigment with ordinary cement.	sq m	165.80
	14B Light shade pigment with white cement	sq m	195.50
	14C Medium shade pigment with 50% white cement and 50% ordinary cement.	sq m	179.40
	14D White cement without any pigment.	sq m	180.45
	14E Light shade pigment with ordinary cement.	sq m	170.85
	14F Ordinary cement without any pigment.	sq m	155.50

S. No.	Description	Unit	Rate ₹
15.	40 mm thick marble chips flooring, rubbed and polished to granolithic finish, under layer 31 mm thick cement concrete 1 : 2 :4 (1 cement : 2 coarse sand : 4 graded stone aggregate. 12.5 mm nominal size) and top layer 9 mm thick with white, black, chocolate, grey, yellow or Baroda green marble chips of sizes from 4 mm to 7 mm nominal size laid in cement marble powder mix 3 : 1 (3 cement: 1 marble powder) by weight in proportion of 4 : 7 (4 cement marble powder : 7 marble chips) by volume including cement slurry etc. complete :		
	15A Dark shade pigment with ordinary cement.	sq m	175.50
	15B Light shade pigment with white cement.	sq m	217.85
	15C Medium shade pigment with 50% white cement and 50% ordinary cement.	sq m	194.85
	15D White cement without any pigment.	sq m	197.55
	15E Light shade pigment with ordinary cement.	sq m	182.70
	15F Ordinary cement without any pigment.	sq m	160.75
16.	40 mm thick marble chips flooring, rubbed and polished to granolithic finish, under layer 28 mm thick cement concrete 1 : 2 : 4 (1 cement : 2 coarse sand : 4 graded stone aggregate 12.5 mm nominal size) and top layer 12 mm thick with white, black, chocolate, grey yellow or Baroda green marble chips of sizes from 7 mm to 10 mm nominal size laid in cement marble powder mix 3 : 1 (3 cement : 1 marble powder) by weight in proportion of 2 : 3 (2 cement marble powder mix : 3 marble chips) by volume including cement slurry etc. complete :		
	16A Dark shade pigment with ordinary cement.	sq m	188.10
	16B Light shade pigment with white cement.	sq m	247.45
	16C Medium shade pigment with 50% white cement and 50% ordinary cement.	sq m	215.20
	16D White cement without any pigment.	sq m	217.40
	16E Light shade pigment with ordinary cement.	sq m	198.15
	16F Ordinary cement without any pigment.	sq m	169.45
17.	Marble chips skirting (upto 30 cm height) rubbed and polished to granolithic finish, top layer 6 mm thick with white, black, chocolate, grey, yellow or Baroda green marble chips of sizes from smallest to 4 mm nominal size laid in cement marble powder mix 3 : 1 (3 cement : 1 marble powder) by weight in proportion of 4 : 7 (4 cement marble powder mix : 7 marble chips) by volume.		
18.	18 mm thick with under layer 12 mm thick cement plaster 1 : 3 (1 cement : 3 coarse sand):		
	18A Dark shade pigment with ordinary cement.	sq m	193.15
	18B Light shade pigment with white cement.	sq m	222.80
	18C Medium shade pigment with 50% white cement and 50% ordinary cement	sq m	206.70
	18D White cement without any pigment.	sq m	208.35
	18E Light shade pigment with ordinary cement.	sq m	198.20
	18F Ordinary cement without any pigment.	sq m	182.95
	18G 21 mm thick with under layer 15 mm thick cement plaster 1 : 3 (1 cement : 3 coarse sand)		
	18H Dark shade pigment with ordinary cement.	sq m	198.85
	18I Light shade pigment with white cement.	sq m	228.55

(Contd.)

S. No.	Description	Unit	Rate ₹
	18J Medium shade pigment with 50% white cement and 50% ordinary cement.	sq m	212.45
	18K White cement without any pigment.	sq m	214.05
	18L Light shade pigment with ordinary cement.	sq m	203.90
	18M Ordinary cement without any pigment.	sq m	188.65
19.	Providing and fixing aluminium strips 40 mm wide and 2 mm thick in joints of terrazo floor.	metre	34.80
20.	Providing and fixing glass strips in joints of terrazo/cement concrete floors :		
	20A 40 mm wide and 4 mm thick.	metre	10.20
	20B 40 mm wide and 6 mm thick.	metre	13.85
21.	Extra for terrazo flooring laid as floor boarders, margins and similar bands exceeding 7.5 cm but not exceeding 30 cm in width.	sq m	4.90
22.	Extra for laying terrazo flooring on staircase treads not exceeding 30 cm in width including cost of forming, nosing etc.	sq m	7.35
23.	Extra for laying terrazo in narrow bands not exceeding 7.5 cm in width.	metre	0.50
24.	Extra for making moulded nosing in terrazo including returned moulded ends and angles to mouldings.	metre	24.50
25.	Special surface finishing to treads, risers and the ends of concrete steps and the like, including form work.	sq m	13.55
26.	Crazy marble stone flooring including filling the gaps with light shade pigment with white cement marble powder mixture (3 parts of white cement: 1 part of marble powder) by weight in proportion of 4 : 7 (4 cement marble powder mix : 7 white, black or white and black marble chips of sizes from 1 mm to 4 mm nominal size by volume) and under layer 25 mm thick cement concrete 1 : 2 : 4 (1 cement : 2 coarse sand : 4 graded stone aggregate 12.5 mm nominal size) rubbing, polishing and cement slurry etc. complete :		
	26A 20 mm thick crazy marble stone white, black or as specified	sq m	504.35
	26B 30 mm thick crazy marble stone white, black or as specified	sq m	548.80
	26C 40 mm thick crazy marble stone white, black or as specified.	sq m	592.30
	C. TILE FLOORING		
27.	Precast terrazo tiles 20 mm thick with marble chips of size upto 6 mm laid in floors, and landings, jointed with neat cement slurry mixed with pigment to match the shade of the tiles including rubbing and polishing complete with precast tiles on 30 mm thick bed of:		
	(1) Lime mortar 1: 1 : 2 (1 lime putty : 1 surkhi: 2 coarse sand)		
	27A Light shade using white cement	sq m	361.65
	27B Medium shade using 50% white cement and 50% ordinary cement	sq m	320.95
	27C Dark shade using ordinary cement.	sq m	285.40
	27D Ordinary cement without any pigment	sq m	264.35
	(2) Lime mortar 1 : 3 (1 lime putty : 3 surkhi)		
	27E Light shade using white cement.	sq m	360.25
	27F Medium shade using 50% white cement and 50% ordinary cement	sq m	379.95

S. No.	Description	Unit	Rate ₹
	27G Dark shade using ordinary cement.	sq m	284.00
	27H Ordinary cement without any pigment.	sq m	262.95
	(3) Lime mortar 1 : 3 (1 lime putty : 3 coarse sand)		
	27I Light shade using white cement.	sq m	362.35
	27J Medium shade using 50% white cement and 50% ordinary cement.	sq m	321.65
	27K Dark shade using ordinary cement.	sq m	286.10
	27L Ordinary cement without any pigment.	sq m	265.05
28.	Precast terrazo tiles 20 mm thick with marble chips of size upto 6 mm laid in floors, and landings, jointed with neat cement slurry mixed with pigment to match the shade of the tiles including rubbing and polishing complete with precast tiles on 20 mm thick bed of cement mortar 1 : 4 (1 cement : 4 coarse sand) :		
	28A Light shade using white cement	sq m	359.55
	28B Medium shade using 50% white cement and 50% ordinary cement	sq m	318.85
	28C Dark shade using ordinary cement.	sq m	283.35
	28D Ordinary cement without any pigment	sq m	262.30
29.	Extra of terrazo tiles are laid in treads of steps not exceeding 30 cm in width.	sq m	8.85
30.	Precast terrazo tiles 20 mm thick with marble chips of sizes upto 6 mm in skirting and risers of steps not exceeding 30 cm in height on 12 mm thick cement plaster 1 : 3 (1 cement : 3 coarse sand) jointed with neat cement slurry mixed with pigment to match the shade of the tiles, including rubbing and polishing complete with tiles of :		
	30A Light shade using white cement.	sq m	416.25
	30B Medium shade using 50% white cement and 50% ordinary cement	sq m	366.80
	30C Dark shade using ordinary cement.	sq m	323.90
	30D Ordinary cement without any pigment.	sq m	302.85
31.	Precast terrazo tiles 20 mm thick with marble chips of sizes upto 6 mm fixed on walls, on 12 mm thick cement plaster 1 : 3 (1 cement: 3 coarse sand) jointed with neat cement slurry mixed with pigment to match the shade of the tiles, including rubbing and polishing complete with tiles of :		
	31A Light shade using white cement.	sq m	409.60
	31B Medium shade using 50% white cement and 50% ordinary cement	sq m	360.15
	31C Dark shade using ordinary cement.	sq m	317.25
	31D Ordinary cement without any pigment.	sq m	296.20
32.	Extra if cut tiles other than half tiles are used in risers of steps, skirting and dado.	sq m	34.00
33.	Chequered terrazo tiles 22 mm thick with marble chips of size upto 6 mm in floors jointed with neat cement slurry mixed with pigment to match the shade of the tiles including rubbing and polishing complete on 28 mm thick bed of:		
	(1) Lime mortar 1 : 1 : 1 (1 lime putty : 1 surkhi : 1 coarse sand)		
	33A Light shade using white cement.	sq m	340.70

(Contd.)

S. No.		Description	Unit	Rate ₹
	33B	Medium shade using 50% white cement and 50% ordinary cement	sq m	332.95
	33C	Dark shade using ordinary cement.	sq m	298.65
	33D	Ordinary cement without any pigment	sq m	277.65
	(2)	Lime mortar 1 : 3 (1 lime putty : 3 coarse sand)		
	33E	Light shade using white cement.	sq m	337.15
	33F	Medium shade using 50% white cement and 50% ordinary cement.	sq m	329.45
	33G	Dark shade using ordinary cement.	sq m	287.80
	33H	Ordinary cement without any pigment	sq m	274.10
34.		Chequered terrazo tiles 22 mm thick with marble chips of size up to 6 mm in floors jointed with neat cement slurry mixed with pigment to match the shade of the tiles including rubbing and polishing complete on 20 mm thick bed of cement mortar 1 : 4 (1 cement : 4 coarse sand) :		
	34A	Light shade using white cement.	sq m	332.70
	34B	Medium shade using 50% white cement, 50% ordinary cement	sq m	326.20
	34C	Dark shade using ordinary cement	sq m	293.10
	34D	Ordinary cement without any pigment	sq m	272.05
35.		Chequered precast cement concrete tiles 22 mm thick with marble chips of size 6 mm in footpath & courtyard jointed with neat cement slurry mixed with pigment to match the shade of tiles including rubbing and cleaning etc. complete on 20 mm thick bed of cement mortar 1 : 4 (1 cement : 4 coarse sand) :		
	35A	Light shade using white cement	sq m	648.00
	35B	Medium shade using 50% white cement 50% grey cement	sq m	711.20
	35C	Dark shade using ordinary cement	sq m	804.00
	35D	Ordinary cement without any pigment	sq m	782.95
36.		Chequered terrazo tiles 30 mm thick with marble chips of sizes upto 6 mm in stairs treads jointed with neat cement slurry mixed with pigment to match the shade of the tiles including rubbing and polishing, rounding of nosing etc. complete on 20 mm thick bed of :		
	(1)	Lime mortar 1 : 1 : 1 (1 lime putty : 1 surkhi : 1 coarse sand)		
	36A	Light shade using white cement.	sq m	362.65
	36B	Medium shade using 50% white cement and 50% ordinary cement.	sq m	353.15
	36C	Dark shade using ordinary cement.	sq m	301.15
	36D	Ordinary cement without any pigment.	sq m	280.10
	(2)	Cement mortar 1 : 4 (1 cement : 4 coarse sand)		
	36E	Light shade using white cement.	sq m	370.25
	36F	Medium shade using 50% white cement and 50% ordinary cement.	sq m	360.70
	36G	Dark shade using ordinary cement.	sq m	308.70
	36H	Ordinary cement without any pigment	sq m	287.65

S. No.	Description	Unit	Rate ₹
37.	Providing and laying in floors matt finish ceramic tiles of 10 mm thickness without warpage, of approved make and colour laid on 20 mm thick cement mortar 1 : 4 (1 cement : 4 coarse sand) including grouting the joints with white cement and matching pigment etc. complete.	sq m	587.85
38.	Providing and fixing glazed screen printed tiles of minimum thickness 5 mm of approved design, colour and shade in skirting, risers of steps and dados on 12 mm thick cement plaster 1 : 3 (1 cement : 3 coarse sand) jointed with white cement slurry mixed with matching pigment etc. complete.	sq m	482.55
39.	Providing and fixing 10 mm thick acid and or alkali resistant tiles of approved make and colour using acid and or alkali resisting mortar bedding and joints filled with acid and or alkali resisting cement as per IS : 4457 complete as per the direction of Engineer-in-Charge :		
(1)	In flooring on a bed of 10 mm thick mortar 1: 4 (1 appropriate cement : 4 coarse sand)		
39A	Acid and alkali resistant tile	sq m	684.10
39B	Acid resistant tile	sq m	684.10
39C	Alkali resistant tile	sq m	684.10
(2)	In dado/skirting on 12 mm thick mortar 1: 4 (1 appropriate cement : 4 coarse sand)		
39D	Acid and alkali resistant tile	sq m	718.55
39E	Acid resistant tile	sq m	718.55
39F	Alkali resistant tile	sq m	718.55
40.	White glazed tiles of minimum thickness 5 mm in skirting, risers of steps and dado on 12 mm thick cement plaster 1: 3 (1 cement : 3 coarse sand) and jointed with white cement slurry and matching pigment etc.	sq m	467.25
41.	Tile work in skirting, risers of steps and dado (upto 2 m height) over 12 mm thick bed of cement mortar 1 : 3 (1 cement: 3 coarse sand) and jointed with grey cement slurry @ 3.3. kg/sq m including pointing in white cement mixed with pigment of matching shade complete :		
(1)	Marble tiles (polished) Raj nagar		
41A	8 mm thick	sq m	661.20
(2)	Ceramic tiles (as per manufactures specifications)		
41B	7.3 mm thick	sq m	617.10
41C	Plain coloured grazed tiles 5 mm thick	sq m	515.05
41D	Factory printed glazed tiles 5 mm thick	sq m	523.30
	D. STONE FLOORING		
42.	Marble stone flooring with 20 mm thick marble stone over 20 mm (average) thick base laid and jointed with grey cement slurry including rubbing and polishing complete with :		

Rate per sq m for base with	
1 : 1 : 1 (1 Lime putty: 1 Surkhi : 1 Coarse sand)	1 : 4 (1 Cement: 4 Coarse sand)

(*Contd.*)

S. No.	Description	Unit	Rate ₹
	(1) **WHITE MARBLE**		
	42A Makrana white first quality	5022.20	5029.75
	42B Makrana White Second quality	2339.10	2346.70
	42C Abu White Makrana	2518.00	2525.55
	42D Abu Panther marble	1208.40	1215.95
	42E Makrana Doongri Adanga	965.65	973.20
	42F Makrana chak Doongri	1099.80	1107.35
	42G Rajnagar plain		971.85
	(2) **BLACK MARBLE**		
	42H Black Zebra Bhainslana	1163.70	1171.25
	42I Black Zebra Kishangarh	1099.80	1107.35
	42J Abu Zebra black	1240.35	1247.90
	42K Makrana dhobi doongri	857.05	884.60
	(3) **GREEN MARBLE**		
	42L Baroda green marble	1176.45	1184.00
	42M Abu green marble	1253.10	1260.70
	42N Bundi green marble	1099.80	1107.35
	(4) **PINK MARBLE**		
	42O Pink plain marble	895.35	902.95
	42P Makrana pink adanga marble	1112.55	1120.15
	42Q Bundi adanga pink marble	812.35	819.90
	(5) **GREY MARBLE**		
	42R Kumari grey marble	959.25	966.80
	42S Bundi grey marble	1035.90	1043.50
	(6) **BROWN MARBLE**		
	42T Bar brown marble	1035.90	1043.50
43.	Extra if pigment is used in the cement slurry to match the shade of the marble slabs.	sq m	2.40
44.	Extra if white cement slurry is used instead of grey cement slurry (in joints of marble stone flooring or tiles).	sq m	4.60
45.	Extra for nosing in marble stone for treads.	metre	58.00
46.	Extra for marble stone flooring in treads of steps, not exceeding 30 cm in width.	sq m	65.70
	E. KOTA STONE FLOORING		
47.	Kota stone slab flooring over 20 mm (average) thick base laid over and jointed with grey cement slurry mixed with pigment to match the shade of the slab including rubbing and polishing complete with :		
		Rate per sq m for base with	
		1 : 1 : 1 (1 Lime putty : 1 Surkhi: 1 Coarse sand)	1 : 4 (1 Cement: 4 Coarse sand)
	47A 25 mm thick	584.00	591.55
	47B 30 mm thick	640.25	647.00
	47C 40 mm thick	651.00	658.55

S. No.	Description	Unit	Rate ₹
48.	Kota stone slabs 25 mm thick in risers of steps, skirting, dado and pillars laid on 12 mm (average) thick cement mortar : 1 : 3 (1 cement : 3 coarse sand) and jointed with grey cement slurry mixed with pigment to match the shade of the slabs, including rubbing and polishing complete.	sq m	528.50
	F. SAND STONE FLOORING		
49.	Supplying sand stone 40 mm thick for flooring, carriage to site and rough chisel dressing :		
	49A Red sand stone	sq m	184.15
	49B White sand stone	sq m	209.80
50.	40 mm thick rough chisel dressed stone flooring over 20 mm (average) thick base with joints finished flush :		
	Rate per sq m for base with		
	1: 1: 1 (1 lime : 1 Surkhi: 1 Coarse sand)		1 : 5 (1 Cement: 5 Coarse sand)
	50A Red sand stone — 246.85		250.30
	50B White sand stone — 272.50		276.00
51.	40 mm thick rough chisel dressed stone flooring over 20 mm (average) thick base including pointing with cement mortar 1 : 2 (1 cement: 2 stone dust) with an admixture of pigment to match the shade of stone with :		
	Rate per sq m for base with		
	1 : 1 : 1 (1 lime : 1 Surkhi: 1 Coarse sand)		1 : 5 (1 Cement: 5 Coarse sand)
	51A Red sand stone — 271.95		275.40
	51B White sand stone — 297.60		301.05
52.	40 mm thick fine dressed stone flooring over 20 mm (average) thick base with joints finished flush :		
	Rate per sq m for base with		
	1 : 1 : 1 (1 lime : 1 Surkhi: 1 Coarse sand)		1 : 5 (1 Cement : 5 Coarse sand)
	52A Red sand stone — 408.85		412.30
	52B White sand stone — 434.50		437.95
53.	40 mm thick fine dressed stone flooring over 20 mm (average) thick base including pointing with cement mortar 1 : 2 (1 cement : 2 stone dust) with an admixture of pigment to match the shade of stone :		
	Rate per sq m for base with		
	1 : 1 : 1 (1 lime : 1 Surkhi : 1 Coarse sand)		1 : 5 (1 Cement: 5 Coarse sand)

(Contd.)

S. No.	Description	Unit	Rate ₹
	53A Red sand stone 433.90		437.40
	53B White sand stone 459.60		463.05
54.	40 mm thick fine dressed and rubbed stone flooring over 20 mm (average) thick base with joints 3 mm thick, side buttered with cement mortar 1 : 2 (1 cement : 2 stone dust) admixed with pigment to match the shade of stone and pointing with same mortar :		
	Rate per sq m for base with 1 : 1 : 1 (1 lime : 1 Surkhi: 1 Coarse sand)		1 : 5 (1 Cement: 5 Coarse sand)
	54A Red sand stone 450.80		454.25
	54B White sand stone 476.45		476.25
55.	40 mm thick fine dressed and rubbed stone flooring over 20 mm (average) thick base with joints 5 mm thick finished flush :		
	Rate per sq m for base with 1 : 1 : 1 (1 lime : 1 Surkhi: 1 Coarse sand)		1 : 5 (1 Cement: 5 Coarse sand)
	55A Red sand stone 430.15		433.60
	55B White sand stone 455.80		459.25
56.	40 mm thick fine dressed and rubbed stone flooring over 20 mm (average) thick base with joints 5 mm thick, including pointing with cement mortar 1 : 2 (1 cement : 2 stone dust) with an admixture of pigment to match the shade of stone :		
	Rate per sq m for base with 1 : 1 : 1 (1 lime 1 Surkhi: 1 Coarse sand)		1 : 5 (1 Cement: 5 Coarse sand)
	56A Red sand stone 465.25		458.70
	56B White sand stone 480.90		484.35
57.	Extra for nosing in steps and treads of kota stone slab.	metre	18.35
58.	Extra for kota stone flooring in steps and treads not exceeding 30 cm in width sq m.	sq m	3.45
59.	Extra for nosing in steps and treads of red or white rough dressed sand stone.	metre	12.20
60.	Extra for red or white rough dressed sand stone flooring in steps and treads not exceeding 30 cm in width.	sq m	2.90
61.	Extra for nosing in steps and treads of red or white sand stone :		
	61A Fine dressed	metre	61.10
	61B Fine dressed and rubbed	metre	76.65

S. No.	Description	Unit	Rate ₹
62.	Extra for red or white sand stone flooring in steps and treads, not exceeding 30 cm in width :		
	62A Fine dressed	sq m	4.85
	62B Fine dressed and rubbed	sq m	12.65
63.	Providing and fixing homogeneous Polyvinyl chloride sheet/tile in flooring and skirting in approved pattern on a smooth and damp proof base using rubber based adhesives of approved quality and manufacturer like Dunlop S-758, Fevicol SR 998 or equivalent including rolling with light wooden roller weighing about 5 kg all complete as directed by Engineer-in-Charge, in approved colour and shade :		
		Rate per sq m with	
		sheet	tile
	63A 1.5 mm thick	286.85	393.30
	63B 2.0 mm thick	325.35	434.10
64.	Rubber sheet flooring plain or marble of required colour on a smooth and damp proof base using rubber adhesive of approved quality including pressing the sheets/tiles with a suitable tool to get a smooth surface all complete as directed by the Engineer-in-Charge :		
	64A 3.2 mm thick	sq m	208.70
	64B 4.80 mm thick	sq m	272.85
	64C 6.40 mm thick	sq m	356.85
	G. WOODEN FLOORING		
65.	25 mm wooden planking, tongued and grooved in flooring including fixing with iron screws complete with :		
	65A Second class teak wood	sq m	1244.25
	65B First class deodar wood	sq m	1119.65
	65C Second class deodar wood	sq m	1016.95
66.	38 mm thick parquet (wood block) flooring of first class teak wood laid over 25 mm thick levelling layer of cement concrete 1 : 2 : 4 (1 cement : 2 coarse sand : 4 stone aggregate 10 mm nominal size) to be paid separately coated with a thin layer of hot bitumen (blown type) @ 2.45 kg per sq m including fixing blocks in position after dipping in hot bitumen (blown type) upto half depth, planed, levelled smooth and finished complete.	sq m	2231.00
67.	Extra for planning the lower surface of wooden planking.	sq m	22.45
68.	Extra for providing and fixing metal strips of 1.6 mm thickness at junctions with other floors :		
	68A 25 mm wide aluminium strip	metre	20.05
	68B 38 mm wide aluminium strip	metre	27.80
69.	Providing and fixing M.S. angle 50 × 50 × 5 mm to act as nosing with lugs of M.S. flat 10 × 5 mm 10 cm long forked at end 60 cm apart (minimum three lugs to be provided) including necessary welding and applying a priming coat of approved primer on exposed surface etc. complete.	kilogram	23.40

(Contd.)

S. No.	*Description*	*Unit*	*Rate* ₹
70.	**Providing and laying 5 mm thick epoxy screeding consisting of araldite G.Y. 257, 100 parts by weight hardener HY 830, 40 parts by weight Hardener HY 850, 20 parts by weight plus quartz sand 900 parts over a primed surface with primer araldite GY 257, 100 parts by weight and hardener HY 840, 50 parts by weight including application of two top coats based on araldite GY 257, 100 parts hardener HY 830, 40 parts hardener HY 850, 20 parts and flow control agent 1 to 3% with acrosil DTO 75, 3 parts complete as per ciba geigy specification including preparation of surface to receive the treatment.**	sq m	912.00

Table 13.11. ROOFING

S. No.	*Description*	*Unit*	*Rate* ₹
	A. ROOFING		
1.	**Providing corrugated G.S. sheet roofing fixed with G.I. J or L hooks, bolts and nuts 8 mm diameter with bitumen and G.I. limpet washers or with G.I. limpet washers filled with white lead and including a coat of approved steel primer and two coats of approved paint on overlapping of sheets complete (upto a pitch of 60 degrees) excluding the cost of purlins, rafters and trusses :**		
	1A 1.60 mm thick with zinc coating not less than 350 gm/m²	sq m	627.70
	1B 1.25 mm thick with zinc coating not less than 350 gm/m²	sq m	506.55
	1C 1.00 mm thick with zinc coating not less than 275 gm/m²	sq m	420.30
	1D 0.80 mm thick with zinc coating not less than 275 gm/m²	sq m	351.25
	1E 0.63 mm thick with zinc coating not less than 275 gm/m²	sq m	292.50
2.	**Extra for providing and fixing corrugated G.S. sheets vertically or to a pitch exceeding 60 degrees.**	sq m	1.95
3.	**Extra for providing and fixing curved C.G.S. sheets in roofing :**		
	3A 0.80 mm thick	sq m	2.40
	3B 0.63 mm thick	sq m	1.95
4.	**Extra for straight cutting in C.G.S. sheet roofing for making opening of area exceeding 40 square decimetre for chimney stacks, sky light etc. :**		
	4A 1.60 mm thick	metre	15.55
	4B 1.25 mm thick	metre	12.30
	4C 1.00 mm thick	metre	9.70
	4D 0.80 mm thick	metre	7.80
	4E 0.63 mm thick	metre	7.80
5.	**Extra for circular cutting in C.G.S. sheet roofing for making opening of area exceeding 40 square decimetre :**		
	5A 1.60 mm thick	metre	84.85
	5B 1.25 mm thick	metre	66.35
	5C 1.00 mm thick	metre	53.10
	5D 0.80 mm thick	metre	42.45
	5E 0.63 mm thick	metre	42.45

S. No.	Description	Unit	Rate ₹
6.	Providing ridges or hips of width 60 cm over all width plain G.S. sheet fixed with G.I.J. or L hooks, bolts and nuts 8 mm dia. G.I. limpet and bitumen washers complete :		
	6A 0.80 mm thick with zinc coating not less than 275 gm/m^2	sq m	219.85
	6B 0.63 mm thick with zinc coating not less than 275 gm/m^2	sq m	187.65
7.	Providing valleys of 90 cm wide overall in plain G.S. sheet fixed with G.I. J or L hooks, bolts and nuts 6 mm dia. G.I. limpet and bitumen washers complete :		
	7A 1.60 mm thick with zinc coating not less than 360 gm/m^2	sq m	449.05
8.	Providing flashing of 40 cm over all width in plain, G.S. sheet fixed with G.I. J or L hooks, bolts and nuts, G.I. limpet and bitumen washer complete, bent to shape and fixed in wall with cement mortar 1 : 3 (1 cement : 3 coarse sand) :		
	8A 1.25 mm thick with zinc coating not less than 350 gm/m^2	sq m	176.90
	8B 1.00 mm thick with zinc coating not less than 275 gm/m^2	sq m	152.95
9.	Providing and fixing 15 cm wide 45 cm over all semi circular plain G.S. sheet gutter with iron brackets 40 × 8 mm size, bolts, nuts and washers etc. including making necessary connections with rain water pipes complete :		
	9A 0.80 mm thick with zinc coating not less than 275 gm/m^2	sq m	188.25
	9B 0.63 mm thick with zinc coating not less than 275 gm/m^2	sq m	161.40
	B. A.C. SHEET ROOFING		
10.	Providing asbestos cement 6 mm thick corrugated sheets roofing and fixing with G.I. J or L hooks, bolts and nuts 8 mm dia. G.I. plain and bitumen wahsers complete excluding the cost of purlins, rafters and trusses : corrugated sheets :		
	10A Upto 60 degrees pitch	sq m	176.75
	10B Above 60 degrees pitch	sq m	178.80
11.	Extra for straight cutting in A.C. corrugated, semi-corrugated 6 mm thick sheet roofing for making openings of area exceeding 40 square decimetre for chimney stacks, skylights etc.	metre	7.80
12.	Extra for circular cutting in A.C. corrugated/semi-corrugated 6 mm thick sheet roofing for making openings of area exceeding 40 square decimetre.	metre	21.50
13.	Extra for providing and fixing wind ties of 40 × 6 mm flat iron section	metre	35.35
14.	Providing and fixing ridges and hips in asbestos cement sheet roofing :		
	14A One piece plain angular ridges	metre	104.40
	14B Serrated or plain wing adjustable ridges	metre	138.40
	14C Close fitting adjustable ridges	metre	181.65
	14D North light adjustable ridges	metre	129.75
	14E Unserrated adjustable hips	metre	139.30
	C. A.C. ACCESSORIES		
15.	Providing and fixing asbestos cement roofing accessories with galvanised iron J or L hooks, bolts and nuts and or G.I. seam bolts and nuts, G.I. plain and bitumen washers complete :		
	15A Apron flashing pieces	metre	99.65
	15B Eave's filler pieces	metre	75.40

(Contd.)

S. No.	Description	Unit	Rate ₹
	15C North light and ventilator curves	metre	182.25
	15D Barge boards	metre	105.20
	15E Ridge finials	pair	69.55
	15F Curved barge boards for north light curves	each	126.20
	15G Roof lights	each	749.45
	15H Expansion joints for ridges	pair	205.80
	15I Expansion joints for north light curves	each	152.45
	15J S type louvers	metre	78.70
16.	Providing flat iron brackets 50 × 3 mm size with necessary bolts, nuts and washers etc. for fixing asbestos cement/G.S. sheets gutters with purlins.	metre	8.85
17.	Providing and fixing asbestos cement drop ends for socketed half round gutters :		
	17A 250 mm/254 mm nominal size with 75 or 100 mm or 150 mm dia drain outlet	each	88.35
	17B 300 mm nominal size with 75 mm or 100 mm or 150 mm dia drain outlet	each	135.05
18.	Providing and fixing asbestos cement drop ends for plain ended eaves or boundary wall gutters :		
	18A 275 × 125 × 175 mm nominal size with 75 or 100 or 150 mm dia outlet	each	87.20
	18B 300 × 150 × 225 mm nominal size with 75 or 100 or 150 mm dia outlet	each	144.35
	18C 450 × 150 × 300 mm nominal size with 75 or 100 or 150 mm dia outlet	each	156.00
	18D 500 × 150 × 250 mm nominal size with 75 or 100 or 150 mm dia outlet	each	165.35
19.	Providing and fixing asbestos cement drop ends for plain ended valley gutters :		
	19A 400 × 125 × 250 mm nominal size with 75 or 100 or 150 mm dia outlet	each	115.20
	19B 450 × 125 × 150 mm nominal size with 75 or 100 or 150 mm dia outlet	each	114.05
	19C 600 × 150 × 225 mm nominal size with 75 or 100 or 150 mm dia outlet	each	180.50
	19D 900 × 200 × 225 mm nominal size with 75 or 100 or 150 mm dia outlet	each	195.70
20.	Providing and fixing asbestos cement stop ends for :		
	(1) Socketed half round eaves gutter :		
	20A 150 mm nominal size	each	21.85
	20B 250/254 mm nominal size	each	30.05
	20C 300 mm nominal size	each	41.70
	(2) Plain ended eaves or boundary wall gutters :		
	20D 275 × 125 × 175 mm nominal size	each	38.20
	20E 300 × 150 × 225 mm nominal size	each	59.20
	20F 450 × 150 × 300 mm nominal size	each	68.55
	20G 500 × 150 × 250 mm nominal size	each	72.05

S. No.		Description	Unit	Rate ₹
	(3)	Plain ended valley gutters :		
	20H	400 × 125 × 250 mm nominal size	each	58.05
	20I	450 × 125 × 150 mm nominal size	each	67.35
	20J	600 × 150 × 225 mm nominal size	each	72.05
	20K	900 × 200 × 225 mm nominal size	each	119.85
21.		Providing and fixing asbestos cement nozzles for :		
	(1)	Socketed half round eaves gutters :		
	21A	150 mm nominal size	each	60.35
	21B	250/254 mm nominal size	each	91.85
	21C	300 mm nominal size	each	137.35
	(2)	Plain ended eaves or boundary wall gutters :		
	21D	275 × 125 × 175 mm nominal size	each	79.00
	21E	300 × 150 × 225 mm nominal size	each	126.85
	21F	450 × 150 × 300 mm nominal size	each	138.50
	21G	500 × 150 × 250 mm nominal size	each	150.20
	(3)	Plain ended valley gutters :		
	21H	450 × 125 × 150 mm nominal size	each	138.50
	21I	600 × 150 × 225 mm nominal size	each	139.70
	21J	900 × 200 × 225 mm nominal size	each	184.00
22.		Providing and fixing asbestos angles for :		
	(1)	Plain ended eaves or boundary wall gutters :		
	22A	275 × 125 × 175 mm nominal size	each	228.35
	22B	300 × 150 × 225 mm nominal size	each	324.00
	22C	450 × 150 × 300 mm nominal size	each	446.50
	22D	500 × 150 × 250 mm nominal size	each	507.15
23.		Painting top of roofs with bitumen of approved quality at 17 kg per 10 sq m impregnated with a coat of coarse sand at 60 cudm per 10 sq m including cleaning the slab surface with brushes and finally with a piece of cloth lightly soaked in kerosene oil complete :		
	23A	With residual type petroleum bitumen of penetration 80/100	sq m	25.15
24.		10 cm thick (average) mud phaska of damped brick earth on roofs laid to slope consolidated and plastered with 25 mm thick mud mortar mixed with bhusa at 35 kg per cum of earth and gobri leaping with mix 1 : 1 (1 clay : 1 cow dung) and covered with flat tile bricks of class designation 100 grouted with cement mortar 1 : 3 (1 cement : 3 fine sand) mixed with 2% of integral water proofing compound by weight of cement and finished neat :		
	24A	With F.P.S. brick tiles	sq m	123.70
25.		Extra for every additional 1 cm thickness of mud phaska.	sq m	2.55
26.		Providing and laying brick tiles of class designation 100 over mumty roofs grouted with cement mortar 1 : 3 (1 cement : 3 fine, sand) mixed with 2% of integral water proofing compound by weight of cement over a 12 mm layer of cement mortar 1 : 3 (1 cement : 3 fine sand) and finished neat :		
	26A	With F.P.S. brick tiles	sq m	108.35

(*Contd.*)

S. No.	Description	Unit	Rate ₹
27.	Providing and laying pressed clay tiles (as per approved pattern 20 mm nominal thickness and of approved size) on roofs jointed with cement mortar 1 : 4 (1 cement : 4 coarse sand) mixed with 2% integral water proofing compound laid over a bed of 20 mm thick cement mortar 1 : 4 (1 cement : 4 coarse sand) and finished neat complete.	sq m	122.30
28.	Lime concrete terracing on roofs average thickness 10 cm laid to fall with 25 mm nominal size brick aggregate and 50% lime mortar 1 : 2 (1 lime putty : 2 surkhi) rammed and finished with gur and belgiri treatment complete including rounding of junctions with parpet wall complete.	sq m	147.15
29.	Lime concrete terracing on roofs, average thickness 10 cm laid to fall with 25 mm nominal size brick aggregate and 50% lime mortar 1 : 2 (1 lime putty : 2 surkhi) rammed and finished with gur and belgiri treatment complete and covered with flat brick tiles of class designation 100 grouted with cement mortar 1 : 3 (1 cement : fine sand) mixed with 2% of integral water proofing compound by weight of cement, over 12 mm layer of cement mortar 1 : 3 (1 cement : 3 fine sand) and finished neat :		
	29A With F.P.S. brick tiles	sq m	259.40
30.	Extra for every additional 0.5 cm thickness of lime concrete terracing.	sq m	7.50
31.	Providing gola 75 × 75 mm in cement concrete 1 : 2 : 4 (1 cement : 2 coarse sand : 4 stone aggregate 10 mm and down gauge) including finishing with cement mortar 1 : 3 (1 cement : 3 fine sand) as per standard design :		
	31A In 75 × 75 mm deep chase	metre	40.90
32.	Making khurras 45 × 45 cm with average minimum thickness of 5 cm cement concrete 1 : 2 : 4 (1 cement : 2 coarse sand : 4 graded stone aggregate of 20 mm nominal size) over P.V.C. sheet 1 m × 1 m × 400 micron, finished with 12 mm cement plaster 1 : 3 (1 cement : 3 coarse sand) and a coat of neat cement rounding the edges and making and finishing the outlet complete.	each	88.20
33.	Providing sand stone slab for roofing and laying them in cement mortar 1 : 4 (1 Cement : 4 coarse sand) over wooden karries or R.C.C. battens (Karries and battens to be paid separately) including pointing the ceiling joints with cement mortar 1 : 3 (1 Cement : 3 fine sand) complete :		
	(1) Red sand stone slab		
	33A 40 mm thick	sq m	206.15
	33B 45 mm thick	sq m	238.95
	33C 50 mm thick	sq m	244.85
	(2) White sand stone slab		
	33D 40 mm thick	sq m	231.80
	33E 45 mm thick	sq m	317.15
	33F 50 mm thick	sq m	323.05
	D. CEILING		
34.	Providing and fixing 20 mm thick wooden planks ceiling (frame work for base to be paid separately) with M.S. screws :		
	34A 2nd class teak wood	sq m	758.05
	34B 1st class deodar wood	sq m	699.75

S. No.	Description	Unit	Rate ₹
35.	Providing and fixing insulating board ceiling of approved quality with necessary nails etc. complete (frame work to be paid separately) :		
	(1) Natural colour insulating board		
	35A 12 mm thick	sq m	209.10
	35B 18 mm thick	sq m	291.10
	(2) White face insulating board		
	35C 12 mm thick	sq m	253.10
	35D 18 mm thick	sq m	357.05
	(3) Flame retardent face insulating board		
	35E 12 mm thick	sq m	265.35
	35F 18 mm thick	sq m	439.85
36.	Providing and fixing hard board sheet ceiling of approved quality with necessary nails etc. complete (frame work to be paid separately) :		
	36A Standard quality boards		
	36B 3 mm thick	sq m	136.75
	36C 4.5 mm thick	sq m	160.05
37.	Providing and fixing flat pressed 3 layer medium density particle board sheet Grade I conforming to IS : 3087 in ceiling with necessary nails etc. complete (frame work to be paid separately) :		
	37A 12 mm thick	sq m	289.60
	37B 18 mm thick	sq m	362.95
38.	Providing and fixing plain A.C. sheet ceiling of approved quality with necessary nails etc. complete (frame work to be paid separately) :		
	38A 4 mm thick	sq m	151.50
	38B 6 mm thick	sq m	195.60
39.	Extra for Circular cutting and waste in ceiling with :		
	39A 2nd class teak wood planks 20 mm thick	metre	125.95
	39B First class deodar wood planks 20 mm thick	metre	118.70
	(1) Natural colour insulating board		
	39C 12 mm thick	metre	57.40
	(2) White face insulating board :		
	39D 12 mm thick	metre	62.85
	39E 18 mm thick	metre	75.80
	(3) Flame retardent face insulating board :		
	39F 12 mm thick	metre	64.40
	39G 18 mm thick	metre	74.25
	(4) Standard quality hard board sheet :		
	39H 3 mm thick	sq m	48.40
	39I 4.5 mm thick	metre	51.30
40.	Extra for providing and fixing ceiling to curved surfaces in narrow widths.	sq m	36.65

(Contd.)

S. No.	Description	Unit	Rate ₹
41.	Providing and fixing false ceiling wit`h 12 mm thick plain/or with design ceiling tiles of BWP type phenol formaldehyde synthetic resin bonded pressed particle board conforming to IS : 3087 finished with a coat of aluminium primer on both sides and edges and two coats of synthetic enamel paint of approved quality on exposed face fixed to a grid made out of anodised aluminium (with 15 micron anodic coating) T-sections 35 × 15 × 1.5 mm size main runners and cross runners 23.5 × 19 × 1.5 mm fixed to main runners placed 600 mm centre to centre both ways so as to form a grid of 600 mm square. The frame work shall be suspended from ceiling by level adjusting hangers of 6 mm dia M.S. rod fixed to roof slab by means of ceiling cleats. The suspenders shall be placed 600 × 1200 mm centre to centre including fixing to the frame with C.P. brase screws and applying a priming coat of zinc chromate yellow primer for steel members complete. (Frame work and suspenders to be paid for separately).	sq m	295.70
42.	Extra for using 12 mm thick semi per forated ceiling tiles instead of 12 mm thick plain ceiling tiles in item above.	sq m	55.55
43.	Extra for providing 3 mm thick transluscent white acrylic plastic sheets of approved quality in false ceiling instead of 12 mm thick plain/or with design particle board ceiling tiles in item above.	sq m	461.05
44.	Providing 10 mm thick plaster of Paris (gypsum anhydrous) ceiling upto a height of 5 m above floor level over first class kail wood strips 25 × 6 mm with 10 mm gap in between and reinforced with rabbit wire mesh fixed to wooden frame (frame work to be paid separately) :		
	44A Flat surfaces	sq m	336.40
	44B Curved surfaces	sq m	365.55
45.	Extra for any sunk or raised mouldings in the plaster of Paris (Gypsum anhydrous) ceiling.	sq m	103.15
46.	Extra for providing plaster of Paris (Gypsum anhydrous) ceiling above 5 metres height from floor level.	sq m per metre height	22.25
47.	Providing and fixing 12 mm thick plaster of Paris (gypsum anhydrous) ceiling tiles upto a height of 5 metres above floor level over wooden frames and rendered smooth with plaster of Paris (frame work to be paid separately).	sq m	199.85
48.	Extra for providing and fixing plaster of paris (Gypsum anhydrous) ceiling tiles beyond 5 metres height from floor level (Height beyond 5 m to be measured for extra payment).	sq m per metre height	10.95
49.	Providing, fixing and applying plaster of paris (POP) false ceiling consisting of frame work made with 50 mm sq M.S. tubes of 18 G thickness as main runner at 600 mm c/c both ways, suspended/ supported with M.S. flats 25 × 4 mm from existing R.C.C. slab including providing and fixing expanded metal of size 5.25 mm × 1.25 mm thickness welded to main runners and applying POP (calcium sluphate semihydrate variety) to the expanded metal of thickness not less than 10 mm finished smooth to line and level including necessary supports scaffolding etc. as required and also including applying a coat of red oxide zinc chromate primer over the M.S. frame work and suspenders complete.	sq m	364.20

S. No.	Description	Unit	Rate ₹
50.	Providing and fixing plaster of paris (POP) false ceiling consisting of frame work made with 50 mm sq M.S. tubes of 18 G thickness as main runners at 600 mm c/c both ways, suspended/supported with M.S. flats 25 × 4 mm from existing R.C.C. slab including providing and fixing minimum 10 mm thick POP (calcium sulphate semihydrate variety) jute reinforced tiles of 600 mm × 600 mm of plain/or of approved design finished smooth to line and level including necessary supports scaffolding etc. as required and also including applying a coat of red oxide zinc chromate primer over the M.S. frame work and suspenders complete.	sq m	987.05
51.	Providing and fixing plain, square edged wooden beading 65 × 12 m section with screws of approved quality for ceilings :		
	51A 2nd class teak wood	metre	43.30
	51B First class deodar wood	metre	36.00
52.	Extra for making chamfered edges of beading.	metre	3.05
53.	Thermal Insulation of roofing with bonded mineral wool, laid over false ceiling with suitable adhesive as per directions of the Engineer-in-charge, 50 mm thick.	sq m	107.10
54.	Thermal Insulation of roofing with Expanded polystyrene fixed with suitable adhesive to the false ceiling as per the directions of the Engineer-in-Charge :		
	(1) With Type N-Normal		
	54A 50 mm thick	sq m	107.40
	(2) With Type SE Self Extinguishing type		
	54B 50 mm thick	sq m	107.40
	E. RAIN WATER SPOUT AND PIPES		
55.	Providing and fixing 100 mm diameter and 60 cm long rain water spout in cement mortar 1 : 4 (1 cement : 4 fine sand) :		
	55A Stone ware spout	each	23.50
56.	Providing and fixing on wall face S.C.I. rain water pipes including filling the joints with spun yarn, soaked in neat cement slurry and cement mortar 1 : 2 (1 cement : 2 fine sand) :		
	56A 100 mm diameter	metre	187.60
	56B 150 mm diameter	metre	358.85
57.	Providing, fixing and embedding cast iron (S&S) class LA. rain water pipes in the masonry, R.C.C. surrounded with 12 mm thick cement mortar of the same mix as that of masonry (lead caulking to be paid for separately :		
	57A 100 mm diameter	metre	203.30
	57B 150 mm diameter	metre	395.25
58.	Providing and fixing M.S. holder bat clamps of approved design to C.I. or S.C.I. rain water pipes embedded in and including cement concrete blocks 10 × 10 × 10 cm of 1 : 2 : 4 mix (1 cement : 2 coarse sand : 4 graded stone aggregate 20 mm nominal size) and cost of cutting holes and making good the walls etc. :		
	58A 100 mm diameter	each	35.90
	58B 150 mm diameter	each	50.35

(Contd.)

S. No.	Description	Unit	Rate ₹
59.	Providing and fixing on wall face C.I. accessories for rain water pipes including filling the joints with spun yarn soaked in neat cement slurry and cement mortar 1 : 2 (1 cement : 2 fine sand):		
	(1) C.I. Plain bend :		
	59A 100 mm diameter	each	80.40
	59B 150 mm diameter	each	156.00
	(2) C.I. head flat or corner type bend :		
	59C 100 mm diameter	each	96.40
	59D 150 mm diameter	each	153.10
	(3) C.I. Plain shoes :		
	59E 100 mm diameter	each	80.40
	59F 150 mm diameter	each	156.00
	(4) C.I. branches (Plain) :		
	59G 100 mm dia single branch	each	124.85
	59H 150 mm dia single branch	each	322.65
	59I 100 mm dia double branch	each	185.95
	(5) C.I. off set (Plain) :		
	59J 100 mm dia. 55 mm projection	each	108.20
	59K 100 mm dia. 75 mm projection	each	119.30
60.	Providing lead caulked joints to sand cast iron rain water pipes and fittings :		
	60A 100 mm dia pipe	each	77.05
	60B 150 mm dia pipe	each	108.00
61.	Providing, fixing and embedding sand cast iron accessories for rain water pipes in the masonry surrounded with 12 mm thick cement mortar of the same mix, as that of masonry (lead caulking will be paid for separately) :		
	61A S.C.I. Plain bend :		
	61B 100 mm diameter	each	99.30
	61C 150 mm diameter	each	236.20
	61D Sand cast iron plain shoes :		
	61E 100 mm diameter	each	85.95
	61F 150 mm diameter	each	155.10
62.	Providing and fixing on wall face asbestos cement rain water pipe including jointing with spun yarn soaked in bitumen and cement mortar 1 : 2 (1 cement : 2 coarse sand) complete :		
	62A 100/101.6 mm diameter	metre	31.95
63.	Providing and fixing for A.C. pipe on wall plugs and standard holder bat clamps comprising of two semi-circular halves of flat iron and cast iron base screwed on wooden plugs :		
	63A 100/101.6 mm diameter	each	37.50
64.	Providing and fixing on wall face asbestos cement fittings for rain water pipes including jointing with spun yarn soaked in bitumen and cement mortar 1 : 2 (1 cement : 2 coarse sand) :		
	(1) Bend of required degree		
	64A 100/101.6 mm dia without door	each	598.85

S. No.	Description	Unit	Rate ₹
64B	100/101.6 mm dia with door	each	40.85
(2)	Off-sets 52.2 mm projection :		
64C	100/101.6 mm diameter	each	45.30
(3)	Junction equal single of required degree :		
64D	100/101.6 mm diameter without door	each	53.85
64E	100/101.6 mm diameter with door	each	64.95
(4)	Junction equal double of required degree :		
64F	100/101.6 mm diameter without door	each	74.55
64G	100/101.6 mm diameter with door	each	80.10
(5)	Standard shoe :		
64H	100/101.6 mm dia	each	45.30
(6)	Hexagonal rain water head :		
64I	400 × 300 mm/408.4 × 304.8 mm, 100/101.6 mm dia.	each	66.40
65.	**Providing and fixing on wall face unplasticised-PVC (working pressure 4 kg per sq cm) rain water pipes conforming to IS : 4985 including jointing with seal ring conforming to IS : 5382 leaving 10 mm gap for thermal expansion :**		
(1)	Single socketed pipes :		
65A	75 mm diameter	each	90.75
65B	110 mm diameter	each	165.90
66.	**Providing and fixing on wall face unplasticised-PVC moulded fittings/ accessories for unplasticised-PVC rain water pipes conforming to IS : 4985 including jointing with seal ring conforming to IS : 5382 leaving 10 mm gap for thermal expansion :**		
(1)	Coupler :		
66A	75 mm	each	65.10
66B	110 mm	each	85.95
(2)	Single Pushfit Coupler :		
66C	75 mm	each	66.20
66D	110 mm	each	96.55
(3)	Single tee with door :		
66E	75 × 75 × 75 mm	each	109.85
66F	110 × 110 × 110 mm	each	165.95
(4)	Single tee without door :		
66G	75 × 75 × 75 mm	each	99.30
66H	110 × 110 × 110 mm	each	153.20
(5)	Bend 87.5° :		
66I	75 mm bend	each	65.65
66J	110 mm bend	each	101.50
(6)	Shoe (Plain) :		
66K	75 mm Shoe	each	118.45
66L	110 mm Shoe	each	212.60
67.	**Providing and fixing unplasticised-PVC pipe clips of approved design to unplasticised-PVC rain water pipes by means of 50 × 50 × 50 mm hard wood plugs, screwed with M.S. screws of required length including cutting brick work and fixing in cement mortar 1 : 4 (1 cement : 4 coarse sand) and making good the wall etc. complete :**		

(*Contd.*)

S. No.	Description	Unit	Rate ₹
	67A 75 mm	each	46.45
	67B 110 mm	each	64.50
68.	Providing and fixing to the inlet mouth of rain water pipe cast iron grating 15 cm diameter and weighing not less than 440 grams.	each	15.85
69.	Providing and fixing at all height false ceiling of 12.5 mm thick tapered edge gypsum board conforming to IS : 2095 including providing and fixing of frame work made of special sections power pressed from M.S. sheet and galvanised in accordance with zinc coating 600 as per IS : 277 and consisting of angle cleats of size 25 mm wide × 16 mm thick with flanges of 22 mm and 37 mm at 1200 mm centre to centre one flange fixed to the ceiling with dash fastner 12.5 mm dia × 40 mm long with 6 mm dia bolts to the angle hangers of 25 × 25 × 5 mm of required length, and other end of angle hanger being fixed with nut and bolts to G.I. channels 45 mm × 15 mm × 0.9 mm running at the rate of 1200 mm centre to centre to which the ceiling section 0.5 mm thick bottom wedge of 80 mm with tapered flanges of 26 mm each having clips of 10.5 mm at 450 mm centre to centre shall be fixed in a direction perpendicular to G.I. channel with connecting clips made out of 2.64 mm dia × 230 mm long G.I. wire at every junction including fixing the gypsum board with ceiling section and perimeter channels 0.5 mm thick 27 mm high having flanges of 20 mm and 30 mm long, the perimeter of ceiling fixed to wall/partition with the help of rawl plugs at 450 mm centre to centre with 25 mm long drive-all screws @ 230 mm interval including jointing and fixing to a flush finish of tapered and square edges of the gypsum board with recommended filler, paper tapes, finisher and two coats of primer suitable for gypsum board as per manufactures specification and also including the coat of making openings for light fittings, grills, diffusers, cutouts made with frame of perimeter channels suitably fixed all complete as per drawing and specification and direction of the Engineer-in-charge but excluding the cost of painting.	sq m	374.70

Table 13.12. FINISHING

S. No.	Description	Unit	Rate ₹
	A. LIME PLASTER		
1.	12 mm lime plaster 1 : 1 : 1 (1 lime putty : 1 surkhi : 1 fine sand).	sq m	38.95
2.	15 mm lime plaster 1 : 1 : 1 (1 lime putty : 1 surkhi : 1 fine sand) on the rough side of single or half brick wall.	sq m	45.35
3.	18 mm lime plaster 1 : 1 : 1 (1 lime putty : 1 surkhi : 1 fine sand) in two coats, under layer 12 mm and top layer 6 mm thick.	sq m	58.75
4.	12 mm lime surkhi plaster 1 : 2 (1 lime putty : 2 surkhi).	sq m	39.90
5.	15 mm lime surkhi plaster 1 : 2 (1 lime putty : 2 surkhi) on rough side of single or half brick wall.	sq m	46.50
6.	18 mm lime surkhi plaster 1 : 2 (1 lime putty : 2 surkhi) in two coats, under layer 12 mm and top layer of 6 mm thick.	sq m	58.25
7.	Lime punning with lime mortar 1 : 1 (1 lime putty : 1 fine sand).	sq m	11.85

S. No.	Description	Unit	Rate ₹
	B. CEMENT PLASTER (IN FINE SAND)		
8.	12 mm cement plaster of mix :		
8A	1 : 4 (1 cement : 4 fine sand)	sq m	41.85
8B	1 : 6 (1 cement : 6 fine sand)	sq m	36.55
9.	15 mm cement plaster on the rough side of single or half brick wall of mix :		
9A	1 : 4 (1 cement : 4 fine sand)	sq m	48.90
9B	1 : 6 (1 cement : 6 fine sand)	sq m	42.50
10.	20 mm cement plaster of mix :		
10A	1 : 4 (1 cement : 4 fine sand)	sq m	59.90
10B	1 : 6 (1 cement : 6 fine sand)	sq m	51.60
	C. CEMENT PLASTER (IN COARSE SAND)		
11.	12 mm cement plaster of mix :		
11A	1 : 4 (1 cement : 4 coarse sand)	sq m	44.95
11B	1 : 6 (1 cement : 6 coarse sand)	sq m	39.60
12.	15 mm cement plaster on rough side of single or half brick wall of mix :		
12A	1 : 4 (1 cement : 4 coarse sand)	sq m	52.55
12B	1 : 6 (1 cement : 6 coarse sand)	sq m	46.20
13.	20 mm cement plaster of mix :		
13A	1 : 4 (1 cement : 4 coarse sand)	sq m	64.70
13B	1 : 6 (1 cement : 6 coarse sand)	sq m	56.40
	D. CEMENT PLASTER WITH A FLOATING COAT OF NEAT CEMENT		
14.	12 mm cement plaster finished with a floating coat of neat cement of mix :		
14A	1 : 3 (1 cement : 3 fine sand)	sq m	58.30
14B	1 : 4 (1 cement : 4 fine sand)	sq m	53.00
15.	15 mm cement plaster on rough side of single or half brick wall finished with a floating coat of neat cement of mix :		
15A	1 : 3 (1 cement : 3 fine sand)	sq m	66.35
15B	1 : 4 (1 cement : 4 fine sand)	sq m	60.00
16.	20 mm cement plaster finished with a floating coat of neat cement of mix :		
16A	1 : 3 (1 cement : 3 fine sand)	sq m	79.30
16B	1 : 4 (1.cement : 4 fine sand)	sq m	71.00
17.	12 mm cement plaster 1 : 3 (1 cement : 3 coarse sand) finished with a floating coat of neat cement.	sq m	61.40
18.	15 mm cement plaster 1 : 3 (1 cement : 3 coarse sand) finished with a floating coat of neat cement on the rough side of single or half brick wall.	sq m	70.05
	E. CEMENT PLASTER IN TWO COATS		
19.	18 mm cement plaster in two coats under layer 12 mm thick cement plaster 1 : 5 (1 cement : 5 coarse sand) finished with a top layer 6 mm thick cement plaster 1 : 6 (1 cement : 6 fine sand).	sq m	60.80

(Contd.)

S. No.	Description	Unit	Rate ₹
20.	18 mm cement plaster in two coats under layer 12 mm thick cement plaster 1 : 5 (1 cement : 5 coarse sand) and a top layer 6 mm thick cement plaster 1 : 3 (1 cement : 3 coarse sand) finished rough with sponge.	sq m	67.70
21.	12 mm cement plaster 1 : 2 (1 cement : 2 stone dust).	sq m	58.40
22.	15 mm cement plaster 1 : 2 (1 cement : 2 stone dust) on the rough side of single or half brick wall.	sq m	68.60
23.	20 mm cement plaster 1 : 2 (1 cement : 2 stone dust).	sq m	85.60
	F. 6 MM CEMENT PLASTER		
24.	6 mm cement plaster to ceiling of mix :		
	24A 1 : 3 (1 cement : 3 fine sand)	sq m	33.00
25.	6 mm cement plaster 1 : 3 (1 cement: 3 fine sand) finished with a floating coat of neat cement and thick coat of Lime wash on top of walls when dry for bearing of R.C.C. slabs and beams.	sq m	45.65
26.	Neat, cement punning :	sq m	11.70
	G. CEMENT LIME PLASTER		
27.	12 mm cement lime plaster of mix :		
	27A 1 : 1 : 6 (1 cement : 1 lime putty : 6 fine sand)	sq m	41.85
	27B 1 : 2 : 9 (1 cement : 2 lime putty : 9 fine sand)	sq m	40.00
28.	15 mm cement lime plaster on rough side of single or half brick wall of mix :		
	28A 1 : 1 : 6 (1 cement : 1 lime putty : 6 fine sand)	sq m	48.80
	28B 1 : 2 : 9 (1 cement : 2 lime putty : 9 fine sand)	sq m	46.60
29.	18 mm cement lime plaster in two coats, under layer 12 mm cement plaster 1 : 5 (1 cement : 5 coarse sand) finished with 6 mm cement lime plaster of mix :		
	29A 1 : 1 : 6 (1 cement : 1 lime putty : 6 fine sand)	sq m	63.60
	H. ROUGH CAST PLASTER		
30.	Rough cast plaster with a mixture of sand and gravel or crushed stone from 6 mm to 10 mm nominal size dashed over and including the fresh plaster in two layers, under layer 12 mm cement plaster 1 : 4 (1 cement : 4 coarse sand) and top layer 10 mm cement plaster 1 : 3 (1 cement : 3 fine sand) mixed with 10% finely grounded hydrated lime by volume of cement :		
	30A Ordinary cement finish using ordinary cement	sq m	107.80
	I. PEBBLE DASH PLASTER		
31.	Pebble dash plaster with a mixture of washed pebble or crushed stone 6 mm to 12.5 mm nominal size dashed over and including fresh plaster in two layers under layer 12 mm cement plaster 1 : 4 (1 cement : 4 coarse sand) and top layer 10 mm cement plaster with cement mortar 1 : 3 (1 cement : 3 fine sand) mixed with 10% finely grounded hydrated lime by volume of cement.	sq m	99.45
32.	Extra for providing and mixing water proofing material in cement plaster work in proportion recommended by the manufacturers :		
	32A 12 mm cement plaster 1 : 3 (1 cement : 3 sand)	sq m	2.40
	32B 12 mm cement plaster 1 : 4 (1 cement : 4 sand)	sq m	1.80
	32C 15 mm cement plaster 1 : 3 (1 cement : 3 sand)	sq m	2.85
	32D 15 mm cement plaster 1 : 4 (1 cement : 4 sand)	sq m	2.10

S. No.		Description	Unit	Rate ₹
	32E	20 mm cement plaster 1 : 3 (1 cement : 3 sand)	sq m	3.65
	32F	20 mm cement plaster 1 : 4 (1 cement : 4 sand)	sq m	2.75
33.		Extra for plastering exterior walls of height more than 10 m from ground level for every additional height of 3 m or part thereof.	sq m	8.90
34.		Extra for plastering on circular work not exceeding 6 m in radius :		
	34A	In one coat	sq m	4.10
	34B	In two coats	sq m	6.30
35.		Extra for plastering done on moulding cornices or architraves including neat finish to line and level :		
	35A	In one coat	sq m	57.80
	35B	In two coats	sq m	95.05
36.		Extra for plastering :		
	36A	Spherical ceiling	sq m	15.30
	36B	Groined ceiling	sq m	16.75
	36C	Flewing soffits	sq m	10.00
37.		Providing and applying plaster of paris putty of 2 mm thickness over plastered surface to prepare the surface even and smooth complete.	sq m	73.55
		J. SUPERIOR PLASTER		
38.		18 mm plastering with terrazo finish rubbed and polished complete, under layer 12 mm thick cement plaster 1 : 3 (1 cement : 3 coarse sand) and top layer 6 mm thick white, black, chocolate, grey, yellow or Baroda green marble chips of 3 mm and down size laid in cement marble powder mix 3 : 1 (3 cement : 1 marble powder) by weight in proportion 4 : 7 (4 cement marble powder mix : 7 marble chips) by volume.	sq m	179.55
39.		Extra if white cement is used instead of ordinary cement in top layer of 18 mm thick plastering with terrazo finish.	sq m	24.35
40.		Extra if colour is added to grey or white cement in top layer of 18 mm plastering with terrazo finish :		
	40A	Red, Chocolate, Orange or buff (yellow) colour	sq m	32.75
	40B	Black colour	sq m	21.75
	40C	Blue or green colour	sq m	24.75
41.		Extra for 18 mm thick terrazo finish marble chips plastering in circular work not exceeding 6 metre radius.	sq m	10.00
		K. ARTIFICIAL RED STONE PLASTER		
42.		18 mm thick artificial red stone plaster consisting of 12 mm under coat of cement plaster 1 : 4 (1 cement: 4 coarse sand) with 6 mm thick finishing coat of cement mortar 1 : 1 : 3 (1 cement marble dust : 3 stone dust) mixed with red oxide to match the shade of red stone.	sq m	123.90
43.		Extra for lining out plaster to imitate stone or concrete blocks walling.	sq m	9.25
		L. PLAIN CEMENT MORTAR BANDS		
44.		12 mm thick plain cement mortar bands in cement mortar 1 : 4 (1 cement : 4 fine sand).		
	44A	Flush Band	cm per metre	0.75
	44B	Sunk Band	cm per metre	0.80
	44C	Raised Band	cm per metre	0.90
	44D	Moulded Band	cm per metre	1.45

(Contd.)

S. No.	Description	Unit	Rate ₹
45.	18 mm thick plain cement mortar band in cement mortar 1 : 4 (1 cement : 4 fine sand) :		
	45A Fulsh Band	cm per metre	0.95
	45B Sunk Band	cm per metre	1.00
	45C Raised Band	cm per metre	1.15
	45D Moulded Band	cm per metre	2.00
	M. POINTING OF BRICK WORK		
46.	18 mm thick moulded cement mortar band in two coats under layer 12 mm thick with cement mortar 1 : 5 (1 cement: 5 coarse sand) top layer 6 mm thick with cement mortar 1 : 4 (1 cement : 4 fine sand).	cm per metre	2.00
47.	Pointing on brick work with cement mortar 1 : 3 (1 cement : 3 fine sand) :		
	47A Flush pointing	sq m	24.00
	47B Ruled pointing	sq m	25.40
	47C Struck or weathered pointing	sq m	30.75
	47D Raised and cut pointing	sq m	39.05
48.	Pointing on brick flooring with cement mortar 1 : 3 (1 cement : 3 fine sand) :		
	48A Flush pointing	sq m	19.65
	48B Ruled pointing	sq m	20.80
49.	Pointing on brick flooring with cement mortar 1 : 4 (1 cement : 4 fine sand) :		
	49A Flush pointing	sq m	18.90
	49B Ruled pointing	sq m	20.05
	N. POINTING ON TILE BRICK WORK		
50.	Pointing on tile brick work with cement lime mortar 1 : 1 : 3 (1 cement : 1 lime putty : 3 fine sand) with an admixture of red oxide to match the shade of tile brick work :		
	50A Flush pointing	sq m	33.25
	50B Ruled pointing	sq m	35.45
51.	Pointing on tile brick work with cement mortar 1: 3 (1 cement : 3 fine sand) :		
	51A Flush pointing	sq m	33.15
	51B Ruled pointing	sq m	34.40
	51C Struck or weathered pointing	sq m	39.60
	O. POINTING ON STONE WORK		
52.	Pointing on stone work with cement mortar 1 : 3 (1 cement : 3 fine sand) :		
	52A Flush pointing	sq m	33.05
	52B Ruled pointing	sq m	35.30
	52C Raised and cut pointing	sq m	59.85
53.	Raised and cut pointing on stone work in white cement mortar 1 : 3 (1 white cement : 3 marble dust).	sq m	73.90
54.	Pointing on white sand stone slab pavement with white cement mortar 1 : 3 (1 white cement : 3 fine sand).		
	54A Flush pointing	sq m	21.15
	54B Ruled pointing	sq m	21.90

S. No.	Description	Unit	Rate ₹
55.	Pointing on stone slab ceiling with cement mortar 1 : 2 (1 cement : 2 fine sand) :		
	55A Flush pointing	sq m	19. 25
	55B Ruled pointing	sq m	20. 35
56.	Extra for pointing on walls on the outside at height more than 10 m from ground level for every additional height of 3 m or part thereof.	sq m	1.65
57.	White washing with lime to give an even shade :		
	57A New work (three or more coats)	sq m	3.60
58.	Satna lime wash on walls one coat.	sq m	1.40
59.	White washing with whiting to give an even shade :		
	59A New work (three or more coats)	sq m	3.60
60.	Colour washing such as green, blue or buff to give an even shade :		
	60A New work (two or more coats) with a base coat of white washing with lime	sq m	4.85
	60B New work (two or more coats) with a base coat of whiting	sq m	4.75
61.	Distempering with dry distemper of approved brand and manufacture (two or more coats) and of required shade on new work, over and including priming coat of whiting to give an even shade.	sq m	15.35
62.	Distempering with oil bound washable distemper of approved brand and manufacture to give an even shade :		
	62A New work (two or more coats) over and including priming coat with cement primer	sq m	26.65
63.	Distempering with 1st quality acrylic washable distemper (ready made) of approved manufacturer and of required shade and colour complete as per manufacturer's specification :		
	63A Two or more coats on new work	sq m	14.60
	63B One or more coats on old work	sq m	8.80
64.	Applying one coat of cement primer of approved brand and manufacture on wall surface :		
	64A Cement primer	sq m	11.20
65.	Finishing walls with water proofing cement paint of approved brand and manufacture and of required shade to give an even shade :		
	65A New work (three or more coats)	sq m	29.85
66.	Applying priming coat :		
	66A With ready mixed pink or grey primer of approved brand and manufacture on wood work (hard and soft wood)	sq m	10.05
	66B With ready mixed aluminium primer of approved brand and manufacture on resinous wood and plywood	sq m	10.65
	66C With ready mixed zinc chromate yellow primer of approved brand and manufacture on steel galvanised iron/steel works	sq m	8.40
	66D With ready mixed zinc chromate yellow primer of approved brand and manufacture on steel work (second coat)	sq m	4.90
67.	Painting with ready mixed paint of approved brand and manufacture in all shades to give an even shade :		
	67A New steel work (two or more coats)	sq m	20.15
	67B New wood work (two or more coats)	sq m	19.75
68.	Painting one thin coat with white lead of approved brand and manufacture on wet or patchy portion of plastered surfaces.	sq m	14.45

(Contd.)

S. No.	Description	Unit	Rate ₹
69.	Finishing with Epoxy paint (two or more coats) at all locations prepared and applied as per manufacturer's specifications including appropriate priming coat, preparation of surface, etc. complete :		
	69A On steel work	sq m	49.35
	69B On concrete work	sq m	49.95
70.	Painting on G.S. sheet with synthetic enamel paint of approved brand and manufacture of required colour to give an even shade :		
	70A New work (two or more coats) including a coat of approved steel primer but excluding a coat of mordant solution	sq m	16.15
71.	Applying a coat of mordant solution on G.S. sheet :		
	71A With a solution of 38 gms of copper acetate in a litre of soft water	sq m	4.35
	71B With a solution made of 13 gms of hydrochloric acid in a solution of 13 gms each of copper chloride, copper nitrate and ammonium chloride dissolved in a litre of soft water	sq m	4.35
72.	Painting (two or more coats) on rain water, soil, waste and vent pipes and fittings with black anticorrosive bitumastic paint approved brand and manufacture over and including a priming of ready mixed zinc chromate yellow primer on new work :		
	72A 100 mm diameter pipes	metre	9.20
	72B 150 mm diameter pipes	metre	13.75
73.	Painting (one or more coats) on rain water, soil, waste and vent pipes and fittings with black anticorrosive bitumastic paint approved brand and manufacture on old work :		
	73A 100 mm diameter pipes	metre	4.15
	73B 150 mm diameter pipes	metre	6.00
74.	Painting (two or more coats) on rain water, soil, waste and vent pipes and fittings with synthetic enamel paint of approved brand and manufacture and required colour over a priming coat of approved steel primer on new work :		
	74A 100 mm diameter pipes	metre	10.45
	74B 150 mm diameter pipes	metre	15.60
75.	Painting with oil type wood preservative of approved brand and manufacture :		
	75A New work (two or more coats)	sq m	7.75
76.	Providing and applying two coats of fire retardent paint FR 881 unthinned on cleaned wood/ply surface @ 3.5 sq m per litre per coat including preparation of base surface as per recommendations of manufacturer to make the surface fire retardant.	sq m	152.75
77.	Coal tarring two coats on new work using 0.16 and 0.12 litre coal tar per sq m in the first coat and second coat respectively.	sq m	7.15
78.	Wall painting with plastic emulsion paint of approved brand and manufacture to give an even shade :		
	78A Two or more coats on new work	sq m	28.35
79.	Painting with synthetic enamel paint of approved brand and manufacture to give an even shade :		
	79A Two or more coats on new work	sq m	20.60

S. No.	Description	Unit	Rate ₹
80.	Painting with synthetic enamel paint of approved brand and manufacture of required colour to give an even shade :		
	80A Two or more coats on new work over an under coat of suitable shade with ordinary paint of approved brand and manufacture	sq m	31.95
81.	Painting with aluminium paint of approved brand and manufacture to give an even shade :		
	81A Two or more coats on new work	sq m	18.95
82.	Painting with acid proof paint of approved brand and manufacture of required colour to give an even shade :		
	82A Two or more coats on new work.	sq m	19.75
83.	Painting with black anti-corrosive bitumastic paint of approved brand and manufacture to give an even shade :		
	83A Two or more coats on new work.	sq m	15.15
84.	Floor painting with floor enamel paint of approved brand and manufacture of required colour to give an even shade :		
	84A Two or more coats on new work.	sq m	22.95
85.	Painting small articles of painted surface and not in conjunction with similar painted work with paint of approved brand and manufacture and of required quality and shade to give an even shade :		
	85A Area not exceeding 0.1 sq m.	each	4.40
	85B Upto 15 cm in width or in girth.	each	4.65
86.	Varnishing with varnish of approved brand and manufacture :		
	86A Two or more coats of glue sizing with copal varnish over an under coat of flatting varnish.	sq m	28.10
	86B One or more coats with copal varnish.	sq m	12.15
	86C Two or more coats glue sizing with spar varnish or an under coat of flatting varnish.	sq m	29.30
	86D One or more coats with spar varnish.	sq m	12.80
87.	French spirit polishing :		
	87A Two or more coats on new works including a coat of wood filler.	sq m	42.90
88.	Polishing on wood work with ready made wax polish of approved brand and manufacture :		
	88A New work	sq m	20.70
89.	Melamine polishing on wood work (one or more coat).	sq m	26.90
90.	Floor polishing on masonry or concrete floors with wax polish of approved brand and manufacture.	sq m	8.95
91.	Lettering with black Japan paint of approved brand and manufacture.	per lettre per cm height	0.55
92.	Varnishing with flatting varnish of approved brand and manufacture one or more coats on old work.	sq m	10.25

(*Contd.*)

S. No.	Description	Unit	Rate ₹
93.	Washed stone grit plaster in two layers, under layer 12 mm cement plaster 1 : 4 (1 cement : 4 coarse sand) furrowing the under layer with scratching tool, applying cement slurry on the under layer @ 2 kg of cement per square metre, top layer 15 mm cement plaster 1 : 1/2 : 2 (1 cement : 1/2 coarse sand : 2 stone chipping 10 mm nominal size) in panels with groove all around as per approved pattern including scrubbing and washing, the top layer with brushes and water to expose the stone chippings, complete as per specification and direction of Engineer-in-charge (Payment for providing grooves shall be made separately).	sq m	144.75
94.	Forming groove of uniform size in the top layer of washed stone grit plaster as per approved pattern using wooden battens, nailed to the under layer including removal of wooden battens, repair to the edges of panels and finishing the groove complete as per specifications and direction of the Engineer-in-charge :		
	94A 15 mm wide and 15 mm deep groove	metre	7.55
	94B 20 mm wide and 15 mm deep groove	metre	7.80
95.	Extra for washed grit plaster on exterior walls of height more than 10 m from ground lever for every additional height of 3 m or part thereof.	sq m	21.80
96.	Extra for washed stone grit plaster on circular work not exceeding 6 m in radius (in two coats).	sq m	13.00
97.	Forming groove of uniform size from 12 × 12 mm and upto 25 × 15 mm in plastered surface as per approved pattern using wooden battens, nailed to the under layer including removal of wooden battens, repairs to the edges of plaster panel and finishing the groove complete as per specifications and direction of the Engineer-in-charge.	metre	7.60
98.	Extra for using white cement in place of ordinary cement in the top layer of the item of washed stone grit plaster.	sq m	60.85

Table 13.13. Repairs of Building

S. No.	Description	Unit	Rate ₹
	A. GENERAL		
1.	Repairs to plaster of thickness 12 mm to 20 mm in patches of area 2.5 sq. metres and under including cutting the patch in proper shape and preparing and plastering the surface of the walls complete including disposal of rubbish to the dumping ground within 50 metres lead :		
	1A With cement mortar 1 : 4 (1 cement : 4 fine sand)	sq m	61.50
	1B With cement mortar 1 : 4 (1 cement : 4 coarse sand)	sq m	58.85
2.	Fixing chowkhats in existing opening including embedding chowkhats in floors or walls cutting masonry for holdfasts embedding hold fasts in cement concrete blocks with cement concrete 1 : 3 : 6 (1 cement : 3 coarse sand : 6 graded stone aggregate 20 mm nominal size) painting two coats of coal tar to sides of chowkhats and making good the damages to walls and floors as required complete including disposal of rubbish to the dumping ground within 50 metres lead :		

S. No.		Description	Unit	Rate ₹
	2A	Door chowkhats	each	188.75
	2B	Window chowkhats	each	114.20
	2C	Clerestory window chowkhats	each	79.60
3.		Making the opening in brick masonry including dismantling fixing chowkhats in floor or walls cutting masonry and fixing holdfasts in cement concrete 1 : 3 : 6 (1 cement : 3 coarse sand : 6 stone aggregate 20 mm nominal size) painting two coats of coal tar to sides of chowkhats and making good the damages to walls and floors complete to match the existing surface :		
	3A	For door	each	242.45
	3B	For window	each	155.50
	3C	For clerestory window	each	97.40
4.		Providing and fixing wooden cleats of size 100 mm × 75 mm × 50 mm to doors and windows with approved fittings including removal of old cleats where necessary including painting, polishing or bees waxing to match the existing shade :		
	4A	2nd class teak wood cleats with brass hinges and screws	each	23.20
	4B	2nd class teak wood cleats with iron hinges and screws	each	17.95
5.		Renewing glass panes, with putty and nails wherever necessary :		
	5A	Glass panes weighing 7.5 kg/sq m.	sq m	239.80
	5B	Glass panes weighing 10 kg/sq m	sq m	280.15
	5C	Glass panes weighing 13.75 kg/sq m	sq m	371.80
	5D	Frosted glass panes weighing 7.5 kg/sq m	sq m	276.50
6.		Renewing glass panes, with wooden fillets wherever necessary :		
	6A	Glass panes weighing 7.5 kg/sq m	sq m	278.55
	6B	Glass panes weighing 10 kg/sq m	sq m	318.90
	6C	Glass panes weighing 13.75 kg/sq m	sq m	410.55
	6D	Frosted glass panes weighing 7.5 kg/sq m	sq m	315.25
7.		Renewing glass panes and refixing existing wooden fillets :		
	7A	Glass panes weighing 7.5 kg/sq m	sq m	236.95
	7B	Glass panes weighing 10 kg/sq m	sq m	277.30
	7C	Glass panes weighing 13.75 kg/sq m	sq m	368.95
	7D	Frosted glass panes weighing 7.5 kg/sq m	sq m	273.60
8.		Supplying and fixing new wooden fillets wherever necessary :		
	8A	2nd class teak wood fillets	metre	10.75
	8B	1st class deodar wood fillets	metre	9.75
	8C	Hollock wood fillets	metre	7.95
9.		Renewal of old putty of glass panes (length).	metre	5.85
10.		Refixing old glass panes with putty and nails.	sq m	75.90
11.		Fixing old glass panes with wooden fillets (excluding cost of fillets).	sq m	54.90
12.		Providing and fixing 16 mm M.S. Fan clamps of standard shape and size in existing R.C.C. slab including cutting chase and making good and painting exposed portion of the clamps complete.	each	57.95

(Contd.)

S. No.	Description	Unit	Rate ₹
13.	Regarding terracing of mud phaska covered with tiles or brick, in cement by dismantling tiles or bricks, removing mud plaster, preparing the surface of mud phaska to proper slope relaying plaster gobri leaping and tiles or bricks, grouted in cement mortar 1 : 3 (1 cement : 3 fine sand) including replacing unserviceable tiles or bricks with new ones and disposal of unserviceable material to the dumping ground (the cost of the new tiles or brick excluded) within 50 metres lead.	sq m	62.95
14.	Replacing sand stone slabs in roofing laid in cement mortar 1 : 4 (1 cement : 4 coarse sand) including necessary repairs and cement pointing with same mortar complete including disposal of rubbish to dumping ground within 50 metres of lead :		
	14A Red sand stone slabs 30 to 40 mm thick	sq m	217.95
	14B Red sand stone slabs 45 mm thick	sq m	251.90
	14C Red stone slabs 50 mm thick	sq m	258.95
	14D White sand stone slabs 30 to 40 mm thick	sq m	243.60
	14E White sand stone slabs 45 mm thick	sq m	330.10
	14F White sand stone slabs 50 mm thick	sq m	337.20
15.	Renewing wooden battens in roofs, including making good the holes in wall and painting with oil type wood preservative of approved brand and manufacture complete including removal of rubbish to the dumping ground within 50 metres lead :		
	15A Sal wood battens	cum	21365.00
	15B 1st class deodar wood battens	cum	31225.00
16.	Renewing wooden beams in roofs including making good the holes in walls and painting with oil type wood preservative of approved brand and manufacture complete including removal of rubbish to the dumping ground within 50 metres lead :		
	(1) Not exceeding 4.00 metres in length.		
	16A Sal wood beams	cum	21885.00
	16B Hollock wood beams	cum	20745.00
	(2) Above 4.00 metres and upto 5.00 metres length.		
	16C Sal wood beams	cum	22150.00
	16D Hollock wood beams	cum	21000.00
17.	Renewing 100 mm dia 2.5 metres long sal wood balli post embedded 60 cm in the ground in a trench 45 cm dia and 75 cm deep filled with cement concrete 1 : 5 : 10 (1 cement : 5 fine sand : 10 stone aggregate 40 mm nominal size) including necessary excavation, cement concrete foundation and painting two coats with oil type wood preservative of approved brand and manufacture complete including disposal of rubbish to the dumping ground within 50 metres lead.	each	185.55
18.	Raking out joints in lime or cement mortar and preparing the surface for repainting or replastering including disposal of rubbish to the dumping ground within 50 metres lead.	sq m	5.05
19.	Extra for making opening or recesses in A.C. corrugated/semi corrugated sheet roofing of girth not more than 1 metre :		
	19A Those not exceeding 100 square centimetres in area	each	7.90
	19B Those exceeding 100 square centimetres but not exceeding 400 square centimetres in area	each	15.20
	19C Those exceeding 400 square centimetres in area	each	21.95

S. No.	Description	Unit	Rate ₹
20.	Flush pointing with cement mortar 1 : 3 (1 cement : 3 fine sand) mixed with 2% of integral water proofing compound by weight of cement for flat tile bricks on top of mud phaska :		
	20A With F.P.S. brick tiles	sq m	13.05
	20B With modular brick tiles	sq m	13.40
21.	Taking out wind ties from roof including cutting out rusted bolts, nuts etc. and removing materials to any distance within compound and stacking.	kg	0.40
22.	Fixing of old wind tie with new fittings including painting two or more coats with anticorrosive bitumastic paint of approved brand and manufacturer over and including priming coat of ready mixed zinc chromate yellow primer of approved brand.	metre	18.60
23.	Renewing bottom rail and/or top runner of collapsible gate including making good all damages and applying priming coat of zinc chromate yellow primer of approved brand and manufacturer.	kg	38.95
24.	Renewing W.I. or M.S. Wheel or roller of steel door or gate and fitting and fixing the same with necessary clamps, nuts and bolts/welding and erection etc. complete :		
	24A Wheel 50 mm dia. and below.	per wheel	41.55
	24B Wheel above 50 mm dia.	per wheel	83.45
	B. Earth work		
25.	*Pumping out water caused by springs, tidal or river seepage, broken water mains or drains and the like.	kilolitre	18.40
	***Note for item no. 13.13.25 :** This pertains to only such pumping of water as is envisaged at the time of tendering and do not include those that need be covered under contractual risk.		
	C. Mud mortar		
26.	Mud mortar.	cum	82.66
	D. Brick work		
27.	Brick work with bricks of class designation 75 in mud mortar.	cum	891.50
28.	Joiring old brick work in metric system with new brick work in cement mortar 1 : 4 (1 cement: 4 coarse sand) in metric system.	sq m	68.15
29.	Joining old brick work in F.P.S. system with new brick work in cement 1 : 4 (1 cement : 4 coarse sand) in metric system.	sq m	70.00
30.	Joining old brick work in F.P.S. system with new brick work in cement mortar 1 : 4 (1 cement : 4 coarse sand) in F.P.S. system.	sq m	77.20
	E. Wood work		
31.	Providing and fixing 25 mm thick shutters for cup board etc.		
	(1) Panelled or panelled and glazed shutters :		
	31A Superior class teak wood including nickel plated bright finished M.S. piano hinges with necessary screws	sq m	1561.35
	31B 1st class teak wood including nickel plated bright finished M.S. piano hinges with necessary screws	sq m	1057.30
	(2) Glazed shutters :		
	31C Superior class teak wood including nickel plated bright finished M.S. piano hinges with necessary screws	sq m	1652.60
	31D 1st class teak wood including nickel plated bright finished M.S. piano hinges with necessary screws	sq m	1159.75

(Contd.)

S. No.	Description	Unit	Rate ₹
32.	Providing and fixing plain jaffri door and window shutters including bright or/and black enamelled M.S. butt hinges with necessary screws 35 × 10 mm laths placed 35 mm apart (frames to be paid separately) including fixing 50 × 12 mm beading complete with :		
	32A Second class teak wood	sq m	1074.90
	32B 1st class deodar wood	sq m	1001.40
33.	Providing and fixing curtain rods of 1.25 mm thick brass plates with two brass brackets fixed with brass screws and wooden plugs etc. wherever necessary complete :		
	33A 12 mm diametre	metre	82.65
	33B 20 mm diametre	metre	87.10
	33C 25 mm diametre	metre	103.75
34.	Providing and fixing M.S. round or square bars at required spacings in wooden frame of windows and clerestory windows.	kg	22.10
35.	Providing and fixing M.S. round or square bars with M.S. flats at required spacings in wooden frames of windows and clerestory windows.	kg	20.60
36.	Providing joists (karries) including hoisting fixing in position and applying wood preservative on unexposed surface etc. complete with :		
	36A Sal wood	cum	21080.00
	36B Hollock wood	cum	19945.00
37.	Providing and fixing for posts, purlins, rafters, post plates etc. including cost of iron nails and spikes required and applying wood preservative on all exposed surfaces :		
	(1) Hollock bailies :		
	37A 80 mm diametre	metre	26.10
	37B 100 mm diametre	metre	32.80
	37C 125 mm diametre	metre	38.35
	37D 150 mm diametre	metre	46.30
38.	Providing and fixing bright finished brass single acting spring hinges with necessary screws etc. complete :		
	38A 150 mm	each	192.10
	38B 125 mm	each	156.55
	38C 100 mm	each	106.55
39.	Providing and fixing bright finished brass double acting spring hinges with necessary screws etc. complete :		
	39A 150 mm	each	285.40
	39B 125 mm	each	197.65
	39C 100 mm	each	166.55
40.	Providing and fixing bright finished brass flush bolts with necessary screws etc. complete :		
	40A 250 mm	each	77.70
	40B 150 mm	each	55.05
	40C 100 mm	each	38.35
41.	Providing and fixing 30 cm long bright finished finger plates 65 × 1.6 mm including necessary screws etc. complete.	each	60.30
42.	Providing and fixing bright finished brass furniture handles.	each	13.90

S. No.	Description	Unit	Rate ₹
43.	Providing and fixing 150 mm bright finished floor brass door stopper with rubber cushion, screws etc. to suit shutter thickness complete.	each	102.50
44.	Providing and fixing bright finished brass hard drawn hooks and eyes :		
	44A 300 mm	each	39.65
	44B 250 mm	each	36.35
	44C 200 mm	each	34.10
	44D 150 mm	each	31.35
	44E 100 mm	each	25.25
45.	Providing and fixing bright finished brass fan light pivot with necessary screws etc. complete.	each	17.90
46.	Providing and fixing 300 mm long bright finished brass chain with hook for fan light including necessary screws etc. complete.	each	13.15
47.	Providing and fixing bright finished brass quadrant stay 300 mm long with necessary screws etc. complete.	each	60.90
48.	Providing and fixing bright finished brass helical door spring (superior quality).	each	168.35
49.	Providing and fixing chromium plated brass butt hinges with necessary screws etc. complete :		
	49A 125 × 70 × 4 mm (ordinary type)	each	61.00
	49B 100 × 70 × 4 mm (ordinary type)	each	50.80
	49C 75 × 65 × 4 mm (heavy type)	each	50.35
	49D 75 × 40 × 2.5 mm (ordinary type)	each	20.90
	49E 50 × 40 × 2.5 mm (ordinary type)	each	12.90
50.	Providing and fixing 85 × 42 mm chromium plated brass pull bolt lock with necessary screws, nuts, bolts and washers etc. complete.	each	102.90
51.	Providing and fixing chromium plated brass door latch with screws etc. complete :		
	51A 300 × 16 × 5 mm	each	84.05
	51B 250 × 16 × 5 mm	each	78.45
52.	Providing and fixing chromium plated brass fan light pivot with necessary screws etc. complete.	each	24.50
53.	Providing and fixing chromium plated brass fan light catch with necessary screws etc. complete.	each	25.80
54.	Providing and fixing 300 mm long chromium plated brass chain with hook for fan light including necessary screws etc. complete.	each	14.90
55.	Providing and fixing chromium plated brass quadrant stays, 300 mm long with necessary screws etc. complete.	each	60.45
56.	Providing and fixing chromium plated brass hasp and staple (safety type) with necessary screws etc. complete :		
	56A 150 mm	each	56.70
	56B 115 mm	each	43.25
	56C 90 mm	each	37.25
	F. ROOFING		
57.	Providing and fixing on wall face S.C.I. rain water pipes including filling the joints with spun yarn, soaked in neat cement slurry and cement mortar 1 : 2 (1 cement : 2 fine sand) :		
	57A 75 mm diameter	metre	150.25

(*Contd.*)

S. No.	Description	Unit	Rate ₹
58.	**Providing, fixing and embedding cast iron (S&S) class LA. rain water pipes in the masonry/R.C.C. surrounded with 12 mm thick cement mortar of the same mix as that of masonry, R.C.C. (lead caulking will be paid for separately):**		
	58A 75 mm diameter	metre	167.85
59.	**Providing and fixing M.S. holder bat clamps of approved design to C.I. or S.C.I. rain water pipes embedded in and including cement concrete blocks 10 × 10 × 10 cm of 1 : 2 : 4 mix (1 cement : 2 coarse sand : 4 graded stone aggregate 20 mm nominal size) and cost of cutting holes and making good the walls etc. :**		
	59A 75 mm diameter	each	35.85
60.	**Providing and fixing on wall face C.I. accessories for rain water pipes including filling the joints with spun yarn soaked in neat cement slurry and cement mortar 1 : 2 (1 cement : 2 fine sand):**		
	(1) C.I. Plain bend :		
	60A 75 mm diameter	each	62.90
	(2) C.I. head flat or corner type bend :		
	60B 75 mm diameter	each	82.25
	(3) C.I. Plain shoes :		
	60C 75 mm diameter	each	62.95
	(4) C.I. branches (Plain) :		
	60D 75 mm dia single branch	each	85.20
	(5) C.I. off set (Plain) :		
	60E 75 mm dia 55 mm projection	each	107.40
	60F 75 mm dia. 75 mm projection	each	90.75
	60G 75 mm dia 115 mm projection	each	96.30
	60H 75 mm dia 150 mm projection	each	101.85
61.	**Providing lead caulked joints to sand cast iron rain water pipes and fittings :**		
	61A 75 mm dia pipe	each	59.95
62.	**Providing, fixing and embedding sand cast iron accessories for rain water pipes in the masonry surrounded with 12 mm thick cement mortar of the same mix, as that of masonry (lead caulking will be paid for separately) :**		
	(1) S.C.I. Plain bend :		
	62A 75 mm diameter	each	82.10
	(2) Sand cast iron plain shoes :		
	62B 75 mm diameter	each	62.10
	G. FINISHING		
63.	**Pointing on brick work with lime surkhi mortar 1 : 2 (1 lime putty : 2 surkhi) :**		
	63A Flush pointing	sq m	22.35
	63B Ruled pointing	sq m	23.65
	63C Struck or weathered pointing	sq m	29.05

S. No.	Description	Unit	Rate ₹
64.	**Pointing on brick work with an admixture of white cement, lime putty, marble dust and stone dust in proportion ¼ : 1 : 1 : 1 (¼ white cement : 1 lime putty : 1 marble dust : 1 stone dust) :**		
	64A Flush pointing	sq m	27.20
	64B Ruled pointing	sq m	28.50
	64C Struck or weathered pointing	sq m	33.90
65.	Pointing on tile brick work with lime mortar 1 : 2 (1 lime putty : 2 surkhi) :		
	65A Flush pointing	sq m	29.95
	65B Ruled pointing	sq m	32.20
	65C Struck or weathered pointing	sq m	37.15
66.	Pointing on tile brick work with an admixture of white cement lime marble dust and stone dust in proportion ¼ : 1 : 1 : 1 (¼ white cement : 1 marble dust : 1 stone dust : 1 lime putty) :		
	66A Flush pointing	sq m	37.35
	66B Ruled pointing	sq m	39.65
	66C Struck or weathered pointing	sq m	44.60
67.	White washing with lime to give an even shade :		
	67A Old work (two or more coats)	sq m	2.15
	67B Old work (one or more coats)	sq m	1.35
68.	White washing with whiting to give an even shade :		
	68A Old work (two or more coats)	sq m	2.20
	68B Old work (one or more coats)	sq m	1.35
69.	Colour washing such as green, blue or buff to give an even shade :		
	69A Old work (two or more coats) with lime	sq m	3.00
	69B Old work (two or more coats) with whiting	sq m	2.95
	69C Old work (one or more coats) with lime	sq m	1.70
	69D Old work (one or more coats) with whiting	sq m	1.70
70.	Removing white or colour wash by scrapping and sand papering and preparing the surface smooth including necessary repairs to scratches etc. complete.	sq m	1.55
71.	Distempering with dry distemper of approved brand and manufacture (one or more coats) and of required shade on old work to give an even shade.	sq m	7.30
72.	Distempering with oil bound washable distemper of approved brand and manufacture to give an even shade :		
	72A Old work (one or more coats)	sq m	9.55
73.	Finishing walls with water proofing cement paint of approved brand and manufacture and of required shade to give an even shade :		
	73A Old work (one or more coats)	sq m	14.60
74.	Removing dry or oil bound distemper by scrapping, sand papering and preparing the surface smooth including necessary repairs to scratches etc. complete.	sq m	2.05
75.	Painting with ready mixed paint of approved brand and manufacture in all shades to give an even shade :		
	75A Old steel work (one or more coats)	sq m	13.05
	75B Old wood work (one more coats)	sq m	12.80

(Contd.)

S. No.	Description	Unit	Rate ₹
76.	Painting on G.S. sheet with synthetic enamel paint of approved brand and manufacture of required colour to give an even shade :		
	76A Old work (one or more coats)	sq m	10.50
77.	Painting (two or more coats) on rain water, soil, waste and vent pipes and fittings with black anticorrosive bitumastic paint of approved brand and manufacture over and including a priming coat of ready mixed zinc chromate yellow primer on new work :		
	77A 50 mm diameter pipes	metre	4.80
	77B 75 mm diameter pipes	metre	6.90
78.	Painting (one or more coats) on rain water, soil, waste and vent pipes and fittings with black anticorrosive bitumastic paint of approved brand and manufacture on old work :		
	78A 50 mm diameter pipes	metre	2.25
	78B 75 mm diameter pipes	metre	3.15
79.	Painting (two or more coats) on rain water, soil, waste and vent pipes and fittings with, aluminium paint of approved brand and manufacture over a priming coat of ready mixed zinc chromate yellow primer on new work:		
	79A 50 mm diameter pipes	metre	5.65
	79B 75 mm diameter pipes	metre	7.85
80.	Painting (one or more coats) on rain water, soil, waste and vent pipes and fittings with synthetic enamel paint of approved brand and manufacture and required colour on old work :		
	80A 50 mm diameter pipes	metre	2.55
	80B 75 mm diameter pipes	metre	3.70
	80C 100 mm diameter pipes	metre	4.75
	80D 150 mm diameter pipes	metre	6.80
81.	Painting with oil type wood preservative of approved brand and manufacture :		
	81A Old work (one or more coats)	sq m	6.05
82.	Coal tarring one coat on old work using 0.12 litre of coal tar per sq m.	sq m	4.50
83.	Wall painting with plastic emulsion paint of approved brand and manufacture to give an even shade :		
	83A One or more coats on old work.	sq m	18.00
84.	Painting with enamel paint of approved brand and manufacture to give an even shade :		
	84A One or more coats on old work.	sq m	13.55
85.	Painting with synthetic enamel paint of approved brand and manufacture of required colour to give an even shade :		
	85A One or more coats on old work.	sq m	14.20
86.	Painting with aluminium paint of approved brand and manufacture to give an even shade :		
	86A One or more coats on old work.	sq m	11.85
87.	Painting with acid proof paint of approved brand and manufacture of required colour to give an even shade :		
	87A One or more coats on old work.	sq m	12.75
88.	Painting with black anti-corrosive bitumastic paint of approved brand and manufacture to give an even shade :		
	88A One or more coats on old work.	sq m	10.00

S. No.	Description	Unit	Rate ₹
89.	**Floor painting with floor enamel paint of approved brand and manufacture of required colour to give an even shade :**		
	89A One or more coats on old work.	sq m	14.70
90.	French spirit polishing :		
	90A One or more coats on old work.	sq m	21.75
91.	Polishing on wood work with ready made wax polish of approved brand and manufacture :		
	91A Old work	sq m	10.55
92.	Re-lettering with black Japan paint of approved brand and manufacture.	per letter per centimetre height	0.35
93.	Painting (one or more coats) with black Japan paint of approved brand and manufacture to give an even shade.	sq m	11.25
	H. SANITARY INSTALLATIONS		
94.	Providing and fixing IInd class teak wood draining board with 65 to 75 mm high skirting and beading, wax polished, supported on a C.I. bracket painted to the required limit complete. The board shall have a fluted surface with smooth finish complete:		
	94A Size 750 × 450 × 25 mm draining board	each	509.50
	94B Size 600 × 450 × 25 mm draining board	each	456.15
95.	Providing and fixing C.P. brass chain and rubber plug complete for sink or wash basin :		
	95A 32 mm dia	each	19.35
	95B 40 mm dia	each	21.55
96.	Providing and fixing rubber plug for sink or wash basin :	each	6.95
97.	Providing and fixing IInd class teak wood draining board with 65 to 75 mm high skirting and beading, wax polished complete. The board shall have a fluted surface with smooth finish complete :		
	97A 750 × 450 × 25 mm size	each	439.85
	97B 600 × 450 × 25 mm size	each	386.50

Table 13.14. Dismantling and Demolishing

S. No.	Description	Unit	Rate ₹
1.	Demolishing lime concrete and disposal of material within 50 metres lead.	cum	59.15
2.	Demolishing cement concrete including disposal of material within 50 metres lead :		
	2A 1 : 3 : 6 or richer mix	cum	169.75
	2B 1 : 4 : 8 or leaner mix	cum	104.45
3.	Demolishing R.C.C. work including stacking of steel bars and disposal of unserviceable material within 50 metres lead.	cum	247.60
4.	Demolishing R.B. work including stacking of steel bars and disposal of unserviceable material within 50 metres lead.	cum	220.95

(Contd.)

S. No.		Description	Unit	Rate ₹
5.		Extra for cutting reinforcement bars in R.C.C. or R.B. work (Payment shall be made on the cross sectional area of R.C.C. or R.B. work).	sq m	94.25
6.		Extra for scrapping, cleaning and straightening reinforcement from R.C.C. or R.B. work.	kg.	0.70
7.		Demolishing brick work including stacking of serviceable material and disposal of unserviceable material within 50 metres lead :		
	7A	In mud mortar	cum	49.00
	7B	In lime mortar with old mughal bricks	cum	123.40
	7C	In lime mortar	cum	59.15
	7D	In cement mortar	cum	143.05
8.		Removing mortar from bricks and cleaning bricks including stacking within a lead of 50 m. (stacks of cleaned bricks shall be measured) :		
	8A	From brick work in mud mortar	1000 nos.	329.95
	8B	From brick work in lime mortar	1000 nos.	388.75
	8C	From brick work in cement mortar	1000 nos.	489.95
9.		Demolishing stone rubble masonry including stacking of serviceable material and disposal of unserviceable material within 50 metres lead :		
	9A	In lime mortar	cum	80.65
	9B	In cement mortar	cum	170.65
10.		Dismantling dressed stone work ashlar face stone work, marble work or precast concrete work including stacking of serviceable and disposal of unserviceable material within 50 metres lead :		
	10A	In lime mortar	cum	102.05
	10B	In cement mortar	cum	199.55
11.		Removing mortar from stones and cleaning stones and concrete articles (net quantity of stacks of cleaned materials will be measured) :		
	11A	In lime mortar	cum	34.20
	11B	In cement mortar	cum	48.90
12.		Dismantling doors, windows and clerestory windows (steel or wood) shutter including chowkhats, architrave, hold-fasts etc. complete and stacking within 50 metres lead :		
	12A	Of area 3 sq. metres and below	each	28.85
	12B	Of area beyond 3 sq. metres	eacg	39.70
13.		Taking out doors, windows and clerestory window shutters (steel or wood) including stacking within 50 metres lead :		
	13A	Of area 3 sq. metres and below	each	11.10
	13B	Of area beyond 3 sq. metres	each	14.75
14.		Dismantling wood work in frames, trusses, purlins and rafters upto 10 metres span and 5 metres height including stacking the material within 50 metres lead :		
	14A	Of sectional area 40 square centimetres and above	cum	352.55
	14B	Of sectional area below 40 square centimetres	metre	1.40

S. No.	Description	Unit	Rate ₹
15.	Extra for dismantling trusses, rafters, purlins etc. of wood work for every additional span of one metre or part thereof beyond 10 metres :		
	15A Of sectional area 40 square centimetres and above	cum per metre span	49.80
	15B Of sectional area below 40 square centimetres	meter per metre span	0.15
16.	Extra for dismantling trusses, rafters, purlins etc. of wood work for every additional height of one metre or part thereof beyond 5 metres :		
	16A Of sectional area 40 square centimetres and above	cum per metre height	69.20
	16B Of sectional area below 40 square centimetres	metre per metre height	0.25
17.	Dismantling steel work in single sections including dismembering and stacking within 50 metres lead in :		
	17A R.S. Joists	kg	0.25
	17B Channels, angles, tees and flats	kg	0.20
18.	Dismantling steel work in built up sections in angles, tees, flats and channels including all gusset plates, bolts, nuts, cutting rivets, welding etc. including dismembering and stacking within 50 metres lead.	kg	0.45
19.	Dismantling steel work in built up sections without dismembering and stacking within 50 metres lead.	kg	0.30
20.	Extra for dismantling trusses, rafters, purlins etc. of steel work for every additional span of one metre or part thereof beyond 10 metres.	kg per metre span	0.05
21.	Extra for dismantling trusses, rafters, purlins etc. of steel work for every additional height of one metre or part thereof beyond 5 metres.	kg per metre height	0.05
22.	Extra for marking of structural steel work required to be reerected.	kg	0.40
23.	Dismantling tile work in floors and roofs laid in cement mortar including stacking material within 50 metres lead :		
	23A For thickness of tiles 10 mm to 25 mm	sq m	5.75
	23B For thickness of tiles above 25 mm and upto 40 mm	sq m	9.10
24.	Demolishing dry brick pitching in floors, drains etc. including stacking serviceable material and disposal of unserviceable material within 50 metres lead.	cum	91.95
25.	Dismantling stone slab flooring laid in cement mortar including stacking of serviceable material and disposal of unserviceable material within 60 metres lead.	sq m	18.70
26.	Demolishing brick tile covering in terracing including stacking of serviceable material and disposal of unserviceable material within 50 metres lead.	sq m	8.45
27.	Demolishing mud phaska in terracing and disposal of material within 50 metres lead.	cum	63.45
28.	Dismantling roofing including ridges, hips valleys and gutters etc., and stacking the material within 50 metres lead of:		
	28A G.S. Sheet	sq m	12.65
	28B Asbestos sheet	sq m	5.95

(Contd.)

S. No.	Description	Unit	Rate ₹
29.	Dismantling stone slab roofing over wooden karries or R.C.C. battens (dismantling karries and battens to be paid for separately) including stacking of serviceable material and disposal of unserviceable material within 50 metres lead.	cum	186.85
30.	Dismantling jack arch roofing and floors including stacking of serviceable material and disposal of unserviceable material within 50 metres lead.	sq m	17.80
31.	Dismantling tiled roofing with battens boarding etc. complete including stacking of serviceable material and disposal of unserviceable material within 50 metres lead.	sq m	14.80
32.	Demolishing thatch roofing including mats, bamboo, jaffari etc. complete including stacking of serviceable material and disposal of unserviceable material within 50 metres lead.	sq m	4.10
33.	Dismantling wooden bailies in posts and struts including stacking within 50 metres lead.	metre	1.45
34.	Dismantling and stacking within 50 metres lead, fencing posts or struts including all earth work and dismantling of concrete etc. in base of :		
	34A 'T' or 'L' iron or pipe	each	21.75
	34B R.C.C.	each	26.20
35.	Cutting bailies or wooden posts of fencing at the point of projection above the concrete or ground and stacking the same within 50 metres lead.	each	2.50
36.	Dismantling barbed wire or flexible wire rope in fencing including making rolls and stacking within 50 metres lead.	kg	2.55
37.	Dismantling wooden trellis work excluding frames but including stacking the serviceable material within 50 metres lead.	sq m	4.80
38.	Dismantling expanded metal or I.R.C. fabrics with necessary battens and beading including stacking the serviceable material within 50 metres lead.	sq m	5.60
39.	Dismantling wooden boardings in lining of walls and partitions, excluding supporting members but including stacking within 50 metres lead :		
	39A Upto 10 mm thick	sq m	4.70
	39B Thickness above 100 mm upto 25 mm	sq m	6.00
	39C Thickness above 25 mm upto 40 mm	sq m	7.15
40.	Dismantling precast concrete or stone slabs in walls, partition walls etc. including stacking within 50 metres lead :		
	40A Thickness upto 40 mm	sq m	20.85
	40B Thickness above 40 mm upto 75 mm	sq m	31.25
41.	Dismantling cement asbestos, Celotax or other hard board ceiling or partition walls including stacking of serviceable materials and disposal of unserviceable materials within 50 metres lead.	sq m	4.50
42.	Dismantling C.I. or asbestos rain water pipe with fittings and clamps including stacking the material within 50 metres lead :		
	42A 75 to 80 mm dia pipe	metre	5.25
	42B 100 mm dia pipe	metre	5.45
	42C 150 mm dia pipe	metre	5.60

S. No.	Description	Unit	Rate ₹
43.	**Dismantling including stacking of serviceable material and disposal of unserviceable material within 50 metres lead :**		
	43A Water bound macadam road	sq m	15.95
	43B Bituminous road	sq m	30.70
44.	**Dismantling G.I. pipes (external work) including excavation and refilling trenches after taking out the pipes, including stacking of pipes within 50 metres lead :**		
	44A 15 mm to 40 mm nominal bore	metre	11.70
	44B Above 40 mm nominal bore	metre	13.90
45.	**Dismantling C.I. pipes including excavation and refilling trenches after taking out the pipes, breaking lead caulked joints, melting of lead and making into blocks including stacking of pipes, lead at site within 50 metre lead :**		
	45A Upto 150 mm diameter	metre	31.20
	45B Above 150 mm dia upto 300 mm dia.	metre	43.90
	45C Above 300 mm diameter	metre	58.30
46.	**Dismantling steel cylinder R.C. pipes including excavation and refilling trenches after taking out the pipes, breaking lead caulked joints, melting of lead and making into blocks including stacking of pipes, lead at site within 50 metres lead :**		
	46A Upto 600 mm diameter	metre	58.30
	46B Above 600 mm diameter	metre	145.05
47.	**Dismantling asbestos cement pressure pipes including excavation and refilling trenches after taking out the pipes and stacking the pipes within 50 metres lead :**		
	47A Upto 150 mm diameter	metre	22.95
	47B Above 150 mm diameter	metre	27.95
48.	Taking out C.I. cover with frame from R.C.C. top slab of manholes of various sizes including demolishing of R.C.C. work and stacking of useful materials near the site and disposal of unserviceable materials into municipal dumps within 50 metres lead.	each	51.35
49.	Taking out C.I. cover with frame from R.C.C. top slab of inspection chambers of various sizes including demolishing of R.C.C. work and stacking of useful materials near the site and disposal of unserviceable materials into municipal dumps within 50 metres lead.	each	30.35
50.	**Dismantling of R.C.C. spun vent shaft including excavating the cement concrete pit completely, taking out the shaft, refilling the excavated gap, stacking the useful materials near the site and disposal of unserviceable materials within 50 metres lead.**	each	358.75
51.	**Dismantling of road gully chamber of various sizes including C.I. grating with frame including stacking of useful materials near the site and disposal of unserviceable materials into municipal dumps within 50 metres lead including refilling the excavated gap.**	each	69.30
52.	Dismantling of flushing cistern of any size including stacking of useful materials near the site and disposal of unserviceable materials within 50 metres lead.	each	77.55
53.	Dismantling of C.I. sluice valve including stacking of useful materials within a lead of 50 metres :		
	53A Upto 150 mm diameter	each	28.35
	53B Above 150 mm diameter	each	96.40

(Contd.)

S. No.	Description	Unit	Rate ₹
54.	Dismantling of spindle fire hydrant including stacking of useful materials within 50 metres lead.	each	57.20
55.	Dismantling of cement concrete platform along with curtain walls and base concrete etc. including stacking of useful materials near the site and disposal of unserviceable materials within 50 metres lead :		
	55A 120 × 120 cm (outside to outside)	each	76.70
	55B 210 × 120 cm (outside to outside)	each	117.70
	55C 320 × 120 cm (outside to outside)	each	166.45
56.	Dismantling old plaster or skirting raking out joints and cleaning the surface for plaster including disposal of rubbish to the dumping ground within 50 metres lead.	sq m	3.80
57.	Dismantling aluminium/gypsum patitions, doors, windows, fixed glazing and false ceiling including disposal of unserviceable surplus material and stacking of serviceable material with in 50 m lead as directed by Engineer-in-charge.	sq m	4.50

Table 13.15. Miscellaneous Building Works

S. No.	Description	Unit	Rate ₹
1.	Making plinth protection 50 mm thick of cement concrete 1 : 3 : 6 (1 cement : 3 coarse sand : 6 graded stone aggregate 20 mm nominal size) over 75 mm bed of dry brick ballast 40 mm nominal size well rammed and consolidated and grouted with fine sand including finishing the top smooth.	sq m	114.05
2.	Making plinth protection with bricks of class designation 75 laid on edge in cement mortar 1 : 6 (1 cement : 6 coarse sand) with 12 mm thick bed of cement mortar 1 : 6 (1 cement : 6 coarse sand) over 75 mm bed of dry brick aggregate 40 mm nominal size rammed, consolidated and grouted with fine sand and the top of bricks pointed with cement mortar 1 : 3 (1 cement : 3 fine sand):		
	2A With F.P.S. bricks	sq m	224.55
3.	Providing and fixing precast reinforced cement urinal partition 105 cm × 60 cm deep and 56 mm thick in cement concrete mix 1 : 2 : 4 (1 cement : 2 coarse sand : 4 graded stone aggregate 6 mm nominal size) reinforced with mild steel bars 6 mm dia at 15 cm centre to centre both ways fixed in walls with cement concrete 1 : 2 : 4 (1 cement : 2 coarse sand : 4 graded stone aggregate 6 mm nominal size) including finishing with 12 mm plastering with terrazo finish rubbed and polished complete, under layer 6 mm thick cement plaster 1 : 3 (1 cement : 3 coarse sand) and top layer 6 mm thick white, black or white and black marble chips of 3 mm and down size laid in cement marble powder mix 3 : 1 (3 cement : 1 marble powder) by weight in proportion of 4 : 7 (4 cement marble powder mix : 7 marble chips) by volume.	each	331.35
4.	Providing and fixing marble slab white Makrana (table rubbed and polished) 105 cm × 60 cm deep × 2.5 cm thick fixed in urinal partition with cement concrete 1 : 2 : 4 (1 cement : 2 coarse sand : 4 graded stone aggregate of 6 mm nominal size) and finished smooth.	sq m	2148.60

S. No.	Description	Unit	Rate ₹
5.	Providing and fixing stone slab table rubbed and polished of size 105 cm × 60 cm deep and 2.5 cm thick fixed in urinal partitions with cement concrete 1 : 2 : 4 (1 cement : 2 coarse sand : 4 stone aggregate 6 mm nominal size) and finished smooth :		
	5A Raj Nagar Marble Stone	sq m	2416.65
	5B Granite Stone of approved shade	sq m	3086.80
6.	Providing and fixing 15 cm high drawer of the cupboard with 12 mm thick base and side planks with wooden handle and 20 × 25 mm runners fixed with screws complete including painting or polishing.		
	NOTE : Overall plan area of the drawer shall be measured :		
	6A Superior class teak wood	sq m	2944.20
	6B First class teak wood	sq m	1985.85
	6C Second class teak wood	sq m	1707.40
	6D First class deodar wood	sq m	1609.60
	6E Second class deodar wood	sq m	1488.35
	6F First class kail wood	sq m	1060.65
	6G Second class kail wood	sq m	962.85
7.	Providing and fixing aluminium strip edging to staircase including fixing with rawl plugs and screws with a thin layer of cement mortar 1 : 3 (1 cement : 3 coarse sand) :		
	7A Size of strip edging 57 × 12 × 3 mm	metre	80.60
	7B Size of strip edging 38 × 12 × 3 mm	metre	103.95
8.	Brick edging 7 cm wide 11.4 cm deep to plinth protection with bricks of class designation 75 including grouting with cement mortar 1 : 4 (1 cement : 4 fine sand).	metre	9.70
9.	Providing and fixing cup board shutters 25 mm thick, with prelaminated flat pressed three layer particle board conforming to IS : 12823 exterior grade (Grade-I Type II) having one side decorative lamination of approved shade and other side balancing lamination including IInd class teak wood lipping of 25 mm wide × 12 mm thick with necessary screws and nickle plated bright finished M.S. piano hinges complete as per direction of the Engineer-in-charge.	sq m	657.05
10.	Providing and fixing cup board shutters with 25 mm thick veenered particle board conforming to IS : 3097 exterior grade (Grade I) of approved make including IInd class teak wood lipping of 25 mm wide × 12 mm thick with necessary screws and nickle plated bright finished M.S. piano hinges complete as per direction of Engineer-in-charge :		
	10A With teak veneering on one side and commercial veneering on other side	sq m	583.75
	10B With commercial veneering on both sides	sq m	406.00
11.	Providing and fixing factory made flush door shutters 30 mm thick made of prelaminated flat pressed three layer particle board conforming to IS : 12823 exterior grade (Grade-I Type II) having one side decorative lamination of approved shade including IInd class teak wood lipping of 30 mm wide × 12 mm thick size with necessary screws and black enamelled M.S. butt hinges complete as per direction of the Engineer-in-charge.	sq m	517.80

(*Contd.*)

S. No.	Description	Unit	Rate ₹
12.	Providing and fixing factory made medium density particle board flush door shutters flat pressed three-layer prelaminated particle board exterior grade, conforming to IS : 3087 grade-I and prelamination conforming to IS : 12823 Grade-I Type II both side decorative matt lamination of approved design, and edges sealed with water resistant paint and lipped with aluminium 'U' type edge beading alround the shutter, including fixing with angle cleat, grip strip, cadmium plated steel screws including fixing of aluminium hinges 100 × 63 × 4 mm etc. complete as per architectural drawing and direction of Engineer-in-charge (cost of 'U' beading and hinges will be paid for separately) :		
	12A 25 mm thick	sq m	988.80
13.	Providing and fixing aluminium U beading of required size to prelaminated/flush door shutter including fixing etc. complete as per direction of Engineer-in-charge.	kg	200.10

Table 13.16. Road Work

S. No.	Description	Unit	Rate ₹
	A. ROADS		
1.	Preparation of subgrade by excavating earth to an average of 22.5 cm depth, dressing to camber and consolidating with road roller including making good the undulations etc. and disposal of surplus earth lead upto 50 metres.	sq m	15.25
2.	Consolidation of subgrade with power road roller of 8 to 12 tonne capacity including making good the undulations etc. with earth or quarry spoils etc. and rerolling the subgrade.	sq m	0.65
3.	Extra for compaction of earth work in embankment under optimum moisture conditions to give at least 95% of the maximum dry density (proctor density).	cum	2.35
4.	Supplying and stacking of graded stone aggregate at site of size range :		
	4A 90 mm to 45 mm	cum	348.10
	4B 63 mm to 45 mm	cum	351.15
	4C 53 mm to 22.4 mm	cum	355.30
5.	Supplying and stacking of over burnt (Jhama) brick aggregate at site of size range :		
	5A 120 mm to 40 mm	cum	246.40
	5B 90 mm to 45 mm	cum	274.15
6.	Laying water bound macadam with specified stone aggregate stone screening and blinding material including screening, sorting, spreading to template and consolidation with power road roller of 8 to 10 tonne capacity etc. complete (payment for stone aggregate, screenings, kankar, moorum and red bajri etc. to be made separately):		
	6A Subbase with stone aggregate 90 mm to 45 mm including stone screening 13.2 mm size.	cum	99.15
	6B Base course with 63 mm to 45 mm size including stone screening 13.2 mm size.	cum	97.55
	6C Base course with 53 mm to 22.4 mm size including stone screening 11.2 mm size.	cum	97.55

S. No.	Description	Unit	Rate ₹
7.	Laying water bound macadam sub-base with brick aggregate and blinding material, earth etc. including screening, sorting and spreading to template and consolidation with light power road-roller etc. complete (payment for brick aggregate and moorum etc. to be made separately) :		
	7A Over burnt (Jhama) brick aggregate 120 mm to 40 mm	cum	64.65
	7B Over burnt (Jhama) brick aggregate 90 mm to 45 mm	cum	64.65
8.	Supplying and stacking of moorum at site.	cum	257.70
9.	Supplying and stacking of red bajri at site.	cum	293.65
10.	Supplying and stacking of stone screenings/chippings at site :		
	10A 13.2 mm nominal size (Type A)	cum	389.25
	10B 11.2 mm nominal size (Type B)	cum	395.10
11.	Spreading 6 mm thick red bajri, watering and rolling complete including preparation of the surface and rolling (Payment for red bajri to be made separately) :		
	11A With road rollar	sq m	1.45
	11B With hand rollar	sq m	1.30
12.	Supplying and laying kerb stone 30 × 20 cm chisel dressed on top and side including fixing in cement mortar 1 : 4 (1 cement : 4 coarse sand) and pointing with cement mortar 1 : 4 (1 cement : 4 coarse sand) including making drainage opening, where required.	metre	107.05
13.	Providing, laying and fixing channel stones 30 × 10 cm chisel dressed on top and side in cement mortar 1 : 4 (1 cement : 4 coarse sand) along the edge of the road, including pointing with cement mortar 1 : 4 (1 cement : 4 coarse sand).	metre	83.55
14.	Brick edging in full brick width and half brick depth including excavation, refilling and disposal of surplus earth lead upto 50 metres:		
	14A With F.P.S. bricks of class designation 75	metre	31.55
15.	Brick edging laid lengthwise with half brick depth including excavation, refilling and disposal of surplus earth lead upto 50 metres:		
	15A With F.P.S. bricks of class designation 75	metre	9.05
16.	Scarifying metalled (water-bound) road surface including disposal of rubbish lead upto 50 m and consolidation of the aggregate received from scarifying with power road roller of 8 to 10 tonne capacity.	sq m	3.35
17.	Making bajri path including preparation of subgrade, supplying and laying brick aggregate of 50 mm nominal size 7.5 cm deep with blinding material consisting of 12 mm moorum and 12 mm red bajri consolidated with road roller.	sq m	37.40
18.	Dry stone pitching 22.5 cm thick including supply of stones and preparing surface complete.	sq m	116.70
19.	Dry brick pitching half brick thick in drains including supply of bricks and preparing the surface complete :		
	19A With F.P.S. bricks of class designation 75	sq m	111.95
20.	Cutting road and making good the same including supply of extra quantities of materials *i.e.* aggregate, moorum screening, red bajri and labour required :		
	20A Bituminous portion	cum	141.00
	20B Water bound macadam.	cum	66.95

(Contd.)

S. No.	*Description*	*Unit*	*Rate* ₹
21.	Cutting bajri paths and making good the same including supply of extra quantities of brick aggregate, moorum and red bajri required.	sq m	25.55
	B. FENCING		
22.	Supplying at site 1.8 m long R.C.C. standard posts with wooden plugs or 6 mm bar nibs.	each	186.55
23.	Supplying at site :		
	23A R.C.C. Standards Struts 2.0 metre long	each	150.20
	23B R.C.C. standard rails 2.25 metre long	each	101.00
	23C R.C.C. standard Pales 1.25 metre long	each	38.35
	23D Welded steel wire fabric of required width rectangular mesh 75 × 25 mm size weight not less than 7.75 kg/Sq m painted with two or more coats of enamel paint of approved shade over a coat of primer (Painting to be paid for separately)	sq m	166.95
24.	Supplying and fixing turn buckles and straining bolts for barbed wire fencing.	each set	48.30
25.	1.2 m high fencing with 1.8 m R.C.C. posts of standard design placed every 3 m apart, embedded in cement concrete blocks, every 15th post, last but one end post and corner post shall be strutted on both sides and end post one side only, provided with nine horizontal lines and two diagonals of barbed wire 9.38 kg per 100 metres (min) between the two posts fitted and fixed with G.I. staples on wooden plugs or G.I. binding wire tied to 6 mm bar nibs fixed while casting the post (cost of R.C.C. posts, struts, earth work and concrete to be paid for separately) :		
	25A With G.I. barbed wire.	metre	33.80
	25B With M.S. barbed wire	metre	31.70
26.	Supplying 30 cm minimum girth sal ballies at site in required length.	metre	13.65
27.	1.2 m high fencing with 1.8 m sal balli posts, 30 cm girth (min) placed every 2.5 m apart embedded in cement concrete blocks and every 15th post, last but one end post and corner post strutted on both sides and end post on one side only, provided with 6 horizontal lines and two diagonals of barbed wire 9.38 kg per 100 metres (min) between two posts fitted and fixed with G.I. staples driven into the posts including two coats of coal tarring of ballies complete (cost of posts, struts, earth work and concrete to be paid for separately) :		
	27A With G.I. barbed wire.	metre	28.20
	27B With M.S. barbed wire	metre	26.60
28.	1.8 m high fencing with 2.5 m sal balli posts, 30 cm girth (min) placed every 2.5 m apart embedded in cement concrete blocks and every 15th post, last but one end post and corner post strutted on both sides and end post on one side only, provided with 9 horizontal lines and two diagonals of barbed wire 9.38 kg per 100 metres (min) between two posts fitted and fixed with G.I. staples driven into the posts including two coats of coal tarring of ballies complete (cost of posts, struts, earth work and concrete to be paid for separately):		
	28A With G.I. barbed wire.	metre	38.20
	28B With M.S. barbed wire.	metre	36.00

S. No.	Description	Unit	Rate ₹
29.	**2.4 m high fencing with 3.3 m sal balli posts, 30 cm girth (min) placed every 2.5 m apart embedded in cement concrete blocks and every 15th post, last but one end post and corner post strutted on both sides and end post on one side only, provided with 12 horizontal lines and two diagonals of barbed wire 9.38 kg per 100 metres (min) between two posts fitted and fixed with G.I. staples driven into the posts including two coats of coal tarring of ballies complete (cost of posts, struts, earth work and concrete to be paid for separately) :**		
	29A G.I. barbed wire	**metre**	**49.10**
	29B M.S. barbed wire.	**metre**	**46.30**
30.	**1.3 metre high concrete rail and pale fencing with 1.8 m R.C.C. posts 2.25 m rails and 1.25 m pales, posts placed at 2.25 m apart embedded in cement concrete blocks 45 × 45 × 70 cm of mix 1 : 5 : 10 (1 cement : 5 fine sand : 10 graded stone aggregate 40 mm nominal size) (Cost of earth work in excavation, concrete work, posts, rails and pales to be paid for separately).**	**metre**	**7.95**
31.	**1.2 m high fencing with 1.8 m angle iron 40 × 40 × 6 mm posts placed every 3 m centre to centre embedded in cement concrete blocks, every 15th post, last but one end post and corner post shall be strutted on both sides and end post on one side only and provided with 9 horizontal lines and two diagonals interwoven with horizontal wires, of barbed wire 9.38 kg per 100 m (minimum) between the two posts fitted and fixed with G.I. staples, turn buckles etc. complete. (Cost of posts, struts, earth work and concrete work to be paid for separately):**		
	31A With G.I. barbed wire.	**metre**	**35.05**
32.	**1.8 m high fencing with 2.4 m angle iron 50 × 50 × 6 mm posts placed every 3 m centre to centre embedded in cement concrete block, every 15th post last but one end post and corner post shall be strutted on both sides and end post on one side only and provided with 12 horizontal lines and two diagonals inter woven with horizontal wires of barbed wire 9.38 kg per 100 m (min) between the two posts and fixed with GI staples, turn buckles etc. complete. (Cost of posts, struts, earth work and concrete to be paid for separately.)**		
	32A With G.I. barbed wire	**metre**	**44.85**
33.	**Supplying at site Angle iron post and strut of required size including bottom to be split and bent at right angle in opposite direction for 10 cm length and drilling holes upto 10 mm dia. etc. complete.**	**kg**	**20.15**
34.	**1.2 m high welded steel wire fabric fencing with 1.8 m posts of specified material and of standard design placed at every 3 m apart embedded in cement concrete blocks 45 × 45 × 60 cm of mix 1 : 5 : 10 (1 cement : 5 fine sand : 10 graded stone aggregate 40 mm nominal size) every 15th post, last but one end post and corner post shall be strutted on both sides and end post on one side only and struts embedded in cement concrete blocks 70 × 45 × 50 cm of the same mix, provided with welded steel wire fabric 0.90 m wide rectangular mesh 75 × 25 mm size weighing not less than 7.75 kg/sq m fixed between the posts fitted and fixed with G.I. staples on wooden plugs or tied to 6 mm bar nibs with G.I. binding wire (cost of posts, welded steel wire fabric, painting, earth work in excavation and concrete to be paid for separately).**	**metre**	**7.95**

(Contd.)

S. No.	Description	Unit	Rate ₹
	C. ROAD SIGNS AND STONES		
35.	Providing and fixing R.C.C. "KEEP LEFT" sign-board of standard design including two or more coats with white zinc paint over a priming coat and lettering with black enamel paint.	each	2487.70
36.	Providing and fixing R.C.C. name board of standard design including painting two or more coats with white zinc paint over priming coat :		
	36A Rectangular with posts.	each	538.45
	36B Flat without post for one direction only	each	845.95
	36C Flat without post for two directions	each	917.85
37.	Engraving letters in hard stone.	per cm height per letter	1.05
38.	Providing and fixing 15 × 15 × 90 cm boundary stone of hard stone with top 30 cm chisel dressed on all four sides and on top (cost of excavation, refilling and concrete etc. to be paid for separately).	each	50.55
39.	Providing and fixing 15 cm dia at top, 20 cm at bottom and 90 cm high precast reinforced cement concrete 1 : 2 : 4 (1 cement : 2 coarse sand : 4 graded stone aggregate 20 mm nominal size) boundary stone as per standard design including finishing smooth with cement mortar 1 : 3 (1 cement : 3 fine sand) (cost of excavation, refilling and concreting to be paid for separately).	each	124.95
40.	Providing and fixing precast reinforced cement concrete 1 : 2 : 4 (1 cement : 2 coarse sand : 4 graded stone aggregate 20 mm nominal size) kilometre stone as per standard design including finishing smooth in 1 : 3 cement mortar (1 cement : 3 fine sand) but excluding the cost of earth work, concrete in foundation, painting and lettering etc. which shall be paid for separately:		
	40A 35 × 111 × 25 cm size.	each	544.55
	40B 50 × 152.5 × 25 cm size.	each	748.35
	40C 35 × 93.5 × 18 cm size.	each	365.55
	D. SURFACE DRESSING		
41.	Surface dressing on new surface with paving bitumen of grade A-90/S-90 of approved quality using 2.25 kg of bitumen per sq m with 1.65 cum of stone chippings 13.2 mm nominal size per 100 sq m of road surface including consolidation with road roller of 6 to 8 tonne capacity etc. complete.	sq m	34.85
42.	Surface dressing on new surface in two coats with bitumen of grade A-90/S-90 of approved quality using 1.8 kg of bitumen per sq m with 1.5 cum of stone chippings 13.2 mm nominal size per 100 sq m of road surface for first coat and 1.1 kg of bitumen per sq m. with 1.00 cu. metre of stone chippings 11.2 mm nominal size per 100 sq m. of road surface for second coat including consolidation of each coat separately with road roller of 6 to 8 tonne capacity etc. complete.	sq m	47.70
43.	Surface dressing on old surface with hot bitumen of grade A-90/S-90 of approved quality using 1.95 kg of bitumen per sq m. with 1.50 cum of stone chippings 11.2 mm nominal size per 100 sq m. of road surface including consolidation with road roller of 6 to 8 tonne capacity, etc. complete.	sq m	28.55

S. No.	Description	Unit	Rate ₹
44.	**Surface dressing one coat on new surface with bitumen of specified grade at a rate of 1.95 kg/sq m. of surface area with 1.5 cum. of stone chippings 13.2 mm nominal size per 100 sq m. of road surface including consolidation with road roller of 6 to 8 tonne capacity, etc. complete :**		
	44A Using bitumen emulsion (minimum 50% bitumen content-RS grade conforming to IS : 8837)	sq m	32.64
	44B Using cut back RC 3 (Rapid curing) bitumen conforming to IS : 217	sq m	41.10
45.	**Surface dressing one coat on old surface with bitumen of specified grade at the rate of 1.22 kg/sq m of surface area with 1.10 cum of stone chippings 11.2 mm nominal size per 100 sq m of road surface including consolidation with road roller of 6 to 8 tonne capacity etc. complete :**		
	45A Using bitumen emulsion (minimum 50% bitumen content-RS grade conforming to IS : 8837)	sq m	20.85
	45B Using cut back RC 3 (Rapid curing) bitumen conforming to IS : 217	sq m	26.10
	E. PRE MIX CARPET		
46.	**Providing and applying tack coat using hot straight run bitumen of grade 80/100 including heating the bitumen, spraying the bitumen with mechanically operated spray unit fitted on bitumen boiler, cleaning and preparing the existing road surface as per specifications :**		
	46A On W.B.M. @ 0.75 kg/sq m.	sq m	7.50
	46B On bituminous surface @ 0.50 kg/sq m.	sq m	5.55
47.	**2 cm premix carpet surfacing with 1.8 cum and 0.90 cum of stone chippings of 13.2 mm size and 11.2 mm size respectively per 100 sq m and 52 kg and 56 kg of hot bitumen per cum of stone chippings of 13.2 mm and 11.2 mm size respectively including a tack coat with hot straight run bitumen including consolidation with road roller of 6 to 9 tonne capacity etc. complete : (tack coat to be paid for separately) :**		
	47A With paving Asphalt 30/40 heated and then mixed with solvent at the rate of 70 grams per kg of asphalt.	sq m	33.50
	47B With paving Asphalt 80/100 heated and then mixed with solvent at the rate of 70 grams per kg of asphalt.	sq m	30.75
	47C With paving Asphalt 60/70 with no solvent	sq m	34.65
48.	**2.5 cm premix carpet surfacing with 2.25 cum and 1.12 cum of stone chippings of 13.2 mm and 11.2 mm size respectively per 100 sq m and 52 kg and 56 kg of hot bitumen per cum of stone chippings of 13.2 mm and 11.2 mm size respectively including a tack coat with hot straight run bitumen including consolidation with road roller of 6 to 9 tonne capacity etc. complete : (tack coat to be paid for separately) :**		
	48A With paving Asphalt 30/40 heated and then mixed with solvent at the rate of 70 grams per kg of asphalt.	sq m	40.80
	48B With paving Asphalt 80/100 heated and then mixed with solvent at the rate of 70 grams per kg of asphalt.	sq m	37.35
	48C With paving Asphalt 60/70 with no solvent	sq m	42.20

(Contd.)

S. No.	Description	Unit	Rate ₹
49.	2 cm premix carpet surfacing with 2.4 cum of stone chippings 11.2 mm nominal size per 100 sq m and bitumen emulsion (Min. 60% bitumen content) of approved quality using 96 kg per cum of chippings including a tack coat of 1 kg bitumen emulsion per sq m of road surface including consolidation with road roller of 6 to 9 tonne capacity etc. complete.	sq m	46.30
50.	2.5 cm premix carpet surfacing with 3 cum of stone chippings 10 mm nominal size per 100 sq m and bitumen emulsion (Min. 60% bitumen contents) of approved quality using 96 kg per cum of chippings including a tack coat of 1 kg bitumen emulsion per sq m of road surface including consolidation with road roller etc. complete.	sq m	53.95
51.	Providing and laying premix bituminous macadam base course with stone aggregate of quality size and grading as specified in CPWD specification and straight run bitumen of grade 80/100 @ 4% by weight of total mix including hot mixing of stone aggregate and bitumen in hot mix plant, transporting mixed material and laying mixed material with paver finisher to the required level and grade, rolling with road roller of 8 to 10 tonne capacity to achieve the required compaction and density :		
	51A 50 mm compacted thickness	cum	1633.00
	51B 75 mm compacted thickness	cum	1633.00
52.	Providing and laying Bitumen Penetration Macadam with hard stone aggregate of quality, size and grading as specified, with bitumen of suitable penetration grade including required key aggregate as specified, spreading coarse aggregate with the help of self propelled/ tipper tail mounted aggregate spreader and applying bitumen by a pressure distributor and then spreading key aggregate with the help of aggregate spreader complete including consolidation with road roller of minimum 8 to 10 tonne capacity to achieve specified values of compaction and surface accuracy :		
	52A For 50 mm compacted thickness using coarse aggregate of size 50-20 mm graded @ 0.60 cum per 10 sq m key aggregate of size 12.5 mm graded @ 0.15 cum per 10 sq m. With paving asphalt 30/40 @ 50 kg/10 sq m	sq m	88.00
	52B For 75 mm compacted thickness in two layers using stone aggregate of size 63-41 mm graded @ 0.90 cum per 10 sq m key aggregate of size 20.0 mm graded @ 0.18 cum per 10 sq m. With paving asphalt 30/40 @ 68 kg/10 sq m	sq m	122.05
53.	Providing and laying 75 mm thick, semi dense asphaltic base course using mineral aggregate satisfying the gradation set out in specifications with 5 percent binder content 80/100 or equivalent (By weight of total mix) with the aid of hot mix plant and paver finisher including rolling with road roller of 8 to 10 tonne capacity to achieve required compaction and density.	cum	1749.15
54.	Providing and laying 4 cm. thick dense bituminous concrete surfacing course using mineral aggregate satisfying the gradation set out in the specifications with 6% binder content 80/100 or equivalent (By weight of total mix) with the aid of hot mix plant and paver finisher including rolling with road roller to achieve the required compaction and density.	cum	2328.90

S. No.	Description	Unit	Rate ₹
	F. MASTIC AND BITUMASTIC SHEET WEARING COARSE		
55.	Providing and laying 25 mm thick bitumen mastic wearing course (as per specifications) with industrial bitumen of grade 85/25 conforming to IS : 702 prepared by using mastic cooker and laid to required level and slope including providing antiskid surface with bitumen precoated fine grained hard stone chipping of approved size at the rate of 0.005 cum per 10 sq m and at approximate spacing of 10 cm centre to centre in both directions, pressed into surface protruding 1 mm to 4 mm over mastic surface, including cleaning the surface, removal of debris etc. all complete.	sq m	194.95
56.	2.5 cm thick bitumastic sheet with hot bitumen of approved quality using stone chippings (60% 12.5 mm nominal size and 40% 10 mm nominal size) @ 1.65 cum per 100 sq m and coarse sand at 1.65 cum per 100 sq m of road surface and with bitumen @ 56 kg/cum of stone chippings and at 128 kg/cum of sand over a tack coat with hot straight run bitumen including consolidation with road roller of 8 to 10 tonne etc. complete, (tack coat to be paid separately) :		
	56A With paving Asphalt 30/40 heated and then mixed with solvent at the rate of 70 grams per kg of asphalt	sq m	55.25
	56B With paving Asphalt 80/100 heated and then mixed with solvent at the rate of 70 grams per kg of asphalt.	sq m	49.45
	56C With paving asphalt 60/70 with no solvent	sq m	57.60
57.	4 cm thick bitumastic sheet with hot bitumen of approved quality using stone chippings (60% 12.5 mm nominal size and 40% 10 mm nominal size) @ 2.60 cum per 100 sq m and coarse sand at 2.60 cum per 100 sq m of road surface and with bitumen @ 56 kg/cum of stone chippings and at 128 kg/cum of sand over a tack coat with hot straight run bitumen including consolidation with road roller of 8 to 10 tonne etc. complete, (tack coat to be paid separately) :		
	57A With paving Asphalt 30/40 heated and then mixed with solvent at the rate of 70 grams per kg of asphalt	sq m	85.05
	57B With paving Asphalt 80/100 heated and then mixed with solvent at the rate of 70 grams per kg of asphalt.	sq m	75.90
	57C With paving asphalt 60/70 with no solvent	sq m	88.75
	G. SEAL COAT		
58.	Providing and laying seal coat of premixed fine aggregate (passing 2.36 mm and retained on 180 micron sieve) with bitumen using 128 kg of bitumen of grade 80/100 bitumen per cum of fine aggregate and 0.60 cum of fine aggregate per 100 sq m of road surface including rolling and finishing with road roller all complete.	sq m	14.55
59.	Providing and laying seal coat over prepared surface of road with bitumen heated in bitumen boiler fitted with the spray set spraying using 98 kg of bitumen of grade 80/100 and blinding surface with 0.90 cum of stone aggregate of 6.7 mm size (Passing 11.2 mm sieve and retained on 2.36 mm sieve) per 100 sq m of road surface including rolling and finishing with power road roller all complete.	sq m	18.60
	H. CONCRETE PAVEMENTS		
60.	Cement concrete 1 : 2 : 4 (1 cement : 2 coarse sand : 4 graded stone aggregate 40 mm nominal size) in pavements, laid to required slope and camber in panels as required including consolidation finishing and tamping complete.	cum	1686.50

(Contd.)

S. No.	Description	Unit	Rate ₹
61.	Providing and laying design mix cement concrete in roads, taxi tracks and runways having a minimum works test beam flexural strength of 30 kg per cm^2, at 28 days using not less than 340 kg of cement per cum of finished concrete, coarse sand and graded stone aggregate of 40 mm nominal size in appropriate proportions as per specified design criteria approved by Engineer-in-charge mechanically vibrated using needle and surface vibrators including steel form work with sturdy M.S. channel sections including curing and providing and filling construction joints and dummy joints with shalijet primer or equivalent including rounding of the edges and filling the grooves 10 × 25 mm deep at top for construction joints and 10 mm × 50 mm deep at top for dummy joints with joint sealing compound (conforming to grade B of IS : 1834) including making necessary arrangements for expansion joints etc. all complete.	cum	1810.45
62.	Extra for providing and mixing hard crete of approved quality and make at the rate of 350 ml per 50 kg of cement bag in cement concrete.	cum	97.20
63.	Providing and fixing in position premoulded joint filler in expansion joints.	per cm depth per cm width per m length	1.45
64.	Providing and laying in position bitumen hot sealing compound for expansion joints etc. :		
	64A Using grade 'A' sealing compound.	per cm depth per cm width per m length	0.60
	I. PAINTING ROAD/RUNWAY MARKINGS		
65.	Painting runway/taxi track/apron marking with adequate no. of coats to give uniform finish with road marking paint of superior make like Goodlas Nerolac Brand No. 452/002 or equivalent as approved by the Engineer-in-charge i/c cleaning the surface of all dirt, scales, oil, grease and other foreign material etc. and lining out complete :		
	65A New work (Two or more coats)	sq m	51.80
	65B Old work (One or more coats)	sq m	31.55
66.	Painting road surface marking with adequate no. of coats to give uniform finish with ready mixed road marking paint confirming to IS : 164, on bituminous surface in white/yellow shade including cleaning the surface of all dirt, scales, oil, grease and foreign material etc. complete :		
	66A New work (Two or more coats)	sq m	33.00
	66B Old work (One or more coats)	sq m	21.10
	J. MISCELLANEOUS		
67.	Making bell mouth opening/entrance of size 100 × 50 × 50 cm for drainage pipe under footpath including providing cement concrete 1 : 3 : 6 (1 cement : 3 coarse sand : 6 graded stone aggregate 20 mm nominal size) for shape of bell mouth including plastering providing and fixing 100 × 50 × 5 cm size precast R.C.C. slab 1 : 2 : 4 (1 cement : 2 coarse sand : 4 graded stone aggregate 12.5 mm nominal size)		

S. No.	Description	Unit	Rate ₹
	reinforced with cold twisted bars reinforcement @ 100 kg per cum of reinforced concrete including plastering with cement mortar 1 : 3 (1 cement : 3 fine sand) of 6 mm thickness on exposed surface of the slab and bell mouth including centring, shuttering and neat cement punning inside the bell mouth etc. all complete.	each	563.25
68.	Providing and fixing Cat's Eye (Glow studs) heavy duty integral stem, reflective, aluminium die cast with elegant finish of size 100 × 100 mm and 20 mm high having a stem of 50 mm (or 12 mm dia. 90 mm long) screwed and nailed to fix into the road surface or at the nosing of the central verge. The road studs should have reflectors fitted on one side of the studs (3 Nos. 7 element or 1 No. 29 element reflector) complete.	each	285.15
69.	Preparation of sub-base road pavement with commercial dry lime (slaked), fly ash stabilised soil with a mix of 3% lime, 12% fly ash and 85% local suitable soil by weight, so as to achieve minimum field C.B.R. of 20 including mixing, rolling with road roller curing etc. all complete :		
	69A Minimum thickness 15 cm.	cum	182.55
70.	Providing and fixing precast lime fly ash concrete blocks 1 : 2 : 3 : 6 (1 lime : 2 fly ash : 3 coarse sand : 6 stone aggregate 20 mm nominal size) including finishing with 10 mm thick cement mortar 1: 3 (1 cement : 3 coarse sand) in foot paths including preparation of sub-grade with a hand rammer, laying 10 mm thick levelling course of fine sand (jamuna sand) and filling the joints with fine sand.	cum	1503.60

Table 13.17. Horticulture and Landscaping

S. No.	Description	Unit	Rate ₹
1.	Trenching in ordinary soil upto a depth of 60 cm including removal and stacking of serviceable materials and then disposing of by spreading and neatly levelling with in a lead of 50 m and making up the trenched area to proper levels by filling with earth or earth mixed with sludge or/and manure before and after flooding trench with water (excluding cost of imported earth, sludge or manure).	cum	7.80
2.	Supplying and stacking of good earth at site including royalty and carriage upto 1 km (earth measured in stacks will be reduced by 20% for payment).	cum	70.45
3.	Supplying and stacking sludge at site including royalty and carriage upto 1 km (sludge measured in stacks will be reduced by 8% for payment).	cum	71.50
4.	Supplying and stacking at site dump manure from Badli or other approved source, including carriage upto 1 km (manure measured in stacks will be reduced by 8% for payment) :		
	4A Screened through sieve of I.S. designation 20 mm	cum	42.25
	4B Screened through sieve of I.S. designation 16 mm	cum	45.85
	4C Screened through sieve of I.S. designation 4.75 mm	cum	48.75
5.	Rough dressing the trenched ground including breaking clods.	100 sq m	15.30

(*Contd.*)

S. No.	Description	Unit	Rate ₹
6.	Uprooting weeds from the trenched area after 10 to 15 days of its flooding with water including disposal of uprooted vegetation.	100 sq m	49.30
7.	Fine dressing the ground.	100 sq m	36.95
8.	Spreading of sludge, dump manure or/and good earth in required thickness (Cost of sludge, dump manure or/and good earth to be paid separately).	cum	5.35
9.	Mixing earth and sludge or manure in proportion specified or directed.	cum	3.60
10.	Grassing with 'Doob' grass including watering and maintenance of the lawn for 30 days or more till the grass forms a thick lawn free from weeds and fit for mowing including supplying good earth if needed (the good earth shall be paid for separately) :		
	10A In rows 15 cm apart in either direction.	100 sq m	55.80
	10B In rows 7.5 cm apart in either direction.	100 sq m	115.90
	10C In rows 5 cm apart in either direction.	100 sq m	177.40
11.	Renovating lawns including weeding, cheeling the grass, forking the ground, top dressing with sludge or manure, mixing the same with forked soil, watering and maintaining the lawn for 30 days or more till the grass forms a thick lawn free from weeds and fit for mowing and disposal of rubbish as directed, including supplying good earth if needed but excluding the cost of sludge or manure (the good earth shall be paid for separately).	100 sq m	341.05
12.	Uprooting rank vegetation and weeds by digging the area to a depth of 60 cm removing all weeds and other growth with roots by forking repeatedly, breaking clods, rough dressing, flooding with water, uprooting fresh growths after 10 to 15 days and then fine dressing for planting new grass, including disposal of all rubbish with all leads and lifts.	100 sq m	606.85
13.	Preparation of beds for hedging and shrubbery by excavating 60 cm deep and trenching the excavated base to a further depth of 30 cm, refilling the excavated earth after breaking clods and mixing with sludge or manure in the ratio of 8 : 1 (8 parts of stacked volume of earth after reduction by 20% : one part of stacked volume of sludge or manure after reduction by 8%), flooding with water, filling with earth if necessary, watering and finally fine dressing, levelling etc. including stacking and disposal of materials declared unserviceable and surplus earth by spreading and levelling as directed, within a lead of 50 m lift upto 1.5 m complete (cost of sludge, manure or extra earth to be paid for separately).	cum	22.00
14.	Digging holes in ordinary soil and refilling the same with the excavated earth mixed with manure or sludge in the ratio of 2 : 1 by volume (2 parts of stacked volume of earth after reduction by 20% : 1 part of stacked volume of manure after reduction by 8%) flooding with water, dressing including removal of rubbish and surplus earth, if any with all leads and lifts (cost of manure, sludge or extra good earth if needed to be paid for separately) :		
	14A Holes 1.2 m dia and 1.2 m deep.	each	92.60
	14B Holes 60 cm dia. and 60 cm deep.	each	12.00

S. No.	*Description*	*Unit*	*Rate* ₹
15.	Half brick circular tree guard in 50 class designation bricks, internal diameter 1.25 metre and height 1.2 metre above ground and 0.20 m below ground bottom two courses laid dry and top three courses in lime mortar 1 : 2 (1 lime putty : 2 surkhi) or cement mortar 1 : 6 (1 cement : 6 fine sand) and the intermediate courses being in dry honey comb masonry as per design complete :		
15A	With F.P.S. Bricks	each	369.35
16.	Providing and fixing M.S. flat iron tree guard 60 cm dia. and 2 m height above ground level formed of 4 nos. 25 × 6 mm and 8 nos. 25 × 3 mm vertical M.S. flats rivetted to 3 nos. 25 × 6 mm M.S. flat iron rings in two halves, bolted together with 8 mm dia. and 30 mm long bolts including painting two coats with paint of approved brand and manufacture over a coat of priming, complete in all respects.	each	806.75
17.	Making tree guard 53 cm dia. and 1.3 m high as per design from empty coal tar drums supplied free by the department including providing and fixing 2 nos. M.S. sheet rings 50 × 0.5 mm with rivets complete in all respects including painting inside and outside of tree guard with :		
17A	A coat of coal tar.	each	54.75
17B	Two or more coats of ready mixed paint of approved quality shade over a priming coat.	each	105.45
18.	Making tree guard 53 cm dia. and 2 m high as per design from empty coal tar drums supplied free by the department including providing and fixing four legs 40 cm long of 30 × 3 mm M.S. flat riveted to tree guard and providing and fixing 2 nos. M.S. sheet rings 50 × 0.5 mm with rivets complete in all respects including painting inside and outside of tree guard with :		
18A	A coat of coal tar.	each	113.30
18B	Two or more coats of ready mixed paint of approved quality and shade over a priming coat.	each	191.45
19.	Edging with bricks laid dry length wise including excavation, refilling, consolidating with hand packing and spreading neatly surplus earth within a lead of 50 m :		
19A	75 class designation		
19B	F.P.S. Bricks	metre	8.45
19C	50 designation		
19D	F.P.S. Bricks.	metre	7.95
20.	Filling mixture of earth and sludge or manure in the desired proportion in trenches, flooding with water and levelling (cost of supplying earth and sludge or manure and mixing excluded).	cum	1.80
21.	Excavation in dumped stones or malba including stacking of serviceable and unserviceable material separately and disposal of unserviceable material lead upto 50 m and lift upto 1.5 m disposed material to be neatly dressed.	cum	50.55
22.	Excavation in bajri path including stacking of serviceable and unserviceable material lead upto 50 m and lift upto 1.5 m disposed material to be neatly dressed.	cum	56.35

(Contd.)

S. No.	Description	Unit	Rate ₹
23.	Excavation in water bound macadam road including stacking the serviceable and unserviceable material separately and disposal of unserviceable material lead upto 50 m and lift upto 1.5 m disposed material to be neatly dressed.	cum	69.30
24.	Flooding the ground with water including making kiaries and dismentling the same.	100 sq m	14.50

Table 13.18. Sanitary Installations

S. No.	Description	Unit	Rate ₹
1.	Providing and fixing white vitreous china water closet squatting pan (Indian type W.C. pan) with 100 mm sand cast Iron P or S trap, 10 litre low level P.V.C. flushing cistern (of approved make) with fittings, C.I./M.S. brackets, 32 mm diameter flush pipe with fittings and clamps, overflow arrangement with specials and mosquito proof coupling of approved municipal design including painting of fittings and brackets, cutting and making good the walls and floors wherever required :		
	1A Long pan pattern W.C. pan of size 580 mm with flush pipe and overflow arrangement	each	1279.75
	1B Orissa pattern W.C. pan of size 580 × 440 mm with integral type foot rests flush pipe and overflow arrangement.	each	1665.25
2.	Providing and fixing white vitreous china pedestal type water closet (European type W.C. pan) with seat and lid. CP brass hinges and rubber buffers, 10 litre low level P.V.C. flushing cistern with fittings, C.I./M.S. brackets 40 mm diameter flush bend with fittings and clamps, overflow arrangement with specials and mosquito proof coupling of approved municipal design complete including painting of fittings and brackets, cutting and making good the walls and floors wherever required :		
	2A W.C. pan with white solid plastic seat and lid	each	1562.40
	2B W.C. pan with black solid plastic seat and lid.	each	1540.15
3.	Providing and fixing white vitreous china pedestal type water closet (European type) with seat and lid, with CP brass hinges and rubber buffers, 10 litre low level flushing cistern with fittings and C.I./M.S. brackets, 40 mm flush bend, overflow arrangement with specials of standard make and mosquito proof coupling of approved municipal design complete including painting of fittings and brackets, cutting and making good the walls and floors wherever required :		
	3A W.C. pan with white solid plastic seat and lid with white vitreous china flushing cistern and C.P. flush bend	each	2458.50
	3B W.C. pan with black solid plastic seat and lid, with white vitreous china flushing cistern and C.P. flush bend.	each	2436.30
4.	Providing and fixing white vitreous china flat back or wall corner type lipped front urinal basin of 430 × 260 × 350 mm and 340 × 410 × 265 mm sizes respectively with automatic flushing cistern with C.I./M.S. brackets standard flush pipe and C.P. brass spreaders with brass unions and G.I. clamps complete, including painting of fittings and brackets, cutting and making good the walls and floors wherever required :		

S. No.	Description	Unit	Rate ₹
4A	One urinal basin with 5 litre P.V.C. automatic flushing cistern	each	1402.35
4B	Range of two urinal basins with 7.5 litre P.V.C. automatic flushing cistern.	each	2468.90
4C	Range of three urinal basins with 7.5 litre P.V.C. automatic flushing cistern.	each	3104.65
4D	Range of four urinal basins with 10 litre P.V.C. automatic flushing cistern.	each	4296.10
5.	Providing and fixing white vitreous china flat back or half stall urinal of 580 × 380 × 350 mm with automatic flushing cistern (of approved make) with fittings, C.I./M.S. brackets standard size C.P. brass flush pipe spreaders with unions and clamps (all in C.P. brass) with waste fitting as per IS : 2556, C.I. trap with outlet grating and other couplings in C.P. brass including painting of fittings and brackets, cutting and making good the walls and floors wherever required :		
5A	Single half stall urinal with 5 litre P.V.C. automatic flushing cistern	each	2755.35
5B	Range of two half stall urinals with 7.5 litre P.V.C. automatic flushing cistern	each	4554.65
5C	Range of three half stall urinals with 10 litre P.V.C automatic flushing cistern	each	6181.15
5D	Range of four half stall urinals with 10 litre P.V.C. automatic flushing cistern	each	7557.90
6.	Providing and fixing one piece construction white vitreous china squatting plate with an brass coupling complete including painting of fittings and brackets, cutting and making good the walls and floors etc. wherever required :		
6A	Single squatting plate with 5 litre P.V.C automatic flushing cistern	each	1733.35
6B	Range of two squatting plates with 7.5 litre P.V.C automatic flushing cistern	each	2692.25
6C	Range of three squatting plates with 10 litre P.V.C automatic flushing cistern	each	3641.75
6D	Range of four squatting plates with 15 litre P.V.C. automatic flushing cistern	each	4479.85
7.	Providing and fixing white vitreous china wash basin with C.I./M.S. brackets, 15 mm C.P. brass pillar taps, 32 mm C.P. brass waste of standard pattern, including painting of fittings and brackets, cutting and making good the walls wherever required :		
7A	Flat back wash basin size 630 × 450 mm with a pair of 15 mm C.P. brass pillar taps.	each	916.95
7B	Flat back wash basin size 630 × 450 mm with a single 15 mm C.P. brass pillar tap.	each	827.05
7C	Flat back wash basin size 550 × 400 mm with a pair of 15 mm C.P. brass pillar taps.	each	768.05
7D	Flat back wash basin size 550 × 400 mm with single 15 mm C.P. brass pillar tap.	each	678.20
7E	Angle back wash basin size 600 × 480 mm with single 15 mm C.P. brass pillar tap.	each	757.05

(Contd.)

S. No.		Description	Unit	Rate ₹
	7F	Angle back wash basin size 400 × 400 mm with single 15 mm C.P. brass pillar tap.	each	629.30
	7G	Flat back wash basin size 450 × 300 mm with single 15 mm C.P. brass pillar tap.	each	568.20
	7H	Surgeon type wash basin of size 660 × 460 mm with a pair of 15 mm C.P. brass pillar taps, with elbow operated levers.	each	1152.50
	7I	Surgeon type wash basin of size 660 × 460 mm with single 15 mm C.P. brass pillar tap with elbow operated levers.	each	1062.60
8.		Add for :		
	8A	Providing 32 mm dia. C.P. brass trap	each	69.90
	8B	Providing 32 mm dia. C.P. brass union.	each	37.70
9.		Providing and fixing white vitreous china pedestal for wash basin completely recessed at the back for the reception of pipes and fittings.	each	532.25
10.		Providing and fixing kitchen sink with C.I. brackets, C.P. brass chain with rubber plug, 40 mm C.P. brass waste complete, including painting the fittings and brackets, cutting and making good the walls wherever required :		
	10A	White glazed fire clay kitchen sink of size 600 × 450 × 250 mm	each	1393.30
11.		Providing and fixing stainless steel kitchen sink as per IS: 13983 with C.I. brackets and stainless steel plug 40 mm including painting of fittings and brackets, cutting and making good the walls wherever required :		
	(1)	Kitchen sink with drain board :		
	11A	510 × 1040 bowl depth 178 mm	each	2066.85
	11B	400 × 915 bowl depth 160 mm	each	1413.60
	11C	500 × 1000 bowl depth 178 mm	each	1413.60
	(2)	Without drain board :		
	11D	610 × 510 bowl depth 200 mm	each	1260.25
	11E	535 × 460 bowl depth 178 mm	each	1198.05
	11F	510 × 432 bowl depth 172 mm	each	1073.60
12.		Providing and fixing white vitreous china laboratory sink with C.I. brackets, C.P. brass chain with rubber plug 40 mm C.P. brass waste and 40 mm C.P. brass trap with necessary C.P. brass unions complete including painting of fittings and brackets, cutting and making good the wall wherever required :		
	12A	Size 450 × 300 × 150 mm	each	912.25
	12B	Size 600 × 450 × 200 mm	each	1709.95
13.		Providing and fixing draining board with C.I./M.S. brackets including painting of brackets, cutting and making good the walls wherever required :		
	13A	White glazed fire clay draining board of size 600 × 450 × 25 mm	each	572.55
	13B	Marble stone draining board of size 600 × 450 × 25 mm	each	492.60
14.		Providing and fixing white vitreous china water closet squatting pan (Indian type) :		
	14A	Long pattern W.C. pan of size 580 mm	each	350.10
	14B	Orissa pattern W.C. pan of size 580 × 440 mm	each	735.70

S. No.	Description	Unit	Rate ₹
15.	Extra for using coloured W.C. pan instead of white W.C. pan :		
	15A Orissa pattern W.C. pan 580 × 440 mm	each	342.20
16.	Providing and fixing white vitreous china pedestal type (European type/wash down type) water closet pan.	each	581.25
17.	Extra for using coloured pedestal type W.C. pan (European type) with low level cistern of same colour instead of white vitreous china W.C. pan and cistern.	each	409.95
18.	Providing and fixing a pair of white vitreous china foot rests of standard pattern for squatting pan water closet :		
	18A 250 × 130 × 30 mm	each pair	88.90
	18B 250 × 125 × 25 mm	each pair	78.90
19.	Providing and fixing 10 litre low level white vitreous china flushing cistern of approved make with fittings such as lead valve less syphon etc. and C.P. brass handle complete.	each	1455.20
20.	Providing and fixing 10 litre low level P.V.C. cistern of approved make with fittings complete.	each	471.85
21.	Providing and fixing 10 litre high level C.I. flushing cistern of approved make with integral fittings such as ball valve G.I. chain and pull complete.	each	489.05
22.	Providing and fixing 5 litre C.I. automatic flushing cistern with fittings.	each	209.65
23.	Providing and fixing 10 litre C.I. automatic flushing cistern with fittings.	each	227.95
24.	Providing and fixing controlled flush, low level cistern made of high density polyethylene/polyethyene, with all fittings complete :		
	24A 10 litre (full flush) capacity-white	each	611.85
	24B 10 litre (full flush) capacity-coloured	each	722.95
	24C 8 litre (full flush) capacity-white	each	584.05
	24D 8 litre (full flush) capacity-coloured	each	917.35
25.	Providing and fixing controlled flush, low level cistern made of vitreous china with all fittings complete :		
	25A 10 litre (full flush) capacity-white	each	964.20
	25B 10 litre (full flush) capacity-coloured	each	1436.40
26.	Providing and fixing solid plastic seat with lid for pedestal type W.C. pan with C.P. brass hinges, rubber buffers etc. complete :		
	26A White solid plastic seat with lid	each	230.30
	26B Black solid plastic seat with lid	each	208.10
27.	Extra for providing coloured other than black solid P.V.C. plastic seat and cover in European type W.C. pan, instead of white plastic seat and cover.	each	111.10
28.	Providing and fixing G.I. chain with G.I. pull.	each	13.20
29.	Providing and fixing G.I. inlet connection for flush pipe connecting with W.C. pan.	each	58.10
30.	Providing and fixing white vitreous china flat back or wall corner type lipped front urinal basin of 430 × 260 × 350 mm and 340 × 410 × 265 mm sizes respectively.	each	324.05
31.	Providing and fixing white glazed fire clay stall urinal of standard size.	each	2719.95

(Contd.)

S. No.	Description	Unit	Rate ₹
32.	**Providing and fixing white vitreous china squatting plate urinal with integral rim longitudinal flush pipe.**	**each**	**636.80**
33.	**Providing and fixing white vitreous china wash basin including making all connections but excluding the cost of fittings :**		
	33A Flat back wash basin of size 630 × 450 mm.	**each**	**547.25**
	33B Flat back wash basin of size 550 × 400 mm.	**each**	**398.40**
	33C Angle back wash basin of size 600 × 480 mm.	**each**	**477.25**
	33D Angle back wash basin of size 400 × 400 mm.	**each**	**349.50**
	33E Flat back wash basin of size 450 × 300 mm.	**each**	**288.40**
	33F Surgeon type wash basin of size 660 × 460 mm.	**each**	**782.80**
34.	**Providing and fixing kitchen sink including making all connections excluding cost of fittings :**		
	34A White glazed fire clay sink of size 600 × 450 × 250 mm.	**each**	**1180.95**
35.	**Providing and fixing white vitreous china laboratory sink including making all connections excluding cost of fittings :**		
	35A Size 450 × 300 × 150 mm.	**each**	**566.60**
	35B Size 600 × 450 × 200 mm.	**each**	**1364.30**
36.	**Providing and fixing C.P. brass waste for sink or wash basin :**		
	36A 32 mm dia	**each**	**51.20**
	36B 40 mm dia	**each**	**57.85**
37.	**Providing and fixing P.V.C. waste pipe for sink or wash basin including P.V.C. waste fittings complete :**		
	(1) Semi rigid pipe		
	37A 32 mm dia	**each**	**23.40**
	37B 40 mm dia	**each**	**25.65**
	(2) Flexible pipe		
	37C 32 mm dia	**each**	**27.85**
	37D 40 mm dia	**each**	**27.85**
38.	**Providing and fixing fisher union for wash basin :**		
	38A 32 mm dia brass union.	**each**	**54.30**
	38B 40 mm dia brass union.	**each**	**64.30**
39.	**Providing and fixing C.P. brass trap for wash basins and sinks :**		
	39A 32 mm dia.	**each**	**78.95**
	39B 40 mm dia.	**each**	**97.85**
40.	**Providing and fixing 100 mm sand cast Iron grating for gully, floor or Nahani trap.**	**each**	**9.20**
41.	**Providing and fixing stainless steel jali (grating) with or without hole for waste pipe for floor/Nahani trap :**		
	41A 75 mm dia weight not less than 70 gms	**each**	**14.75**
	41B 100 mm dia. weight not less than 100 gms.	**each**	**15.85**
42.	**Providing and fixing plastic moulded jali of required colour and shade for floor/nahani trap :**		
	42A Circular type	**each**	**42.50**
	42B Rectangular with openable circular lid	**each**	**52.50**
43.	**Providing and fixing in position 32 mm diameter G.I. flush pipe for high level flushing cistern complete including cutting and making good the walls and floors.**	**each**	**240.90**

S. No.	Description	Unit	Rate ₹
44.	**Providing and fixing in position 25 mm diameter mosquito proof coupling of approved municipal design.**	**each**	**14.45**
45.	**Providing and fixing 600 × 450 mm bevelled edge mirror of superior glass (of approved quality) complete with 6 mm thick hard board ground fixed to wooden cleats with C.P. brass screws and washers complete.**	**each**	**327.35**
46.	**Providing and fixing mirror of required shape and size with plastic moulded frame of approved make and shade with 6 mm thick hard board backing :**		
	46A Circular shape 450 mm dia.	**each**	**257.80**
	46B Rectangular shape 453 × 357 mm	**each**	**216.80**
	46C Oval shape 450 × 350 mm (outer dimensions)	**each**	**238.75**
	46D Rectangular shape 1500 × 450 mm	**each**	**725.35**
47.	**Providing and fixing 600 × 120 × 5 mm glass shelf with edges rounded off supported on anodised aluminium angle frame with C.P. brass brackets and guard rail complete fixed with 40 mm long screws, rawl plugs etc. complete.**	**each**	**127.00**
48.	**Providing and fixing towel rail complete with brackets fixed to wooden cleats with C.P. brass screws :**		
	48A C.P. Brass towel rail with two C.P. brass brackets.	**each**	**131.25**
	48B 600 × 20 mm size	**each**	**123.45**
49.	**Providing and fixing toilet paper holder :**		
	49A C.P. brass	**each**	**69.05**
	49B Vitreous china	**each**	**101.60**
50.	**Providing and fixing soil, waste and vent pipes :**		
	(1) 100 mm dia. :		
	50A Sand cast iron S&S pipe	**metre**	**196.95**
	50B Centrifugally cast (spun) iron S&S pipe	**metre**	**210.05**
	(2) 75 mm diameter :		
	50C Sand cast iron S&S pipe	**metre**	**161.55**
	50D Centrifugally cast (spun) iron S&S pipe	**metre**	**180.75**
	(3) 50 mm dia		
	50E Sand cast iron S&S pipe	**metre**	**137.20**
	50F Centrifugally cast (spun) iron S&S pipe	**metre**	**138.00**
51.	**Providing and filling the joints with spun yarn cement slurry and cement mortar 1 : 2 (1 cement : 2 fine sand) in S.C.I./C.I. pipes :**		
	51A 50 mm dia pipe	**metre**	**10.40**
	51B 75 mm dia pipe	**metre**	**14.65**
	51C 100 mm dia pipe	**metre**	**17.20**
52.	**Providing and fixing M.S. holder-bat clamps of approved design to Sand Cast iron/cast iron (spun) pipe embedded in and including cement concrete blocks 10 × 10 × 10 cm of 1 : 2 : 4 mix (1 cement : 2 coarse sand : 4 graded stone aggregate 20 mm nominal size) including cost of cutting holes and making good the walls etc. :**		
	52A For 100 mm dia. pipe	**each**	**36.40**
	52B For 75 mm dia. pipe	**each**	**36.40**
	52C For 50 mm dia. pipe.	**each**	**34.95**

(Contd.)

S. No.	Description	Unit	Rate ₹
53.	**Providing and fixing bend of required degree with access door, insertion rubber washer 3 mm thick, bolts and nuts complete :**		
	(1) 100 mm :		
	53A Sand cast iron S&S	each	123.75
	53B Centrifugally cast (spun) iron S&S	each	109.30
	(2) 75 mm dia :		
	53C Sand cast iron S&S	each	102.10
	53D Centrifugally cast (spun) iron S&S	each	89.85
	(3) 50 mm :		
	53E Sand cast iron S&S	each	81.30
	53F Centrifugally cast (spun) iron S&S	each	84.65
54.	**Providing and fixing plain bend of required degree :**		
	(1) 100 mm :		
	54A Sand cast iron S&S	each	99.30
	54B Centrifugally cast (spun) iron S&S	each	99.30
	(2) 75 mm :		
	54C Sand cast iron S&S	each	82.10
	54D Centrifugally cast (spun) iron S&S	each	82.10
	(3) 50 mm :		
	54E Sand cast iron S&S	each	62.40
	54F Centrifugally cast (spun) iron S&S	each	65.75
55.	**Providing and fixing heel rest sanitary bend :**		
	(1) 100 mm dia :		
	55A Sand cast iron S&S	each	113.75
	55B Centrifugally cast (spun) iron S&S	each	108.20
	(2) 75 mm :		
	55C Sand cast iron S&S	each	94.30
	55D Centrifugally cast (spun) iron S&S	each	95.45
	(3) 50 mm :		
	55E Sand cast iron S&S	each	76.85
	55F Centrifugally cast (spun) iron S&S	each	77.95
56.	**Providing and fixing double equal junction of required degree with access door, insertion rubber washer 3 mm thick, bolts and nuts complete :**		
	(1) 100 × 100 × 100 × 100 mm :		
	56A Sand cast iron S&S	each	243.65
	56B Centrifugally cast (spun) iron S&S	each	230.30
	(2) 75 × 75 × 75 × 75 mm :		
	56C Sand cast iron S&S	each	188.75
	56D Centrifugally cast (spun) iron S&S	each	174.30
	(3) 50 × 50 × 50 × 50 mm :		
	56E Sand cast iron S&S	each	156.85
	56F Centrifugally cast (spun) iron S&S	each	119.10

S. No.	Description	Unit	Rate ₹
57.	**Providing and fixing double equal plain junction of required degree :**		
	(1) 100 × 100 × 100 × 100 mm :		
	57A Sand cast iron S&S	each	211.50
	57B Centrifugally cast (spun) iron S&S	each	200.40
	(2) 75 × 75 × 75 × 75 mm :		
	57C Sand cast iron S&S	each	157.65
	57D Centrifugally cast (spun) iron S&S	each	143.20
	(3) 50 × 50 × 50 × 50 mm :		
	57E Sand cast iron S&S	each	122.40
	57F Centrifugally cast (spun) iron S&S	each	92.40
58.	**Providing and fixing single equal plain junction of required degree with access door, insertion rubber washer 3 mm thick, bolts and nuts complete :**		
	(1) 100 × 100 × 100 mm		
	58A Sand cast iron S&S	each	182.60
	58B Centrifugally cast (spun) iron S&S	each	183.75
	(2) 75 × 75 × 75 mm		
	58C Sand cast iron S&S	each	136.55
	58D Centrifugally cast (spun) iron S&S	each	137.65
	(3) 50 × 50 × 50 mm		
	58E Sand cast iron S&S	each	96.85
	58F Centrifugally cast (spun) iron S&S	each	117.95
59.	**Providing and fixing single equal plain junction of required degree :**		
	(1) 100 × 100 × 100 mm		
	59A Sand cast iron S&S	each	154.85
	59B Centrifugally cast (spun) iron S&S	each	155.95
	(2) 75 × 75 × 75 mm		
	59C Sand cast iron S&S	each	98.75
	59D Centrifugally cast (spun) iron S&S	each	112.10
	(3) 50 × 50 × 50 mm		
	59E Sand cast iron S&S	each	83.50
	59F Centrifugally cast (spun) iron S&S	each	84.65
60.	**Providing and fixing double unequal junction of required degree with access door, insertion rubber washer 3 mm thick, bolts and nuts complete :**		
	(1) 100 × 100 × 75 × 75 mm		
	60A Sand cast iron S&S	each	167.05
	60B Centrifugally cast (spun) iron S&S	each	217.05
	(2) 100 × 100 × 50 × 50 mm		
	60C Sand cast iron S&S	each	195.95
	60D Centrifugally cast (spun) iron S&S	each	184.85
	(3) 75 × 75 × 50 × 50 mm		
	60E Sand cast iron S&S	each	163.20
	60F Centrifugally cast (spun) iron S&S	each	77.65

(Contd.)

S. No.	Description	Unit	Rate ₹
61.	Providing and fixing double unequal plain junction of required degree :		
(1)	100 × 100 × 75 × 75 mm		
61A	Sand cast iron S&S	each	151.50
61B	Centrifugally cast (spun) iron S&S	each	193.75
(2)	100 × 100 × 50 × 50 mm		
61C	Sand cast iron S&S	each	151.50
61D	Centrifugally cast (spun) iron S&S	each	174.85
(3)	75 × 75 × 50 × 50 mm		
61E	Sand cast iron S&S	each	122.10
61F	Centrifugally cast (spun) iron S&S	each	65.45
62.	Providing and fixing single unequal junction of required degree with access door, insertion rubber washer 3 mm thick, bolts and nuts complete :		
(1)	100 × 100 × 75 mm		
62A	Sand cast iron S&S	each	180.40
62B	Centrifugally cast (spun) iron S&S	each	180.40
(2)	100 × 100 × 50 mm		
62C	Sand cast iron S&S	each	180.40
62D	Centrifugally cast (spun) iron S&S	each	180.40
(3)	75 × 75 × 50 mm		
62E	Sand cast iron S&S	each	136.55
62F	Centrifugally cast (spun) iron S&S	each	136.55
63.	Providing and fixing single unequal plain junction of required degree :		
(1)	100 × 100 × 75 mm		
63A	Sand cast iron S&S	each	153.75
63B	Centrifugally cast (spun) iron S&S	each	153.75
(2)	100 × 100 × 50 mm		
63C	Sand cast iron S&S	each	153.75
63D	Centrifugally cast (spun) iron S&S	each	153.75
(3)	75 × 75 × 50 mm		
63E	Sand cast iron S&S	each	111.00
63F	Centrifugally cast (spun) iron S&S	each	117.65
64.	Providing and fixing double equal plain invert branch of required degree :		
(1)	100 × 100 × 100 × 100 mm		
64A	Sand cast iron S&S	each	210.40
64B	Centrifugally cast (spun) iron S&S	each	100.40
(2)	75 × 75 × 75 × 75 mm		
64C	Sand cast iron S&S	each	160.95
64D	Centrifugally cast (spun) iron S&S	each	93.20
(3)	50 × 50 × 50 × 50 mm		
64E	Sand cast iron S&S	each	136.85
64F	Centrifugally cast (spun) iron S&S	each	70.20

S. No.		Description	Unit	Rate ₹
65.		**Providing and fixing single equal plain invert branch of required degree :**		
	(1)	100 × 100 × 100 mm		
	65A	Sand cast iron S&S	each	179.30
	65B	Centrifugally cast (spun) iron S&S	each	75.95
	(2)	75 × 75 × 75 mm		
	65C	Sand cast iron S&S	each	131.00
	65D	Centrifugally cast (spun) iron S&S	each	64.15
	(3)	50 × 50 × 50 mm		
	65E	Sand cast iron S&S	each	103.50
	65F	Centrifugally cast (spun) iron S&S	each	45.10
66.		**Providing and fixing double unequal invert branch of required degree :**		
	(1)	100 × 100 × 75 × 75 mm		
	66A	Sand cast iron S&S	each	230.40
	66B	Centrifugally cast (spun) iron S&S	each	100.40
	(2)	100 × 100 × 50 × 50 mm		
	66C	Sand cast iron S&S	each	230.40
	66D	Centrifugally cast (spun) iron S&S	each	93.75
	(3)	75 × 75 × 50 × 50 mm		
	66E	Sand cast iron S&S	each	195.40
	66F	Centrifugally cast (spun) iron S&S	each	68.75
67.		**Providing and fixing single unequal plain invert branch of required degree :**		
	(1)	100 × 100 × 75 mm		
	67A	Sand cast iron S&S	each	162.60
	67B	Centrifugally cast (spun) iron S&S	each	163.75
	(2)	100 × 100 × 50 mm		
	67C	Sand cast iron S&S	each	160.40
	67D	Centrifugally cast (spun) iron S&S	each	163.75
	(3)	75 × 75 × 50 mm		
	67E	Sand cast iron S&S	each	117.65
	67F	Centrifugally cast (spun) iron S&S	each	55.45
68.		**Providing and fixing sand cast iron S&S off sets :**		
	(1)	76 mm off sets		
	68A	With 50 mm dia. pipe	each	107.65
	68B	With 75 mm dia. pipe	each	121.00
	68C	With 100 mm dia. pipe	each	160.95
	(2)	114 mm off sets		
	68D	With 50 mm dia. pipe	each	115.95
	68E	With 75 mm dia. pipe	each	124.85
	68F	With 100 mm dia. pipe	each	158.20
	(3)	152 mm off sets		
	68G	With 50 mm dia. pipe	each	97.55
	68H	With 75 mm dia. pipe	each	127.55
	68I	With 100 mm dia. pipe	each	157.55

(Contd.)

S. No.		Description	Unit	Rate
69.		**Providing and fixing centrifugally cast (spun) iron S&S off sets :**		
	(1)	**75 mm off sets**		
	69A	**With 50 mm dia. pipe**		
	69B	**With 75 mm dia. pipe**	**each**	**96.**
	(2)	**150 mm off sets**		
	69C	**With 50 mm dia. pipe**	**each**	**15.30**
	69D	**With 75 mm dia. pipe**	**each**	**7.55**
	67E	**With 100 mm dia. pipe**	**each**	**55**
70.		**Providing and fixing door piece, insertion rubber washer 3 mm thick, bolts & nuts complete :**		
	(1)	**100 mm**		
	70A	**Sand cast iron S&S**	**each**	**152.65**
	70B	**Centrifugally cast (spun) iron S&S**	**each**	**153.75**
	(2)	**75 mm**		
	70C	**Sand cast iron S&S**	**each**	**123.20**
	70D	**Centrifugally cast (spun) iron S&S**	**each**	**124.30**
	(3)	**50 mm**		
	70E	**Sand cast iron S&S**	**each**	**97.95**
71.		**Providing and fixing terminal guard :**		
	(1)	**100 mm**		
	71A	**Sand cast iron S&S**	**each**	**73.75**
	71B	**Centrifugally cast (spun) iron S&S**	**each**	**83.75**
	(2)	**75 mm**		
	71C	**Sand cast iron S&S**	**each**	**59.85**
	71D	**Centrifugally cast (spun) iron S&S**	**each**	**68.75**
	(3)	**50 mm**		
	71E	**Sand cast iron S&S**	**each**	**47.95**
	71F	**Centrifugally cast (spun) iron S&S**	**each**	**55.75**
72.		**Providing and fixing collar :**		
	(1)	**100 mm**		
	72A	**Sand cast iron S&S**	**each**	**60.40**
	72B	**Centrifugally cast (spun) iron S&S**	**each**	**60.40**
	(2)	**75 mm**		
	72C	**Sand cast iron S&S**	**each**	**51.00**
	72D	**Centrifugally cast (spun) iron S&S**	**each**	**51.00**
	(3)	**50 mm**		
	72E	**Sand cast iron S&S**	**each**	**41.30**
	72F	**Centrifugally cast (spun) iron S&S**	**each**	**41.30**
73.		**Providing and fixing 50 mm dia pass over pipe :**		
	73A	**Sand cast iron S&S**	**each**	**133.50**
	73B	**Centrifugally cast (spun) iron S&S**	**each**	**133.50**
74.		**Providing lead caulked joints to sand cast iron/centrifugally cast (spun) iron pipes and fittings of diameter :**		
	74A	**100 mm**	**each**	**77.05**
	74B	**75 mm**	**each**	**66.15**
	74C	**50 mm**	**each**	**54.00**

S. No.	Description	Unit	Rate ₹
75.	Providing and fixing M.S. stays and clamps for sand cast iron/ centrifugally cast (spun) iron pipes of diameter :		
	75A 100 mm	each	22.65
	75B 75 mm	each	21.00
	75C 50 mm	each	19.10
76.	Providing and fixing sand cast iron trap of self cleansing design with sand cast iron screwed down or hinged grating with or without vent arm complete, including cost of cutting and making good the walls and floors :		
	76A 100 mm inlet and 100 mm outlet	each	240.40
	76B 100 mm inlet and 75 mm outlet	each	207.05
	76C 100 mm inlet and 50 mm outlet	each	190.40
77.	Cutting chases in brick masonry walls for following diameter sand cast iron/centrifugally cast (spun) iron pipes and making good the same with cement concrete 1 : 3 : 6 (1 cement : 3 coarse sand : 6 graded stone aggregate 12.5 mm nominal size) including necessary plaster and pointing in cement mortar 1 : 4 (1 cement : 4 coarse sand) :		
	77A 100 mm dia	metre	80.45
	77B 75 mm dia	metre	44.25
	77C 50 mm dia	metre	36.20
78.	Painting C.I. cistern with bitumastic or any other anti-corrosive paint inside and white paint over a coat of zinc chromate yellow primer (of approved quality) on the outside surface of the cistern flush pipe, other fittings, etc. complete for new work.	each	122.95
79.	Re-painting C.I. cistern with bitumastic or any other anti-corrosive paint inside and white paint on the outside surface of the cistern, flush pipe, other fittings, etc. complete including polishing of wooden seat and lid and cleaning of W.C. pan with acid wherever necessary.	each	82.70
80.	Repainting C.I. cistern with synthetic enamel paint of approved colour brand and manufacture on the outside surface of cistern flush pipe, other fittings etc. complete.	each	42.10
81.	Painting sand cast iron/centrifugally cast (spun) iron soil, waste vent pipes and fittings with paint of any colour such as chocolate grey, or buff etc. over a coat of primer (of approved quality) for new work :		
	81A 50 mm diameter pipe	metre	6.20
	81B 100 mm diameter pipe	metre	10.90
	81C 75 mm diameter pipe	metre	8.35
82.	Repainting sand cast iron/centrifugally cast iron (spun) iron, soil, waste, vent pipes and fittings with paint of any colour such as chocolate, grey or buff etc. :		
	82A 50 mm diameter pipe	metre	2.90
	82B 100 mm diameter pipe	metre	5.25
	82C 75 mm diameter pipe	metre	3.95
83.	Repainting bath tub of size 1700 × 730 × 430 mm with enamel paint.	each	122.15

(Contd.)

S. No.	Description	Unit	Rate ₹
84.	Providing and Fixing vitreous china dual purpose colset suitable for use as squatting pan or European type water closet (Anglo Indian W.C. pan) with seat lid with C.P. brass hinges and rubber buffers, 10 litre low level flushing cistern with fitting and brackets, 40 mm flush bend 20 mm overflow pipe with specials of standard make and mosquito proof coupling of approved municipal design complete, including painting of fittings and brackets, cutting and making good the walls and floors wherever required :		
	84A White vitreous china dual purpose WC pan with white solid plastic seat and lid with white vitreous china flushing cistern and C.P. flush bend.	each	1631.75

Table 13.19. Water Supply

S. No.	Description	Unit	Rate ₹
	A. G.I. Pipes and fittings		
1.	Providing and fixing G.I. pipes complete with G.I. fittings and clamps, including cutting and making good the walls etc. (internal work) :		
	(1) Exposed on wall		
	1A 15 mm dia. nominal bore	metre	53.90
	1B 20 mm dia. nominal bore	metre	62.15
	1C 25 mm dia. nominal bore	metre	81.75
	1D 32 mm dia. nominal bore	metre	101.85
	1E 40 mm dia. nominal bore	metre	117.85
	1F 50 mm dia. nominal bore	metre	158.05
	(2) Concealed pipe including painting with anti corrosive bitumastic paint, cutting chases and making good the wall		
	1G 15 mm dia nominal bore	metre	50.00
	1H 20 mm dia nominal bore	metre	56.50
2.	Providing and fixing G.I. pipes complete with G.I. fittings including trenching and refilling etc. (external work) :		
	2A 15 mm dia. nominal bore	metre	49.80
	2B 20 mm dia. nominal bore	metre	56.50
	2C 25 mm dia. nominal bore	metre	75.55
	2D 32 mm dia. nominal bore	metre	93.35
	2E 40 mm dia. nominal bore	metre	104.60
	2F 50 mm dia. nominal bore	metre	139.10
	2G 65 mm dia. nominal bore	metre	174.00
	2H 80 mm dia. nominal bore	metre	229.60
	2I 100 mm nominal bore	metre	374.80
	2J 150 mm nominal bore	metre	588.15
3.	Making connection of G.I. distribution branch with G.I. main of following sizes by providing and fixing tee, including cutting and threading the pipe etc. complete :		
	3A 25 to 40 mm nominal bore	each	95.70
	3B 50 to 80 mm nominal bore	each	172.95
	3C 100 to 150 mm nominal bore	each	401.80

S.No.		Description	Unit	Rate ₹
4.		**Fixing water meter and stop cock in G.I. pipe line including cutting and threading the pipe and making long screws etc. complete (cost of water meter and stop cock to be paid separately).**	each	78.50
		B. BRASS FITTINGS		
5.		**Providing and fixing brass bib cock of approved quality :**		
	5A	15 mm nominal bore	each	77.10
	5B	20 mm nominal bore	each	94.65
	5C	25 mm nominal bore	each	144.30
6.		**Providing and fixing brass stop cock of approved quality :**		
	6A	15 mm nominal bore	each	84.90
	6B	20 mm nominal bore	each	94.65
	6C	25 mm nominal bore	each	142.10
	6D	32 mm nominal bore	each	162.95
7.		**Providing and fixing brass gate valve with C.I. wheel of approved quality (screwed end) :**		
	7A	25 mm nominal bore	each	151.00
	7B	32 mm nominal bore	each	207.40
	7C	40 mm nominal bore	each	252.60
	7D	50 mm nominal bore	each	397.85
	7E	65 mm nominal bore	each	514.15
	7F	80 mm nominal bore	each	804.70
8.		**Providing and fixing ball valve (brass) of approved quality complete :**		
	(1)	High or low pressure with plastic floats		
	8A	15 mm nominal bore	each	102.00
	8B	20 mm nominal bore	each	166.30
	8C	25 mm nominal bore	each	186.20
9.		**Providing and fixing gun metal non-return valve of approved quality (screwed end) :**		
	(1)	25 mm nominal bore		
	9A	Horizontal	each	174.85
	9B	Vertical	each	139.30
	(2)	32 mm nominal bore		
	9C	Horizontal	each	291.20
	9D	Vertical	each	180.10
	(3)	40 mm nominal bore		
	9E	Horizontal	each	394.20
	9F	Vertical	each	230.85
	(4)	50 mm nominal bore		
	9G	Horizontal	each	586.15
	9H	Vertical	each	308.40
	(5)	65 mm nominal bore		
	9I	Horizontal	each	979.10
	9J	Vertical	each	786.90
	(6)	80 mm nominal bore		
	9K	Horizontal	each	1341.05
	9L	Vertical	each	1062.20

(Contd.)

S. No.	Description	Unit	Rate ₹
	(7) 100 mm nominal bore		
	9M Horizontal	each	1402.95
	9N Vertical	each	1286.30
10.	Providing and fixing brass ferrule with C.I. mouth cover including boring and tapping the main :		
	10A 15 mm nominal bore	each	80.00
	10B 20 mm nominal bore	each	121.95
	10C 25 mm nominal bore	each	165.95
11.	Providing and fixing unplasticised PVC connection pipe with brass unions :		
	(1) 30 cm length		
	11A 15 mm nominal bore	each	21.85
	11B 20 mm nominal bore	each	28.50
	(2) 45 cm length :		
	11C 15 mm nominal bore	each	28.20
	11D 20 mm nominal bore	each	37.10
12.	Providing and fixing CP. brass shower rose with 15 or 20 mm inlet :		
	12A 100 mm diameter	each	20.75
	12B 150 mm diameter	each	32.65
	C. C.I. PIPES AND SPECIALS		
13.	Laying in position centrifugally cast (spun) iron S&S or flanged pipes.	quintal	26.30
14.	Laying in position S&S or flanged C.I. special such as tees, bends, collars, tapers and caps etc.	quintal	54.15
15.	Providing and laying S&S centrifugally cast iron pipes (class LA).	quintal	1698.45
16.	Providing and laying S&S C.I. standard specials such as tees, bends, collars, tapers, caps etc. (Heavy class) :		
	16A Upto 300 mm dia	quintal	1580.20
	16B Over 300 mm dia	quintal	1769.10
17.	Providing and laying flanged C.I. standard specials such as tees, bends, collars, tapers, caps etc. (Heavy class) :		
	17A Upto 300 mm dia	quintal	1704.65
	17B Over 300 mm dia	quintal	1891.30
18.	Providing and laying S&S C.I. non standard specials (Heavy class) :		
	18A Upto 300 mm dia	quintal	1897.40
	18B Over 300 mm dia	quintal	2060.70
19.	Providing and laying flanged C.I. non standard specials (Heavy type) :		
	19A Upto 300 mm dia	quintal	2010.70
	19B Over 300 mm dia	quintal	2182.95
20.	Providing and laying S&S centrifugally cast (spun) iron pipes (Class LA) :		
	20A 80 mm dia. pipe	metre	273.45
	20B 100 mm dia. pipe	metre	348.30
	20C 125 mm dia. pipe	metre	455.40
	20D 150 mm dia. pipe	metre	565.80
	20E 200 mm dia. pipe	metre	826.05
	20F 250 mm dia. pipe	metre	1115.05

S. No.	Description	Unit	Rate ₹
20G	300 mm dia. pipe	metre	1439.70
20H	350 mm dia. pipe	metre	1812.65
20I	400 mm dia. pipe	metre	2202.80
20J	450 mm dia. pipe	metre	2659.30
20K	500 mm dia. pipe	metre	3116.80
20L	600 mm dia. pipe	metre	4154.80
21.	Providing and laying S&S C.I. standard bends (Heavy class) :		
21A	80 mm diameter C.I. bend 90°	each	284.45
21B	80 mm diameter C.I. bend 45°	each	284.45
21C	80 mm diameter C.I. bend 22 1/2°	each	252.85
21D	80 mm diameter C.I. bend 11 1/4°	each	237.05
21E	100 mm diameter C.I. bend 90°	each	379.25
21F	100 mm diameter C.I. bend 45°	each	379.25
21G	100 mm diameter C.I. bend 22 1/2°	each	331.85
21H	100 mm diameter C.I. bend 11 1/4°	each	300.25
21I	125 mm diameter C.I. bend 90°	each	521.45
21J	125 mm diameter C.I. bend 45°	each	505.65
21K	125 mm diameter C.I. bend 22 1/2°	each	426.65
21L	125 mm diameter C.I. bend 11 1/4°	each	395.05
21M	150 mm diameter C.I. bend 90°	each	679.50
21N	150 mm diameter C.I. bend 45°	each	647.90
21O	150 mm diameter C.I. bend 22 1/2°	each	553.05
21P	150 mm diameter C.I. bend 11 1/4°	each	505.65
21Q	200 mm diameter C.I. bend 90°	each	1058.75
21R	200 mm diameter C.I. bend 45°	each	979.75
21S	200 mm diameter C.I. bend 22 1/2°	each	837.50
21T	200 mm diameter C.I. bend 11 1/4°	each	758.50
21U	250 mm diameter C.I. bend 90°	each	1548.60
21V	250 mm diameter CI. bend 45°	each	1406.35
21W	250 mm diameter C.I. bend 22 1/2°	each	1185.15
21X	250 mm diameter C.I. bend 11 1/4°	each	1058.75
21Y	300 mm diameter C.I. bend 90°	each	2133.25
21Z	300 mm diameter C.I. bend 45°	each	1912.05
21AA	300 mm diameter C.I. bend 22 1/2°	each	1580.20
21BB	300 mm diameter C.I. bend 11 1/4°	each	406.35
22.	Providing and laying S&S C.I. standard tees (Heavy class) :		
22A	80 × 80 mm C.I. tee	each	363.45
22B	100 × 80 mm C.I. tee	each	442.45
22C	100 × 100 mm CI. tee	each	474.05
22D	125 × 80 mm C.I. tee	each	568.90
22E	125 × 100 mm C.I. tee	each	600.45
22F	125 × 125 mm C.I. tee	each	647.90
22G	150 × 80 mm C.I. tee	each	711.10
22H	150 × 100 mm C.I. tee	each	742.70
22I	150 × 125 mm C.I. tee	each	790.10

(Contd.)

S. No.	Description	Unit	Rate ₹
22J	150 × 150 mm C.I. tee	each	837.50
22K	200 × 80 mm C.I. tee	each	1058.75
22L	200 × 100 mm C.I. tee	each	1090.35
22M	200 × 125 mm C.I. tee	each	1121.95
22N	200 × 150 mm C.I. tee	each	1169.35
22O	200 × 200 mm C.I. tee	each	1279.95
22P	250 × 80 mm C.I. tee	each	1485.40
22Q	250 × 100 mm C.I. tee	each	1517.00
22R	250 × 125 mm C.I. tee	each	1564.40
22S	250 × 150 mm C.I. tee	each	1611.80
22T	250 × 200 mm C.I. tee	each	1706.60
22U	250 × 250 mm C.I. tee	each	1833.05
22V	300 × 80 mm C.I. tee	each	2022.65
22W	300 × 100 mm C.I. tee	each	2038.45
22X	300 × 125 mm C.I. tee	each	2085.85
22Y	300 × 150 mm C.I. tee	each	2117.45
22Z	300 × 200 mm C.I. tee	each	2243.90
22AA	300 × 250 mm C.I. tee	each	2370.30
22BB	300 × 300 mm C.I. tee	each	2512.50
23.	Providing and laying S&S C.I. crosses (Heavy class) :		
23A	80 × 80 × 80 × 80 mm C.I. cross	each	474.05
23B	100 × 100 × 100 × 100 mm C.I. cross	each	616.30
23C	125 × 125 × 125 × 125 mm C.I. cross	each	821.70
23D	150 × 150 × 150 × 150 mm C.I. cross	each	1058.75
23E	200 × 200 × 200 × 200 mm C.I. cross	each	1611.80
23F	250 × 250 × 250 × 250 mm C.I. cross	each	2291.30
23G	300 × 300 × 300 × 300 mm C.I. cross	each	3113.00
24.	Providing and laying S&S C.I. standard tapers with larger end socketed (heavy class) :		
24A	100 × 80 mm C.I. taper	each	252.85
24B	125 × 80 mm C.I. taper	each	331.85
24C	125 × 100 mm C.I. taper	each	363.45
24D	150 × 80 mm C.I. taper	each	426.65
24E	150 × 100 mm C.I. taper	each	442.45
24F	150 × 125 mm C.I. taper	each	489.85
24G	200 × 100 mm C.I. taper	each	632.10
24H	200 × 125 mm C.I. taper	each	663.65
24I	200 × 150 mm C.I. taper	each	711.10
24J	250 × 125 mm C.I. taper	each	884.90
24K	250 × 150 mm C.I. taper	each	932.30
24L	250 × 200 mm C.I. taper	each	1042.95
24M	300 × 150 mm C.I. taper	each	1264.15
24N	300 × 200 mm C.I. taper	each	1390.60
24O	300 × 250 mm C.I. taper	each	1532.80

S. No.	Description	Unit	Rate ₹
25.	Providing and laying S&S C.I. standard tapers with smaller end socketed (Heavy class) :		
25A	100 × 80 mm C.I. taper	each	252.85
25B	125 × 80 mm C.I. taper	each	300.25
25C	125 × 100 mm C.I. taper	each	331.85
25D	150 × 80 mm C.I. taper	each	363.45
25E	150 × 100 mm C.I. taper	each	395.05
25F	150 × 125 mm C.I. taper	each	458.25
25G	200 × 100 mm C.I. taper	each	537.25
25H	200 × 125 mm C.I. taper	each	600.45
25I	200 × 150 mm C.I. taper	each	663.65
25J	250 × 125 mm C.I. taper	each	774.30
25K	250 × 150 mm C.I. taper	each	837.50
25L	250 × 200 mm C.I. taper	each	1090.35
25M	300 × 150 mm C.I. taper	each	1106.15
25N	300 × 200 mm C.I. taper	each	1264.15
25O	300 × 250 mm C.I. taper	each	1469.60
25P	350 × 200 mm C.I. taper	each	1627.55
25Q	350 × 250 mm C.I. taper	each	1839.85
25R	350 × 300 mm C.I. taper	each	2087.50
25S	400 × 250 mm C.I. taper	each	2282.10
25T	400 × 300 mm C.I. taper	each	2547.45
25U	400 × 350 mm C.I. taper	each	2848.20
26V	450 × 350 mm C.I. taper	each	3131.25
25W	450 × 400 mm C.I. taper	each	3449.70
25X	500 × 350 mm C.I. taper	each	3432.00
25Y	500 × 400 mm C.I. taper	each	3750.45
25Z	500 × 450 mm C.I, taper	each	4068.85
25AA	600 × 400 mm C.I. taper	each	4829.55
25BB	600 × 450 mm C.I. taper	each	5183.35
25CC	600 × 500 mm C.I. taper	each	5661.00
26.	Providing and laying C.I. double socket collars (Heavy class) :		
26A	80 mm C.I. collar	each	221.20
26B	100 mm C.I. collar	each	268.65
26C	125 mm C.I. collar	each	347.65
26D	150 mm C.I. collar	each	442.45
26E	200 mm C.I. collar	each	632.10
26F	250 mm C.I. collar	each	869.10
26G	300 mm CI. collar	each	1121.95
27.	Providing and laying C.I. plugs (heavy class) :		
27A	80 mm C.I. plug	each	47.40
27B	100 mm C.I. plug	each	63.20
27C	125 mm C.I. plug	each	94.80
27D	150 mm C.I. plug	each	142.20
27E	200 mm C.I. plug	each	221.20

(Contd.)

S. No.	Description	Unit	Rate ₹
	27F 250 mm C.I. plug	each	347.65
	27G 300 mm C.I. plug	each	474.05
28.	Providing and laying C.I. caps (Heavy class) :		
	28A 80 mm C.I. cap	each	110.60
	28B 100 mm C.I. cap	each	142.20
	28C 125 mm C.I. cap	each	189.65
	28D 150 mm C.I. cap	each	237.05
	28E 200 mm C.I. cap	each	379.25
	28F 250 mm C.I. cap	each	537.25
	28G 300 mm C.I. cap	each	726.90
29.	Providing and laying double flanged C.I. bends (Heavy class) :		
	29A 80 mm dia. C.I. bend 90°	each	221.60
	29B 80 mm dia C.I. bend 45°	each	238.65
	29C 100 mm dia. C.I. bend 90°	each	289.80
	29D 100 mm dia. C.I. bend 45°	each	306.85
	29E 125 mm dia. C.I. bend 90°	each	392.05
	29F 125 mm dia C.I. bend 45°	each	426.15
	29G 150 mm dia C.I. bend 90°	each	528.45
	29H 150 mm dia C.I. bend 45°	each	579.60
	29I 200 mm dia C.I. bend 90°	each	835.25
	29J 200 mm dia C.I. bend 45°	each	920.50
	29K 250 mm dia C.I. bend 90°	each	1227.35
	29L 250 mm dia C.I. bend 45°	each	1363.70
	29M 300 mm dia C.I. bend 90°	each	1704.65
	29N 300 mm dia C.I. bend 45°	each	1909.20
30.	Providing and laying double flanged C.I. duck foot bends 90° (Heavy class) :		
	30A 80 mm dia. bend	each	357.95
	30B 100 mm dia. bend	each	443.20
	30C 125 mm dia. bend	each	613.65
	30D 150 mm dia. bend	each	801.15
	30E 200 mm dia. bend	each	1261.45
	30F 250 mm dia. bend	each	1892.15
	30G 300 mm dia. bend	each	2659.25
31.	Providing and laying double flanged C.I. tees (Heavy class) :		
	31A 80 × 80 mm C.I. tee	each	357.95
	31B 100 × 80 mm C.I. tee	each	426.15
	31C 100 × 100 mm G.I. tee	each	443.20
	31D 125 × 80 mm C.I. tee	each	545.50
	31E 125 × 100 mm C.I. tee	each	579.60
	31F 125 × 125 mm C.I. tee	each	613.65
	31G 150 × 80 mm C.I. tee	each	698.90
	31H 150 × 100 mm C.I. tee	each	715.95
	31I 150 × 125 mm C.I. tee	each	767.05
	32J 150 × 150 mm C.I. tee	each	801.15

S. No.	Description	Unit	Rate ₹
31K	200 × 80 mm C.I. tee	each	1056.85
31L	200 × 100 mm C.I. tee	each	1073.90
31M	200 × 125 mm C.I. tee	each	1125.05
31N	200 × 150 mm C.I. tee	each	1159.15
31O	200 × 200 mm C.I. tee	each	1261.45
31P	250 × 80 mm C.I. tee	each	1517.10
31Q	250 × 100 mm C.I. tee	each	1534.15
31R	250 × 125 mm C.I. tee	each	1585.30
31S	250 × 150 mm C.I. tee	each	1636.45
31T	250 × 200 mm C.I. tee	each	1738.75
31U	250 × 250 mm C.I. tee	each	1858.05
31V	300 × 80 mm C.I. tee	each	2079.65
31W	300 × 100 mm C.I. tee	each	2113.75
31X	300 × 125 mm C.I. tee	each	2147.85
31Y	300 × 150 mm C.I. tee	each	2198.95
31Z	300 × 200 mm C.I. tee	each	2318.30
31AA	300 × 250 mm C.I. tee	each	2437.60
31BB	300 × 300 mm C.I. tee	each	2574.00
32.	Providing and laying double flanged C.I. crosses (Heavy class) :		
32A	80 × 80 × 80 × 80 mm C.I. cross	each	460.25
32B	100 × 100 × 100 × 100 mm C.I. cross	each	579.60
32C	125 × 125 × 125 × 125 mm C.I. cross	each	784.15
32D	150 × 150 × 150 × 150 mm C.I. cross	each	1022.80
32E	200 × 200 × 200 × 200 mm C.I. cross	each	1585.30
32F	250 × 250 × 250 × 250 mm C.I. cross	each	2301.25
32G	300 × 300 × 300 × 300 mm C.I. cross	each	3170.60
33.	Providing and laying double flanged C.I. tapers (Heavy class) :		
33A	100 × 80 mm C.I. taper	each	204.55
33B	125 × 80 mm C.I. taper	each	340.90
33C	125 × 100 mm C.I. taper	each	375.00
33D	150 × 80 mm C.I. taper	each	392.05
33E	150 × 100 mm C.I. taper	each	426.15
33F	150 × 125 mm C.I. taper	each	460.25
33G	200 × 100 mm C.I. taper	each	528.45
33H	200 × 125 mm C.I. taper	each	579.60
33I	200 × 150 mm C.I. taper	each	630.70
33J	250 × 125 mm C.I. taper	each	698.90
33K	250 × 150 mm C.I. taper	each	750.05
33L	250 × 200 mm C.I. taper	each	852.30
33M	300 × 150 mm C.I. taper	each	869.35
33N	300 × 200 mm C.I. taper	each	988.70
33O	300 × 250 mm C.I. taper	each	1108.00
34.	Providing and laying C.I. flanged socketed tail pieces (Heavy class) :		
34A	80 mm C.I. flanged socket	each	221.60
34B	100 mm C.I. flanged socket	each	272.75

(*Contd.*)

S. No.		Description	Unit	Rate ₹
	34C	125 mm C.I. flanged socket	each	340.90
	34D	150 mm C.I. flanged socket	each	443.20
	34E	200 mm C.I. flanged socket	each	460.25
	34F	250 mm C.I. flanged socket	each	1056.85
	34G	300 mm C.I. flanged socket	each	1346.65
35.		Providing and laying C.I. flanged spigot tail pieces (Heavy class) :		
	35A	80 mm C.I. flanged spigot	each	204.55
	35B	100 mm C.I. flanged spigot	each	238.65
	35C	125 mm C.I. flanged spigot	each	323.90
	35D	150 mm C.I. flanged spigot	each	392.05
	35E	200 mm CI. flanged spigot	each	664.80
	35F	250 mm C.I. flanged spigot	each	903.45
	35G	300 mm C.I. flanged spigot	each	1159.15
36.		Providing lead caulked joints to spun iron or C.I. pipes and specials including testing of joints but excluding the cost of pig lead :		
	36A	80 mm diametre pipe	each	45.40
	36B	100 mm diametre pipe	each	49.25
	36C	125 mm diametre pipe	each	71.50
	36D	150 mm diametre pipe	each	73.70
	36E	200 mm diametre pipe	each	97.80
	36F	250 mm diametre pipe	each	121.70
	36G	300 mm diametre pipe	each	146.55
37.		Supplying pig lead at site of work.	quintal	4448.00
38.		Providing flanged joints to double flanged C.I. pipes and specials including testing of joints :		
	38A	80 mm diametre pipe	each	43.70
	38B	100 mm diametre pipe	each	76.35
	38C	125 mm diametre pipe	each	77.45
	38D	150 mm diametre pipe	each	104.85
	38E	200 mm diametre pipe	each	131.50
	37F	250 mm diametre pipe	each	196.35
	38G	300 mm diametre pipe	each	204.15
		D. C.I. SLUICE VALVES, FIRE HYDRANTS AND FIXTURES		
39.		Providing and fixing C.I. sluice valves (with cap) complete with bolts, nuts, rubber insertions etc. (the tail pieces if required will be paid separately) :		
	(1)	80 mm diametre		
	39A	Class I	each	1328.30
	39B	Class II	each	1453.45
	(2)	100 mm diametre		
	39C	Class I	each	1789.40
	39D	Class II	each	1957.50
	(3)	125 mm diametre		
	39E	Class I	each	2187.45
	39F	Class II	each	2394.40

S. No.	Description	Unit	Rate ₹
	(4) 150 mm diametre		
	39G Class I	each	2696.05
	39H Class II	each	2948.65
	(5) 200 mm diametre		
	39I Class I	each	4666.60
	39J Class II	each	5116.75
	(6) 250 mm diametre		
	39K Class I	each	6978.90
	39L Class II	each	6544.70
	(7) 300 mm diametre		
	39M Class I	each	8721.75
	39N Class II	each	9574.90
40.	Constructing masonry Chamber 30 × 30 × 50 cm, inside with 75 class designation brick work in cement mortar 1 : 5 (1 cement : 5 fine sand) for stop cock, with C.I. surface box 100 × 100 × 75 mm (inside) with hinged cover fixed in cement concrete slab 1 : 2 : 4 mix (1 cement : 2 coarse sand : 4 graded stone aggregate 20 mm nominal size) necessary excavation foundation concrete 1 : 5 : 10 (1 cement : 5 fine sand : 10 graded stone aggregate 40 mm nominal size) and inside plastering with cement mortar 1 : 3 (1 cement : 3 coarse sand) 12 mm thick finished with a floating coat of neat cement complete as per standard design :		
	40A With F.P.S. bricks	each	331.40
41.	Constructing masonry Chamber 60 × 60 × 75 cm, inside with 75 class designation brick work in cement mortar 1 : 5 (1 cement : 5 fine sand) for sluice valve, with C.I. surface box 100 mm. top diameter, 160 mm bottom diameter and 180 mm deep (inside) with chained lid and RCC top slab 1 : 2 : 4 mix (1 cement : 2 coarse sand : 4 graded stone aggregate 20 mm nominal size) necessary excavation foundation concrete 1 : 5 : 10 (1 cement : 5 fine sand : 10 graded stone aggregate 40 mm nominal size) and inside plastering with cement mortar 1 : 3 (1 cement : 3 coarse sand) 12 mm thick finished with a floating coat of neat cement complete as per standard design :		
	41A With F.P.S. bricks	each	1901.85
42.	Constructing masonry Chamber 90 × 90 × 100 cm, inside with 75 class designation brick work in cement mortar 1 : 5 (1 cement : 5 fine sand) for sluice valve, with C.I. surface box 100 mm. top diameter, 160 mm bottom diameter and 180 mm deep (inside) with chained lid and RCC top slab 1 : 2 : 4 mix (1 cement : 2 coarse sand : 4 graded stone aggregate 20 mm nominal size) necessary excavation foundation concrete 1 : 5 : 10 (1 cement : 5 fine sand : 10 graded stone aggregate 40 mm nominal size) and inside plastering with cement mortar 1 : 3 (1 cement : 3 coarse sand) 12 mm thick finished with a floating coat of neat cement complete as per standard design :		
	42A With F.P.S. bricks	each	3247.10

(Contd.)

S. No.	Description	Unit	Rate ₹
43.	Constructing masonry Chamber 120 × 120 × 100 cm, inside with 75 class designation brick work in cement mortar 1 : 5 (1 cement : 5 fine sand) for sluice valve, with C.I. surface box 100 mm. top diameter, 160 mm bottom diameter and 180 mm deep (inside) with chained lid and RCC top slab 1 : 2 : 4 mix (1 cement : 2 coarse sand : 4 graded stone aggregate 20 mm nominal size) necessary excavation foundation concrete 1 : 5 : 10 (1 cement : 5 fine sand : 10 graded stone aggregate 40 mm nominal size) and inside plastering with cement mortar 1 : 3 (1 cement : 3 coarse sand) 12 mm thick finished with a floating coat of neat cement complete as per standard design :		
	43A With F.P.S. bricks	each	4485.55
44.	Constructing masonry Chamber 60 × 60 × 75 cm, inside with 75 class designation brick work in cement mortar 1 : 5 (1 cement: 5 fine sand) for fire hydrants, with C.I. surface box 350 × 350 mm. top and 165 mm deep (inside) with chained lid and RCC top slab 1 : 2 : 4 mix (1 cement : 2 coarse sand : 4 graded stone aggregate 20 mm nominal size) necessary excavation foundation concrete 1 : 5 : 10 (1 cement : 5 fine sand : 10 graded stone aggregate 40 mm nominal size) and inside plastering with cement mortar 1 : 3 (1 cement : 3 coarse sand) 12 mm thick finished with a floating coat of neat cement complete as per standard design :		
	44A With F.P.S. bricks	each	1946.20
45.	Constructing masonry Chamber 60 × 45 × 50 cm, inside with 75 class designation brick work in cement mortar 1 : 5 (1 cement : 5 fine sand) for water meter complete with C.I. double flap surface box 400 × 200 × 200 mm. (inside) with locking arrangement and RCC top slab 1 : 2 : 4 mix (1 cement : 2 coarse sand : 4 graded stone aggregate 20 mm nominal size) necessary excavation foundation concrete 1 : 5 : 10 (1 cement : 5 fine sand : 10 graded stone aggregate 40 mm nominal size) and inside plastering with cement mortar 1 : 3 (1 cement : 3 coarse sand) 12 mm thick finished with a floating coat of neat cement complete as per standard design :		
	45A With F.P.S. bricks	each	1778.20
46.	Painting G.I. pipes and fittings with white paint over a ready mixed priming coat, both of approved quality for new work :		
	46A 15 mm diameter pipe.	metre	2.75
	46B 20 mm diameter pipe.	metre	3.25
	46C 25 mm diameter pipe.	metre	4.25
	46D 32 mm diameter pipe.	metre	5.05
	46E 40 mm diameter pipe.	metre	6.10
	46F 50 mm diameter pipe.	metre	7.05
47.	Repainting G.I. pipes and fittings with white paint of approved :		
	47A 15 mm diameter pipe.	metre	1.35
	47B 20 mm diameter pipe.	metre	1.60
	47C 25 mm diameter pipe	metre	2.05
	47D 32 mm diameter pipe	metre	2.40
	47E 40 mm diameter pipe	metre	2.80
	47F 50 mm diameter pipe	metre	3.30

S. No.	Description	Unit	Rate ₹
48.	**Painting G.I. pipes and fittings with two coats of anti-corrosive bitumastic paint of approved quality :**		
	48A 15 mm diameter pipes	metre	1.50
	48B 20 mm diameter pipes	metre	1.75
	48C 25 mm diameter pipes	metre	2.25
	48D 32 mm diameter pipes	metre	2.65
	48E 40 mm diameter pipes	metre	3.05
	48F 50 mm diameter pipes	metre	3.60
	48G 65 mm diameter pipes	metre	4.45
	48H 80 mm diameter pipes	metre	5.15
49.	**Providing and filling sand of grading zone V or coarser grade alround the G.I. pipes in external work :**		
	49A 15 mm dia. pipe.	metre	13.85
	49B 20 mm dia. pipe.	metre	14.00
	49C 25 mm dia. pipe.	metre	14.40
	49D 32 mm dia. pipe.	metre	14.75
	49E 40 mm dia. pipe.	metre	14.95
	49F 50 mm dia. pipe.	metre	15.50
	49G 65 mm dia. pipe.	metre	24.50
	49H 80 mm dia. pipe.	metre	25.25
	49I 100 mm dia. pipe.	metre	26.75
	49J 150 mm dia. pipe.	metre	39.85
50.	**Boring with 100 mm diameter casting pipe for hand pump/tube well in all soils except ordinary hard rocks requiring blasting including removing the casing pipe after the hand pipe/tube well is lowered and tested :**		
	50A Upto 6 metres depth	metre	95.35
	50B Beyond 6 m and upto 12 m depth	metre	114.30
	50C Beyond 12 m and upto 18 m depth	metre	134.35
51.	**Providing and placing in position filters of 40 mm diameter G.I. pipe with brass strainer of approved quality.**	metre	252.60
52.	**Providing and fixing to filter and lowering to proper levels 40 mm G.I. pipe for tube well including cleaning and priming the tube well.**	metre	102.25
53.	**Providing and placing in position hand pump of approved quality for 40 mm diameter G.I. pipe complete with all accessories.**	each	363.60
54.	**Providing and fixing G.I. Union in G.I. pipe including cutting and threading the pipe and making long screws etc. complete (new work) :**		
	54A 15 mm nominal bore	each	36.95
	54B 20 mm nominal bore	each	42.50
	54C 25 mm nominal bore	each	48.05
	54D 32 mm nominal bore	each	53.60
	54E 40 mm nominal bore	each	64.70
	54F 50 mm nominal bore	each	101.35
	54G 65 mm nominal bore	each	135.80
	54H 80 mm nominal bore	each	164.70
	54I 100 mm nominal bore	each	306.65
	54J 150 mm nominal bore	each	939.90

(Contd.)

S. No.	Description	Unit	Rate ₹
55.	Providing and fixing G.I. Union in existing G.I. pipe line, cutting and threading the pipe and making long screws including excavation, refilling the earth or cutting of wall and making good the same complete wherever required :		
	55A 15 mm nominal bore.	each	79.70
	55B 20 mm nominal bore.	each	85.25
	55C 25 mm nominal bore.	each	90.80
	55D 32 mm nominal bore.	each	96.35
	55E 40 mm nominal bore.	each	107.50
	55F 50 mm nominal bore.	each	159.70
	55G 65 mm nominal bore.	each	194.15
	55H 80 mm nominal bore.	each	223.00
56.	Providing and placing on terrace (at all floor levels) polyethylene water storage tank of approved brand and manufacture with cover and suitable locking arrangement and making necessary holes for inlet, outlet and overflow pipes but without fittings and the base support for tank.	per litre capacity	4.10
	E. C.P. BRASS FITTINGS		
57.	Providing and fixing C.P. brass bib cock of approved quality conforming to IS : 8931 :		
	57A 15 mm nominal bore	each	168.10
58.	Providing and fixing C.P. brass long nose bib cock of approved quality conforming to IS standards and weighing not less than 810 gms :		
	58A 15 mm nominal bore	each	196.50
59.	Providing and fixing C.P. brass long body bib cock of approved quality conforming to IS standards and weighing not less than 690 gms :		
	59A 15 mm nominal bore	each	224.00
60.	Providing and fixing C.P. brass stop cock (concealed) of standard design and of approved make conforming to IS : 8931 :		
	60A 15 mm nominal bore	each	203.65
61.	Providing and fixing C.P. brass angle valve for basin mixer and gyser points of approved quality conforming to IS : 8931 :		
	61A 15 mm nominal bore	each	151.30
62.	Providing and fixing C.P. brass close hole basin mixer pillar tap of approved quality and make, weighing not less than 1.970 kg :		
	62A 15 mm nominal bore of standard back type	each	616.20
	F. PVC/PTMT FITTINGS		
63.	Providing and fixing P.T.M.T (An Engineering thermoplastic) bib cock of approved quality colour and make :		
	63A 15 mm nominal size, 86 mm long, 102 mm high and 43 mm wide with 12 mm seat dia and replaceable washers, weighing not less than 90 gms.	each	84.90
	63B 15 mm nominal size, 122 mm long, 110 mm high and 43 mm wide with 12 mm seat dia. and replaceable washers, weighing not less than 105 gms.	each	102.65
	63C 15 mm nominal size, 180 mm long, 110 mm high and 43 mm wide with 12 mm seat dia. and replaceable washers, weighing not less than 126 gms.	each	118.20

S. No.	Description	Unit	Rate ₹
64.	Providing and fixing P.T.M.T. (An Engineering thermoplastic) stop cock of approved quality colour and make :		
	64A 15 mm nominal size, 86 mm long, 90 mm high and 43 mm wide with 12 mm seat dia. and replaceable washers, weighing not less than 95 gms.	each	84.90
	64B 15 mm nominal size, 86 mm long, (F/T) 90 mm high and 43 mm wide with 12 mm seat dia. and replaceable washers, weighing not less than 95 gms.	each	84.90
	64C 20 mm nominal size, 89 mm long, 86 mm high and 43 mm wide with 12 mm seat dia. and replaceable washers, weighing not less than 95 gms.	each	94.90
65.	Providing and fixing P.T.M.T. (An Engineering thermoplastic) pillar cock of approved quality colour and make :		
	65A 15 mm nominal size, 107 mm long, 131 mm high and 43 mm wide with 12 mm seat dia and replaceable washers, weighing not less than 120 gms.	each	125.75
66.	Providing and fixing P.T.M.T. (An Engineering thermoplastic), push cock of approved quality colour and make :		
	66A 15 mm nominal size, with 20 mm B.S.P. female threads, 100 mm long, 57 mm high and 33 mm wide with 12 mm seat dia and replaceable washers, weighing not less than 75 gms.	each	74.90
	66B 15 mm nominal size, with 12 mm B.S.P. female threads, 80 mm long, 30 mm high and 30 mm wide with 12 mm seat dia and replaceable washers, weighing not less than 47 gms.	each	62.65
67.	Providing and fixing P.T.M.T. (An Engineering thermoplastic) grating of approved quality, colour and make :		
	(1) Circular type :		
	67A 100 mm nominal dia 12 mm high, domed shape conforming to I.S. standards and weighing not less than 25 gms.	each	24.75
	67B 125 mm nominal dia., 15 mm high domed shape conforming to I.S. standards and weighing not less than 40 gms.	each	32.50
	67C 125 mm nominal dia., 14 mm high, domed shape with 31 mm waste hole conforming to I.S. standards and weighing not less than 40 gms.	each	32.50
	(2) Rectangular type with openable circular lid :		
	67D 150 mm nominal size square, 18 mm high with 100 mm dia. of the inner hinged round grating domed shape conforming to I.S. standards, weighing not less than 110 gms.	each	35.85
	67E 150 mm nominal size square, 18 mm high with 100 mm dia. of the inner of hinged round grating domed shape with 31 mm waste hole conforming to I.S. standards, weighing not less than 100 gms.	each	30.30
	G. AIR VALVE AND WATER METER (BULK TYPE)		
68.	Providing and fixing C.I. double acting air valve of approved quality with bolts, nuts, rubber insertions etc. complete (The tail pieces, tapers etc. if required will be paid separately) :		
	68A 50 mm dia	each	2825.15
	68B 80 mm dia	each	3936.15
	68C 100 mm dia	each	4747.30

(Contd.)

S. No.		*Description*	*Unit*	*Rate* ₹
69.		**Providing and fixing enclosed type water meter (bulk type) conforming to IS : 2373 and tested by Municipal Board complete with bolts, nuts, rubber insertions etc. (The tail pieces if required will be paid separately) :**		
	69A	**80 mm dia nominal bore**	each	168.35
	69B	**100 mm dia nominal bore**	each	251.85
	69C	**150 mm dia nominal bore**	each	337.40
	69D	**200 mm dia nominal bore**	each	452.95
70.		**Providing and fixing C.I. dirt box strainer for bulk type water meter with nuts, bolts, rubber insertions etc. complete conforming to IS : 2373 :**		
	70A	**80 mm dia**	each	236.55
	70B	**100 mm dia**	each	359.40
	70C	**150 mm dia**	each	482.80
	70D	**200 mm dia**	each	644.60

Table 13.20. Drainage

S. No.		*Description*	*Unit*	*Rate* ₹
		NOTE: The rates given for all the items under sub-head 'Drainage' are applicable to work executed in soils above sub-soil water level. Extra allowance has to be made for work under sub-soil water level.		
		A. STONE WARE PIPES AND FITTINGS		
1.		**Providing, laying and jointing glazed stoneware pipes grade 'A' with stiff mixture of cement mortar in the proportion of 1 : 1 (1 cement : 1 fine sand) including testing of joints etc. complete :**		
	1A	**100 mm diameter**	metre	74.05
	1B	**150 mm diameter**	metre	105.80
	1C	**200 mm diameter**	metre	143.80
	1D	**230 mm diameter**	metre	163.75
	1E	**250 mm diameter**	metre	185.05
2.		**Providing, laying and jointing glazed stoneware pipes grade 'A' with stiff mixture of cement mortar in the proportion of 1 : 3 (1 cement : 3 fine sand) including testing of joints etc. complete :**		
	2A	**100 mm diameter**	metre	71.10
	2B	**150 mm diameter**	metre	101.50
	2C	**200 mm diameter**	metre	137.95
3.		**Providing and laying cement concrete 1 : 5 : 10 (1 cement : 5 coarse sand : 10 graded stone aggregate 40 mm nominal size) alround S.W. pipes including bed concrete as per standard design :**		
	3A	**100 mm diameter S.W. pipe**	metre	197.90
	3B	**150 mm diameter S.W. pipe**	metre	242.05
	3C	**200 mm diameter S.W. pipe**	metre	282.15
	3D	**230 mm diameter S.W. pipe**	metre	308.90
	3E	**250 mm diameter S.W. pipe**	metre	326.25

S. No.	Description	Unit	Rate ₹
4.	Providing and laying cement concrete 1 : 5 : 10 (1 cement : 5 coarse sand : 10 graded stone aggregate 40 mm nominal size) upto haunches of S.W. pipes including bed concrete as per standard design :		
	4A 100 mm diameter S.W. pipe	metre	94.05
	4B 150 mm diameter S.W. pipe	metre	152.45
	4C 200 mm diameter S.W. pipe	metre	179.20
	4D 230 mm diameter S.W. pipe	metre	196.55
	4E 250 mm diameter S.W. pipe	metre	208.60
5.	Providing and fixing square-mouth S.W. gully trap grade 'A' complete with C.I. grating brick masonry chamber with bricks of class designation 75 and water tight C.I. cover with frame of 300 × 300 mm size (inside) the weight of cover to be not less than 4.50 kg and frame to be not less than 2.70 kg as per standard design :		
	(1) 100 × 100 mm size P type		
	5A With F.P.S. bricks	each	436.00
	(2) 125 × 100 mm size P type		
	5B With F.P.S. bricks	each	448.20
	(3) 150 × 100 mm size P type		
	5C With F.P.S. bricks	each	445.05
	(4) 180 × 100 mm size P type		
	5D With F.P.S. bricks	each	474.45
	(5) 180 × 150 mm size P type		
	5E With F.P.S. bricks	each	488.65
6.	Dismantling of old S.W. pipes including breaking of joints and bed concrete stacking of useful materials near the site within 50 m lead and disposal of unserviceable materials into municipal dumps :		
	6A 100 mm diameter	metre	6.15
	6B 150 mm diameter	metre	6.80
	6C 200 mm diameter	metre	7.20
	6D 230 mm diameter	metre	7.45
	6E 250 mm diameter	metre	7.65
	6F 300 mm diameter	metre	8.10
	6G 350 mm diameter	metre	9.30
	6H 400 mm diameter	metre	10.20
	6I 450 mm diameter	metre	10.60
7.	Providing and laying non-pressure NP2 class (light duty) R.C.C. pipes with collars jointed with stiff mixture of cement mortar in the proportion of 1 : 2 (1 cement : 2 fine sand) including testing of joints etc. complete :		
	7A 100 mm dia. R.C.C. pipe	metre	122.10
	7B 150 mm dia. R.C.C. pipe	metre	140.65
	7C 250 mm dia. R.C.C. pipe	metre	179.90
	7D 300 mm dia. R.C.C. pipe	metre	233.50
	7E 450 mm dia. R.C.C. pipe	metre	366.05
	7F 500 mm dia. R.C.C. pipe	metre	429.55
	7G 600 mm dia. R.C.C. pipe	metre	564.45
	7H 700 mm dia. R.C.C. pipe	metre	649.50
	7I 800 mm dia. R.C.C. pipe	metre	829.35
	7J 900 mm dia. R.C.C. pipe	metre	1003.40
	7K 1000 mm dia. R.C.C. pipe	metre	1254.50

(Contd.)

S. No.		Description	Unit	Rate ₹
	7L	1100 mm dia. R.C.C. pipe	metre	1529.20
	7M	1200 mm dia. R.C.C. pipe	metre	1649.80
8.		Constructing brick masonry manhole with 75 class designation bricks in cement mortar 1 : 4 (1 cement : 4 coarse sand) R.C.C. top slab with 1 : 2 : 4 mix (1 cement : 2 coarse sand : 4 graded stone aggregate 20 mm nominal size), foundation concrete 1 : 4 : 8 mix (1 cement : 4 coarse sand : 8 graded stone aggregate 40 mm nominal size) inside plastering 12 mm thick with cement mortar 1 : 3 (1 cement : 3 coarse sand) finished with floating coat of neat cement and making channels in cement concrete 1 : 2 : 4 (1 cement : 2 coarse sand : 4 graded stone aggregate 20 mm nominal size) finished with a floating coat of neat cement complete as per standard design :		
	(1)	Inside size 90 × 80 cm and 45 cm deep including C.I. cover with frame (light duty) 455 × 610 mm internal diamensions total weight of cover and frame to be not less than 38 kg (weight of cover 23 kg and weight of frame 15 kg)		
	8A	With F.P.S. bricks	each	2453.95
	(2)	Inside size 90 × 80 cm and 60 cm deep including C.I. cover with frame (light duty) 455 × 610 mm internal diamensions total weight of cover and frame to be not less than 38 kg (weight of cover 23 kg and weight of frame 15 kg)		
	8B	With F.P.S. bricks	each	2672.10
	(3)	Inside size 120 × 90 cm and 90 cm deep including C.I. cover with frame (medium duty) 500 mm internal diameter, total weight of cover and frame to be not less than 116 kg (weight of cover 58 kg and weight of frame 58 kg)		
	8C	With F.P.S. bricks	each	4822.70
	(4)	Inside size 120 × 90 cm and 90 cm deep including C.I. cover with frame (heavy duty) 560 mm internal diameter, total weight of cover and frame to be not less than 208 kg (weight of cover 108 kg and weight of frame 100 kg)		
	8D	With F.P.S. bricks	each	6023.60
9.		Extra for depth for manholes :		
	(1)	Size 90 × 80 cm		
	9A	With F.P.S. bricks	metre	1441.65
	(2)	Size 120 × 90 cm		
	9B	With F.P.S. bricks	metre	1727.40
10.		Constructing brick masonry circular type manhole 0.91 m internal dia at bottom and 0.56 m dia at top with 75 class designation F.P.S. bricks in cement mortar 1 : 4 (1 cement : 4 coarse sand), inside cement plaster 12 mm thick with cement mortar 1 : 3 (1 cement : 3 coarse sand) finished with a floating coat of neat cement, foundation concrete 1 : 3 : 6 mix (1 cement : 3 coarse sand : 6 graded stone aggregate 40 mm nominal size), and making necessary channel in cement concrete 1 : 2 : 4 (1 cement : 2 coarse sand : 4 graded stone aggregate 20 mm nominal size) finished with a floating coat of neat cement all complete as per standard design :		
	10A	0.91 m deep with S.F.R.C. cover and frame (heavy duty, HD-20 grade designation) 560 mm internal diameter conforming to I.S. 12592, total weight of cover and frame to be not less than 182 kg, fixed in cement concrete 1 : 2 : 4 (1 cement : 2		

S. No.		Description	Unit	Rate ₹
		coarse sand : 4 graded stone aggregate 20 mm nominal size) including centering shuttering all complete, (Excavation, foot rests and 12 mm thick cement plaster at the external surface shall be paid for separately)	each	3167.85
	10B	1.67 m deep with S.F.R.C. cover and frame (heavy duty, HD-20 grade designation) 560 mm internal diameter conforming to I.S. 12592, total weight of cover and frame to be not less than 182 kg, fixed in cement concrete 1 : 2 : 4 (1 cement : 2 coarse sand : 4 graded stone aggregate 20 mm nominal size) including centering shuttering all complete. (Excavation, foot rests and 12 mm thick cement plaster at the external surface shall be paid for separately)	each	4227.35
11.		Extra depth for circular type manhole 0.91 m internal dia (at bottom) with F.P.S. bricks :		
	11A	Beyond 0.91 m to 1.67 m	metre	1394.05
12.		Constructing brick masonry circular manhole 1.22 m internal dia at bottom and 0.56 m dia at top with 75 class designation F.P.S. brick in cement mortar 1 : 4 (1 cement : 4 coarse sand) inside cement plaster 12 mm thick with cement mortar 1 : 3 (1 cement : 3 coarse sand) finished with a floating coat of neat cement foundation concrete 1 : 3 : 6 (1 cement : 3 coarse sand : 6 graded stone aggregate 40 mm nominal size) and making necessary channel in cement concrete 1 : 2 : 4 (1 cement : 2 coarse sand : 4 graded stone aggregate 20 mm nominal size) finished with a floating coat of neat cement all complete as per standard design :		
	12A	1.68 m deep with SFRC Cover and frame (heavy duty HD-20 grade designation) 560 mm internal diameter conforming to IS : 12592, total weight of cover and frame to be not less than 182 kg fixed in cement concrete 1 : 2 : 4 (1 cement : 2 coarse sand : 4 graded stone aggregate 20 mm nominal size) including centering shuttering all complete. (Excavation, foot rests and 12 mm thick cement plaster at the external surface shall be paid for separately)	each	4695.25
	12B	2.29 m deep with SFRC Cover and frame (heavy duty HD-20 grade designation) 560 mm internal diameter conforming to IS : 12592, total weight of cover and frame to be not less than 182 kg, fixed in cement concrete 1 : 2 : 4 (1 cement : 2 coarse sand : 4 graded stone aggregate 20 mm nominal size) including centering shuttering all complete. (Excavation, foot rests and 12 mm thick cement plaster at the external surface shall be paid for separately)	each	5794.80
13.		Extra depth for circular type manhole 1.22 m internal dia (at bottom) with F.P.S. bricks :		
	13A	Beyond 1.68 m to 2.29 m	metre	1802.55
14.		Constructing brick masonary circular manhole 1.52 m internal dia at bottom and 0.56 m dia at top with 75 class designation F.P.S. brick in cement mortar 1 : 4 (1 cement : 4 coarse sand) inside cement plaster 12 mm thick with cement mortar 1 : 3 (1 cement : 3 coarse sand) finished with a floating coat of neat cement, foundation concrete 1 : 3 : 6 (1 cement: 3 coarse sand : 6 graded stone aggregate 40 mm nominal size) and making necessary channel in cement concrete 1 : 2 : 4 (1 cement: 2 coarse sand: 4 graded stoen aggregate 20 mm		

(*Contd.*)

S. No.	Description	Unit	Rate ₹
	nominal size) finished with a floating coat of neat cement all complete as per standard design :		
	14A 2.30 m deep with SFRC Cover and frame (heavy duty HD-20 grade designation) 560 mm internal diameter conforming to IS : 12592, total weight of cover and frame to be not less than 182 kg fixed in cement concrete 1 : 2 : 4 (1 cement : 2 coarse sand : 4 graded stone aggregate 20 mm nominal size) including centering shuttering all complete. (Excavation, foot rests and 12 mm thick cement plaster at the external surface shall be paid for separately)	each	8667.90
	14B 4.18 m deep with SFRC Cover and frame (heavy duty HD-20 grade designation) 560 mm internal diameter conforming to IS : 12592, total weight of cover and frame to be not less than 182 kg. fixed in cement concrete 1 : 2 : 4 (1 cement : 2 coarse sand : 4 graded stone aggregate 20 mm nominal size) including centering shuttering all complete : with F.P.S. bricks. (Excavation, foot rests and 12 mm thick cement plaster at the external surface shall be paid for separately)	each	16730.15
15.	Extra depth for circular type manhole 1.52 m internal dia (at bottom) with F.P.S. bricks :		
	15A Beyond 2.30 m	metre	4288.45
16.	Providing M.S. foot rests including fixing in manholes with 20 × 20 × 10 cm cement concrete blocks 1 : 3 : 6 (1 cement : 3 coarse sand : 6 graded stone aggregate 20 mm nominal size) as per standard design :		
	16A With 20 × 20 mm square bar	each	72.75
	16B With 20 mm diameter round bar	each	61.35
17.	Providing orange colour safety foot rest of minimum 6 mm thick plastic encapsulated as per IS : 10910 on 12 mm dia steel bar conforming to IS : 1786 having minimum cross section as 23 mm × 25 mm and over all minimum length 263 mm and width as 165 mm with minimum 112 mm space between protruded legs having 2 mm tread on top surface by ribbing or chequering besides necessary and adequate anchoring projections on tail length on 138 mm as per standard drawing and suitable to withstand the bend test and chemical resistance test as per specifications and having manufacture's permanent identification mark to be visible even after fixing, including fixing in manholes with 30 × 20 × 15 cm cement concrete block 1 : 3 : 6 (1 cement : 3 coarse sand : 6 graded stone aggregate 20 mm nominal size) complete as per design.	each	113.70
18.	Replacement of M.S. foot rests in manholes including dismantling concrete blocks and fixing with 20 × 20 × 10 cm cement concrete blocks 1 : 3 : 6 (1 cement : 3 coarse sand : 6 graded stone aggregate 20 mm nominal size) :		
	18A With 20 × 20 mm square bar	each	83.00
	18B With 20 mm diameter round bar	each	71.60
19.	Supplying and fixing C.I. cover without frame for manholes :		
	19A 455 × 610 mm rectangular C.I. cover (light duty) the weight of the cover to be not less than 23 kg.	each	324.10
	19B 500 mm diameter C.I. cover (medium duty) the weight of the cover to be not less than 58 kg.	each	905.65
	19C 560 mm diameter C.I. cover (heavy duty) the weight of the cover to be not less than 108 kg.	each	1351.65

S. No.	Description	Unit	Rate ₹
20.	**Providing and fixing in position precast R.C.C. manhole cover and frame of required shape and approved quality :**		
(1)	**LD-2.5 :**		
20A	**Rectangular shape 600 × 450 mm internal dimensions**	**each**	**670.85**
20B	**Square shape 350 mm internal dimensions**	**each**	**951.75**
20C	**Circular shape 450 mm internal diameter**	**each**	**1118.40**
(2)	**MD-10 :**		
20D	**Square shape 500 mm internal dimension**	**each**	**753.85**
20E	**Circular shape 500 mm internal diameter**	**each**	**1481.35**
(3)	**HD-20 :**		
20F	**Circular shape 560 mm internal diameter**	**each**	**1904.30**
(4)	**EHD-35 :**		
20G	**Circular shape 560 mm internal dia.**	**each**	**2293.15**
21.	**Supplying and fixing C.I. cover 300 × 300 mm without frame for gully trap (standard pattern) the weight of cover to be not less than 4.5 kg.**	**each**	**81.60**
22.	**Making connection of drain or sewer line with existing manhole including breaking into and making good the walls, floors with cement concrete 1 : 2 : 4 mix (1 cement : 2 coarse sand : 4 graded stone aggregate 20 mm nominal size) cement plastered on both sides with cement mortar 1 : 3 (1 cement : 3 coarse sand) finished with a floating coat of neat cement and making necessary channels for the drain etc. complete :**		
22A	**For pipes 100 to 230 mm diameter**	**each**	**89.20**
22B	**For pipes 250 to 300 mm diameter**	**each**	**110.65**
22C	**For pipes 350 to 450 mm diameter**	**each**	**163.20**
23.	**Providing sand cast iron drop connection externally for 60 cm drop from branch sewer line to main sewer manhole including inspection and cleaning eye with chain and lid, sand cast iron drop pipe and bend encased alround with cement concrete 1 : 5 : 10 (1 cement : 5 fine sand : 10 graded stone aggregate 40 mm nominal size) with all centring and shuttering required, cutting holes in walls and making good with brick work in cement mortar 1 : 5 (1 cement : 5 fine sand) plastered with cement mortar 1 : 3 (1 cement : 3 coarse sand) on inside of the manhole wall lead caulked joints between sand cast iron pipes and fittings, stiff cement mortar 1 : 1 (1 cement : 1 fine sand) joints between sand cast iron tee and S.W. pipe, making required channels complete as per standard design and specifications :**		
23A	**100 mm dia. sand cast iron drop connection**	**each**	**1678.65**
23B	**150 mm dia. sand cast iron drop connection**	**each**	**2774.45**
24.	**Extra for depths beyond 60 cm of sand cast iron drop connection complete :**		
24A	**For 100 mm dia. sand cast iron drop connection**	**metre**	**620.00**
24B	**For 150 mm dia. sand cast iron drop connection**	**metre**	**996.20**
25.	**Dismantling of manhole including R.C.C. top slab, C.I. cover with frame including stacking of useful materials near the site and disposal of unserviceable materials into municipal dumps within 50 m lead :**		
25A	**Rectangular manhole 90 × 80 cm and 45 cm deep**	**each**	**179.10**

(Contd.)

S. No.		Description	Unit	Rate ₹
	25B	Rectangular manhole 120 × 90 cm and 90 cm deep	each	313.40
	25C	Rectangular arch type manhole 140 × 90 cm and 2.45 m deep	each	588.40
	25D	Circular manhole 122 cm diameter and 1.68 m deep	each	452.40
26.		Extra for depth of manholes dismantled :		
	26A	Rectangular manhole 90 × 80 cm and 45 cm deep	metre	142.70
	26B	Rectangular manhole 120 × 90 cm and 90 cm deep	metre	169.90
	26C	Rectangular arch type manhole 140 × 90 cm and 2.45 m deep (upto 4.25 m depth)	metre	137.00
	26D	Circular manhole 122 cm diameter and 1.68 m deep (upto 2.29 m depth)	metre	298.70
27.		Raising manhole cover and frame slab to required level including dismantling existing slab and making good the damage as required (Raising depth of manhole to be paid separately) :		
	27A	Rectangular manhole 90 × 80 cm with rectangular cover 600 × 450 mm of grade LD-2.5	each	415.40
	27B	Rectangular manhole 120 × 90 cm with circular cover 500 mm dia of grade MD-10	each	647.75
	27C	Rectangular manhole 120 × 90 cm with circular cover 560 mm dia of grade HD-20	each	602.85
	27D	Circular manhole 140 cm dia with circular cover 600 mm dia of grade EHD-35	each	475.85
28.		Providing R.C.C. spun vent shaft with cowl 140 mm and 200 mm internal and external dia respectively at top 300 and 450 mm internal and external dia respectively, at bottom and 9.10 m overall length, bottom 1.25 m below ground level fixed in a pit 90 cm × 90 cm × 150 cm with cement concrete 1 : 4 : 8 (1 cement : 4 coarse sand : 8 graded stone aggregate 20 mm nominal size) 25 cm in bed and 20 cm alround with top 15 cm in cement concrete 1 : 2 : 4 (1 cement : 2 coarse sand : 4 graded stone aggregate 20 mm nominal size) junction of vent shaft and concrete grouted with cement mortar 1 : 1 (1 cement : 1 fine sand) including making connection with sewer manhole with 150 mm diametre cement concrete pipe of required length complete as per standard design.	each	6288.40
29.		Constructing brick masonry road gully chamber 50 × 45 × 60 cm with bricks of class designation 75 in cement mortar 1 : 5 (1 cement : 5 fine sand) including 500 × 450 mm precast R.C.C. horizontal grating with frame complete as per standard design :		
	29A	With F.P.S. bricks	each	1274.80
30.		Constructing brick masonry road gully chamber 45 × 45 × 77.5 cm with bricks of class designation 75 in cement mortar 1 : 5 (1 cement : 5 fine sand) with precast R.C.C. vertical grating complete as per standard design :		
	30A	With F.P.S. bricks	each	1360.05
31.		Constructing brick masonry road gully chamber 110 × 50 × 77.5 cm with bricks of class designation 75 in cement mortar 1 : 5 (1 cement : 5 fine sand) including 500 × 450 mm precast R.C.C. horizontal grating with frame and vertical grating complete as per standard design :		
	31A	With F.P.S. bricks	each	2517.55

S. No.	Description	Unit	Rate ₹
32.	Constructing brick masonry chamber for underground C.I. inspection chamber and bends with 75 class designation bricks in cement mortar 1 : 5 (1 cement : 5 fine sand) C.I. cover with frame (light duty) 455 × 610 mm internal dimensions, total weight of cover with frame to be not less than 38 kg (weight of cover 23 kg and weight of frame 15 kg) R.C.C. top slab with 1 : 2 : 4 mix (1 cement : 2 coarse sand : 4 graded stone aggregate 20 mm nominal size) foundation concrete 1 : 5 : 10 (1 cement : 5 fine sand : 10 graded stone aggregate 40 mm nominal size), inside plastering 12 mm thick with cement mortar 1 : 3 (1 cement : 3 coarse sand) finished smooth with a floating coat of neat cement on walls and bed concrete etc. complete as per standard design :		
	(1) Inside dimensions 455 × 610 mm and 45 cm deep for single pipe line :		
32A	With F.P.S. bricks	each	1305.35
	(2) Inside dimensions 500 × 700 mm and 45 cm deep for pipe line with one or two inlets :		
32B	With F.P.S. bricks	each	1525.45
	(3) Inside dimensions 600 × 850 mm and 45 cm deep for pipe line with three or more inlets :		
32C	With F.P.S. bricks	each	1770.05
33.	Extra for depth beyond 45 cm of brick masonry chamber :		
	(1) For 455 × 610 mm size		
33A	With F.P.S. bricks	metre	999.05
	(2) For 500 × 700 mm size		
33B	With F.P.S. bricks	metre	1090.05
	(3) For 600 × 850 mm size		
33C	With F.P.S. bricks	metre	1269.60
34.	Constructing brick masonry open surface drain with bricks of class designation 75 in cement mortar 1 : 4 (1 cement : 4 fine sand) including earth excavation, 10 cm thick bed concrete 1 : 5 : 10 (1 cement : 5 fine sand : 10 graded stone aggregate 40 mm nominal size) and 25 mm thick cement concrete 1 : 2 : 4 (1 cement : 2 coarse sand : 4 graded stone aggregate 12.5 mm nominal size) for filling haunches including 12 mm cement plaster 1 : 4 (1 cement : 4 coarse sand) with a floating coat of neat cement inside the drain, its top and exposed side including disposal of surplus earth complete as per standard design :		
	(1) 10 cm drain 20 cm average depth		
34A	With F.P.S. bricks	metre	160.40
	(2) 15 cm drain 20 cm average depth		
34B	With F.P.S. bricks	metre	169.60
	(3) 25 cm drain 30 cm average depth		
34C	With F.P.S. bricks	metre	231.85

(Contd.)

S. No.	Description	Unit	Rate ₹
35.	Constructing grease trap 80 × 40 × 46 cm (inside) with one brick thick brick masonry wall with inlet and outlet drain with bricks of class designation 75 in cement mortar 1 : 4 (1 cement : 4 fine sand) plastered 12 mm thick with 1 : 4 (1 cement : 4 coarse sand) finished with a floating coat of neat cement on inside and exposed surfaces having two stone baffled walls 34.5 cm deep and third one 19 cm deep, each 40 mm thick and 45 cm long embedded 2.5 cm on either side in brick masonry, 40 mm thick 100 × 60 cm stone cover and 7.5 cm thick bed concrete 1 : 5 : 10 (1 cement : 5 fine sand : 10 graded stone aggregate 40 mm nominal size) with 40 mm flooring in cement concrete 1 : 2 : 4 (1 cement : 2 coarse sand : 4 graded stone aggregate 12.5 mm nominal size) with a floating coat of neat cement including all earth excavation, refilling and disposal of surplus earth complete as per standard design :		
	35A With F.P.S. bricks	each	987.75
36.	Making soak pit 2.5 m diameter 3.0 metre deep with 45 × 45 cm dry brick honey comb shaft with bricks of class designation 75 and S.W. drain pipe 100 mm diameter, 1.8 m long complete as per standard design :		
	36A With F.P.S. bricks	each	5629.25
37.	Constructing soak pit 1.20 × 1.20 × 1.20 m filled with brickbats including S.W. drain pipe 100 mm diameter and 1.20 m long complete as per standard design.	each	702.10
38.	Providing and fixing S.W. intercepting trap in manholes with stiff mixture of cement mortar 1 : 1 (1 cement : 1 fine sand) including testing of joints etc. complete :		
	38A 100 mm dia	each	128.05
	38B 150 mm dia	each	203.65

Table 13.21. MISCELLANEOUS

S. No.	Description	Unit	Rate ₹
1.	Cutting holes upto 30 × 30 cm in walls including making good the same :		
	1A With F.P.S. bricks	each	49.70
2.	Cutting holes upto 15 × 15 cm in R.C.C. floors and roofs for passing drain pipe etc. and repairing the hole after insertion of drain pipe etc. with cement concrete 1 : 2 : 4 (1 cement : 2 coarse sand : 4 graded stone aggregate 20 mm nominal size) including finishing complete so as to make it leak proof.	each	45.00
3.	Making chases upto 7.5 × 7.5 cm in walls including making good after housing G.I. pipe etc.	metre	19.15
4.	Making hole upto 20 × 20 cm and embedding pipes upto 150 mm diameter in masonary and filling with cement concrete 1 : 3 : 6 (1 cement : 3 coarse sand : 6 graded stone aggregate 20 mm nominal size) including disposal of malba.	metre	61.25
5.	Disinfecting C.I. water mains by flushing with water containing bleaching powder at 0.5 gms per litre of water and cleaning the same with fresh water, operation to be repeated three times including getting the sample of water from the disinfected main tested in the municipal laboratory :		

S. No.	Description	Unit	Rate ₹
5A	80 mm diametre C.I. pipe	100 metre	146.10
5B	100 mm diametre C.I. pipe	100 metre	188.45
5C	125 mm diametre C.I. pipe	100 metre	245.40
5D	150 mm diametre C.I. pipe	100 metre	297.60
5E	200 mm diametre C.I. pipe	100 metre	402.95
5F	250 mm diametre C.I. pipe	100 metre	513.70
5G	300 mm diametre C.I. pipe	100 metre	580.25
5H	350 mm diametre C.I. pipe	100 metre	650.45
5I	400 mm diametre C.I. pipe	100 metre	726.65
5J	450 mm diametre C.I. pipe	100 metre	804.95
5K	500 mm diametre C.I. pipe	100 metre	888.95
5L	600 mm diametre C.I. pipe	100 metre	1063.50
6.	Extra for every operation of disinfecting the C.I. main by flushing with water containing bleaching powder at 0.5 gms per litre of water and cleaning the same with fresh water, including getting the samples of water tested in the municipal laboratory :		
6A	80 mm diametre C.I. pipe.	100 metre	53.45
6B	100 mm diametre C.I. pipe.	100 metre	65.95
6C	125 mm diametre C.I. pipe.	100 metre	81.75
6D	150 mm diametre C.I. pipe.	100 metre	96.60
6E	200 mm diametre C.I. pipe.	100 metre	152.20
6F	250 mm diametre C.I. pipe.	100 metre	175.40
6G	300 mm diametre C.I. pipe.	100 metre	197.80
6H	350 mm diametre C.I. pipe.	100 metre	234.60
6I	400 mm diametre C.I. pipe.	100 metre	272.00
6J	450 mm diametre C.I. pipe.	100 metre	311.30
6K	500 mm diametre C.I. pipe.	100 metre	351.15
6L	600 mm diametre C.I. pipe.	100 metre	433.80
7.	Dismantling old C.I. pipes including excavation and refilling trenches after taking out the pipes, breaking lead caulked joints, melting of lead and making into blocks including stacking of pipes at site lead upto 50 metre :		
7A	80 mm diametre C.I. pipe.	metre	47.00
7B	100 mm diametre C.I. pipe.	metre	48.60
7C	125 mm diametre C.I. pipe.	metre	50.00
7D	150 mm diametre C.I. pipe.	metre	51.50
7E	200 mm diametre C.I. pipe.	metre	57.05
7F	250 mm diametre C.I. pipe.	metre	62.40
7G	300 mm diametre C.I. pipe.	metre	66.75
7H	350 mm diametre C.I. pipe.	metre	69.40
7I	400 mm diametre C.I. pipe.	metre	74.30
7J	450 mm diametre C.I. pipe.	metre	77.95
7K	500 mm diametre C.I. pipe.	metre	81.00
7L	600 nun diametre C.I. pipe.	metre	86.05

(Contd.)

S. No.	Description	Unit	Rate ₹
8.	Labour for cutting C.I. pipe with steel saw :		
	8A 80 mm diametre C.I. pipe.	each cut	12.75
	8B 100 mm diametre C.I. pipe.	each cut	17.20
	8C 125 mm diametre C.I. pipe.	each cut	24.05
	8D 150 mm diametre C.I. pipe.	each cut	32.40
	8E 200 mm diametre C.I. pipe.	each cut	43.25
	8F 250 mm diametre C.I. pipe.	each cut	53.50
	8G 300 mm diametre C.I. pipe.	each cut	64.35
	8H 350 mm diametre C.I. pipe.	each cut	74.60
	8I 400 mm diametre C.I. pipe.	each cut	85.35
	8J 450 mm diametre C.I. pipe.	each cut	95.70
	8K 500 mm diametre C.I. pipe.	each cut	106.45
	8L 600 mm diametre C.I. pipe.	each cut	126.45
9.	Supplying and stacking of hard stone (for stone pitching) 22.5 cm thick at site.	cum	310.55
10.	Dry stone pitching 22.5 cm thick laid in courses and required profile with hammer dressed stones having no side less than 15 cm, with minimum depth of 20 cm including preparing the bedding surface etc. all complete.	sq m	51.55
11.	75 mm thick back filling for pitching including supplying of required materials and consolidation etc. complete with :		
	11A Moorum	sq m	20.60
	11B Stone aggregate 20 mm nominal size	sq m	30.70
	11C Stone aggregate 40 mm nominal size	sq m	28.40

Table 13.22. Pile Work

S. No.	Description	Unit	Rate ₹
	A. PILE WORK		
1.	Providing, driving and installing driven cast-in-situ reinforced cement concrete piles of specified diameter and length below the pile cap in cement concrete 1 : 2 : 4 (1 cement : 2 coarse sand : 4 graded stone aggregate 20 mm nominal size), to carry safe working load not less than specified, excluding the cost of steel reinforcement but including the cost of shoe and the length of pile to be embedded in the pile cap etc. all complete. (Length of pile for payment shall be measured from top of shoe to the bottom of pile cap) :		
	1A 400 mm dia. piles	metre	534.35
	1B 450 mm dia. piles	metre	657.60
	1C 500 mm dia. piles	metre	794.80
	1D 550 mm dia. piles	metre	946.75

S. No.	*Description*	*Unit*	*Rate* ₹
2.	**Boring, providing and installing bored cast-in-situ reinforced cement concrete pile of specified diametre and length below the pile cap in cement concrete 1 : 1½ : 3 (1 cement : ½ coarse sand : 3 graded stone aggregate of 20 mm nominal size), to carry a safe working load not less than specified, excluding the cost of steel reinforcement but including the cost of boring with casing and/or bentonite solution and the length of the pile to be embedded in the pile cap. (Length of pile for payment shall be measured upto bottom of pile cap) :**		
	2A 300 mm dia. piles	metre	246.40
	2B 400 mm dia. piles	metre	438.95
	2C 450 mm dia. piles	metre	555.65
	2D 600 mm dia. piles	metre	987.95
3.	**Boring, Providing and installing cast in situ single under reamed piles of specified diametre and length below pile cap in cement concrete piles with mix 1 : 1½ : 3 (1 cement : ½ coarse sand : 3 graded stone aggregate 20 mm nominal size), to carry a safe working load not less than specified, excluding the cost of steel reinfrocement but including the cost of boring with bentonite solution and the length of the pile to be embedded in pile cap. (Length of pile for payment shall be measured upto the bottom of pile cap) :**		
	3A 300 mm dia. piles	metre	283.50
	3B 400 mm dia. piles	metre	537.05
	3C 450 mm dia. piles	metre	692.10
	3D 550 mm dia. piles	metre	822.40
4.	**Extra over item no. 23.2.4 for boring, providing and installing cast in situ double under reamed piles, instead of single under ream of specified diameter and length. (Only the quantity of extra bulbs are to be paid).**	metre	291.50
5.	**Providing, driving and installing driven Pre-cast reinforced cement concrete piles of specified diameter and length below the pile cap in cement concrete 1 : 1 : 5 : 3 (1 cement : 1.5 coarse sand : 3 graded stone aggregate 20 mm nominal size). Subject to a minimum cement content of 430 kg per cum of concrete to carry safe working load not less than specified. With a central through preformed hole with M.S. black pipe of dia, 40 mm for grouting with cement sand grouting of mix 1 : 2 (1 cement : 2 coarse sand) under sufficient positive pressure to ensure complete filling including centring, shuttering, driving and removing the steel casing pipe and lifting casing etc. complete but exculding the cost of steel reinforcement. (Length of pile for payment shall be measured from top of the shoe to the bottom of pile cap) :**		
	5A 400 mm dia.	metre	641.35
	5B 450 mm dia.	metre	872.35
	5C 500 mm dia.	metre	644.95
	5D 550 mm dia.	metre	1154.30
	B. TESTS		
6.	**Vertical load testing of piles in accordance with IS: 2911 (Part IV) including installation of loading plateform and preparation of pile head or construction of test cap and dismantling of test cap after test etc. complete as per specification and the direction of Engineer-in-charge.**		

(Contd.)

S. No.		Description	Unit	Rate ₹
			Rate per test	
			initial test	Routine test
	6A	Single pile		
	6B	Upto 50 tonne capacity pile	19109.20	11443.30
	6C	Above 50 tonne and upto 100 tonne capacity pile.	28663.80	17164.95
7.		Group to two or more piles.		
			Rate per test	
			initial test	Routine test
	7A	Upto 50 tonne capacity	38218.40	22886.60
8.		Cyclic vertical load testing of pile in accordance with IS Code of practice IS : 2911 (part IV) including preparation of pile head etc for :		
	(1)	Single pile		
	8A	Upto 50 tonne capacity pile	per test	111443.00
	8B	Above 50 tonne and upto 100 tonne capacity pile.	per test	17164.95
	(2)	Group of two piles.		
	8C	Upto 50 tonne capacity each.	per test	22886.60
9.		Lateral load testing of single pile in accordance with IS Code of practice IS : 2911 (Part IV) for determining safe allowable lateral load on pile :		
	9A	Upto 50 tonne capacity pile	pet test	11110.00
	9B	Above 50 tonne and upto 100 tonne Capacity piles.	pet test	16665.00

Table 13.23. Aluminium Work

S. No.		Description	Unit	Rate ₹
1.		Providing and fixing anodised aluminium work for doors, windows, ventilators and partitions with extruded built up standard tubular and other sections of approved make conforming to IS : 733 and IS : 1285, anodised transparent or dyed to required shade according to IS : 1868. (Minimum anodic coating of grade AC 15), fixed with rawl plugs and screws or with fixing clips, or with expansion hold fastners including necessary filling up of gaps at junctions, at top, bottom and sides with required PVC/neoprene felt etc. Aluminium sections shall be smooth, rust free, straight, mitred and jointed mechanically wherever required including cleat angle, Aluminium snap beading for glazing/panelling, C.P. brass/stainless steel screws, all complete as per architectural drawings and the directions of Engineer-in-charge. (Glazing and panelling to be paid for separately.) :		
	1A	For fixed portion	kg	174.70
	1B	For shutters of doors, windows and ventilators including providing and fixing hinges/pivots and making provision for fixing of fittings wherever required including the cost of PVC/neoprene gasket required (Fittings shall be paid for separately.)	kg	183.80

S. No.	Description	Unit	Rate ₹
2.	Providing and fixing 12 mm thick prelaminated three layer medium density (exterior grade) particle board Grade I, Type II conforming to IS : 12823 bonded with phenol formaldehyde synthetic resin, of approved brand and manufacture in panelling fixed in aluminium doors, windows shutters and partition frames with C.P. brass/ stainless steel screws etc. complete as per architectural drawings and directions of Engineer-in-charge :		
	2A Pre-laminated particle board with decorative lamination on one side and balancing lamination on other side.	sq m	254.20
	2B Pre-laminated particle board with decorative lamination on both sides.	sq m	794.30
3.	Providing and fixing glazing in aluminium door, window, ventilator shutters and partitions etc. with PVC/neoprene gasket etc. complete as per the architectural drawings and the directions of Engineer-in-charge. (Cost of aluminium snap beading shall be paid in basic item.) :		
	3A With glass panes of 4.0 mm thickness (weight not less than 10.0 kg/sq m)	sq m	352.45
	3B With glass panes of 5.50 mm thickness (weight not less than 13.75 kg/sq m)	sq m	444.65
4.	Providing and fixing double action hydraulic floor spring of approved brand and manufacture (conforming to IS : 6315) for aluminium doors including cost of cutting floors as required, embedding in floors and cover plates etc. complete as per the direction of Engineer-in-charge.	each	891.35
5.	Providing and fixing anodised aluminium work (with minimum 15 micron uniform anodic coating) consisting of tee/angle sections, of approved make conforming to IS : 733 in frames of false ceiling including aluminium angle cleats with necessary C.P. brass/stainless steel sunk screws, aluminium perimeter angles fixed to wall with rawl plugs @ 450 mm centre to centre and fixing the frame work to level adjusting hangers (6 mm dia. M.S. rods) with necessary cadmium plated machine screws all complete as per approved architectural drawings and direction of the Engineer-in-charge (level adjusting hangers, ceiling cleats and expansion hold fastners to be paid for separately).	kg	214.15
6.	Providing and fixing level adjusting hangers of 6 mm dia. M.S. rods (upto 1200 mm length) fixed to roof slabs by means of M.S. angle ceiling cleats 40 × 40 × 5 mm size 40 mm long and expansion hold fastners 12.5 mm dia. 40 mm long including applying priming coat of zinc chromate yellow primer for steel members complete.	each	54.10
7.	Providing and fixing machine moulded anodised aluminium covering of approved pattern and design, made out of machine cut aluminium sheet and machine holed for receiving screws, over expansion joints on vertical surfaces/ceilings with full threaded, cadmium plated steel screws 4 mm dia. stem, 30 mm long and aluminium washers 2 mm thick, 15 mm dia. at a staggered pitch of 200 mm cenre to centre including drilling holes in the receiving surface and providing expandable plastic sleeves in holes etc. complete. (Anodising on the aluminium sheet and washers to be 15 micron thick) :		
	7A Made out of 170 mm wide anodised aluminium sheet 2.5 mm thick.	kg	178.05
	7B Made out of 210 mm wide anodised aluminium sheet 2.5 mm thick.	kg	178.05

(Contd.)

Table 13.24. WATER PROOFING

S. No.	*Description*	*Unit*	*Rate* ₹
1.	**Providing and laying integral cement based treatment for water proofing on horizontal surface at all levels as all levels as directed by Engineer-in-charge and consisting of :**		
	(I) 1st layer of 20 mm thick approved and specified rough stone slab over a 25 mm thick base of cement mortar 1 : 3 (1 cement : 3 coarse sand) mixed with water proofing compound conforming to IS : 2645 in the recommended proportion, Joints sealed and grouted with cement slurry mixed with water proofing compound conforming to IS : 2645 in proportion recommended by the manufacturer.		
	(II) 2nd layer of 25 mm thick cement mortar 1 : 3 (1 cement : 3 coarse sand) mixed with water proofing compound in recommended proportions.		
	(III) Finishing top with stone aggregate of 10 mm to 12 mm nominal size spreading @ 8 cum/sq m thoroughly embedded in the 2nd layer.		
	1A Using rough kota stone.	sq m	398.40
	1B Using rough red sand stone.	sq m	404.35
2.	**Providing and laying integral cement based treatment for water proofing on the vertical surface by fixing specified stone slab 20 mm thick with cement slurry mixed with water proofing compound conforming to IS : 2645 in recommended proportion with a gap of 20 mm (minimum) between stone slabs and the receiving surfaces and filling the gaps with neat cement slurry mixed with water proofing compound and finishing the exterior of stone slab with cement mortor 1 : 4 (1 cement : 4 coarse sand) 20 mm thick with neat cement punning mixed with water proofing compound in recommended proportion complete at all levels and as directed by Engineer-in-charge :**		
	2A Using rough kota stone	sq m	460.60
	2B Using rough red sand stone.	sq m	466.70
3.	**Providing and laying water proofing treatment to vertical and horizontal surfaces of depressed portions of W.C., kitchen and the like consisting of :**		
	(*i*) Ist course of applying cement slurry @ 4.4 kg/sq m mixed with water proofing compound conforming to IS : 2645 in recommended proportions.		
	(*ii*) IInd course of 20 mm cement plaster 1 : 3 (1 cement : 3 coarse sand) mixed with water proofing compound in recommended proportion.		
	(*iii*) IIIrd course of applying blown or/residual bitumen applied hot at 1.7 kg per sq m of area.		
	(*iv*) IVth course of 400 micron thick PVC sheet. (Overlaps at joints of PVC sheet should be 100 mm wide and pasted to each other with bitumen @ 1.7 kg/sq m.)	sq m	171.70
4.	**Providing and Placing in position suitable PVC water stops for construction/expansion joints between two RCC members and fixed to the reinforcement with binding wire before pouring concrete etc. complete :**		
	4A Serrated with central bulb (225 mm wide, 8-11 mm thick)	metre	281.55
	4B Dumb bell with central bulb (180 mm wide, 8 mm thick)	metre	253.80
	4C Kickers (320 mm wide, 5 mm thick)	metre	446.00

S. No.	Description	Unit	Rate ₹
5.	Providing and laying in situ five course water proofing treatment with glass fibre tissue reinforced bitumen over roof consisting of first coat of bitumen primer @ 0.40 kg per sq m, 2nd and 4th courses of bonding material @ 1.60 kg per sq m, which shall consist of blown type bitumen of grade 85/25 conforming to IS : 702, third layer of glass fibre tissue course as specified, fifth, the top most layer of stone grit 6 mm and down size or pea-sized gravel spread @ 6 dm^3 per sq m including preparation of surface excluding grading for slope etc. complete.	sq m	88.10
6.	Providing and laying in situ seven course water proofing treatment with glass fibre tissue reinforced bitumen over roof consisting of first coat of bitumen primer @ 0.40 kg per sq m, 2nd, 4th and 6th courses of bonding material @ 1.60 kg per sq m, which shall consist of blown type bitumen of grade 85/25 conforming to IS : 702, third and fifth layers of glass fibre tissue course as specified, seventh, the top most layer of stone grit 6 mm and down size or pea-sized gravel spread @ 6 dm^3 per sq m, including preparation of surface excluding grading for slope etc. complete.	sq m	136.80
7.	Providing and laying in situ nine course water proofing treatment with glass fibre tissue reinforced bitumen over roof consisting of first coat of bitumen primer @ 0.40 kg per sq m, 2nd, 4th, 6th, 8th courses of bonding material @ 1.60 kg per sq m, which shall consist of blown type bitumen of grade 85/25 conforming to IS : 702, third, fifth and seventh courses of glass fibre tissue, as specified, ninth, the top most layer of stone grit 6 mm and down size or pea-sized gravel spread @ 6 dm^3 per sq m including preparation of surface excluding grading for slope etc. complete.	sq m	184.85
8.	Providing and laying integral cement based water proofing treatment including preparation of surface as required for treatment of roofs, balconies, terraces etc. consisting of following operations : (*a*) Applying and grouting a slurry coat of neat cement using 2.75 kg/sq m. of cement admixed with proprietary water proofing compound conforming to IS : 2645 over the RCC slab including cleaning the surface before treatment. (*b*) Laying cement concrete using broken bricks/brick bats 25 mm to 100 mm size with 50% of cement mortar 1: 5 (1 cement : 5 coarse sand) admixed with proprietary water proofing compound conforming to IS : 2645 over 20 mm thick layer of cement mortar of mix 1 : 5 (1 cement : 5 coarse sand) admixed with proprietary water proofing compound conforming to IS : 2645 to required slope and treating similarly the adjoining walls upto 300 mm height including rounding of junctions of walls and slabs. (*c*) After two days of proper curing applying a second coat of cement slurry admixed with proprietary water proofing compound conforming to IS : 2645. (*d*) Finishing the surface with 20 mm thick jointless cement mortar of mix 1 : 4 (1 cement : 4 coarse sand) admixed with proprietary water proofing compound conforming to IS : 2645 and finally finishing the surface with trowel with neat cement slurry and making of 300 × 300 mm square. (*e*) The whole terrace so finished shall be flooded with water for a minimum period of two weeks for curing and for final test. All above operations to be done in order and as directed and specified by the Engineer-in-Charge.		

(*Contd.*)

S. No.	Description	Unit	Rate ₹
	8A With average thickness of 120 mm and minimum thickness at khurra as 65 mm.	sq m	253.85
9.	Providing and laying four courses water proofing treatment with bitumen felt over roofs consisting of first and third courses of blown or/and residual bitumen applied hot at 1.45 kg per square metre of area for each course, second course of roofing felt type 3 grade-I (hessian based self finished bitumen fait) and fourth and final course of stone grit 6 mm and down size or pea-sized gravel spread at 6 cubic diametre per square metre including preparation of surface but excluding grading complete with :		
	9A Bitumen felt (hessian base) type 3 grade I Blown or/and residual bitumen applied hot 1.45	sq m	83.90
10.	Providing and laying six courses water proofing treatment with bitumen felt over roofs consisting of first, third and fifth courses of blown or/and residual bitumen applied hot at 1.45, 1.20 and 1.45 kg per square metre of area respectively, second and fourth courses of roofing felt type 3 grade-I (Hessian based self finished bitumen felt) and sixth and final course of stone grit 6 mm and down size or pea sized gravel spread at 6 cubic dm per sq m including preparation of surface but excluding grading, complete.	sq m	137.60
11.	Providing and laying six courses water proofing treatment with bitumen felt over roofs consisting of first, third and fifth courses of blown or/and residual bitumen applied hot at 1.45, 1.20 and 1.70 Kg per square metre of area respectively, second and fourth courses of roofing felt type 2 grade-I (fibre base self finished bitumen felt) six and final courses of stone grit 6 mm and down size or pea sized gravel spread at 6 dm cubic per sq m including preparation of surface, excluding grading, complete.	sq m	185.60
12.	Providing and laying six courses water proofing treatment with bitumen felt over roofs consisting of first, third and fifth courses of blown or/and residual bitumen applied hot at 1.45, 1.20 and 1.70 kg per square metre of area respectively, second and fourth courses of roofing felt type 2 grade-II (glass fibre base self finished bitumen felt) and sixth and final course of stone grit 6 mm and down size or pea sized gravel spread at 6 cubic, dm per sq m including preparation of surface but excluding grading, complete.	sq m	185.70
13.	Supplying and applying bitumenous solution primer on roof and/or wall surface at 0.24 litre per sq m.	sq m	7.30
14.	Deduct for omitting in water proofing treatment final course of spreading stone grit 6 mm down size or pea sized gravel :		
	14A at 6 cubic dm per sq m	sq m	4.90
	14B at 8 cubic dm per sq m	sq m	6.30
15.	Grading roof for water proofing treatment with :		
	15A Lime concrete with 20 mm nominal size brick aggregate and 50% lime mortar 1 : 2 (1 lime putty : 2 surkhi)	cum	1456.00
	15B Cement concrete 1 : 2 : 4 (1 cement : 2 coarse sand : 4 graded stone aggregate 20 mm nominal size)	cum	1718.70
	15C Cement mortar 1 : 3 (1 cement : 3 coarse sand)	cum	2703.70
	15D Cement mortar 1 : 4 (1 cement : 4 coarse sand)	cum	2333.85

14

Coefficients for Cement Consumption

Table 14.1. MORTARS

S. No.	Description	Unit	Quantity of cement to be used per unit quantity of work (Quintals)
	A. CEMENT MORTAR		
14.1.1	Cement mortar 1 : 1 (1 cement : 1 fine sand)	cum	10.20
14.1.2	Cement mortar 1 : 2 (1 cement : 2 fine sand)	cum	6.80
14.1.3	Cement mortar 1 : 3 (1 cement : 3 fine sand)	cum	5.10
14.1.4	Cement mortar 1 : 4 (1 cement : 4 fine sand)	cum	3.80
14.1.5	Cement mortar 1 : 5 (1 cement : 5 fine sand)	cum	3.10
14.1.6	Cement mortar 1 : 6 (1 cement : 6 fine sand)	cum	2.50
14.1.7	Cement mortar 1 : 2 (1 cement : 2 coarse sand)	cum	6.80
14.1.8	Cement mortar 1 : 3 (1 cement : 3 coarse sand)	cum	5.10
14.1.9	Cement mortar 1 : 4 (1 cement : 4 coarse sand)	cum	3.80
14.1.10	Cement mortar 1 : 5 (1 cement : 5 coarse sand)	cum	3.10
14.1.11	Cement mortar 1 : 6 (1 cement : 6 coarse sand)	cum	2.50
14.1.12	Cement mortar 1 : 2 (1 cement : 2 stone dust)	cum	6.80
14.1.13	Cement mortar 1 : 2 (1 cement : 2 marble dust)	cum	6.80
14.1.14	Cement mortar 1 : 5 (1 cement : 5 marble dust)	cum	3.10
14.1.15	Cement mortar 1 : 1 : 3 (1 cement : 1 marble dust : 3 stone dust)	cum	3.80
14.1.16	White cement Lime mortar 1/4 : 1 : 1 : 1 (1/4 White cement : 1 lime putty : 1 stone dust : 1 marble dust)	cum	1.60*
14.1.17	White cement mortar 1 : 2 (1 White cement : 2 marble dust)	cum	6.80*
14.1.18	White cement mortar 1 : 3 (1 White cement : 3 Marble dust)	cum	5.10*
14.1.19	White cement mortar 1 : 5 (1 White cement : 5 marble dust)	cum	3.10*
	B. CEMENT LIME MORTAR		
14.1.20	Cement lime mortar 1 : 1 : 3 (1 cement : 1 lime putty : 3 fine sand)	cum	4.10
14.1.21	Cement lime mortar 1 : 1 : 6 (1 cement : 1 lime putty : 6 fine sand)	cum	2.50
14.1.22	Cement lime mortar 1 : 1 : 7 (1 cement : 1 lime putty : 7 fine sand)	cum	2.20

(Contd.)

14.1.23	Cement lime mortar 1 : 1 : 8 (1 cement : 2 lime putty : 8 fine sand)	cum	1.90
14.1.24	Cement lime mortar 1 : 2 : 9 (1 cement : 2 lime putty : 9 fine sand)	cum	1.70
14.1.25	Cement lime mortar 1 : 1 : 3 (1 cement : 1 lime putty : 3 coarse sand)	cum	4.10
14.1.26	Cement lime mortar 1 : 1 : 6 (1 cement : 1 lime putty : 6 coarse sand)	cum	2.50
14.1.27	Cement lime mortar 1 : 3 : 12 (1 cement : 3 lime putty : 12 fine sand)	cum	1.30
14.1.28	Cement lime mortar 1 : 3 (1 cement : 3 coarse sand with 10% addition of class 'C' lime)	cum	5.10

Table 14.2. CONCRETE WORK

S. No.	*Description*	*Unit*	*Quantity of cement to be used per unit quantity of work (Quintals)*
	A. GENERAL		
14.2.1	**Providing and laying in position cement concrete of specified grade excluding the cost of centring and shuttering-All work upto plinth level :**		
	1A 1 : 1 : 2 (1 cement : 1 coarse sand : 2 graded stone aggregate 20 mm nominal size)	cum	6.10
	1B 1 : 1.5 : 3 (1 Cement : 1.5 coarse sand : 3 graded stone aggregate 20 mm nominal size)	cum	4.00
	1C 1 : 2 : 4 (1 Cement : 2 coarse sand : 4 graded stone aggregate 20 mm nominal size)	cum	3.20
	1D 1 : 2 : 4 (1 Cement : 2 coarse sand : 4 graded stone aggregate 40 mm nominal size)	cum	3.20
	1E 1 : 3 : 6 (1 Cement : 3 coarse sand : 6 graded stone aggregate 20 mm nominal size)	cum	2.20
	1F 1 : 3 : 6 (1 Cement : 3 coarse sand : 6 graded stone aggregate 40 mm nominal size)	cum	2.20
	1G 1 : 3 : 6 (1 Cement : 3 fine sand : 6 graded stone aggregate 40 mm nominal size)	cum	2.20
	1H 1 : 4 : 8 (1 Cement : 4 coarse sand : 8 graded stone aggregate 40 mm nominal size)	cum	1.70
	1I 1 : 4 : 8 (1 Cement : 4 fine sand : 8 graded stone aggregate 40 mm nominal size)	cum	1.70
	1J 1 : 5 : 10 (1 cement : 5 coarse sand : 10 graded stone aggregate 40 mm nominal size)	cum	1.30
	1K 1 : 5 : 10 (1 cement : 5 fine sand : 10 graded stone aggregate 40 mm nominal size)	cum	1.30

14.2.2	Providing and laying cement concrete in retaining walls, return walls, walls (any thickness) including attached pilasters, columns, piers, abutments, pillars, posts, struts, buttresses, string or lacing courses, parapets, coping, bed blocks, anchor blocks, plain window sills, fillets etc. upto floor five level, excluding the cost of centring and shuttering :		
	2A 1 : 1 : 2 (1 Cement : 1 coarse sand : 2 graded stone aggregate 20 mm nominal size)	cum	6.10
	2B 1 : 1.5 : 3 (1 Cement : 1.5 coarse sand : 3 graded stone aggregate 20 mm nominal size)	cum	4.00
	2C 1 : 2 : 4 (1 Cement : 2 coarse sand : 4 graded stone aggregate 20 mm nominal size)	cum	3.20
	2D 1 : 2 : 4 (1 Cement : 2 coarse sand : 4 graded stone aggregate 40 mm nominal size)	cum	3.20
	2E 1 : 3 : 6 (1 Cement : 3 coarse sand : 6 graded stone aggregate 20 mm nominal size)	cum	2.20
	2F 1 : 3 : 6 (1 Cement : 3 coarse sand : 6 graded stone aggregate 40 mm nominal size)	cum	2.20
	2G 1 : 3 : 6 (1 Cement : 3 fine sand : 6 graded stone aggregate 40 mm nominal size)	cum	2.20
	2H 1 : 4 : 8 (1 Cement : 4 coarse sand : 8 graded stone aggregate 40 mm nominal size)	cum	1.70
	2I 1 : 4 : 8 (1 Cement : 4 fine sand : 8 graded stone aggregate 40 mm nominal size)	cum	1.70
	2J 1 : 5 : 10 (1 Cement : 5 coarse sand : 10 graded stone aggregate 40 mm nominal size)	cum	1.30
	2K 1 : 5 : 10 (1 Cement : 5 fine sand : 10 graded stone aggregate 40 mm nominal size)	cum	1.30
14.2.3	Providing and laying cement concrete in kerbs, steps and the like at or near ground level excluding the cost of centring, shuttering and finishing :		
	3A 1 : 2 : 4 (1 cement : 2 coarse sand : 4 grade stone aggregate 20 mm nominal size)	cum	3.20
	3B 1 : 3 : 6 (1 cement : 3 coarse sand : 6 graded stone aggregate 20 mm nominal size)	cum	2.20
	B. CEMENT CONCRETE (PRECAST)		
14.2.4	Providing and fixing upto floor five level precast cement concrete string of lacing courses, copings, bed plates, anchor blocks, plain window sills, shelves, louvers, steps, stair cases, etc. including hoisting and setting in position with cement mortar 1 : 3 (1 cement : 3 coarse sand) cost of required centring, shuttering and finishing smooth with 6 mm thick cement plaster 1 : 3 (1 cement : 3 fine sand) on exposed surfaces complete :		
	4A 1 : 2 : 4 (1 cement : 2 coarse sand : 4 graded stone aggregate 20 mm nominal size)	cum	3.80
	4B 1 : 3 : 6 (1 cement : 3 coarse sand : 6 graded stone aggregate 20 mm nominal size)	cum	2.80
14.2.5	Providing and fixing at or near ground level precast cement concrete in kerbs, edgings etc. as per approved pattern and setting in position with cement mortar 1 : 3 (1 cement : 3 coarse sand) including the cost of required centring, shuttering and finishing smooth with 6 mm thick cement plaster 1 : 3 (1 cement : 3 fine sand) on exposed surfaces complete :		

(*Contd.*)

	5A 1 : 2 : 4 (1 cement : 2 coarse sand : 4 graded stone aggregate 20 mm nominal size)	cum	3.62
14.2.6	Providing and fixing upto floor five level precast cement concrete solid block including hoisting and setting in position with cement mortar 1 : 3 (1 cement : 3 coarse sand) cost of required centring, shuttering and finishing smooth with 6 mm thick cement plaster 1 : 3 (1 cement : 3 fine sand) on exposed surfaces complete :		
	6A 1 : 2 : 4 (1 cement : 2 coarse sand : 4 graded stone aggregate 20 mm nominal size)	cum	4.13
	6B 1 : 3 : 6 (1 cement : 3 coarse sand : 6 graded stone aggregate 20 mm nominal size)	cum	3.13
14.2.7	Providing and fixing upto floor five level precast cement concrete hollow block including hoisting and setting in position with cement mortar 1 : 3 (1 cement : 3 coarse sand) including the cost of required centring, shuttering and finishing smooth with 6 mm thick cement plaster 1 : 3 (1 cement : 3 fine sand) on exposed surfaces complete :		
	7A 1 : 2 : 4 (1 cement : 2 coarse sand : 4 graded stone aggregate 20 mm nominal size)	cum	2.466
	7B 1 : 3 : 6 (1 cement : 3 coarse sand : 6 graded stone aggregate 20 mm nominal size)	cum	2.006
	C. DAMP-PROOF COURSE		
14.2.8	Providing and laying damp-proof Course 40 mm thick with cement concrete 1 : 2 : 4 (1 cement : 2 coarse sand : 4 graded stone aggregate 12.5 mm nominal size).	sq m	0.13
14.2.9	Providing and laying damp-proof Course 50 mm thick with cement concrete 1 : 2 : 4 (1 cement : 2 coarse sand : 4 graded stone aggregate 20 mm nominal size).	sq m	0.16

Table 14.3. REINFORCED CEMENT CONCRETE

S. No.	*Description of item of work*	*Unit*	*Quantity of cement to be used per unit quantity of work (Quintals)*
	A. CAST-IN-SITU		
14.3.1	Providing and laying in position specified grade of reinforced cement concrete excluding the cost of centring, shuttering, finishing and reinforcement-All work upto plinth level :		
	1A 1 : 1 : 2 (1 cement : 1 coarse sand : 2 graded stone aggregate 20 mm nominal size)	cum	6.10
	1B 1 : 1.5 : 3 (1 cement : 1.5 coarse sand : 3 graded stone aggregate 20 mm nominal size)	cum	4.00
	1C 1 : 2 : 4 (1 cement : 2 coarse sand : 4 graded stone aggregate 20 mm nominal size)	cum	3.20
14.3.2	Reinforced cement concrete work in walls (any thickness), including attached pilasters, buttresses, plinth and string courses, fillets, columns, pillars, piers, abutments, posts and struts, etc. upto floor five level excluding cost of centring, shuttering, finishing and reinforcement :		

	2A 1 : 1 : 2 (1 cement : 1 coarse sand : 2 graded stone aggregate 20 mm nominal size)	cum	6.10
	2B 1 : 1.5 : 3 (1 cement : 1.5 coarse sand : 3 graded stone aggregate 20 mm nominal size)	cum	4.00
	2C 1 : 2 : 4 (1 cement : 2 coarse sand : 4 graded stone aggregate 20 mm nominal size)	cum	3.20
14.3.3	Reinforced cement concrete work in beams, suspended floors, roofs having slope upto 15°, landings, balconies, shelves, chajjas, lintels, bands, plain window sills, staircases and spiral stair cases upto floor five level excluding the cost of centring, shuttering, finishing and reinforcement with 1 : 2 : 4 (1 cement : 2 coarse sand : 4 graded stone aggregate 20 mm nominal size).	cum	3.20
14.3.4	Providing and laying upto floor five level reinforced cement concrete in kerbs, steps and the like excluding the cost of centring, shuttering, finishing and reinforcement with 1 : 2 : 4 (1 cement : 2 coarse sand : 4 graded stone aggregate 20 mm nominal size).	cum	3.20
14.3.5	Reinforced cement concrete work in arches, archribs, domes, vaults, shells, folded plate and roofs having slope more than 15° upto floor five level excluding the cost of centring, shuttering, finishing and reinforcement with 1 : 2 : 4 (1 cement : 2 coarse sand : 4 graded stone aggregate 20 mm nominal size).	cum	3.20
14.3.6	Reinforced cement concrete work in chimneys, shafts, upto floor five level excluding the cost of centring, shuttering, finishing and reinforcement with 1 : 2 : 4 (1 cement : 2 coarse sand : 4 graded stone aggregate 20 mm nominal size).	cum	3.20
14.3.7	Reinforced cement concrete work in well-steining excluding the cost of centring, shuttering, finishing and reinforcement with 1 : 2 : 4 (1 cement : 2 coarse sand : 4 graded stone aggregate 20 mm nominal size).	cum	3.20
14.3.8	Reinforced cement concrete work in Vertical and Horizontal fins individually or forming box louvers and facias upto floor five level excluding the cost of centring, shuttering, finishing and reinforcement with 1 : 2 : 4 (1 cement : 2 coarse sand : 4 graded stone aggregate 20 mm nominal size).	cum	3.20
	B. PRE-CAST R.C.C.		
14.3.9	Providing, hoisting and fixing upto floor five level precast reinforced cement concrete work in string courses, bands, copings, bed plates, anchor blocks, plain window sills and the like including the cost of required centring, shuttering, finishing smooth with 6 mm thick cement plaster 1 : 3 (1 cement : 3 fine sand) on exposed surfaces complete but excluding cost of reinforcement with 1 : 2 : 4 (1 cement : 2 coarse sand : 4 graded stone aggregate 20 mm nominal size).	cum	3.80
14.3.10	Providing, hoisting and fixing upto floor five level precast reinforced cement concrete in small lintels not exceeding 1.5 m clear span upto floor five level including the cost of required centring, shuttering and finishing smooth with 6 mm thick cement plaster 1 : 3 (1 cement : 3 fine sand) on exposed surfaces but excluding the cost of reinforcement with 1 : 2 : 4 (1 cement : 2 coarse sand : 4 graded stone aggregate 20 mm nominal size).	cum	3.77

(Contd.)

14.3.11	Providing, hoisting and fixing upto floor five level precast reinforced cement concrete in mouldings as in cornices, windows sills etc. including the cost of required centring, shuttering and finishing smooth with 6 mm thick cement plaster 1 : 3 (1 cement : 3 fine sand) on exposed surfaces complete but excluding the cost of reinforcement with 1 : 2 : 4 (1 cement : 2 coarse sand : 4 graded stone aggregate 20 mm nominal size).	cum	3.80
14.3.12	Providing, hoisting and fixing upto floor five level precast reinforced cement concrete in lintels, beams and bressumers including setting in cement mortar 1 : 3 (1 cement : 3 coarse sand) the cost of required centring and shuttering and finishing smooth with 6 mm thick cement plaster 1 : 3 (1 cement : 3 fine sand) on exposed surfaces but excluding the cost of reinforcement with 1 : 2 : 4 (1 cement : 2 coarse sand : 4 graded stone aggregate 20 mm nominal size).	cum	3.49
14.3.13	Providing, hoisting and fixing upto floor five level precast reinforced cement concrete in shelves including setting in cement mortar 1 : 3 (1 cement : 3 coarse sand) the cost of required centring, shuttering and finishing with neat cement punning on exposed surfaces but excluding the cost of reinforcement with 1 : 2 : 4 (1 cement : 2 coarse sand : 4 graded stone aggregate 12.5 mm nominal size).	cum	3.80
14.3.14	Providing, hoisting and fixing upto floor five level precast reinforced cement concrete in vertical and horizontal fins individually or forming box louvers setting in cement mortar 1 : 2 (1 cement : 2 coarse sand) including the cost of required centring, shuttering and finishing smooth with 6 mm thick cement plaster 1 : 3 (1 cement : 3 fine sand) on exposed surfaces complete but excluding the cost of reinforcement with 1 : 2 : 4 (1 cement : 2 coarse sand : 4 graded stone aggregate 20 mm nominal size).	cum	4.73
14.3.15	Providing, precast cement concrete Jali 1 : 2 : 4 (1 cement : 2 coarse sand : 4 stone aggregate 6 mm nominal size) reinforced with 1.6 mm dia mild steel wire including roughening cleaning, fixing and finishing in cement mortar 1 : 3 (1 cement : 3 fine sand) etc. complete excluding plastering of the jambs, sills and soffits :		
	15A 50 mm thick	sq m	1.64*
	15B 40 mm thick	sq m	1.64*
	15C 25 mm thick	sq m	1.64*
	C. ENCASING ROLLED STEEL SECTION		
14.3.16	Encasing rolled steel sections, in beams and columns, with cement concrete 1 : 2 : 4 (1 cement : 2 coarse sand : 4 stone aggregate 12.5 mm nominal size) including centring and shuttering complete but excluding cost of reinforcement.	cum	3.20
14.3.17	Encasing rolled steel section in grillages with cement concrete 1 : 2 : 4 (1 cement : 2 coarse sand : 4 stone aggregate 12.5 mm nominal size) including centring and shuttering but excluding cost of expanded metal and hangers.	cum	3.20
	D. MISCELLANEOUS		
14.3.18	Deduct for omitting in R.C.C. work smooth finishing of the exposed surface with 6 mm thick cement mortar 1 : 3 (1 cement : 3 fine sand).	100 sq m	3.67

*Cement for fixing only.

14.3.19	Extra for rendering smooth the top of suspended floors, landings and staircases (treads and risers) with cement mortar 1 : 2 (1 cement : 2 coarse sand) including a floating coat of neat cement and protecting the surface with a layer of 7.5 cm of earth laid over 15 mm of fine sand in case of suspended floor and bricks laid in mud mortar in case of landings and steps including subsequent removal and cleaning of the same.	100 sq m	4.17
14.3.20	Providing and filling in position bitumen mix filler of Proportion 80 kg of hot bitumen 1 kg of cement and 0.25 cubicmetre of coarse sand for expansion joints.	per cm depth per cm width per 100 m length	0.00032
14.3.21	Providing reinforced cement concrete eaves board 25 mm thick and 15 cm to 30 cm wide excluding the cost of centring, shuttering, finishing and reinforcement with 1: 2 : 4 mix (1 cement : 2 course sand : 4 graded stone aggregate 10 mm nominal size) upto floor two level.	cum	3.20
	E. DESIGN MIX CONCRETE		
14.3.22	Providing and laying in position machine batched, machine mixed and machine vibrated design mix cement concrete of specified grade for reinforced cement concrete structural elements, excluding the cost of centring, shuttering, finishing and reinforcement-M-20 grade reinforced cement concrete :		
	22A All work upto plinth level	cum	3.83*
	22B All work from plinth level upto floor V level.	cum	3.83*
	22C Walls, columns, pillars, posts and struts	cum	3.83*
	22D Beams, plinth beams, girders, bressumers, cantilevers, Suspended floors lintels roofs and staircases including spiral staircases, shelves etc.	cum	3.83*
14.3.23	Add or deduct for providing richer or leaner mixes respectively at all floor levels :		
	23A Providing M-25 grade R.C.C. instead of M-20 grade R.C.C.	cum	0.27*
	23B Providing M-30 grade R.C.C. instead of M-20 grade R.C.C.	cum	0.37*
	23C Providing M-35 grade R.C.C. instead of M-20 grade R.C.C.	cum	0.45*
	23D Providing M-15 grade R.C.C. instead of M-20 grade R.C.C.	cum	(–) 0.63*
14.3.24	Providing and placing in position precast reinforced cement concrete waffle units square or rectangular as per design and shape for floors and roofs in 1 : 1½ : 3 (1 cement : 1½ coarse sand : 3 graded stone aggregate 10 mm nominal size) including flush or deep ruled pointing at joints in cement mortar 1 : 2 (1 Cement : 2 fine sand), making necessary holes of required sizes for carrying through service lines etc., providing steel wire handles for lifting etc., form work in precasting, handling, hoisting, centering and erection complete for all floor levels but excluding the cost of reinforcement and steel wire.	cum	4.16

* Actual weight for design mix will be worked out taking into consideration the cement requirement as per particular design mix.

Table 14.4. BRICK WORK

S. No.	*Description of item of work*	*Unit*	*Quantity of cement to be used per unit quantity of work (Quintals)*
	A. GENERAL		
14.4.1	Brick work with bricks of class designation 75 in foundations and plinth in :		
	1A Cement lime mortar 1 : 1 : 6 (1 cement : 1 lime putty : 6 fine sand)	cum	0.625
	1B Cement lime mortar 1 : 2 : 9 (1 cement : 2 lime putty : 9 fine sand)	cum	0.425
	1C Cement lime mortar 1 : 1 : 6 (1 cement : 1 lime putty : 6 coarse sand)	cum	0.625
	1D Cement mortar 1 : 4 (1 cement : 4 fine sand)	cum	0.950
	1E Cement mortar 1 : 6 (1 cement : 6 fine sand)	cum	0.625
	1F Cement mortar 1 : 4 (1 cement : 4 coarse sand)	cum	0.950
	1G Cement mortar 1 : 6 (1 cement : 6 coarse sand)	cum	0.625
14.4.2	Constructing tharry with bricks of class designation 75 laid on edge in cement mortar 1 : 4 (1 cement : 4 coarse sand), cement pointing 1 : 2 (1 cement : 2 fine sand) including necessary excavation and 10 cm bed of cement concrete 1 : 5 : 10 (1 cement : 5 fine sand : 10 graded stone aggregate 40 mm nominal size) complete.	100 sq m	31.28
14.4.3	Providing half brick masonry with bricks of class designation 75 in cement mortar 1 : 3 (1 cement : 3 coarse sand) in superstructure for closing cavity 5 to 7.5 cm wide in cavity wall complete with 10 cm/11.4 cm wide bitumen felt type 3 grade 1.	100 metre	3.86
14.4.4	Brick work 7 cm thick with bricks of class designation 75 in cement mortar 1 : 3 (1 cement : 3 coarse sand) in superstructure.	100 sq m	9.23
14.4.5	Brick work 7 cm thick with bricks of class designation 50 in cement mortar 1 : 3 (1 cement : 3 coarse sand) in superstructure.	100 sq m	9.23
14.4.6	Brick work in plain arches in superstructure including centring and shuttering complete for span upto 6 metres with :		
	6A Bricks of class designation 75 in cement mortar 1 : 3 (1 cement : 3 coarse sand)	cum	1.28
14.4.7	Brick work in gauged arches in superstructure in cement mortar 1 : 4 (1 cement: 4 coarse sand) including centring and shuttering complete, span upto 6 metres with :		
	7A Bricks of class designation 75	cum	0.95
	7B Bricks of class designation 50	cum	0.95
	B. HALF BRICK MASONRY		
14.4.8	Half brick masonry with bricks of class designation 75 in foundations and plinth in :		
	8A Cement mortar 1 : 3 (1 cement : 3 coarse sand)	100 sq m	14.28
	8B Cement mortar 1 : 4 (1 cement : 4 coarse sand)	100 sq m	10.64
14.4.9	Providing brick band 10 cm/7.0 cm thick 5 cm/5.7 cm projected from wall face, in bricks of class designation 75 laid in cement mortar 1 : 4 (1 cement : 4 coarse sand).	100 meter	0.380

	C. BRICK TILE WORK		
14.4.10	Tile brick masonry with tile bricks of class designation 100 in foundation and plinth in :		
	10A Cement lime mortar 1 : 1 : 6 (1 cement : 1 lime putty : 6 fine sand)	cum	1.00
	10B Cement lime mortar 1 : 1 : 6 (1 cement : 1 lime putty : 6 coarse sand)	cum	1.00
	10C Cement mortar 1 : 4 (1 cement : 4 fine sand)	cum	1.52
	10D Cement mortar 1 : 6 (1 cement : 6 fine sand).	cum	1.00
	10E Cement mortar 1 : 4 (1 cement : 4 coarse sand)	cum	1.52
	10F Cement mortar 1 : 6 (1 cement : 6 coarse sand)	cum	1.00
14.4.11	Tile brick masonry with tile bricks of class designation 100 in plain arch work in superstructure in cement mortar 1 : 4 (1 cement : 4 coarse sand) including centring and shuttering complete.	cum	1.33
14.4.12	Tile brick masonry with tile bricks of class designation 100 in gauged arch work in superstructure in cement mortar 1 : 4 (1 cement : 4 coarse sand) including centring and shuttering complete. cum 1.33		
14.4.13	Tile brick masonry work 5 cm thick with tile bricks of class designation 100 in cement mortar 1 : 3 (1 cement : 3 coarse sand) in superstructure.	100 sq m	7.65
	D. HONEY COMB WORK		
14.4.14	Honey-comb brick work 10/11.4 cm thick with bricks of class designation 75 in cement mortar 1 : 4 (1 cement : 4 coarse sand).	100 sq m	6.56
	E. MOULDING AND CORNICES,		
14.4.15	Providing 10 cm/7.0 cm thick and 5 cm/5.7 cm projected string course with bricks of class designation 75 in cement mortar 1 : 4 (1 cement : 4 coarse sand).	100 metre	0.38
14.4.16	Moulding and cornices with brick masonry in cement mortar 1 : 4 (1 cement : 4 coarse sand) girth to be measured in cm and length in running metre.	100 metre per cm girth	0.0353
	F. EXPOSED BRICK WORK		
14.4.17	Brick work with selected bricks of class designation 75 in exposed brick work including making horizontal and vertical grooves 10 mm wide 12 mm deep complete from ground level upto plinth level in cement mortar 1 : 6 (1 cement : 6 fine sand).	cum	0.625
14.4.18	Brick work with selected bricks of class designation 75 in exposed brick work including making horizontal and vertical grooves 10 mm wide 12 mm deep complete from ground level upto plinth level in cement mortar 1 : 6 (1 cement : 6 coarse sand).	cum	0.625
14.4.19	Brick work with machine moulded bricks of class designation 75 in exposed brick work including making horizontal and vertical grooves 10 mm wide 12 mm deep complete from ground level upto plinth level in cement mortar 1 : 6 (1 cement : 6 fine sand).	cum	0.55
14.4.20	Brick work with machine moulded bricks of class designation 75 in exposed brick work including making horizontal and vertical grooves 10 mm wide 12 mm deep complete from ground level upto plinth level in cement mortar 1 : 6 (1 cement : 6 coarse sand).	cum	0.55
14.4.21	Brick work with clay flyash bricks of class designation 75 in superstructure above plinth level to floor five level in :		
	21A Cement lime mortar 1 : 1 : 6 (1 cement : 1 lime putty : 6 fine sand)	cum	0.625

(Contd.)

	21B Cement lime mortar 1 : 2 : 9 (1 cement : 2 lime putty : 9 fine sand)	cum	0.425
	21C Cement lime mortar 1 : 1 : 6 (1 cement : 1 lime putty : 6 coarse sand)	cum	0.625
	21D Cement mortar 1 : 4 (1 cement : 4 fine sand)	cum	0.950
	21E Cement mortar 1 : 6 (1 cement : 6 fine sand)	cum	0.625
	21F Cement mortar 1 : 4 (1 cement : 4 coarse sand)	cum	0.950
	21G Cement mortar 1 : 6 (1 cement : 6 coarse sand)	cum	0.625

Table 14.5. Stone Work

S. No.	*Description of item of work*	*Unit*	*Quantity of cement to be used per unit quantity of work (Quintals)*
	A. RANDOM RUBBLE MASONRY		
14.5.1	Random rubble masonry with hard stone in foundation and plinth including levelling up with cement concrete 1 : 6 : 12 (1 cement : 6 coarse sand : 12 graded stone aggregate 20 mm nominal size) at plinth level with :		
	1A Cement mortar 1 : 6 (1 cement : 6 coarse sand)	cum	0.825
	1B Cement mortar 1 : 6 (1 cement : 6 fine sand)	cum	0.825
	1C Cement lime mortar 1 : 1 : 8 (1 cement : 1 lime putty : 8 fine sand)	cum	0.627
	B. COURSED RUBBLE MASONRY		
14.5.2	Coursed rubble masonry (first sort) with hard stone in foundation and plinth with :		
	2A Cement mortar 1 : 6 (1 cement : 6 coarse sand)	cum	0.750
	2B Cement mortar 1 : 6 (1 cement : 6 fine sand)	cum	0.750
	2C Cement lime mortar 1 : 1 : 8 (1 cement : 1 lime putty : 8 fine sand)	cum	0.570
14.5.3	Coursed rubble masonry (second sort) with hard stone in foundation and plinth with :		
	3A Cement mortar 1 : 6 (1 cement : 6 coarse sand)	cum	0.750
	3B Cement mortar 1 : 6 (1 cement : 6 fine sand)	cum	0.750
	3C Cement lime mortar 1 : 1 : 8 (1 cement : 1 lime putty : 8 fine sand)	cum	0.570
14.5.4	Stone work in plain ashlar in super structure upto floor five level in cement mortar 1 : 6 (1 cement : 6 coarse sand) including pointing with cement mortar 1 : 2 (1 white cement : 2 stone dust) with an admixture of pigment matching the stone shade :		
	4A Red sand stone	cum	0.54
	4B White sand stone	cum	0.54
14.5.5	Stone work plain ashlar in arches in cement mortar 1 : 3 (1 cement : 3 coarse sand) including centring, shuttering and pointing with white cement mortar 1 : 2 (1 white cement : 2 stone dust) with an admixture of pigment matching the stone shade :		
	5A Red sand stone	cum	1.07
	5B White sand stone	cum	1.07

14.5.6	Stone work plain ashlar in domes in cement mortar 1 : 3 (1 cement : 3 coarse sand) including centring, shuttering and pointing with white cement mortar 1 : 2 (1 white cement : 2 stone dust) with an admixture of pigment matching the stone shade :		
	6A Red sand stone	cum	1.07
	6B White sand stone	cum	1.07
14.5.7	Stone work ashlar punched (ordinary) in superstructure upto floor five level in cement mortar 1 : 6 (1 white cement : 6 coarse sand) including pointing with cement mortar 1 : 2 (1 cement : 2 stone dust) with an admixture of pigment matching the stone shade :		
	7A Red sand stone	cum	0.54
	7B White sand stone	cum	0.54
14.5.8	Stone work sunk or moulded or sunk and to moulded upto floor five level in cement mortar 1 : 6 (1 cement : 6 coarse sand) including pointing with white cement mortar 1 : 2 (1 white cement : 2 stone dust) with an admixture of pigment matching the stone shade :		
	8A Red sand stone	cum	0.54
	8B White sand stone	cum	0.54
14.5.9	Stone work for wall lining etc. (veneer work) over 12 mm thick bed of cement lime mortar 1 : 1 : 6 (1 cement : 1 lime putty : 6 fine sand) including pointing in white cement mortar 1 : 2 (1 white cement : 2 stone dust) with an admixture of pigment matching the stone shade : (To be secured to the backing by means of cramps which shall be paid for separately).	100 sq m	4.53 1.56*
14.5.10	Providing and fixing gun metal cramps of required shape for anchoring stone wall lining to the backing or securing adjacent stones in stone wall lining in cement mortar 1 : 2 (1 cement : 2 fine sand) including making the necessary chases :		
	10A 25 × 6 mm – 30 cm long	each	0.007
	10B 15 × 6 mm – 16.5 cm long	each	0.007
14.5.11	Providing and fixing stone dowels 10 × 5 × 2.50 cm cut to double wedge shape as per design in cement mortar 1 : 2 (1 cement : 2 fine sand) including making the necessary chases.	each	0.007
14.5.12	Providing and fixing copper pins 7.5 cm long 6 mm diameter for securing adjacent stones in stone wall lining in cement mortar 1 : 2 (1 cement : 2 fine sand) including making the necessary chases.	each	0.007
14.5.13	Providing and fixing sloping chajja of stone 40 mm thick and upto 80 cm wide beyond the wall as measured along the slope in cement mortar 1 : 4 (1 cement : 4 coarse sand) with 12 mm diameter anchoring steel bar 45 cm long fixed in each stone and supported on and including with bricks cove of class designation 75 in cement mortar 1 : 4 (1 cement : 4 coarse sand) including pointing in cement mortar 1 : 2 (1 white cement : 2 stone dust) with an admixture of pigment matching the stone shade :		
	(1) Red sand stone :		
	13A With F.P.S. bricks	100 sq m	5.59
	(2) White sand stone :		
	13B With F.P.S. bricks	100 sq m	5.59

(Contd.)

14.5.14	Providing and fixing horizontal chajja of stone 40 mm thick and upto 80 cm projection in cement mortar 1 : 4 (1 cement : 4 coarse sand) including pointing in white cement mortar 1 : 2 (1 white cement : 2 stone dust) with an admixture of pigment matching the stone shade.	100 sq m	4.94 0.03*
14.5.15	30 mm red sand stone sun-shade (chisel-dressed) supported on red sand stone brackets, fixed in walls with cement mortar 1 : 4 (1 cement : 4 coarse sand) including finishing complete.	100 sq m	2.19
14.5.16	Providing and fixing red sand stone brackets 55 × 22.5 × 45 cm sunk and moulded including providing and fixing with 4 Nos. gun metal cramp 25 × 6 mm. 30 cm long and dowel bars 7.5 cm long 6 mm dia as per design.	100 nos.	3.02
14.5.17	Stone work, plain in copings, cornices, string courses and plinth courses, in cement mortar 1 : 6 (1 cement : 6 coarse sand) including pointing with white cement mortar 1 : 2 (1 white cement : 2 stone dust) with an admixture of pigment matching the stone shade.	cum	0.54
14.5.18	30 mm thick red sand stone shelves fixed in walls in cement mortar 1 : 3 (1 cement : 3 coarse sand) including finishing complete.	100 sq m	1.64
14.5.19	30 mm thick red sand stone shelves (chisel dressed) supported on 40 × 40 × 6 mm T or angle iron brackets 0.75 m apart fixed on 15 × 10 × 10 cm blocks of cement concrete 1 : 3 : 6 (1 cement : 3 coarse sand : 6 graded stone aggregate 20 mm nominal size).	100 sq m	0.55
14.5.20	30 mm thick red sand stone shelves (chisel dressed) supported on precast reinforced cement concrete brackets 1 : 2 : 4 (1 cement : 2 coarse sand : 4 graded stone aggregate 12.5 mm nominal size) fixed 0.75 m apart in walls with cement mortar 1 : 4 (1 cement : 4 coarse sand) with section of the bracket 5 × 10 cm at the wall and tapering to 5 × 5 cm at the free end with a loop reinforcement of one 10 mm diameter bar per bracket.	100 sq m	4.30
14.5.21	Wall lining butch work with Dholpur stone 40 mm thick rough facing on the exposed surface with stone strips of minimum length 230 mm and required width including embedding every tenth layer and bottom most layer in masonry or concrete after making necessary chases of size 75 × 75 mm and by providing layer of 75 mm thick strips i/c 12 mm thick bed of cement mortar 1 : 3 (1 cement : 3 coarsie sand) i/c ruled pointing in cement mortar 1 : 2 (1 white cement : 2 stone dust) with an admixture of pigment to match the shade of stone complete as per direction of Engineer-in-charge.	100 sq m	15.50 1.70*
14.5.22	Stone work for wall lining etc. (Veneer work) over 12 mm thick bed of cement mortar 1 : 3 (1 cement: 3 coarse sand) and jointed with grey cement slurry @ 3.30 kg/sq m. including rubbing and polishing complete. (To be secured to the backing by means of cramps which shall be paid for separately) : **22A** Kota stone slabs rough chiselled **22B** 25 mm thick	100 sq m	13.744
14.5.23	Stone tile work for wall lining with special adhesive like araldite or equivalent over 12 mm thick bed of cement mortar 1 : 3 (1 cement : 3 coarse sand) including pointing in white cement with an admixture of pigment to match the stone shade : **23A** 8 mm thick (mirror polished and machine cut edge) **23B** Granite black stone	100 sq m	10.44 1.70*

*White Cement

Table 14.6. Marble Work

S. No.	*Description of item of work*	*Unit*	*Quantity of cement to be used per unit quantity of work (Quintals)*
14.6.1	Marble work (table rubbed and polished) for wall lining (veneer work) in cement mortar 1 : 3 (1 cement: 3 coarse sand) including pointing with white cement mortar 1 : 2 (1 white cement : 2 marble dust) with an admixture of pigment to match the marble shade : (To be secured to the backing by means of cramps which shall be paid for separately) :		
	(1) White Marble—Raj Nagar Plain		
	1A 18 mm thick	100 sq m	8.67 + 1.70
	1B 30 mm thick	100 sq m	8.67 + 1.70
14.6.2	Providing and fixing 20 mm thick mirror polished, machine cut for kitchen platforms, vanity counters facias and similar locations of required size of approved shade colour and texture laid over 20 mm thick base cement mortar 1 : 4 (1 cement : 4 coarse sand) with joints treated with white cement, mixed with matching pigment, epoxy touch ups, including rubbing, curing etc. complete at all levels :		
	(1) Abu plain white marble		
	2A Area of each slab upto 0.10 sq m.	100 sq m	2.85
	2B Area of each slab over 0.10 sq m but upto 0.20 sq m	100 sq m	5.70
	2C Area of each slab over 0.2 sq m but upto 0.5 sq m	100 sq m	5.32
	(2) Abu plain white		
	2D Area of each slab over 0.5 sq m but upto 1.0 sq m	100 sq m	5.32
	(3) Abu plain white		
	2E Area of each slab over 1.0 sq m but upto 2.0 sq m	100 sq m	5.13
	(4) Abu plain white		
14.6.3	Extra for fixing marble/granite stone over and above corresponding basic item in facia and drops of width upto 150 mm with expoxy resin based (Araldite or equivalent) adhesive including cleaning etc. complete.	100 metres	1.27
14.6.4	Providing and fixing cramps of required size and shapes in RCC/ CC with cement mortar 1 : 2 (1 cement : 2 fine sand) including drilling necessary hole in stones and embedding the cramp in the hole (fastener to be paid separately) :		
	4A Gunmetal cramps	kg.	0.0635
	4B Stainless steel cramps	kg.	0.0701
14.6.5	Providing and fixing gun metal cramps 25 × 6 mm, 30 cm long as per design in cement mortar 1 : 2 (1 cement : 2 fine sand) including making necessary chases.	each	0.007
14.6.6	Providing and fixing gun metal cramps 25 × 6 mm, 30 cm long as per design in cement mortar 1 : 2 (1 cement : 2 fine sand) including making necessary chases.	each	0.007
14.6.7	Providing and fixing copper 7.5 cm long of 6 mm diameter in cement mortar 1 : 2 (1 cement : 2 fine sand) including making necessary chases.	each	0.007

(Contd.)

14.6.8	Providing and fixing stone dowel 10 × 5 × 2.5 cm cut to double wedge shape as per design, in cement mortar 1 : 2 (1 cement : 2 fine sand) including making necessary chases.	each	0.007
14.6.9	Stone tile (polished) work for wall lining over 12 mm thick bed of cement mortar 1 : 3 (1 cement : 3 coarse sand) and cement slurry @ 3.3 kg/sq m including pointing in white cement complete:		
	(1) Doongri Adanga marble :		
	9A 20 mm thick	100 sq m	10.44 + 1.70*

*White Cement

Table 14.7. Wood Work

S. No.	*Description of item of work*	*Unit*	*Quantity of cement to be used per unit quantity of work (Quintals)*
14.7.1	Providing 2nd class 50 × 50 × 50 mm teak wood plugs including cutting brick work and fixing in cement mortar 1 : 3 (1 cement : 3 sand).	100 nos.	0.01
14.7.2	Providing and fixing of (all kinds and thickness except jamb lining) wooden lining and wooden plugs complete with necessary screws.	100 sq m	0.055
14.7.3	Providing and fixing 25 mm plain Second class teak wood skirting with necessary screws priming coat on unexposed surfaces.	100 sq m	0.17
14.7.4	Providing and fixing 19 mm thick 150 mm wide pelmet with curtain rod and bracket including fixing with 25 × 3 mm M.S. flat 10 cm long and plug etc. complete.	per 100 metre	0.01
14.7.5	Providing and fixing curtain road with brackets, plugs etc.	per 100 metre	0.01
14.7.6	Providing and fixing iron or Aluminium brackets.	100 nos.	0.66
14.7.7	Providing 40 × 3 mm flat iron hold fast 40 cm long including fixing to frame with 10 mm dia. bolts nuts and wooden plugs and embedding in cement concrete block 30 × 10 × 15 cm 1 : 3 : 6 mix (1 cement : 3 sand : 6 graded stone aggregate 20 mm nominal size).	100 nos.	1.10

Table 14.8. Steel Work

S. No.	*Description of item of work*	*Unit*	*Quantity of cement to be used per unit quantity of work (Quintals)*
14.8.1	Providing and fixing M.S. sheet sliding shutter/garage door/rooling shutters.	100 sq m	0.35
14.8.2	Providing and fixing steel glazed doors, windows and ventilators of standard rolled steel sections, joints mitred and welded with 15 × 3 mm lugs 10 cm long embedded in cement concrete blocks 15 cm × 10 cm × 10 cm size, of 1 : 3 : 6 (1 cement: 3 sand :		

	6 graded stone aggregate 20 mm nominal size) or with wooden plugs and screws or rawl plugs and screws or with fixing clips or with bolts and nuts including providing and fixing of glass panes with glazing clips and specials metal sash putty or metal beading with screws.	100 sq m	1.30
14.8.3	Providing and fixing T Iron frames for doors, windows and ventilators, of mild steel tee sections, joints mitred and welded with 15 × 3 mm lugs 10 cm long embedded in cement concrete blocks 15 cm × 10 cm × 10 cm size, of 1 : 3 : 6 (1 cement : 3 sand : 6 graded stone aggregate 20 mm nominal size).	100 kgs.	0.11
14.8.4	Providing and fixing 20 × 6 mm mild steel 15 cm long clamps for securing chick tops.	100 nos.	0.05
14.8.5	Providing and fixing mild steel rings of 6 mm round bar and 40 mm internal dia for fastening ropes of chicks.	100 nos.	0.05

Table 14.9. Flooring

S. No.	*Description of item of work*	*Unit*	*Quantity of cement to be used per unit quantity of work (Quintals)*
	A. BRICK FLOORING (WITH MODULAR/FPS BRICKS)		
14.9.1	In cement mortar 1 : 4 (1 cement : 4 coarse sand) including cement slurry.	sq m	0.1850
14.9.2	In cement mortar 1 : 6 (1 cement : 6 fine sand) including cement slurry.	sq m	0.1285
	B. CEMENT CONCRETE FLOORING		
14.9.3	Flooring 1 : 2 : 4 (1 cement : 2 sand : 4 graded stone aggregate) finished with a floating coat of neat cement including cement slurry but excluding cost of nosing of edges and strips etc. but excluding cost of nosing of steps etc. complete :		
	3A 25 mm thick with 12.5 mm nominal size stone aggregate	sq m	0.1220
	3B 40 mm thick with 20 mm nominal size stone aggregate	sq m	0.17
	3C 50 mm thick with 20 mm nominal size stone aggregate	sq m	0.202
	3D 75 mm thick with 20 mm nominal size stone aggregate	sq m	0.282
14.9.4	40 mm thick red oxide flooring under layer 30 mm thick cement concrete 1 : 2 : 4 (1 cement : 2 sand : 4 graded stone aggregate 12.5 mm nominal size) and top layer of 10 mm thick plaster of cement red oxide mix (using 3.5 kg of red oxide of iron per 50 kg. of cement) 1 : 3 (1 cement : 3 coarse sand) finished with a floating coat of neat cement red oxide mix of same proportion including cement slurry but excluding the cost of nosing of steps etc. complete.	sq m	0.219
14.9.5	52 mm thick with metallic concrete hardner topping under layer of cement concrete 1 : 2 : 4 (1 cement : 2 sand : 4 graded stone aggregate 20 mm nominal size) and top layer of 12 mm thick metallic concrete hardner consisting of mix 1 : 2 (1 cement : 2 stone aggregate 6 mm nominal size) by volume with which metallic hardening compound of approved quality is mixed in the ratio of 4 : 1 (4 parts of cement : 1 part of metallic floor hardening compound of approved quality by weight including cement slurry but excluding the cost of nosing of steps etc. complete :		

(*Contd.*)

	5A 52 mm thick with 40 mm thick under layer	sq m	0.231
	5B 62 mm thick with 50 mm thick under layer	sq m	0.263
14.9.6	Cement plaster skirting (upto 30 cm height) with cement mortar 1 : 3 (1 cement : 3 coarse sand) finished with a floating coat of neat cement :		
	6A 18 mm thick	sq m	0.14
	6B 21 mm thick	sq m	0.1551
14.9.7	Red oxide plaster skirting (upto 30 height) with top layer of 6 mm thick plaster of cement mix, using 3.5 kg of red oxide of iron per 50 kg of cement in mortar 1 : 3 (1 cement : 3 coarse sand) finished with a floating coat of cement red oxide mix of same proportion including cement slurry complete :		
	7A 18 mm thick with under layer 12 mm thick cement plaster 1 : 3 (1 cement : 3 coarse sand)	sq m	0.1302
	7B 21 mm thick with under layer 15 mm thick cement plaster 1 : 3 (1 cement : 3 coarse sand)	sq m	0.1444
14.9.8	Pavement with 1 : 2 : 4 (1 cement : 2 coarse sand : 4 graded stone aggregate 20 mm nominal size) including finishing complete.	cum	3.20
	C. TERRAZO FLOORING		
14.9.9	40 mm thick marble chips flooring rubbed and polished to granolithic finish, under layer 34 mm thick cement concrete 1 : 2 : 4 (1 cement : 2 coarse sand : 4 graded stone aggregate 12.5 mm nominal size) and top layer 6 mm thick with white, black, chocolate, grey, yellow or baroda green marble chips of sizes 1 mm to 4 mm nominal size laid in cement marble powder mix 3 : 1 (3 cement : 1 marble powder) by weight in proportion of 4 : 7 (4 cement marble powder mix : 7 marble chips) by volume including cement slurry etc. complete :		
	9A Dark shade/light shade pigment or without any pigment with ordinary cement	sq m	0.1695
	9B Light shade pigment or without any pigment with white cement	sq m	0.129 0.0405*
	9C Medium shade pigment with approximately 50% white cement and 50% ordinary cement	sq m	0.1492 0.0202*
14.9.10	40 mm thick marble chips flooring rubbed and polished to granolithic finish, under layer 31 mm thick cement concrete 1 : 2 : 4 (1 cement : 2 coarse sand : 4 graded stone aggregate 12.5 mm nominal size) and top layer 9 mm thick with white, black, chocolate, grey, yellow or baroda green marble chips of sizes 4 mm to 7 mm nominal size laid in cement marble powder mix 3 : 1 (3 cement : 1 marble powder) by weight in proportion of 4 : 7 (4 cement marble powder mix : 7 marble chips) by volume including cement slurry etc. complete :		
	10A Dark or light shade pigment or without any pigment with ordinary cement	sq m	0.1783
	10B Light shade pigment or without any pigment with white cement	sq m	0.1205 0.0578*
	10C Medius shade pigment with 50% ordinary cement and 50% white cement	sq m	0.1494

14.9.11	40 mm thick marble chips flooring rubbed and polished to granolithic finish, under layer 28 mm thick cement concrete 1 : 2 : 4 (1 cement : 2 coarse sand : 4 graded stone aggregate 12.5 mm nominal size) and top layer 12 mm thick with white, black, chocolate, grey, yellow or baroda green marble chips of sizes 7 mm to 10 mm nominal size laid in cement marble powder mix 3 : 1 (3 cement : 1 marble powder) by weight in proportion of 2 : 3 (2 cement marble powder mix : 3 marble chips) by volume including cement slurry etc. complete :		
	11A Dark shade/light shade pigment or without any pigment with ordinary cement	sq m	0.1907
	11B Light shade pigment or any without any pigment with white cement	sq m	0.1097 0.081*
	11C Medium shade pigment with 50% white cement and 50% ordinary cement	sq m	0.1502 0.0405*
14.9.12	Marble chips skirting (upto 30 cm height) rubbed and polished to granolithic finish, top layer 6 mm thick with white, black, chocolate, grey, yellow or baroda greert marble chips of sizes from smallest to 4 mm nominal size laid in cement marble powder mix 3 : 1 (3 cement : 1 marble powder) by weight in proportion of 4 : 7 (4 cement marble pewder mix : 7 marble chips) by volume :		
	(1) 18 mm thick with under layer 12 mm thick, cement plaster 1 : 3 (1 cement : 3 coarse sand)		
	12A Dark shade/light shade pigment or without any pigment with ordinary cement	sq m	0.1292
	12B Light shade pigment or no pigment with white cement	sq m	0.0887 0.0405*
	12C Medium shade pigment with 50% white cement and 50% ordinary cement	sq m	0.109 0.0203*
	(2) 21 mm thick with under layer 15 mm thick, cement plaster 1 : 3 (1 cement : 3 coarse sand)		
	12D Dark shade/light shade pigment or without any pigment with ordinary cement	sq m	0.1435
	12E Light shade pigment or no pigment with white cement	sq m	0.1030 0.0405*
	12F Medium shade pigment with 50% white cement and 50% ordinary cement	sq m	0.1230 0.0203*
14.9.13	Special surface finishing to treads, risers and ends of concrete steps and like.	sq m	0.0220
14.9.14	Crazy marble stone flooring including filling the gaps with cement marble chips mixture (3 parts of cement : 1 part of marble powder) by weight in the proportion of 4 : 7 (4 cement marble powder mix : 7 marble chips) by volume and under layer of 25 mm thick cement concrete 1 : 2 : 4 (1 cement : 2 sand : 4 graded stone aggregate 12.5 mm nominal size) rubbing, polishing and cement slurry etc. complete :		
	14A 20 mm thick	sq m	0.1200 0.0405*
	14B 30 mm thick	sq m	0.1200 0.0610*
	14C 40 mm thick	sq m	0.1200 0.0810*

(Contd.)

	D. TILE FLOORING		
14.9.15	Precast terrazo tiles 20 mm thick with white black or white and black marble chips of sizes upto 6 mm laid in floors, treads of steps and landings, jointed with neat cement slurry mixed with pigment to match the shade of the tiles including rubbing and polishing complete with precast tiles on 30 mm thick bed of :		
	15A Lime mortar 1 : 1 : 2 or 1 : 3 Light shade using white cement	sq m	0.044 0.044*
	15B Medium shade using 50% white cement and 50% ordinary cement	sq m	0.0660 0.0220*
	15C Dark shade or without pigment using ordinary cement	sq m	0.0880
14.9.16	Precast terrazo tiles 20 mm thick with marble chips of sizes upto 6 mm in skirting and risers of steps not exceeding 30 cm in height and on walls, laid on 12 mm thick cement plaster 1 : 3 (1 cement : 3 sand) jointed with neat cement slurry :		
	16A Light shade using white cement	sq m	0.0734 0.066*
	16B Medium shade using 50% white cement and 50% ordinary cement	sq m	0.1064 0.033*
	16C Dark shade or without any pigment using ordinary cement	sq m	0.1394
	E. CHEQUERED TERRAZO TILE FLOORING		
14.9.17	Chequered terrazo tiles 22 mm thick with marble chips of sizes upto 6 mm in floors, jointed with neat cement slurry mixed with pigment to match the shade of the tiles including rubbing, polishing, complete on 28 mm thick bed of lime mortar 1 : 1 : 2 or 1 : 3 :		
	17A Light shade using white cement	sq m	0.044 0.048*
	17B Medium shade using 50% white cement and 50% ordinary cement	sq m	0.068 0.024*
	17C Dark shade or without any pigment using ordinary cement	sq m	0.092
14.9.18	Chequered terrazo tiles 30 mm thick with marble chips upto 6 mm in stairs, treads jointed with neat cement slurry mixed with pigment to match the shade of the tiles including rubbing, polishing, rounding of nosing etc. complete on 20 mm thick bed of :		
	(1) Lime mortar 1 : 1 : 1 (1 lime putty : 1 surkhi : 1 coarse sand)		
	18A Light shade using white cement	sq m	0.044 0.066*
	18B Medium shade using 50% white cement and 50% ordinary cement	sq m	0.077 0.033*
	18C Dark shade or without any pigment using ordinary cement	sq m	0.110
	(2) Cement mortar 1 : 4 (1 cement : 4 coarse sand)		

	18D Light shade using white cement	sq m	0.1291 0.066*
	18E Medium shades using 50% white cement and 50% ordinary cement	sq m	0.1621 0.033*
	18F Dark shade or without any pigment using ordinary cement	sq m	0.1951
14.9.19	White glazed tiles 5.6 or 7 mm thick in flooring treads risers of steps skirting and dado on 12 mm thick cement plaster 1 : 3 (1 cement : 3 sand) in base and jointed with white cement slurry etc.	sq m	0.0942 0.0250*
14.9.20	Providing and fixing 50 mm internal and external angles of glazed tiles.	metre	0.0052 0.0012*
	F. MARBLE STONE FLOORING		
14.9.21	Marble stone slab flooring with 20 mm thick marble stone over 20 mm thick base of lime mortar 1 : 1 : 1 (1 lime putty : 1 surkhi : 1 sand) and jointed with ordinary cement slurry etc. (all marble slabs) :		
	21A 20 mm thick	sq m	0.050
	21B 30 mm thick	sq m	0.0512
	21C 40 mm thick	sq m	0.0536
14.9.22	Marble stone slab flooring with 20 mm thick marble stone over 20 mm thick base of cement mortar 1 : 4 (1 cement : 4 sand) and jointed with ordinary cement slurry etc. (all marble slabs) :		
	22A 20 mm thick	sq m	0.13512
	22B 30 mm thick	sq m	0.1363
	22C 40 mm thick	sq m	0.1387
14.9.23	Extra if white cement slurry is used instead of ordinary cement slurry in joints of marble stone flooring.	sq m	0.0076*
14.9.24	Marble slab 30 mm thick in risers of steps, skirting, dado, wall and pillars, laid on 12 mm thick cement mortar 1 : 3 (1 cement : 3 sand) and jointed with ordinary cement slurry.	sq m	0.1234
	G. KOTA STONE FLOORING		
14.9.25	Kota stone slab flooring over 20 mm thick base lime mortar 1 : 1 : 1 (1 lime putty : 1 surkhi : 1 sand) and jointed with neat cement slurry etc.		
	25A 25 mm thick	sq m	0.0640
	25B 30 mm thick	sq m	0.0680
	25C 40 mm thick	sq m	0.0760
14.9.26	Kota stone slab flooring over 20 mm thick base of cement mortar 1 : 4 (1 cement : 4 sand) and jointed with neat cement slurry etc.		
	26A 25 mm thick	sq m	0.1491
	26B 30 mm thick	sq m	0.1531
	26C 40 mm thick	sq m	0.1611
14.9.27	Kota stone slab 25 mm thick in risers of steps, skirting dado and pillar, laid on 12 mm thick cement mortar 1 : 3 (1 cement : 3 sand) and jointed with neat cement slurry etc.	sq m	0.1374

(Contd.)

	H. SAND STONE FLOORING		
14.9.28	40 mm thick sand stone flooring over 20 mm thick base of cement mortar 1 : 5 (1 cement : 5 sand) with joints finished flush.	sq m	0.0775
14.9.29	40 mm thick sand stone flooring over 20 mm thick base of cement mortar 1 : 5 (1 cement : 5 sand) including pointing with cement mortar 1 : 2 (1 cement : 2 stone dust).	sq m	0.0931
14.9.30	40 mm thick sand stone flooring over 20 mm thick base of lime mortar 1 : 1 : 1 (1 lime : 1 surkhi : 1 sand) including pointing with cement mortar 1 : 2 (1 cement : 2 stone dust).	sq m	0.0156
14.9.31	40 mm thick fine dressed and rubbed stone flooring over 20 mm thick base of cement mortar 1 : 5 (1 cement : 5 sand) with joints 5 mm thick finished flush.	sq m	0.0828
14.9.32	40 mm thick fine dressed and rubbed stone flooring over 20 mm thick base of cement mortar 1 : 5 (1 cement : 5 sand) with joints 5 mm thick including pointing with cement mortar 1 : 2 (1 cement : 2 stone dust).	sq m	0.0984
14.9.33	Precast terrazo tiles 20 mm thick with marble chips of sizes upto 6 mm laid in floors and landings jointed with neat cement slurry mixed with pigment to match the shade of the tiles, including rubbing and polishing with precast tiles on 20 mm thick bed of cement mortar 1 : 4 (1 cement : 4 coarse sand) :		
	33A Light shade using white cement	sq m	0.129 0.044*
	33B Medium shade using 50% white cement and 50% ordinary cement	sq m	0.151 0.022
	33C Dark shade or no shade using ordinary cement	sq m	0.173
14.9.34	Chequered terrazo tiles 22 mm thick with marble chips of sizes upto 6 mm in floors jointed with neat cement slurry on 20 mm thick bed of cement mortar 1 : 4 (1 cement : 4 coarse sand) :		
	34A Light shade using white cement	sq m	0.129 0.044*
	34B Medium shade using 50% white cement and 50% ordinary cement	sq m	0.151 0.022*
	34C Dark shade or no shade using ordinary cement	sq m	0.173
14.9.35	Providing and laying in floors matt finish ceramic tiles 10 mm thick laid on 20 mm thick cement 1 : 4 (1 cement : 4 coarse sand) including grouting joints with white cement.	sq m	0.1242 0.025*
14.9.36	Providing and laying acid and alkali resistant tiles using acid and alkali resisting mortar bedding and jointing filled with acid/ alkali resistant cement :		
	36A In floors on a bed of 10 mm thick acid proof cement mortar 1 : 4 (1 acid proof cement : 4 sand)	sq m	0.0786**
	36B In dados on 12 mm thick acid proof cement mortar 1 : 4 (1 acid proof cement : 4 sand)	sq m	0.0862**
14.9.37	Tile work in skirting, risers of steps and dado on 12 mm thick bed of cement mortar 1 : 3 (1 cement : 3 sand) jointed with grey cement slurry @ 3.3. kg/sq m including pointing in white cement mixed with pigment.	sq m	0.1044 0.025*

* White Cement

** Acid alkali resistant cement

Table 14.10. Roofing

S. No.	*Description*	*Unit*	*Quantity of cement to be used per unit quantity of work (Quintals)*
14.10.1	10 cm thick (average) mud phuska of damped brick earth on roofs laid to slope consolidated and plastered with 25 mm thick mud mortar mixed with bhusa at 35 kgs, per cubic metre of earth and gobri leaping with mix 1 : 1 (1 clay : 1 cow dung) and covered with flat brick tiles grouted with cement mortar 1 : 3 (1 cement : 3 fine sand) and finished neat :		
	1A With F.P.S. brick tiles.	100 sq m	3.11
14.10.2	Providing and laying brick tiles over mumty roof grouted with cement mortar 1 : 3 (1 cement : 3 fine sand) over 12 mm layer of cement mortar 1 : 3 (1 cement : 3 fine sand) and finished neat :		
	2A With F.P.S. brick tiles	100 sq m	9.13
14.10.3	Lime concrete terracing on roofs average thickness 10 cm laid to fall with 25 mm nominal size brick ballast and 50% lime mortar 1 : 2 (1 lime putty : 2 surkhi) rammed and finished with gur and belgri treatment complete and covered with flat brick tiles of designation 100 grouted with cement mortar 1 : 3 (1 cement : 3 fine sand) over 12 mm layer of cement mortar 1 : 3 (1 cement : 3 fine sand) and finished neat :		
	3A With F.P.S. brick tiles	100 sq m	9.13
14.10.4	Providing and laying pressed clay tiles as approved pattern 20 mm nominal thickness and of approved size on roofs jointed with cement mortar 1 : 4 (1 cement : 4 coarse sand) mixed with 2% integral water proofing compound laid over a bed of 20 mm thick cement mortar 1 : 4 (1 cement : 4 coarse sand) and finished neat complete.	100 sq m	19.76
14.10.5	Providing gola 75 × 75 mm in cement concrete 1 : 2 : 4 (1 cement : 2 coarse sand : 4 graded stone ballast 10 mm nominal size) including finishing with cement mortar 1 : 3 (1 cement : 3 fine sand).	metre	0.031
14.10.6	Making Khurras 45 × 45 cm with average minimum thickness of 5 cm of cement concrete 1 : 2 : 4 (1 cement : 2 coarse sand : 4 graded stone aggregate of 20 mm nominal size) finished with 12 mm cement plaster 1 : 3 (1 cement : 3 coarse sand) and a coat of neat cement rounding the edges and making and finishing the outlet complete.	each	0.0116
14.10.7	Providing stone slabs for roofing and laying them in cement mortar 1 : 4 (1 cement : 4 coarse sand) over wooden karries of RCC battens (Karries and battens to be paid separately) including pointing the ceiling with cement mortar 1 : 3 (1 cement : 3 fine sand) :		
	7A 40 mm thick slab	100 sq m	0.67
	7B 45 mm thick slab	100 sq m	0.76
	7C 50 mm thick slab	100 sq m	0.80

(*Contd.*)

14.10.8	Providing and fixing on wall face C.I. rain water pipes including filling the joints with spun yarn, soaked in neat cement slurry and cement mortar 1 : 2 (1 cement : 2 fine sand) :		
	8A 75 mm dia. pipe	100 metre	0.066
	8B 100 mm dia. pipe	100 metre	0.088
	8C 150 mm dia. pipe	100 metre	0.132
14.10.9	Providing and fixing M.S. holder bat clamps of approved design to C.I. or S.C.I. pipes (of any diameter) embedded in and including cement concrete blocks 10 × 10 × 10 cm of 1 : 2 : 4 mix (1 cement : 2 coarse sand : 4 graded stone aggregate 20 mm nominal size) and cost of including holes and making good the walls etc.	each	0.0032
14.10.10	Providing and fixing on wall face C.I. accessories for rain water pipes including filling the joints with spun yarn soaked in neat cement slurry and cement mortar 1 : 2 (1 cement : 2 fine sand) :		
	10A 75 mm dia. C.I. plain bend	each	0.0026
	10B 100 mm dia. C.I. plain bend	each	0.0031
	10C 150 mm dia. C.I. plain bend	each	0.0051
	10D 75 mm dia. C.I. head flat or corner type corner type	each	0.0015
	10E 100 cm dia. C.I. head flat or corner type	each	0.0015
	10F 150 mm C.I. head flat or corner type	each	0.0026
	10G 75 mm dia. C.I. plain shoe	each	0.0015
	10H 100 mm dia. C.I. plain shoe	each	0.0015
	10I 150 mm dia. C.I. plain shoe	each	0.0026
	10J 75 mm dia. C.I. single branch (plain)	each	0.0026
	10K 100 mm dia. C.I. single branch (plain)	each	0.0051
	10L 150 mm dia. C.I. single branch (plain)	each	0.0051
	10M 75 mm dia. C.I. double branch (plain)	each	0.0039
	10N 100 mm dia. C.I. double branch (plain)	each	0.0046
	10O C.I. off sets (plain) 75 mm dia. 55 mm projection	each	0.0026
	10P C.I. off sets (plain) 75 mm dia. 75 mm projection	each	0.0026
	10Q C.I. off sets (plain) 75 mm dia. 115 mm projection	each	0.0026
	10R C.I. off sets (plain) 75 mm dia. 150 mm projection	each	0.0026
	10S C.I. off sets (plain) 100 mm dia. 55 mm projection	each	0.0031
	10T C.I. off sets (plain) 100 mm dia. 75 mm projection	each	0.003
14.10.11	Providing, fixing and embedding sand cast iron rain water pipes on wall face in the masonry surrounded with 12 mm thick cement mortar of the same mix as that of masonry :		
	11A 75 mm dia. pipe	100 metre	0.035
	11B 100 mm dia. pipe	100 metre	0.047
	11C 150 mm dia. pipe	100 metre	0.070
14.10.12	Providing, fixing and embedding sand cast iron accessories for rain water pipes in masonry surrounded with 12 mm thick cement mortar of the same mix as that of masonry :		
	12A S.C.I. plain bend 75 mm dia.	each	0.0026
	12B S.C.I. plain bend 100 mm dia.	each	0.0031
	12C S.C.I. plain bend 150 mm dia.	each	0.0051
	12D S.C.I. plain shoe 75 mm dia.	each	0.0015

Item	Sub	Description	Unit	50 mm	80 mm	100 mm
	12E	S.C.I. plain shoe 100 mm dia.	each			0.0015
	12F	S.C.I. plain shoe 150 mm dia.	each			0.0026
14.10.13		Providing and fixing on wall face asbestos cement rain water pipes including jointing with spun yarn soaked in bitumen and cement mortar 1 : 2 (1 cement : 2 coarse sand) complete :				
	13A	50 mm dia.	100 metre			0.075
	13B	80 mm dia.	100 metre			0.125
	13C	100 mm dia.	100 metre			0.150
14.10.14		Providing and fixing for A.C. pipe (of any diameter) wall plugs and standard holder bat clamps comprising of two semi-circular halves of flat and cast iron base screwed on wooden plugs.	each			0.0002
14.10.15		Providing and fixing on wall face asbestos cement fittings for rain water pipe including jointing with spun yarn soaked in bitumen and cement mortar 1 : 2 (1 cement : 2 coarse sand) :		50 mm	80 mm	100 mm
	15A	Bend of required degree with door or without door	each	0.0036	0.0058	0.0073
	15B	offset 52.2 mm projection	each	0.0029	0.0045	0.0058
	15C	Offset 76.2 mm projection	each	0.0029	0.0045	0.0058
	15D	Offset 114.3 mm projection	each	0.0029	0.0045	0.0058
	15E	Offset 152.4 mm projection	each	0.0029	0.0045	0.0058
	15F	Offset 228.6 mm projection	each	0.0029	0.0045	0.0058
	15G	Offset 304.8 mm projection	each	—	0.0045	0.0058
	15H	Offset 457.2 mm projection	each	—	0.0045	0.0058
	15I	Offset 609.6 mm projection	each	—	—	0.0058
	15J	Junction equal single of required degree with or without door	each	0.0036	0.0058	0.0073
	15K	Junction equal, double with or without door of required degree	each	0.0054	0.0087	0.011
	15L	Standard shoe.	each	0.0020	0.0029	0.0029
	15M	Hexagonal rainwater head :				
	15N	250 × 200 mm, 80 mm dia or 100 mm dia.	each			0.0029
	15O	300 × 250 mm, 80 mm dia or 100 mm dia.	each			0.0029
	15P	400 × 300 mm, 100 mm dia	each			0.0029
	15Q	Pentagonal rain water head 230 × 200 mm, 80 or 100 mm dia.	each			0.0029
14.10.16		Grading roof for water proofing treatment with :				
	16A	C.C. 1 : 2 : 4 (1 cement : 2 coarse sand : 4 stone aggregate 20 mm nominal size)	cum			3.20
	16B	Cement mortar 1 : 3	cum			5.10
	16C	Cement mortar 1 : 4	cum			3.80

Table 14.11. FINISHING

S. No.	*Description*	*Unit*	*Quantity of cement to be used per unit quantity of work (Quintals)*
	A. CEMENT PLASTER		
14.11.1	12 mm 1 : 4 (1 cement : 4 sand)	100 sq m	5.47
14.11.2	12 mm 1 : 6 (1 cement : 6 sand)	100 sq m	3.60
14.11.3	15 mm 1 : 4 (1 cement : 4 sand)	100 sq m	6.54
14.11.4	15 mm 1 : 6 (1 cement : 6 sand)	100 sq m	4.30
14.11.5	20 mm 1 : 4 (1 cement : 4 sand)	100 sq m	8.51
14.11.6	20 mm 1 : 6 (1 cement : 6 sand)	100 sq m	5.60
	B. CEMENT PLASTER WITH A FLOATING COAT OF NEAT CEMENT		
14.11.7	12 mm 1 : 3 (1 cement : 3 sand)	100 sq m	9.54
14.11.8	12 mm 1 : 4 (1 cement : 4 sand)	100 sq m	7.67
14.11.9	15 mm 1 : 3 (1 cement : 3 sand)	100 sq m	10.97
14.11.10	15 mm 1 : 4 (1 cement : 4 sand)	100 sq m	8.74
14.11.11	20 mm 1 : 3 (1 cement : 3 sand)	100 sq m	13.62
14.11.12	20 mm 1 : 4 (1 cement : 4 sand)	100 sq m	10.71
	C. CEMENT PLASTER IN TWO COATS		
14.11.13	18 mm cement plaster in two coats under layer 12 mm cement plaster 1 : 5 (1 cement : 5 sand) and top layer 6 mm thick cement plaster 1 : 6 (1 cement : 6 sand)	100 sq m	6.26
14.11.14	18 mm cement plaster in two coats under layer 12 mm cement plaster 1 : 5 (1 cement : 5 sand) and top layer 6 mm thick cement plaster 1 : 3 (1 cement : 3 sand)	100 sq m	8.13
14.11.15	12 mm cement plaster 1 : 2 (1 cement : 2 stone dust)	100 sq m	9.79
14.11.16	15 mm cement plaster 1 : 2 (1 cement : 2 stone dust)	100 sq m	11.70
14.11.17	20 mm cement plaster 1 : 2 (1 cement : 2 stone dust)	100 sq m	15.23
	D. 6 MM CEMENT PLASTER		
14.11.18	6 mm cement plaster to ceiling 1 : 4 (1 cement : 4 sand)	100 sq m	2.74
14.11.19	6 mm cement plaster to ceiling 1 : 3 (1 cement : 3 sand) finished with a floating coat of neat cement	100 sq m	5.87
14.11.20	Neat cement punning	100 sq m	2.20
	E. CEMENT LIME PLASTER		
14.11.21	12 mm 1 : 1 : 6 (1 cement : 1 lime putty : 6 sand)	100 sq m	3.60
14.11.22	12 mm 1 : 2 : 9 (1 cement : 2 lime putty : 9 sand)	100 sq m	2.45
14.11.23	15 mm 1 : 1 : 6 (1 cement : 1 lime putty : 6 sand)	100 sq m	4.30
14.11.24	15 mm 1 : 2 : 9 (1 cement : 2 lime putty : 9 sand)	100 sq m	2.92
14.11.25	18 mm in two coats under layer 12 mm cement plaster 1 : 5 (1 cement : 5 sand) finished with 6 mm cement lime plaster 1 : 1 : 6 (1 cement : 1 lime putty : 6 sand)	100 sq m	6.26

	F. ROUGH CAST PLASTER		
14.11.26	**Rough cast plaster with a mixture of sand and gravel or crushed stone from 2.36 mm to 12.5 mm nominal size dashed over and including the fresh plaster in two layers top layer 10 mm cement plaster 1 : 3 (1 cement : 3 sand) mixed with 10% finely grounded hydrated lime by volume of cement and under layer 12 mm cement plaster :**		
	(1) 1 : 4 (1 cement : 4 sand)		
	26A With ordinary cement finish using ordinary cement	**100 sq m**	**11.59**
	(2) 1 : 5 (1 cement : 5 sand)		
	26B With ordinary cement finish or cement and pigment finish	**100 sq m**	**10.58**
	26C With white cement and pigment finish	**100 sq m**	**4.46 6.12***
	G. PEBBLE DASH PLASTER		
14.11.27	**Pebble dash plaster with a mixture of washed pebble or crushed stone 6 mm to 12.5 mm nominal size dashed over and including fresh plaster in two layers, top layer 10 mm cement plaster 1 : 3 (1 cement : 3 sand) mix with 10% finely grounded hydrated lime and under layer 12 mm cement plaster :**		
	27A 1 : 4 (1 cement : 4 sand)	**100 sq m**	**11.59**
	27B 1 : 5 (1 cement : 5 sand)	**100 sq m**	**10.58**
	27C 1 : 6 (1 cement : 6 sand)	**100 sq m**	**9.72**
	H. SUPERIOR PLASTER		
14.11.28	**18 mm plaster with terrazo finish rubbed and polished complete, under layer 12 mm cement plaster 1 : 3 (1 cement : 3 sand) and top layer 6 mm thick white, black, chocolate, grey, yellow or Baroda green marble chips of size 3 mm and down size laid in cement marble powder mix 3 : 1 (3 cement : 1 marble powder) by weight in proportion of 4 : 7 (4 cement marble powder mix : 7 marble ships) by volume.**	**100 sq m**	**11.64**
14.11.29	**Extra if white cement is used instead of ordinary cement in top layer of 18 mm plastering with terrazo finish.**	**100 sq m**	**4.30 7.34**
	I. ARTIFICIAL RED STONE MARBLE SHADE PLASTER		
14.11.30	**18 mm thick consisting of 12 mm thick under layer of cement plaster 1 : 4 (1 cement : 4 sand) with 6 mm thick finishing coat of cement mortar 1 : 1 : 3 (1 cement : 1 marble dust : 3 stone dust) mixed with red oxide.**	**100 sq m**	**9.47**
14.11.31	**18 mm thick consisting of 12 mm thick under layer of cement plaster 1 : 4 (1 cement : 4 sand) with 6 mm thick middle coat of Makrana lime plaster with lime : marble particle and stone dust in ratio 2 : 1 : 1.**	**100 sq m**	**5.47**
	J. PLAIN OR MOULDED CEMENT MORTAR BANDS		
14.11.32	**12 mm thick in cement mortar 1: 4 (1 cement : 4 sand) all types**	**100 metre 1 cm wide**	**0.053**
14.11.33	**18 mm thick in cement mortar 1:4 (1 cement : 4 sand) all types**	**100 metre 1 cm wide**	**0.076**
14.11.34	**18 mm thick in two coats under layer 12 mm thick with cement mortar 1 : 5 (1 cement : 5 sand) top layer 6 mm thick with cement mortar 1 : 4 (1 cement : 4 sand)**	**100 metre 1 cm wide**	**0.07**

(Contd.)

	K. POINTING ON BRICK WORK		
14.11.35	Flush or ruled or cut or weather pointing on brick work with cement mortar 1 : 3 (1 cement : 3 sand)	100 sq m	1.53
14.11.36	Raised and cut pointing on brick work with cement mortar 1 : 3 1 cement : 3 sand)	100 sq m	2.04
14.11.37	Flush or ruled or cut or weather pointing on brick work with lime mortar 1 : 1 : 3 (1 cement : 1 lime putty : 3 sand)	100 sq m	1.23
14.11.38	Flush or ruled pointing on brick flooring with cement mortar 1 : 3 (1 cement : 3 sand)	100 sq m	1.02
14.11.39	Flush or ruled pointing on brick flooring with cement mortar 1 : 4 (1 cement : 4 sand)	100 sq m	0.76
	L. POINTING ON BRICK TILE WORK		
14.11.40	Flush or ruled or cut or weather pointing on brick tile work with cement mortar 1 : 3 (1 cement : 3 sand)	100 sq m	2.35
14.11.41	Flush or ruled or cut or weather pointing on tile brick work with lime mortar 1 : 1 : 3 (1 cement : 1 lime putty : 3 sand)	100 sq m	1.89
	M. POINTING ON STONE WORK		
14.11.42	Flush or ruled pointing on stone work with cement mortar 1 : 3 (1 cement : 3 sand)	100 sq m	1.17
14.11.43	Raised and cut pointing on stone work with cement mortar 1 : 3 (1 cement : 3 sand)	100 sq m	2.35
14.11.44	Raised and cut pointing on stone work with white cement mortar 1 : 3 (1 white cement : 3 sand)	100 sq m	2.35*
14.11.45	Flush or ruled pointing on stone slabs ceiling with cement mortar 1 : 2 (1 cement : 2 sand)	100 sq m	0.68
14.11.46	Washed stone grit plaster in two layers, under layer 12 mm thick with cement mortar 1 : 4 (1 cement : 4 sand) and top layer 15 mm thick cement plaster 1 : 0.5 : 2 (1 cement : 0.5 sand : 2 stone chipping 10 mm nominal size) including applying cement slurry on the under layer @ 2 kg of cement per sq m.	100 sq m	1.767
	NOTE : Cement consumption for pointing is same for FPS and Modular bricks.		

* White Cement

Table 14.12. Repairs to Building

S. No.	*Description*	*Unit*	*Quantity of cement to be used per unit quantity of work (Quintals)*
14.12.1	Repairs to plaster in patches of 2.5 square metre and under including cutting the patch in proper shape and preparing and plastering the surface of the walls :		
	1A With cement mortar 1 : 4 (1 cement : 4 sand)	100 sq m	6.95
	1B With cement lime mortar 1 : 1 : 7 (cement : lime putty : 7 sand)	100 sq m	4.03
14.12.2	Fixing chowkhats in opening including embedding chowkhat in floor, cutting masonry for fold fasts embedding hold fasts in cement concrete block with cement concrete 1 : 3 : 6 (1 cement : 3 sand : 6 graded stone aggregate 20 mm nominal size) including making good the walls :		

	2A Door chowkhats	each	0.12
	2B Windows chowkhats	each	0.06
	2C Clerestory window chowkhats	each	0.03
14.12.3	Providing and fixing M.S. fan clamps of standard shape and size in existing R.C.C. slab including cutting chase and making good.	each	0.016
14.12.4	Regarding terracing of mud phuska covered with tiles or bricks in cement by dismantling tiles or bricks, removing mud plaster, preparing the surface of mud phuska to proper slope relaying mud plaster gobri leaping and tiles or bricks grouted in cement mortar 1 : 3 (1 cement : 3 sand).	100 sq m	3.11
14.12.5	Replacing sand stone slabs in roofing laid in cement mortar 1 : 4 (1 cement : sand) including necessary repairs and cement pointing with same mortar complete :		
	5A 30 to 40 mm thick	100 sq m	0.668
	5B 45 mm thick	100 sq m	0.744
	5C 50 mm thick	100 sq m	0.78
14.12.6	Renewing wooden battens in roofs, including making good the holes in walls.	cum	0.36
14.12.7	Renewing wooden beams not exceeding 4.0 metres in length in roofs including making good the holes in walls.	cum	0.13
14.12.8	Renewing wooden beams (above 4 metres and up to 5 metres length in roofs including making good the holes in walls.	cum	0.11
14.12.9	Renewing 100 mm dia. 2.5 metres long salwood balli post embedded 60 mm in the ground in a trench 45 cm dia and 75 cm deep filled with cement concrete 1 : 5 : 10 (1 cement : 5 sand : 10 stone aggregate 40 mm nominal size)	each	0.15
14.12.10	Flush pointing with cement mortar 1 : 3 (1 cement : 3 fine sand) on top of brick tiles		
	10A With F.P.S. brick tiles	100 sq m	0.76

Table 14.13. Miscellaneous Building Works

S. No.	*Description*	*Unit*	*Quantity of cement to be used per unit quantity of work (Quintals)*
14.13.1	Making plinth protection 50 mm thick of cement concrete 1 : 3 : 6 (1 cement : 3 sand : 6 graded stone aggregate 20 mm nominal size) over 75 mm bed of dry brick ballast consolidated and grouted with fine sand including finishing the top smooth.	sq m	0.110
14.13.2	Making plinth protection with bricks on edge in cement mortar 1 : 6 (1 cement : 6 sand) and laid on 12 mm thick CM. 1 : 6 (1 cement : 6 sand) over 7.5 cm bed of dry brick aggregate 40 mm nominal size rammed, consolidated and grouted with fine sand and top of bricks pointed with cement mortar 1 : 3 (1 cement : 3 sand).	sq m	0.118

(Contd.)

14.13.3	**Providing and fixing precast reinforced cement concrete urinal partition over all size 105 cm × 60 cm deep and 55 mm thick in cement concrete mix 1 : 2 : 4 (1 cement : 2 coarse sand : 4 graded stone aggregate 6 mm nominal size) reinforced with mild steel bars 6 mm dia at 15 cm centre to centre both ways fixed in walls with cement concrete 1 : 2 : 4 (1 cement : 2 coarse sand : 4 grades stone aggregate 6 mm nominal size) including finishing with 6 mm thick terrazo plaster 1 : 2 (1 part of cement : 2 parts of marble chips of 3 mm thick cement plaster 1 : 3 (1 cement : 3 coarse sand) including finishing complete.**	**each**	**0.18**
14.13.4	**Providing and fixing marble slab white markana 105 × 60 × 2.5 cm thick fixed in urinal partition with cement concrete 1 : 2 : 4 (1 cement : 2 coarse sand : 4 graded stone aggregate 6 mm nominal size) finished smooth.**	**sq m**	**0.016**
14.13.5	**Providing and fixing stone slab table rubbed and polished of size 105 cm × 60 cm deep and 2.5 cm thick fixed in urinal partitions with cement concrete 1 : 2 : 4 (1 cement : 2 coarse sand : 4 stone aggregate 6 mm nominal size) and finished smooth :**		
	5A Raj Nagar Marble Stone	**each**	**0.016**
	5B Granite Stone of approved shade	**each**	**0.016**
14.13.6	**Constructing 90 × 200 × 45 cm deep cupboard with 7.5 × 5 cm frame, 25 mm thick wooden partitions and shelves supported on 25 × 25 mm wooden runners 50 × 20 mm architraves and 25 mm dia wooden curtain rods mounted on wooden brackets, complete including painting or polishing.**	**each**	**0.13***
14.13.7	**Providing and fixing aluminium strip edging to stair case including fixing with rawl-plug and screws with a thin layer of cement mortar 1 : 3 (1 cement : 3 sand) size of strip 57 × 12 × 3 mm or 38 × 12 × 3 mm.**	**metre**	**0.0113**

* White cement

Table 14.14. Road Work

S. No.	*Description of item of work*	*Unit*	*Quantity of cement to be used per unit quantity of work (Quintals)*
	A. FENCING		
14.14.1	**Supplying and laying kerb stone 30 × 20 cm chisel dressed on top and side including fixing in cement mortar 1 : 4 (1 cement : 4 coarse sand) and pointing with cement mortar 1 : 4 (1 cement : 4 fine sand) including making drainage opening, where required.**	**100 metres**	**1.50**
14.14.2	**Providing, laying and fixing channel stones 30 × 10 cm chisel dressed on top and side in cement mortar 1 : 4 (1 cement : 4 coarse sand) along the edge of the road, including pointing with cement mortar 1 : 4 (1 cement : 4 coarse sand).**	**100 metres**	**0.83**
14.14.3	**Supplying at site 1.8 m long R.C.C. standard posts with wooden plugs or 6 mm bar nibs.**	**100 nos.**	**15.59**
14.14.4	**Supplying at site :**		
	4A R.C.C. Standards struts 2.0 metre long	**100 nos.**	**10.80**
	4B R.C.C. Standard rails 2.25 metre long	**100 nos.**	**4.84**
	4C R.C.C. Standard pales 1.25 metre long	**100 nos.**	**1.50**

	B. ROAD SIGNS AND STONES		
14.14.5	Providing and fixing R.C.C. "KEEP LEFT" sign-board of standard design including two or more coats with white zinc paint over a priming coat and lettering with black enamel paint.	each	0.558
14.14.6	Providing and fixing R.C.C. name board of standard design including painting two or more coats with white zinc paint over priming coat :		
	6A Rectangular with posts.	each	0.169
	6B Flat without post for one direction only	each	0.4988
	6C Flat without post for two directions	each	0.544
14.14.7	Providing and fixing 15 cm dia at top 20 cm at bottom and 90 cm high precast reinforced cement concrete 1 : 2 : 4 (1 cement : 2 coarse sand : 4 graded stone aggregate 20 mm nominal size) boundary stone as per standard design including finishing smooth with cement mortar 1 : 3 (1 cement : 3 fine sand) (cost of excavation, refilling and concreting to be paid for separately).	each	0.082
14.14.8	Providing and fixing precast reinforced cement concrete 1 : 2 : 4 (1 cement : 2 coarse sand : 4 graded stone aggregate 20 mm nominal size) kilometre stone as per standard design including finishing smooth in 1 : 3 cement mortar (1 cement : 3 fine sand) but excluding the cost of earth work, concrete in foundation, painting and lettering etc. which shall be paid for separately :		
	8A 35 × 111 × 25 cm size.	each	0.37
	8B 50 × 152.5 × 25 cm size.	each	0.698
	8C 35 × 93.5 × 18 cm size.	each	0.23
	C. CONCRETE PAVEMENTS		
14.14.9	Cement concrete 1 : 2 : 4 (1 cement : 2 coarse sand : 4 graded stone aggregate 40 mm nominal size) in pavements, laid to required slope and camber in panels as required including consolidation finishing and tamping complete.	cum	3.20
14.14.10	Making bell mouth opening/entrance of size 100 × 50 × 50 cm for drainage pipe under footpath including providing cement concrete 1 : 3 : 6 (1 cement : 3 coarse sand : 6 graded stone aggregate 20 mm nominal size) for shape of bell mouth including plastering providing and fixing 100 × 50 × 5 cm size precast R.C.C. slab 1 : 2 : 4 (1 cement : 2 coarse sand : 4 graded stone aggregate 12.5 mm nominal size) reinforced with cold twisted bars reinforcement @ 100 kg per cum of reinforced concrete including plastering with cement mortar 1 : 3 (1 cement : 3 fine sand) of 6 mm thickness on exposed surface of the slab and bell mouth including centring, shuttering and neat cement punning inside the bell mouth etc. all complete.	10 nos.	6.60

Table 14.15. Sanitary Installations

S. No.	*Description*	*Unit*	*Quantity of cement to be used per unit quantity of work (Quintals)*
	A. SANITARY FITTINGS (Complete items)		
14.15.1	Fixing long pan pattern on Orissa pattern squatting pan or pedestal type water closet 10 litre flushing cistern and brackets, G.I. flush pipe or bend with specials and mosquito proof coupling complete including cutting and making good the walls and floors.	each	0.05
14.15.2	Fixing vitreous china flat back or wall corner type, lipped front, urinal basin of 430 × 260 × 350 mm and 340 × 410 × 265 mm size respectively with automatic C.I. flushing cistern with fittings, brackets standard size pipe and spreaders with brass union and G.I. clamps complete, including painting of cistern and fittings, cutting and making good the walls and floors :		
	2A One urinal basin with 5 litre P.V.C. automatic flushing cistern	each	0.025
	2B Range of two urinal basins with 7.5 litre P.V.C. automatic flushing cistern	each	0.04
	2C Range of three urinals with 7.5 litre P.V.C. automatic flushing cistern	each	0.067
	2D Range of four urinal with 10 litre P.V.C. automatic flushing cistern	each	0.095
14.15.3	Fixing white glazed fire clay half stall urinal with automatic C.I. flushing cistern with fittings, C.I. brackets, standard size C.P. brass flush pipe and spreaders with unions and clamps, C.I. trap with outlet grating and the couplings in C.P. brass including painting of cistern and fittings, cutting and making good the walls and floors :		
	3A Single stall urinal with 5 litre P.V.C. automatic flushing cistern	each	0.051
	3B Range of two stall urinals with 7.5 litre P.V.C. automatic flushing cistern	each	0.102
	3C Range of three stall urinals with 10 litre P.V.C. automatic flushing cistern	each	0.153
	3D Range of four stall urinals with 15 litre P.V.C. automatic flushing cistern	each	0.203
14.15.4	Fixing one piece construction white vitreous china squatting plate urinal with an integral longitudinal flushing pipe, automatic flushing cistern with fittings, M.S. brackets, standard size, G.I. flush pipe for back and front flush with standard spreader pipes with fittings, G.I. clamps, and coupling in C.P. brass complete, including painting the cistern and fittings and making good the walls and floors :		
	4A Single squatting plate with 5 litre P.V.C. automatic flushing cistern	each	0.051
	4B Range of squatting plates with 7.5 litre C.I. automatic flushing cistern	each	0.102
	4C Range of three squatting plates with 10 litre C.I. automatic flushing cistern	each	0.153

	4D Range of four squatting plates with 15 litre C.I. automatic flushing cistern	each	0.203
14.15.5	Fixing wash basin with brackets, pillar taps, rubber plug, waste of standard pattern and unions complete including cutting and making good the walls.	each	0.25
14.15.6	Fixing white vitreous chaina pedestal for wash-basin completely recessed at the back for reception of pipes and fittings.	each	0.016*
14.15.7	Fixing sink with brackets, 40 mm rubber plug, brass chain, waste, with necessary unions complete including cutting and making good the walls.	each	0.025
14.15.8	Fixing draining board with skirting and beading, with brackets painted white complete including cutting and making good the walls.	each	0.014
	B. SANITARY FITTINGS (Items separately ordered)		
14.15.9	Fixing long pan pattern or Orissa pattern squatting, or pedestal type W.C. pan.	each	0.025
14.15.10	Fixing a pair of white glazed vitreous chaina foot rests of standard pattern for Indian type W.C. pan.	each	0.005
14.15.11	Fixing flat back or wall corner type lipped front urinal basin of 430 × 260 × 350 mm and 340 × 410 × 265 mm.	each	0.01
14.15.12	Fixing white glazed fire clay stall urinal of standard size	each	0.02
14.15.13	Fixing white vitreous chaina squatting plate urinal with integral longitudinal flush pipe.	each	0.02
14.15.14	Fixing wash basin including making all connections excluding cost of fittings.	each	0.015
14.15.15	Fixing sink including making all connections complete.	each	0.015
14.15.16	Fixing in position 32 mm diameter galvanised steel telescopic flush pipe complete including cutting and making good the walls and floor.	each	0.01
	C. SAND CAST IRON CENTRIFUGALLY CAST (SPUN) IRON PIPE AND FITTINGS		
14.15.17	Fixing M.S. holder bat clamp to 100 mm or 75 mm or 50 mm dia sand cast iron centrifugally cast (spun) iron pipe embedded in cement concrete blocks 10 × 10 × 10 cm of cement concrete 1 : 2 : 4 (1 cement : 2 sand : 4 stone aggregate) including cost of cutting holes and making good the wall etc.	each	0.005
14.15.18	Fixing M.S. stays and clamps for 100 mm or 75 mm or 50 mm diameter sand cast iron centrifugally cast (spun) iron pipe.	each	0.005
14.15.19	Fixing sand cast iron trap of self cleansing design with sand cast iron screwed down or hinged grating with or without vent arm complete including cost of cutting and making good the walls and floor :		
	19A 100 mm in let and 100 mm outlet	each	0.025
	19B 100 mm in let and 75 mm outlet	each	0.025
	19C 100 mm in let and 50 mm outlet	each	0.025
14.15.20	Cutting chase in brick masonry walls for fixing 100 mm diameter sand cast iron/centrifugally cast (spun) iron pipes and making good the same with cement concrete 1 : 3 : 6 (1 cement : 3 sand : 6 stone aggregate) including necessary plaster and pointing in cement mortar 1 : 4 (1 cement : 4 sand) :		
	20A 100 mm dia pipe	100 metre	5.40
	20B 75 mm dia	100 metre	3.70
	20C 50 mm dia	100 metre	1.87

Table 14.16. Water Supply

S. No.	*Description*	*Unit*	*Quantity of cement to be used per unit quantity of work (Quintals)*
14.16.1	Providing and fixing G.I. pipes complete with G.I. fitting and clamps including cutting and making good the walls etc. (internal work) :		
	(1) Exposed on walls		
	1A 15 mm dia	100 metres	0.05
	1B 20 mm dia	100 metres	0.06
	1C 25 mm dia	100 metres	0.07
	1D 32 mm dia	100 metres	0.075
	1E 40 mm dia	100 metres	0.08
	1F 50 mm dia	100 metres	0.08
	1G Concealed pipe including ceiling chases and making good the walls 15, 20 mm nominal bore.	100 metres	0.88
14.16.2	Constructing brick masonry chamber 30 × 30 × 50 cm inside with F.P.S. bricks of class designation 75 in cement mortar 1 : 5 (1 cement : 5 sand) for stop cock with C.I. surface box 100 × 100 × 75 cm (inside) with hinged cover fixed in cement concrete slab 1 : 2 : 4 mix (1 cement : 2 sand : 4 graded stone ballast 20 mm nominal size) necessary excavation, foundation concrete 1 : 5 : 10 mix (1 cement : 5 sand : 10 graded stone ballast 40 mm nominal size) and inside plastering with cement mortar 1 : 3 (1 cement : 3 sand) 12 mm thick finished with a floating coat of neat cement.	each	0.26
14.16.3	Constructing brick masonry chamber 60 × 60 × 75 cm inside with F.P.S. bricks of class designation 75 in cement mortar 1 : 5 (1 cement : 5 sand) for sluice valve with C.I. surface box 100 mm top diameter, 160 mm bottom diameter and 180 mm deep (inside) with chained lid and R.C.C. top slab 1 : 2 : 4 mix (1 cement : 2 sand : 4 graded stone ballast 20 mm nominal size) necessary excavation, foundation concrete 1 : 5 : 10 mix (1 cement : 5 sand : 10 graded stone ballast 40 mm nominal size) and inside plastering with cement mortar 1 : 3 (1 cement : 3 sand) 12 mm thick finished with a floating coat of neat cement complete.	each	1.44
14.16.4	Constructing brick masonry chamber 90 × 90 × 100 cm inside with F.P.S. bricks of class designation 75 in cement mortar 1 : 5 (1 cement : 5 sand) for sluice valve with C.I. surface box 100 mm top diameter, 160 mm bottom diameter and 180 mm deep (inside) with chained lid and R.C.C. top slab 1 : 2 : 4 mix (1 cement : 2 sand : 4 graded stone ballast 20 mm nominal size) necessary excavation, foundation concrete 1 : 5 : 10 mix (1 cement : 5 sand : 10 graded stone ballast 40 mm nominal size) and inside plastering with cement mortar 1 : 3 (1 cement : 3 sand) 12 mm thick finished with a floating coat of neat cement complete.	each	2.48
14.16.5	Constructing brick masonry chamber 120 × 120 × 100 cm inside with F.P.S. bricks of class designation 75 in cement mortar 1 : 5 (1 cement : 5 sand) for sluice valve with C.I. surface box 100 mm top diameter, 160 mm bottom diameter and 180 mm deep (inside)		

	with chained lid and R.C.C. top slab 1 : 2 : 4 mix (1 cement : 2 sand : 4 graded stone ballast 20 mm nominal size) necessary excavation, foundation concrete 1 : 5 : 10 mix (1 cement : 5 sand : 10 graded stone ballast 40 mm nominal size) and inside plastering with cement mortar 1 : 3 (1 cement : 3 sand) 12 mm thick finished with a floating coat of neat cement complete.	each	3.50
14.16.6	Constructing brick masonry chamber 60 × 60 × 75 cm inside with F.P.S. bricks of class designation 75 in cement mortar 1 : 5 (1 cement : 5 sand) for fire hydrants with C.I. surface box 350 × 550 mm top and 165 mm deep (inside) with chained lid and R.C.C. top slab 1 : 2 : 4 mix (1 cement : 2 sand : 4 graded stone ballast 20 mm nominal size) necessary excavation, foundation concrete 1 : 5 : 10 mix (1 cement : 5 sand : 10 graded stone ballast 40 mm nominal size) and inside plastering with cement mortar 1 : 3 (1 cement : 3 sand) 12 mm thick finished with a floating coat of neat cement.	each	1.30
14.16.7	Constructing brick masonry chamber 60 × 45 × 50 cm inside with F.P.S. bricks of class designation 75 in cement mortar 1 : 5 (1 cement : 5 sand) for water meter complete with C.I. double flap surface box 400 × 200 × 200 mm (inside) with locking arrangement and R.C.C. top slab 1 : 2 : 4 mix (1 cement : 2 sand : 4 graded stone ballast 20 mm nominal size) necessary excavation, foundation concrete 1 : 5 : 10 mix (1 cement : 5 sand : 10 graded stone ballast 40 mm nominal size) and inside plastering with cement mortar 1 : 3 (1 cement : 3 sand) 12 mm thick finished with a floating coat of neat cement complete.	each	1.34

Table 14.17. DRAINAGE

S. No.	*Description*	*Unit*	*Quantity of cement to be used per unit quantity of work (Quintals)*
14.17.1	Jointing glazed stone ware pipe grade 'A' with stiff mixture of cement mortar in the proportion of 1 : 1 (cement : 1 sand) :		
	1A 100 mm dia	100 meter	2.17
	1B 150 mm dia	100 meter	3.23
	1C 200 mm dia	100 meter	4.33
	1D 230 mm dia	100 meter	4.87
	1E 250 mm dia	100 meter	5.40
14.17.2	Jointing glazed stone ware pipe grade 'A' with stiff mixture of cement mortar in the proportion of 1 : 3 (cement : 3 sand) :		
	2A 100 mm dia	100 meter	1.07
	2B 150 mm dia	100 meter	1.60
	2C 200 mm dia	100 meter	2.13
	2D 230 mm dia	100 meter	2.40
	2E 250 mm dia	100 meter	2.67
14.17.3	Laying cement concrete 1 : 5 : 10 (1 cement : 5 sand : 10 graded stone aggregate 40 mm nominal size) alround S.W. pipe including bed concrete as per standard design :		

(Contd.)

	3A 100 mm dia. S.W. pipe	100 metre	19.24
	3B 150 mm dia. S.W. pipe	100 metre	23.53
	3C 200 mm dia. S.W. pipe	100 metre	27.43
	3D 230 mm dia. S.W. pipe	100 metre	30.03
	3E 250 mm dia. S.W. pipe	100 metre	31.72
14.17.4	Laying cement concrete 1 : 5 : 10 (1 cement : 5 sand : 10 graded stone aggregate 40 mm nominal size) upto haunches of S.W. pipe including bed concrete as per standard design :		
	4A 100 mm dia. S.W. pipe	100 metre	9.14
	4B 150 mm dia. S.W. pipe	100 metre	14.82
	4C 200 mm dia. S.W. pipe	100 metre	17.42
	4D 230 mm dia. S.W. pipe	100 metre	19.11
	4E 250 mm dia. S.W. pipe	100 metre	20.28
14.17.5	Fixing square mouth S.W. gully trap grade 'A' complete with C.I. grating brick masonry chamber with F.P.S. bricks of class designation 75 and water tight C.I. cover with frame of 300 × 300 mm size (inside) the weight of cover to be not less than 4.50 kg and frame to be not less than 2.70 kg :		
	5A 100 × 100 mm size, P type gully trap	each	0.27
	5B 125 × 100 mm size, P, Q, or S type gully trap	each	0.27
	5C 150 × 100 mm size, P or S type gully trap	each	0.26
	5D 180 ×100 mm size, P type gully trap	each	0.26
	5E 180 × 150 mm size, P or S type gully trap	each	0.25
14.17.6	Laying light duty non pressure NP2 or PI class R.C.C. Pipes with collars jointed with stiff mixture of cement mortar in the proportion of 1 : 2 (1 cement : 2 sand) including testing of joints etc.		
	6A 100 mm dia. R.C.C. pipe (NP2) or P1	100 metre	0.5
	6B 150 mm dia. R.C.C. pipe (NP2) or P1	100 metre	0.6
	6C 250 mm dia. R.C.C. pipe (NP2) or P1	100 metre	0.9
	6D 300 mm dia. R.C.C. pipe (NP2) or P1	100 metre	1.10
	6E 450 mm dia. R.C.C. pipe (NP2) or P1	100 metre	2.40
	6F 500 mm dia. R.C.C. pipe (NP2) or P1	100 metre	2.60
	6G 600 mm dia. R.C.C. pipe (NP2) or P1	100 metre	3.20
	6H 700 mm dia. R.C.C. pipe (NP2) or P1	100 metre	3.70
	6I 800 mm dia. R.C.C. pipes(NP2) or P1	100 metre	4.20
	6J 900 mm dia. R.C.C. pipe (NP2) or P1	100 metre	4.90
	6K 1000 mm dia. R.C.C. pipe (NP2) or P1	100 metre	5.50
	6L 1100 mm dia. R.C.C. pipe (NP2) or P1	100 metre	6.10
	6M 1200 mm dia. R.C.C. pipe (NP2) or P1	100 metre	6.80
14.17.7	Constructing brick masonry manhole with F.P.S. bricks of class designation 75 in cement mortar 1 : 4 (1 cement : 4 sand) top slab with 1 : 2 : 4 mix (1 cement : 2 sand : 4 graded stone aggregate 20 mm nominal size) foundation concrete 1 : 4 : 8 (1 cement : 4 sand : 8 graded stone aggregate 40 mm nominal size) inside plastering 12 mm thick with cement mortar 1 : 3 (1 cement : 3 sand) finished with floating coat of neat cement and making channels in cement concrete 1 : 2 : 4 mix (1 cement : 2 sand : 4 graded stone aggregate 20 mm nominal size) finished with a floating coat of neat cement complete :		

	7A Inside size 90 × 80 cm and 45 deep including C.I. Cover with frame 455 × 610 mm internal dimensions.	each	2.31
	7B Inside size 90 × 80 cm and 60 deep including C.I. Cover with frame 455 × 610 mm internal dimensions.	each	2.49
	7C Inside size 1.2 m × 90 cm and 90 cm deep including C.I. Cover and frame 500 mm internal diameter.	each	3.82
	7D Inside size 1.2 m × 90 cm and 90 cm deep including C.I. Cover and frame 560 mm internal diameter.	each	3.78
	(1) Extra for depth for manholes :		
	7E Size 90 × 80 cm	metre	1.26
	7F Size 1.2 m × 90 cm	metre	1.52
14.17.8	Constructing brick masonry arched type manhole 1.4 m × 90 cm inside size with 75 class designation brick in cement mortar 1 : 4 (1 cement : 4 sand) arch work with F.P.S. bricks of class designation 75 in cement mortar 1 : 3 (1 cement : 3 sand) inside cement plastering 12 mm thick with cement cortar 1 : 3 (1 cement: 3 sand) finished with a floating coat of neat cement upto height of crown level of arch above the benching level and cement pointed with cement mortar 1 : 2 (1 cement : 2 sand) for remaining portion R.C.C. top slab 1 : 2 : 4 (1 cement : 2 sand : 4 graded stone aggregate 20 mm nominal size) foundation concrete 1 : 4 : 8 (1 cement : 4 sand : 8 graded stone aggregate 40 mm nominal size) and making channel in cement concrete 1 : 2 : 4 mix (1 cement : 2 sand : 4 graded stone aggregate 20 mm nominal size) finished with a floating coat of neat cement complete :		
	8A 2.45 m deep with C.I. cover and frame 500 mm internal diameter	each	6.34
	8B 2.45 m deep with C.I. cover and frame 560 mm internal diameter	each	6.31
	8C 4.25 m deep with C.I. cover and frame 500 mm internal diameter	each	8.45
	8D 4.25 m deep with C.I. cover and frame 560 mm internal diameter	each	8.42
	8E 9.75 m deep with C.I. cover and frame 500 mm internal diameter	each	18.91
	8F 9.75 m deep with C.I. cover and frame 560 mm internal diameter	each	18.88
14.17.9	Extra for depth for manholes :		
	9A From 2.45 m to 4.25 m	metre	1.17
	9B Beyond 4.25 m to 9.75 m	metre	1.90
	9C Beyond 9.75 metres	metre	2.35
14.17.10	Constructing brick masonry circular type manhole 0.91 internal diameter at bottom and 0.56 m dia. at top with F.P.S. brick of class designation 75 in cement mortar 1 : 4 (1 cement : 4 sand) inside cement plaster 12 mm thick with cement mortar 1 : 3 (1 cement: 3 sand) finished with a floating coat of neat cement R.C.C. top slab 1 : 2 : 4 (1 cement : 2 sand : 4 graded stone aggregate 20 mm nominal size) foundation concrete 1 : 3 : 6 (1 cement : 3 sand : 6 graded stone aggregate 40 mm nominal size) and making channel in cement concrete 1 : 2 : 4 mix (1 cement : 2 sand : 4 graded stone aggregate 20 mm nominal size) finished with a floating coat of neat cement complete :		

(*Contd.*)

	10A 0.91 m deep with SFRC cover and frame 560 mm internal diameter	each	2.75
	10B 1.67 m deep with SFRC cover and frame 560 mm internal diameter	each	3.61
14.17.11	Constructing brick masonry circular type manhole 1.22 internal diameter at bottom and 0.56 m dia. at top with F.P.S. brick of class designation 75 in cement mortar 1 : 4 (1 cement : 4 sand) inside cement plaster 12 mm thick with cement mortar 1 : 3 (1 cement : 3 sand) finished with a floating coat of neat cement R.C.C. top slab 1 : 2 : 4 (1 cement : 2 sand : 4 graded stone aggregate 20 mm nominal size) foundation concrete 1 : 3 : 6 (1 cement : 3 sand : 6 graded stone aggregate 40 mm nominal size) and making channel in cement concrete 1 : 2 : 4 mix (1 cement : 2 sand : 4 graded stone aggregate 20 mm nominal size) finished with a floating coat of neat cement complete :		
	11A 1.68 m deep with SFRC cover and frame 560 mm internal diameter	each	5.39
	11B 2.29 m deep with SFRC cover and frame 560 mm internal diameter	each	6.27
14.17.12	Constructing brick masonry circular type manhole 1.52 internal diameter at bottom and 0.56 m dia. at top with F.P.S. brick of class designation 75 in cement mortar 1 : 4 (1 cement : 4 sand) inside cement plaster 12 mm thick with cement mortar 1 : 3 (1 cement : 3 sand) finished with a floating coat of neat cement R.C.C. top slab 1 : 2 : 4 (1 cement : 2 sand : 4 graded stone aggregate 20 mm nominal size) foundation concrete 1 : 3 : 6 (1 cement : 3 sand : 6 graded stone aggregate 40 mm nominal size) and making channel in cement concrete 1 : 2 : 4 mix (1 cement : 2 sand : 4 graded stone aggregate 20 mm nominal size) finished with a floating coat of neat cement complete :		
	12A 2.30 m deep with SFRC cover and frame 560 mm internal diameter	each	10.86
	12B 4.18 m deep with SFRC cover and frame 560 mm internal diameter	each	16.71
14.17.13	Extra for depth for circular type manholes :		
	13A 0.91 m internal dia (at bottom) beyond 0.91 to 1.67 m.	metre	1.13
	13B 1.22 m internal dia. (at bottom) beyond 1.682 to 2.29 m.	metre	1.44
	13C 1.52 m internal dia (at bottom) beyond 2.30 to 4.18 m.	metre	3.11
14.17.14	Providing M.S. footrests including fixing in manholes with 20 × 20 × 10 cm cement concrete blocks 1 : 3 : 6 (1 cement : 3 sand : 6 graded stone aggregate 20 mm nominal size):		
	14A With 20 × 20 mm square bar	100 nos.	0.88
	14B With 20 mm dia round bar	100 nos.	0.88
14.17.15	Providing and fixing safety foot rest plastic encapsulated 12 mm dia. bars fixing in 30 × 20 × 15 cm cement concrete blocks 1 : 3 : 6 (1 cement : 3 sand : 6 graded stone aggregate 20 mm nominal size).	100 nos.	1.98
14.17.16	Replacement of M.S. footrests in manholes including dismantling concrete block and with 20 × 20 × 10 cm cement concrete blocks 1 : 3 : 6 (1 cement : 3 sand : 6 graded stone aggregate 20 mm nominal size) :		
	16A With 20 × 20 mm square bar	100 nos.	0.88
	16B With 20 mm dia round bar	100 nos.	0.88

14.17.17	Providing and fixing in position precast R.C.C. manhole cover and frame of required shape and approved quality :		
	(1) LD—2.5		
	17A Rectangular shape 600 × 450 mm internal diamensions	each	0.128
	17B Square shape 350 mm internal diamensions	each	0.096
	17C Circular shape 450 mm internal diametre	each	0.096
	(2) MD—10		
	17D Square shape 500 mm internal diamensions	each	0.128
	17E Circular shape 500 mm internal diametre	each	0.096
	(3) HD—20		
	17F Circular shape 560 mm internal diametre	each	0.096
	(4) EHD—35		
	17G Circular shape 560 mm internal diametre	each	0.096
14.17.18	Making connection of drain or sewer line with existing manhole, including breaking into and making good the walls or floors with cement concrete 1 : 2 : 4 (1 cement : 2 sand : 4 graded stone aggregate 20 mm nominal size) cement plastered on both sides with cement mortar 1 : 3 (1 cement : 3 sand) finished with a floating coat of neat cement and making necessary channels for the drain :		
	18A For pipes 100 to 230 mm diameter	each	0.056
	18B For pipes 250 to 300 mm diameter	each	0.095
	18C For pipes 350 to 450 mm diameter	each	0.153
14.17.19	Providing sand cast iron drop connections externally for 60 cm drop from branch sewer line to main sewer manhole including inspections and cleaning eye with chain and lid, sand cast iron drop pipe and bend encased alround with cement concrete 1 : 5 : 10 (1 cement : 5 sand : 10 graded stone aggregate 40 mm nominal size) cutting holes in walls and making good with brick work in cement mortar 1 : 5 (1 cement : 5 sand), plastered with cement mortar 1 : 3 (1 cement : 3 sand) stiff cement mortar 1 : 1 (1 cement : 1 sand) joints between sand cast iron tee and S.W. pipe making required channels complete :		
	19A 100 mm dia sand cast iron drop connection	each	0.34
	19B 150 mm dia sand cast iron drop connection	each	0.46
14.17.20	Extra for depth beyond 60 cm of sand cast iron drop connection complete :		
	20A For 100 mm dia sand cast iron drop connection	metre	0.21
	20B For 150 mm dia sand cast iron drop connection	metre	0.26
14.17.21	Providing R.C.C. spun vent shaft with cowl, 140 mm and 200 mm internal and external dia. respectively at top, 300 and 450 mm internal and external dia respectively at bottom and 9.10 m over all length, bottom 1.25 m below ground level fixed in a pit 90 × 90 cm 1.5 m with cement concrete 1 : 4 : 8 (1 cement : 4 sand : 8 graded stone aggregate 40 mm nominal size) 25 cm in bed and 20 cm alround with top 15 in cement concrete 1 : 2 : 4 (1 cement : 2 sand : 4 graded stone aggregate 20 mm nominal size) junction of vent shaft and concrete grounted with cement mortar 1 : 1 (1 cement : 1 sand) including making connection with sewer manhole with 150 mm dia. cement concrete pipe of required length complete as per standard design.	each	1.89

(Contd.)

14.17.22	Constructing brick masonry road gully chamber 50 × 45 × 60 cm with F.P.S. bricks of class designation 75 including 500 × 450 mm C.I. horizontal grating with frame complete as per standard design.	each	0.88
14.17.23	Constructing brick masonry road gully chamber 45 × 45 × 77.5 cm with F.P.S. bricks of class designation 75 with vertical grating complete as per standard design.	each	0.91
14.17.24	Constructing brick masonry road gully chamber 110 × 50 × 77.5 cm with F.P.S. bricks of class designation 75 including 500 × 450 mm C.I. horizontal grating with frame and vertical grating complete as per standard design.	each	1.60
14.17.25	Constructing brick masonry chamber for underground C.I. inspection chamber and bends with F.P.S. bricks of class designation 75 in cement mortar 1 : 5 (1 cement : 5 sand) C.I. cover with frame (light duty) 455 × 610 mm internal dimensions, total weight of cover with frame to be not less than 38 kg (weight of cover 23 kg and weight of frame 15 kg) R.C.C. top slab with 1 : 2 : 4 (1 cement : 2 sand : 4 graded stone aggregate 20 mm nominal size) foundation concrete 1 : 5 : 10 (1 cement : 5 sand : 10 graded stone aggregate 40 mm nominal size) inside plastering 12 mm thick with cement mortar 1 : 3 (1 cement : 3 sand) finished smooth with a floating coat of neat cement on wall and bed concrete etc. complete as per standard design :		
	25A Inside dimension 455 × 610 mm and 45 cm deep for single pipe line	each	0.86
	25B Inside dimension 500 × 700 mm and 45 cm deep for pipe line with one or two inlets.	each	1.02
	25C Inside dimension 600 × 850 mm and 45 cm deep for pipe line with three or more inlets.	each	1.27
14.17.26	Extra for depth beyond 45 for brick masonry chamber with F.P.S. bricks of class designation 75 :		
	26A 455 × 610 mm size	metre	0.75
	26B 500 × 700 mm size	metre	0.82
	26C 600 × 850 mm size	metre	0.96
14.17.27	Constructing brick masonry open surface drain with F.P.S. bricks of class designation 75 in cement mortar 1 : 4 (1 cement : 4 sand) including earth excavation 10 cm thick bed concrete 1 : 5 : 10 (1 cement : 5 sand : 10 graded stone aggregate 40 mm nominal size) and 25 mm thick cement concrete 1 : 2 : 4 (1 cement : 2 sand : 4 graded stone aggregate 12.5 mm nominal size) for filling haunches including 12 mm cement plaster 1 : 4 (1 cement : 4 sand) with a floating coat of neat cement inside the drain, its top and exposed side :		
	27A 10 cm drain 20 cm average depth	10 metres	16.12
	27B 15 cm drain 20 cm average depth	10 metres	17.86
	27C 25 cm drain 30 cm average depth	10 metres	23.74
14.17.28	Constructing brick masonry open surface drain with F.P.S. bricks of class designation 75 in cement mortar 1 : 4 (1 cement : 4 sand) including earth excavation with semi circular S.W. glazed channel fixed with cement mortar 1 : 1 (1 cement : 1 sand) over a bed of 10 cm thick cement concrete 1 : 5 : 10 (1 cement : 5 sand : 10 graded stone aggregate 40 mm nominal size) including filling spaces under edges with cement concrete 1 : 2 : 4		

	(1 cement : 2 sand : 4 graded stone aggregate 12.5 mm nominal size) and 12 mm cement plaster 1 : 4 (1 cement : 4 sand) with a floating coat of neat cement over exposed surfaces of masonry :		
	28A 10 cm drain 20 cm average depth with 10 cm S.W. glazed channel	100 metres	15.94
	28B 15 cm drain 20 cm average depth with 15 cm S.W. glazed channel	100 metres	16.79
	28C 25 cm drain 30 cm average depth with 25 em S.W. glazed channel	100 metres	21.88
14.17.29	Extra for every additional one cm average depth of drain (for all diameters).	100 metres cm depth	0.37
14.17.30	Constructing grease trap 80 × 40 × 46 cm (inside) with 20 cm thick brick masonry walls with F.P.S. bricks of class designation 75 with inlet and outlet drain in cement mortar 1 : 4 (1 cement : 4 sand) plastered 12 mm thick with 1 : 4 cement mortar (1 cement : 4 sand) finished with floating coat of neat cement, on inside and exposed surfaces, having two stone baffle walls 34.5 cm deep and one 19 cm deep 40 mm thick and 45 cm long embedded 2.5 cm on either side in brick masonry 40 mm thick 100 × 60 cm stone cover and 7.5 cm thick bed concrete 1 : 5 : 10 (1 cement : 5 sand : 10 graded stone aggregate 40 mm nominal size) with 40 mm flooring in cement concrete 1 : 2 : 4 (1 cement : 2 sand : 4 graded stone aggregate 20 mm nominal size) finished with a floating coat of neat cement	one trap	0.69
14.17.31	Making soak pit 2.50 m in diameter 3 m deep with 45 × 45 cm dry brick honey comb shaft in F.P.S. bricks and S.W. drain pipe 100 mm diameter 1.8 m long complete.	each	0.072
14.17.32	Providing and fixing SW intercepting trap in marbles with stiff mixture of cement mortar 1 : 1 (1 cement : 1 fine sand) including testing of joints etc. complete :		
	32A 100 mm dia.	each	0.013
	32B 150 mm dia.	each	0.019

Table 14.18. Miscellaneous

S. No.	*Description of item of work*	*Unit*	*Quantity of cement to be used per unit quantity of work (Quintals)*
14.18.1	Cutting holes upto 30 × 30 cm in wall with F.P.S. bricks including making good the same.	100 holes	2.92
14.18.2	Cutting holes upto 15 × 15 cm in R.C.C. floors and roofs for passing pipe etc. and repairing the hole after insertion of drain pipe etc. with cement concrete 1 : 2 : 4 (1 cement : 2 sand : 4 graded stone aggregate 20 mm nominal size) including finishing complete.	100 holes	0.70
14.18.3	Making chases upto 7.5 × 7.5 cm in walls including making good after housing G.I. pipe etc.	100 metres	0.88
14.18.4	Making hole upto 20 × 20 cm and embedding pipes upto 150 diameter in masonry and filling with cement concrete 1 : 3 : 6 (1 cement : 3 sand : 6 graded stone aggregate 20 mm nominal size)	100 metres	4.90

Coefficient for Bitumen Consumption

Table 14.19. Road Work

S. No.	*Description of item of work*	*Unit*	*Quantity of bitumen to be used per unit quantity of work (Quintals)*
	A. SURFACE DRESSING		
14.19.1	Surface dressing on new surface with paving bitumen A-90/S-90 of approved quality using 2.25 kg of bitumen per sq m with 1.65 cum of stone chippings 13.2 mm nominal size per 100 sq m of road surface including consolidation with power road roller of 6 to 8 tonne capacity etc. complete.	sq m	0.0225
14.19.2	Surface dressing on new surface in two coats with bitumen A-90/S-90 of approved quality using 1.8 kg of bitumen per sq m with 1.5 cum of stone chippings 13.2 mm nominal size per 100 sq m of road surface for first coat and 1.1 kg of bitumen per sq m with 1.00 cum of stone chippings 11.2 mm nominal size per 100 sq m of road surface for second coat including consolidation of each coat separately with power road roller of 6 to 8 tonne capacity etc. complete.	sq m	0.029
14.19.3	Surface dressing on old surface with hot bitumen A-90/S-90 of approved quality using 1.95 kg of bitumen per sq m with 1.50 cum of stone chippings 11.2 mm nominal size per 100 sq m. of road surface including consolidation with power road roller of 6 to 8 tonne capacity etc. complete.	sq m	0.0195
14.19.4	Surface dressing one coat on new surface with bitumen of specified grade at a rate of 1.95 kg/sq m of surface area with 1.5 cum of stone chippings 13.2 mm nominal size per 100 sq m of road surface including consolidation with road roller, etc. complete :		
	4A Using bitumen emulsion (minimum 50% bitumen content—RS grade conforming to IS : 8837)	sq m	0.0195
	4B Using cut back RC 3 (Rapid curing) bitumen conforming to IS : 217	sq m	0.0195
14.19.5	Surface dressing one coat on old surface with bitumen of specified grade at the rate of 1.22 kg/sq m surface area with 1.10 cum of stone chippings 11.2 mm nominal size per 100 sq m of road surface including consolidation with road roller, etc. complete :		
	5A Using bitumen emulsion (minimum 50% bitumen content—RS grade conforming to IS : 8837)	sq m	0.0122
	5B Using cut back RC 3 (Rapid curing) power road roller of 6 to 8 tonne capacity conforming to IS : 217	sq m	0.0122
	B. PRE MIX CARPET		
14.19.6	Providing and applying tack coat using hot straight run bitumen of grade 80/100 including heating the bitumen, spraying the bitumen with mechanically operated spray unit fitted on bitumen boiler, cleaning and preparing the existing road surface as per specifications :		
	6A On W.B.M. @ 0.75 kg/sq m.	sq m	0.0075
	6B On bituminous surface @ 0.50 kg/sq m.	sq m	0.0050

14.19.7	2 cm premix carpet surfacing with 1.8 cum and 0.90 cum of stone chippings 13.2 mm size and 11.2 mm size respectively per 100 sq m and 52 kg and 56 kg of hot bitumen per cum of stone chippings 13.2 mm and 11.2 mm size respectively including a tack coat with hot straight run bitumen including consolidation with power road roller of 6 to 9 tonne capacity etc. complete : (tack coat to be paid separately) :		
	7A With paving Asphalt 30/40 heated and then mixed with solvent at the rate of 70 grams per kg of asphalt.	sq m	0.0144
	7B With paving Asphalt 80/100 heated and then mixed with solvent at the rate of 70 grams per kg of asphalt.	sq m	0.0144
	7C With paving Asphalt 60/70 with no solvent	sq m	0.0144
14.19.8	2.5 cm premix carpet surfacing with 2.25 cum and 1.12 cum of stone chippings 13.2 mm and 11.2 mm size respectively per 100 sq m and 52 kg and 56 kg of hot bitumen per cum of stone chippings 13.2 mm and 11.2 mm size respectively including a tack coat with hot straight run bitumen including consolidation with power road roller of 6 to 9 tonne capacity etc. complete : (tack coat to be paid separately) :		
	8A With paving Asphalt 30/40 heated and then mixed with solvent at the rate of 70 grams per kg of asphalt.	sq m	0.018
	8B With paving Asphalt 80/100 heated and then mixed with solvent at the rate of 70 grams per kg of asphalt.	sq m	0.018
	8C With paving Asphalt 60/70 with no solvent	sq m	0.018
14.19.9	2 cm premix carpet surfacing with 2.4 cum of stone chippings 11.2 mm nominal size per 100 sq m and bitumen emulsion (Min. 60% bitumen contents) of approved quality using 96 kg per cum of chippings including a tack coat of 1 kg bitumen emulsion per sq m of road, surface including consolidation with power road roller etc. complete.	sq m	0.033
14.19.10	2.5 cm premix carpet surfacing with 3 cum of stone chippings 10 mm nominal size per 100 sq m and bitumen emulsion (Min. 60% bitumen contents) of approved quality using 96 kg per cum of chippings including a tack coat of 1 kg bitumen emulsion per sq m of road surface including consolidation with power road roller etc. complete.	sq m	0.0388
14.19.11	Providing and laying premix bituminous macadam base course with stone aggregate of quality size and grading as specified in CPWD specification and straight run bitumen of grade 80/100 @ 4% by weight of total mix including hot mixing of stone aggregate and bitumen in hot mix plant, transporting mixed material and laying mixed material with paver finisher to the required level and grade, rolling by power road roller of 8 to 10 tonne capacity to achieve the required compaction and density :		
	11A 50 mm compacted thickness	cum	0.88
	11B 75 mm compacted thickness	cum	0.88
14.19.12	Providing and laying Bitumen Penetration Macadam with hard stone aggregate of quality, size and grading as specified, with bitumen of suitable penetration grade including required key aggregate as specified, spreading coarse aggregate with the help of self propelled/tipper tail mounted aggregate spreader and applying bitumen by a pressure distributor and then spreading key aggregate with the help of aggregate spreader complete including consolidation with power road roller of minimum 8 to 10 tonne capacity to achieve specified values of compactive strength and surface accuracy :		

(Contd.)

	12A For 50 mm compacted thickness using coarse aggregate of size 50-20 mm @ 0.60 cum per 10 sq m graded, key aggregate of size 12.5 mm graded @ 0.15 cum per 10 sq m. With paving asphalt 30/40 @ 50 kg/10 sq m	sq m	0.05
	12B For 75 mm compacted thickness in two layers using stone aggregate of size 63-41 mm @ 0.90 cum per 10 sq m key aggregate of size 20.0 mm graded @ 0.18 cum per 10 sq m. With paving asphalt 30/40 @ 68 kg/10 sq m	sq m	0.068
14.19.13	Providing and laying 75 mm thick, semi dense asphaltic base course using mineral aggregate satisfying the gradation set out in specification with 5 percent binder content 80/100 or quivalent (By weight of total mix) with the aid of hot mix plant and paver finisher including rolling with power road roller of 8 to 10 tonne capacity to achieve required compaction and density.	cum	1.180
14.19.14	Providing and laying 4 cm. thick dense bituminous concrete surfacing course using mineral aggregate satisfying the gradation set out in the specification with 6% binder content 80/100 or equivalent (By weight of total mix) with the aid of hot mix plant and paver finisher including rolling with power road roller to achieve the required compaction and density etc. all complete.	cum	1.416
	C. MASTIC AND BITUMASTIC SHEET WEARING COARSE		
14.19.15	Providing and laying 25 mm thick bitumen mastic wearing course (as per specification) with industrial bitumen of grade 85/25 conforming to IS : 702 prepared by using mastic cooker and laid to required level and slope including providing antiskid surface with bitumen precoated fine grained hard stone chipping of approved size at the rate of 0.005 cum per 10 sq m and at approximate spacing of 10 cm centre to centre in both directions, pressed into surface protruded 1 mm to 4 mm over mastic surface, including cleaning the surface, removal of debris etc. all complete.	sq m	0.0879
14.19.16	2.5 cm thick bitumastic sheet with hot bitumen of approved quality using stone chippings (60% 12.5 mm nominal size and 40% 10 mm nominal size) @ 1.65 cum per 100 sq m and coarse sand at 1.65 cum per 100 sq m of road surface and with bitumen @ 56 kg/cum of stone chippings and at 128 kg/cum of sand over a tack coat with hot straight run bitumen including consolidation with road roller etc. complete, (tack coat to be paid separately) :		
	16A With paving Asphalt 30/40 heated and then mixed with solvent at the rate of 70 grams per kg of asphalt	sq m	0.0303
	16B With paving Asphalt 80/100 heated and then mixed with solvent at the rate of 70 grams per kg of asphalt.	sq m	0.0303
	16C With paving asphalt 60/70 with no solvent.	sq m	0.0303
14.19.17	4 cm thick bitumastic sheet with hot bitumen of approved quality using stone chippings (60% 12.5 mm nominal size and 40% 10 mm nominal size) @ 2.60 cum per 100 sq m and coarse sand at 2.60 cum per 100 sq m of road surface and with bitumen @ 56 kg/cum of stone chippings and at 128 kg/cum of sand over a tack coat with hot straight run bitumen including consolidation with road roller etc. complete, (tack coat to be paid separately) :		
	17A With paving Asphalt 30/40 heated and then mixed with solvent at the rate of 70 grams per kg of asphalt	sq m	0.0479

	17B With paving Asphalt 80/100 heated and then mixed with solvent at the rate of 70 grams per kg of asphalt.	sq m	0.00768
	17C With paving asphalt 60/70 with no solvent	sq m	0.0479
	D. SEAL COAT		
14.19.18	**Providing and laying seal coat of premixed fine aggregate (passing 2.36 mm and retained on 180 micron sieve) with bitumen using 128 kg of 80/100 bitumen per cum of fine aggregate and 0.60 cum of fine aggregate per 100 sq m of road surface complete.**	sq m	0.00768
14.19.19	**Providing and laying seal coat over prep ıred surface of road with bitumen heated in bitumen boiler fitted with spray set using 98 kg of bitumen of 80/100 grade and blinding one surface with 0.90 cum of stone aggregate of 6.7 mm size) (Passing 11.2 mm sieve and retained on 2.36 mm sieve) per 100 sq m of road surface including rolling and finishing with power road roller complete.**	sq m	0.0098
	***Note for item no. 17.59 and 17.60**—item to be operated only with the prior approved of CE concerned.		

Part—II

CONTRACTS AND ACCOUNTS

Part—II

CONTRACTS AND ACCOUNTS

1

Contracts and Tender

1.1. CONTRACTS DATA FROM THE REMOTEST ANTIQUITY

In ancient Greek, when structures were built, Greek law laid down certain relationships between the contractor and the owner. They had certain rules and regulations. Such rules and regulations and other conditions of contracts are still prevailing today with certain modifications. At that period also contractors were required to hire sufficient skilled and unskilled persons, qualified worksmen. They were required to give the guarantee of the quality of works. Penalties were prescribed for failure or delay of the works. Payments were made in installments as per the progress of the works. These things are existing today also.

As per Indian Contract Act of 1872 "Contract" is an agreement between competent parties, enforceable at law whereby each acquires a right to what is promised by the other. Two persons can have any sort of agreement, they may promise to each other but unless such promises are enforceable at law they form no contract. Hence it should be noted that every contract is an agreement enforceable by law but every agreement is not necessarily a contract.

The term contractor means a person, syndicate or firm that has made such an undertaking for execution or for services in connection with civil works.

1.2. ESSENTIALS OF CONTRACT

Following are the essential requirements for formation of a contract. These have been recognised universally:

(1) Legally competent parties. (2) A lawful subject matter.

(3) Proper and valid considerations.

(4) Genuine agreement signed by both the parties.

Engineering contract is a contract concerning to engineering project. It is also a type of business agreement. As per Indian Contract Act parties involved into a contract must be legally competent. Infants, lunatics, drunken people are not competent. There is no hard and fast rule that two persons doing engineering contract with each other should not have any close relations or blood relation but still as far as possible it should be avoided. In certain states "a wife cannot contract to her husband", such rules are existing, though they are legally competent parties. The contract should be on a lawful subject matter which is enforceable at law. These contracts must not violate state or union territory, *i.e.* if a contract has been made in one state it will be invalid for other state. There should be proper consideration between a contractor and owner whether Government Organisation or private party. In absence of these considerations it becomes very difficult to execute the work properly. In engineering contracts there are mutual promises. The contractor promises to execute the works properly, to perform the works faithfully. Similarly it is the duty of the owner to make the payments when due. Further a contract must be genuine. Things should be clear. There should not be any misrepresentations or fraud. The contract agreement is not valid unless until signed by both the parties.

The contracts may be divided into two classes *viz.* "Special Contract or Sealed Contract" and "Simple Contract or Open Tender Contract". Sealed contracts are invited for big and important works and they are in writing and hence requires no considerations," for their validity. They are opened on scheduled date and in the presence of the contractors who have given tender or their representatives. Their presence is not essential but it is desirable that the contractor or his representatives may be present when the tenders are opened. A simple contract or open contract may be in oral talks between the engineer and contractor or it may be in writing also. It is generally used for small work.

For a contract to be valid there must be an offer from owner to get the work executed and similarly there must be an acceptance from the contractor to execute the work as per laid terms and conditions. Both the offer and acceptance must be definite and legal.

Considerations and its meaning-when at the desire of the promiser, the promisee or any other person has done or abstained from doing or does or abstains from doing or promises to do or to abstrain from doing some thing, such act of abstinence or promises is called "consideration" for the promise. In other words; if the agreement for transfer provides for certain acts or things to be done by transferee in addition to providing the price in monetary terms, the value of such acts or things will also form part of "apparent consideration".

1.3. FREE CONSENT

Free consent is the consent which has been obtained by the free will of the parties involved in contract, out of their own accord. A consent is said to free when it is not carried out by any of the following:

(1) **Coercion.** It is the utterness of threat to commit an act forbidden by the Indian Penal Code to induce someone to enter into a contract.

(2) **Duress.** It is the fear caused by the threat of a bodily harm.

(3) **Undue influence.** It is an influence which compels a person to do something which he would not have done if he had been a free agent. The relation between the parties is such that one of the parties having taken an unfair advantage is in a position to dominate the will of the other.

(4) **Fraud.** Related to an absence of a honest belief and a wicked mind. It also includes false statement made by parties.

(5) **Mis Representation.** *i.e.* incorrect statement unknown to all the parties involved in contract that materially affects the contract. For example, though water is supplied to the contractor but it is mentioned in document that contractor will have to make his own arrangement of water for construction work. It is mis representation. Another example time period given for work is too less and then time granted is extended with escalation.

(6) **Mistakes.** It is an error made in contract document that may lead to mis representation or may affect contract. The mistake can be either by one party of contract or by both the parties. This mistake is called bilateral.

1.4. TYPE OF CONTRACTS

There are many ways of getting a work executed in contract system; the work is got executed through an agency called contractor, who arranges all materials, labour, equipments etc. for the completion of the work in time. The main idea behind any contract system is

(*i*) To get lowest total cost of contruction.

(*ii*) To achieve greatest speed of construction to have minimum indirect expenditure.

(*iii*) To have best workmanship and

(*iv*) To have future business between owner and contractor based upon previous experiences. These different system of contracts are listed below:

Each method has its own merits and demerits.

(1) Lump-sum contract.
(2) Cost plus a fixed percentage contract.
(3) Cost plus a fixed fee contract.
(4) Target contract.
(5) Item rate contract (B 2-system).
(6) Percentage rate contract (B 1-system).
(7) Labour contract.
(8) Joint venture contract.
(9) Turn-key projects.
(10) Indirect lump-sum contract for flats or bunglows.
(11) Bot system.

(1) **Lump-sum Contract.** This is an offer by a contractor, that he undertakes the execution of a specific work for a definite lump-sum amount and to complete the same within specified time period. The detailed drawings and detailed specifications are supplied to the contractor by the owner *i.e.* department or private agency having capital to get the work executed. It is duty of contractor to complete the work as per drawings and specifications supplied and as per terms and conditions agreed upon. On the completion of the work; the work is checked as per drawings and specifications and if approved; the amount is paid to the contractor. Hence quantities of various items are not measured. The difficulty arises when enginer-in-charge or owner makes certain changes in the drawings and specifications. Further some contractors also have tendency to use cheap materials of construction to reduce the cost of that work so as to earn maximum profit. In this type of system, contractor takes the risk of unfavourable circumstances, he therefore quotes a good percentage so that he may be sure of his profit whatever may happen. Hence cost of work becomes very high. Therefore this type of system of contract have become obsolete where it is possible to measure the quantities. In civil engineering works this system has totally become obsolete expect for a few works where work can not be measured, for example, construction of some decorative piece; or construction of some sculpture etc. where labour cost involved is very high and quantity measurement has no relation with its work this lump-sum system of contract is used.

(2) **Cost plus fixed percentage contract.** Under this type of system of contract, contractor furnishes all labour and material necessary to complete the work for actual cost of work plus an agreed percentage of the said cost as the profit of the contractor. This percentage profit is fixed. Hence due to this fixed percentage of profit of actual work; contractor always tries to increase the cost of project. No doubt the speed and quality of work is maintained but there is always tremendous wastage of various materials used in construction. This consequently increases the cost of project and hence the profit of contractor making project more costly. This type of system of contract has become obsolete now-a-days and used only in case of emergency works.

(3) **Cost plus a fixed fee.** This was implemented to modify the above method; to control the tendency of contractor to increase the cost of project unnecessarily. This is similar to cost plus fixed percentage of actual cost except this fixed percentage is converted to fixed fee irrespective of the actual cost. In this system contractor gets a fixed amount in the form of profit, what so ever may be the cost of work. Due to fix amount of profit contractor always tries to complete the job earliest possible so that he can get himself involved in other contract. Here work progress is maintained properly quality of materials used also maintained but workmanship quality is not, as contractor is a always in hurry to complete work early. Smaller the completion time; more will be profit as contractor can execute more jobs in lesser period of

time. However this system of contract is still better than cost plus fixed percentage, still this method could not become very popular and hence not used in general.

(4) **Target system of contract.** This is a slight modification over cost plus fixed fee contract system. Under this system, the contractor is paid a fixed fee on a prime cost bases for the work performed under the contract and in addition he receives a percentage on saving effected against either a prior agreed estimated total cost on a target value arrived; without changing the specification. It was presumed that contractor due to proper management of work and labour can reduce the cost of work consequently earning more profit and making structure economical. The desire for extra gain encourages the contractor to use his skill and experience in keeping the cost as low as possible.

But due to continuous increase in the prices of materials and labour and due to other reasons; it is rather very difficult to save the amount from earlier estimated cost. Rather it has been experienced that the cost of work is always more than the estimated cost and hence no extra earning is possible what so ever skill may be used. Due to this reason; this method of contract system is not getting popularity.

(5) **Item-Rate Contract (B 2-system).** In item rate contract the contractor undertakes the execution or construction of a work on the item rate basis. The amount the contractor receives depends upon quantities of various items of works executed. In this system; bill of quantities is prepared mentioning various items of construction and their quantities; contractors bidding contract are required to quote the rates of various items mentioned in bill of quantity with the stipulation that work will be subjected to measurement and payments are made at the unit price quoted. This particular system is called item rate contract. The difficulty with this system is; it is rather difficult to scrutinize the tenders submitted by various bidders; hence modified. In modified system of item rate contract; the department generally quotes various items of construction along with their quantities and rates. The bidders *i.e.* contractors are required to quote various percentages at which he wants to execute that item. As such for each item a separate percentage is quoted. This system of contract is called as 'percent item rate contract' system. This system was very popular in P.W.D. and still used many times. This system is also called B 2-system of contract in P.W.D.

Schedule A

Item No.	*Quantities estimated but may be more or less*	*Item of work*	*Estimated Rates*		*Unit*	*Total amount according to estimated quantities*
			In figures ₹ *Ps.*	*In words*		
		As per Separate Sheet Attached				

Department Hand Book

Note 1. All work shall be carried out as per other specifications of the Division or as directed.

Note 2. Rates quoted include clearance of sit (Prior to commencement of work and at its close in all respects and hold good for work under all conditions, site moisture, weather etc.

Signature of contractor Sinature of $\frac{\text{Executive Engineer}}{\text{Assistant Engineer}}$

Note. To be continued on additional sheets if found necessary.

When the quantities of various items are not available; then there was practice to adopt item rate contract system. The drawback in this system, as the quantities of various items are not known. The contractor always gives higher rates for those item quantities which are likely to increase and low rates for those likely to be decreased. The same is found in percentage item rate contract. The contractor quotes higher percentage for items likely to increase and lower percentage for items likely to be decreased. This results in unbalanced contract. Therefore this type of contract system should be avoided as far as possible. Unless until detailed estimate is made; quantities of different items are evaluated correctly and got ascertained that there will not be more than five-percent variation in each quantity maintaining the overall cost variation less than 5 percent only; this contract system should not be used.

(6) **Percentage rate contract (B 1-system).** This system of contract is very popular and common now-a-days. Most of the works either in P.W.D. or private organisation are undertaken with this system only. In this system detailed estimate is prepared and contractors are required to quote single percentage either higher or lower at which he wants to execute

Schedule B

S. No.	*Particulars*	*Quantity*
1.	Cement in plastic bags	76.75 MT 1527 bags
2.	120 mm dia hume pipes NP-2 class. 20 running meters *i.e.* 8 number of 2.5 m each	Per one meter running

Rates at which the material will be charged to the contractor			*Place of delivery*
Unit	*In figure*	*In words*	
Per one MT	1800.00	Rupee one thousand eight hundred only	at departmental store
Per one meter running	1400.00	Rupee one thousand four hundred only	at departmental store

Note 1. The person of firm submitting the tender should see that the rate in the above schedule are filled up by the Executive Engineer-in-charge on issue of the form prior to the submission of the tender.

Note 2. The contractor should furnish the account of all materials before placing demand for further material and furnish full account of all Department. If any material remained unused with the contractor, he should return the same to the Department. In the event of non return of such material recovery at penal rate of twice the issued rate with S.T. and G.T. will have to be effected from the contractor.

Note 3. Wastage of steel to be borne entirely by the contractor.

Signature of contractor Signature of $\frac{\text{Executive Engineer}}{\text{Assistant Engineer}}$

this job. As such all item rates are changed with the same percentage; hence tender generally does remains balanced and scrutinity becomes comparatively very easy. Now-a-days materials like cement and steel are supplied by the department hence chances of manipulation becomes still less. Most of the engineering contracts are performed with this method only. The rate of recovery of material is given in schedule A. It helps the contractor to decide his rates to be quoted for item involved with use of these materials.

(7) **Labour contract.** This is the most common system of construction for private individual building; particularly in small cities and big towns. Under this system of contract; the contractor arranges all necessary labour; tools and plants and equipments required for. The construction and all the materials required are supplied by the owner. This type of system of contract is also particularly suitable for those cases where the owner or Government departments is in a privileged position to by large quantities of materials at cheap rates. This system is very common for small and private works. Most of the private dwellings are given on a labour contract only and the owner arranges all the materials required for construction. Generally owner also appoints some engineer to supervise the work to maintain the quality and to economise the cost of construction at a fixed fee or percentage of actual cost of construction as supervision charges.

(8) **Joint Venture Contract.** This system of contracting has developed due to tremendous increase in the size of work or due to development of specialised persons for certain specialised job. In case of important and big projects, it is rather difficult to individual contractor to complete the work in specified period of construction. Further different specialist firms have developed who can undertake such work at a reasonable rate with less time for its construction. Hence it was thought and then decided to divide the whole work into different parts either on the basis of amount of work involved or on the basis of special type of work with which a specific firm may be familiar. Hence the work was divided into different contractors and hence joint venture system of contract developed. The firm joint venture system involved six competing construction firms headed into line under one management at the construction of Hoover Dam. The system has become very popular and common now. In a building itself different works are given to different specialists firms under a main contractor and work is got done efficiently and early. Wiremen; plumber etc. are specialist persons for these jobs. Similarly gangs for concreting work are very popular in India. Their jobs is only to do concreting of various elements of reinforced concrete work.

(9) **Turn-key projects.** Now-a-days in civil engineering construction for certain type of works; turn-key system of contract/project has become very common. This system was used during the construction of apartments and flats. The person who wants a flat; is required to complete the paper work and transaction work and then enter into his own house simply by turning the key *i.e.* opening the door.

In this system; the contractor is required to prepare the project including its planning, designing; estimation and execution. Once the project is complete the whole project work is handed over to the owner. Most of the elevated storage reservoirs (ESR) are constructed by turn-key-project system only.

(10) **A new method of contract has developed in India now-a-days.** This is an indirect type of lump-sum contract. In this system a rate of construction per square meter of plinth area is decided jointly by owner and contractor or builder. The specifications are generally fixed or decided jointly and based on these specifications a rate per sq. meter plinth area excluding land cost is decided. This rate includes the contractors profit. Once this agreement is made contractor or builder develops or constructs a bungalow on owners land and payments are made by owner to the contractor or builder at a regular interval at various stages of

construction. Many times even the drawings; specifications and rates are fixed by builder, owner asks builder/contractor to construct/develop the plot.

This system is becoming very popular in India. In big cities or towns; most of the bungalows are constructed with this type of system of contract. Here the owner fully gets relieved of all problems come across during construction.

(11) **BOT *i.e.* Built operate and transfer.** This is a new system in which land is acquired by Govt. and contractor is asked to built the civil works, operate it by collecting some fee from its users to collect the cost of construction and once the cost is collected, to transfer it to the owner *i.e.* Government. No investment is made by government under this system. Drawings, estimates are prepared by Government and contractor is required to execute the work as per designs and specifications given by Engineer. No payment is made to the contractor. All expenditures incurred are to be made by contractor. In return he is authorised to collect some charges as specified by government from the users of that civil work and once the cost is recovered by contractor, the site is transferred from contractor to department *i.e.* department takes possession of that site. The security however is provided to the contractor by Government regarding law and order problems if any.

Mostly Bridges and Roads are constructed and developed by this particular system of contract.

These are the various systems of getting a work constructed and executed. Each method has its speciality in itself and can be used effectively as per the prevailing conditions.

1.5. LABOUR CO-OPERATIVE SOCIETY

In most of the states; labour co-operative societies have been formed; and generally it is a practice to award contract for an amount less than ₹ 1.00 lakh to these labour co-operative societies without calling the tenders and at the estimated rates based on divisional schedule of rates, brought upto date. While awarding the works; class of society is taken into consideration and these classes are formed based on capacity of that society to undertake, their work. Based on the financial status, managerial and technical capacity and staff; these labour co-operative societies in general classified as:

Class A : Maximum eligibility upto ₹ 1,00,000.00

Class B : Maximum eligibility upto ₹ 50,000.00

Class C : Maximum eligibility upto ₹ 20,000.00

These labour co-operative societies are generally exempted from the production of solvency certificate for getting registered but are required to produce a certificate from the District Deputy Register/District federation regarding its capacity and financial resources. Chairman of that labour co-operative society is generally resulted for dealing with. The number of works allotted to one society is generally restricted to three only.

1.6. REGISTRATION OF CONTRACTOR

Each contractor is required to get himself registered to various departments where he is interested to work. In case of Government contract these contractors get themselves registered to Government and hence called as government contractor; however one should not get confused by the meaning Government contractor. These contractors are not serving the Government as an employee but are entitled to do Government jobs if awarded.

The various classes of contractor in general and amount upto which works can be taken by them and other details are given below in tabular form.

S. No.	Class of contractor	Amount up to which works can be taken (Lakh)	Minimum solvency (Lakh)	Annual turn over (average of last three years) (Lakh)	Estimated cost of works in hand during current year (Lakh)
1.	I	Without limit	30.00	75.00	150.00
2.	II	300.00	15.00	50.00	100.00
3.	III	100.00	5.00	25.00	50.00
4.	IV	50.00	2.50	15.00	30.00
5.	V	15.00	0.75	5.00	10.00
6.	VI	5.00	0.50	2.00	4.00
7.	VII	2.00	0.20	0.50	1.00

The contractor are also classified in some department in a method depending upon the amount upto which they can undertake the work given below:

Class	*Amount upto which works can be taken*
A1	Without limit
A	upto ₹ 100.00 lakh
B+	upto ₹ 60.00 lakh
B	upto ₹ 30.00 lakh
B1	upto ₹ 15.00 lakh
C	upto ₹ 5.00 lakh
D	upto ₹ 2.00 lakh
E	upto ₹ 0.00 lakh

To get a contractor to be registered under certain class, he has to apply to the competent authority. He is further required to submit following documents along with the application:

(1) Solvency certificate for an appropriate amount.

(2) Attested copy of deed of partnership and power of attorney on stamp paper.

(3) Current Income tax clearance certificate.

(4) Works certificate for all works performed during last three years and for works in progress.

(5) Undertaking (for class I and class II) for employment of the staff.

(6) Application in duplicate with all documents.

(7) Attested photo of all partners if any.

Latest revision has been made in this regard and some new rules have been implemented. The Engineer contractors now-a-days have been permitted for registration for class VI *i.e.* for works cost upto ₹ 5 lakh without producing solvency certificate.

Prescribed Application Form for Registration as Contractor:

(1) Name of applicant with full postal address.

(2) Detail of firm *i.e.* whether partnership deed, Hindu undivided family, individual etc.

(3) Name of person holding power of attorney.

(4) Name of sole proprietors/partners with particulars.

(5) Name of Bankers with full address.

(6) Place of Business.

(7) Class in which registration sought.

(8) Whether contractor desires to deposit lump-sum money for securing exemptions from EMD or will pay EMD with each tender.

(9) List of works executed during last three years (contractor is required to furnish all details like works, its location, cost, stage of construction etc.).

(10) List of Tools and Plants possessed by him.

(11) Technical qualification of contractor, his partner and employees working under him.

(12) Has the applicant or his partner black listed by the govt. in the past.

(13) Whether registered with other department, state, organisation (if yes give list).

(14) Upto date income tax clearance certificate enclosed or not.

(15) Amount of solvency certificate enclosed.

I/we certify that I/we have not been and will not get myself/ourself registered as contractor in the department under more than one name.

Date : Signature of applicant with address

Pre-qualification of Contractor. Sometimes jobs are awarded on the basis of the quotations received from 'selected tenderer', which means tenders are invited from a group of known reputed contractors who are considered suitable for that job. This method is known as 'Pre-qualification' and saves a lot of time on the part of the employer, consultant and contractor. Sometimes, for special type of jobs, it is mentioned in the advertisement that specialist contractors having considerable experience alone apply. In order to judge the capability of contractor for that job employer asks contractor to furnish relevant data and it is obligatory on the part of the contractor to supply all such informations required to the employer and obliq. Sometimes department or consultants or owner have their own list of empanelled contractors those have already worked with them. The distribution of tender papers is then restricted to these contractors only. This, no doubt saves a considerable time but at the same time reprive other good contractors to tender the works, and show their capabilities. Sometimes for a very specialised job only one specialised firm is consulted and job is awarded by due negotiations. This is of course common in private works, however objectionable in government jobs. The possibility of malpractice can not be totally avoided in prequalification.

1.7. CONDITIONS OF CONTRACT

While preparing a contract agreement or agreement deed; certain conditions are laid down which are binding to the contractor as well as owner, it is mainly to avoid dispute during the progress of work if any. These conditions of contract though remain same for all works in general, but then changes in certain cases from person to person and also depends on type of work and amount of work to be executed. The certain basic principles have to be strictly adhered to while preparing the contract agreement. Variation in these conditions are liable to be challenged by either of the parties. If there are minor variations, they are generally accepted by both but for major decisions; the matter is solved jointly. If there is a wide variation in the cost; the matter is referred to higher authorities for approval.

There are two types of conditions that are generally made in tender document.

(1) General conditions of contract. (2) Special conditions of contract (Particular).

The general conditions are those which do not affect the work. These are obligatory bindings on the contractor whilst special conditions are based on type of work and the conditions vary from work to work.

A few general conditions of contract are as tasted below:

(1) Work should be executed as per the drawings and specifications mentioned in agreement bond. There should be no modification in design; drawing etc. from those given in notice inviting tender.

(2) Period allotted for that work should not change. Only when it may become essential to change the period due to unavoidable reasons or natural calamities; it may be changed but only with due permission from higher authorities.

(3) It is obligatory that it is the responsibility of contractor to clear the site, to give medical aid to labour if required and to give free access to departmental engineers at site.

(4) Contractor is bound to pay minimum wages to the labour as per Workmens Compensation Act.

(5) There should be no flaw in agreement deed. It is usual practice in case of large works to get agreement scrutinised from law department so that legal aspect of the agreement are taken care of.

(6) Contractor can not assign or sublet the work to other contractor. Only for special type of works this can be done but only with due permission of engineer in charge.

(7) It is responsibility of engineer incharge to see that proper payments as per progress of works are made to contractor. He is also required to see that work progress is maintained by the contractor maintaining the quality as per specifications.

(8) Dismantling of works not approved by the engineer if any and construction of new one, dismantling defective work is contractors job. No extra payment is made for dismantling and reconstruction of dismantled work to the contractor.

(9) It is responsibility of contractor to provide potable water to the labours employed by him.

(10) The contractor is required to make his own arrangement for electric power at his own cost and no claim can be made in this behalf. The layout and method of laying lines and wiring and the nature of connected leads must be approved by engineer incharge.

(11) In case of errors, omissions and discrepancies; and doubts the matter should be referred to competent authorities and the decision of competent authorities shall be final and binding on the contractor.

(12) All the materials excavated is of the government or of owner and should be disposed of as directed by the competent authorities as Deputy Engineer or Executive Engineer as the case may be.

All these conditions are binding on the parties involved in agreement deed. Along with these some other special condition can be laid down which are binding on both the parties. These special conditions depend on type of work and amount and quality of work. A few examples of these special conditions are:

(1) The concrete used is of grade M 30 and contractor is required to get a mix designed from an approved laboratory before concreting is made.

(2) Concrete should be compacted only be 60 mm diameter and 600 mm long needle vibrator giving 5000-6000 vibration per minute.

(3) Through stone of size as mentioned in drawings should only be used at a spacing shown in drawings.

1.8. CONTRACT DOCUMENTS

The contract documents in general consist of following items.

(1) Title page giving the detailed location of site; division/circle issuing tender, type of tender and type of work to be performed.

(2) Index-page giving content of contract documents.

(3) Tender notice.

(4) Special conditions of contract including schedule A and B.

Schedule A—is bill of quantities specifying the quantity of various items involved in that work and rates in case of B1 tender.

Schedule B—is list of materials to be supplied by the department and their recovery rate.

(5) Detailed specification all items of works.

(6) Detailed Drawings. (7) Deed of pledge.

This contract documents called agreement deed is always in written/typed on required stamp paper duly signed by the owner as well as contractor. Each page of this deed is to be signed by both the parties. Generally three to four copies of the agreement are prepared and distributed as below.

(1) One copy along with attested copy to higher authority. Higher authorities sometimes the agreement and returns original copy to engineer incharge and retain one attested copy for record.

(2) One copy is kept in locker and is taken out only in case of dispute if required by a court of law.

(3) One copy is issued to accountant general.

(4) One copy is given to the contractor duplicate copies of contract documents can be held if required.

1.9. PERFORMANCE OF CONTRACT

Pèrformance of contract means to deposit a sum equal to security deposit with the department and to sign performance bond for a value mentioned in tender notice. It is on a form approved by engineer, architect viz. government bond. Government security. It remains in the custody of architector department till the defect liability period is over.

1.10. BREACH OF CONTRACT

In every contract system; generally two parties are involved. These parties in civil engineering are contractor and owner when each acquires a right what is promised by other. If one of party fails to perform or fulfil his obligations, under the contract; it results into breach of contract which may lead to determination or termination of contract. It causes a loss to one party that gives an immediate cause of action and a right to damages as compensation for loss occurring from the breach.

As far as determination of contract by owner or employer; this can be done under following conditions:

(1) Default on behalf of contractor like

(*a*) Contractor loses the job for any reason known to him only.

(*b*) If contractor suspends the work and does not start again even after receiving notice.

(*c*) Does not maintain the progress and quality inspite of several notices.

(*d*) Does not dismantle and reconstruct the faulty work pointed out by department.

(*e*) Sublets part of the work to other contractor without prior permission.

(2) **Bankuptcy.** If contractor becomes bankrupt. Under such condition; owner takes the work in possession like materials and machineries laying at site. The owner however is required to make payment of materials and equipment at site. No payment however is made to contractor in any form.

Sometimes there is breach of contract from owner also. It is fundamental right of contractor also to recover the damages that have caused him due to breach of contract, not because of his fault. He will have to be put in the same position; where he could have been if had completed the work as per contract deed. Contractor is therefore entitle to cover the loss of profit on full job. He is also entitled to get interest on his capital invested for period of determination of the profit amount depending upon whether the breach is their before starting of work or part work has been executed.

In case contractor commits breach of contract; the employer is also entitled completing or correcting the contractors balance work.

Finally; it is to be noted that aggrieved party will have to prove that he has suffered loss on account of wrong action of other party.

1.11. PAYMENT OF BILLS TO CONTRACTOR

Like contractors responsibility to complete the work as per drawings; specifications and conditions of contract; it is responsibility of department to make the payments of the bills submitted by contractor as and when these are due. Generally two types of bill are submitted by the contractor.

(1) According to progress of work contractor submits his bill called as running bill or Running account bill generally known as RA-1; RA-2; RA-3 *i.e.* running account bill No. 1, running account bill No. 2, running account bill No. 3 and so on. Generally 5 to 6 running bills are submitted during the whole work.

(2) After the completion of work the contractor submits the final bill for payment of remaining amount except S.D. which is paid only after one monsoon season or size months after completion of work which even is later.

For the representation of running bills; measurements are taken in measurement books (called MB) for the works already completed till that particular date and market on drawings. Abstract sheet clearly indicating the quantity of each item completed. Its rate and amount of that item and total cost of work executed is also prepared. This amount is further increased or decreased depending upon percentage quoted in percent rate contract.

From this amount reached various deductions are made. These deductions are:

(1) Deduction or advances given to contractor if any.

(2) Security deposit money (part) if full S.D. is not deposited by contractor. If contractor has made payment S.D. in the beginning before the start the work no deduction is made.

(3) Cost of materials supplied by department to contractor as per schedule A.

(4) Income tax @ 2% of the amount of running bill and this amount is directly remitted to income tax department through bank/treasury challan and a copy of counter foil is given to contractor for submission of his return to income tax department.

(5) Sales tax if applicable at the prevailing rate and the amount is remitted to sales tax department.

Each running bill is then duly signed by contractor; engineer-in-charge who has made the measurements before the bill is submitted to appropriate authority for payment. Each running bill must be given certain reference number and the same should be mentioned in next successive running bill. An example to illustrate it is given it is given here with.

1.12. ADVANCES TO CONTRACTOR

Once a work order is given to contractor after completing all necessary formalities like deposition of S.D. signing agreement deed etc.; mostly contractors as involved in other contract work also may not have sufficient funds available with them to start the actual work. Hence contractors request to the owner for payment of some advance amount against the work which is further deducted from the running bill. These advances paid are called as mobilization advance or material advance or secured advance etc. These advances are paid to raise the initial finance needed by the contractor to mobilise the work smoothy and to have and maintain regular progress of the work.

'Secured Advance' is a term applied specifically to an advance made on the security of materials brought at the site of work; to a contractor whose contract is for the completed item of works. 'Mobilisation advance' is a term applied specifically to an advance made to the contractor to mobilise the work in the initial period as the funds required in initial period are comparatively large. This mobilization advance vary from 5 percent to 10 percent and in special cases upto 15 percent of estimated cost of work. Material advance against the material brought at site is generally given 50 percent to 70 percent of the cost of materials brought at the site.

The practice of material advance now-a-days is always avoided as there is always possibility of thefts of the material from the site. These advances paid to the contractor are deducted from his first running bill only so that the S.D. remains with the department as guarantees of quality of work from the contractor.

Temporary advance is an advance given temporarily by the disbursing officer to a subordinate officer to enable him to make payments of specific jobs like muster rolls or other vouchers while which have already been passed for payments. The account of this is also maintained in a proforma used for imprest. The amount of temporary advance must be closed as early as possible. The basic differences between imprest and temporary advance are:

(1) The imprest is recouped from time to time and is a fixed amount whereas the temporary advance can not be recouped and it is not a fixed mainly; it depends on payments to be made.

(2) The payment from imprest are not required to be sanctioned in advance whereas temporary advance is given against sanctioned payment.

(3) The imprest money can be used for various job or items whilst the temporary can be used for specified work; payment of which has already been sanctioned.

1.13. TENDER

Tender is an invitation from the owner to the contractor to execute some work at specified cost in specified time and published in the form of tender notice in newspapers; notice boards; gussets etc. according to the cost of works.

These tenders may be invited by two classes viz.

(1) Open tenders (2) Sealed tenders

Sealed tenders are invited for big and important works and they are in writing and hence requires wide publicity and no considerations for their validity. These tenders are opened on scheduled date and scheduled time in the presence of contractors who have submitted tender or their representatives. The presence of contractor or his representative during the opening of the tender is not essential but it is always desirable. An open tender is an oral talk between the engineer and contractor for certain small job to be performed. This may be in writing also. However this is also required to be published to have good competition so as to economise the cost of that work. It is generally used for small works.

For a contract to be valid; there must be an offer from owner in the form of tender notice to get some specified work to be executed and similarly there must be an acceptance from the contractor to execute the work. Both the offer and acceptance must be definite and legal.

1.14. TENDER NOTICE

It is an offer from the department engineer to various contractors to undertake some specific job at some specified terms and conditions and to complete that job in specified period. Tender notice published must give sufficient informations to the contractor so that there should be no ambiguity to the contractor. It should contain following informations :

(1) Estimated amount of the works and category of contractors entitled to tender for the work.

(2) The place where and the time when the contract documents can be seen and blank forms of tender obtained; also the amount to be paid for such forms of tender.

(3) The place where and date on which and time when tenders are to be submitted and are to be opened.

(4) The amount of Earnest money required and amount and nature of security deposit to be paid on acceptance of tender.

(5) The period during which the work is to be completed.

(6) With whom or what authority the acceptance of the tender will rest.

(7) The necessity of attaching the tender a list of documents accompanying the tender; signed by the contractor.

(8) Name of work and its location.

A few tender notices for various type of works are given below : for some special works where suficient and capable agencies are not available to perform the work and where the cost of the work is very high. Global tenders (International level) are invited to undertake that job. One of this type of global tender is also given here with. Various terms used in tender notices are dealt later on.

Tender Notice

Sealed percentage Tenders in B-1 form are invited on behalf of Chief Engineer for the work mentioned below from the contractors Registered with P.W.D. in Class III and above or Registered with C.P.W.D., Railway and M.E.S. in appropriate class.

S. No.	*Description*	*Detail*
1.	Name of work	Industrial Area, Ph-11. Deepening and widening existing nalla including providing built up section and remodelling/construction of addition C.D. works
2.	Estimated cost	₹ 93,74,474/-
3.	Earnest money deposit (By demand draft)	₹ 93,750/-
4.	Date of receipt of Pre-qualification form	2.6.98
5.	Period of issue of blank tender forms upto 15.00 hrs. only on all working days	26.4.98 to 09.6.98
6.	Cost of tender forms	
	(*i*) In cash	₹ 1500/-
	(*ii*) By post	₹ 1550/- Non refundable
7.	Last date of submission of sealed offers	16.6.93 upto 15.00 hrs.
8.	Place of submission of sealed tenders	Office of the Chief Engineer

Important Notes

(1) Earnest Money be paid in the form of Demand Draft only drawn in favours of "The Executive Engineer, Division on any scheduled/Nationalised Bank.

(2) Submission of offers in two envelopes system shall be followed as under :

(*a*) *First Envelope :* Contained Demand Draft towards E.M.D.

(*b*) *Second Envelope :* Technical/Price bid.

(3) Any other information can be had from the office of the Executive Engineer, division on specific request during office hours on all working days.

(4) Blank tender forms will be issued to the pre-qualified contractors only.

(5) Right to reject any or all the offers without assigning any reason thereof is reserved by the competent authority.

Sd/-
Executive Engineer
Division

ZILLA PARISHAD

Works Department No. 1

Tender Notice for Purchase of Cement

Zilla Parishad invites Tenders Notices from producing companies and company's authorised distributors, in sealed envelopes in tender notice form for fixing the rates of cement and for purchase of cement for the period 01.6.93 to 31.5.94 the company distributors should have authorised company's distributorship certificate. They should attach it with tender document.

Details of Tender Notice

1.	Qualification	Cement producing company or company's authorised distributors.
2.	Details for supply of cement	O.P.C. cement/ISI 269 Mark/1979/43 grade (50 kgs bags)
3.	Quantity of cement	5,000 Metric Tons.
4.	Approximate price for supply	₹ 1,10,00,000- (one crore ten lacs only)
5.	Place, where tender forms are available and price of form	Executive Engineer works division, Zilla Parishad Office ₹ 500/- (Five hundred only), Non-refundable or Tender Notice forms available for ₹ 500/- (In Demand draft non-refundable in the name of Chief Accounts and Finance Officer, Zilla Parishad).
6.	Advance amount	₹ 1,00,000/- (One lack only).
7.	Deposit amount	₹ 2,50,000/- (Two lacks fifty thousand only)
8.	Blank Tender Document selling period	Date : 24.5.93 to 29.5.93
9.	Last date for submission and opening of tender documents	Tender documents will be accepted till 07.6.93 at 14.00 hrs. If possible will be opened on the same day.

Note : Please note that Tender Notices demanded by Postal Order or send through post will not be accepted. Interested supplier companies/authorised distributors have been provided terms and conditions sample with the Tender document. Requirement of cement quantity possible may increase or decrease by 25%. Rate of cement will be unchangeable upto 31.5.94, the last date of Tender notice. Cement supply should be made to ten talukas in the jurisdiction of Zilla Parishad such as :

(1) Block Development Officer panchayat samiti. (2) Deputy Engineer Zilla Parishad Sub Division (Works). (3) Deputy Engineering Zilla Parishad Sub Division Godown and at the

place where stocking facility is available. Willing cement producing companies or cement distributors should mention single rate (including octroi, sales tax, transportation upto talukas godown, loading, unloading and stocking). Please note that rates mentioned for different duration or in any other form will not be accepted. Cement supply is expected as per demand of work at taluka places and to authorised officers at district places. This supply should be made available as per terms and conditions.

Tenders, setting terms will not be accepted. Chief Executive Officer Zilla Parishad may reject tender without mentioning any reason. Tender rates will be applicable from passing the tender to the end of period mentioned. For more details contact during working days and in working time to Executive Engineer, works department No. 1, Zilla Parishad.

Executive Engineer — Sd/-

Works Department — Chief Executive Officer

Zilla Parishad. — Zilla Parishad

Tender Notice

(1) Sealed Tenders in duplicate are invited for Special repairs for the buildings of 'Officers' Quarters at Bombay. The estimated cost is ₹ 26,80,000.00 only Established and reputed firms/ contractors having necessary resources, equipments and experience of having executed two or more similar type of works, individually costing not less than 50 percent of the estimated cost, need tender for the work.

(2) Tender forms can be obtained from the Manager, Premises Department, Division, on payment of ₹ 200/- per set which amount is not refundable under any circumstances. The tender forms will be issued only to those who furnish written request with information about the names and addresses of their Bankers and Clients with the name of works, duration and the authority under whom it was executed along with documentary evidence. Tender forms will be issued between 11.00 a.m. to 5.00 p.m. on all working days upto 24th May 1993.

(3) Tenders in prescribed forms in duplicate, superscribing the name of work on sealed envelope and addressed to manager will be received by him upto 2.00 p.m. on 31st May 1993 and shall be opened at 3.00 p.m. on the same day in presence of the authorised representatives of the tenders, who choose to remain present.

(4) The Manager reserves the right to accept or reject any or all tenders without assigning any reason thereof.

Press Notice

The Executive Engineer, Construction Division P.W.D. invites sealed item rate tenders from approved and eligible contractors of P.W.D., provided they have satisfactorily completed three similar works individually costing not less than ₹ 1 crore each during the last five years, upto 3.00 p.m. on 21.5.93 for the following works :

S. No.	*Name of work*	*Construction of 44 nos. type I and 104 nos. type II Qrts. at IGNOU at Maidan Garhi.*
1.	Estimated cost	Approx. ₹ 3.29 crores.
	Time allowed for completion of work	18 (Eighteen) months.
	Name of work	*Construction of 66 nos. type III and 30 nos. type IV and 20 nos. type V. Qrts. at ...*
2.	Estimated cost	Approx. ₹ 4.03 crores.
	Time allowed for completion of work	18 (Eighteen) months.

Tenders will be opened at 3.30 p.m. on the same day.

Earnest money amounting to ₹ 20,000.00 each should be deposited in the Bank and receipt challan must accompany each tender. Tenders of the contractor who do not deposit the earnest money through Treasury Challan or guaranteed by the Bank in favour of the Executive Engineer, Construction Division in the prescribed form, will be summarily rejected.

Conditions and forms of tenders can be had from the Executive Engineer, Construction Division from 11.00 a.m. to 4.00 p.m. on all working days on payment of ₹ 150.00 each (not refundable) upto 17.5.93.

Sd/-

Executive Engineer

Construction Division

1.15. VARIOUS TERMS USED IN TENDER NOTICES

(1) **Estimated Cost.** It is cost of that work estimated on the basis of drawings and specifications. While inviting tender; it is essential to have detailed idea regarding cost of that work as earnest money deposit (EMD) and security deposit (SD) depend upon this estimated cost of construction. Further class of contractor who can bid the tender also depends upon this estimated cost only in general and in Government job in particular. The capacity of a contractor to undertake some work depends upon his current financial position and number of works in hand.

(2) **Earnest Money Deposit (EMD).** While submitting any tender, the contractor is required to deposit certain amount with tender document to the department as a guarantee that if his tender is accepted; he may not refuse to work. In case of refusal this amount is forfeited. This amount of deposit is called Earnest Money Deposit (EMD). Earnest Money of the contractor whose tenders have not been accepted is refundable. The amount of earnest money to be deposited with the tender should be sufficient large to be a security against loss in case of contractor is failing to complete the contract documents and furnish the required security within the appointed time, after the acceptance of his tender as the case may be. The amount of earnest money in general is 1 percent to 2 percent of estimated cost of works. According to PWD Maharashtra as per 1984 documents it is equal to an amount as shown below :

S. No.	*Estimated amount of work put to tender*	*Earnest Money*
1.	Upto 1 crore	1 per cent
2.	Above 1 crores and upto 2 crores	3/4 per cent subject to a minimum of ₹ 1 lakh
3.	Above 2 crores	1/2 per cent subject to a minimum of ₹ 1.5 lakh

This can be increased if considered necessary as justifiable under certain peculiar circumstances.

A contractor fails to complete the contract document after its acceptance, it is publicised for removal of is name from the list of approved contractor.

(3) **Security Deposit.** On acceptance of the tender, contractor has to deposit some amount with the department before work order is issued. It is to have a check on the contractor so that he fulfills all the terms and conditions laid down in the contract and maintains quality and work satisfactorily. If he fails to do so; part or whole money deposited is forfeited by the department. This amount deposited as security against quality is called Security Deposit *i.e.* S.D. It is generally 5 to 10 percent of estimated cost of work and is inclusive of E.M.D. which is deposited by contractor along with the tender documents. In case of some faulty construction; if contractor refuses to demolish and reconstruct; the same can be done by the department

from security deposit money. No security deposit is made in case of contract is for supply of material as supplied material itself becomes a security. This security deposit is refundable to the contractor after a specific period of time after completion of the project. This period is generally six month or one mansoon season after completion of the project which ever is more. No interest is paid on S.D.

Many a time when the cost of the project work is large; it is deducted in installments from the running bill of the contractor, generally 50 percent amount of S.D., contractor is required to deposit in advance and remaining 50 percent is deducted from 2-4 running amount bills as the case may be.

As per P.W.D. Maharashtra following is amount of deposit as S.D.

Security Deposit

S. No.	*Particular*	*Percentage*	*Subject to minimum (₹)*
1.	Earth work for contract upto estimated cost of		
	(*a*) ₹ 10,000/- 4 to 6%	—	
	(*b*) ₹ 10,000 to ₹ 50,000/-	3 to 5%	500
	(*c*) ₹ 50,001 to ₹ 1,00,000/-	2 to 4%	2000
	(*d*) Over ₹ 1,00,000/-	2%	2000
2.	Other work		
	(*a*) Upto ₹ 20,000/-	5 to 7%	—
	(*b*) ₹ 20,000/- to ₹ 50,000/-	4 to 6%	1200
	(*c*) ₹ 50,000/- to ₹ 1,00,000/-	3 to 5%	2500
	(*d*) Over 1 lakh	2 to 4%	

(4) **Defect Liability Period.** The S.D. is refunded only after this period. This is the period during which; there may be possibility that the work executed by contractor may show defect. It is generally six months or one mansoon which ever is more.

(5) **Time Period of Work.** This time period allotted for any work is based on type of work, various items involved; time required for each item of work; total estimated cost of work. This varies from a few days in case of supply of materials to a few years in case of construction work of very large amount. In general it is about 15 days to 3 months for supply of materials and 6 months to 18 months for construction work of appropriate amount and size.

(6) **Cost of Tender Form.** Each tender is made available to contractor by making payment to the department as the cost of tender form. This is basically to curtail fissiparous tendencies of contractor and secondly to recover the expenditure incurred in the form of advertisement and printing cost of tender documents. Department issuing tender form is not supposed to earn profit in the form of tender form; but department is supposed to recover its cost.

(7) **Duration of Project.** It is also an important aspect of tender. The Escalation charges are generally not paid for first 12 months *i.e.* after the start of the works. Different type of civil works need different duration *i.e.* time limit for its completion. For example, a road work needs less time in comparison to building. Further depending upon cost, a particular type of work also needs different duration for its construction. A building cost ₹ 50.00 lacks will need less time than that of a building having a cost of ₹5.00 crore. Therefore this duration of project also becomes an important item of tender. It depends on various factor such as type of work type of labour required and their availability; curing period in case of R.C. works, weather conditions, infrastructure required and available and so many other factors.

1.16. INVITATION OF TENDERS

There are three ways in which tenders can be invited.

(1) Private Invitation (2) Public Notice (3) Negotiable Tender

This depends upon type of work *i.e.* Government or Private. In case of private work generally known contractors are invited and asked to submit their tender in prescribed proforma and by discussion and negotiation one of the contractor is awarded that job. Of course, all necessary formalities are required to be completed to avoid any dispute or problem existing later on. However in Government job wide publicity is required to be made so that each registered and qualified contractor can bid his offer. This method opens chances for new contractors. Earlier contractors used to be non-technical persons having little or no knowledge of that job; tremendous problems have erupt due to this. But now-a-days qualified and technical persons having technical degree have entered in the field of contract. This has saved a lot of unnecessity disputable problem. The work in case of public notice is generally given to contractor bidding lowest amount. For small works generally petty contractors are insisted and by negotiations the work is given to that contractor. In case of construction of private individual work; labour contract is given generally by mutual negotiations only.

1.17. TIME SCHEDULE FOR CALLING OF TENDERS

Every tender published need sufficient time to be given to contractor to submit his bid. It depends on estimated cost of the work. As per P.W.D. Government of Maharashtra following are the time limit for first call and second call.

S. No.	*Particular of work*	*Period of notice for first call*	*Period of notice for second and subsequent calls*
1.	Works costing up to 50,000	15 days	10 days
2.	₹ 5,000 to ₹ 5 lakhs	30 days	15 days
3.	Above ₹ 5 lakhs	Six weeks	30 days

Officer concerned are allowed to reduce notice period upto 20 days (in case of 30 days) in the case of second and subsequent calls, after recording the reason, therefore.

The minimum time gap between the last date of issue of the tender form and the date for receiving and opening of tenders is generally as under and in no case; the tender form be issued during the gap period.

S. No.	*Particular of work*	*Time gap*
1.	For all works; the acceptance of tenders of which is within the competence of Suptt. Engineer and below.	4 days
2.	For all works; the acceptance of tenders of which is within the competence of Chief Engineer.	7 days

1.18. TENDER DOCUMENTS

Before the work is given on contract; an agreement is prepared. This agreement should have following documents attached to make it valid; further each paper of this document must have signature of both parties *i.e.* owner (department engineer or competent authorty issuing tender) and contractor undertaking that work. These documents are issued to contractor in the form of tender form containing all the informations and conditions. It also includes drawings and specifications to have an idea regarding the work for which the tender is issued. These tender document include :

(1) ***Title page :*** Title page should have title of work to be performed; reference member location of site and issuing authority of tender.

(2) ***Index page :*** Giving list of contents in serial order with page number.

(3) Printed form of agreement duly completed as necessary.

(4) Brief tender notice as published earlier in the prescribed form.

(5) Detailed notice to contractor in prescribed form (tender notice).

(6) A complete set of drawings showing the general dimensions of the work proposed and so far as necessary, details of various parts as per specified rules.

(7) Additional instruction to tender if any.

(8) Statement of design details if required.

(9) General specifications.

(10) Detailed specifications for all items involved and other items.

(11) Special specifications for concrete work.

(12) General conditions of contract. (13) Special conditions if any.

(14) Statement of machinery available with the contractor and machineries available with owner that can be given to contractor on hire for specified job with details of their charges; terms and conditions.

(15) A certificate to the effect that the estimate made and the plans on which the tenders are based have been carefully examined and that change are called for the reason to be specified.

(16) Declaration of contractor. (17) Schedule B. (18) Schedule B1.

Along with these documents a few more attachments are sometimes made necessary by the department. These details are like:

(1) Contractor is asked to submit a list of machineries in his possession that can be used for that job. It is also a point of consideration to award the contract.

(2) Proof of previous experiences. (3) Technical staff employed by contractor.

(4) Total works in hand with the contractor.

(5) Income tax clearance certificate.

(6) Details of work of similar type and magnitude of work carried out by contractor.

1.19. TWO-ENVELOPE-SYSTEM

The system of submitting tender documents is also called as two envelope-system as; two envelopes are used by bidder.

These two envelopes used contain :

(1) One envelope is used to put the DD or Bank challan or treasury challan of amount equal to EMD required for that job and marked.

(2) Second big envelope sealed contains tender bid of that contractor for that specified job.

These two envelopes are again put in a third big size envelope duly pasted. When contractor submits this to the department; the department opens the big envelope and then opens small envelope containing EMD receipt. The competent authority checks whether the amount is equal to that mentioned in tender notice and in case the amount is not equal to that required as per tender notice the tender is treated as void. The amount of EMD is then transferred to the account department and other big envelope having tender bid is marked time and date of seals of bid, seals are checked; these seals must be intact and then put into safe custody till the opening of the tender.

Such a system adopted and used in practice is called as two envelope system, very common in P.W.D., C.P.W.D. and other government department involved in construction work.

1.20. PREPARATION AND SUBMISSION OF TENDER

The bidder who is interested to execute the job, submits his tender to the department. Once the tender notice is issued by the department, various contractors; interested for that job, procure it from department after making payment of cost of tender form. These contractors study the tender document visits and inspects the site; decide individually at what particular rate the tender can be executed earning reasonable profit. Generally two envelope system explained above is adopted. The tender documents along with earnest money deposit is submitted to department in time as mentioned in tender notice and a receipt of acknowledgment is duly received.

1.21. SCRUTINY OF TENDER AND ACCEPTANCE

Once various tenders received by the department; next job is to scrutinize them. It is mainly to have minimum cost of project maintaining good quality work. Following factors are considered while doing scrutiny.

(1) Name of contractor and his registration.

(2) Earnest Money Deposit DD or challan whether attached, if this is not submitted the tender is rejected immediately.

(3) Previous experience of contractor for similar jobs if any and total experience.

(4) His previous record of works executed.

(5) Financial position.

(6) Machineries available with him in relation to the work to be performed.

(7) Man power; skilled and unskilled available with him.

(8) Rates quoted or percent rate quoted.

Earlier was practice to award tender to a contractor; has quoted minimum rates. But now-a-days along with his percentage rate; other factors given above are also considered. Now-a-days qualified engineers have entered into the field of contractor and it has been experienced that there are always less problems as engineering contractors can easily understand the drawings and specifications and knows the importance of quality control. This has also become point of consideration while doing scrutiny and award of tenders.

A comparative statement is prepared of contractors bid submitted and minimum bid with his previous expense is taken into consideration; final decision is made. In case department feels, that contractor in consideration is not reliable; contractor; having second lowest bid is taken for consideration. If required by the department, or owner, the bidder is required to produce evidences of experience, ability and financial standing as well as statement of plant and machinery. The person whose tender is accepted is required to execute an agreement bond to completed the work as per terms and conditions mentioned in tender deed. He is required to start the work; immediately after issue of work order.

The acceptance of contract to a contractor is issued clearly indicating the details of work; its site; cost and rate quoted by bidder. The contractor then informs department; its acceptance and submits security deposit sign agreement deed; gets work order and starts the work.

Ring Formation

It has become a practice by contractors to form a close circuit ring and to prevent other contractors to enter into the competition. A few contractors join together and get works distributed. For example, if a department or owner has invited tender for four works; then four contractor will form a ring and each will submit four tender, one for each work. The contractors get works distributed in advance and quotes very higher rate for works not to be executed by them. It means if 4 contractor A, B, C and D are tendering for four works P, Q, R and S then contractor A will submit four tenders one for each, however he will quote very high rates for three jobs for ex. P, Q and R and will quote lower rate for S. Similar other contractors will do the same and each will get a work at comparatively higher rate. These contractors involved in ring, keep a watch to see that no other contractor submits his tender. This type of system promotes unhealthy competition, and increase cost of project. This type of ring formation should be curbed. Owners or departments are required to check it and to avoid this.

1.22. REVOCATION OF TENDER

A tender becomes a contract if it is accepted. The right to reject one or all the tender without assigning any reason is the right of the owner or department. Similarly, before a tender is opened and accepted; bidder has right to withdraw his tender due to any reason known to bidder only. Section 4 and 5 of Indian Contract Act permits withdrawal of tender by the contractor. This is called as 'Revocation of Tender'. However it is permissible only before the opening and acceptance of tender and not later on. Once tender is opened and accepted, contractor has no right to get his tender revocated.

1.23. EXTRA ITEMS

Extra items are those which are not mentioned in the estimate and had to be provided as per the directives of the competent authority. Executive Engineer in PWD/CPWD are authorised to sanction the execution of and the rates to be paid for; extra item of works; not provided for in regular tender accepted by higher authorities by themselves or by their subordinate officers subject to the following conditions :

(1) The amount of an individual item does not exceed ₹ 10,000/- and total cost is within the amount upto which Executive Engineer is competent to accept.

(2) The rate to be fixed; mutually agreed between engineer-in-charge and contractor if rate is not given in schedule of rate.

(3) If no rate is available in current schedule of rate; it is to be analysed; before finally fixed.

(4) If cost of any extra items exceeds ₹ 10,000/- approval from S.E. or other higher competent authority is required.

(5) No extra item should be got executed from contractor on oral orders or in anticipation of sanction by the competent authority.

(6) The rate of extra item be scrutinised by the divisional accountant before they are accepted and sanctioned by the competent authority.

(7) No extra item rate list can be sanctioned against price work tender.

Many times contractor refuses to execute extra works if not included in tender and having lower rate in schedule of rates. Under such conditions either contractor is offered higher rates and as such new contract is required to be executed. These extra items are found due to:

(1) Impractical planning and extra items are required to make construction possible.

(2) Changes made by owner due to some reasons.

(3) Due to unforeseen circumstances.

(4) Certain items are not drawn on drawings by mistake and later on required to be executed.

1.24. ADDITION AND ALTERATIONS

During the process of preparation of drawings and estimates; it is always a good practice to take into account each item of that work accurately. There should be no ambiguity in specification and no omissions in drawing. As these, some time create problem in execution or become a point of dispute between contractor and engineer. However the engineer incharge reserves the right to make any changes in, Omission from, and addition to or substitution for; the original design drawings and specifications and instruction as are necessary in the opinion of the engineer in charge during progress of work and which may be given to the contractor in writing duly signed by engineer. Such changes are deemed to have formed as work included in the original tender and it is binding to the contractor to carry out such works. The time of completion if required can be extended proportionately and rates for more additional items are given as per schedule of rates. However while making alteration in drawings in general and specifications in particular care should be taken so that there will not be considerable change in the cost of that work; further it may not be objectionable of contractor. In case of dispute the matter is generally referred to superintending engineer of that circle and is final binding on to the contractor. In case of any alteration; addition or substitution if employment of additional labour, material and equipment is required; the claim revision of rates must be specified by contractors within 7 days from the receipt of order. The Engineer-in-charge may revise the rates if found justified. In no circumstance, however contractor has any right to suspend the work due to non-settlement of rates of items. Similarly in the case of curtailment of work, contractor has right to claim compensation as he is likely to loose his profit.

1.25. DEFECTS

It is responsibility of contractor to execute work as per drawings and specifications. Engineer-in-charge if finds any defective work not executed as per condition of contract; can order the contractor to dismantle and reconstruct the defective part. It is customary to contractor to dismantle that part and reconstruct it as per directive of the engineer-in-charge. No claim for dismantling and reconstruction can be made by the contractor. In case contractor refuses to dismantle and reconstruct; engineer-in-charge has right to get the work dismantled and reconstructed on behalf of the department. The expenditure incurred will be deducted either from the running bill of contractor or from remaining bill of contractor or from security deposit as the case may be. This if required can be publicised to black list the contractor for further work. Further if the same is repeated; the department reserves the right to terminate the tender giving due notices to the contractor. Under such condition if the remaining work is less; department can take that work executed by employing labour or as the case may be and the amount can be debited from security deposit of the contractor. If remaining work is enough; department can get that work executed through some other agency (contractor) and S.D. of earlier contractor is forfeited.

1.26. LIQUIDATED DAMAGE

It is an amount of compensation payable by a contractor to the owner due to delayed construction. This amount of compensation is not related with real damage. In case, contractor fails to complete the work within prescribed time as mentioned in tender deed the contractors is required to pay to the owner a sum stated in the tender as liquidated damage for such default. It is not a penalty as imposed per day for delay. This liquidated damage does not relieve the contractor from his obligations and liabilities under the contract. In case if the work or premise is used by owner before its completion, the amount of liquidated damage is reduced in proportion in which the value of the part has been utilised. However this reduction is permissible only if owner or Government has issued the certificate of works occupancy.

1.27. UNLIQUIDATED DAMAGE

This is known as ordinary damage having relation with the actual damage done. When a contract is broken, the party who suffers by such breach is entitled to receive from the party who has broken the contract.

1.28. ESCALATION OF RATES

Once the agreement deed is signed; work order is issued, contractor is required to complete job at specified rates in given project duration. He is not entitled to claim higher rates than those mentioned in tender deed, due to rise in market price of materials or labour. But with present inflation rate; it has become difficult to contractors to complete job, particularly when work is very large involving considerable time period. Hence to overcome this difficulty, contractor either quotes higher rates or asks for escalation. In absence of this many times contractor either abandons the work, stop the work or goes slow. Hence to overcome this; now-a-days contractor is allowed to take benefit of escalation and hence escalation clause is introduced in agreement in agreement deed. It is therefore now in practice to mention the rate of all important materials like cement; steel; wood; brick; pipes, fixtures in the agreement so as to decide escalation later on.

The central government has also approved formula for escalation of materials and labour. These are stated below :

For materials :

$$V_m = 0.7[0.88\ V - C - S]\ \frac{W_1 - W_{10}}{W_{10}}$$

where V_m = Variation in material cost *i.e.* increase or decrease in the amount in rupee to be paid or recovered.

V = Value of work done during the period under reckoning encluding advances on materials if any.

C = Cost of cement used in work.

S = Cost of steel used in work.

C and S are calculated by multiplying the quantity consumed and basic rate fixed by the department. In case contractor procures these materials no deduction is made in above formulae.

W_1 = Average all India whole-sale price Index for all commodities for the period under reckoning as published.

W_{10} = Average all India wholesale Index for all commodities during the month of opening of the tender as published.

For labours :

$$V_L = 0.3[0.88\ V - C - S]\ \frac{I - I_0}{I_0}$$

where V_L = Variation in labour cost *i.e.* decrease in amount of rupees to be paid or recovered.

V, C and S same as stated above.

I = Average all India consumer price index number for industrial worker declared by Labour Bureau; Government of India as published, during the period under reckoning.

I_0 = All India consumer price index number for industrial worker declared by Labour Bureau, Government of India as published, during the month of the tender.

Note : In case the bill is submitted prior to 15th day of a particular month; index for that month is not considered to arrive at average indices.

Now-a-days escalation charges are also claimed by contractor for delay in the work due to departmental reason. Many times it happens that department does not supply materials like cement and steel in time; hence work is heldup and delayed. Similarly payment is delayed; the contractor stops the work and period of execution gets delayed. Under such condition; due to delay; the price index increases; material cost increases and overhead expenses of contractor also increases. As such he claims for escalation charges. He claims that if delay from contractor side is penalised then department should also pay escalation for delay of work due to departmental fault.

A few more formulaes under by different organisations are as listed below :

(1) **Escalation for Labour**

$$V_L = \left\{\frac{W}{100}\right\} Y \left\{\frac{L_1 - L_{10}}{L_{10}}\right\}$$

where V_L = Variation in labour cost.

W = Cost of works done.

Y = Component of labour as expressed as percent of total value of works.

L_1 = Consumer price index for industrial worker at the time of execution.

L_{10} = Consumer price index for industrial worker at the time of base period *i.e.* time of submission of tender.

(2) **Escalation for material cost and fuel etc.**

$$V = 0.75 \frac{P \times R}{100} \left(\frac{I - I_0}{I_0}\right)$$

where V = Increase or decrease in the price of works done

P = Percentage of compound labour, material lubricant as specified (can be used for labour also).

R = Value of works done during the quarter for which price escalation is being paid or deducted.

I = Indeces for consumer price index at the time of execution of work.

I_0 = Price index at the time of submission of tender.

(3) $$VLM = (0.88\,R - C)\,\frac{I - I_0}{I_0}$$

where VLM = Variation in the amount to be claimed or refunded.

R = Work done for period under consideration.

C = Total amount of controlled material used for work (supplied by department).

I and I_0 = Price index as given earlier.

Other considerations are :

(1) No escalation is paid generally for first 12 months or that portion of works executed during that first 12 months (for very big works).

(2) Escalation clauses are not applicable where value of work is less than certain specified amount say ₹ 25 lack.

(3) Materials supplied by department are not considered for escalation.

(4) No price increase or decrease made effective if not more than ± 5% of the said price.

(5) Price escalation clause is not applicable if the work is not completed in the stipulated time period or authorised extension of time. Some time some departments mention special clause of escalation under such condition it is very essential to take all points into considerations while deciding such special clauses.

1.29. SUB LETTING

As per contract deed and contract Act; a contractor assigned a work can not sub let or assign whole or part of that work to any other contractor without written permission from the engineer-in-charge. This is permitted only under certain special condition when the original contractor has become ill or undergone some treatment which makes him unable to execute the job; however the responsibility of original contractor regarding quality work can not be avoided.

Sub-letting of work to petty contractor for some specialised job is a common feature. Generally main contractor assigns concreting work to some gangs specialised for the job; or electrical fittings, plumbing etc. are assigned to other contractor; such subletting is not in written form; but it is however permitted as the other party is not directly involved in contract deed.

1.30. INSPECTION OF WORK

The engineer-in-charge of site is required to visit the site regularly and inspect the quality and progress of work and to instruct contractor time to time as and when required in case of defective construction. Engineer-in-charge must ask the contractor to dismantle and reconstruct that defective part at his own cost and no claim should be made by contractor for this. In case of refusal of contractor, the engineer-in-charge should get the work done and to recover the expenditure increased from contractor or can deduct this amount from his running bill. It is the responsibility of contractor or his representative to provide free access to department engineer at site as and when he visits. The engineer-in-charge is required to maintain his daily diary; maintaining the work progress record.

1.31. ARBITRATION

Arbitration means settlement of dispute between two parties involved; generally contractor and owner. This settlement is generally, done not by court of law but by a few persons having complete knowledge of that work and deputed by parties involved. These person or persons appointed to settle the dispute are called 'Arbitrator' and process of setting dispute is called 'Arbitration'. Arbitrator gives decision on the basis of evidences available; inquiries made and his own skill and knowledge. His decision is generally accepted by both the parties and also incorporated into the decree of the court if required *i.e.* if earlier decision is not accepted by either of the parties and if matter is referred to court of law. Aribtrator has to take such decision which must be correct and acceptable by both the parties.

The essential requirement for a person to work as an arbitrator is that :

(1) He is in a quasi judicial position, therefore, the first essential requisite in persons occupying that post is judicial impartiality and freedom from partiality and freedom from bias.

(2) He should be honest; impartial and disinterested in any of the parties involved.

(3) He must be qualified person having thorough knowledge of that subject matter under dispute.

(4) He must be a person of high integrity and unshakable faith in justice.

Arbitration Act. It is an act to consolidate and amend the law relating to Arbitration. This act called as Arbitration Act 1940 extends to whole India except Jammu and Kashmir. According to this act amended upto date; an arbitrator has following five powers:

(1) To administer Oath to the parties and witnesses appearing.

(2) To state a special case for the opinion of the court or any question of law involved, or state the award wholly or in part, in the form of a special case of such question for the opinion of the court.

(3) To make the award conditional or in the alternative.

(4) To correct in an award any clerical mistake or error arising from the accidental slip or omission.

(5) To administer to any party to the arbitration interrogatories as may in the opinion of the arbitrator, be necessary.

According to Arbitration Act, 1940; various kinds of arbitrator are :

(1) Arbitration with no intervention of court of law.

(2) Arbitration with intervention of court of law but with no suit under pending.

(3) Arbitration in suits.

According the Arbitration Act, 1940, Clause 25; the procedure adopted for settlement of dispute in civil engineering contract consist of following steps :

(1) Appointment of arbitrator by higher competent authority within 30 days after receiving complete detailed grievances and claim from contractor. Contractor is required to 'Submit his statement of facts' within 90 days *i.e.* period of limitation.

(2) Preparation and submission of case for Arbitration. All documents are required to be submitted to Arbitrator. These documents consist of agreement deed; drawings; specifications; conditions of contract and the grievances and claims in the form of 'statement of facts' and the bills; vouchers corresponding to dispute.

(3) Hearing of the case by arbitrator as per provisions in the Act. Both parties are permitted to plead their case with due arguments by other. Arbitrator requires to hear both the sides pleading and then to scrutinise and examine all documents. The total direction for this hearing should be completed within four months.

(4) *Issue of Award :* Arbitrator later on; going through all details give the decision. The award should be obtained by parties on non-judicial stamp paper. Once the award is issued by Arbitrator his duty and authority ceases. He can not make any second award.

(5) Finally is the filling of award *i.e.* if the decision is acceptable by both the parties; the award is written on stamp-paper and then duly signed by Arbitrator; both the parties involved and witnesses. This if required can be filed in court of law to its validity.

If the decision is not acceptable by either party; then the party has right to file a suit in court of law for further necessary action and then matter is resolved in court of law only by the regular judicially procedure.

As such Arbitration is an expensive way of settling the dispute between owner and contractor. As far as possible matter is solved at very first or second level only. In extreme cases matter is referred to court. The judiciary procedure and law takes very long time hence people to avoid it.

"Tribunal" is the term applied to either the sole arbitrator or the panel of arbitrators conducting the arbitration and it is of comfort to the parties to be able to choose a tribunal in whom they have confidence. That is why it is important for the parties to endeavour to agree the sole arbitrator or, as the case may be, to appoint their party arbitrator otherwise they will have someone appointed leaving with essentially no scope for objection. In case of panel of arbitrators; it consists of three persons—one appointed by each party and third is appointed as chairman jointly. The chairman has special right to cast his vote in the event of disagreement.

Arbitration has been around for a long time. It has been suggested that it was a method of dispute resolution during the Egyptian Civilization, but it was certainly used by the ancient Greeks and Romans. Traders at the medieval fairs in England and on the continent adopted arbitration to settle their differences regarding price or quality. Over a period of time arbitration became more widespread and is being used to settle an increasing variety of disputes and by the late 17th century it was considered necessary to put it on a more formal footing. The first English arbitration act was made in 1698.

The benefits of arbitration become widely acknowledged and by the end of the 19th century, international arbitration procedures were established for settlement of disputes between countries. International business had developed in magnitude and complexity during the 19th century, to an extend that in 1920, the international Chamber of Commerce was founded to promote regularise trade and investment. It is widely specified in International Construction Contracts. The intention of ICC was to provide a universally acceptable procedure to overcome the diversity in arbitration practice concern regarding the disparities between and, often, the inadequacy of law on arbitration; gave rise to the formation of the United Nations Commission on Trade and Law and Model Law on International Commercial Arbitration which was adopted in 1985 and has been widely adopted by most of the countries. It can not be defined that the diversity worldwide can cause difficulties as regards the deciding of international disputes, but such difficulties are certainly no greater than if the dispute is settled through litigation.

Litigations : Litigations in construction industries are increasing very large. Many of the problems can be solved by means of an Arbitration act; however, in most of cases they are not. Therefore litigations are increasing many fold. In most of the countries litigations and not arbitration is preferred. The main reason behind can be that arbitrators are also biassed; or the parties involved in may not be getting satisfactory results through a process of arbitration. In construction industry there are mainly two possible causes for litigation, bad construction or bad contractual arrangements.

The improper specification is one of the reason for arbitration which leads to litigations. A current practice to prepare specifications is cut and paste through computer. It makes so many mistakes that reading to a amicable solution through arbitration becomes difficult if not impossible. Moreover specifications is a very important document of contract process which is given least attention. Many countries have prepared standard specifications, but these specification can not be followed for all type of construction works. An experienced contractor, especially, a wity one, will spot weaknesses in the specification that can be exploited.

There is another factor in the propensity to litigation—the relation between the engineer representing the designer on behalf of the building owner on the one hand, and on the other, the contractor. Under the contract, the engineer has to approve quite specifically much of that is done on the site, and has the power to direct the contractor to proceed in a particular manner, or even to remove work deemed to be unsatisfactory. This has to be well documented. All this is as it should be; but sometimes the correspondences between the engineer and contractor becomes progressively more acrimonious. At that stage, it becomes difficult to parties to have cool discussion to reach to a mutually acceptable solution. Threats are made, and eventually, the parties proceed to arbitration or litigation. In U.K. steps have been taken to obviate it. Many contracts now require the appointment of an adjudicator at the beginning of construction. As soon as there is disagreement; before matter develops into a formal dispute, the adjudicator steps in and takes a provisional decision. This allows the work to progress unhindered by soured relations. Later on, if either party is dissatisfied with the adjudicator's decision, it can proceed to arbitration.

1.32. SPECIFICATIONS

Specification embrace endless details, ranging over a scope which cannot possibly be converted in any text book. Certain fundamental ideas have been dealt herewith in brief.

Legally the specifications form an integral part of the construction contract. It describes the work and materials to be used in construction in details. It indicates the nature, character and the form of the finished work and prescribe the special characteristics of the materials which can to be used therein, more particularly about the data not shown on drawings.

A combination of drawings and specifications gives the contractor the complete idea about the work he has to perform and materials he has to use in the construction.

Specifications in general should be definite and explicit. These should be lucidly written in the simplest possible language with clauses in a logical order. The description should be exact and complete. A common fault in specifications is indefiniteness of description, arising because of not having actual idea of work and materials or due to obscurity in the language used. Words like "Proper" or "Insufficient" which do not give or "As far as possible" clear idea should be written by an experienced engineer who has complete ideas of construction further they should be concise as far as possible, because fewer words will involve less risk of legal difficulties as this being an legal document.

Specifications are generally of two types :

(*i*) General or brief specifications or (*ii*) Detailed specifications.

General specifications states the clauses of work to be employed in various parts of the building or other work. These specifications only serve as the guideline to the person preparing estimate or designing the work. Hence though they are attached to the contract document but do not form the part of the contract document to be challenged in law.

Detailed specifications law down the rules with regard the quality of material and workmanship. These form a part of the contract document. Being beyond scope of this book.

1.33. INDIAN CONTRACT ACT, 1872

Important provisions and terms relating purchase and construction of contracts are :

(*a*) When one person signifies to another his willingness to do or to abstain from doing anything, with a view to obtaining the assent of that either to such act or abstinence, he is said to make a proposal.

(*b*) When a person to whom the proposal is made, signifies his assent thereto, the proposal is said to be accepted. A proposal when accepted, becomes a promise.

(*c*) Every promise and every set of promises, forming the consideration for each other, is an agreement.

(*d*) An agreement not enforceable by law is said to be void.

(*e*) An agreement enforceable by law is a contract.

(*f*) A contract which ceases to be enforceable by law becomes void when it ceases to be enforceable.

Communication, Acceptance and Revocation of Proposals

The communication of proposals, the acceptance of proposals, and the revocation of proposals and acceptances, respectively, are deemed to be made by any act or omission of the party proposing, accepting or revoking, by which he intends to communicate such proposal, acceptance or revocation, or which has the effect of communicating it. Communication is complete as follows :

(*a*) Communication of a proposal is complete when it comes to the knowledge of the person to whom it is made.

(*b*) Communication of an acceptance is complete when it comes to the knowledge of the proposer.

(*c*) Communication of a revocation is complete, when it comes to the knowledge of the person against whom it is made.

A proposal may be revoked at any time before the communication of its acceptance is complete as against the proposer, but not afterwards. An acceptance may be revoked at any time before the communication of the acceptance as against the acceptor, but not afterwards. A proposal is revoked :

(*a*) by the communication of notice of revocation by the proposer to the other party.

(*b*) by the lapse of the time prescribed in such proposal for its acceptance, or, if no time is so prescribed, by the lapse of a reasonable time, without communication of the acceptance.

(*c*) by the failure of the acceptor to fulfil a condition precedent to acceptance.

(*d*) by the death or insanity of the proposer, if the fact of the death or insanity comes to the knowledge of the acceptor before acceptance.

Acceptance must be absolute. In order to convert a proposal into a promise the acceptance must be absolute and unqualified.

Acceptance by performing conditions or receiving consideration. Perforamance of the conditions of a proposal, for the acceptance of any consideration for a reciprocal promise which may be offered with a proposal, is an acceptance of the proposal.

What Agreement are Controls ? All agreements are contracts if they are made by the free consent of parties competent to contract, for a lawful consideration and with a lawful object, and are not hereby, expressly declared to be void.

What consideration and objects are lawful ? The consideration or object of an agreement is lawful, unless it is forbidden by law, or

- is of such nature that, if permitted it would defeat the provisions of any law or is fraudulent or
- the court regards it as immoral, or opposed to public policy.

In each of the above cases, the consideration or object of agreement is said to be unlawful. Every agreement of which the object or consideration is unlawful is void.

Obligation of parties to contracts. The parties to a contract must either perform, or offer to perform, their respective promises, unless such performance is dispensed with or excused under the provisions of this Act, or of any other law.

1.34. COMPENSATION OF LOSS OR DAMAGE CAUSED BY BREACH OF CONTRACT

When a contract has been broken, the party who suffers by such breach is entitled to receive, from the party who has broken the contract, compensation for any loss or damage caused to him thereby, which naturally arose in the usual course of things from such breach. Such compensation is not to be given for any remote and indirect loss or damage sustained by reason of the breach. When a contract has been broken, if a sum is named in the contract as the amount be paid in case of such breach, or if the contract contains any other stipulation by way of penalty, the party complaining of the breach is entitled to receive reasonable compensation not exceeding the amount so named or, as the case may be, the penalty stipulated for.

2

P.W.D. System of Accounts, Works and Travelling Allowance

2.1. NECESSITY OF ACCOUNTS

In day to day working of an individual or a family so far as his expenses are concerned, they have necessarily to be related to his individual means or that of his family. In the case of a State or Central Government the expenditure has to be planned well ahead of the financial year concerned so that an effective control is exercised on the expenditure of various departments of the Government. The expenditure has further to be related to the expected revenue receipts/income of the State. This exercise is known as budgetting and the session of the Centre or the State in which the budget is passed is known as budget session.

2.2. BOOKS OF REFERENCE AND CODE

Accounts are the backbones for the satisfactory execution of any project. Maintenance of accounts starts even before the project is taken in hand and the finalisation of accounts is the last item before closing the project. Some of the reference books are as below.

(A) Central Publications :

1. Fundamental Rules.
2. The Civil Service Rules.
3. Minimum Wages Act.
4. Trade Union Act.
5. Payment and Wages Act.
6. Payment of Gratuity Act and Central Rules.
7. Employees Provident Funds and Miscellaneous Provident Act 1952.
8. Financial Rules and Treasury Rules.
9. Public Works Department Code.
10. Accounts Code, Vol. I and Vol. II.
11. Treasury Rules.

(B) State Publications :

1. Departmental Financial Rules. The book contains financial and accounts procedure rules supplementary to the general financial rules.

2. Manual of Orders. Each state P.W.D. and as well as each branch of such P.W.D. maintains its own Manual. These manuals are primarily supplementary to the code and provide detailed instructions particularly in matters peculiar to the department concerned.

3. Public Works Department Code. In addition to the Central Code on the subject each State has its own code which defines the functions of the executive and administrative ways of the department.

2.3. DIFFERENT CLASSES OF ESTABLISHMENT IN THE P.W.D.

The following are the different categories of establishment in the Public Works Department :

1. Basic or Regular Establishment : (*i*) Permanent (*ii*) Quasi (*iii*) Temporary.
2. Workcharged or Project Establishment.

These establishments are briefly described below :

1. Basic or Regular Establishment

(*i*) **Permanent**

Table 2.1 gives the basic establishment of a division along with main duties of each branch.

Table 2.1

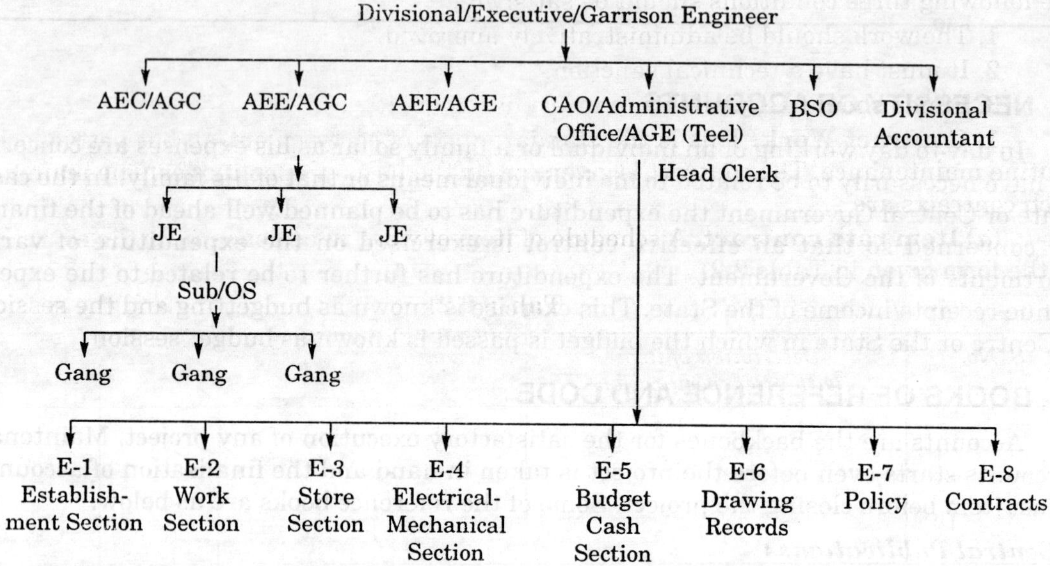

Note : The division into E-1 to E-8 section is based on the M.E.S. organisation but essentially other departments are also similarly organised and known as indicated within the brackets though the nomenclature E-1, E-2 etc., is not used.

E-7 section deals with policy and hence does not exist in the Divisional/Garrison Engineer's Office.

In the above establishment persons holding substantive posts form the permanent establishment.

(*ii*) **Quasi Permanent Establishment.** Due to ever-increasing work load of the divisional office, say on account of projects taken in hand from time to time, additional staff is, therefore, recruited to handle the increased load. Till such time that the basic cadre is recruited, this staff remains as temporary establishment. However, such of the temporary staff whose work has been found satisfactory for at least three years and there is no likelihood of their being retrenched due to reduction in work load is appointed as Quasi Permanent. It is a class between temporary and permanent establishments.

(*iii*) **Temporary.** This has been explained in 2 above.

2. Work Charged Establishment. The Establishment recruited primarily for work associated with the project in the division is termed as 'work charged establishment'. All personnel employed in addition to the basic establishment comes under this category.

2.4. DIFFERENT METHODS OF CARRYING OUT WORKS

Works executed by the Public Works Department can be broadly divided into two categories namely :

1. Original Works and
2. Repairs or Maintenance Works (A.R.M.W. and S.R.)

1. Original Works. Depending upon the type of work original work falls under, three categories, namely :

(*a*) Minor Works and (*b*) Major Works (*c*) Projects.

2. Repairs or Maintenance Works. This consists of the work executed for keeping the structure in proper working condition. No administrative approval is required for carrying out the maintenance works as funds are allotted on the basis of earlier budget grants, on percentages basis, on the total expenditure, year of construction and type of construction (temporary/permanent). Whatever may be the category of work before any work is executed the following three conditions should be satisfied :

1. The work should be administratively approved.
2. It must have a technical sanction.
3. Funds should be available to meet the expenditure.

1. Contract Work. This is the standard form of carrying out all but petty works and routine maintenance. The contract is given out on the basis of open tender. The main types of such contracts are :

(*a*) **Item rate contract.** A schedule of item of work to be done under the contract is as in the form given in Table 2.2.

Table 2.2

S. No.	*Description of item with brief specification*	*Quantity*	*Unit*	*Rate*	*Amount*
				Total	₹

All columns of the schedule are prepared by the department except columns 5 and 6 which are filled by the tendering party.

(*b*) **Lumpsum Contract.** In this type of contract full details of the work along with detailed drawings and specifications are given and the tendering party undertakes to complete the job within the specified period at the rate quoted.

(*c*) **Combination of item rate and lumpsum.** Where the contractor undertakes to get job done on the lumpsum contract basis and at the same time quotes the rate in the schedule of rates provided in the tender to regulate the rate of payment in respect of additions and alternations.

(*d*) **Contract based on fixed percentage above/below the current standard schedule of rates.** Schedule of quantity is blank and the bidder only gives his bid as percentage above/below the standard schedule rates under reference.

2. Place Work System

This system is adopted for small jobs at the current scheduled rates at the direction of the Engineer-in-charge. In remote areas sometimes contractors to undertake a job are not forthcoming while local people are available for small jobs. Sometimes if this work is found economical (the rates tendered by bidder being higher) and the Piece Work is converted into a Bond or Contract Agreement.

3. By Departmental Labour

This is the only method available for carrying out mixed jobs and maintenance. Some of the major projects (such as projects in Border Roads) are entirely carried out by departmental engaged labour. Almost all the cement concrete work in the Highway departments is carried out departmentally. Most of the track laying and maintenance work in railways is carried out by departmental labour. The comparative cost is higher but proper quality control is easier. The system also saves time.

2.5. TRAVELLING ALLOWANCE

2.5.1. Introduction

Travelling Allowance (TA) is a compensatory allowance granted to a employee to cover expenses incurred by him while travelling in companies interest. The policy is that TA should not become a source of income or profit to servants. These allowances are as per pay scales raised from time to time. Therefore these should be taken as guidelines only.

2.5.2. Travel Entitlements

The employees drawing basic pay plus NPA plus Stagnation Increment of ₹ 5100 and above are allowed travel by first class AC; those drawing between ₹ 2800-5099 are allowed AC II tier/first class; those drawing between ₹ 1400-2799 are allowed travel by first class/AC chair car, or by AC II tier when first class/AC chair car is not available in direct trains, and those drawing pay below ₹ 1400 are allowed to travel by second class. Officers in receipt of pay of ₹ 5100 and above may, at their discretion, travel by air on tour/transfer. Apart from this, non-entitled officers are also allowed to travel by air under certain specified provisions. No official below the level of Secretary to Government of India is presently entitled to travel first class by air either within or outside the country while on tour.

Top Executives	=	Air first (J) class/AC I class train
Senior Executives and Executives in pay scales of ₹ 3700-5000 and above.	=	Air economy (Y) class in case of domestic flights and business/club class in case of foreign flights/ AC I class train
Executives in pay below ₹ 3700-5000	=	Air economy class/AC II Tier train
Supervisory Staff	=	AC II Tier train
Supporting Staff	=	First class train/AC III Tier train
Auxiliary Staff	=	Sleeper Class Train

In case of road travel between places connected by rail, travel by any means may be allowed provided the total fare does not exceed the train fare by the entitled class. In case of places not connected by rail, all Executives should be allowed travel by AC bus/AC taxi. Supervisory/Supporting Staff should be allowed travel by deluxe/express buses and Auxiliary Staff by ordinary bus. The eligibility for air travel deliberately so as to curtail loss of official time incurred during train/road travel while on tour. This will also reduce the amount of DA which is paid for the entire duration of the tour. While no changes are necessary in entitlements for travel by sea, to convert the existing entitlements which are based on monthly emoluments to a rank-based system, we recommend that in case of journeys by sea or river steamer, officers of the status of Executives and above should be allowed travel by highest class. Supervisory and supporting Staff should be allowed travel by lower class if there are more than two classes. Auxiliary staff should be allowed to travel by the lowest class.

2.5.3. Daily Allowance

Daily allowance is a uniform allowance for each day of absence from headquarters on duty to a place beyond a radius of 8 kilometres, which is intended to cover the ordinary daily expenses incurred by a servant away from his headquarters while on tour. Due to inflation, these rates have now become unrealistic and are not adequate to meet the incidental expenditure incurred by servants on tour. It is also a fact that in a new place with attendant language problems, unfamiliarity with routes of public transport etc., an employee has to perforce use scooter/taxi which proves to be quite expensive. Further, with improved hotel entitlement being recommended elsewhere, the expenditure on food would also go up which may not be compensated by merely neutralising the effect of inflation on the existing rates. Presently, the TA/DA rates are fixed on the basis of pay plus Non Practising Allowance plus Stagnation Increments. The categories and rates for travelling allowance and daily allowance areas under:

S. No.	*Category*	*Daily Allowance**			
		A-1 class cities Hotel / Non-Hotel Rates	*A class cities & specially expensive localities Hotel / Non-Hotel Rates*	*B-1 class cities and expensive cities Hotel / Non-Hotel Rates*	*Others Hotel / Non-Hotel Rates*
1.	Top Executives & Sr. Executives	₹ 400/200	₹ 320/160	₹ 240/120	₹ 160/80
2.	Executives	₹ 350/150	₹ 280/120	₹ 210/90	₹ 140/60
3.	Supervisory Staff	₹ 225/125	₹ 180/100	₹ 135/75	₹ 90/50
4.	Supporting Staff	₹ 190/100	₹ 150/80	₹ 115/60	₹ 75/40
5.	Auxiliary Staff	₹ 150/75	₹ 120/60	₹ 90/45	₹ 60/30

* These are to be taken as per policies prevailing.

It is clarified that hotel rates will be admissible only in case a servant stays in a properly licensed hotel, charging a regular tariff. In all other cases, including stay in government/ public sector/private guest houses, etc. the Non-Hotel Rates will apply. In order to prevent any erosion in these rates on account of inflationary pressures it is further recommend that consideration of these rates of TA/DA whenever the all India Consumer Price Index increases to the extent of fifty per cent should be taken.

CATEGORY	ACCOMMODATION			
Top Executives & Sr. Executives	*Reimbursement of actual expenditure incurred towards normal single room rent in a hotel of a category not above 5 star.*			
Executives	*Normal single room in a hotel of a category not above 3 star.*			
	A-1 class cities	*A class cities & specially expensive localities*	*B-1 class cities & specially expensive localities*	*Others*
Supervisory Staff	Any hotel room up to ₹ 200* per day	Any hotel room up to ₹ 260* per day	Any hotel room up to ₹ 220 per day	Any hotel room up to ₹ 150 per day
Supporting Staff	Any hotel room up to ₹ 225 per day	Any hotel room up to ₹ 190 per day	Any hotel room up to ₹ 160 per day	Any hotel room up to ₹ 90 per day
Auxiliary Staff	Any hotel room up to ₹ 195 per day	Any hotel room up to ₹ 150 per day	Any hotel room up to ₹ 90 per day	Any hotel room up to ₹ 70 per day

*Rates be revised as her prevailing norms only.

2.5.4. Provision Regarding Travel in Staff Car with Family Members while on Official Tour

Presently, an officer proceeding on tour in a staff car can, in exceptional cases and with prior approval of an officer of the level of senior executive, take his family members along with him but for this facility he has to pay a prescribed amount.

2.5.5. Transfer Grant and Packing Allowance

The Packing Allowance and Lumpsum transfer grant should be merged and called 'Composite Transfer Grant'. The quantum of this grant is equal to one month's basic salary. Packing Allowance and Lumpsum Transfer Grant are only available in case of transfer between two stations located at a minimum distance of 20 kilometres from each other. 'Composite Transfer Grant' @ one month's basic pay should invariably be paid in case of all transfers involving a change in station, irrespective of the distance between the new and old station. However, in cases of transfer within the same city wherein a change of residence is necessitated solely on account of the transfer, Composite Transfer Grant equal to 1/3rd of the monthly basic salary of the transferred employee may be paid.

2.5.6. Transport of Personal Effects on Transfer

Presently, personal effects transported by road between places connected by rail are only reimbursed to the extent of actual expenditure or 1¼ times of the amount admissible for transport by goods train for the maximum admissible quantity, whichever is less. Frequently rail wagons are not available or there are some genuine practical difficulties due to which a government official on transfer is forced to transport his personal effects by road. As transportation by road is costlier, the employee on transfer has to incur additional expenditure from his pocket.

2.5.7. Transport Allowance

We have observed that on account of various factors like unprecedented growth of city limits, increase in volume of traffic and nonavailability of residential accommodation at reasonable rents near offices which are usually located in the heart of the city, there has been an unprecedented increase in the commutation time between residences and place of work. This affects the work environment in offices adversely as employees spend much of their energy in commuting and are, therefore, not able to concentrate properly on official work. While government has allowed journeys between residence and place of work by official car to executives of the rank of Joint Secretary and above on payment of an monthly amount, the

Table 2.3. Range of Conveyance Allowance*

Name of the PSU/BANK	*Executives*	*Supervisory*	*Workmen*	*Others*
Gujarat State Fertiliser Company Ltd.	₹ 2180-1280	₹ 725-530	₹ 705-505	₹ 215
NTPC Ltd.	₹ 1460-240	₹ 235-180	₹ 225-150	—
Coal India Ltd.	₹ 1200	₹ 950	₹ 330	₹ 190
Tehri Hydro Development Corpn. Ltd.	₹ 1100-375	₹ 280	₹ 175	₹ 120
Project and Equipment Corpn. of India Limited/State Trading Corpn. of India.	₹ 1060-1000 ₹ 370 (Car) ₹ 175 (Scooter) (Other Mode)	—	₹ 340 (Two Wheeler) ₹ 150 (Other Mode)	—
Indian Railway Construction Co.	₹ 900-800	₹ 350-300	₹ 300-250	₹ 250-200
Cement Corpn. of India Ltd.	₹ 850	₹ 220-125	₹ 150-125	₹ 100
Mica Trading Corpn. of India Ltd.	₹ 800 (car) ₹ 275 (Scooter) ₹ 115 (if no vehicle)	₹ 255-110	₹ 255-110	₹ 255-110

Madras Fertilizers Ltd.	₹ 750	₹ 300	₹ 300	₹ 150
Bharat Yantra Nigam	₹ 650-600 (Car) ₹ 225-135 (Two Wheeler)	₹ 100-50	₹ 65-50	₹ 65-50
Indian Telephones Industries Ltd.	₹ 650-225	—	—	—
EPI Ltd.	₹ 650-450	₹ 250-175	—	—
Bharat Electronics Ltd.	₹ 650 (in case of Car) ₹ 225 (in case of Scooter)	₹ 225-120	₹ 125-85	₹ 50
North Eastern Handicrafts/Handlooms Development Corpn. Ltd.	₹ 650-₹ 600	₹ 200-175	₹ 175-150	₹ 140-115
Hindustan Fertilizer Corporn. Ltd.	₹ 525	₹ 175	₹ 100	₹ 45
Paradeep Phosphates Ltd.	₹ 500-350	₹ 175	₹ 120	₹ 45
Engineers India Ltd.	₹ 450-400	₹ 175-150	₹ 150-100	₹ 40
Bongaigaon Refinery and Petrochemicals Ltd.	₹ 450-400	₹ 175-150	₹ 150-125	₹125-100
National Textiles Corp./Rail India Technical and Economic Services Ltd.	₹ 450-400	₹ 175-150	₹ 150-100	₹ 40
Hindustan Petroleum Corp. Ltd.	₹ 450-300	₹ 190-140	—	—
Bharat Aluminium Ltd.	₹ 400 (car) ₹ 175-100 (two wheeler)	₹ 150-100		
Hindustan Salts Ltd./Rural Electrification Corpn. Ltd.	₹ 450-400	₹ 175-150	₹ 150-100	₹.40
Indian Overseas Bank	₹ 350-175 (₹ 300-100 in case no vehicle is kept)	—	—	—
State Bank of Hyderabad	₹ 350-125 (₹ 200-100 in case no vehicle is kept)	₹ 175-125	—	—

* Varies from time to time with the revision of salary and cost index.

same needs to be further expanded and liberalised, especially in the context of the public sector and private sector practice of either providing a company car or a liberal petrol allowance to its executives. Details of such allowances are indicated in Table 2.3.

The Executives, Supervisors and the category of Supporting and Auxiliary staff may be given transport allowance at the monthly rates of ₹ 800, ₹ 400 and ₹ 100 respectively in places classified as A1 and A cities. In all other places transport allowance at the rate of ₹ 400 for Executives, ₹ 200 for Supervisors and ₹ 75 for Support and Auxiliary staff should be taken account.

2.6. CORRELATION BETWEEN WORKS AND ACCOUNTS

Funds are allotted for the execution of works on the basis of the Administrative Approval of the work and the schedule of demand for the financial year under consideration. The financial year of the country is from 1st April to 31st March. The forecast for works-in-progress and expected to be taken in hand by the Works Department is made in the month of July of the preceding year. In October 1st, changes-in-grants is initiated and in the month of December second and final change is made. The purpose of this is to enable the demands to be consolidated on the basis of overall availability during the budget session between February to April. It would thus be clear that the funds for any work are based on the works and overall control of expenditure can only be exercised by maintaining separate construction accounts for each work. This establishes the correlation between Works and Accounts.

Further control is exercised on the expenditure in respect of the various items of administrative approval by segregating the expenditure in respect of individual items of the Administrative Approval. Not only the overall expenditure should be within the sanctioned amount but also the expenditure on individual item of the Administrative Approval is controlled. So far as audit requirement is concerned control on these primary elements is not required. Moreover in the case of works executed through contract agencies a further division of expenditure is not feasible because the contractor is paid on the basis of the total quantities of each item of work of the Administrative approval and hence no further correlation between Works and Accounts is possible.

In the case of works executed departmentally expenditure is further split into the following sub-heads in respect of each item of the Administrative approval.

(*a*) **Stores (constructed material).** For work study and cost analysis purpose the quantity of each material incorporated in each item of work is recorded.

(*b*) **Labour.** The time spent by each type of labour is noted.

Maintenance of accounts under the sub-heads mentioned above thus serves the following purpose, particularly in works executed by departmental labour :

(*i*) For compilation of data for works study and cost control.

(*ii*) For verification of output constants leading to revision/modification of existing schedule of rates *i.e.* for revision of analysis of rates.

(*iii*) To have an independent and permanent record of payment and production.

The above brings home the correlation which exists between Works and Accounts.

2.7. MANUAL OF ORDERS

In addition to Public Works Department Code, each branch of the P.W.D. maintains its own manual. The manuals serve as a supplement to the code. They contain the powers, jurisdiction and limits of expenditure of the various government officers. They also contain rules and orders on subjects particular to each department.

2.8. DEPARTMENTAL FINANCIAL RULES

This contains the financial and accounts procedure rules which are special to the Public Works Department. These rules are supplementary to the general financial rules of the Government.

In general it deals with the working procedure of P.W.D. It lays down the rules for maintaining records of work done and payments made. It also deals with the procedure of stores material.

2.9. ORGANISATION OF PUBLIC WORKS DEPARTMENT

2.9.1. Introduction

The various engineering departments of the government responsible for construction and maintenance of public works such as buildings, roads, canals, health and electrical installations, are known as Public Works Departments. The main branches of this department are :

1. Public Works Department—Buildings and Roads Branch. The department is responsible for construction of buildings and roads of the centre or state as the case may be.

2. Public Works Department—Irrigation Branch. The department is responsible for constitution and maintenance of irrigation system of the state comprising of :

(*i*) Dams (*ii*) Canal headworks (*iii*) Irrigation channels.

Note. In the case of the construction of major dams autonomous boards are constituted where senior engineers of the department are sent on deputation.

3. Public Works Department—Local-self Government. (Engineering Department). Also known as Public Health Department. The department deals with the water supply and sewage disposal works.

4. Electricity Department. The department deals with the construction of generation and distribution of electricity. On account of the large expansion in the production and distribution system, this department now functions as Electricity Department, such as DESU (Delhi Electric Supply Undertaking), UPESD, HESB, PESB, etc. The other departments of the Government are :

(*a*) **The Railway Department.** Though this engages the largest number of Engineers (Civil, Electrical and Mechanical) yet it does not strictly fall in the category of PWD. The accounting procedure is however, the same with slight modification to suit the needs of the department. For example, an imprest in the PWD means the standing advance given to Junior Engineer to meet his day-to-day requirements and is recouped at regular intervals. The term "impres" in the railways denotes the tool box containing specified number and types of track fittings from which the engineer draws his daily requirements. The fittings thus used are replaced/recouped from time to time.

(*b*) **Military Engineer Services.** This engineering department of the Government is responsible to the Engineer-in-Chief for construction and maintenance of defence works. The working of the department is, however, very much similar to the working of other PWD's.

2.9.2. Administrative setup of Public Works Department

Table 2.4 gives the normal setup of the department of the Centre or the State as the case may be.

2.9.3. The Function of Chief Engineer

The Chief Engineer, who is the technical and administrative head of the department is responsible to the Secretary to Government for efficient running of the department. As a technical head he is exercises control, primarily technical, in the execution of the projects and maintenance of works. He submits budget proposals to the government in respect of all original and maintenance works in his jurisdiction and exercises control over the expenditure in collaboration with the Accountant General of the State or Controller and Auditor General in the case of Centre. In the case of M.E.S. he controls accounts in collaboration with the Controller of Defence Accounts of the concerned command. Depending upon the progress of the works he initiates demand of additional funds or surrender of the existing funds. As administrative head he controls employment, transfer, leave and discipline of the staff. He usually represents the department in the recruitment of gazetted staff in the Selection Boards such as U.P.S.C's or State Service Commissions. In case of recruitment of subordinate staff he arrange their selection. As head of the organisation he enjoys the following financial and administrative powers/authority :

(*a*) **Financial**

(*i*) Administrative approval of works other than buildings upto ₹ 1,25,000, in respect of buildings and roads which do not fall under any other administrative control. This limit varies from state to state as well as from time to time.

(*ii*) **Acceptance of tenders for works by contract**—Full powers.

Table 2.4. Minister

(There may be one or more ministers. For example at the Centre, Works and Housing are under one minister, while Power is under the other and Water Resources under another.)

SECRETARY

(A senior technical person or IAS/PCS Officer)

CHIEF ENGINEER

Sometimes there are a number of Chief Engineers in which case the seniormost Chief Engineer who is responsible to the Government for all the works in his jurisdiction is designated as Engineer-in Chief. In other cases, other Chief Engineers are designated as Additional CEs.

Superintending Engineer Circle I | S.E. Circle II | S.E. Circle III etc.

(There are 3 to 4 SF's under a CE)

Divisional Engineer/EE/GE | EE/GE | EE/GE | EE/GE | EE/GE

(There are 4 to 6 divisions in a circle)

AEE/AE/SDO | AEE/AE/SDO | AEE/AE/SDO | AEE/AE/SDO

(There are 4 to 6 sub-divisions in a division)

JE (I) | JE (II) | JE (III) | JE (IV)

There are 4 to 6 Junior Engineers and Section Officers in a subdivision.

(*iii*) **Sanction/Approval of estimates for repair** — Full powers

(*iv*) **Sanction Deposit Works** — Full powers

(*v*) Purchase of livestock, repair of articles under the head 'T & P' excluding purchase of motor vehicle. — ₹ 30,000 at any one time.

(*b*) **Technical**

(*i*) To accord technical sanction for original work and repairs. — upto 5% in excess of the administratively approved amount.

2.9.4. Functions of Superintending Engineer

He is responsible to the Chief Engineer for the following in respect of his circle :

(*a*) Administrative and technical control of the circle.

(*b*) Exercises financial control over execution of original and repair works.

(*c*) Carries out from time to time and as on required basis inspections of works in his jurisdiction.

(*d*) Arranges procurement of the stores required and transfer/disposal of surplus stores.

(*e*) Carries out inspection of offices of all divisions under him and checks for their proper working. A report of such inspections is submitted to the Chief Engineer.

(*f*) Exercises administrative control in respect of recruitment, transfer and discipline of all subordinate staff in his circle except Circle Office Superintendent, Head Draftsman and Accountants.

(*g*) Keeps himself informed about the progress of works in his circle and bottlenecks. For this purpose he holds monthly meeting with the Divisional Engineer and contractors. He exercises the following financial and administrative powers/authority :

(*a*) **Financial**

(*i*) Administrative approval of works other than residential accommodation upto ₹ 1,10,000.

(*ii*) Acceptance of tenders by contract upto ₹ 15 lacs.

(*iii*) Acceptance of purchase or manufacture material, tools and plant for use on works or for running and maintenance of machines and equipment within the sanctioned allotment. He holds full powers for that.

(*iv*) Sanction of deposit works upto ₹ 1,10,000.

(*b*) **Technical.** To accord technical sanction for original works upto ₹ 100,000 and for maintenance and repairs upto ₹ 1,400,000 at a time.

Note : In the Military Engineering Services, the civilian cadre is designated as Superintending Engineer and the Army Cadre of the Service as Commander Works Engineer (CWE).

2.9.5. Functions of Divisional Officer/Executive Garrison Engineer

The Divisional Engineer/Executive Engineer is responsible to the Superintending Engineer for administrative and technical control of his division. In particular his main duties are :

(*i*) To see that no work is taken in hand without administrative approval, allotment of funds and technical sanction.

(*ii*) To exercise effective quality control and quantity control to see that the specifications laid down are strictly adhered to and that the progress is commensurate with the scheduled time.

(*iii*) To see that the contractor's accounts are properly maintained and are regularly submitted to the Competent Financial Authority concerned, To carry out these duties the Divisional Accountant is attached to his division as financial advisor and representative of the Accountant General. In the case of M.E.S. the Unit Accountant does similar duties and is a representative of the CDA (Controller of Defence Accounts).

(*iv*) As drawing and disbursing officer of the division he draws money from the concerned treasury and makes payment to the contractor and labour and office establishment against funds placed by the Government in the concerned treasuries.

(*v*) Carries out inspection of the offices of AEE/AE/SDO atleast once a year and submits reports thereof to the Superintending Engineer.

(*vi*) Inspection of works-in-progress and site checking of measurements entered by the Junior Engineer in the Measurement Books (MBs).

(*vii*) Ensures that all tools, plant and machinery in the subdivisions are properly maintained and utilised.

The Divisional Officer exercises the following financial and administrative powers/ authority.

(*a*) **Financial**

(*i*) Acceptance of tender for work by contract upto ₹ 1,50,000.

(*ii*) Order piece works for works and repairs upto ₹ 1,10,000 at the current schedule of rates.

(*iii*) Sanctioning temporary increase in reserve limit of divisional stock upto 10% over the sanctioned scale laid down for the division.

(*b*) **Technical.** To accord technical sanction for original works and repair works upto ₹ 1,10,000 at a time.

2.9.6. Functions of AEE/AGE/AE/SDO

Assistant Executive Engineer (AEE), Assistant Garrison Engineer (AGE), Assistant Engineer (AE), Sub-divisional Officer (SDO), is responsible to the Executive Engineer for efficient management and execution of works in his sub-division. He is correctly designated as the engineer-in-charge of the works. He carries out the following duties :

(*i*) Arranges stock, execution, progress and completion of all original works and repairs in the sub-division.

(*ii*) Carries out regular check of works in progress and ensures quality and quantity control over the works. Quality control is exercised by ensuring execution of works according to design plan and specification. Quantity control is exercised by checking the progress from time to time with respect to CPM/Bar Charts as the case may be.

(*iii*) Maintains construction accounts of works in his subdivision.

(*iv*) Carries out percentage checks of measurements recorded by the junior engineer in the MBs.

(*v*) Carries out physical verification of all the standard Measurement Books in the subdivision once a year.

(*vi*) Exercises proper care and control for safe custody of cash and stores.

(*vii*) Carries out physical verification of all stores including tools, plant, equipment and machinery at least once a year. A certificate to the effect that the verification has been done is entered on the body of the relevant ledgers and report of verification submitted to the Divisional Engineer.

(*viii*) Checks muster rolls in respect of daily engaged labour and casual rolls in respect of casual labour.

(*ix*) Maintains accounts of all the works in his charge and submits the same to the Divisional Engineer. Even when the disbursing officer is the Divisional Engineer he maintains close liaison with the Divisional Accountant/Unit Accountant for proper maintenance of the Construction Accounts.

(*x*) Maintains all buildings/Roads/Irrigation Works and other structures efficiently and keeps relevant documents up-to-date.

(*xi*) Reports to the Divisional Engineer any unusual occurrence or damage to Government assets in his charge.

(*xii*) Exercises administrative control of the office and field staff in the subdivision.

2.9.7. Functions of Junior Engineer (JE)/Sectional Officer/Overseer

The Junior Engineer is responsible to the Sub-Divisional Officer/Engineer-in-Charge in respect to the works under his charge. In particular his duties consist of the following :

(*i*) Supervision of all works in his charge executed through contractor or departmentally.

(*ii*) Arranges labour for departmental works.

(*iii*) Maintains attendance of departmentally employed daily labour on muster roll and of casual labour on casual labour roll either directly or through the field staff consisting of sub overseer or mate. Daily report is submitted to the SDO.

(*iv*) Takes measurements of all works in the Measurement Books.

(*v*) Exercises direct control in respect of specifications and progress of works under his charge.

(*vi*) Prepares running bills and final bills of all works in his charge. According to the contract agreement, the contractor is supposed to submit his bill but in actual practice the Divisional Officer waves this requirement for efficient running of the subdivision and hence the bills are prepared by the Junior Engineer.

(*vii*) Prepares pay bills of the work charged establishment of his section.

(*viii*) Carries out field survey of proposed projects and ground tracing (Dagbailing) of structures/constructions on the ground.

(*ix*) Prepares estimates for all types of works in the section.

(*x*) Reports any unusual/special event to the Engineer in-charge.

(*xi*) Carries out check of tools plants, furniture and fittings of inspection houses, rest houses and other departmental buildings and arranges collection of rents and revenue due to Government.

(*xii*) Carries out half yearly checks of all stores in his charge and submits reports thereof to the Sub-divisional Officer.

(*xiii*) Carries out annual inspection of all structures in his charge and submits report of such inspection to the Engineer in-Charge.

(*xiv*) Maintains accounts of his imprest and arranges its recoupment at fixed intervals.

(*xv*) Initiates disposal of unserviceable stock, tools and plants in the form of survey report.

2.9.8. Duties of Junior Engineer

(*a*) **Duties in Planning**

1. Preparation of Preliminary Estimate, and Detailed Estimate.
2. Preparation of N.I.T.
3. Checking of additional items, extra items, and variations in estimated quantities.
4. Test check of measurements.
5. Planning of works.
6. Preparations of Schedule of rates, specifications and analysis of rates.
7. Examination of amendments, deviations and special conditions of contracts.
8. Fixing and Revision of minimum fair wages.
9. Inspection of works and detailed examination of expenditure.
10. Preparation of simple designs and drawings.

(*b*) **Duties in Construction**

1. Land Acquisition.
2. Execution of works, according to drawings, design specifications and conditions of contract.
3. Checking Layout of works, and materials of site.
4. Issue of stores.
5. Labour welfare.

6. Keeping progress of works.
7. Measuring the works and preparation of contractor's bill.
8. Making Recovery statements.
9. Reporting of all accidents and thefts.
10. Keeping inspection book, order book.
11. Keeping Record of materials obtained from dismantling.
12. Giving completion Report.
13. Handling over of works for maintenance after completion.
14. Helping the department in arbitration.

(*c*) **Duties in Maintenance**

1. Taking over the charge of computed Buildings.
2. Maintenance of capital register.
3. Preparation of estimates (AR and MO; work charged staff; material; SR. works), and additions and alterations.
4. Allotment Register (Possession Report; Vacation Report and inventory of houses).
5. Record of work charged staff.
6. Maintenance of complaint book, suggestion book, daily task diary of workers and materials used.
7. Record of dismantled material (serviceable and unserviceable).
8. Furniture record (Receipt and Issue).
9. Material account (Receipt and Issue).
10. Tools and Plants.
11. Correspondences Record.
12. Periodical Returns.
13. Inspection Record of Buildings.
14. Preparation of Standard Measurement Books.
15. Execution of works.

(*d*) **Handing over of Charges**

(*a*) **Planning.** Handing over of Estimates; N.I.T. extra item, statements, additional item statements, drawings, designs, specifications, schedule of rates, analysis of rates, reports about the works.

(*b*) **Construction.** Handing over of specifications, drawings, designs, contract documents, estimates, additional items; variations record; list of tools and plants; list of stores, recovery documents; MB's; Road Metal account; surplus stores, unsettled claims of contractors/suppliers; record of work charged establishments, List of level books, indent books, field books; progress repprts; account of advances paid; recovery statements; imprest account, Labour reports, accident reports, record of materials obtained; inspection books, order book and other correspondences.

(*c*) **Maintenance.** Handing over of record of A.R. and M.O. works, S.R. works etc. Estimates, drawings designs, specifications, capital register; allotment register; inventories; work charged record; complaint books, suggestion books, inspection register; dismentled material account, store account; furniture account, tools and plants account, M.B. S.M.B's and transfer entry books, and other correspondences.

2.9.9. Accounts Branch

The accounts branch is headed by the Divisional Accountant who is an adviser to the Divisional Engineer and represents the Accountant General. In the case of MES he is known as Unit Accountant (UA) and performs functions similar to that of the Divisional Accountant. He represents the CDA (Controller of Defence Accounts) of the command concerned.

The following duties are performed by the Accounts Branch :

1. Compilation of accounts of the division.

2. Advising the Divisional Engineers in matters concerning accounts, budget estimates and financial rules and regulation in day-to-day operation.

3. Keeps a watch on the financial transactions of the unit and carries out pre-audit of all payment vouchers in the Division. If he feels certain transactions are irregular he records his opinions for consideration of the Divisional Engineer. The Divisional Engineer can overrule such advise but in that situation he takes full responsibility for the transaction.

4. Carries out post audit of payments made by subordinate officer (AEE/AGE/AE/SDO) where such officers have been delegated the powers of drawing and disbursing.

5. Checks the payments with reference to the individual items of the administrative approval.

6. Scrutinises draft contract agreements in respect of financial property of the same.

7. The Divisional Cashier, who does not belong to accounts department, works under the guidance and instructions of the Divisional Accountant. The cashier belongs to the regular establishment of the Division and maintains the following financial documents :

(*a*) Pass Books. (*b*) Leave Accounts.
(*c*) Register of Receipts. (*d*) Register of Unpaid Wages.
(*e*) Register of Security. (*f*) Cheque Books and Cash Books.

8. Reviews MB's of the sub-division from time to time and brings irregularity, if any, to the notice of the Divisional Engineer.

9. Prepares/Scrutinises and certifies the money expenditure return with respect to the cash book entries.

10. Prepares record for arbitration and legal cases of the division. In the case of MES this job is done by the contract/surveyor of works branch (E.8).

11. Checks TA bills and other account vouchers of the division before they are passed for payment.

12. Scrutinises the comparative statement before the same is placed before the Divisional Engineer.

13. The Divisional Accountant/Unit Accountant is in short the financial advisor of the Divisional Engineer although his advise may at times be ignored by the Divisional Engineer in which case he takes full responsibility for the transaction.

2.9.10. Drawing Branch

The branch is headed by the Head Draftsman (E-6 branch in the case of M.E.S.). This branch performs the following duties :

1. Maintains records and distribution of all drawing and mathematical instruments of the Division.

2. Maintains and keeps upto-date all the road registers and road graphs and drawings of all constructed structures in the division. The final bill of any new construction is not passed till such time the relevant entry has been made in the connected register and verified by the Drawing Branch.

3. Prepares project drawings and detailed working drawings of all the works in the division.

4. Maintains departmental library.

2.9.11. Correspondence Branch

The office superintendent/Divisional head clerk is responsible to the Executive Engineer in all matters concerning general correspondence, establishment and discipline. In the M.E.S., this is known as E-1 section.

The following functions are carried out by the section :

(1) Receiving, opening, sorting and distribution of dak.

(2) Deals with all confidential work such as confidential reports of the establishment, despatching cases and other confidential matter.

(3) Handles all establishment matters such as :

(*i*) Recruiting. (*ii*) Promotions and transfer

(*iii*) Salary bills. (*iv*) T.A. Bills. (*v*) Welfare.

(4) Deals with cases involving Workmen Compensation Act.

(5) Maintains diary, indexing, filing, arrear statement, correction slip, reference books, typing and despatching.

(6) Maintains confidential reports and Service Books. In addition to the above functions, which deal with establishment, the following additional duties in respect of works, cash and policy and contract are also performed in the Public Works Department. In M.E.S. organisation these functions are carried out by the following branches :

Works	E-2 Section
Cash	E-5 Section
Policy	E-7 Section
Contract	E-8 Section

Thus the additional duties in addition to the establishment section are :

(1) Upkeep and handling of cash book and other financial documents dealt with under duties of Divisional Accountant in respect of the cashier. The cashier is thus under the dual control of the Divisional Accountant and the Head Clerk.

(2) Issue and receipt of money received on behalf of the Government.

(3) Issue notes of tender, tender form and prepare tender agreement.

(4) Reservation of rest houses and connected correspondence.

(5) Compilation and submission of Reports and Return.

(6) Deal with correspondence relating to estimate of works.

(7) Procure stores for Divisional stock. (In the case of MES, there is separate stores organisation under Barracks and Stores office).

2.9.12. Revenue Branch

This branch is in Irrigation Department only. Deputy Revenue Officer/Deputy Collector/ Senior Tahsildar is incharge of this branch which performs the following duties :

1. Collection of canal dues from users.

2. Demarcation of areas availing canal-irrigation facilities.

3. Maintenance of register of the cultivator/farmers along with the amounts to be paid by each.

2.9.13. P.W.D. Establishment

In the M.E.S., two additional establishment exist. One of these is independent and works directly under the Chief Engineer of the command. Their usefulness has since been appreciated and they have been added to the C.P.W.D. establishment as well. These two establishments are S.W. (Surveyor of Works) and T.E. (Technical Examination).

2.10. P.W.D. SYSTEM OF ACCOUNTS

2.10.1. System of Accounts

(*a*) **Civil Accounting System.** Under this system :

(*i*) All receipts are deposited into the Treasury on which the station is based.

(*ii*) All money required for distribution/payment is drawn from the Treasury on presentation of bills.

(*iii*) Monthly return giving abstract of transaction is submitted to the Accountant General by the Treasury.

(*b*) **P.W.D. According System.** Under this system the Government intimates the Accountant General the names of the drawing and disbursing officers and the head of the Department namely the Chief Engineer intimates the monthly limit of cash that can be placed at the disposal of the drawing and disbursing officers. The drawing and disbursing officer issues cheques for contractor's payment or draws cash against the assignment. At the end of the month the drawing and disbursing officer submits the closed cash book alongwith all the connected vouchers to the Accountant General/Controller of Defence Accounts as the case may be.

(*c*) **Fresh Account System.** The system is similar to the P.W.D. system of accounting with slight variation to suit the departmental condition.

2.10.2. Classification of Transactions

In order to have an effective control on the spending of the Government departments, all the transactions are divided into the following four divisions, namely :

1. Capital 2. Revenue 3. Remittance 4. Debit.

2.10.3. Heads of Accounts

All monetary transactions are primarily divided into two categories namely :

(*i*) Receipts, and (*ii*) Expenditure.

Separate heads of accounts therefore exist for these two categories.

From the year 1974-75 a scientific three digit classification has been introduced in accounting.

The important features of this classification are illustrated in Table 2.5.

Table 2.5. Three Digits Classification of Accounts.

General Services | Social and Community Service | Economic Services

(Heads of Accounts grouped under three Sectors)

SECTOR

Public Works | Education | Housing | etc. | etc.

(Major heads under each sector)

MAJOR HEAD

MINOR HEAD

SUBHEAD

DETAILED HEAD

(Under each Major head are minor head, subheads and detailed heads.)

All monetary transaction in Public Works Department can be classified as shown in Table 2.6.

For the Public Works, Major heads for Receipts Revenue is 059.

The minor heads are :

1. Non-residential buildings. 2. Rent. 3. Other Receipts.

Detailed heads for other receipts are :

(*i*) Sale proceeds of dead stock, waste papers or other items the cost of which is met from office expenses.

(*ii*) Other items.

Thus the rent realised for as non-residential building will be deposited into the treasury under the head 059 — Public Works (2).

Table 2.6. Grouping of Transactions in P.W.D.

Major Head	*Block Allotted*	*Remarks*
Receipt	020 to 199	I. There is a difference of 200 between the block numbers of revenue head and receipt head between capital outlay head and revenue head.
Expenditure		
Revenue Side	211 to 399	
Capital Side	411 to 597	
Public Debt		
Loan Allowances	611 to 799	
Public Account	801 to 899	
Contingency Fund	800	

Table 2.7 gives further classification in respect of the receipt and expenditure heads.

Table 2.7. Receipt and Expenditure Heads.

Department	*Receipt Head*	*Expenditure Head*		*Remarks*
		Revenue	*Capital outlay*	
Education	077	277	477	There is a change of 2 in the first digit, the second and third digits being the same.
Housing	080	280	480	
Roads and Bridges	137	337	537	

Similarly money realised from the auction of unserviceable material will be deposited under the head 059—Public Works 3 (*i*).

Major Head expenditure revenue is 259—Public Works. There is no sub-major head and the minor heads are :

(1) Construction of non-residential buildings

(2) Direction and administration. (3) Planning and Research.

(4) Maintenance. (5) Furniture.

Thus ₹ 5000 spent on planning and research will be chargeable to the head 259—Public Works (3).

Table 2.8. Sectional Classification forMajor Heads

S. No.	*Classification*	*Method of Denoting*
1.	Sectors	Denoted by Capital Letters in separate series (*i*) Revenue Receipt (*ii*) Revenue Expenditure (*iii*) Capital Outlay
2.	Sub-Sectors	Denoted by small alphabets within brackets
3.	Major Head	Denoted by Code No.
4.	Minor Head	Denoted by small alphabet within brackets
5.	Sub-Head	Denoted by Arabic numbers within brackets such as (1), (2) etc.
6.	Detail Heads	Standard objects of expenditure to indicate nature of expenditure. Table 2.7 gives the details of the items termed as SOE's
7.	Plan Scheme	Denoted by Code Nos.

Table 2.9. List of Standard Objects of Expenditure (SOE)

S. No.	*Particulars*	*Remarks*	*S. No.*	*Particulars*	*Remarks*
1.	Salaries		15.	Tools and equipment	
2.	Wages		16.	Motor Vehicle	
3.	Travel Expenditure		17.	Maintenance	
4.	Office Expenditure		18.	Investment	
5.	Payment for professional and special services		19.	Material & Supplies	
			20.	Interest	
6.	Rent, taxes etc.		21.	Pension/Gratuity	
7.	Publication		22.	Depreciation	
8.	Advertising		23.	Inter account transfer	
9.	Grants-in-aid		24.	Write off/Losses	
10.	Scholarship		25.	Suspense	
11.	Hospitability expenses		26.	Dietary charges	
12.	Secret Service		27.	Medicines	
13.	Major Works (over 1 lac)		28.	Other charges	
14.	Minor Works (below 1 lac)				

Details of other major heads can be had from booklets available in the Divisional offices.

As an additional example let us take Education.

Major head for Revenue Receipt is 077.

The sub-major heads are :

A. Primary *B.* Secondary *C.* Special *D.* Pre-university.

The minor heads are :

1. Tuition and Examination fee 2. Textbooks.

Thus money received for the sale of Secondary class books by the government will be deposited into the Government treasury under the head 077-Education—B—(2).

Note. On the basis of the recommendations of the Second Report of the team of Reform in the structure of Account Heads, the Comptroller and Auditor General of India has prescribed the list of major and minor heads of accounts for classification of transaction of Union, States and Union Territories of Government. This has been done with the approval of the President of India and comes into effect from 1 April, 1974 *i.e.* for the financial year for 1974-75. As a result of this the Major and Minor Head of classification given in Appendix 2 to PWD Accounts code has been modified. For ready reference, some of the heads existing under the old system and the present are given in Table 2.10.

Table 2.10. Statement of Earlier Major Heads and Minor Heads and the Revised Heads

Heads of Accounts prior to 1.4.74	*Heads of Accounts after 1.4.74*
V—Taxes on income other than corporate tax	021 — Taxes on income other than Corporate Tax.
xxxvii — Public Works	059 — Public Works
Receipts for works	083 — Housing
	059 — Public Works
Recoveries of Expenditure	083 — Public Works
Miscellaneous	137 — Roads and Bridges
xxxiv/xxx — Irrigation, embankment and drainage works	133 — Irrigation
xxxvi — Electricity schemes	131 — Water and Power Development Scheme
	134 — Power Projects
xlii — Aviation	136 — Civil Aviation
45 — Electricity Scheme	334 — Power Projects
50 — Public Works	259 — Public Works
52 — Capital outlay on public works	Deleted
71 — Misc.	265 — Other Administrative Services
Rent, Rates and Taxes	766 — Loans to Govt. Servants
P — Loans and Advances	843 — Civil Deposits
T — Deposits and Advances	805 — State Provident Funds
State Provident Funds G.P. Fund	A – Civil Fund, G.P. Fund D – Other P. Funds WCP Funds

2.11. CASH

2.11.1. Introduction

All the financial transactions in the Division or Disbursing sub-division are entered in the cash book of the Division or sub-division as the case may be. An abstract of all such transactions is prepared at the close of the month in which all the entries of the cash book are shown. In some departments two cash books are maintained, when the cash book of the month is closed it is sent to the Divisional Office/Accountant General/CDA for post-audit and transactions pertaining to the succeeding months are entered in the second cash book.

A typical cash book form (PPWA Form 1) is given in Table 2.11.

The term cash includes the following :

(*i*) Legal tender coins (*ii*) Currency notes

(*iii*) Deposits-at-call receipts of government banks and demand drafts.

(*iv*) Accepted private cheques.

Table 2.11. Cash Book Form C.P.W.A. — Form 1.

Cash Book of Shri 'A' Executive Engineer..........Divn. for the Month of 7/2001.

Receipts				*Payment*				
Date of Receipts July 2001	*From whom received*	*Amount*	*Classification of Receipt*	*Date of Payment*	*Voucher No. Paid*	*To whom*	*Bank or Treasury Cash No. of Amount / Cheque*	*Classification of Charges*
1st	Opening balance							
	Details of Balance : Cash Temporary Impress to	Total		By Closing Balance ₹ ...				The balance at the closing of the book at end of month should be the same in receipt and payment side.

Note : 1. Undisbursed pay of staff is kept in a subsidiary cash book and is not included in the opening cash balance.

2. Post-Office Savings Bank Pass Book balance and service postage stamps are not included the opening cash balance.

3. Fine is credited of the same work.

2.11.2. Treasury Challans

When any money is deposited into government treasury or sub-treasury in Form 32-A shown in Table 2.12 the following particulars are given in the form.

(*i*) Nature of payment.

(*ii*) Person/Officer on whose account payment is made.

This challan is prepared in duplicate. One copy is retained in the treasury for record and the other is returned to the depositor duly signed.

Table 2.12. Treasury Challan (Form 32-A)

Challan of cash paid with the State/Reserve Bank of India

By Whom Tendered	*To be filled in by the remitter*		*To be filled in by the Departmental Officer or the Treasury*		
	Name (or designation) and address of the person on whose behalf money to paid.	Full particulars of the remittance and of authority (if any)	Amount	Head of Account	Order to the Bank **Dated :** Signature and full designation of the officer ordering the money to be paid in.

Signature................

(Sd)

Accountant.............

Treasury Officer/Agent

Treasurer..................

2.11.3. Imprest Account

In order to carry out petty purchases for satisfactory execution of the work efficiently the disbursing officer sanctions a standing advance upto a maximum of ₹ 1000 at a time. Usually such advance is kept upto ₹ 250. The subordinate concerned submits details of expenditure by the 25th of every month in Form C.P.W.A.-2 along with supporting vouchers. The expenditure thus incurred during the month is recouped in the beginning of the month so that the amount of the permanent imprest is restricted in the beginning of the month.

2.11.4. Temporary Advance

In addition to the Imprest Account described above temporary advances are given by the Divisional Engineer to the Sub-divisional Officer against passed vouchers for making payment at site to muster roll labour or casual labour. The account of such advance is submitted to the Divisional Officer immediately after the disbursement is made.

2.11.5. Construction Accounts

Construction Account is maintained by the Divisional Engineer/GE/AEE/AE/SDO to exercise, financial control over the expenditure. It gives the financial position of this and gives at a glance the booked expenditure and expected liabilities. These accounts are compiled as below :

(*a*) **Expenditure.** The expenditure in respect of any job consists of the following :

(*i*) Paid bills (*ii*) Stores received for the work from the store.

(*iii*) Accepted book debits (*iv*) Any credits which may have been received.

(*b*) **Liabilities.** An order for execution of any work or for the provision of stores is a liability till the clearance of the bill. The following expected payments form the liabilities :

(*i*) Work order to the contract for the execution of the work. This order is initially a liability. As running payments are made the amount paid comes under the expenditure head and the liability is reduced by that amount.

(*ii*) Order for supply of stores.

(*iii*) Estimated cost of services ordered from other departments.

(*iv*) Wage bill of labour.

(*c*) **Credits.** The principles applicable to liability hold good for expected credits

(*d*) **General.** Separate folios of construction accounts are operated for

(*i*) Each item of a major work. (*ii*) Each item of a minor work.

(*iii*) Each minor head under sub-head.

These folios are grouped by budget heads and kept in the cover. If desired, separate covers may be used for major heads.

At the end of the month, each folio is closed. These accounts are sent to the accounts branch for scrutiny. The expenditure return is compiled after the abstract has been verified by the Accounts branch with respect to the cash book entries.

A typical form for construction accounts used in the Military Engineering service is given in Table 2.13.

2.11.6. Schedule of Demands

Schedule of demands is an annual return submitted in the prescribed form asking for funds for both original work (in progress and expected to be taken in hand) and maintenance repair.

In the case of original works (projects, major work) the demands for fund is based on the expected expenditure during the financial year under reference. In the case of minor works,

however, back allotment is placed as lumpsum at the disposal of the departmental head and usually only such works, are sanctioned as can be completed within the same financial year. However, if any minor works is not completed within the financial year, the additional minor works for the new year would include the balance of previous year's work.

Table 2.13. Form for Construction Accounts

Expenditure

Item	*Date*	*Particulars*	*Voucher*		*Labour*	*Payments to contr-actors*	*Materials*	*Transport*	*Other charges*	*Credits*	*Running Total*
			No.	*Date*							
	Grand Total										

Liabilities and Expected Credits					*Booked expend-iture*	*Contractors Accounts*			*Initial*	*Remarks*
Liability incurred or credits cancelled		*Liabilities cancelled or credits expected*		*Net liabilities outstanding running total*	*Liabili-ties running total Col. 11+ Col. 16*	*Charges against*	*Recoveries from*	*Running total*		
Order No.	*Amount*	*Order No.*	*Amount*							

Table 2.14. Schedule of Demand for Major Work-in-Progress

S. No.	*Minor head and detailed Head*	*Name and locality of work*	*Amount of estimate as approved administ-ratively*	*Anticipated expenditure in the current year*	*Total antici-pated expen-diture to the end of current year*	*Amount required next year*	*No. and date of the authority for work*

Table 2.15. Schedule of Demands for New Major Work

New Major Work Administrative approval for which has been accorded/Necessity accepted.

S. No.	*Minor and Detailed heads*	*Order of priority*	*Locality and name of work*	*Anticipated expenditure in the current year*	*Amount required next year*	*Remarks*

2.12. STORES

2.12.1. Introduction

For the execution of any Civil Engineering project, the following resources apart from the manpower are required :

(1) Construction stores (2) Tools and plant

(3) Vehicles (4) Plant, machinery and equipment.

The success of any project thus depends on the proper procurement, utilisation, upkeep and transfer/disposal of resources not required for the project.

Proper maintenance of stores is as important as maintenance of cash. Proper maintenance of stores is, therefore, absolutely necessary.

2.12.2. Safe Custody of Stores

The Divisional Engineer is ultimately, responsible for initial procurement, its safe custody, proper storage, distribution and disposal of surplus stores. In the Public Works Department the divisional stores is normally held by Junior Engineer. He is responsible to the Divisional Engineer for safe custody and proper distribution and accounting and submission of reports and returns.

Apart from the divisional store, every subdivision holds stores for its day-to-day work, usually drawn from the divisional stores. The sub-divisional officer usually makes one of the Junior Engineer or a sub-overseer as incharge for the sub-divisional stores.

2.12.3. Classification of Stores

All stores can be classified under the following two categories namely :

(1) Stock (2) Directly charged to works.

Stores procured for general use of construction work and maintenance work are initially kept under suspense head of the stock and issued to the required jobs on the basis of indents. Debit for such stores is raised against the job for which these stores have been issued and credit given to the suspense head of the stock.

In the case of projects, the requirement of stores is very large and a separate organisation is normally required to take charge of the stores transactions. Such stores, which are procured for specific projects are known as Material-at-Site Stores. Their cost is directly debited to the project. The difference in the cost of procurement and supply rate to the contractor is also directly adjusted in the project accounts. The term 'Material-at-Site' does not mean that such project material is necessarily stored at the project site.

2.12.4. The accounting and control of construction stores can be divided into the same two categories under which stores are classified as namely

(1) Stores for Specific Works and (2) Stores for Divisional stock.

The above two categories are dealt with in this article separately.

1. **Stores for Specific Works.** As soon as procurement action for stores is initiated, it amounts to a financial commitment. It, therefore, follows that such action should be taken when the administrative approval for the work has been accorded and funds for the same have been allotted. However, as soon as the possibility of any project materialising is visualised planning has to be started. For example exploring accurately of different categories of stores and collection of information in respect of their rates may be started in anticipation of the allotment of the funds.

On receipt of the stores, the officer in charge of stores (normally a Junior Engineer) prepares receipts voucher in triplicate. The allocation against the work is given in the vouchers. Two copies of the receipt voucher are sent to the Divisional Engineer. One copy is retained by the Divisional Engineer and the second copy is returned to the SDO/JE after recording therein the estimated cost of stores on the basis of which liability is booked in the construction accounts of the work concerned. On receipt of the bill, the same is processed in the normal manner. When the bill is paid the liability is cancelled and corresponding amount is added to the expenditure column. Thus the total of the expenditure plus liability remain unchanged. When stores are purchased from private agency, no separate receipt voucher is required. The entry of the stores is certified in the bill itself and amount paid debited to the work.

All stores received for a specific work are entered in the Material-at-Site register. One page is allotted for each article. The issue rate for such stores is fixed by the divisional engineer from actual procurement cost without percentage addition for overheads as is done for stock stores. When it is desired to book expenditure in respect of various items of the work on separate folio in the construction account, material account is opened. This account is maintained on the ordinary construction account form. The cost of bulk receipt is entered as debit and the value of issue is entered as credit. The account is closed on completion of the job.

In the case of important projects, all stores issued directly to the work and the amount of such issue are kept for atleast two years, after the completion of the work. The account of such stores, showing the total quantity of stores received and incorporated in the work is subject to audit. At the close of the project the material account is cleared and statement of surplus stores is prepared. Such stores have to be cleared before the accounts of the project are finally settled and the project closed. The surplus stores are disposed off in one of the following ways :

(*a*) **By Transfer to the Divisional Stock.** In this case the cost of carriage and handling from site to divisional stock is debited to the project. Such a transfer is subject to the condition that the stores would be utilised within the next six months and that the holding limit of the stock would not be exceeded.

(*b*) By transfer to another project.

(*c*) By public auction.

Funds realised by disposal of surplus materials are credited to the work. The profit or loss consequent upon disposal of such surplus material is credited/debited to the work to balance the material account.

2. **Stores for Divisional Stock.** Direct financial control over the expenditure entailed in efficient handling, safe custody and proper maintenance of divisional stock is exercised by means of stores overheads estimates. Such estimates are sanctioned by the higher engineer and provide the basis for allowance for overheads to be made, when fixing stock book rate for stores held in divisional stocks.

The following accounts and records are maintained in connection with stock transaction :

(*a*) **Stock Register.** This shows daily receipts and issues of items and is closed annually. The register is kept by the store-keeper.

(*b*) **Stock Purchase Register.** This register shows how stock book rate for each item is calculated. It is maintained by the Divisional Engineer.

(*c*) Stores-in-hand Ledger. (*d*) Quarterly Stock Summary.

The estimate to cover the cash of operating the divisional stock is prepared annually by the Divisional Engineer/GE and sanctioned by SE/CWE. This estimate covers the following expenses :

(*i*) Wages of casual and muster roll labour, engaged in the maintenance of stores at site.
(*ii*) Cost of handling stores.
(*iii*) Cost of repairs and maintenance of divisional store building,
(*iv*) Cost of wastage of stores in stock.
(*v*) Cost of repairs and overhaul of stores in stock where applicable.
(*vi*) Cost of packing/unpacking of stores where necessary.
(*vii*) Other miscellaneous and minor expenditure.

2.13. STOCK

2.13.1. Introduction

As already explained in chapter 5 all stores in the civil engineering construction can primarily be divided into stock and project stores. The term stock by usage does not only cover the stores held in the divisional store godown primarily for meeting day-to-day requirement of the division *i.e.* for normal repairs/maintenance and such works but also includes the complete stores organisation. This organisation comprises of :

(*i*) Permanent, temporary personnel and casual and muster roll labour.

(*ii*) Building structure and storage arrangements for receipts holding and issue of stores from the divisional stock.

(*iii*) Watch and ward arrangements. (*iv*) Fire fighting arrangements.

Stores are accounted for more or less on the same lines as cash though the system of accounting has to be different primarily on account of the fact that a number of varieties of items are involved.

2.13.2. Articles in Stock/Inventory of Store

A number of articles are held in stock depending upon the average consumption in the previous year. The holding of construction and other consumable stores in the divisional store serves the following purposes :

(*a*) Articles of daily use, particularly for maintenance work and repair carried out departmentally, are readily available.

(*b*) Controlled construction stores such as steel cement bricks etc., which the contractor may not be able to procure from the open trade source because of short supply, are readily available. The bid of the contractor for undertaking the work become lower.

(*c*) Before any material is accepted in the store, it is inspected from the point of view of its quality. The chances of inferior material being incorporated in the work are thereby considerably reduced.

In order that the accounting of stores may be done satisfactorily and articles may be readily identified and located, materials of similar nature are grouped under different subheads on the lines shown in Table 2.16.

Table 2.16. Grouping of Stores in the Divisional Stock

S. No.	*Sub-head of stock*	*Name of articles/materials*
1.	Building materials	Cement, lime, brick, timber, M.S. bar. C.G.I. sheets, Asbestos sheets, etc.
2.	Painting Store	Turpentine oil, paints, etc.
3.	House Fittings/sanitary Fittings	Watercloset Seats, Wash hand basin, Towel rail, etc.
4.	Miscellaneous Stores	Baskets, tree guards, shuttering planks, etc.
5.	Brick-kiln material	Sheets for chimneys, coat
6.	Fuel	Kerosene oil woodfuel, charcoal, etc.
7.	Small stores	Hinges, Handles, Nails, Rivets, Screws, etc.

Under each of the above subheads, an inventory displaying the name of the articles held under the subhead in the sub-stock is maintained. This list is termed as inventory of stores. Apart from such an inventory which gives the holdings in the sub-stock at a glance a tally card is placed where individual item is stored.

2.13.3. Reserve Stock Limit

The purpose of the divisional stock is to have a stock of such articles ready in hand which are required for day-to-day use. The articles to be stored and the quantity of such articles are fixed on the basis of previous year's consumption and on the expected store requirement for minor and major works. In the case of projects, the stores are procured and accounted for separately as project stores and their account maintained as Material-at-site Account.

The following factors determine the store-holding limit of a Divisional Stock.

(*a*) The procurement of stores from trade channels of Government depots may take as much as six month. Hence a minimum of say 3 month requirement and a maximum of six months should be stocked.

Table 2.17. Inventory of Stores under Sub-head Building Material

S. No.	*Name of Article*	*Upper Holding Limit*	*Mim. Reserve Limit*	*Balanced Held*	*Date*
1.	Cement				
2.	Lime				
3.	Bricks				
	(*i*) I class (*ii*) II class				
4.	M.S. Bars				
	(*i*) 6 mm ϕ (*ii*) 10 mm ϕ				
	(*iii*) 12 mm f				
	(*iv*) 16 mm ϕ etc.				
5.	C.G.I. sheets				
	(*i*) Size (*ii*) Size				
6.	Asbestos Sheets				
	(*i*) Size (*ii*) Size				

(*b*) Huge quantity of articles if not consumed within a reasonable period of 6 months are likely to deteriorate. The quantity of such stores should therefore be restricted to 3—6 months requirement.

(*c*) Stores held in stock is a blocked money and hence the value of such stock should be the minimum.

(*d*) Large quantities of stores need larger accommodation, larger establishment to handle receipts, holding and issue of stores and larger expenditure in watch and ward and security arrangements.

Table 2.18. Tally Card

(Upper Holding Limit.......Reserve Limit.......)

Date	*Quantity Received*	*Quantity Issued*	*Balance*

Taking the above factors into consideration the Superintending Engineer, fixes the maximum limit of amount upto which materials can be kept in a division. The limit thus fixed is known as the *Reserve Stock Limits*. This limit for a division is fixed every year. Holding stores in excess of this reserve limit is a serious audit objection.

The Superintending Engineer may, however, increase such a limit in special cases when he feels that the work load of the Division has been increased by a number of minor and major works. This increased limit for a specified period is known as Temporary Reserve Limit.

Apart from and in addition to Reserve stock limit in some of the Department effective measures are taken to ensure availability of stores in the Divisional stock. For this purpose a minimum and maximum holding limits of each article of day-to-day requirement is fixed. In fact, the Reserve Stock limit itself represents the total value of the upper holding limit.

The purpose of the minimum holding limit is to ensure that before this limit is reached procurement action is initiated.

2.13.4. Quantity Account of Stores

The stores are as important as cash and hence by and large an effective check on the receipts, holding and issue of stores is necessary. All transactions pertaining to receipt and issue of stores are entered by the Junior Engineer incharge of stores daily in the same way as recording entries in the cash book. The register is closed monthly on a date fixed by the Divisional Engineer and forwarded to the divisional officer more or less in the same manner as copy of the cash book. In the case of stores, however, only the abstract is forwarded.

The day-to-day transactions are maintained in the form as shown in Table 2.19.

Table 2.19. Stock Register

Division.........
Sub-Division.........
Station..........

Month of.........

Date	*Reference to M.B. for receipts and indent for issues*	*Source of recipt receipt or to whom issued*	*Head of Account*	*Name of Article*					
				Cement	*Steel*	*Timber*	*Paint*	*etc.*	
Balance Brought Forward Receipts during Month Total Receipts Grand Total **Issues** Total of issues Balance C/O.									

2.13.5. Balance Return of Stock

In addition to the monthly abstract of receipt and issues, which the Engineer-in-charge sends every month to the Divisional Officer in the form shown in Table 6.5. The Divisional Engineer prepares a half yearly statement from the monthly record every month from the sub-division.

The purpose of monthly and half yearly returns is to provide an independent check on the transaction in the Divisional and Sub-divisional stores.

2.13.6. Stock Action for Verification

The Superintending Engineer or other senior officer (Deputy Chief Engineer, Chief Engineer etc. may carry out test check of the divisional stock at any time with a view to verify the physical holding with the book balance. Similarly the Divisional Engineer may carry out a test verification of any item in the Divisional store or in the sub-divisional store.

Shortage or surplus during such checks are reconciled at the spot in the manner given below :

(*a*) **Articles found surplus.** The quantity by which the articles is found surplus is taken on stock and credited to the head "Reverse Receipt". The reason for surplus has to be explained by the store holder.

(*b*) **Articles found short.** The quantity by which the article is found short is issued and the cost thereof debited to the head "Suspense head" Miscellaneous Advances. The shortage is treated as loss and matter is investigated.

2.13.7. Writing off Losses in Stock

If it is found that the loss has occurred inspite of taking all the precautions and that nobody is to be blamed, a loss statement is initiated to which the finding of the stock taking officer and the report of investigation is attached. The loss is finally written off under orders of the competent authority. Various officers of the Department have the authority for writing off such losses. In case the loss is due to negligence, theft or fraud, the responsibility is fixed on the person responsible and disciplinary/departmental action including recovery of full/part value of the loss is made.

Table 2.20. Half Yearly Balance Return of Stock

Division........
Sub-Division..........
Station.......... Period.........

S. No.	*Names of article*	*Units*	*Issue Rates*	*Balance Brought forward*	*Receipts*	*Issues*	*Closing Balance*	*Divisional storeholder Signature*	*Divisional Engineer's Signature*

2.13.8. Stock-Taking of Stores

To ensure proper utilisation of stores all the stores held in Divisional stock are verified once in a year. This verification is carried out in two ways. Firstly is the audit verification.

This is carried out under the control of the Accountant General/Controller of Defence Accounts as the case may be. This audit party carries out the following verification of the stocks.

(*a*) All the book balances at the end of previous audit are accounted for.

(*b*) All receipts are limited with the Measurement Book No. and page.

(*c*) All receipts and issue vouchers are entered in the same sequence in which the transactions take place.

(*d*) All stores issued to contractors, the cost of which is to be recovered from him are marked as such in the indent as well as in the stock book.

(*e*) Physical stock taking has been carried out and recorded on the relevant ledgers and that surpluses and discrepencies noted are adjusted according to the procedure laid down. Secondly the entries in stock of the Division are checked up once a year. The stock taking team records the physical ground balances irrespective of the book balance and discrepancies are reconciled as described in Art. 2.11.6.

In addition to the verification of the ground balance, this party may look into the following as well :

(*a*) Half yearly stock taking by the stockholder has been carried out and certificate to this effect at the end of the ledger.

(*b*) Surprise checks of stores have also been carried on.

(*c*) The divisional and sub-divisional stores in respect of any article are checked in the divisional and sub-divisional stores at the same time.

(*d*) If certain categories of store have not been used in the preceding six months or are not likely to be used during the near six months, disposal action should be initiated.

2.13.9. Tools and Plant

Like stores, tools and plant are also classified under the following two categories, namely :

1. Tools and plant required for normal maintenance and minor or major works.
2. Tools and plant procured for a project work or for a specified purpose. The cost of such articles directly charged to the work concerned.

Table 2.21. Account of Receipt of Tools and Plant

Division..........
Sub-Division..........
Station.............. Month..........

Date	*Source of receipt with particulars*	*Names of articles with classification*					*To be filled in the Divisional office Reference to voucher no. addjustment of value.*
		Road Rollers	*Tar boilers*	*Sledge Hammers and so on*			

(Sd.) Sub Divisional Officer

Except in M.E.S. where the construction equipment such as tools, plant, machinery vehicles are maintained by the E/M Section, scientific and engineering instruments by the E-6, section (Drawing branch) and furniture and general stores by the Barracks and stores section, tools and plant includes plant, machinery, vehicles, tools, surveying instruments, engineering instrument, furniture and similar stock.

Tables 2.21 and 2.22 show typical forms for receipts and issue of tools and plant.

On receipt of an item of tools and plant it is entered in the form for receipt which is prepared in triplicate, one copy is retained by the store keeper and the other two copies are sent to the Sub-divisional Officer for posting in the tools and plant register.

The Sub-divisional Officer carries out the posting in his ledger and gives reference of the page on which entered in both the copies and sends one copy to the Divisional Engineer. The suppliers bill is passed for payment on the basis of these entries in the relevent register.

Table 2.22. Account of Issues of Tools and Plant

Division..........Sub-Division..........Station..........

Date	*To whom issued with particulars*	*Name of articles with classification*	*To be filled in Divisional office*
			Reference to recovery of value

(Sd.) Sub-Divisional Officer

Similarly all issues are recorded in the tools and plant issue register. Tools and plant sent out from the subdivision for repair or lent to other division is also treated as issue and entered in the form. The abstract of all issued is submitted to the Divisional Officer every month.

Table 2.23 shows tools and plant register in which a consolidated account of receipts, issues and balance is maintained. The form is in three parts. First part shows article in hand, second part shows article temporarily let out or sent for repairs and the third part shows shortages awaiting adjustment.

Table 2.23. Head and Sub-Head of Tools and Plant

S. No.	*Head*	*Sub-Head*	*Example*	*Remarks*
1.	Plant and Machinery	(*i*) Fixed (*ii*) Movable	Stone, Crusher Shaper etc.	
		(*iii*) Locomotives and Rolling Stock	Welding plant, Compressor Wagon, Trolley, Engine	
		(*iv*) Vehicle	Trucks, Jeeps, Car Boat, Pontoons	
		(*v*) Boat Bridging and Navigation Equipment		
		(*vi*) Road making plant	Road Roller, Making plant Stand	
2.	Tools	(*i*) Fixed (*ii*) Movable	Vice, hammer	
		(*iii*) Hand Tools	Pliers, tapes, wrench	
3.	Scientific Apparatus	(*i*) Scientific apparatus	Thermometer	
		(*ii*) Mathematical Drawing Instruments	Pentograph, drawing board	
		(*iii*) Surveying Instruments	Theodolite, Compass, Level	
		(*iv*) Electrical Instruments	Electric motors	
		(*v*) Other Energy instruments	Voltameter	
		(*vi*) Matrics	Water meter, Electric Meter	
4.	Furniture	(*i*) Office	Chair Table,	
		(*ii*) Residential and Rest House	Wash Basin, Cots, Towel Stand	
		(*iii*) Camp Equipment	Folding chair, Folding table, Camp Cot	
5.	Hospital Equipment	(*i*) Furniture	Dention Chair, Operation table	
		(*ii*) Plant (Equipment)	Sterilising Plant, X-ray Plant	
6.	Live Stock	(*iii*) Instruments	Forceps, Measure glass, Syranges, Horses, Camels, Donkeys	

2.13.10. Preparation of Survey Report

Table 2.24 shows form for initiating survey report.

Table 2.24. Survey Report Form

Division..........

Sub-Division.........

Location..........

Number or Quantity	*Description of article*	*Book Value*		*Date of Record*	*Remarks by the Officer-in-Chief*	*Remarks or orders of Divisional Officer*	*Order of S.E.*
		Rate	*Amount*				

Submitted to the Supervising Engineer for order

(Sd.) Divisions Engineer

Returned to the Divisional Officer for necessary action as per order above.

In case the Divisional Officer is competent to sanction the survey report he would sanction it himself instead of sending to the J.E.

Just as accounting procedure for stores (stock) is as important as that of cash (Every store being equivalent to cash) the tools and plant are as important as stores or as cash. The points of differences between the accounting procedure of stock and tools and plants is given in Table 2.25.

Table 2.25. Difference between Account of Stock and Tools and Plant

S. No.	*Item of Comparison*	*Stock*	*Tools and Plant*
1.	Head of Accounts	Suspense head 'stock' or directly changed to work.	Final head, Machinery and equipment directly to work.
2.	Mode of keeping Accounts	Both quality and value are kept.	Only quantity accounts are kept.
3.	Closing of register	Closed half yearly.	Closed yearly ending September.
4.	Adjustment of loss, Stock or Short stores	Material found short is charged off and deducted to Misc. P.W. Advances.	Articles continue to be borne on account book of until written off.
5.	Adjustment of Surplus stores	Value of Surplus stock is credited to revenue and articles taken on charge as under receipt.	Articles found surplus are taken as the basis of Supporting receipts without affecting the Final value.

2.13.11. Road Metal Register

It is normal practice to stock road metal on the road side berm and issue from time to time to the road work on as required basis. The advantages of this system are :

(*i*) The material is supplied at the road side where it is actually required for road work and the delay is avoided there by saving the cost of loading/unloading the transportation.

(*ii*) No separate watch and ward or storage space is required as the gang keeps a watch over the material along its beat.

The main disadvantage is that it is difficult to keep a continuous watch over the entire road length. This is taken care of by holding the gang-mates responsible for the safety of road side material and secondly, making it obligatory in the form of submission of monthly road return showing the following information in respect of road metal :

1. Name of Road 2. KM. No.

3. Nature of road metal, quantity carried over from last month Receipts during the month issues during the month balance at the end of month.

The bill of labour (muster roll casual as well as regular labour) is not passed for payment unless it is supported by material statement.

The inspecting officer carries out surprised check of the material at site with the entry on the road metal register.

Table 2.26 shows the form on which monthly road material return is submitted by the Junior Engineer incharge of the highway section.

Table 2.26. Statement of Receipts, Issues and Balance of Road Metal

Division..........
Sub-Division..........
Location..........
Name of the Road.......... Month of.........

No. of Kilo- metre	*Name of Metal*	*Opening Balance C.M.*	*Receipts during the month*	*Total C.M.*	*Expenditure during the month*	*Closing Balance*	*Actual checked by Measurement*	*Remark*

When fresh supply of material is received at site, the quantity received is entered on the MB and forms the basis for payment of the supplies bill.

When material is found surplus it is taken as receipt. The quantity found short is shown in red under the remark column and is carried forward till the loss is recovered or it is written off with the approval of the competent authority.

Table 2.27 shows indenting for construction stores.

Table 2.27. Indent for Stores

Book No.......... Indent No.......... Date..........
Division..........
Sub-Division.......... Station..........
Name of the Work.......... Name of the Contractor..........
No. of Contruction Aspects or Works..........

S. No.	*Description of Material*	*Unit*	*Quantity*	*Remarks*

The material should be delivered..........

Sd/- AEE/SDO

Note : The undersigned has been complied as per quality shown. Receive the material and enter in.

(Sd.) Supply Officer

M.B. No.......... Pay.......... Recovery Officer..........

2.13.12. Material Charged Directly to Works

Material used on works is obtained from the following two sources :

(*a*) From the Divisional stock on indents.

(*b*) Directly from the trade.

(*c*) Material obtained from the divisional stock on indents.

The indent is prepared in triplicate.

The following points should be scrutinised by the officer preparing the indent.

1. Quantity of material is clearly specified.

2. Head of account is indicated.

3. Name of work as per administrative approval is correctly shown :

(*d*) Directly from the trades.

Stores purchased directly from the trade is debited directly to the work head concerned.

2.14. WORKS

2.14.1. Introduction

The main purpose of having works and accounts procedure is to execute works which satisfy the following conditions :

(*a*) The structure should be technically sound. This is achieved by according technical sanction for each work or part thereof. At site quality of work is ensured by :

(*i*) Checking/inspecting the execution with respect to detailed specification in respect of material and workman ship.

(*ii*) Passing the work in stages.

(*iii*) Rectification of defective work.

(*b*) The work should be completed in specified period.

This is achieved by :

(*i*) Specifying period of completion and incorporation of penalty clause in the condition of contract for delay in the completion of project.

(*ii*) Having bar charts and CPM and PERT methods of work programming to ensure completion on time.

(*c*) Expenditure planned for the year should not be exceeded. This is achieved by fixing allotment for the financial year.

(*d*) The total expenditure on the completion of the work should not exceed the planned amount. This is achieved by according administrative approval in respect of each item of the work.

The various provisions of the works and accounting procedures have been developed primarily to satisfy the aforesaid requirements. The various agencies which undertake the execution of works have their own rules, prescribed forms of various reports and returns etc. As the present book has been written for general use of students the rules, regulations and form of reports and returns have been dealt in a general way instead of adhering to the central or state PWD forms.

2.14.2. Categories of Works

The various categories of works are shown in Table 2.28.

Table 2.28. Categories of Works

- Original Works
  - New Works
  - Special Repair Works
  - Addition and/or Alteration to existing works (excluding minor works)
- Repair Works (Maintenance)
  - Normal Maintenance
  - Special Repairs
  - Addition and/or Alteration under minor works

Note. 1. The categorisation and scope of special repair varies from state to state and department to department. It also depends upon the nature of such repair. For example, special repair necessiated almost every year due to the damage caused by monsoon in the hilly region of the Himalayas (termed as SRMD, special repair, monsoon damages) fall under the maintenance/repair of the road concerned. In the same department extensive repairs to a large structural complex would fall under the category of original works.

2.14.3. Classification of Works

Table 2.29 gives normal classification of works based on the completion cost.

Table 2.29. Works

- Project (work exceeding ₹1,50,000)
- Major works (work exceeding ₹ 1,20,000/ ₹ 1,50,000)
- Minor (work below ₹ 1,20,000/ ₹ 1,50,000)
- Petty (work costing below ₹ 1,25,000)

Note. 1. It has already been brought out in Article 7.2 that the classification of normal work differs from state to state and department to department. In view of the continuous increasing in the cost of living, proposals for increasing the present limit of ₹1,20,000 to ₹ 1,50,000 has been already initiated.

2. The scope of minor works varies from department to department as well as from time to time. About 30 years back in MES, for example, works below ₹ 15,000 were termed as minor works. In course of time this limit was raised to ₹ 1,20,000 and would in the near future go to ₹ 1,50,000.

2.14.4. Conditions for Taking Work in Hand

Before any work is taken in hand the following five requirements should be fulfilled :

(1) Administrative approval is obtained by the competent Administrative authority.

(2) Funds have been allotted by the competent Financial Authority.

(3) Technical sanction is accorded by the competent Engineering Authority.

(4) Land acquisition proceedings have been completed, compensation paid, and possession of land taken over.

(5) Work order has been placed by the competent Engineering Authority.

2.14.5. Methods of Carrying out Works

Works are carried out primarily by the following two methods :

(*a*) Through Contract Agency. (*b*) Departmentally by employing D.E.L.

(*c*) Departmentally by engaging labour through contract agency.

2.14.6. Different Types of Contracts

The different types of contracts are :

1. Item rate contract.
2. Lumpsum contract.
3. Scheduled contract.
4. Combination of lumpsum plus scheduled rate.
5. Percentage contract.

The above types are briefly described below :

1. **Item Rate Contract.** In this system of contract the schedule of quantity shown in Table 2.30 is the basis of allotting the work. The schedule is prepared from the estimate of the work in which the rate column is filled by the tenderer and normally the party whose quotation is the lowest is allotted the job.

Table 2.30. Schedule of Quantities (Schedule B)

S. No.	*Description of the Item*	*Quantity*	*Unity*	*Rate*	*Cost*
1.	Earthwork is excavated in hours	—	—		
2.	etc.				
3.					
4.					
5.					
			Total		

2. **Lumpsum Contract.** Complete description of the work along with detailed specification and details of working drawings and schedule of stores is supplied with the tender form and the contractor undertakes to complete the job for a specified sum. The advantage of this type of contract is that the payments are simplified. No measurement for running or final bills is necessary. However, the drawback in the system is that any modification or deviation has to be carried out by means of an amendment which may not be acceptable or agreed to by the contractor.

3. **Scheduled Rate.** This is similar to item rate contract as the contractor undertakes the execution of work at approved schedule of rates plus a fixed percentage higher or lower as the case may be. Payment is made on the basis of actual quantity of each item or supplies made. The payment is made on the basis of through rates wherein the rate tendered includes cost of labour and material. Payment may be done on the basis of free supply of materials.

4. **Combination of Lumpsum plus Schedule Rate.** Under this type of contract, a fixed sum is agreed to on the completion of a particular job and additions or alterations are carried out on the basis of current schedule of rates.

5. **Percentage Contract.** In this type of contract approximate value of work is indicated along with brief description and drawings (where applicable) and the tenderer bids his percentage above or below the current schedule of rates. No schedule of quantity is given. This type of contract is particularly suitable for 'Term contract' where the works involved cannot be indicated or for periodical services (white washing, colour washing etc.). In the MES this is the only method of allotting work of repairs to defence buildings in cantonements.

2.14.7. Allotment of Work

Work is normally allotted to the contractor on the basis of properly advertised notice calling tenders for the work. The party which quotes the lowest is normally allotted the work. In case the work is allotted to other than the lowest party the officer who accepts such a tender has to record reasons for doing so. In case the reasons recorded by him are not convincing it would result in a serious audit objection by the Financial Authority which may result in disciplinary/departmental action against the person concerned.

2.14.8. Quotation and Tender/Preparation, Receipt and Acceptance

In order to select a suitable party for execution of any work, the Divisional Engineer invites quotations plain paper to which non-judicial stamp may or may not be affixed. No contract agreement is executed between the department and the contractor and work is paid for the basis of actual measurement. No earnest money or security deposit is required. This type of contract is allotted for carrying out urgent works/petty works where the amount involved is below ₹ 50,000.

In all other cases, work is allotted on the basis of 'tenders' invited after giving reasonable publicity to the same.

The work involved in allotting the work by inviting tenders can be broadly divided into two types namely :

1. Pre-tender action, and 2. Post-Tender action.

The pre-tender action involves the following :

(*a*) Preparation of contract documents. (*b*) Issue of Notice inviting tenders.

Post tender action involves :

(*a*) Opening of tenders. (*b*) Acceptance of tenders.

1. Pre-tender action

(*a*) Preparation of contract document.

The following documents are prepared before tenders are invited :

(*i*) Layout plan of the area showing the location of the work.

(*ii*) Complete set of drawings including working drawings.

(*iii*) Schedule of stores specifying clearly the stores which would be issued, the place of issue and the issue rate.

(*iv*) Schedule of T & P along with the place of delivery and the condition of hire charges.

(*v*) General condition of contract.

(*vi*) General and particular specifications.

(*vii*) Mode of running payments and method of depositing security.

The above documents are scrutinised from the financial point of view by the Divisional Accountant/Unit Accountant by the works/branch contract branch/SW in respect of other details.

It is usual to indicate the competent authority for the acceptance of the tender. It should further be specified that the competent authority reserves the right to reject any or all the tenders without assigning any reason.

(*b*) Issue of notice inviting tenders when administrative approval has been accorded and funds for the work have been allotted; notice of tender along with the information detailed in articles 2.14.4 is invited. Wide publicity commensurate to the cost of the work as detailed in Table 2.31 is given.

2. Post Tender Action

(*a*) **Opening of tenders.** The day, date and time of opening of tenders along with the time upto which sealed tenders from parties may be accepted *i.e.* specified in the notices of tenders. Normally the time fixed for opening is on the same day upto which tenders may be received. Allowance is made to the receipt by post and hence the time for opening is usually after normal postal delivery of the station. At any rate tenders received by post are considered as tenders in time if the party can establish beyond doubt the quotation have been posted before the same were opened. The Divisional Engineer nominates two officers of his district to open the tenders and all the contractors are invited to observe the opening.

(*b*) **Acceptance of tenders.** See Art. 2.14.8.

Table 2.31. Publicity required for Tender Notice

S. No.	*Amount of work*	*Method of Publicity*
1.	Above ₹ 1,50,000	(*a*) 3 Weeks notice through leading dailies. (*b*) Individually to registered contractors. (*c*) Other Division of the Deptt. and local office.
2.	Between ₹ 1,20,000 and ₹ 1,50,000	(*a*) 2 Weeks notice. (*b*) As for (*b*) and (*c*).
3.	Between ₹ 1,10,000 and ₹ 1,20,000	(*a*) Ten days notice. (*b*) As for 1 (*a*) and (*c*).

2.14.9. Contract Agreement

The Contract Agreement is an undertaking by the President of India and the party whose tender has been accepted for fulfilment of the terms and conditions laid therein. In short the contractor gives an undertaking to execute the work according to drawing and specification along with such other instructions as the Engineer-in-Charge or Senior inspecting officer may issue from time to time. The party further agrees to complete the work within the period fixed in the notice of calling for tenders and in the event of delay the party is liable to be penalised upto 10% of the value of the contract or to the employment of debitable agency. The Executive Engineer who represents the President of India binds the Government to pay the party for the work done according to the terms and conditions given in the Contract Agreement.

The following basic principles have to be strictly adhered to while preparing the Contract Agreement. Variation of these conditions particularly if the same are favourable to the contractor are liable to be challenged by other prospective parties who had submitted the tenders or by the department itself or by the Audit party.

1. There should be no modification in respect of design, drawing and specification form those given in the notice inviting tenders.
2. The scope of the work should not be changed.
3. Period of completion should not be changed.

While preparing the draft agreement the following precautions should be taken :

(*i*) There should be no ambiguity in the terms and conditions which may be taken advantage of by the contractor.

(*ii*) The date of starting should be clearly specified usually it is the date on which work order is received by the contractor or his representative or the date on which possession of the site is given whichever is later.

(*iii*) No work should be allowed to be started till the Contract Agreement is signed by the contractor.

(*iv*) As far as possible there should be no correction, or other interpolation in the Contract Agreement. If it is unavoidable such corrections should be jointly attested by the Executive Engineer and the contractor.

(*v*) All relevant drawings, such as site plan, working drawings, and various schedules forming part of the contract agreement should be free from flaws so that the same may not be disputed in a court of law. In the case of large works it is usual to get the agreement scrutinised from the "Legal Rememberencer" so that the legal aspects of the agreement are taken care of.

(*vi*) Workmen Compensation Act, Minimum Wages Act should be referred to in the Contract Agreement so that the contractor is bound to act on the same.

Only printed form of contract deed should be used. It should not be necessary, to add any typed material. In the event it becomes necessary, prior permission from the Superintending Engineer should be obtained.

When the tenders are accepted by the Executive Engineer, three copies of the agreement are prepared and distributed as below :

1. One copy along with attested copy is sent to the Superintending Engineer who scrutinises the agreement and returns the original to the Executive Engineer and retains the attested copy for his record.

2. One copy under lock and key is kept with Executive Engineer and is not taken out except when required in a court of law.

3. One copy to Accountant General/CDA.

In case the contractor asks for one set he is given the same on payment. When the tenders are accepted by the Superintending Engineer, four copies of agreement are prepared in the first instance.

Some of the important contract clauses of general application are given below :

1. Obligatory on the part of the contractor to get the sample of material approved and kept in the project museum for further reference.

2. Obligatory to get the work passed in stages.

3. Dismantling of defective work at contractor's risk and cost.

4. Imposition of a maximum of 10% of the cost of the work for delaying in the completion of work at the rate of 1% per week.

5. Incompleted work to be executed departmentally or through debitable agencies.

6. Change in the quantity of work under written orders of the Executive Engineer within the prescribed limits depending upon the type of the contract.

7. Extension time for completion of work to be applied within a week of the cause of hindrance giving full reasons thereof. Extension of time is allowed by the authority who accepts the tender.

8. In case of any dispute, the case be referred to the Arbitrator appointed under the rules within 30 days of the preparations of the final bill.

2.14.10. Work Orders

When order to start the work is given to the contractor on the basis of open tenders invited for the same, the contractor is intimated in writing by a registered letter that his tender has been accepted and he should attend the Divisional Office to sign the Contract Agreement. After the Contract Agreement has been signed he is instructed to take over the possession of the site and take the work in hand. He is further informed that for purpose of completion of the work, the date of start shall be taken as the date of his receipt of the letter under reference or the date on which the site has been handed over irrespective of the actual date of starting the work. However, when the work is allotted on the basis of Piece-work System order to start the work is given in the form given in Table 2.32.

Terms and Conditions of Work Order

1. Work to execute according to instructions of Engineer-in-charge as per PWD specifications.

2. The work may be terminated at any time by the Engineer-in-charge.

3. The contractor may withdraw his acceptance of the work.

4. The contractor should submit his bill for payment in respect of the work done during the preceding month.

5. Payment under Workmen's Compensation Act 1924, will be paid by the Government to the concerned party the cost of which may be recovered from the payments due to the contractor.

Order for work specified herein is given to Shri..........(contractor) to be executed on the condition given here as :

Table 2.32. Work Order Form

Division..........

Sub-Division..........

H.Q..........

S. No.	*Particular of Work*	*Rate*	*Per*	*Remarks*
1.	Earth work in excavation over areas including its disposal and dressing, etc.			

Sd/- Contractor

Sd/- Divisional Engineer

6. No workman/labour below 12 years of age shall be employed.

7. The contractor shall be paid for the work actually executed.

2.15. PAYMENT FOR WORKS

2.15.1. Daily Labour/D.E.L.

When a work of short duration and of non-recurring nature involving engagement of skilled, semi-skilled or unskilled labour/workers is to be executed daily or departmentally engaged labour is employed. The main features of this system are :

1. The attendance of such labour is marked on the muster roll form in which the name of the labour along with the father's name and trade of labour is given. (See Table 2.33).

2. The Divisional Engineer normally exercises control over engagement of labour on muster roll by maintaining a register in the Division, with the Divisional Accountant in which details are recorded as shown in Table 2.36.

3. The attendance of engaged labour is recorded daily and the person recording such attendance initials and totals of the person present daily. The inspecting officer EE/AE/SDO/JE checks the physical attendance without any prior notice.

4. No labour below 14 years of age is employed.

5. Muster roll are closed for payment every week, fortnight or latest every month.

6. Only one muster roll is used for a specific work against all sanction (there may be any number of continuation sheets against such sanction).

7. The attendance is marked at work site where the muster roll is kept readily available. No duplicate record is maintained.

8. Payment is made by the AEE/AGE/SDO in the presence of the concerned subordinate.

The amount paid and the amount remaining unpaid and transferred to the register of unpaid wages are both recorded (See Part II of Table 2.33). Part II may or may not be operated, however, separate register of unpaid wages is invariably kept.

Table 2.33. Muster Roll Form

Division......
Sub-Division......
Location......
Name of work.......

Cash Book...... Vr. No....... Dated......

S. No.	*Name*	*Father's Name*	*Trade*	*Dates*	*Total*	*Rate*	*Amount*	*Dated initial and remarks of the officer making payment. Signature / LTI allotted is recorded.*
1. 2. 3. etc.								

Daily Total	
Initial of Subordinate	
Marking attendance	
Initial of Inspection officer	

Passed for ₹......
Signature of (EE/AEE/SDO)

Table 2.34. Part II Register of Unpaid Work

Month and period to which arrear relates	*Sl. No. as per Muster Roll*	*Name*	*Father's Name*	*Amount Due*	*Amount paid*	*Dated initial of officer making payment*
			Total			

Arrear as per this Muster Roll

S. No. as per muster roll	*Name*	*Father's Name*	*Amount due*	*Amount paid*	*Dated initial of the officer making payment*
		Grand Total	₹		

Amount paid as arrear of previous Muster Roll. ₹
Balance Carried to Next Muster Roll.

Table 2.35. Part III

Description of work	*Quantity*	*Deduct work already included in previous muster roll*	*Balance*	*Rate*

M.B. No.............. Date of measurement

9. The work done is recorded in the Measurement Book as well as in Part III of the muster roll and rate of work arrived at. In case the work is not susceptible to measurement, remarks to indicate the same are recorded.

Table 2.36. Muster Roll Register

S. No.	*Date*	*Name of work*	*Period for which Sanctioned (Days)*	*Nos. Sanctioned (alongwith trade)*	*Remarks*

Note : Maintenance of this register is not an audit requirement but it is usual practice to have one in the Divisional Office.

2.15.2. Casual Labour

Sometimes it is not possible for the sub-ordinate at work site to get sanction for employment of labour on muster roll. Examples for such situation are :

Table 2.37. Casual Labour Roll

Division....... Cash Book Vr. No..........Date...........
Sub-Division.......
Location.......
Name of the work.......
Period.......

Numbers Employed	*Trade*	*Period (in days)*	*Rate*	*Amount*	*Dated initials and remarks of paying officer*	*Quantity of work done with reference to recorded measurement if any*	*Work to which chargeable*

Total ₹..........
Deduct unpaid..........

Net Pay ₹ ....
Total amount paid in ₹.......... Signature AEE/AGE/AE/SDO

(*a*) Road block due to slip in a hilly area.
(*b*) Breach in a canal.

The work has to be taken in hand immediately to avoid traffic jam and inconveniences to the passengers or to avoid loss of water and inconvenience to the public.

The attendance of the labour employed is recorded by the Junior Engineer in his diary and daily report is sent to the AEE/AGE/AE/SDO, on the completion of the job, payment bill is prepared in the form shown in Table 2.37.

In M.E.S. however, the term casual labour denotes such labour whose services are required for a comparatively longer duration (more than one month). The Garrison Engineer sanctions their employment and the pay bill is prepared as that of other works charged establishment.

Work done in any division by the casual labour is taken into consideration while recruiting labour for regular maintenance.

2.15.3. Payment of Work Charged Establishment

Sanction for work charged establishment is given in the same way as for regular temporary personnel but except for recruitment of a few skilled categories involving high monthly rates of payment the Division/Garrison Engineer is usually the appointing authority subject to availability of the funds.

In the case of large projects, the entire establishment of the project is work charged and the power of appointing various categories rests with various authorities as in the case of regular/temporary establishment.

The bills are prepared in the form given in Table 2.38 on monthly basis.

When a number of persons are appointed on work charged basis against different works, it is normal practice to prepare separate bills for each work.

2.15.4. Labour Engaged Through Contractor

The working of the various works departments shows that as far as possible labour on muster roll needs to be discouraged and therefore every Divisional Engineer adopts his own method of discouraging such labour. As for muster rolls for normal maintenance work are concerned some of the Chief Engineers lay down the maximum amount which should not exceed on such labour.

Sometimes for work of comparatively short duration, local labour is not available or as only available through a contractor/agent. In such cases, payment is made directly to the contractor instead paying to the individual labour. The department is not bothered about the particular of individual labour but a report in respect of the type and number of daily labour employed and the quantity of work done is sent daily to the Engineer-in-charge. This compiled report forms the basis of payment along with the measurements recorded in the M.B. (Both these evidently have to agree). To avoid disputes at a later date the daily report is got signed by the contractor as a token of his acceptance.

The payment is made to the contractor in one of the following ways :

(*a*) On the basis of work done at previously settled rates.

(*b*) On the basis of labourers actually employed. The profit of the contractor is either included in the rates of payment of the labour or in lumpsum or on percentage basis.

2.15.5. Measurement Book, Inspection, Checking and Measurement

Measurement Book. Measurement book forms the basis of all payments which can be measured. In other words it forms the original record of all work/supplies which are susceptible of measurement. The works/supplies include all contractor's maintenance, repair done through departmental labour or through contractor. All supplies made by contractor are entered in the Measurement Book. The quantities thus entered are calculated, totalled and payments made.

Table 2.38. Paybill of Work Charged Establishment

Division........ Month of Payments....... Cash Vr. No.......
Sub-Division....... Location....... Bill for the month of.......

S. No.	*Name of incumbent (Name to be written group-wise and sanction no. and date to be recorded against each group in red ink)*	*Designation*	*Period*	*Rate*	*Amount due (In case more than one work is involved, the total of each work to be entered in red ink*	*Amounts Paid*	*Dated acknow-ledgement, Payee*	*Dated initials of the officer making payment*

Total amount paid on work.......

1. Certified that all persons for whom wages have been drawn in this bill have been actually employed during the month for the work shown and were employed on the work for which sanctioned.

Pav....... GE/EE (Sd)/- AEE/AGE/AE/SDO

Checked (Divisional/Unit Accountant)

Table 2.39. Recording of Measurement in the MBs

Recording of bills for work done	*Recording measurements for supply of materials*
(*i*) Name of the work as given in the AA	(*i*) Name of the supplies as given in W.O.
(*ii*) Location of the work	(*ii*) No. and date of agreement or W.O.
(*iii*) Name of the contract	(*iii*) Purpose of the supply *i.e.* Stock/Direct issue to work (give name of work)/ Direct issue etc.
(*iv*) No. and date of Contract Agreement	(*iv*) Date of supplies specified in S.O./W.O.
(*v*) Date of order to start work	(*v*) Date of completion of supply
(*vi*) Date of completion of the work (in case of running bill write work-in-progress)	(*vi*) Date of measurement
(*vii*) Date of measurement	

Table 2.40 shows a typical page of Measurement Book.

Table 2.40. Page of a MB

Date of Commencement.........

Date of Complete.........

Date of Measurement.........

S.No.	*Particular of Works No.*	*C*	*B*	*D*	*Contents*

Abstract of cost.

Date : (Sd)/J.E.

In addition to the ordinary/common measurement book described above the following records are also entered in books known as measurement books. Such measurement books are :

1. Standard Measurement Book and 2. Check Measurement Book.

1. **Standard Measurement Books.** Periodical services such as white-washing, colour washing, painting, distempering etc. of a building are carried out at regular intervals. If every time detailed measurements are made it would involve considerable time and energy. This difficulty has been won over by preparing standard measurement books in respect of all such buildings. The measurement pertaining to the normal periodical services are entered in the measurement book by a senior J.E./O.S. and accuracy of the measurements is certified by the A.E.E./A.G.E./A.E./S.D.O. concerned. The calculation of various periodical services are scrutinised and certified as correct by the Divisional/Unit Accountant. Subsequently only the quantity of work done as recorded in the bill of the contractor and certificate of the work having been carried out as per standard measurement book and according to the specification.

2. **Check Measurement Book.** Check Measurement Book is issued to the A.E.E./A.G.E./ A.E./S.D.O. for the purpose of carrying out test check in respect of measurement of a work carried out by the Junior Engineer/Overseer. At the end of the measurement the following certificate is given by the officer recording such measurement.

"Check measurement recorded by me in Check Measurement Book No.........Page No...... The J.E./S.O. concerned was/was not present when check measurements were made."

To eliminate chances of double payment, no payment is made on the basis of measurement recorded in the Check Measurement Book.

When the cost of work exceed ₹ 5,000, the measurements are checked at site by the Divisional/Garrison Engineer and the A.E.E./A.G.E./A.E./S.D.O. The percentage of such checks depends upon the value of work and importance of the project and varies from 5% for E.E./ G.E. to 25% for A.E.E./A.G.E.

In the M.E.S. and certain State P.W.D. the per cent check to be carried out by senior officer is specified and such checks are recorded on the main measurement book instead of keeping a separate Check Measurement Book.

The limit of variation between the original measurements and the test measurements usually permitted are :

1% in case of original work, 5% in case of repair work and 10% in case of earth work.

2.15.6. Payment to Contractors and Suppliers

Payments to contractors and suppliers may be classified as shown in Table 2.41.

Table 2.41

Bill for Payment to Contractors and Suppliers

- First and Final Bill (Table 19.38)
- Running Account Bill (Table 19.39)
- Account for Secured Advance (Table 19.40)
- Running Account Bill (Table 19.41)
- Final Bill (Table 19.42)

Table 2.42. First and Final Bill (CPWD) Form 2.

Division...... Sub-Division......

(To be used when a single payment is made for a job or contract, *i.e.* only on its completion)

Name of the work......... Cash Book Voucher No......... Date..........

Name of contractor or supplier	*Items of work*	*Reference to recorded measurement and date*	*Date of*		*Quantity*	*Unit*	*Rate*	*Amount*	*Total Amount payable*		*Payees dated signature*	*Dated signature of witness*	*Dated Certificate of Disbursement*	
			Orders to commence work	*Completion of work*					*In figures*	*In words*			*Mode of payment*	*Paid by me*

M.B. No......... Pay......... Date.........

Pay ₹......... (Rupees.........)

For use in AG's Office

Reviewed

(Accounts Clerk) Divisional Accountant Audited Supdt. Gazetted Officer

Table 2.43. Running Account Bill (CPWD Form 26)

(Final payments must invariably be made in form printed on yellow paper which should not be used intermediated payment).

Division......... Sub-Division.........

Cash Book Voucher No......... Date.........

Name of contractor.........

Name of work.........

Serial No. of this bill.........

No. and date of previous bill for this work.........

Reference to Agreement No.........

Date of written order to commence work

Date of actual completion of work.........

I—ACCOUNTS OF WORK EXECUTED

Item of work	*Unit*	*Rate*	*Quantity executed up-to-date as per M.B....*	*Payment on the basis of actual measurement*		*Remarks*
				Up-to-date	*Since previous bill*	

II—CERTIFICATES AND SIGNATURES

1. The measurements on which entries in columns 1 to 6 of Account of I are based, were made by.........on........., and are recorded at page.........of Measurement Book No.........

2. Certificate regarding actual execution of work.

Dated signature of officer preparing the bill.............

Dated signature of officer authorising payment.........

Dated signature of contractor.................

III—MEMORANDUM OF PAYMENTS

1. Total value of the work actually measured.
2. Total upto date advance payments for works not yet measured.
3. Total upto date secured advances.
4. Total of items (1 + 2 + 3).
5. Deduct : Amount with held
   (*a*) From previous bill as per Running Account Bill. (*b*) From this bill.
6. Balance (Item 4.5).
7. Total amount of payment already made.
8. Payments now to be made, as detailed below :
   (*a*) By recovery of amounts creditable to this work.
   Total 5 (*b*) + 8 (*a*)
   (*b*) By recovery of amounts creditable to work.

(*c*) By cheque.

Total of 8 $(b + c)$.

Pay ₹.................. (by cheque)

Dated initials of disbursing officer..........

Received ₹.........(Rupees..................) as above memorandum on account of this work.

Stamp

Signature of contractor.........

Paid by me *vide* Cheque No................. Date.........

Dated initials of person actually making the payment.........

IV—REMARKS

For use in Divisional Officer

Checked

Accounts Clerk — Divisional Accountant

For use in AG's Office

Audited — Reviewed

Auditor — Superintendent — Gazetted Officer

Table 2.44. Account of Security (CPWD Form 26-A)

Division.........

Sub-Division.........

Name of contractor.........

Name of work.........

Serial No. of the Bill to which the account pertains.........

Reference to Agreement.............................. Cash Voucher No.........Date.........

Account of secured advances allowed on the security of materials brought to site.

Quantity outstanding from previous bill	Deduce:—Quantity utilised in work measured since previous bill	Quantity outstanding including brought to site since previous bill	Full rate as assessed by the Divisional office	Description of materials	Unit	Reduced rate at which advance is made	Up-to-date amount of advance	Reference to Divisional Officer's written orders authorising the Adv.	Reasons for non-clearance of Advance when outstanding for more than 3 months

Total amount outstanding as per the accounts.........(C)

Deduct : Amount outstanding as per entry.........(C).........of the Annexure to the previous bill

Net amount since previous bill (in words) Rupees.........

Dated signatures of officer preparing the bill...............

Dated signatures of officer authorising payment............

Table 2.45. (CPWD Form 27-A)

RUNNING ACCOUNT

Cash Book Vr. No.................. Name of Contractor................
Name of work.................. Serial No. of Bill................
No. and date of previous bill................. Reference to Agreement...........
Date of written order to commence work.............

I—ACCOUNT OF WORK

1. Approximate Value of work upto date
2. Valve of measure work
3. Deduct amount total work held
4. Balance upto date (1 + 2 – 3)
5. Deduct intermediate payment
6. Intermediate payment now to be made (4-5)
7. Amount of secured Advance
8. Total payment now to be made

(*a*) By recovery of amount creditable to this work
(*b*) By recovery of amounts creditable to other work (*c*) By cheque

II—ACCOUNT OF SECURED ADVANCE ALLOWED OR SCRUTINY OF MATERIALS BROUGHT TO SITE

Quantity outstanding from previous bill	*Deduct utilised in work*	*Quantity outstanding*	*Full rate as assessed by Divisional officer*	*Description of materials*	*Unit*	*Reduced rate at which advance is made*	*Up-to-date amount of advance*	*Reference to Divisional Officer's written order*	*Reasons for non-clearance of Advance when outstanding for more than 3 months*

Total outstanding as per this account
Amount outstanding as per previous bill
Net amount since previous bill (in words) Rupees.............

Ill—CERTIFICATE AND SIGNATURE

I have certified that

1. Value of work done upto date is not less than...........
2. Detailed measurement was made by me ₹............on at page No............M.B.
3. Quantity of material have actually been brought at site............signature of contractor Signature of officer preparing the bill

Pay (₹...........)

Dated signature of the officer authorising the payment..................

IV. ACQUITTANCE

Received (₹...........) as an intermediate payment in connection with the contract to above.

Stamp

Full Signature of Contractor............

Witness

Paid by me $\frac{\text{Cash}}{\text{Cheque}}$

Dated initials of the person actually making the payment..........

V. REMARKS

For use in Divisional Office

Checked A/C Clerk — Divisional Accountant

For use in A.G.'s Office

Audited — Reviewed

Auditor — Supdt. — Gazetted Officer

Table 2.46. (CPWD Form 27-B)

FINAL BILL

(To be used for "Final payment" to contractors on lumpsum contracts)

Cash Book Vr............No........... Dated...........

Name of Contractor........... Name of work...........

Serial No. of this Bill........... No. and date of previous bill for this work

Reference to Agreement........... Date of written order to commence work....

Date of actual completion of work............

I. ACCOUNT OF WORK EXECUTED

Sub-work	*Rate*	*Unit (lumpsum for each)*	*Up-to-date*		*Remark*
			Quantity	*Amount*	

II and III as for Form 27-A, Table 19.40

IV. ACQUITTANCE

Received Rupees....as above in full settlement of all demands on account of the contract.

Stamp

....

Full Signature

Dated initials of person actually making payment

Rank

Paid by me $\frac{\text{Cash}}{\text{Cheque}}$

V. REMARKS

Checked — For use in Divisional Office — Divisional Account

A/Clerk — For use in A.G.'s Office

Audited

Auditor — Supdt. — Gazetted officer

3

Safety Engineering in Construction

3.1. INTRODUCTION

Construction has been an important part of man's activities since the men came out of cave. Construction has been considered as one of the biggest industry in India. Various constructions made are either below the ground, in the form of basements etc. or above ground. Construction is also made under water or in the space. Total investment in India since independence has been more than total invested during 150 years before independence. As per five years plan investment, in construction sector is of the order of about 40 to 45 percent to total outlay.

When such a quantum of works are executed; so much financial investment is made, accidents are unavoidable; but then it is prime-necessary to minimise it; to take safety precautions which are essential and need of today. It has been said of a certain section of a rail road that every tie laid represents the loss of one human life, the life of a worker on the gang that built the rail road. During earlier of construction, it was common practice to presume, that following construction will cause life of one person either labour or other person involved in construction of site.

(1) Double storey construction (2) Two floors of a multi-storey building

(3) About one kilometer of tunnel (4) One person for each bridge constructed.

As such construction is a high accident prone industry. It has been further invstigated that more than 10 million workers receive injuries in the course of one year throughout the world. Based on world trend, it is estimated that accident rate in construction is about three times the rate in the manufacturing/fabrication sector. There were 640000 accidents in construction 1983; when the employment in industry was about 3574000 about 16% employees suffered injury. So far proper records have not been maintained in India regarding injuries and accidents those take place every year. However no country can accept loss of life as a price to pay for construction. Accident prevention to be made as an essential part of the programme of the contractor who expects to enjoy a successful career in this particular activity.

The various types of occupational accidents that occur in construction industry are :

(1) Exposure either for environmental condition like temperature or contact with potentially harmful substances like dust etc.

(2) Contact with electric current.

(3) Over exertion; stressed body movements.

(4) Struck by or striking against object or material at the site during construction.

(5) Falling from height or at the same level including slipping.

(6) Caught in machine or material.

(7) Rubbed or abraded by object like machineries or materials or temporary and permanent structures.

(8) Powered vehicle accidents.

These accidents cause following diseases :

(1) Un-necessary cause mental stress;

(2) Deafness, decompression sickness; skin diseases Hernea;

(3) Bursitis, muscle strain;

(4) Cancer etc.

As far as the safety of workers is, concerned, Factory act and Mines act are in prevailing in India; but they are legally not applicable to construction accidents as construction is not yet recognised as an industry. Further contract workers are not deemed to be governed under the factories act.

Therefore today there is need of accident prevention programme on every project in order to reduce the cost of construction measured in terms of

(1) Human lives sacrificed (2) Injuries to workers of any extent

(3) Loss of damage to equipment (4) Loss of time during and after construction accident

(5) Compensation, insurance cost to worker if expire at work site, during construction period.

3.2. INDIRECT ACCIDENT COSTS

Due to accident at any construction site there are injuries to one or more workers which may lead to the death of one or more workers. No doubt the compensation in the form of insurance is paid to the worker; medical assistance is granted; still there are always certain indirect expenses in any form; the contractor has to bear. These losses can not be covered by insurance or compensation are called indirect cost and include the following :

(1) Cost of lost time of injured employee and that of other employees who either stop the work due to accident or those who are employed for first aid and after assistance to that injured person.

(2) Cost of supervisory staff in assisting that injured employee involved in investigations for cause of accident and preparing accident report.

(3) Cost lost due to damaged equipment or damage of other property material etc.

(4) Cost due to delayed progress of the work due to accident.

(5) Cost of payment of wages to the injured person, during the period of the injury; the labour or worker could not attend his duties.

(6) Cost due to slowing down the work of other workers/employees due to accident, as there is always a tendency to take extra unnecessary precaution by each worker after the accident; hence works of other employees also slow down and suffer.

Studies have shown that loss due to indirect cost is about four times that of loss of direct cost. As such it is always necessary to take safety measures to avoid accidents.

3.3. SAFETY AND HEALTH

Special features have been made by construction industry which adversely influence the safety and health of workers. Special problems that arise at construction sites are due to following reasons :

(1) Short time duration of work sites to labourer.

(2) Seasonal employment.

(3) Extensive and exhaustive use of migrant labour.

(4) Extensive sub-contractiang practice.

(5) Effect of weather. (6) Overtime working. (7) Competitive tendering.

Due to these reasons, workers change at every stage, safety measures are not adopted, further, no training is given to the workers; hence accidents take place.

There is always a tendency in most of the construction sites to work unusual long hours during span of good weather to make up for time lost in bad weather. Sometimes due to need to finish certain operation as these can not be stopped such concreting; workers are required to work for extra time; even during night also. This also causes accidents, contractor also always tries to get more work done from migrant labours.

At present; bye laws framed by municipalities and corporation take care of safety in construction industry. Safety codes are framed by almost all municipalities and corporation which are applicable to that territory. Government departments either Central or State have also prepared safety codes for safety of workers involved in construction industry. But these provisions are inadequate and there is no enforcing machinery to check whether safety codes are observed or not. Hence as such though the death rate probably is the highest in construction industry but no record is available rather it is also doubtful whether such authentic record has been made some where by some one else or not.

A balanced health and safety policy should include the following :

(1) Safe and healthy working conditions for workers at construction site.

(2) Training of employees, workers regularly.

(3) To comply with safety codes laws and regulations for the protection of health, safety and environment.

(4) Safety instruments and materials must be used during construction.

(5) Ill workers should not be employed, children should also be not employed to at construction site.

(6) Unnecessary persons should not be allowed at construction site.

(7) Enforcing contractor, management to employ safety precautions, safety codes before execution of any work is started.

(8) Regular medical check up of workers.

(9) Application of systematic safety training programme.

The objectives behind all there safety measures, precautions, safety code are :

(1) To minimise incidents and accidents.

(2) Identification and elimination of risks before losses occur.

(3) Devloping confidence in workers.

(4) Avoiding loss of time, life, machinery and of course work.

All construction equipment/machine entail risk. Safety of worker or any other person while using any construction equipment/machine in general and special or heavy equipment/ machine in particular is an important aspect of construction. It is necessary to give considerable attention to this factor. There are cases of casualties up to the extent of fatal accidents during improper use of heavy machines like bulldozer or cranes etc. Safety planning in advance protects worker and public and develops in confidence in worker making him safe and free of all worries. Accidents in general are always due to multiple mistakes of workers and other persons or due to negligence. These both can be avoided if little precautions are taken into considerations. Each equipment/machine to be used should be properly studied before put into use. The operator should be trained before he is asked to work on it. If all these precautions are taken into consideration, fatal accidents can be minimized considerably creating confidence in workers.

3.4. ACCIDENT PREVENTION PROGRAMME

An accident prevention programme must be started on every construction site in order to reduce the cost of construction in terms of human life and injuries; damage materials and machineries and equipments and loss of time. It is therefore essential to correct useful informations about the accidents which have taken place at various construction sites; their reason. For this it is further necessary to evolve a proper accident monitoring system that can collect the relevant information from the persons concerned. The system should have positive thinking, that the aim is the prevention of accidents. An organisation chart of .'safety department' is given herewith in Fig. 3.1.

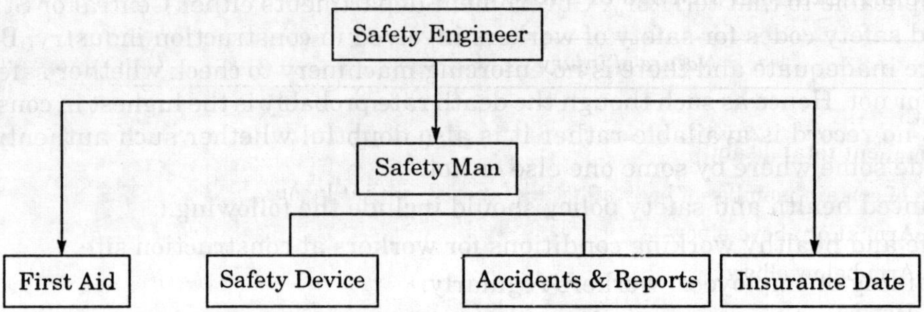

Fig. 3.1. Organisation chart and Safety Department.

Next step in accident prevention programme is thorough examination of construction equipments and machineries and their maintenance property in safe condition. Many accidents take place only due to faulty design and poor maintenance of construction equipments. Workers using machine must also be trained properly and be equipped with safety devices for safe procedure of works. Supervision by experience supervisor and proper training can go a long way in preventing most of the accidents. Management can play a very important and efficient role in accident prevention. Many times it has been seen that management itself do not pay much and proper attention to the safety programme for the sake of their own interest of increasing the production. This is not a good practice. Management must see that safety codes are followed and implemented.

Every accident that results is a personal injury of any form and must be reported and investigated and remedial measures must be taken. Investigation will also reveal that further efforts may be expected to achieve improvement in the safety performance.

Every site whether large or small must have adequate facilities for rendering first aid to injured employees. If an employee has suffered a serious temporary disabling injury or a permanent disability, it must be made compulsory to that employer to exercise every effort to rehabitate that employee.

3.5. TERMS USED

(*a*) **Injury-Frequency Rate.** The injury frequency rate is defined as the number of workers disabling injuries per 10^6. man hours worked. A disabling injury means an injury which causes a loss of working time beyond the day; shift or turn during which the injury received.

$$\text{Injury frequency rate} = \frac{\text{Number of disabling injuries} \times 10^6}{\text{No. of man hours worked}}$$

Injury frequency rate does not take into account the time lost because of an injury.

(*b*) **Injury Severity Rate.** It is defined as the number of days of lost time because of injuries per 1000 man hours worked. The standard scales for lost time resulting from death or permanent disability is given in Table 3.1. If an injury causes the death or permanent disability of a worker the number of days of lost time used for that worker should be taken from this table even though a worker who loses several fingers in an accident and later on returns to work, total disability be only considered. The severity rate in terms of equation is expressed as

$$\text{Injury – Severity rate} = \frac{\text{No. of days lost} \times 1000}{\text{No. of man hours worked}}$$

Table 3.1. Standard Scale of Time Charges for Various Injuries

S. No.	*Nature of injury*	*Time charge days*
1.	Death	6000
2.	Permanent total disability	6000
3.	Loss of certain member of body affecting function of that labour	
	(*a*) Arm at or above elbow	4570
	(*b*) Arm below elbow	3600
	(*c*) Hand	3000
	(*d*) Thumb	600
	(*e*) Any one finger	300
	(*f*) Two fingers of same hand	750
	(*g*) Three fingers of same hand	1200
	(*h*) Four fingers of same hand	1800
	(*i*) Thumb and one finger of same hand	1200
	(*j*) Thumb and two fingers of same hand	1500
	(*k*) Thumb and three fingers of same hand	2000
	(*l*) Thumb and four fingers of same hand	2400
	(*m*) Leg at or above knee	4500
	(*n*) Leg below knee	3000
	(*o*) Foot at ankle	2400
	(*p*) Great toe	300
	(*q*) 2 Great toes	600
	(*r*) 1 eye loss of sight	1800
	(*s*) Both eyes loss of sight	6000
	(*t*) 1 ear loss of hearing	600
	(*u*) Both ears, loss of hearing	3000

Table 3.2. Injuries Deemed to Result in Permanent/Partial Disablement

S. No.	*Injury*	*Percentage of loss of earing capacity*
1.	Loss of both hands	100
2.	Loss of a hand and a foot	100
3.	Loss of sight	100
4.	Very severe disfigurement of face	100
5.	Absolute deafness	100
6.	Double amputation to leg or thigh and other foot	100
7.	Amputation through shoulder joint	90
8.	Loss of a hand or thumb and four fingers of one hand	60
9.	Loss of thumb	30
10.	Loss of four fingers of one hand	50
11.	Loss of three fingers of one hand	30
12.	Loss of 2 fingers of one hand	20
13.	Amputation of both feet	90
14.	Loss of all toes of both feet	40
15.	Amputation below the knee	40
16.	Loss of one eye	40
17.	Loss of vision of one eye	30
18.	Loss of index finger	14
19.	Loss of middle finger	12
20.	Loss of right or left little finger	7
21.	Loss of right or left great toe	14
22.	Loss of any other toe	3
23.	Two toes of one foot excluding great toe	5
24.	Three toes of one foot excluding great toe	6
25.	Four toes of one foot excluding great toe	9

Injury Index—The injury index is expressed as

$$\text{Injury index} = \frac{\text{Frequency rate} \times \text{severity rate}}{1000}$$

Example. *A contractor who had employed 200 men, for 50 week extracting work for 40 hrs. a week on certain site had 8 disabling injuries. What is his injury frequency rate. Also calculate injury severity rate if these injuries had resulted in a loss of total 90 day from work. Also calculate injury index.*

Solution.

$$\text{Injury frequency rate} = \frac{\text{No. of disabling injuries} \times 10^6}{\text{No. of man hr. worked}} = \frac{8 \times 10^6}{200 \times 40 \times 50} = 20 \text{ per year}$$

$$\text{Injury severity rate} = \frac{\text{No. of days lost} \times 1000}{\text{No. of man hr. worked}}] = \frac{90 \times 1000}{200 \times 40 \times 50}$$

$$= 0.225 \quad i.e. \; 22.5 \text{ percent}$$

$$\text{The injury index} = \frac{\text{Frequency rate} \times \text{severity rate}}{1000} = \frac{20 \times 0.225}{1000} = 0.0045.$$

3.6. CLASSIFICATION OF CONSTRUCTION ACCIDENTS

Extensive studies carried out show that main causes of construction accidents may be grouped as follows :

(1) Uncontrollable contact between men and equipment or between men and material such as cranes, trucks; material storages etc.

(2) Failure of temporary structures such as scaffoldings, forms, ladders, cofferdams etc.

(3) Inherent engineering hazards; such as the use of explosives, toxic gases; toxic dusts etc.

(4) Unsafe practice of individual workers or personal hazards resulting from the carelessness of workers.

These can be avoided if proper precautions are taken. As per provisions of Factories Act 1948; accidents in general are classified into 5 categories *viz.*

(1) **Minor Accidents.** Accidents which made the worker disabled for less than 48 hours come under this category.

(2) **Reportable Accidents.** If an accident causes worker disabled such that he can not work for more than 48 hours the accident is classified as reportable accident. Such accidents must be reported.

(3) **Fatal Accident.** Results in a death of a worker.

(4) Accidents which causes poisoning and

(5) Dangerous occurrence.

All the accidents mentioned above except No. 1 must be reported and investigated. The report must include following details.

(1) Name of organisation and department of working.

(2) Date of accident. (3) Name of injured person.

(4) Home address of employee. (5) Time of the accident.

(6) Name of the supervisor. (7) First aid given

(8) (*a*) Details about previous disability of worker if any.

(*b*) If yes, whether investigation about accidents conducted.

(*c*) Report of investigation.

(9) Name of person who first reported about the accident along with witness.

(10) Investigation report.

(11) Certificate about disobedience to follow the safety rules on the part of management and worker.

This report prepared should be signed by appropriate authority.

3.7. LIST OF POSSIBLE ACCIDENTS IN CASE OF BUILDING WORKS

(1) **Excavation.** Earth sliding, falling of worker due to slippery area in case of water logged area, Blasted material may hit worker in case of excavation by blasting and snacks/scorpian may bite if found during excavation.

(2) **Concreting.** Framework may fall or fail, steel cage may collapse, slipping of formworks, plumb-bob may hit person at lower level, concrete bucket or metal pan may fall down, labourer or worker may slip from any position and fall below in case of slab particularly, ladder may slip erected for worker.

(3) **Masonry work and plastering.** Brick may fall down, failure of scaffolding, props, bambooes may break, hammer may fall.

(4) **Plumbing works.** Chiesel, hammer etc. may fall on persons working at lower level.

(5) **Painting works.** Ladder may slip, ropes may get cut.

(6) **Truck working.** While going reverse may hit ladder on which a person may be working, vehicle may slip or overturn, brakes may fail.

4 Report Writing

4.1. INTRODUCTION

Project report normally forms the basis of the administrative approval of any project. The administrative approval is the primary commitment by the competent authority for taking the work in hand. However according to the fundamental principles of accounting, no work can be taken in hand unless funds for the project have been alloted and technical sanction for various elements of the project has been accorded. Sometimes in the case of top priority projects, the pre-requisites of a project *i.e.* administrative approval and the allotment of funds, may be ignored but technical sanction which is a guarantee by the competent engineering authority in respect of the technical soundness of the work, should be ensured before work be taken in hand. Works executed with one administrative approval and allotment of funds would form audit objection against the project authorities. These objections would be settled in due course when covering administrative approval is accorded and funds are alloted. However a work which has been executed without technical sanction can strictly speaking not be settled by the issue of technical sanction because the irregularity committed is such that the issue of subsequent or covering sanction does not carry any weight. Fortunately, this technical complication is beyond the appreciation of audit authorities and the subsequent issue of technical (covering) sanction is considered by the audit as adequate to settle the objection.

The issue of the administrative approval, which is the principal requirement of any project is normally based on the detailed estimate the preparation of which requires considerable field data collection followed by the design based on the collected field data. In fact the so called project report is the survey report. Salient features of which are given in article 12.2.

4.2. SURVEY REPORT OF THE PROJECT

The survey report is based on the field work and office design work which includes detailed estimate of the project including phasing out if and when required. The survey itself may consist of selection of site and preparation of the site plan and layout plan of the various components proposed in the project complex. In the case of road, railway or canal project the survey may consist of reconnaissance, preliminary and detailed one. All the above classes of surveys may be conducted but in the case of self-evident alignment only detailed survey may be necessary.

The field work done by the survey party in respect of the finally selected alignment is consolidated and the following features of the complex are highlighted :

1. **Ground details of the area.** In the case of building complex located in a comparatively small area general description of the place with respect to known places or land marks and topography are given. In the case of road, railway, canal etc. ground details of the alignment along with the standards *i.e.* formation width, road land, etc. are given along with location of bridges and culverts. Factors leading to the selection of site and design data in respect of the proposed bridge are given.

The detailed estimate of the project forms one of the appendices along with the supporting details such as site plan showing location and relative position of various units, working drawing and brief design details of these units and calculation of quantities. For example, project report in respect of a highway project would consist of the following :

1. **Introduction.** A summary from the initiation of the proposal to the finalisation of the alignment along with brief description of the route and the various surveys carried out which lead to the finalisation of the particular route.

2. Geometric standards of the proposed highway including traffic survey, design speed, type and width of pavement, shoulder grade, curvature and sight distances.

3. Salient features of the proposed alignment starting from starting station and ending at the terminal station. Factors leading to the ruling gradient along with the horizontal and vertical control points may be included in this.

4. Foundation conditions including soil classification and various strata as well as statement showing swamps and marshy areas if coming in the alignment,

5. Drainage including weather conditions prevalent during the year and suggested general drainage scheme of the project.

6. Availability of road material.

7. Permanent road land along with general condition of open areas, houses, and other built up areas along with their approximate valuation as indicated under the head land compensation in the detailed estimate.

8. **Special feature of the Project.** Under this heading may be included all such information which may be of importance from the point of view of the project but may not have been included under any of the headings indicated earlier.

Construction Nuisance. Noise, vibrations, dust, illumination particularly during night working are the nuisances found in almost all the construction sites. These all problems are due to use of heavy machines in case of pile driving, blasting and mucking etc. which cannot be avoided. It is therefore essential to a contractor to take some steps to control them and to safeguard the health of workers at the site. Precautions taken will also reduce the possibilities of accidents as noise may make someone to deaf and dumb. Such worker may not be able to listen and therefore some fatal accident can occur due to it.

Conclusion. Under this the total estimated cost of the project specifying separately the amount earmarked for compensation of property of various types to be acquired for the highway and contingencies is specified and request.for according administrative approval of the project along with specific demand of allotment of funds for the year and preferably break up of allotment of funds for the various years is made. The basis for arriving at the cost of the project is also specified. At the end the officer initiating the project report signs the report giving the designation and date of signing. A list of appendices, annexures and enclosures is also given.

4.3. ANNEXURES TO THE PROJECT REPORT

The project report or the technical report in respect of the project is primarily meant for the administrative authority to have a general idea of the project, its usefulness and total cost involved. The administrative authority would normally be having quite a few of such projects under consideration and hence while according administrative approval to a particular project a comparative study of the various projects under consideration is made. The information given in the report should therefore on the one hand be comprehensive enough to lime light all salient features of the project and at the same time it should be brief enough so that irrelevant data and information from the point of view of the administrative authority is not supplied. On the other hand, before the report is submitted to the administrative authority, the engineer authority has to satisfy itself about the feasibility and technical soundness of the project as well as reliability of the cost indicated therein. To meet the view point of the administrative authority as well as to be self sufficient in respect of the technical details, it is common practice to provide sufficient details as annexures to the technical report or in the case of highway project to the survey report. The number and details of such annexures will depend on the characteristic features of the particular project. In case the project is that of a highway, the supporting details provided as annexures to the project report are :

1. Index plan.
2. Site plan.
3. Longitudinal section along with estimate of quantities of earthwork.
4. Cross section.
5. Details of protective works (specially in the case of hill roads) consisting of retaining walls, breast walls, parapet walls etc.
6. Drainage details along with a list of proposed bridges and culverts with their location size, length and design particulars.
7. Availability of road material.
8. Design details including traffic consideration.
9. Bridge design or other structure design details if the project includes bridges or other major structure.
10. Land acquisition and land compensation schedule.
11. Estimate of cost of the project.

The above annexures are briefly described below :

1. Index plan. The purpose of index plan is to give the relative position of the proposed highway with respect to the surrounding area and connecting highways. For example if the proposed highway connects Delhi and Ambala, the index plan will include not only the states along which the highway is to pass namely Delhi and Haryana in this case but also the adjoining states along with the existing means of communications *i.e.* existing roads, railways, navigation channels and important towns along the highway and also in the adjoining area.

2. The site plan. This may be carried over a number of consecutive sheets and shows on plan the complete highway alignment including details of curves, drainage crossings, protective works, rail road crossings, soil classification and other connected details. All cities, towns and villages along the alignment along with important features are shown in this plan. In fact it is a comprehensive plan which gives all the details of the highway except the grades and cross sections for which separate sets of drawings are prepared.

3. Longitudinal section along with estimated quantity of earthwork. This is drawn on the basis of the level line run along the centre of the proposed alignment and the proposed formation level fixed on the basis of the proposed grade. Normally one km length of the highway is shown in a sheet although sometimes the L-section is prepared in the form of a continuous roll by pasting various continuation sheets. This longitudinal section along with the supporting cross sections is used to compute the quantities of earthwork in filling and excavation and is normally tabulated at the bottom of the sheet as shown in Fig. 4.1.

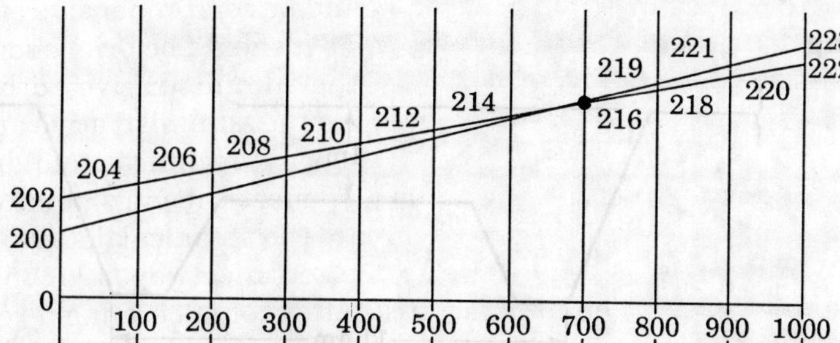

	0	100	200	300	400	500	600	700	800	900	1000
Earthwork in Cutting (m^3)								620	1240	1240	
Earthwork in Embankment (m^3)	2880	3535	4280	4770	4770	4770	2385				
Height of Embankment, h (m)	2.0	2.0	2.5	3.0	3.0	3.0	0				
Depth of Cutting (m)									1.0	1.0	1.0
Formation Level	202	204	206	208	210	212	214	216	218	220	222
Ground Level R.D.	202	202	203	205	207	209	211	216	219	221	223

0 100 200 300 400 500 600 700 800 900 1000 metres

Fig. 4.1. Longitudinal Section

4. Cross-section. Although longitudinal section and cross section are shown on separate continuation sheets as separate sets of drawing. It is common practice in the department to combine the results of the two in the form given in Fig. 4.1. The cross sections are used as supporting documents to check the calculation of earthwork shown in the longitudinal sheet as shown in the calculation.

$$x_0 = \left(\frac{11.4 + 11.4 + 6}{2}\right) \times 2 = 28.8 \text{ m}^2 \qquad x_0 = 28.8 \text{ m}^2$$

chainage 100 :

x_1 same as at x_0 $\qquad x_1 = 28.8 \text{ m}^2$

$$x_2 \text{ Height} = 2.5 \text{ m } x_2 = \left(\frac{11.4 + 11.4 + 7.5}{2}\right) \times 2.5 = 37.9 \text{ m}^2$$

$$x_3 \text{ Height} = 3 \text{ m } x_3 = \left(\frac{11.4 + 11.4 + 9}{2}\right) \times 3 = 47.7 \text{ m}^3$$

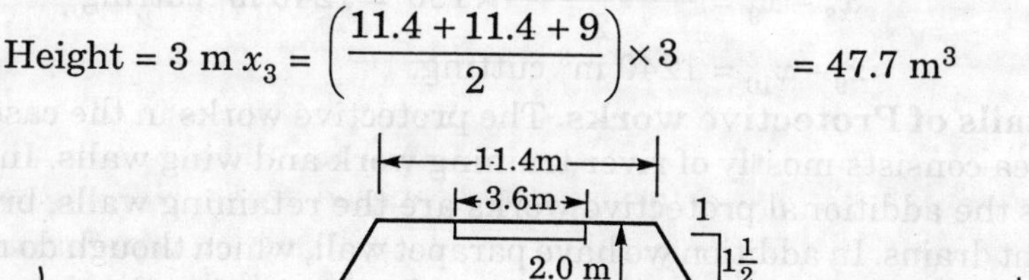

Fig. 4.2 (*a*)

x_4, x_5, 6_6 Height 3 m ; $x_4, x_5, x_6 = 47.7 \text{ m}^2$, $x_7 = 0$.

Cutting

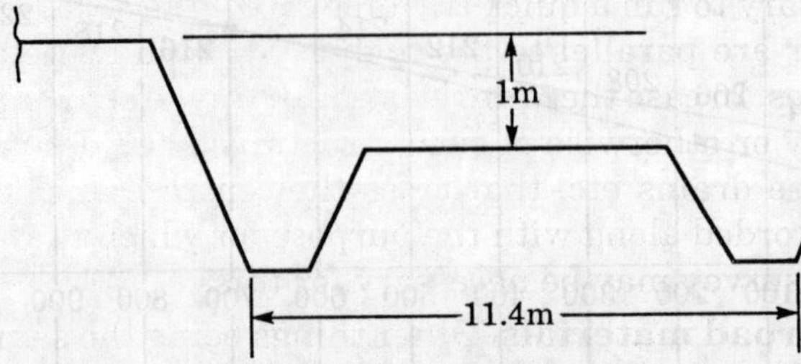

Fig. 4.2 (b)

$$x_8 = x_9 = x_{10} : \text{Depth of cutting} = 1 \text{ m}$$

$$x_8 = \left(\frac{11.4 + 11.4 + 2}{2}\right) \times 1 = \frac{24.8}{2} = 12.4 \text{ m}^2$$

$$x_8 = x_9 = x_{10} = 12.4 \text{ m}^2.$$

Reference : L-section (Fig. 4.1) and cross section (Fig. 4.2).

Calculation of Quantities of Earthwork

(*a*) Earthwork in embankment

$$x_0 - x_1 = \left(\frac{28.8 + 28.8}{2}\right) \times 100 = 2880 \text{ m}^3$$

$$x_1 - x_2 = \left(\frac{28.8 + 37.90}{2}\right) \times 100 = \frac{66.70}{2} \times 100 = 3535 \text{ m}^3$$

$$x_2 - x_3 = \left(\frac{37.90 + 47.70}{2}\right) \times 100 = 42.80 \times 100 = 4280 \text{ m}^3$$

$$x_3 - x_4 = 47.70 \times 100 = 4770 \text{ m}^3$$

$$x_4 - x_5 = 47.70 \times 100 = 4770 \text{ m}^3$$

$$x_5 - x_6 = 47.70 \times 100 = 4770 \text{ m}^3$$

$$x_6 - x_7 = \frac{47.70 + 0}{2} \times 100 = 23.85 \times 100 = 2385 \text{ m}^3$$

$$x_7 - x_8 = \frac{0 + 12.4}{2} \times 100 = 6.2 \times 100 = 620 \text{ m}^3 \text{ cutting}$$

$$x_8 - x_9 = \frac{12.4 + 12.4}{2} \times 100 = 1240 \text{ m}^3 \text{ cutting}$$

$$x_9 - x_{10} = 1240 \text{ m}^3 \text{ cutting.}$$

5. Details of Protective works. The protective works in the case of highway over flat and rocky area consists mostly of river training work and wing walls. In the case of highways in hilly areas the additional protective works are the retaining walls, breast wall, side drains and catchment drains. In addition we have parapet wall, which though do not give any protection to the road, yet are a very desirable feature, firstly, to give the driver a sense of security against falling into the *khud* and secondly, to prevent any direct load coming on the retaining wall in the *khud* side. The retaining walls are designed only for pressure due to retaining the filling.

6. Drainage Detail. Enough information must be recorded to enable the designer to provide adequately for the drainage flow. This will ordinarily require an approximate determination of the drainage area and the nature of run off whether fast, medium or slow. It may sometimes be necessary to run a quick traverse round the area. Highest flood levels in all the streams that cross or are parallel to the highway should be determined or ascertained from available local sources. In case there are existing drainage structures or existing highways or railways, the adequacy or otherwise of such structures should be ascertained. All private drains, field drains, house drains etc. that cross the centre line or affect the design of the proposed highway are recorded along with the purpose for which they are constructed. Sometimes a special drainage survey may be necessary for this.

7. Availability of road materials. Other things being the same preference is given to an alignment along which stone quarries or rocks are available. However, the nature of the rocks and the quantity of stone which these rocks are capable of yielding should also be studied to enable the Engineer authority to weigh the advantage gained from the existence of road building materials along the alignment. The availability of construction materials for road construction does not only help in reducing the cost of construction but also reduce subsequently the cost of maintenance of the highway.

8. Design details including traffic consideration. Normally the class of highway for which location survey is to be done including preparation of detailed estimate is determined before hand on the basis of the following :

(*i*) Expected traffic on the highway (*ii*) Strategic importance of the highway

(*iii*) Expected increase in traffic due to opening of potential commercial areas such as forest resources, lime stone quarries, expected mines.

The above factors having been taken into consideration the highway design reduces to the pavement design for which the following factors will have to be considered by the designer.

(*a*) "Whether the traffic, soil and climate conditions call for the construction of a flexible or rigid pavement for the proposed highway.

(*b*) Expected traffic intensity and the type of traffic expected,

(*c*) Soil classification of the subgrade.

(d) Prevalent moisture condition. (*e*) Frost condition.

9. Design of bridge and other Structures. Highway bridges are classified as major bridges, minor bridges and bridges and culverts. Normally bridge of span over 50 metres come under the category of major bridges and planning design and construction of such bridges is separated from the main highway project. Bridges between 15 metres and 50 metres span come under the category of minor bridges. The design and planning of such bridges is normally done along with the main highway project but the project Engineer normally gets the same approved by the competent Engineer authority. For bridges below 15 metre span the Engineer incharge of the highway project normally does the planning, design and execution himself. Other connected structure with the project are also dealt with on the same lines as different categories of bridges depending upon the relative importance of the proposed structure.

In case highway crosses any railway canal or other communication systems, the bridge design and execution is done by the authority in charge of that system and cost thereof is debited to the project.

10. Land acquisition and land compensation details. Legally no ground work connected with the execution of the highway project can be taken in hand without obtaining legal rights over the road land. This is done by acquiring the land required for the highway by either paying compensation for the private property thus acquired by arranging transfer of land in case the same belongs to other department or ministry of the Government.

11. Estimate of cost of the Project. One single factor which is said to have the greatest influence on the project is the cost. The administrative approval, so far as the administration is concerned, is an authority to incur the amount of expenditure to the extent of its approval within the limitation of the allotment of funds. The value of this amount is arrived at by working out the details of the various items of work involved in the project and determining the probable rate in each item of work. In respect of certain items of work such as earthwork in excavation or earthwork in embankment the quantities are straightly calculated from the longitudinal sections and cross section. As regard other items of work such as concrete work, masonry work, protective work etc., detailed specifications in respect of these items have to be framed before the rate of the item can be determined.

Equipment planning. Use of construction equipment on site is unavoidable as on today. No civil engineering work can be executed without using construction equipment/ machinary one type or the other. It is therefore essential to know the type of equipment and machineries required for type of project works. Equipment either can be purchased or borrowed on lease or on rent. Therefore study of equipment economics is essentially required to be studies before a final project report is made and submitted. Engineer/contractor though do this but not from financial or other consideration.

Equipment Economics. It is an important factor while purchasing an equipment. Purchasing of Equipment involves a large expense. A contractor/owner is required to invest a good amount for its purchase. Unless the purchase is justified, it may not be worthwhile to purchase it. More over contractor losses interest which he would have earned by putting this amount as securities. Though equipment can be purchase or hired on a rent with an option to purchase it later on. However every contractor would like to purchase if he can afford as in this case the equipment is available as and when required. It reduces his dependency on others. But justification of its purchase is very essential. The life of equipment, its type *i.e.* standard or special, amount involved, interest loss, its utility for one project/work or more projects/works, downtime cost, obsolescence cost etc are many factors required to be taken into consideration before a final decision is made. In case equipment is purchased with hard cash if available with contractor, he loses interest on it. In case if he takes loan to purchase it, contractor is required to pay interest on amount borrowed as a loan. As such he is required to make an analysis how much he is going to spent on it and how much he is likely to earn. If earning is more than investment, it may be advisable to purchase else one should get it rented.

For example if an equipment cost ₹ 50.00 Lacks having a useful life of as 5 years (may be in hours also), now either the contractor can use his hard cash available with him'to purchase it or he can borrow a loan of about 80% cost *i.e.* ₹ 40.00 Lacks from any financing body to purchase it. In case if contractor uses his hard cash, he is losing a compound interest of about ₹ 22 to ₹ 23 in a span of 5 years with an approximate rate of interest of 7.5 to 8%. In case he borrows loan, he in general will be required to pay an interest of about ₹ 20 to ₹ 22 Lacks on an amount of ₹ 40.0 Lacks, moreover he is also losing interest on ₹ 10 lacks which he has put to borrow the equipment. As such contractor has to spent/invest an approximate amount of ₹ 75.0 Lacks to make equipment available to his work. Now question arises whether this much expenditure is justified? Whether contractor is going to earn more than the amount spent in a span of 5 years? Will there be no down time cost? Whether no new equipment is likely to come in market making it obsolete? Here equipment economics play an important role in decision making.

Part—III

VALUATION OF IMMOVABLE PROPERTIES

1

Valuation and Its Concept

1.1. GLOSSARY OF TERMS

Abnormal sale. A sale that is not typical of what is happening in the market place.

Absorption rate. An estimate of the rate at which a particular classification of properties for sale or lease can be successful marketed in a given area : it is often requested in a feasibility study or an appraisal in connection with a request for financing.

Abstraction. A method of valuing land in which an appraiser establishes a typical ratio of site value to total property value from comparable improved properties. This ratio is then applied to the total value of the property being appraisal to estimate the value of the land. Also called the allocation or extraction method.

Accessibility. The ease with which a person can enter or exit a particular tract of land.

Accession. The transfer of ownership of fixtures or land as a result of the attachment of those fixtures or land to another's property.

Accrued depreciation. The difference between an improvement's reproduction or replacement cost and its market value as of the date of the appraisal. It represents the total depreciation accumulated since the improvement was constructed.

Accumulated depreciation. (*See* accrued depreciation).

Acreage property. A large and, for the most part, unimproved tract of land : such land is often used for agricultural purposes.

Actual age. The number of years that have elapsed since construction was completed. Also called chronological or historical age.

Adjacent land. Land physically located close to or near another parcel of land.

Adjusted sales price. The estimated sales prices of a comparable property after additions and/or subtractions have been made to the actual sales price to allow for differences between the comparables and the subject property.

Adjustments. The dollar value or percentage amounts added to or subtracted from the sales price of a comparable property to arrive at an indicated value for the property being appraised (subject property). Real estate elements of comparison typically are adjusted in the following order : property rights, financing terms, conditions of sale, market conditions, location, and physical characteristics.

Ad valorem. A tax based on value. Real property tax is an ad valorem tax based on the assessed valuation of the property.

Adverse possession. The acquiring of title to real property owned by another by means of open, actual, continuous, and hostile possession for a statutory period of time.

After-tax cash flow (ATCF). The cash flow remaining after debt service and ordinary income tax on operations are subtracted from net operating income.

Age-life depreciation. An appraisal method of computing accrued depreciation. Under this method, depreciation is estimated by multiplying the reproduction or replacement cost by the ratio of the improvement's effective age to total economic life.

Air rights. The legal right to use and occupy the space above a particular parcel of real estate; air rights can be transferred legally through selling them, leasing them and, in some instances, creating an easement.

Amenities. Features that enhance the value or desirability of real estate. Amenities may be tangible (such as a swimming pool) or intangible (such as a good view).

Amortization. The repayment or retiring of debt through scheduled, systematic repayment of principal over a set period.

Amortization schedule. A schedule that shows the amounts of principal and interest incurred and paid at each time period of a scheduled, systematic repayment of principal.

Anchor tenant. The major store within a shopping center that attracts or generates traffic for the facility. Anchors are strategically placed to maximize sales for all tenants. The type of anchor depends on the type of shopping center (*e.g.*, a supermarket is a typical anchor for a neighbourhood shopping center) whereas a major chain or department store is a typical anchor for a regional shopping mail.

Annual debt service. The total mortgage payments required in one year in regard to a particular loan.

Annual loan constant. The ratio of annual debt service or yearly loan payment to the original principal on the loan.

Annuity. A series of cash flows in which an equal payment occurs at regular or fixed intervals. Also sometimes used to refer to a series of equal payments that change according to a predictable pattern [*e.g.*, increasing by a fixed dollar amount each year (straight-line annuity) or increasing by a constant percentage each year (constant-ratio annuity)]. Formulas can be used to find the present value or future value of these later annuities.

Annuity in advance. A series of cash flows in which an equal payment occurs at the beginning of each period.

Anticipation. The appraisal principle that states that value is created by the expectation of benefits, to be received in the future.

Appraisal. The act or process of developing an opinion of value.

Appraisal principles. Concepts that provide the rationale of market behaviour, which affects value. Appraisal principles include anticipation, change, supply and demand, substitution, and balance.

Appraisal process. The step-by-step analysis undertaken by an appraiser for the purpose of accurately developing an opinion of value.

Appraisal report. A report, written or oral, that contains the results of an appraisal. A standard written report usually contains the following pieces of information : the definition of value to be applied, the estimate and effective date of the valuation, certifications and limiting conditions, description of the property and rights being appraised, supporting data, justification to support the value estimate, consideration of each of the three approaches, and the reconciliation. Oral reports should also include the above information when appropriate.

Appraiser. A person who possesses the education, training, and experience necessary to accurately render an opinion as to the value of real estate.

Appreciation. An increase in the value of an asset over some period of time, opposite of depreciation.

Approaches to value. Various methods typically used by an appraiser in preparing an appraisal report. Of the three traditional approaches to value, the cost approach bases value on the reproduction or replacement cost of the improvements, less depreciation, plus the value of the land. The income approach bases value on the capitalization of future cash flows from a property at an acceptable market rate. The market approach (or sales comparison approach) bases value on a comparative analysis of recent sales prices of similar properties, after making adjustment for seller concessions, time and any differences in the properties.

Appurtenances. Items that have been affixed to a property and thus have become an inherent part of the property. Such items usually pass with the property when title is transferred although they are not part of the property (*e.g.*, easements, water rights, condominium parking stalls).

Arbitrator. One who mediates a dispute.

Arm's-length transaction. A transaction occurring in a competitive market with reasonable exposure under conditions requisite to a fair sale, with a willing buyer and seller each acting prudently, knowledgeably, and for self-interest. An arm's-length transaction assumes that neither buyer nor seller is under undue duress.

Asking price. The price at which the owner offers to sell.

Assessed value. The value or worth of a property on which ad valorem taxes are based.

Assessment. A valuation of real property for tax purposes in which the assessed value of the property is determined.

Assessment ratio. The ratio of assessed value to full market value as set by the taxing authority; used by the tax assessor in determining the amount of property tax due on a parcel of real estate.

Average deviation. A number arrived at by finding the average of a set of numbers, adding the absolute difference of this average with each value and then dividing this sum by the total number of values in the set. Average deviation gives an indication of the variation in the set of numbers.

B. Ratio of building value to total value.

Balance. The appraisal principle that states that property value is a function of contrasting, opposing, or interacting elements and their state of equilibrium.

Band of investment. An appraisal technique used in the income approach where the overall rate is derived from the weighted-average rates attributable to the components of a capital investment. The technique can be based on mortgage-equity components or land-building components. Note, however, that the term is often used to refer *only* to the mortgage-equity approach. In this case, the overall rate is found by a weighted average of the mortgage loan constant and the equity dividend rate.

Base rent. The minimum rent stipulated in a lease. It is typically associated with leases that also specify some sort of overage rent.

Basic employment. Employment in basic industry.

Basic industry. An industry that attracts income from outside the community; opposite of a non-basic industry, which is a support industry for a basic industry.

Basic point. One one-hundredth (1/100) of 1 percent. Used to indicate a change in interest rates. For example, if interest rates rise from 10 percent to 11 percent, then the increase would be 100 basis points.

Before-tax cash flow (BTCF). The cash flow remaining after deduction of debt service (principal and interest) and any other cash outflows from net operating income. BTCF considers all cash flows that could affect the investor except federal income taxes. For example, leasing commissions and the cost of tenant improvements would be subtracted in calculating BTCF. Also referred to as pretax cash flow.

Blanket mortgage. A loan secured by more than one property or lot. It is commonly used in construction financing for subdivision or condominium development.

Book value. The amount at which property is carried on the books of a company. It usually equals the original cost less accounting depreciation plus any additions to capital.

Borrower. One who has temporarily used funds from another through the use of debt financing.

Break-down method. A method of estimating accrued depreciation in which each cause of depreciation is analysed and measured separately. The different types of depreciation are then added to find the total depreciation.

Break-even point. The point where the property's effective gross income is equal to the sum of its typical operating expenses plus debt service (principal and interest). This indicates the point-of-zero, before-tax cash flow.

Buffer zone. A strip of land separating one type of zoning from another. A buffer zone will sometimes be left vacant as a buffer from land uses that are incompatible.

Building capitalization rate (R_B). The ratio of the building income to building value. In the income approach to value, the rate is used in both the band of investment and residual techniques to convert income into estimated value.

Building codes. Rules and ordinances created by a municipal government to regulate the design, construction, quality, use, occupancy, location, and maintenance of buildings to provide minimum standards to safeguard public welfare. Building codes are a part of a state's police power and are enforced by inspections and the issuance of building permits and certificates of occupancy.

Building ratio. The ratio of building value to total property value; used in band of investment techniques in the income approach to appraisal.

Building residual technique. A method used to find property value in the income approach when the value of land and net operating income are known. The income attributable to land is subtracted from the net operating income to find the income attributable to improvements. This figure is then capitalized and added to the land value to estimate the property value.

Building restrictions. Limitations and regulations placed on a property that control the type and size of structures that can be constructed; examples would include zoning ordinances and deed restriction.

Bundle of rights. A concept that describes real property by the legal rights associated with owning the property. It specifies rights such as the rights to sell, lease, occupy, and trade and property. The buyer in a sales transaction typically purchase the legal rights previously held by the seller, except those that are reserved or limited in the sale.

Business risk. The risk associated with unknown future variability in rents, vacancies, or operating expenses.

Buy down. A lump-sum payment to the lender that reduces the monthly payment of the borrower; it is sometimes used by developers to lower the effective interest rate on the buyer's loan. The cost of the buydown is usually reflected in the purchase price.

Buyer's market. A situation in which supply in the marketplace is greater than demand.

Capital gain. The gain arising from the resale of a capital asset. The capital gain equals the net proceeds from the sale minus the adjusted basis (original cost minus depreciation) of the asset. As of 1987, capital gains are taxed at the same rate as ordinary income. However, limits do exist on the- amount of capital loss allowed to offset ordinary income.

Capital loss. The loss arising when the net proceeds from the sale of a capital asset do not equal the adjusted basis (original cost minus depreciation) of the asset. Limits do exist on the amount of capital loss allowed to offset ordinary income.

Capitalisation. A technique used in the income approach to convert income into an estimate of value. See direct capitalisation *and* yield capitalisation.

Capitalisation rate. A rate used in the income approach to convert income into value; it equals the ratio of the net operating income to the property value or sales price. The rate reflects market conditions, property characteristics, risk, etc. Also called a cap rate.

Capitalise. In *approach,* the process of determining an opinion of value based on the income produced by the property. The value can be estimated by yield capitalisation or by direct capitalisation. In *tax accounting* including the cost of an item in the depreciable basis of the property as opposed to including the item as a current expense.

Cash equivalency. The process that adjusts, the sales price of a comparable with a typical financing to reflect a sales price with typical market financing. This is necessary because any premium that results from a typical financing is not part of the value of the real property; the financing premium is intangible personal property.

Cash flow. The periodic income or loss arising from operations of the property; it is the income remaining after expenses and debt service are subtracted. This after-tax cash flow also subtracts income taxes.

Central business district (CBD). A city's down-town area, which contains the business and governmental activities of the area.

Central tendency. The tendency of values in a set of numbers to cluster around a certain point in a frequency distribution; measures of central tendency are the mean, median and mode.

Certificate of reasonable value (CRV). A certificate issued by the Veterans Administration that states an estimate of the value of the property being appraised; a CRV must be issued on any property in which VA financing is used.

Change. The appraisal principle that states that the cause and effect of economic and social forces are constantly causing property values to be in transition.

Chattels real. All interests in real estate that do not constitute a freehold or fee estate in land such as leasehold estates.

Chronological age. The true age of an item; also called actual age.

Classifical theory. A theory of value popular in the 1700s that based the value of an item on the cost of production. Scarcity, and utility were also believed to affect value.

Collection loss. A loss of income incurred when payment is not collected from tenants.

Commercial property. Properties used for business purposes.

Common elements. The part of the land and buildings in a condominium form of ownership that is jointly owned and used with other unit owners.

Comparables. Properties used to determine an estimate of value for a subject property. Such properties have been recently sold or leased and are similar to the property being evaluated. Comparables need not be identical to the subject but should be similar or relatively easy to adjust for differences in comparison. Also called comps.

Comparative unit method. A method used to estimate building costs in which components of the building are totaled on a unit basis, such as dollars per square foot or cubic foot of area, and are based on known costs of similar structures adjusted for time and physical differences.

Competition. An appraisal principle that states that competition is a function of supply and demand.

Compound growth. The process of increasing in value by a certain percentage each period.

Compound interest. Interest based on the original principal plus all accrued interest incurred before that time period. Each interest payment is added to the principal; the following period's interest is then multiplied by that sum to find the current interest incurred.

Concessions. A service or discount given to prospective tenants to induce them to lease specific properties.

Condemnation. The exercise of the power of eminent domain by the government (*i.e.*, the right of the Government to take private property for public use).

Condition of sale. An element of comparison in the sales comparison approach that refers to the motivations of the buyer and seller in a sales transaction. Examples include the relationship between buyer and seller, financial needs of buyer and seller (a "quick" sale) and lack of exposure on the market.

Condominium. A form of ownership in which persons hold fee simple title to individual units within the building and an undivided interest in common areas.

Condominium conversion. The process of converting rental property, such as an apartment building, into a condominium form of ownership.

Conformity. An appraisal principle that states that value is created when components of a property are in harmony with its surroundings.

Consequential damages. The financial compensation made to a person who has suffered loss or injury as a result of a breach of contract that could not reasonably have been prevented.

Consistent use. An appraisal concept that states that land and improvements to that land must be valued on the same basis; improvements to the land must contribute to the land value to have any value themselves.

Constant amortization mortgage. A mortgage that requires equal periodic principal payments. Because the interest decreases as the loan is amortized, total payments decrease over the loan term.

Construction cost. The expenses incurred to build a structure including direct costs of labour and materials plus the contractor's indirect costs (such as taxes and interest).

Constructive notice. The legal presumption that a person is responsible for knowing certain facts that may be discovered by diligence or inquiry into the public records.

Consumer Price Index (CPI). A statistical measure of the change in price levels of a predetermined mix of consumer goods and services; often used as a means of adjusting rental payments in a lease.

Contract rent. The actual rent specified in a lease.

Contractor's overhead. Direct costs other than costs of material and labour (*e.g.*, job supervisor costs, contractor's insurance, and worker's compensation).

Contribution. The appraisal principle that states that the worth of a particular component is measured by the amount it contributes to the value of the whole property, regardless of the actual cost of the component the value of the component may be measured as the amount by which its absence would detract from the entire property value.

Conversion. The transformation of an income-producing property into another use.

Convertible mortgage. A mortgage in which the lender may be convert mortgage interests into equity interests at some time during the life of the loan in lieu of or by decreasing cash amortization payments.

Cooperative ownership. A form of ownership in which each resident of a cooperative apartment building or housing corporation has purchased shares in a corporation that holds title to the building. The individual pays a proportionate share of operating expenses and debt service on the building owned by the corporation based on the amount of stock held in the corporation. In return for stock in the corporation, the individual receives a lease granting occupancy of a specific unit in the building.

Corner influence. The effect on value when a property line abuts the intersection of two streets; the value may be greater or less than inside lots depending on the utility associated with being located on a corner.

Corporation. In legal terms, an organisation that acts as a single legal entity in performing certain activities; corporate status is held separately from the individual involved.

Cost approach. One of three traditional approaches to value in appraisal theory. In the cost approach, value is based on the estimated land value plus the current cost to reproduce or replace the existing structure, deducting for all accrued depreciation in the property.

Cost service index. A regional table of factors used to convert historical costs into current costs.

Cost-of-living index. A summary of general consumer prices through time.

CPI adjustment. An adjustment used in lease in which the rent payment is periodically adjusted by a percentage of the increase in the Consumer Price Index (CPI); the CPI adjustment is used to help protect the lessor from unexpected increases in inflation.

Curable. Reasonable and economically feasible to cure refers to an item of physical deterioration and functional obsolescence in which the cost to cure the item is less than or the same as the anticipated increase in value after the item is cured.

Curable functional obsolescence. A defect caused by a flaw in the structure, material, or design in which the cost to cure the item is less than or the same as the anticipated increase in value after the item is cured.

Curable physical deterioration. An item in need of repair; deferred maintenance. To be curable, the cost of curing the item must be reasonable and economically feasible.

Current use. The use for which a property is presently designated; it may or may not be the highest and best use.

Date of value. The date of which the value of a property is estimated in an appraisal report, it is not necessarily the same as the date of the report.

Debt coverage ratio (DCR). The ratio of annual net operating income to annual debt service; often used as a criterion in underwriting income property loans.

Debt equity ratio. The relationship between the total amount of the loan and the invested capital (equity) of the owner(s).

Debt service. The dollar amount of the annual loan payment.

Dedication. A voluntary transfer of privately owned property for some public use.

Deed. A written, legal instrument by which an estate or ownership interest in real property is conveyed by a grantor to a grantee when it is executed and delivered. Many different types of deeds exist; the main difference being the covenant made by the grantor (*e.g.*, warranty deeds, grant deeds, executor's deed, quitclaim deed).

Deed of trust. A legal instrument, similar to a mortgage, that conveys title to property to a third party trustee; the deed of trust secures an obligation owed by the borrower to the lender.

Deed restriction. A clause in the deed of a property that limits the property's use.

Default ratio. A ratio that divides the effective gross income by the sum of the operating expenses plus the mortgage payment; a ratio of less than 1 means that the property is not generating enough income to service the mortgage payment.

Deferred annuity. A stream of cash flows that begins at some time in the future.

Deferred maintenance. Items in need of repair because the maintenance has been postponed resulting in physical depreciation or loss in value of a building; this type of depreciation is usually curable.

Demand. The quantity of real property desired at a certain price or rent at a specific time in a given market.

Demographic data. Data regarding the population and its changes; specifically regarding the population size, density, and distribution (among others).

Demolition costs. The expenses incurred to tear down and remove the improvements on a parcel of land; demolition costs may be considered in highest and best use analysis.

Density of land development. The number of building units or occupants per unit of land area (acre, square mile); allowable density is commonly specified in zoning ordinances.

Depreciable. Property subject to wear and tear and used in a trade or business or held for the production of income; land personal residences are not depreciable.

Depreciation. A loss in property value from any cause; the difference between reproduction cost or replacement cost and market value. In appraisal, depreciation is divided into three classes; physical deterioration, functional obsolescence, and external obsolescence. The term *depreciation* is also used to refer to tax depreciation, which is a deduction from NOI {see net operating income) when calculating taxable income. Tax depreciation is a function of the current tax law and not necessarily related to actual depreciation in the value of the asset.

Depth tables. Uniform percentage tables that indicate the proportion of site value attributable to each additional amount of depth in the lot; typically used in urban areas where lot depths are often similar.

Design and layout. The architectural arrangement of a property; if not up to current standards, design and layout may cause functional obsolescence.

Developer. One who organises and supervises the construction of improvements in an attempt to put land to its most profitable use.

Developer's profit. The sum of money a developer expects to receive in addition to costs for the time and effort, coordination, and risk-bearing necessary to develop a real estate. That portion associated with creation of the real estate by a developer is referred to as developers profit. *See* entrepreneurial profit.

Direct capitalisation. In the income approach, the method used to convert a *single* year's income into an estimate of property value. This can be accomplished by dividing the net operating income by a market-derived overall capitalisation rate or by multiplying the income by a market-derived income multiplier.

Direct costs. Costs for labour and materials, including contractor's overhead and profit. Also called hard costs.

Direct reduction mortgage. A mortgage in which both principal and interest are paid in periodic, usually equal, installments adequate for amortization over the loan's term.

Discount. (1) The fee paid at the origination of a debt for the use of capital during that period and commonly deducted from the principal when the funds are advanced. (2) Conversion of future payments to a present value with the use of a discount rate. *See* discounted cash flow analysis.

Discounted cash flow analysis. In general, the use of discounting in appraisal or investment analysis to calculate a present value, net present value, IRR, or other measures that consider the time value of money; A procedure in which anticipated future cash flows are discounted to a net present value by the appropriate yield rate based on the assumption that benefits received in the future are worth less than benefits received now due to the time value of money.

Discount points. A fee paid to a lender at the origination of a loan where one discount point equals 1 percent of the principal of the loan.

Discount rate. Used in the income approach; a compound-interest rate used to convert expected future cash flows into a present value. It should represent the rate of return necessary to attract investment capital.

Dispersion. The degree of scatter of values in a set of numbers; usually measured from a central value.

Dominant estate. The estate that derives benefit from the servient estate in an easement. For example, an easement road passes over an owner's land (servient estate) to another parcel of land (dominant estate).

Dwelling. A structure designed for occupancy as living quarters.

Dwelling units. A room or rooms, containing a single kitchen and constituting an independent unit for living space of a single family; dwelling units do not include hotel or motel rooms.

Easement. A legal interest in real property that conveys use or enjoyment but not ownership of the property.

Easement in gross. A limited right of one person to use another's property when the right is not created for the benefit of land owned by the owner of the easement, such right is not attached to any particular estate or land, nor is it transferred through the conveyance of title. Examples would include pipelines and telephone lines.

Economic age-life method. A method of estimating accrued depreciation in which the ratio of effective age to total economic life is multiplied by the reproduction or replacement cost to calculate the accrued depreciation.

Economic base analysis. An analysis of the economic activity of a community that enables it to attract income frm outside its boundaries. The relationship between basic and non-basic employment is used to predict population, income or other variables that affect real estate values or land utilisation.

Economic depreciation. Loss of value from all causes outside the boundaries of the property itself.

Economic force. In appraisal theory, one type of force that affects property value; it includes factors such as supply and demand, employment, wage levels, industrial exapansion, and availability of mortgage credit.

Economic life. The time span during which improvements to real property contribute to value (*i.e.*, the time in which income is expected to exceed operating expenses).

Economic rent. In appraisal practice this is considered synonymous with market rent.

Effective age. The age of a property based on its condition and utility or wear and tear; it may be more or less than the actual age.

Effective annual rate. The annual interest rate that is equivalent to a nominal annual rate that is compounded more frequently than annually. For example, if the nominal rate is 12 percent compounded monthly, the effective annual rate is $[1 + (.12 + 12)]^{12} - 1 = 12.68$ percent.

Effective gross income (EGI). The income from all operations of real property less an adjustment : vacancy and collection looses.

Effective gross income multiplier (EGIM). The ratio of sales price or value no effective gross income.

Efficiency ratio. The ratio between a building's net leasable area and gross area.

Egress. The means by which a person leaves or exits a property; the opposite of in-gress.

Elements of comparison. A categorisation of property characteristics that cause real estate prices to vary. Examples include; property rights, financing terms, conditions of sale, date of sale (or market conditions), location, and physical characteristics.

Emblements. A growing crop that is produced annually and is considered personal property.

Eminent domain. The Government right to take private property for public use upon the payment of just compensation to the property owner.

Encroachment. A part of real estate that physically intrudes on, overlaps, or trespasses on the property of another.

Encumbered. The legal term applied to a property that has attached to it a claim, lien, charge, or liability.

Encumbrance. An interest or claim against the land of another that burdens or takes away from the value of the property. Mortgages, taxes, and easements are considered encumbrances.

Entrepreneurial profit. The sum of money an Entrepreneur expects to receive in addition to costs for the time and effort, coordination, and risk-bearing necessary to create a project. That portion associated with creation of the real estate by a developer is referred to as developer's profit. Properties that also include an operating business may include additional entrepreneurial profit that is reflected in the going-concern value of the property. (*See* going-concern value),

Environmental forces. In appraisal theory, one of four categories of forces that affect property value; Environmental forces include climate, location, topography, natural barriers, and transportation systems.

Environmental regulations. The Environmental Protection Agency, created by the federal Government, sets standards to control air, water, and noise pollution and other environmental conditions.

Equity. The owner's interest in property above all claims and liens against it. The term is often used to refer to the amount an investor initially invests in a project (*e.g.*, the difference between the acquisition cost and the net proceeds from debt financing).

Equity buildup. Refers to the increase in the owner's equity over time due to any repayment of principal on the loan and any increase in the value of the property. The owner receives the benefit of this equity buildup when the property is sold.

Equity dividend. The result of subtracting debt service (principal and interest) from NOI (*See* net operating income). This will equal before-tax cash flow if there are no other cash outflows. (*See* before-tax cash flow).

Equity dividend rate (R_E). The ratio of before-tax cash flow to the equity investment. Also called equity capitalisation rate and cash on cash return.

Equity kicker. An equity interest in a property given to the mortgage lender.

Equity residual. A technique used to find property value in the income approach when the value of the mortgage and net operating income are known. The annual debt service is substracted from the net operating income to find the income attributable to equity. This figure is then capitalised and added to the value of the mortgage to find the property value.

Equity yield rate (Y_E). A rate of return on equity capital; the equity investor's internal rate of return based on before-tax cash flows and the equity investment.

Escalation clause. A clause appearing in a contract in which the price or rent is based on some event or index. It is used to help offset increases in operating expenses.

Escheat. The government right to transfer property ownership to the state when the owner dies without a will or any ascertainable heirs.

Evaluation. An analysis of a parcel of real estate in which a value estimate is not necessarily required. The study may be based on the nature, quality or utility of an interest in the parcel or the entire parcel.

Excess land. On an unimproved site, land that is not needed to accommodate a site's highest and best use. On an improved site, the surplus land that is not needed to serve or support the existing improvement.

Excess rent. The amount of contract rent over market rent; probably created by a favourable lease with a locational advantage, unusual management, or lease origination in a stronger market.

Exculpatory clause. A clause that limits the recourse of one party against another in the event of default by limiting recovery to the property only.

Expense ratio. The ratio of annual operating expenses to potential gross income or effective gross income.

Expense stop. In a lease, a dollar amount (usually expressed on a per-square-foot basis) above which the tenant agrees to pay operating expenses; helps protect the lessor from unexpected increases in expenses from inflation or other factors. The amount paid by the tenant is said to "pass through" to the tenant. (*See* passthrough).

Exponential change. An increase by a certain percentage each period as opposed to a straight-line change, which increases by a constant dollar amount each period. Synonymous with compound change or constant ratio change.

External obsolescence. A defect caused by negative influences outside the property itself; it is not considered curable. Also called economic obsolescence.

Externality. The appraisal principle that states that forces outside a property's boundaries may have a positive or negative effect on its value.

Extrapolation. The process of forecasting future trends based on current and past data patterns and relationships. Assumes that the same economic factors that affected past trends are likely to continue over the forecasting period.

Face amount. The value of a security as set fourth in the document itself; the par value as shown on the document as opposed to the real value or market value, which may differ if interest rates have changed.

Feasibility analysis. An analysis of the ability of a project to satisfy the economic objectives of the investor.

Fee appraiser. A person who charges a fee for rendering an opinion of value rather than basing compensation on the derived value.

Fee simple estate. Ownership of a property that is unencumbered by any other interest or estate.

Fee simple value. The value of the fee simple estate.

Final estimate of value. A range of value or a single dollar amount given in an appraisal report that is derived by reconciling various approaches to value.

Financial leverage. The use of debt to purchase real estate; the effect on an investor's return may be positive or negative.

Financial management rate of return (FMRR). A variant of the internal rate of return in which negative cash flows are discounted to a present value at a safe rate (liquid rate) and positive cash flows are compounded forward to the end of the holding period at a reinvestment rate (run-of-the-mill rate). The FMRR is the rate that equates the present value to the future value of the positive cash flows.

Financial risk. Uncertainty caused by financing an investment.

Financial statements. A formal composite statement that reflects the financial status and net worth of an individual or entity as of a specified date; usually classifies assets, liabilities, income, and expenses.

Financially feasible. A project that satisfies the economic objectives of the investor.

Financing costs. The expense incurred to acquire capital to finance a project in mortgages, often charged up front in the form of points.

First mortgage. A mortgage that has priority as a lien over all other mortgages. In cases of foreclosure, the first mortgage will be repaid plus legal expenses before other mortgages are satisfied.

Fixed expenses. Operating expenses that do not vary with the occupancy level.

Fixed-rate mortgage. A loan in which the interest rate is constant over the term of the loan.

Fixture. Personal property that becomes real property because of the manner in which it is affixed, the character of the item, and the intention of the tenant who attached the item.

Flat rental. A rent specified in a lease that remains constant throughout the lease term.

Foreclosure. A legal process in which a default in payment or other terms of the mortgage note causes the property used as security for the mortgage to be sold to satisfy the debt; the title in the mortgage is passed to either the holder of the mortgage or to a third party.

Form report. A specific format for presenting an appraisal report; typically required by financial institutions, insurance companies, and government agencies.

Free and clear. Real property that is free of any liens, mortgages, or other encumbrances.

Front foot. A measurement of land that abuts the street line or other landmark, such as a river or lake; typically used for lots of near uniform depth in urban areas.

Frontage. The linear distance of land that abuts a lake, river, street, or highway.

Fully amortised loan. A loan with equal, periodic payments that allow for both principal and interest to be recovered over the term of the loan.

Functional obsolescence. (*See* curable functional obsolescence *and* incurable functional obsolescence).

Future benefits. In appraisal, anticipated positive cash flows or appreciation in property value; a premise of the income approach.

Gentrification. A process in which neighbourhood properties are purchased and renovated or rehabilitated.

Going-concern value. Value created by a business operation; includes an intangible value that is not considered as a part of the real estate.

Government forces. In appraisal theory, one of four forces thought to affect real estate value; includes government controls and regulations, public services, zoning, and building codes (among others).

Graduated-payment mortgage (GPM). A loan in which payments start low and increase over the term of the loan. It is designed to help borrowers match payments with projected increases in income.

Graduated rental. Rent that graduates (usually increases) periodically during a lease term based on changes specified in the lease.

Grantee. One to whom property is transferred by deed, trust instrument, or other document.

Grantor. One who transfers property to another by deed, trust instrument, or other document.

Graphic analysis. A method used in sensitivity analysis in which one variable is changed and the effect of this change on a second variable is plotted on a graphy. By visually analysing the graph the appraiser may be able to better determine if assumptions used in the appraisal are realistic.

Gross income. Total income from the operation of a property before operating expenses are deducted; effective gross income also subtracts an allowance for vacancy and collection loss whereas potential gross income does not. "Other income" from sources such as vending machines is also included in gross income.

Gross income multiplier (GIM). The ratio of sales price or value to annual potential or effective gross income. Also called gross rent multiplier.

Gross leasable area (GLA). The total floor area designed for the occupancy of tenants; it does not include common areas.

Gross lease. A lease which specifies that all or most property charges must be paid by the lessor (or landlord).

Gross living area. Residential space measured by finished and habitable above-grade areas.

Ground lease. A lease that grants the right to use and occupy the land only.

Ground rent. Rent paid for the right to use and occupy land.

Highest and best use. The use that maximizes return to the land. Highest and best use must meet four criteria; it must be physically possible, financially feasible, legally permissible, and maximally productive.

Holding period. The time span over which a property is owned.

Improved site. A parcel of land that has been modified or developed for use in constructing improvements.

Improvement. A structure or building permanently attached to the land.

Improvement ratio. A ratio that compares the value of the improvements to the total value of property.

Income approach. One of the three approaches to value in appraisal theory; property value is estimated based on the property's anticipated future benefits. Also called the income capitalisation approach.

Income capitalisation. A method used in the income approach to convert income to a value estimate by either dividing a single income figure by the appropriate capitalisation rate or by discounting the reversion and annual cash flows for the holding period at the appropriate yield rate.

Increasing and decreasing returns, principle of. An economic principle that states that the addition of more factors of production will increase the output up to a certain point, which is the point of the asset's maximum value.

Incurable functional obsolescence. A defect that is caused by a deficiency or super-adequacy in the structure, materials, or design and layout of a structure; the defect is deemed incurable if the cost to cure the defect is greater than the anticipated increase in value after the defect is cured.

Incurable physical deterioration. A defect caused by physical wear and tear on the building that is considered unreasonable or uneconomic to correct.

Index lease. A lease that specifies rent adjustments based on the change in a specific index (*e.g.*, the CPI index).

Indirect costs. Construction expenses for items other than labour and materials (*e.g.*, financing, taxes, administrative costs, etc.). Also called soft costs.

Industrial property. Land and buildings used for manufacturing, processing, assembly, and storage of products or natural resources.

Inflation index. A time series trend that tracks the erosion of the purchasing power of currency.

Infrastructure. The core of development in a building or complex that serves as the source of utilities, and support services.

Ingress. Access or entrance into land; opposite of egress.

Inside lot. A lot located between the corner lots or a specific block.

Insurable value. The value of a property for insurance purposes.

Interest. (1) The cost of using money; a return on capital; (2) A type of extent of ownership.

Interest expense. The periodic cost incurred through a debt.

Interest-only loan. A loan in which only interest is paid during the term of the loan and principal is recovered in a balloon payment at the loan maturity.

Interest rate. A rate of return on capital; the cost of using money. Also known as a term loan.

Interest rate risk. The uncertainty caused by a variation in interest rates.

Interim use. A highest and best use expected to change in the future although the future use is not currently financially or physically possible.

Internal rate of return (IRR). The annualised rate of return on capital that equates the value of cash returns over time with the cash invested; the discount rate that makes the net present value of an investment equal to zero.

Interpolation. The estimation of a value within a range of data in a set of numbers.

Investment analysis. An analysis of a proposed real estate investment for the purpose of determining the feasibility of the project for a particular investor. The focus is often on the relationship between acquisition price and anticipated future benefits.

Investment value. The value of a property to a particular investor.

Joint tenancy. Joint ownership by two or more persons with right of survivorship in which each person has an identical interest and right of possession.

Junior mortgage. A loan with less priority than the first mortgage as a lien in case of foreclosure. It may be first, second, or third, etc. loan.

Just compensation. Fair and reasonable compensation to both the private owner of property and the public when property is taken for public use through condemnation.

Land. The earth's surface and natural resources in their original state.

Land building ratio. The ratio between the total land space and the gross building area.

Land capitalisation rate (R_L). The ratio of the land income to land value; it is used in the income approach in residual techniques to convert income into estimated value.

Land ratio (L). The ratio of land value to total property value.

Land residual technique. A technique used to find property value in the income approach when the value of the building and net operating income are known. The income attributable to the building is subtracted from the net operating income to find the income attributable to the land. This figure is then capitalised and added to the building value to find the total property value.

Land use. The utilisation of a site to produce revenue or other benefits.

Land utilisation studies. An analysis of the potential uses of a parcel of land and a determination of the highest and best use for that parcel.

Landlocked. A parcel of land that belongs to one person and is completely surrounded by land belonging to another.

Landlord. One who leases a property to another. Also called lessor.

Lease. A contract that transfers the rights of possession of a property from the owner to another for a specific period of time in return for a specified rent.

Leased fee estate. An ownership interest held by a landlord in which the right to use and occupy a property has been conveyed by lease to another.

Leasehold estate. An ownership interest held by a tenant in which the right to use and occupy a property has been conveyed to the tenant by lease.

Leasehold value. The value of a lease present when the market rental value is greater than the contract rent.

Legal description. A description of a parcel of land complete enough to allow a competent surveyor to locate the exact boundaries of the land.

Legally non-conforming use. A use that was once legal but no longer conforms to the zoning in which it is located; this usually occurs due to zoning changes.

Legally persmissible. That which is allowable by law. To be the highest and best use of a site, the use must be legally permissible.

Lessee. One who uses and occupies a property under a lease agreement; a tenant.

Lessor. One who holds property title and rents the property to another under a lease agreement; a landlord.

Letter report. A shortened appraisal report that states the conclusions of the appraisers investigation and analysis. It typically contains an identification of the property, purpose of the appraisal, a description of the analysis, the date of valuation, and limiting conditions. Much of the data and reasoning are omitted.

Leverage. The process of increasing purchasing power by using borrowed funds (debt) to acquire real estate. The debt may increase or decrease the rate of return on the investment.

License. A formal agreement from a constituted authority that allows an activity to be conducted. A lein is the right to retain lawful possession of the property or another until the owner fulfills a legal duty to the person holding the property. A mortgage is an example of common lein. It is thus defines a right of detaining. The property of another until some claim is satisfied.

Lien. A charge created by agreement or law against a property as the security for a debt.

Life estate. An estate limited to the lifetime of a designated party and conveys the rights to use, occupy, and control the property.

Limited common elements. Items in a multiunit project that are available for use by one or more but not all units (*e.g.*, parking stalls or storage units).

Limiting conditions. Specifications in an appraisal report that restrict the assumptions in the report to certain situations (*e.g.*, date and use of the appraisal, definition of value, definition of surveys used or not used).

Linear regression. The analysis of one or more independent variables and their effect on a single dependent variable.

Linkage. The time-distance relationship between a property or neighbourhood and other destinations or originations.

Liquidity. The ease of selling an asset for cash.

Listing price. The asking price at which a property is listed for sale, it does not necessarily equal the market value.

Loan balance. The amount of principal left to be paid on a loan at a specified period of time; it equals the present value of future payments.

Loan constant. (*See* mortgage loan constant.)

Loan term. The number of periods over which a loan will be held.

Loan-to-value ratio (M). The ratio of the loan principal to the total value of the property.

Location. The time-distance relationship (linkage) between a property or neighbourhood and all other origins and destinations.

Lot. Land within a set of defined boundaries. Also called a parcel, plot or tract.

Maintenance. Procedures and expenditures necessary to keep a property in operating condition.

Maintenance fee. The payments made by the individual owners in a condominium to the home-owner's association for expenses incurred in the maintenance and upkeep of the common areas.

Management fee. A fee paid for the administration and supervision of a property.

Manufactured housing. Residential buildings that are partially assembled or completely assembled before being placed on a permanent site.

Market analysis. An analysis of trends in market conditions (such as location, competition, and demand unit) that affect a property and value.

Market approach. One of the three approaches to value in appraisal theory; value is estimated by comparing sales of similar properties sold recently to the subject property and adjusting the comparable sales for differences in characteristics to indicate a final value estimate for the subject property.

Market conditions. Characteristics of the market such as vacancy rates, interest rates, employment levels, etc.

Market rent. The rent income a property would most probably command if offered in the competitive market.

Market segmentation. An analysis of submarkets within a larger market.

Market value. The cash value of a property to a well informed, typical buyers in an open market. The most probable price a property should bring in a competitive and open market under all conditions requisite to a fair sale, with the buyer and seller each acting prudently and knowledgeably and assuming the price is not affected by undue stimulus.

Marketability study. An analysis of the ability of a property to be absorbed, sold, or leased under current or anticipated market conditions.

Mass appraisal. An estimate of value for a large number of properties as of given date; similar properties are valued in a uniform manner by property types with standard methodology.

Maximally productive. One of four criteria in highest and best use analysis, it states that a use is the highest and best use if it produces the highest value or price.

Mercantilism. A theory of value popular in the eighteenth and nineteenth centuries that stated that wealth is associated with a nation's power. It focused on maintaining a favourable balance of trade through strong economic controls to accumulate gold.

Metes-and-bounds method. A legal description of land in which land boundaries are referred to by a point of beginning (POB) a line in a specified direction from this point (metes), and a point of change in direction in the boundary (boundary) until the line has returned to the point of beginning.

Minimum lot size. A provision in a zoning ordinance that stipulates the minimum dimensions of a lot necessary for construction of a building.

Mode. The most frequent value in a set of numbers.

Modified economic age-life method. A method of estimating accrued depreciation in which the ratio of effective age to total economic life is multiplied by the reproduction or replacement cost minus curable physical and functional obsolescence to calculate the accrued depreciation.

Monument. A natural or artificial visible object that is fixed in place and used by surveyors to establish real estate boundaries.

Mortgage. A legal document in which real estate is named as the security or collateral for the repayment of the loan.

Mortgage equity analysis. An analysis of income-producing property that studies the effect of mortgage terms and equity requirements on the property value.

Mortgage interest. The cost of borrowing money through a mortgage; the rate can be fixed or variable.

Mortgage loan constant (R_M). The ratio of annual debt service to principal of the loan.

Mortgage payment (PMT). The outlay made to decrease the principal and/or interest on a mortgage.

Mortgage. One who advances funds for a mortgage loan; the lender.

Mortgagor. One who gives a mortgage as security for a loan; the borrower.

Most probable selling price. The most likely price at which a property should sell if exposed in a competitive market for a reasonable period of time, under the market conditions at the date of the appraisal (*See* market value).

Multifamily. A structure that is architecturally intended for habitation by more than one family.

Multiple regression analysis. A statistical analysis that measures the influence of two or more independent variables on one dependent variable. Often used in mass appraisal of single family residences.

Narrative report. The most common and complete type of appraisal report; it includes an introduction, assumptions of the appraisal, presentation and analysis of data and addenda.

Negative amortisation. The results of a loan payment that is less than the interest charged per period; in effect, the loan balance increases each period by the amount of interest unpaid. This generally occurs in mortgages with initially low payments that increase at some point in time.

Negative cash flow. An expenditure or payment given to another party; occurs when operating expenses are greater than operating income.

Negative externalities. Forces from outside the property's boundaries that cause the property value of decrease.

Negative leverage. The result of borrowing at a cost of capital that exceeds the return on capital causing the return on equity to decrease.

Neighbourhood. An area characterised by complementary land uses.

Neighbourhood boundaries. Borders that surround the area that influences the value of a subject property; may coincide with changes in prevailing land use, occupant characteristics, or physical characteristics.

Neighbourhood life cycle. The changes that occur in a neighbourhood over time; the cycle is defined by four stages; growth, stability, decline, and revitalisation.

Neoclassical theory. A theory of value popular in the late nineteenth and early twentieth centuries that stressed supply and demand as factors for determining value.

Net income multiplier (NIM). The ratio of the property value or sales price to its net operating income for a given year. It is the reciprocal of the overall capitalisation rate.

Net income ratio (NIR). The ratio of net operating income to effective gross income.

Net lease. A lease in which the tenant pays expenses such as property taxes, insurance and maintenance. Sometimes referred to as a net lease.

Net leasable area. Floor space that can be rented to tenants; the space available for rent; generally excludes common areas.

Net operating income (NOI). The income remaining after deducting all operating expenses and vacancy and collection loss from total potential income.

Net present value (NPV). The discounted value of all future cash flows minus the initial cash outlay. A discount rate must be specified to calculate a NPV.

Net proceeds. Cash received after all liens and expenses have been paid.

Net net net lease. A lease to which the tenant pays taxes, insurance and maintenance. (*See* net lease).

Nominal interest rate (I). A stated annual rate of interest.

Non-basic industry. A service or support industry in an area; the opposite of a basic industry, which generates income from outside the area.

Note. A legal document that acknowledges a promise to pay a specified debt.

Obsolescence. A loss in value resulting from defects in design or forces outside the boundaries of a property; may be either functional or external.

Occupancy. The level of units leased.

Office building. A building used primarily by companies to conduct business.

Offsite improvements. Physical improvements that affect the use and the value of a parcel of land but are not directly located on the land; examples for residential real estate would include streets, curbs, and open space.

Onsite improvements. Physical improvements that are constructed within the boundaries of a parcel of land (*e.g.*, buildings, structures, and other support facilities installed within the boundaries of the property).

Open-end mortgage. A loan that allows the mortgagor to borrow additional sums based on specified conditions, such as minimum asset to debt ratios.

Open space. Land that has not been improved with buildings; such land is often left by a developer in a subdivision for recreational use and enjoyment by all the property owners.

Operating expense ratio (OER). The atio of total operating expenses to effective gross income.

Operating expenses. Expenditures necessary to maintain the real property and continue the production of income.

Opportunity cost. The cost of options for gone or opportunities not chosen.

Option. A legal contract that allows one to buy, sell, or lease real property within a specified time limit under specified terms.

Oral report. A complete unwritten appraisal report; it must be based on the same facts and conclusions as a written report.

Ordinary annuity. A level annuity for which all payments are received at the end of the period.

Ordinary income. Income that is subject to income taxes at the owner's income tax rate.

Original cost. The actual cost of a property to its present owner.

Overage. (*See* overage rent.)

Overage rent. A rent paid in addition to a fixed base rent; it is usually based on a variable figure such as a percent of sales or an index.

Overall capitalisation rate (R_O). The ratio of net operating income from a single year or average of several years to sales price or property value.

Overall yield rate (Y_O). The yeild rate based on the NOI and resale proceeds (reversion). The discount rate that equates the present value of the NOI and resale proceeds with the purchase price. Sometimes referred to as a free-and-clear yield because it does not consider financing.

Parking ratio. The number of available parking spaces divided by a unit of rentable area, usually per 1,000 square feet of rentable area.

Partial release. A mortgage clause in a blanket mortgage in which the lender agrees to release certain parcels from the mortgage lien upon payment by the mortgagor; frequently found in tract development construction loans.

Participation mortgage. A loan in which the lender shares part of the income or resale proceeds from a property in return for a reduction in periodic loan repayments.

Partnership. A business arrangement in which two or more persons co-own a business.

Partnership interest. An ownership interest in a partnership.

Passthrough. The tax advantage of a partnership or real estate investment trust that permits cash flows and deductions, especially depreciation, to "pass through" the legal structure of the partnership directly to the individual investors. The transfer of specified operating expenses to the tenant to be paid based on the terms of the lease. For example, the lease may specify that property taxes are passed through to the tenant to be paid.

Payback period. The time required for cumulative income from an investment to equal the amount initially invested. Usually calculated to the next whole year.

Percentage lease. A lease that specifies a rent based on some percent of sales from the property, usually in addition to a base rent; frequently used in retail properties.

Percentage rent. Rent based on a percent of sales from the property. (*See* percentage lease.)

Personal property. Items not permanently affixed to real estate and not considered real property. Personal property can be tangible (such as furniture and fixtures) or intangible (such as a premium paid for below-market financing or going concern value).

Physical age-life method. A method of estimating incurable physical deterioration in which the deterioration is calculated by multiplying the ratio of effective age divided by the total physical life of the item by the reproduction or replacement cost of the item minus any curable physical deterioration already charged. (*See* incurable physical deterioration).

Physical characteristics. The tangible aspects of real estate.

Planned unit development (PUD). A zoning classification for a subdivision that sets a density limit and allows the dwelling units to be clustered to provide for common open space.

Plat. A map showing and identifying the location of land that has been subdivided into individual lots.

Plottage. An increment of value that results when extra utility is created by combining two or more sites under a single ownership.

Police power. The government right to regulate property to protect public safety, health, morals, and general welfare.

Positive leverage. The result of borrowing of a cost of capital less than the return on capital causing the return on equity to increase.

Potential gross income (PGI). The total operating income produced by a real property assuming no vacancies or collection losses.

Potential gross income multiplier (PGIM). The ratio of sales price or value to the potential gross income.

Presales. A sale by a developer that occurs before construction.

Present value (PV). The current worth of a payment or payments based on the time value of money future payments are discounted to an equivalent current value by a discount rate based on the premise that cash flows received sooner are more valuable than cash flows received later.

Present value of annuity (a_n). The current worth of a level stream of future cash flows discounted to the present time period at a specified discount rate; column 5 of the compound interest tables in Appendix B. Also called present value interest factor annuity.

Present value of one factor ($1/s_n$). The current worth of a payment to be received in the future, the future payment is discounted to the current value through the present value of one factor which can be found in compound interest tables (*e.g.*, Column 4 in Appendix B). Also called reversion factor, present value interest factor.

Price. The amount of money paid or asked for in exhange for an item.

Primary data. Information gathered by the appraiser that is not available in a published source.

Principal (loan). The amount of capital borrowed or remaining to be paid on an investment. Also refers to that portion of a loan payment that reduces the balance of the loan.

Principle (appraisal). The interactive factors that affect property value includes concepts such as supply and demand substitution, conformity balance, and externalities.

Pro-forma statement. Financial statements that show future expected cash flows.

Profitability index (PI). The ratio of the present value of a cash flow to the initial cash outlay. A discount rate must be specified.

Profit. The right to remove something from the land of another.

Profits. The amount by which the proceeds of a transaction exceed the expenses.

Projected income. The amount of net cash flow forecasted for a future period; may be used in the income approach.

Property. Anything in which there is ownership; may refer to real property or personal property.

Property insurance. Protection by an owner/user against the risk of a certain loss or disastrous event.

Property management. The process of overseeing the financial, physical, and administrative aspects of property operations.

Property manager. One who oversees the operational activities of a property; including the leasing, marketing, maintenance, and the administration.

Property residual technique. A historical term for estimating the property value by discounting the expected future NOI and the expected proceeds from sale of the property. This term is a mis because there is no true "residual" component as in other residual techniques. This technique is just a form of discounted cash flow analysis.

Property rights. The privileges associated with the ownership of real estate; includes rights such as the right to sell, lease, occupy, or use. Such rights may be divided independently of the real estate itself.

Property tax. An ad valorem tax issued by the government based on the assessed value of property.

Property value. The worth of a property; a property may have several different values depending on the interest or use involved (*See* market value, investment value, insurable value, assessed value, leased fee value *and* going-concern value.)

Proprietary lease. In a multiunit building, the lease a corporation provides to the stockholders that allows them to use a specific unit under the conditions specified.

Range of value. In an appraisal report, the confidence interval in which the final estimate of a property's value may lie.

Raw land. Land that has not been improved.

Real estate. The physical land and structures affixed to it. Usually differentiated from real property, which refers to the ownership rights in real estate.

Real estate taxes. A levy issued to the property owner by the government based on the assessed value of the property.

Real property. The bundle of rights inherent in the ownership of real estate. District from personal property.

Reappraisal lease. A lease that contains a provision providing for the amount of the rent to be based on the appraised value of the property.

Reconciliation. In the appraisal process, the analysis of value indications from different appraisal approaches to arrive at a final value estimate.

Reconstructed operating statement. A document that states estimated future income and expenses of a property in the proper format for appraisal purposes.

Regional shopping center. An enclosed shopping area comprised of numerous stores including national and regional chains; such centers are located in areas with populations in excess of 250,000.

Remainder. A future possessory interest in real estate that becomes effective upon the termination of another estate in that property.

Remaining economic life. The estimated time period during which operating income will be greater than operating expenses; the period over which improvements will continue to contribute to property value.

Renewal options. A lease clause that allows the lessee to extend the lease under specified terms for a certain period of time.

Rentup. The process of finding tenants for a new building.

Repairs. Minor alterations required to keep a building in operating condition.

Replacement cost. The cost to construct a building with equivalent utility at current prices, materials, standards, design, and layout.

Reproduction cost. The cost to construct an exact duplicate of a building at current prices using the same materials, standards, design, layout and quality, and embodying all the subject's deficiencies, superadequacies, and obsolescence.

Resale. Sale of a property at the termination of the holding period.

Reserve for replacement. An accounting allowance to provide for the maintenance and replacement of short-lived items.

Residential area. A locality characterised by residential use.

Residential property. Units used for dwelling purposes, not of a transient nature.

Residential area. A locality characterised by residential use.

Residual. Value or income attributable to a component, such as financial, physical, or legal estate components, after deducting an amount necessary to meet a required return on the other component.

Residual income. Income attributable to a component after the known income from other components is deducted from the total income.

Residual techniques. Processes used in the income approach in which the unknown income from one component is derived by subtracting the known income from another component from the net operating income. The derived (residual) income is then capitalised to find the value of the corresponding component. Can be used for land-building or mortgage-equity components.

Retail. Use of a property characterised by the sale of merchandise (*e.g.*, shopping areas).

Return of capital. The recovery of invested funds over time, either through net operating income or resale.

Returns on capital. Income that provides a rate of return to the investor on capital that has been invested. Analogous to an interest rate or IRR.

Reverse annuity mortgage. A loan for homeowners who owe little or nothing on their homes; typically allows owners to borrow against the value of their home in periodic payments to the borrower so that a supplemental income is provided.

Reversion. A lessor's right to possess leased property at the termination of a lease. Also refers generally to sale of a property at the end of a holding period.

Reversionary value. (1) The worth of a lessor's right to possess leased property at the termination of the lease. (2) The value of a property at the end of a holding period.

Review appraiser. An appraiser who inspects the reports of other appraisers to determine the validity of the conclusions and data given in the report.

Rezoning. A change or amendment to a zoning map.

Risk. Uncertainty arising from the probability that events will not occur as expected.

Sale price. The amount of money paid or asked for in a specific transaction; the sale price may include non-realty items such as personal property or a financing premium.

Sales adjustment grid. A grid used in the sales comparison approach in which the elements of comparison are listed by line for the subject property and comparable properties; it allows an easy comparison of different properties for adjustment to find the value of the subject property.

Sales comparison approach. One of the three approaches to value in appraisal theory; value is estimated by comparing similar properties that have sold recently to the subject property.

Sandwich estate. An estate that arises from a sandwich lease.

Sandwich lease. A sublease that occurs when a lessee leases a property to another and becomes a lessor.

Second mortgage. A loan that is subordinate to the first mortgage; a type of junior mortgage.

Secondary data. Data that are obtained from published sources and have not been collected by the appraiser.

Secondary mortgage market. A market that exists for the sale and purchase of existing mortgages; it provides more liquidity for the mortgage market.

Senior mortgage. A loan given precedence over another loan. In case of foreclosure, the senior mortgage will be fulfilled first.

Sequence of adjustments. In the sales comparison approach, adjustments to comparable characteristics should be made in the following order to find the appropriate value of the subject property; property rights, financing terms, conditions of sale, market conditions, location, and physical characteristics.

Severance damage. In an eminent domain proceeding in which part of a real property interest is taken for public use; it is a loss in market value of the remainder that arises as a result of the taking. It is compensable to the owner.

Shared appreciation mortgage. Participation loan in which the lender receives part of the increase in property value at the time or resale.

Shopping center. A building that contains several retail stores, typically with one or more large department, discount or grocery stores and a common parking area.

Single-family unit. A structure intended and used for occupancy by one family.

Single purpose property. A property whose highest and best use is unique to that site; land value in this case is based on the highest and best use of the property, regardless of the most likely use.

Sinking fund ($1/S_n$). An account in which equal installments of funds are periodically deposited to accumulate enough money to replace an asset or reach a specified target sum; usually assumes compound interest.

Site. A plot of land improved for a specific purpose.

Social characteristics. (*See* social forces.)

Special assessment. A tax imposed only against those parcels of reality that will benefit from a proposed public improvement.

Special purpose property. A property appropriate for only one use or a very limited number of uses; its highest and best use will probably be continued at the current use, or the improvements will be demolished.

Sepculative use. Property held primarily for future sale, value is based on the future heighest and best use.

Standard deviation. The square root of the arithmetic mean of the squares of the deviations from the arithmetic mean of the frequency distribution; it measures the extent of variability in a frequency distribution. It is often used as a measure of risk.

Standing stock. The amount of real estate that has already been built, it is one indication of the supply of real estate.

Straight-line capitalisation. A method of developing an overall capitalisation rate; the capitalisation rate is calculated by adding an allowance for return of capital to the discount rate (return on capital). The allowance for return of capital assumes the capital is recaptured *evenly* over the holding period or economic life of the property. For example, if the economic life of the property is 50 years, the allowance for return of capital will be 1/50, or 2 percent. With a 10-percent discount rate the overall capitalisation rate is 12 percent. This method, which is not commonly used today, implicity assumes that the property's income is declining each year.

Strip center. A commercial use of real estate, such as a neighbourhood shopping center in which the buildings are adjoining and narrow in depth relative to their length.

Structure. Any constructed improvement including buildings, kiosks, garages, fencing, and enclosures.

Subdivision. A large plot of land divided into smaller lots for sale or lease.

Subdivision regulations. A local ordinance that establishes minimum standards to be met before a subdivision will be approved for development; regulations include width of streets, size of lots, and drainage requirements.

Subject building. The building being appraised.

Subject property. The property being appraised.

Sublease. An agreement in which the tenant (lessee) leases the property or part of the property to a third party, thus becoming a lessor.

Subleasehold. The property interest associated with a sublease.

Submarkets. A further division of a market based on the preferences of buyers and sellers.

Subordinate. That which takes less precedence than another.

Subordinated mortgage. A loan that takes less precedence (junior) to another loan.

Subordinate clause. A mortgage clause that gives priority to a subsequent mortgage.

Substitution. The appraisal principle that states a buyer will pay no more for a property than the cost of obtaining an equally desirable substitute.

Super adequacy. A type of functional obsolescence caused by a structural component that is too large or of a higher quality than what is needed for the highest and best use of the property; an item the cost of which exceeds its value; an over-improvement.

Supply. The quantity of a product available on the market at a particular time as a function of different prices.

Supply and demand. In appraisal, a principle that states that the value of a property depends on the quantity and price of the property type available in the market, and on the number of market participants and the price they are willing to pay.

Supply and demand study. An analysis of the availability and desire for a specific type of property.

Surplus productivity. The net income that remains after the costs of labour, capital, and coordination have been deducted from total income.

Tax depreciation. The loss in value of a building due to wear and tear, which is allowed to be subtracted from income and sale proceeds under tax law.

Tax shelter. The ability of a property of shield income from taxes, usually through accounting losses arising from interest deductions and depreciation.

Taxable income. On income-producing properties, net operating income minus depreciation and interest; should not be confused with after-tax income or before-tax cash flow.

Tenancy by the entireties. An equal indivisible estate held by a husband and wife in which neither has a disposable interest in the property during the lifetime of the other, except by joint action; the property passes to the survivor upon death of one spouse.

Tenancy in common. An indivisible estate held by two or more persons who may have equal or unequal interests; the property passes to the heirs and not the survivor(s) on the death of one.

Tenant. One who exclusively occupies or holds a property through a lease; a lessee.

Tenant improvements. In construction projects, the installation of finished tenant space by lessee or lessor; also may refer to fixed improvements installed and paid for by a lessee.

Terminal capitalisation rate. The capitalisation rate used to estimate the resale price for a property at the end of a holding period; it equals the estimated net operating income at the time of sale (or one year after the year of sale) divided by the sale price. The NOI for the year *following* the year of sale is often used when estimating value with a terminal capitalisation rate because this is the *first* year of NOI for the buyer.

Time-sharing. A sale of limited undivided ownership interests in a property in which each purchaser receives a deed conveying title to the unit for a specific period of time.

Topography. The features and contour of the land.

Trade area. A defined geographic area from which a business attracts the majority of its customers.

Trade fixtures. A type of personal property that is owned and attached to a rented space by the *tenant* and is used in conducting business; it is differentiated from a regular fixture, which is part of the real estate, by the manner in which it is affixed, the character of the item, and the intention of the tenant who attached the item. Whereas regular fixtures are real property, trade fixtures remain personal property.

Trend analysis. A study of changes in the environment of a property used particularly in the income approach to help forecast future changes in property income, sales price, and occupancy rates.

Trustee. One who holds property in trust for another and controls legal title to property under a trust agreement.

Trustor. One for whom property is held under a trust agreement.

Under improved land. Land that, due to the fact it is not being used under its highest and best use, does not generate the maximum amount of income that could be generated.

Unit-in-place method. A method of estimating building costs in which total building cost is estimated by summing prices for various building components as installed based on specific units of use such as square footage or cubic footage. Also called the segregated cost method.

Useful life. The period of time over which a property is expected to remain economically feasible to the investor.

Utilities. Operating sendees required by a developed area, usually provided by public companies (*e.g.*, electricity, telephone, water, and gas).

Vacancies. Space available for rent that is not occupied.

Vacancy allowance. In the income approach, a deduction from potential gross income for current or expected future space not rented due to tenant turnover or to lack demand.

Vacancy and collection loss. (*See* vacancy allowance *and* collection loss.)

Valuation. The process of estimating a defined value of an identified interest in a specific parcel of real estate as of a given date.

Value (V). The monetary worth of rights arising from property ownership.

Value in exchange. The value of a property in a typical market; market value.

Value in use. The value of a property based on a specific use. This may differ from market value when the use is specialised and there is a limited market for the property based on that use.

Variable expense. An operating expense that varies with the occupancy or use level of a property.

Variance. In *statistics*, the arithmetic mean of the squares of the deviations from the arithmetic mean of the frequency distribution; it measures the extent of variability in a frequency distribution. In zoning, official permission to depart from the requirements of a zoning ordinance.

Volume of new construction. The amount of property that has recently been built; it is one indication of the supply of real estate.

Wear and tear. Physical deterioration of property due to weathering, aging, and use.

Wraparound mortgage. A loan in which the lender takes over payments of a previous mortgage and in turn provides a mortgage in the amount of the previous mortgage plus an additional amount. It is subordinate to the previous loan.

Yield. The rate of return on an investment. Could be an overall yield for the property (Y_O), a yield for the equity investor (Y_E), or a yield for the lender (Y_M).

Yield capitalisation. A method used in the income approach to determine property value by discounting future cash flows at an appropriate discount rate (yield rate) that reflects the rate of return required by investors. The approach may or may not explicitly consider financing. (*See* discounted cash flow analysis).

Zoning. An application of police power; a legal mechanism for local governments to regulate land use and density of development for privately owned real property.

Zoning restrictions. (*See* zoning). Restrictions may be placed on issues such as height, density, use, or development of properties.

1.2. GENERAL

Individual universally exercise daily the art of valuation without realising that, each exchange of property, of what so ever nature and character, involves an appraisal which at least is an elementary valuation, each exchange of property involves an estimate of the relative worth of the item exchanged. In ordinary trade, value is estimated by the utmost instinctive decision that the price quoted is fair or unfair.

From the down of civilisation, land has been found to have a value for its capacity to provide the essentials of life like food, cloth and shelter. It has been recognised even at the time of difference in value of two plots by the trial and error when people found that the produce from one plot per acre more than that of other, the greater productivity of some lands made them scarce and part of fertile land used to be exchanged for a big chunk of follow land. In older days there was a barter system whereby one commodity was exchanged for other, the equivalent depending again upon the law of supply and demand. There was also a practice in our country where the service of an individual or of a family were valued against a price of land, the person or the family receiving land in exchange for the services to the land lord, or to the state. This process went on till the introduction of money as the medium of exchange comes into existence.

In the past, kings used to appoint experts to evaluate precious stones, diamond, gold etc. The value was determined by them on the basis of their experience without detailed and critical analysis of facts and circumstances. The present day regalement is however critical analysis of facts and circumstances under which, evaluation of value of any commodity is made.

Real Estate: Land is an immovable property and is therefore referred to as the real estate or real property or realty. The word estate is derived from Latin word, meaning status and in early times, it was meant to indicate the status of the person in the society. Subsequently the person who owned the land was referred to as the estate holder. Thus the real property is defined as a thing which can be owned or held. The thing may either by corporeal or incorporeal. The term real estate is defined in the Tenth Five Year Plan as Land including the air above it and ground below it and any building or structure on it. It is also referred to as Realty.

Types of Real Estate are :

Residential Real Estate

Commercial Real Estate and

Industrial Real Estate.

Asset : Asset means an item which is advantageous or well worth to have. An asset can be tangible or intangible. Land, building, plant and machineries, farms, Jewellery etc. are tangible assets. The intangible assets are a good will in business, rights to a branch name or monogram; technological know how etc.

Some times Lend-lease companies or banks etc. use a term Non Performing Asset (NPA). It is a term used by these companies, banks and other for the defaulter's asset which were originally pledged to lenders at the time of grant of loans.

1.3. VALUATION CONCEPT

Valuation in general is defined as the art of estimating the fair monetary measures of the desirability of ownership of specific property for specific purpose. For each property the value must be expressed in terms of some recognised medium of exchange, usually in the monetary units of country in which the property is located. For international exchange purposes, the unit of worth adapted is generally an internationally accepted money unit such as Dollar or Pound or many times in terms of Gold.

In most uses of the terms 'Value' as applied to property is a sense of worth, a desirability of ownership or possession or the exchangeability of property as it can be measured in terms of Dollar, Pounds or other monetary unit. The fundamental basis of the value of any specific property is the present worth to the present owner or to the would be purchaser or the probable future services expected from the property during its probable future productive life in service.

It is essential to be made clear that valuation is altogether different from costing, because value is an assessed worth of an asset in context of a specific purpose and at particular time period. This purpose determines the variety of factors that influence an asset's value and since number of these factors stem directly from a given state of economy prevailing at that time, the valuation becomes purpose oriented and time frame related exercise. Costing is qualitative; it is a exact science; where most of the parameters are well defined *viz.* material cost, transportation cost, labour cost, administration etc., and these parameters is well defined and cost calculation methods are well known and properly defined. Therefore there is a different in valuation and costing.

1.4. VALUE

There are a large number of definitions of value of any asset or property but none of them are convincing. Person change its meaning, they interpret it as per their requirements or to give maximum benefit to his client in case of engineering valuation. The various meanings of value are :

1. The transaction, which takes place between buyer and a seller and binds them legally or otherwise, decides what we call as the exchange value. However the word 'exchange' is not being used in practice.

2. Amount of money, which a willing purchaser is ready to part with for a certain commodity, offered by a willing seller and the transaction takes at that price emerges the concept of value. Sometimes, in certain cases, the cost of a commodity or a property may be the value of the property. However value of the commodity or the property may not be the cost of the property. Value of any thing means its worth or qualities as also the qualities inherent in the thing on which its utility or worth depends. It is said a price is a fact and the value is an estimate of what the price ought to be.

1.4.1. Value Dependent Factors

Property value differs according to the following factors :

1. Value depends on place, time, circumstances and purpose.

2. Economic solicitations such as depressions and booms.

3. Supply and demand.

Value of any asset differs based on its location *i.e.* values differs from place to place and in the same city from one locality to other locality. The property in the suburbs will be less valuable then the property in cities. Value also very with passage of time. The value of land in one year in a certain locality may not be the same as the value in another year. A property will have different yields satisfying willing purchasers in different years and thus will give different values. Hence it is essential to record the date as on which valuation is made. In an ever-changing economic situation the factor assumes a great importance. The purpose and circumstances under which the valuation is to make are also very important factors. For instance, it is the cost of replacing the property, which is damaged or destroyed. For advancing a loan, it is based on the risk involved. For investment, it is the amount on which an adequate return can be derived in future. In tax valuation it is the price, which a willing seller would receive from equally willing but not too anxious buyers, in an atmosphere of informality and competition.

The ability to pay for a commodity is dependent to an extent, on the amount of money in circulation. When money is freely available, prices remain high. When money is scarce, prices remain low. When trade is brisk, money circulates rapidly. This affects values. It also leads to demand for commodities. Effective demand is largely dependent on the purchasing power of the consumer; supply means the amount available for transfer to other people. The supply of certain commodities can be altered if required. The supply of land can not be increased; however its supply for construction can be increased by long term policies of land reclamation. Considerable land was reclaimed for Bombay city. The Novel Base in Willington Island, Cochin was also expanded by land reclamation. There can be reverse also; a land can also be diminished by disastrous floods or due to some other reason.

Demand and supply are important factor and play a vital role in valuation of property market. Demand and supply are in fact equated in any particular time by some level of price. Other things being equal at any given time, any increase in demand or decrease in supply will cause price to rise, conversely any decrease in demand or increase in supply will cause price to fall.

Therefore the concept of value is very easy to understood but difficult of define exactly which will serve the purpose for all requirements. An expert, therefore, before deciders the value of immovable property for a particular purpose, study the property not only from inspection of its physical condition, also studies its potentiality from the angle of existing laws and acts. Similarly an expert will have to study the various economic factors such as interest rates for quilt edged recruits, government securities, bank rates and the in country.

Once the concept of value is clear in the mind of valuer, then only he will be in a position to use his judgement for deciding the various values with due regard to all the factors mentioned above and can analyse the different cases required for valuation purpose.

Immovable property means any land or any building or a part of a building and includes where any land or any building or part of a building is to be transferred together with any machinery plant, furniture, fittings or other things also.

1.4.2. Considerations and its Meaning

When at the desire of the promisor, the promise or any other person has done a abstained from doing or does or obtains from doing, or promises to do or to abstain from doing something, such act of abstinence or promises is called a consideration for the promise. In other words if the agreement for 1.41 transfer provides for certain acts or things to be done by the transferee in addition to providing the price in monetary terms, the value of such acts or things will also form part of "apparent consideration".

1.4.3. Essential Qualification for Value

In order that a commodity can have value, it must possess three essential qualifications, namely :

1. It must possess utility.
2. It must by scarce.
3. It must be transferable or marketable, not to be confused with portable.

It is necessary that all these essential must go hand in hand and in absence of any of them, the commodity will have no value, as air possesses utility but not scarce and hence it has no economical value. Similarly rotten apples may be scarce but since they have no utility hence have no value. A property has got a value because it satisfies all the three essential requirements.

Value has to be found out assuming that there is an open market in which the property is being sold.

1.4.4. Various Definitions of Value

A straight forward judicial definition of the term value is "it is price at which property will sell in the perverting market without a forced sale between willing buyers and willing sellers, both having reasonable knowledge of the property and the market therefore" it is also called as Fair Value. Various other definitions are given below it varies with the purpose.

Market Value. Market value is the value established in a public market by exchanges between willing sellers and willing buyers. The market value fluctuates, with the degree of willingness of the buyer and the seller and with the conditions of the sale. In market value, the market forces play a predominant role. There are various alternative options available to buyer as well as to seller. In such a situation, if there are no overriding reasons to force any decision for a buyer or seller *i.e.* buying and selling both acts is not influenced by any uncommon market conditions *i.e.* hyper inflation or undue, uncommon depression; then the value at which an exchange takes place is termed as a Fair Market Value.

Replacement Value. Replacement value refers to that of a property determined on the basis of what it would cost usually at the current price level to replace the property or its service with at least equally satisfactory and comparable property and service.

Relative Value. Relative value becomes an issue in company amalgamations and absorptions. Actual market value may be quite un-important in such instances even though it forms the basis of the calculation. The vital question is how to arrive at the relative values of the respective enterprises so that a just settlement my be concluded.

Real Value or Value to the Owner. It envisages the intrinsic value to the owners as long term investment rather than the immediate realisation which is characteristic of market value. It is equivalent to the amount of loss, which the owner would suffer if he was deprived of his property. This concept is not inconsistent with the willing buyer and willing seller doctrine.

Economic Value. It is difficult to define economic value at the same time unpredictable. The two terms 'economic value' and 'Value' though seem to be alike at first sight are not so as they convey different sense in every respect. Satisfaction of an individual is given more emphasis in economical value. It would be best to define it in terms of relative satisfaction that individual and groups obtain from tangible and intangible goods and services. The measurement of economic value is also no less important for it enables one to determine the economic value of a thing being exchanged, "The scale of measurement of economic value is partly determined by the formal and informal market place in which exchanges take place, and partly by individual attitudes towards property and wealth".

Appraisal Value. The ultimate purpose behind the valuation of a property is to find out its acceptable fair value. A fair market value, when arrived at, puts to an end all the horse-trading and the consequent struggles. Fair value is the end product of appraisal value. Appraisal value is ordinarily expressed in terms of reproduction cost less accumulated depreciation.

Liquidated Value. It is an estimate of the sum, which the holder of the shares would be expected to receive in the event of the company being voluntarily wound up. It is a striking departure from the other values, each of which is based upon the concept of continuity of a going concern.

If we want to know the actual value of any property, which it can fetch, it will be approximately its liquidated value. When a company goes into liquidation, its character as a going concern ceases, having scattered into assets and liabilities to be disposed of ultimately individually or in lots. The realisation on the liquidation will be according to the worth of the assets of the going concern. However this may not be an exactly precise, all time true statement since due to some forced sale; mainly because of urgency. The value realised may not be, truly speaking a fair market value. Thus it is apparent that the liquidation value has a distinct relationship with the market value. If any difference is found between the two values, liquidation and market, it is largely due to peculiar circumstances under which the exchange takes place and suitable adjustment will have to be made.

Social Value. Social value is, and can become, a measurement in accordance with a scale agreed to by a group of individual.

Ethical Value. Depending upon the moral and religious rules and customs of society one lives in, ethical value is closely related to social value. The scale of ethical value measures our principles, attitudes and actions and all of us are aware of the relative position of our own principles and actions on the ethical value scale of society.

Aesthetic Value. Buildings designed by Architects fetch better price. For superior designed and constructed building, market value is often more than cost, by as much as 10 percent. Promoter's profit is relevant for valuation of flats but not for isolated buildings. Actual cost is not the same as value. The cost of reproduction on the date of completion is more than actual incurred. The difference is an account of increase in cost index.

Speculation Value. Some properties have future secret prospects, if one could visualize it. This is referred as speculative value.

Forced Sale Value. In case of bank loans, Bank insists that the applicant must give a collateral security on equitable mortgage to the desired valour. The loan limit sometimes depends upon the security. At a later date due to inevitable circumstances, if the applicant fails to repay the loan along with interest the banks has first right to sale the property, which was given to them as security on auction. Or otherwise the applicant is forced to sell the property due to the urgent and absolute necessity. This value is called as Forced sale value. Since the demand is less and also sentimental reasons are also attached, generally the forced sale value is less when compared to the market value.

Reversionary Value. It is the value of an asset to the owner after the expiry of lease period. As and after the expiry of lease period, the property is reverted back to the owner; the owner gets some advantages. This is called reversionary value.

Discounted Value. When owner and purchaser enter into the sale agreement some times consideration is given on the date of agreement and partly on subsequent dates. In such cases the payments to be made on subsequent dates are required to be discounted so as to reflect the considerations on the date of agreement. This is called discounted value. An interest of 8% is provided for it.

Book Value. It is value an asset as shown in accounts book. This is value on that particular day arrived by deducting total depreciation till date from its value on the date of its purchase.

Depreciated Value. This is equal to book value theoretically as for accounting is concerned. However it is used to arrive at efficient economic value.

Face Value. It is price paid to purchase it.

Insurance Value. It is the net replacement cost, keeping in mind depreciated condition of the asset.

Potential Value. It is the value of an asset could fetch if sold in open market at a later date due to its increased potentiality.

Assessed Value. Value of machinery realised on sale when its useful span of life is over, but has not become useless.

Scrap or Junk Value. Value of any asset particularly that of machine, realised when it becomes absolutely useless except for sale as Junk. It also applies to built up properties, have outlived, their useful life and in such cases the value of old materials of such building less cost of demolition, represents the scrap value or break up value. It is also known as demolition value.

Earning Value. It is the present value of a property, which will start yielding an income in future.

Potential Value. The land has got an internet value which may go on increasing due to passage of time or due to same alternative use fetching more return. This inherent value is known as potential value.

Distress Value. When a property is sold at a lower price than that which can be obtained for it in an open market, it is said to have distress value it may be due to :

(1) Financial difficulty to the owner

(2) Indirect benefit to purchaser

(3) Panic due to war, riots, floods etc.

Monopoly Value. Following the law of demand and supply as the number of available plots in a locality goes on decreasing, the value of land goes on increasing, and a time comes when very few plots remain in the market. The fancy price demanded by the owner for those few remaining plots is known as monopoly value. The owner has whole sole monopoly to sell them at a reasonable high cost.

Sentimental Value. The fancy is higher price, which an owner demands due to his attached sentiments with the property, is called sentimental value. It does not have any relationship with market value. There may not be any purchasers for that property with that higher price, but it is certainly higher to the owner. This value is called as sentimental value even some time purchaser purchases an asset at a higher rate mainly due to his sentiments attached to that property.

Going Concern Value. It means value of the business as a whole. The concept involves valuation of a continuing enterprise from which allocation or apportionment's of overall going concern value may be made to constituent parts, as they contribute to the whole, but none of the components of themselves constitute market value. A going concern is usually sold with land and building, plant and machinery, stock in trade and unionised and management employees of the undertaking with continuity of service and full protection of their existing terms and conditions of service, which includes gratuity pension, per requisites and other benefits.

Guide Line Value. The trade line value is fixed by the registrar's office for the purpose of fixing stamp duty and the value should not be used for assessing the present value or market value. In many cases, the guide line rate is more than the prevailing rate.

Forced Sale Value. It is the value of property when sold under pressure or under certain influence. This value is always different from market value. The factors affect sale values are:

(1) If the property is auctioned by the bank it must be borne in mind:

(*a*) If this property is purchased through the auction, the buyer has to pay the entire sum in white and he has to complete the transaction within a short period and

(*b*) For the entire value he has to pay stamp duty.

(2) Since the present owner owns the property for quite a long period, they may enjoy many bidders to quote the rate.

(3) Negative sentiments also pay a major role while purchasing by the third man.

(4) Experiences and past history reveals that the suit filed property will yield only a less price when compared to the real market.

Because of the above facts forced sale value is always about 75 to 85 percent of market value.

Time Related Value. Conditions in a given market or general economic conditions are normally subject to variety of changes. During a given period of time the changes go through a sort of pattern either up or down. These patterns for that period of time are termed as 'market trend'. But when changes are very large, they become unpredictable. Then the value of that asset is defined on a particular date. The valuer is required to determine the worth of a given asset at a given period of time : this is called as a 'Time Related Value'.

Purpose Oriented Value. An asset is basically a useful object. Its utility to the owner or user or purchaser depends to a great extent on the circumstances of its use, its potential of care, its durable life etc. The tax laying authorities determine the levy of various tax percentages based on purpose of the property likely to be used. The lending institutes see the properly from different visions and as per purpose the loan is decided. Purchasing a flat or a Car of ₹ 5 Lac has different meaning whereas both are assets. Hence value of any asset depends upon purpose for which it is going to be used. A flat or a shop of same value will have different income depending upon. Therefore when a value is assessed based on its purpose : it is called purpose oriented value.

1.5. MARKET VALUE

For each property the value is expressed in terms of some recognised medium of exchange usually in the momentary units. The market value of particular property may be defined as that amount of money, which at every given time can be obtained for the property from the person able and willing to purchase it. This may be more or less than actual value of property on the basis of theoretical calculations. For example if a old premise may fetch a net rent of ₹ 1000/- per annum hence taking into consideration a rate of interest of 5% the value of property comes to be 1000 × 100/5 = ₹ 20000/- only; whilst market value of that property may be more than this.

It means the "Market Value" of any land or building or both or any other asset is estimated as price, which in the opinion of the assessing authority such asset would fetch if sold in open market. The meaning of the market value of the property would mean that the amount, which could reasonably be expected for the property if the same is sold by a willing seller to a guanine purchaser and pre-supposes the knowledge, situation and circumstance of the property in question. If it is to assess for the purpose of taxation, market value of the property has to be considered as the basis for assessment and the fact that a specific property has a special value to a particular person should not be taken into consideration. Such market value is called as ordinary market value.

If a property is to be acquired by the government for any public purpose under the law of Eminent Domain, the nodule to assess market value should be based on highest and best value with all the potentials, because the owner has to be compensated for the 'Entire Loss' of his property and therefore the valuation should be on the basis of fair market value based on highest and best value including all potentials.

Social value, ethical value and economic value invariably make a tremendous impact on the market value. In all activities, small or big, important or un-important mans guiding factors or his sentiments, emotions and passions and this is no exception to his purchase or sale deals. In property valuation, factors like availability of place of worship cultural groups or centres, higher educational facilities do certainly count. In relatively economically and socially backward countries, caste and regions are also required to be taken into account to assess market value. It will not be wrong to say, that these factors rather dictate the market value of many premises. A genuine efficient and energetic valuer therefore is required to take these factors also in consideration while allocating a property in question.

Risk and uncertainly are also important factor that effect market value. Since expectations about future conditions form an integral part of value, one must test the reliability and consistency of these future expectations. The degree of specific risk and general understanding will depend upon the nature of goods or services with reference to the prevailing social, economical and political conditions.

Essential Characteristics of Market Value. The essential characteristics for any asset for market value are:

1. Vender must be willing to sell.

2. Purchaser must be willing to purchase and must be a prudent one who can put the land to the most beneficial use.

3. No compulsion on either in the transactions.

4. Urgent necessity to purchase or sale to be discarded.

5. Disinclination of vendor to be ignored.

6. Sentimental value to the vendor will have place.

7. Present and future uses known as potentials are to be taken into account.

1.6. VALUER

Valuation is the art or process of estimating or assessing value of some asset, depending on the circumstances of the case and purpose for which valuation is needed at a given time, place and under specified market conditions. An expert who does this job of assessment is known as valuer provided he has right to do it. Therefore a registered valuer is an authorised and expert witness in the eyes of laws. The function of valuer is therefore to assess the actual value of specified property on specified date, acceptable to each and every person in question. The function of valuer is therefore not simply for the benefit of the parties, but also and perhaps, primarily for the assistance of the court by defining with precision the area beyond which, without the leave of the court and consequential amendments of the pleasing, the conflict must not be allowed to extend. The valuer should therefore make certain that all available facts have been marshalled before making final valuation. The essential requirements for a guanine valuer are:

(1) He must have thorough knowledge of estimation of cost and materials required for any construction in case of immovable property.

(2) He must have knowledge of latest know how of construction materials and construction techniques.

(3) He must have knowledge of various laws and acts like easement law, land acquisition, and town planning act etc. He is supposed to be acquainted with central and local Government Taxation Policy.

(4) The valuer must be able to make on organised study of the best available information's on the subject of valuation.

(5) He must accept the responsibility as valuer and must adhere to the standard if excellence. He must not be biased and at the same time must have ethical sense. It means he must recognise his responsibilities for preparation of a document, which has got legal bearing and his duties to the public, Government or Tax authorities and courts.

(6) Valuation work demands a professional skill. A valuer therefore should be conscientious, highly trained, and energetic and should have a strong sense of integrity. Curiosity with a habit of putting nose for unearthing hidden values will make a valuer, a good valuer.

The valuer must bear in mind that the valuation is dependent on various factors such as land economics, demand and supply, use and utility and many such other factors of economics and not only the engineering or architecture. The property is a bundle or rights of land and building's the value of 'Right' in that property which gives the value. It is one, who possesses wealth, possesses certain rights, which makes him to enjoy the right of use and enjoy that property. It is the possession of this right that constitutes the property. These property rights are not material things but merely express the relation.

Almost all the valuations are required for legal purposes. Therefore the valuer is required to choose a method of valuation depending upon the purpose for which the property is being valued. Therefore the valuer's judgement is a very important part in valuation. The valuer has to occupy the position of the expert witness in the courts. He is not only committed to information on facts but also to express his opinion on the valuation. The valuer must know that his first duty is to assist the court in deciding the case. An expert witness should always give nothing but the truth in court of law. He must be ready for cross-examination.

A valuer must keep in mind that "Render more services than you are paid soon you will find that you are paid more than what you render". The law of increasing return takes care of this.

1.6.1. Types of Valuer

There are four types of valuers:

(1) Self styled valuers.

(2) Valuers approved by certain Banks—They are called as panel valuer or panel Engineers.

(3) Valuers approved by the institution of valuers. They are given title as approved valuers (Fellow Valuers or Associate Valuers).

(4) Valuers register with Income Tax Department (Central Board of Direct Taxes). They are called as Registered valuers or Government approved valuers.

Valuation *i.e.* appraisal ceases to be professional when the valuer is dictated by client, employer or Government. The valuer's independence is necessary for true honest reporting of the assignment.

There is a very Veg term used by valuer *i.e.* Government Approved valuer. It is very difficult to say that Mr. X is a government approved valuer. There are various government departments. Then there are departments either under the control of central Government or State Government or Local Government bodies. All these department solicit the services of valuers for one reason or the other. All these department maintain a panel of valuers with them for specific purpose and ask services for any of them. Though these valuers work for Government, though they can not be defined as Government approved valuer as the panel of valuers with Government is also modified or changed as per requirement. However it is essential to a person to have one of the following qualification to work as a registered or approved valuer to a firm. These are:

(1) A degree in Civil Engineering or Architecture or town planning from a recognised University.

(2) Post graduate degree in valuation from recognised University.

(3) Possesses a qualification recognised by Central Government for recruitment to superior services or posts under Central Government in the field of Civil Engineering, Architecture or Town Planning.

Surveyors and Loss assessors who normally work for insurance claims are not valuers. They are simply to assess the cost of the damages with a view to re-instate the assets *i.e.* what it costs to re-instate.

1.6.2. Role of a Professional Valuer

A valuer is highly skilled professional, who with matured technical expertise and skill prepares a valuation of the worth of land, buildings, plant and machinery or possessions for specific purpose.

The scope of his work is very wide and extends from residential property to large estates, factories, offices, shops, plant and machinery of every kind.

Some say that valuation is an art, others, and it is a science. In fact it is delightful and exciting blending of both. The art of judgement and foreseeing required in the process of valuation has to be based on scientific analysis of available data, to arrive at practical, applicable and acceptable valuation. It is a fact that valuation process is most delicate and soundly based requiring balance of judgement to decide tricky based requiring balance of judgement to decide tricky issues with several options and variable parameters.

The professional valuer is in utmost demand now to cater this emerging situation especially in the following two fields:

(1) Valuation of Real Estate (2) Valuation of Plant and Machinery

1.7. VALUE—PRICE AND COST

Cost is a fact, price is a policy and value an opinion.

These terms are often confused by many. Price is the amount of money paid to the seller by the purchaser of the property whilst cost is the price paid plus all other expenses incurred by the purchaser in the acquisition of the property. The term actual cost, original cost and historical cost are used to indicate the outlay which was made by either the present owner or by owner who first purchased or built the property for use in normal function. However in valuation original cost usually means the investment made in property by the owner who first used the property when it was new with land, however original cost is taken to mean the price by the present owner.

The cost of property is not necessarily be equal to its value. On the other hand, cost is considered as evidence of value and in establishing the value of the property. It is necessary to investigate both the original cost and replacement cost. It is usually safe to consider that the value of property to the owner was at least equal to its cost at the moment he took its possession.

'Wealth' is synonymous with economic goods. Wealth consists of all those commodities which are exchangeable. In order to be classified as wealth; it must possess utility; scarcity and transferability (not portability) it is a relative term.

In general, 'value' of a property is its worth for which that can be sold by a seller if he is ready to sell and purchased by buyer provided he is willing and able to purchase that. If these conditions are not existing value has got no meaning.

1.8. CAPITAL GAINS

When any immovable property is sold/transferred by any individual or a member of Hindu undivided family, any profit or gains arising from the transfer of capital asset is immovable property is called capital gains. The hard cash received due to probate is called treated as capital gains. It is chargeable to Income Tax under the head 'Capital Gains' and is deemed to be the income of the previous year in which the transfer took place (as her section 45 of Income Tax act.). The income chargeable under the head capital gains is computed by deducting the full value of the consideration received of accruing as a result of the transfer of the capital assets the following amounts *viz*.

(*i*) Expenditure incurred wholly and exclusively in connection with such transfer.

(*ii*) The cost of acquisition of the asset, the cost of improvement there of and multiplied by cost inflation index.

(*iii*) (*a*) Income tax assessment (*b*) Capital gains tax
(*c*) Wealth and gift tax (*d*) Land and building tax
(*e*) Municipal tax and octroy (*f*) Other taxes if any (*g*) Gift tax

(*iv*) To get solvency certificate.

1.9. OBJECT OF VALUATION

The main objects of valuation are:

(1) When a person wants to sell his property or when a purchaser wishes to purchase property; both are found interested to have an idea about its value; before final decision is taken.

(2) When a property is to be rented; its valuation is required. A rent of about 5 to 8 percent of its valuation is considered to be feasible.

(3) It become essential to valuate the property for fixation of different types of taxes.

(4) For insurance of property; the premium depends on its value hence valuation is made.

(5) When government acquires a private property in the interest of public; its compensation is given to the owner; hence valuation becomes essential under such conditions.

(6) When a matter regarding property dispute is taken to the court, to determine court fee and other details its valuation becomes essential.

(7) In case to companies; private sector works; to prepare balance auditors need idea about assets; hence valuation existing property is made and assets are fixed.

(8) When a person wants a loan against the security of his asset, it is called as a mortgage loan. For ascertaining the present value of such assets, it is essential to evaluate it.

(9) Betterment charges—To develop certain area for its betterment, the owners of houses of that area are required to pay additional taxes to authorities. These extra or additional taxes are known as betterment charges. This depends on the value of the property as such owner should know the value of his asset prior and after the development of that area.

(10) Reinstatement—In case property owner wishes to reinstate his property, the valuation of asset becomes essential, possible use of old materials should be taken into account.

(11) Some time a property has future secret prospects; of course if one would visualise it this is referred as speculation value or speculation.

(12) Other reason is for partition or for dissolution of firms.

(13) Valuation is essential to find the depreciation value of the asset. Hence to decide upon the depreciation of any asset its value is required to be known.

(14) Valuation of other items like jewellery is very essential for its allotment to different family members. One may also remember that it is essential to obtain a qualified valuers report if jewellery in house hold worth is in excess of rupees five lakh.

(15) When two different companies decide to amalgamate, or one company takes over the business of another; there is always a need to bring in more finance. In such situations, while approaching a lending institutions if valuer report is attached, proposal are speedily processed.

(16) Through the price of building or Machinery depreciated; the value of land in general always appreciates, hence while doing valuation of premise; it is always essential to know the value of total premise and not of a part. It is always possible that the value of an individual may be decreasing but of total premise may be increasing.

(17) International accounting standards expect that a true picture of a company is reflected by its balance sheet of its financial accounts. It is also essential for intending investors, existing share holders, lending Institutions, company's own bankers etc. to know real worth of that enterprise. For this period revaluation of company's assets is necessary to project the updated picture.

(18) In a global market; the currency fluctuations plays a major role in financial planning. Therefore today all the companies small or big, always find it in their interest to obtain revaluation of their plant and Machinery assets, especially those of foreign origin. It is always a good practice to obtain revaluation certificate periodically, at least once in three to five years duration for machines of foreign origin.

(19) When advance payments are required to be made against works contract; it is very essential to have idea about work completed to make advance payment against work completed.

(20) For claiming duty drawback and export incentives; it is desirable to substantiate the claim with the help of valuers report, preferably from valuer who is also chartered Engineer.

(21) In case of collaboration with an overseas foreign firm; it is essential to have the existing assets revalue and incorporate their correct value in the books to ensure proper financial perspectives.

(22) If a second hand machine is imported, it is better to have invoice of revalued assessment of machine duly certified by authorised valuer. It will reduce the custom duty and will save time and money for person having purchased second hand machine as well as of custom authorities.

(23) Even during Auction of any property a minimum value is required to be defined. It is essential to management as well as various persons concerned like share holders or persons involved like purchaser, seller, Government etc. Even when public limited concern decides to dispose some of its capital goods, or sell some scrap material, valuation is very essential to avoid later on disputes or problems may arise later on.

(24) To quality for concession Granted under small scale Industry rules, a certification by a qualified valuer regarding the capital employed in plant and machinery becomes very helpful.

(25) Valuation is also essential if a property is required to be liquidated. The liquidator has to decide as to what price the company assets would fetch at current market rate.

(26) A charitable trust or a co-op. society is also required to have a qualified valuers report for seeking permission for disposing the capital goods, assets like building, machinery etc. from the charity commissioner.

(27) Immigration officers who scrutinize visa applications to some prosperous countries like USA; find out the applicants financial and family stakes in the country of his/her origin; hence valuation certificate some time becomes essential.

(28) In case of Divorce, cases becomes complicated when sizeable assets are involved and where emotional and pecuniary values get mixed up. A qualified valuer can help to sort out matters to the satisfaction of parties.

1.10. FACTORS AFFECTING VALUE OF AN ASSET

The value of any asset depends on many factors. An expert valuer should study these factors properly before deciding the value of any property. Those are:

(1) **Price Index.** Present market rate of various material, labour, machinery etc. must be known to a valuer. This further depends upon quality and availability, supply and demand and other.

(2) **Location of Property.** It affects a lot on value of that property, a piece of land may cost ₹ 10 per sq. meter to ₹ 5000 or more per square meter depending upon its location, either area wise or town wise similarity a building cost may vary from ₹ 3500 to ₹ 4000 per sq. meter to ₹ 30,000/- per sq. meter or more depending up on its location, all other factors remaining the same.

(3) Demand and supply also affect the value of property to a considerable extent.

(4) Return that can be fetched from the property is also a factor affecting its value. A building having more life and fetching more rent costs more.

(5) Useful remaining life of that asset, its conditions of maintenance and repair, scrap or salvage it is likely to have after its useful life is over, are a few other factors affect its value.

(6) Functional use value, flexible utility *i.e.* possibilities of alterations of its occupancy also affect its value. The time and date, the valuation is made also has got significance effect on the value of the property.

(7) Neighbourhood conditions.

(8) Any easement right developed during the period.

(9) Local bylaws restricting addition, alteration of building.

(10) Outlook and elevation of building.

(11) Space utilisation and services.

1.11. TYPES OF VALUATIONS

There are various types of valuation; adopted depending upon its object. There are:

(1) Ordinary Valuation. In ordinary exchange of property; the value is determined by the judgement of the seller and the buyer, each taking into account the knowledge of the property, the prevailing exchange conditions for such property and his own exigencies and those of the other party. By the process of barter; the seller and buyer finally agree upon the sale price. In the majority of cases, only a few simple mathematical computations are involved. Such ordinary valuations are made authoritatively and bindings only through acceptance of the terms of exchange by both the seller and the purchaser of the property.

(2) Formal Valuation. In formal valuation of property, the value is determined by judgement of specially qualified valuators. Such valuations may be for use in property sell or for many other purposes, such as taxing property; securing loans; determining rents and establishing fair commodity prices. The formal valuation is not computed by mathematical formula but is fixed by expert judgement. However, mathematical computations of varying degree of complexity often are required; these computations may be technical or non-technical.

(3) Engineering Valuation. It is the art or estimating the value of specific properties where professional engineering knowledge on and judgement are essential. Examples of such property valuations are valuation of mines, factories, industrial plants, machineries, etc.; and other all kind of public utilities.

Laws which affect the value of a property:

(1) Transfer of property of Act, 1872

(2) Indian easement Act, 1882

(3) Land acquisition Act, 1894 and chapter xx-c of Income Tax Act.

(4) Urban Land Tax Act.

(5) Lease and Rent Control Act.

(6) Ceiling and Regulation Act.

(7) Town and Country Planning Act.

(8) Tenants Act.

(9) Income Tax Act.

(10) Sale of Property Tax.

All these acts and a few more are dealt briefly in last chapter.

1.12. ENVIRONMENT AND VALUATION

Impacts of human activities and environment controls have been causing pollution of our environment. The effect of environment on valuation has been noticed many times. People do not purchase property if located in poor environment. It clearly indicates that there is a certain defined effect of existing property under consideration. Environments also effect the materials of construction in due course. The best example to quote is "Tajmahal" one of the wonderful structure on this earth. The surrounding environment effect is noticed and therefore corrective steps have been taken by government. The effect is mainly due to air pollution of materials or other pollutions like water pollution, noise pollution etc. on the surrounding of the property.

Effect of air pollution on materials may be manifested in following ways:

(1) Soiling	(2) Abrasion	(3) Chemical reaction	(4) Embitterment
(5) Fading	(6) Weakening	(7) Disintegration	(8) Discoloration
(9) Darkening	(10) Corrosion	(11) Etching	(12) Structural failure

Effect of pollution on the cost of structure may be direct or indirect durability of structure is tested; it is a test of effect of environment on life and quality of structural elements and materials used in construction. Air pollution got following effects on materials.

(1) Deposition (2) Soiling (3) Hardening and weakening

(4) Chocking of ducts and transfer points.

Dust particles present in air pollutes environment tremendously and its effect on human body is well experienced by every body. Its effect on buildings is also well known. If some one wishes to sell his building, he always gets the building under consideration white/colour washed, it is simply to look building in good condition *i.e.* to show that structure is maintained properly to hide bad patches if any. This all is done to fetch more value of the building. To summarise therefore it can be said that valuer should have to be expertise and must mature their knowledge of environment aspect while valuating any building. It is more essential in case of industrial structures and buildings of historical and architectural heritage.

1.13. REAL ESTATE VALUATION

Valuations of Real Estate are required for a variety of purposes and brief outline shows respective considerations.

(*a*) **Mortgage.** In the majority of house purchases, buyers need to borrow money to meet present day prices. Sources of finance are banks and local authorities.

The valuer will make a critical appraisal of the property, taking into account the nature of the location and proximity to amenities. He will estimate the age and take into account the character, design, plan decorative and structural value of property. He will carry out an academic valuation where appropriate by calculating the floor area in order to arrive at an estimated building cost, allowing for essential repairs and adding the value of the site. He will examine his recent sales records to find comparable and finally make his written report to the mortgage (the Lender) giving his recommendations.

(*b*) **Insurance.** Dwellings are subject to hazards such as fire, storm and flood, hence the need to protect them with insurance. They may be partially damaged or totally destroyed but at least there remains the value of the site. Consequently, the valuer is called upon to advice as to re-building and replacement costs, to which he will add a percentage to cover professional fees for the services of architects and surveyors necessary for the re-building and site clearance. With insurance the valuer must keep up to date with building costs.

(*c*) **Rating.** Local bodies levy appropriate taxes to the property, dewlling as a return for various infrastructure obligations extended to the locality. This includes education, roads, sewers and a variety of other outgoings necessary to maintain the system. The property tax is based on rateable value. These rateable values are made by the assessor of municipal authority. These values are somewhat hypothetical and are open to criticism and appeal. Apart therefore from the Civil Servant, valuers in private practice are asked to advise as to the accuracy of these assessments, especially taking into account changing environment and circumstances. They may be called upon to appear on behalf of their clients at the local appellate Court to argue the case and endeavour to obtain appropriate reductions in rates and taxes.

(*d*) **Probate—Official Proving of Will.** When people die, leaving property, the estate may be liable to Capital Transfer Tax as per the law of land, in which event the solicitor of the deceased will seek a valuation of the dwelling and appropriate contents, for submission when obtaining probate. Values may be with vacant possession, tenanted or part possession and the valuer in private practice must be prepared to argue his case and go to appeal if necessary.

(*e*) **Sale and Purchase.** The valuer must be able to value property on behalf of vendors, and he can also be retained to act for purchasers. In the former case, he will explore the potential, seeking the highest possible valuation for his client, whilst in the latter there is a natural tendency to be more conservative. However, judicious balance is necessary in each case.

The basis of valuation under this heading is similar to that outlined under "Mortgage" and at the same time, if the vendor client purchased the property in recent years, to that purchase price can be added the cost of improvements plus the calculated appreciation as a further addition on current open market value. In addition, the valuer will advise the vendor as to the right price for negotiations.

(*f*) **Compulsory Acquisition for Public Purpose.** From time to time, Government or local authorities decide to carry out planned city development including such works as new highways, roads, airports or improvements to existing facilities which require the acquisition from private owners of whole or part of the land and buildings which they own and or occupy. The interests of these land owners must be protected and proper compensation assured. The valuer must know the Land Acquisition Acts and how to interpret them in each case.

It will be appreciated that the valuation field is indeed a wide one requiring that the valuation field is indeed a wide one requiring extensive knowledge, expertise and experience, and is one where a sound professional study and involvement is essential. It will be seen that there, are two sides of the fence, the government or local authority employee as opposed to the valuer in private practice. The opportunities are considerable and the qualified valuer is able, if he so chooses, to gain experience in both spheres during his practising life.

(*g*) **Direct Tax Acts.** Under the Direct Tax Acts valuation is required under Chapter XXC (Pre-emptive right of purchase) of Income Tax Act which is now applicable throughout India when sale price of immovable property exceeds Rupees Ten Lakhs. Even valuations are required for Capital Gains Tax, Wealth Tax, and Gift Tax etc.

(*h*) **Financial Valuations.** Financial valuations are carried out for a variety of reasons including, amongst others, balance sheet purposes, bank loans and other funding activities, company takeovers and mergers, compulsory purchase, and taxation. In essence, the valuer is required to assess the true worth of a company of its real estate in its present location and role, as part of the existing business.

Following a valuation, the specialist valuer may be instructed to negotiate on behalf of his client. Therefore, in addition to his technical knowledge and valuation skills, an understanding of company law and other relevant legislation is vital.

(*i*) **Easement Right.** When a property is burdened with an easement right such as right of light and air, right of support, right of passage etc., it will be have an adverse effect on the value of the property. It is always prudent to make a physical verification of the property by inspection thereof to ensure that there are no adverse claims against the property by holders of dominant heritage claiming easement rights.

(*j*) **Rent Control Act.** All states in our country have there own rent control act with certain revisions and modifications. This act is mainly to avoid by taking undue advantages by anti social elements and detrimental both to the landlord as well as tenant. The Bombay rent control act 1984 though has ended by March 1998 still in enforce in Maharashtra.

1.14. PLANT AND MACHINERY VALUATION

When one pauses to reflect upon the immense variety of plant at work in our factories, producing vast array of products, ranging from miniature printed circuits to ocean going cargo ships, the prospect of becoming a plant valuer must surely be both challenging and exciting.

There is a saying that 'the wealth of any great industrial nation lies within the boundary walls of its factories and manufacturing plants'. How many careers offer one the opportunity of unlocking the doors, contained within those walls, and inspecting, without encumbrance, the detailed workings of the plant which produces the Nations' Wealth!

Valuation of plant and machinery is required for insurance, financial and market purposes etc. Let us now consider the approach to each of these aspects of plant valuation.

(*a*) **Insurance.** Valuations for insurance purposes are undertaken in order to establish the value of all property which is intended to be covered by a policy of insurance. The valuation is carried out by compiling an inventory of the plant, machinery and all other contents (excluding stock and materials-in-trade) which is at risk in the factory, and then pricing the items on the basis of either reinstatement with new or in-dimity, according to the requirements of the client.

All the insurance policies have certain stipulation, and this must be meticulously studied and any conditions which will affect the valuation must be taken into account in arriving at the figures shown in the final report to the client.

Preparing an insurance valuation, so that bother under-insurance and over-insurance are avoided, is a complex task requiring not only an understanding of plant in the factory, but also a thorough knowledge of insurance principles and law.

Many firms of specialist valuers offer a comprehensive loss assessing service, which entails compiling and settling claims in respect of bother material damage and also loss of profits.

(*b*) **Financial Valuations.** Financial valuations are carried out for a variety of reasons including, amongst others, balance sheet purposes, bank loans and other funding activities, company takeovers and mergers, compulsory purchase, and taxation. In essence, the valuer is required to assess the true worth for a company of its plant and machinery in its present location and role, as part of the existing business.

Following a valuation, the specialist valuer may well be instructed to negotiate on behalf of his client; therefore, in addition to his technical knowledge and valuation skills, an understanding of company law and other relevant legislation is vital.

Financial valuation is undoubtedly the most demanding aspect of plant valuation, utilising most of the valuer's skills and often resulting in vast sums of money changing hands.

(*c*) **Valuation for Disposal.** Plant and machinery generally becomes available for disposal following rationalisation or modernisation programmes and in cases of company insolvency. When valuation advice is sought in such cases, the valuer is required to be fully conversant with price levels and market trends, and a thorough knowledge of the practice and structure of the industry in question is essential.

Plant may be sold by private treaty, tender or auction sale and advice in respect of the best method of disposal will usually be required.

Following valuation for open market purposes, firms of specialist valuers are often instructed to undertake the disposal of plant and machinery, and the plant valuer, in his capacity as auctioneer, will manage the sale, including organising conducting the presentation of the machinery, drafting and organising the advertising programme preparing the sale catalogue and overseeing the supervision of viewing and delivery of lots.

Auctioneering skills can only be learned from experience, but the auctioneer must be completely conversant with legislation governing the sale of goods.

(*d*) **Deciding Equity at the Time of Foreign Collaboration.** Due to liberalisation there is inward flow of foreign exchange and many companies enter into collaboration with foreign companies. The valuation of assets plays an important role in deciding share of foreign company.

Although the valuation is not an exact science, the opinions expressed are based on

(*i*) Information made available

(*ii*) His experience in the filed and

(*iii*) His versatile and sagacious perception of complex factors influencing his assignment.

A professional approach of valuer demands that valuer's certificate should reflect the reality rather than somebody's suggestions.

1.15. FEES FOR VALUATION

The fee to be charged for valuation of any asset is a matter between the valuer and his client. The kind of services provided by valuer, the quality of his work, the amount of trust and confidence a valuer has in market, the overall reputation which a professional valuer has been able to establish for himself in the field and many other such factors decide the quantum of a fee a valuer can earn. Worldwide it is unethical and unprofessional to accept fees in a form of commission, rebate, brokerage or similar such norms. However as per wealth tax rules, the fee to be charged by a registered valuer for valuation of any asset should not exceed the amount calculated at the following rates.

(1) (*a*) On the first 50000 rupee of the asset a value 1/2 percent of the value.

(*b*) On the next 1 lakh rupee of the asset a value 1/4 percent of the value,

(*c*) On the balance of the asset as value 1/8 percent of the value.

(2) When two or more assets are required to be valued by a registered valuer at the instance of an assesse, all such assets shall be deemed to constitute a single asset for the purposes of calculating the fees payable to such registered valuer.

(3) Where the amount of fees calculated in accordance is less than ₹ 50/-, the registered valuer can charge a minimum of ₹ 50 as his fee.

These above rules are prescribed for wealth tax assessment only and therefore can not be standardized. The fee charge can differ from one valuer to other depending upon his reputation in market. However, it is desirable to link the fees with the total meadays invested for doing the site inspection, research work and analysis for arriving at assessed value. But it is always a good practice to fix the schedule of fees well in advance and as a lump sum amount for specially described assignment and to avoid ambiguities before the completion of assignment.

Many a times it can be decided as certain percentage or lump sum amount based upon

(*i*) The amount of award granted by courts to valuer's client in a litigation for which the valuer worked or

(*ii*) Reduction in taxation likely to be obtained by clients through valuation work or

(*iii*) Sale value realised for assets sold or

(*iv*) Amount of financial loan/aid/subsidy to be obtained by valuers client for which valuation exercise has been ordered or

(*v*) Arriving at value, suggested/requested/opined by his client *i.e.* value which is suitable and convenient to some one.

1.16. FREEHOLD AND LEASE HOLD PROPERTIES

An asset or a property may be freehold or leasehold. A free hold property implies that the owner of the property is in absolute and perpetual possession of it. He can fetch return on this property for infinite time unless it is sold or given on lease to some other person in consideration. It is the highest form of ownership and owner of free hold property can do whatsoever he likes. He can use that property for himself or can sent. He is the wholesale owner of the property and can develop as per rules and regulation prevailing at that area.

Lease hold property is one which is given on lease for a specified period of time with certain specified terms and conditions by the owner having free hold rights. In return the free holder of property gets certain amount for granting lease. This is called granting property on lease. Even government also gives some property on lease to other persons to use it for certain specified period of time.

The person who takes the lease is called lessor or the lease holder and owner who grants lease is known as lessor.

1.17. EASEMENT RIGHT

It is a right to a person to get light and ventilation both 'horizontally'. The word horizontally is more important. It is illustrated by an example. On plot a building has been constructed, double storied and construction is a butting the property line, while the plot B is still vacant. After a few years is person having in possession plot B. If starts construction; then owner of plot B can not force to owner of plot A to close the windows; rather same other space in between plot A and B will have to be provided by B; so that light and ventilation of Plot A is not obstructed horizontally. This is called 'Easement Act' owner of plot B had to take objection in the beginning itself; further no more objection was received earlier as time period has passed by owner of adjoin plot was enjoying the light or ventilation thought the opening at the side of plot B; it is his right to ask owner of plot B to have some open space it is his easement right.

This is very important from valuation point of view, as such the value of property of B reduces to some exhalant due to this easement Act.

The subject like valuation can not be left in such small member of pages. The valuer must have knowledge of life tables valuation table used; before he does valuation of any property further various acts prepared by government; the knowledge of these acts is must to a valuer.

SOME USEFUL ABBREVIATIONS IN VALUATION

- AIV — Associate in Institution of Valuers.
- BM — Bench Mark/Branch Manager.
- B.A. No. — Building Approval Number.
- CAB — Capital Adequacy Ratio.
- CBDT — Central Board of Direct Taxes.
- CPWD — Central Public Works Department.
- DCF — Discounted Cash Flow.
- DRT — Debt Recovery Tribunal.
- DTP — Director of Town Planning.
- DTCP — Director of Town and Country Planning.
- EC — Encumbrance Certificate.
- EM — Equitable Mortgage.
- FAR — Floor Area Ratio.
- FERA — Foreign Exchange Regulation Act.
- FIV — Fellowship of Institution of Valuers.
- FMB — Field Measurement Book.
- FMV — Fair Market Value.
- FSI — Floor Space index.
- GIS — Geographical Information System.
- GLR — Guide Line Rate.
- GMR — Gross Maintainable Rent.
- IRDA — Insurance Regulation and Development Authority.
- IT — Income Tax.

- ITO Income Tax Officer.
- LLL Land Locked Land.
- LSR Legal Security Report.
- NA Non Agriculture.
- NMR Net Maintainable Report.
- NOC No Objection Certificate.
- NPA Non Performing Assets.
- OD Over Draft.
- OS No. Original Suit Number.
- PC Plot Coverage.
- PLR Prime Lending Rate.
- RCOP No. Rent Control Original Petition Number.
- RS No. Resurvey Number.
- SF No. Survey Field Number.
- SLR Statutory Liquidity Ratio.
- TS No. Town Survey Number.
- UDS Un Divided Share.
- VAO Village Administrative Officer.
- VA Valuation Officer.
- WDV Written Down Value.

2

Engineering Economics

2.1. GENERAL

Economics is a study of men as they live, move and think in the ordinary business of life. It is a study of economic problems of the people living in a community. It studies those activities of social, real and normal human beings those are related to wealth. Economics is an art as well as an science. A property can be valued either on higher side or on lower side to some extent. This is an art. How to assess property value on either side to certain extent, is a science.

Economics is a science which studies human behaviour as a relationship between ends and scarce means which have alternative uses. Ends imply objectives or wants of a man which are never ending whereas scarces available are limited. As such economics can be defined as to meet the maximum wants or objectives with available scarce resources.

The knowledge of engineering economics to an engineer in general and valuer in a particular is very essential. There are cases where property worth very high is sold at a very less cost. The value of property many a times decreases or increases in a very small period of time. This all depends on demand and supply; need of person having some asset in possession, funds available with the purchaser and many other factors. Therefore the knowledge of engineering economics. Net present value, likely charges in market; government policies etc. is very essential to a valuer.

There are three qualities of human being which are studied in economics. These are:

(1) They are the member of society. It is a true fact. Every individual person is a member of the society.

(2) They must be real human beings. It is also true. To an imaginary person; theories of economics can not be related.

(3) Human beings involved are normal persons; economic theory applied to them.

All these human beings are related to wealth and economics deals or studies with human beings and wealth which are always scarce. Consumption of wealth, production of wealth, exchange of wealth, distribution of wealth etc. are all such matters that are related to economics and consequently to valuation.

Economics laws contain a clause "other things being equal" which is totally wrong. It is assumed that from a given set of facts, certain conclusions can be drawn, if no other changes take place in the meantime. Other things are not equal always and consequently therefore in economics, a definite conclusion cannot be predicted from a given set of facts. Even the given set of facts can change at any time and therefore economic laws are hypothetical as their truth and operation depends upon a large number of factors which are variable and imperfectly as certainable. A property valuated as very high today many not have same value tomorrow also. It has happened many a times. A property worth of millions of rupee have become of little use next day due to natural calamities or due to some other reason. Therefore the knowledge of economics and economic problem is very essential to a valuer. A few terms used in economics and affect value of an asset are given herewith.

(1) **Goods.** Any material which satisfy human wants are goods. These goods are either free goods such as water in ocean or sand in desert as they are available more than required. Other are economic goods, the supply of which is scarce in relation to demand. These goods are transferable and in possession of a man. Moreover it has a utility value and can be exchanged. Earlier there was a trend of change of commodity as per needs. These goods have marketability.

(2) **Price.** Value expressed in terms of money is called price. Earlier was practice to value what in terms of rice. Now a days the media of exchange is gold or currency.

(3) **Wealth.** It is synonymous with economic goods. Wealth consists of all such commodities which are exchangeable. In order to classify as wealth, a thing must possess the follow three qualities:

(*i*) It must have utility.

(*ii*) It must be scarce.

(*iii*) It must be transferable.

The wealth may be

(*a*) Personal or private

(*b*) Collective or common wealth.

(*c*) National wealth.

(*d*) Cosmopolitan or International wealth.

(4) **Wants.** It is a desire supported by ability and willingness to satisfy. The three essential requirement of any want or desire to purchase, ability to satisfy and willingness to spare means for the purchase. Now a days a tendency of hording things has developed. Whether a man is in need or not, he simply purchases for future shortages likely to occur as one presumes. The value of assets or buildings in getting appreciated very fast. This may be one of the reason. Many times houses are purchased by persons and kept vacant. They do not need it but preserves it as an investment. The value of property is therefore affected by wants also. There are examples persons are in possession of number of houses at different cities. These houses remain vacant for years together. Caretakers are appointed. They enjoy these properties. This also increases value of property unnecessarily. Black money in market increases wants and prices of buildings get increased.

(5) **Demand and Supply.** Demand and supply are the two words on which whole economics depend. Both are related to each other. If one is more other goes down. Demand means the amount of a commodity which people are willing to buy at that price. Supply is the quantity of a commodity which is offered for sale at a particular price. Stock is the quantity of goods

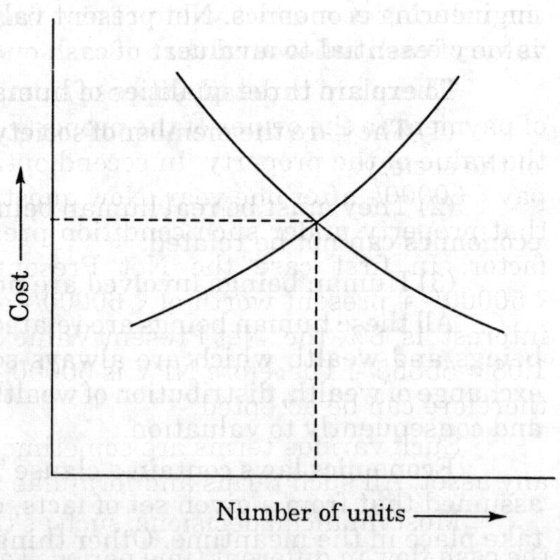

More supply less demand prices to go down
Less supply more demand prices to go high
A balance where demand and supply are same prices remain stable

Fig. 2.1. Supply-demand balance.

that could be sold while the supply is the quantity of goods that would be sold at a given price and hence supply can not be more than that of stocks. While the demand and supply move inversely; the supply and price move together.

The value of any property much more depends upon supply and demand. If number of houses to be sold are more than demand. The value automatically goes down. The fluctuation in the value of property is mainly due unbalance in demand and supply. If the demand and supply are same; the price remains stable if the supply is more; it means that there is more demand; however these two do not match and therefore prices increases.

(6) **Rights and Duties.** Rights necessarily imply corresponding duties. Rights and duties are two wheels of a cart. Without one, other can not survive. One can not enjoy his rights unless he recognises similar rights available to others. The right of one citizen implies the duty of another. If a citizen has certain rights, it is his duty to recognise that other person also has similar rights to enjoy. Rights may be moral or legal. Moral rights are recognised and enforced by public opinion and customs but can not be enforced by the authorities, while legal rights have support of government rules and regulations. Easement act is enforced legal right to enjoy natural resources like sun, wind etc. The value of a property is affected by rights and duties enforced either by public opinion or by authorities.

(7) **Inflation.** It is a very important factor in economics. Inflation also affects the value of any asset considerably. Inflation gives idea about surplus money available in market in the form of black money. It un-necessarily increases price index and value of property. More the inflation, more the surplus and therefore prices shoot up as a person having surplus money never objects to pay more. Therefore, it is very essential to control inflation. It affect national economy also considerably.

2.2. ENGINEERING ECONOMY

Study of engineering economy is very essential to a valuer. The time value of money plays a very important role in valuation of asset. Various interest theories help in assessing the value. Net present value of any financial decision is the difference between the present value of cash inflow and that of cash out flow. Wealth is defined as net present value.

To explain in detail, suppose a person wants to purchase a property. He gives two options of payment to the owner of the property. In option he is ready to pay ₹ 100000/- as on today as the value of the property. In second option he says to pay ₹ 50000/- as on today and ready to pay ₹ 60000/- after one year. Now question arises which offer the owner should accept to sell that property under such condition present value; he is likely to get becomes an important factor. In first case the Net Present Value (NPV) is ₹ 100000/-. In second case NPV is ₹ 50000/- + present worth of ₹ 60000/- at certain specified rate of interest. If current rate of interest is 8% the Net Present Value of ₹ 60000/- is $60000/(1 + i) = 60000/1 + 0.08 = 60000/1.08 = 55555$/-. Therefore NPV is $50000 + 55555 = 105555$/-. This is more than ₹ 100000/- and therefore can be accepted.

Such various terms are sometimes required to be considered while evaluating value of any asset. All such terms and formulae used are given in subsequent pages.

Most financial decisions, such as the purchase of assets; procurement of funds etc. affect the cash flow in different time period. To quote an example if a fixed asset is purchased, it will require an immediate cash outflow and will generate cash flows during many future years. The recognisition of the time value of money and risk are extremely vital in financial decision making. The welfare of owner would be maximised when NPV is created by making a financial decision.

If p = Present value of ₹ 1 to be recovered after n years at a rate of interest i

F = Future value of ₹ 1 at the end of n years invested at a discounting rate of i

n = number of years under consideration

i = Rate of interest or rate of return expected or discounting rate of interest

R = Sinking fund *i.e.* an amount to be invested at the end of each year for n years at a rate of interest of i to recover ₹ 1 at the end of n years also called as Annuity.

S = Total amount to be recovered at the end of n years if ₹ 1/- is invested at the end of each year at a rate of interest i.

If $n = \infty$

Then asset is supposed to have income for perpetuity *i.e.* for infinite life time.

(1) **Compound value of a lump sum**

$$F_n = P(1 + i)^n$$

$(1 + i)^n$ is called compound value factor $(CVF)_{in}$

If an amount of ₹ 1000 is put for 5 years at a rate of interest of 9%.

$$F_g = 1000\,(1 + 0.09)^5 = ₹\ 1538.62$$

$$= 1000\,(CVF)_{in} = ₹\ 1538.62$$

This $(CVF)_n$ can be referred from Table. However due to availability and use of calculator, these can be calculated easily.

(2) **Present value of a lump sum**

It can be said that present worth of ₹ 1

1 can be calculated using formulae

$$P = \frac{F}{(1+i)^n} = F\left\{\frac{1}{(1+i)^n}\right\}$$

The factor $\frac{1}{(1+i)^n}$ is called net present value of ₹ 1 likely to receive after n years at a rate of interest i. This factor is $(PVF)_{n,i}$ *i.e.* present value factor.

Suppose an investor wants to find out present value of ₹ 50000/- to be received after 15 years at a rate of interest of 9%. Then

$$p = \frac{₹\ 50000}{(1+0.09)^{15}} = ₹\ 13750/-$$

$$= ₹\ 50000\,(PVF)_{15,9} = ₹\ 50000 \times 0.275 = ₹\ 13750/-$$

(3) **Compound Value of an Annuity.** An annuity is a fixed payment (or receipt) at the end of each year for a specific number of years. The EMI *i.e.* equal monthly instalments calculated by financing agency such as loan is an annuity. Sinking fund is also an annuity. The expression for sinking fund is given in sinking fund method of depreciation in the chapter Depreciation.

$$S = R\left\{\frac{(1+i)^n - 1}{i}\right\} = F_n = R(CVAF_{ni})$$

$\left\{\frac{(1+i)^n - 1}{i}\right\}$ is called as compound value factor of an annuity $(CVAF_{ni})$. It means if an amount of R is put aside every year for n years at a rate of interest i, it will accumulate to F_n or S

i.e. total amount to be recovered at the end of n year at a rate of interest i. If an amount of ₹ 1 is invested at the end of each year, similarly

$$R = S\left\{\frac{i}{(1+i)^n - 1}\right\}$$

The factor $\left\{\frac{1}{(1+i)^n - 1}\right\}$ is called sinking fund factor *i.e.* $(SFF)_{n,i}$. This *SFF* indicates that an amount to be invested at the end of each year for n years at a rate of interest i to recover ₹ 1/- at the end of n years. It can be said that an amount of annuity to be put at the end of each year to receive ₹ 1 at the end of period under consideration.

(4) **Compound Value of an Annuity Due.** Value of an annuity due is similar to that of compound value of an annuity. In case of present value of an annuity, the amount of annuity is paid at the end of each year whereas if this annuity is paid in the beginning of each year; it called as compound value of an annuity due and calculated as

$$F_n = S = R\left\{\frac{(1+i)^n - 1}{i}\right\}(1+i) = R(CVAF_{n,i})(1+i)$$

(5) **Present Value of an Annuity.** An investor may have an opportunity to receive a constant periodic amount (an annuity) for certain number of years. The present value of such amount is calculated by aggregating all the present values to get the total present value of the annuity.

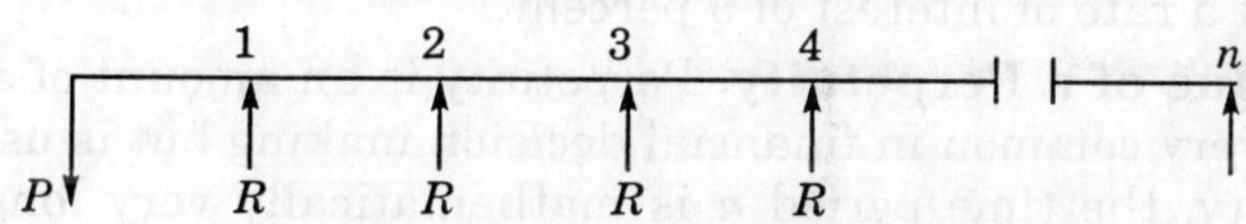

$$\therefore \quad P = \frac{R}{(1+i)} + \frac{R}{(1+i)^2} + \frac{R}{(1+i)^3} + \ldots \frac{R}{(1+i)^n}$$

$$\therefore \quad P = R\left(\frac{1}{i} - \frac{1}{i(1+i)^n}\right)$$

$$\therefore \quad PV = R(PVAF_{ni})$$

(6) **Present Value of an Annuity Due.** It is similar to present value of an annuity except that in case of present value of annuity the amount is received at the end of each year whereas in case of present value of an annuity due the amount is received in the beginning of the year as shown below:

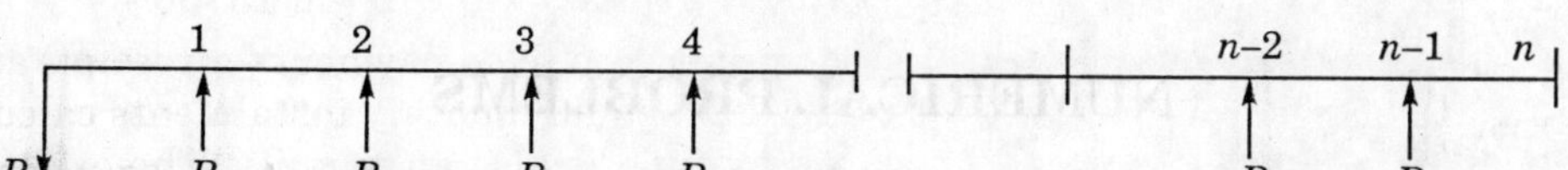

$$\therefore \quad P = R + \frac{R}{(1+i)} + \frac{R}{(1+i)^2} \ldots\ldots \frac{R}{(1+i)^{n-1}}$$

$$\therefore \quad P = R\left\{\frac{1-(1+i)^{-n}}{i}\right\}(1+i) = R\left\{\frac{1}{i} - \frac{1}{(1+i)^n}\right\}(1+i)$$

$$= R\{PVAF_{n,i}\}(1+i)$$

(7) **Capital Recovery and Loan Amortisation.** If an investment is made as on today for a given period time with certain specified rate of interest; one would like to know the annual income he would get. Capital recovery is the annuity of an investment for a specified

time at a given rate of interest. For example if an amount of ₹ 10000/- is invested today for a period of 4 years at a rate of interest of 10%. Then

$$R = P\left\{\frac{i(1+i)^n}{(1+i)^n - 1}\right\} = 10000\left\{\frac{0.1(1.1)^4}{(1.1)^4 - 1}\right\} = ₹\ 3155/-$$

This indicates that an amount of ₹ 3155/- one will get at the end of each year for 4 years.

This $\left\{\frac{i(1+i)^n}{(1+i)^n - 1}\right\}$ is called as capital recovery factor ($CRF_{n,i}$). It is inverse of present value factor of an annuity or present value annuity factor ($PVAF_{n,i}$). Capital recovery factor helps in the preparation of a Loan Amortization (*i.e.* loan repayment) schedule.

For example if ₹ 10000/- is borrowed at a rate of 9 percent for 3 years. Then this ₹ 10000/- can be repaid in 3 instalment, one at the end of each year and the amount required to paid is

$$R = 1000\left\{\frac{0.09(1.09)^3}{(1.09)^3 - 1}\right\}$$

or
$$= 10000\left\{\frac{1}{PVAF_{3,9}}\right\} = \frac{10000}{2.531} = ₹\ 3951/-$$

It means a sum of ₹ 3951/- is required to be made as repayment to amortize a loan of ₹ 10000/- for 3 years at a rate of interest of 9 percent.

(8) **Present Value of a Perpetuity.** Perpetuity is an amount of annuity that occurs indefinitely. It is not very common in financial decision making but is useful sometimes. By definition in perpetuity, the time period n is mathematically very long *i.e.* upto infinity. Therefore the equation present value of annuity reduces to

$$P = R\left\{\frac{1}{i} + \frac{1}{i(1+i)^n}\right\} = R\left\{\frac{1}{i} + \frac{1}{\infty}\right\} = \frac{R}{i}$$

It means if a person invest a sum of ₹ P, he will receive an amount R for infinite period of time, *i.e.* if an amount of ₹ 10000/- is invested at a rate of interest of 10% then,

$$R = 10000 \times 0.1 = ₹\ 1000/-$$

The person will receive ₹ 1000/- every year for infinite years. Or in other words to receive ₹ 1000/- for perpetuity, one has to invest ₹ 10000/- with a rate of interest of 10 percent for very long period, say of n years when $n \to \infty$.

NUMERICAL PROBLEMS

Q. 1. *Your grandfather is 70 years old and possesses a total saving of ₹ 100000/-. He expects to survive for another 10 years. He places his saving in a Bank that gives him a rate of return of 9 percent per annum. He wants to have sum amount at the end of each year such that after ten years the balance should become zero. What amount he is likely to get the end of each year.*

Sol.

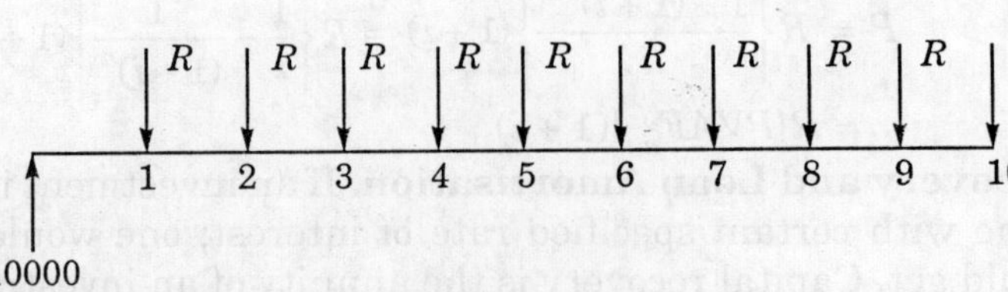

$$P = R\left\{\frac{(1+i)^n - 1}{i(1+i)^n}\right\}$$

or
$$R = P\left\{\frac{i(1+i)^n}{(1+i)^n - 1}\right\}$$

$$= 10000\left\{\frac{0.09\times(1.09)^{10}}{(1.09)^{10} - 1}\right\} = 10000\left\{\frac{0.09\times 2.367}{2.367 - 1}\right\}$$

$= ₹\ 15586/-$ **Ans.**

Q. 2. *One buys a house for ₹ 6 lakh and immediately make a cash payment of ₹ 2 lakh. The remaining amount he finances at a rate of interest of 12.5 percent per annum for 15 years with equal annual instalments. How much is the amount of annual instalment?*

Sol.

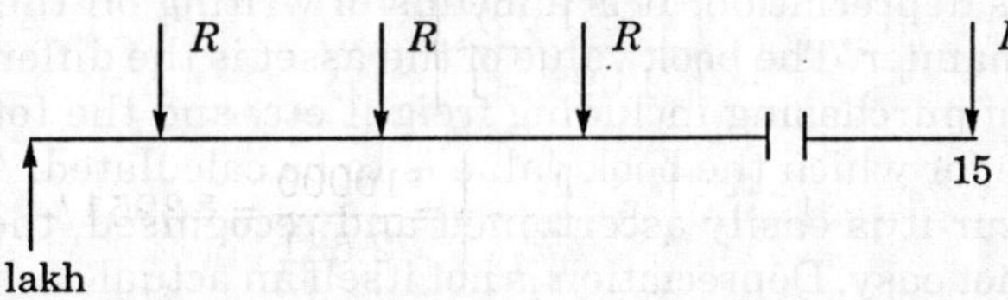

$$R = 400000\left\{\frac{i(1+i)^n}{(1+i)^n - 1}\right\} = 400000\left\{\frac{0.125\times(1.125)^{15}}{(1.125)^{15} - 1}\right\} = ₹\ 60328/-$$ **Ans.**

Q. 3. *Find the amount of sinking fund to be paid annually at a discounting rate of 8% to receive an amount of ₹ 2 lakh after 10 years.*

Sol.
$$R = S\left\{\frac{i}{(1+i)^n - 1}\right\} = 200000\left\{\frac{0.08}{(1.08)^{10} - 1}\right\}$$

$= ₹\ 13793/-$ **Ans.**

3

Depreciation

3.1. GENERAL

Every asset (Property) whether fixed or movable has got certain useful life. Its book value goes on decreasing with time. This decrease in book value of an asset with use or age or obsolescence is defined as depreciation. It is a means of writing off the cost of the asset in a rational and systematic manner. The book value of the asset is the difference between the cost of the asset on the date of purchasing including freight etc. and the total depreciation made against asset to that date for which the book value is to be calculated. Although the fact that depreciation does not occur it is easily ascertained and recognised, the determination of its magnitude in advance is not easy. Depreciation is not itself an actual cash flow, it is an artificial allocation.

3.2. PURPOSES OF DEPRECIATION

Because property generally decreases in value, it is desirable to consider the effect that this depreciation has on engineering projects. To be depreciable, property.

(1) must be used in business or held for production of income.

(2) Have a useful life longer than one year and

(3) Be some thing that wears out decay, is used up, become obsolete, or loose value from natural causes.

Primary it is necessary to consider depreciation for two reasons:

(1) To provide for the recovery of capital over time that has been invested in physical property.

(2) To enable the cost of depreciation to be charged to the cost of producing products or services that result from the use of property. Depreciation cost is deductible in computing profits on which income taxes are paid.

3.3. VARIOUS MEANINGS OF DEPRECIATION

There are different technical meanings attached to the ward Depreciation based on four basic concepts. These are:

(1) **Decrease in Value.** This concept implies that if the value of one asset is some way computed at two different dates; then depreciation, regardless of what combination of causes may possibly have been responsible for the value charge, is the difference in the value at the later from that of the earlier date.

(2) **Amortized Cost.** This in fact is the accounting concept of depreciation. From the view point of accounting, the cost of an asset is a prepaid operating expense to be apportioned appropriately among the years of its life by some more or less systematic procedure. It should be un-ambiguously emphasized that it is cost, not value that is apportioned in orthodox

accounting. Depreciation accounting is a system of accounting in which depreciation *i.e.* total present cost less salvage value is distributed over the estimated useful life of the asset in a systematic and rational manner. It is a process of allocation and not of valuation. Depreciation for the year is the portion of the total change under such a system that is allocated to the year. Although the allocation may properly take into account occurrence during the year, it is not intended to be a measurement of all such occurrences. Although the common phrase Book Value to describe the difference between the cost of an asset and the total of the depreciation changes made to date against the asset, this difference is more accurately described as "unamortized cost".

(3) **Appraisal concept of Depreciation.** Many appraisal of old assets are based on replacement cost. A replacement cost appraisal should answer the question. "What could one afford to pay for this asset in comparison with the most economical new one. An upper limit on the value to its owner of an old asset may be determined by considering the cost of reproducing its service with the most economical new asset available for performing the same service. The most economical new substitute asset may have many advantages over an existing old asset such as longer life expectancy, lower annual disbursements for operation and maintenance, increased receipts from sale of product or service. The deduction from the cost of the hypothetical new substitute asset should be a measure in money terms of all of these advantages of the existing old asset.

In the language of appraisal, this deduction is called depreciation. Appraisal depreciation, therefore, should mean the value inferiority at some particular date *i.e.* the date of appraisal, of one asset, the existing old one being appraised, to another asset, a hypothetical new one used as the basis for valuation. This concept implies two assets and the measurement of their two values at one date.

(4) **Impaired Serviceableness.** As machine becomes older, they are often unable to hold as close tolerances as when they were new. Similarly, the strength of structure may be impaired by the decay of timber members or the corrosion of metal members. Again it should be emphasized that this is not a value concept at all. Impaired serviceableness may result in decrease in value, but there are many other common reasons for decrease in value. Assets that are physically as good as new are not necessarily as valuable as they were new. They may have higher operation and maintenance cost; they will nearly have shorter life expectancy, service conditions may have changed, more economical alternative methods may have become available. This all is called absolescence cost.

3.4. VARIOUS TERMS USED IN DEPRECIATION

Various terms like salvage value, depreciable base, accrued depreciation etc. are defined briefly in subsequence paragraph.

The salvage value of a property is the net sum (actual) or (estimated) over and above the cost removal and sale, realised for it when it is disposed off by its owner.

Salvage value of an equipment is its market value if put in market for sale before its useful life is over. It may be equal to its book value as books of account. Scrap value is the value of equipment once its useful life is over and equipment theoretically has become useless or cannot be used for its intended use. Many a time salvage value and scrap value are assumed to be same which as per my opinion is not correct. Salvage value depends upon many factors, more important being how it is maintained. It can be more or less than its book value depending upon its maintenance, obsolescence, downtime, market demand etc. Scrap value however depends upon its material content and utility of that material. Many a time scrap value is negative, it means a contractor/owner is required invest from his pocket to dispose it off.

The term depreciation base is the original cost, the replacement cost, the value or any similar amount, which is to be allocated or adjusted for depreciation. The depreciation base is inclusive of salvage value. The term depreciable base is employed to designate the depreciation base less salvage value.

Annuity. It is the net instalment of annual or periodical payment for repayment of the capital amount invested in a property for a specified period. Annuity is paid either in the beginning of the year or at the end of the year or period of instalment. When it is paid in the beginning, it is called annuity due and when it is paid in the end of each period or at the end of the year it is called as annuity certain. When it is receivable for an indefinite period, it is known as perpetual annuity. When it commences after a few years from the actual date of capital investment it is known as deferred annuity. Its importance is to calculate the yearly or periodic instalment for loan or mortgage.

Accrued Depreciation. The term accrued depreciation has been used to measure a total depreciation from a given base from date now to the date of valuation or inquiry.

(*i*) In estimating present value form the evidence of replacement cost, accrued depreciation as assumed to be the difference between the estimated replacement cost now and the determined present value of the existing property.

(*ii*) When the original cost is used as the starting point accrued depreciation is assured to be the difference between the original cost and the present value.

(*iii*) In the accounting sense accrued depreciation is the sum motion of the annual depreciation allocation recorded is the books of account to date for the property in question.

Numerically this accrued depreciation may differ.

The 'annual depreciation' is the depreciation during a year of its useful life, *i.e.* the decrease value during the year. Theoretical depreciation is a depreciation estimated without given reasonable consideration to the several factors which effect the depreciation such as age, physical condition, future usefulness of the asset etc. whilst 'actual depreciation' is the estimate of depreciation made after considering all factors which influence it. Actual depreciation cannot be estimated without accurate knowledge of the physical condition of service of the asset.

Obsolescence. This is very important factor in case of valuation of buildings in general and valuation of machineries and equipments in particular. The continuous improvements in the design of equipments result in lower production cost. As such one who is owning and using old equipment looses his profit. For example if a new concrete mixer has come in market and if it takes less time for good mixing of concrete by say about 10 percent, a person who is using old mixer looses 10 percent from his profit as market cost per cubic meter of concrete may remain same or it may get reduced by 10 percent to both the user. This loss of 10 percent to a person using old machine is called as obsolescence. This happens in buildings also particularly in pre fabricated constructions. Obsolescence therefore should not be overlooked while assessing the value of a building.

3.5. TYPES OF DEPRECIATION

Depreciation is decrease in value of an asset, have several causes, some of which are very difficult to predict or anticipate.

(1) **Normal Depreciation.** Various type of Normal depreciations are as shown below

(*a*) **Physical.** This type of depreciation occurs due to the following reasons:

(*i*) Wear and Tear (*ii*) Physical Decay

(*iii*) Accidental (*iv*) Neglected Maintenance

(*b*) **Functional.** This is due to

(*i*) Inadequate or (*ii*) Obsolescence

Physical depreciation is mainly due to the lessening of the physical ability of a property to produce results. Its common causes are wear and deterioration. These cause operation and maintenance cause to increase and output to decrease. As a result profit decreases. Physical deterioration is mainly a function of time and use. Functional depreciation also called as obsolescence, is comparatively more difficult to determine. It is decrease in value due to the lessening in the demand for the function that the property/machinery was designed to render. This lessening may be brought about in many ways. Styles change, population centres shift, more efficient machines are produced or markets are saturated. Increased demand may mean that an existing machine is no longer able to produce the required volume or number of items; hence the existing machine has to be replaced by new machine so as to withstand market competition. Thus inadequacy is a cause of functional depreciation.

(2) Depreciation due to change in price level in almost impossible to predict and therefore is seldom accounted for in economy studies. When price level rises during inflationary periods, even if all the capital invested at the time of original purchase are recovered. This recovered capital may not be sufficient to provide an identical replacement. Although there has been a recovery of the invested capital, the capital has decreased in value. Thus it is the capital, not the property thus has depreciated. Inflecting annual depreciation to compensate for this phenomenon is not permitted in determining profits for income tax purposes. This is some times referred as "depletion".

(3) Depreciation due to accidents mainly due to negligence or due to structural defects or diminution of supply (natural gas, water etc.) is called as contingent depreciation.

Difference between depreciation and obsolescence. Depreciation is a physical loss in the value of property due to its use, wear and tear where as obsolescence is the loss in the value of property or profit from that asset due to change in design, fashion, utility or any other similar reason. Change in design of machine improves efficiency or reduces cost of production but a person already in possession of old machinery is bound to use that machinery till new one is purchased. As such his margins of profit decreases or the value of old machinery goes down, this is called obsolescence. Depreciation varies as per its use, age of the property where as obsolescence does not depend on its use or age. It is possible to find the depreciation. Various methods are available to find depreciation but there is no full proof method available to calculate obsolescence cost. Obsolescence depends on development of R and D facilities, a machine may become obsolete in a very short span of life, the same is not true for depreciation.

3.6. METHODS OF DEPRECIATION

There are certain requirements of a Depreciation method. There are various methods to find the depreciation of any asset. However, what so ever method may be used, it should fulfil the following requirements from standpoint of management.

(1) It should not be too complex.

(2) It should provide for the recovery of invested capital as rapidly as is consistent with the economic facts involved, known and computed salvage should agree if possible.

(3) It should accept by the internal revenue service, if the method is also to be used for determining government income taxes.

(4) It must assure that the book value will be reasonably close to the market value at any time.

These requirements are somewhat difficult to meet. As a result of these, numerous methods have been derived based on some hypothesis regarding loss of an asset value versus time and in an attempt to solve the complex problem in a reasonably simple and satisfactory manner. The method adopted for depreciation, is however expected to provide recovery of capital and the proper assignment of depreciation cost over the estimated life of the asset. The amount claimed of depreciation in a given year is influenced by an asset value, estimated life, salvage value, date in service and the method of calculating the depreciation. But equally important a depreciation method should account properly for the flow of capital funds that are recovered and which there by reduce the amount of capital remaining invested in a project. The recovery funds thus are available to the firm for other use or investment. Finally, the method used must permit the proper evaluation of the profitability of an investment being considered in an engineering economy study.

3.6.1. Method of Depreciation Calculation

In general, the many well-known methods of depreciation may be classified into following groups:

(A) Those not involving use of interest

(1) Straight line method (2) Modified straight line method

(3) Sum of the year digit (SOYD) method

(B) Sinking fund method based on interest theory

(C) Other Methods

(*i*) Declining balance method (*ii*) Double declining balance method

(*iii*) Declining balance method with switchover to straight line

(*iv*) Annuity charging method (*v*) Insurance policy method

(D) Appraisal method (E) Realistic method

All these methods are dealt herewith in detail.

Amortization. When the payment of debt is made by a series of equal periodic payments, it is known as amortization.

(A) 1. **Straight Line Method.** The basic concept of the straight line method is that as long as the service period and salvage value on which the depreciation allocation is based remain uncharged, the depreciation provision remain the same for each unit of service rendered. However when the probable line of an asset is changed, so to the year 10 years after having being used for the past 7 years, the graph representing accrued accounting depreciation between zero age and age of retirement is two straight line segments, each with a different slopes but joined at age 7. Nevertheless, this method is still regarded as straight line method.

A variation of the straight-line method is the multiple straight lines. A multiple straight line results when there is a charge in the estimated probable life or salvage value from that used the first year. This change in factors could result from a planned programme or from the re-estimate of the factors. Under a planned programme, a shorter service life and smaller salvage value would be used in the period of early service than would be used following a planned change in these factors. The intent of such planning is to achieve depreciation allocation in early life greater than would result from using the find service life throughout all service periods. By frequent increase in the estimated probable service life, the multiple straight-line methods would produce results somewhat similar to those obtained by use of the declining balance method.

By definition of the straight line method if,

B = Depreciation base including salvage value (This base may be the original cost, other cost or a value which is to be allocated).

Bd = Depreciable base *i.e.* amount to be allocated this is depreciation base less estimated salvage value

V_s = Salvage value

D = Annual depreciation allocation

N = Probable service life of asset in years.

Then $$Bd = B - V_s$$

and $$D = \frac{B - V_s}{n} = \frac{Bd}{n}$$

If B_x = unallocated portion of the depreciation base which is unallocated to age x and X = age of property in years.

Then $$B_x = B - \frac{Bd}{n}x = Bd\left[1 + \frac{x}{n}\right] + V_s$$

$$B_x = \left[\frac{n - x}{n}\right]BD + V_s$$

This formula helps to find the book value of an asset having useful life of n years at any period of x years.

2. **Modified Straight Line Method.** This method is slight modification method over multiple straight line method and is based on the recommendations of plant and machinery committee 1974. This committee has recommended that equipment can be depreciated in two parts, depreciation first 50 percent of allocated base in first 40 percent of useful life and remaining 50 percent of allocated base in remaining 60 percent life. It means if allocated base of 10000/- is to be depreciation in a total period of 10 years than ₹ 5000/- should be depreciated in first 4 years and remaining ₹ 5000/- in remaining 6 years. This means the annual depreciation in first 4 years shall be equal to 1250 and the same in reaming 6 years shall be ₹ 833.33 per annum.

3. **Sum of Digit Method.** The sum of the year (SOYD) method of depreciation is an Arbitrary method of allocation in which the depreciation base is held constant and the yearly rate is decreased. If the life of any equipment is 6 years, then sum of digit is equal to 1 + 2 + 3 + 4 + 5 + 6 = 21. The denominator of Fraction depreciation is taken equal to 21. The depreciation allocation for the first through the sixth years are found by multiplying the depreciable base by the series of fractions 6/21, 5/21, 4/21, 3/21, 2/21 and 1/21 *i.e.* to say depreciation during first year: $6/21 \times D_b$

Depreciation during third year: $\frac{4}{21} \times D_b$ and so on

Similarity Depreciation during first year: $\frac{6}{21} D_b$

Total depreciation in two years: $\frac{6}{21} D_b + \frac{5}{21} D_b = \frac{11}{21} D_b$

Total depreciation in 3 years: $\left[\frac{6}{21} + \frac{5}{21} + \frac{4}{21}\right] D_b = \frac{15}{21} D_b = \frac{5}{7} D_b$ and so on.

(B) **Based on Interest Theories**

Sinking Fund Method. This method of depreciation is now used in cost accounting by only a few enterprises, although did enjoy in the past a certain popularity in the public utility field. This method is still used extensively in engineering economy studies as a basis of selection of alternate proposals. In the sinking fund method of depreciation, the total allocation of the depreciable base to any date is equal to the corresponding accumulation of annual payments to the sinking fund and compound interest thereon.

Sinking fund is an annual payment, which is accumulated during the life of the asset so as to replace the asset after its useful life is over at some stated rate of interest.

The book value of the asset at any time is the first cost of the asset minus the amount accumulated in the imaginary fund up to date. This method is also known as present worth method since the book value at any time is equal to the present worth of the uniform annual cost of capital recovery for the remaining year of life plus the present worth of the prospective salvage value.

Mathematical development of the sinking fund method. If R is the annual equal year and payment is sinking fund at the end of each year and I is annual rate of interest.

If amount accumulated at the end of 1st year = R then amount accumulated at the end of 2nd year = $R + R + R_{xi} = R + R(1 + i)$.

Amount accumulated at the end or 3rd year = $R + \{R + R(1 + i)\} + \{R + R(1 + i)\}$

$$= R + R(1 + i) + R(1 + I)^2$$

Amount accumulated at the end of 4th year = $R + R(1 + i) + R(1 + i)^2 + R(1 + i)^3$.

Therefore

Amount accumulated at the end of n year $= R + R(1 + i) + R(1 + i)^2 + R(1 + i)^3$

$$= -R(1 + i)^{n-1}.$$

This total amount deposited will be equal to depreciable base, *i.e.* depreciation base minus salvage value = B_d.

$$B_d = R + R(1 + i) + R(1 + i)^2 + R(1 + i)^3 + \ldots R(1 + i)^{n-1} \quad \ldots(1)$$

Multiply both the sides by $(1 + i)$

$$B_d(1 + i) = R(1 + i) + R(1 + i)^2 + R(1 + i)^3 \ldots R(1 + i)^{n-1} + (1 + i)^n \quad \ldots(2)$$

Subtracting Eq. (1) from Eq. (2).

$$B_d\, i = R(1 + i)^n - R$$

$$R\{(1 + i)^n - 1\} = B_d\, i$$

$$R = \frac{B_d \times i}{(1+i)^n - 1} = B_d \frac{i}{(1+i)^n - 1} = \left\{\frac{i}{(1+i)^n - 1}\right\} B_d \quad \ldots(3)$$

This gives the amount of equal annual year end payment to the sinking fund for a depreciable base B_d.

The accumulation in the fund at any year and is represented by S_x which is found by equation.

$$S_x = B_d \frac{(1+i)^x - 1}{(1+i)^n - 1} \quad \ldots(4)$$

The unallocated base B_x is equal to the depreciable base new, since the accumulation in the sinking fund (accrued depreciation) plus the salvage value as,

$$B_x = B_d - S_x + V_s$$

$$B_d - B_d \frac{(1+i)^x - 1}{(1+i)^n - 1} + V_s$$

$$= B_d = \left\{ \frac{(1+i)^n + (1+i)^x}{(1+i)^n - 1} \right\} + V_s \qquad ...(5)$$

(C) **1. Declining Balance Method.** In the declining balance method a fixed percentage of depreciation is applied to the unallocated balance of the base. Therefore, it results the declining balance method closely parallels the sum of the digits method.

The formula for the unallocated base of the property at any age by this method is

$$B_x = B(1-f)^x \qquad ...(1)$$

where B = depreciation base, including the salvage V_s

B_x = Unallocated base at age x

f = the period (annual) rate of depreciation.

Although the expression $(1-f)^x$ is always less than unity and depreciation eases as the age x increases, it does not equal zero until x equals infinity. Hence, the accrued book depreciation of a property by the declining balance method theoretically would never reach 100 percent of the base.

If finite ending of it can be achieved by case of a salvage value *i.e.* equation (1) may be written in terms of the salvage value and the service life is n years.

$$V_s = B(1-f)^n \qquad ...(2)$$

By use of the salvage value and a probable life 'n' of the property, it is possible to determine f; for this equation (2) reduce to

$$f = 1 - \sqrt[n]{\frac{V_s}{B}}$$

2. Double Declining Balance Method. The method is similar to declining balance method; but declines at a rate double of declining balance method. Hence percentage by which depreciation taken place in

$$P = 2\left[1 - \left(\frac{V_s}{B}\right)^{1/n}\right]$$

It is illustrated by example later on.

Comparison of Different Method. Comparison of different method of depreciation is as shown in Fig. the straight line method gives uniform depreciation of the cost throughout its useful life. The declining balance method and sum of year's digit method give a greater depreciation in the early years of life than in the later years. The sinking fund method gives smaller depreciation in the early years of life than in the final years. Modified straight-line method gives slightly greater depreciation in the first 50% life of equipment and less in remaining 50% life.

Book values with the sinking fund method are always greater than they would be with straight-line method as the rate of the recovery of capital is slower in the early years of life of asset. The sinking fund method of depreciation is not used much now.

Depreciation *v/s* useful life. Books value *v/s* useful life and book value *v/s* depreciation curve can be plotted to compare different methods.

Example. Find the value at the end of year equipment by each method cost. ₹ 25,000 expected useful 6 years and salvage value ₹ 4000.

Solution. (*i*) **Straight line method:**

Depreciation base = 25,000

Salvage value = 4000

$\therefore$ Depreciable base $B_d = B - V_s$

$\therefore$ $B_d = 25000 - 4000 = 21000$

$\therefore$ Annual depreciation $= \dfrac{21,000}{6} = 3500$

Results are shown in tabular form below:

Table 3.1

Year	*Depreciation during this year*	*Total depreciation*	*Book value*	*Remarks*
0	00	00	25,000	
1	3500	3500	21,500	
2	3500	7000	18,000	
3	3500	10,500	14,500	
4	3500	14,000	11,000	
5	3500	17,500	7,500	
6	3500	21,000	4,000	Salvage values

(*ii*) **Declining balance method:**

Percentage of depreciation

$$P = 1 - \left[\frac{V_s}{B}\right]^{1/n} \quad \text{refer equation}$$

$$\therefore \quad P = 1 - \left[\frac{4000}{25,000}\right]^{1/6} = 26.4, \textit{ i.e. } 26.4\%$$

Results shown in tabular form.

Table 3.2

Year	*Depreciation during this year*	*Total depreciation*	*Book value*	*Remarks*
0	—	—	25000	25000 × 0.264 = 6600
1	6600	6600	18400	18400 × 0.264 = 4857.60
2	4857.60	11457.60	13542.40	
	(26.4% of book value at the end of one year)			
3	3575.20	15032.80	9967.20	
4	2631.30	17664.10	7335.90	
5	1936.70	19600.80	7335.90	
6	1425.40	21026.20	3973.82	
	1399.20	21000.00	4000.00	
			Actual as $V_s = 4000$ given	
			$\therefore$ $B_d = 21000$	
			and $D = 21000 = 19600.8$	

(*iii*) **Double declining balances method:**

$$\text{Here} \quad P = 2 \times \left\{1 - \left[\frac{V_s}{B}\right]^{1/n}\right\} = 0.528, \textit{ i.e. } 52.8\%$$

Results are shown in Table 4.3.

Table 3.3

Year	*Depreciation during this year*	*Total depreciation*	*Book value*	*Remarks*
0	—	—	25000	Cost of equipment
1	13200	13200	11800	25000 × 0.528 = 13200
2	6230	19430	5569.60	11800 × 0.528 = 6230
3	1570	21000	4000	Cannot be less than V_s
4	—	21000	4000	
5	—	21000	4000	
6	—	21000	4000	Salvage value

(*iv*) **Sum of digit method.** $\Sigma N = 1 + 2 + 3 + 4 + 5 + 6 = 21$

Results shown in Table 3.4.

Table 3.4

Year	B_d	*Coefficient of depreciation for the year*	*Depreciation*	*Book value*	*Remarks*
0	21000	—	—	25000	
1	21000	6/21	6000	19000	
2	21000	5/21	5000	14000	
3	21000	4/21	4000	10000	
4	21000	3/21	3000	7000	
5	21000	2/21	2000	5000	
6	21000	1/21	1000	4000	Salvage value

(*v*) **Modified straight line method.** Salvage value is already given otherwise it is taken equal to 10% of cost of equipment 50% of cost of equipment 50% of

$$\therefore \quad B = 25000 \; V_s = 400, B_d = 21000$$

this amount *i.e.* 10500 will depreciate in first 4% of its useful life, *i.e.* in 2.4 years, *i.e.* 2 years 5 months (29 months) and remaining amount *i.e.* 1050 in remaining 60 of period, *i.e.* 3.6 years, *i.e.* 3 years and 7 months (43 months). Results are shown in tabular form.

Table 3.5

Year	*Depreciation during this year*	*Total depreciation*	*Book value*	*Remarks*
0	—	—	25000	—
1	4375	4375	20625	$\frac{10500}{29} \times 12 = 4375$
2	4375	8750	16250	—
3	3519	12269	12731	$\frac{10500}{29} \times 5 + \frac{10500}{43} \times 7$ = 1810 + 1709 = 3519
4	2930	15199	9801	$\frac{10500}{29} \times 12 = 2930$
5	2930	18129	6871	—
6	2930	21059	3941	App. equal to book value

(*vi*) **Sinking fund method :**

$$\therefore \quad R = B_d \frac{i}{(1+i)^n - 1} \text{ refer eq.}$$

$$\therefore \quad R = 21000 \times \frac{0.04}{(1+0.04)^6} - 1$$

If i = 4% annual rate of interest = ₹ 3166

Results are tabulated as under:

Table 3.6

End of year	*Annual sinking fund*	*Interest on total sinking (fund (CI.5) @ 4% per annum)*	*Depreciation during that year (2 + 3)*	*Total depreciation*	*Book value*	*Remarks*
0	—	—	—	—	25000	
1	3166	—	3166	3166	21834	
2	3166	126 (3166 × 0.04) = 126	3292	6458	18.542	3166 + 3292 = 6458
3	3166	258 (6458 × 0.04)	3424	9882	15118	6458 + 3424 = 9882
4	3166	395	3561	13443	11557	
5	3166	538	3704	17147	7833	
6	3166	686	3852	20999	4001	equal to salvage value

Q. *A building stands on a free hold plot of land measures 600 sq m yields a gross rent of ₹ 1000/- per month. The price of land is ₹ 75/- per sq m. The estimated future life of building is 12 years but is expected to extend by another 16 years if structural and other repairs costing ₹ 16000/- are immediately carried out. The total amount of outgoing is 25 percent of the gross rent. The owner requires 7% return on land 11% return on building with 6% redemption of capital. Find out whether it will be advisable to spend the above cost of repairs from investment point of view.*

Sol. (*i*) Present value of ₹ 1 per annum allowing 11% interest on capital and 6% as redemption of capital = 5.91 for 12 years.

(*ii*) Present value of ₹ 1 per annum allowing 11% interest on building and 6% as redemption for 12 + 16 = 28 years = 8.03.

(*iii*) Present value of ₹ 1 recoverable at the end of 12 years @ 7% = 0.44.

(*iv*) Present value of ₹ 1 recoverable at the end of 12 + 16 = 28 years @ 7% rate of interest = 0.15.

gross rent = 1000 × 12 per annum = ₹ 12000/- per annum.

Outgoing @ 25% = 0.25 × 12000 = 3000/-

∴ Net return = ₹ 9000/- = per annum.

∴ Cost of land = 600 × 75 = ₹ 45000/-

Value Before Repairs. Capitalised values of building at 11% and 6% interest are 900 × 5.91 = 53100 deferred value of land deafened for 12 years @ 7% = 45000 × 0.44 = 19800.

∴ Total value of property = 53100 + 19500 = 72500/-

Value After Repairs. Capitalised value of building for 28 years.

@ 11% and 6% = 9000 × 8.03 = 72270/-

Deferred value of land for 28 years @ 7% = 45000 × 0.15 = 6750

∴ Total value of property = 72270 + 6750 = 73020

∴ Difference between after repairs and before repair values = 73020 – 72270 = 150.

The difference is negligible where he will have to spent ₹ 16000/- on repairs for improvement and benefit is only ₹ 150/- hence advised not to repair and sell it as it is.

The owner of a building gets a net annual rent 3500/-. The future life of the building is estimated 12 years. But if recommended repairs are carried out immediately at on estimated cost of ₹ 30,000/-, it is expected to lost for 30 years.

Assuming the rate of interest as 8% determine where it is economical to carry out the recommended repairs to the building leave as it is.

Depreciation of Buildings. The depreciations of the buildings depend upon the relationship between the age of the building and its total expected life. The total life expected depends upon the type of construction of building as under:

(A) RCC framed structure — 80 years

(B) RCC roofed load having structure — 60 to 70 years

(C) R.B. slabbed load bearing structure — 50 years

(D) ACC/GIC sheet roofed structure — 40 years

(E) Country tiled/thatched roofing — 10 years

The sinking fund method or straight-line methods are used to find the depreciated value of building. However the rate of annual depreciation can also be taken as equal to 100/- life span of asset. As such for R.C.C. structure the rate of annual depreciation will be equal to 100/80 *i.e.* 1.25%. Most of the engineering department at various state uses the following formula for depreciation, accordingly.

$$D = \frac{P(1-i)^n}{100}$$

where D = Depreciated value

P = Cost at present market rate

i = Fixed percentage for depreciation

N = Number of years, the building had been constructed *i.e.* previous life of building it has served its function or survived.

Some department have also adopted another formula as given below:

$$D = \frac{\text{Previous life of building}}{\text{Total expected life of building}} \times \text{present cost} \times \frac{9}{10} \text{ of building}$$

Depreciation is a complex phenomenon affected by market trends, fair and reasonable cost expected at the time Valuation. The depreciation of building can be verified by mode of construction, settlement of foundation, cracks in walls, condition of flooring, joist, beams and posts decay due to white ants and so on. Condition of roof, sanitary facilities, rapier and maintenance also effect the depreciation of buildings.

Depreciation of building also concerns several factors must important of which are structural strength of building materials used standard of construction and class of building. Thus depreciation pays a very important role while vaulting a building.

Modified method of depreciation. Author during the National Seminar on Valuation of Movable and Immovable Assets held at Goa on 28th to 30th Dec. 1992 had suggested a method to find the depreciation of building.

Suggested method of depreciation is on the basis of previous life of building and remaining future expected life, which depends on soundness and quality of building on the date of valuation. It means a building 50 years old may have its future life of only 10 years if not maintained property or may serve for another 40 years or more if maintained property and put in sound condition. Hence the depreciation of building should be applied in proportion of its previous life and expected future life. If a building is m years old and expected to serve for another n years then the building be depreciated by an amount of $m/(m + n) \times$ depreciable base. Depreciable base = present cost of construction – salvage. This is illustrated by example.

Example. *A building was constructed 40 years ago and is till existing in sound condition and hence can be presumed to serve for another 70 years. Find the depreciation of building if today's cost of construction of similar building is ₹ 250000/- assume salvage value 10% of present construction cost.*

Sol. Depreciation base = 2,50,000 – 25,000 = 2,25,000

$\therefore$ Today's total depreciation of building $= \dfrac{40}{40 + 70} \times 2{,}25{,}000 =$ ₹ 81,818/-

$\therefore$ Today's value of building = 250000 – 81818 = 168182

i.e. approximate 1.70 lakh.

Problem 1. *Mr. 'A' has purchased a land of 1,00,000 m² for ₹ 25/- sq m. He formed a labour after allotting 25% of the space for roads, parks etc. the rest of the land he segregated into plots of 1500 sq m each. He has spent 5% towards developments. He expects 50% profit margin and what is the price of each plot?*

Sol.

(A) Total Area	= 1,00,000 m^2
Area spent for roads 25%	= 25,000 m^2
Area/Plot	= 75,000 m^2
Number of plots 75,000/1,500	= 1,500 m^2
(B) Total area	= 50 Nos.
Purchased Rate	= 1,00,000 m^2
Purchased Value	= ₹ 25/sq m
Cost of development 5%	= ₹ 25,00,000
Total Cost	= ₹ 1,25,000
Cost/Plot (26,25,000/50)	= ₹ 52,500
Expected profit 50%	= ₹ 26,250
Price/Plot	= ₹ 78,750
Rate/sq m 78,750/1,500	= ₹ 52.50/sq m

Problem 2. *An R.C.C. roofed residential building of 120 sq m was constructed 10 years be assuming replacement value as ₹ 4,000/sq m and rate of depreciation as calculate the depreciation value and depreciated value (or present value) by strait line method and constant %age method.*

Sol.

(A) **Straight Line Method:**

$$D = C - S / n$$

D = Annual Depreciation

C = Replacement Value = 120 × 4000 = ₹ 4,80,000

S = Scrap Value 10% (assumed) = ₹ 48,000

N = Life of Building = 50 years

D = 4,80,000 – 48,000/50 = 8,460/year

D for 10 year 8640 × 10 (Depn. Value) = ₹ 86,400

Depreciated value 4,80,400 = ₹ 3,93,600/-

Note : This can be also worked out like this Depreciation %age

= Age/Life (100 – 10%)

= 10/50 × 90 = 18%

Depreciation Value 18% of 4,80,00 = ₹ 86,400

Depreciated Value 4,80,000 – 86,400 = ₹ 3,93,600/-

(B) **Constant %age Method:**

Depreciated Value D = $P(1 - r/100)^n$

P = Replacement Value = 120 × 4000 = ₹ 4,80,000

R = Constant %age depreciation = 2%

N = Age of the building = 10 years

Depreciated value = 480,000 $(1 - 2/100)^{10}$

= 4,80,000 × 0.8171 = ₹ 3,92,195/-

∴ Depreciated Value = 4,80,000 – 392195 = ₹ 87,805/-

3.7. OTHER METHODS OF DEPRECIATION

(1) **Insurance Policy Method.** In this method an amount is paid to insurance companies in the form of premium for endowment policy purchased, whereby the insurance company undertakes to pay a stated sum at the end of a given period. It is a type of sinking fund method. However in this method if something goes wrong, insurance company pays full amount assured in between also.

(2) **Revaluation Method.** In this method, the assets are revalued each year and resulting depreciation is changed to profit of the concern or firm. This method is useful to those assets which constantly change and the life of which uncertain. Even when configuration changes rapidly, this method can be applied. It can be used to electronics goods in general and computers in particular as on today.

(3) **Annuity Charging Method.** Here the interest is charged on the cost of the machine or the asset every year on the book value, but the rate of depreciation remains constant every year if

C = Cost of Machine

S = Scrap/salvage value of the machine

N = Useful life of machine under consideration

i = Rate of interest in fraction

R = Rate of depreciation

If the value of machine after one year become C_1

Then $R = Ci + C = C_1 = C(1 + r) - C_1$

Similarity the value of machine after 2 years in C_2

Then $R = C_1 i + C_1 - C_2 = C_1(1 + i) - C_2$

Thus the formula comes to = $\dfrac{\{C(1+i)^n - S\}^i}{\{1+(1+i)^n\}}$.

By substituting the different values in the formula, rate of depreciation can be worked out.

$$R = \frac{\{C(1+i)^n - S\}^i}{\{1+(1+i)^n\}}$$

(4) **The Retirement Method.** As per this method, the whole original cost of the asset is charged to depreciation expenses in the year in which it is being retired. Part of the total cost from current expenses while the asset remains is service, is not written off. This method is based on service life of the asset in terms of time and used for small machineries only that too in a small firm.

3.8. DEPLETION

When natural resources are consumed, their quantity decreases. This decrease in quantity can not be recovered as it can not be manufactured. For example as limestone is being used to produce cement; the resources of limestone quarries are decreasing, and these resources which are natural can not be produced. This decrease in value of natural resources with usage is called as depletion. A good example as on today is teak wood. Though one is ready to put any amount for teak wood shutters and frames; but due to heavy reduction in resources, the teak wood is not available to fabricate timber doors. The resources have diminished and therefore the value of teak wood has come down. The cost of depreciation can be replaced; the material can be replaced in case of depreciation; but the some can not be done in depletion. Therefore in the actual operation of many natural resources, business; the depletion fund created are used to acquire new properties to give continuity to the enterprise. Another good example is stone quarries. When no more stone is left to quarry *i.e.* total rock mass has been quarried; either the quarry site is changed or the machineries are sold and new business is started as the available machinery can not be used for any other job. Depletion in terms of value can be calculated using following formula.

If depletion for the year under consideration is = S
Cost of property = P
No. of units likely to be produced = N
Units sold during the year under consideration = n

Then $S = \dfrac{P \times n}{N}$

Other Numerical Problems

Problem 3. *A Building of 12 × 16 m is situated in a plot of 20 × 15 sq m. The plinth area rate including building water supply, drainage and electricals is ₹ 4,500/sq m. The year of strutting is 1968. Present value of land is ₹ 500/sq m. Assuming a %age of depreciation as 1.5%. Calculate the present value (Depreciated value) of the property. Date of valuation is March 1998.*

A. Value of land:

Extent of land 20 × 15	= 300 sq m
Rate of land	= ₹ 500/sq m
Value of land 300 × 500	= ₹ 1,50,000

B. Value of Building:

Size of the Building		= 12 × 16
Plinth area		= 192 sq m
Replacement unit rate of construction		= ₹ 4,500/sq m
Replacement value 192 × 4500		= ₹ 8,64,000
Rate of depreciation	r =	1.5
Age of the building (1998-1968)	n =	30 years
Depreciated value of the Building		= $P(1 - r/100)^n$
		= $8,64,000(1 - 1.5/100)^{30}$
		= 8,64,000 × 0.6355
		= ₹ 5,49,036/-

C. Total value:

A.	Value of land	= ₹ 1,50,000
B.	Depreciated value of Building	= ₹ 5,49,036
C.	Total Value	= ₹ 6,99,036

Problem 4. *A building was constructed 8 years before at a cost of 8,00,000. As per schedule of rates, the value has increased by 35% over the original cost consider labour and material cost, what is the present value of the building per annum depreciation is 2%.*

	Cost 8 years back	= ₹ 8,00,000
	Today value increased by 35%	= ₹ 2,80,000
	Replacement value today	= ₹ 10,80,000
	Value of depreciation	= 2%
	Age of the building	= 8 years
	Present value of depreciated value	= 0.02 × 8 × 1080 on 172800
∴	Present value of property	= ₹ 907200 **Ans.**

Problem 5. *The plinth area of the building constructed 15 years back is 150 sq m. The replacement rate is ₹ 5000/sq m total life is estimated for 50 years.*

Calculate the depreciated value as on date

(*i*) By straight line adopting 10% as the salvage value.

(*ii*) By constant %age adopting r = 2%

Plinth area of the building	= 150 sq m
Replacement rate	= 5000/sq m
Replacement value 150 × 5000	= ₹ 7,50,000
Age	= 15 years
Life	= 50 years
Rate of depreciation	= 2%

A. Depreciated value by straight line method:

$$D = C - S/n$$

C =	Replacement Value	= ₹ 7,50,000
S =	Salvage Value 10%	= ₹ 75,000
N =	Total life	= 50 years
	Depreciation value per year	= 75,50,000 – 75,000/50
		= ₹ 13,500

Depreciated for 15 years = ₹ 2,02,500
Depreciated value = ₹ 5,47,500

B. Depreciated value by constant %age method:

$$D = P(1 - r/100)^n$$

P = Replacement value = ₹ 7,50,000
R = Rate of depreciation = 2%
N = Age of the building = 15 years
= $7,50,000\ (1 - 2/100)^{15}$
= 5,53,927

Problem 6. *A building of 200 sq m is situated in a plot of 400 sq m. The replacement rate of construction is ₹ 4,500/sq m and the unit rate of land in the locality is ₹ 500/sq m. The outgoes is 5% of the value of the building per annum. Assume 9% as net return on value of building and 6% on the land value. Calculate the net rent and standard rent.*

A. Extent of plot = 400 sq m
Unit rate of land = ₹ 4,500/sq m
Value of land = ₹ 2,00,000

B. Plinth area of Building = 200 sq m
Replacement rate = ₹ 4,500/sq m
Replacement Value = ₹ 9,00,000

C. Net Return:
For land = 2,00,000 × 6/100 = ₹ 12,000
For building = 9,00,000 × 9/100 = ₹ 81,000
Total Net Return = ₹ 93,000

D. Outgoes
5% of value of building 0.5 × 9,00,000 =

E. Gross Return : Net Return + Outgoes =

F. Standard Rent/Month =

Problem 7. *A building fetches a monthly rent of 10,000 per month. The outgoes are annual repairs. ₹9,000 insurance. ₹500, annual sinking fund : ₹1,500 management charges is ₹ 1,000. Adopting the year of purchase as 8,33, calculate the cost.*

Monthly rent = ₹ 10,000
Yearly rent (Gross Return) = ₹ 1,20,000

Outgoes:
Annual Repairs : ₹ 9,000
Insurance : ₹ 500
Sinking Fund : ₹ 1,500
Management Charges : ₹ 1,000

Total : ₹ 12,000 = ₹ 12,000

Net Return = Gross Return – Outgoes = ₹ 1,08,000
Capital cost = Net Return × Years purchase = ₹ 1,08,000 × 8.33
= ₹ 8,99,640

Problem 8. *A residential building of 55 sq m area was constructed at a cost of ₹.1,75,000. It is proposed to construct a building 62.5 sq m. Plinth area in the same locality allowing 5% for escalation of prices and 7.5% for changes in design. Find the approximate estimated cost of the proposed building.*

A. Existing Building = 55 sq m
Plinth area = ₹ 1,75,000
Cost of building = ₹ 1,75,000
∴ Unit rate of construction, 1,75,000/55 = ₹ 3,182

B. Proposed Building
Plinth area = 62.5 sq m
Escalation for prices = 5.0%
Increase due to design = 7.5%
Total increase = 12.5%
Unit rate of existing building = ₹ 3,182
Unit rate of proposed building
After considering the increase = 3,182 × 1.125 = 3,580/sq m
Estimated cost of new building = 62.5 × 3580 = ₹ 2,23,750

Problem 9. *An old building was purchased by a person for ₹ 80,000. Calculate the coefficient of sinking fund, amount of sinking fund and yearly instalment of sinking fund the future life of the building is 20 years. Rate of interest is 5% and scrap value taken as 10% of the cost of purchase.*

$$I = s \times i/(1 + 1)^n - 1$$

Purchase value = ₹ 80,000
Scrap Value 10% = ₹ 8,000
Net value (or value of sinking fund) S = ₹ 72,000
Future life of building (n) = 20 years
Rate of interest (i) = 5% (0.05)
Co-efficient of sinking fund $I_c = i/(1 + 1)^n - 1$
$= 0.05/(1 + 0.05)^{20} - 1$
$= 0.05/(1.05)^{20} - 1 = 0.05/1.6533$
$= 0.03$
I = yearly instalment $= S \times I_c$
$= 72{,}000 \times 0.03$
= ₹ 2,160

Answer:
Co-efficient of sinking fund = 0.03
Amount of sinking fund = ₹ 72,000
Yearly instalment = ₹ 2,160

Problem 10. *The total value of the property is 4,00,000. Outgoes ₹ 6,000. If the rate of return is 9%, calculate the standard rent.*

A. Net return
Total Value = ₹ 4,00,000
Rate of return = 9%
Net return = 4,00,000 × 9/100 = 36,000

B.	Outgoes	= ₹ 6,000
C.	Gross Return = Net Return + Outgoes	= 36,000 + 6,000 = 42,000
D.	Monthly Rent (or Standard Rent)	= 42,000/12 = ₹ 3,500

Problem 11. *A property fetches a rent of 3,500 p.m. The outgoes is ₹ 6,000. If the rate of return is 9%, calculate the capital cost.*

Monthly Rent	= 3,500 p.m.
Annual Rent	= 42,000
Outgoes	= ₹ 6,000
Net Return = Gross Return – Outgoes	= ₹ 36,000
Capital Cost = Net Return × Years Purchase	= 36,000 × 100/9 = ₹ 4,00,000

Problem 12. *The cost of land is ₹ 2,00,000 and the cost of building is ₹ 2,25,000. If rate of return is 8%, what is the standard rent and that could be collected from torent assuming the outgoes as ₹ 14,000.*

Total Value:	
Value of property	
Land	= ₹ 2,00,000
Building	= ₹ 2,25,000
Total Value	= ₹ 4,25,000
Net Return	
Total value	= ₹ 4,25,000
Rate of return	= 8%
Net return	= 4,25,000 × 8/100 = ₹ 34,000
Outgoes	= ₹ 14,000
Gross Return = Net Rent + Outgoes	= ₹ 48,000
Monthly Rent	= ₹ 4,000

Problem 13. *The monthly rent of a property is ₹ 4,000. Outgoes is ₹ 14,000. If the year purchase is 12.5%, what is the capital cost.*

Monthly Rent	= ₹ 4,000
Annual Rent (Gross)	= ₹ 48,000
Outgoes	= ₹ 14,000
Net Return = Gross Rent – Outgoes	= ₹ 34,000
Capital cost = Net Return × Year purchase	= 34,000 × 12.5 = ₹ 4,25,000

Problem 14. *A property is let out at a monthly rent of ₹ 1,500. If the outgoings are taken at 30% of Gross annual rent and if the owner of the property expects a return.*

Monthly Rent (Gross)	= ₹ 1,500
Annual Rent 1,500 × 12 (G.I.)	= ₹ 18,000
Outgoings 30%	= ₹ 5,400
Net Income 18,000 – 5,400	= ₹ 12,600 (Gross – Outgoing)
Rate of interest	= 12%
Years purchase 100/12	= 8.33%
Capitalised value N.I. × Y.P.	= ₹ 1,04,958
Say	= ₹ 1,05,000

Problem 15. *The size of the plot is 20 × 12 cm. Cost of the land is ₹ 400 / sq m. Area the building 140 m^2. Replacement rate is ₹ 5,000 / m^2. The present value of supply, sanitary and electrical arrangements is ₹ 50,000. Allowing a depreciation of 1.5% per year, calculate the fair rent.*

Adopt rate of return as 9%. Age of the building is 15 years.

A. Land:

Size of the plot = 20 × 12 m

Extent of the plot = 240 sq m

Rate/m^2 = ₹ 400

Value of plot 240 × 400 = ₹ 96,000 (A)

B. Depreciated Value of the Building = $P(1 - r/100)^n$

Plinth area = 140 m^2

Replacement Rate = ₹ 5,000/m^2

Replacement Value = ₹ 7,00,000

Age n = 15 years

Rate of depreciation r = 1.5 = 7,00,000 $(1 - 1.5/100)^{15}$

= 5,58,009

C. Present Value of Services = ₹ 50,000

D. Total Value

Land = ₹ 96,000

Building = ₹ 5,58,009

Services = ₹ 50,000

Total = ₹ 7,04,009

E. Fair Rent

Total Value = ₹ 7,04,009

Rate of Return = 9%

Fair Rent/Year = 9/100 × 7,04,009 = ₹ 63,631

Fair Rent/Month = 63,631/12 = ₹ 5,280

Problem 16. *A building is constructed at the cost of ₹ 3,50,000 in a plot of 220 sq m area. The cost of land is ₹ 450 / m^2. Calculate net rent and gross rent of the property if expenditure on all outgoings including sinking fund is 5% of cost of construction and the cost of land. Assume 10% as net return on the cost of construction and 5% on the land cost.*

A. Total value

Extent of the plot = 220 sq m

Unit rate of land = ₹ 450/sq m

Value of land 220 × 450 = ₹ 99,000

Cost of building = ₹ 3,50,000

Value of property = ₹ 4,49,000

B. Net Return:

(*i*) for land @ 5% as rate of return

99,000 × 5/100 = ₹ 4,900

(*ii*) for building @ 10% as rate of return

3,50,000 × 10/100 = ₹ 35,000

(*iii*) Total Net Rent = ₹ 39,950

C. Outgoings = 5% of cost of construction and

The value of land 5/100 × 4,49,000 = ₹ 22,450

D. Gross return = Net Return + Outgoings

Gross Rent = 39,950 + 22,450 = ₹ 62,400

E. Gross Rent = 62,400 = ₹ 5,200

Problem 17. *A building of 800 sq m plinth area is on a plot of area 2000 sq m the building is rented for ₹ 12,000 per month. Cost of the land is ₹ 2,000 per sq m. Taking all outgoings as 35% of gross income per annum and net yield as 6% find the value of the property.*

A. Plinth area of the building = 800/sq m

Plot area = 2,000 sq m

Unit rate of land = ₹ 2,000 sq m

Hence the value of land 2000 × 2000 = ₹ 40,00,000

B. Monthly rent = ₹ 12,000

Yearly rent (Gross Rent) = ₹ 1,44,000

Outgoings 35% of Gross Income

1,44,000 × 0.35 = ₹ 50,400

C. Gross Return = Net Return + Outgoings

Net Return = Gross Return – Outgoings = 1,44,000 – 50,400 = ₹ 93,600

D. Capitalised value at the net yield of 6% = Net Return × Year's Purchase

= 93,600 × 100/6 = ₹ 15,60,000

Normally the rent is for the entire property. In the problem the cost of the land is given additionally. Hence it is assumed that the rent given is only for the building.

Total value of the property

Value of land = ₹ 40,00,000

Capitalised value of building = ₹ 15,60,000

Total = ₹ 55,60,000

Problem 18. *A person has invested ₹ 50,000 a plot and ₹ 1,50,000 on construction of a building over it, expecting 6% return. Assuming the cost of annual repairs to be ₹ 1,000 and other outgoings to be 30% of gross rent, calculate reasonable rent, of the annual sinking fund co-efficient is 0.01 (i.e. One paise per rupee).*

Net Rent

Value of plot = ₹ 50,000

Value of Building = ₹ 1,50,000

Total value of capital cost = ₹ 2,00,000

Rate of return = 6%

Net Rent = 2,00,000 × 6/100 = ₹ 12,000

Outgoings:

Annual Repairs = 1,000

Sinking Fund Co-efficient = 0.01

Sinking Fund 0.01 × 2,00,000 = 2,000

Total outgoes 1000 + 2000 = ₹ 3,000

Net Rent + Outgoes (A.R. + S.F.) = 12,000 + 3,000 = ₹ 15,000

Other Outgoings = 30% of Gross

Outgoings = ₹ 100

Net Rent = ₹ 70

If the net rent is ₹ 70 then the gross rent is ₹ 100. If the net rent is ₹ 15,000 the gross rent is

100/70 × 15,000 = 21,429

Standard Rent/Month	= 21,429/12 = ₹ 1,786
Check:	
Monthly Rent	= 1,786
Yearly Rent	= 1,786 × 12 = ₹ 21,432
Outgoes:	
30% of 21,432	= ₹ 6,430
Sinking Fund	= ₹ 2,000
Annual Repairs	= ₹ 1,000
	= ₹ 9,430
Net Rent = Gross Rent – Outgoes	= 21,432 – 9,430 = ₹ 12,002
Capitalised Value @ 6% as rate of return	= ₹ 12,002 × 100/6 = ₹ 2,00,033

Problem 19. *A building of total cost ₹ 10,00,000 has been constructed in a plot of 12 × 18 m. The prevailing market rate of plot is ₹ 1100 / sq m. If the expenditure on all outgoings is ₹ 40,000 per annum, determine the net rent and gross rent. Assume the rate of return as 6% on building and 4% for land.*

A.	Extent of land 12 × 18 m	= 216 sq m
	Unit rate of land	= ₹ 1,100/sq m
	Value of Building	= ₹ 2,37,600
B.	Value of Building	= ₹ 10,00,000
C.	Net return	
	Land	= 2,37,600 × 4/100 = ₹ 9,504
	Building	= 10,00,000 × 6/100 = ₹ 60,00,000
	Total Net Return/Year	= ₹ 69,504
	Monthly net rent 69,504/12	= ₹ 5,792
D.	Gross Return	= ₹ 69,504
	Net return	= ₹ 40,000
	Gross Return/Year	= ₹ 1,09,504
	Monthly Gross Rent	= ₹ 9,125

Problem 20. *In a plot of 25 × 30 m, a building of four flats has been constructed for a cost of ₹ 20,00,000. The unit rate of land is ₹ 810 / sq m. The value of sanitary, water supply and other services is ₹ 5,00,000. The owner expects 9% as rate of return. Calculate the standard rent of each flat assuming.*

(*i*) The life of the building as 60 years and sinking fund will be created on 45 interest.

(*ii*) Annual repairs cost at 1% of the cost of construction.

(*iii*) Other outgoings including taxes at 30% of the net return.

A.	Land:	
	Extent of land 25 × 30	= 750 sq m
	Unit rate of land	= ₹ 810/sq m
	Value of land 750 × 810	= ₹ 6,07,500

B. Building:

Value of Building alone	=	₹ 20,00,000
Value of services	=	₹ 5,00,000
Total value of building	=	₹ 25,00,000

C. Capital cost:

Land	=	₹ 6,07,500
Building	=	₹ 25,00,000
Capital cost	=	₹ 31,07,500

D. Net Return:

Capital cost	=	₹ 31,07,500
Rate of return	=	9%
Rate of return	=	31,07,500 × 9/100
Net Return (Rent)	=	₹ 2,79,675

E. Outgoes:

(*i*)	Annual Repairs 1% of 25,00,000	=	₹ 25,000
(*ii*)	Outgoings including taxes 30% of 2,79,675	=	₹ 83,903
(*iii*)	Sinking fund	=	₹ 10,505

$S = 25,00,000$

$I = 4\%$

$N = 60$

$L = Si(1 - I)^n - 1$

(*iv*)	Total outgoes	=	₹ 1,19,408

F. Gross Rent:

Gross Rent	=	Net Rent + Outgoes
Net Rent	=	₹ 2,79,675
Outgoes	=	₹ 1,19,408
Gross Rent	=	₹ 3,99,083
Standard Rent/Month–4 flats	=	3,99,083/12 = ₹ 33,257
Standard Rent/each flat	=	₹ 33,257/4 = ₹ 8,314

4 Years Purchase

4.1. INTRODUCTION

Years purchase is a very important term used in valuation of properties. Without knowing years purchase *i.e.* *YP* it is difficult to assess value of any asset in general and rental method in particular. Though this method is used mainly for rental method, however other methods also need it. Therefore before various methods are dealt, it is essential to understand years purchase, its concepts and use. Therefore *YP* has been dealt in detail in subsequent articles.

4.2. YEARS PURCHASE

It is a multiplier factor multiplied to net annual income from a property to get capitalised value of the income. This capitalised value is also called value of that property. For a certain free hold property if net rent is ₹ 1800/- per year and if 5 percent is regarded a reasonable return on capital invested in it, the estimated value of perpetual property will be 1800 × 100/*i* = 1800 × 100/5 = ₹ 36000 (Thirty six thousand only). This 100/*i* *i.e.* 20 is called as years purchase for perpetual property. This multiplier is known as the present value of ₹ 1.00 per annum invested with specified rate of interest for specified period.

When the income form the property is perpetual, the appropriate *Y.P.* can be found simply by dividing 100 by the prevailing rate of interest *i.e.* reasonable return on capital invested *i.e.* *YP* = 100/interest rate = 100/-, hence in above case *YP* = 20. But where the income is receivable for a limited period only, the finding of the appropriate figure of *Y.P.* involves use of valuation tables or relevant mathematical for mule. The reason being in such of cases, investor has to set aside a portion of his income in the form of sinking fund to recover the cost after expiry of useful life of property. If no such provision is made, the investor looses both the capital and income at the end of useful life period *Y.P.* is some what reduced in such cases.

Therefore for $Y.P. = \dfrac{100}{i + S}$

where i is rate of interest or also called as rate of return expected on investment and

S is sinking fund *i.e.* equal annual year and payment to replace ₹ 100 at the end of given period.

$$S = \frac{i}{(1+i)^n - 1}$$

Where n is useful life of that of asset. This formula of *Y.P.* is based on sinking fund having been invested at the same rate of interest as return expected on investment. This formula is applicable when the amount of sinking fund is invested in the same enterprise or at elsewhere, where the interest received is equal to return expected on investment. Such sinking funds accumulate at lower rate of interest. If sinking fund is invested at other rate of interest then,

$$Y.P. = \frac{100}{i + S_1} \text{ where } S_1 = \frac{t_1}{(1 + i_1)^n - 1}$$

This is called dual rate of interest.

This particular *Y.P.* is calculated using dual rate of interest and generally used when the sinking fund is invested at other place and not in the same enterprise, hence rate of interest will be different in general. These two interests can also be same. This investment can also be made for a different time period n_1, less than n.

In case of properties if leased the *Y.P.* is calculated taking into consideration lessees interest *Y.P.* in case of leased property is

$$Y.P. = \frac{1}{i + S} \text{ where } S = \frac{t}{(1 + i)^n - 1}$$

if property is perpetual *i.e.* having n = 999 years or infinite.

$$S = 0 \quad \therefore \quad Y.P. = \frac{1}{i}$$

If property is given on lease for a period of n_1 years then

$$Y.P. = \frac{1}{i + S_1} \text{ where } S_1 = \frac{i}{(1 + i)^{n_1} - 1}$$

If property is given on lease for infinite period then also S_1 = 100 *i.e.* when a lease is given for infinite time, it can be treated as good as freehold property and *Y.P.* can be calculated by using formula *Y.P.* = 100% therefore infinite period of lease.

Y.P. for lessee = Y.P. lessor = Y.P.

Year purchase for free hold and lease hold Properties

Properties. **In case of infinite period of lease, a property holder enjoys right of the property for indefinite time; it means he enjoys that property of his own of perpetual natural and *Y.P.* is therefore calculated as explained above. However in case of property is leased for a short duration *i.e.* 30 years or 50; both the lessee and the lessor have their own interest in that asset and therefore the value of property for both these persons will be different depending upon their interest and period, these two parties can enjoy it. This has been dealt in detail in article of valuation of lease held properties *Y.P.* for properties having limited useful life (*i.e.* not perpetual one) (Single rate).**

This is the present value of a series of ₹ 1 payable at the end of each year in future for n years at i rate of compound interest. This is also denoted in general by the expression *Y.P.*

The present worth of ₹ 1/- to be paid in n years from now of rate of return is t percent is called present value of ₹ 1/- it is remembered that a rupee to day is worth more than at a future date, it is obvious that this value is always less than 1. This present value also called as single payment present worth factor and is equal to = $1/(1 + i)^n$.

$$\therefore \quad PV = \frac{1}{(1 + i)^n}$$

Now we have to sum this for n years

$$\therefore \quad YP = \frac{1}{(1 + i)^1} + \frac{1}{(1 + i)^2} + \frac{1}{(1 + i)^3} - \frac{1}{(1 + i)^{n-1}} + \frac{1}{(1 + i)^n}$$

this is a geometric progression and the sum of this series.

$$YP = \frac{\dfrac{1}{(1+i)}\left\{\dfrac{1}{(1+i)^n} - 1\right\}}{\dfrac{1}{(1+i)^{-n}}} = \frac{\dfrac{1}{(1+i)}\left\{\dfrac{1-(1+t)^n}{(1+i)^n}\right\}}{\dfrac{1-(1+i)}{(1+i)^{-1}}}$$

$$= \frac{1-(1+i)^n - 1}{(1+i)^n} = \frac{1}{t} - \frac{1}{(1+i)^n} = \frac{1}{t}\left\{1 - \frac{1}{(1+i)^n}\right\}$$

$$\therefore \quad YP = \frac{1}{i}\{1-(PV)\}$$

This is applicable for properties not in perpetual, having limited life and in which no provision has been made for sinking fund separately.

Ex-years purchase for 5 years @ 10%

$$= \frac{1}{i}\left\{1 - \frac{1}{(1+i)^n}\right\} = \frac{1}{0.1}\left\{1 - \frac{1}{(1+0.1)^5}\right\} = \frac{1-0.6209}{0.1} = 3.7908$$

This means that if ₹ 3.7908 was deposited in a bank or elsewhere today the investor would be entitled to receive ₹ 1/- per annum for 5 years @ 10% interest compounded.

The income ₹ 1 per annum serves two purposes:

(*a*) it provides interest at 10 percent on the sum outstanding

(*b*) it provides sinking fund to replace ₹ 3.79.

Thus over 5 years the investor receives a return on the capital and also a return of the capital.

***YP* with sinking fund it's is sinking fund then**

$$S = \frac{i}{(1+i)^{n-1}} \text{ as explained earliest}$$

$$\therefore \quad Y = (1+i)^n - 1 = \frac{i}{s} \text{ or } (1+i)^n = \frac{i}{s} + 1 \frac{i+s}{s}$$

$$\therefore \quad YP = \frac{1}{i}\left\{1 - \frac{i}{(1+i)^n}\right\} \text{ but } = (1+i)^n = \frac{t+s}{s}$$

$$\therefore \quad YP = \frac{1}{i}\left\{i \frac{1}{\dfrac{i+s}{s}}\right\} = \frac{1}{t}\left\{1 - \frac{s}{i+s}\right\} = \frac{1}{t}\left\{\frac{i+s-s}{i+s}\right\} = \frac{1}{i+s}$$

This *YP* represent the value to day of the right to receive ₹ 1 per annum at the end of each year for a given number of years.

Example. *Find a value of a building premise, earning a net rent of ₹ 5000 / - per annum. Other conditions are as given below:*

(1) *Property is receivable and simple rate of interest is assumed.*

(2) *Property is perpetual and net yield expected is 6 percent.*

(3) *Property is receivable with dual interest on property being 6 percent and sinking fund 3%.*

(4) *Life of Building can be presumed as 50 years.*

Solution.

(1) In this case $Y.P. = 100/6 = 16.66$

Value of premise = 5000 × 16.66 = ₹ 83333/-

(2) This is a case of single interest rate.

$$S = \frac{0.06}{(1+0.06)^{50} - 1} = 0.003446$$

$$Y.P. = \frac{100}{6+0.3446} = 15.76$$

Value of property = 15.76 × 5000 = ₹ 78815

(3) In third case dual rate of interest are given

$$S = \frac{0.03}{(1+0.03)^{50} - 1} = 0.0089$$

$$Y.P. = \frac{100}{6} + .89 = 14.51$$

Value of property = 14.51 × 5000 = ₹ 72569/- **Ans.**

This shows that in dual rate of interest value of property is less compared to single rate of interest. The reason being; at a lower rate of sinking fund; bigger sum have to be set aside annually.

To calculate *Y.P.* depending upon security and type of premise return expected is based on rate of interest. The different rates considered are given below:

	Particular	*Rate of Interest*
(1)	Ground rent *i.e.* rent of bare land; no Building constructed on it for well-secured land	5 to 6 percent of land cost
	Unsecured rent	6 to 7 percent of land cost
(2)	Residential Houses Permanent building	
	1st class	6 to 7 percent of building and land
	2nd class const.	7 to 8 percent of building and land
	Semi permanent (average)	7 to 8% of Building and land cost.
	Temporary residential building	9 to 10% of cost
	Flats	8 to 11%
(3)	Commercial Buildings; Shops and Business Premises.	7 to 9%
(4)	Godowns and Warehouses	7 to 9%
(5)	Industrial Premises	8 to 11%

These interest rates are given for free hold property being more secured; for lease hold property where rate is more; security is less, higher rate of interest is considered. In practice 1% higher rate is provided.

Freehold Property. The term free hold implies to a property which the owner holds absolutely in his possession. Physically or the receiver rent arising from it from leaser and tercancies which have been created out of the free hold interest. It is the highest form of ownership having full security hence possess more value. The owner of property also called as freeholder of the property, can do whatever he likes of it. He has right to rent it; sell it, or develop it. He can further leave it to other also. In short he is at full liberty to do according to his choice of course as per the rules. Only government; in the interest of public can force free holder to either to sell to govt. or govt. can get its possession. The free holders of property while doing some sort of construction or alteration has no repute to interfere with the rights of others.

Leasehold Property. The term implies to a property, which is held in lease for a specific term of years; subject to payment of an annual rent and to the observance of convenants contained in the lease. A free holder can grant lease of his property to some other for certain period with certain specified conditions. The free holder or the person who grants the lease is called 'Lessor' and a person who takes it as Lessee or leaseholder.

A property is generally leased for a period of 30 years or 99 years as the case may be, the residential buildings are leased for short period also. The main forms of leases as (1) Building lease (2) Occupation leases.

In case of building lease a land is leased by owner to lessee and lessee construct building and uses it for a specified period of lease. Once lease period expires; the property *i.e.* Building and land is reverted back to the owner. Ground rent is only paid by lessee. This lease is generally for a period of 99 years to 999 years; 99 years being more common. In occupation lease building constructed by owner and land is leased with a specified amount for a specified period. The lease period are generally 3 to 21 years depending upon type of building. For residential building periods is less while for commercial building it is more up to 30 years also.

Outgoing. To maintain the annual income from a property, some expenses are required to be made. There expenses in cured to maintain the property are called outgoings. These outgoings when reduced from gross-rent gives net rent. Principal outgoings considered for land and building are as given below. There are also called as deductions.

(*a*) **Taxes.** An owner of property has to pay taxes such as Municipal taxes, water taxes, income tax. Property tax etc. These various form 15 to 20 percent of gross rent. This is the major amount an owner has to spend.

(*b*) **Insurance.** As per act each and every property in possession should be insured, it becomes essential when a loan is fetched against that property, or bank guarantee, or security is required against payment. A premium paid for insurance is considered as an investment on the property. Provision of $\frac{1}{2}$ to 1 percent of gross rent is required to be made for premium of insurance.

(*c*) **Sinking Fund.** A portion of yearly yield or income is set a side for reinstatement of capital after its useful life is over, it is also considered as an outgoing. It is essential in property if not perpetual like equipments, machinery's etc.

(*d*) **Collection Charges.** In case of big premises it is not possible to owner having other good business; to collect rent by himself. He appoints some persons to collect it further this person appointed is paid from rent, hence considered as expenditure. About 2 to 4% of gross rent is considered as collection and management charges.

(*e*) **Vacancies and Bed Depth.** It is experienced that some of the persons have tendency not to pay and a part premise many times remain vacant hence earning nothing out of it. A provision for such term is also required to be made. It has been experienced that 1 to 2% of gross rent is always lost either due vacant premise or due to bed depth. In case of Hostels, the possibility of vacancies cannot be avoided.

(*f*) **Repairs and Maintenance.** A property is to be kept in good condition needs, proper maintenance and annual repairs like whitewash, colourwash etc.; annually. Generally 1 to 4% of construction cost or 10 to 12% of gross rent is provided for repair and maintenance of premise.

All these deductions of expenses made on property are called outgoing. Gross rent minus outgoing is called net return of premise.

Net rent = Gross rent – Deductions

i.e. Net rent = Gross rent – Outgoings.

Example. *A man has purchased a leasehold properly for ₹ 150000/- which produces a net income of ₹ 15000/- per annual. The lease has 30 years to run. What sum should be placed annually in a sinking fund which will accumulate at 3% compound interest so that he redeems his purchase money at the termination of his lease. What rate of interest did the purchaser of the property obtain for his capital?*

Sol. (*i*) A net income of ₹ 15000/- per annum for 30 years—a terminate income for 30 years after which reversion

$$\therefore \quad S \text{ is sinking fund} = \frac{i}{(1+i)^n - 1}$$

where $i_1 = 3\%$ $n = 30$ years

$$S = \frac{0.03}{(1+0.03)^{30} - 1} = 0.02102$$

(Amount to be deposited to redeem ₹ l)

∴ Annual sinking fund to redeem ₹ 150000/- after 30 years = 0.02102 × 150000

= ₹ 3180/- **Ans.**

(*ii*) $Y.P.$ of property sold $= \dfrac{150000}{15000} = 10$

If i is rate of interest for dual rate of interest $Y.P. = \dfrac{1}{i+S}$

$$\therefore \quad 10 = 1 - \frac{1}{i + 0.02102}$$

$$\therefore \quad i = \frac{1}{10} + 0.2102 = 0.0997898 = 9.97898\% \textbf{ Ans.}$$

Question. *Years purchase for flats is less. Why?*

Answer. The reason is that, flats have a higher rate of interest, moreover land is not owned by single person. It is a property of all apartment owners. As such it is less secured in comparison to individual house. As *Y.P.* is inversely proportion to that of return expected; it is less.

5

Methods of Valuation

5.1. GENERAL

As explained earlier, valuation is defined as present monetary value of real premises or real estate. The word 'Real' is very important. Valuation of any asset not in existence has got no meaning. The method of valuation for different type of properties or assets differs.

5.2. METHODS OF VALUATION

The methods available to evaluate any property are as given below:

(1) Valuation from life *i.e.* present book value, generally used for construction equipment (A method of Depreciation).

(2) Rental method of valuation generally applied to flats, bungalows.

(3) Land and building method also called as income capitalization method.

(4) Evidence method based on comparison tendencies also called as comparable sales method.

(5) Reproduction cost method.

(6) Global valuation method.

(7) Break up value method.

A valuer prior to valuing any property must examine and collect following details about it:

(1) Location of property with reference to road width, its frontage etc.

(2) Shape and size of property.

(3) Whether owned by singly or co-owner property particularly the plot.

(4) Whether lease hold or free hold.

(5) Restrictions of local byelaws for or leasehold converted into free hold construction thereon if any.

(6) Permissible maximum construction thereon.

(7) Whether Commercial, Residential or Industrial.

(8) Restriction of sale or lease deed if any.

(9) Land rates fixed by authorities like district magistrate or corporation etc.

(10) Sale transactions for that particular type of land during the years to arrive to some realistic value.

(11) Whether the land falls in contonment area or not and as such old grant/or lease hold for number of year. It can be achieved by Search-Report.

(12) Whether earlier registered documents contain provision for grant of sale permissible prior to sale.

(13) Whether any easement right exists.

(14) Probable future development of that locality under consideration.

(15) Any other information if available regarding land such as filled up land, water logged land etc.; regarding building; its year of construction, its life as on today and future expected life by judgement depending upon its maintenance etc.

(16) Whether all the taxes are paid till the date of valuation.

(1) **Valuation from Life.** This method is generally used for equipments but also used for buildings in general. In this method depreciated value of asset is calculated assuming that the cost of building consists of both building and land as used in case of flats. For example if a flat was purchased about 10 years back and if the same flat is available as on today with certain rate per square meter with similar specifications, than the cost of flat is calculated assuming as constructed recently only. The value of flat is then calculated depreciating this cost for 10 years with appropriate method of depreciation. This cost is called as present value of that flat under consideration.

Q.1. *Find present value of a flat 15 years old but is in good condition. Present rate of sale of similar flat in that locality is ₹ 10000/- per square meter, and build up area of flat is 95 square meter.*

Sol. The present value of similar flat is ₹ 100000 × 95 = ₹ 9.5 Lacs

The flat is 15 years old and building is maintained in good condition. Assuming a total life of building as 70 years

$$\text{Percent Depreciation in 15 years} = \frac{15}{70} \times 100 = 21.43\%$$

$$\text{Therefore present value of flat} = 9500000 - 0.2143 \times 950000$$

$$= ₹\ 7.46 \text{ Lacs} \quad \textbf{Ans.}$$

Q.2. *A person has purchased a flat for ₹ 10 lacs. The expected life of flat is 40 years. What amount he should set aside at a rate of interest of 8 percent to receive his expenditure to get new flat purchased after expiry of useful life of flat.*

Sol. $$R = S\left\{\frac{i}{(1+i)^n - 1}\right\} \quad \text{Assuming salvage value = zero}$$

$$R = 1000000\left\{\frac{0.08}{(1+0.08)^{40} - 1}\right\} = ₹\ 3860/\text{- per year} \quad \textbf{Ans.}$$

Q.3. *In Q.2, if he presumes that after 40 years ₹ 10 lacs will not be sufficient to purchase similar flat. As such he wants to put a fund set aside for 20 years and accumulates this as fixed deposit for next 20 years. He expects a rate of return of 8 percent in both the cases and wants to have an amount of ₹ 25 lacs after 40 years. What amount he should keep aside for first 20 years.*

Sol.

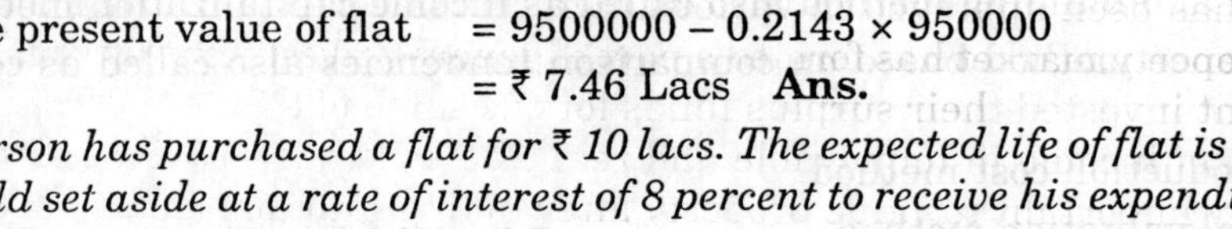

$$P_1 = \frac{2500000}{(1+i)^n} = \frac{2500000}{(1+0.08)^{20}} = ₹\ 5.36 \text{ lacs}$$

This amount is required to be deposited in the form of sinking fund.

$$\therefore \quad R = P \times \frac{i}{(1+i)^n - 1}$$

$$= 536000 \times \frac{0.08}{(1+0.08)^{20} - 1} = ₹\ 11713/- \quad \textbf{Ans.}$$

(2) **Rental Method of Valuation.** This method is used for big premises like flats, hotels, and hostels, offices from which income can be produced or likely to be produced from the property. These methods consists of ascertaining net rent per annum from the asset and multiplying this to years purchase. Hence procedure consists of:

(*a*) To find out gross rent likely to be received from the asset.

(*b*) To find out goings *i.e.* deduction: These are expenses incurred on the asset in the form of taxes, insurance etc., as explained in subsequent paragraph.

(*c*) To find net rent *i.e.* gross rent minus outgoing.

(*d*) To decide present value of Rupees one per annum received in perpetuity *i.e. Y.P.* bases on required rate of interest. This depends on type of asset and other condition. The different rate applicable for various properties has been given in article of years purchase.

(*e*) To assess values of property by multiply net income per annum to *Y.P.*

This method has been further illustrated by a few examples. This method is also called as capitalised income method of valuation.

This method of valuation, is one of the most important methods to evaluate the market price and has been approved in various high courts decision. During the last more than one decade, property market has formed a part of general investment market and people have to a great extent invested their surplus funds for the same of their safely and good return and for realization of income in immovable and real estate. It has therefore, becomes very essential and equally important to value property after taking into consideration, the income approach and hence the importance of the method. There are very clear principles of valuation where buildings are in possession of tenants and they cannot be evicted or the rent payable by them enhanced in accordance with the provision of rent control Act, the only appropriate method of valuation is to capitalise the annual rental by certain number of years purchase.

In this method land and building constitute one unit and the value of entire unit is determined it means, it is assumed that full FSI/FAR has been utilised.

Q.1. *A piece of land measuring 5 acres is let for ₹ 75/- per acre per month on a 99 years lease. The lessee has built a permanent building on the site. What is the value of the owner's interest (An interest rate of 6% can be assumed for calculation purposes and all the taxes etc. to be borne by the lessee).*

Sol. Given the rent ₹ 75/- per month/Are as Net rent:

Total rent per annum = 75 × 5 × 12 = ₹ 4500/- per annum

Years purchase for leasehold, as per table can be calculated.

Considering rate of interest as 6% for period of 99 years = 100/6 = 16.6

Value of the property = 4500 × 16.6 = ₹ 74750/- **Ans.**

Q.2. *5 Areas of land is let on lease for 99 years for ₹ 5/- per acre per month. The lessee has constructed temporary dwellings on the land. The lessee is liable for tenant's taxes on the land and the owner's taxes can be taken as 9%.*

Sol. Here land has been given on lease, a temporary dwelling has been built up and hence land cannot be considered fully secured. Anyhow considering fully secured land, a rate of interest 6% has been assumed.

Y.P. as per 6% rate for 99 years for leased hold case = 16.6

Value of property = 273 × 16.6 = ₹ 4525/- **Ans.**

Q.3. *Make computations for the value of a premises consisting of an office block let for ₹ 400/- per month inclusive of all taxes and electric charges up to ₹ 50/- per month. The office block was constructed only few months back and is in very good condition. The rent is fair as compared to other buildings in the locality.*

Sol. Gross rent of premises = ₹ 400.

Deduction:

(*i*) Taxes @ 15% ₹ 60/- p.m.

(*ii*) Insurance Charges ₹ 8/- p.m.

(*iii*) Collection Charges @ 2% ₹ 8/- p.m.

(*iv*) Vacancies and bed debts @ 2% ₹ 8/- p.m.

(*v*) Repairs and Maintenance @ 3% ₹ 12/- p.m.

(*vi*) Electric charges Given ₹ 50/- p.m.

Total deduction = ₹ 146/- per month

Net rent = 400 – 146 = 254/- per month

₹ 254 × 12 per annum = ₹ 3048/- per annum

Office Block has been constructed just a few months back and hence a rate of interest 7% shall be considered.

Y.P. considering free hold interest for @ 7% = 100/7

$$\text{Value of property} = \frac{₹\ 3048 \times 100}{7} = ₹\ 43540/-\quad \textbf{Ans.}$$

Q.4. *A plot of land measuring 4 acres is let (for 99 years lease) on a ground rent which is four times secured since the lessee has constructed a permanent residential building over it and is in very good condition. The fair rent (Rack rent) for this type of premises is ₹ 12000/- per annum. Compute the value of the landowner's interest:*

(a) When owners share of taxes is 10%.

(b) When all the taxes are borne by the lessee.

Sol. The fair rent Rack rent *i.e.* rate of land + Building on it = ₹ 12000/- per annum.

We know that:

$$\frac{\text{Rack rent}}{\text{Ground rent}} = x, \text{ where '}x\text{' is said to be number by which Ground rent is secured.}$$

In given problem ground rent is secured 4 times *i.e.* $x = 4$

Ground rent = 12000/4 = ₹ 3000/- per annum.

(*a*) Owner's share of taxes is 10%. It is assumed that this 10% is inclusive of all taxes, Insurance etc.

$$\text{Net rent} = 3000 - \frac{3000 \times 10}{100} = ₹\ 2700/-$$

Y.P. from charts for lease hold interest of 5% as property is secured one – 100/5 = 20

Value of land = 2700 × 20 = ₹ 54000/-

(*b*) If all taxes are borne by lessee than

Value of property = 3000 × 20 = ₹ 60000/-

Q.5. *A premises (ware house) is let on ₹ 1200/- per month inclusive of all taxes and is in very good condition. However the fair rent is ₹ 1600/- per month in the locality. How much Govt. should pay to the owner for acquiring the premises.*

Sol. The premise was let for ₹ 1200/- per month whilst fair rent is ₹ 1600/- per month, inclusive of all taxes.

Deduction :

Taxes @ 15%
Insurance @ 2%
Collection charges @ 2%
Vacancies and debts @ 2%
Repairs and Maintenance @ 4%
Total = 25%

Net rent considering 1200/- per as to rent

$$= 1200 - \frac{25 \times 1200}{900} = 1200 - 300 = ₹\ 900/-$$

Considering ₹ 1600/- p.m. as the rent.

Net rent = 1600 = 16 × 25 = 1600 – 400 = ₹ 1200/-

For warehouse a rate of interest = 7% is assumed

Y.P. for free hold interest = 100/7

Value of premises for Net Rent 900/- per month = 900 × 12 × 100/7 = ₹ 1,54,300/-

and Value of premises for Net Rent 900/- per month = 1200 × 12 × 100/7 = ₹ 2,05,500/-

As at present the premise has been let on lower rent, after certain years no owner would like to pay very much excess money of ₹ 205500/- compared to old rent *i.e.* lower rent. No one would like to purchase the premise at higher price or value.

Hence a fair deal will be an average or in between two and hence considering this fact a fair deal will for ₹ 175000/-.

Fair value of premises = ₹ 175000/- **Ans.**

Short Comings of This Method. With today's contract conditions there is always scope of doubts and drawback in this particular method of valuation, particularly to the owner. These are:

(1) The owner always has a fear that ultimately the tenants may become owner under the prevailing political situations and in force of fact progressive legislation.

(2) He always possesses a risk of damage of his assets and as such no security of capital.

(3) No certainty of realisation of rental income in view of large scale day to day litigation.

(4) Liquidity of investment is not possible to be created in short period and at low last.

(5) Rising of loans against house property is quite cumbersome and involves many complications like compulsory registration of mortgage deed etc.

(6) The investment in house property requires efficient management, which is expensive and also not easily available.

(7) Life of building is also not assured due to degenerating quality of materials like cement etc.

(8) Problem of local, state and central taxes.

(9) Liquidation of capital and collection of sinking fund.

(3) **Land and Building Method of Valuation.** In this method the valuation of land and part building constructed over it are made separately and the value of that asset is made by adding them. If building does not exist then only land is evaluated.

"A track of land is defined geographically as a specific area of the earth's surface, its characteristics embrace all reasonable stable on vertically above and below. This area including those of the atmosphere, the soil and underlying geology, the hydrology, the plant and animal population and the results of the post and present human activity". The land being a scarce resource is limited. It cannot be produced. It therefore differs in its value from most of other assets. Value of land depends upon the use to which it is put and also the intensity of development.

Evidently a derivation of the land rate by comparison with actual sale instances is the best method. For arriving to an appropriate value, knowledge of factors in founding the land rate and the extent to which each of these factors affects the land rate are essential. It is easy to understand the contribution of various factors at different stages in development in general and that of urban development in particular if we follow the growth of development of town or village and analyse the sale instances over a long period.

The principles to be follow for valuation of land some enumerated principles by experience and learned values are:

(1) Recent sale instance of land in the neighbourhood.

(2) Income yielding capacity and state of the money market.

(3) Value depends on supply and demand.

(4) Land value generally appreciates with time but in rare occasion, it decreases due to serious sustaining social turmoil like ware earthquake, water logging etc.

(5) Land value is based on the most advantageous way in which the land can be put to use by a prudent prospective buyer to realise the full potential of the land.

(6) Land, which may probably be used for building purposes, must not be valued as agricultural land.

(7) In case of leasehold land, all restrictions imposed by the landlord on the use of the land are to be taken into account.

(8) Market price is not a conclusive test of real value in all the cases. Future market value is dependent on the perception of the prudent prospective buyer and is different from the actual sellers price or buyer's price.

The factors that affect the value of an asset in valuation by land and building method are explained below:

(1) Valuation of land is based on its utility. This utility is affected by various factors. These are:

(*a*) **Floor**—space index or floor area ratio.

(*b*) **Shape of land**—rectangular land cost more than other shape.

(*c*) **Frontage/Depth ratio**—A frontage/Depth ratio of 1.2 to 1.8 is preferred for residential building. A land with large depth costs less due to more loss of space for movement.

Similarly more frontages restrict planning of building particularly residential building. More frontages are always desirable at commercial *i.e.* shopping area as more number of shops can have road frontage.

(2) **Situation of property**—A locality based on its use can be classified as:

(A) Residential (B) Commercial (C) Industrial (D) Mixed

This locality based on standard of living is further classified as posh, HIG, MIG, LIG slum etc. The locality based on environmental condition is further classified as highly polluted and none polluted *i.e.* health.

These all factors affect the value of land. In general a property or land located in busy market area always cost more.

(3) Size of plot or land is also one of the factor land cost per unit area of smaller plot is always more, however very small plots have very low cost per unit area. In general more the size of plot more will be cost, however, when land is sold for development of some colony, then it is sold at a rate of per unit Hector and then it cost less.

(4) Restriction on transfer of land such as leasehold and free hold effect land cost.

(5) Land cost is also effected by urban land ceiling act, easement act etc.

(6) Return frontage or End Plots—End plots generally have two sides open; hence costly. Proper light and ventilation can be held in End plots hence cost more.

(7) Vista Land, having a front road hence due to a general front view may cost more.

Recess Land and Recessed. Recess land is that portion of a land, which has no frontage, obviously value of such recessed land is less than the land, which has a frontage. If the depth of recessed land is more than one and half times the width of the belt in which it lies; it is called Recessed-Recess land. In general the cost of recess land is taken as three-forth of normal land having frontage and that of recessed recess land is taken as one-half of normal land. This is shown in Fig. 5.1.

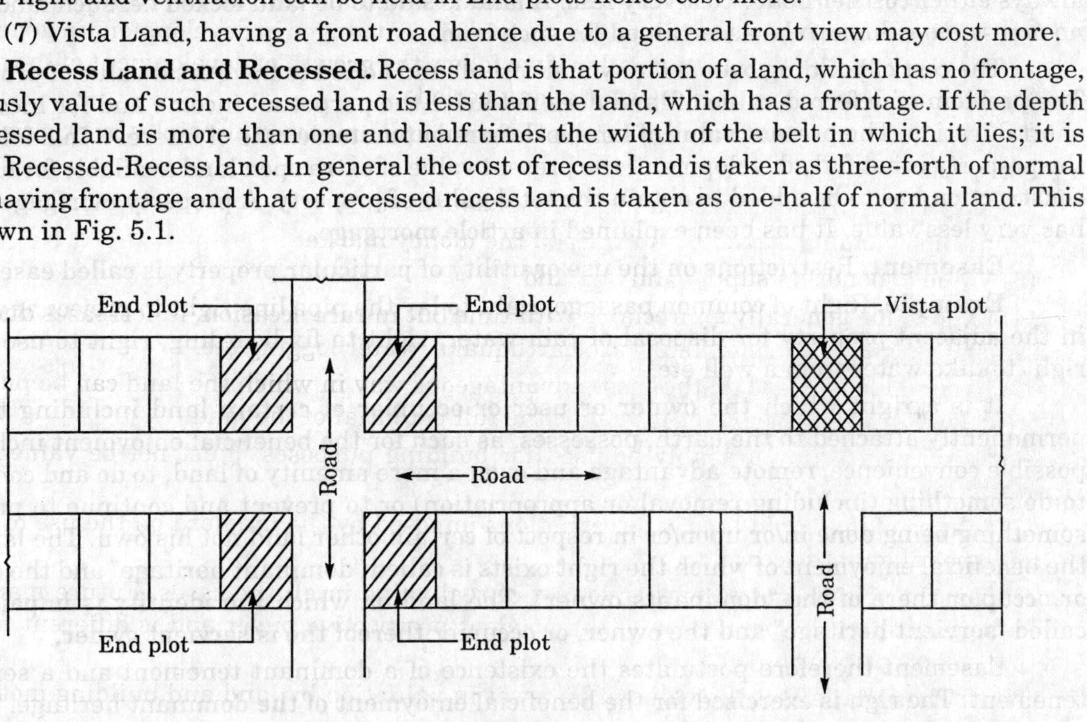

Fig. 5.1

As shown in Fig. 5.2 A plot *ABCDEFGH* has part *CDEF* has a frontage of *FE*, whilst land *ABCFGH* has no frontage. Further length *AC* is more than 1.5 times the width of recessed land *i.e. AH*. Hence portion *BCEG* is called as recessed land and portion *ABGH* is called as recessed-recess land having value comparably very less. The cost of such land further depends on its length *AD*, more the length *AC* less will be value of the land.

A land is said to be "Land Locked", where there is no access available from any road. No value of such land can be ascertained.

Along with these, there are many factors such as social; cultural, religious etc., which also affect value of a property. Colonies developed for one particular class of community either cost less or very large. Buster land is one, which landed for huts or for temporary buildings. To evacuate such building is difficult and because these are rented on a very small rent are

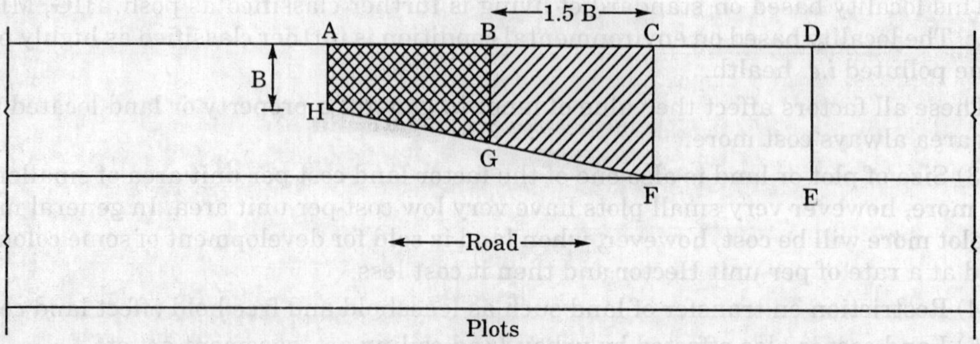

Fig. 5.2

always either costlier hence cost very less. A land is said to be land locked *i.e.* such land have no access; no value can be ascertained for such land.

The cost of building over it if any and cost of land added to have total value of property. The problem of deferred value of land does not arise the perpetual income and for income of short duration. The present value of land is deferred at suitable rate of interest. In addition if the property is not fully development; the present value of extra open land available for further construction has to be added to obtain the total value of property. A property mortgaged also has very less value. It has been explained in article mortgage.

Easement. Restrictions on the use or utility of particular property is called easement.

Example. Right of common passage, right to lay the pipe line right to project anything in the adjacent property for disposal of rain water, right to fix boarding, right to use toilet right to take water from a well etc.

It is a right which the owner or user or occupier of certain land including things permanently attached to the earth, possesses, as such for the beneficial enjoyment including possible convenience, remote advantage and even a mere amenity of land, to do and continue to do something (including removal or appropriation) or to prevent and continue to prevent something being done in/or upon/or in respect of certain other land not his own. The land for the beneficial enjoyment of which the right exists is called "dominant heritage" and the owner or occupier there of the "dominants owner". The land on which the identity is impaired is called "servient heritage" and the owner, or occupier thereof the is servient owner.

Easement therefore postulates the existence of a dominant tenement and a servient tenement. The righ is exercised for the beneficial enjoyment of the dominant heritage. These are not purely personal rights. There can be no easement between landlord and tenant. The Indian Easement Act, 1982; defining all these is called Indian easement act and is applicable to a few States.

A right to carry carts over a road passage does not divide dominant servient Tenements. Hence every resident on the road can be turn be both a dominant and a servient tenement.

Reassessment right however always affect the value of property, it decreases in general valuer therefore must have thorough knowledge of easement Act preferably of state referred to.

A few examples are hereby illustrated to explain this method in details.

Belting method of Valuation of Land. This method of valuation is often used for valuation of land by comparing the value of adjoining plots. Example illustrates this also.

Q. 1. *Valuate the land shown in Fig. 5.3. With the following data : land to a depth of 30 m in the area is valued at ₹ 50/- per m² and second belt value is three fourth of first belt value.*

Recess. Land if any can be valued at 3/4th of the belt value.

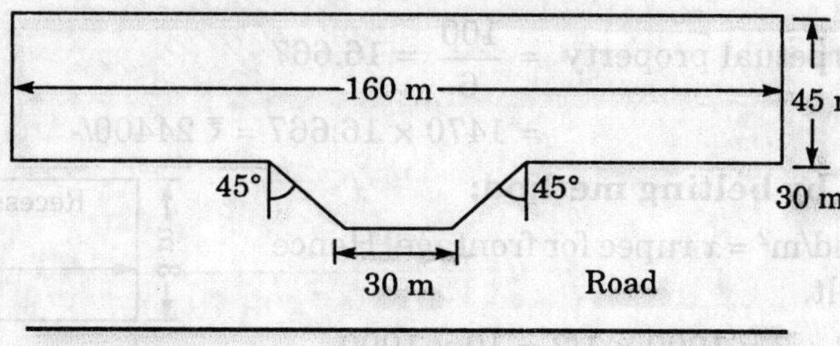

Fig. 5.3

Sol. The existing plot and their effective areas are shown below.

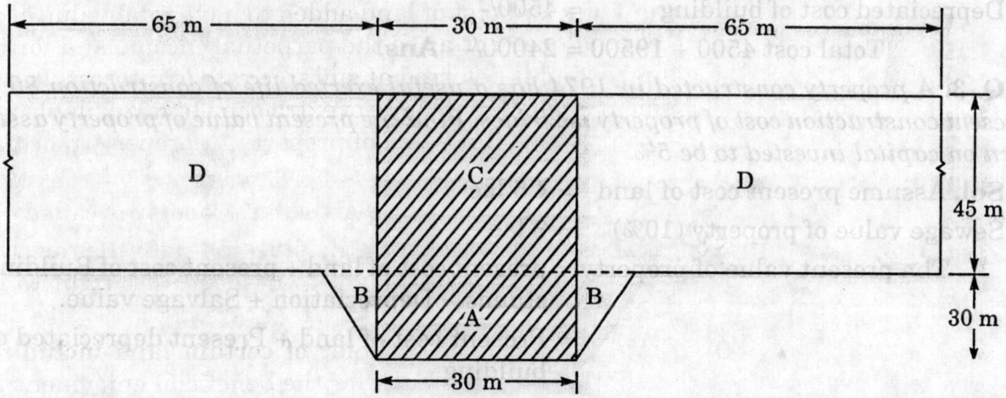

Fig. 5.4

A is frontage land *B* is recess land; *C* is second belt and *D* is recessed land of 2nd belt.

∴ Effective area of $A = 30 \times 30 = 900 \text{ m}^2$

$$B = \frac{30 \times 30}{2} \times 2 \times \frac{3}{4} = 675 \text{ m}^2$$

$$C = 30 \times 45 \times \frac{3}{4} = 1012.5 \text{ m}^2$$

$$D = 65 \times 45 \frac{3}{4} \times \frac{3}{4} \times 2 = 3290.6 \text{ m}^2$$

∴ Total effective area 5878.1 sq m

∴ Value of land = 5878.1 × 50 = ₹ 293905/- **Ans.**

Q. 2. *What is the value of a property constructed over a plot of land 3m frontage by 3 m deep having a shop erected there on and let for ₹ 175 inclusive of taxes per month. The depreciated value of the building is ₹ 4500, land in the vicinity to a depth of 10 m is worth ₹ 1000/- per m² value of recess land if any can be taken as 1/2 of belt value.*

Method 1. Rental Method of Valuation:

The gross rent/year of shop = 175 × 12 = ₹ 2100/- per year

If outgoing 30%

So net rent $= ₹\left(2100 - \dfrac{2100 \times 30}{100}\right) = ₹\ 1470$

Y.P. @ 6% for perpetual property $= \dfrac{100}{6} = 16.667$

Value of shop $= 1470 \times 16.667 = ₹\ 24400/-$

Method 2. Cost by belting method:

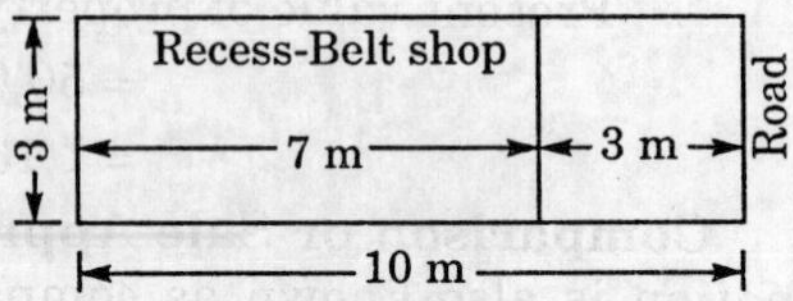

Fig. 5.5

Let the cost of land/m^2 = x rupee for frontage. Hence to find cost of recess belt.

$$X \times 3 + 7 \times 1000 \times 1/2 = 10 \times 1000$$

$$X = 2166.17 \text{ m}^2$$

$$\text{Value of plot} = 6500/3 \times 3 \times 3 = 19500/-$$

Depreciated cost of building = 4500/-

Total cost 4500 + 19500 = 24000/- **Ans.**

Q. 3. *A property constructed in 1974 has a useful exerted life of construction 80 years. The present construction cost of property is 20 lacs. Find the present value of property assuming a return on capital invested to be 5%.*

Sol. Assume present cost of land = ₹ 5 lac

Sewage value of property (10%) = 2 lac

The present value of property = present cost of land + present cost of Building as it stands – Depreciation + Salvage value.

= Present cost of land + Present depreciated cost of building

Present cost of land = ₹ 5 (lacs given)

Present salvage value = ₹ 2 lac (assumed 10%)

Present cost of Building = ₹ 20 lac (given)

Depreciation of Property:

(1) R is sinking fund @ 5% per annum then for 80 years

$$R = \frac{i}{(1+i)^n - 1} \times 20{,}000$$

$$R = \frac{0.05}{(1+0.05)^{80} - 1} \times 20{,}000 = 2059.30$$

The today's life of building is 22 years (in 1996).

$\therefore$ Amount receivable including of interest of ₹ 1.00 annum at the rate of 5% interest for 22 years.

$$R = \frac{(1+i)^n - 1}{1} = \frac{(1+0.05)^{22} - 1}{0.05} = 38.50$$

$\therefore$ The value of accumulated elated fund for 22 years. Due to sinking fund deposit.

$= 2059.30 \times 38.50 = ₹\ 79294.00$

The amount ₹ 79294.00 will compound for next 58 years *i.e.* remaining life to building and is equal

$$= (1 + i)^n \times 79394 = (1 + 0.05)^{58} \times 79294 = 13,43444.00$$

This is taken as depreciation of building

∴ Present Value of Building excluding salvage

= 20,00,000 – 13,43,444 = ₹ 6,56,556/-

∴ Present value of property

= 50,00,000 + 20,000,000 – 13,43,444 + 2,00,000

= ₹ 13,56,556 = ₹ 13.60 lac **Ans.**

Comparison or Sale Approach Method. Comparison or sale approach methods of valuation is also known as comparable sale instance method and consist of taking into consideration the process released at the sale of similar property in the locality at about the date of valuation. This method is mostly used for vacant land. The price fixed should have relation to the price paid within reasonable time in bonafied transactions of the land acquired or lands adjacent to the land which possess similar advantages, evidences derived from sales or comparable lands and analysis of such sale instances. An important factor to be taken into consideration is that the evidence of market value from sales must be capable of comparison. The comparison must take into account not only what is to be valued *i.e.* the value to be disregarded and those to be taken into account but also the qualities of the land or buildings and all the intrinsic circumstances.

As such in this method sale of one like has to be compared with the sale of another like. For example if one has sale instance of or lease hold property, it cannot be applied in case of free hold property. Similarly sale instance of a single owned property cannot be made applicable or comparable to a jointly owned property. Another essential requirement in this method is all efforts are essentially required to be made to collect the sale instances as near to the point of time as possible.

Comparison in this method, regarding physical aspect, social aspect and market aspect is necessary. Physical aspect would include size, shape, floor area, built-up area, location, construction and specifications, aesthetic, frontage, function adequacy, expected future life, state of maintenance, surround area, locality of that area, type of people residing in nearby areas and so on social aspect include environment teeters, neighbourhood qualities, anticipated future life of social balance etc. Market aspect would take into account present rent level, future expected rent level, present sale price anticipated future sale price, demand and supply etc.

While doing comparison and applying this method, valuer doing this job must have knowledge of rent control Act, Land control act, properly control act, cost ceiling, state laws, municipal building bye laws, Labour Laws and Regulations Market. Fluctuating interest rates, and various other acts and laws applicable to it. Government Policy and its attitude and the trend of its legislation towards its immovable properties are required to be watched with.

This method is however tricky and requires good experience in its application. This method is based on market approach. This approach consists of the collection of sale amounts or offered prices of comparable properties, their comparison and then to come to a certain appropriate figure as value of that property. However this is a job of expert valuer.

Comparable selling method is the best method for valuing lands *i.e.* price paid within a reasonable time of the relevant date. The comparison in this regard must be in respect of lands, which are:

(*i*) Similar in character to the land in question

(*ii*) Reasonably proximate to that land and

(*iii*) Having similar amenities and advantages and those sales transactions must have taken place on a date, which is proximate to the relevant date.

The sales must also have taken place genuinely in an open market and all speculative transactions must be excluded. The price obtained for small piece of land cannot be adopted for a land having a bigger area.

Evidence Method of Valuation. This method of valuation is based on evidence available and general market condition. It is used mainly for tedious jobs.

Valuation of Business Premises. Valuation of business premieres is rather a tedious job and in values many calculation. Factors allocating are:

(*i*) Nature of interest and what particular business involved.

(*ii*) Property details like plinth area, specification, life, maintenance level, location etc.

(*iii*) Fair rent at which property can be fetched.

The valuation is done by Rental method of valuation or land and building method of valuation. Evidence available are also studies and then real value of property is calculated. It is possible that the value of property may be more or less than actual market value of property. The period decision is taken considering sellers interest, purchaser's interest by proper negotiation.

Development Method Valuation. In this method a developer and promoters are assumed to earn some profit in the form of return on their capital investment. As such in this method are value is as ascertained by adding a marginal profit on cost of construction. In case the construction work is in progress; an estimation of cost is made on future probable date of completion of work and a profit is added to achieve the value of that asset.

The term reproduction cost is used to indicate estimated cost of producing the similar house with same specifications at prevailing rate of construction. However a margin of profit is required to be taken into consideration. Many a times due to natural calamities also a house is required to be constructed; here also the cost involve in construction of similar house is called as reproduction cost. This is called as development method of valuation.

Accounts Method of Valuation. Under this method, the expenditure incurred on construction is actually calculated by summing up the payments under different vouchers made for material, labour, sundries etc. Actually this method is more accurate and more reliable; however one has to be very particular and punctual in maintaining date wise actual accounts along with the bills/vouchers and receipts etc.

Selection of Method. There are various methods of valuation of an asset and each method is used under specific condition. Since most of the valuations are made for financial institution like banks, generally land and building method is used for valuation of properties as owner of property and banks are quite comfortable and can understand this easily.

Rent capitalization method *i.e.* Rental method of valuation is used for those properties which are fully rented is tenanted. The size of such properties is generally large and consist of number of flats or houses rented. In some specific cases like flats/apartments or houses in townships.

Comparable sale method is used to assess fair market value for various purposed including valuation for Banks.

This method is however effective only when comparables are available in market. Profit method is used for properties like hotels, cinema theatres; however in case of bank loans;

there properties are also valued by land and building method as financial bodies are rarely interested in profit earned. Moreover in case of NPA, financial bodies cannot do that business to collect their dues. Residual method of valuation also called as development method of valuation is used for the properties having latent potential for development or for properties whose net value can be increased by capital expenditure as other methods in such cases cannot give fair market value. Base land are used by builders and promoters and do valuation with this method only. Accounts method of valuation is used for book value only and to show assets of a firm in the credited accounts.

Q. 1. *A plot measuring 4 are is let for 99 years lease on a ground rent of ₹ 200/-. The lessees has constructed the building (Shops) and in turns gets a rent of ₹ 1800/- p.m. complete the lessees and lessor interest.*

Sol. Given date

For lessee interest (assuring all taxes borne by lessee)

Ground rent = 200 × 12 = ₹ 2400 p.a.

Net rent = ₹ 2400 Ps.

Let the interest rate be @ 5% as it is well secured

Y.P. for 99 years @ 5% *i.e.* 19.84

Lessor interest	= 2400 × 19.84	= 47700/-
Lessee's interest	= Gross rent	= 1800 × 12 = 21600/- p.a.
Outgoings	= repairs 10%	= 2160
Municipal taxes 12%		= 2592
Collection and management 2%		= 432
Vacancies and bed debt 2%		= 432
Insurance 2%		= 432
Rent of load 2%		= 2400
Total		= 8418

Net rent = 21600 – 8418 = 13182/-

Net rate of interest be 8% as these are shops. As the question is stipulated about the unexpired life taken equal to 99 years. Assume sinking fund 3 percent.

Y.P. @ 8% and 3% for 99 years 12.24 (from table)

Lessee's interest = 13182 × 12.24 = 161000/-

Q. 2. *A lease to B a plot of land in 1930 on following terms*

1930-1943	*₹ 50/- p.m.*
1944-53	*₹ 63/- p.m.*
1954-63	*₹ 68/ p.m.*
1964-76	*₹ 73/- p.m.*

All taxes are to be paid by lessee.

Lessee is to erect structure worth at least ₹ 10000 and to fill up the taxes. After the expiry of lease this structure is reverted to the lesser. The area of land in 4 acre land at the same road is selling for ₹ 24000 per area. Building have already erected costing ₹ 40000/- it can be assumed that the value of land will not fall below the present value. What is the interest value of lessee in the year 1942.

Assuming the rate of interest as 5% as the rent in well secured.

Y.P. @ 5% for 1 year is 0.952

Net rent during 1942-43 = 50 × 12 = 600/- p.a.
Owners interest – 600 × 0.952 = 572
Net rent during 1944-53 = 63 × 12 = 756
Y.P. @ 5% for 10 years depended 1 year = (7.722 – 0.952) = 6.770
Owners Interest = 756 × 6.77 = 5130
Net rent during 1954-63 = 68 × 12 = 816
Y.P. @ 5% for 10 years deferred 11 years 5.1
Owner interest = 816 × 5.1 = 4160
Net rent during 1964-76 = 73 × 12 = 876/- p.a.
Y.P. for 13 years defused 21 years = 3.372
Owners interest = 816 × 3.372 = 2920
Owners interest during 1942-1976 = 1+ 2 + 3 + 4
= 573 + 5130 + 4160 + 2920 = ₹ 12782/-
Reversionary value = P.V. of ₹ 1 receivable
After 34 years @ 5% × (cost land cost of bed)
Cost of land = 4 × 24000 = 96000
Cost of Building = 40000
Total = 136000
Reversionary value = 0.19 × 13600 = 21
Total lessees interest as on 1942 = ₹ 12782 + 20100 = 32882

Q. 3. *Under what situation you will use the under mentioned method of valuation.*

(1) Rental Method (2) Land and Bldg. Method (3) Both above Method.

Rental Method: When

(*i*) Land is fully utilised (*ii*) Fair rent is available

Land and Building:

(*i*) When part of land is used only for construction.

(*ii*) When due to any reason rent is very small and value of land is high.

(*iii*) When building is in poor condition and land can be sold at reasonable price.

Both above Method:

(*i*) When part of land is used and building is in good rental value.

(*ii*) Due to development of a locality the cost of land increase and land is available for sale as a part.

Q. 4. *Find the value of a lease hold shop for 99 years of which 75 years are unexpired at the ground rent of ₹ 150/- per annum. It was let 5 years ago on a 21 years lease at ₹ 1200/- p.a. to a well-established firm and as it is an important market where values are increasing rapidly. It is considered that it will be worth ₹ 1800/- p.a. On full repining lease at the end of present term.*

Sol. (A property leasehold has lessees interest whilst for freehold interest are calculate lessees interest).

Gross rent for 21 – 5 = 16 years = 1200 p.a.
Gross rent for 75 – 16 = 59 years = 1800 p.a.
If overall outgoings are taken as 35%
Net rent for 16 years = 1200 – 420 = ₹ 780/- p.a.

And net rent for reaming 59 years = 1800 – 630 = 1170/- p.a.

If sinking fund rate is taken 4%

Y.P. for 59 years @ = 7.94786

Value for 59 years = 3.21 × 1170 = 3760

Total value of property = 6200 + 3760 = ₹ 9960/-

Q. 5. *A lease hold shop premises for the remainder of the lease having 20 years unexpired the period a rent of ₹ 200/- p.m. And has the right at the expiration of the lease to review the lease at the rate same rent for a further perused 20 years provided to the act the time of renewal pays a premium of ₹ 40000/-. The net rack rent rental value of the property is ₹ 2000 p.m. What is the present value of lessees interest.*

Sol. From question it is clear that the shop has been constructed by lessees. Lessee's interest, is to be determined and hence single rate of interest will have to be considered.

Net rack rent = ₹ 2000/- *i.e.* fair rent

Lease rent = ₹ 200/- p.m.

Lessees Beneficial rent = 2000 – 200 = 1800/- p.m. = 21600/- p.a.

Y.P. for 20 years @ 8% = 9.818

Lessee's interest for first 20 years = 21600 × 9.818 = ₹ 212000 ...(A)

Y.P. 20 years deferred for 20 years @ 8% = 11.925 – 9.818 = 2.107

Lessee's interest for next 20 years = 21600 × 2.107 = 45500 ...(B)

Present value of premium = 40000 × Present Value of ₹ 1 receivable after 20 years
= 40000 × 0.37089 = 15000 ...(C)

Present value of property = A + B + C
= 212000 + 45500 + 15000 = ₹ 272500

Q. 6. *Assess the present value of a residential property situated in the suburb of a city. The detail of which are given below:*

(a) Free hold property two storied, newly constructed building plinth area 200 square meters on a plot of having 700 square meters of area...meter area.

(b) Two plots of vacant land situated nearly have been sold recently of the following prices.

$$\frac{\textit{Plot No. 1}: 144\ m^2 \ \textit{for ₹ 25000}}{\textit{Plot No. 2}: 360\ m^2 \ \textit{for ₹ 55000}}$$

(c) The ground floor of the building is let to a tenant for residential purpose at a rent of ₹ 750/- p.m. Inclusive of municipal taxes. The accommodation in the first floor is similar to ground floor and occupied by the owner for residence.

(d) The building is in Burnt bricks built structure with RCC roof; floors are finished with mosaic tiles. Door and window are of wood.

(e) The municipal taxes for three month amount to ₹ 350/- the repairs are carried out by the owner.

Sol. Gross rent = ₹ 750/- p.m. per floor
= ₹ 750 × 12 p.a. per floor = ₹ 750 × 12 × 2 p.a.
= ₹ 18000 p.a.

Outgoing :	Repair		12%
	Vacancies and bed debts		1%
	Insurance		2%
	Others		2%
	Total		17%

Outgoing at the rate 17% = 3060

Municipal taxes 350 × 4 = 1400

Total outgoing = ₹ 4460/- p.a.

Net rent = 18000 – 4460 = 13540/- p.a.

Assuring @ 6% and life perpetuity as building is well built and is in good condition

***Y.P.* @ 6% for** = 16.16

Value of Building = 13540 × 16.16 = ₹ 225700/-

Value of land – Rate of first plot = 25000/144 = ₹ 173/m^2

Rate of second plot = 55000/360 = ₹ 153/m^2

This shows that plot size as increase the rate decrease.

Taking a rate of ₹ 125/m^2

The value of plot 125 × 700 = 87500/-

Built up area in 200 m^2

Value of this plot = 200 × 125 = 25000/-

Value of land = 87500 – 25000 = 62500/-

Value of premises (Residential Property) = Cost of land + Cost of Building

= 62500 + 225700 = ₹ 288200/-

Examples

Q. 7. *A RCC building fetchers a gross rent of ₹ 4000/- per annum. The expected future life of structure is 50 years. The total outgoings in the form of various taxes are 25% of gross rent. The rate of interest for sinking fund is 6% and that for capitalization is 5%. Find value of property.*

Sol. Given gross Income = ₹ 4000/- p.a.

Gross-outgoing @ 25% = 25/100 × 4000 = 1000

Net Income 4000 – 1000 = ₹ 3000/-

$$Y.P. = \frac{1}{t+s}$$

where $t = 5\%$ and $s = \dfrac{t_1}{(1+t_1)^n - 1} = \dfrac{0.06}{(1+0.06)^{50} - 1} = 0.003446$

$$\therefore \quad Y.P. = \frac{1}{0.05 + 0.003446} = 18.7$$

∴ Capitalised values of property = ₹ 3000 × 18.7 = ₹ 56100.00 **Ans.**

Q. 8. *What will be the value of the property fetchers a not rent of ₹ 6000/- per annum at the rate of interest of 10%. The sinking fund was to be collected at 0.5 paisa per rupee.*

Sol. Given $\frac{10}{100} = 0.1$

Sinking fund installment $S = 0.5/1N = 0.005.$

$$Y.P = \frac{1}{t+s} = \frac{1}{0.1+0.005} = 9.52$$

∴ Value of property = 6000 × 9.52 = ₹ 57120/-

Q. 9. *A newly contracted building cost ₹ 225000/- plot measuring 300 square meter. Found monthly rent.*

(i) Rate of land is ₹ 50/- per square meter.

(ii) Return expected on cost of land and building is 8%.

(iii) Expected life of building 60 years.

(iv) Rate of inherent for sinking fund is 3%.

(v) Scrap value is 10% of construction cost.

(vi) Outgoing 3%.

Sol. Cost of building = ₹ 225000/-

Cost of land = 50 × 300 = 15000

∴ Total cost 225000 + 15000 = 240000/-

Return expected = 8% on total cost $= \frac{8}{100} \times 24000 = 19200/-$

∴ Net rent = ₹ 19200/-

Sinking fund = Construction cost – Scrap value

= 225000 – 22500 = 202500

∴ Sinking fund installment $= \frac{t \times s}{(1+t)^n - 1} = \frac{0.08 \times 202500}{(1+0.003)^{60} - 1} = 1242$

If gross rent = R ∴ Outgoings = $0.3R$

∴ $R - 0.3R - 1242 = 19200$

∴ $0.7R = 20442$

R = ₹ 429203/-

∴ Rent per month $= \frac{₹\ 29203}{12}$ = ₹ 2433/50 per month

Q. 10. *Valuate a property (land + building) using the following*

Salvage value = ₹ *1000*

Original cost = ₹ *1,00,000*

Rate of interest permitted = *4%*

Overall expected life = *40 years*

Future expected life = *30 years*

The building is erected over a plot of land 4 × 4 in and the land in the vicinity to a depth of 15 m worth ₹ 500 per m² (value of recess land if any can be taken as 3/4 of bell value).

Sol. Salvage value = ₹ 1000

Bd = Depreciable base = 100000 – 1000 = ₹ 99000/-

$t = 0.004$, $n = 40$, $x = 40 - 30 = 10$

$$Bx = Bd\left\{\frac{(1+0.04)^{40} - 1(1+0.04)^{10}}{(1+0.004)^{30} - 1}\right\} + 1000 = ₹\ 89000/-$$

The building is erected over a plot of land as shown

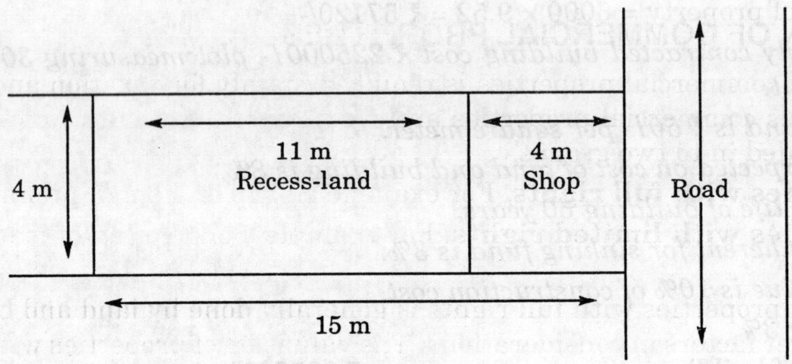

Cost of land is calculated by belting method

Let cost of land per sqm $= x$

$\therefore$ $4x \times 11.500 \times 3/4 = 15 \times 500$

$x = 844/\text{m}^2$

$\therefore$ Cost of land $4 \times 4 \times 4 \times 844$ = ₹ 13504/-

$\therefore$ Value of property = 89000 + 13504 = ₹ 101504/- **Ans.**

Q. 11. *A plot 10 m wide and 60 m long has got roads on both front and rear. The front side is commercial and has a meter value of ₹ 6000/- sq m where as rear side is residential with a market value of ₹ 2000/- sq m. How to arrive at market value of plot?*

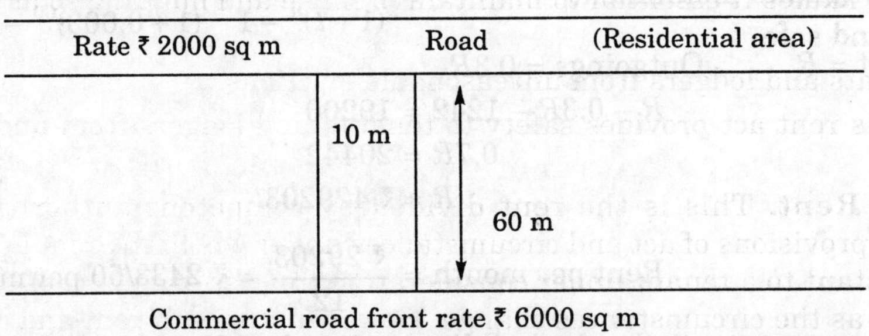

Sol. Belting method with half plot on each belt will have to be applied.

(A) Plot 10 m × 30 m having approach from commercial road

(*i*) Area of first Belt : 10 m × 20 m = 200 sq m

(*ii*) Area of 2nd Belt : 10 m × 10 m = 100 sq m

Total = 300 sq m

$\therefore$ Cost of land of first belt = 200 × 600 = 12 lacs

Cost of second belt = 100 × 6000 × 3/4 = 4.5 lacs

Total = 16.5 lacs

(B) Rear plot will also have same belt and belt area

Cost of first belt $= 200 \times 2000 = 4$ lacs

Cost of second belt $= 100 \times 200 \times 3/4 = 1.5$ lacs

Total = 5.5 lacs

$\therefore$ Total cost of land $= 16.5 + 5.5$

= 22 lacs **Ans.**

5.3. VALUATION OF COMMERCIAL PROPERTIES

Valuation of commercial properties is required mainly for taxation and market value. In most of the cases commercial properties are exempted from wealth tax. The commercial properties are divided in to two groups.

(1) **Properties with full rights.** For example a shop or a small premise.

(2) **Properties with limited rights.** For example a shop or an office in a multi story building.

Valuation of properties with full rights is generally done by land and building method taking FSI and other factors in considerations. The valuation of properties with limited rights is done either by rental method of valuation or by composite methods.

5.4. STANDARD RENT

The transfer of property at defines the rights of owner as well as those of tenants. Though this is act passed by central government, however every state government as invited directly or indirectly. They also have formed rent restriction act. This rent restriction act has its jurisdiction only in the particular state where it exists, whereas transfer of property act is applicable through out India. There acts are amended from time to time as per requirements. The objectives of this act are:

(1) To control the rents and rates of hotels, lodging houses, guest houses etc.

(2) This act makes it essential to maintain premise and building so as inmates should feel comfortable and safe.

(3) To tenants and lodgers from unreasonable evictions.

As such this rent act provides safety to tenants and lodgers from undue harassment from owners.

Standard Rent. This is the rent divided by competent authorities taking into consideration the provisions of act and circumstances under which the rent is fixed. Standard rent remains constant to a tenant under consideration. In case of change of tenant; standard rent also changes as the circumstances change. However standard rent and contractual rent differ mostly. Standard rend is generally low, however it is always beneficial not to get any rent fixed by court based on rent act, as it favours tenants; landlord never gives any attention as it is very difficult to maintain premise. However now a days rent control act has been revised and modified as such landlord does not loose much.

The rent control act is not applicable to government or local authorities.

Process of Fixing Standard Rent. It is fixed by a standard procedure as given below:

(1) In case tenant feels that he is paying more rent then he submits an application to court for fixing the standard rent. Justification is also required to be attached through report by a Competent Engineer.

(2) Owner of the house is also required to submit his say duly certified by a Competent Engineer.

(3) Court then based on facts submitted by both the parties decides the rent of the premises under consideration.

However in case of dispute, either of the parties have right to go to higher court. In between the proceeding, the tenant has right to withdraw the case if some agreement could be reached.

Method to Calculate Standard Rent. There are two methods to calculate standard rent; comparative method and investment method.

In case of comparative method; the rent is fixed comparing the rent of similar property in that locality; taking into considerations the carpet area, rent of similarly building in two same locality, type of construction; life of structure; specifications used etc. However this method gives very approximate rent as with so many factors, hence final conclusion can not be drawn.

In case of investment method; standard rent is calculated by deducting outgoings from return on investment made. Return on investment made depends upon type of premise, locality, specifications etc. Cost of construction depends upon many factors, however it should be realistic one. In case of flats it also depends upon floor at which the flat is.

5.5. VALUATION TABLES

Before embarking on any method of valuation it is necessary that a study of the tools used in valuation techniques be understood. The development of these is based on the principle that a rupee today is worth more than one rupee at a future date due to interest that involves in future happening in economic terms over a period of time. All investment terms must be governed as per the economic conditions.

'Interest' can be defined as money paid for the use of money. A property constructed by one is rented to other at certain specific rent. This rent is the return in the form of interest on his investment. The cost of money (*i.e.* interest) varies with the amount of risk involved and with the size and duration of the loan. The interest rate varies from time to time and mainly controlled by Government. However in private sector it varies from time to time, place to place and as per demand and supply urgency and necessity of money. The rate of interest includes the compensation risk and loss, inflation, revise charges etc. it is generally expressed as per annum.

If P = Total value of ₹ 1 at the end of n years invested at the rate of interest i

$Q = PV$ = Present value of present worth of R_1 1/- to be recovered after n years at a rate of interest t

R = The amount to be invested at the end of each year for n year at a rate of interest t to recover ₹ 1/- at the end of n years.

S = Total amount to be recovered at the end of n years if ₹ 1/- is invested every year for n years at a rate of interest t.

Then,

$$P = (1+t)^n$$

$$Q = (1+t)^{-n} = \frac{1}{(1+t)^n}$$

$$R = \frac{t}{(1+t)^n - 1}$$

$$S = \frac{(1+t)^n - 1}{t}$$

The table is in following proforme used:

Valuation Table

Single Payment		*Annuities (uniform series payment)*	
Compound amount P	*Present value or present worth Q or PV*	*Sinking fund R*	*Compound amount S*
$(1+t)^n$	$\dfrac{1}{(1+t)^n}$	$\dfrac{t}{(1+t)^n-1}$	$\dfrac{(1+t)^n-1}{t}$

5.6. REAL ESTATE VALUATION REPORT

A report in general is a device to communicate facts, informations and data etc. together with opinion and advice if called for. The process of writing of a valuation report in general starts only after the completion of process of valuation. A valuation report requires a sound technical knowledge and skill including analysis of data and informations collected and then conclusions drawn. It also includes opinions and advices if asked, defined clearly, effectively, effeciently and convincingly.

The physical appearance of a report together with its format, style of presentation, analysis of informations and data collected and reaching to fund conclusion mentioning value of property and advice and suggestion given, all play an important role in understanding the technical contents of valuation report. The report should be specific, defined in clear words with no ambiguity or scope for different interpretations. Effective use of words be made. A report should be so arranged that a client who is not an engineer can easily understand it, can easily refer to any particular part of a report at any time without any difficulty. It should be systematic and methodical. It should be in a logical sequence with simple, short and complete sentences. Forwarding letter, though does not form a part of report but should be attached with report referring identification of property being valued and the purpose of valuation.

Before a valuation report is made, site inspection must be made. Maximum possible data and informations must be collected from clients and other persons nearby the actual sites. The documents should be studied in detail. The base deed if any should be checked, counter checked with lease period and expiry of lease. Record of Government and Municipal offices city Survey office, Talathi office should be made or consulted regarding informations about survey no. area, tenure title ownership, occupancy, encumbrances if any as recorded etc. Building bye laws regarding permissible built up area and open spaces and actual construction made at site should also be studied thoroughly. Type of structure, year of construction, materials used, improvements made if any, year of improvement made, depreciations etc. are should be studied before reaching a final value. Cost Index is also one of the important factor in valuation report to find depreciated value of property in general and wealth day in particular.

A format generally used to submit valuation report of flat is given herewith. Every valuer can have his own format, havever it should be clear and specific.

Format for Valuation of Flats

S. No.	*Description*	*Remarks*
I.	**General**	
1.	Purpose of Valuation	...
2.	Date of Valuation	...
3.	Name of the owner (as reported) and address	...
4.	Document produced for perusal	...
II.	**Apartment Building**	
1.	Nature of the Apartment	...
2.	Location	...
	T.S. No.	...
	Block No.	...
	Ward No.	...
	Village/Municipality/Corporation	...
	Door No., Street or road (Pin code)	...
3.	Description of the Locality Residential Commercial/Mixed	...
4.	Year of Construction	...
5.	Number of Floors	...
6.	Type of Structure	...
7.	Number of Dwelling Units in the Building	...
8.	Quality of Construction	...
9.	Appearance of the Building	...
10.	Maintenance of the Building	...
11.	Facilities Available Lift	...
	Protected Water Supply	...
	Underground Sewerage	...
	Alround Compound Wall is Existing?	...
	Pavement is laid around the Building?	...
III.	**Flat**	
1.	The floor in which the flat is situated	...
2.	Door No. of the Flat	...
3.	Specification of the Flat	...
	Roof	...
	Flooring...	...
	Doors	...
	Windows	...
	Fittings ...	...
4.	House Tax	...
	Assessment No.	...
	Tax Amount	...
	In the Name of	... ₹
5.	Electricity Service Connection No.	...
	Meter Card is in the Name of	...Sri.
6.	How is the maintenance of the Flat?	...
7.	Sale Deed executed in the name of	...Sri
8.	What is the undivided area of Land as per Sale Deed.	...
9.	What is the plinth area of the Flat?	...

10.	What is the floor Space Index (Approx.)	...
11.	What is Carpet Area of the Flat?	...
12.	Is it Posh/I Class/Medium/Ordinary?	...
13.	Is it being used for Residential or Commercial?	...
14.	Is it Owner-occupied or tenanted?	...
15.	If tenanted, what is the monthly rent?	... ₹
IV.	**General**	
1.	How is the Marketability?	...
2.	What are the factors favouring for an extra Potential Value ?	...
3.	Any negative factors are observed which affect the market value in general?	...
V.	**Rate**	
1.	After analysing the comparable sale instances, what is the composite rate for a similar flat with same specification in the adjoining locality?	...
2.	Assuming it is a new construction, what is the adopted basic composite rate of the flat under valuation after comparing with the specifications and other factors with the flat under comparison (give Details)	...
3.	Breakup for the Rate:	
	(*i*) Building + Services	₹
	(*ii*) Land + Others	₹
VI.	**Composite Rate adopted after Depreciation:**	
(*a*).	Depreciated Building Rate	
	Replacement cost of Flat with Services (V(3)I)	₹
	Age of the Building	
	Life of the Building estimated	
	Depreciation %age assuming the Salvage Value as 10%	...
(*b*).	Total Composite Rate arrived for valuation	
	Depreciated Building Rate VI (*a*)	... ₹
	Rate for Land and Others V(3) (*ii*)	... ₹
	Total Composite Rate	... ₹

Valuation Details

S. No.	*Description No.*	*Qty.*	*Rate per*	*Estimated Value ₹*
1.	Present value of the flat	...		
2.	Ward robes	...		
3.	Showcases/almirahs	...		
4	Kitchen arrangements	...		
5.	Superfine finish	...		
6.	Interior Decoration	...		
7.	Electricity desposits Electrical fittings, etc.	...		
8.	Extra collapsible gates/grill works etc.	...		
9.	Potential Value if any	...		
10.		...		
11.		...		
	Total	...		

Certificate

1. It is hereby certified that the present value of the flat as discussed above is in my opinion ₹ ....(Rupees...).
2. The property was inspected on .... in the presence of .... Mr.....................
3. Value varies with the purpose and date. This certificate is not to be referred if the purpose is different other than mentioned in this report.
4. The connected Title Deed for the subject flat in the opinion of this valuer is the dated .... registered as a documents in .... Registrars office with registration No. ....

Place :

Date : Govt. approved valuer

5.7. IDENTIFICATION OF PROPERTY FOR VALUATION

Assessment Register TSI from Municipal Council/Committee.

Affidavit

The Main Job of Valuer is to identify or match the property physically with the Documents submitted by the client.

1. If there is government allotted property or property in a well-defined colony (approved), then there must be some numbers for that particular plot. In that case valuer must ask for the whole site plan of that colony and compare the plot/property by taking the start from Road/street.
2. In other case where the house numbers are not allotted but the property is located in city/town/village in the locality, then the all four sides may be compared with deed by asking from the neighbourhood.

	Site as per deed	Site as per actual
North		
South		
East		
West		

Valuer should visit the property throughly and ask from the residents of that property about the ownership. Sometimes the property is rented out which may create problem for the financing institute on later stages. Some clients only want to mortgage their property because they were unable to get the property vacated.

3. In case of flats, floor number may be added like if property is on 4th floor we can give names of the owners of 3rd and 5th floor.
4. In case of land or big size properties copy of latha/masavi is needed. In the latha/masavi Musteel Number, Kila Number, Khasra Number are very much clear. In that case property is located by that number.
5. In all other cases the property can be only verified by latitude and longitude. This is the precise method by which property can be located any time any where on the earth.

Various programmes like Google Earth, Yahoo Map etc. are available for this purpose. Moreover GPS is also useful for this.

6

Valuation of Lease Holds Properties

6.1. GENERAL

As per "The transfer of property Act" a lease of immovable property is a transfer of right to enjoy such property, made for a certain time (express or implied) or in perpetuity, in consideration of a price paid or promised, or of money a share of crops, service or any other thing of value, to be rendered periodically or on specified occasions to the transfer by the transferee, who accepts the transfer on such items. The transferor is called the lessor; the transferee is called the lessees. The price is called as the premium and the money, share, service or other thing to be rendered is called as the rent, it may be payable periodically or at specified times.

It can also be defined as "contract between owner (lessor) and the tenant or any other person whom the right to use is granted (lessee) to possess and use the land, building or property or any other thing for a specified time upon payment of an agreed rent as per specified terms and conditions (covenants) stipulated before hand and mutually agreed upon by the lessor and lessee in respect of property in question lease of machine plants and machineries can also be given.

The full bundles of rights inherent in the property with free hold tenure may further be divided by a lease or leaser so as to create two or more interest in the property like lesser interest, lessee's interest sub lessees interest etc. The lesser in some considerations surrenders part of such bundles of rights vested with him to the lessee retaining the right to repossess the property at the end of the lease term called 'reversion'. After the expiry of the stipulated lease it is obligatory on the part of lessee to let lessor hold over the property failing which, the lessee will be treated as sufferance.

Features of a Lease. As explained above, a lease is a grant of property for use for a specific time by lessor or lessee. The considerations being usually the payment of premium and or rent. In any case, certain rights are conferred on the lessee by the lessor. The essential features of a lease are:

(1) In a lease, there is a transfer of an interest in the immovable property. If the property in question is not in "Exclusive possession" with the grantee and the subject matter is in the control and possession of the grantor, then it is not a lease.

(2) If during the continuance of the lease any accretion is made to the property, such accretion is deemed to be comprised in the lease.

(3) A lease is transferable and perusable.

(4) A lease can be terminated by forfeiture Else it can only be terminated as per classes of "Transfer of property Act (eight different ways enumerated in section" III of transfer of property act to terminate the lease).

(5) The lessees' interest is not liable to be defeated by a subsequent transfer of the leased property.

(6) A lessee is entitled to maintain a suit in his own name against trespassers and strangers.

(7) Death of either party does not affect a lease.

A lease of an immovable property can be made from year to year or for any term exceeding one year or reserving a yearly rent only by a registered instrument. In any other case it can be made either by a registered instrument by or an oral agreement accompanied by delivery of possession. This instrument however should be executed by both the parties *i.e.* lessor and lessee.

6.2. TYPES OF LEASE

There are five principal forms of lease:

(1) Building or land lease
(2) Occupational lease
(3) Perpetual lease
(4) Sub-lease
(5) Life lease *i.e.* lease for life
(6) Equipment lease

(1) **Building or Land Lease.** Many times, an owner of any land, if not in a position to construct a building on his own plot gives his open land to another person on lease on payment, which is called as ground rent; lessee can erect building and develop the property. Buildings are repairs and maintained by lessee and outgoing are also paid by lessee. Various terms and conditions are specified and agreed upon by all the parties involved. Such ground rent is called as secured ground rent. A ground rent without any building erected on it is called unsecured ground rent. Ground rent is well secured by means of improvement of land and lessor not suspected to capital gain tax except with lease with premiums. In respect of carrying out the improvement, the alternate provisions may be that the lessee to remove the building at his own cost after the expiry of lease resting the land to its original position to lessor free of cost or on payment of its value of the relevant time, the value to be fixed by mutually agreed method. In some cases lessee sells the freehold right to lessee.

Building leases are generally granted for a period of 99 years or may be for different periods. However a long period is generally considered feasible to enable the lessee to recover his capital invested in improvement of the land. On the expiry of lease period. The land and the building erected on it are reverted back to the lesser.

(2) **Occupational Lease.** Under this lease both land and building are given on lease. The term of lease therefore is generally short this term varies from 3 to 5 years of short duration to a maximum of 20 to 30 years for residential building shops are generally leased out for a period 14 to 21 years and there may be clause of reversion in lease deed. The duration of term therefore depends upon the type of property.

If the lease rent is equal to full rent of the land and building together, then the rent is called as 'Rack Rent' and if is less than full rental value is called as 'Head rent'.

There should not be much difference in rack rent and head rent, however if lease holder has carried out some additional construction or have made some alterations and improvements which are likely to affect the value of property, the difference between rack rent and head rent can be large. Many a times lessee gives some lump sum amount to lesser and therefore pays less rent to accommodate this lump sum amount given before property is leased, then also the difference is found large. Improvement or development of surrounding area also causes appreciation of property value. This also causes a large difference in rack rent and head rent.

If such conditions are visualised by lesser, he leases out his property at a rising rent basis. This means he grants lease with a condition that rent shall be increased by certain laid down terms and conditions. This rent which increases with time is called rising rent. However this is decided by mutual consent of lesser and lessee and once finalised becomes binding to both.

Though the lease period in case of occupational lease is short, the chances of the property reverting back to the lessor are remote due to rent contract Act under which eviction is difficult. While ascertaining the fair market value of such properties, it should therefore be noted then an intending purchaser could purchase only such rights the lessor has in the property readily available. This lease many times therefore are granted for certain specified occupation, so that if occupation is changed lease gets terminated and it becomes relatively easy to get property evicted.

(3) **Perpetual Lease.** This is a continuous and permanent transaction of property for perpetuity initially the agreement is made for a short duration and later on with good experiences and relations, the same lease is renovated for perpetuity.

(4) **Sub-Lease.** A lessee may grant a lease to another person for a shorter duration time than his own lease. Such a transaction is called sub lease. The rent charged by lessee from sub-lessee may be more or less than the original rent charged. The name ground rent recovered under sub-lease is called "Improved grount rent".

The duration of sub-lease is always less than the original lease if both the periods are same; it no longer remains as sub lease. It is then called as 'Assignment'.

(5) **Life Lease.** This type of lease is for life term of the lessee. In this type of lease, the lease comes to an end after the death of lessee. This type of lease is generally adopted for land only; however this type of lease is not in existence in our country.

(6) **Equipment Lease.** A lease is an agreement between lessee (user of equipment on rent) and lesser (one who is the owner of equipment) for the use of an equipment on certain terms and conditions mutually accepted and made in a written form duly signed by both and registered to be valid in the court of law. It is a legal document and mostly non cancelable. The lessee pays an amount as acceptable to lesser and will use equipment/machine for specified period. It is his responsibility to maintain equipment in good and working condition. At the end of lease period, the equipment/machine is reverted back to the owner. In many a cases it has been found that lessee purchases the equipment from lesser after expiry of lease Period making payment to the lesser at a price decided by the consent of both the parties involved *i.e.* lesser and lessee.

6.3. TERMINATION OF LEASE

A lease of on immovable property can be terminated in the following cases:

(1) By efflux of the time *i.e.* the lease automatically get terminated on the last date of the term No formalities are required to be made.

(2) By the happening of an event *i.e.* if conditional lease is granted and conditional event occurs then lease gets terminated. For example if lease is made for 21 years or life time then the lease shall get terminated automatically on the happening of any of one event.

(3) **Merger**—the lease terminates when the right of the lessee merges in that of the lessor on the whole property. The same person cannot be a landlord and a tenant of the same property at the same time in the same right.

(4) **By express**—surrender *i.e.* lessee gives up his interest under the lease to the lessor by mutual agreement between them. No formalities are required except delivery of possession from lessee or lessor.

(5) By implied surrender *i.e.* if the lessee accepts from the lessor a new lease of the leased property, to take effect during the continuance of the existing lease, this is an implied surrender of the former lease and such lease determines thereupon.

(6) **By Forfeiture**—A lease determines forfeiture if the lessee breaks an express condition which provides that on breach there of. It is necessary in such case to give a notice to the lessee of his intention to determine the lease. Thereafter landlord *i.e.* loser can maintain a suit for possession, provided he does not waive his right.

6.4. VALUATION OF LEASE HOLDS PROPERTIES

The difference in the value of free hold properties and leasehold property is a well-known accepted fact. A heavily encumbered lease holds property with various restrictions has less value than that of a similar property without any restriction. Therefore while valuing a lease hold property, it is necessary to ascertain its fair market value for all the vested interest combined together and then the appropriate appointment should be done between the lessor and lessee so as to evaluate their respective shares of appointed interest. The interest of lessor, lessee and sub lessee are different and value of property though for them is also different.

Laser's Interest. The lessor's interest in the leased out property is the present market value (PMV) of the rights to the lessor to waive the restrictions imposed by the lease agreement and, as such can be divided up to following two heads, namely—

(1) Capitalised value of the lease rent for the unexpired period of lease and

(2) Present value of reversion to the property at the expiry of the lease period subject to the terms and conditions of the lease deed.

Lessee's Interest. The lessee's interest in the lease hold property is—

(1) Capitalised value of the net yield from the property for unexpired expired period of lease. It is also called as 'Profit rental'.

(2) Interest on the cost of improvement if any as per covenants of the lease agreement. The lessee's interest is not a perpetual one but is a waste interest. Hence it would be valued at a dual rate of interest, one to provide for yield on its investment and the other for recipient for his capital invested for the improvement.

Sub Lessees Interest. The sub lessee is bounded by all the covenants of main lease. The sub lessee's interest is less secured and therefore his interest is capitalised at a higher interest rate than that adopted for head lessee's interest.

Different rates of interest are applied to different level of ownership. This is only a redistribution of risks of rights to income under the terms of lease agreement. However, it is required to study the legal aspects of lease and the laws prevailing in respective state where the property is situated.

6.5. LIABILITIES

In case of lease hold properties lesser and lessee have certain liabilities as per prevailing rules and regulations. Similarly both have certain rights in the lease hold properties under considerations. These are given in subsequent paragraphs.

Lesser. It is usual practice by lesser, granting lease of his assets to lessee to hid a few things of that property. It is basically wrong. Once a lease of property is granted, he should handover possession to lessee at the same time it should be clear in his mind that as long as lessee is paying rent and performing his conditioning mentioned in that lease documents, he has right to enjoy the property peacefully. The lessee also has rights to construct some portion if he feels so and if bye laws prevailing permits. Similarly at the time of termination of lease *i.e.* either after completion of lease period or if lessee due to some reason or the other wants to return the property to lesser, the lease can remove fittings if any provided by him; however he is required to handover property to lesser in the same conditions as it was before the lease was granted. However in case of natural calamities beyond the control of men, the lessee can handover property even earlier also *i.e.* before the expiry of lease period and without carrying out the repairs as it was beyond his power to avoid destrution of property. The lessee has right to sub lease the property with due permission of lesser or to mortgage the asset or transfer and assign rights to other person for only remaining period of lease.

Lessee. He is also required to not to hide any thing he intends to do later on. He is also bound to restore and maintain property as it was when lessee was granted. However with usage and life of structure; a few wears and tears are allowed. He is also required to pay rent or agreed amount in time. He is further required to give possession to lesser *i.e.* owner after expiry of lease period. He is not authorised to change the functional use of property. A house leased for residential purposes can not be used for commercial purposes else the lease gets broken and lesser has each and every right to get his property reverted back before expiry of lease period.

6.6. LEASE AND LICENSEE

As per Indian easement act 1982 Section 52, license is a right to do or to continue to do something in or upon the immovable property of the grantor. The person who has right to grant license is called licensor and the person to whom the license is granted is known as licensee. The two terms lease and license differ in many respect. In case of lease, rights are transferred to do any thing whereas in case of license only two parties involved are concerned. For example if a lease is granted for house lessee can do all the alterations and modifications and no body can object whereas if license is granted, he has limitations for the purposes for which this is granted. A lease can be sub leased *i.e.* transferable whereas license is not. Lease granted to a person gets automatically transferred to his son whereas a license can not be. License can be cancelled at any time but lease can not be. It is not revocable. Lease documents are required to be registered as per transfer of property act. In case of lease interests are transferable; this is not possible in case of license.

6.7. METHODS OF VALUATION OF LEASE HOLD PROPERTIES

There are two methods vaulting the leasehold properties.

Method 1: In this the property is values as free hold property and this value is apportioned between the lessor lessee and sub less as per their respective interest.

Method 2: In this method, value is determined separately for lessor and lessee taking their own-interest in to considerations.

This has been illustrated by a few examples.

Q.1. *Premise was given on lease for 33 years in 1970 at a rent of ₹ 600/- per month with a premium of ₹ 25000/- find the interest of the lessor, and lessee as on 1980. A net return for similar property in 1980 was ₹ 1100/- per month.*

Sol. Lessee's Interest: The profit enjoyed by the lessee = 1100 – 600 = ₹ 500/- he will receive this for a period of (33 – 10) = 23 years. Assuming a rate of interest on this return at a rate of 7.5 percent for annum.

The capitalised income due to this with a rate interest of 7.5 percents and assuming a rate of interest of 5% for redemption of capital (Sinking fund).

$$Y.P. = \frac{1}{t + s}$$

where $s = \dfrac{1}{\dfrac{(1 + t_1)^n - 1}{t_1}}$

here let $t = 0.75, t_1 = 0.05, n = 33$ years

$$s = \frac{1}{\dfrac{(1 + 0.05)^{23} - 1}{0.05}} = 0.024$$

$$Y.P. = \frac{1}{0.075 + 0.024} = 10.09$$

Capitalised value for lessee = 50 × 12 × 10.09 = ₹ 60540/-

The premium of ₹ 25000/- has not been taken into account since it was paid 10 years back in consideration of the reduced rent.

Lesser Interest. Lessors interest comprises of

(*i*) During the lease period

(*ii*) After the expiry of lease

(*i*) During the lease period the lessors interest is limited to receive the rent @ ₹ 600/- per month or ₹ 7200/- per annum for the unexpired period of lease is 33 – 10 = 23 years.

The net rent is to be capitalised for 23 years and the rate of capitalisation will be less then what is adopted for lessee's interest.

The rate of interest is taken 7.5 – 1 = 6.5%

Y.P. for 23 years @ 6.5% on capital and redemption

$$= \frac{1}{0.065 + s}$$

where $s = \dfrac{1}{\dfrac{(1 + 0.065)^{23} - 1}{0.065}} = 0.01996$

$$\therefore \quad Y.P. = \frac{1}{0.065 + 0.01996} = 11.77$$

∴ Capital value = ₹ 7200 × 11.71 = ₹ 84744/-

After expiry of the lease, the lessor *i.e.* owner will get ₹1100 per month or ₹ 13200/- per annum for remaining period of life. This is capitalised in perpetuity, assuming that the property in question has a future life of about 50 years. Rate of interest for capitalising the reversion is generally higher and assumed to be equal to 7%.

$$\therefore \quad Y.P. = \frac{100}{7} = 14.286$$

∴ Capitalised value = ₹ 13200 × 14.286 = 188575/-

The lessor will get his income only after the expiry of remaining lease period *i.e.* 23 years. Differing the value for 23 years its value.

$$= \frac{1}{(1 + t_1)^n} \times 188575 = \frac{1}{(1 + 0.07)^{23}} \times 188575 = 39779/-$$

∴ Lessor Interest = 84774 + 39779 = ₹ 1,24,553/-

∴ Value as freehold = 1,88,575/-

The sum of lessee's interest and lessee's interest = 60540 + 124553 = 185093/-

Thus there is a difference when a lease hold property is valued as lease hold or free hold.

If compensation is required to be given then it should be given in the ratio of 1,24,553 and 60,540 *i.e.* 2.057 : 1 to lessor and lessee.

Q.2. *A plot of land has been given on building lease on a ground rent of ₹ 4000/- per annum. The lease is for 99 years and the unexpired period of lease is 30 years after which the property shall be reverted back to the lessor.*

If the present market value of similar free hold property (lessors interest + lessees interest) ₹ 6,00,000/- what is the present value of the lessors interest in the property.

Sol. The lessor's interest in the property is:

(1) The net income of ₹ 40,000/- per year for remaining period of lease is 30 years and

(2) After the expiry of lease the lessor will also get his property reverted back which has a present value of ₹ 6,00,000/-.

Present value of ₹ 40,000/- per annum at a rate of interest of 6% for 30 years.

$$= \frac{(1+t_1)^n - 1}{t(1+t_1)^n} \times \text{ net income per annum}$$

$$\therefore \quad P.V. = \left\{\frac{(1+0.06)^{30} - 1}{0.06 \times (1+0.06)^{30}}\right\} \times 40,000 = 5,50,593/-$$

Present value of ₹ 6,00,000/- @ 6.6%

$$\text{Receivable for 30 years} = F\left\{\frac{1}{t(1+t_1)^n}\right\} = 6,00,000\left\{\frac{1}{t(1+0.065)^{30}}\right\} = ₹\ 1,04,466/-$$

Present value of lessors interest in the property = ₹ 5,50,593 + ₹ 1,04,466/-

= ₹ 6,55,059/- = ₹ 6,55,060/-

Y.P. for infinite period of lease

$$Y.P. = \frac{1}{1+s^1}$$

when $s^1 = \dfrac{1}{\dfrac{(1+i_1)^{n_1} - 1}{i_1}}$ when n_1 = unexpired period of lease = $n - t$

when t = expired period of lease if $n = 0$

$$s_1 = \text{Lim} \frac{1}{N - \dfrac{(1+i)^{n_1} - 1}{i}} = \frac{1}{x}$$

$$Y.P. = \frac{1}{1+s_1} = \frac{1}{i}$$

Therefore for an infinite period of lease *Y.P.* for lease = *Y.P.* for lessee = 1/*i*.

7

Mortgage

7.1. MEANING OF MORTGAGE

Mortgage means to pledge a property against security. For example if a person having a property of certain worth, and if in need of money, can pledge his property to other person as a security and can fetch some amount, part of the value of property. The essential condition is that a person having a property must be willing to pledge and has got capacity to return the amount within a specified period, with specified rate of interest; and other person is willing to have that property as a security and has an amount to give. This is called as mortgage. The person by whom the property is mortgaged is called mortgager and a person to whom the property is pledged is called mortgagee.

The mortgager retains the right to recover his property freed from the charge created by the mortgagees on replacement of the amount due to mortgages. This is called "Equity of redemption".

As a general rule, a mortgage is a sound form of investment offering reasonable security and a fair rate of interest, and although the mortgagee dead probably stipulate for replacement at the end of six months it is annual for loan, to continue for a very much longer period.

Remedies. If the mortgager defaults in payment of interest an observance of the covements of the mortgagee has the following remedies against the property:

(1) Right to sell the property as per Law of Property Act. Mortages will have to pay the surpluses amount if any to mortgagee.

(2) He may apply to the court for a foreclosure order, which will have the effect of distinguishing the mortgagor's equity of redemption.

(3) He may at any time take personal possession of the income from the property, and after paying all necessary outgoings may apply balance to pay interest on the mortgage debt, including arrears if any. The surplus if any, must be paid to the mortgagers or applied to reducing the mortgage debt.

(4) Under the law of property act mortgagee may appoint a receiver to collect the income from property and apply it to the purpose indicated above in clause 3 including payment of the receivers commission.

It is evident that these remedies will be effective only where in case I and II, the market value of property exceeds the amount due to the mortgager whereas in case III and IV the net income from property, after paying all outgoing and annual charges having priority to the mortgage, is sufficient to discharge the annual interest on the loan with a margin to cover possible arrears if of interest. As per sections 54 of Transfer of Property Act. A mortgage is the transfer of an interest in specific immovable property for the purpose of securing the payment of money advanced or to be advanced by way of loan, an existing or future debt of the performance of an engagement which may give rise to a pecuniary liability.

Although the property itself in the mortgagee's principal security, it is usual for the mortgage deed to include a personal movement by the mortgager to repay the loan. This may be reinforced by a personal guarantee of some third party so that in addition to the remedies above, there is part of action on the personal covement.

7.2. FACTORS TO BE CONSIDERED

Factors to be considered while mortgaging property are:

(1) Speculative value of property must be ascertained it is important to a mortgager as well as to mortgagee.

(2) Risk factor—There is possibility that a mortgager will get it back and is the real owner of property. It is generally 1/2 to 2/3 *i.e.* depending on conditions of the value of property, amount is given.

(3) Removable part if any in property are taken into consideration. Removable part should not be mortgaged as far as possible.

(4) Mortgage deed should be prepared in writing and be signed by both mortgager and mortgagee both should have one copy of mortgagee deed with them.

In India mortgage act is effective and all documents be made, as per this act. Unless until proper mortgage deed is prepared it is not legal. Property mortgaged legally through court is called legal mortgage wise if in writing with mutual understanding it is called equitable mortgage.

It is important to note that mortgage operates as a transfer or all interest in land, which is given as security. But the interest, which is equity, passes to the mortgagee, is not ownership or domination which not with standing the mortgage, resides in the mortgager. The right of mortgagee is only an accusing right, which is included merely to ensure the due payment of the debt.

7.3. CLASSIFICATION OF MORTGAGES

As per transfer of property Act, mortages are classified as:

(1) Simple Mortgage
(2) Mortgage by conditional sale
(3) Use Fructuary Mortgage
(4) English Mortgage
(5) Equitable Mortgage
(6) Anomalous Mortgage

(1) **Simple Mortgage.** It is defined as where without delivering the possession of the mortgaged property, the mortgager binds him personally to pay other mortgage money and agrees expressly or initially, that in the event of his failure to pay according to his contract the mortgagee shall have a right to cause the mortgaged property to be sold and the proceeds of sale is to be applied so far as may be necessary, in payment of the mortgage money, this transaction is called a simple mortgage.

In simple mortgage, the mortgagee is not put into possession of the property pledged to him. He has neither, therefore the right to satisfy the debt out of the rents and profit, nor can be required the absolute ownership of mortgaged property of fore closure.

Therefore in simple mortgage the security for a debt is two fold (*i*) the personal obligation and (*ii*) The property, and it should be noted that a personal covenant carries with it by necessary implication a power of sale. As such there are two fold remedies. One arising out of the breach to repay and second by sale of hypothetical through court. The word cause the mortgaged property to be simply that the property has to be sold only through the intervention of court.

Therefore the general characteristics of simple mortgage are:

(1) There must be a loan (2) There is a personal liability to pay

(3) Possession is not delivered (4) There is no foreclosure

(5) No power to private sale but sale through court.

(2) **Mortgage by Conditional Sale.** When the mortgagee ostensibly sells the mortgaged property on conditions that

(*a*) On default of payment of mortgage money on a certain date, the sell shall become absolute or

(*b*) On such payment being made the sale shall be void or

(*c*) On such payment being made the buyer shall transfer the property to the seller.

This transaction is called as Mortgage by condition sale and the mortgagee is mortgaged by conditional sale provided that no such transactions shall be deemed to be mortgage, unless this condition is embodied in the document, which effect or profits to affect the sale. This is a mortgage in which the ostensible sale is conditional and included simply as a security for the debt. Personal liability is not an essential ingredient of a mortgage by conditional sale. The mortgagee right to the recent mortgagee money is limited to the mortgaged property. This works the essential differences between simple mortgage and mortgage by conditional sale.

The general characteristics to mortgage by conditional sale are:

(1) The mortgager ostensibly sells the mortgaged property. The transaction has the appearance of a sale, but is really not a sale.

(2) The condition is that the sale shall be absolute in default of payment on a particular date or the sale shall be void on such pay met and the property retransferred.

(3) The remedy of the mortgagee is by foreclosure and not by sale.

(4) It must be created by one document and not by two documents *i.e.* one for sale and another for purchaser.

(5) It must be registered instrument.

(3) **Use Fructuary Mortgage.** When the mortgager delivers possession expressly or by implication binds him to deliver possession of the mortgaged property to the mortgagee, and such possession until payment of mortgage money or partly in being interest and partly in the payment of the mortgage money the transaction is called as use fructuary mortgage and mortgagee as use fructuary mortgager. Other features of this are:

(*a*) The mortgagee takes possession of the mortgaged property on the understanding that he will pay himself out of the rents and profit.

(*b*) No time limit is fixed for the mortgage money becoming due or being paid.

(*c*) The mortgagee can not see either for sale or for fore closures.

(*d*) There is no personal liability on the mortgagor.

(4) **English Mortgage.** Where the mortgagee finds him to repay the mortgage property on a certain date and transfers the mortgaged property absolutely to the mortgages, but subject to a provision, that he will transfer it to the mortgagor upon payment of the mortgage money as agrees. This transaction is called English mortgage. There are three essential conditions for English mortgage. These are (1) That the mortgagor should find himself to pay the mortgage money on a certain day (2) That the property mortgaged should be transferred absolutely to mortgagee and (3) That such absolute transfer is made subject to a provision that the mortgagee will reconvene the property to the mortgage money on the appointed day.

The general characteristics of English mortgage are:

(*i*) It is accompanied by delivery of possession.

(*ii*) There is personal convenant to pay the amount.

(*iii*) It is affected by absolute transfer of property with a provision for re-transfer in case of repayment of the amount.

(*iv*) The remedy is by way of sale and not by fore closure.

(*v*) The power of sale out of court *viz* private sale is conferred on certain persons under certain circumstances (section 69).

(5) **Equitable Mortgage.** Where a person in any of the following towns namely Calcutta, Chennai, Mumbai and Kanpur and in any other town which the state Government concerned by Notification in the official Gazette, specify in the behalf delivers to a credit or the agent documents of title to immovable property, with intent to create a security there on, the transaction is called as Equitable Mortgage by deposit of title deed. The requisition of a mortgage by deposit of title are (*i*) debt (*ii*) a deposit of title deed (*iii*) an intention that deeds shall be securely for the debt.

The characteristics of equitable mortgage are :

(*i*) It is created in the town only those notified by state government from time to time. Presently it is created only at Bombay, Madras & Calcutta.

(*ii*) It is affected by the deposit of documents retaining to title. There is no delivery of possession of the property.

(*iii*) The deposit is by the way of security for existing or future debt.

(*iv*) No registration is required.

(*v*) Remedy is by sale and not fore closure.

(*vi*) All provisions that apply to simple mortgage also apply to this an equitable mortgage.

(6) **Anomalous Mortgage.** A mortgage which is not a simple mortgage by conditional sale, as unfructuary mortgage, as English mortgage or a mortgage by deposit of the deeds within the meaning of the transfer of Property Act, is called as an Anomalous mortgage. The remedy of this mortgage is either by sale or for closure as the terms permit.

7.4. SALIENT FEATURES

Salient features of mortgaged properties are:

(1) **Redemption.** In the mortgage deed the mortgagor agree to repay the loan and when loan is fully repaid, he has got a power to recover his property back from the mortgagee. This is also termed as equity of redemption.

(2) **Amount of loan.** 50 to 60 percent of capitalised value is safe limit for loan.

(3) **Insurance.** It is always desirable to get the property insured for both the parties *i.e.* mortgagor and mortgagee.

(4) **Lease hold property.** It is possible to have a mortgage deed for lease hold property also. But in such cases, it is essential to take care to see that amount of remaining loan does not exceed the value of the property. It is therefore essential to value such property periodically.

(5) **Period of loan.** The period of repayment of loan is generally more and therefore the property must stand as security for the loan over a longer period of time. This must be taken care of for mortgage purposes.

(6) **Subsequent mortgage.** A property can be mortgaged more than once. In such cares the first registered mortgage deed will have first claim then the subsequent mortgage deed. Therefore the subsequent mortgagees must be careful in deciding the amount of loan against property.

(7) **Third party guarantee.** Normally, the mortgagee is more interested in recovery of his loan rather than the possession of the mortgagees property. Therefore sometimes a personal guarantee from a reputed party is included called third party guarantee for refund of the loan however this party does not refund the loan.

7.5. PURPOSES FOR VALUATION FOR MORTGAGE OF PROPERTIES

The properties are mortgaged for the purpose of obtaining loans, for offering collateral securities, creating interest or keeping lien. There are various types of mortgages such as simple mortgage, mortgage by conditional sale, usefructuary mortgage, English, mortgage, mortgage by deposit of title deeds, anomalous mortgage. Each type differs from one another. While valuing properties for mortgage or under mortgage, the valuer should bear in mind following points:

(*i*) Mortgager may be a Bank, public body, co-operative society or financial institution. The purpose of mortgage indicates to what extent the property is mortgaged. For example in case of apartments the mortgagees equitable to the value of Apartment and the whole building is not covered. In case of flats and apartments or any parcel of property, equitable mortgage terms are normally applied. Valour should consider the terms clearly and adopt appropriate values. A valuer generally comes across the equitable mortgage and while the Banks got the deed deposited while getting the property valued prior to give advance to the party concerned. A valuer is expected to consider all the details of property in such cases prier to grant of his certificate to the party concerned for determination of its market value.

(*ii*) Where a property already mortgage is to be valued then it is important to note that mortgage property is treated as encumbered in the open mark and therefore an appropriate percentage should be deducted from the value.

(*iii*) The rights of mortgage over the property, in case the mortgagee fails to fulfill the mortgage deed condition are clearly mentioned. If the mortgage is a private body then the interest payable to other financial institutions constituted under laws, will have predominance over recoveries. The liabilities of taxation will also be recovered predominantly. If proper information is not obtained, then it will be difficult for the values to assess the value of property devoid of such interest and liabilities.

(*iv*) It is advisable to obtain a detailed title report from legal advisers before taking any steps for valuation.

The process or the method to find the value of mortgaged property is not different. The net income multiplied by years purchase generally gives value of the asset. This is a rental method of valuation. However land and building method can also be used to find value of any asset. The net income likely to occur from this property should be calculated very carefully and should always be on safer side. Materials which are portable or those can be removed easily should not be taken into consideration for valuation purposes like fans, electrical appliances, shutters of cupboards, folding dining tables etc.

Q.1. *Assess the amount which a mortgager can offer for free hold residential property, which is let to 59 tannest at a total monthly rental of ₹ 1250/- inclusive of municipal taxes amounted to ₹ 430/- per quarter External repairs are carried out by land lord and in addition. The following outgoing is also born by him.*

(1) Salaries of watchmen ₹ 800/-p.a.

(2) Average Electricity charges ₹ 700/- p.a.

Besides above it is expected that an expenditure of ₹ 10000/- will be made by the landlord at the end of 10 years for replacement of doors and windows.

Sol. Gross rent = 1250 × 12 = ₹ 15000/- p.a.

Outgoings: Repair and Maintenance 10%	₹ 1500/-
Municipal taxes (as given) 430 × 4	₹ 1720/-
Bed debts and vacancies 4%	₹ 600/-

Insurance 2%	₹ 300/-
Salary of watchman (Given)	₹ 800/-
Average Electricity charges	₹ 700/-
Management and collection charges %	₹ 300/-
Total	₹ 5920/-

Net rent = 15000 – 5920 = ₹ 9080/- p.a.

Assuming rate of interest, as this is a residential flat as 8% and life to perpetuity if properly maintained and repair are carried out.

Y.P. @ 8% and 3% for perpetuity 12.248.

Owners interest = 9080 × 12.248 = ₹ 111500/-

After 10 years of ₹ 10000 has to be invested for the replacement of doors and windows.

Present value of ₹ 1000 @ 5%

= 10000 × Present value of ₹ 1 @ 5%

= 10000 × .614 = ₹ 6140

Net owners interest = 111500 – 6140 = ₹ 105360

For mortgagee 2/3 amount can be given as loan keeping 1/3rd as margin of security. Net amount for which it can be mortgage = 105360 × 2/3 = ₹ 70000/- **Ans.**

Example. *A commercial building is based for 30 years at ₹ 70,000/- per annum, all express are to borne by the lesser.*

Period expired 10 years.

The present rental value is ₹ 3.5 lacs per annum value the property for mortgage purpose for free holds interest. Advice the amount he can expect as mortgage more.

Solution. Unexpired period of lease = 10 years

Lease rent – net ₹ 70,000/-

Y.P. for 10 years @ 6% = 6.14

Value of ₹ 70,000 = 70,000 × 6.14 = ₹ 4,29,800/-

Reversion of full rental value present rent ₹ 3,50,000/-

Y.P. in perpetuity at 6% per annum deferred for 10 years is 9.3%

Reversionary value = 3,50,000 × 9.3 = 32,55,000/-

Total free hold value 429800 + 3255000 = 3684800/-

In case mortgage amount is limited to 60% of the value, the amount he can avail will be approximately ₹ 22 lacs.

8

Acts and Laws Related to Construction and Valuation of Property

8.1. INTRODUCTION

A person or institution or trust/society or a person/organisation lending loan, builder/promoter/developer or any other person involved directly or indirectly is interested to know what acts and laws are prevailing and how these acts and laws affect the cost of construction and consequently later on its value. Even when money is required to be borrowed or when a financing organisation lends loan; it becomes essential to have security of money invested. Many a time work under construction is heldup due to one reason or the other. Properties put to sell in market are stayed. All these happens mainly due to disputes or incomplete knowledge of laws and acts. It is therefore essential to have knowledge of acts and laws prevailing for construction and valuation. These laws decide the cost of construction as well as value of the asset if put in market for sell or for mortgage etc. All these acts related are given here briefly only to acquint the valuer about these. These acts have been and are modified and revised as when found necessary by competent authorities and as such can not be given in detail. However each and every act has been dealt in subsequent paragraphs. Some other acts which are not related to construction and valuation are also given as they affect it indirectly; moreover many a times during valuation or during disputes between parties involved; they give guidelines and are required to be considered.

These laws and acts have been modified and revised many a times as per requirement and necessity felt by government. It is a continuously process. It is therefore essential to a value to go in details of each and every act and law with latest amendments prevailing at that time and required to be taken into consideration at the time of valuation.

A few acts given are restricted to Maharashtra state only; however other states may also be having similar acts prevailing in that state. To acquint students with such acts; they are also given herewith.

8.2. THE FACTORIES ACT 1948

The Indian factories act was passed first time in 1881. Then thereafter it was amended many times. The present act functioning was passed in 1948 after various amendments. This act is applicable to all the factories employing 10 or more workers and using any type of power. The main object of this act is to consolidate and amend laws for regulating labour in the factories in India. According to this act no worker of age less than 18 should be employed. Further this act also classifies calendar year; week, day.

According to this act 'Factory' means a premise wherein 10 or more workers are working or were working on any day of the preceding 12 months, and in any part of which, a manufacturing process is being carried on with the aid of power.

Following are the main features of the factories Act:

(1) The act specifies that permission from the appropriate authorities must be sought before a factory is started.

(2) Act also prescribes various provisions for maintaining health of workers. Cleanliness, ventilator, lighting, drinking water facilities, toilets etc. must be provided as per the norms. The temperature inside the factory where workers are working must be maintained within tolerance limit. Provision for fresh air-circulation, humidification, must be made. Over-crowding should be avoided.

(3) Factories act also dictates that safety provisions for workers must be made from machineries and works. Safety measures must be made available against dangerous, toxic fumes and gases. Provisions for fire-fighting system must be available for safety.

(4) Welfare provisions like working facility, sitting facility, first-aid appliances, canteen, shelter, rest rooms, lunch rooms, creches etc. must be made available according to the factory act depending upon number of workers.

(5) Hours of works, holidays, overtime wages, restriction on the double employment, employment of women etc. norms must be applied. Workers should not be allowed to work more than 48 hrs. in a week and 9 hours in a day.

(6) It also restricts that no child, who has not completed his age 14th year, shall be allowed to work in a factory. Further fitness certificate must be granted by a doctor before a child is appointed. Further they should not be permitted to work during night hours. Further he should not be allowed to work for more than 4–5 hours a day.

(7) Regular leave with wages shall be granted as per the provisions and rules and regulations. Medical leave should also be granted if any worker suffers from any disease specified in the schedule which makes worker impossible to attend the work.

(8) Those violates the provision of factory act should be penalised accordingly. Authorities reserve the right to shut down the factory under such circumstances.

(9) Other provisions made are that the workers should work sincerely. Workers have no right to willfully interfere with or misuse any appliance, convenience or any other thing provided in a factory for the purpose of securing health, safety or welfare of the workers. Workers are required to follow the provisions of act, otherwise they are also liable to be punished.

8.3. THE WORKERS COMPENSATION ACT

This act was implemented to make provision of compensation to the workers if injured during working in the factory due to accident. This protect worker from unnecessary hardship arising from accident. This act was made in 1923 and came into force from July 1, 1924. This has been amended many times and finally drafted in 1962.

Accordingly to this act if any worker gets injured causing him partial or fully disabled to work; or dies during working in his working hours in the factory; he or his dependent as the case may be; must get compensation. This compensation is generally in terms of monetary given to him or his dependent or in the form of recruitment of one of his dependent. Along with this; the worker should also be provided the expenses incurred for medical treatment. The amount of compensation depends upon (*a*) The pay of the worker concerned and (*b*) The extent of injury. The act classifies injury under four categories.

(*i*) Causing death

(*ii*) Causing permanent total disablement

(*iii*) Causing permanent partial disablement

(*iv*) Causing temporary disablement.

The amount of compensation is given in Table 8.1. Further the percentage of loss of earning capacity for various injuries deemed to result in partial/permanent disablement is given in article safety engineering of chapter.

Table 8.1

Compensation to workers heaving monthly wages from ₹ 400 upto ₹ 1000 from May, 1976.

Monthly Wage workman		*Amount of compensation*		*Half monthly payment as compensation for temporary disablement ₹ (Half of the monthly wages)*
More than	*But not more than*	*Death*	*Permanent total disablement*	
400	500	21000	29400	118.75
501	600	21600	30240	135.00
601	700	23000	32340	148.75
701	800	24000	33600	160.00
801	900	27000	37800	168.75
901	1000	30000	42000	175.00

8.4. THE EMPLOYEES STATE INSURANCE ACT, 1948

This act is brought into force; as many times it was found that worker's compensation act of 1924 fails to function. The examples are:

(*a*) It has been found that due to lack of finance available to the worker; he fails to file a case under court of law.

(*b*) The worker does not have knowledge of acts and other rules as such whatever compensation is given by employer; he accepts.

Though these deficiencies have been overcome by amendment in 1938; still contains certain loop holes like all disease are not listed in compensation act; also during his sickness; worker does not get any amount for his medical treatment. This employees state insurance act, 1948 takes care of all such items. According to this act; each and every worker working in a factory must be insured according to his work and working conditions for any accident if occurs in factory. The worker as well as employer are required to contribute to this fund. The record is maintained by corporation as well as by employer. The corporation appoints inspector for the inquiries and other details. The benefits that a person got insured under this act gets are like sickness benefit, maternity benefit, disablement benefit, dependents benefit, medical benefit funeral benefit etc. as power the provisions of corporation.

8.5. THE INDUSTRIAL DISPUTE ACT, 1947

This act was made inforceable for any sort of industrial dispute between employers and workmen; workmen and workmen connected with the employment and nonemployment or with the conditions of labour of any person. The basic reason for industrial dispute between labour and capital resulting in strikes and lockout. Low wages, non-payment of bonus, non-payment of overtime, medical etc. Favourism, exploitation, improper working conditions etc. are various reasons for industrial disputes. The various type of strikes called by workers are general strike, sitdown strike, tool down strike, go-slow strike, sympathetic strike etc.

Many times it also causes lock-out of factory, Gherao, picketing also take place which forces employer to seek police help. Various methods are adopted to resolve disputes are:

(*a*) Collective bargaining between two parties involved.

(*b*) Conciliation and mediation—a mediator is involved.

(*c*) Arbitration may be voluntary or compulsory.

As individual can not afford to fight for his right; collectively all the workers of that factory can ask employer for their benefit; if required can go to the court.

8.6. INDIAN TRADE UNION ACT

As individual can not fight for his right; unions were made where all workers are member of that union and fight collectively for their right and betterment for themselves keeping interest of employer as well as of factory. The Indian trade unions are registered bodies of trade unions. Employers are required to recognise these unions, failing which matter is taken to labour court appointed by the government.

Unions collect membership fee from employees without any interference by the management. The collected amount is used for establishment and to meet recurring expenditure. The fund is also used for specific purposes as laid down by act. This amount is audited every year. It is also responsibility of unions that it case of strike, peace is required to be maintained so that there will not be any loss to the factory.

The first trade union in India was formed in Madras in 1918. The all Indian Trade Union Congress (AITUC) came into existence in 1920 and The Trade Union Act was passed in 1926 which gave a legal status and recognition to these trade unions. This act was further amended in 1947 and 1964. Various major trade unions working in India are AITUC; Indian National Trade Union Congress (INTUC), Hind Mazdoor Sabha (HMS), United Trade Union Congress (UTUC) and Bhartiya Mazdoor Sang (BMS). There are various small trade unions also. All these unions come under trade union act and has to follows the norms laid down by this Act.

8.7. THE EMPLOYEES PROVIDENT FUND ACT

This act passed mainly to protect the welfare of the family members of that worker. Accordingly to this act; some fixed amount depending upon wages of the worker is deducted from salary of the worker monthly contributed to provident fund. This amount of provident fund is refunded to that workers after his retirement. This is basically to meet his expenses and his dependent during their old age. In certain cases equal amount is contributed by the employee and then it is called as contributory provident fund. According to this act; an interest on the total amount contributed in his account is also given and added to workers provident fund. In case of emergency worker can take loan from this amount or can have partly amount refunded after completion of 15 years of service. According to the act employer can not use this money for any purpose of the factory. In most of his amount is credited to government account under the name of the worker *i.e.* the amount remains under the control of the government.

8.8. THE MINIMUM WAGES ACT, 1948

This act was passed in 1948. This act dictates terms that no worker or employee should be paid an amount less than that required for survival of that worker. The worker must be in a position to fulfill his minimum needs of bread, shelter and clothing. This act is applicable to almost all the employees whether in industry or elsewhere. Further this act empowers the government central as well as state government to fix minimum rates. These rates are modified by time to time as per market index rate. This act also decides the wages to be given for overtime; piece work etc. The minimum wage consists of basic rate of wage and cost of living allowance and cash value of essential commodities. Provisions made in the act to appoint a competent authority to calculate the cost of living index. This act has brought uniformity in the standard of fixation of wages. A wage board for important industries to ensure equal pay for equal work has also been appointed by government of India. Accordingly to this act every employee as well employer are required to maintain the account of wages paid and received. Labour courts; industrial tribunals and conciliation courts home made important contribution in their field.

8.9. THE ARBITRATION ACT, 1940

Arbitration is the settlement of dispute by the decision not of a regular and ordinary court of law but of one or more persons chosen by the parties themselves who are called arbitrators. 'Arbitration act' is an act to consolidate and amend the law relating to arbitration. This act is called as arbitration act 1940. It extrends to the whole of India except the State of Jammu and Kashmir. The arbitrator should be an independent person or persons and must have knowledge of that subject matter. As per this act arbitrator has powers to give judgement or can refer the matter to court of law for opinion. He has right to correct clerical mistake or accidental slip or omission if any. According to this various types of arbitration are:

(*a*) Arbitration without intervention of court

(*b*) Arbitration with intervention of court where there is no suit pending

(*c*) Arbitration in suits.

Arbitration clause 25 lays down that a contractor can not have recourse to a count for redress of his grievances, unless he has exhausted the channel of arbitration as set in this clause. There is a set procedure to treat cases of arbitration as laid down in the Arbitration act 1940 and must be followed in case of disputes.

8.10. SALE OF GOODS ACT, 1930

Law of sale goods was originally embodied in Section 76 to 123 of the Indian Contract Act, 1872. However as the provisions of the sections were found inadequate to meet the complexities of growing mercantile transactions, the said sections were replaced and "Sale of Goods Act, 1930" took its birth. It is well known that our sale of goods act 1930 is based upon and is largely reproduction of the English sale of goods Act, 1893 and in principles of law of sale of goods in both the countries is now the same.

The sale of goods act applies only to movable goods other than actionable (claims) and money and not to immovable which are governed by the Transfer of Property Act, 1882. Actionable claim means "those in action" thing in action, it means the person has a right to recover a thing by suit but does not have the enjoyment of thing.

Goods may be (*i*) existing or (*ii*) future existing goods are further classified as (*a*) Specific Goods and (*b*) as curtained or Generic Goods.

Specific Goods means goods identified and agreed upon at the time of contract of sale *i.e.* mode. These goods are already in existence and are physically present in some Person's possession and ownership. For example, a specific car or a specific watch. Generic or as curtained Goods are indicated by description and not specifically identified for example 1 kg of oil or a few kg of oils with mercantile. Future goods means goods to be manufactured or purchased or acquired by the seller after making of the contract of sale. These goods do not exist at the time of contract of sale, but subsequently comes into existence.

A contract of sale of goods is a contract where seller transfers or agrees to transfer the property in goods to the buyer for a price. Such a sale may be conditional or absolute. A contract of sale of goods may be either a sale or an agreement to sell.

Formalities of this contract are:

(1) Offer and acceptance (2) Delivery (3) Price (4) Goods

Property means general property in goods and not merely a special property. General property means ownership of the goods and special property means special interest in the goods under the sale of goods act. Property under this act means ownership transfer of property, thus is transfer of ownership in the goods and not nearly specific interest in the goods. The term is important as transfer of property determines transfer of risks from seller to buyer.

8.11. THE LAND ACQUISITION ACT, 1984

To provided certain public purposes/uses such as Educational/Health/Transport Irrigation/Housing/Buildings and communication etc. land would be needed for serving the public at large. All lands are not owned by the Government and under the Constitution, right to make property by the citizen is ensured. Then how do we get the land for above purposes when needed by the Govt./Semi-Govt.

The Land Acquisition Act of 1894 has been enacted for the only purpose of acquiring the private lands whether open or built-up by adopting the regular proposal in this regard.

Main provisions of this Act, stipulates that when any piece, of land whether open or builtup (consisting with structure already built) is needed for any public purpose and if that public proposal is approved by the Govt. then Govt. would issue orders for acquiring the land describing the detailed schedule with the identity of land with its Survey No., Plot No., village and its area as recorded in the Revenue Record of the particular village.

After following the entire procedure stiupulated under the Act in various sections, the award has to be declared by the Special Land Acquisition Officer appointed for this purposes by mentioning in the award the compensation payable as per market value as on notified date to the land owner/his bonafide representative. If the compensation is not acceptable to the owner, then he can accept the same under protest and file a claim to enhance compensation in the District Court within prescribed time limit. If the Court is convinced about the claim filled by the owner, then court passes order to grant enhancement of the compensation and orders the Acquiring Body to pay the enhancement as per order.

Entire procedure under this Act is totally democratic and at every stage the owner has right to lodge his say in writing before the Special Land Acquisition Officer. If the owner feels that the acquisition proposed is not justifiable for public purposes, then he can challenge the same before the High Court feels the same as mentioned by the owner, the acquisition stands cancelled.

The act also provides or empower the Govt. to initiate the acquisition for the private Institutions, which are registered under the Trust Act and Societies Act and are delivering public purposes whether if may be in the Educational or Health field.

The benefit of this Act is that any land whether open or built can be acquired by the Government for public purposes.

8.12. THE URBAN LAND (CEILING AND REGULATION) ACT, 1976

This Act has been introduced by the Central Govt. all over India, with a view to have restrictions on the holding of land by each individual in the cities/agglomerations prescribed in the schedule of the Act. In Maharashtra, there are nine agglomerations, where such restriction is imposed in the cities like (1) Mumbai, (2) Thane, (3) Kalyan-Dombivali-Ulhas Nagar, (4) Pune, (5) Solapur, (6) Nasik, (7) Sangli-Miraj, (8) Kolhapur, (9) Nagpur.

Under this Act there are three categories, which gives the quantum of areas in each agglomeration which can be held by the individual. These categories are (*A*) 500 sq m. (*B*) 1000 sqm. (C) 1500 sqm. "*A*" category is applicable to Mumbai, while "*B*" is for Pune, Thane, Kalyan and "*C*" is for Solapur, Sangli-Miraj etc.

The Act clear cutly spells out that if the land determined is more than the prescribed limit of category *A, B, C* then the residual land stands excess.

This excess land under the law stands acquired without any choice of the owner. He would be entitled for payment of compensation as prescribed under the law. In this law the compensation is not payable immediately on taking over of the surplus land, but initially the amount is determined under the law is payable, while residual would be given in terms of the bonds which can be cashed after 20 years.

The Act also provides the exemption of surplus land to the owner on the ground of gift to the public purposes to the private institutions which are registered under the Society Act and Trust Act.

The Act also provides the exemption under the pretext of the housing schemes sponsored by norms prescribed under the law by the Govt. from time to time. Some of the schemes implemented under this law, consists of Anand Nagar on the Paud Road, Sakal Nagar, near Baner Road and such other schemes seen as advertised in the paper.

Main intention of this law is to curb the speculation of land hoarding by the private individual and make available the surplus land to large public for housing purposes.

8.13. TRANSFER OF DEVELOPMENT RIGHT (TDR)

Modified Development Control (DC) rules for Pune introducing transfer of development rights (TDR) accommodation reservation and specific norms on off-street parking at residential, institutional, government or semi-government and commercial buildings have been sanctioned by the Maharashtra Government.

The other salient features of the modified DC rules are grant of special powers to the Municipal Commissioner for alternating reservations in case of public utilities, and permission for construction up to four per cent of total area on hill top-hill slope and in green zones.

Specific norms on revised area and height limitations for industrial buildings have been framed. Roads on which shops will be permitted too have been listed in the modified DC rules.

The latest sanction to major modification introducing TDR and accommodation reservation for the first time in municipal limits. These modifications are introduced to speed up acquisition of reserved lands.

The provisions for TDR entitles the owner of a land reserved for public purpose to and award of Floor Space Index (FSI) in the form of a Development Right Certificate (DRC) which he may use for himself or transfer to any other person.

This is subject to onwer's undertaking to develop or construct the specified public amenity on part of the land and surrendering that portion free of cost to cost to the PMC. The owner will be issued a DRC on the remaining land only after satisfactory compliance of the conditions prescribed by the municipal authority.

The city has been divided into three zones—'*A*' comprising civic wards in congested areas, '*B*' comprising civic wards in semi-congested areas and '*C*' comprising civic wards in non-congested areas.

Specific rules have been framed to ensure proper utilisation of the DRCs. Subject to the conditions land down in these rules the DRC originating from zone '*A*' can be used in zone '*B*' or '*C*'. A DRC originating from zone '*B*' may be used in either zone '*B*' or in zone '*C*' while a DRC originating from zone '*C*' can be used only in zone '*C*'.

However, the DRCs shall not be used on plots for housing schemes for slum dwellers for which additional FSI is permissible and the areas where permission FSI is less than 1.0 also, the DRC shall not be used on plots fronting specified arterial roads upto a depth of 30 meters in zone '*s*' only.

Table 8.2. Revised area, hight limitations for industrial buildings

Plot size (square meters)	*Maximum built-up area (%)*	*Minimum marginal open space m*	*Minimum side rear marginal space, m*	*Minimum width of plot in mtrs.*	*Maximum FSI*	*Maximum number of storeys*
300 to 500	50	6	3	15	1	3
501 to 1000	50	6	4	20	1	3
10001 to 2500	50	6	4.5	25	1	3
2501 to 5000	50	6	6	35	1	3
5000 and above	50	6	6	50	1	3

Under accommodation reservation, sites designated for dispensaries, maternity homes and hospitals, in congested areas may be allowed to be developed for mixed use provided that owners of such properties give required built-up area for the amenities to the satisfaction of the P.M.C.

Owners fulfilling this condition may avail additional FSI up to 40 per cent of the total plot area or the actual constructed area to be handed over to the PMC, whichever is less.

The PMC may acquire, develop and maintain the amenity as a reservation or the owner may be permitted to develop the amenity subject to his handling over to the corporation free of charge a built-up area of specified percentage for the amenity. Similar conditions and rules with minor modification will apply to shopping centres, children's play ground, parks and gradients, cultural centres, fire brigade and industrial use.

Specific norms have been framed for off street parking at residential, institutional, government or semi-government, industrial and commercial buildings. Thus, providing adequate space for parking specified number of four-wheelers, two-wheelers and cycles, will henceforth be mandatory at all buildings in both congested and non-congested areas.

Further, the modified DC rules empower the Municipal Commissioner to alter reservations in case of public utilities provided that, where a site is designated for a specific purpose in the development plan (DP), he with prior approval of the government may permit the designation for schools and their playground, the Commissioner may interchange their use.

This was being done to speed up the alteration processes. Thus, the Municipal Commissioner will not be subject to the lengthy procedures of sanctions from civic sub-committees and elected general body, and calling for objections from citizens.

Construction of swimming pools, sports centres amusement parks, health clubs, cafeteria and canteens, will be allowed on hilltop-hill slopes and in green zones provided the maximum floor space area does not exceed four per cent of the total plot area, with only ground floor without stilts.

Constructions at petrol pumps will henceforth be permitted for providing allied services only.

The new rules will help the PMC in expediting the implementation of the development plan. Since 1987, when the development plan was approved, only 15 per cent of land reserved for providing civic amenities could be utilised.

The new rules offers a pragmatic choice to landowners whose land had been reserved for projects offering civic amenities. Earlier, the administration acquired the land after paying due consideration to the landowner. Under the new rules, the land-owners have the option of retaining, a major portion of the land (upto 85 per cent) by developing the required facility at their expense and handing it over to the PMC.

8.14. ENVIRONMENTAL PROTECTION ACT, 1986

After Bhopal disaster in 1984 claiming 300 lives or so, the Central Govt. enacted the Environmental Protection Act in May, 1986. It came force in whole of India on 19th November, 1986.

Concern over the state of environment has grown the world ever since the sixties. The decline in environmental quality has been evidenced by increasing pollution, loss of vegetal cover and biological diversity, excessive concentrations of harmful chemicals in the ambient atmosphere and in food chains, growing risks of environmental accidents and threats to life support systems. The world community's resolve to protect and enhance the environmental quality found expression in the decisions taken at the United Nations Conference on the Human Environment held in Stockholm in June, 1972. Government of India participated in the Conference and strongly voiced the environmental concerns. While several measures have been taken for environmental protection both before and after the Conference, the need for a general legislation further to implement the decisions of the conference has become increasingly evident.

Although there are existing laws dealing directly or indirectly with several Environmental matters, it is necessary to have a general legislation for environmental protection. Existing laws generally focus on specific types of pollution or on specific categories of hazardous substances. Some major areas of environmental hazards are not covered. There exist uncovered gaps in areas of major environmental hazards. There are inadequate linkages in handling matters of industrial and environmental safety. Control mechanisms to guard against slow, insidious build up of hazardous substances, especially new chemicals, for an authority which can assume the lead role for studying planning and implementing long term requirements of environmental safety and to give direction to and co-ordinate a system of speedy and adequate response to emergency situations threatening the environment.

In view what has been stated above, there is urgent need for the enactment of a general legislation on environmental protection which inter alia, should enable of an authority or authorities with adequate powers for environmental protection, regulation of discharge environmental pollutants and handling of hazardous substances, speedy response in the event of accidents, threatening environment and deterrent punishment to those who endanger human environment, safety and health.

The act seeks to achieve the above objectives.

8.14.1. Power to Central Government to take Measures to Protect and Improve Environment

(*a*) The central Government shall have the power to take all such measures as it deems necessary or expedient for the purpose of protecting and improving the quality of the environment and preventing controlling and abating environmental pollution.

(*b*) In particular measures may include the following:

(*i*) Planning and executing of a nation-wide programme for the prevention, control and abatement of environmental pollution;

(*ii*) Laying down standards for the quality of environment is its various aspects;

(*iii*) Laying down standards for emission or discharge of environmental pollutants from various sources whatsoever;

(*iv*) Restriction in which any industries, operations or processes shall not be carried out or shall be carried out subject to certain safeguards;

(*v*) Layking down procedure and safeguards for the prevention of accidents which may cause environmental pollution and remedial measures for such accidents;

(*vi*) Laying down procedures and safeguards for the handling of hazardous substances;

(*vii*) Examination of such manufacturing processes, materials as are likely to cause environmental pollution;

(*viii*) Carrying out and sponsoring investigations and research relating to problems of environmental pollution;

(*ix*) Inspection of any premises, plan, equipment, etc. to take steps for the prevention, control and abatement of environmental pollution;

(*x*) Establishment or recognition of environmental laboratories and institutes to carry out the functions entrusted to such environmental laboratories and institutes under this Act;

(*xi*) Collection and dissemination of information in respect of matters relating to environmental pollution;

(*xii*) Preparation of manuals, codes or guides relating to the prevention, control and abatement of environmental pollution;

(*xiii*) Such other matters, as the Central Government deems necessary for the purpose of securing the effective implementation of provisions of this Act.

The Central Government may, (if it considers it necessary) constitute an authority for the purpose of exercising and performing such of the powers and functions (including the power to issue directions).

8.14.2. Power to Give Directions

The Central Government may issue directions is writing to any person, officer or any authority who shall be bound to comply with such directions.

(*a*) The closure, prohibition or regulation or any industry, operation or processor.

(*b*) Stoppage or regulation of the supply of electricity or water or any other service.

8.14.3. Rules to Regulate Environmental Pollution

The Central Government may, make rules in respect of:

(*a*) The Standards of quality of air, water or soil for various areas and purposes;

(*b*) The maximum allowable limits of concentration of various environmental pollutants (including noise) for different areas;

(*c*) The procedures and safeguards for the handling of hazardous substances;

(*d*) The prohibition and restrictions on the handling of hazardous substances in different areas; etc.

8.14.4. Prevention, Control and Abatement of Environmental Pollution

(*a*) No person carrying on any industry, operation or process shall discharge or emit any environmental pollutant in excess of standard prescribed.

(*b*) No person shall handle or cause to be handled any hazardous substance except after complying with such safeguards as may be prescribed.

(*c*) Furnishing of information to authorities and agencies responsible for such discharge and the person incharge of the place at which any accident or other unforeseen act or event occur the person will forth with:

(*i*) Intimate the fact of such occurrence

(*ii*) Be bound, if called upon, the render all assistance, to such authorities.

(*d*) On receipt of information shall, as early as practicable cause such remedial measures to be taken as are necessary to prevent or mitigate the environmental pollution.

(*e*) The expenses, if any may be recovered as arrears of land revenue or of public demand.

8.14.5. Powers of Entry and Inspection

Any person empowered by the Central Government in this behalf shall have a right to enter, at all reasonable times:

(*a*) For determining whether, and if, so in what manner, any such functions are to be performed or whether provisions of this Act or the permission granted under this Act is being or has been complied with;

(*b*) For the purpose of examining and testing any equipment, industrial plant, record, register, document or any other material object or for conducting a search of any building in which he has reasons to believe that an offence under this Act of the rules made thereunder has been or is being or is about to be committed and for seizing any such equipment, industrial plant, record register, document or other material object it may furnish, evidence of the commission of an offence punishable under this Act.

(*c*) Every person carrying on any industry, operation or process or handling any hazardous substances shall be bound to render all assistance to the person empowered by Central Government and if he fails to do so shall be guilty of an offence under this Act.

(*d*) If any person willfully delays or obstructs any person empowered by the Central Government he shall be guilty of an offence under this Act.

8.14.6. Power to Make Sample and Procedure to be followed in Connection therewith

The Central Government or any office empowered by it in this behalf, shall have power take for the purpose of analysis, samples of air, water soil or other substance from any factory, premises of other place in such manner as may be prescribed.

8.14.7. Environmental Laboratories

(*a*) The Central Government may establish/recognise one or more laboratories or institutes as environmental laboratories to carry out the functions entrusted to an environmental laboratory.

(*b*) Make rules specifying the function of the environmental laboratory.

(*c*) The procedure for the submission to the said laboratory of samples of air, water soil or other substance for analysis or tests, the form of the laboratory report thereon and the fees payable for such report.

8.14.8. Penalty for Contravention of the Provisions of Act

(*a*) Whoever do not comply with provisions of this act is punishable with imprisonment for a term which may be upto five years or with fine which may extend to one lakh rupees, or with both and in case the failure or contravention continues, with additional fine which may extend to five thousand rupees for every day.

(*b*) If the failure or contravention referred continues beyond a period of one year and date of conviction, the offender shall be punishable with imprisonment for a term, which may extend to seven years.

8.15. INDIAN ELECTRICITY ACT AND ELECTRICITY RULES

The Indian electricity act was passed in 1910 to the supply of electricity to all the consumers who apply for it. This act was passed to supply electricity to all the consumers who apply for it and to control and regularise electric supply.

According to this act all electric supply lines must be provided with safety devices used for this purpose. Accordingly on person except a license holder shall be allowed to use or generate or transmit energy more than 250 watts and 100 volts. As per the act central electricity boards, state electricity boards have been developed which consists of persons from government, boards, railways, mines and I.S.I. The jobs of these boards are to make rules and regulation to regulate generation, transmission, use and supply of electricity. According to this act any person interfering with meters; or misusing the powers of involved in the light and building is liable of the punishment as per norms of the act.

This act also classifies the voltage lines as low, medium, high or extra high depending upon the voltage. This acts permits any electricity inspector to enter any premise and inspect the works. This act also dictates the ruler of testing of installation and connections; switch board installation, variation in voltage, variation in frequency; reading of meters and cut-outs and connection with the earth. Electricity rules have been flamed in 1956 for strict implementation of Act, 1910.

8.16. THE BOILER ACT

This act was passed in 1923. This act makes the registration and regular inspection of all boilers compulsory except for those in ships, or those which are under the control of Railways and defence department. This act dictates that a boiler can not be used under any circumstance, unless it is registered. Further a boiler can not be used at a pressure higher than what is prescribed by the authority. A person holding certificate of competency only can operate the boiler. The boiler operator also at the same time must get ensured that it has been registered. Before he operates; he must get checked its parts and fittings. Various fittings and appliances must be checked for its working pressure.

8.17. APPRENTICE ACT, 1961

This act was passed in 1961 to train the person for a period varying from 2 years to 3 years before they are put to actual production job. This training is exhaustive and sufficiently long. This is called as apprentices training and extracts are called as apprentices. As per this act apprentices must be taught guidance and supervision of experts. The aim of this act is to overcome unemployment problem and to help young and promising technicians for entrepreneurship. Though this act was passed in 1961 but has been implemented since 1963. This act made it compulsory on the part of employer in 217 specified industries to engage apprentices in 138 trades. This act restricts that children below the age of 14 years should not be allowed to join the course. If a factory or concern in having more than 500 workers or employees, then that concern must have separate training centre Quota has been fixed for reserved categories for this apprentice training. Apprentices are also paid stipend as per the norms given in the act and modified time to time. The main advantage of this act are that it caters to the need of trained hand and increases production. It also improves the quality of work and reduces production cost. It also reduces wastages.

8.18. MINES ACT, 1952

This act has been passed mainly to safeguard the interest of mine workers. This act also lays certain norms like minimum wages, safety measures, working hours etc. to the mine workers.

8.19. LAND CEILING ACT

The urban land (Ceiling and Regulations) Act, 1976, known as Act No. 33 of 1976 under the article 252 of the constitution resolution come into force on 17 February, 1976 with retrospective effect of applications for all the transactions or transfers on or after 17.02.1975. Since that the law is constantly getting amended and may continue to amend.

The objective of imposing this act is for imposing ceiling on urban property as realised necessity by various state government. It was to control the disorderly development of urban areas with respective growth of population and increasing urbanisation. The urban land ceiling (ULC) Act has created as impact on values of properties and therefore on valuation also this act restricts and regulates transfer and use of urban property. The sellers and purchasers are required as per this act to file an application and affidavits under various sections, even if a seller has land lesser than the ceiling limits prescribed and the purchaser has more land than the ceiling limit.

Articles:

(1) Provision of village sites or the extension, planned development or improvement of existing village sites.

(2) The provision of land for town or rural planning.

(3) The provision of land for planned development of land from public funds in pursuance of any scheme or policy of government and subsequent disposal thereof in whole or in part by lease, assignments or outright sale with the object of securing further development as planned.

(4) The provision of land for a corporation owned or controlled by the state. Tenant lands for old structures constructed before 1970.

(5) Provision of land for residential purposes to the poor or landless or to the persons residing in areas affected by natural calamities, or to persons displaced or affected by the implementation of any scheme undertaken by government, any local authority or a corporation or controlled by the state.

(6) The provision of land for carrying out any educational, housing, health or slum clearance scheme sponsored by Government or any authority established by Government for carrying out any such scheme or with a prior approval of appropriate Government, by a local authority, or a society, registered under the Society Registration Act, 1860 or under the corresponding law for the time being in force in a state or a co-operative relating to pertain societies the time being in force in any state.

(7) Provision of land for any other scheme of development sponsored Government or with the prior approved of appropriate government by a authority.

(8) Provision of any premises or building for locating a public office.

There are state amendments to this Claus and the base is becoming broader and broader to include several purposes in this definition.

Similarly all State Governments have almost unanimously made amendments their respective State laws, improvement in Trust Act, Regional and Town Planning Acts, Industrial Development Acts, and Highways Acts, narrowing down the scope for differences. The various court ruling have sealed the probable loopholes and the Land Acquisition Act as on this comprehensive more than ever before.

Once a State Government for competent authority has decided to acquire any land including built-up structures for any public purpose, the gazette notification is published to declare the intentions. The data of Gazette notifications lays a pivotal role in valuations. There is a stipulated time limit of three years within which the authority has to take concrete steps otherwise the date is lapsed. However such authority has a power to publish fish gazette notification and in that case the pivotal date is extended to date if fresh notification.

There is also an obligation on authority of make proper surveys, to assess the fair market values of such properties to be acquired. The compensation payable is usefully decided on the basis of average rent of the property for five years preceding the date of notification and in absence, if found necessary, call for rent records from' municipalities or Corporations for comparable rents of five years in adjoining areas. The survey is most important as it exactly notes the dimensions, the land use, tenancies, the unoccupied areas and even between tenant, and landlords. The use on the date of notification plays an important role. If the market value is specially high in consequence of the land being put to a use which is unlawful or contrary to public policy, that use is disregarded and the market value is deemed to be the market value of and if put to ordinary use.

If owner has erected or re-erected any structure other than mentioned in survey after the date of notification then value of that structure is disregarded. However if any improvements are made to the land which are as per the proposal for improvements in consequence to the lands under acquisition, such improvements are considered while adopting the market value.

The lands are acquired for various purposes such as road widening, slum improvement, any Town Planning Scheme sewerage disposal, flood relief etc. However the existing land use on the date of notification (provided it is lawful and in line with public policy) is taken into consideration and the basis of the future land use is disregarded.

A valuer, while deterring the fair market value, of such properties, should consider the following stages:

(1) The survey sheet mentioning dimensions, structures, names of tenants, and the prevailing land use.

(2) The date of notification in official gazette, date of order of acquisition and award issued by competent authority. In case the date of acquisition is lapsed whether fresh notification is issued or not.

(3) Any additions and alterations done after the date of notification should be disregarded. However any improvements made with the pricier permission of the competent authority within then notification period may be considered.

(4) Rents of five years received or receivable as prevailing rents in the vicinity should be taken into account. In case of unoccupied areas or areas free of rent given to nearest relatives should be considered on the basis of prevailing rents in the vicinity.

(5) An average or gross rents thus obtained from records for five years should be considered and l/5th of such gross rent should be deducted in case of Municipal taxes, insurance, collection charges and repairs and maintenance, expenses are not known. However, if proper accounts are maintained then actual expenses should only be considered to arrive at actual net rent.

(6) In case of any fruit trees are standing then a fair assessment depending upon their life yield and further life may be added in the value of property.

(7) Note down the actual land use and adopt proper years purchase to capitalise the value.

(8) In case of rental valuation, reversionary value of land is disregarded. However, in land and building method the land values should be added to the depreciated values of structures.

The purpose of valuation also plays an important role. If a valuer is asked to advise on the fair and reasonable market value of the properties to be acquired then his course of action should be as laid down above. However in the case where the property is already in process or acquired then the value should be determined from the award of compensation (received or receivable) after deducting the interest payable for the period from the date of notification and the date of payment of compensation. However 15% solarium (whether awarded or not) on the market value as on the day of notification should be added. The awards issues normally take into account the various incidental charges etc. these charges should be deducted from the award. In absence a reasonable percentage between 15 to 20% may be deducted from the compensation.

It is generally observed that the valuation for taxation purposes differs from valuation for acquisition purposes. The tax laws a constantly amended and issuing various directives and sometimes steps and method. Such amendments have been made to simplify the procedures and avoid probable litigation and loss of time. Therefore several aspects could be ignored. A valuer should take a judicious decision in adopting the course while working out valuation for taxation purposes. If he observes that there is a difference (not more than 15%) between the two values adopted by different methods, then the average value should be certified as fair and reasonable value.

It is important to note here that a person aggrieved may ask for high valuation for compensation purposes for lands in acquisition. He may need such valuation to be recorded in court matters. At the same time the same person may ask the valuer to produce a report indicating far less value asking advantage of the subjuris matter for above all and therefore valuer should be careful in finding out the market value since practice and the courts (if observations are recorded) may initiate lawful proceedings against the valuer.

8.20. TRANSFER OF PROPERTY ACT : 1882 (ACT NO. 4 OF 1882) AMENDED UPTO 24TH AUGUST, 1984

The Transfer of Property Act is extended to all States of India. Basic purposes of this act is to regulate the transfer of property whether movable or immovable. The transfer of property means an act by which a living associations or body of individuals, conveys property in present or in future to one or more other living persons, or to himself and one or more living persons and "To Transfer Property" is to perform such act. We are primarily concerned with immovable properties.

The immovable property means the property which is "Attached to the earth" means

(*a*) Rooted in the earth as in the case of trees and shrubs,

(*b*) Embedded in the earth as in the case of walls and building,

(*c*) Attached to what is so embedded for the permanent beneficial enjoyment of that to which it is attached.

The transfer of property is done by sale, mortgagee, gift, lease or any other negotiable instruments of transfer. The transfer of property by gift has religious sanction and it differs from religion to religion. All other means of transfer have common code of conduct. The rights of property are generally two types : (1) lease hold and (2) free hold.

A lease hold right may vary form fraction of a year to perpetuity of 30 years and above. Whereas the free hold right vary from any number of years from 99 to 999 years. Similarly in agricultural lands the same is further classified into (1) Bhoomidhari means one who holds land and (2) Bhoomiswami means who owns the land. Like in rented properties the owners enjoy rights of benefits for a consideration whereas the tenant hold tenancy rights it is beneficial enjoyment payable to the owners. There are various laws governing these rights and they differ from State to State depending upon the accepted practices in the respective societies.

The transfer of property act has been amended and it practically covers all the aspects of transfer. Wherever there is any other law having rules for transfer of properties such provisions are read in the line and with the same express meaning of the Transfer of Property Act and subject to certain conditions ruling beneficial use in the public interest, all rules and regulations mentioned in the said acts, (for examples Urban Land Ceiling Act) are to be read in the meaning and context of the Transfer of Property Act.

The Indian Registration Act governing the procedure of registration and the stamp duty is also closely related with this act Valuation is required for the purpose of assessing stamp duty and also assessing the value consideration to transferer or transferee. Values fourths two purposes is based on the broader principles of valuation. Various State Governments have made it mandatory to adopt the values proposed by their town planners in the form of indices for particular periods in different agglomerations. It is generally observed that actual sale values are considerably high or low in each transaction. However it is general tendency to mention less value for transfer of property purposes and adopt the value on the basis of indices for stamp duty purposes.

There are generally two parts for every transfer. One is an agreement or will and second is the actual document of transfer for registration purposes. Here also religion plays important role. For example in Hindu law oral partition by akarta is acceptable whereas in other religions the cases are different.

It is vital for every transaction that the transferer holds good and marketable title over the property to be transferred. The transferor hold such rights, as karta, as constituted power of attorney, as lessor, as assigner, as liquidate, as inheritor, etc. To establish the transferor's position in those regards, he has to establish cretins documents such as sale deeds, gift deeds documents should bear the same identity through earlier documentation. It is generally for more than a certain period and even if they are available it becomes virtually counter such difficulties, there is a provision possession it is lawful, uninterrupted possession of the property for more than 12 years. This provision entitles the possessor to act as transferer. However, there are certain exceptions like government lands which are excluded from this provision. For registration of deed or transfer, several no objection certificate and clearances are necessary. Various departments such as income tax, city survey corporations or improvement trust etc. and competent authorities such as Town Planning authorities under ULC act etc. have their own procedures to be adopted. Even though every such department and authority has income tax department, to control evasion of the improvement trust to control terms and conditions of leases and various building permits accorded, ULC Act to control the concentration of urbanisable lands in the hand of few, city survey and nazul departments to regulate registrations in their respective records etc. It is normally seen that the various laid down procedures of the departments have several conflicting things, which creates chaos and harassment to the parties of the transfer apart from the money and time required.

It is ironical to note that a transferee has to satisfy himself about the title, rights and interest of the transferer and transferee in turn undertakes to indemnify the transfer to any defects found in later course time. It is invariably a slip shod method and by the time such defects are observed transferee is left with claiming the compensation through lengthy legal battles.

Other salient features of this Transfer of Property Act are:

(1) The sections 53A and 54 of Transfer of Property Act deal with the transfer of immovable property.

(2) According to the Section 54 of Transfer of Property Act, the sale is a transfer of ownership in exchange for a price paid or promised or part paid and part promised. The transfer of immovable, property of the value more than ₹ 100/- should be made only through a registered instrument. The sale is complete as soon as the deed is registered. The property does not pass or the ownership is not transferred until the registration is effected. But once the registration is effected the title relates to the date of execution.

(3) The Section 53A of Transfer of Property Act dealing with the part performance protects the buyers' interest. This gives a shield to a buyer from the possible frauds of a seller. For the application of Section 53A of the application of Section 53A of Transfer of Property Act the following conditions should be satisfied:

(*i*) There should be contract to transfer for an immovable property for a consideration.

(*ii*) There should be written agreement and its terms can be well ascertained with reasonable certainty.

(*iii*) The transferee in part performance of the contract has taken the possession of the property or any part thereof.

(*iv*) The transferee has done some act in furtherance of the contract.

(*v*) The transferee is ready and willing to perform his part of the contract.

(5) The Section 53A while protecting the rights of the buyer does not give the buyer the title of flat. The transfer of property can take place only on completion of the registration as per section 54 of Transfer of Property Act.

(6) Let us see the effect of these Acts in respect of wealth tax liabilities of flat owners.

(7) One of the methods to own a flat is to form a co-operative house building society having the persons interested in having a flat as members. The society then constructs and allots the flats to the members on the land purchased by the society. By virtue of being a member of the co-operative society, the fiat allotted get the right to use the flats and sell their flats. In the case of sale of a flat by a member only a change of names are made in the records of the society and no transfer documents are made no transfer documents are made and registered with the registrar of assurance. This is done probably to avoid tax liabilities.

(8) Another method adopted to own a flat is that a developer or a builder purchases the land and construct the building comprising of flats and make agreements for sale of different types of flats to the intending buyers. On taking payments from various buyers he hands over the possession of the fiats to actually these transfers of rights are to be registered under Transfer of Property Act. But in order to avoid the stamp duty this is normally deferred indefinitely.

(9) In an yet another method the developer constructs a building as per the agreement with the prospective owners of the flats. The undivided share of the land is transferred by the landowners only and registered. Whereas the only and registered. Whereas the building is concerned no restoration takes place as the building is contructed on a building contract with an individual owner. This is mainly done with a view to avoid stamp duty on the building cost. Generally it is the prospective owners are not identified at the start of the project. As such entering into contract for construction. This is done to avoid double stamp duty on the building portion. The undivided share of the land is also sold directly by owners (and not by the develops) and not by the developers) through the power of attorney received by the developers from the owners.

(10) Main objective in delaying the registration and avoiding the registration and avoiding the registration is to avoid the stamp duty and tax liabilities. The people try to defer and avoid the transfer, by not registering the transfer as required under Section 54 of Transfer of Property Act. By not registering, the transferee does not become the legal owner, the transferee has been taking the advantage of the legal flaw to avoid the capital gain and the wealth tax liability.

(11) When the documents of transfer is not registered, the legal owner is the promoter or the co-operative society. Though they are the legal owners, the user of the flats enjoy the maximum right. The value of the rights at the hands of the transferors as well as their tax liability is much less.

(12) In order to make the real owners to pay the taxes by the flat owners who enjoy the maximum rights are made liable to pay the taxes are made liable to pay the taxes by amending the Sections 2(*m*)(*iii*) of Wealth Tax Act and Section 2(47)(*v*) and (*vi*) and 27 Income Tax Acts w.e.f. 01.04.1988.

(13) As per these amendments the transfer means to include the part performance of contract. In other works the non-registration does not come in the way of making the owners to pay the tax. The real users and owners have become liable to pay taxes.

8.21. MAHARASHTRA OWNERSHIP FLATS ACT, 1963

This act specifies regulation of the promotion of construction, sale management and transfer of properties. This act also specifies certain guide lines and conditions to be followed both by the promotor and buyer. The salient features and this act are:

(1) The promoter/builder will have to refund the amount received by him from the buyer, with interest; for failure to give possession within specified time or future time if allowed.

(2) The nature extent and description of common area and facilities and limited common areas and facilities if any, and the percentage of individual interest in the common areas and facilities appertaining to flat greed to be sold.

(3) After plans and specifications are disclosed no alterations or additions are allowed without the consent of persons who have agreed to take the flats, and defects noticed within three years are to be rectified at the builders cost.

Chapter xx-c of I.T. Act

Income Tax Act, 1961 has a total of 23 chapters out of these, chapter xx-c deals with the purchase of immovable properties by Central Government in certain cases of transfer.

It is believed that investment in real estates provide junk of unaccounted Black Money. Therefore Government of India in 1972 added a chapter xx-A to the I.T. Act to counteract evasion of tax. According to this act Government was authorised to go ahead with acquisition of properties owned by private bodies if those properties were under valued by more than 15% in a sale. However this particular act could not become effective due to following difficulties.

(1) To prove the intentions of transfer involving Black Money.

(2) To prove the suspected under valuation of properties.

(3) To arrive at the fair market value there of therefore the provision of chapter xx-c was introduced in 1986. The main object of this chapter is that power has been vested with the Central Government to a pre-emptive (means frost priority) right to purchase immovable properties which are offered for sale in the market at the price agreed between transferor and trasferee. This provision is applicable to the properties have value more than 10 lakhs. The main objective of this clause was to curb the use of black money in real estate business and to prevent evasion of capital gains tax, wealth tax. The provision of this chapter came into existence from 01.10.1996 and has 15 sections and applicable to towns and cities approved by Central

Government throughout seven appropriate authorities which consist of three members, two of them being members of the Indian I.T. Service Group-A holding post of commissioner of I.T. or equivalent higher post of one of the Central Government Engineering Services Group-A of the rants Chief Engineer equivalent.

There are certain merits and demerits of this Act. The main advantage is that a person whose property is purchased by government will get this money duplicate from Government without any anxiety and apprehension. Where the main demerits is genuine prospective buyer may loose his opportunity of purchase it.

8.22. MAHARASHTRA REGIONAL AND TOWN PLANNING ACT, 1960 (THE M.R. AND T.P. ACT, 1966)

This act is intended to plan, control use of land not only in delineated areas of various cities, but of the entire state by preparing development plan considering present and future needs.

According to this act first "base map" giving complete details of the existing residential, commercial, industrial, educational and recreational facilities is prepared. On this 'base map' proposed development plan which will cater the needs of projected population for next two decades is marked. This development plan shall cater for the basic amenities and facilities such as school, play grounds, gardens, shopping centres road net work etc.

The draft development plan catering various needs a published for inviting suggestions/ objections. After carefully studying and making due modifications, the plan is finalised and submitted to the Government for sanction. After the sanction by the Government, the plan gets statutory backing for implementation.

The manner, in which development plan for a city is prepared, on the similar lines. Development plans for different regions of the state are prepared so as to integrate development of the state.

For providing many amenities like school, play grounds, parks etc. land is required. The beauty of this act lies in inherent acquisition of land by pulling out the entire land under the scheme and redistribution of the same to each of the landowner by reducing the proportionate land required for amenities.

Rules for plot sizes, built up area, FSI etc. For orderly development of city, the local body of the city has to make rules and regulations regarding permissible built up area, plot sizes, laying of roads in the colony layout, floor space index etc.

The act also provides for the selection of New Town sites for the accommodation of the increased and projected population in the fast growing urban areas like Pimpri-Chinchwad near Pune.

8.23. THE MAHARASHTRA HOUSING AND AREA DEVELOPMENT ACT, 1976

As a result of rapid growth in urban areas, development in the rural areas around cities is taking place. If haphazard growth in these areas is not checked, may lead to problems in future. At the same time, government is not in a position to provide huge funds required to construct houses for people of different income groups. To overcome these difficulties/problems, the government has set up different "Area Development Boards" in 5 different divisions, with head offices located at Bombay, Pune, Nagpur, Aurangabad, Amarawati and Nashik.

The main function of these boards is to acquire and develop the land and also construct the housing tenements for various income groups as per the norms laid down by the Govt. and HUDCO (India). By constituting these Boards, it has become possible and easy to have housing stock for all income groups. This body has also borrowing powers to have the financial outlay for their yearly programme and that they should not depend upon the State funds. Infect for state it is not possible to have this tremendous outlay for housing and area development when other important functions of the state require lot of funds.

Provisions have been made in the act, so as to have control over complete administrations, accounts, implementation and such other matters.

Examples of these Boards can be seen from the colonies they have developed in Mumbai, Pune and elsewhere in the State. In Pune, Agarkar, Nagar, Laxmi, Nagar Gokhale Nagar, Phule Nagar at Yerawada colonies have been developed by the Pune Board. In Mumbai also large number of colonies have been developed by the Board known as Pant Nagar, Kannamwar Nagar, at vadre large number of Govt. Quarters are constructed.

One more important area is developed by the Board near Aurangabad at Walunj. This is large complex developed to suit the large scale development carried out by Industrial Establishments like Bajaj Auto etc.

8.24. THE BOMBAY METROPOLITAN REGIONAL DEVELOPMENT AUTHORITY, 1974

Taking recourse to the Maharashtra Regional and Town Planning Act, 1966, the State Govt, prepared the Regional Plan for Bombay Metropolitan Region in the year 1970. Looking to the rapid growth of Greater Mumbai, within the jurisdiction of the Mumbai Mahapalika and also out said the Mahapalika area just adjacent to it, the Regional Plan proposal suggested the constitution of Authority for implementation of the proposals in the Region. If this is not done constitution of Authority for implementation of the proposals in the Region. If this is not done the rapid development of large scale slum areas would grow and the city would become the victim of the population explosion.

Considering this suggestion, the State Govt. Immediately enacted the "Bombay Metropolitan Regional Development Authority, 1974". It mainly empowers the State to constitute this authority under the head of Chief Metropolitan Commissioner and under his administrative control all other wings for acquisition of land, its development by providing infrastructure load development sub-division of land, planning the building comprising of housing tenements for various income groups, provision of water supply, open spaces and sites for amenities like school, playground shopping complexes etc.

Besides this function, the authority has to exercise its control over all the lands included within the jurisdiction of the authority for its use and development. It must be unconformity with the proposals of the Regional Plan and no deviation is permissible on any account. Secondly, it is the planning authority for preparation of small area development plans for the different villages or countryside areas included within the jurisdiction of the Regional plan. This authority has the powers on the lines of Municipal Corporation for removing/pulling down the unauthorised development taking place in the Region. In fact this is the authority in the region, area development, provision of basic infrastructure such as water supply drainage, roads, amenities and facilities, construction of various buildings for providing tenements for various income groups. In fact a full fledge development on the neighbourhood, power to recover the property tax, in-spite of the developing the sites etc. This authority can recommend the Govt. for constituting Municipal Council or Corporation for further perpetual looking after the area so developed for its maintenance etc. As an example in this case, the New Mumbai Municipal Corporation is constituted recently for the areas around Vashi and such other villages developed in the Mumbai Metropolitan Region.

This Act has the jurisdiction in only areas included in the Bombay Metropolitan Region plan, sanctioned by the Govt. in 1974.

8.25. SARFAESI ACT, 2002

SARFAESI act *i.e.,* Securitization and Re-construction of Financial Assets and Enforcement of Security Interest Act, 2002 was introduced in 2002 with main objectives to provide quick and effective remedy to banks and financial institutions to posses auction and to liquidate secured assets to recover their lawful dues from their borrowers. This act further comprises of various sections dealing with different provisions. It is mainly to curb the tendencies of borrowers, not to make repayment of loan and later on declare firm to be liquidated. Once an installment is not paid, the term loan account becomes Non-performing Assets *i.e.,* NPA. If the successive installments are not paid, there is a default. Under such cases to help banks and financial institutions, this act has been introduced. However, there are a few lacunas in this act also, but it is a certainly a good instrument and can be used to recover lawful dues from borrower.

8.26. RIGHT TO INFORMATION (RTI) ACT, 2005

This is an act to provide for setting out practical regime of right to information for citizens to secure access to information under the control of public authorities in order to promote transparency and accountability in the working of every public authority. The act extends to whole of India except State of J & K as J & K has its own RTI Act, 2009. Under the provision of this act, every citizen has right to call for information from a public authority which is required to furnish information expeditiously or within 30 days from the date of information asked for. This act also requires every public authority to computerize their record for wide dissemination and to pro-actively publish certain categories of information so that the citizens need minimum resources to request for information formally.

For several decades, government authorities and other public servants were able to hide information, documents, records etc. from the public as they were not accountable to the general public. The RTI act 2005 has made it possible to ask for information from any public authority and authorities are required to furnish information asked for within 30 days of request.

However there is certain information which cannot be supplied if there disclosure is likely to affect the sovereignty and integrity of state or nation, security, strategic, scientific or economic interest of the state or nation or lead to incitement of an offence do not come under this act. Information which has been expressly forbidden to be published by any court of law or tribunal or the disclosure of which may constitute contempt of court also do not come under this act. Other information which would cause breach of privileges of parliament or state assembly, trade secrets , intellectual property, information received in confidence from foreign government and some other information which are required to be kept secret m the interest of nation also do not come under this act.

Valuers can make use of this act to gather information, documents and records from government and public authorities like banks, financial institutions and others to benefit their clients and society at large.

8.27. WEALTH AND WEALTH TAX

Wealth is the abundance of valuable resources or material possessions. The word wealth is derived from the old English *weal*, which is from an Indo-European word stem. An individual, community, region or country that possesses an abundance of such possessions or resources is known as wealthy.

The concept of wealth is of significance in all areas of economics, and clearly so for growth economics and development economics. Yet the meaning of wealth is context-dependent and there is no universally agreed upon definition. At the most general level, economists may define wealth as "anything of value" which captures both the subjective nature of the idea and the idea that it is not a fixed or static concept. Various definitions and concepts of wealth have been asserted by various individuals and in different contexts. Defining wealth can be a normative process with various ethical implications, since often wealth maximization is seen as a goal or is thought to be a normative principle of its own.

Wealth tax Act came into existence from April 01, 1957 and it extends to whole of India. Wealth tax is charged on the net wealth of assesses. It is charged for every assessment year in respect of net wealth accumulated under specified assets as per this act. Wealth tax is charged in the hands of individuals, HUFs and all private and public companies on the net wealth as on 31st March of each year under consideration. It is charged as 1% of the amount by which net wealth exceeds by ₹ 30 Lakhs. However following assesses are excluded from this act :

1. Companies registered under companies' act 1956.
2. Co-operative societies
3. Social clubs
4. Political parties
5. Mutual funds coming under Income tax act:

Net wealth includes values of all assets including deemed assets but excluding exempt assets as defined in this act and after deduction there from of the debts which are incurred in relation to such assets. Assets exempted are:

1. Property held under the charitable or religious trust.
2. One house or part of a house belonging to an individual/HUF irrespective of value of house.
3. A plot of land not exceeding 500 Sq. Meter belonging to an individual/HUF.
4. Any heirloom jewelery in possession of ruler.
5. Assets and money brought in India by any person of Indian Origin or Indian Citizen, from any other with an intention to settle in India, permanently.

8.28. INTERNATIONAL FINANCIAL REPORTING STANDARDS

International Financial Reporting Standards *i.e.* IFRS is a set of accounting standards developed by an independent organization called International Accounting Standard Board (IASB) to provide a global framework for public companies to prepare and disclose their financial statements. The earlier accounting system IAS *i.e.* International Accounting Standards has been replaced by IFRS and has been accepted by most of the countries including India.

The idea behind it is to increase disclosure of information on assets and liabilities and decrease asymmetry of information between managers and investors. The actual fair value is given where possibilities of misleading is minimized considerably.

8.29. REAL ESTATE REGULATION BILL

There is a rapid growth in real estate and to safeguard interest of home buyers as well as builders and promoters, Government have brought a Real Estate Regulation Bill 2011 (Regulation and Development) to establish a regulatory mechanism for real estate. There is different opinion of this bill. However this bill is yet to be finalized and passed in parliament to become an act. The views of government, builder, consumer and other experts are varying in nature but each and every one involved is interested to get this bill passed to make real estate system transparent.

8.30. VALUATION REPORT

Valuation report by a qualified and approved valuer is required to be prepared. Hence while preparing a valuation report it is essential to contain the following information in report.

(1) Fair description and proper location of the assets which are the subject of the valuation giving clearly identification, comments with reference to legal rights and restrictions in ownership if any.

(2) The purpose of valuation should be clearly worded and stated in the beginning of report.

(3) The limiting conditions like (*a*) hypothetical valuation (*b*) fractional valuation (*c*) Initial opinion subject to revision etc. should be clearly stated.

(4) Terms used under reference should be clearly defined and explained.

(5) Method used for valuation; its description should be stated.

(6) The factors influencing the analysis, opinion and conclusions must be clearly reported. These should not be misleading. There should be no ambiguity involved.

(7) Declaration of disinterestedness of the concerned valuer is a statutory need and must form a part of the report.

(8) Signature and name of valuer or valuers as the case may be; must be a part of the valuation report. Without signature, report is not a valid one.

(9) Original documents available for inspection must be enlisted properly after perusal. If not available, must be recorded in report.

(10) Xerox copies of the originals, duly certified must be attached to the report under consideration.

(11) If some assumptions are made by valuer, they must be recorded as annexure to the valuation report and be certified by valuer.

(12) Clients name should also be recorded in report.

There are certain institution; have their own format of valuation report. In such cases, valuer should submit his report in prescribed format; however he should check that no point is missing which may mislead the report. Overall valuation report should make it obvious as to what has led him to his assessment.

Valuation under normal circumstances is to provide security to financial organisation in care of loans or to purchase assets. Valuation under their act is made for making recovery from the mortgaged/hypothecated assets of loan granted by banks or other financial institutions. Valuation in normal cases is done before asset is mortgaged/hypothecated or purchased while valuation under this act is done after mortgaged and when borrowers account becomes Non Perforcing Asset (NPA).

9 Miscellaneous Topics

9.1. VALUATION ACCORDING TO PURPOSES

The valuers are generally appointed to evaluate any property for one of the following reasons:

(1) Tax purposes

(*a*) Income tax (*b*) Capital gain tax (*c*) Wealth and Gift tax

(*d*) Land and building tax (*e*) Municipal taxes

(2) Loan purposes from financing institutions like from nationalised banks. HDFC, LIC etc. Particularly for construction of residential commercial or industrial units.

(3) For business purposes

(*a*) for sale and purchase (*b*) for rent fixation (*c*) for insurance

(*d*) for partition (*e*) for dissolution of firms

(*f*) for court fee and stamp duty (*g*) for acquisition (*h*) for mortgage

(*i*) for registration

The usual method of valuating any property is same except a few considerations depending upon purpose. If one has to get evaluate his property for tax purposes, he likes to show the value of that property minimum, contradictory if he has to sleuth same, he tunes per very high value. However a responsibility of a guanine valuer is to value the property must appropriately taking into considerations all possible factors in subsequent paragraphs, how a properly should be evaluated according to its purpose is explained briefly.

(1) **Tax—Purposes :**

(*a*) **Income Tax.** On the construction or acquisition of the property or a house the owner is required to submit the details of expenditure incurred on the acquisition or construction of the property to income tax department. If the assessing officer is satisfied with the details of expenditure then there is no necessity of valuation but if he suspects that the expenditure shown is not correct and unaccounted money has been used in the construction, then he may demand a valuation from registered valuer or refer the case to the valuation cell of the department. Such valuation is in fact the estimation of the cost of existing structure to determine the probable expenditure on the construction. The valuer do such valuation on the basis of plinth area rates of CPWD or local PWD using cost index extra and additional items are worked out separately on the basis of schedule of rates.

(*b*) **Capital Gain Tax.** Capital gain tax is charged when a property is sold with financial gain in this method the value of property is determined on the date of its acquire taking into considerations all additions and alterations made in the property and then present value is determined and corrected as per difference of inflation index issued by income tax department between the year of acquisition and the year of assessment or transaction. This value is deducted from sale value for capital gain.

(*c*) **Wealth and Gift Taxes.** Central board of direct taxes has laid down a detailed procedure in wealth tax rules in schedule for calculating the value of the property and it should be followed to find value for wealth and gift tax. This procedure is based on rent capitalisation method of valuation.

(*d*) **Land and Building Tax.** This tax is imposed by some state governments on the market value of the land and building. It is similar to wealth tax. It is imposed on the premises that the persons who are having the property vaulting more than certain limit and collected for upliftment of down trodden. The property is valued by both methods as land and building method and rental method and the value is assessed on 1st April of the assessing year. The cost of building is taken as per to (PWD) plinth area rate taking cost index into consideration and land value is assessed, as per market rate.

(*e*) **Municipal tax (Property Tax).** The municipal or corporation charges property tax for providing following service to the public.

(1) **General Tax—**for fire, lighting roads, gardens, play ground, parks etc.

(2) **Water Tax—**street watering, common public taps, fire hydrants etc.

(3) **Conservancy and Drainage Tax—**public latrine, scavenging, general and special sanitary chess, sewer lines.

The tax is charged on the basis of rateable value of the property *i.e.*, gross annual return minus repairs. It is valued as per assessment code for valuation of properties in the municipal corporation published by Indian Institute of Public Administration, New Delhi.

(2) **Loan Purposes.** The financial institutions advance loans for construction of house, industrial or commercial unit etc. In such cases requirements of the institution such as clear title of the land, approved plan from local body etc. must be fulfilled. The valuer is required to submit a forecase estimate and not the valuation of building detailed break estimate is required to be submitted. After the sanction of loan, the amount is advanced in parts as per the progress of construction works and a certificate regarding it is required to be submitted to the institution. The financial institutions do not advance the full loan but only a part amount as sectored. The property is also mortgaged, by the financing institution. The valuation at a later date if required then it is made by one of the various methods available to value and property.

(3) **For Business Purposes.** Many times businessmen need working capital for expanding the business for various reasons. The property is also required to be vaulted for various other reasons as explained earlier. When loan is advanced for working capital and expanding business, the financial institution demands the valuation and papers of the property of the person to mortgage the property. In such cases reversionary value of land and reconstruction value of building may be applied on plinth area rate basis with due consideration of age, life and depreciation. If the building is rented then rent capitalisation method may be used but the comparatively higher value may be taken. The financial institutions do not advance the loan amount equal to valuation but almost half the amount of valuation.

In case of sale and purchase, the sale value is decided by negotiation between parts or through the property dealer depending upon the trend in the locality, need of purchaser and seller, objects of purchaser etc. In case valuer is concerned he is required to examine the title of the property, age life of structure, condition of structure, repairs and maintenance, needed encumber some on the property, prevailing rates of land, free and built in etc. After collecting all these data a judgement is required to be made to final the fair market value of that property. It is the likely value to give an idea about which the property may be transacted.

A case of Fixation of rent comes when the Government or corporation or institution etc. hires the property. The rent is fixed as a certain percentage of interest in the investment. The interest is fixed by the concerned of Government in such cases the land value is taken and the reconstruction value of the building with due consideration of depreciation based on plinth area rates is worked out and the total value is determined. The annual rent is worked out as a certain percentage of this amount and on this amount the taxes, repair charges and collection charges are added. It is called gross annual rent.

For insurance of any premise, vehicle machinery etc. for less and damages, the owner is required to declare the amount of property to be insured. At the time of loss of the Insurance Company get the survey conducted of the loss and gets the valuation of the property and the loss. In case insurance is done for lesser amount then the companies pay proportional amount of the loss. In such cases the reproduction method with depreciation is used.

For partition of properties land and building method may be used. The same method can also be used for dissolution of firms.

For court fee and stamp duty rent capitalisation method or land and building method as the case may be, is used. And building method is generally assumed to be appropriate in case of valuation for property acquisition. For mortgage works land and building method is generally used. Land and building method based on plinth area rate method is generally used for registration of transfer of property. The land values are fixed by the Government from time to time and building value is worked out by land and building method of valuation.

These are the various methods in general adopted to find the value of any property according to its purpose.

9.2. VALUATION OF VARIOUS ASSETS

Valuation of Flats. In case of flats or apartments, the superstructure is conveyed to the buyer and the land is conveyed to all the buyers jointly. Only undivided share of the land apportioned to the flat is conveyed to the particular flat. These land attached to the flat does not belong to the flat owner but to a group to all flat owners. The various parts of the building like foundation, terrace, staircase, lobby, lift etc. have to be considered to serve all the flats. In view of the co-operative nature of the ownership of same parts of the property, its valuation is different from independent buildings in which the owner enjoys the land and building as a whole.

There are various methods of valuation as explained earlier. All the methods can be applied to flat with little difference. Land and building method can be applied to flats which have been completed and ready for occupation or for have been completed and ready for occupation or for flats which under use. In this method the undivided share of land apportioned to the flat is separately assessed and to this, the value of building component of the flat is determined and added allowing suitable dedication towards depreciation. The value of flats already completed and in use can also be assessed by comparing sale instances. However care should be taken to ensure that the comparable sale conforms to the specification, functional services, available open space, parking facilities, facilities like playground, number of floors, nature of ownership of land free hold or lease hold, monthly contribution to be paid to the association, future life terms of payment and any other comparable factors. Suitable adjustments which the value of the flat to be assessed and the flat that is being compared. In some cases the built-up area specified by the promoter will be more than what is available physically and the promoter will not give the working details. However the sale deed will show the extent specified by the promoter.

Rent capitalisation method is generally more suitable for flats which are in use and for those used for commercial purposes. The value is assessed by capitalising the net annual income. Development method of valuation is generally used for flats under construction and likely to take some time for their completion. In this method, the probable investment likely to be made for the project is estimate and to this the reasonable percentage of developers profit is added. This gives the value, which the developer should realise on sale. However this figure will reflect a few years after commencement of the project and the mode of payment will also be in instalment during the period of construction. Hence proper discount has to be given to the amount with appropriate rate of interest.

Valuation of Bare Plot(Land): Valuation of land in general can be defined as valuation of bare plot to be used for immovable property like building and that of agricultural land to be used for agricultural purpose.

Land gets broadly further classified as:

(1) Residential Housing Land.

(2) Commercial Land.

(3) Industrial Land.

(4) Institutional Land, and the like.

(1) Residential Housing Land: Residential Housing Land is such a type of land, where the land is solely used for developing and construction of residential housing colonies or group houses which are developed by either the state authority or equally by private owners or co-operative housing societies and the like.

(2) Institutional Land: Schools, Colleges, Hostels, Hospitals, Training Centres, Libraries, Convention Halls etc., can be termed as Institutional land sites and the areas of such land site's are always larger ones in better acreages coverings to accommodate group usages for collective purposes of a particular type of activity or activities.

(3) Commercial Land: Such types of lands are in major towns and cities and cosmopolitan cities as well, and are used for business purposes such as commercial complexes, shopping malls and shopping complexes, office complexes etc. to supplement the economic growth of such major towns and cities apart from providing other commercial and civic facilities and thus fullfil the required needs of the people of the locality living nearby as also provide commercial connectivity and activity to the adjoining areas with other distantly located locations.

(3) Industrial Lands: Various agencies of Government and private bodies have been developing industries for which lands required are earmarked either inside the town or city limits or on its borders. They are of following categories:

(*a*) Land for industries developed by Central Government or their undertakings and industries put up on such lands with government funds.

(*b*) Land for industries developed by State Governments or their undertakings and industries put up on such lands with State Government funds.

(*c*) Land for industries purpose developed by private agencies.

(*d*) Industrial land plots approved by Government in a mixed type locality.

In case of valuation of bare plot to be used for development of residential or commercial purpose, the most important document is its conversion from agricultural to non agricultural use else it cannot be used for building purpose. Similarly in case of land acquisition for road widening or other purpose, its legality is to be checked in detail. Other data and documents to be collected and verified are:

- Sale deed and approved layout.
- Verification and Inspection of boundary stones of plot as per approved layout.

- Land use certificate and master plan of that area as developed by appropriate authorities.
- Conversion letter.
- Site visit to check all details with the help of compass is also essential.
- Current Photographs.
- Market rate and rates as per sub-registrar office.

Once all these details are collected and verified, valuer should write a detailed description of property, its measurements, location, direction, area etc. and then only should prepare valuation report to reach to a value of that land under consideration.

Valuation of land as appears very easy but it is really a tedious and challenging job as every owner wants to fetch maximum return giving various reasons. Various challenges and intricacies involved in valuation of land and its characteristics, shape and size, legality, rates, boundaries, non-agricultural conversion, identification, original owner, lease documents if any and so on.

9.3. VALUATION OF COMMERCIAL COMPLEX

Commercial properties consists of

(*a*) movable assets like machineries and furnitures

(*b*) immovable assets like land and buildings.

All these yield income which can or cannot be bifurcated. Thus value of commercial property depends upon earning capacity of the property. Hence average gross income has to be worked out and compared with similar property. Entertainment catering, storage, trade, offices, utility services etc. are a few a categories come under commercial properties.

For rented properties, maintainable rent or actual rent which ever is more can be taken for valuation. For lodges, cinema theatres/hotels, if leased out, rental method can be adopted. If is an owner run property, the net income can be capitalised by adopting profit and loss method after accounting for outgoings, maintenance cost and sinking fund for equipments and furniture and other movables.

Following methods can be only for valuating commercial properties:

(1) Comparable sale instance method for sale of the property

(2) Profit and loss method for owner run establishment

(3) Income capitalisation method (yield method) for long leased property and or properties mainly intended for tenanting.

(4) In very old building, rental method for future life expectancy and reversionary value of land after the expiry of the life of the old building.

Still the depressing effects are required to be considered while valuing badly managed commercial premises. Usually the difference between the value, evaluated by physical method and rental method should be with in 15 percent barring distressed sales.

9.4. VALUATION OF TIME-SHARE PROPERTIES

With real estate becoming less and less affordable, a new concept of time-share ownership has developed. Ownership of a particular property or a flat (*i.e.* a unit) according to this concept is held for a specified period of time during a year.

Ownership concept has gradually evolved over the years. Historically, it was for a parcel of land measured by meters with no consideration for height scarce and tall building were constructed with better technology, ownership included the height factor. This was the second dimension. There was still only one owner the building and one dead. As cities become more congested and accommodation more scarce and unaffordable at reasonable price, the concept of ownership flats was introduced. This was the third dimension each flat had a different owner and there was different deed for each flat.

In the time-share area, which we are not about to enter, the concept of time has been introduced. Time is going to become the fourth dimension. The deed will probably show ownership of a flat on a time basis, say on a weakly, basis or a few weeks in a year, which will be specified in the deed.

The concept of time-sharing was initially introduced some times in the mid 1960's at a resort in the French. The concept was adopted by developers of roses and hill stations in Europe and America. Many investors say it as a chance to own a second. Home in holiday resort where holidays could be cheap, as no exorbitant hotel charges had to be paid. Promoters were also enthusiastic as it paved the way for a practically 100% occupancy rate as compared to a yearly average of 70 to 80 percent normally occupancy rates in see sides and hill resorts. In India a few developers started such time share ownership sometimes in the early and mid 1980 however has not come very popular so far because of certain practical difficulties. However it is likely to become successful in due course of period.

Timeshare ownership can be of two types, in one case, the promoter runs the business and lets the owner use the premises as per agreement for a specific time of the year. This agreement may be for a period of about 20 years or so, once the period is over the entire property is reverted back to the original developer. This type of deed is referred as "Right to use" ownership it is a type of learn on long term basis. The property is however maintained by developer. The second type commonly referred to as "ownership type" consist of the owner buying the interest in real estate and the owner receives title interest etc. He is allowed to sell or lease as per rules pertaining to other real estate. The benefits of this type of ownership are obvious there is an opportunity to build equity and to be able to sell or dispose of the property as per the owner choice.

The advantage of this type to the owner or developer is the higher cash flow due to marketing of the individual time share and probably better price than if the entire property was sold in one block. It is an accepted and well-relaised fact of valuation that if a large ownership interest is broken into smaller units, the similar unit normally produces a higher unit sale price. The purchaser on the other hand is benefited to the extent that he gets relatively chapter accommodation in the future at today's rate marking a lump sum payment once.

However there is restricted market in such time share properties, but it creates a unique valuation problem as each timeshare is different from the next.

9.5. BUILDING COST INDEX

Building cost index is a number which shows the resultant effect of the cost of building materials *viz.* steel, cement bricks tiles wood, labour etc. which have got varying effect in their own field, on the cost of building, it is number which gives on indication of the relative increase or decrease in cost of certain item or commodity with respect to the cost of certain base. It is also defined as the unit increase or decrease which may not have happened in the price of a certain year with reference to the price of some previous year known as "Base Year". The building cost index of base year is taken as 100 for comparison basis. This mean if building cost index after two years of base year in 120 means prices of all materials, labour etc. on average gone high by 20 percent with reference to base year.

It is one of the several methods available for estimating the cost of construction as reproduction cost. Plinth area rate method is quick simple and less time consuming and easily understood by non-technical persons also. The PWD give cost index for various years with reference to base year.

In any construction 10 percent of the various items contribute to a larger percentage of the cost and remaining of the other items attribute only balance of the cost. Hence it is enough if the cost of cement, steel bricks, sand aggregate timber and on labour part mason, carpenter and bar—bender is considered. The requirement of the building materials and labour and their contribution in the cost of construction have been worked out based on the actual observations made during the construction of different types of buildings. The percentage contribution of various building materials and labour is known as weightage. Hence by multiplying with the weightage to the prevailing market price of a commodity and dividing by the market piece of the very same material during base period, cost index can be computed.

For Example : If rate as on 1.1.1992 for 1000 bricks was ₹ 600/-

and rate as on 1.1.1992 for brick is ₹ 650/-

And permissible weightage for bricks = 16.00

$$\text{Cost index for 1.1.1993} = \frac{650 \times 16}{600} + 100 = 117.33$$

In this way the cost index is calculated for various essential items. It is then added and average is calculated to find cost index for plinth area rate. The weightage (approximate) given to various essential materials is as given below:

Bricks	—	11.00
Steel	—	20.00
Aggregate	—	5.00
Sand	—	4.50
Cement	—	20.00
Mason	—	8.5
Carpenter	—	4.0
Beldar/coolie	—	11.00
Timber	—	11.00
Total		100.00

The weightage however varies slightly depending upon year variation in the price and other factors, hence required to be modified. The overall total however remains only 100.

9.6. STANDARD RENT

It is a rent charged by public organisation especially for residential buildings from their employees. It is some fixed proportion of cost of building and land. Presently this also called as standard license fee.

Standard rent is considered as the reasonable rent fixed by competent authority rent controller under rent control act the word reasonable is very important. The owner or landlord always demands maximum rent and he justifies it to be reassembles. Where as tenant likes to pay minimum and he feels that to be reasonable on the basis of services provided to him by land lord and his capacity to pay from his income. Tenants, particularly service class people are hard pressed person, they are subjected to more exploitation as they need immediate shelter on transfer etc. the government duty is to check this exploitation tendency, and to fix a reasonable rent. The landlords feel to fetch a return on their investment equal to the amount they would have got if the amount had been put else where at certain interest rate, *i.e.* about 12 percent return on money invested. This can not be possible at least in residential buildings. The investment is generally made to develop his assets and interest in terms of return is not taken into consideration. A reasonable return is certainly expected but not equivalent to interest. The interest in case of un-secured investment can be further high to the order of 24% to 60% but then the security of the investment goes down tremendously.

The property constitutes of two parts (1) land and (2) building. Land is limited and as it becomes more and more scarce, however building cost does not appreciate to that extent. Bare land precedes no return unless a building is erected on it. Rent is paid for the services and facilities provided in a house. A house without amenities like shelf cooking platform, fans etc. will fetch less rent than a house provided with all these amenities. The standard rent is calculated by following methods.

(1) **Standard rent on the basis of usable floor area.** This method is based on area given on rent. The necessary usable area required for different come group like LIG, MIG etc. is decided by expert committee. This committee also decides the specifications of such houses. The rent paying capacity is based on the monthly or annual income of these people likely to reside in the house. This income is taken as base for deciding standard rent. The superfluous expenditure of person rented is not taken into consideration. This is calculated as given below. This standard rent now a days is also called as standard license fee and this method is applicable mainly for government owned quarters given on rent to their employees.

(*i*) **For building owned by government:**

If (*a*) annual equivalent of amount spent on construction.

(*b*) outgoings like taxes, repairs and maintenance, Insurance premium etc.

and (*c*) annual equivalent of capital (may or may not) invested for additions or alternator.

$$\text{Standard licence fee} = \frac{a+b+c}{12}$$

(*ii*) If for building given on lease than if

(*a*) Amount paid annually for lease,

(*b*) Outgoings in the form of taxes etc.

and (*c*) Capital investments for addition or alterations.

$$\text{Then standard licence fee} = \frac{A + b + \text{annual equivalent of } c \text{ at a rate } i}{12} - 1$$

(2) **Standard rent on the basis of return on investment.** The valuation of each building for this method is done for the services and necessary specifications ignoring the superfluous items such as decorative and unnecessary expensive items. It encourages people to go for cheap and economical houses and discourage for superfluous expenditure. A fair rate of interest on investment may be fixed. A return of 6 to 8 percent on investment can be considered as a standard rent. This return can be increased up to 10 to 12 percent for building other than residential. Usual practice is to fix standard rent equivalent to 6 percent of building cost inclusive of all amenities and 3 percent of land cost. The half rate of interest on land is cost is generally proposed with the view that land does not depreciate at all and appreciation on its value is much more than the building.

The standard rent fixed so can be revised after every three years as per the consumer's price index.

Renting of house on rent higher than the standard rent must be made a criminal offence. Moreover the evacuation of the premise should be made easy on demand for personal use or in the absence of cordial relations between the owner and the tenant, the tenant under such condition will not have any objection to vacate as he will be sure to get another house on standard rent. The owner of the house will also change standard rent, as he will know that he cannot get higher rent. The standard rent therefore should be fixed for all the houses whether self occupied or rented and this rent should form the basis of all taxation.

9.7. RENT CONTROL BILL

Rent Restriction Act. Also known, as rent act exists in various stales. This act has been introduced mainly as means of social legislation and have been utilised to empower sates either to curtail or enlarge the rights and obligations of landlords and tenants. Every state has formed its own-rent act as per constitution of India, and is similar in nature. The main aim of rent act is to give protection to tenants against their landlords in respect to rents, evictions and repairs. However there were many drawbacks and short coming, a bill has been made by central government called as rent control bill mainly to remove short comings of the act and to give justice both *i.e.* to the landlord as well as to be tenant.

The salient lectures of this bill are:

(1) The rent act is applicable to cities and towns having population more than 3 lacs of people.

(2) The co-operative housing societies are exempted from the rent act.

(3) The standard rent fixed once shall be liable to be revised after every 3 years.

(4) The standard rent includes cost of maintenance; hence landlord will be able to maintain the property in good conditions.

(5) The eviction of tenant for bonafied use of landlord is permissible. In case of dispute the matter can be referred to rent tribunals for quick and speed disposal and cannot be taken to civil court.

9.8. TYPES OF RENT

Virtual Rent. It is actually a full rental value, *i.e.* it is an addition of rent decided plus effect duc to premium of any end effect of additions made by the lessee if any.

Fair Rent. It is actually a rent of on premises ought to be; whether paid more or less. For example if a property fetch a rent of ₹ 500/- per month whilst actually paid to the owner is ₹ 400/- p.m. than ₹ 500/- p.m. is a fair rent, whilst ₹ 400/- p.m. is a virtual rent. Virtual rent may be fair rent but not always. Further in valuating any property by rental method, fair rent should be taken into consideration and not virtual one.

Ground Rent. The ground rent represents the rental value of a bare site at the time the lease is granted. It is of two types; secured and unsecured, secured means some building has been constructed over it, hence property secured; otherwise unsecured. In case of secured ground rent; depending on rent, it is further denoted by so many times ground rent is secured, for instance if ground rent of a land is ₹ 150/- per month, later on a building is constructed and rent fixed is ₹ 1500/- p.m. hence in second case property is said to be secured by 10 times.

Rack Rent. Where the rent reserved under an occupation lease represents the full rental value of land and buildings; or near it; it is called rack-rent *i.e.* Rack-rent is total of building rent and land rent.

Improved Rent. If a property leased by one is rental to third party at rent higher than what the lessee is paying to lesser, this higher rent is known as improved rent. The rent paid by lessee is called Head rent. Hence lessee is getting a profit of it, this called profit rent.

∴ Profit rent = Improved rent – Head rent

9.9. LIFE CYCLE COST ASSESSMENT OF BUILDING

Life Cycle Cost (LCC) is the total discounted rupee cost of owning, operating, maintaining, repairing replacing and disposing of a structure/building over a period of time. Life Cycle Cost Analysis (LCCA) is an economic evaluation technique that determines the total cost of owning and maintaining an asset over a stipulated period of time. This stipulated period of time is called as study period.

The investment by the promoter/developer/builder for construction is called construction cost. This investment made is called capital expenditure. Time Value of money should also be considered while calculating Direct Construction Cost (DCC) alongwith interest paid on money borrowed/used for construction. The interest rate can vary from Prime landing rates (always higher) of the commercial banks to as low as given by housing financial organisation to industrial owner. However these rates do not vary more and therefore an average rate of interest is taken into consideration over the construction period. More the period of construction more the amount of interest one has likely to pay as such construction period should be as small as possible. This is Interest During Construction (IDC).

Developer/Promoter/Builder sells the building (may be apartment) and recovers his investment made in the form of Principal including interest and Profit. He always prefers to have early return of invested capital. Less the period of construction less the amount of interest as such this can be indirectly treated as saving in rental charges due to decrease in period of construction.

∴ Net construction cost

= Direct construction cost + Interest during construction

– saving in rental charges due to less period of construction

NCC = DCC + IDC – Saving in R.C.

The expenses possible to occur in future years during the functional life of building includes repairs and maintenance, salvage, replacement of part if any. These possible expenses in future are brought down to its base year (*i.e.* year of commencement of work) and then added to NCC to give Net Present Worth (NPW) of the investment on the building over the period of study. The rate at which these future expenses are brought down *i.e.* discount rate is generally equal to the rate of inflation in the market. If this inflation is neglected it is called real discount rate. However at present the inflation varies between 8 to 10 percent and therefore real discount rate is never considered. Nominal discount rate is also many a times to considered. Nominal discount rate takes fluctuation of inflation rate into consideration.

Based on all these factors the Life Cycle Cost (LCC) of a building is calculated as given below:

LCC = NCC + DFE

= DCC + IDC – Saving in RC + DFE

where NCC = Net Construction Cost

DCC = Direct Construction Cost

IDC = Interest During Construction

RC = Rental Charges

DFE = Discounted Future Expenses

If fact, LCC is not the actual cost incurred for the building. It is an assessed value of the building considering the actual cost incurred at present for construction of the building combined with the possible future costs necessary to keep the building functional over its period of life expectancy. LCC could be used as an indicator of the return of investment for the structure. It is a useful technique of comparing proposals for the same structure offered to be built using different design and construction technologies. As such the improvement of technology could be well assessed with respect to their feasibility in terms of investment.

LCC therefore is an indicator towards the possible value/worth of the building at the base year (*i.e.* year of construction) study considering all the components of initial cost and future cost. Since the building loans are long term soft loan; it is desirable that the buildings are valued on the basis of LCC for mortgage purposes. This will indicate fairly the actual value of property under consideration. It has been observed that real estate property always appreciates with time. The increased value of property will allow more loan to be borrowed.

10

Valuation of Other Assets

10.1. GENERAL

Other than immovable properties like building and land, valuation of various other assets is also required to be made. Various other assets, valued are grouped in following subsequent paragraphs briefly.

(1) Urban Land and Building
(2) Agricultural Land
(3) Plants and Machineries
(4) Gem and Jewellery
(5) Coffee Plantation, Tea Plantation, Rubber Plantation and Cardamom Plantation
(6) Forests
(7) Mines and Queries
(8) Stocks, Shares, Debentures, Security Shares
(9) Works of Art
(10) Life Interest, Reversions and Interest in Expectancy.

10.2. VALUATION OF PLANT AND MACHINERIES

A machine is a living entity, like an individual. When provided with power, performs certain functions for which the same has been designed. All these machines and plants are required to be maintained to have good performance from them. Like a human being, machines also need care and attention. Machines also have certain span of economically productive life during these works usefully, efficiently. As per prevailing needs machines are designed to work under various environmental conditions. Large varieties of materials are used to manufacture or fabricate them. These machines are also required to be insured. Persons use various machine articles from them, sell them in market and earn their bread. Persons also manufacture, modify. The machines to reduce the cost of production. Once machines become obsolete there useful life is over; these are discarded or sold as scrap.

The machines are always subject to accidents or damage due to various reasons. There these machines are required to be insured so that in case of damage, the owner can purchase other machinery and can earn his bread. For insurance, it is essential to know its value and therefore it is required to evaluate the value of that plant and machinery to be ensured. Moreover when machine is required to be sold, it again becomes necessary to pay its fair market value where both seller and buyer may agree upon to do their transition. For a work while valuation exercises to start, the post working life history of the machine and knowledge of certain parameters, the valour is able to calculate the present market value of machine. Its other important details can be held from manufacturer or from some other agency having knowledge of that machine.

The valuation of machine and plant can be done in following steps.

(1) To decide the problem *i.e.* to decide the purpose for which valuation is to be made. The name of machine/plant, its locations name of owner, the purpose for which the machine/plant is used, available market if any and other such details are collected.

(2) Next step consists of collecting the post history of the machine in question. Its total useful life, present life, type of service taken, working environment, maintenance schedule, number of users, whether purchased new or used one, machine specification, model name, makers name, purchase cost etc. repairs if any undertaken, major or minor, depreciation rate adopted its insurance value, book value as per plant register, outstanding debts if any, etc. are also collected.

(3) The information regarding following items is collected:

(*a*) Appreciation factor or cost index rise due to yearly increase in cost of materials.

(*b*) Lowering of value of money due to machine getting obsolete.

(*c*) A factor due to sophistication in design due to advancement in technology or other reasons.

(4) The value of a new similar machine is then obtained from supplier or by some other methods. This value is called as replacement value.

(5) The value of the machine and plant is then worked out by an expert valuer involved in valuation of machineries and plant.

Now a days it has become very essential to evaluate the plants and machineries and therefore various valuers have come up with this particular job of valuation only.

10.3. VALUATION OF AGRICULTURAL LANDS

The meaning of agricultural land means lands which are used or are capable of being used for raising any valuable plant or trees or any other purpose of forming. A land fit for cultivation and not converted in to non agricultural, whether cultivated or not, including garden land, orchārd land (used for fruit bearing trees) etc. come in to category of agricultural land. The quality of soil is one of the most important factor that affects the value of agricultural land. For example an agricultural land with black cotton soil with sufficient water available may have maximum value whereas waste land of little use for agricultural purpose may have minimum value.

Agricultural sector is the largest one in India. The use of modern techniques and development of new and useful agricultural machineries have opened new vistas in agricultural production and productive creating thereby new wealth with the resulting enhancement in the value of agricultural assets.

The valuation of agricultural land and other agricultural assets like horticultural, fishery etc. is mainly done for the purpose of capital gains taxes, transfer sells, insurance, compulsory acquisition etc. The purpose for which valuation is carries out is greatly manifested on the valuation approach to be followed. The parameters to be considered in agricultural valuation are many depending upon the agro climatic conditions, type of forming crops, cropping patterns, and fertility management's and its location.

A land, which is near to the town, having proper approaches, power and water has a higher value. Vicinity of .land in question from the National Highway, State Highway, Major District Roads, other District Roads, Village road etc. greatly influences its value. The size and shape of the farm, provision of irrigation, facility of transportation, proximity of market for the land produce, availability of electricity, economics of land produce etc. are the cardinal points which affect the value of an agricultural land. Along with these, following factors also affect the value of an agricultural land.

(1) Water logging of land if any, its extent and area of water logged patches.

(2) Appropriate area deduction for high tension transmission tower (S) if any (11 kV/ 33 kV/66 kV).

(3) Valuation of farm houses (if any), done separately.

(4) Valuation of fence if existing.

(5) Description and valuation of horticultural assets if any.

(6) **Land situation.** If land is existing with in 8 km of local limits of municipality or cantonment board, are subjected to levy tax on selling or transfer.

(7) Valuation of well, tube well if any.

(8) If the prospective conversion of farm for non-agricultural purpose is contemplated, then development plans zoning, permissible FSI, municipal regulations to arrive at the net area after plotting, consideration of severance if any.

The valuation of land is generally done by capitalisation method of valuation taking into considerations all above points.

Valuation of Gold and Jewellery. Gold is a precious metal having international market Jewelleries are made using gold and other precious stones and are very popular. Throughout the world Ladies particularly are very fond of use of gold and jewelleries. It is a status symbol also. It is popular amongst rich as well as medium class due its beauty, attractive yellow colour, brightness, and softness, non-affected by chemical and non-perishable one. Being a metal of international repute. Can be enclosed in any part of the world with equal value. The valuation of such a precious item is done by expert values having expertise knowledge of this field its value is determined for tax purpose or when the same is collected from someone as money in the form of gold and jewelleries.

Valuation of Mines. India has an abundant deposit of various mineral resources. There are various reasons to evaluate these mines fully of various mineral resources. The most important reasons are purchase/Sale Speculation/Mortgage/Taxation/Leasing of mineral properties etc. Acquisition of mines, dissolution of partnership deed if any, litigation, estate valuation bank loans, and financial statements, auction bidding etc. are various reasons. The value of these mines depends on following:

(1) Assured recoverable content of the area and its qualify.

(2) Cost of production and future projected price of mineral products.

(3) Risk mining.

(4) Remoteness, its approaches, availability of power and supply and availability of water, fuel transportation.

(5) Environmental sensitiveness and general activity of that area.

(6) Track-record of the exploration Geologists.

(7) General economic, political climate taxing statuses illegitimate influence (if any) and police protection.

(8) Supply and cost of labour.

(9) Mining history of the region, profits and difficulties met.

(10) Presence of valuable mineral or metals.

There are various methods like statistical or probabilistic method, price/earning multiple methods, Hoskolds method *i.e.* explicit reinvestment rate of return method, discounted cash flow (DCF) method and so on. However DCF method is more common and used in practice to find the value of a mine. However this is beyond scope of this book and therefore is not dealt herewith.

The value of mines and queries depends upon the quality and the quantity of materials that can be queried from. The amount involved, the machineries required to query the mines are required to be taken in to consideration while valuating mines. The approaches, market, demand of raw materials, power supply etc. are various factors those affect the value of mines and queries. Risk factor involved is also one of the important factor in its valuation.

10.4. VALUATION OF SHARES

The wealth of primitive man was determined by the land he owned and the stock of precious metal and gems he possessed. Today wealth includes real estate, bank deposit and balance, stock of precious metal and gems, antiques and rare paintings ownership of business enterprise and more impatient investment in stocks and shares. Investment in share has become important in industrial world and shares an equal weightage with that of agriculture,

Valuation of share has two dimensions. One is the value as perceived by an individual investor who has no controlling interest in the company and who values its worth in terms of returns it offers and its potential to appreciate in the near or distant future. The record is more relevant where the owner of shares has also the controlling interest in the company. The value of share is determined as earning per share (EPS) per annum. The valuations of shares of business houses need an in-depth study of the assets of the company's and each asset needs an individual treatment from the point of view of valuation. Liabilities of company also affect share value tremendously; however this is not dealt here in detail, as this valuation is not related to real estate valuation.

Works of Arts. Valuation of such articles is a much specialised job. Persons having knowledge, involved in this field can only do this type of valuation. Here material cost involved is very less in comparison to labour, skill involved and mental satisfaction.

A-1 Useful Tables and Technical Data

Table 1. I.S. Soil Classification (IS : 1498–1970) (Including Field Identification and Description)

Major Divisions			*Group symbol*	*Typical Names*	*Visual Examination*	*Dry Strength*	*Wet and Manipulated*	*Thread (Fine Material)*	*Dilatancy Test*
COARSE-GRAINED SOILS More than half of material is larger than 75-micron sieve size*	GRAVELS (g) More than half of coarse fraction is larger than 4.75 mm sieve size (For visual classification, the 5 mm size may be used an equivalent to the 4.75 mm sieve size)	*Clean Gravels* (Little or no fines)	GW	Well graded gravel, gravel-sand mixtures, little or no fines	Hard, smooth well-rounded gravel, containing 1/3 sand	None	Not applicable	Not possible to roll	Not applicable
			GP	Poorly graded gravels or gravel-sand mixtures, little or no fines	Maximum size 50 mm (2″), predominant size 12 mm-25 mm (1/2″–1″) smooth, well-rounded about 20% sand	None	Not applicable	Not possible to roll	Not applicable
		Gravel with fines (Appreciable amount of fines)	GM	Silty gravels, poorly graded gravel, sand-silt mixtures	Gravel about 70%, maximum size 60 mm (2½″). Predominant size 20 mm-38 mm (3/4″ – 1½″) moderately silty	None to slight	Fines-practically non-plastic	Thread less than 6 mm (1/4″) diameter not possible	Not applicable
			GC	Clayey gravels, poorly graded gravel-sand-silt mixtures Welpressibility	Maximum size gravel 60 mm (2½″), predominant size 10 mm-20 mm (3/8″–3/4″) appreciable percentage of clay binder	Medium to high	Fines—moderately to highly plastic	Possible to roll the thread, gritty to touch when broken dry Not applicable	

*The 75-micron sieve size is about the smallest particle visible to the naked eye

(Contd.)

Table 1. I.S. Soil Classification (IS : 1498–1970) (Including Field Identification and Description)

Major Divisions			*Group symbol*	*Typical Names*	*Visual Examination*	*Dry Strength*	*Wet and Manipulated*	*Thread (Fine Material)*	*Dilatancy Test*
COARSE-GRAINED SOILS More than half of material is larger than 75-micron sieve size	SANDS (S) More than half of coarse fraction is smaller than 4.75 mm sieve size (For visual classification, the 5 mm size may be used as equivalent to the 4.75 mm sieve size)	*Clean Sand*	SW	Well-graded sands, gravelly sands little or no fines	About 20% gravel 38 mm (1½″) maximum size, sand well-rounded and hard	None	Not applicable	Not possible to roll	Not applicable
			SP	Poorly graded sands or gravelly sands, little or no fines	Sand poorly graded predominantly coarse, slightly silty	None	Not applicable	Not possible to roll	Not applicable
		Sands with fines (Appreciable amount of fines)	SM	Silty sands, poorly graded sand-silt mixtures	Sand very fine, large portion of silt about 10%, gravel 20 mm (3/4″) size	None to slight	Practically non-plastic	Thread less than 6 mm (1/4″) diameter not possible to roll	Not applicable
			SC	Clayey sands, poorly graded sand clay mixtures	About 50–60% sand with fair clay binders up to about 10%, pea size gravel	Medium to slight	Fines—moderately to highly plastic	Possible to roll the thread, gritty and coarse when broken dry	Not applicable

Table 1. I.S. Soil Classification (IS : 1498–1970) (Including Field Identification and Description)

Major Divisions		*Group symbol*	*Typical Names*	*Visual Examination*	*Dry Strength*	*Wet and Manipulated*	*Thread (Fine Material)*	*Dilatancy Test*
FINE-GRAINED SOILS More than half of material is smaller than 75-micron sieve size	SILTS (M), CLAYS (C) *i/c* Organic Silts (O) With low compressibility ; liquid limit-less than 35	ML	Inorganic silts and very fine sands, rock flour, silty or clayey fine sand or clayey silts with none to low plasticity	Predominantly silt with traces of clay and excess of fine sands	None to slight	Practically non-plastic	Possible to roll thread 6 mm (1/4") with high moisture, coarse texture	Quick to slow
		CL	Inorganic clay, gravelly clays, sandy clays, silty clays, lean clays of low plasticity	More than half sand and silt, rest about 30–40%	Medium to high	Very plastic	Possible to roll thread, slightly gritty when broken dry	Nil to very slow
		OL	Organic silts of low plasticity	Silt, organic, strong odour of decayed mater, slightly plastic	None to slight	Slightly plastic	Possible to roll thread, weak and coarse in texture	Slow
	SILTS (M), CLAYS (C) *i/c* Organic Silts (O) With medium compressibility; liquid limit-greater than 35 and less than 50	MI	Inorganic silts, silty or clayey fine sands, or clayey silts of medium plasticity	Silt with slight clay and fine sands	Low	Moderately plastic	Possible to roll thread	Quick to slow
		CI	Inorganic clays, gravelly clays, sandy clays, silty clays, lean clays of medium plasticity	Fine sand-10-20%, slightly silty, and rest is all clay	Medium to high	Highly plastic	Possible to roll thread, smooth feel when broken dry	—
		OI	Organic silts and organic silty clays of medium plasticity	Silt, organic matter, strong odour moderately plastic	Low to medium	Moderately plastic	Possible to roll thread	Slow

(Contd.)

Table 1. I.S. Soil Classification (IS : 1498–1970) (Including Field Identification and Description)

Major Divisions			*Group symbol*	*Typical Names*	*Visual Examination*	*Dry Strength*	*Wet and Manipulated*	*Thread (Fine Material)*	*Dilatancy Test*
FINE-GRAINED SOILS More than half of material is smaller than 75-micron sieve size	SILTS (M), AND CLAYS (C) *i/c* Organic Clays (O)	With high compressibility ; liquid limit-greater than 50	MI	Inorganic silts of high compressibility, micaceous or diatomaceous fine sandy or silty soils, elastic silts	Silt, elastic, slightly clay and moderately plastic	None to slight	Slightly plastic	Coarse textured thread with high percentage of moisture	Slow to nil
			CH	Inorganic clays of high plasticity, fat clays	Clay, fat high percentage of ultra clay sand and silt, not more than 10 to 15%	Very high	Very plastic	Fine textured thread, high strength when broken dry	Nil
			OH	Organic clays of medium to high plasticity	Clay, organic, slightly organic odour, very plastic, no coarse material	Medium to high	Moderately to very plastic	Possible to roll thread, fine texture	Nil to very slow
High organic soil			Pt	Peat and other highly organic soils with very high compressibility	Very fibrous, strong organic odour, black in colour	Low to medium	Fibrous and highly organic very plastic	Possible to roll a rough-textured thread with high moixture	Not applicable

Note : Boundary classification.

Soil possessing characteristics of two groups are designated by combination of group symbols.

For example : GW-GC, well graded gravel and mixture with clay binder.

Table 2. British and Indian Equivalent of American Sieves

United States A.S.T.M.E.11/26	*Great Britain B.S. 410*	*I.S. Sieve No.*
2 inches	2 inches	50 mm
1½ "	1½ "	40 mm
3/4 "	3/4 "	20 mm
3/8 "	3/8 "	10 mm
3/16 "	3/16 "	4.75 mm
7	6	2.80 mm
10	8	2.00 mm
12	10	1.60 mm
14	12	1.40 mm
16	14	1.18 mm
18	16	1.00 mm
30	25	600 μ
35	30	500 μ
40	36	425 μ
45	44	355 μ
60	60	250 μ
70	72	212 μ
80	85	180 μ
100	100	150 μ
120	120	125 μ
170	170	90 μ
200	200	75 μ
325	350	45 μ

Pile Formulae

(*i*) **Sander's Pile Formula** $Q_{dy} = \dfrac{W_H \times H}{S}$

where W_H = Height of the ram

H = Height of fall.

Q_{dy} = Bearing capacity Q_d of a point bearing pile.

S = Average penetration of the pile under the last few blows of hammer.

(*ii*) **Sander's Modified Pile Formula**

$$Q_{dy} = \frac{W_H \times H}{S + c}$$

Here the term c represents additional penetration. For hammer driven pile it is taken equal to 2.5 cm and for steam hammer pile = 0.254 cm.

(*iii*) **Engineering News Formula**

$$Q_a = \frac{6.7 W_H \times H}{S + c}$$ where H and S are in cm.

Foundations and their Stability

Foundations on Sand and Gravel on Main Cohesionless Soils

$$q_f = p_0(N_q - 1) + \gamma \frac{B}{2} N_y + p$$ (For strip foundation)

$$q_f = p_0(N_q - 1) + 0.4\ \gamma B N_y + p$$ (For square of circular foundation)

where q_f = Ultimate bearing capacity.

p_0 = Effective pressure on over bardar Soil at foundation level.

N_q, N_y = Bearing capacity factors. (See Fig. 2.1)

B = Width of foundation.

γ = Density of soil.

The bearing capacity factors for shallow foundation are given in Fig. 1.

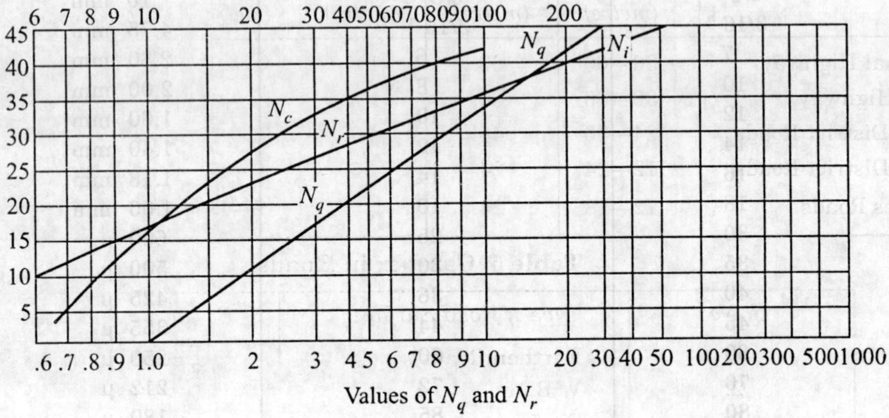

Fig. 1. Terzaghi's bearing capacity factor of shallow foundation ($D > B$)

Table 3. Allowable Bearing Capacity of Various Types of Soil

Case 1. Foundation below 3 m width or rock surface.

Nature of Rock	*Bearing Value T/m²*
Massive hard igneous rocks	Exceeds Safe working 500 Stress on concrete
Schist or slates	400
Interbedded hard mud stone	300
Hard unweathed chalk	200
Clay slate and soft mud	100

Case 2. Foundation in non-cohesive soil at depth below G.L. greater than 75 cm.

Nature of Soil	*Bearing values for foundations of width (T/m²)*		
	1 m	2 m	3 m
Very dense gravel	60	50	40
Dense sand	35—60	30—50	25—40
Medium dense sand	15—35	10—30	10—25
Loose sand	5—15	5—10	5—10

Case 3. Foundation in cohesive soils depth below G.L. greater than 1 cm.

Nature of Soil	*Bearing values for foundation of width (T/m²)*		
	1 m	2 m	3 m
Hard boulder clay	80	60	40
Very stiff boulder clay	40—80	30—50	15—25
Stiff fissured clays	20—40	15—25	7.5—12.5
Firm consolidated clays	10—20	7.5—20	5—7.5
Soft consolidated clay	5—10	25—5	Negligible

Roads

Table 4. Width of Formation

Road classification	*Open areas and agricultural country*				*Urban (building) and industrial area*
	Normal width (metre)	*Building line (metre)*	*Central line (metre)*	*Normal width (metre)*	*Building (set back) line. Width of strip beyond road boundary (metre)*
National Highway	30—60	60	132	24—60	3—6
State Highway	30—60	60	132	24—60	3—6
Major District Roads	24—30	48	90	12—18	3
Other District Roads	12—24	24	36	9—15	—
Villages Roads	12—18	24	30	9—15	—

Table 5. Camber in Roads

S. No.	*Type of Road Surface*	*Camber recommended*
1.	Earthen Roads	1 in 20 to 1 in 24
2.	W.B.M.	1 in 30 to 1 in 48
3.	Surface painted	1 in 36 to 1 in 48
4.	Other bituminous roads	1 in 48 to 1 in 60
5.	Concrete roads	1 in 60 to 1 in 72

Table 6. Ruling Gradient Recommended by I.R.C.

Nature of terrain	*Ruling gradient*	*Limiting gradient*	*Exceptional gradient in length not exceeding 75 m per/cm*
Plains	1 in 30	1 in 20	1 in 15
Hills	1 in 20	1 in 15	1 in 12

Table 7. Extra Widening of Roads

Radius in metre	*Extra width*				
	In plains or Rolling Terrain	*Radius in metre*	*Hilly single lane*	*Radius in metre*	*Two lane Hilly*
Upto 60	0.9	14—20	1.5	30—40	1.5
60 to 150	0.6	20—30	1.2	40—60	1.2
151 to 300	0.3	30—60	0.9	60—100	0.9
Over 300	nil	60—150	0.6	100—150	0.6
		Above 150	Nil	Above 150	Nil

Table 8. Minimum Length of Transition Curves

Design Radius in metres \ Speed	*Minimum transition lengths for various speed in metres*									
	Flat Country						*Hill Road*			
	35	40	50	65	80	100	20	25	30	50
15							40			
20							40	40		
30							20	30	50	
50							—	20	30	
60	50	50	50				—	—	30	50
80	—	—	—				—	—	20	50
90	40	50	50				—	—	20	30
100	—	—	40	60			—	—	—	20
400	—	—	—	30	60	110				
500	—	—	—	30	50	90				
1000	—	—	—	—	30	50				
1500	—	—	—	—	—	30				
2000	—	—	—	—	—	30				

Table 9. Right of Way

S. No.	Classification of the road	*Right of way (Width in metres approx.)*			
		Open area		*Built up and Industrial areas*	
		Normal	*Range*	*Normal*	*Range*
1.	National and State highways	30.5 m	(30.5—61)	24.4 m	24.40—61
2.	Major District Roads	24.4 m	(24.4—30.5)	12.2 m	12.2—18.4
3.	Other District Roads	12.2 m	(12.2—24.4)	9.15 m	9.15—15.25
4.	Village Roads	12.2 m	(12.2—18.3)	9.15 m	9.15—15.25

Table 10. Formation Width

S. No.	*Highway Classification*	*Formation width in plain and rolling areas*	*Formation width in hilly areas*
1.	National Highway		
	(*i*) Single lane	12 m	(*i*) 6.25 m. This may be reduced to 5.85 m in rocky stretches
	(*ii*) Two lane	12 m	(*ii*) 8.8 m. This may be reduced to 8.0 m in rocky stretches.
2.	State Highway	—Do—	—Do—
3.	Major District Road	9 m desirable 8.5 m minimum	4.75 m. This may be reduced to 4.35 m in rocky stretches.
4.	Other Distt. Road	—Do—	—Do—
5.	Village Roads	7.5 m desirable 6 m minimum	4 m. This may be reduced to 3.6 m in rocky stretches.

Table 11. Road Width

S. No.	*Daily tonnage per day*	*No. of lanes*	*Road width*
1.	(Light to medium traffic) 1000 tonnes	One	3.6 metres (for concrete pavements 3 m)
2.	Heavy traffic 1001—1500	One	3.6 metres 3 m for concrete pavement with 0.9 metre gravel shoulders
3.	Very heavy traffic, above 1500	One	5.4 metres with gravel beams or 6 metres.

Table 12. Classification and Crossing Characteristics

S. No.	*Category of Road*	*Width of Carriageway*		*Type of Pavements*		*Minimum Width of gates at right angles to C.L. of track*	*Maximum length of Guard Rail*
		Between gates	*Outside gates within 30 m from gate*	*Between gates*	*Outside gates*		
1.	**Class I Road** (*a*) National Highway (*b*) State Highway (*c*) Important roads with in municipal limits (*d*) Road in and around towns	As per col. 7	7 m	Same as outside the railway boundary. If the surface outside is cement concrete black topped surface may be provided.	Same as that of existing road. If the existing surface is not black topped, should be done up to a distance of 30 m beyond each gate.		2 m more than the width of the crossing
2.	**Class II Roads** (*a*) MDR and ODR (*b*) Unimportant municipal roads (*c*) Roads within non-municipal towns (*d*) Other surface roads		5.5 m				
3.	**Class III Road** (*a*) Earth road (*b*) Cart track		3.75 m				
4.	**Class IV Road**		2 m				

(*Contd.*)

S. No.	*Position of gates with respect to carriageway*	*Minimum distance of gates from the C.L. of the nearest rail track*	*Width of road formation outside the gates upto 30 m beyond the gates*	*Length and Gradients*		*Angle of crossing between C.L. of track and the road*
				Between gates	*Outside gates*	
1.	Gates may be swing gates, lifting gates or movable barriers. They should be at right angles to C.L. of the road. On class IV, road, stakes shall be fixed between the gate posts to prevent passage of road vehicles	This should be 3 m (9′ 6″) on broad gauge and 2.5 m (8′) on metre gauge	Width of carriage way immediately outside the gate plus 5 metres	Level	Level upto 15 m beyond gates and flatter than 1 to 40 beyond	Not lower than 45° except with the permission of the railway board
2.	—Do—	—Do—	—Do—	—Do—	Level upto 8 m beyond gates and flatter than 1 in 30 beyond	—Do—
3.	—Do—	—Do—	—Do—	—Do—	Level upto 8 m beyond gates and flatter than 1 in 20 beyond	—Do—
4.	—Do—	—Do—	Suitable width subject to 3 m being the minimum		Flatter than 1 in 15	—Do—

S. No.	*Minimum radius of curvature*		*Sight distance*		*Minimum straight length of road outside gate*	*Traffic Warning Board*	
	Plain and Rolling	*Hilly country*	*Plain or rolling area*	*Hilly country*		*Plain or rolling*	*Hilly road*
1.	250	90 m	120 m	60 m	30 m	120 m	60 m
	(For National and State Highway) For other categories of roads, the best possible radius having regard to safety of the road traffic should be adopted.						
2.			90 m	50 m	22.5 m	90 m	50 m
3.			40 m	27 m	15 m	40 m	30 m
4.			—	—	—	Gates should be painted white	

Gate Lodge Distance Minimum		*Wicket gates for foot passenger*	*Provision of light on gates at night*		*Remark*
From C.L. of nearest rail	*From edge of carriageway*		*Light as observed by road user*	*Light as observed by driver*	
6 m	6 m	To be provided except where over bridge is provided	Red when either gate is closed white when open to road	Red when gates are closed across the railway track	
6 m	6 m	—Do—	—Do—	—Do—	
6 m	3 m	Need not be provided	Same as for I & II except that reflectors may be used as an alternate to lamps		
6 m	3 m	—Do—	—Do—		

Table 13. Characteristics of Flexible and Rigid Pavements

S. No.	*Characteristics*	*Flexible Pavements*	*Rigid Pavements*	*Remark*
1.	Effect of loading (*a*) Normal loading (*b*) Excessive loading	Adjusts itself to loading by undergoing elastic deformation Yields to excessive stresses resulting in local depression of surface	Tends to act as a beam or cantilever and resists deformation Ruptures by producing a crack on the surface	
2.	Temperature effect	Does not produce any stresses	Heavy temperature stresses are produced	
3.	After effect of heavy loading	The surface has self-healing properties as it deforms elastically	The damage caused to the surface under heavy loading is of a permanent nature	

Use of CBR Values in Design

The CBR values in design curve (based in IRC : 37—1970) is given in Fig. 2.

The curves are used for design purpose for the following manner :

The CBR value is projected on one of the curves (*A, B, C, D, E, F*) and the point of intersection is further projected on the ordinate giving the total pavement thickness. The division of the total thickness into the various layers is made depending upon the availability of different materials and their known CBR values, so as to make the most economical combination.

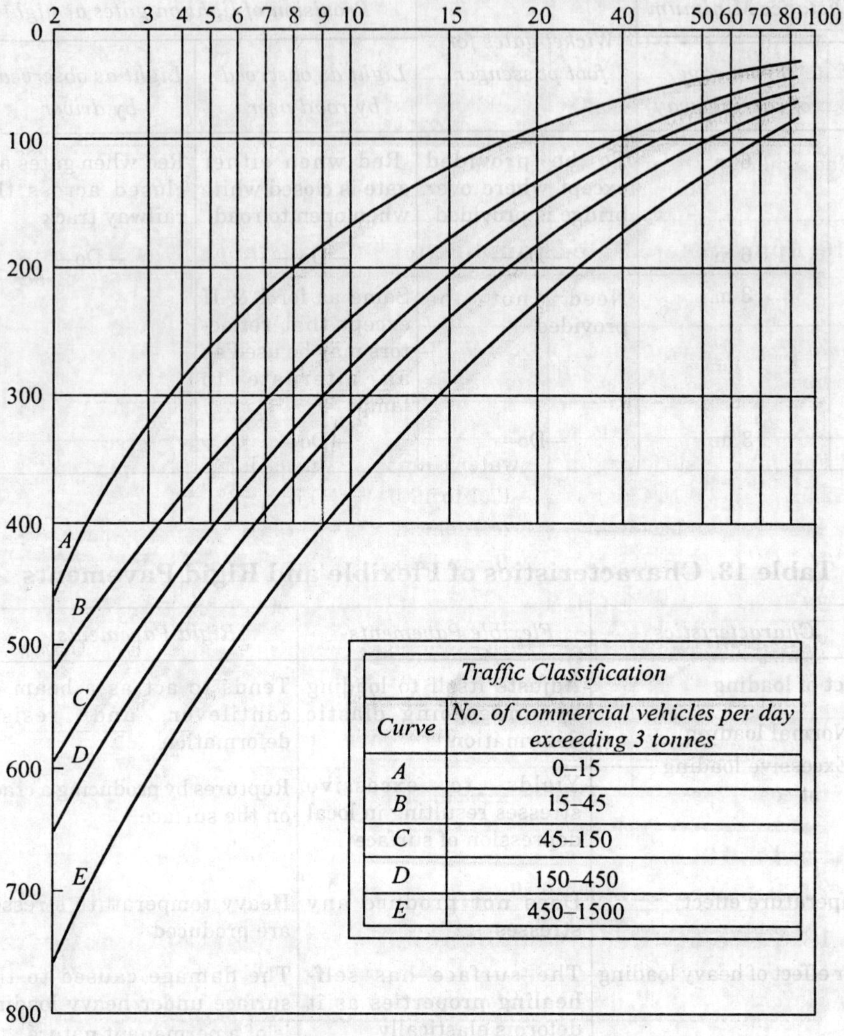

Fig. 2. CBR curves for flexible pavement design.

Table 14. Physical Requirements of Aggregate for Coverage of Surface Dressing

S. No.	*Test*	*Permissible value*
1.	Abrasion value	
	(*a*) Using Los Angeles machine	Max. 30 per cent
	(*b*) Aggregate Impact value	Max. 30 per cent
2.	Stripping value	Max. 25 per cent
3.	Water absorption	Max. 1 per cent (except in case of slag)
4.	Soundness, per cent loss with sodium sulphate for five cycles	Max. 12 per cent
5.	Unit weight or bulk density	Minimum 1120 kg/m^2 (In case of slag only)

Table 15. Gradation Requirements of Aggregates for Coverage of Surface Dressing

S. No.	*Purpose*	*Specification*
1.	Surfacing WBM first coat	100 per cent passing through 20 mm square mesh sieve and retained on 10 mm square mesh sieve
2.	Renewal coat 10 mm	100 per cent passing through 12.5 mm square mesh sieve and retained on 6.3 mm square mesh sieve

Table 16. Approximate Rate of Application of Bituminous Materials and Aggregates

S. No.	*Aggregates*		*Binder*			
	Normal size in mm	*Quantity per 10 m^2 in m^2*	*Straight run buitumen per 10 m^2 in kg*	*Road tar per 10 m^2 in kg*	*Cut back per 10 m^2 in kg*	*Emulsion per 10 m^2 in kg*
1.	I. For	surfacing	water bound	macadam	Surface	—
	12.5	0.14 to 0.5	17.1 to 19.5	17.1 to 22	19.5 to 22	
	II. For	subsequent	or renewal	coats		
	10.0	0.09 to 0.11	9.8 to 12.5	12.2 to 17.1	9.8 to 12.2	—
2.	10 to 2.8	0.08	—	—	—	9.8 to 12.2

Table 17. Gradation Requirements of Aggregates for Coverage of Surface Dressing for Two Coats

S. No.	*Purpose*	*Specifications*
1.	For first coat 12 mm	Passing through 18 mm square mesh sieve and retained on 9 mm square mesh sieve.
2.	For second coat 9 mm	Passing through 12 mm square mesh sieve and retained on 6 mm square mesh sieve.

Table 18. Viscosity Requirement and Requirements of Quantity of Primers

Type of Surface	*Standard tar viscosity of primer at 60°*	*Quantity per 10 m^2 kg*
Low porosity	0—5	7.3 to 9.8
Medium porosity	6—12	9.8 to 12.2
High porosity	16—32	12.2 to 14.6

The following materials are used for prime coats :

SC-1 and SC-2 ; MC-0 ; MC-1 and MC-2 ; RT-1, RT-2 and RT-3.

Table 19. Physical Requirements of Aggregates for Coverage of Surface Dressing

S. No.	*Test*	*Permissible Value*
1.	Abrasion test	
	(*a*) Using Los Angeles abrasion value	Max. 40 per cent
	(*b*) Aggregate impact value	Max. 30 per cent
2.	Stripping values	Max. 25 per cent
3.	Soundness with sodium sulphate for five cycles	Max. 12 per cent
4.	Weight or bulk density	1120 kg/m^2 (In case of slag)

Table 20. Gradation Requirements for Coarse Aggregate for Various Compacted Thicknesses

Percent passing Sieve No.	*Compacted thickness*	
	50 mm	*75 mm*
63 mm	—	100
50 mm	100	—
38 mm	—	35–70
25 mm	35–70	—
19 mm	—	0—15
12 mm	0—15	
9 mm	—	
No. 4 ASTM	—	
No. 8 ASTM	0—5	0—5

Table 21. Requirements of Coarse Aggregate for Various Compacted Thicknesses

Compacted thickness	*Quantity*
50 mm	0.60 m^2 per 10 m^2
75 mm	0.90 m^2 per 10 m^2

Table 22. Gradation Requirements for Key Aggregate

% Passing Sieve No.	*Compacted thickness*	
	50 mm	75 mm
38 mm	—	—
25 mm	—	100
19 mm	100	35–70
12 mm	35—70	—
9 mm	—	0—15
ASTM No. 4	0—15	—
ASTM No. 8	0—5	0—5

Table 23. Requirements of Key Aggregate

Compacted thickness	*Quantity cu metre per 10 m^2*
50 mm	0.15
75 mm	0.18

Table 24. Requirements of Material for Seal Coat

Material	*Size*	*Quantity required for 10 m^2*
Chipping	9 mm, passing 12 mm and retained on 6 mm square mesh	0.09 to 0.11 m^2
Binder	I. Straight run bitumen or II. Road tar of suitable grade	9.8 to 12 kg

Table 25. Requirements of Binder for Bituminous Penetration Macadam

Compacted thickness	*Binder*	*Quantity in kg per 10 m²*
50 mm	(*i*) Straight run bitumen	50
	(*ii*) Road tar RT-4/RT-5	60—65
75 mm	(*i*) Straight run bitumen	68
	(*ii*) Road tar RT–4/RT–5	82—88

Table 26. Physical Requirements of Aggregate for Bituminous Bound Macadam

S. No.	*Test*	*Permissible value*		*Remark*
		Base course	*Binder course*	
1.	Aggregate impact value	35 pc	30 pc	
2.	Los Angeles abrasion value maximum	50 pc	40 pc	
3.	Weight per cu m minimum	1120	1120	for slag only
4.	Loss with sodium sulphate for 5 cycles maximum	12 pc	12 pc	
5.	Stripping Test maximum	25 pc	25 pc	

Table 27. Quantity of Materials Required for 10 m² of Road Surface

Materials	*Quantity required for compound thickness of 50 mm*	*Quantity required for compacted thickness of 75*
Aggregates	0.60 to 0.75 m²	0.90 to 1.10 m³

Table 28. Requirements of Binder for Tack Coat for 10 m² Surface

For bitumen treated surface 5 to 7.5 kg	For untreated water bound macadam surface 7.5 to 10 kg

Table 29. Quantity of Aggregates Required per 10 m² of Road Surface

S. No.	*Material required*	*Quantity per 10 m²*
1.	*For Carpet :*	
	(*a*) Coarse aggregate—1.25 mm size passing IS 20 mm square mesh retained on IS 10 mm square mesh	0.18 m³
	(*b*) Coarse aggregates—10 mm size; passing IS 12.5 mm square mesh, retained on IS 6.3 mm square mesh	0.09 m³
	Total	0.27 m³
2.	*For Seal Coat :*	
	(*a*) Low rain fall areas (under 150 cm per year) Medium coarse sand (fineness modulus of more than 2.5) or fine grit passing sieve No. 1.70 mm and retained on IS sieve No. 180 micron	0.06 m²
	(*b*) High rainfall area Coarse aggregate—6.3 mm size passing IS 10 mm square mesh, retained on IS sieve 2.36 mm mesh	0.09 m²

Table 30. Quantity of Binder Required per 10 m² of Road Surface

S. No.	*Material required*	*Quantity per 10 m²*
1.	*For tack coat :*	
	(*a*) On water bound macadam surface	7.3 to 9.8 kg
	(*b*) On an existing top back surface	4.9 to 7.3 kg
2.	*For premixing :*	
	(*a*) For 12.5 mm size coarse aggregate	9.5 kg @ 56 kg per m³
	(*b*) For 13 mm size coarse aggregate	5.1 kg @ 56 kg per m³
3.	*For Seal Coat :*	
	(*a*) For low rainfall areas (Under 150 cm per year)	6.8 kg
	(*b*) For high rainfall areas (over 150 cm per year)	9.8 kg

Table 31. Quantity of Aggregates Required per 10 m² of Road Surface

S. No.	Material required	Quantity per 10 m²
1.	*For Carpet*	
	(*a*) Coarse aggregate 12.5 mm size passing IS 20 mm square mesh and retained on IS 10 square mesh.	0.18 m³
	(*b*) Coarse aggregate 10 mm size passing IS 12.5 mm sq. mesh and retained on IS 6.3 mm sq. mesh.	0.09 m³
		0.27 cu m
2.	*For Seal Coat*	
	Medium coarse sand of fine quantity (passing IS Sieve No. 1.70 mm and retained on IS Sieve No. 180 micron.	0.06 m³

Table 32. Quantity of Binder Required per 10 m² of Surface

S. No.	Material required	Quantity per 10 m²
1.	For priming coat (on WBM surface)	12.2 to 14.7 kg.
2.	For tack coat (on an existing black top surface)	7.3 to 9.8 kg.
3.	For seal coat	9.8 kg.
4.	For premixing	19.7 kg @ 72 kg per m³

Rigid Pavements

(*i*) **The Westergaard Formulas**—Due to modern construction technique the road bed is made to optimum density and there is uniformity of compaction across entire roadway. Substantial shoulders are provided. The drainage is also very effective and therefore the sub-grade gives proper support to the pavement slab. The slab acts as an elastic plate supported on continuous but yielding support. Therefore deflection of the slab due to applied wheel load is accompanied by equal deformation of subgrade. Therefore the deflection is dependent on the stiffness of slab and stiffness of the subgrade. According to Westergaard, the deflection is a function of the relative stiffness of the slab to that of the subgrade called the radius of relative stiffness. The radius of relative stiffness.

$$l \text{ in cm} = \sqrt{\frac{Ed^3}{12(1-\mu^2)k}}$$

where, E = Modulus of elasticity of the concrete kg/cm²

d = Slab thickness cm.

μ = Poisson's ratio for the concrete.

k = Sub-grade modulus kg/cm³

Values of l are given in table 33 for various values of k and d, with $E = 2.80 \times 10^5$ kg/cm² and μ = 0.15.

Table 33. Radius of Relative Stiffness l in cm

k Subgrade Modulus	*d = 15 cm*	*d = 18 cm*	*d = 21 cm*	*d = 24 cm*	*d = 27 cm*	*d = 30 cm*
2	79.67	91.34	102.53	113.34	123.80	133.98
4	66.99	76.81	86.28	95.30	104.11	112.67
6	60.53	69.40	77.91	86.12	94.07	101.80
8	56.33	64.59	72.50	80.14	87.54	94.74
10	53.28	61.08	68.57	75.79	82.79	89.60
12	50.90	56.36	65.51	72.41	79.10	85.61
14	48.98	56.15	63.04	69.68	76.11	82.37
16	47.37	54.31	60.97	67.39	73.61	79.67
18	46.00	52.74	59.20	65.43	71.48	77.35
20	44.80	51.36	57.66	63.73	69.62	75.34

The radius a of wheel-load distribution on a slab corner loading shown in Fig. 3 is given in graph Fig. 4.

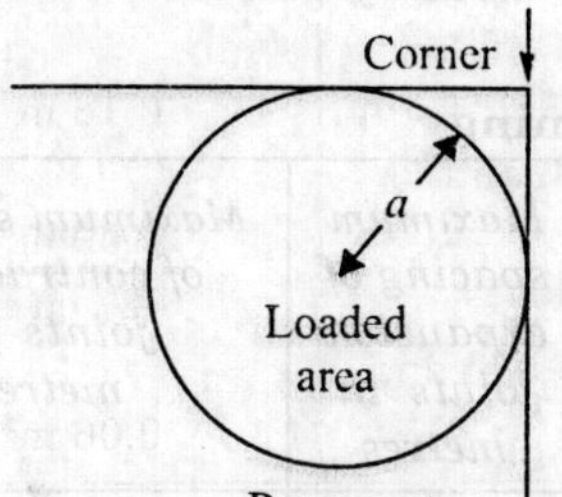

Fig. 3

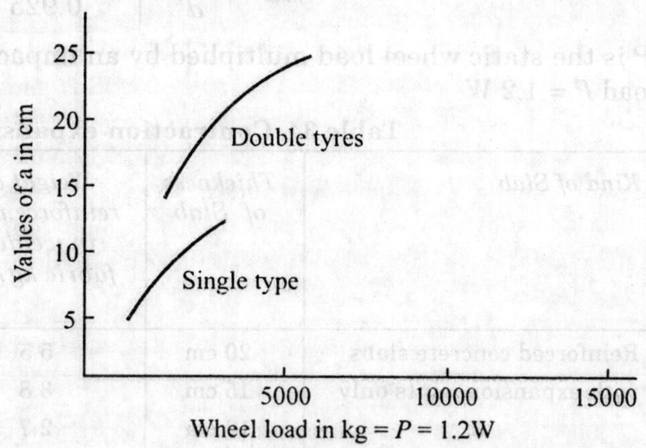

Fig. 4

When the load is applied away from edges, *i.e.* interior loading, the maximum bending moment is positive and causes tension at the bottom. The stress intensity is highly concentrated at the load position. Similar is the case for edge loading condition. In case of interior loading the stress acts radially from the load and is uniform in all directions. In case of edge loading, the maximum stress is parallel to the edge of the slab.

In case of interior loading, the area on which the stress is concentrated is known as resisting section and the equivalent radius of resisting section.

$$b = \sqrt{1.6 + d^2} - 0.675\,d$$

where d is the thickness of pavement.

In case of corner loading, the maximum tensile stress occurs along the bisector of the corner at a distance

$$D = 2.38\sqrt{al}$$

Westergaard's equations as obtained from using theory of thin plates resting on elastic foundation are :

(*a*) For edge loading, $\sigma_{max} = \dfrac{0.51\,P}{d^1}\left[4\log_{10}\left(\dfrac{l}{b}\right) + 0.359\right]$

(*b*) For corner loading, $\sigma_{max} = \dfrac{3\,P}{d^2}\left[1 - \left(\dfrac{a\sqrt{2}}{l}\right)^{0.6}\right]$

(*c*) For interior loading, $\sigma_{max} = \dfrac{0.3162\,P}{d^2}\left[4\log_{10}\left(\dfrac{l}{b}\right) + 1.069\right]$

(*ii*) **Picket's Equation**—Upward warping of the slab corner due to differential temperature and moisture content in top and bottom of the slab reduces subgrade support and therefore there will be increase in stress in the concrete. For these reasons the derived expressions by Westergaard have been modified to semi-empirical formulas which have given results in close agreement with stresses measured in field. The modified formulas as suggested by Gerald Picket also known as Picket's equations are given below :

For protected corners, $\sigma_{max} = \dfrac{3.36\,P}{d^2}\left[1 - \dfrac{\sqrt{a/l}}{0.925 + 0.22a/l}\right]$

For unprotected corners, $\sigma_{max} = \dfrac{4.2\,P}{d^2}\left[1 - \dfrac{\sqrt{a/l}}{0.925 + 0.22a/l}\right]$

where P is the static wheel load multiplied by an impact factor usually 1.2. If W is the static wheel load $P = 1.2\,W$

Table 34. Contraction-expansion Joining

S. No.	Kind of Slab	Thickness of Slab	Weight of reinforcement in welded fabric kg/m^2	Maximum spacing of expansion joints in metres	Maximum spacing of contraction joints in metres
1.	Reinforced concrete slabs	20 cm	5.5	37	
	with expansion joints only	15 cm	3.8	25	
		10 cm	2.7	12.5	
2.	Reinforced concrete slabs	20 cm	3.8	45	15
	with expansion and dummy	15 cm	2.7	37	13
	contraction joints	10 cm	2.2	30	7.5
3.	Uncracked concrete	20 cm	—	37	4.5
	slabs	15 cm	—	27	4.5
		10 cm	—	27	4.5

Table 35. Width of Carriageway, Shoulder and Roadway (Based on IRC : 52—1973)

S. No.	Highway Classification	Carriageway width in metres	Shoulder width in metres	Roadway width in metres
1.	National Highways			
	(*i*) Single lane	3.75	2 × 1.25	6.25
	(*ii*) Double lane	7.0	2 × 0.9	8.8
2.	Major District Roads	3.75	2 × 0.5	4.75
3.	Other District Roads	3.75	2 × 0.5	4.75
4.	Village Roads	3.00	2 × 0.5	4.00

Note : (*i*) The roadway widths given above are exclusive of parapet (usual width 0.6 m) and side drain (usual width 0.6 m). These should be provided in addition to the shoulders as necessary.

(*ii*) In hard rocky stretches, the width of shoulder may be reduced by 0.4 m on either side on double lane roads and 0.2 m in other cases.

Table 36. Minimum Right of Way in Metres

Highway Classification	Right of way width	
	Normal	Exceptional
(*a*) National Highways/State Highways	24	18
(*b*) Major District Roads	18	15
(*c*) Other District Roads	15	12
(*d*) Village Roads	9	9

Airports

Table 37. Characteristics of Principal Transport Aircrafts

S. No.	*Designation*	*Manufacture*	*Cruising speed (kmph)*	*Take-off distance (metre)*	*Landing distance (m)*	*Fuel capacity (litres)*	*Max take-off gross wt. (kg)*	*Wing area (sq m)*
1.	150	Cessna	180	420	300	130	700	15.7
2.	PA-30B	Piper	300	450	540	450	1600	17.8
3.	DC-3	Douglas	340	830	800	8000	16000	96.7
4.	DC-9-20	Douglas	880	1800	1500	14000	38000	92.5
5.	DC-6B	Douglas	500	1200	1000	25000	45000	146
6.	990-A	Convair	800	3000	1500	75000	110,000	225.0
7.	DC-8-10	Douglas	800	3000	1500	85000	120,000	277.3
8.	727-200	Boeing	800	1800	1400	36000	70,000	165
9.	707-120B	Boeing	800	2400	2000	85000	110,000	243
10.	707-320	Boeing	800	3000	2100	120,000	140,000	300
11.	747	Boeing	1000	3000	2000	—	300,000	—
12.	SST	Boeing	3000	2250	2000	—	300,000	—

Note : Cruising speed is the speed of aircraft with respect to the ground when the aircraft is flying at its maximum speed.

Now-a-days speed of aircraft is expressed in terms of ratio of its speed to that of sound. This speed is expressed in terms of Mach. Thus the speed of Russian M. Gs (about 2500 kmph) can be stated as 2.1 Mach.

Table 38. I.C.A.O. Classification of Airports (Runway Length)

Code	*Runway lengths is metres*
A	2500
B	2150—2500
C	1800—2150
D	1500—1800
E	1280—1500
F	1080—1280
G	980—1080

Table 39. I.C.A.O. Classification of Airports (Pavement strength)

Code	*Single isolated wheel load in kg.*	*Tyre pressure kg/m²*
1	45,360	8.4
2	34,020	7.0
3	27,220	7.0
4	20,410	7.0
5	13,610	6.0
6	6,869	4.90
7	2,270	2.90

Table 40. Runway Geometric Standards (I.C.A.O.)

Airport classi-fication	*Basic length of main runway in metres*	*Maximum width of runway in metres*	*Maximum width of taxiway in metres*	*Approach surface slopes*		*Maximum Longitudinal gradient%*	*Maximum effective gradient%*	*Maximum transverse gradient%*
				Instrument runway	*Non-instru-ment runway*			
A	2500 or above	45	23	1 : 50	1 : 40	1.25	1.0	1.5
B	2150-2500	45	23	1 : 50	1 : 40	1.25	1.0	1.5
C	1800-2150	45	23	1 : 50	1 : 40	1.5	1.0	1.5
D	1500-1800	45	18	1 : 50	1 : 40	1.5	1.0	1.5
E	1280-1500	45	15	1 : 50	1 : 30	1.5	1.0	1.5
F	1080-1280	30	12.5	1 : 50	1 : 30	1.5	1.0	1.5
G	900-1080	30	12.5	1 : 50	1 : 25	1.5	1.0	1.5

Note. 1. The basic runway length is for sea-level elevation. Correlation should be applied for temperature and elevation. The maximum effective gradient is obtained by dividing the maximum difference in runway centre line elevation by total length of the runway.

2. Maximum width of landing strip for all these classes is 150 metres for Non-Instrumental Runways and 300 metres for Instrumental Runways.

3. Rate of change of grade for all classes : 0.3% for 30 metres of vertical curves.

4. Sight distances : Any two points 3 metres above the runway must be mutually visible within distance of half the runway length.

5. Grading beyond runway ends 60 metres on either side.

6. Shoulders Transverse Grade : 75 metres from runway centre line 2.5% maximum, remaining maximum.

Table 41. Runway, Taxiway Width and Lateral Clearance Recommendations

Maximum standard	*VFR (Visual Flight Rules) Airports*	*General utility Airports**		*All other Airports*	
		A	*B*	*Runway length 960 m to 1220 m*	*Runway length above 1220 m*
Width of Landing strip, metre	30	45	60	120	150
Runway, metre	15	22.5	30	30	45
Taxiway, metre	6	12	12	15	22.5
Taxiway centre line to Run-way centre, line, metre	30	60	67.5	75	120
Parallel Taxiway centre line, metre	—	—	—	60	90
Aircraft parking area, metre	—	30	30	52.5	75
Obstacle, metre	—	22.5	22.5	30	60
Runway, centre line to Aircraft					
Parking area, metre	42	90	97.5	127.5	195
Obstacle, metre	30	37.5	37.5	60	75
Run way centre line to Building line, metre					
(*a*) Instrument Runway	—	—	—	225	225
(*b*) Non-instrument Runway	60	90	96	150	225

*A = Less than 1500 metre elevation and less than 25 kmph cross wind 95% of time.

B = Greater than 1506 metre elevation and greater than 25 kmph cross wind 5% of time.

Table 42. Minimum Surface and Base Course Thickness for Different ESWL (As recommended by Corps of Engineers, USA)

Load 1000 kg ESWL	*Thickness of surfacing (base course 80% CBR*	*Base Thickness*	*Total Thickness*	*Thickness of surface (base course 100% CBR*	*Base Thickness*	*Total Thickness*
4.50	5 cm	15 cm	20 cm	5 cm	15 cm	20 cm
9.0	5 cm	15 cm	20 cm	5 cm	15 cm	20 cm
13.50	7.5 cm	15 cm	22.5 cm	5 cm	15 cm	20 cm
18.00	7.5 cm	15 cm	22.5 cm	5 cm	15 cm	20 cm
22.5	7.5 cm	15 cm	22.5 cm	5 cm	15 cm	20 cm
27.0	10 cm	15 cm	25 cm	7.5 cm	15 cm	22.5 cm
31.5	10 cm	15 cm	25 cm	7.5 cm	15 cm	22.5 cm

Table 43. Landing Area for Helicopter

S.No.	*Designation of Helicopter*	*Size of landing area*
1.	Single Engined	
	(*i*) 2700 kg weight (VFR)	Square of 22.5 metres or circle of equivalent area
	(*ii*) 6800 kg (VFR)	Square of 30 metres or circle of equivalent area
		60 m × 120 m.
2.	Multi-engined (IFR)	

Railways

F.F. Rail Section. (See Fig. 5).

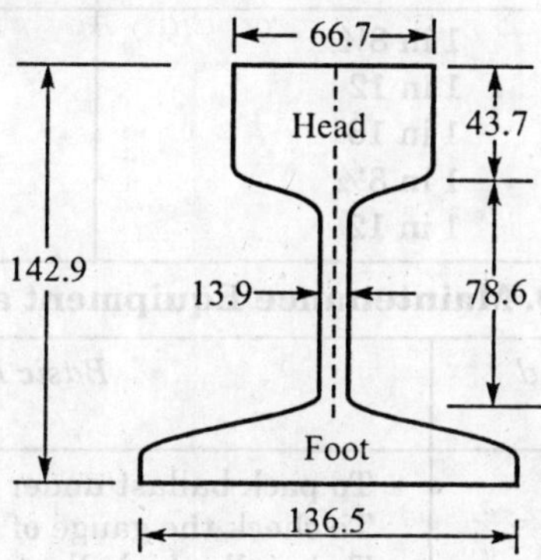

Fig. 5. F.F. Rail.

Table 44. Approximate Average Quantity of Ballast per km Length

S. No.	*Track particular*	*Gauge*	*Sleeper Density*	*Depth of Cushion*	*quantity of ballast cm. per km.*
1.	Double line	B.G.	M + 6	25 cm	2600 m^3
2.	Single line	B.G.	M + 6	25 cm	1300 m^3
3.	Double line	M.G.	M + 6	20 cm	1800 m^3
4.	Single line	M.G.	M + 6	20 cm	900 m^3
5.	Single line	M.G.	M + 3	20 cm	510 m^3

Table 45. Gauges of Railway in the World

S. No.	*Classification of Gauge*	*Gauge in metres*
1.	Standard Gauge	1.435
2.	Broad Gauge	1.676
3.	Broad Gauge	1.524
4.	Cape Gauge	1.067
5.	Metre Gauge	1.000
6.	Other Gauges	Different Gauge

Table 46. Gauges of Railway in India

S. No.	*Nomenclature of Gauge*	*Gauge in metre*	*(% of total Approximately)*
1.	B.G.	1.676	53%
2.	M.G.	1.000	40%
3.	N.G.	0.762 }	
4.	N.G.	0.610 }	7% app.

Table 47. Minimum Formation Widths on Indian Railways

S. No.	*Particular of formation*	*Track particular*	*Formation width in metres*
1.	Embankment	Single	6.10
2.	Excavation	Single	5.49
3.	Embankment	Double	10.82
4.	Excavation	Double	10.06

Table 48. Standard Length of Tongue Rail

Gauge	*Crossing Number*	*Length of tongue rail in metres*
B.G.	1 in 8½	4.72
B.G.	1 in 12	6.4
B.G.	1 in 16	9.76
M.G.	1 in 8½	3.96
M.G.	1 in 12	5.49

Table 49. Maintenance Equipment and Tools

S. No.	*Name of hand tools and Mechanical appliance*	*Basic Function*
1.	Beater-cum-pick axe	To pack ballast under sleeper
2.	Rail gauge	To check the gauge of track
3.	Shovel	To handle the ballast
4.	Ballast screen	To screen out ballast
5.	Crow bars	To correct track alignment
6.	Rail tongs	To lift rails
7.	Jim crow or rail bender	To bend the rails
8.	Cant board	To provide cant on curves
9.	Splice rail	To indicate level of outer and inner rails on curves
10.	Adzes	To do adzing of wooden sleepers
11.	Mallet or wooden hammer	To sound the sleepers for packing
12.	Sledge hammer	To assist in heavy cutting work
13.	Claw bar	To remove dog spikes out of sleepers
14.	Lifting jack	To lift portion of track
15.	Electric tie-tampers	To place ballast under sleeper
16.	Vibration tampers	Functions same as electric tamper but easier to handle
17.	Track liner	To correct considerable variation in alignment efficiently.

Table 50. Prescribed Details for Level Crossing

S. No.	Classification	Width of gates in metres	Maximum grades of approach
1.	Special class	7.3 to 9.1	1 in 40
2.	Class A	7.3	1 in 30
3.	Class B	3.7	1 in 30
4.	Class C	3.7	1 in 20
5.	Class D	1.8	1 in 20

Table 51.

S. No.	Name of station	Name of railway	Length of platform in metres
1.	Sonepur	N.E.R.	736
2.	Bezwada	S.R.	674
3.	Jhansi	E.R.	617
4.	Dakor	W.R.	448

Table 52. Height of Passenger Platform

S. No.	Type of platform	Height of platform over rail level		
		B.G.	M.G.	N.G.
1.	Rail level	0.00 m	0.00 m	0.00 m
2.	Low level	0.45 m	—	—
3.	High level	0.76—0.84 m	0.31—0.41m	0.23—0.41 m

Passenger Platform. (See Fig. 6).

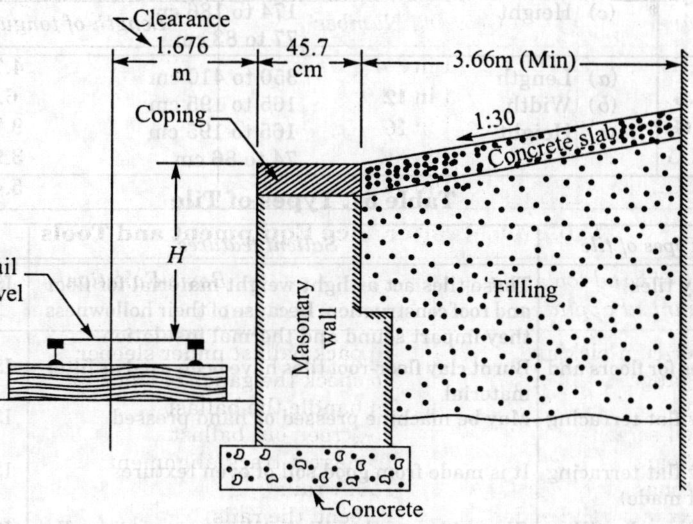

Fig. 6

Table 53. Distance between C.L. of Track and Adjacent Structure

S. No.	Platform classification	Minimum horizontal distance between C.L. of Track and any structure in metre		
		B.G.	M.G.	N.G.
1.	Passenger platform	5.33 m	5.00 m	4.88 m
2.	Goods platform	4.72 m	3.18 m	3.05 m

Building Materials

Table 54. (Based on IS : 1077—1976)

Class Designation	Average compressive strength			
	Not less than		Less than	
	kg/cm²	*N/mm²*	*kgf/cm²*	*N/mm²*
350	350	35	400	40
300	300	30	350	35
250	250	25	300	30
200	200	20	250	25
175	175	17.5	200	20
150	150	15	175	17.5
125	125	12.5	150	15
100	100	10	125	12.5
75	75	7.5	100	10
50	50	5	75	7.5
35	35	3.5	50	5

Table 55. Standard Size of Bricks

Length in cm	*Width in cm*	*Height in cm*
19	9	9
19	9	4

Table 56. Tolerances per 20 Bricks

Sub-class A	(*a*) Length (*b*) Width (*c*) Height	368 to 392 174 to 186 174 to 186 cm 77 to 83 cm	(380 ± 17 cm) (180 ± 6 cm) (80 ± 6 cm) (80 ± 3 cm)
Sub-class B	(*a*) Length (*b*) Width (*c*) Height	350 to 410 cm 165 to 195 cm 165 to 195 cm 74 to 86 cm	(38 ± 30 cm) (180 ± 15 cm) (80 ± 5 cm) (80 ± 6 cm)

Table 57. Types of Tile

S. No.	*Types of tile*	*Salient features*	*ISI code reference*
1.	Hollow clay tiles	These tiles act as light weight material for floor and roof construction. Because of their hollowness they impart sound and thermal insulation	IS : 3951 (Part I)–1975
2.	Hollow tiles for floors and roofs	Burnt clay floor-roof tiles have been used as filter material	IS : 3951 (Part ID)–1975
3.	Burnt clay flat terracing tiles	May be machine pressed or hand pressed	IS : 2690 (Part I)–1975
4.	Burnt clay flat terracing tiles (hand made)	It is made from good soil of even textures	IS : 2690 (Part II)–1975
5.	Clay ridge and ceiling tiles	Clay ridge and ceiling tiles were originally manufactured in Mangalore	IS : 1464–1973
6.	Structural hollow clay floor tiles	Used for structural floor and roof construction	IS : 3951–1967
7.	Polystyrene walls tiles	Useful for use in interior surfaces	IS : 3463–1966
8.	PVC (vinyl) asbestos floor tiles	These tiles give decorative finish to the floor	IS : 3461–1966
9.	Ceramic unglazed vitreous acid resistant	Used for floor and tank lumps	IS : 4457–1967
10.	Glazed earth and wall tiles	These tiles are used in finishing floors and walls of kitchen	IS : 777–1970

Table 58. ISI Classification of Lime

S. No.	*Name of constituent*	*Class A*	*Class B*		*Class C*	
		Per cent	*% slaked*	*% unslaked*	*% slaked*	*% unslaked*
1.	Calcium and magnesium oxide					
	(*a*) Maximum	60	70	70	85	85
	(*b*) Minimum	70	—	—	—	—
2.	Silica aluminium and ferricoxide minimum	25	15	15	—	—
3.	Insoluble portion of HCl	2	2	3	—	—
4.	Loss on ignition (Max)					
	(*a*) Lumps of lime	—	5	5	—	—
	(*b*) Ground lime	—	20	20	—	—
5.	CO_2 minimum	5	5	5	5	5

Table 59. Mix Proportions for Lime Mortar

S. No.	*Description of mortar*	*Lime*	*Cement*	*Lime pozzolana mix*	*Pozzolana*	*Sand*	*Compressive strength 28 days k/m^2*	*Hardening time after completion of work*
1.	Lime cement	1C	1	—	—	6	30 to 50	14
2.	Lime cement	2B	1	—	—	9	20 to 30	14
3.	Lime pozzolana mixture	—	—	1	—	1.5	30 to 50	14
4.	Lime cement	3B or 3C	1	—	—	12	7 to 15	14
5.	Hydraulic lime	1A	—	—	—	2	—	14
6.	Lime pozzolana	1C	—	—	—	2	7 to 15	14
7.	Lime	1B	—	—	—	3	5 to 7	28

Table 60. Physical Requirements of Masonry Cement

S. No.	*Characteristics*		*Requirement*
1.	**Fineness**		
	Residue on 45 micron IS sieve (max)		15%
2.	**Setting time**		
		Initial (Min.)	90 minutes
		Final (Max.)	24 hours
3.	**Soundness**		
	(*i*) Le Chatelier expansion (Max.)		10 mm
	(*ii*) Anti-clave expansion (Max.)		1%
4.	Compressive	7 days	25 kg/cm^2
	Strength	28 days	50 kg/cm^2

Table 61. ISI Specification for Different Types of Cement

S. No.	*Name of test property*	*Ordinary Cement*	*Rapid Hardening Cement*	*Low Heat Portland Cement*	*Portland blast Furnace Slag Cement*	*Portland Porrolena Cement*	*Masonary Cement*	*Remarks*
1.	Fineness test							
	(*i*) Max residue on IS sieve No. 9%	10	5	—	10	5	—	
	(*ii*) Specific surface	2250	3260	3200	2250	3000	5000	
2.	Setting test lime							
	(*i*) Initial (minutes)	30	30	30	30	30	90	
	(*ii*) Final (minutes)	600	600	600	600	600	24 hrs.	
3.	Soundness LeChatelier Max. (mm)	10	10	10	10	10	10	
	Autoclave Max. (%)	0.5	0.5	0.5	0.5	0.1	1.0	
4.	Compressive strength (kg/cm^2)							
	1 day	—	115	—	—	—	—	
	3 days	115	210	70	115	—	—	
	7 days	175	—	—	175	148	25	
	28 days	—	—	265	—	—	50	
5.	Tensile strength kg/cm^2 (Min.)							
	1 day	—	20	—	—	—	—	
	3 days	20	30	—	20	—	—	
	7 days	25	—	—	25	—	—	
6.	Heat of Hydration per gm.							
	7 days	—	—	65 calories	—	—	—	
	28 days	—	—	75 calories	—	—	—	
7.	Chemical composition	1. $\frac{\text{Alumina}}{\text{Iron Oxide}} < 0.66$ 2. Manganese < 5% 3. Sulphur (SO_4) < 275% 4. Less due to ignition 4% 5. Insoluble residue < 1.5% 6. $\frac{\text{Lime}}{\text{Silica}} < 1.02$ > 0.66	Same as ordinary cement	% of line after action with SO_3 < 2.4 silica + 1.2 aluminium + 0 to iron oxide ≯ 1.9 Al silica + 1.2 times Al + 0.65 times iron oxide. Rest same as ordinary cement.	(*i*) Silica dioxide 27 to 32% (*ii*) Iron oxide 0 to 1% (*iii*) Calcium oxide 0 to 19% (*iv*) Magnesium oxide 0 to 17% (*v*) Manganese oxide 0 to 2%	(*i*) Loss of ignition < 5% (*ii*) Magnesia < 5% (*iii*) Sulphur anhydride 2 to 7.5%		

Table 62. Determination of Fineness Modulus of Sand

ISI Sieve No.	*% retained on Sieve*	*Cumulative % retained on Sieve*
480	4	4
240	10	14
120	15	29
60	30	59
30	35	94
9	6	100
	Total	300

Fineness Module = $\frac{300}{100}$ = 3

Table 63. Uses of Different Types of Indian Timber

S. No.	*Name of Timber*	*Works for which used*
1.	Teak	High class furniture, agriculture complements, ship building, railway sleepers building construction, musical instruments
2.	Sal	Railway sleepers, building construction, furniture, ship building
3.	Deodar	Railway sleepers, building construction.
4.	Toon	Furniture, musical instruments.
5.	Kail	Railway sleepers.
6.	Rose wood	Furniture.
7.	Bamboo	Rafters and poles
8.	Chir	Packing boxes.
9.	Babul	Wheels
10.	Simul	Well curbs.

Table 64. Composition of Solders

S. No.	*Type of Solder*	*% of*		*Remarks*
		Lead	*Tin*	
1.	Soft solder	37	63	Used sheet metal works. Melting range 150 to 350°C.
2.	Medium solder	50	50	Temp, range 350—500°C.
3.	Plumbers' solder	70	30	} Hard solders having range of 500 to 900°C.
4.	Electricians' solder	5	42	

Table 65. Engineering Properties and Use of Different Steel.

S. No.	*Nomenclature of Steel*	*Engineering Properties*	*Uses*
1.	Cast iron	C 2 to 4.5% Sp. gr. 7.2 Ultimate compressive strength 1500 kg/m^2 does not rust.	Used for making cots, base plate, railways etc.
2.	Wrought iron	C 0.15 to 0.25% Sp.Gr. 7.70 Ultimate compressive strength 2000 kg/m^2 Ultimate tensile strength 3750 kg/cm does not rust easily.	Used for making plain and corrugated sheets and small pipes and for making electromagnets
3.	Low carbon or mild steel	C 0.5 to 0.6% Sp. gr. 7.8 Ultimate compressive strength 4750 kg/cm^2 Ultimate tensile strength 5500 kg/cm	Used for making beams, girders, angle iron, T and I section M.S. rods are used in R.C.C. work.
4.	High carbon or Hard steel	C 0.6 to 1.7% Sp. Gr. 7.9 Ultimate compressive strength 1200 to 25000 kg/cm^2 Ultimate tensile strength 8000 to 16000 kg/cm^2. Rusts readily	Used for making tools and cutlery, machines parts subjected to shocks and vibration.
5.	High tensile steel	C < 0.3% Ultimate tensile strength upto 7000 kg/cm^2 Yield stress upto 3300 kg/cm^2	Used for prestressed concrete work.
6.	Spring steel	C 0.6 to 1.7%	Suitable for springs.
7.	Plain carbon, tool steel		
	(*a*) Chisel steel	C 0.3 to 0.4% Cr 2% Ni and Tungsten 2 to 3%	
	(*b*) Shear steel	C 0.85% Vanadium 1%	Used for making chisel, punch, coal cutter pickaxe.
	(*c*) Die steel	C 0.6%, Ni 1%	Used for making die.
8.	High speed steel	C 0.6 to 0.7%	
	(*a*) Tungsten high speed steel	Tungsten 12 to 18% Cr 4% Vanadium 1%	Used for cutters, turning and boring steel
	(*b*) Molybdenum high speed steel	C 0.75% Molybdenum 8.54 Cr 4% Vanadium 1% Tungsten 1.5%	—Do—

S. No.	Nomenclature of Steel	Engineering Properties	Uses
	(c) Tungsten molybdenum high speed steel	C 0.8% Tungsten 5.75% Molybdenum 4.5% Cr. 4% Vanadium 1.5%	—Do—
9.	Nickel steel	C 0.25—0.4% Cr. 1.5% Ni 3 to 3.5%	For making armour plates, boiler plates with 3.6% Ni, it is known as invar used for pendulum of clocks.
10.	Manganese steel	A very hard steel Armagnetic	For rails under heavy traffic or on curve.
11.	Vanadium steel	Hard and cut resisting	Used for axle, spring and propeller shafts.
12.	Chromium steel	% of Cr < 2% High percentage makes steel brittle	Ball bearing, file, safe, cutting tools and projections.

Table 66. Characteristics of Wrought Aluminium and Alloys

Material Symbol	Composition %	Characteristics	Available forms	Uses
PIB	Cu < 0.5, Si < 0.3, Fe < 0.4 ; Mn < 0.03, Zn < 0.1. (Cu + Si + Fe + Mn + Zn) < 0.5	High purity Al (99.5% Al)	Sheet, plates rods	Food and chemical plant. Electrical conductors and reflectors
PIC	Cu < 0.6, Si < 0.5, Fe < 0.7 Mn < 0.1 (Cu + Si + Fe + Mn + Zn) < 1.0	Commercially pure Al (99% Al)	—do—	Breeding, packing and cooking utensils
NP3	Cu < 0.1, Si < 0.6, Fe < 0.7 M 1 to 1.5	Al alloy. Stronger and harder than PIC. Has good weldability	—do—	Building sheet, sheet metal
PN4	Cu < 0.10, Mg 17 to 28 Si < 0.7, Fe < 0.7, Mn < 0.5 Cr < 0.25	Al alloy. Strength increases with Mg content	Sheet, rods,	Panelling and structures exposed to marine atmosphere
NP6	Cu < 0.1, Mg 4.5 to 5.5 Si < 0.7, Fe < 0.7, Mn < 1.0, Cr < 0.3	Al alloy. Highly resistive to corrosion	Sheet, tube roads,	Ship building and other applications
NP8	Cu < 0.1, Hg 4 to 4.9 Si < 0.4, Fe < 0.7 Mn 0.5 to 1.0 Cr < 0.25	Al alloy. Highly resistive to corrosion	Plate, forging	—do—
HP20	Cu 0.15 to 0.4, Mg 8 to 1.2 Si 0.4 to 0.8 Fe < 0.7 Mn 0.2 to 0.8, Cr 1.5 to 0.35	Al alloy medium strength corrosion resistant	Sheet, plate forging	General structural and architectural application
HP30	Cu < 0.1, Mg, 0.4 to 1.4 Si 0.4 to 1.3, Fe < 0.6, Mn 0.4 to 1.0, Cu < 0.3	A medium strength alloy. Corrosion resistant and weldable	Sheet, plate tube	Structural engineering
HP14	Cu 3.5 to 4.5, Mg, 0.4 to 1.2, Si 0.2 to 0.7, Fe < 0.7 Mg 0.4 to 1.0	Strong aluminium alloy having good ductility	Tube forging wire rod	Stressed components of aircraft
HP15	Cu 3.8 to 9.8, Mg 0.2 to 0.8 Si 0.5 to 0.9, Fe < 0.7 Mn 0.3 to 1.2	Strong ductility. Al alloy	Sheet plate tube, wire and forging	Stressed aircraft components

Note. The symbolic representation by letters is as below :

B : Bolts and screw stock
PC : Clad plate
P : Plate
N : Not-heat-treatable alloy
H : Heat treatable alloy.

Table 67. Requirement for R.C. Cutback Bitumen

S. No.	*Characteristics*	*RC-0*	*RC-1*	*RC-2*	*RC-3*	*RC-4*	*RC-5*	*Remark*
1.	Saybolt Furol viscosity in sees							Tests 3 and 4 are on residue from distillates upto 360°C
	(*a*) 75°C	75 to 100	—	—	—	—	—	
	(*b*) 50°C	—	76—106	—	—	—	—	
	(*c*) 60°C	—	—	75 to 150	250 to 500	125 to 250	300 to 600	
	(*d*) 82°C	—	—					
2.	Flash point (Min)°C	—		26.5	26.5	26.5	26.5	
3.	Penetration at 25°C 100 gm, 5 sec 1/100 cm	80 to 120	80 to 120	80 to 120	80 to 120	80 to 120	80 to 120	
4.	Ductility at 25°C (Min)	100	100	100	100	100	100	

Table 68. Requirement for MC Cutback Bitumen

S. No.	*Characteristics*	*MC-0*	*MC-1*	*MC-2*	*MC-3*	*MC-4*	*MC-5*	*Remark*
1.	Saybolt Furol viscosity in seconds							Tests 3 and 4 are on residue from distillate upto 360°C
	(*a*) 25°C	75 to 150	—	—	—	—	—	
	(*b*) 50°C	—	75 to 150	—	—	—	—	
	(*c*) 60°C	—	—	100 to 200	—	—	—	
	(*d*) 82°C	—	—	—	250 to 500	125 to 250	300 to 600	
2.	Flash point (Min) in °C	38	38	65.5	65.5	65.5	65.5	
3.	Penetration @ 25°C 5 secs, in 1/100 cm	120 to 300	120 to 300	120 to 300	120 to 300	120 to 300	120 to 300	
4.	Ductility at 25°C in cm (Min)	100	100	100	100	100	100	

Table 69. Requirement of S.C. Cutback Bitumen

S. No.	*Characteristics*	*SC-0*	*SC-1*	*SC-2*	*SC-3*	*SC-4*	*SC-5*	*Remark*
1.	Saybolt Furol viscosity in secs at							Test 4 is on residence from distillate upto 360°C
	(*a*) 25°C	75 to 150	—	—	—	—	—	
	(*b*) 50°C	—	75 to 125	—	—	—	—	
	(*c*) 60°C	—	—	100 to 200	250 to 500	—	—	
	(*d*) 82°C	—	—	—	—	125 to 500	300 to 600	
2.	Water % by vol. (Max)	0.5	0.5	—	—	—	—	
3.	Flash point (Min) °C	65.5	65.5	79.4	93.3	107	121	
4.	Ductility at 25°C m cm (Min)	100	100	100	100	100	100	

Table 70. Requirement of Road Tar

S. No.	*Characteristics*	*Limits for Grades*					*Remarks*
		RT-1	*RT-2*	*RT-3*	*RT-4*	*RT-5*	
1.	Viscosity						
	(*a*) Temp. of Tar °C						
	(*b*) Viscosity in Tar						
2.	Softening point						
3.	Softening point of residue Max °C						
4.	Water % by vol. (Max.)						
5.	Sp. gr. at 25°C						

Table 71. Requirement of Bitumen Emulsion

S. No.	*Characteristics*	*Rapid Setting RS*	*Medium Setting MS*	*Slow Setting SS*	*Remark*
1.	Viscosity by Standard Saybolt Furol viscosymeter in secs at 25°C	20—100	20—100	20—100	
2.	Water content % by weight	Not more than		45	
3.	Settlement, 5 days % (Max)	3	3	3	
4.	Cement mixing test % (Max)	—	—	2	
5.	Sieve test, % (Max)	0.10	0.10	0.10	

Concrete Technology

Table 72. Permissible Stresses in Concrete (IS : 456—1978)

Grade of Concrete	*All values in N/mm²* *Permissible Stress in Compression*		*Permissible stress in Bond (Average for plain bars in tension*
	Bending σ_{cbc}	*Direct* σ_{cc}	τ_{pd}
M10	3	2.5	—
M15	5	4	0.6
M20	7	5	0.8
M25	8.5	6	1.9
M30	10	8	1.0
M35	11.5	9	1.0
M40	13	10	1.2

Note. The load stress given in Col. 4, shall be measured by 25% for bars in compressive.

Table 73. Percentage of Water for Gauging Cement Paste and 1 to 3 Cement and Standard Sand Mortar

Percentage of Water				
Required to give standard penetration of 5 to 7 mm from bottom of Vicat mould	*To be used for gauging cement paste for test for soundness (0.78 P)%*	*To be used for gauging cement paste for setting tensile tests (0.85 P)%*	*To be used for gauging 1 to 3 cement and standard sand mortar for tensile straight* $\frac{0.78\,P + 2.5}{4}\%$	*Remark*
33.0	25.7	28.0	8.9	
32.5	25.4	27.6	8.9	
32.0	25.0	27.3	8.8	
31.5	24.5	26.6	8.6	
31.1	24.2	26.4	8.6	
30.5	23.8	23.9	8.5	
30.0	23.4	25.5	8.4	
29.0	22.6	24.6	8.2	
28.5	22.2	24.2	8.1	
28.0	21.8	23.8	8.0	
27.5	21.5	23.4	7.9	
27.0	21.1	22.9	7.8	
26.5	20.7	22.5	7.7	
26.0	20.3	22.1	7.6	

Table 74. ASTM Requirements for Chemical Composition of Cements

Requirements	*Types of cement*				
	I	*II*	*III*	*IV*	*V*
SiO_2					
Silicon Dioxide (Min) %	—	21.0	—	—	—
Al_2O_3 (Max) %	—	6.0	—	—	—
Fe_2O_3 Max %	—	6.0	—	6.5	—
MgO (Max) %					
SO_3	5.0	5.0	5.0	5.0	5.0
(*i*) When 3 CaO, Al_2O_3 is 8% or less (Max) %	2.5	2.5	3.0	2.3	2.3
(*ii*) When $3CaO \cdot Al_2O_3$ is more than 8% (Max) %	3.0	—	3.0	—	—
Loss of ignition (Max) %	3.0	3.3	3.0	2.3	3
Insoluble residue (Max) %	0.75	0.75	3.75	0.75	0.75
($3CaO$, SiO_2) Tricalcium	—	50	—	35	50
Silicate, ($2CaO$, SiO_2) Dicalcium	—	—	—	40	—
silicate, $3CaO$, Al_2O_3 Tricalcium					
Aluminate	—	8	15	7	50

ASTM classification of portland cement is as below.

Type I. For general concrete work when types II, III, IV & IV are not required

Type II. For use where concrete is exposed to moderate sulphate action.

Type III. For use where high early strength is required.

Type IV. For use where low heat of hydration is required.

Type V. For use where high sulphate resistance is required.

Table 75. Properties of Ordinary Portland and High Alumina Cement

Test	*Ordinary Portland Cement*	*High Alumina Cement*
Fineness of grinding specific surface sq. cm per gram not less than	2250	2250
Setting Time		
Initial setting time $\nless$	45 minutes	30 minute
Initial setting time $\ngtr$		6 hours
Final setting time $\ngtr$	10 hours	2 hrs. after initial set
Soundness		
Le Chatelier test expansion after 1 hour boiling mm	10	5
After 3 hours boiling mm	—	1
Compressive strength kg/cm^2		
After 1 day $\nless$	150 day	300 kg/cm^2
After 3 day $\nless$	—Do—	350 kg/cm^2 and to show increase over 4 on day strength

Table 76. Relative Properties of Various Types of Cement

S. No.	Type of cement	Tensile strength kg/cm^2			Compressive strength kg/cm^2			Setting time $m\ m/s^2$		Soundness exp. in mm Le Chetelier expansion	Residue < %	Heat evolution in 7 days cal/gm	% of main compounds		
		1 day	3 days	7 days	1 day	3 days	7 days	Initial	Final				Trisilicate	Disilicate	Aluminium
1.	Portland cement (ordinary)	—	20	25	—	115	175	30	600	10	10	85	40	30	11
2.	Rapid Hardening	20	30	—	115	210	—	30	600	10	5	100	50	20	10
3.	Blast Furnace	—	20	25	—	115	175	30	600	10	—		—	—	—
4.	Low Heat	—	—	—	—	70	115	60	600	10	—	65	25	45	5
5.	High Alumina	—	—	—	400	490	—	120–320	Not more than 120 mm after initial set	—	8	90	—	—	—

Table 77. Maximum Fineness Modulus (Permissible)

Amount of total aggregate per quintal of cement	Fineness modulus for max. aggregate size of	
cum	20 mm	40 mm
0.23	5.1	5.8
0.29	4.9	5.6
0.35	4.8	5.5
0.41	4.7	5.4
0.46	4.6	5.3
0.51	4.5	5.2

Table 78. Estimated Relation Between the Minimum and Average Crushing Strength of Works Cubes for Different Work Conditions

Condition	Minimum strengths as % of average strength
Very good control	75
Fair control	60
Power control	40

Table 79. Internal Dimension of Slump Test Moulds

S. No.	Details	Dimension (mm)	Tolerance (mm)
1.	Bottom diameter	200	+ 3, – 1.5
2.	Top diameter	100	+ 3, – 1.5
3.	Hight	300	± 1.5

Table 80. Strength Requirements of Concrete

Grade of concrete	*Compressive strength of 15 cm cube at 28 days after mixing, conducted in accordance with IS : 516—1959 kg / cm²*	
	Preliminary test minimum	*Works test minimum*
M 100	135	100
M 150	200	150
M 200	260	200
M 250	320	250
M 300	380	300
M 350	440	350
M 400	500	400

Table 81. Quantities of Materials for Various Mixes to Obtain One cum of Compacted Material

Maximum size of course aggregate	*Normal mix by volume*	*Quantity of materials required*		
		Cement lag	*Fine aggregate cum*	*Course aggregate cum*
20 mm	1 : 1 : 2	11.7	0.407	0.814
	1 : 1.2 : 2.4	10.1	0.420	0.840
	1 : 1.5 : 3	8.5	0.440	0.880
10 mm	1 : 2 : 3	7.7	0.533	0.795
40 mm	1 : 1.5 : 4.5	6.7	0.348	1.044

Table 82. Weight of Immersion Vibrator

Size of Vibrator mm (outside diameter)	*Weight in kg*
25	1
35	2
40	2
50	3
60	4
65	5
70	6

Table 83. Size Capacity and Rating of Vibrating Table

Length in m	*Breadth in m*	*Capacity in tonnes*	*Output rating in kW*
1	1	0.25	0.75
1	1	1.0	1.5
2	1	0.5	0.75
2	1	1	1.5
3	1	1.5	2.2

Table 84. Details of Vibrators

Designation	*Type of vibrator*	*Capacity of the power unit in kW*	*Weight of vibrating body in kg*	*Remarks*
FDC—200	Fixed directly coupled	0.2	10—25	
MDC—200	—	0.2	10—25	
MF—400	—	0.4	25—40	

Table 85. Size of Transit Mixers

Designation	*Nominal Capacity*	
	Mixer (min) m²	*Aligator (min) m³*
3 TM	3	3.75
4 TM	4	5.00
3 TM	5	6.25
6 TM	6	7.5

Table 86. Specification of Plaster Recommended by the Code of Practice

S. No.	*No. of coats of plaster*	*Situation*	*Mix proportion by vol. (cement : lime : sand)*	*Thickness*
1.	Single coat	External and internal	1 : 0 : 3 1 : 0 : 4 1 : 0 : 6 1 : 1 : 6 1 : 2 : 9	10 to 15 mm
2.	Two coats plaster			
	(*a*) Backing coat	External and internal	1 : 0 : 3 1 : 0 : 4 1 : 0 : 6 1 : 0 : 6	10 to 12 mm
	(*b*) Finishing coat	—Do—	1 : 0 : 3 to 6 1 : 1 : 6 1 : 2 : 9	3 to 8 mm
3.	Three coat plaster	Very rough surface both internal and external		
		(*a*) Base coat	1 : 0 : 3 1 : 0 : 4 1 : 0 : 6	10 to 15 mm
		(*b*) Second coat	1 : 0 : 3 to 6 1 : 1 : 6 1 : 2 : 9	3 to 8 mm
		(*c*) Finishing coat	Fat lime and fire sand or marble dust in equal proportion	3 to 5 mm

Table 87. Spacing of Joints

S. No.	*Kind of state*	*Thickness of slab*	*Weight of reinforce-ments in welded fabric kg/m*	*Max. spacing if expansion joint in metres*	*Max. spacing of contraction joints in metres*
1.	RCC slab without expansion joints	20 cm 15 cm 10 cm	5.5 3.8 2.7	37 25 12.5	— — —
2.	RCC slab with expansion joint	20 cm 15 cm 10 cm	3.8 2.7 2.2	45 37 30	15 13 7.5
3.	Uncracked concrete slab	20 cm 15 cm 10 cm	— — —	37 27 27	4.5 4.5 4.5

Cement and Bitumen Consumption Statement

The cost of material varies from time to time, the quantity of material used for various categories of work remain constant and serves as a very important guide for analysis of rates in the early stages and for checking the store statements in the final stages. The most important material which needs greater amount of quality and quantity control is cement. C.P.W.D. has, therefore, prepared a detailed cement consumption statement for various items of work. Some of these constants are given below with some constants for bitumen. The list is only illustrative and not comprehensive. For detailed information all India Schedule of rates issued by C.P.W.D should invariably be referred to.

Table 88. Cement Consumption Statement

S. No.	*Item of work*	*Unit*	*Quantity of cement per unit quantity of work (Quintals)*
1.	Cement Mortar		
	1 : 1 (Cement Sand)	m^3	10.20
	1 : 2 (Cement Sand)	m^3	6.80
	1 : 3 (Cement Sand)	m^3	5.10
	1 : 4 (Cement Sand)	m^3	3.8
	1 : 5 (Cement Sand)	m^3	3.1
	1 : 6 (Cement Sand)	m^3	2.5
2.	Cement Concrete		
	1 : 1 : 2 (Cement: Sand : graded Sand)	m^2	6.10
	1 : 2 : 4 (Cement: Sand : graded Sand)	m^2	3.20
	1 : 3 : 6 (Cement: Sand : graded Sand)	m^2	2.20
	1 : 4 : 8 (Cement: Sand : graded Sand)	m^2	1.70
	1 : 5 : 10 (Cement: Sand : graded Sand)	m^2	1.30
	1 : 6 : 12 (Cement: Sand : graded Sand)	m^2	1.10
3.	D.P.C.		
	1 : 2 : 4 25 mm thick	m^3	0.08
	40 25 mm thick	m^3	0.13
	50 25 mm thick	m^2	0.16
4.	R.C.C. Work Cast in Situ	m^2	3.20
	R.C.C. Work Cast in Precast		
	1 : 2 : 4 beam, column	m^2	3.20
	1 : 2 : 4 beam with (1 : 3 cement: sand) rendering the card board 25 mm and 15 to 30 cm thick	m^2	6.28

(Contd.)

S. No.	*Item of work*	*Unit*	*Quantity of cement per unit quantity of work (Quintals)*
5.	Brick work	m^2	6.28
	1 : 3	"	1.12
	1 : 4	"	0.84
	1 : 5	"	0.68
	1 : 6	"	0.55
6.	R.R. Masonry		
	Cement mortar 1 : 6	m^2	0.75
	Cement mortar 1 : 1 : 8		
	(cement : lime putty : sand)	"	1.07
7.	Ashlar Masonry	m^2	
	1 : 6 with 1 : 2 (cement : sand dust pointing)	"	0.54
	13 : 3 m^2		1.07
8.	Brick Flooring		
	1 : 4 (Cement : Fine Sand) including cement slurry	m^2	0.185
	1 : 6 "	"	0.1285
9.	Cement Concrete Flooring		
	1 : 2 : 4 25 mm thick	"	0.1220
	40 " "	"	0.17
	50 " "	"	0.202
	75 " "	"	0.282
10.	Terrazo Flooring 40 mm thick marble chip flooring under layer of 100 mm thick (1 : 2 : 4) cement concrete laid on marble powder 3 : 1 (3 cement : 1 marble powder) by weight by proportion of 4 : 7 (4 cement marble powder mix : 7 marble chips) by volume including cement slurry etc. complete.	"	0.1695
11.	Tile Flooring		
	Precast terrazo tile 50 mm thick		
	Lime mortar 1 : 1 : 2 or 1 : 3	"	0.044
12.	Cement Plaster		
	12 mm 1 : 3	100 m^2	7.34
	12 mm 1 : 4	"	5.47
	12 mm 1 : 6	"	4.46
	10 mm 1 : 6	"	3.00
	15 mm 1 : 3	"	8.77
	" 1 : 4	"	6.54
	" 1 : 5	"	5.33
	" 1 : 6	"	4.30
	20 mm 1 : 3	"	11.40

Note. Cement consumption is independent of

(*i*) Whether fine/coarse sand is used

(*ii*) Whether 20 mm/40 mm nominal size aggregate is used

(*iii*) Whether stone/brick aggregate is used.

S. No.	Item of work	Unit	Quantity of cement per unit quantity of work (Quintals)
	" 1 : 4	"	8.50
	" 1 : 5	"	6.94
	" 1 : 6	"	5.60
13.	Pointing on brickwork		
	Weather Pointing 1 : 3	100 m^2	1.53
	Raised and Cast 1 : 3	"	2.35
	Flush or Ruled 1 : 1 : 3	"	1.23
	(cement : lime putty : sand)	"	
	Flush or Ruled 1 : 4	"	0.76
	" 1 : 6	"	0.50

Table 89. Bitumen Consumption Statement

S. No.	Description of work	Unit	Quantity of Bitumen in Quintals
1.	Painting one coat with Bitumen 5.90, 2.25 kg/m^2 with 1.65 m^3 of stone aggregate 12.5 mm per 100 m^2	sq m	0.0225
2.	Painting two coats. 2 kg/m^2 bitumen with 1.5 m^3 stone aggregate 12.5 mm size per 100 m^2 for first coat and 1 kg/m^2 with 9 m^3 of stone aggregate 10 mm size per 100 m^2.	"	0.03
3.	Painting one coat with bitumen emulsion (minimum 50% bitumen contents) of approved quality using 2.25 kg/m^2 of bitumen emulsion with 1.5 m^3 of stone aggregate 12.5 mm size per 100 m^2 of road surface.	m^2	0.0225
4.	Painting two coats with bitumen emulsion using 2 kg/m^2 of bitumen emulsion with 1.35 m^3 of stone aggregate 12.5 m on nominal size per 100 sq m for the first coat and 1 kg/m^3 of emulsion with 0.9 m^3 stone aggregate 10 mm nominal size per 100 sq m for the second coat.	m^3	0.03
5.	2 cm permix carpet surface with 2.5 m^3 of stone aggregate 10 mm nominal size per 100 m^3 of bitumen emulsion (Min 60% bitumen contents) of approved quality using 9 kg m^3 of aggregate including a lack coat of 1kg bitumen emulsion per m^3 of road surface.	m^2	0.033
6.	Seal coat with paving bitumen S-90 using 1.5 kg of bitumen per m^2 with 1.05 m^2 of stone aggregate 10 mm nominal size per 100 m^2 of road surface.	m^2	0.025
7.	Seal coat with bitumen emulsion (minimum 50% bitumen contents) of approved quality using 1.5 kg of bitumen per m^3 with 1.05 m^3 of stone aggregate 10 mm nominal size per 100 m^2.	m^2	0.025
8.	4 cm thick bitumen concrete surfacing using stone aggregate 3.8 m^3 (60% 20 mm nominal size and 40% 12.5 mm nominal size) per 100 m^2 and coarse sand at 1.9 m^3 per 100 sq m premixed with hot cut back bitumen of approved quantity at 56 kg per m^3 of stone aggregate and 28 kg per m^3 of sand over tack coat of 0.75 kg per m^3 including finishing complete.	m^2	0.581
9.	2.5 cm bitumastic sheet with hot cut back bitumen using stone aggregate (60% 12.5 mm nominal size and 40% 12 mm nominal size) at 1.65 m^3 per 100 sq m coarse sand at 1.65 m^3 per 100 sq m bitumen at 56 kg per cum of aggregate and 128 kg per m^3 of sand over a tack coat of 0.75 kg per sq m complete.	m^2	0.0379
10.	Painting two coats with paving bitumen using 2 kg per sq m with 1.5 m^3 stone aggregate 12.5 mm nominal size per 100 sq m of road surface for first coat and 1 kg of bitumen per 100 sq m for second coat complete.	m^2	0.03

Labour Output Constants

Labour output constants (Based on IS : 7272, part 1, 1974) and quantities of materials required for different items of works.

(A) Labour output constants—Analysis of rates is the basis for getting the work done and payment thereof. Although in the case of all the major works, contract is given on the basis of quoted rates (normally the lowest quoted rates) yet before inviting tenders considerable amount of field work has to be done.

The various stages involved are :

(*i*) Initiation of the proposal.

(*ii*) Acceptance in principle by the Competent Administrative Authority.

(*iii*) Preparation of the detailed estimate for Administrative Approval.

The estimate for obtaining Administrative Approval has to be as accurate as possible since the expenditure of the entire project is governed by this approval.

The rates on which the estimate is based should be as realistic as possible so that the tendered amount of the work falls with in its Administrative approval. For this purpose rates of different items are fixed as Standard Schedule of Rates based on the output constants, quantities of materials for different items of work, and the rates for labour and materials.

The output constants and the materials required for different items of work do not change from time to time though the rates of labour and materials go on changing with the change in the general price index.

Labour output constants and materials required for different items of work are given in this chapter while approximate current rates of material and labour for Delhi are dealt with in Chapter 16.

Tables given below give labour output constants.

Table 90. Labour Output Constants (Items of Work)

S. No.	*Description of work*	*Unit*	*Labour*	*Recommended constant (Days)*	*Remark*
1.	Excavation and Earthwork	cum	Mate	0.06	Extra
			Mazdoor	0.62	refilling
	(*a*) Excavation over areas upto				in layer
	1.5 m and removal.	cum	Mate	0.06	Mate 0.02
			Mazdoor	0.60	Mazdoor 0.25
	(*b*) Excavation in trenches.	cum	Mate	0.06	Bhisti 0.02
			Mazdoor	0.5	
2.	Concrete				
	(*a*) Hand mixed C.C.	cum	Mason	0.1	
			Mazdoor	2.13	
			Bhisti	0.7	
	(*b*) Hand mixed L.C.	cum	Mason	0.1	
			Mazdoor	2.65	
			Bhisti	0.8	
			Bullock with Driver	0.15	

S. No.	Description of work	Unit	Labour	Recommended constant (Days)	Remark
	(*c*) R.C.C. Work	cum	Mason	0.24	
			Mazdoor	0.25	
			Bhisti	0.90	
			Mixer operator	0.07	
			Mixer	0.07	
			Vibrator	0.07	
3.	Mortars				
	(*a*) Cement mortar any mix. By hand.	cum	Mazdoor	0.75	
			Bhisti	0.07	
	(*b*) Cement, lime, sand any mix.	cum	Mazdoor	1.33	
			Bhisti	0.1	
			Bullock with driver	0.33	
4.	Brick work (walls)				
	(*a*) Exceding one brick thick. Cement : Lime mortar	cum	Mason	0.94	Labour for mixing will be extra in all types of lime work
			Mazdoor	1.8	
			Bhisti	0.2	
	(*b*) One brick thick. Cement : Lime mortar	sq m	Mason	0.25	
			Mazdoor	0.4	
			Bhisti	0.1	
	(*c*) Half brick in 'Cement mortar'	sq m	Mason	0.12	
			Mazdoor	0.2	
			Bhisti	0.07	
	(*d*) Tile work in Superstructure in cement mortar	sq m	Mason	1.8	
			Mazdoor	1.8	
			Bhisti	0.2	
5.	Form work Fabrication and erection				
	(*a*) Columns and walls	cum	Carpenter	0.25	
			Mazdoor	0.20	
	(*b*) Suspended floors/roofs	sq m	Carpenter	0.23	
			Mazdoor	0.20	
	(*c*) Sides and soffits of beams	sq m	Carpenter	0.30	
6.	Reinforcement Bar reinforcement complete	Quintal	Bar bender	1.0	
			Mazdoor	1.0	
7.	Plastering and Pointing				
	(*a*) 15 mm thick cement plaster	Quintal	Mason	0.08	
			Mazdoor	0.1	
			Bhisti	0.1	
	(*b*) Struck pointing to brickwork cement mortar	Quintal	Mason	0.08	
			Mazdoor	0.1	
			Bhisti	0.1	

(*Contd.*)

S. No.	Description of work	Unit	Labour	Recommended constant (Days)	Remark
8.	Paving and floor finish				
	(*a*) 40 mm thick floor finish, P.C.C.	Quintal	Mason	0.08	Labour for mixing concrete will be each for (*a*) and (*b*)
			Mazdoor	0.12	
			Bhisti	0.1	
	(*b*) 40 mm thick terrazo flooring				
	(*i*) Laying	Quintal	Mason	0.22	
			Mazdoor	0.22	
			Bhisti	0.01	
	(*ii*) Cutting, grinding and polishing	Quintal	Mazdoor	0.5	
			Machine	0.4	
9.	Damp proof course				
	(*a*) 40 mm thick P.C.C.	sq m	Mason	0.1	
			Mazdoor	0.1	
			Bhisti	0.01	
	(*b*) 20 mm thick P.C.C.	sq m	Mason	0.1	
			Mazdoor	0.1	
			Bhisti	0.01	
10.	Joinery				
	(*a*) Door and window chaukhats	cum	Carpenter	20.0	
			Mazdoor	2.0	
	(*b*) 40 mm thick door or window shutters	sq m	Carpenter	0.9	
			Mazdoor	0.1	
	(*c*) Fixing ready made shutters	sq m	Carpenter	0.25	
			Mazdoor	0.25	
11.	Glazing Fixing glass panes on steel or wood	sq m	Glazier	0.2	
			Mazdoor	0.01	
12.	Painting and Polishing	sq m	Painter	0.35	
13.	White washing and colour washing				
	(*a*) Three coats on new surface	sq m	Washer	0.02	
			Mazdoor	0.01	
	(*b*) Two coats colour washing over one under coat white wash on new work	sq m	Washer	0.03	
			Mazdoor	0.01	
	(*c*) White wash one coat on old or new work.	sq m	Washer	0.02	
	(*d*) Distempering with dry distemper 3 coats on new surface including a priming coat.	sq m	Painter	0.08	
			Mazdoor	0.04	
14.	Terraced roofing				
	(*a*) 10 cm thick mud phuska including one layer of tile and gobar leeping	sq m	Mason	0.13	
			Mazdoor	0.36	
			Bhisti	0.11	
	(*b*) 10 cm thick lime concrete terracing	sq m	Mason	0.1	
			Mazdoor	0.37	
			Bhisti	0.15	

Table 91. Labour Output Constants (Quantity of Work per day)

S. No.	*Description of item*	*Quantity of Work per day*	*Remarks*
1.	**Mason**		
	(*i*) Lime concrete	10 cum	20 to 30
	(*ii*) Cement concrete 1 : 5 : 10	10 cum	sq m
	(*iii*) c.c. in R.C.C. 1 : 2 : 4	3 cum	
	(*iv*) Brick work in foundations	2 cum	
	(*v*) Brick work in superstructure	1.5 cum	
	(*vi*) Brick work in arches	1 cum	
	(*vii*) Half brick work in partitions	8 sq m	
	(*viii*) Tile work in superstructure	0.5 cum	
	(*ix*) 40 mm thick D.P.C.	10 sq m	
	(*x*) Stone work ashlar type	0.25 cum	
	(*xi*) Stone work random rubble	1.0 cum	
	(*xii*) Marble work	0.05 cum	
	(*xiii*) Brick flooring	15 sq m	
	(*xiv*) P.C.C. flooring	8 to 10 sq m	
	(*xv*) Terrazo flooring	4 to 5 sq m	
	(*xvi*) Marble flooring	1 to 2 sq m	
	(*xvii*) Stone flooring	4 to 5 sq m	
	(*xviii*) Mud phuska	8 sq m	
	(*xix*) Lime concrete terracing	10 sq m	
	(*xx*) 15 mm thick plaster	10 sq m	
	(*xxi*) Pointing	10 sq m	
	(*xxii*) Punning	20 sq m	
	(*xxiii*) R. B. Work	4 to 5 sq m	
	(*xxiv*) Tile roofing	5 sq m	
	(*xxv*) Three coats white or colour washing on new surface	50 sq m	
	(*xxvi*) Two coats white washing on new surface	100 sq m	
2.	**Carpenter**		
	(*i*) Timbering in trenches open type	300 to 400 sq m	
	(*ii*) Centering and shuttering	4 to 8 sq m	
	(*iii*) Door and window chaukhat	0.05 cum	
	(*iv*) Door and window shutter	1 sq m	
	(*v*) Jafri work	1 sq m	
	(*vi*) Pelmets	5 sq m	
	(*vii*) Jali work	5 sq m	
	(*viii*) Wooden floors	0.5 sq m	
	(*ix*) A.C. sheet roof	8 sq m	
	(*x*) Ceiling work	2 sq m	
	(*xi*) Fixing shutters	4 sq m	
	(*xii*) Fixing glass panes	5 sq m	
	(*xiii*) Wooden marking	2 to 4 sq m	

(*Contd.*)

S. No.	Description of Item	Quantity of Work per day	Remarks
3.	**Painter**		
	(*i*) Distempering on now surface	20 sq m	
	(*ii*) Wood preservative on new wood work	50 sq m	
	(*iii*) Painting wood work with priming coat	20 sq m	
	(*iv*) Painting new wood work with two coats along with priming coat	10 sq m	
	(*v*) Painting old wood work with one coat	30 sq m	
	(*vi*) Varnishing new wood work complete	20 sq m	
	(*vii*) Polishing new wood work complete	5 sq m	
	(*viii*) Applying one coat of bitumen on D.P.C.	50 sq m	
4.	**Blacksmith**		
	(*i*) M.S. Bars, bending, binding and placing in position	100 kg.	
	(*ii*) Structural steel work	200 kg.	
5.	**Mazdoor**		
	(*i*) Earthwork in trenches	2 to 3 cum	
	(*ii*) Earthwork in filling	5 to 10 cum	
	(*iii*) Concrete work in foundations	0.4 cum	
	(*iv*) Concrete work in R.C.C.	0.3 cum	
	(*v*) Mixing cement mortar	3 cum	
	(*vi*) Delivering bricks	4000 No.	
	(*vii*) Breaking brick ballast 25 mm size	0.8 cum	
	(*viii*) Breaking stone ballast 40 mm size	0.5 cum	
	(*ix*) Excavation in rock	1 cum	
	(*x*) Delivering mortar	5 cum	

3. Quantities of materials required for different items of work.

Table 92. Lime Mortar (Unit 1 cum)

S. No.	Description	Lime putty cum	Sand cum	Surkhi cum	Ash cum	Remarks
1.	Lime putty 1 : 1 (Lime putty : sand)	0.7 (46 kg)	0.7	—	—	(*a*) For cu. m of mortar ; 1.42 cum of dry material is required.
2.	Lime mortar 1 : 1 : 1 (Lime putty : Surkhi : sand)	0.473 (284 kg)	0.473	0.473	—	(*b*) 1 cum lime patty is equal to 600 kg of unbalanced lime.
3.	Lime mortar 1 : 1 : 1 (Lime putty : ash : sand)	0.473 (284 kg)	0.473	—	0.473	(*c*) Material is calculated according to proportion

Table 93. Cement Mortar (Unit 1 cum)

S. No.	*Description*	*Cement (cum)*	*Sand (cum)*	*Remarks*
1.	Cement mortar 1 : 1 (Cement : Sand)	0.71 (21.3 bags)	0.71	(*a*) For 1 cum of mortar 1 : 1, 1 : 2, 1 : 3 : 1.42 cum of dry mortar is required.
2.	Cement mortar 1 : 2 (Cement : sand)	0.473 (14.2 bags)	0.946	(*b*) For 1 cum of mortar of 1 : 4, 1 : 5, 1 : 6, 1.3 cum of dry material is required.
3.	Cement mortar 1 : 3 (Cement : Sand)	0.355 (10.6 bags)	1.065	(*c*) 1 cum cement is equally 300 bags (1430 kg).
4.	Cement mortar 1 : 4 (Cement : Sand)	0.26 (7.8 bags)	1.04	(*d*) Material is calculated according to proportion.
5.	Cement mortar 1 : 5 (Cement : Sand)	0.217 (6.5 bags)	1.08	
6.	Cement mortar 1 : 6 (Cement : Sand)	0.176 (5.0 bags)	1.124	

Table 94. Cement Lime Mortar (unit 1 cum)

S. No.	*Description*	*Cement cum*	*Lime putty (cum)*	*Sand (cum)*	*Remarks*
1.	Cement lime mortar 1 : 1 : 6 (cement : lime putty : sand)	0.177 (5.3 bags)	0.177 (106 kg)	1.06	1. For 1 cum mortar 1.42 cum of dry material is required.
2.	Cement lime mortar 1 : 1 : 7 (cement : lime putty : sand)	0.158 (4.7 bags)	0.158 (95 kg)	1.10	2. Material is calculated according to proportion
3.	Cement lime mortar 1 : 1 : 8 (cement : lime putty : sand)	0.142	0.142	1.13	

Note. 1. For 1 cum of mud mortar, 1–10 cum of dry mud is required.

2. For blasting 10 cum of hard rock 6.42 kg of powder and 7 No. of fuses are required. (7 No. of holes are drilled).

3. Wooden materials are used 16 times in trenches for timbering.

Table 95. Lime Concrete (Unit 1 cum)

S. No.	*Description*	*Lime putty*	*Sand cum*	*Coarse Agg. cum*	*Ash or surkhi cum*	*Remarks*
1.	Lime concrete 1 : 6 (Lime putty : sand)	0.142 (85 kg)	0.426	1.00	—	40% lime mortar is used 1 cum of coarse of aggregate is used.
2.	Lime concrete 1 : 1 : 1 (lime : ash : sand)	0.19	1.00	0.19		

Table 96. Cement Concrete (Unit 1 cum)

S. No.	Description	Cement cum	Sand cum	Coarse Aggregate cum	Remarks
1.	Cement concrete 1 : 2 : 4 (cement : sand : coarse aggregate)	0.22 (6.6 bags)	0.44	0.88	For 1 cum of finished concrete 1.54 cum of dry material is required.
2.	Cement concrete 1 : 3 : 6	0.154 (4.6 bags)	0.462	0.924	
3.	Cement concrete 1 : 4 : 8	0.118 (3.5 bags)	0.472	0.944	
4.	Cement concrete 1 : 5 : 10	0.096 (2.8 bags)	0.48	0.96	
5.	Cement concrete 1 : 6 : 12	0.08 (2.4 bags)	0.48	0.96	

Note. 1. Timber will become unserviceable after being used 16 times in centre and shuttering for R.C.C. work.

2. D.P.C. 40 mm thick, with cement concrete 1 : 2 : 4 mix, 100 sq m, 24.32 bags of cement are required.

3. R.C.C. work 1 : 1½ : 3 mix, for cum of concrete 3 bags of cement are required.

4. R.C.C work 1 : 1 : 2 mix, for one cum of concrete 12.8 bags of cement are required.

5. For cement slurry on R.C.C. slab, 3.75 kg. per sq m of cement is required.

6. Rendering smooth the tops of suspended floors with cement mortar 1 : 2 mix, including floating coat of neat cement, 8 bags of cement are required for 100 sq m of surface area.

Table 97. Brick Work (Unit 1 cum)

S. No.	Description	Brick (No.)	Cement (bags)	Sand (cum)	Remarks
1.	Brick work 1 : 3 mortar (cement : sand)	500	2.60	0.25	By volume 25% of cement mortar is used.
2.	Brick work 1 : 4 mix	500	1.95	0.25	By volume 30% cement mortar is used.
3.	Brick work 1 : 5	500	1.60	0.25	
4.	Brick work 1 : 6	500	1.30	0.25	
5.	Half brick masonry 1 : 3 (unit sq m)	55	2.60	0.025	By volume 45% of cement mortar is used.
6.	Brick tile masonry 1 : 6	950	1.60	0.32	
7.	R.B. work in roofs 1 : 2 mix	420	6.40	0.43	

Note. 1. Honeycomb brickwork in cement mortar 1 : 4 : 11 bags of cement are required for 100 sq m.

2. Joining old brickwork with new brickwork, in cement mortar 1 : 3, 4 bags of cement are required for 100 sq m.

3. Tile brickwork 5 cm thick in cement mortar 1 : 3, 7 bags are required for 100 sq m.

Table 98. Stone Work (Unit 1 cum)

S. No.	Description	Stone (cum)	Cement bags	Sand cum	Remarks
1.	R.R. masonry in cement mortar 1 : 6 (cement : sand)	1.0	0.86	0.37	
2.	C.R. masonry in cement mortar 1 : 6	1.6	1.6	0.32	
3.	Stone work in plain ashlar 1 : 6 (cement : sand)	1.3	1.00	0.20	
4.	Stone work for wall lining etc. (Veneer work) 60 mm thick in cement mortar (unit sq m)	1 sq m	0.20	0.02	

Note. 1. Marble work in steps, in cement mortar 1 : 4, 1.5 bags of cement are required for 1 sq m.

2. Marble work for wall lining, 4 cm thick, in cement mortar 1 : 3, 20.5 bags of cement are required for 100 sq m.

3. Fixing 4 cm thick jali, in cement mortar 1 : 2, 7 bags of cement are required for 100 sq m.

4. 50 × 50 × 50 mm wood plugs, fixing in cement mortar 1 : 3, 0.02 bag of cement are required for 100 No.

5. Fixing 20 × 6 mm, mild steel 15 cm long clamps, for securing chick tops 1 bag of cement is required for 100 No.

Table 99. Flooring (Unit 1 sq m)

S. No.	*Description*	*Brick No.*	*Cement bags*	*Sand cum*	*Coarse Agg. 20 mm (cum)*	*Marble chips*	*Remarks*
1.	Brick flooring in cement mortar 1 : 6	50	0.15	0.03	—	—	—
2.	40 mm thick concrete flooring 1 : 2 : 4, finished with floating coat of neat cement	—	0.30	0.018	0.35	—	—
3.	40 mm thick marble chips flooring, under layer 30 mm cement concrete 1 : 2 : 4 and top layer 9 mm thick marble chips mortar	—	0.30	0.014	0.028	14 kg	Marble powder 2 kg.

Note. 1. 20 mm cement plaster skirting upto 30 cm height with cement mortar 1 : 3, finished with a floating cost of neat cement, 23 bags of cement are required for 100 sq. m.

2. Marble chips skirting upto 30 cm height, top layer 6 mm thick marble chips, 29 bags of cement are required for 100 sq m.

3. Marble stone slab flooring, 25 mm thick, over 20 mm thick base of cement mortar 1 : 4, 27 bags of cement are required for 100 sq. m.

4. Kota stone slab flooring, 25 mm thick, 30 bags of cement are required for 100 sq. m laid over 20 mm base of cement mortar 1 : 4.

5. 40 mm sand stone flooring, over 20 mm thick base of cement mortar 1 : 5, 15 bags of cement are required for 100 sq m.

6. Floating coat of cement, 202 kg. of cement is required for 1 sq m.

Table 100. Finishing (Unit 100 sq m)

S. No.	*Description*	*Cement bags*	*Sand cum*	*Remarks*
1.	6 mm thick cement plaster 1 : 3	7.40	0.74	0.70 cum of mortar
2.	12 mm thick cement plaster 1 : 6	7.20	1.44	1.44 cum of mortar
3.	20 mm thick cement plaster 1 : 6	11.20	2.24	2.22 cum of mortar
4.	Neat cement punning	4.40	—	
5.	Brick pointing on stone work with cement mortar 1 : 3	3.00	0.30	0.30 cum of mortar
6.	Flush pointing on brickwork with cement mortar 1 : 6	1.00	0.20	0.20 cum of mortar
7.	18 mm plaster with terrazo finish under layer 12 mm cement plaster 1 : 3 and top layer 6 mm marble chips mortar	23.30	1.47	2.16 cum of mortar

Table 101. Miscellaneous Building Work

S. No.	*Description of Item*	*Unit*	*Cement bags*	*Remarks*
1.	Repair to plaster with cement mortar 1 : 4	100 sq m	14.00	
2.	Fixing door chaukhats with openings	Each	0.24	
3.	Mud phuska of terracing	100 sq m	11.40	
4.	Fixing M.S., Fan clamps	Each	0.03	
5.	Rough cast or pebble dash plaster	100 sq m	19.20	
6.	Plinth protection	100 sq m	17.20	
7.	Laying kerb stone 30 × 20 cm	100 m	3.00	
8.	Fixing R.C.C. posts in concrete	100 Nos.	180.00	
9.	Fixing road Signs	Each	1.0	
10.	Cement concrete 1 : 2 : 4 in pavements	cum	6.60	
11.	Fixing Indian pattern W.C. complete	Each	0.1	
12.	Fixing flat back or wall corner type urinal	Each	0.10	
13.	Floating S.W. pipe 100 mm dia.	100 m	0.05	
14.	Laying cement concrete 1 : 5 : 10 round S.W. pipe including bed concrete for 100 dia.	Each	4.30	
15.	Constructing brick masonry manhole 90 × 80 × 60 cm	Each	0.50	
16.	Constructing circular manhole 1.4 m internal diameter, 2.45 m deep	Each	4.40	
17.	Constructing brick masonry open surface drain 10 cm 20 cm deep	100 m	3.45	

Table 102. Finish Work (White Washing Distempering and Painting etc.)

S. No.	*Description of item*	*Material*	*Units*	*Quantity*	*Remarks*
1.	White washing on new work (3 coats)	Lime	sq m	3 kg	
2.	White washing on old work (2 coats)	Lime	sq m	2 kg	
3.	White washing on old work (1 coat)	Lime	sq m	1 kg	
4.	Distemper on new work	1. Whiting	1 sq m	0.1 kg	
		2. Distemper	1 sq m	0.15 kg	
5.	Distemper on old work	Distemper	1 sq m	0.1 kg	
6.	Cement paint on new work (3 coats)	Cement paint	1 sq m	0.2 kg	
7.	Cement paint on old work	Cement paint	1 sq m	0.2 kg	
8.	Painting with oil type preservative on new work	Oil preservative	sq m	0.1 litre	
9.	Painting with oil type preservative on old work	Oil preservative	sq m	0.08 litre	
10.	Priming coat on wood work	Ready mixed	sq m	0.08 litre	
11.	Priming coat on steel	Ready mixed primer	sq m	0.08 litre	
12.	Priming coat, plastered surface	Ready mixed primer	sq m	0.10 litre	
13.	Painting on new wood work (2 coats)	Ready mixed primer	sq m	1.12 litre	
14.	Painting on old work	Ready mixed primer	sq m	0.06 litre	
15.	Varnishing on old work	Copal varnish	sq m.	0.08 litre	
16.	Varnishing on new wood work (2 coats)	1. Flatting varnish	sq m	0.08 litre	
		2. Copal varnish	sq m	0.08 litre	
17.	Polishing with wax polish on new work	wax polish	sq m	0.05 kg	

S. No.	Description of item	Material	Units	Quantity	Remarks
18.	Polishing with wax polish on old work	Wax polish	sq m	0.02 kg	
19.	French spirit polishing on new work	1. Spirit	sq m	0.15 litre	
		2. Shellac	sq m	0.2 litre	
20.	French spirit polishing on old work	1. spirit	sq m.	0.08 litre	
		2. shellac	sq m	0.01 litre	
21.	Painting G.I. sheets on new work	Ready mixed paint	sq m	0.08 litre	
22.	Painting G.I. sheets on old work	Ready mixed paint	sq m	0.04 litre	

Plain and Reinforced Concrete

Table 103. Grades of Concrete (IS : 456—2000)

Grade Designation	*28 day Compression strength N/mm^2*
M10	10
M15	15
M20	20
M25	25
M30	30
M35	35
M40	40
M45	45
M50	50
M55	55
M60	60
M65	65
M70	70
M75	75
M80	80

Table 104. Properties of Nominal Mix Concrete

Grade of concrete	*Total quantity of dry aggregate per 50 kg of cement (Max) kg*	*Proportion of face aggregate to coarse aggregate (By Mass)*	*Quantity of water per 50 kg of cement (Max)*
M5	800	generally 1 : 2 but subject to an upper limit of 1 : 1½ and lower limit of 1 : 2½	60
M7.5	625		45
M10	480		34
M15	350		32
M20	250		30

Table 105. Permissible Stresses in Concrete (All Values in N/mm²)

Grade of concrete	*Permissible stresses in compression*		*Permissible stress in Bond*
	Bending σ_{cbc}	*Direct* σ_{cc}	C_{pd}
M10	3.0	2.5	—
M15	5.0	4.0	0.6
M20	7.0	5.0	0.8
M25	8.5	6.0	0.9
M30	10.0	8.0	1.0
M35	11.5	9.0	1.1
M40	13.0	10.0	1.2
M45	14.5	11.0	1.3
M50	16.0	12.0	1.4

Table 106. Permissible Shear in Concrete

	Permissible shear stress in concrete τ_c N/mm^2, *grade of concrete*					
$100A_s/bd$	*M15*	*M20*	*M25*	*M30*	*M35*	*M40*
0.25	0.22	0.22	0.23	0.23	0.23	0.23
0.50	0.29	0.30	0.31	0.31	0.31	0.32
0.75	0.34	0.35	0.36	0.37	0.37	0.38
1.0	0.37	0.39	0.40	0.41	0.42	0.42
1.25	0.40	0.42	0.44	0.45	0.45	0.46
1.50	0.42	0.45	0.46	0.48	0.49	0.49
1.75	0.44	0.47	0.49	0.50	0.52	0.52
2.0	0.44	0.49	0.51	0.53	0.54	0.55
2.25	0.44	0.51	0.53	0.55	0.56	0.57
2.5	0.44	0.51	0.55	0.57	0.58	0.60
2.75	0.44	0.51	0.56	0.58	0.60	0.62
3.00 and above	0.44	0.51	0.57	0.60	0.62	0.63

Bending Coefficients for Slabs (See Table 107)

B.M. coefficients for slabs spanning in two directions at right angles, simply supported on four sides.

The maximum moments per unit width are given by the equation

$$M_x = \alpha_x w l_x^2 \text{ and } M_y = \alpha_y w l_x^2$$

Table 107

l_y/l_x	1.0	1.1	1.2	1.3	1.4	1.5	1.75	2.0	2.5	3.0
α_x	0.062	0.074	0.084	0.093	0.099	0.104	0.113	0.118	0.122	0.124
α_y	0.062	0.061	0.059	0.055	0.051	0.046	0.037	0.029	0.020	0.014

Table 108. Effective Length of Compression Member

Degrees of restraint	*Symbol*	*Theoretical value of effective length*	*Recommended value of effective length*
Held in position and restrained against rotation	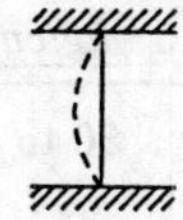	0.5 *l*	0.65 *l*
Held in position at both end, restrained against rotation at one end		0.7 *l*	0.8 *l*
Held in position at both ends but not restrained against rotation	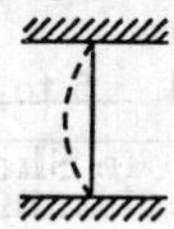	1.0 *l*	1.0 *l*
Effectively held in position against rotation at one end, at the other end restrained against rotation but not held in position	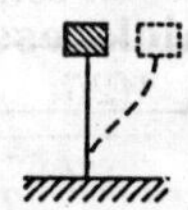	1.0 *l*	1.2 *l*
Held in position and restrained against rotation at one end, at the other and partially restrained against rotation	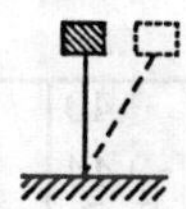	—	1.5 *l*
Held in position at one end but not restrained against rotation and not held in position at other end	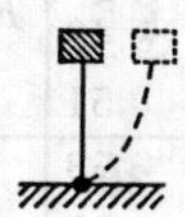	2.00 *l*	2.00 *l*
Held in position and restrained against rotation at one end but not held in position against the other end		2.00 *l*	2.00 *l*

Table 109. Mix Proportions for Lime Mortar

S. No.	*Description of mortar*	*Lime*	*Maximum part by volume*				*Compressive strength of mortar at 28 days kg cm²*	*Hardening time after completion of the work in days*
			Conc.	*Lime pozzolana*	*Poz-zolana*	*Sand*		
1.	Lime cement	1C	1	—	—	6	30 to 50	14
2.	Lime cement	2B	1	—	—	9	20 to 30	14
3.	Lime pozzolana mixture	—		1		1.5	30 to 50	14
4.	Lime cement	3B or 3C	1	—	—	12	7 to 15	14
5.	Hydraulic lime	1A	—	—	—	2	—	14
6.	Lime pozzolana	IC	—	—	1	2	7 to 15	14
7.	Lime	1B	—	—	—	3	5 to 7	28

Table 110. Basic Compressive Strength of Masonry Mortar

S. No.	*Description of mortar*	*Parts by volume*	*Compressive strength of mortor at 28 day kg/cm²*	*Hardening time after completion of the work in days*	*Basic stress a kg/cm²*
1.	Cement : Sand	1 : 6	30 to 50	14	3 to 4.1
2.	Cement : Lime : Sand	1 : 3 : 12	7 to 15	14	0.5 to 1
3.	Cement : Lime : Sand	1 : 2 : 9	20 to 30	14	2 to 4
4.	Hydraulic Lime : Sand	1 : 2	—	—	—
5.	Lime Pozzolana : Sand	1 : 2	7 to 15	14	0.5 to 1.0
6.	Lime : Sand	1 : 3	5 to 7	28	0.4 to 0.5

Note. The table is valid and slenderness ratio of 6 and loading with zero eccentricity.

Table 111. Maximum Thickness of External Walls

Storey above ground	*Height of wall above ground (metres)*		*Length of wall (metres)*	*Thickness of wall in cm*							
	Not exceeding	*Exceeding*		*Basement Floor*	*Ground Floor*	*1st Floor*	*2nd Floor*	*3rd Floor*	*4th Floor*	*5th Floor*	*6th Floor*
1	3.5	5.0	any	40	30	—	—	—	—	—	—
1	5.0	6.5	any	50	40	—					
2	—	6.5	under 10	30	20	20					
2	6.5	9.5	under 10	40	30	30	—	—	—	—	—
2	6.5	9.5	over 10	50	40	30	—	—	—	—	—
3	10	1.35	under 10	50	40	30	30	—	—	—	—
8	10	1.35	over 10	60	50	40	30	20	—	—	—
4	13.5	18	under 10	60	50	40	30	30	—	—	—
4	13.5	18	over 10	70	60	50	40	30	—	—	—
6	20	27.5	under 10	80	70	60	50	40	40	30	—
6	20	27.5	over 0	90	80	70	60	50	40	30	—
7	23.5	32.0	under 10	90	80	70	60	50	40	40	30
7	23.5	32.0	over 10	100	90	80	70	60	50	40	30

Table 112. Mortar for Different Plasters

Situation	Mix proportion				Class of lime used	Thickness in mm	Remarks
	Cement	*Lime*	*Surkhi or pozzolana*	*Sand*			
A. Single coat plaster							Type C
							Fat Lime
1. External plaster							
(*a*) Below DPC	1	1	0	6	B or C	10 to 15	Type A and
(*b*) Above DPC	1	2	0	9			Type B
	0	1	0	3			Hydrated
	0	1	1	1–2	B or C		Lime
	1	0	0	2—3			
	1	0	1	1—2			
2. Internal plaster	1	2	0	9	B or C	10 to 15	
Also is low or medium	1	3	0	12			
cost houses and	0	1	0	2–3	A	10 to 15	
buildings	0	1	1	1—2			
	1	0	0	2—3	B or C	10 to 15	
	1	0	1	1—2			
B. Two coat plaster	Baking	coat					
3. External plaster	1	1	0	6	B or C	15	
	1	0	0	3			
	Finishing	coat					
	1	1	0	6	B or C	3 to 15	
	1	2	0	9			
4. Internal plaster of	Backing	coat					
superior finish	1	1	0	6	B or C	15	
	1	0	0	3			
	Finishing	coat					
	1	1	0	6	B or C	3 to 10	
C. Three coat plaster	Rendering or building course as in (4) above						
5. Internal plaster required even and smooth surface	Finishing coat, Fat lime and ground sand or marble dust in equal proportion				C	Less than 3 mm	

Guidelines for Building Drawing

The purpose of a building drawing is to give adequate information to the site engineer and his field staff so that the layout of the structure at site and construction of the various components in respect of their respecting locations and sizes may be facilitated without reference to the planned design details. This information is given with the help of the following drawings :

(*i*) Plan (*ii*) Elevation and

(*iii*) Sections along the required plane or planes.

(*i*) **Plan.** Plan or the top view is obtained by imagining that the structure is cut by a horizontal plane at the sill of the window and upper portion is removed. The projection of the remaining portion on the horizontal portion below the building gives the plan the top view. The invisible portion between the plane at which the horizontal section is taken and the foundation below ground level is indicated by dotted lines.

(*ii*) **Elevation.** Elevation may be front or side or both depending upon the requirements. Whatever portion of the building is visible above the ground is projected on a vertical plane behind the structure as first angle projection. Hidden parts are shown by dotted lines.

(*iii*) **Section.** Such details of the structure as are not available from the top view or front/side views are obtained by means of section. The direction along which the section is cut and details given are indicated by means of arrow. If the details of the top view are required, the section is cut along the elevation, the portion opposite the arrow is imagined to be removed and remaining portion of the structure is projected on the horizontal plane. Similarly if the details of front view or side view are required, the section is cut on the plan (top view), the portion opposite the arrow is imagined to be removed and the remaining portion of the structure is projected on the concerned vertical plane.

Normally top view, front view and sectional views are required to provide complete construction details to the site engineer.

Conventional Signs for Different Constructional Details in a Building

Standard signs normally adopted in building drawings for showing various constructional details are given in Fig. 1. These are in addition to the normal conventional signs adopted by the Survey of India for depicting various features and normally used for survey drawings only.

Conventional signs for constructional details in a building drawing.

S. No.	*Description of item*	*Symbol*
1.	Ground level	
2.	Sand filling	
3.	Ramned KHOA	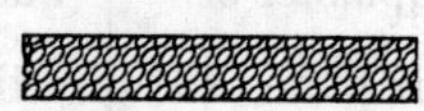
4.	Lime terrace	
5.	Plain cement concrete P.C.C	
6.	Reinforce cement concrete R.C.C	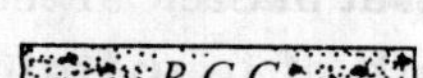
7.	Brick work	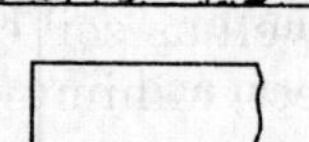
8.	Plaster	
9.	Floor finish	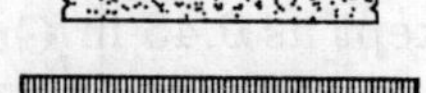
10.	Timber	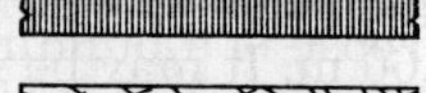
11.	Glass	
12.	Water level	

Fig. 1

Guidelines for Planning a House

Standard by-laws are available for planning of a house with respect to permissible area of the plot that can be covered. The local corporation, municipalities and city boards present their own by-laws which have to be satisfied before any building plan may be sanctioned. However the general features given below take care of all such by-laws.

1. **Maximum Covered Area.** Table 113 gives permissible covered area for various plots.

Table 113. Permissible Covered Area

S. No.	*Classification of plot*	*Area of plot m^2*	*Covered area permissible % of area of plot*
1.	Type A	> 1000	33
2.	" B	501—1000	40
3.	" C	201—500	50
4.	" D	< 200	60

Some local bodies in towns allow coverage of upto 66% of plot area.

2. **Minimum set back.** Table 114 gives minimum set back.

Table 114. Minimum Set back.

Front M	*Sides M*	*Back M*
0.3	1.5	4.5

Some local bodies prescribe more frontage.

3. **Components of a residential building.** A residential house has normally the following components :

(*i*) Drawing room (*ii*) Bed room (*iii*) Guest room
(*iv*) Dining room (*v*) Kitchen (*vi*) Store
(*vii*) Bath (*viii*) Water closet (*ix*) Front and rear verandah
(*x*) Stair case of the building if double storeyed.

Note. In modern practice dining and drawing rooms are combined. They are separated by sliding curtain. Residential buildings for academicians and those of legal profession should have a separate study room say (3.60 m × 4.2 m).

4. **Carpet area.** Carpet area varies from 50 to 65% of the plinth area.

5. **Depth of foundations.** Depth of foundation depends on the loading, and type of foundation as well as soil characteristics. However in order that the foundation is free from weathering effect, minimum depth of foundation should be 1 metre.

6. **Plinth level.** The height of plinth depends upon the nature of the adjoining ground especially with respect to drainage and flood level. This height varies from 0.30 m-0.60 m usually it is kept as 0.45 m.

7. **Height of ceiling.** For main rooms of the building the height should be between 3.30 m and 3.60 m. It may be reduced to 3.00 m for bath and W.C.

8. **Wall thickness.** For single storey house, thickness of brick walls should be one brick (20 cm) and for double storey house one and a half brick (30 cm).

9. **Double storeyed building.** The total floor area provided by a double storeyed building costs between 80 and 85 per cent of the cost of equivalent floor area provided by a single

storeyed house. It is therefore economical to have two or three storeyed houses. In view of the fact that available land for house construction is limited, the only way to meet ever increasing demand of housing is to resort to multistoreyed buildings.

10. **Geometry of the house.** As a rule it is more economical to have a square plan than an oblong one. The area occupied by the walls of an along house may be 25% larger than the corresponding area occupied by a square building. The house built on square plan keeps the house comparatively cooler in summer and warmer in winter. The square house is more cosy and comfortable.

11. **Orientation of the building.** In a modern housing complex in the urban areas, the architect or the engineer has very little flexibility to decide the orientation of the building. When the area is developed for housing, the roads, sewers, water supply main lines and electric lines are already laid. The frontage of the house has to fit in with the front road and except to locate the building such that the by-laws regarding the covered area and the setbacks from front, back and sides, there is no 'flexibility available, for the orientation of the building. However, where certain flexibility is available, such as in locating a farm house or an isolated building, the following points may be kept in view.

(*i*) The orientation of the building should be such that maximum benefit is obtained from sun and air.

(*ii*) As far as possible the house should face south, in the northern hemisphere so that low altitude sun is available during winter.

(*iii*) In places subjected to westerly winds the building should face east to get protection from westerly winds. Otherwise as a rule the house should face the direction in which wind blows for most of the time during the year.

12. **Ventilation of the building.** The purpose of ventilation is to permit fresh air to come inside the rooms and to remove stagnant air, smoke and odour.

For effective ventilation the total area of doors and windows, should be 25 per cent of the total floor area, 12½ % may be provided for windows. In addition to this ventilators should have 4% of the floor area.

Generally ventilators are placed 15 to 30 cm below the ceiling.

Chimney or smoke outlet is provided in kitchen for escape of smoke. The modern house, however, caters for space for gas cylinder, and the question of smoke outlet does not arise.

13. **Rooms, location and common size.** The common size and desirable location of various components of a residential building are given in Table 115.

Table 115. Common Sizes and Location of Various Components of a Residential Building

S. No.	*Particulars of the building component*	*Common size*	*Location and other characteristics*
1.	Living room or drawing room	4.20 m × 4.80 m to 5.4 m to 7.2 m	This is the most important part of the building complex. It is used as sitting place for family members and for visitors. It should be directly approachable from the front verandah and connected to the dining room when it is separately located. It should be well lighted and ventilated.
2.	Dining room	3.6 m × 4.2 m to 4.2 m × 4.8 m	It should be connected to the drawing room as well as the kitchen. Modern houses have combined drawing and dining rooms, separated by sliding curtain.

S. No.	Particulars of the building component	Common size	Location and other characteristics
3.	Bed room	3.0 m × 3.6 m to 4.2 m × 4.8 m	The location should provide privacy and proper ventilation. At least one wall should be exposed to the atmosphere for proper lighting and ventilation.
4.	Office room/study room/guest room	3.0 m × 3.6 m	Should be at one end of the front varandah disconnected from other rooms. Some times it serves as guest room. However, where it is to be used as a guest room, it should have an attached bath and W.C.
5.	Store room	2.5 m × 2.5 m to 3.0 m × 3.0 m	It should be adjacent to the kitchen with a number of built in rakes and shelves.
6.	Pantry	2.5 m × 3.0 m	It is used for keeping cooked food. For ordinary family, the built in cup boards and shelves serves the purpose of pantry as well.
7.	Bath and W.C.	1.8 m × 1.8 m to 1.8 m × 2.5 m 1.2 m × 1.8 m 1.2 m × 1.2 m	For combined bath and W.C. For separate bath For separate W.C. In modern houses W.C. and bath are in the same room attached to each bed room. Separate bath and W.C. have the advantage that both of them can be used at the same time.
8.	Kitchen	2.5 m × 3.9 m to 3.0 m × 3.0 m	It should be located in the rear of the building and connected to pantry, and dinning room. It should have one approach from the rear verandah or from outside. It should be properly ventilated. It should be fitted with sink for washing utensils and rack for plates.

Fabrication, Erection and Detailing of Steel Structure

Introduction. Users of structural steel base their design, fabrication, and erection on various hand books which are based on the existing standards for hot rolled steel sections.

IS : 800—1962 lays down code of practice for use of structural steel in general building construction. The code is divided into the following seven sections :

1. General.
2. Loads.
3. Permissible stresses.
4. Design.
5. Fabrication.
6. Erection.
7. Steel work tenders and contracts.

The ISI has also brought out Hand Book for structural engineer. The matter contained in this book from the point of view of maximum convenience in using the handbook in the design office is a great asset.

The contents of this book have been grouped as follows :

Section A. Structural shapes and other steel products.

Section B. Beams, channels and compound sections used as girder.

Section C. Angles, single and double.

Section D. Beam, channels and other compound sections used as columns.

Some of the salient features of this handbook are :

(*i*) In arriving at the various gauge distances, the largest possible size of the rivets have been taken care of. In case of beams, the rivet gauge have been kept the same, irrespective of the width of the flange. This enables the use of multiple punches in fabricating shops since the same punch can be used for a number of beam sections. The gauge distances in webs, in case of beams and channels have been given for guidance only. The actual gauge distance will depend on the type of end connections.

(*ii*) The rivet gauge distances can be changed upon the rivet size. This is to be done with the specific understanding between the design office and the fabricator.

(*iii*) The allowable loads given in the handbook are for beams and channels used as girders. Adequate lateral supports for the compression flange is understood.

(*iv*) The mean thickness of flanges has been worked out on the basis of the gross area of each flange. This gross area of each flange is taken to be equal to the area of the additional plate plus the area of the flange of each section. Where channels have been used for the top flanges, only web area of the channel is included in computing the gross area of the flange.

(*v*) The diameter of the rivet hole is taken to be 1.6 mm $\left(\frac{1}{16}\text{ in}\right)$ more than the normal diameter of the rivet as per fabrication and design office practice in the country. The practice in the continent is however to assume the diameter of the hole to be 1 mm larger than the nominal diameter of the rivet. This practice has been followed in the handbook.

Fabrication of Steel Structure. IS : 800—1962 lays down code of practice for fabrication of steel structure. Salient features of these recommendations are :

1. **Straightening.** All material shall be straight, unless required to be curvilinear form, and free from twists. If necessary, it shall be straightened and/or flattened by pressure.

2. **Clearances.** The erection clearance for cleated ends of members connecting steel to steel shall not be greater than 20 mm at each end. In case of beams without web cleats, erection clearance shall be below 3 mm. Wherefrom practical considerations, greater clearance is required, suitably designed seatings should be provided.

Unless otherwise specified, in cases where black bolts are used, the holes may be 2.0 mm greater than the diameter of the bolts.

3. **Cutting.** Shearing, cropping or sawing may be used for cutting. For mild steel only gas cutting is permissible by mechanically controlled torch. In case of high tensile steel gas cutting may be adopted provided special care is taken to leave sufficient metal to be removed by machining so that all metal that has been hardened by flame is removed.

Hand flame cutting may be resorted to only when approved by the inspector.

No loads shall be transmitted into metal through a gas cut surface except where the material is subsequently joined by welding.

4. **Holing.** When holes have to be drilled through more than one thickness of material they shall as far as possible be drilled only after the members have been assembled and tightly clamped or bolted together.

Punching before assembly may be permitted if the holes are punched 3 mm less in diameter than the required size and reamed after assembly to the full diameter. The thickness of material punched shall be below 16 mm.

In case when holes are drilled through two or more separate parts in one operation, such parts shall be separated after drilling and burrs shall be removed. In connecting angles and plates holes may be punched full size through material of less than 13 mm thickness.

Finished holes shall be no more than 1.5 mm or 2.0 mm (as the case may be, depending on whether the diameter of the rivet or bolt is less than or more than 25 mm) in diameter larger than the diameter of the rivet or black bolt passing through them.

Holes for turned and fitted bolts shall be drilled to a diameter equal to the nominal diameter of the shank or barrel.

Holes for rivets or bolts shall not be formed by a gas cutting process.

5. **Assembly.** The component parts during assembly shall neither be twised or otherwise damaged and shall be so assembled that the specified camber is maintained.

6. **Riveting.** Rivets, when driven, shall completely fill the holes. When counter-sunk, the counter-sinking shall be fully filled by the rivet. Proudness of the countersunk head, if any, shall be dressed off flush.

Whenever practicable, machine riveting shall be carried out by using machines of the steady pressure type.

Special care shall be taken in heating and driving long rivets.

7. **Bolting.** Washer, where required, shall be tapered or otherwise suitably shaped, to give the heads and nuts of bolts a satisfactory bearing.

The treaded portion of each bolt shall project through the nut at least one thread.

8. **Welding.** Welding shall be carried out in accordance with the relevant standard. Standards (refer class 39.1 and 39.2, IS 800—1962).

9. **Machinary of Butts, Caps and Bases.** In column caps and bases, the ends of shafts together with attached gussets, angles, channels, etc., after riveting together, should be accurately machined not only the parts connected buttover the entire surface of contact.

The column ends need not be machined if sufficient gussets and rivets are provided to transmit the entire loading.

Ends of bearing stiffeners shall be machined on ground to fit tightly at both top and bottom.

10. **Slab bases and caps.** A bearing face which is to be grouted direct to a foundation need not be machined if such a face is true and parallel to the upper face.

Slab bases and caps shall be accurately machined over the bearing surfaces and shall be in effective contact with the end of the Stanchion.

Holes shall be provided in Stanchion bases when required for the escape of air, to facilitate grouting.

11. **Solid Round Steel Columns.** Where slabs are welded in position, the reduced end of the shaft shall be kept just sufficiently short to accommodate a fillet weld around the hole without weld metal being proud of the slab else the caps and bases may be welded direct to the column without boring or shouldering.

All bearing surfaces of slabs intended for metal to metal contacts shall be machined perpendicular to shaft.

12. **Painting.** All surfaces shall be dried and thoroughly cleaned to remove all loose scales and loose rust before they are painted, oiled or otherwise treated. Surfaces which are inaccessible after assembly, though not in contact, shall receive the full specified protective treatment before assembly.

When surfaces are to be welded, the steel shall not be painted or metal coated within a suitable distance of any edge to be coated, if the paint specified or the metal coating be harmful to welders or repair the quality of the welds.

Parts to be encased in concrete shall not be painted or oiled.

13. **Marking.** Each component of steel work shall be distinctly marked before delivery and shall bear such other marks as well facilitate erection.

14. **Shop Erection.** The steel work shall be temporarily shop erected complete so that accuracy of fit may be checked before despatch.

15. **Packing.** All projecting plates or bars and all ends of members at joints shall be stiffened, all straight bars and plates shall be bundled, all screwed ends and machined surfaces shall be suitably packed.

16. **Inspection and Testing.** Inspection shall be made at the place of manufacture prior to despatch. The manufacturer shall guarantee compliance with the specified provisions.

Any component of structure found not to comply with the specified provisions, shall be liable to rejection. Defects which may appear during fabrication shall be made good according to the procedure laid down.

The manufacturer shall supply all gauges and templates required for testing, checking and inspection.

Erection of Steel Structures. IS : 800—1962 lays down code of practice for erection of steel structures. Salient features of these recommendations are :

1. **Plant and Equipment.** The suitability and capacity of all plant and equipment used for erection shall be to the satisfaction of Engineer-in-charge.

2. **Storing and Handling.** The storage and handling of structural steel should be done in such way that it is subjected to minimum stresses and damage.

3. **Setting out.** Positioning, levelling and plumbing of steel components shall be such that every part of structure is placed accurately in accordance with the approved drawings and to the satisfaction of the Engineer.

4. **Security During Erection.** During erection of steel work, when required, shall be temporarily braced to provide for all load to be carried by the structure during erection.

Permanent bolting riveting or welding shall not be done until proper alignment has been finally checked and approved.

5. **Field Connections.** Rivets driven at site shall be driven with the same care as those driven in the shop.

Field assembly and welding shall be carried out in accordance with the requirements for shop fabrication.

Where steel has been delivered painted, the paint shall be removed for a distance of at least 50 mm on either side of the joints before field welding.

6. **Painting after Erection.** All surfaces to be painted shall be dry and thoroughly cleaned before painting of steel.

After erection specified protective treatment shall be completed.

Where metal coating has been given to the steel, such coating shall be completed on site so as to be continuous over any welds and site rivets or bolts. Bolts which have been galvanised or similarly treated are exempted from this requirement.

Surfaces which will be inaccessible after site assembly shall receive the full specified protective treatment before assembly.

7. Bedding of stanchion bases, bedding and encasing of grillage beams and bearing of beams and girders.

(*i*) Bedding of stanchion and bearings of beams and girders on stone, brick or concrete (Plain or Reinforced)

This operation shall not be carried out for multistoreyed buildings until a sufficient number of bottom length of stanchions has been properly lined, levelled and plumbed and sufficient beams are in position.

The operation shall not be carried out until steelwork has been finally plumbed during which stanchion bases shall be supported on steel wedges. Immediately before grouting, the space under the steel shall be thoroughly cleaned. One of the following methods shall be adopted.

(*a*) Use of neat portland cement grout to a thickness below 25 mm.

(*b*) Use of portland cement mortar to a thickness of between 25 mm and 50 mm. The mortar shall not be weaker than 1 : 2 (cement : sand)

(*c*) Use of portland cement mortar mixed as dry as possible with a thickness greater than 50 mm and mortar richer than 1 : 2 (cement to fine aggregate) consolidation shall be carried out by ramming with a suitable blunt hammer against properly fixed supports till the space is completely filled.

(*ii*) Bedding of grillage beams on concrete (Plain or Reinforced).

The space between two layers of grillage beams shall be filled with grout or mortar as specified for stanchions bases.

Bedding between stanchion base plates and top tier of grillage beam with cement mortar shall not be permitted unless specially designed to limit the stresses in the mortar to permissible limits.

(*iii*) Grouting of grillage shall not be done till the first lengths of stanchions have been plumbed, aligned and levelled.

(*iv*) Encasing of steel work in foundations and fillings between grillage beams Grillage beams and all steel in foundations shall be solidly encased in dense concrete with a minimum cover of 100 mm.

Detailing of Steel Structures. Detailing of material required for erection of steel structure is necessary for the following :

(*i*) **For Provisioning of Construction Stores.** As is well known practice in Construction Projects that before the erection is started 2/3 of the stores required should be at site and 1/3 in sight. Long before starting the field work in a project, therefore store provisioning has to be initiated. In order that the material procured is suitably provisioned, details of material required have to be worked out. On the other hand, sometimes the designer has to modify his design taking into consideration the sections already available on the basis of earlier *ad hoc* procurement or easily available as surplus stores from another project which may have been closed or where such stores may be surplus to its requirement as a result of over provisioning or because of change of modification in the design.

(*ii*) **For Obtaining Administrative Approval for the Project.** The Administrative Approval of the project is based on the detailed estimate of the works. In the case of steel structure, the bulk of the expenditure is on the procurement of the construction stores. Hence need for working out and detailing the steel components. Sometimes, however, to expediate Administrative Approval, the estimate of cost is based on the plinth area basis. This basis is arrived out from known construction cost of similar steel structures.

(*iii*) **Site Fabrication.** Before the fabricator can start site erection, the details of the components required for site fabrication of the structure must be detailed and known to the fabricator. This aspect is therefore a very important part of site erection. In the case of major project involving complicated fabrication work, the contractor normally allots the work to

another agency which is responsible for preparation of detailed fabrication drawings and yet the same approved by the consultant detailed by the owner/user. The fabricator gets his payment on the basis of such fabrication drawings as are approved for erection by the consultant. The payment is made on the basis of approved tonnage fabricated. The contractor himself gets the payment on the basis of tonnage detailed and worked out in the fabrication drawings and so is the payment for fabrication drawings made for preparation of the detailed working drawings.

Before the material can be detailed, working drawing illustrating all the details have to be prepared. These details are based on the design drawings prepared by the Engineer Consultant. The detailed drawings have therefore to be approved by the consultant before the stores statement can be supplied to the contractor for site fabrication.

Table 116. Detailing of Materials

S. No.	*Section*	*Length*	*Nos. Reqd.*	*Weight in kgs.* *Unit Wt.*	*Total Wt.*	*Remarks*
1.	PL—200 × 10th	7320	1	78.50	114.90	
2.	MB—600	7024	1	122.60	861.15	
3.	" "	6390	1	122.60	783.40	
4.	" "	5758	1	122.60	705.93	
5.	MB—450	4824	1	72.40	349.25	
6.	" "	4192	1	72.40	303.50	
7.	" "	3656	1	72.40	264.70	
8.	" "	3122	1	72.40	226.05	
9.	MC—300	933	1	35.80	33.40	
10.	" "	933	1	35.80	33.40	
11.	" "	732	1	35.80	26.20	
12.	" "	732	1	35.80	26.20	
13.	" "	1480	1	35.80	53.00	
14.	MC—200	928	1	22.10	20.50	
15.	PL—200 × 10th	409	4	78.50	25.70	
16.	16 ϕ STUD	75	15	1.60	1.80	
17.	MC—200	820	4	22.10	72.50	
18.	PL—200 × 10th	844	9	78.50	119.25	
19.	PL—200 × 10th	600	3	78.50	28.25	
20.	PL—200 × 10th	11751	2	78.50		
21.	PL—875 × 12th	11911	2	94.20	369.00	
22.	PL—400 × 10th	2623	1	78.50	1963.53	
23.	PL—836 × 10th	2623	2	78.50	82.35	
24.	PL—400 × 10th	1245	1	78.50	344.30	
25.	PL—2000 × 10th	7350	1	78.50	39.10	
26.	PL—2000 × 10th	6150	1	78.50	1153.95	
27.	PL—2000 × 10th	4950	1	78.50	965.55	
28.	PL—2000 × 10th	3750	1	78.50	777.15	
29.	PL—2000 × 10th	2550	1	78.50	588.75	
30.	PL—1481 × 10th	1350	1	78.50	400.35	
					156.95	
					10890.02	
					10890.19	10890 kg.

Detailing of R.C.C. Structure

Introduction. Detailing of R.C.C. structures has become a very specialised job in view of large number of R.C.C. structures that have revolutionised the construction industry. Two fold purpose served by detailing are :

(*i*) For determination of size and quality of reinforcement bars.

(*ii*) For fabrication of reinforcement bars into the exact profile (full size) in which these bars are placed at site before pouring of concrete. For this purpose it is necessary to have a schedule of reinforcement where in the shape of various bars including, binding and bending details are given. Before preparing such details the following guide lines should be known to the fabricator.

(*iii*) Steel reinforcement is worked out on the actual requirement including hooks, cranks, overlaps etc. For purpose of providing of steel however, allowance for wastage due to cutting to smaller sizes has to be made 25% extra may be allowed for this. This wastage can be considerably reduced, particularly in the case of heavy sections if the available market sections are taken into consideration at the design stage and during preparation of fabrication drawings by the fabricator. However, in the absence of detailed drawings the requirement of mild steel for reinforcement may be calculated as per Table 117.

Table 117. Calculation of Steel

S. No.	*R.C.C. Component*	*Steel as % of Concrete*
1.	Beams	1 to 2
2.	Columns	1 to 5
3.	Lintels, Slab etc.	0.7 to 1
4.	Foundation and footing	0.5 to 0.8

(*iv*) The length of a hook may be taken as 9 dia. The total length of straight bar hooked at both ends may be taken as L + 18 dia (See Fig 8 *a*)

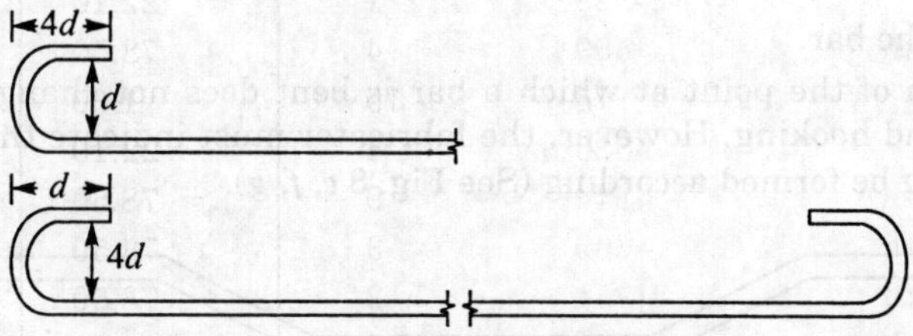

(*a*)

Total length of hooked bar = $L + 18d$.

(*v*) Additional length for one bar bent up at 45° (See Fig. 8 *b*)

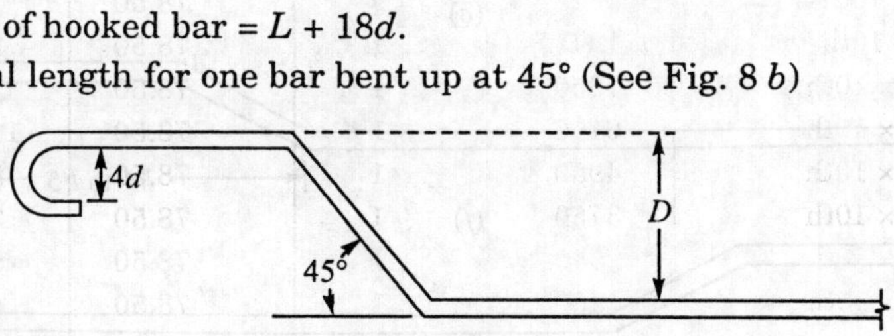

(*b*)

The increase in length.

$$= \text{Difference in length between hypotenuse and the bar}$$

$$= \frac{D}{\sin 45^\circ} - D$$

$$= 1.42D - D = 0.42D$$

For two bent up bars at 45°, additional length = $0.42 \times 2D = 0.84D$.

where D = depth.

(*vi*) The additional length for one bar bent up at 30° (See Fig. 8 *c*).

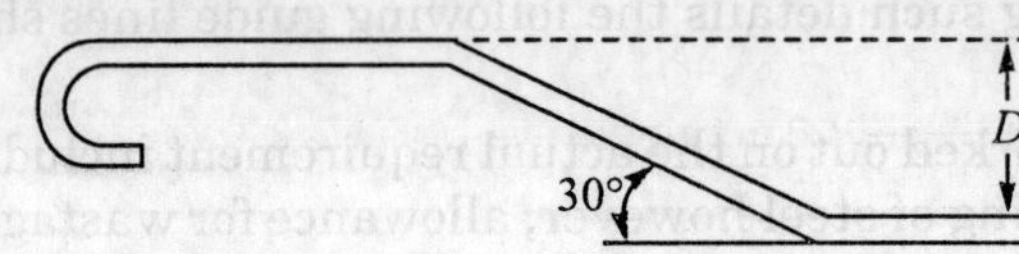

(c)

The increase in length.

$$= \text{Difference in length between hypotenuse and the base}$$

$$= \frac{D}{\sin 30} - \frac{D}{\tan 30^\circ} = 2 - 1.73\,D = 0.27D \text{ say } 0.3D.$$

For a bar cranked up at 30° at both ends, the increase in length = $2 \times 0.3D = 0.6D$.

(*vii*) Overlap at joint. (See Fig. 8 *d*).

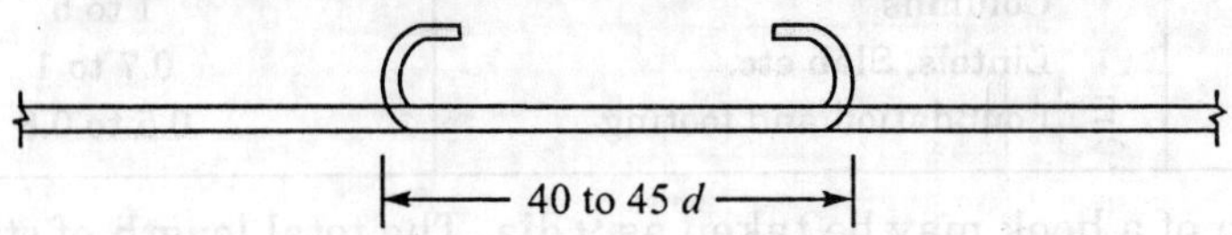

(*d*)

Additional length due to overlap = $(40 + 18)d = 58d$

where d = diameter of the bar.

Note. The location of the point at which a bar is bent does not change the additional length calculated for cranking and hooking. However, the fabricator must indicate the position of bending so that the bench for bending be formed according (See Fig. 8 *e, f, g*).

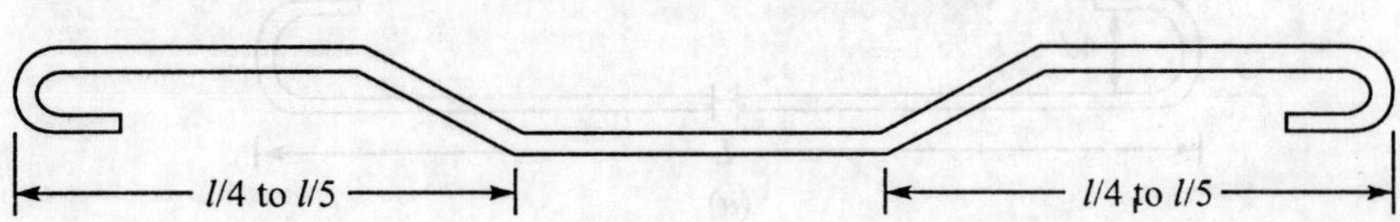

(*e*)

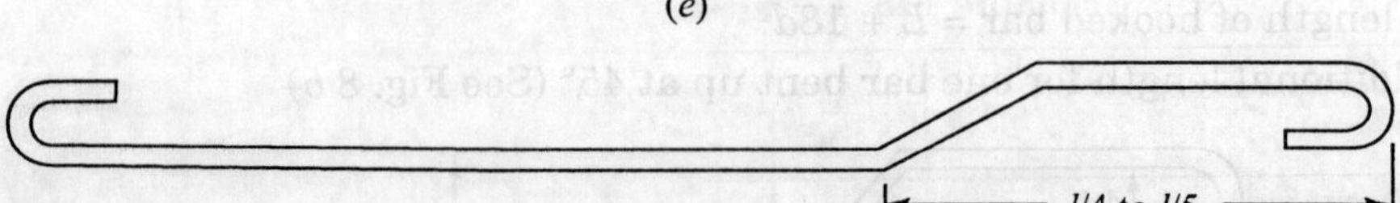

(*f*)

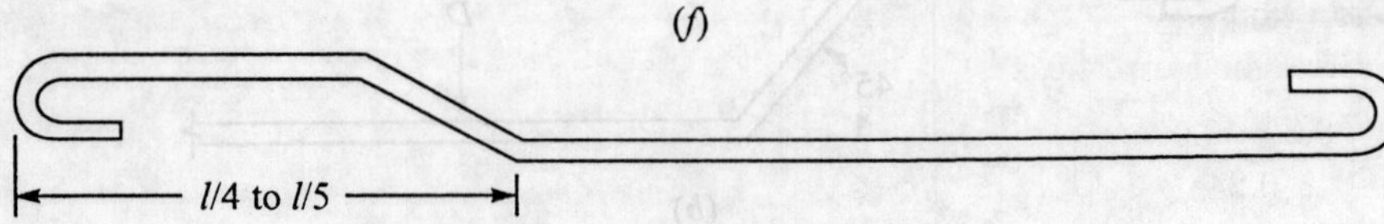

(*g*)

Fig. 8

Schedule of Reinforcement. Schedule of reinforcement for some of the typical cases are given below. The fabricator or detailer for reinforcement prepares these schedules on the basis of which reinforcement bars are bent at site.

Example 1. *Prepare schedule of reinforcement for a R.C.C. slab given in Fig. 9.*

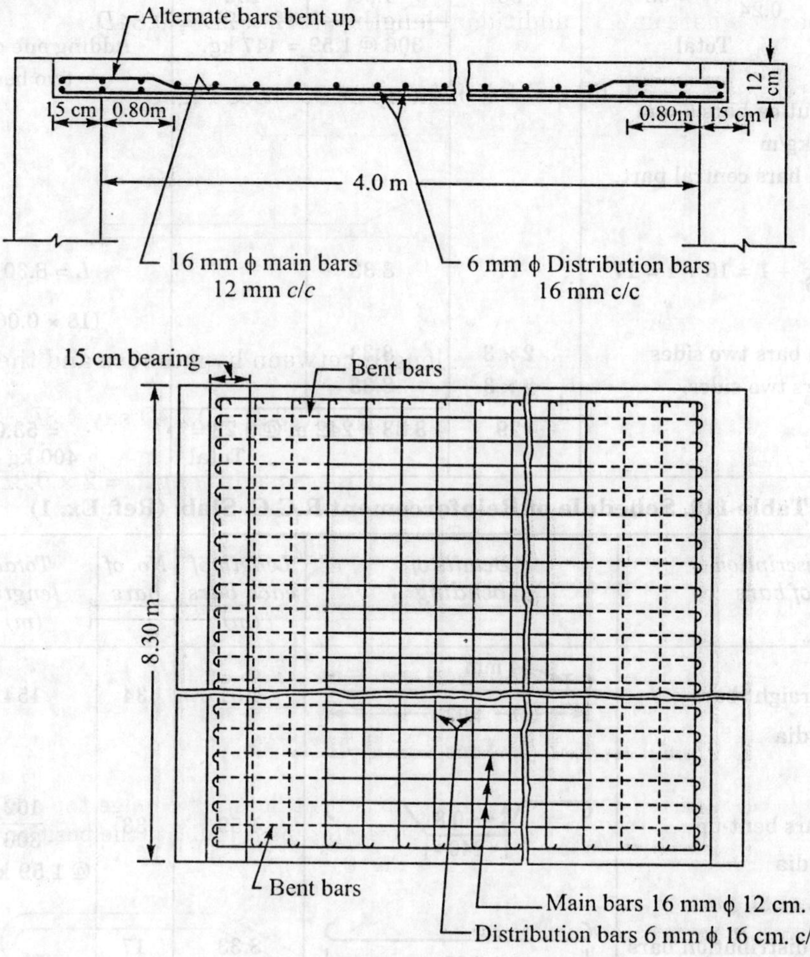

Fig. 9

Table 118. Details of Reinforcement

S. No.	*Particulars of bar*	*No.*	*Length (m)*	*Quantity (m)*	*Remarks*
1.	(*i*) Main bars 16 mm @ 1.59 kg/m. Straight bars 24 c.c. $\left(\frac{8.30-0.08}{0.24}+1\right)=34$	34	4.51	154	L = 4 + 0.15 × 2 – 2 × 0.04 (side over – 2 hooks) = 4.22 + 18 × 0.016 = 4.22 + 0.288 = 4.51

(*Contd.*)

S. No.	*Particulars of bar*	*No.*	*Length (m)*	*Quantity (m)*	*Remarks*
	(*ii*) Bent up bars. $\frac{8.30-0.08}{0.24}=33$	33	4.59	152	
	Total		306 @ 1.59 = 447 kg.		Adding one depth (8 cm) two bent ups.
2.	Distribution bars 6 mm @ 0.22 kg/m Bottom bars central part. 16 mm. No $\frac{2.4}{0.16}+1=16+1=17$	17	8.33		$L = 8.30 - 0.08 + (18 \times 0.006) = 8.33$
	Bottom bars two sides	2 × 3	8.33		
	Top bars two sides.	2 × 3	8.33		
		29	8.33 = 242 m @ 0.22 =	Total	= 53.00 kg. 400 kg = 5.0 q.

Table 119. Schedule of Reinforcement R.C.C. Slab; (Ref. Ex. 1)

S. No.	*Description of bars*	*Details of bending*	*Length of each bars (m)*	*No. of bars*	*Total length (m)*	*Weight kg*
1.	Main straight bars 16 mm dia	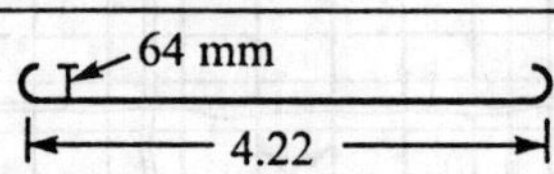	4.51	34	154	
2.	Main bars bent-up 16 mm dia	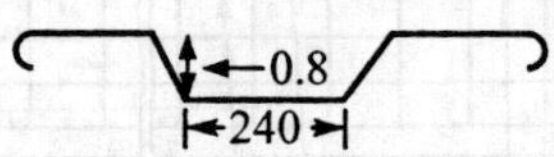	4.59	33	152 306 @ 1.59 kg/m	447 kg.
3.	Bottom distribution bars 6 mm ϕ central portion	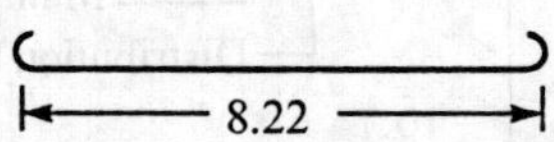	8.33	17		
4.	Bottom distribution bars 6 mm ϕ Two sides	9.9	8.33	6		
5.	Top distribution bars 6 mm ϕ Two sides	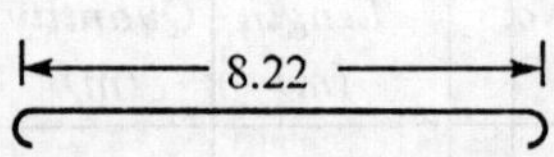	8.33	6		
			8.33	29	242 @ .22 kg/m	530 kg.
					Total =	500 kg.

Example 2. *Prepare schedule of reinforcement for a R.C.C. Beam 90 cm × 40 cm in section from the given drawing (Fig. 10)*

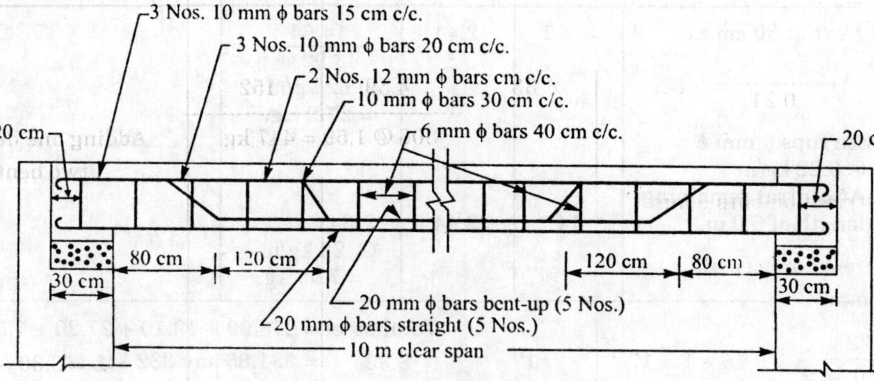

Fig. 10

Table 120. Details of Reinforcement

S. No.	Particulars of bars	No.	Length (m)	Quantity (m)	Remarks
1.	**Main Bars**				
	(i) 20 m dia straight bars @ 2.47 kg/m.	5	10.88	54.40	L = 10.60 – 2 end cover + 2 hooks = 10.60 – 0.08 + (18 × 0.020) = 10.52 + 0.360 = 10.88
	(ii) 20 mm dia bent up bars @ 2.47 kg/m	5	11.63	58.15	L = 10.60 – 2 end covers + 2 hooks + one depth = 10.60 – 0.08 + (18 × 0.02) + 0.75 = 10.52 + 0.36 + 0.75 = 11.63
				112.55 @ 2.47 = 278 kg.	
	(iii) 12 mm dia. top bars @ 0.89 kg/m.	2	10.74	21.48 @ 0.89 **= 19.1 kg.**	L = 10.60 – 2 end covers + 2 hooks = 10.60 – 0.08 + (18 × 0.012) = 10.52 + 0.36 = 10.74 m.
2.	**Stirrups**				
	(i) 10 mm φ @ 0.62 kg/m At end 15 cm c.c.	3 × 2	2.44	14.64	L = (75 × 2 + 32 × 2 cm + 30 cm extra)
	(ii) Next at 20 cm c.c.	3 × 2	2.44	14.64	= 150 + 64 + 30 = 244 cm = 2.44 m

(Contd.)

S. No.	Particulars of bars	No	Length (m)	Quantity (m)	Remarks
	(*iii*) Next at 30 cm c.c.	3 × 2	2.44	14.64 43.92 @ 0.62 kg/m **= 27.2 kg.**	
	(*iv*) Stirrups 6 mm ϕ @ 0.22 kg/m At central remaining length of 6.0 m.	14	2.44	34.2 m @ .22 kg/m = 7.55 kg.	

Total steel = 278.00 + 19.10 + 27.20 + 7.55 = 331.85 say 332 kg.

Table 121. Schedule of Reinforcement for R.C.C. Beam. (Example 2)

S. No.	Description of bars	Details of bending	Length of each bars (m)	No. of bars	Total length (m)	Weight (kg)
1.	Main straight-bars 20 mm dia	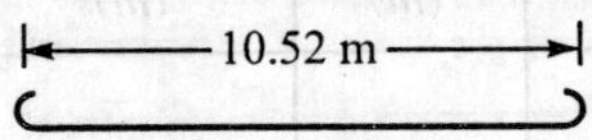	10.88	5	54.40	
2.	Main bent-up bars 20 mm dia	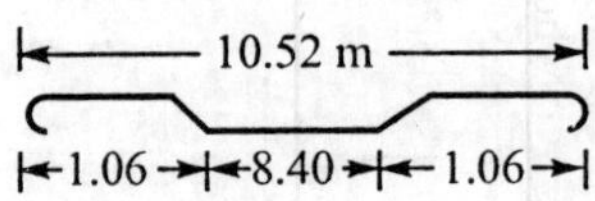	11.65	3 } 5	58.15 112.55 @247 kg/m	278.00
3.	Main bent-up bars 20 mm dia	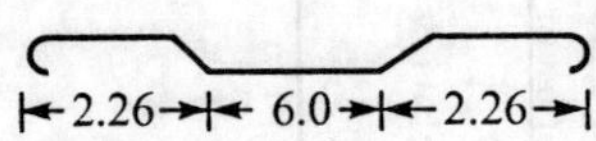	11.65	2		
4.	Top straight-bars 12 mm dia	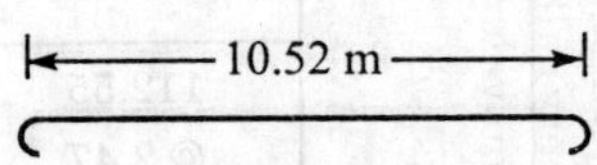	10.74	2	21.41 @ 0.89 kg/m	19.10
5.	(*i*) Stirrups 10 mm ϕ	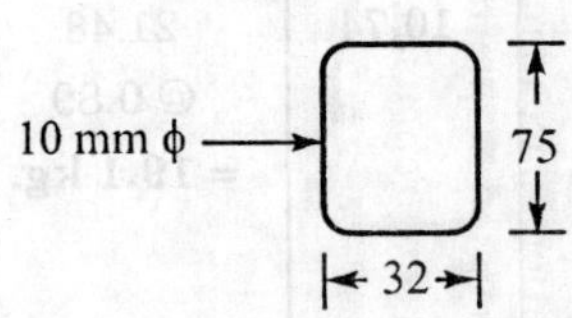	2.44	18	43.93 @ 0.62 kg/m	27.20
	(*ii*) Stirrups 6 mm ϕ	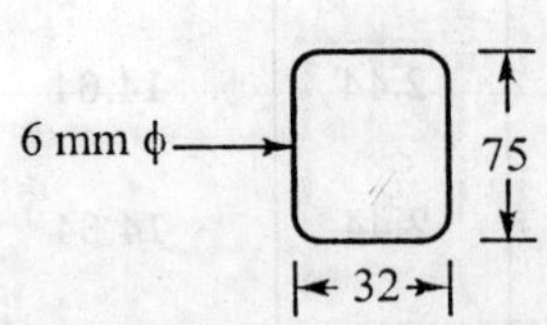	2.44	14	34.2 @ 22 kg/m.	7.55
					Total = Say =	331.85 3320 kg.

Table 122. Live Loads on Floors

S. No.	Loading Class No.	Types of floors	Minimum Live Loads per kg/m² of Floor Area	Alternative Minimum Live Load
1.	200	Floors in dwelling houses, tenements, hospital wards, bed rooms and private sitting rooms in hostels, and dormitories	200	Subject to a minimum total load of 2.5 times the values in col. 4 for any given slab panel and 6 times the values in col. 4 for any given beam. This total load shall be assumed uniformly distributed on the entire area of the slab panel or the entire length of the beam. (applies to S. No. 1–5)
2.	250	Office floors other than entrance halls, floors of light workrooms	*250—400	
3.	300	Floors of banking halls, office entrance halls and reading rooms	300	
4.	400	Shop floors used for the display and sale of merchandise; floors of work-rooms generally ; floors of classrooms in schools, floors or places of assembly with fixed seating, restaurants; circulation space in machinery halls, power stations, etc. where not occupied by plant or equivalent.	400	
5.	500	Floors of warehouses, workshops, factories and other buildings or parts of buildings of similar category for light weight loads; office floors for storage and filing purposes; floors of places of assembly without fixed seating, public rooms in hotels, dance halls, waiting halls, etc.	500	
6.	750	Floors of warehouses, workshops, factories and other buildings or parts of buildings of similar category for medium-weight loads	750	—
7.	1000	Floors of warehouses, workshops, factories and other buildings or parts of buildings of similar category for heavy-weight loads floors of book stores and libraries, roofs and pavement lights over basements projecting under the public footpath	1000	—
8.	Garage, Light	Floors used for garages for vehicles not exceeding 2-5 tonnes gross weight :		The worst combination of actual wheel loads, whichever is greater.
		Slabs	400	
		Beams	250	The worst combination of actual wheel loads, whichever is greater.

*The lower value of 250 kg/m² should be taken where separate storage facilities are provided and the higher value of 400 kg/m² should be taken where such provisions are lacking.

S. No.	Loading Class No.	Types of floors	Minimum Live Loads per kg/m² of Floor Area	Alternative Minimum Live Load
9.	Garage, Heavy	Floors used for garages for vehicles not exceeding 4 tonnes gross weight	750	Subject to a minimum of one and a half times maximum wheel load but not less than 900 kg considered to be distributed over 75 cm square.
10.	Stairs	Stairs, landings and corridors for class 200 loading but not liable to over-crowding	300	Subject to a minimum of 130 kg concentrated load at the unsupported end of each step for stairs constructed out of structurally independent cantilever steps.
		Stairs, landings and corridors for class 200 loading but liable to overcrowding, and for all other classes	500	
11.	Balcony	Balconies not liable to overcrowdings :		
		For class 200 loading	300	—
		For all other classes	500	—
		Balconies liable to overcrowding	500	—

Note 1 : A reference to a 'floor' includes a reference to any part of that floor, and a reference to 'slabs' includes boarding and beams or ribs spaced not further apart than one metre between centres, and a reference to 'beams' means all other beams and ribs.

Note 2 : Under loading class No. 250, the reference to 'light workrooms' envisages rooms in which some light machines for example, sewing machines used by milliners or tailors) are operated without a central power-driven unit, that is, the machines are independently operated, either by hand or by small motors. Under loading class No. 400, the reference to 'workrooms' generally envisages the installation of machines operated with a central-driven unit, with the individual machines being belt driven.

Note 3 : 'Fixed seating' implies that the removal of the seating and the use of the space for other purposes is improbable. The maximum likely load in this case is, therefore, closely controlled.

Note 4 : The loading in workshops, warehouses and factories varies considerably and so three loadings under the terms 'light', 'medium' and 'heavy' are introduced in order to allow for more economical designs but the terms have no special meaning in themselves other than the live load for which the relevent floor is designed. It is, however, important particularly in the case of heavy weight loads, to assess the actual loads to ensure that they are not in excess of 1000 kg/m²; in cases where they are in excess, the design shall be based on the actual loading.

Note 5 : The load classification for stairs, corridors, balconies and landings provide for the fact that these often serve several occupancies and are used for transporting the furniture and goods.

Table 123. Live Loads on Roofs

S. No.	*Type of Roof*	*Live Load Measured on Plan*	*Minimum Live Load Measured on Plan*
1.	Flat, sloping or curved roof with slopes up to and including 10 degrees :		
	(*a*) Access provided	150 kg/m^2	375 kg uniformly distributed over any span of one metre width of the roof slab and 900 kg uniformly distributed over the span in the case of all beams.
	(*b*) Access not provided, except for maintenance	75 kg/m^2	190 kg uniformly distributed over any span of one metre width of the roof slab and 450 kg. uniformly distributed over the span in the case of beams.
2.	Sloping roof with slope greater than 10 degrees	(*a*) For roof membrane, sheets or purlins—75 kg/m^2 less 2 kg/m^2 for every degree increase in slope over 10 degrees (*b*) For members supporting the roof membrane and roof purlines, such as trusses, beams, girders, etc.—2/3 of load in (*a*). (*c*) Loads in (*a*) and (*b*) do not include loads due to snow, rain, dust collection, etc., and the effects of such loads shall be appropriately considered	Subject to a minimum of 40 kg/m^2
3.	Curved roofs with slope at springing greater than 10 degrees	$(75 - 345\,\gamma^2)$ kg/m^2 where $\gamma = \frac{h}{l}$ h = the height of the highest point of the structure measured from its springing ; and l = chord width of the roof if singly curved and shorter of the two sides, if doubly curved.	Subject to a minimum of 40 kg/m^2

Note : For special types of roofs with highly permeable and absorbent material, the contingency of roof material increasing in weight due to absorption of moisture shall be provided for.

Table 124. Shape (in Plan) Factors

Plan Shape of the Structure	*Factors*		
	Ratio of Height to Base Width 0.4	*Ratio of Height to Base Width 4.8*	*Ratio of Height to Base Width 8 or over*
Circular	0.7	0.7	0.7
Octagonal	0.8	0.9	1.0
Square (wind perpendicular to diagonal)	0.8	0.9	1.0
Square (wind perpendicular to face)	1.0	1.15	1.3

Note 1 : In the case of projections above the general roof level, the base width shall be taken as th width of the construction where it rises from the surface of the roof ; and the height governir the ratio of height to base width shall be that from the roof surface to the top of the constructio

Note 2 : The division of wind load into that acting on windward and leeward sides shall be the same a that for rectangular buildings as affected by the openings.

Table 125. Wind Pressures on Roofs (Wind Normal to Ridge)

Slope of Roof on Windward Side (α)	*External Wind Pressure*	
	Windward Slope	*Leeward Slope*
0°	– 1.00 p	– 0.50 p
10°	– 0.70 p	– 0.50 p
20°	– 0.40 p	– 0.50 p
30°	– 0.10 p	– 0.50 p
40°	+ 0.10 p	– 0.50 p
50°	+ 0.30 p	– 0.50 p
60°	+ 0.40 p	– 0.50 p
70°	+ 0.50 p	– 0.50 p
80°	+ 0.50 p	– 0.50 p
90°	+ 0.50 p	– 0.50 p

Note 1 : In the above table, plus (+) means an external positive pressure on the roof normal to th surface of the roof and minus (–) means an external suction on the roof normal to the surfa of the roof.

Note 2 : The wind pressures to be assumed over intermediate roof slopes may be interpolated linearl

Note 3 : In the case of a flat roof, windward slope means windward half of the roof and leeward slo means leeward half of the roof.

S. No.	Types of Rocks and Soils	Presumptive Safe Bearing Capacity kg/cm^2	Remarks
	(a) Rocks		
1.	Rocks (hard) without lamination and defects, for example, granite, trap and diorite	33	—
2.	Laminated rocks, for example, sandstone and limestone sound condition	16.5	—
3.	Residual deposits of shattered and broken bed rock and hard shale, cemented material	9.0	—
4.	Soft rock	4.5	—
	(b) Non-cohesive Soils		
5.	Gravel, sand and gravel, compact and offering high resistance to penetration when excavated by tools	4.5	*See Note 1*
6.	Coarse sand, compact and dry	4.5	Dry means that the ground water level is at a depth not less than the width of foundation below the base of the foundation.
7.	Medium sand, compact and dry	2.5	—
8.	Fine sand, silt (dry lumps easily pulverized by the fingers)	1.5	—
9.	Loose gravel or sand gravel mixture ; loose coarse to medium sand, dry	2.5	*See Note 1*
10.	Fine sand, loose and dry	1.0	—
	(c) Cohesive Soils		
11.	Soft shale, hard or stiff clay in deep bed, dry	4.5	This ground is susceptible long term consolidation settlement

S. No.	*Types of Rocks and Soils*	*Presumptive Safe Bearing Capacity* kg/cm^2	*Remarks*
12.	Medium clay, readily indented with a thumb nail	2.5	—
13.	Moist clay and sand clay mixture which can be indented with strong thumb pressure	1.5	—
14.	Soft clay indented with moderate thumb pressure	1.0	—
15.	Very soft clay which can be penetrated several centimetres with the thumb	0.5	—
16.	Black cotton soil or other shrinkable or expansive clay in dry condition (50 per cent saturation)	—	*See Note 2.* To be determined after investigation.
	(*d*) *Peat*		
17.	Peat	—	*See Notes 2 and 3.* To be determined after investigation.
	(*e*) *Made-Up Ground*		
18.	Fills or made-up ground	—	*See Notes 1 and 4.* To be determined after investigation.

Note 1 : Compactness or looseness of non-cohesive materials may be determined by driving a wooden picket of dimensions 5 cm × 5 cm × 70 cm with a sharp point. The picket shall be pushed vertically into the soil by the full weight of a person and if the penetration of the picket exceeds 20 cm, the loose state shall be assumed to exist.

Note 2 : No generalized values for presumptive safe bearing capacities can be given for these types of soils. In such area, adequate site investigation shall be carried out and expert advice shall be sought.

Note 3 : Peat may occur in a very soft spongy condition or may be quite firm and compact. While ultimate bearing capacity may be high in the compact cases very large consolidation settlements occur even under small pressures and the movements continue for decades.

Note 4 : The strength of made-up ground depends on the nature of the material, its depth and age, and the methods used for consolidating it.

Note 5 : The presumptive safe bearing values may be increased by an amount equal to weight of the material (virgin soil) removed from above the bearing level, that is, the base of the foundation.

Note 6 : For non-cohesive soils, the presumptive safe bearing value shall be reduced by 50 per cent if the watertable is above or near the bearing surface of the soil. If the watertable is below the bearing surface of the soil at a distance at least equal to the width of the foundation, no such reduction shall apply. For intermediate depths of the watertable, proportional reduction of the presumptive safe bearing value may be made.

Table 127. Thickness of Footings

S. No.	*Types of Footings*	*Thickness of Footings*	*Remarks*
1.	Masonry	(*a*) ≮ 25 cm (*b*) twice the maximum projection from the face of the wall	Select the greater of the two values
2.	Plain Concrete :		
	For normal structures	(*a*) ≮ 20 cm	
		(*b*) twice the maximum offset	Foot footings resting on soil
		(*c*) ≮ 30 cm	For footings resting on top of pile
	For lightly loaded structures	(*a*) ≮ 15 cm	Resting on soil
		(*b*) ≮ 20 cm	Resting on pile
3.	Reinforced Concrete	(*a*) ≮ 12 cm	Resting on soil
		(*b*) ≮ 30 cm	Resting on pile

Table 128. Choice of Piles

S. No.	*Site Conditions*	*Choice of Pile*	*Remarks*
1.	Coarse sand or gravel	Driven precast or cast in *situ* piles	Develops point bearing and frictional resistance
2.	Firm stratum with soft material below	Provide enlarged base for the pile with piles spaced sufficiently apart	Bearing capacity will be improved
3.	Fine sand and silt (saturated)	Driven cast *in situ* piles	—
4.	Expensive soils and poor soils of shallow depths overlying firm soils strata	Short bored piles with enlarged base	Base shall rest on stable zone

Note : The choice of the timber piles (treated or untreated) depends on site conditions (water tables).

Table 129. Ultimate Bearing Capacity of Pile Groups

S. No.	*Description*	*Ultimate Bearing Capacity of Pile Groups*
1.	Piles drawn into clay or silty soil	Less than $n \times b$
2.	Cast in *situ* piles resting on hard strata	Equal to $n \times b$
3.	Driven piles in loose sandy soil	Greater than $n \times b$

where n = number of piles in the group,
and b = ultimate bearing capacity of individual pile.

Table 130. Permissible Stresses for Grade I Timber

Permissible Stresses (kg/cm²)	*Location*	*Group A*	*Group B*	*Group C*
Bending and tension along grain	Inside locations	182	123	84
	Outside locations	152	102	70
	Wet locations	120	81	60
Shear	Horizontal all locations*	12	9	6
	Along grain all locations**	17	13	9
Compression parallel to grain	Inside locations	120	70	64
	Outside locations	106	63	56
	Wet locations	88	58	46
Compression perpendicular to grain	Inside locations	60	22	22
	Outside locations	46	18	17
	Wet locations	38	15	14

*The values of horizontal shears to be used only for beams.

**In all other cases shear along grain to be used.

Table 131. Effective Height

S. No.	Condition of Support	Wall		Columns	
		Effective Height	Fig. No.	Effective Height	Fig. No.
1.	Adequate lateral support and partial rotational restraint at top and bottom. For example, where the floor (or roof) has a direction of span at right angles to the wall, so that the reaction to the load of the floor or roof is provided by the walls ; or where the concrete floors have a bearing on walls irrespective of the direction of the span.	0.75 *H*	32.12	0.85 *H*	32.13
2.	Adequate lateral support and partial rotational restraint at either top or bottom, and lateral restraint at other end. For example, fully braced construction which is itself adequately supported and incorporates (*a*) timber floors immediately below or above a reinforced concrete floor, and (*b*) roof trusses above a reinforced concrete floor or the like.	0.85 *H*	1.00 *H*		
3.	Adequate lateral support at top, and bottom where the floors (or roofs) have a direction of span parallel with the wall, top and bottom, and do not bear on it, or fully braced construction which is itself adequately supported and which incorporates roof trusses and timber upper storey floors.	1.00 *H*	1.00 *H*		
4.	Adequate lateral support and partial rotational restraint at bottom and not lateral support or rotational restraint at the top where the wall has no lateral support at top (construction not fully anchored or not fully braced).	1.50 *H*	32.12	2.00 *H*	32.13
5.	Free standing non-load bearing members.	2.00 *H*		2.00 *H*	

Note 1 : H is the height of wall or column between centres of support or the centre of support to the point near the footing, where the thickness of wall or column is minimum.

Note 2 : Where there is discontinuity in bound, due to damp-roof course or other materials. *H* should be measured from the discontinuity and the condition of end restraint at the discontinuity shall be taken as one of the lateral supports only.

Note 3 : A stable concrete element, such as a footing or a floor (irrespective of the direction of span) having bearing on or supporting a wall or column may be considered to provide partial restraint. In the case of roofs, the partial rotational restraint shall be assumed to be provided only when the direction of span is at right angles to the direction of wall or column.

Note 4 : In the case of a column, the effective heights for both of its sides shall be considered taking into account the conditions of support at the ends.

Note 5 : When assessing effective height, floors not adequately anchored to walls shall not be considered as providing lateral support to such walls.

Note 6 : Where a load-bearing pier is bonded to a wall whose thickness is at least two-thirds of the horizontal dimension of that pier, measured at right angles to the length of the wall and so as to include the thickness of that wall ($t_w = 2/3t_p$), that pier and the portion of the wall to which it is bonded may be treated as a wall.

Table 132. Effective Length of Walls

S. No.	*Conditions of Support*	*Effective Length*
1.	Where a wall is continuous and supported by cross walls or buttresses and there is no opening within one-eighth of the wall height h or H (whichever is less from the face of the supporting wall or buttress.	0.8 L
2.	Where a wall is supported by a buttress or cross wall at one end and continuous with buttress or cross wall supports at the other end.	1.0 L
3.	Where a wall is supported at each end by a buttress or a cross wall.	1.0 L
4.	Where the wall is free at one end and supported by a buttress or cross wall at the other end.	1.5 L

where L = the length of wall from or between centres of piers, buttresses or cross walls ;
H = the actual height of the wall between centres of adequate lateral supports and
h = the effective height of the wall.

A-2

Building Cost Index

Consumer Price Index (CPA) is an statistical measure of the change in price levels of a predetermined mix of consumer. Goods and services and often used as a means of adjusting rental payments of lease. And cost of living index is a summary of general consumer prices through time.

Similarly Building Cost Index (BCI) is a number which shows the resultant effect of cost of building materials *viz.* steel, cement, bricks, tiles, wood, labour etc. which have got varying effect in their own fields on the cost of building. It is defined as the unit increase or decrease (which have not happened till date) in the price of a certain year with reference to the price of same previous year known as base year. The building cost index of base year is taken as 100 for comparison basis.

The CPWD has been fixing the cost index from time to time. The CPWD has fixed base years as 1955, 1970, 1976, 1992 and 2002. If cost index as on 10.04.1980 was 180 in comparison to its base year of 01.10.1976; it indicates that cost of construction has increased by 80 percent cost index gives an idea in increase or decrease (which likely to occur never) in construction cost with reference to base year. This is due to increase in cost of materials, labour, transportation and many other factors involved in construction. The cost index of different places varies considerably. It is mainly due to either availability of labour at a very low cost or the material is required to be transported at a considerable distance, this increase transportation cost of material thereby increasing the cost index. Many a time due to non availability of labour ; labour force is also required to be moved at a construction site. This increases cost of labour ; moreover labour force is required to be provided by meals etc. along with other expenses. This also increases cost index at a particular place under consideration.

The cost index as on 1998/99 of a few places in India is given below :

S. No.	*Place*	*State*	*Month / year*	*Cost Index*
1.	Delhi	Central Province	6/99	162
2.	Bombay	Maharashtra	6/97	200
3.	Chennai	Andhra Pradesh	6/99	191
4.	Calcutta	Bental	6/99	211
5.	Hydrabad	Andhra Pradesh	6/98	168
6.	Raichur	Andhra Pradesh	6/97	178
7.	Warangal	Andhra Pradesh	6/98	161
8.	Itanagar	Arunachal Pradesh	6/98	250
9.	Patna	Bihar	6/98	205
10.	Panaji	Goa	6/98	188

11.	Ahmedabad	Gujrat	6/98	165
12.	Baroda	Gujrat	6/97	155
13.	Surat	Gujrat	6/98	171
14.	Ambala	Haryana	1/98	143
15.	Simla	Himachal Pradesh	6/96	178
16.	Jammu	Jammu & Kashmir	10/97	156
17.	Srinagar	Jammu & Kashmir	10/97	188
18.	Banglore	Karnataka	6/98	187
19.	Mysore	Karnataka	6/98	179
20.	Trichur	Kerala	6/98	208
21.	Earnakulam	Kerala	6/98	216
22.	Bhopal	Madhya Pradesh	6/98	163
23.	Gwalior	Madhya Pradesh	6/98	160
24.	Indore	Madhya Pradesh	6/98	164
25.	Jabalpur	Madhya Pradesh	6/98	168
26.	Aurangabad	Maharashtra	1/97	176
27.	Nagpur	Maharashtra	1/98	163
28.	Pune	Maharashtra	1/99	195
29.	Nashik	Maharashtra	1/97	176
30.	Imphal	Manipur	6/98	233
31.	Shillong	Meghalaya	6/98	230
32.	Kohima	Nagaland	6/98	259
33.	Bhubaneshwar	Orissa	1/98	180
34.	Amritsar	Punjab	6/98	155
35.	Jaipur	Rajasthan	6/98	153
36.	Jodhpur	Rajasthan	6/98	144
37.	Gangtok	Sikkim	6/98	185
38.	Coimbatore	Tamilnadu	6/99	203
39.	Pondicherry	Tamilnadu	6/99	179
40.	Agartala	Tripura	6/98	262
41.	Agra	Uttar Pradesh	6/97	164
42.	Lucknow	Uttar Pradesh	6/97	167
43.	Varanasi	Uttar Pradesh	1/98	172
44.	Andaman, Nicobar	Union Territory	6/99	235
45.	Chandigarh	Union Territory	6/96	140
46.	Lakshdweep	Union Territory	12/92	377

The formula by which cost index is calculated over plinth area rates has following weightages for different materials of construction and labour involved. An approximate weightage in general considered are given here.

(*a*)	Cement	12.5 to 15%
(*b*)	Stone aggregate	5 to 6.5%
(*c*)	Coarse sand	2 to 3.00%
(*d*)	Steel	18 to 20%
(*e*)	Labour	28 to 25.00%
(*f*)	Bricks	6 to 8.00%
(*g*)	Flooring items	3 to 4.00%
(*h*)	Paints	2 to 3.00%
(*i*)	Ply & Wood	4 to 5.00%
(*j*)	Pipes	2 to 2.50%
(*k*)	Lamps and Fan	3 to 3.50%
(*l*)	Wires and Cables	2 to 4.00%
(*m*)	Electric machines	2 to 2.50%
	Total	100.00%

Thus said cost index is based on the market rates of basic items specially like cement, steel, stone grit, sand, bricks and labour as well as other building items.

A-3

Additional Important Tables

Table 1. Rough Estimation for Cost of Buildings

S.No.	Name of Items	Percentage of total cost
1.	Labour	30 to 35
2.	Cost of materials	70 to 65
3.	Foundation upto and including plinth	15 to 20
4.	Superstructure	80 to 85
5.	Second storey	75 to 85 of I storey
6.	Direct and overhead cost :	
	(*a*) Direct on actual work	85
	(*b*) Overhead cost due to establishment, supervision, incidental etc.	15
7.	Sanitation and electrification :	
	(*a*) Sanitary and water supply	7 to 9
	(*b*) Electric installations without fans	7
	(*c*) Electric fans	5
8.	Cost break-up of different parts :	
	(*a*) Earthwork in excavation and filling	½ to 1
	(*b*) Foundation concreting	4 to 6
	(*c*) Damp proof course	1
	(*d*) Brick work	34
	(*e*) Roofing	20
	(*f*) Doors and windows	16
	(*g*) Plastering and pointing	10
	(*h*) White and colour washing, painting	2
	(*i*) Miscellaneous	4
9.	Cost of material and labour :	
	(*a*) Bricks	25
	(*b*) Cement	10
	(*c*) Steel bars	10
	(*d*) Timber	15
	(*e*) Lime	5
	(*f*) Labour	30
	(*g*) Miscellaneous	5
10.	Material required on plinth area basis for single storey buildings :	
	(*a*) Brick	500 Nos. per sq m of plinth area.
	(*b*) Cement	1.5 bags per sq m of plinth area.
	(*c*) Steel bars	12 kg. per sq m of plinth area.
	(*d*) Coal for burning bricks	1.5 quintals per sq m of plinth area
11.	Annual repair and maintenance	1 to 1½% of capital cost of building.

Table 2. Approximate Area, Cubic Spaces for Different Types of Buildings

Type of building	*Floor area per head sq m*	*Cubic space per head sq m*	*Verandah area per cent*	*Area occupied by wall per cent*
Residential	2.5 to 3.0	9	10 to 20	15 to 20
School	1.0 to 2.0	4.2	10 to 20	15 to 20
Hostel	7.0 to 10.0	30	25 to 35	15 to 20
Hospital	8.0 to 10.0	30	25 to 35	15 to 20
Factory	2.5 to 3.0	9 to 12	25 to 35	10
Office building	2.5 to 3.0	12 to 15	25 to 35	10

Note. For residential building the liveable area known as carpet area should be 50 to 70% of the plinth area.

Table 3. Size of Rooms in Residential Plot

Room	*Standard type in metres*	*Ordinary type in metres*
Drawing room	4.2 × 4.8	5.2 × 4.8 (drawing and dining)
Dining room	4.2 × 4.3	—
Bed room	4.2 × 4.8	3.0 × 4.2
Office room	3.0 × 3.6	—
Guest room	3.0 × 3.6	—
Kitchen	3.0 × 3.0	2.5 × 3.0
Store	3.0 × 3.0	2.5 × 2.5
Pantry	2.5 × 3.0	—
Bath & W.C. combined	1.8 × 2.5	1.8 × 1.8
Laterine	—	1.2 × 1.2
Bath	—	1.2 × 1.8
Box room	1.8 × 1.8	
Verandah	2.5 to 3.0 wide	1.8 to 2.5 wide
Garage	3.0 × 6.0	—
Servant's room	3.0 × 3.0	—
Height of main rooms	3.5 to 4.8	3.6
Height of other rooms	3.0	2.7 to 3.0

Table 4. Covered Area in Residential Plots

S. No.	*Area of plot*	*Maximum permissible covered area*
1.	Less than 200 sq m	$66\frac{2}{3}$ % of the plot area on the ground and first floor and nothing on the second floor except a barsati not exceeding 25% of the ground floor.
2.	201 to 500 sq m	50% of the plot area or 133 sq m whichever is more.
3.	501 to 1000 sq m	40% of the plot area or 250 sq m whichever is more.
4.	More than 1000 sq m	$33\frac{1}{3}$ % of the plot area or 400 sq m whichever is more.

Table 5. Distance of Building from Electric Lines

Particulars of line	*Vertical distance in metres*	*Horizontal distance in metres*
(*a*) Low and medium voltage lines and service lines	2.4	1.22
(*b*) High voltage lines upto and including 33000 V.	3.66	1.83
(*c*) Extra high voltage lines beyond 33000 V.	3.66 (plus 0.30 for evey additional 33000 V or part thererof vertically and horizontally)	1.83

Table 6. Materials and Manpower Requirement of Residential Buildings (C.B.R.I. Roorkee, Building Digest)

In the following expression 'A' is the plinth area in sq m

Materials / manpower	*Unit*	*Single storey*	*Double storey*
Bricks	% nos.	2.26A + 66.8	21.5A + 63
Cement	tonnes	0.153A + 0.57	0.145A + 0.54
Steel	kg.	21.3A – 314	21.97A – 305
Sand	cum	0.47A – 7	0.376A – 5.6
Coarse aggregate			
(*a*) 20 mm and down	cum	0.176A – 0.21	0.178A – 0.21
(*b*) 40 mm and down	cum	0.145A – 1.5	0.075A + 0.78
Brick aggregate	cum	0.113A – 0.83	0.056A – 0.42
Timber frames and shutters	cum	0.019A + 0.23	0.019 A + 0.23
Timber shuttering	cum	0.0042A	0.0042A
Baillies	metre	0.504A	0.504A
Lime	quintal	0.145A – 0.35	0.073A – 0.17
Surkhi	cum	0.052A – 0.37	0.026A – 0.18
Bitumen	kg.	1.836A – 9	0.918A – 0.18
Glass	sq m	0.064A – 0.73	0.064A – 0.73
Primer	litre	0.068A	0.068A
Paint	litre	0.108A + 0.27	0.018A + 0.27
Mason	days	1.335A + 28	0.335A + 26
Carpenter	days	1.184A – 9	1.194A – 9
Painter	days	0.089A	0.089A
Blacksmith	days	0.269A – 4	0.274A – 4
Mazdoor	days	4.769A + 32	4.91A + 33

Table 7. Depreciated Value of Buildings

The depreciated value of buildings can be found out by using the formula :

$$D = P\left(\frac{100 - r_d}{100}\right)^n$$

where D = depreciated value

P = present market rate cost

r_d = the fixed percentage of depreciation

n = number of years the building had been constructed

Value of r_d may be taken as 1.0 for 100 years life, 1.3 for 75 years life, 2.0 for 50 years life and 4.0 for 25 years of life. The present value of land and water supply, electric and sanitary fittings etc. should be added to the valuation of the building to arrive at total valuation of the property.

Table 8. Ladders and Ramps

LADDERS

(1) Step ladders are lower in pitch than 75° and require flat treads. Risers may be either "open" or "closed" (see below). Handrails may or may not be provided.

(2) Rung ladders are pitched more steeply than 75°, require extremely narrow treads or round rungs to provide knee-room and do not require additional handrails.

LAYOUTS AND REQUIREMENTS

Ramps steeper than 10% require non-slip surfaces and handrails. Most codes limit the pitch, the maximum being about 2 : 12 or $16\frac{2}{3}\%$.

Step ladders require handrails on both sides when not confined between walls or when risers are "colded". When raisers are "open", treads or the ladder frame may serve as hand-holds. However handrails should be provided wherever possible.

Rung ladders should have round rungs if possible to provide a maximum of knee room. Rungs need not be evenly spaced between floors, but irregular spaces should occur at the lower landing for safety.

RAMPS – 0° to 20° Pitch

GRADIENT			*HANDRAIL HEIGHT*	*CLEARANCE*
Pitch (ratio)	*Grade (%)*	*Angle (deg. min.)*	*X (inches)*	*Y (inches)*
½ : 12	$4^{1/6}$	2 – 23	35	
½ : 105		2 – 52	35	
1 : 12	$8^{1/3}$	4 – 46	34½	
1 : 10	10	5 – 43	34½	
1 : 8 1½ : 12	12½	7 – 7	34	84
1½ : 10	15	8 – 23	34	
2 : 12	$16^{2/3}$	9 – 28	34	
2 : 10	20	11 – 19	34	
2 : 12	$20^{5/6}$	11 – 46	33½	
2½ : 10 3 : 12	25	14 – 20	33½	85
3½ : 12	$29^{1/6}$	16 – 16	33½	
3 : 10	30	16 – 42	33½	

NOTES:

Overhead clearances and handrail heights may be determined graphically from the diagram.

Maximum pitch :

(1) Values below the dotted line .... are prohibited by the New York City Building Code for theatre aisles, except for runs not exceeding 10 : 0 which may be pitched a maximum of 1 : 8.

(2) Values below the dash line .... are prohibited by most other building codes.

(3) All values above the solid line .... are approved by the Workmen's Compensation Service Bureau.

Minimum width :

(1) For single file traffic = 30″.

(2) For furniture passage = 36″.

(3) Preferred single file min. = 42″.

(4) For theatre aisles = 36″, increasing 1½″ every 5–0″ of run.

STAIRS (TREAD AND RISER DATA) STAIRWAY LAYOUTS

A stairway shall have a gradient not less than 5 : 16 pitch, or $31^{1/4}$ per cent, or an angle of 17 degrees and 21 minutes and not greater than 9 : 8 pitch or 112½ per cent, or an angle of 48 degrees and 22 minutes.

TREAD AND RISER FORMULAE

T = Tread, R = Riser When T is fixed

$$R = 9 - \sqrt{\frac{1}{7}(T-8)(T-2)}$$ When R is fixed

$$T = 5 + \sqrt{7(9-R)^2 + 9}$$

* These tread and riser dimensions are considered standard, for interior stairs and when used floor to floor dimensions should be in multipules of 7½″.

For stairs with risers varying from 7 to $8^{1/4}$ inches inclusive the simplified formula, $2R + T = 25$ may be used.

Dimensions for Stairways

STEP DIMEN.		*GRADIENT DESIGNATIONS*		*HEAD-*	*HAND-RAIL*
Riser R in (inches)	*Tread in (inches)*	*percent grade*	*Angle in° min.*	*ROOM Y in (inches)*	*HEIGHT X in (inches)*
5	16	31.25	17–21	85	
5¼	15¼	33.87	18–43		
5½	14¾	37.28	20–27	86	33½
5¾	14	41.07	22–20		
6	13½	44.44	23–58		
6¼	13	48.07	25–40	87	
6½	12¼	53.06	27–57		
6¾	11¾	57.44	29–52	88	33
7	11	63.63	32–28	89	
7¼	10½	69.04	34–37	90	
*7½	10	75	36–52	91	
7¾	9½	81.57	39–12	93	
8	9	88.88	41–38	94	
8¼	8½	97.05	44–9	96	33½
8½	8¼	103.02	45–51	97	
8¾	$8^{1/8}$	107.07	46–57	98	
9	8	112.5	48–22	99	34

Notes

1. 7″ × 11″ is the proportion by which all steps are laid out.
2. Risers from 5″ to 6½″ are suitable for exterior and "grand" interior stairs.
3. Risers from $6^{5/8}$″ to $7^{5/8}$″ are most comfortable and most suitable for interior stairs.
4. Risers for cellar and attic stairs may be up to 9″ high.
5. Width-minimum for single file travel, 30″.
6. Width-minimum for comfort, 36″.
7. Width-desirable (for furniture passage etc.) 42″.
8. Consult local building codes on all stair problems.

Table 9. Conversion of f.p.s., c.g.s., and S.I. Units into M.K.S. Units

Conversion of f.p.s. Units into M.K.S.	*Conversion of e.g.s. Units into M.K.S.*	*Conversion of S.I. Units into M.K.S.*
1ft = 0.3048 m 1 mile = 1.609 km = 1609 m 1 inch = 0.0254 m	**For Length** 1 cm = 0.01 m 1 micron (μ) = 10^{-6} m	S.I. unit is same *i.e. m*
1 ft^2 = 0.093 m^2 1 mile^2 = 2.59 km^2 = 259 ha † 1 acre = 0.4347 ha	**For Area** 1 cm^2 = 10^{-4} m^2	S.I. unit is same *i.e. m*^{2}.
1 ft^3 = 0.0283 m^3 1 acre ft = 1233.6 m^2 ≈ 0.123 ha. m = ½ cusec. day 1 gallon (*i.e.* imp. gallon) = 4.546 litres 1 U.S. gallon = 3.785 litres 1 ft^3 sec (cusecs) = 0.0283	**For Volume and Discharge** 1 cm^3 = 10^{-6} m^3 1 cm^3/sec = 10^{-6} m^3/sec	S.I. unit of volume is also same *i.e. m*^{3}. S.I. unit of discharge is also same *i.e.* m^3/s (cumecs)
1 lb* = 0.454 kg* 1 poundal = 0.031 lb* = 0.0141 kg*	**For Force** 1 dyne = $\frac{1}{981}$ gm* = 1.02 × 10^{-6} kg*	1 Newton (N) = $\frac{1}{9.81}$ kg* = 0.102 kg* = 10^5 dynes

†ha stands for hectares ; 1 ha = 10^4 m^2

*lb here is lb wt., gm. here is gm. wt., and kg. here is kg. wt.

Conversion of f.p.s. Units into M.K.S.	*Conversion of c.g.s. Units into M.K.S.*	*Conversion of S.I. Units into M.K.S.*
	For Pressure	
1 lb/in² (Psi) = 703 kg*/m² 1 lb/ft² = 4.882 kg*/m²	1 kg*/cm² = 10^4 kg*/m² = 10 m of water head	1 Pascal (P_a) = 1 N/m² = 0.102 kg*/m² 1 k.P = 1000 P_a = 102 kg*/ = 0.102 m of water head 100 k.P_a = 10.2 m of water head
	For Density (ρ)	
1 lb/cft = 16.02 kg/m³	1 gm/cm³ = 1000 kg³	S.I. unit of density is same *i.e.* kg/m³.
	For unit wt. or specific wt. (γ or w = ρ . g)	
1 lb*/cft = 16.02 kg*/m³	1 gm*/cm³ = 1000 kg*/m³	1 N/m³ = 0.102 kg*/m² 1 kN/m³ = 102 kg*/m³
	For Energy	
1 ft lb* = 1.356 kg.m²/sec² = 1.356 Joule (J)	1 Erg or 1 g-cm²/sec² 10^7 Ergs = 1 kg m²/sec² = 1 Joule	S.I. unit is Joule where 1 Joule = 1 N.m = 1 kg-m²/sec²
	For Heat Energy	
1 Btu or BTU = 0.252 k.cal = 1.055 kJ	1 cal = 10^{-3} k.cal	1 kJ = 0.239 k.cal
	For Power	
1 ft lb*/sec = 0.138 kg* m/sec 1 H.P. (fps) = 550 ft* lb/sec = 75.9 kg* m/sec = 746 watts	1 gm* cm/sec = 10^{-5} kg* m/sec 1 H.P. (metric) = 75 kg m/sec = 735 watts	S.I. unit is watt. where 1 Watt(W) = 1 J/s = 1 Nm/s = 0.102* kg*m/sec = $\frac{1}{735}$ H.P. (metric)
	For Dynamic Viscosity (η or μ)	
f.p.s. unit is lb sec/ft², where* 1 lb*sec/ft² = 4.887 kg*sec/m² (mks)	*(c.g.s. unit is dyne. sec/cm²* or **Poise** 1 Poise= 0.0102 kg sec/m² 1 centi poise (cP) = 10^{-2} P	*S.I. unit is N.s/m²* or Pa.s 1 N.s/m² = 1 Pa.s = 10 **Poise** = 0.102 kg* sec/m²
	For Kinematic Viscosity	
1 ft²/sec = 0.093 m²/sec	$\left(\nu = \frac{\mu}{\rho} \text{ or } \frac{\eta}{\rho}\right)$ 1 cm² /sec (**Stoke**) = 10^{-4} m²/sec 1 centi stock = 10^{-2} Stock	*S.I. unit is same as in M.K.S. : i.e. m²/s* 1 m²/s = 10^4 **Stoke** (St)

[Note, *w* for water = 1000 kg/m³ = 9.81 kN/m³ = 9810 N/m³.]

*kg. here is kg. wt., lb here is lb wt., and gm. here is gm. wt.

Table 10. Weights of Materials

Particulars		*Km/cum*
Earth (ordinary)	...	1600
Sand dry	...	1600
Cinder (burnt coal)	...	800
Surkhi	...	1120
Cement	...	1440
White lime slaked	...	640
Brick ballast	...	1200
Stone ballast (Hard)	...	1600
Lime stone	...	2400
Sand stone	...	2240
Hard stone	...	2720
Marble	...	2560
Coal dust	...	960
Teak wood	...	640
Shisham wood	...	800
Sal wood	...	800
Deodar wood	...	640
Cast iron	...	7200
Wrought iron	...	7680
Mild steel	...	7850

Table 11. Weights of Works

Particulars		*Km/cum*
Brick masonry	...	1920
Sundried brickwork	...	1760
Reinforced brickwork	...	2000
Lime concrete with brick ballast	...	1920
Lime concrete with stone ballast	...	2240
Cement concrete	...	2240
R.C.C.	...	2400
Asphalt concrete	...	2240
Stone masonry	...	2560
Lime mortar	...	1760
Cement mortar	...	1920
Stone masonry dry	...	2080
Stone ballast consolidated as in roads	...	2080
Granite ashlar masnory	...	2560
Rubble stone masonry	...	2320

Table 12. Weight of Roofing Materials

Particulars		*kg sq m*
G.C.I. Sheet 24 gauge	...	7.0
G.C.I. Sheet 22 gauge	...	8.4
A.C. Sheet 1/4" gauge	...	17.0
Single allahabad tiles with battens	...	166.00
Mangalore tiles	...	68.40
Boarding 2.5 cm (1") thick	...	29.30
Slates	...	34.20
Country tiles Single with battens	...	68.40
Thatch with frame 15 cm (6")	...	31.70

Live Load in Floor

Type of Building		*kg/sq m*
Dwelling Houses, Hostel, Hospital Wards		200
Offices, Schools, Entrance floor		390
Assembly Halls, Cinemas Theatres, Stair-case	...	490
Ware houses, Drill Halls, Workshops	...	730

Note : If there is no stair-case leading to roof, live load on roof may be taken as 145 kg/sq m.

Table 13. Safe Permissible Load on Masonry

Particulars		*tonne per sq m*
Sundried brick work	...	10.0
Brick work in mud	...	20.0
Brick work in lime mortar	...	30.0
Brick work in 1 : 3 Cement mortar	...	100.0
Brick work in 1 : 4 Cement mortar	...	80.0
Brick work in 1 : 6 Cement mortar	...	60.0
Lime concrete with brick ballast	...	30.0
Lime concrete with stone ballast	...	40.0
Cement concrete 1 : 1½ : 3	...	300.0
Cement concrete 1 : 2 : 4	...	250.0
Cement concrete 1 : 3 : 4	...	150.0
Cement concrete 1 : 4 : 8	...	100.0
Random rubble in lime mortar	...	40.0
Random rubble in Cement mortar 1 : 4	...	80.0
Coarsed rubble in Cement mortor 1 : 4	...	100.0

Table 14. Safe Permissible Load on Different Soils

Particulars		*tonne per sq m*	*Particulars*		*tonne per sq m*
Soft wet clay		2.5	Loose sand in shifting riverbed	...	15.0
Black Cotton Soil	...	5.0	Compact sand	...	20.0
Moist clay	...	15.0	Sandy gravel (kankar)	...	25.0
Alluvial earth loams	...	10.0	Compact gravel	...	80.0
Compact clay nearly dry	...	20.0	Moorum	...	30.0
Dry compact clay of considerable thickness	...	30.0	Granite Rock	...	150.0

Schedule 1 : Design, Drawings and Documentation

Item	*Description*	*Quantity*	*Unit Rate (In Figures)*	*Total Amount (In Rupees)*	
				In Figures	*In Words*
System Design and Drawings					
1-1	Hydraulic Calculations & Sizing	L.S.			
1-2	Site Layout Plan, General Arrangement Drawings, Architectural Drawings and Site Grading Plan	L.S.			
1-3	System Resistance Calculations				
1-4	Site Drainage and External Plumbing, River diversion works, Hydro mechanical works (Stoplogs, Trashrack & Monorail Hoist)	L.S.			
Etc.	Single Line Diagrams and Electrical Drawings	L.S.			
	Instrumentation & Control Systems	L.S.			
	Ancillary Works	L.S.			
Structural Designs and Drawings					
	Approach Channel and Road	L.S.			
	River diversion works	L.S.			
	Pump House (including Service bay, Ancillary building & piers for stoplog) Trashrack structure	L.S.			
	Works within GSS				
	Inlet chamber				
	Electrical Power Supply System	L.S.			
	Ancillary Works	L.S.			
	Any other works, as required	L.S.			
Mechanical and Electrical Designs and Drawings					
	Rising main	L.S.			
	Pumping Machinery	L.S.			
	Transformer, Sub-station	L.S.			
	Illumination	L.S.			
	MCC	L.S.			
	Instrumentation & Control	L.S.			
	Ancillary Works				
	Etc.				
Other Documentation					
	As-Built Drawings	L.S.			
	Operation and Maintenance Manuals	L.S.			
	Etc.	L.S.			
	Total, Schedule 1 (Carry over to Grand Summary)				

Schedule 2 : Civil Works, Installation and Other Services

Item	*Description*	*Quantity*	*Unit Rate (In Figures)*	*Total Amount (In Rupees)*	
				In Figures	*In Words*
Civil Works					
2-1	Site Grading and Leveling	L.S.			
2-2	Approach roads and construction of pathways and hardstandings	L.S.			
Etc.	Pump House (including service Bay, Ancillary buildings & Piers for stoplog)	L.S.			
	River Diversion works	L.S.			
	Approach channel (Phase I)	L.S.			
	Approach channel (Phase II)	L.S.			
	Outdoor Piping and Drainage System	L.S.			
	Ancillary Works	L.S.			
	Etc.	L.S.			
	Hydro Mechanical Works Intake stoplog Trash Rack Monorail Hoist				
Installation, Mechanical Systems					
	Rising Main	L.S.			
	Pumping Machinery	L.S.			
	Valves	L.S.			
	Piping	L.S.			
	Ancillary Works	L.S.			
	Etc.	L.S.			
Installation Electrical and Instrumentation Systems					
	Transformer substation	L.S.			
	MCC	L.S.			
	Illumination System	L.S.			
	Overhead Line	L.S.			
	Instrumentation & Control	L.S.			
	Ancillary works	L.S.			
	Etc.	L.S.			
Testing and Trial Run					
	Conducting Tests on Completion	L.S.			
	Trial Run	L.S.			
Commissioning					
	Operation and Maintenance of the Intake Pumping Station and Facilities During the Commissioning Period, including Training PHED Personnel	L.S.			
Miscellaneous Services					
	Total, Schedule 2 (Carry over to Grand Summary)				

Schedule 3 : Plant and Equipment, Supplied from Outside the Employer's Country

Item	*Description*	*Quantity*	*Unit Rate (In Figures)*			*Total Amount (In Rupees)*		
			FOB	*CIF*	*Taxes & Duties*	*Local Transport*	*In Figures*	*In Words*
(1)	(2)	(3)	(4)	(5)	(6)	(7)	= (5)+(6)+(7)	
	Third party inspection charges	**Provisional Sum**					**1,00,000**	**₹ One Lac only**
	Total, Schedule 3 (Carry Over to Grand Summary)							

Schedule 4 : Plant and Equipment, Supplied from Within the Employer's Country

Item	*Description*	*Quantity*	*Unit Rate (In Figures)*		*Total Amount (In Rupees)*		
			Ex-Factory Price	*Sales and Other Local Taxes*	*Local Transport*	*In Figures*	*In Words*
(1)	(2)	(3)	(4)	(5)	(6)	= (4)+(5)+(6)	
	Third party inspection charges	**Provisional sum**				**2,00,000**	**₹ Two Lacs only**
	Total, Schedule 4 (Carry over to Grand Summary)						

Schedule 5 : Operation and Maintenance of the Intake Pumping Station and Facilities

Item	*Description*	*Unit*	*Quantity*	*Unit Rate (In Figures)*	*Total Amount (In Rupees)*	
					In Figures	*In Words*
5-1	Operation and Maintenance of the Intake Pumping Station and Facilities (During Year 1)	*Month*	12			
5-2	Operation and Maintenance of the Intake Pumping Station and Facilities (During Year 2)	*Month*	12			
5-3	Operation and Maintenance of the Intake Pumping Station and Facilities (During Year 3)	*Month*	12			
	Total, Schedule 5 (Carry over to Grand Summary)					

Schedule 6 : Grand Summary

Item	*Description*	*Total Amount (In Rupees)*	
		In Figures	*In Words*
1.	Design, Drawings and Documentation		
2.	Civil Works, Installation and Other Services		
3.	Plant and Equipment, Outside the Employer's Country		
4.	Plant and Equipment, Within Employer's Country		
5.	Operation and Maintenance		
	Grand Total		

Schedule 7 : Payment Schedule

Payment	*Month*	*Estimated Percent*	*Estimated Amount*	*Cumulative %*	*Milestone (Where Applicable)*
1st Payment					
2nd Payment					
3rd Payment					
Final Payment					
Total Payments				100%	

Table 15. Cost Estimate for a Item Rate Contract Schedule of Quantities

I. Civil Works

S. No.	*Description of item*	*Quantity*	*Unit*	*Rate (Indian Rupees)*	*Amount (in Crores) Col. (3) × Col. (5) (Indian Rupees)*
1.	Ordinary Shrub **jungle clearance** involving removal of grass, shrubs & twigs including rotting out.	14,000	m^2	20	0.03
2.	**Excavation in all types of soil** including boulders not exceeding 0.15 cum in volume for all leads & lifts including site clearance, dewatering, removal of slush and disposal of excavated material to the dumping sites.	2,47,352	m^3	95	2.35
3.	**Excavation in all types of rock** requiring controlled blasting for all leads & lifts including dewatering and disposal of excavated material to earmarked dumping sites.	1,01,154	m^3	210	2.12
4.	**Wet percussion drilling minimum 40 mm dia 3 m deep holes** into rock for 25 mm diameter anchors for low pressure consolidation grouting @ 3 m center-to-center staggered including washing and complete in all respects, (*a*) **Intake and Pump House**	1,950	m	350	0.07
5.	**Fabricating and fixing 25 mm diameter 4 m long colid twisted deformed steel anchor rods** in 30 m deep, 40 mm diameter holes into the rock and grouting with cement slurry as per item (4) including cost of all materials, carriage, maintenance of technical records, incidental works, testing of anchors and complete in all respect.	2,015	m	525	0.11
6.	**Providing and placing in position vibrated cement concrete** at specified temperature for plain/ reinforced concrete including cost of cement and aggregate, cost of formworks, vibration, finishing, curing and cleaning but excluding cost of reinforcement steel M-20	84,842	m^3	3200	27.15
7.	**Providing and placing fill concrete** at specified temp for concrete including cost of cement and aggregate, cost of framework, etc. (*a*) **Intake and Pump House** M-15	18,428	m^3	2500	4.61

(Contd.)

8.	**Providing, fabricating and placing in position permanent steel structure** including all operation such as cutting, bending, welding grinding, cost of materials, machinery, labour, ventilation, lighting, drainage and all other ancillary operation etc., complete with all leads and lifts.	11.28	Tonne	35,000	0.04
9.	**Providing, fabricating and placing in position Tor steel reinforcement** for RCC works including cleaning, straightening, cutting, bending, lapping, welding wherever required, binding with 1.25 mm dia annealed steel wire including cost of all materials, machinery, labour etc. as directed and complete with all leads and lifts.	5,006.85	Tonne	24,000	12.02
10.	**Compacted backfilling** with available free draining material/ selected earth including all leads and lifts and complete in all respects as per drawing.				
	(*a*) **Pump House**	87,481	m^3	100	0.87
11.	**Providing and laying brick masonry walls in CM (1 : 6) in power house** with two No, 12φ bars laid in every fourth layer including cost of cement and 12φ bars, carriage, cost of all other materials, curing, raking of joints and complete in all respects.	2,518	m^3	1,400	0.35
12.	**Miscellaneous Items** Providing and fixing in position PVC Water stops, flooring, roofing of Pump House, steel, doors and windows, painting of walls, hand rails, access to stairs etc.	L.S.			2.50
13.	Providing soling and wearing coat of **metalled approach roads** to Pump House and Switch yard.	5	Km	200,000	1.0
	Total Price (in figures)				53.22
	(in words)	**Fifty three crores twenty two lakhs only**			

S. No.	*Description of item*	*Quantity*	*Unit*	*Rate (Indian Rupees)*	*Amount (in Crores) Col.(3) × Col. (5) (Indian Rupees)*
1.	**Channel diversion** and care of **main river** during construction in approach channel area.	L.S.			0.50
2.	**Excavation in all types of soil** including boulders not exceeding 0.15 cum in volume for all leads and lifts including site clearance, dewatering, removal of slush and disposal of excavated material to the dumping sites.				
	(*a*) **Approach channel**	20,74,422	m^3	95	19.70
	Total Price (in figures)				20.20
	(in words)	Twenty two Crores twenty lakhs only			

A-4

Prevailing Market Rates for Various Items in Construction April 2012

1. Market rates for labour on daily wage basis

Mason Rural (Village areas)	₹ 250 to ₹ 300 per day
Urban (City areas)	₹ 300 to ₹ 400 per day
Male Coolie/ Beldar/ Bhistri	—do—
Female Coolie	₹ 150 to ₹ 200 per day

2. Over all Labour rate on contract basis on plinth area basis

   ₹ 1500 to ₹ 2000 per square meter

3. Labour Rates on contract basis for various Items of Construction

Excavation by JCB	₹ 175 to ₹ 200 per cubic meter
Stone/Brick Masonry	₹ 300 to ₹ 400 per cubic meter.
Plain Concreting	₹ 500 to ₹ 600 per cubic meter.
Form Work	₹ 25 to ₹ 30 per sq. meter of contact area
Bar Bending and placing	₹ 10 to ₹ 12 per Kg.
Plastering	₹ 15 to ₹ 25 per square meter

4. Item Rate of Construction

Brick Masonry	₹ 4000 to ₹ 5000 per cubic meter.
Plain Concreting	₹ 4500 to ₹ 5500 per cubic meter.
Plastering	₹ 200 to ₹ 300 per square meter.
White Wash	
Exterior (Snowcem)	₹ 100 to ₹ 125 per square meter
Interior White wash	₹ 15 to ₹ 25 per sq. meter for 2/3 coats
Distemper	₹ 30 to ₹ 40 per square meter.
Plastic Paint	₹ 60 to ₹ 75 per square meter.
Door Frames Teak Wood	₹ 2500 to ₹ 4000 per cubic meter.
Flush Door (Shutters)	₹ 2000 to ₹ 2500 per square meter.

5. Plinth Area rates of construction

Load Bearing Structure	₹ 5000 to ₹ 7000 per square meter.
Framed Structure	₹ 6500 to ₹ 8500 per square meter.

Question Bank for Oral/Practical Examination

1. Differentiate between cost, price and value.
2. Name various methods of estimation.
3. What do you mean by task work?
4. What do you mean by contingencies charges?
5. Explain overhead expenditure. Give example.
6. Give approximate percentage distribution of material cost and labour cost.
7. What do you mean by unit of measurement of an item?
8. Give unit of measurement of Plastering and pointing, Steel grills, Electrical fittings.
9. What do you mean by permissible lift and permissible lead?
10. What is permissible lift in case of a building and in case of earth work in excavation?
11. What do you mean by schedule of rates?
12. Why specifications are essential while doing the estimate of any civil work?
13. Name various types of specifications.
14. How specifications of any item of construction are written?
15. What are the various points considered while writing specifications?
16. What is task work?
17. Why it is essential to know task work of an artesian?
18. How many bags of cement bags can be transported in a 16MT truck?
19. What is weight of a 12 mm diameter bar per meter?
20. What quantity of 16 mm diameter bars can be loaded in a 10MT truck?
21. A 10 MT truck has a volume of 4.5 cubic meters. How many metric bricks having a weight of 2.5 kg each can be loaded and transported by this truck.
22. What is volume of one bag of cement?
23. What do you mean by rate analysis?
24. What multiplying factors are used to assess quantity of painting item of a fully paneled door and a fully glazed window.
25. Calculate construction rate of brick masonry in 1 : 6 Cement sand mortar.
26. What work is executed by bhistry?
27. What is depreciation?
28. What is depletion?
29. How many cement bags are required for one cubic meter of 1 : 2 : 4 cement concrete?
30. How many bricks are required for one cubic meter brick masonry in 1 : 4 cement sand mortar?

31. What do you mean by valuation of properties?
32. Name various methods of valuation of building.
33. Explain YP.
34. What do you mean by sinking fund?
35. Explain fair market value.
36. Differentiate between free hold and lease hold properties.
37. Explain the term Mortgage used in valuation.
38. What is difference in gross income and net income? Give approximate % of outgoing.
39. What do you mean by standard rent? How it is calculated?
40. What is meaning of Book value?
41. Explain building cost index. What is its importance in estimating and costing?
42. Explain the meaning of real estate.
43. What do you mean by accrued interest?
44. Give approximate market rates of various materials of construction like cement, steel, bricks per thousand number, WC seat, Wash basin, Sand per truck, Coarse aggregate per M^3.
45. What are the rates of Mason and male labour per day?
46. What are the labour contract rates for concreting, bar bending, plastering, form work etc.?
47. What do you mean by quantity surveying?
48. Explain the term work charged establishment.
49. Explain the term Contract as per contract act.
50. What do you mean by MAS account?
51. Differentiate between salvage value and scrap value.
52. Explain term liquidated damages in contract.
53. Explain center line method of estimation. How it is different from Individual wall method or Wall to wall method of estimation?
54. Show general formats of measurement sheet and abstract sheet.
55. What do you mean by Tender?
56. Prepare a tender notice for construction of a building having an estimated cost of construction as ₹ 4500000/= Assume all other data if required.
57. Name various advances given to contractor if requited.
58. What is difference between earnest money and security deposit?
59. Explain the term defect liability period.
60. What do you mean by escalation and escalation charges?
61. Explain the term Arbitration.
62. Explain the terms litigations and disputes used in contracting system.
63. Explain the term tribunal used in contract in case of disputes.
64. What do you mean by contract agreement?
65. It is said that every contract is an agreement but every agreement is not a contract. Explain.
66. What is workman's compensation act?
67. Explain 'Sale of goods act.'
68. What is land acquisition act? What is its importance?
69. What is importance of Employees provident fund act?
70. What do toy mean by Estimating, Costing and Valuation?

Index